Essentials of Understanding Psychology

2024 RELEASE

Robert S. Feldman

University of Massachusetts Amherst

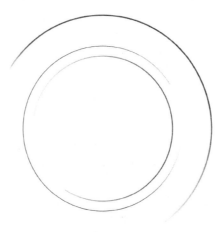

Mc
Graw
Hill

ESSENTIALS OF UNDERSTANDING PSYCHOLOGY, 2024 RELEASE

Published by McGraw Hill LLC, 1325 Avenue of the Americas, New York, NY 10019. Copyright ©2024 by McGraw Hill LLC. All rights reserved. Printed in the United States of America. Previous editions ©2021, 2019, and 2017. No part of this publication may be reproduced or distributed in any form or by any means, or stored in a database or retrieval system, without the prior written consent of McGraw Hill LLC, including, but not limited to, in any network or other electronic storage or transmission, or broadcast for distance learning.

Some ancillaries, including electronic and print components, may not be available to customers outside the United States.

This book is printed on acid-free paper.

1 2 3 4 5 6 7 8 9 LWI 29 28 27 26 25 24

ISBN 978-1-264-19795-8 (bound)
MHID 1-264-19795-0 (bound)
ISBN 978-1-264-67760-3 (loose-leaf)
MHID 1-264-67760-X (loose-leaf)

Executive Portfolio Manager: *Ryan Treat*
Senior Product Development Manager: *Dawn Groundwater*
Senior Product Developer: *Erin DeHeck*
Marketing Manager: *Isfa Syed*
Content Project Managers: *Mary E. Powers* (core), *Jodi Banowetz* (assessment)
Manufacturing Project Manager: *Sandy Ludovissy*
Designer: *Beth Blech*
Content Licensing Specialist: *Carrie Burger*
Cover Image: *Wavebreakmedia/Shutterstock*
Compositor: *Aptara®, Inc.*

All credits appearing on page or at the end of the book are considered to be an extension of the copyright page.

Library of Congress Cataloging-in-Publication Data

Names: Feldman, Robert S. (Robert Stephen), 1947- author.
Title: Essential of understanding psychology / Robert S. Feldman,
    University of Massachusetts Amherst.
Description: 2024 Release. | New York, NY : McGraw Hill LLC, [2025] |
    Includes index.
Identifiers: LCCN 2023032395 (print) | LCCN 2023032396 (ebook) | ISBN
    9781264197958 (hardcover) | ISBN 9781264677603 (spiral bound) | ISBN
    9781264676859 (ebook) | ISBN 9781264679386 (ebook other)
Subjects: LCSH: Psychology.
Classification: LCC BF121 .F337 2025 (print) | LCC BF121 (ebook) | DDC
    150–dc23/eng/20230809
LC record available at https://lccn.loc.gov/2023032395
LC ebook record available at https://lccn.loc.gov/2023032396

The Internet addresses listed in the text were accurate at the time of publication. The inclusion of a website does not indicate an endorsement by the authors or McGraw Hill LLC, and McGraw Hill LLC does not guarantee the accuracy of the information presented at these sites.

Dedication
To
Kathy

About the Author

ROBERT S. FELDMAN is Professor of Psychological and Brain Sciences and Senior Advisor to the Chancellor at the University of Massachusetts Amherst. A recipient of the College Distinguished Teacher Award, he teaches psychology classes ranging in size from 15 to nearly 500 students. During the course of more than three decades as a college instructor, he has taught undergraduate and graduate courses at Mount Holyoke College, Wesleyan University, and Virginia Commonwealth University in addition to the University of Massachusetts.

Professor Feldman, who initiated the Minority Mentoring Program at the University of Massachusetts, also has served as a Hewlett Teaching Fellow and Senior Online Teaching Fellow. He initiated distance-learning courses in psychology at the University of Massachusetts.

A Fellow of the American Psychological Association, the Association for Psychological Science, and the American Association for the Advancement of Science, Professor Feldman received a BA with High Honors from Wesleyan University and an MS and PhD from the University of Wisconsin-Madison. He is a winner of a Fulbright Senior Research Scholar and Lecturer Award and the Distinguished Alumnus Award from Wesleyan. He is past President of the Federation of Associations in Behavioral and Brain Sciences Foundation, which advocates for the field of psychology, and is on the board of the Social Psychology Network. He also chairs the McGraw Hill Learning Science Advisory Board. He has written and edited more than 250 books, book chapters, and scientific articles. He has edited *Applications of Nonverbal Behavioral Theory and Research, Improving the First Year of College: Research and Practice,* and most recently, *Learning Science: Theory Research and Practice.* He is also author of *P.O.W.E.R. Learning: Strategies for Success in College and Life.*

His textbooks, which have been used by more than 2 million students around the world, have been translated into Spanish, French, Portuguese, Dutch, German, Italian, Arabic, Chinese, Korean, and Japanese. His research interests include deception and honesty in everyday life, work that he described in *The Liar in Your Life,* a trade book published in 2009. His research has been supported by grants from the National Institute of Mental Health and the National Institute on Disabilities and Rehabilitation Research.

Professor Feldman loves music, is an enthusiastic pianist, and enjoys cooking and traveling. He is a member of the University of Massachusetts Amherst Foundation Board and former Chair of the Board of Directors of New England Public Media, representing the major public broadcasting and streaming outlets in western New England. He and his wife, also a psychologist, live in the Pioneer Valley of Massachusetts in a home overlooking the Holyoke mountain range.

Brief Contents

Mc Graw Hill **connect**

McGraw Hill Education Psychology APA Documentation Style Guide

Contents

DGLimages/Shutterstock

Mladen Zivkovic/Shutterstock

CHAPTER 4

States of Consciousness 129

Odua Images/Shutterstock

wavebreakmedia/Shutterstock

Photodisc/Getty Images

Blend Images/Getty Images

CHAPTER 8

Motivation and Emotion 290

wavebreakmedia/Shutterstock

Santypan/Shutterstock

Prostock-studio/Shutterstock

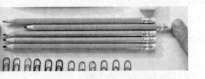
Andrey_Popov/Shutterstock

CHAPTER 12

Psychological Disorders 455

bernardbodo/Getty Images

Agencja Fotograficzna Caro/
Alamy Stock Photo

Mc Graw Hill **connect**

McGraw Hill Education Psychology APA Documentation Style Guide

Guide to Diversity, Equity, and Inclusion in *Essentials of Understanding Psychology*

Material in this text is based on research drawn from journals, books, and other sources that represent the diversity of the field of psychology–both in terms of subject matter and the diversity of authors. For example, following is a sampling of journals used in writing *Essentials of Understanding Psychology:*

African Journal of Psychiatry, American Anthropologist, American Journal of Community Psychology, American Journal on Mental Retardation, American Sociological Review, Annual Review of Sociology, Anxiety, Stress & Coping: An International Journal, Archives of Sexual Behavior, Archives of Women's Mental Health, Asian Journal of Psychiatry, Chinese Journal of Clinical Psychology, Chinese Journal of Psychology, Community Mental Health Journal, Community, Work & Family, Cultural Diversity and Ethnic Minority Psychology, Culture & Psychology, Culture, Medicine, and Psychiatry: An International Journal of Cross-Cultural Health Research, Diversity and Ethnic Minority Psychology, Early Years: An International Journal of Research and Development, Ethnic and Racial Studies, European Archives of Psychiatry and Clinical Neuroscience, European Journal of Psychological Assessment, European Journal of Psychotraumatology, European Journal of Social Psychology, European Journal of Training and Development, European Neuropsychopharmacology, European Psychiatry, European Psychologist, European Review of Applied Psychology, Family & Community Health, Health Care for Women International, International Journal of Comparative Psychology, International Journal of Cross-Cultural Management, International Journal of Dream Research, International Journal of Eating Disorders, International Journal of Emergency Mental Health, International Journal of Group Psychotherapy, International Journal of Human Development, International Journal of Inclusive Education, International Journal of Intercultural Relations, International Journal of Jungian Studies, International Journal of Mental Health, Journal of Black Psychology, Journal of Community & Applied Social Psychology, Journal of Cross-Cultural Psychology, Journal of Diversity in Higher Education, Journal of Ethnic and Cultural Diversity in Social Work, Journal of Psychology in Africa, Journal of Russian & East European Psychology, Journal of Sociology, Journal of the International Neuropsychological Society, Psychology of Popular Media Culture, Quality & Quantity: International Journal of Methodology, Sex Roles, Sexuality & Culture, Stress and Health: Journal of the International Society for the Investigation of Stress, Transcultural Psychiatry, and *Women's Health.*

Moreover, *Essentials of Understanding Psychology* includes a substantial number of studies that have been conducted by researchers who are members of traditionally underrepresented groups, as well as research that involves experimental participants who are members of traditionally underrepresented groups and/or represent diverse national and international cultures. Specifically, here is a chapter-by-chapter sampling of studies and researchers who exemplify the diversity of the field of psychology and who are represented in this book:

Chapter 1: Introduction to Psychology

- Diversity science and cross-cultural psychological subfields (Neblett, 2019)

- Issues relating to gender and racial representation in the field of psychology (Clay, 2017; Fowler et al., 2018; Frost et al., 2019; Marulanda & Radtke, 2019; Wiedman, 2019; American Psychological Association, 2020; Lin et al., 2020)

- Gender pay gap in the psychological professions (Clay, 2017; Wiedman, 2019; Gruber et al., 2021)

- Impact and implications of the lack of diversity on psychology as a profession (Stevens, 2015; Stewart et al., 2017; Andoh, 2021)

- Dominance of United States-based psychologists (IJzerman et al., 2021)

- Founding mothers of psychology including Margaret Floy Washburn, Leta Stetter Hollingworth, Mary Calkins, Karen Horney, June Etta Downey, Anna Freud, and Mamie Phipps Clark (Hollingworth, 1943/1990; Denmark & Fernandez, 1993; Furumoto & Scarborough, 2002; Lal, 2002; Butler, 2009; Galdi, 2015; American Psychological Association, 2021)

- Prejudice and discrimination of early psychologists and the American Psychological Association's 2021 apology for systemic inequity, racism, discrimination, and denigration of people of color (American Psychology Association, 2021a, 2021b; Cummings Center for the History of Psychology, 2021)

- Importance of representation in survey research (Davern, 2013; Engel et al., 2015; Nedelec, 2017)

- Drawbacks of survey research including issue of respondents who do not want to admit atypical, minority, or socially undesirable attitudes (Zitner, 2021; King, 2022)

- Ethnographic research focused on understanding the attitudes and values of a culture (Ayón et al., 2020; Graham et al., 2020; Soundy & Heneghan, 2022)

- Random assignment and diversity of participants in experimental groups

- Research showing that the harm experienced by Black college students who encounter online discrimination on social media is reduced if White college students intervene and publicly express antiracist support (Hurd et al., 2022)

- Use of Western, Educated, Industrialized, Rich, and Democratic (WEIRD) participants in research and the need to ensure diversity of research participants (Schulz et al., 2018; Alper & Yilmaz, 2019; Kupferschmidt, 2019)

- Requirements of the National Institute of Mental Health and National Science Foundation for experiments to address issues of diverse populations (Hruschka et al., 2018; Sierra-Mercado & Lazaro-Munoz, 2018)

- Problems with diversity of MTurk participants and its impact on research findings (Stewart et al., 2015; Toich et al., 2022; Burnette et al., 2022)

Chapter 2: Neuroscience and Behavior

- Impact of genetics on a range of traits including sexual orientation (Barbaro et al., 2017; Wertz et al., 2019; Flint, 2022)

- Research showing tissue changes in the part of the cortex related to sensation in the fingertips when a person learns Braille (Makin & Flor, 2020; Bacon & Brinton, 2021)

- Cultural neuroscience and its examination of individualistic and collectivist orientations Nakagawa et al., 2019)

- Research showing an association between collectivism and the density of white matter in certain regions of the brain (Nakagawa et al., 2019).

- Differences in male and female brain lateralization, weight, and processing (Joel & McCarthy, 2017; Goyal et al., 2019; Schmied et al., 2020; Swanson et al., 2020; Carpita et al., 2021; Kurth et al., 2021)

- Gender differences in socialization and environmental influences

- Evidence of varying volumes of gray matter in and thickness of the cortex for high- and low-income adolescents (Mackey et al., 2015; Dufford et al., 2019; Hair et al., 2022)

- Lack of diversity in participant pools for brain research

- Limitations of brain studies due to lack of race or ethnicity data (Qu et al., 2021)

Chapter 3. Sensation and Perception

- Gender differences in rates of color blindness

- Sensitivity to different sound frequencies by age

- Teenagers setting ring tones to frequencies too high for older adults to hear and businesses using high-frequency sounds to discourage teenage loitering (Moreno-Gómez et al., 2017; Winberg, 2019)

- Use of echolocation by people with impaired vision (Thaler, 2015; Salles et al, 2019; Susler et al., 2022)

- Ability of research participants to identify sex of a volunteer by the volunteer's smell (Flohr et al., 2017; Parma et al., 2017; Sorokowski et al., 2019)

- Women's ability to identify their babies by smell (Flohr et al., 2017; Parma et al., 2017; Sorokowski et al., 2019)

- Declines in smell abilities by age (Tucker, 2022)

- Research suggesting the ability of gay men to identify whether a t-shirt had been worn by a gay or straight man by smell and the ability of lesbian women to distinguish the smell of other lesbian women (Martins et al., 2005; Mahmut & Croy, 2019; Zietsch, 2021)

- Japanese flavor of umami (Nakamura et al., 2011; Cecchini et al., 2019; Qi et al., 2022)

- Gender differences in susceptibility to pain (Park, 2011; Berke et al., 2017; Pester et al., 2022)

- Racial bias in how medical providers react to patient pain and how reports of pain from people of color can be minimized (Driscoll et al., 2021; Mende-Siedlecki et al., 2021)

- Gate-control theory explanation for cultural differences in the experience of pain (Vasudeva et al., 2015; Penlington et al., 2019)

- Acupuncture as a traditional Chinese pain treatment (Khedr et al., 2017; Wang et al., 2022)

- Consistency of perceptual principles across diverse cultures (Kemp et al., 2022)

- Culture in which a person is raised influences their perception of the world (Segall et al.,1966; Fujita et al., 2017)

- Cultural differences in the ability to reproduce a "devil's tuning fork" (Deregowski, 1973)

- Impact of variations in learning and experience in producing cross-cultural differences in perception (Hudson, 1960; deBruïne et al., 2018; Phillips, 2019)

Chapter 4: States of Consciousness

- Research gap in racial, ethnic, and cross-cultural differences in the amount of time people spend in sleep stages (Rao et al., 2009; Ahn et al., 2021)

- Use of Guatemalan worry dolls as sleep aides (Abrams, 2017)

- Gender differences in the speed in which men and women fall asleep, the length and depth of sleep, and the frequency of waking at night (Monk et al., 2011; Petersen, 2011; Jonasdottir et al., 2021)

- Changes in sleep requirements by age (Monk et al., 2011; Petersen, 2011; Jonasdottir et al., 2021)

- Racial disparities in quality of sleep (Ahn et al., 2021; Cheng et al., 2021)
- COVID-19 aggravation of existing racial disparities in sleep (Scarpelli et al., 2021)
- Quality of sleep for individuals in rich and poor countries and developed and underdeveloped countries (Rao et al., 2021)
- Experience of nightmares after the George Floyd murder (Reks et al., 2017; Bulkeley, 2020)
- Prevalence of insomnia among women and older adults (Abrams, 2017; Ong, 2017; Hallit et al., 2019; Abrams, 2021)
- Racial disparities in insomnia as a result of discrimination and systematic racism (Johnson et al., 2016; Chang et al., 2021)
- Prevalence of sleep apnea by gender, age, and race (Spilsbury et al., 2015; Ratz et al., 2018)
- *Siesta* and *inemuri* as cultural examples of napping (Abrams, 2017; Egan et al., 2017)
- Consistency in patterns of happiness across cultures (Golder & Macy, 2011)
- Use of meditation in Eastern religions
- Increase in the use of meditation by women (Laughlin, 2018; Clarke et al., 2018; Priyanka, 2021)
- Examples of people from Sioux, Aztec, and Hasidic Jewish cultures seeking to alter their states of consciousness (Bartocci, 2004; Ember & Carolus, 2017; Greene, 2020)
- Rates of binge drinking by gender and age (Holzhauer et al., 2017; Wilsnack et al., 2018; Esser et al., 2021; Centers for Disease Control and Prevention, 2021)
- Cultural and ethnic differences in alcohol consumption and physical reactions to alcohol (McCabe et al., 2019; Harris et al., 2021)
- Pronounced rate of opioid overdose deaths among Black individuals as a result of systemic challenges in health care, employment, and other societal impediments (Kamp & Wernau, 2021; Larochelle et al., 2021)
- Use of marijuana by age (Johnston et al., 2016; Miech et al., 2021)
- Impact of heavy marijuana use on testosterone production and sperm count (Rossato et al., 2008)

Chapter 5: Learning

- Racism sustained through classical conditioning (Dang et al., 2015)
- Different cultures' preferences for teaching styles and how those approaches affect how people learn (Sternberg, 2011; Rogoff et al, 2017)
- Cultural differences in relational and analytical learning styles (Adams et al., 2007; Armstrong et al., 2021; Adams, 2022)
- Forced immigration and academic success (Ogbu, 2003; Foster, 2005; Klinger et al., 2018)

Chapter 6: Memory

- Relationship between implicit memory and prejudice (Enge et al., 2015; Lucas et al., 2019; O'Shea et al., 2020)
- Other-race effect phenomenon in which people have more difficulty recognizing and recalling faces of people of other races than people of their own race (Yaros et al., 2019; Marsh, 2021; McKone et al., 2021)
- Classic research on schemas showing the power of racial prejudice to influence the reliability of memory (Allport & Postman, 1958; Brigard et al., 2017; Pelletier & Drozda-Senkowska, 2020)
- Characteristics of an accused person such as race, age, and accents, and their influence on eyewitness memories (Maeder & Ewanation, 2018; Cantone et al., 2019)
- Age and influences to the susceptibility of memories (Wright et al., 2015; Saywitz et al., 2019; Perez et al., 2022)
- Early research suggesting preliterate cultures had strong motivation for memory recall (Daftary & Meri, 2002; Berntsen & Rubin, 2004)
- Examples of feats of memory in poetry singers in the Balkans and among Hebrew scholars (Strathern & Stewart, 2003; Rubin et al., 2007; Seamon et al., 2010; Song et al., 2019)
- Similarities of basic memory processes across cultures
- Cultural differences in framing of information, learning, and recall strategies (Mack, 2003; Wang & Conway, 2006; Rubin et al., 2007; Goyal et al., 2019; Gutchess & Boduroglu, 2019; Gutchess et al., 2021)
- Foreign language recall as examples of proactive interference and retroactive interference
- Rates of Alzheimer's disease among non-Hispanic Black and Hispanic Americans (Alzheimer's Association, 2022)
- Use of the keyword technique to remember words in foreign languages (Miyatsu & McDaniel, 2019; Al-Faris & Jasmin, 2021)

Chapter 7: Thinking, Language, and Intelligence

- High agreement within cultures about prototypes (Rosch & Mervis, 1975)
- Prototype examples in Eastern and Western cultures
- Ability of concepts and prototypes to perpetuate racial prejudice (Bastart et al., 2021)
- Annual causes of children's death by age (Leonhardt, 2021)
- Extension of the illusion of explanatory depth to political beliefs and attitudes (Fernbach et al., 2013; Vitriol & Marsh, 2018; Gaviria & Corredor, 2021)

- Vietnamese legend of monks guarding three towers and 64 rings and the Tower of Hanoi puzzle presented as examples of problem solving
- Ability of people in collectivist cultures to solve problems involving interdependence and connection (Leung & Chiu, 2010; Wen et al., 2013; Arieli & Sagiv, 2018; Sagiv & Schwartz, 2022)
- Proficiency of people in individualist cultures in solving problems involving autonomy (Leung & Chiu, 2010; Wen et al., 2013; Arieli & Sagiv, 2018; Sagiv & Schwartz, 2022)
- Gender stereotypes around creativity and their association to masculine traits (Proudfoot & Fath, 2021; Taylor & Barbot, 2021; Trapido, 2022)
- Changes in creativity over the lifespan (Gopnik et al., 2015; Gopnik & Griffiths, 2017; Hui et al., 2019)
- Identification of 869 phonemes among all world languages (Redford, 2017; Shinohara & Iverson, 2021)
- Differences in phonemes as a reason learning other languages is difficult (Redford, 2017; Shinohara & Iverson, 2021)
- Babbling in infants who are unable to hear and are exposed to sign language (Shehata-Dieler et al., 2013; Elmlinger et al., 2019; Persson et al., 2021)
- Critical periods for learning a second language (Shafer & Garrido-Nag, 2007; Choubsaz & Gheitury, 2017; Hartshorne et al., 2018)
- Vocabulary of Inuit people as an example of the linguistic-relativity hypothesis (Tsukasaki & Ishii, 2004; Stam, 2015; Bohnemeyer, 2020)
- Russian, Icelandic, Kuuk Thaayorre, and Piraha language differences (Boroditsky, 2010; Fuhrman et al., 2011)
- Research on the relationship between health and language (Llabre, 2021)
- Hispanic paradox (Valencia et al., 2021; Llabre, 2021)
- Relationship between bilingualism and executive functioning and cognitive flexibility (Christoffels et al., 2015; Hartanto & Yang, 2019; Hartanto et al., 2019; Nichols et al., 2020; Lowe et al., 2021; Paap, 2021)
- Physical changes to the brain in bilingual speakers (Legault et al., 2019; Voits et al., 2022)
- Statistics on the numbers of nonnative English speakers in the United States and prevalence of people in the United States who speak a language other than English at home (Shin & Kominski, 2010; Federal Interagency Forum on Child and Family Statistics, 2019; Zeigler & Camarota, 2019)
- Effectiveness of bilingual and immersion educational programs (Wildavsky, 2000; Grivet et al., 2021)
- Psychological impact of biculturalism (Benet-Martínez et al., 2006; Tadmor, 2007; Schwartz et al., 2019; MacDonald, 2022)

- Navigation techniques used by Marshall Island sailors as demonstration of intelligence (Tingley, 2016)
- Cultural differences in defining intelligence (Crowne, 2013; Blackwell et al., 2015; Chao et al., 2017)
- Declines in fluid intelligence over the lifespan (Ackerman, 2011; Pezoulas et al., 2017; Taylor & Bisson, 2020)
- Political controversy around emotional intelligence (Strauss, 2021; Goldstein, 2022)
- Critique of adaptive testing suggesting it may discriminate against lower socioeconomic test takers and increase the digital divide (Levine, 2011; Nisbett, 2020; O'Connell & Marks, 2021)
- Statistics on prevalence of intellectual disabilities (Patrick et al., 2021)
- Education for All Handicapped Children Act and promotion of mainstreaming (Reiner, 2018; De Bruin, 2019)
- Success of intellectually gifted individuals (Sternberg et al., 2011; Strenze, 2015; Bucaille et al., 2021)
- City and rural backgrounds as examples of environmental determinants of intelligence
- Racial and cultural differences in intelligence test outcomes and bias in standardized testing (Suzuki et al., 2011; Loehlin et al., 2015; Rezai-Rashti & Lingard, 2021)
- Challenges in developing culture-fair IQ tests (Fagan & Holland, 2009; Rizzi & Posthuma, 2013; Hagmann-von Arx et al, 2018)
- Role of systemic racism in traditional IQ testing (Nisbett, 2020; O'Connell & Marks, 2021)
- Discussion of the validity of genetic causes in differences between races in IQ scores (Tosto et al., 2017; Toto et al., 2019; Quinn et al., 2022)

Chapter 8: Motivation and Emotion

- Discussion of an ironman athlete with down syndrome (Streeter, 2020; Chan, 2021)
- Variety in the ideal body image across cultures (Franko & Roehrig, 2011; Lin et al., 2015)
- Discussion of how cultural influences and individual habits play important roles in determining when, what, and how much we eat (Leeman et al., 2011; Gu et al., 2017; Lincoln & Nguyen, 2022)
- Connection between eating behavior and systemic racism, including chronic stress from racism and unequal access to healthcare (Aaron & Stanford, 2021; Mackey et al., 2022)
- Socioeconomic factors and access to affordable, healthy, and nutritious foods (Aaron & Stanford, 2021; Mackey et al., 2022)
- Eating disorders and age (National Eating Disorders Association, 2019)
- Prevalence of eating disorders by gender (Striegel-Moore & Bulik, 2007; Arcelus et al., 2011)

- Prevalence of eating disorders in developed and Westernized countries (Milos et al., 2017; Saul et al., 2022)

- Differences in male and female sex drives (Baumeister & Stillman, 2006; Leiblum & Chivers, 2007; Carvalho & Nobre, 2011; Meston & Stanton, 2019; Lan et al., 2021)

- Gender differences in the frequency of masturbation and changes over the lifespan (Oliver & Hyde, 1993; Pinkerton et al., 2002; Das, Parish, & Laumann, 2009; Cooper & Klein, 2018; Barrett & Burgess, 2020)

- Definition of heterosexuality, homosexuality, and bisexuality and statistics on the percentage of males and females engaging in gay or lesbian experiences (Gates, 2017; Newport, 2018; McCarthy, 2019)

- Double standard for women regarding sex outside of marriage (Lyons et al., 2011; Penhollow et al., 2017; Guo, 2019)

- Changes in the number of women having sex outside of marriage over the past 50 years (Horowitz et al., 2019; Manning, 2020)

- Increase in the incidence of premarital sexual intercourse among men (Guttmacher Institute, 2012; Lindberg et al., 2019)

- Generational attitudes toward sex outside of marriage (Horowitz et al., 2019)

- Views toward sex outside of marriage by culture (Singh et al., 2000; Majumdar, 2018)

- Rates of sexual activity by age (Ingraham, 2019; NORC, 2021)

- Prevalence of homosexuality and bisexuality (Gates, 2017; Newport, 2018; McCarthy, 2019)

- Kinsey scale of sexual behavior (Kinsey et al., 1948)

- Biological and genetic factors influencing sexual orientation (Gooren, 2006; LeVay, 2011; Servick, 2014; Burri et al., 2015; Sanders et al., 2021; Reardon, 2021)

- Prejudice and discrimination faced by lesbian, gay, and bisexual people (Moody et al., 2018; Goldhammer et al., 2019; Guz et al., 2021)

- Definition of transgender and gender fluid

- Prevalence of transgender people in the United States (Bazelon, 2022; Ghorayshi, 2022)

- Gender confirmation surgery (Lobato, Koff, & Manenti, 2006; Richards, 2011; Gorton & Erickson-Schroth, 2017)

- Politics surrounding transgender issues (Turban et al., 2021; Ghorayshi, 2022)

- Transgender restroom discussion (Steinmetz, 2015; Callahan & Zukowski, 2019)

- Definition of intersex (Roen, 2019; Monro et al., 2021)

- Gender and time spent with friends (Johnson, 2004; Semykina & Linz, 2007; Hofer et al., 2017)

- Gender differences in the display of need for power (Schultheiss & Schiepe-Tiska, 2013; Sibunruang et al., 2015; Hofer & Busch, 2019)

- Differences in descriptions of emotions across cultures including descriptions of s*chadenfreude, hagaii,* and *musu* (Dasborough & Harvey, 2017; Lange & Boecker, 2019; Nia & Otto, 2021)

- Racial bias in artificial intelligence and unconscious biases encoded into software (Rhue, 2019; Schwemmer et al., 2020)

- Six basic universal emotions across cultures (Ekman, 2007)

- Research on an isolated community of people in New Guinea that demonstrated a universal ability to identify basic emotions (Ekman, 1972; Ekman, 1994b; Matsumoto, 2002)

- Facial-affect program as an explanation for why people across cultures express emotions similarly (Kendler et al., 2008; Krumhuber & Scherer, 2011; Fernández-Sotos et al., 2021)

- Heterogeneity in facial expressions among the Hadza people of Tanzania (Barrett et al., 2019; Gendron et al., 2020; Barrett, 2021)

Chapter 9: Development

- Genetic differences of males and females

- Prevalence of sickle cell disease among Black or African American babies (Wills, 2013; Pecker & Lanzkron, 2021)

- Tay-Sachs disease in Jews of Eastern European ancestry (McPartland, 2016; Zhang et al., 2019; Flotte et al., 2022)

- Male and female differences in height and weight over the lifespan (National Center for Health Statistics, 2000)

- Differences in the ways in which mothers and fathers interact with their children (Bureau et al., 2017; Lin et al., 2019; Amodia-Bidakowska et al., 2020)

- Cultural influences on children's styles of play (Drewes, 2005; Rentzou et al., 2019; Hughes, 2021)

- Child-rearing styles in the US versus Japan (Jones, 2007; Pinquart & Kauser, 2017)

- Adjustment and achievement among children with immigrant parents (Organization for Economic Cooperation and Development, 2018; Suárez-Orozco & Suárez-Orozco, 2018)

- Critique of Erik Erikson's stages of psychosocial development relating to greater emphasis on male development than female

- Difficulty of reaching the formal operational stage in cultures less technically oriented than Western societies (Keating & Clark, 1980; Super, 1980; Genovese, 2006)

- Role of culture in Vygotsky's theory of cognitive development (Vygotsky, 1926/1997; Vasileva & Balyasnikova, 2019; Erbil, 2020)

- Ethnic and cultural diversity of adolescents as a group (Frey, 2018)

- Impact of early and late maturation for boys and girls (Mensah et al., 2013; Natsuaki et al., 2015; Weir, 2016; Park et al., 2017; Sadeh et al., 2019; Copeland et al., 2019)
- Cross-cultural research and the difficulty of generalizing Kohlberg's theory of moral development (Stey et al., 2013; Buon et al., 2017; Mathes, 2019)
- Gender differences in views toward moral behavior (Gilligan, 1996; Walker & Frimer, 2009; Capraro & Sippel, 2017; Moheghi et al., 2020)
- Carol Gilligan's morality of caring for women (Gilliganb, 1996)
- Outsized impact of screen time on mental health problems for girls (Twenge et al., 2022)
- The role of male- and female-oriented concepts in the development of identity (Gilligan, 2004)
- Cultural differences when children leave their parents' homes
- Gender differences in rates of death by suicide and in suicide attempts (Yildiz et al., 2019; Centers for Disease Control and Prevention, 2022)
- Statistics on race and suicide rates and risk of suicide (Ramchand et al., 2021; Centers for Disease Control and Prevention, 2022)
- Increased risk of suicide for lesbian, gay, bisexual, and transgender teens (Centers for Disease Control and Prevention, 2022)
- Cultural rites of passage into adulthood (Selsky, 1997; Magida, 2006; Forth, 2018; Wiseman, 2019)
- Male bias in occurrence of coming-of-age ceremonies
- Relationship between cultural acceptance of old age and the level of difficulty women experience with menopause (Beyene et al., 2007; Espinola et al., 2017; Bullivant Ngati Pikiao et al., 2021)
- Gender differences in aging during emerging and middle adulthood (Jackson et al., 2009; Kuosmanen et al., 2016)
- Divorce-rate acceleration across the globe ((Park & Raymo, 2013; Olson & DeFrain, 2014; Luscomb, 2018; Zahl-Olsen et al., 2019; McGinty, 2019)
- Prevalence of single-parent families in the United States by race and ethnicity (Sarsour et al., 2011; U.S. Bureau of the Census, 2022)
- Consistency of data across racial and ethnic groups that shows the likelihood that a single-family household is led by the mother versus a father (Sarsour et al., 2011; U.S. Bureau of the Census, 2022)
- Rates of employment for women with children (U.S. Bureau of Labor Statistics, 2022)
- Traditional gender roles in marriages (Damaske, 2011; Hwang et al., 2019)
- Division of household labor in gay and lesbian relationships (Miller, 2018)

- Women's "second shift" (Hochschild & Machung, 2012; Brailey & Slatton, 2019; Organisation for Economic Co-operation and Development, 2022)
- Cognitive functioning and age (Johnson & Deary, 2011; Tse et al., 2019; Mulas et al., 2021)
- Memory loss in older adults in cultures where older adults are held in high esteem (Dixon et al., 2007; Pinal et al., 2015)
- Impact of a person's sex and age on how they respond to death (Clark & Kaufer, 2018; Corr, 2020; Tyrrell et al., 2021)

Chapter 10: Personality

- Gender differences in male and female development according to Freud's theory of psychosocial development
- Critique of Freudian theories for viewing women as inferior to men and for a lack of diversity in his research population (Grünbaum, 2015; Shapira-Berman, 2019)
- Examples of mother, female, and male archetypes (Potash, 2015; Vaughn Becker & Neuberg, 2019; Roesler & Ulyet, 2021)
- Karen Horney as the first feminist psychologist (Horney, 1937; Coolidge et al., 2011; Forsythe, 2019)
- Importance of cultural factors in determination of personality (Jones, 2006; Horney, 2000)
- Consistency of the Big Five personality traits across cultures (Saucier & Srivastava, 2015; Bouvard & Roulin, 2017; Hall et al., 2019; John, 2021)
- Influence of cultural factors on the development of self-esteem (Cheng & Kwan, 2008; Chin, 2015)
- Controversies around the use of race and ethnicity to create test norms (Pedraza & Mungas, 2008; Nettles, 2019; Payne & Hannay, 2021)
- Racial differences in test results for the General Aptitude Test Battery (Galef, 2001; Starr, 2022)
- Use of race-based norming in the evaluation of concussions and dementia claims of Black athletes in the National Football League (Fleming, 2000; Possin et al., 2021)

Chapter 11: Health Psychology: Stress, Coping, and Well-Being

- Veterans and posttraumatic stress disorder (U.S. Department of Veterans Affairs, 2021; Sokol et al., 2021; Mohatt et al., 2022)
- Rates of suicide for military veterans versus nonveterans (U.S. Department of Veterans Affairs, 2021; Sokol et al., 2021; Mohatt et al., 2022)
- Type A behavior patterns and likelihood of developing coronary heart disease in men (Korotkov et al., 2011; Schneiderman et al., 2019; Heine & Weiss, 2021)

- Lack of research on Type A behaviors and coronary heart disease in women

- Increased likelihood of Black Americans to die from smoking-related illnesses (Minică, 2017; Kamimura et al., 2018; Erzurumluoglu et al., 2019)

- Racial disparities in quality of health care

- Trends in teenage smoking by education grade (Johnston et al. 2022)

- Racial health disparities in the US (Caratala & Maxwell, 2020; Nafiu et al., 2020; Centers for Disease Control and Prevention, 2022; Kelly, 2022; Sun et al., 2022)

- Relationship between socioeconomic status and health care outcomes (Population & Public Health, 2020; Kelly, 2022)

- Influence of racial, ethnic, and cultural discrimination on health outcomes including the biased belief that African Americans patients are less susceptible to pain (Hoffman et al., 2016; Kelly, 2022)

- Increased likelihood of people of color becoming infected with COVID and unequal treatments for physical and mental health issues for people of color during the COVID pandemic (Gollust et al., 2022; Thomeer et al., 2022; Willems et al., 2022)

- Economic cost of health disparities (Center for Medicare Advocacy, 2022)

- Systemic racism highlighted by the pandemic and increased number of hate crimes, including anti-Asian and anti-Semitic crimes, during the pandemic (American Psychological Association, 2020; Lee, 2022; Jones, 2022)

- Disproportionate rates of hospitalization and death from COVID for Black and Hispanic people (Aubrey, 2020; Moyer, 2021)

- Ways in which the pandemic intensified existing inequalities such as access to technology (Atske & Perrin, 2021).

- Disproportionate rates of stress for Hispanic, Black, and Asian adults during the pandemic (American Psychological Association, 2021)

- Gender differences in the use of patient-centered communications (Bertakis et al., 2009; Shin et al., 2015)

- Difficulties in providing medical advice to patients whose native language is not English (Al Shamsi et al., 2020)

- Cultural values and expectations contribution to communication barriers between patients and physicians (Brooks et al., 2019)

- Happiness, gender, and race (Cummings, 2019; Eternod, 2021)

- Happiness and economic prosperity (Whillans et al., 2017; Whillians & Dunn, 2019; Killingsworth, 2021; Tauseef, 2022)

Chapter 12: Psychological Disorders

- The New Testament, the Koran, the Talmud, and the Book of Mormon as sources of societal ideals

- Sociocultural perspective's assumption that society and culture shape abnormal behavior

- Higher levels of diagnoses of schizophrenia spectrum disorder among members of less affluent socioeconomic groups (Ridley et al., 2020)

- Racial disparity in involuntary hospitalization (Ridley et al., 2020)

- Increased likelihood of people in lower income brackets to suffer from depression or anxiety (Treatment Advocacy Center, 2016; Novasky & Rosales, 2020)

- Stigma of a gender dysphoria label (Kamens, 2011; Kleinplatz et al., 2013)

- Increased likelihood of women to experience major depression and discussion of possible environmental and biological reasons (Sarubin et al., 2017; Ojagbemi et al., 2018; Santomauro et al., 2021)

- High proportion of people with antisocial personalities coming from lower socioeconomic groups (Chen et al., 2011; Singh, 2022)

- Depression, anxiety, and behavioral disorders by age (Centers for Disease Control and Prevention, 2019; U.S. Department of Health and Human Services, 2019)

- Prevalence of psychological and substance-use disorders in people across the globe (Ritchie & Roser 2018)

- Effect of economic disparities on psychological treatment (Jacob et al., 2007; Wang et al., 2007; Scott et al., 2018)

- Surveys showing the varying incidence of major depression from culture to culture (Arifin et al., 2018; De Los Reyes et al., 2019)

- DSM-5-TR as a reflection of Western culture in the early years of the 21st century

- Relationship between rates of psychological disturbance across the world and the rates of gun violence (Budenz et al., 2018; Leander et al., 2019; Yelderman et al., 2019)

- Role of culture in determining what behavior should be labeled "abnormal" (Jacob, 2014; Allen & Becker, 2019; Langa & Gone, 2020)

- Cultural factors influencing specific symptoms of schizophrenia spectrum disorder (Watters, 2010; Munro et al., 2017; Fadus et al., 2019)

- Disorders unique to specific cultures (Cohen et al., 1999; Adams & Dzokoto, 2007; Ebigbo et al., 2015; Ustun, 2022)

- Differences between explanations for psychological disorders in different cultures (Lee et al., 2007; Watters, 2010; McRobbie, 2018)

Chapter 13: Treatment of Psychological Disorders

- Peace, shanti, and shalom as phrases repeated when trying to achieve a state of relaxation
- Spiritual component of Alcoholics Anonymous programs (Dodes, 2015; Glaser, 2015; Kelly et al., 2020)
- Importance of taking environmental and cultural backgrounds into account during treatment for psychological disorders (Pottick et al., 2007; Hillier, 2018; Ameen & Kahn, 2020)
- Deinstitutionalization proponents' goal to ensure proper treatment for patients while maintaining their civil rights (Pow et al., 2015; Hudson, 2019; Brown, 2022)
- Lack of adequate mental healthcare as a worldwide problem (Thornicroft et al., 2017; Keynejad et al., 2021; Singla, 2021)
- Percentage of the population in low-, middle-, and higher-income countries that receive treatment for major depression (Thornicroft et al., 2017; Keynejad et al., 2021; Singla, 2021)
- Cultural stigma as one reason why people are discouraged from seeking mental health treatment (Lu et al., 2021; Wijeratne et al., 2021)
- Lack of well-trained providers in poverty-stricken areas (Lu et al., 2021; Wijeratne et al., 2021)

Chapter 14: Social Psychology

- Likelihood of being persuaded by people with whom we share a personal or social identity (Ooms et al., 2019; Eberhardt, 2022; Hastall et al., 2022)
- Consistency of the formation of first impressions across cultures (Pretsch et al., 2013; Murphy et al., 2019; Murphy & Hall, 2021; Hester et al., 2021)
- Assumed-similarity bias discounting the diversity of people in the world (Kouros & Papp, 2019; Carson & Kouros, 2022)
- Prevalence of the fundamental attribution error in Western cultures (Flick & Schweitzer, 2021)
- Nazi officer participation in the Holocaust as an example of obedience to authority
- Concepts of stereotype, prejudice, and discrimination
- Discussion and examples of racism, modern racism, the self-fulfilling prophecy, and stereotype vulnerability (Pearson et al., 2007; Pager & Shepherd, 2008; Blanton et al., 2015; Leskinen et al., 2015; Tappin et al., 2017; Peters et al., 2019; Jeffries & Reed, 2021; Waite, 2021; Yu & Hyun, 2021)
- Psychological toll of discrimination (Ozier et al., 2019; Torres et al., 2022)
- Behavior of parents, other adults, and peers shaping children's feelings about members of various groups (Quinn et al., 2018; Matsuda et al., 2020; Waxman, 2021)
- Overt and covert discrimination (Ozier et al., 2019; Ozturk & Berber, 2022)

- Transmission of stereotypes through media (Scharrer & Ramasubramanian, 2015; Jin et al., 2019; Ash et al., 2022)
- Social identity theory and slogans such as "gay pride" and "Black is beautiful" (Hogg, 2006; Kahn et al., 2017; Edwards et al., 2019; Steffens et al., 2021)
- Ingroup and outgroup prejudice (Tajfel & Turner, 2004; Ratner et al., 2014; Berry et al., 2021; Kawakami et al., 2022)
- Social neuroscience focus on understanding prejudice (Todorov et al., 2011; Kasemsap, 2017; Kavaliers et al., 2019; Ford & Young, 2021)
- Research on changes in the amygdala that suggest culturally learned societal messages about race (Lieberman, 2007; Nelson, 2013; Singh et al., 2022)
- Impact of discrimination on functional connectivity (Han et al., 2021)
- Perpetuation of race-based health disparities through discrimination (Geugies et al., 2019)
- Implicit Association Test as a measure of prejudice (Blanton et al., 2015; Roberts et al., 2017; McConnell & Rydell, 2019; Schimmack, 2021)
- Clear implicit biases revealed through IAT test results (Westgate et al., 2015; Axt et al., 2021; Hong et al., 2022)
- Changes in implicit bias since 2007 related to sexuality and race (Charlesworth & Banaji, 2019)
- Strategies psychologists have developed to reduce prejudice and discrimination (Zhao et al., 2019; Cook, 2021; Mullangi & Jagsi, 2019; Naidoo et al., 2021; White et al., 2021; Kalla et al., 2021; Lee et al., 2022;; Petzel & Casad, 2022; Simms et al., 2023)
- Gender differences in the characteristics men and women value in friendships and in mates (Sprecher & Regan, 2002; Williams et al., 2022)
- Likelihood of heterosexual and same-sex couples meeting online (Rosenfeld & Thomas, 2012; Rosenfeld et al., 2019)
- Definition and impact of microaggressions over the long term (Williams, 2019; Harmon, 2020; Abrams, 2021; Smith & Griffiths, 2022)
- Increasing opportunities to interact with people who are different from you racially, ethnically, and culturally due to technological advances
- Shifting demographics in the percentage of people who are of African, Latin American, Asian, and Arabic ancestry in the United States (Cohn & Caumont, 2016; Pappano, 2019; Velez & Jessup-Anger, 2022)
- Population trends suggesting the United States will not have any single racial or ethnic majority by 2055 (Cohn & Caumont, 2016; U.S. Census Bureau, 2017, 2019)
- Immigration statistics (Lazear, 2017)

- Discussion of Intersectionality (DeBlaere, Watsonk, & Langrehr, 2018; Mays & Ghavami, 2018)
- How the subtleties of language affect how people think about themselves and members of particular groups (Forson, 2018)
- Race as a social construction (Zuberi, Patterson, & Stewart, 2015; Gross & Weiss, 2018)
- Definition of race and ethnicity and their impact on our view of others and ourselves and our everyday behavior (Mannarini, Talò, & Rochira, 2017; Park et al., 2018)
- Psychological implications of use of gender neutral pronouns
- Difference between gender identity and sexual orientation
- Definition of culture and multiculturalism (Wan & Chiu, 2011; Han & Ma, 2015; Bornstein & Lansford, 2019)
- Transmission of culture from one generation to another in both spoken and written form (Wan & Chiu, 2011; Han & Ma, 2015; Bornstein & Lansford, 2019)
- Psychology's past focus on only universal principles of human behavior, thereby ignoring the role of culture and its current understanding of the consequences of culture (Triandis, 2011; Rosenblatt, 2013; Gercama & Jones, 2020)
- Collectivist and individualist cultures (Nguyen, Le, & Boles, 2010; Arpaci, Baloğlu, & Kesici, 2018)

- Relationship between cultural perceptions underlying academic success and scholastic motivation (Chen & Zhang, 2011; Fetvadjiev et al., 2018; Wu et al., 2018)
- Norms of equality and equity in individualist and collectivist cultures (Boarini, Laslier, & Robin, 2009; Okely, Weiss, & Gale, 2018)
- Interdependent and independent views of self in individualist and collectivist cultures (Markus & Kitayama, 2003, 2010; Levine et al., 2016; Andersen, 2017)
- Homicide rate for Black Americans (Lepore, 2009; Associated Press, 2011; Rosenfeld et al., 2017)
- Regional differences within cultures (Nisbett & Cohen, 1996; Anwar, Fry, & Grigaityté, 2018; Hornsveld et al, 2018)
- Views of aggression in different cultures (Brown, 1986; Bonta, 1997; Lambert, 1971; Dernbach & Marshall, 2001)
- Levels of aggression in males and females (Whiting, 1965; Segall, 1988; Bosson & Vandello, 2011; Slotboom, Hendriks, & Verbruggen, 2011; Bass et al., 2018; Aimé et al., 2018)
- Anti-immigrant rhetoric (Lazear, 2017)
- Statistical reality of the immigrant population in the US (López & Bialik, 2017; Houri & Sullivan, 2019; Radford, 2019)
- Benefits of increased intercultural interaction (Deutsch, 1994; Nowak et al., 2010; Adler & Aycan, 2018)

Mc Graw Hill connect®

A complete course platform

Connect enables you to build deeper connections with your students through cohesive digital content and tools, creating engaging learning experiences. We are committed to providing you with the right resources and tools to support all your students along their personal learning journeys.

65%
Less Time Grading

Laptop: Getty Images; Woman/dog: George Doyle/Getty Images

Every learner is unique

In Connect, instructors can assign an adaptive reading experience with SmartBook® 2.0. Rooted in advanced learning science principles, SmartBook 2.0 delivers each student a personalized experience, focusing students on their learning gaps, ensuring that the time they spend studying is time well spent. **mheducation.com/highered/connect/smartbook**

Study anytime, anywhere

Encourage your students to download the free ReadAnywhere® app so they can access their online eBook, SmartBook® 2.0, or Adaptive Learning Assignments when it's convenient, even when they're offline. And since the app automatically syncs with their Connect account, all of their work is available every time they open it. Find out more at **mheducation.com/readanywhere**

"I really liked this app— it made it easy to study when you don't have your textbook in front of you."

Jordan Cunningham, a student at *Eastern Washington University*

Effective tools for efficient studying

Connect is designed to help students be more productive with simple, flexible, intuitive tools that maximize study time and meet students' individual learning needs. Get learning that works for everyone with Connect.

Education for all

McGraw Hill works directly with Accessibility Services departments and faculty to meet the learning needs of all students. Please contact your Accessibility Services Office, and ask them to email **accessibility@mheducation.com**, or visit **mheducation.com/about/accessibility** for more information.

Affordable solutions, added value

Make technology work for you with LMS integration for single sign-on access, mobile access to the digital textbook, and reports to quickly show you how each of your students is doing. And with our Inclusive Access program, you can provide all these tools at the lowest available market price to your students. Ask your McGraw Hill representative for more information.

Solutions for your challenges

A product isn't a solution. Real solutions are affordable, reliable, and come with training and ongoing support when you need it and how you want it. Visit **supportateverystep.com** for videos and resources both you and your students can use throughout the term.

Updated and relevant content

Our new Evergreen delivery model provides the most current and relevant content for your course, hassle-free. Content, tools, and technology updates are delivered directly to your existing McGraw Hill Connect® course. Engage students and freshen up assignments with up-to-date coverage of select topics and assessments, all without having to switch editions or build a new course.

Preface

Students First

If I were to encapsulate my goals in writing *Essentials of Understanding Psychology*, as well as my teaching philosophy, this is what I would say: **Students First**.

I believe that an effective introduction to a discipline must be oriented to students: informing them, engaging them, and exciting them about the field and helping them connect it to their world. It needs to embody the principles of contemporary learning science and present the material in a way that draws students into the field and stimulates their thinking. *Essentials of Understanding Psychology*, with its focus on **Students First**, seeks to promote success by engaging students' attention and informing them about the field, which results in students deeply learning the course content and–equally important to me–becoming excited about the field of psychology.

To achieve my **Students First** goals, *Essentials of Understanding Psychology*, includes a rich array of features, described below.

MODULAR ORGANIZATION

Each chapter of *Essentials of Understanding Psychology* is divided into three to five manageable, self-contained sections, called modules, that include learning outcomes and assessment opportunities. Thus, rather than facing a long and potentially daunting chapter, students encounter material that has been organized into manageable portions, which psychological research has found is the optimal way to learn.

CONNECT: A PERSONALIZED EXPERIENCE THAT LEADS TO IMPROVED LEARNING AND RESULTS

McGraw Hill's Connect® is a digital assignment and assessment platform that strengthens the link between faculty, students, and course work, helping everyone accomplish more in less time. Connect for *Essentials of Understanding Psychology* includes assignable and assessable videos, quizzes, exercises, and interactivities, all associated with learning objectives. Interactive assignments and videos allow students to experience and apply their understanding of psychology to the world with fun and stimulating activities.

SMARTBOOK™

SmartBook McGraw Hill's SmartBook helps students distinguish the concepts they know from the concepts they don't, while pinpointing the concepts they are about to forget. SmartBook's real-time reports help both students and instructors identify the concepts that require more attention, making study sessions and class time more efficient. SmartBook is optimized for mobile and tablet use and is accessible for students with disabilities. Content-wise, measurable and observable learning objectives help improve student outcomes. SmartBook personalizes learning to individual student needs, continually adapting to pinpoint knowledge gaps and focus learning on topics that need the most attention. Study time is more productive and, as a result, students are better prepared for class and coursework.

For instructors, SmartBook tracks student progress and provides insights that can guide teaching strategies. For students, SmartBook makes study more efficient by highlighting where in the chapter to focus, asking review questions, and pointing students to resources until they understand.

Connect's assignments help students contextualize what they've learned through application, so they can better understand the material and think critically. SmartBook will create a personalized study path customized to individual student needs. Finally, Connect reports deliver information regarding performance, study behavior, and effort, so instructors can quickly identify students who are having issues, or focus on material that the class hasn't mastered.

Evergreen Content and technology are ever-changing, and it is important for you to keep your course up to date with the latest information and assessments. That's why we want to deliver the most current and relevant content for your course, hassle-free.

Essentials of Understanding Psychology is moving to an Evergreen delivery model, which means it has content, tools, and technology that is updated and relevant, with updates delivered directly to your existing McGraw Hill Connect® course. Engage students and freshen up assignments with up-to-date coverage of select topics and assessments, all without having to switch releases or build a new course.

Powerful Reporting Whether a class is face-to-face, hybrid, or entirely online, McGraw Hill's Connect provides the tools needed to reduce the amount of time and energy that instructors must spend to administer their courses. Easy-to-use course management tools allow instructors to spend less time administering and more time teaching, while reports allow students to monitor their progress and optimize study time.

- The At-Risk Student Report provides instructors with one-click access to a dashboard that identifies students who are at risk of dropping out of the course due to low engagement levels.

- The Category Analysis Report details student performance relative to specific learning objectives and goals, including APA Learning Goals and Outcomes and levels of Bloom's taxonomy.

- The SmartBook Reports allow instructors and students to easily monitor progress and pinpoint areas of weakness, giving each student a personalized study plan to achieve success.

Building Student Critical Thinking Skills At the apply and analyze levels of Bloom's taxonomy, **Scientific Reasoning Activities** found in Connect offer in-depth arguments to sharpen students' critical thinking skills and prepare them to be more discerning consumers of psychology in their everyday lives. For each chapter, there are multiple sets of arguments accompanied by auto-graded assessments requiring students to think critically about claims presented as facts. These exercises can also be used in Connect as group activities or for discussion.

Power of Process guides students through the process of critical reading, analysis, and writing. Faculty can select or upload their own content, such as journal articles, and assign analysis strategies to gain insight into students' application of the scientific method. For students, Power of Process offers a guided visual approach to exercising critical thinking strategies to apply before, during, and after reading published research. Additionally, utilizing the relevant and engaging research articles built into Power of Process, students are supported in becoming critical consumers of research.

Power of Process for
PSYCHOLOGY

With the help of **Thematic Relevancy Modules for Introductory Psychology**, students will be able to see how psychology relates to their everyday lives. Developed by a diverse group of authors, the modules are found in Connect both as a standalone eBook and assignable in Smartbook. Each module supports an APA theme and complements the introductory psychology narrative. Thematic Relevancy Modules follow a consistent framework to support student learning. Each module opens with a real-world example, describes how psychology applies, provides easy-to read content related to the topic, and concludes with suggestions for how students can apply what they learned to their own lives. The modules also include links to relevant videos, and auto-graded assessment questions for each module are assignable within Connect. The Thematic Relevancy Modules are available in Connect at no additional cost.

PROMOTING STUDENT ACTIVE ENGAGEMENT

Students First also means activities that contribute to success in the course. This edition includes application-based activities and a writing assignment tool.

Application-Based Activities are highly interactive, automatically graded, online learn-by-doing exercises that provide students a safe space to apply their knowledge and problem-solving skills to real-world scenarios. Each scenario addresses key concepts and skills that students must use to work through and solve course-specific problems, resulting in improved critical thinking and development of relevant workplace skills. Topics include the following:

- Drugs and their effects on the brain
- Ethics in research
- Female sexual anatomy
- Gender identity
- Homologous structures
- Male sexual anatomy
- Observational learning
- Reinforcement and punishment

- Research design
- States of consciousness
- Stages of memory
- Stages of sleep
- Structures and functions of the brain
- Theories of emotion
- Theories of motivation
- Types of love
- Types of memory

Available within McGraw Hill Connect®, the **Writing Assignment** tool delivers a learning experience to help students improve written communication skills and conceptual understanding. Assign, monitor, grade, and provide feedback on writing more efficiently and effectively.

At the Remember and Understand levels of Bloom's taxonomy, **Concept Clips** help students break down key themes and difficult concepts in psychology. Using easy-to-understand analogies, visual cues, audio, and colorful animation, Concept Clips make psychology meaningful to everyday life. Topics include replication of research, social facilitation, and hypothesis and theories. New for this revision, Concept Clips feature a more modern visual style, updated scripts and assessment items, and enhanced accessibility.

Interactivities, assignable through Connect, engage students with content through experiential activities. New and updated activities include: Understanding Correlations, Heuristics, Gardner's Theory of Multiple Intelligences, Sexual Anatomy, Sexually Transmitted Infections, Personality Assessment Cognitive Dissonance, Explicit and Implicit Bias, and First Impressions and Attraction.

At the Understand and Apply levels of Bloom's taxonomy, **NewsFlash** exercises, powered by Connect, tie current news stories to key psychological principles and learning objectives. After interacting with a contemporary news story, students are assessed on their ability to make the connection between real life and research findings. NewsFlash is

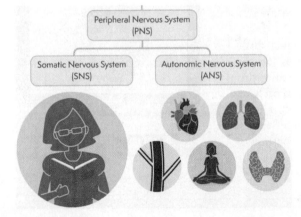

updated regularly and uses expert sources to cover a wide range of topics, including emotion, personality, stress, drugs, COVID-19, ableism, disability, social justice, stigma, bias, inclusion, gender, and LGBTQA+, among others. Through the connection of psychology to students' own lives, concepts become more relevant and understandable.

The McGraw Hill Immersive Brain Program provides opportunities for students to learn about the brain and its connection to behavior through interaction. Embedded within the *Essentials of Understanding Psychology* ebook, SmartBook, and ReadAnwhere App are three-dimensional, dynamic figures of the brain. Students have the opportunity to navigate within these dynamic figures to explore key structures and functions to support their understanding of key concepts. Sample figures include:

- Lobes of the Brain
- The Neuron
- The Adolescent Brain
- Alzheimer's Disease and the Brain
- Infant Attachment and the Brain

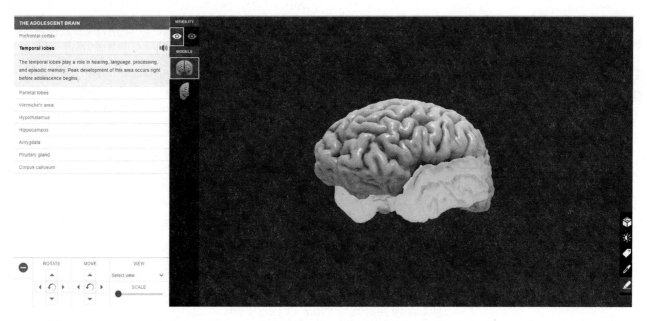

Additionally, Brain Lab Activities as assignable as Application-Based Activities through Connect. These activities, which incorporate the dynamic brain figures, allow student to practice with and apply their understanding of the brain's structures and functions. Sample Lab Activities include:

- Reaction Time
- Classical Conditioning
- Stereotypes and Prejudice
- Fight or Flight
- Memory Creation and Retention
- Morality

Introductory Psychology videos show psychological concepts in action. New to this release are: Neuroscience of Language, Neuroscience of ADHD, Neuroscience of Anxiety, Treating ADHD with Therapy, Neuroscience of Love, History of Psychology, The, Naturalistic Observation in Psychology, The Usefulness of Psychological Research, The Birth of Epigenetics: the Agouti Mouse Study, Conformity–Are You Like a 3 or 7 Year Old?

Psychology at Work videos, assignable and assessable within McGraw Hill Connect™, highlight nine careers in which knowledge of psychology is beneficial in the workplace. Each video introduces a person at work who specifies how knowledge gained from taking introductory psychology in college is applied to the work environment.

Student Tools: Mastering the Material

Student success in psychology means mastering the material at a deep level. These are some additional tools embedded in *Essentials of Understanding Psychology* that help students maximize their performance:

> **! Study Alert**
> Differentiate the stages of sleep (stage 1, stage 2, stage 3, and REM sleep), which produce different brain-wave patterns.

STUDY ALERTS

Throughout, marginal notes point out important and difficult concepts and topics. These Study Alerts offer suggestions for learning the material effectively and for studying for tests.

APPLYING PSYCHOLOGY IN THE 21ST CENTURY

These features—all new in this edition—highlight the relevance of psychology by presenting current and potential applications of psychological theory and research findings to real-world problems. For example, one of the *Applying Psychology in the 21st Century* features focuses on the effects isolation had on people's lives during the COVID-19 pandemic.

APPLYING PSYCHOLOGY IN THE 21ST CENTURY

STRESS, CORONAVIRUS, AND YOUNG AMERICANS' MENTAL HEALTH

Are you feeling stressed out, perhaps more than some of the adults around you seem to feel? How did the coronavirus pandemic affect your level of stress? Significantly? If so, you're not alone. Many others of the current generation of college students report feeling the same way, and the stress took a toll on their mental health.

Even before the pandemic, a report by the **American Psychological Association (2018)** detailed the findings of an online survey of over 3,500 adults (plus an additional 300 teens between 15 and 17 years old) investigating their perceived stress levels and mental health. Sixty-four percent of adults reported feeling stressed over money and work. Among Americans aged 15 to 21 (known as Generation Z), 30% reported feeling significantly stressed by housing insecurity, while fully a third were stressed by personal debt. Alarmingly, 28% reported hunger or food insecurity as ongoing sources of stress in their lives.

FROM THE PERSPECTIVE OF...

Every chapter includes questions to help students connect psychological concepts with career realities. Called *From the Perspective of...*, this feature helps students understand how psychology relates to various career fields.

From the perspective of...

An Educator How might you use the findings in sleep research to maximize student learning?

Andersen Ross/Blend Images/Getty Images

EXPLORING DIVERSITY

In addition to substantial coverage of material relevant to diversity, including the images that accompany the text, every set of modules also includes at least one special section devoted to an aspect of racial, ethnic, gender, or cultural diversity. These sections highlight the ways in which psychology informs (and is informed by) issues relating to the increasing multiculturalism of our global society. For example, one *Exploring Diversity* section discusses the importance of choosing research participants who are representative of all humans.

# Exploring Diversity

Choosing Participants Who Represent *All* Humans

When Latané and Darley, both college professors, decided who would participate in their experiment, they turned to the people most easily available: college students. Using college students as participants has advantages as well as drawbacks. The big benefit is that because most research occurs in university settings, college students are readily available. Typically, they cost the researcher very little: They participate for either extra course credit or a relatively small payment.

The problem is that college students may not represent the general population adequately. In fact, undergraduate research participants are typically a special group of people: Relative to the general population, college students tend to be from **W**estern, **E**ducated, **I**ndustrialized, **R**ich, and **D**emocratic cultures. That description forms the acronym WEIRD, which led one researcher to apply the nickname to research participants (Schulz et al., 2018; Alper & Yilmaz, 2019; Kupferschmidt, 2019).

NEUROSCIENCE IN YOUR LIFE

This feature emphasizes the importance of neuroscientific research within the various subfields of the discipline and in students' lives. Representative brain scans, with both caption and textual explanation, illustrate significant neuroscientific findings that increasingly influence the field of psychology. For example, one *Neuroscience in Your Life* feature explores resilience and how it is reflected in the functioning of the brain.

NEUROSCIENCE IN YOUR LIFE: MENTAL HEALTH AND THE BRAIN AFTER COVID

Physical health and mental health are closely intertwined, partly because they both relate to brain health. COVID-19 gives a great example of these interrelationships. About 30% of COVID survivors have experienced depression, posttraumatic distress, and other psychological symptoms for weeks or even months after recovering from the virus. Neuroscience studies show how these symptoms are linked to the structure and function of the brain. One study of COVID survivors found that greater levels of depressive symptoms and distress 2–3 months after COVID were associated with smaller brain volumes and unhealthy white matter tracts (bundles of nerve fibers that connect parts of the brain) in regions linked to mood and anxiety disorders in other studies (Benedetti et al., 2021).

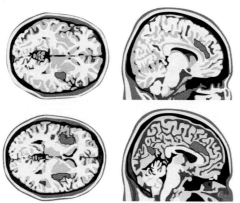

The brain regions shown in orange have been linked to depression, posttraumatic stress disorders, and other mental health conditions. In COVID survivors, higher symptoms of depression (top row) and distress (bottom row) were associated with smaller volumes in those brain regions.

Student Learning: How Key Content and Concepts Have Been Updated

Essentials of Understanding Psychology provides broad coverage of the field of psychology, including the theories, research, and applications that form the core of the discipline. Along with the traditional areas of psychology–neuroscience, sensation and perception, states of consciousness, learning, memory, cognition, human development, personality, psychological disorders and treatment, and social psychology–the applied topics of gender and sexuality and health psychology receive extensive attention.

The new release continues its commitment to extensive coverage of diversity and inclusion. A concluding module called "Diversity, Equity, Inclusion, and Culture" in the Social Psychology chapter addresses questions of how diversity affects individual behavior, how we observe and understand other people, and how our understandings (and misunderstandings) of our differences can lead to cooperation and/or conflict. Throughout the book, the examples and photos reflect the range of people and the settings in which they live, not only in the United States but across the world. Moreover, gender-neutral wording has been used throughout the entire text.

In addition, *Essentials of Understanding Psychology* contains a significant amount of new and updated features and content. Hundreds of new citations have been added, and most of them refer to articles and books published in the past 2 to 3 years. Moreover, a special effort has been made to include research that has been conducted by underrepresented researchers, as well as studies that include experimental participants who themselves are members of underrepresented groups.

The following list of new and revised topics and textual changes provides a good indication of the content's currency and *Student First* focus:

Chapter 1. Introduction

- Added a new Prologue and Epilogue on the psychological implications of the Maui wildfires
- Changed the *environmental psychology* term to *climate and environmental psychology,* and modified the definition to emphasize the work of psychologists on climate change issues
- Discussed the increasing focus on climate change and environment by psychologists
- Discussed the increased focus on diversity, equity, and inclusion by psychologists
- Discussed the increase in cross-disciplinary work by psychologists
- Discussed the role of counseling psychologists in helping with pandemic-related problems and current events such as gun violence
- Added a discussion of diversity science to the expanding boundaries of psychology's scope
- Defined and described diversity science
- Added new statistics on the number of psychologists
- Added a new section on issues of diversity in the field of psychology
- Added new statistics on racial composition in the field of psychology

- Added a discussion of the limitations experienced by female psychologists, including their access to publishing and grants
- Added a discussion of women's challenges exacerbated by the pandemic
- Added a discussion of the dominance of U.S. researchers and its drawbacks
- Added a new figure on workforce demographics and race/ethnicity
- Added a new figure on the top skills of psychology major graduates
- Added a reference to ancient Chinese precursors of psychological concepts
- Added Mamie Phipps Clark in the history of women in early years of psychology
- Added a new section on the history of psychology and people of color
- Added a description of prejudice and discrimination in early psychology
- Added the APA apology to people of color for the past racism of the field
- Added the APA pledge to aid in dismantling systemic racism and ending health disparities
- Added a new *Neuroscience in Your Life* feature on "The Brain in Space"
- Added a new figure on the physical changes to astronauts' brains after spaceflight

- Revised the *Applying Psychology in the 21st Century* feature to include modern societal problems including COVID-19, social media, terrorism, and climate change, among others
- Added an example of flawed surveys that underestimated support for Donald Trump before the 2016 presidential election
- Introduced and described ethnographic research, including its advantages and disadvantages
- Added a discussion of the Hispanic cultural practice of holding a *quinceañera* when a girl reaches the age of 15
- Changed the example of the difficulty of matching from gender to age, given the potential fluidity of gender
- Added material on the generality of bystander effect exemplified by studies using nonhumans
- Added further support for concerns about the replicability of findings in psychology
- Added coverage of the importance of gender, racial, and ethnic diversity in psychological research
- Discussed the use of placebos in the development of COVID-19 vaccines
- Revised the discussion on assessing whether research results are presented fairly

Chapter 2. Neuroscience and Behavior

- Added a new Prologue and Epilogue on person whose spinal cord was severed in an accident but whose condition improved with a computer chip implant
- Revised the section on mirror neurons, emphasizing the role of imitation and removing references to higher-order interpretation of others' behavior
- Updated the section on human diversity and the brain, including origins of differences
- Added research on women's brains, which are more interconnected than men's, perhaps leading to differences in multitasking capabilities
- Updated the description of Neuropixels research methodology
- Added material on the percentage of neuronal turnover due to neurogenesis
- Added material on the limitations of neuroscience studies that don't take race and ethnicity into account
- Discussed the production of dopamine and online addictions
- Discussed endorphin release and addiction to opioids and heroin
- Removed the designation of the pituitary gland as the "master" gland
- Added a new estimate of the number of synapses
- Added a new *Applying Psychology in the 21st Century* feature on mind uploading
- Added material on using brain-scanning techniques to identify the content of people's thoughts
- Added material on personality changes as side effects of brain implants
- Deleted the top-brain, bottom-brain distinction

Chapter 3. Sensation and Perception

- Added a new Prologue and Epilogue on a person who lost their sense of smell
- Added a new definition of chronic pain
- Added new statistics on the cost of chronic pain
- Added material on racial and ethnic disparities in the treatment of pain

- Clarified the definition of nondigital camera
- Clarified the description of depth perception and cultural differences
- Redrew Figure 8 for a more realistic image in terms of race
- Clarified the example of a batter's success in hitting a pitched ball
- Changed the wording of the sentence with every third letter missing
- Clarified the caption for the figure of zeros and eights
- Revised the number of discernable colors to 10 million
- Revised the scenario of a woman whose taste abilities were disrupted
- Added material on the sensitivity of the sense of smell in nonhumans
- Added material on the use of dogs to identify COVID cases in humans
- Discussed the failure of efforts to replicate extrasensory perception results
- Added a new *Applying Psychology in the 21st Century* feature on smells emitted by humans
- Added material on acupuncture as a means of pain relief
- Added material on similarities across cultures in the identification of star constellations

Chapter 4. States of Consciousness

- Added a new Prologue and Epilogue on the surgical treatment of addiction
- Added material comparing the experience of consciousness across cultures
- Added material on different brain wave patterns in different types of daydreaming
- Added material and a figure on racial differences and disparities in sleep quantity, including insomnia
- Added material on sleep difficulties during the pandemic worldwide
- Added material on the increase in nightmares related to the pandemic
- Added material on findings about more emotional dreams among those most affected by the pandemic
- Added evolutionary evidence for the importance of sleep found in organisms lacking a brain
- Added coverage of the association of long-term COVID and sleep disorders

- Added a reference to the use of *siesta* to label afternoon naps in Hispanic cultures (and adopted by English-speakers)
- Added material on the racial disparities that were exacerbated during the COVID pandemic
- Discussed the importance of not "chasing sleep"
- Added material on the link between daydreaming and creativity
- Added new statistics on the use of meditation, including the increase during the pandemic
- Added new statistics on opioid deaths, noting that this is the highest level ever recorded
- Added statistics on race disparities in opioid deaths
- Noted the role of COVID in the surging opioid epidemic
- Clarified the definition of binge drinking
- Added new statistics on per-capita alcohol drinking
- Discussed alternate states of consciousness in other cultures
- Added material on the increase in dreams about racial injustice following the George Floyd protests
- Added material on cultural explanations about the importance of sleep (e.g., Mayan worry dolls)
- Added material on the Japanese practice of *inemuri* related to napping
- Added material on the incidence of sleep apnea by sex and race
- Discussed sudden unexpected infant death (SUID)
- Added a new delineation of the four reasons why we sleep
- Added material on the percentage of emotion-laden words noted in a Brazilian dream study
- Added a new *Applying Psychology in the 21st Century* feature on advertisers inserting product placements using dream-induction techniques
- Added material on the combination of hypnosis and virtual reality to manage pain
- Added survey data on altered states of consciousness through trance states across cultures

- Added material on the Western practices that reflect a search for altered states of consciousness such as mediation, use of unprescribed drugs, and extreme exercise
- Added material on the racial differences in brain-wave patterns during sleep
- Added material on the use of LSD and other hallucinogens as treatment for psychological disorders
- Added material on personalized circadian medicine

Chapter 5. Learning

- Added a new Prologue and Epilogue on how reinforcement is used to promote good driving skills and save money
- Added a new *Applying Psychology in the 21st Century* feature on using dogs to identify people with the COVID-19 virus
- Added material on concerns around the extent and depth of conditioning of Little Albert
- Added material on how racism can be sustained by the classical conditioning processes
- Refined the discussion of shaping as exemplified by textbooks
- Refined the example of negative reinforcement relating to the application of ointment
- Corrected the name of Jason Bautista in the example of modeling of behavior
- Added a study of online encounters of groups with diverging viewpoints and the association with an increased likelihood of actual real-world aggression
- Refined the conclusions about the negative consequences of viewing violent video games

Chapter 6. Memory

- Added a new Prologue and Epilogue on a woman who experienced highly superior autobiographical memory (HSAM)
- Added an example of how the smell of sunscreen can evoke the memory of beach vacations
- Added a discussion of the other-race effect (ORE) and how it affects memories of people of other versus the same race

- Added a discussion of how the characteristics of an accused person such as race, age, and accent affect eyewitness memories
- Added a discussion of fake news and how it interacts with the recollection of information consistent with prior beliefs
- Added a discussion of false memories and COVID-19 vaccination information
- Added a new *Applying Psychology in the 21st Century* feature on creating and erasing false memories
- Included new Alzheimer's disease incidence figures
- Added information on racial differences in the incidence of Alzheimer's disease
- Included the ranking of Alzheimer's disease as a cause of death among U.S. adults
- Discussed false confessions as an example of false memories
- Added material on the value of forgetting
- Added a discussion of the accuracy of autobiographical memories related to high-impact events
- Added an example of the cross-cultural recollection of details and how it is affected by initial encoding of culturally salient information
- Added information on children's less proficient language skills as a source of memory deficiencies
- Discussed the tip-of-the-tongue phenomenon as only a partial failure of recall
- Discussed the inaccuracy of flashbulb memories
- Added the key term of *Wernicke-Korsakoff syndrome*
- Refined the description of claims that memory enhancers are effective in cases of memory impairment such as Alzheimer's disease

Chapter 7: Thinking, Language, and Intelligence

- Added a new Prologue and Epilogue on thought-reading using brain scanning
- Used the term *Inuit* rather than *Eskimo*
- Added material on cultural differences in prototypes

- Added an example of concepts and prototypes perpetuating discrimination
- Added material on the use of machine learning to spot patterns in data
- Added material on the availability heuristic and the COVID pandemic
- Added a new figure on the likelihood of children's death from common causes compared with COVID
- Added material on the illusion of explanatory depth
- Added Wordle as an example of an arrangement problem
- Added material on physicians' use of heuristics in determining infant delivery modality (vaginal versus cesarean)
- Added material on algorithmic bias in artificial intelligence
- Added clarity in naming for inducing structure problems
- Added material on collectivistic and individualistic cultures and problem solving
- Used COVID to demonstrate inaccurate evaluation of solutions and explain confirmation bias
- Added material on the acceptance of fake news caused by embrace of intuition rather than science
- Added material on the illusory truth effect in fake news evaluation
- Discussed cognitive immunization as a way to address fake news
- Introduced material on the Russian invasion of Ukraine to demonstrate cognitive immunization
- Discussed creativity as a quality driven by vision and curiosity
- Added a new *Neuroscience in Your Life* feature on comedic expertise and the brain
- Added a discussion of the lack of systematic gender differences in creativity and the continuing bias that associates creativity with stereotypic "male" traits
- Added material on creativity among people with autism spectrum syndrome
- Added a new *Applying Psychology in the 21st Century* feature on language hypothesis to explain cardiovascular health benefits of speaking Spanish

- Added new examples of the semantic features of words
- Added material on colony-specific communication greetings in naked mole-rats
- Added material on the critical period for second-language acquisition
- Additional material on distinguishing between human languages and gibberish
- Added material on executive function and bilingualism
- Added new statistics on the number of non-English speakers in the United States
- Added a new figure showing percentages of non-English speakers in the United States
- Added a new example of Gardner's spatial intelligence using architect Frank Gehry
- Added a new example of Gardner's bodily kinesthetic intelligence using basketball star LeBron James
- Added material on the loss of emotional intelligence during prolonged COVID-19 lockdowns
- Changed the reliability/validity example of SAT subtest to the math section
- Added new statistics on the number of people classified with an intellectual disability
- Discussed why *mental retardation* is an outmoded term that fosters stereotypes
- Introduced a new key term of *fetal alcohol spectrum disorder* to replace the old term of *fetal alcohol syndrome*
- Added new material on the incidence of fetal alcohol spectrum disorder
- Refined the discussion of racial differences in IQ
- Added the new *Exploring Diversity* section on developing a culture-fair IQ test
- Discussed cultural bias in testing
- Changed age of origin of intellectual disabilities to before age 22
- Added digital SAT and GRE General examples of computer-administered adaptive testing
- Refined the discussion of IQ, genetics, and the environment
- Linked criticism of the bell curve to factors associated with systemic racism

- Revised the epilogue and added new reflection questions

Chapter 8: Motivation and Emotion

- Added a new Prologue and Epilogue on a person with Down syndrome who completed a triathlon
- Refined the sensation-seeking questionnaire
- Added boredom as a reason for seeking stimulation
- Added material on the challenge and hindrance stressors affecting motivation in the workplace
- Added material on the predominance of hindrance stressors during the pandemic
- Clarified the requirement of meeting all prior sets of needs before moving to higher level needs according to Maslow
- Refined the critical thinking/review question on intrinsic and extrinsic motivation
- Added a new vignette on the relationship between eating and emotional needs
- Added new statistics on the prevalence of obesity
- Discussed changes in metabolism during the life span
- Added material on obesity and systemic racism
- Clarified the prevalence of anorexia in males
- Added new statistics on the prevalence of eating disorders
- Added material on the increase in the prevalence of eating disorders due to the pandemic
- Discussed social media as a cause of eating disorders
- Added material on TikTok algorithms and exposure to weight-loss videos
- Updated contact information to find eating disorder support
- Added techniques for losing weight, such as having a plan with clear objectives
- Updated the definition of masturbation
- Added material on pandemic-related increases in masturbation
- Added material on gender differences in masturbation
- Clarified the terminology for sex outside of marriage

- Clarified the double standard for sex outside of marriage
- Added statistics on the acceptability of cohabitation
- Added a new figure on attitudes toward sex outside of marriage
- Discussed cultural differences in attitudes toward sex outside of marriage
- Revised the description of sexual orientation
- Revised the definition of homosexuality
- Revised the definition of bisexuality
- Updated statistics on gay, lesbian, and bisexual populations
- Added material on hormonal exposure and sexuality
- Added material on gender fluidity
- Added statistics on the transgender population
- Discussed the increase in self-identification as transgender
- Discussed the politicization of transgender issues
- Discussed growth mindset and academic success
- Modernized the vignette about emotions associated with admission to college
- Added a new *Applying Psychology in the 21st Century* feature on artificial intelligence and emotion
- Added new a *Neuroscience in Your Life* feature on age and regulating emotions
- Added research on heterogeneity in the way facial expressions express emotion
- Added new epilogue reflection questions on motivation and emotion

Chapter 9: Development

- Added a new Prologue and Epilogue about an athlete in late adulthood
- Revised the list of characteristics most affected by heredity
- Added an example about Stephen Curry
- Added the term *sickle cell disease*
- Added new statistics on sickle cell anemia
- Added material on COVID-19 food supply chain disruptions in low- and middle-income countries

- Discussed neonatal abstinence syndrome
- Discussed the increase in neonatal addiction due to the opioid crisis
- Added material on the prevalence of fetal alcohol syndrome disorder
- Expanded the discussion of screen time guidelines
- Added statistics on child-care arrangements
- Added a new vignette reflecting adolescent anxieties
- Changed the age for when puberty begins in girls
- Added material on challenges associated with early and late maturation
- Added a new *Applying Psychology in the 21st Century* feature on the impact of screen time
- Discussed screen time recommendations that have been criticized for not taking into account the nature of the screen time
- Added data on boomerang children during COVID-19
- Added statistics on suicide prevalence
- Changed the terminology of "committing suicide" to "death by suicide"
- Added material on race, ethnicity, and suicide
- Added a new figure on suicide rates by race and ethnicity
- Added material on COVID-19 and increases in suicidal thoughts
- Added information on 988, the national suicide prevention hotline
- Added additional signs of a potential suicide
- Updated the statistics on single-parent households
- Added material on racial differences in the prevalence of single-parent households
- Updated statistics on mothers working outside of the home
- Added material on the division of household chores among gay and lesbian couples
- Revised the discussion of the second shift
- Added statistics on the prevalence of Alzheimer's disease
- Added a new *Neuroscience in Your Life* feature on how to be a SuperAger
- Added new epilogue reflection questions on development and aging

Chapter 10. Personality
- Added a new Prologue and Epilogue on imposter Anna Chapman
- Refined the language in Figure 3 on defense mechanisms
- Revised the example of the mother archetype of Mother Earth
- Added a new *Applying Psychology in the 21st Century* feature on the degree to which personality traits are apparent to others
- Added an example of online profiles curated on TikTok videos
- Added Gandhi as an example of humanistic virtuousness
- Added material on the discontinuance of race-based norming
- Added an example of Black NFL players and the evaluation of concussions
- Added questions regarding the scientific integrity of Eysenck's work

Chapter 11. Health Psychology: Stress, Coping, and Well-Being
- Added a new Prologue and Epilogue on one woman's reaction to the COVID pandemic
- Added new statistics on the incidence of PTSD in military veterans
- Added new statistics on the incidence of mass shootings
- Added new statistics on the number of killings due to mass shootings
- Added a new section on the coronavirus pandemic
- Added statistics on the number of deaths due to COVID worldwide and in the United States
- Added a discussion of the greater effects of negative versus positive life events
- Added a discussion of the treatment of PTSD with MDMA
- Added a discussion of the relationship between positive events and later well-being among people with depression
- Added a new section on mass shootings and gun violence
- Added material on stress and mass murders statistics
- Added statistics on the success of quitting smoking

- Added new vaping statistics
- Added a discussion of the efforts to ban Juul products
- Added a discussion of antismoking message fatigue
- Added a new *Exploring Diversity* section on health disparities
- Added a discussion of stress and the pandemic
- Added a discussion of COVID and mental health
- Added a new *Neuroscience in Your Life* feature on brain changes due to COVID
- Added a discussion of COVID and loneliness, social isolation, and social support
- Added a new *Applying Psychology in the 21st Century* feature on the value of social support from strangers
- Added a discussion of vaccine hesitancy
- Added a discussion of learning loss due to the pandemic
- Added a discussion of happiness as associated with improvements in health
- Added a discussion of telehealth
- Added a discussion indicating that happy people are not always happy
- Clarified the relationship between happiness and income level

Chapter 12. Psychological Disorders
- Added a new Prologue and Epilogue about a person experiencing hallucinations
- Added updates on sociocultural explanations of disorders
- Added data on the prevalence of mental illness among the homeless
- Added a discussion of the publication of the DSM-5-TR
- Added a discussion of links between income, depression, and anxiety
- Added a new *Applying Psychology in the 21st Century* feature on the rise in mental health issues in teenagers
- Added a discussion of trauma as a cause of borderline personality disorder
- Added a discussion of a new DSM disorder: prolonged grief disorder
- Added new statistics on the incidence of autism

- Added a nongendered explanation of anxiety as a learned response to stress
- Updated statistics on the financial cost of depression in terms of lost productivity
- Added new statistics on the prevalence of depression
- Added a new *Neuroscience in Your Life* feature on psychological disorders and the brain
- Removed the discussion of Asperger's syndrome
- Added a discussion of gender differences in the prevalence of autism
- Added directions to call 988 if experiencing thoughts of self-harm
- Added a discussion of mass murderers and psychological disturbance
- Revised the figures on the worldwide incidence of depression
- Addressed concerns raised about the Rosenhan study results
- Addressed the change in the incidence of depression
- Added a discussion of the rise in depression due to the COVID pandemic
- Added a discussion of postpartum depression
- Added new incidence figures for major depression in adolescents
- Added new incidence figures for ADHD
- Refined the definition of xenophobia
- Added a discussion of government panel recommendations on routine screening for depression and anxiety

Chapter 13. Treatment of Psychological Disorders

- Added a new Prologue and Epilogue on personalized deep brain stimulation treatment for depression
- Added statistics on the prevalence of seeking treatment
- Discussed questions around the scientific integrity of Eysenck's work
- Updated statistics on the use of antidepressant drugs
- Added a new *Applying Psychology in the 21st Century* feature on the

use of psychedelic drugs in treatment
- Discussed the effectiveness and popularity of online therapy postpandemic
- Discussed the difficulty of building rapport during online therapy
- Discussed the issue of licensing across state lines for therapists providing online therapy
- Discussed the future of online therapy
- Added a section on newer forms of brain stimulation
- Added a discussion of mental health treatment remaining out of reach for much of the world's population
- Discussed barriers to mental health treatment
- Updated statistics on the mental health status of homeless people
- Discussed the use of group therapy and psychedelic drugs
- Updated electroconvulsive treatment details
- Added a new learning objective relating to online therapy
- Added a new *Neuroscience in Your Life* feature on brain activity and treatment effectiveness

Chapter 14. Social Psychology

- Added a new Prologue and Epilogue on those who have stepped up to offer help during the war in Ukraine
- Added a new module on diversity, equity, inclusion, and culture
- Added new examples of influencers in social media, including those who seek to change attitudes
- Added a discussion on the importance of sharing social identity on persuasiveness
- Updated the "need for cognition" questionnaire
- Added an example of Donald Trump and the persistence of impressions
- Added a discussion of authority figures, personal stories, and persuasiveness related to COVID vaccine compliance
- Added a discussion of attitude change and reactance

- Added an example of door-in-the-face strategy related to blood donation requests
- Added a discussion of reasons for social media use
- Added a discussion of online gaming and friendships
- Added a discussion of increases in social media use during the pandemic
- Discussed cross-cultural findings on sex differences in mate preference
- Removed material on cross-cultural differences in the importance of love in marriage
- Added a discussion of microaggressions couched as compliments or questions
- Added a new *Applying Psychology in the 21st Century* feature on chemistry in relationships
- Added a new figure about meeting online for heterosexual couples
- Updated conclusions regarding the likelihood of meeting online for heterosexual couples
- Added data on the frequency of microaggressions in a sample of Black adolescents
- Updated the discussion of the Sandy Hook school shooting to one on the Uvalde school shooting
- Introduced the term *racism*
- Updated the statistics on violence in the United States
- Added a new section on the language of diversity
- Added new material on collectivism and individualism
- Added a new section on how people view themselves within a culture
- Added new material on the cultural aspect of violence
- Added new material on immigrants
- Added a new *Becoming an Informed Consumer of Psychology* feature on reducing war, promoting peace, and creating a just world

McGraw Hill Psychology APA Documentation Style Guide

- Updated based on the 7th edition of the *Publication of the American Psychological Association.*

Supporting Instructors with Technology

McGraw Hill offers additional technology tools for instructors to develop and tailor the course they want to teach. They include the following:

REMOTE PROCTORING

New remote proctoring and browser-locking capabilities are seamlessly integrated within Connect to offer more control over the integrity of online assessments. Instructors can enable security options that restrict browser activity, monitor student behavior, and verify the identity of each student. Instant and detailed reporting gives instructors an at-a-glance view of potential concerns, thereby avoiding personal bias and supporting evidence-based claims.

POLLING

Every learner has unique needs. Uncover where and when you're needed with the new Polling tool in McGraw Hill Connect®! Polling allows you to discover where students are in real time. Engage students and help them create connections with your course content while gaining valuable insight during lectures. Leverage polling data to deliver personalized instruction when and where it is needed most.

TAILOR YOUR COURSE

Easily rearrange chapters, combine material from other content sources, and quickly upload content you have written, such as your course syllabus or teaching notes, using McGraw Hill's **Create.** Find the content you need by searching through thousands of leading McGraw Hill textbooks. Arrange your book to fit your teaching style. Create even allows you to personalize your book's appearance by selecting the cover and adding your name, school, and course information. Order a Create book, and you will receive a complimentary print review copy in 3 to 5 business days or a complimentary electronic review copy via email in about an hour. Experience how McGraw Hill empowers you to teach */your* students *your* way: http://create.mheducation.com.

TRUSTED SERVICE AND SUPPORT

McGraw Hill's Connect offers comprehensive service, support, and training throughout every phase of your implementation. If you're looking for some guidance on how to use Connect or want to learn tips and tricks from super users, you can find tutorials as you work. Our Digital Faculty Consultants and Student Ambassadors offer insight into how to achieve the results you want with Connect.

INTEGRATION WITH YOUR LEARNING MANAGEMENT SYSTEM

McGraw Hill integrates your digital products from McGraw Hill with your school learning management system (LMS) for quick and easy access to best-in-class content and learning tools. Build an effective digital course, enroll students with ease, and discover how powerful digital teaching can be.

Available with Connect, integration is a pairing between an institution's LMS and Connect at the assignment level. It shares assignment information, grades and calendar items from Connect into the LMS automatically, creating an easy-to-manage course for instructors and simple navigation for students. Our assignment-level integration is available with **Blackboard Learn**, **Canvas by Instructure,** and **Brightspace by D2L,** giving you access to registration, attendance, assignments, grades, and course resources in real time, in one location.

INSTRUCTOR SUPPLEMENTS

Instructor's Manual The instructor's manual provides a wide variety of tools and resources for presenting the course, including learning objectives and ideas for lectures and discussions.

Test Bank and Test Builder By increasing the rigor of the test bank development process, McGraw Hill has raised the bar for student assessment. Organized by chapter, the questions are designed to test factual, conceptual, and applied understanding. All test questions are available within Test Builder software.

Available within Connect, Test Builder is a cloud-based tool that enables instructors to format tests that can be printed or administered within a Learning Management System. Test Builder offers a modern, streamlined interface for easy content configuration that matches course needs, without requiring a download. Test Builder enables instructors to:

- Access all test bank content from a particular title
- Easily pinpoint the most relevant content through robust filtering options
- Manipulate the order of questions or scramble questions and/or answers
- Pin questions to a specific location within a test
- Determine their preferred treatment of algorithmic questions
- Choose the layout and spacing
- Add instructions and configure default settings

PowerPoint Presentations The PowerPoint presentations, which are WCAG compliant, highlight the key points of the chapter and include supporting visuals. All of the slides can be modified to meet individual needs.

Image Gallery The Image Gallery features the complete set of downloadable figures and tables from the text. These can be easily embedded by instructors into their own PowerPoint slides.

Acknowledgments

One of the central features of *Essentials of Understanding Psychology* is the involvement of professionals as well as students in the review process. The *Essentials of Understanding Psychology* has relied heavily–and benefited substantially–from the advice of many instructors and students from a wide range of backgrounds. Among the colleagues who provided specific support are the following:

Richard Bernstein, Broward College

Jessica Carpenter, Elgin Community College

Deborah Dartnell, West Chester University

Eric Jackson, University of New Mexico

Heather Jennings, Mercer County Community College

Candace Lapan, Wingate University

Catherine Matson, Wilbur Wright College

Laura Otrimski, Edgecomb Community College

Eirini Papafratzeska, Mercer County Community College

Michele Poulos, East Coast Polytechnic Institute

Lora Vasiliauskas, Virginia Western Community College

Christi Young, Southwest Michigan College

Special thanks go to Vonetta Dotson of Georgia State University. Vonetta drafted the *Neuroscience in Your Life* features, bringing a deft touch to complex material and making connections with students' lives.

In addition to those mentioned above, many teachers along my educational path have shaped my thinking. I was introduced to psychology at Wesleyan University, where several committed and inspiring teachers–in particular, Karl Scheibe–conveyed their sense of excitement about the field and made its relevance clear to me. Karl epitomizes the teacher-scholar combination to which I aspire, and I continue to marvel at my good fortune in having such a role model.

By the time I left Wesleyan, I could envision no other career but that of psychologist. Although the nature of the University of Wisconsin, where I did my graduate work, could not have been more different from the much smaller Wesleyan, the excitement and inspiration were similar. Again, a cadre of excellent teachers–led, especially, by the late Vernon Allen–molded my thinking and taught me to appreciate the beauty and science of the discipline of psychology.

My colleagues and students at the University of Massachusetts Amherst provide ongoing intellectual stimulation, and I thank them for making the university such a fine place to work. Several people also provided extraordinary research and editorial help. In particular, I am especially grateful to my superb graduate students, past and present, including Erik Coats, Ben Happ, Sara Levine, Chris Poirier, Jim Tyler, and Matt Zimbler. John Bickford, in particular, provided invaluable editorial input that has enhanced the content considerably. Finally, I am grateful to Michelle Goncalves, whose hard work and dedication helped immeasurably on just about everything involving this material.

I offer great thanks to the McGraw Hill editorial and marketing teams. Thanks especially to Ryan Treat, Katie Stevens, and the entire psychology editorial team (Best Team Award winners), who provided encouragement and support as I worked on this revision. I also thank award-winning marketing specialists A. J. Laferrera and Isfa Syed for their enthusiasm and commitment to this project. I am in awe of the psych team's enthusiasm, commitment, and never-ending good ideas. Finally, the upper management of McGraw Hill has provided me with ongoing support, encouragement, and inspiration, and I especially thank Mike Ryan, president of the Higher Education group, and Simon Allen, CEO of McGraw Hill. I thank these folks not only for their superb professionalism, but also for their friendship.

I am very grateful to Susan Messer, product developer on this release. Susan did a superb job of managing a myriad of details (as well as me), bringing motivation, intelligence, and a fine literary sense to the project. Furthermore, Dawn Groundwater, senior product development manager, provided coordination and the solutions to many seemingly-intractable problems. Finally, every reader of this book owes a debt to Rhona Robbin and Judith Kromm, developmental editors for earlier iterations. Their relentless pursuit of excellence formed the essence of this book, and they taught me a great deal about the craft and art of writing.

Central to the design and production process were Danielle Clement, Mary Powers, Carrie Burger, and Beth Blech, key members of the production group. I am proud to be a part of this world-class McGraw Hill team.

Finally, I remain completely indebted to my family. My parents, Leah Brochstein and Saul Feldman, provided a lifetime foundation of love and support, and I continue to see their influence in every corner of my life. My extended family also plays a central role in my life. They include, more or less in order of age, my nieces and nephews, my terrific brother, my brothers- and sisters-in-law, and the late Ethel Radler. My mother-in-law, the late Mary Evans Vorwerk, had an important influence on this book, and I remain ever grateful to her.

Ultimately, my children, Jonathan, Joshua, and Sarah; my daughters-in-law Leigh and Julie; my son-in-law Jeffrey; my grandsons Alex and Miles; my granddaughters Naomi, Lilia, Rose, and Marina; and my wife, Katherine, remain the focal points of my life. I thank them, with immense love, and thank my lucky stars that they are in my life.

Robert S. Feldman
Amherst, Massachusetts

Making the Grade: A Practical Guide to Smarter Studying

No matter why you are taking introductory psychology, it's a safe bet you're interested in maximizing your understanding of the material and getting a good grade. And you want to accomplish these goals as quickly and efficiently as possible.

Good news: Several subfields of psychology have identified different ways to help you learn and remember material you will study throughout college. Here's my guarantee to you: If you learn and follow the guidelines in each of these areas, you'll become a better student and get better grades. Always remember that *good students are made, not born.*

Adopt a General Study Strategy: Using the P.O.W.E.R. Framework

Psychologists have devised several excellent techniques to improve study skills. One of the best, based on a substantial body of research, is "P.O.W.E.R," or *Prepare, Organize, Work, Evaluate,* and *Rethink.*

The **P.O.W.E.R.** system entails the following steps:

- **Prepare.** In *Essentials of Understanding Psychology,* 2024 Release, read the broad questions called *Learning Outcomes* to *Prepare* yourself for the material that follows. *Learning Outcomes* are at the start of each chapter and each module.

- **Organize.** The *Organize* stage involves developing a mental roadmap of where you are headed. *Essentials of Understanding Psychology* includes an outline at the beginning of each chapter. Read it to get an idea of what topics are covered and how they are organized.

- **Work.** Because of your effort in the *Prepare* and *Organize* stages, the *Work* stage will be easier. You know what questions the material will answer based on the *Learning Outcomes,* and you know how it is organized based on the outline. Read everything in the content, including the material in boxes and the margins, to fully understand the material.

- **Evaluate.** *Evaluate* provides the opportunity to determine how effectively you have mastered the material. In *Essentials of Understanding Psychology,* questions at the end of each module offer a rapid check of your understanding of the material. *Evaluate* your progress to assess your degree of mastery.

- **Rethink.** This final stage, *Rethink,* entails reanalyzing, reviewing, questioning, and challenging assumptions. Rethinking allows you to consider how the material fits with other information you have already learned. Every major section of *Essentials of Understanding Psychology* ends with a *Rethink* section. Answering its thought-provoking questions will help you think about the material at a deeper level.

Using the P.O.W.E.R. framework will help you maximize the efficiency and effectiveness of your study. In addition, the P.O.W.E.R. framework can be applied beyond the classroom, helping you to achieve success in your career and life.

Comstock/Stockbyte/Getty Images

Manage Your Time

Managing your time as you study is a central aspect of academic success. But remember: The goal of time management is to permit us to make informed choices about how we use our time. Use these time management procedures to harness time for your own advantage.

SET YOUR PRIORITIES. First, determine your priorities. *Priorities* are the tasks and activities you need and want to do, rank-ordered from most important to least important.

The best procedure is to start off by identifying priorities for an entire term. What do you need to accomplish? Rather than making these goals too general, make them specific, such as, "studying 10 hours before each chemistry exam."

IDENTIFY YOUR PRIME TIME. Are you a morning person or do you prefer studying later at night? Being aware of the time or times of day when you can do your best work will help you plan and schedule your time most effectively.

MASTER THE MOMENT. Here's what you'll need to organize your time:

- A *master calendar* that shows all the weeks of the term on one page. It should include every week of the term and seven days per week. On the master calendar, note the due date of every assignment and test you will have. Also include important activities from your personal life, drawn from your list of priorities. Add some free time for yourself.

- A *weekly timetable* that shows the days of the week across the top and the hours, from 6:00 A.M. to midnight, along the side. Fill in the times of all your fixed, prescheduled activities—the times that your classes meet, when you have to be at work, the times you have to pick up your child at day care, and any other recurring appointments. Add assignment due dates, tests, and any other activities on the appropriate days of the week. Then add blocks of time necessary to prepare for those events.

- A *daily to-do list* using a small calendar or your smartphone. List all the things that you intend to do during the day and their priority. Start with the things you *must* do and that have fixed times, such as classes and work schedules. Then add in the other things that you *should* accomplish, such as researching an upcoming paper or finishing a lab report. Finally, list things that are a low priority, such as taking in a new movie.

CONTROL YOUR TIME. If you follow the schedules that you've prepared, you've taken the most important steps in time management. Things, however, always seem to take longer than planned.

When inevitable surprises occur, there are several ways to take control of your days to follow your intended schedule:

- **Say no.** You don't have to agree to every favor that others ask of you.

- **Get away from it all.** Adopt a specific spot to call your own, such as a corner desk in a secluded nook in the library. If you use it enough, your body and mind will automatically get into study mode as soon as you get there.

- **Enjoy the sounds of silence.** Studies suggest that we are able to concentrate most when our environment is silent. Experiment and work in silence for a few days. You may find that you get more done in less time than you would in a more distracting environment.

- **Take an e-break.** Take an e-break and shut down your communication sources for some period of time. Phone calls, text messages, IMs, and e-mail can be saved on a phone or computer. They'll wait.

Stockbyte/Getty Images

- **Expect the unexpected.** You'll never be able to escape from unexpected interruptions and surprises that require your attention. But by trying to anticipate them and thinking about how you'll react to them, you can position yourself to react effectively when they do occur.

Take Good Notes in Class

Let's consider some of the basic principles of notetaking:

- **Identify the instructor's—and your—goals for the course.** The information you get during the first day of class and through the syllabus is critical. In addition to the instructor's goals, you should have your own. How will the information from the course help you to enhance your knowledge, improve yourself as a person, achieve your goals?

- **Complete assignments before coming to class.**

- **Listen for the key ideas.** Listen for such phrases as "you need to know . . . ," "the most important thing to consider . . . ," "there are four problems with this approach . . . ," and—a big one—"this will be on the test . . . "; phrases like these should cause you to sit up and take notice. Also, if an instructor says the same thing in several ways, the material being discussed is important.

- **Use short, abbreviated phrases—not full sentences—when taking notes.**

- **Pay attention to PowerPoint slides or what is displayed in class on overhead projectors, whiteboards, or chalk boards. Remember these tips:**

  - Listening is more important than seeing.

  - Don't copy everything that is on every slide.

  - Remember that key points on slides are . . . key points.

  - Check to see if the presentation slides are available online.

  - Remember that presentation slides are not the same as good notes for a class.

F64/Photodisc/Getty Images

Memorize Efficiently

Here's a key principle of effective memorization: Memorize what you need to memorize. *Forget about the rest.*

You have your choice of dozens of techniques of memorization. Also, feel free to devise your own strategies or add those that have worked for you in the past.

REHEARSAL. Say it aloud: rehearsal. Think of this word in terms of its three syllables: re–hear–sal. If you're scratching your head about why you should do this, it's to illustrate the point of *rehearsal:* to transfer material that you encounter into long-term memory.

MNEMONICS. This odd word (pronounced with the "m" silent—"neh MON ix") describes formal techniques used to make material more readily remembered.

Among the most common mnemonics are the following:

- **Acronyms.** *Acronyms* are words or phrases formed by the first letters of a series of terms. For example, Roy G. Biv helps people to remember the colors of the spectrum (red, orange, yellow, green, blue, indigo, and violet).

- **Acrostics.** *Acrostics* are sentences in which the first letters spell out something that needs to be recalled. The benefits of acrostics are similar to those of acronyms.

- **Rhymes and jingles.** "Thirty days hath September, April, June, and November." If you know the rest of the rhyme, you're familiar with one of the most commonly used mnemonic jingles in the English language.

Study for Tests Strategically

Here are some guidelines that can help you do your best on tests:

KNOW WHAT YOU ARE PREPARING FOR. To find out about an upcoming test, ask if it is a "test," an "exam," a "quiz," or something else. These names imply different things. In addition, each kind of test question requires a somewhat different style of preparation.

- **Essay questions.** The best approach to studying for an essay test involves four steps:

  1. Reread your class notes and any notes you've made on assigned readings that will be covered on the upcoming exam. Also go through the readings themselves, reviewing underlined or highlighted material and marginal notes.

  2. Think of likely exam questions. Some instructors give lists of possible essay topics; if yours does, focus on this list and think of other possibilities.

  3. Answer each potential essay question–aloud. You can also write down the main points that any answer should cover.

  4. After you've answered the questions, look at the notes and readings again. If you feel confident that you've answered specific questions adequately, check them off. If you had trouble with some questions, review that material immediately. Then repeat step 3, answering the questions again.

- **Multiple-choice, true-false, and matching questions.** Studying for multiple-choice, true-false, and matching questions requires attention to the details. Write down important facts on index cards: They're portable and available all the time, and the act of creating them helps drive the material into your memory.

- **Short-answer and fill-in questions.** Short-answer and fill-in questions are similar to essays in that they require you to recall key pieces of information, but they don't demand that you integrate or compare different types of information. Consequently, the focus of your study should be on the recall of specific, detailed information.

Rubberball/Getty Images

TEST YOURSELF. When you believe you've mastered the material, test yourself on it. You can create a test for yourself, in writing, making its form as close as possible to what you expect the actual test to be.

DEAL WITH TEST ANXIETY. What does the anticipation of a test do to you? *Test anxiety* is a temporary condition characterized by fears and concerns about test-taking. You'll never eliminate test anxiety completely, nor do you want to. A little bit of nervousness can energize us, making us more attentive and vigilant.

On the other hand, for some students, anxiety can spiral into the kind of paralyzing fear that makes their minds go blank. There are several ways to keep this from happening to you:

- *Prepare thoroughly.*
- *Take a realistic view of the test.*
- *Learn relaxation techniques.*
- *Visualize success.*

Klaus Vedfelt/Getty Images

CHAPTER 1
Introduction to Psychology

LEARNING OUTCOMES FOR CHAPTER 1

LO 4-1 What major issues confront psychologists conducting research?

PROLOGUE *INFERNO IN HAWAII*

A small brush fire that started on the outskirts of the historic Hawaiian town of Lahaina soon transformed into a relentless inferno. Propelled by gale-force winds, the fire consumed the entire town in less than a day. Scores of people perished in what was the deadliest U.S. wildfire in more than a century. The town was eradicated.

But in the face of such death and destruction, the best of humanity was also on display. Many stepped in to aid those who had lost their loved ones and homes, helping them pick up the pieces of their shattered lives.

Although the catastrophic wildfires that destroyed the town of Lahaina in Hawaii killed scores of people, the help provided to surviving victims of the fires also demonstrated the best of humanity.
Rick Bowmer/AP Photo

LOOKING *Ahead*

Although the wildfire that consumed Lahaina began as an environmental tragedy, it also produced significant psychological consequences. Consider, for example, the ways in which different kinds of psychologists considered the effects of the disaster:

- Psychologists who study the biology underlying behavior would examine changes in the functioning of peoples' bodies as they reacted to the emergency.

- Learning and memory psychologists might examine what people later remembered about the disaster.

- Psychologists who study thinking processes would consider how people view risks, such as those related to living in an area prone to extreme weather events, and how they calculate the ways in which such risks apply to them personally.

- Developmental psychologists, who study people at various stages of life, might examine how age was related to the stress that fire survivors experienced.

- Health psychologists would examine the ways in which experiencing the disaster might be linked to later illness.

- Clinical and counseling psychologists, who provide therapy for psychological disorders, might help survivors deal with the guilt they experienced because they survived while many others did not.

- Social psychologists, who study questions concerning interpersonal interaction, would try to understand why some people came forth to demonstrate heroism and helpfulness while others did not help at all.

As you'll see, the field of psychology addresses questions like these—and many, many more. In this chapter, we begin our examination of psychology, the types of psychologists, and the various roles psychologists play.

Module 1
Psychologists at Work

Psychology is the scientific study of behavior and mental processes. The simplicity of this definition is in some ways deceiving, concealing ongoing debates about how broad the scope of psychology should be. Should psychologists limit themselves to the study of outward, observable behavior? Is it possible to scientifically study thinking? Should the field encompass the study of such diverse topics as physical and mental health, perception, dreaming, and motivation? Is it appropriate to focus solely on human behavior, or should the behavior of other species be included?

Most psychologists would argue that the field should be receptive to a variety of viewpoints and approaches. Consequently, the phrase *behavior and mental processes* in the definition of psychology must be understood to mean many things: It encompasses not just what people do but also their thoughts, emotions, perceptions, reasoning processes, memories, and even the biological activities that maintain bodily functioning.

Psychologists try to describe, predict, and explain human behavior and mental processes, as well as help to change and improve the lives of people and the world in which they live. They use scientific methods to find answers that are far more valid and legitimate than those resulting from intuition and speculation, which are often inaccurate (see Figure 1).

LEARNING OUTCOMES

LO 1-1 What is the science of psychology?

LO 1-2 What are the major specialties in the field of psychology?

LO 1-3 Where do psychologists work?

psychology The scientific study of behavior and mental processes. (Module 1)

FIGURE 1 The scientific method is the basis of all psychological research and is used to find valid answers. Test your knowledge of psychology by answering these questions.

Source: Adapted from Bensley, Alan D. & Lilienfield, Scott O. (2017). Psychological misconceptions: Recent scientific advances and unresolved issues. *Current Directions in Psychological Science, 26*(4), 377–382, and Lamal, P. A. (1979). College students' common beliefs about psychology. *Teaching of Psychology, 6*, 155–158.

Psychological Truths?

To test your knowledge of psychology, try answering the following questions:

1. Infants love their mothers primarily because their mothers fulfill their basic biological needs, such as providing food. True or false?

2. The greater the intelligence someone generally has, the poorer their social skills. True or false?

3. The best way to ensure that a desired behavior will continue after training is completed is to reward that behavior every single time it occurs during training rather than rewarding it only periodically. True or false?

4. People with schizophrenia have at least two distinct personalities. True or false?

5. Parents should do everything they can to ensure their children have high self-esteem and a strong sense that they are highly competent. True or false?

6. Children's IQ scores have little to do with how well they do in school. True or false?

7. Eyewitness testimony is typically surprisingly accurate. True or false?

8. Once people reach old age, their leisure activities change radically. True or false?

9. Most people would refuse to give painful electric shocks to other people. True or false?

10. People who talk about suicide are unlikely to actually try to kill themselves. True or false?

Scoring: The truth about each of these items: They are all false. Based on psychological research, each of these "facts" has been proven untrue. You will learn the reasons why as we explore what psychologists have discovered about human behavior.

The Subfields of Psychology: Psychology's Family Tree

As the study of psychology has grown, it has given rise to a number of subfields (described in Figure 2). The subfields of psychology can be likened to an extended family, with assorted nieces and nephews, aunts and uncles, and cousins who, although they may not interact on a day-to-day basis, are related to one another because they

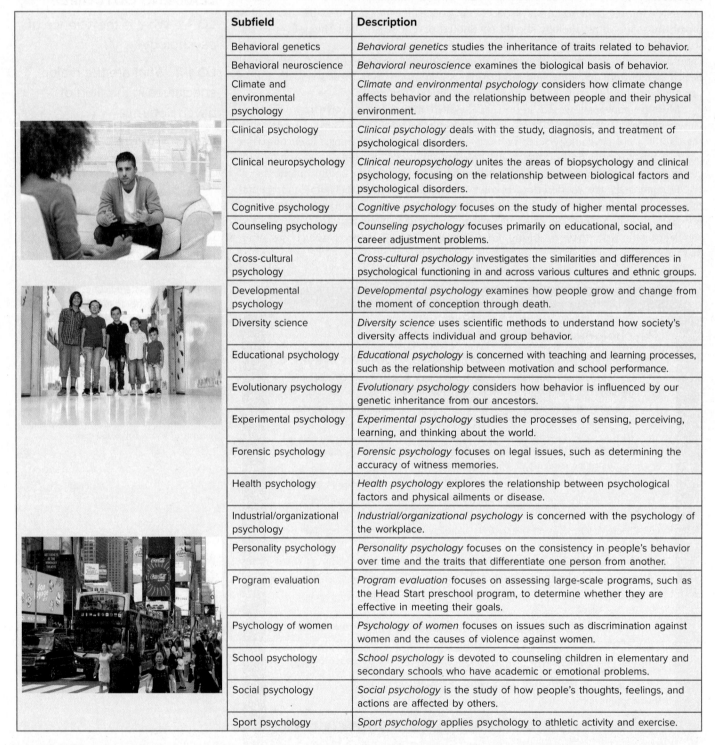

Subfield	Description
Behavioral genetics	*Behavioral genetics* studies the inheritance of traits related to behavior.
Behavioral neuroscience	*Behavioral neuroscience* examines the biological basis of behavior.
Climate and environmental psychology	*Climate and environmental psychology* considers how climate change affects behavior and the relationship between people and their physical environment.
Clinical psychology	*Clinical psychology* deals with the study, diagnosis, and treatment of psychological disorders.
Clinical neuropsychology	*Clinical neuropsychology* unites the areas of biopsychology and clinical psychology, focusing on the relationship between biological factors and psychological disorders.
Cognitive psychology	*Cognitive psychology* focuses on the study of higher mental processes.
Counseling psychology	*Counseling psychology* focuses primarily on educational, social, and career adjustment problems.
Cross-cultural psychology	*Cross-cultural psychology* investigates the similarities and differences in psychological functioning in and across various cultures and ethnic groups.
Developmental psychology	*Developmental psychology* examines how people grow and change from the moment of conception through death.
Diversity science	*Diversity science* uses scientific methods to understand how society's diversity affects individual and group behavior.
Educational psychology	*Educational psychology* is concerned with teaching and learning processes, such as the relationship between motivation and school performance.
Evolutionary psychology	*Evolutionary psychology* considers how behavior is influenced by our genetic inheritance from our ancestors.
Experimental psychology	*Experimental psychology* studies the processes of sensing, perceiving, learning, and thinking about the world.
Forensic psychology	*Forensic psychology* focuses on legal issues, such as determining the accuracy of witness memories.
Health psychology	*Health psychology* explores the relationship between psychological factors and physical ailments or disease.
Industrial/organizational psychology	*Industrial/organizational psychology* is concerned with the psychology of the workplace.
Personality psychology	*Personality psychology* focuses on the consistency in people's behavior over time and the traits that differentiate one person from another.
Program evaluation	*Program evaluation* focuses on assessing large-scale programs, such as the Head Start preschool program, to determine whether they are effective in meeting their goals.
Psychology of women	*Psychology of women* focuses on issues such as discrimination against women and the causes of violence against women.
School psychology	*School psychology* is devoted to counseling children in elementary and secondary schools who have academic or emotional problems.
Social psychology	*Social psychology* is the study of how people's thoughts, feelings, and actions are affected by others.
Sport psychology	*Sport psychology* applies psychology to athletic activity and exercise.

FIGURE 2 The major subfields of psychology.

Photos: (Top): ESB Professional/Shutterstock; (Middle): Zurijeta/Shutterstock; (Bottom): Alexandre Tziripouloff/Shutterstock

share a common goal: understanding behavior. One way to identify the key subfields is to look at some of the basic questions about behavior that they address.

WHAT ARE THE BIOLOGICAL FOUNDATIONS OF BEHAVIOR?

In the most fundamental sense, people are biological organisms. *Behavioral neuroscience* is the subfield of psychology that focuses on how the brain and the nervous system, as well as other biological aspects of the body, determine behavior.

Thus, neuroscientists consider how our body influences our behavior. For example, they may examine the link between specific sites in the brain and the muscular tremors of people affected by Parkinson's disease or attempt to determine how our emotions are related to physical sensations.

HOW DO PEOPLE SENSE, PERCEIVE, LEARN, AND THINK ABOUT THE WORLD?

If you have ever wondered why you are susceptible to optical illusions, how your body registers pain, or how to make the most of your study time, an experimental psychologist can answer your questions. *Experimental psychology* is the branch of psychology that studies the processes of sensing, perceiving, learning, and thinking about the world. (The term *experimental psychologist* is somewhat misleading: Psychologists in every specialty area use experimental techniques.)

Several subspecialties of experimental psychology have become specialties in their own right. One is *cognitive psychology*, which focuses on higher mental processes, including thinking, memory, reasoning, problem solving, judging, decision making, and language.

WHAT ARE THE SOURCES OF CHANGE AND STABILITY IN BEHAVIOR ACROSS THE LIFE SPAN?

A baby producing their first smile . . . taking their first step . . . saying their first word. These universal milestones in development are also singularly special and unique for each person. *Developmental psychology* studies how people grow and change from the moment of conception through death. *Personality psychology* focuses on the consistency in people's behavior across their lives, as well as the traits that differentiate one person from another.

HOW DO PSYCHOLOGICAL FACTORS AFFECT PHYSICAL AND MENTAL HEALTH?

Frequent depression, stress, and fears that prevent people from carrying out their normal activities are topics that interest health psychologists, clinical psychologists, and counseling psychologists. *Health psychology* explores the relationship between psychological factors and physical ailments or disease. For example, health psychologists are interested in assessing how long-term stress (a psychological factor) can affect physical health and in identifying ways to promote behavior that brings about good health (Proyer et al., 2013; Sauter & Hurell, 2017; Raque et al., 2021).

Clinical psychology deals with the study, diagnosis, and treatment of psychological disorders. Clinical psychologists are trained to diagnose and treat problems that range from the crises of everyday life, such as unhappiness over the breakup of a relationship, to more extreme conditions, such as profound, lingering depression. Some clinical psychologists also research and investigate issues that vary from identifying the early signs of psychological disturbance to studying the relationship between family communication patterns and psychological disorders.

Like clinical psychologists, counseling psychologists deal with people's psychological problems, but the problems they deal with are more specific. *Counseling psychology* focuses primarily on educational, social, and career adjustment problems. Almost every college has a center staffed with counseling psychologists. This is where students can

Study Alert

The subfields of psychology allow psychologists to explain the same behavior in multiple ways. Review Figure 2 for a summary of the subfields.

get advice on the kinds of jobs they might be best suited for, on methods of studying effectively, and on strategies for resolving everyday difficulties, such as problems with roommates or anxiety related to the COVID-19 pandemic or gun violence. Many large business organizations also employ counseling psychologists to help employees with work-related problems.

HOW DO OUR SOCIAL NETWORKS AFFECT BEHAVIOR?

Our complex networks of social interrelationships are the focus for many subfields of psychology. For example, *social psychology* is the study of how people's thoughts, feelings, and actions are affected by others. Social psychologists concentrate on such diverse topics as human aggression, liking and loving, persuasion, and conformity.

Cross-cultural psychology investigates the similarities and differences in psychological functioning in and across various cultures and ethnic groups. For example, cross-cultural psychologists examine how cultures differ in their use of punishment during child rearing.

EXPANDING PSYCHOLOGY'S FRONTIERS

The boundaries of the science of psychology are constantly growing. Four newer members of the field's family tree—evolutionary psychology, behavioral genetics, clinical neuropsychology, and diversity science—have sparked particular excitement and debate within psychology.

Evolutionary Psychology *Evolutionary psychology* considers how behavior is influenced by our genetic inheritance from our ancestors. The evolutionary approach suggests that the chemical coding of information in our cells not only determines traits such as hair color and race but also holds the key to understanding a broad variety of behaviors that helped our ancestors survive and reproduce.

Evolutionary psychology stems from Charles Darwin's arguments in his ground-breaking 1859 book, *On the Origin of Species*. Darwin suggested that a process of natural selection leads to the survival of the fittest and the development of traits that enable a species to adapt to its environment.

Evolutionary psychologists take Darwin's arguments a step further. They argue that our genetic inheritance determines not only physical traits such as skin and eye color but certain personality traits and social behaviors as well. For example, evolutionary psychologists suggest that behavior such as shyness, jealousy, and cross-cultural similarities in qualities desired in potential mates are at least partially determined by genetics, presumably because such behavior helped increase the survival rate of humans' ancient relatives (Lewis et al., 2017; Bhogal, Farrelly, & Galbraith, 2019; McCauley et al., 2022).

Although they are increasingly popular, evolutionary explanations of behavior have stirred controversy. By suggesting that many significant behaviors unfold automatically because they are wired into the human species, evolutionary approaches minimize the role of environmental and social forces. Still, the evolutionary approach has stimulated a significant amount of research on how our biological inheritance influences our traits and behaviors (Mesoudi, 2011; Flannelly, 2017; Al-Shawaf, Lewis, & Buss, 2018).

Behavioral Genetics Another rapidly growing area in psychology focuses on the biological mechanisms, such as genes and chromosomes, that enable inherited behavior to unfold. *Behavioral genetics* seeks to understand how we might inherit certain behavioral traits and how the environment influences whether we actually display such traits (Maxson, 2013; Vukasović & Bratko, 2015; Krüger, Korsten, & Hoffman, 2017; Harden, 2021).

Clinical Neuropsychology *Clinical neuropsychology* unites the areas of neuroscience and clinical psychology: It focuses on the origin of psychological disorders in biological factors. Building on advances in our understanding of the structure and chemistry of the brain, this specialty has already led to promising new treatments for psychological disorders as well as debates over the use of medication to control behavior (Craig, 2017; Kasten el al., 2021).

Diversity Science Psychologists who study *diversity science* use scientific methods to understand how society's diversity affects individual and group behavior. Diversity science takes a broad view of diversity, considering race, ethnicity, gender, sexual orientation, religion, people with disabilities, economic class, age, and other variables. Psychologists who apply this orientation have a variety of specialties, but they all use scientific methods to study traditionally underrepresented groups, with the goal of reducing racism, prejudice, and discrimination as well as exploring the structures of society that support inequality (Neblett, 2019).

Working at Psychology

Help Wanted: Assistant professor at a small liberal arts college. Teach undergraduate courses in introductory psychology and courses in specialty areas of cognitive psychology, perception, and learning. Strong commitment to quality teaching, as well as evidence of scholarship and research productivity, necessary.

Help Wanted: Industrial-organizational consulting psychologist. International firm seeks psychologists for full-time career positions as consultants to management. Candidates must have the ability to establish a rapport with senior business executives and help them find innovative and practical solutions to problems concerning people and organizations.

Help Wanted: Clinical psychologist. PhD, internship experience, and license required. Comprehensive clinic seeks psychologist to work with children and adults providing individual and group therapy, psychological evaluations, crisis intervention, and development of behavior treatment plans on multidisciplinary team.

As these job ads suggest, psychologists are employed in a variety of settings. Many doctoral-level psychologists are employed by institutions of higher learning (universities and colleges) or are self-employed, usually working as private practitioners treating clients (see Figure 3). Other work sites include hospitals, clinics, mental health centers,

FIGURE 3 The breakdown of where U.S. psychologists (who have a PhD or PsyD) work.
Source: Stamm et al., 2016.

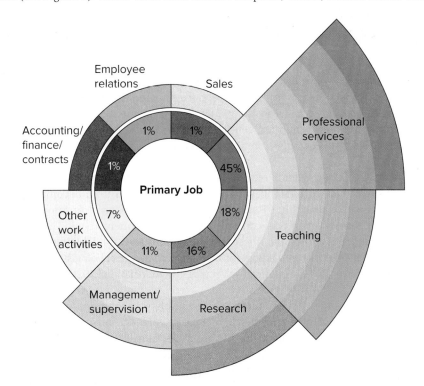

counseling centers, government human-services organizations, businesses, schools, and even prisons. Psychologists are employed in the military, working with soldiers, veterans, and their families, and they work for the federal government in the U.S. Department of Homeland Security, fighting terrorism. Psychologists who specialize in program evaluation are increasingly employed by foundations that want to assess the value of programs they fund (Moscoso et al., 2013; American Psychological Association, 2016; Urban & Linver, 2019).

Most psychologists, though, work in academic settings, allowing them to combine the three major roles played by psychologists in society: teacher, scientist, and clinical practitioner. Many psychology professors are also actively involved in research or in serving clients. Whatever the particular job site, however, psychologists share a commitment to improving individual lives as well as society in general. In addition, whatever their specialization and subfield, psychologists tend to be happy with their work. In fact, those with doctoral degrees are more likely to report job satisfaction than doctoral degree holders in other fields (Conroy, Lin, & Christidis, 2019; Lin et al., 2021).

Moreover, keep in mind that professionals from a variety of occupations use the findings of psychologists. To get a glimpse into how nonpsychologists use psychology in their professions, see the feature titled "From the Perspective of . . ." throughout the text.

From the perspective of...

An Educator Imagine that a classroom teacher wants to improve the performance of a 10-year-old student who is not doing well in math. What branches of psychology might the teacher draw on to get ideas about how to help the student?

Andersen Ross/Blend Images/Getty Images

PSYCHOLOGISTS: A STATISTICAL PORTRAIT

Although there is no "average" psychologist in terms of personal characteristics, we can draw a statistical portrait of the field. Around 180,000 psychologists are working today in the United States, but they are outnumbered by psychologists in other countries. Although most research is conducted in the United States, psychologists in other countries are increasingly influential in adding to the knowledge base and practices of psychology (Rees & Seaton, 2011; Takooshian et al., 2016; Bureau of Labor Statistics, 2022).

In the United States, women outnumber men in the field, a big change from earlier years when women faced bias and were actively discouraged from becoming psychologists. Today, women make up 70% of the psychology workforce. And looking at the educational pipeline, women will continue to outnumber men: about 75% of psychology graduate students are female. Those in the field are actively debating whether and how to seek balance in the percentage of men and women psychologists (Varma, 2018; Marulanda & Radtke, 2019; American Psychological Association, 2020).

Challenges of Diversity in Psychology Despite the higher proportion of women in the field, they still lag behind men when it comes to salaries, career advancement, and high-status positions within the field. For example, female psychologists working in

4-year colleges and medical schools earn, on average, 82.7% of what males make. Furthermore, because they often face gender bias, more academic service requirements, and greater family demands than males, women tend to publish less, their work is referred to less by other scientists, and they hold fewer research grants (Clay, 2017; Weidman, 2019; Gruber et al., 2021).

Moreover, the COVID-19 pandemic amplified some of the impediments that female psychologists frequently face. For example, women were more likely than men to be the primary breadwinner in single-parent households, thereby facing greater family demands than men and experiencing subsequent drops in productivity (Thayer, 2021).

Another challenge regarding diversity in psychology is that the majority of psychologists in the United States are White. Only around 16% of all professionally active psychologists are members of racial minority groups. Specifically, the composition is 6% Hispanic, 4% Black/African American, 4% Asian, 2% other, and 84% White. On the other hand, racial and ethnic minorities represent 26% of psychologists age 35 and younger, so the numbers are increasing (see Figure 4; Lin, Conroy & Ghaness, 2020). Although the numbers of minority individuals entering the field are far greater than they were a decade ago and continue to grow, the numbers have not kept up with the dramatic growth of the minority population at large (American Psychological Association, 2018, 2020; Lin, Stamm, & Christidis, 2018; Frost et al., 2019).

The underrepresentation of racial and ethnic minorities among psychologists is significant for several reasons. First, the field of psychology is diminished by a lack of the diverse perspectives and talents that minority-group members can provide. Furthermore, minority-group psychologists serve as role models for members of minority communities, and their underrepresentation in the profession might deter other minority-group members from entering the field. Finally, because members of

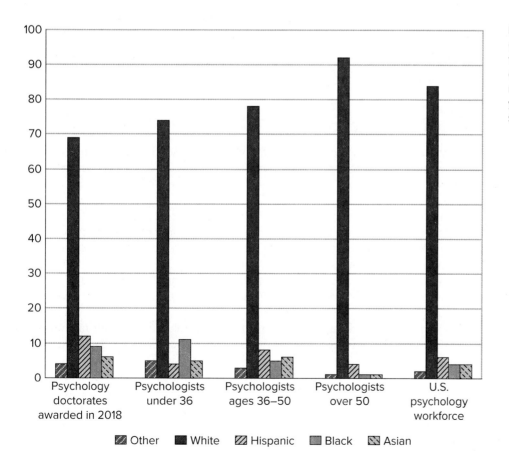

FIGURE 4 Psychology's workforce demographics. Although psychology's workforce is still largely White, the proportion of psychologists from racial and ethnic minority groups is growing among younger age groups.
Source: Lin et al., 2020.

minority groups often prefer to receive psychological therapy from treatment providers of their own race or ethnic group, the rarity of minority psychologists can discourage some members of minority groups from seeking treatment (Stevens, 2015; Stewart et al., 2017; Andoh, 2021).

One more diversity challenge involves the dominance of psychologists who are located in the United States. Even though those who live in the United States represent a relatively small proportion of the world's population, the scientific journals for the field of psychology disproportionately publish U.S. authors, and the research they report is most often conducted on people in the United States. Given the vast differences in cultures across the world, the lack of diversity among psychology researchers and participants limits our ability to attain a full understanding of human behavior (Ijzerman et al., 2021).

THE EDUCATION OF A PSYCHOLOGIST

How do people become psychologists? The most common route is a long one. Most psychologists have a doctorate, either a *PhD* (doctor of philosophy) or, less frequently, a *PsyD* (doctor of psychology). The PhD is a research degree that requires a dissertation based on an original investigation. The PsyD is obtained by psychologists who want to focus on the treatment of psychological disorders. Note that psychologists are distinct from psychiatrists, who have a medical degree and specialize in the diagnosis and treatment of psychological disorders, often using treatments that involve the prescription of drugs.

Both the PhD and the PsyD typically take 4 or 5 years of work past the bachelor's level. Some fields of psychology involve education beyond the doctorate. For instance, doctoral-level clinical psychologists, who deal with people with psychological disorders, typically spend an additional year doing an internship.

About a third of people working in the field of psychology have a master's degree as their highest degree, which they earn after 2 or 3 years of graduate work. These psychologists teach, provide therapy, conduct research, or work in specialized programs dealing with drug abuse or crisis intervention. Some work in universities, government, and business, collecting and analyzing data.

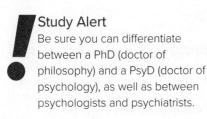

Study Alert

Be sure you can differentiate between a PhD (doctor of philosophy) and a PsyD (doctor of psychology), as well as between psychologists and psychiatrists.

CAREERS FOR PSYCHOLOGY MAJORS

Although some psychology majors head for graduate school in psychology or an unrelated field, the majority join the workforce immediately after graduation. Most report that the jobs they take after graduation are related to their psychology background.

An undergraduate major in psychology provides excellent preparation for a variety of occupations. Because undergraduates who specialize in psychology develop good analytical skills, are trained to think critically, and are able to synthesize and evaluate information well, employers in business, industry, and the government value their preparation. Furthermore, undergraduate psychology majors hold a variety of specific skills that employers find valuable (see Figure 5; American Psychological Association 2011, 2021; Geher, 2019).

The most common areas of employment for psychology majors are in the social services, including working as administrators, serving as counselors, and providing direct care. Some 20% of recipients of bachelor's degrees in psychology work in the social services or in some other form of public affairs. In addition, psychology majors often enter the fields of education or business or work for federal, state, and local governments (see Figure 6; Rajecki & Borden, 2011; Sternberg, 2017; American Psychological Association, 2021).

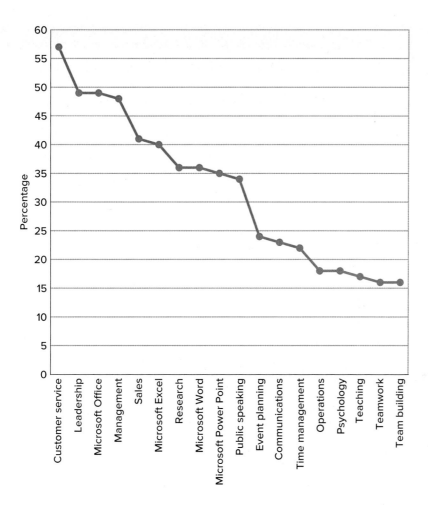

FIGURE 5 Top Skills of Psychology Majors. An undergraduate psychology major provides many of the skills that future employers are seeking.

Source: Conroy et al., 2021.

Positions Obtained by Psychology Majors

Business Fields	Education/Academic Fields	Social Fields
Administrative assistant	Administrator	Activities director
Advertising sales representative	Alumni director	Behavioral specialist
Affirmative action officer	Child-care provider	Career counselor
Benefits manager	Child-care worker/supervisor	Case worker
Claims specialist	Data manager	Child protection worker
Community relations officer	Financial aid counselor	Clinical coordinator
Customer relations coordinator	Fundraiser Laboratory assistant	Community outreach worker
Data manager	Parent/family educator	Corrections officer
Employee counselor	School teacher	Counselor assistant
Employee recruiter	Public opinion surveyor	Crisis intervention counselor
Human resources coordinator/manager/specialist	Research assistant	Employment counselor
Labor relations manager/specialist	Teaching assistant	Group home attendant
Loan officer		Mental health assistant
Management trainee		Occupational therapist
Marketing specialist		Probation officer
Personnel manager/officer		Program manager
Product and services researcher		Rehabilitation counselor
Programs/events coordinator		Residence counselor
Public relations specialist		Social service assistant Social worker
Retail sales manager		Substance abuse counselor
Sales representative		Victims' advocate
Special features writer		Youth counselor
Staff training and development specialist		
Trainer		

FIGURE 6 Although many psychology majors pursue employment in social services, a background in psychology can prepare one for many professions outside the social services field. What is it about the science and art of psychology that make it such a versatile field?

Sources: Adapted from Kuther, 2003; Landrum, 2018; and Geher, 2019.

RECAP/EVALUATE/RETHINK

RECAP

LO 1-1 What is the science of psychology?

- Psychology is the scientific study of behavior and mental processes, encompassing not just what people do but also their biological activities, feelings, perceptions, memory, reasoning, and thoughts.

LO 1-2 What are the major specialties in the field of psychology?

- Behavioral neuroscientists focus on the biological basis of behavior, and experimental psychologists study the processes of sensing, perceiving, learning, and thinking about the world.
- Cognitive psychology, an outgrowth of experimental psychology, studies higher mental processes, including memory, knowing, thinking, reasoning, problem solving, judging, decision making, and language.
- Climate and environmental psychology considers how climate change affects behavior and the relationship between people and their physical environment.
- Developmental psychologists study how people grow and change throughout the life span.

- Personality psychologists consider the consistency and change in an individual's behavior, as well as the individual differences that distinguish one person's behavior from another's.
- Health psychologists study psychological factors that affect physical disease, whereas clinical psychologists consider the study, diagnosis, and treatment of abnormal behavior. Counseling psychologists focus on educational, social, and career adjustment problems.
- Social psychology is the study of how people's thoughts, feelings, and actions are affected by others.
- Cross-cultural psychology examines the similarities and differences in psychological functioning among various cultures.
- Other increasingly important fields are evolutionary psychology, behavioral genetics, clinical neuropsychology, and diversity science.

LO 1-3 Where do psychologists work?

- Psychologists are employed in a variety of settings. Although the primary sites of employment are private practice and colleges, many psychologists are found in hospitals, clinics, community mental health centers, and counseling centers.

EVALUATE

Match each subfield of psychology with the issues or questions posed below.

a. Behavioral neuroscience
b. Experimental psychology
c. Cognitive psychology
d. Developmental psychology
e. Personality psychology
f. Health psychology
g. Clinical psychology
h. Counseling psychology
i. Educational psychology
j. School psychology
k. Social psychology
l. Industrial psychology

1. Richa, a college freshman, is worried about her grades. She needs to learn better organizational skills and study habits to cope with the demands of college.
2. At what age do children generally begin to acquire an emotional attachment to their fathers?
3. It is thought that pornographic films that depict violence against women may prompt aggressive behavior in some men.
4. What chemicals are released in the human body as a result of a stressful event? What are their effects on behavior?
5. Luis is unique in his manner of responding to crisis situations, with an even temperament and a positive outlook.
6. The teachers of 8-year-old Omie are concerned that he has recently begun to withdraw socially and to show little interest in schoolwork.
7. Janetta's job is demanding and stressful. She wonders if her lifestyle is making her more prone to certain illnesses, such as cancer and heart disease.
8. A psychologist is intrigued by the fact that some people are much more sensitive to painful stimuli than others are.
9. A strong fear of crowds leads a college student to seek treatment for their problem.
10. What mental strategies are involved in solving complex word problems?
11. What teaching methods most effectively motivate elementary school students to successfully accomplish academic tasks?
12. Jessica is asked to develop a management strategy that will encourage safer work practices in an assembly plant.

RETHINK

Do you think intuition and common sense are sufficient for understanding why people act the way they do? In what ways is a scientific approach appropriate for studying human behavior?

Answers to Evaluate Questions

a-4; b-8; c-10; d-2; e-5; f-7; g-9; h-1; i-11; j-6; k-3; l-12

KEY TERM

psychology

Module 2
A Science Evolves: The Past, the Present, and the Future

LEARNING OUTCOMES

LO 2-1 What are the origins of psychology?

LO 2-2 What are the major approaches in contemporary psychology?

LO 2-3 What are psychology's key issues and controversies?

LO 2-4 What is the future of psychology likely to hold?

Seven thousand years ago, people assumed that psychological problems were caused by evil spirits. To allow those spirits to escape from a person's body, ancient healers chipped a hole in a patient's skull with crude instruments–a procedure called *trephining*.

According to the 17th-century philosopher René Descartes, nerves were hollow tubes through which "animal spirits" conducted impulses in the same way that water is transmitted through a pipe. When a person put a finger too close to a fire, heat was transmitted to the brain through the tubes.

Franz Josef Gall, an 18th-century physician, argued that a trained observer could discern intelligence, moral character, and other basic personality characteristics from the shape and number of bumps on a person's skull. His theory gave rise to the field of phrenology, employed by hundreds of practitioners in the 19th century.

Although these explanations might sound far-fetched, in their own times they represented the most advanced thinking about what might be called the psychology of the era. Our understanding of behavior has progressed tremendously since the 18th century, but most of the advances have been recent. As sciences go, psychology is one of the new kids on the block. (For highlights in the development of the field, see Figure 1.)

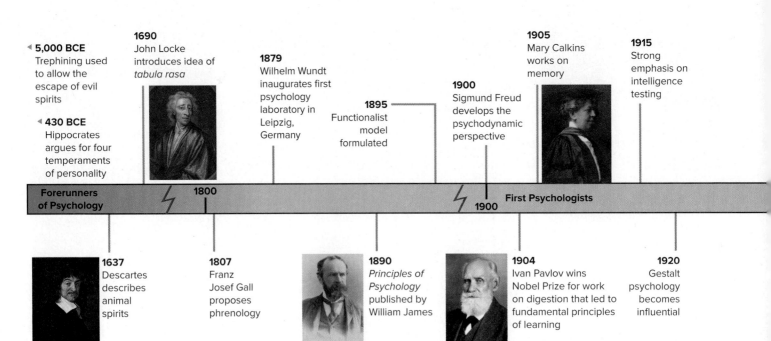

FIGURE 1 This time line illustrates major milestones in the development of psychology.

(Descartes): Everett - Art/Shutterstock; (Locke): National Gallery of Art; (James): National Portrait Gallery, Smithsonian Institution; (Pavlov): Pictorial Press Ltd/Alamy Stock Photo; (Calkins): The Schlesinger Library, Radcliffe Institute, Harvard University; (Watson): Granger Historical Picture Archive/Alamy Stock Photo; (Clark): Pictorial Press Ltd/Alamy Stock Photo; (Maslow): Bettmann/Getty Images; (Piaget): Gado Images/Alamy Stock Photo; (Loftus): ©Elizabeth Loftus; (Eberhardt): Chris Farber/Getty Images

The Roots of Psychology

We can trace psychology's roots back to the ancient philosophers. For example, Greeks considered the mind to be a suitable topic for scholarly contemplation, and early Chinese philosophers believed that the heart was the center of understanding.

Later philosophers argued for hundreds of years about some of the questions psychologists grapple with today. For example, the 17th-century British philosopher John Locke believed that children were born into the world with minds like "blank slates" (*tabula rasa* in Latin) and that their experiences determined what kind of adults they would become. His views contrasted with those of Plato and Descartes, who argued that some knowledge was inborn in humans.

However, the formal beginning of psychology as a scientific discipline is generally considered to be in the late 19th century, when Wilhelm Wundt, in Leipzig, Germany, established the first experimental laboratory devoted to psychological phenomena. At about the same time, William James was setting up his laboratory in Cambridge, Massachusetts.

When Wundt set up his laboratory in 1879, his aim was to study the building blocks of the mind. He considered psychology to be the study of conscious experience. His perspective, which came to be known as **structuralism,** focused on uncovering the fundamental mental components of perception, consciousness, thinking, emotions, and other kinds of mental states and activities.

To determine how basic sensory processes shape our understanding of the world, Wundt and other structuralists used a procedure called introspection. **Introspection** is a procedure in which people are presented with a stimulus—such as an image or sentence—and asked to describe, in their own words and in as much detail as they

Structuralism focuses on uncovering the fundamental mental components of consciousness, thinking, and other mental states and activities.

Wayhome Studio/Shutterstock

structuralism Wundt's approach, which focuses on uncovering the fundamental mental components of consciousness, thinking, and other kinds of mental states and activities. (Module 2)

introspection A procedure in which people are presented with a stimulus—such as an image or sentence—and asked to describe, in their own words and in as much detail as they can, what they were experiencing. (Module 2)

1924
John B. Watson, an early behaviorist, publishes *Behaviorism*

1928
Leta Stetter Hollingworth publishes work on adolescence

1947
Mamie Phipps Clark studies effects of segregation in Black preschool children

1951
Carl Rogers publishes *Client-Centered Therapy*, helping to establish the humanistic perspective

1953
B. F. Skinner publishes *Science and Human Behavior*, advocating the behavioral perspective

1954
Abraham Maslow publishes *Motivation and Personality*, developing the concept of self-actualization

1957
Leon Festinger publishes *A Theory of Cognitive Dissonance*, producing a major impact on social psychology

1969
Arguments regarding the genetic basis of IQ fuel lingering controversies

1980
Jean Piaget, an influential developmental psychologist, dies

1981 David Hubel and Torsten Wiesel win Nobel Prize for work on vision cells in the brain

1985
Increasing emphasis on cognitive perspective

2020
Subfields such as clinical neuropsychology, environmental psychology, and health psychology develop

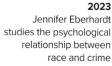

2000
Elizabeth Loftus does pioneering work on false memory and eyewitness testimony

2023
Jennifer Eberhardt studies the psychological relationship between race and crime

2020
Considerable advances in neuroscience and new applications with the potential to improve the human condition

Modern Psychology

2000

How do people make choices from an array of possibilities? Introspection sought to determine how individuals could analyze and articulate their internal thought processes when they were making a decision.

Obradovic/E+/Getty Images

could, what they were experiencing. Wundt argued that by analyzing people's reports, psychologists could come to a better understanding of the structure of the mind.

Over time, psychologists challenged Wundt's approach. They became increasingly dissatisfied with the assumption that introspection could reveal the structure of the mind. Introspection was not a truly scientific technique because there were few ways an outside observer could confirm the accuracy of others' introspections. Moreover, people had difficulty describing some kinds of inner experiences, such as emotional responses. Those drawbacks led to the development of new approaches, which largely replaced structuralism.

The perspective that replaced structuralism is known as functionalism. Rather than focusing on the mind's structure, **functionalism** concentrated on what the mind *does* and how behavior *functions*. Functionalists, whose perspective became prominent in the early 1900s, asked what role behavior plays in allowing people to adapt to their environments. For example, a functionalist might examine the function of the emotion of fear in preparing us to deal with emergency situations.

William James, an American psychologist, led the functionalist movement. Functionalists examined how people satisfy their needs through their behavior. The functionalists also discussed how our stream of consciousness—the flow of thoughts in our conscious minds—permits us to adapt to our environment. The American educator John Dewey drew on functionalism to develop the field of school psychology, proposing ways to best meet students' educational needs.

Another important reaction to structuralism was the development of Gestalt psychology in the early 1900s. **Gestalt (geh-SHTALLT) psychology** emphasizes how perception is organized. Instead of considering the individual parts that make up thinking, Gestalt psychologists took the opposite tack, studying how people consider individual elements together as units or wholes. Led by German scientists such as Hermann Ebbinghaus and Max Wertheimer, Gestalt psychologists proposed that "The whole is different from the sum of its parts," meaning that our perception, or understanding, of objects is greater and more meaningful than the individual elements that

functionalism An early approach to psychology that concentrated on what the mind does—the functions of mental activity—and the role of behavior in allowing people to adapt to their environments. (Module 2)

Gestalt (geh-SHTALLT) laws of organization A series of principles that describe how we organize bits and pieces of information into meaningful wholes. (Modules 2, 11)

make up our perceptions. Gestalt psychologists have made substantial contributions to our understanding of perception.

WOMEN IN PSYCHOLOGY: FOUNDING MOTHERS

As in many scientific fields, social prejudices hindered women's participation in the early development of psychology. For example, many universities would not admit women to their graduate psychology programs in the early 1900s.

Despite the hurdles they faced, women made notable contributions to psychology, although their impact on the field was largely overlooked until recently. For example, Margaret Floy Washburn (1871-1939) was the first woman to receive a doctorate in psychology, and she did important work on animal behavior. Leta Stetter Hollingworth (1886-1939) was one of the first psychologists to focus on child development and on women's issues. She collected data to refute the view, popular in the early 1900s, that women's abilities periodically declined during parts of the menstrual cycle (Hollingworth, 1943/1990; Denmark & Fernandez, 1993; Furumoto & Scarborough, 2002; American Psychological Association, 2021).

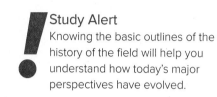

Study Alert

Knowing the basic outlines of the history of the field will help you understand how today's major perspectives have evolved.

Mary Calkins (1863-1930), who studied memory in the early part of the 20th century, became the first female president of the American Psychological Association, which at the time was the dominant association of psychologists. Karen Horney (pronounced "HORN-eye") (1885-1952) focused on the social and cultural factors behind personality, and she also founded the *American Journal of Psychoanalysis*. June Etta Downey (1875-1932) spearheaded the study of personality traits and became the first woman to head a psychology department at a state university. Anna Freud (1895-1982), the daughter of Sigmund Freud, also made notable contributions to the treatment of abnormal behavior, and Mamie Phipps Clark (1917-1983) carried out pioneering work on how children of color grew to recognize racial differences (Lal, 2002; Galdi, 2015).

Mamie Phipps Clark conducted significant and influential research during the 1950s. A Black social psychologist, Clark studied racial identification and self-esteem of preschool children. Her research, conducted with her husband Kenneth Clark, influenced several school-desegregation court cases, including the famous Supreme Court ruling in *Brown vs. Board of Education* in 1954 (Butler, 2009).

PEOPLE OF COLOR AND THE HISTORY OF PSYCHOLOGY

For much of its history, the field of psychology was dominated by White males. Furthermore, along with members of other disciplines, early psychologists reflected the prejudice and discrimination against people of color in society at large, which not only harmed people of color who sought entry to the field, but significantly impeded the development of psychology as a discipline. For example, many early psychologists subscribed to notions derived from Darwin's evolutionary theory that focused on the notion of "survival of the fittest." That focus led to discredited ideas of White superiority and theories of eugenics, a perspective that proposed that some races were inherently inferior due to physical limitations, such as having "primitive brains" (Cummings Center for the History of Psychology, 2021).

However, as the field developed, more people of color became psychologists. Furthermore, the Civil Rights movement that began in the 1960s influenced psychologists to address issues of prejudice and discrimination and reject earlier notions of White superiority. Consequently, the field began to embrace the centrality of issues involving diversity, equity, and inclusion.

In addressing the racism of prior generations of psychologists, the American Psychological Association (APA) issued a formal apology in 2021. The apology cited the involvement of psychologists in systemic inequities, racism, discrimination, and denigration of people of color. Moreover, the APA pledged to aid in dismantling systemic racism and to work toward ending psychological and physical health disparities (APA, 2021a, 2021b).

Today's Five Major Perspectives

! Study Alert
Use Figure 2 to differentiate the five perspectives, which are important because they provide a foundation for every topic covered throughout the text.

The men and women who laid the foundations of psychology shared a common goal: to explain and understand behavior using scientific methods. Seeking to achieve the same goal, the tens of thousands of psychologists who followed those early pioneers embraced–and often rejected–a variety of broad perspectives.

The perspectives of psychology offer distinct outlooks and emphasize different factors. Just as we can use more than one map to find our way around a particular region–for instance, a map that shows roads and highways and another map that shows major landmarks–psychologists developed a variety of approaches to understanding behavior. When considered jointly, the different perspectives provide the means to explain behavior in its amazing variety.

Today, the field of psychology includes five major perspectives (summarized in Figure 2). These broad perspectives emphasize different aspects of behavior and mental processes, and each takes our understanding of behavior in a somewhat different direction.

THE NEUROSCIENCE PERSPECTIVE: BLOOD, SWEAT, AND FEARS

neuroscience perspective The approach that views behavior from the perspective of the brain, the nervous system, and other biological functions. (Module 2)

When we get down to the basics, humans are animals made of skin and bones. The **neuroscience perspective** considers how people and nonhumans function biologically: how individual nerve cells are joined together, how the inheritance of certain characteristics from parents and other ancestors influences behavior, how the functioning of the body affects hopes and fears, which behaviors are instinctual, and so forth. Even more complex kinds of behaviors, such as a baby's response to strangers, are viewed as having critical biological components by psychologists who embrace the neuroscience perspective. This perspective includes the study of heredity and evolution, which considers how heredity may influence behavior, and behavioral neuroscience, which examines how the brain and the nervous system affect behavior.

Because every behavior ultimately can be broken down into its biological components, the neuroscience perspective has broad appeal. Psychologists who subscribe to this perspective have made major contributions to the understanding and betterment of human life, ranging from cures for certain types of deafness to drug treatments for

Neuroscience
Views behavior from the perspective of biological functioning

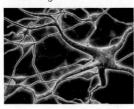

Cognitive
Examines how people understand and think about the world

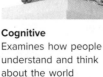

Behavioral
Focuses on observable behavior

Humanistic
Contends that people can control their behavior and that they naturally try to reach their full potential

Psychodynamic
Believes behavior is motivated by inner, unconscious forces over which a person has little control

FIGURE 2 The major perspectives of psychology.

(Neuroscience): Alfred Pasieka/Science Photo Library/Alamy Stock Photo; (Cognitive): Les Byerley/Shutterstock; (Behavioral): Ariel Skelley/Blend Images LLC; (Humanistic): fizkes/Shutterstock; (Psychodynamic): Athanasia Nomikou/Shutterstock

people with severe mental disorders. Furthermore, advances in methods for examining the anatomy and functioning of the brain have permitted the neuroscientific perspective to extend its influence across a broad range of subfields in psychology. (We'll see examples of these methods throughout this book in the *Neuroscience in Your Life* feature.)

NEUROSCIENCE IN YOUR LIFE: THE BRAIN IN SPACE

Is outer space the next frontier for studying the human brain?

Neuroscientists have long known that environmental stressors found on planet Earth, such as pollution and crowding, can significantly affect the way your brain functions. But more recently, they've expanded their focus beyond Earth to include outer space. Neuroscientists are studying the ways medical conditions, mental health disorders, and environmental stressors affect the structure and functioning of the brain—even when the environment happens to be outer space (Frantzdis et al., 2019; Popova et al., 2020).

For example, a group of neuroscientists gave magnetic resonance imaging (MRI) scans to a group of astronauts before and after they spent 6 months on the International Space Station. One change they found after spaceflight was an expansion of the brain's fluid-filled chambers, which are called ventricles. Since enlargement of the ventricles often signals loss of brain volume or other types of damage to the brain, these results add to scientific evidence that space poses a risk to astronauts' brain health (Barisano et al., 2022).

Other studies help to explain *why* this change might occur: The space environment exposes astronauts to very low gravity—called microgravity—and radiation. Astronauts also spend long periods isolated in small, confined spaces. These characteristics of space flight shift the position of the brain within the skull, change the volume of parts of the brain, and increase the buildup of fluid. Now neuroscientists at NASA and other organizations are seeking methods to minimize or prevent these negative effects and make it safer for astronauts to travel to the International Space Station, the moon, and even Mars.

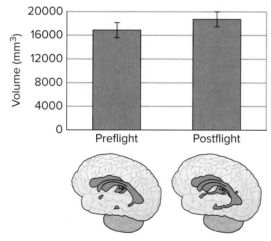

The bar graph shows the average size of astronauts' lateral ventricles, the largest fluid-filled chambers in the brain, before and after spending 6 months on the International Space Station. The images are based on averaging the brain map of each individual astronaut to show the size and shape of the lateral ventricles, shown in orange, before and after spaceflight. You can see from the bar graph and the brain images that the ventricles were larger after spaceflight.
Source: Barisano et al., 2022.

THE PSYCHODYNAMIC PERSPECTIVE: UNDERSTANDING THE INNER PERSON

To many people who have never taken a psychology course, psychology begins and ends with the psychodynamic perspective. Proponents of the **psychodynamic perspective**

psychodynamic perspective The approach based on the view that behavior is motivated by unconscious inner forces over which the individual has little control. (Module 2)

Sigmund Freud
Chronicle/Alamy Stock Photo

behavioral perspective The approach that suggests that observable, external behavior, which can be objectively measured, should be the focus of study. (Module 2, 37)

argue that behavior is motivated by inner forces and conflicts about which we have little awareness or control. They view dreams and slips of the tongue as indications of what a person is truly feeling within a seething cauldron of unconscious psychic activity.

The origins of the psychodynamic view are linked to one person: Sigmund Freud. Freud was an Austrian physician in the early 1900s whose ideas about unconscious determinants of behavior had a revolutionary effect on 20th-century thinking, not just in psychology but in related fields as well. Although some of the original Freudian principles have been roundly criticized, the contemporary psychodynamic perspective has provided a means not only to understand and treat some kinds of psychological disorders but also to understand everyday phenomena such as prejudice and aggression.

THE BEHAVIORAL PERSPECTIVE: OBSERVING THE OUTER PERSON

Whereas the neuroscience and psychodynamic approaches look at what is inside people to determine the causes of their behavior, the behavioral perspective takes a different approach. Proponents of the behavioral perspective rejected psychology's early emphasis on the internal workings of the mind and brain. Instead, the **behavioral perspective** suggests that the focus should be on external behavior that can be directly observed and measured objectively.

John B. Watson was the first major American psychologist to use a behavioral approach. Working in the 1920s, Watson believed that one could gain a complete understanding of behavior by studying the environment in which a person operated.

In fact, Watson believed rather optimistically that it was possible to bring about any desired type of behavior by controlling a person's environment. This philosophy is clear in his own words: "Give me a dozen healthy infants, well-formed, and my own specified world to bring them up in and I'll guarantee to take any one at random and train him to become any type of specialist I might select—doctor, lawyer, artist, merchant-chief, and yes, even beggar-man and thief, regardless of his talents, penchants, tendencies, abilities, vocations and race of his ancestors" (Watson, 1924).

The behavioral perspective was championed by B. F. Skinner, a pioneer in the field. Much of our understanding of how people learn new behaviors is based on the behavioral perspective. As we will see, the behavioral perspective crops up along every byway of psychology. Along with its influence in the area of learning processes, this perspective has made contributions in such diverse areas as treating mental disorders, curbing aggression, resolving sexual problems, and ending drug addiction (Schlinger, 2011; Ruiz, 2015; Fryling, 2017).

THE COGNITIVE PERSPECTIVE: IDENTIFYING THE ROOTS OF UNDERSTANDING

cognitive perspective The approach that focuses on how people think, understand, and know about the world. (Module 2, 37)

Efforts to understand behavior lead some psychologists straight into the mind. Evolving in part from structuralism and in part as a reaction to behaviorism, which focused so heavily on observable behavior and the environment, the **cognitive perspective** focuses on how people think, understand, and know about the world. The emphasis is on learning how people comprehend and represent the outside world within themselves and how our ways of thinking about the world influence our behavior.

Many psychologists who adhere to the cognitive perspective compare human thinking to the workings of a computer, which takes in information and transforms, stores, and retrieves it. In their view, thinking is *information processing*.

Psychologists who rely on the cognitive perspective ask questions on subjects ranging from how people make decisions to whether a person can watch television and study at the same time. The common elements that link cognitive approaches are an emphasis on how people understand and think about the world and an interest in describing the patterns and irregularities in the operation of our minds.

From the perspective of...

A Health-Care Provider How can a basic understanding of psychology improve your job performance in the health-care industry?

Tetra Images/Getty Images

THE HUMANISTIC PERSPECTIVE: THE UNIQUE QUALITIES OF THE HUMAN SPECIES

The humanistic perspective rejects the view that behavior is determined largely by automatically unfolding biological forces, unconscious processes, or the external world around us. Instead, the **humanistic perspective** suggests that all individuals naturally strive to grow, develop, and be in control of their lives and behavior. Humanistic psychologists maintain that each of us has the capacity to seek and reach fulfillment.

According to Carl Rogers and Abraham Maslow, who were central figures in the development of the humanistic perspective, people actively strive to reach their full potential. The emphasis of the humanistic perspective is on *free will*, the ability to freely make decisions about one's own behavior and life. The notion of free will stands in contrast to *determinism*, which sees behavior as caused, or determined, by things beyond a person's control.

The humanistic perspective assumes that people have the ability to make their own choices about their behavior rather than relying on societal standards. More than any other approach, it stresses the role of psychology in enriching people's lives and helping them achieve self-fulfillment. By reminding psychologists of their commitment to the individual person in society, the humanistic perspective has been an important influence (Linley, 2013; Hayes, 2015; DeRobertis & Bland, 2019; DeRobertis, 2021).

Don't let the abstract qualities of the broad approaches we have discussed lull you into thinking that they are purely theoretical: These perspectives underlie ongoing work of a practical nature, as we discuss throughout this book. To start seeing how psychology can improve everyday life, read the *Applying Psychology in the 21st Century* feature.

humanistic perspective The approach that suggests that all individuals naturally strive to grow, develop, and be in control of their lives and behavior. (Module 2, 37)

APPLYING PSYCHOLOGY IN THE 21ST CENTURY

PSYCHOLOGY MATTERS

"Investigators search for clues at site of suicide bombing."

"Anti-vaxxers claim COVID is a hoax."

"Use of social media sites TikTok and Instagram are associated with teenage depression."

"Black suspect in robbery dies after clash with police."

"Young Americans sue federal government for failing to limit climate change, thereby depriving them of a climate system capable of sustaining human life."

A quick review of any day's news headlines reminds us that the world is beset by a variety of stubborn problems that resist easy solutions. At the same time, a considerable number of psychologists are devoting their energies and expertise to addressing these problems and improving the human condition. Let's consider some of the ways in which psychology has addressed and helped work toward solutions to major societal problems:

Concerns about climate change have led to a surge of interest in environmental psychology.

Design Pics/PunchStock

- *Why did a substantial minority of people believe that COVID-19 vaccines were harmful, with some even denying the existence of the pandemic?* Not only did the pandemic upend many peoples' lives, it also led to substantial disagreements about the cause of the pandemic and how to treat the virus. Mandates about wearing protective masks, lock-downs, and quarantines produced a wide range of reactions–from acceptance to complete rejection–that complicated public-health responses to the pandemic. Research psychologists sought to understand the reasons for such varied responses, and those who provide mental health support developed new treatment techniques to alleviate the anxiety and depression that many people experienced (Caviccioli et al., 2021; Favreau et al., 2021; Ranot, 2021).

- *What are the roots of racism in the United States?* Psychologists have discovered that even subtle forms of prejudice and discrimination can cause significant harm in recipients. Furthermore, they have learned that people who sincerely believe themselves to not be racist still harbor unconscious racist thoughts that can translate into discriminatory behavior. On the positive side, they are developing strategies that break down racial barriers and heal the hurt and stigma of decades of racism (Fisher et al., 2017; David & Derthick, 2018; Shrikant et al., 2022).

- *How is social media changing the way we live?* Social-networking media such as Facebook, TikTok, Instagram, and Twitter have changed the way people communicate and the way news spreads around the world. How do these social media platforms affect the way people relate to each other? How do they affect our perceptions of world events and even our own emotions? Psychologists are examining the motivations behind social networking, its influence on individuals and social institutions, and possible beneficial applications of the technology (Zyoud et al., 2018; Parent, Gobble, & Rochlen, 2019; Valkenbeurg, Meier, & Beyes, 2022).

- *How is information about climate change affecting the way people interact with the environment?* Psychologists are applying their knowledge and skills to addressing environmental issues. How can we encourage behavior that will benefit rather than harm the environment? How do people learn and understand the causes of climate change? How do changes in temperature affect people's lives and psychological health? Work by psychologists will increasingly influence these vital questions (Abeles et al., 2019; Xiang et al., 2019).

- *What are the causes of terrorism?* What motivates suicide bombers? Are they psychologically disordered, or can their behavior be seen as a rational response to a particular system of beliefs? As we'll see when we discuss psychological disorders, psychologists are gaining an understanding of the factors that lead people to embrace suicide and to engage in terrorism to further a cause in which they deeply believe (Theriault, Krause, & Young, 2017; Choma et al., 2018; Leder, Schlegel, & Schütz, 2021).

- *What gives people satisfaction with life and a sense of well being?* Research has found that during difficult economic times, it's important to understand that wealth and possessions don't make people happy. Instead, happiness comes from enjoying life's little moments and finding purpose and meaning in what you do (Crespo & Mesurado, 2015; Jin & Kim, 2017; Etxeberria, Etxebarria, & Urdaneta, 2019).

These topics represent just a few of the issues that psychologists address daily. To further explore the many ways that psychology has an impact on everyday life, check out the American Psychological Association (APA) website, at www.apa.org, which features psychological applications in everyday life.

RETHINK

- What do *you* think are the major problems affecting society today?
- What are the psychological issues involved in these problems, and how might psychologists help find solutions to them?

Psychology's Key Issues and Controversies

As you consider the many topics and perspectives that make up psychology, ranging from a narrow focus on minute biochemical influences on behavior to a broad focus on social behaviors, you might find yourself thinking that the discipline lacks cohesion. However, the field is more unified than a first glimpse might suggest. For one thing, no matter what topical area a psychologist specializes in, they rely primarily on one of the five major perspectives. For example, a developmental psychologist who specializes in the study of children could make use of the cognitive perspective or the psychodynamic perspective or any of the other major perspectives.

Psychologists also agree on what the key issues of the field are (see Figure 3). Although there are major arguments regarding how best to address and resolve the key

Issue	Neuroscience	Cognitive	Behavioral	Humanistic	Psychodynamic
Nature (heredity) vs. nurture (environment)	Nature (heredity)	Both	Nurture (environment)	Nurture (environment)	Nature (heredity)
Conscious vs. unconscious determinants of behavior	Unconscious	Both	Conscious	Conscious	Unconscious
Observable behavior vs. internal mental processes	Internal emphasis	Internal emphasis	Observable emphasis	Internal emphasis	Internal emphasis
Free will vs. determinism	Determinism	Free will	Determinism	Free will	Determinism
Individual differences vs. universal principles	Universal emphasis	Individual emphasis	Both	Individual emphasis	Universal emphasis

FIGURE 3 Key issues in psychology and the positions taken by psychologists subscribing to the five major perspectives of psychology.
(Neuroscience): Alfred Pasieka/Science Photo Library/Alamy Stock Photo; (Cognitive): Les Byerley/Shutterstock; (Behavioral): Ariel Skelley/Blend Images LLC; (Humanistic): fizkes/Shutterstock; (Psychodynamic): Athanasia Nomikou/Shutterstock

issues, psychology is a unified science because psychologists of all perspectives agree that the issues must be addressed if the field is going to advance. As you contemplate these key issues, try not to think of them in "either/or" terms. Instead, consider the opposing viewpoints on each issue as the opposite ends of a continuum, with the positions of individual psychologists typically falling somewhere between the two ends.

Issue 1: *Nature (heredity) versus nurture (environment).* How much of people's behavior is due to their genetically determined nature (heredity), and how much is due to nurture, the influences of the physical and social environment in which a child is raised? Furthermore, what is the interplay between heredity and environment? These questions have deep philosophical and historical roots, and they are involved in many topics in psychology.

A psychologist's take on this issue depends partly on which major perspective they subscribe to. For example, developmental psychologists whose focus is on how people grow and change throughout the course of their lives may be most interested in learning more about hereditary influences if they follow a neuroscience perspective. In contrast, developmental psychologists who are proponents of the behavioral perspective are more likely to focus on environment (Moffitt, Caspi, & Rutter, 2006; Barrett, 2011).

However, every psychologist would agree that neither nature nor nurture alone is the sole determinant of behavior; rather, it is a combination of the two. In a sense, then, the real controversy involves how much of our behavior is caused by heredity and how much is caused by environmental influences.

Issue 2: *Conscious versus unconscious causes of behavior.* How much of our behavior is produced by forces of which we are fully aware, and how much is due to unconscious activity—mental processes that are not accessible to the conscious mind? This question represents one of the great controversies in the field of psychology. For example, clinical psychologists adopting a psychodynamic perspective argue that psychological disorders are brought about by unconscious factors, whereas psychologists employing the cognitive perspective suggest that psychological disorders largely are the result of faulty thinking processes.

Issue 3: *Observable behavior versus internal mental processes.* Should psychology concentrate solely on behavior that can be seen by outside observers, or should it focus on unseen thinking processes? Some psychologists, particularly those relying on the

Study Alert
Use Figure 3 to learn the key issues that underlie every subfield of psychology.

behavioral perspective, contend that the only legitimate source of information for psychologists is behavior that can be observed directly. Other psychologists, building on the cognitive perspective, argue that what goes on inside a person's mind is critical to understanding behavior, and so we must concern ourselves with mental processes.

Issue 4: *Free will versus determinism.* How much of our behavior is a matter of **free will** (choices made freely by an individual), and how much is subject to **determinism,** the notion that behavior is largely produced by factors beyond people's willful control? An issue long debated by philosophers, the free-will/determinism argument is also central to the field of psychology (Goto et al., 2015; Moynihan, Igou, & van Tilburg, 2017; Allakhverdov, 2019).

free will The idea that behavior is caused primarily by choices that are made freely by the individual. (Module 2)

determinism The idea that people's behavior is produced primarily by factors outside of their willful control. (Module 2)

For example, some psychologists who specialize in psychological disorders argue that people make intentional choices and that those who display so-called abnormal behavior should be considered responsible for their actions. Other psychologists disagree and contend that such individuals are the victims of forces beyond their control. The position psychologists take on this issue has important implications for the way they treat psychological disorders, especially in deciding whether treatment should be forced on people who don't want it.

Issue 5: *Individual differences versus universal principles.* Specifically, how much of behavior is due to the unique and special qualities or each person–the individual differences that characterize them–compared with how much stems from the culture and society in which people live, reflecting universal principles that underlie the behavior of all humans? Psychologists who rely on the neuroscience perspective tend to look for universal principles of behavior, such as how the nervous system operates or the way certain hormones automatically prime us for sexual activity. Such psychologists concentrate on the similarities in our behavioral destinies despite vast differences in our upbringing. In contrast, psychologists who employ the humanistic perspective focus more on the uniqueness of every individual. They consider every person's behavior a reflection of distinct and special individual qualities.

The question of the degree to which psychologists can identify universal principles that apply to all people has taken on new significance in light of the tremendous demographic changes now occurring in the United States and around the world. As we discuss next, these changes raise new and critical issues for the discipline of psychology in the 21st century.

From the perspective of...

A Social Worker Imagine that you have a caseload of clients who come from diverse cultures, ethnicities, and races. How might you consider their diverse backgrounds when assisting them?

Sam Edwards/OJO Images/age fotostock

Psychology's Future

We have examined psychology's foundations, but what does the future hold for the discipline? Although the course of scientific development is notoriously difficult to predict, several trends seem likely:

- As its knowledge base grows, psychology will become increasingly specialized, and new perspectives will evolve. For example, our growing understanding of the brain and the nervous system, combined with scientific advances in genetics and gene therapy, will allow psychologists to focus on *prevention* of psychological disorders rather than only on their treatment (Cuijpers et al., 2008; Goldstein, Ross, & De Luca, 2019).

- The evolving sophistication of neuroscientific approaches is likely to have an increasing influence over other branches of psychology. For instance, social psychologists already are increasing their understanding of social behaviors such as persuasion by using brain scans as part of an evolving field known as *social neuroscience.* Furthermore, as neuroscientific techniques become more sophisticated, there will be new ways of applying that knowledge, as we discuss in *Neuroscience in Your Life* (Cacioppo & Decety, 2009; Di Ieva et al., 2015; Mattan, Kubota, & Cloutier, 2017).

- Psychology's influence on issues of public interest also will grow. The major problems of our time—such as violence, terrorism, racial and ethnic prejudice, poverty, and environmental changes, and technological disasters—have important psychological components. Already, psychology has had significant influences on social policy, informing lawmakers' decision making, a trend that is likely to increase (Zimbardo, 2004; Dweck, 2017; Fiske, 2017).

- Psychologists will follow increasingly strict ethical and moral guidelines. When it was revealed in 2015 that several psychologists participated in the interrogation and torture of military prisoners in the aftermath of the 9/11 terrorist attacks and that some of the leaders of the American Psychological Association (APA) were aware of these activities, a national scandal ensued. As a consequence, the APA adopted strict new guidelines that prohibit psychologists from participating in national security interrogations. In addition, psychologists are barred from working at the Guantánamo base in Cuba and at CIA black sites (Risen, 2015; Fink, 2017).

- The public's view of psychology will become more informed. Surveys show that the public at large does not fully understand the scientific underpinnings of the field. However, as the field itself embraces such practices as using scientific evidence to choose the best treatments for psychological disorders, psychology's reputation will grow (Lilienfeld, 2012; Ferguson, 2015).

- Finally, as the population becomes more diverse, issues of diversity—embodied in the study of racial, ethnic, linguistic, and cultural factors—will become more important to psychologists providing services and doing research. The result will be a field that can provide an understanding of *human* behavior in its broadest sense (Quintana et al., 2006; Richmond et al., 2015).

RECAP/EVALUATE/RETHINK

RECAP

LO 2-1 What are the origins of psychology?

- Wilhelm Wundt laid the foundation of psychology in 1879, when he opened his laboratory in Germany.
- Early perspectives that guided the work of psychologists were structuralism, functionalism, and Gestalt theory.

LO 2-2 What are the major approaches in contemporary psychology?

- The neuroscience approach focuses on the biological components of the behavior of people and animals.

- The psychodynamic perspective suggests that powerful, unconscious inner forces and conflicts about which people have little or no awareness are the primary determinants of behavior.
- The behavioral perspective deemphasizes internal processes and concentrates instead on observable, measurable behavior, suggesting that understanding and control of a person's environment are sufficient to fully explain and modify behavior.
- Cognitive approaches to behavior consider how people know, understand, and think about the world.
- The humanistic perspective emphasizes that people are uniquely inclined toward psychological growth and

higher levels of functioning and that they will strive to reach their full potential.

LO 2-3 What are psychology's key issues and controversies?

- Psychology's key issues and controversies center on how much of human behavior is a product of nature or nurture, conscious or unconscious thoughts, observable actions or internal mental processes, free will or determinism, and individual differences or universal principles.

LO 2-4 What is the future of psychology likely to hold?

- Psychology will become increasingly specialized, will pay greater attention to prevention instead of just treatment, will become more and more concerned with the public interest, and will take the growing diversity of the country's population into account more fully.

EVALUATE

1. Wundt described psychology as the study of conscious experience, a perspective he called _____.
2. Early psychologists studied the mind by asking people to describe what they were experiencing when exposed to various stimuli. This procedure was known as _____.
3. The statement "In order to study human behavior, we must consider the whole of perception rather than its component parts" might be made by a person subscribing to which perspective of psychology?

4. Jeanne's therapist asks her to recount a violent dream she recently experienced in order to gain insight into the unconscious forces affecting her behavior. Jeanne's therapist is working from a _____ perspective.
5. "It is behavior that can be observed that should be studied, not the suspected inner workings of the mind." This statement was most likely made by someone with which perspective?
   a. cognitive perspective
   b. neuroscience perspective
   c. humanistic perspective
   d. behavioral perspective
6. "My therapist is wonderful! He always points out my positive traits. He dwells on my uniqueness and strength as an individual. I feel much more confident about myself—as if I'm really growing and reaching my potential." The therapist being described most likely follows a _____ perspective.
7. In the nature-nurture issue, nature refers to heredity, and nurture refers to the _____.

RETHINK

Focusing on one of the five major perspectives in use today (i.e., neuroscience, psychodynamic, behavioral, cognitive, and humanistic), can you describe the kinds of research questions and studies that researchers using that perspective might pursue?

Answers to Evaluate Questions

1. structuralism; 2. introspection; 3. Gestalt; 4. psychodynamic; 5. d. Behavioral perspective; 6. humanistic; 7. environment

KEY TERMS

structuralism	Gestalt (geh-SHTALLT) psychology	psychodynamic perspective	humanistic perspective
introspection		behavioral perspective	free will
functionalism	neuroscience perspective	cognitive perspective	determinism

Module 3
Research in Psychology

The Scientific Method

Do "Birds of a feather flock together" or is it "Opposites attract"? "Two heads are better than one" or "If you want a thing done well, do it yourself"? And how about, "The more the merrier" versus "Two's company, three's a crowd"?

If we were to rely on common sense to understand behavior, we'd have considerable difficulty–especially because commonsense views are often contradictory. In fact, one of the major undertakings for the field of psychology is to develop suppositions about behavior and to determine which of those suppositions are accurate (Ferguson, 2015).

Psychologists–as well as scientists in other disciplines–meet the challenge of posing appropriate questions and properly answering them by relying on the scientific method. The **scientific method** is the approach used by psychologists to systematically acquire knowledge and understanding about behavior and other phenomena of interest. As illustrated in Figure 1, it consists of four main steps: (1) identifying questions of interest, (2) formulating an explanation, (3) carrying out research designed to support or refute the explanation, and (4) communicating the findings.

THEORIES: SPECIFYING BROAD EXPLANATIONS

In using the scientific method, psychologists start by identifying questions of interest. We have all been curious at some time about our observations of everyday behavior. If you have ever asked yourself why a particular teacher is so easily annoyed, why a

LEARNING OUTCOMES

LO 3-1 What is the scientific method?

LO 3-2 What role do theories and hypotheses play in psychological research?

LO 3-3 What research methods do psychologists use?

LO 3-4 How do psychologists establish cause-and-effect relationships in research studies?

! **Study Alert**
Use Figure 1 to remember the four steps of the scientific method (identifying questions, formulating an explanation, carrying out research, and communicating the findings).

scientific method The approach through which psychologists systematically acquire knowledge and understanding about behavior and other phenomena of interest. (Module 3)

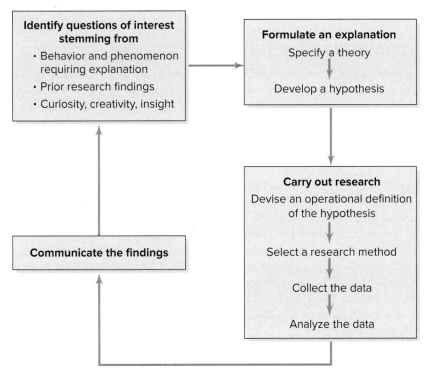

FIGURE 1 The scientific method, which encompasses the process of identifying, asking, and answering questions, is used by psychologists and by researchers from every other scientific discipline to come to an understanding about the world. What do you think are the advantages of this method?

friend is always late for appointments, or how your dog understands your commands, you have been formulating questions about behavior.

Psychologists, too, ask questions about the nature and causes of behavior. They may want to explore explanations for everyday behaviors or for various phenomena. They may also pose questions that build on findings from their previous research or from research carried out by other psychologists. Or they may produce new questions that are based on curiosity, creativity, or insight.

theories Broad explanations and predictions concerning observations of interest. (Module 3)

After a question has been identified, the next step in the scientific method is to develop a theory to explain the observed phenomenon. **Theories** are broad explanations and predictions concerning observations of interest. They provide a framework for understanding the relationships among a set of otherwise unorganized facts or principles.

All of us have developed our own informal theories of human behavior, such as "People are basically good" or "People's behavior is usually motivated by self-interest." However, psychologists' theories are more formal and focused. They are established on the basis of a careful study of the psychological literature to identify earlier relevant research and previously formulated theories, as well as psychologists' general knowledge of the field.

Growing out of the diverse approaches employed by psychologists, theories vary both in their breadth and in their level of detail. For example, one theory might seek to explain and predict a phenomenon as broad as emotional experience. A narrower theory might attempt to explain why people display the emotion of fear nonverbally after receiving a threat (Smith et al., 2017; Gruber et al., 2019; Reisenzein, 2021).

Psychologists Bibb Latané and John Darley, responding to the failure of bystanders to intervene when Kitty Genovese was murdered in New York, developed what they called a theory of *diffusion of responsibility* (Latané & Darley, 1970). According to their theory, the greater the number of bystanders or witnesses to an event that calls for helping behavior, the more the responsibility for helping is perceived to be shared by all the bystanders. Thus, the greater the number of bystanders in an emergency situation, the smaller the share of the responsibility each person feels—and the less likely that any single person will come forward to help.

HYPOTHESES: CRAFTING TESTABLE PREDICTIONS

Although the diffusion of responsibility theory seems to make sense, it represented only the beginning phase of Latané and Darley's investigative process. Their next step was to devise a way to test their theory. To do this, they needed to create a hypothesis. A **hypothesis** is a prediction stated in a way that allows it to be tested. Hypotheses stem from theories; they help test the underlying soundness of theories.

hypothesis A prediction, stemming from a theory, stated in a way that allows it to be tested. (Module 3)

In the same way that we develop our own broad theories about the world, we also construct hypotheses about events and behavior. Those hypotheses can range from trivialities (such as why your English instructor wears those weirdly colored shirts) to more meaningful matters (such as the best way to study for a test). Although we rarely test these hypotheses systematically, we do try to determine whether they are right. Perhaps we try comparing two strategies: cramming the night before an exam versus spreading out our study over several nights. By assessing which approach yields better test performance, we have created a way to compare the two strategies.

operational definition The translation of a hypothesis into specific, testable procedures that can be measured and observed. (Module 3)

A hypothesis must be stated in a way that will allow it to be tested, which involves creating an operational definition. An **operational definition** is the translation of a hypothesis into specific, testable procedures that can be measured and observed in an experiment.

There is no single way to go about devising an operational definition for a hypothesis; it depends on logic, the equipment and facilities available, the psychological perspective being employed, and ultimately the creativity of the researcher. For example, one researcher might develop a hypothesis that uses as an operational definition of "fear" an increase in heart rate. In contrast, another psychologist might use as an operational definition of "fear" a written response to the question "How much fear are you experiencing at this moment?"

Latané and Darley's hypothesis was a straightforward prediction from their more general theory of diffusion of responsibility: The more people who witness an emergency situation, the less likely it is that help will be given to a victim. They could, of course, have chosen another hypothesis (try to think of one!), but their initial formulation seemed to offer the most direct test of the theory.

Psychologists rely on formal theories and hypotheses for many reasons. For one thing, theories and hypotheses allow them to make sense of unorganized, separate observations and bits of data. They permit them to place observations and data within a coherent framework. In addition, theories and hypotheses allow psychologists to move beyond known facts and make deductions about unexplained phenomena and develop ideas for future investigation (Barrett & Russell, 2015; Haig, 2018; Laplane et al., 2019).

In short, the scientific method, with its emphasis on theories and hypotheses, helps psychologists pose appropriate questions. With properly stated questions in hand, psychologists then can choose from a variety of research methods to find answers.

> **! Study Alert**
> Remember that a theory is a broad explanation, whereas a hypothesis is a more narrow prediction.

Psychological Research

Research—systematic inquiry aimed at the discovery of new knowledge—is a central ingredient of the scientific method in psychology. It provides the key to understanding the degree to which hypotheses (and the theories behind them) are accurate.

Just as we can apply different theories and hypotheses to explain the same phenomena, we can use a number of alternative methods to conduct research. As we consider the major tools that psychologists use to conduct research, keep in mind that their relevance extends beyond testing and evaluating hypotheses in psychology. All of us carry out elementary forms of research on our own. For instance, a supervisor might evaluate an employee's performance; a physician might systematically test the effects of different doses of a drug on a patient; a salesperson might compare different persuasive strategies. Each of these situations draws on the research practices we are about to discuss.

Descriptive Research

Let's begin by considering several types of *descriptive research* designed to systematically investigate a person, group, or patterns of behavior. These methods include archival research, naturalistic observation, survey research, and case studies.

ARCHIVAL RESEARCH

Suppose that, like the psychologists Latané and Darley (1970), you were interested in finding out more about emergency situations in which bystanders did not provide help. One of the first places you might turn to could be historical accounts. By searching newspaper records, for example, you might find support for the notion that a decrease in helping behavior historically has accompanied an increase in the number of bystanders.

Using newspaper articles is an example of archival research. In **archival research,** existing data, such as census documents, college records, online databases, and newspaper articles, are examined to test a hypothesis. For example, college transcripts, stored by colleges for every student, may be analyzed and used to determine whether there are gender differences in academic performance. Similarly, social media sites such as Facebook and Twitter provide huge pools of data from millions of users that researchers can use—though this practice raises serious privacy issues (Fisher & Barnes-Farrell, 2013; Kosinski et al., 2015; Haji & Stock, 2021).

archival research Research in which existing data, such as census documents, college records, and newspaper articles, are examined to test a hypothesis. (Module 3)

Archival research is a relatively inexpensive means of testing a hypothesis because someone else has already collected the basic data. Of course, the use of existing data has several drawbacks. For one thing, the data may not be in a form that allows the researcher to test a hypothesis fully. The information could be incomplete, or it could have been collected haphazardly (Zickar, 2015; Tully & Carr, 2021).

Most attempts at archival research are hampered by the simple fact that records with the necessary information may not exist. In these instances, researchers often turn to another research method: naturalistic observation.

NATURALISTIC OBSERVATION

naturalistic observation Research in which an investigator simply observes some naturally occurring behavior and does not make a change in the situation. (Module 3)

In **naturalistic observation,** the investigator observes some naturally occurring behavior and does not make a change in the situation. For example, a researcher investigating helping behavior might observe the kind of help given to victims in a high-crime area of a city. The important point to remember about naturalistic observation is that the researcher simply records what occurs, making no modification in the situation that is being observed (Haas et al., 2015; Wilson & Joye, 2017; Smith & Pinter-Wollman, 2021).

Although the advantage of naturalistic observation is obvious—we get a sample of what people do in their "natural habitat"—there is also an important drawback: the inability to control any of the factors of interest. For example, we might find so few naturally occurring instances of helping behavior that we would be unable to draw any conclusions. Because naturalistic observation prevents researchers from making changes in a situation, they must wait until the appropriate conditions occur. Furthermore, if people know they are being watched, they may alter their reactions and produce behavior that is not truly representative.

SURVEY RESEARCH

survey research Research in which people chosen to represent a larger population are asked a series of questions about their behavior, thoughts, or attitudes. (Module 3)

There is no more straightforward way of finding out what people think, feel, and do than asking them directly. For this reason, surveys are an important research method. In **survey research,** a *sample* of people chosen to represent a larger group of interest (a *population*) is asked a series of questions about their behavior, thoughts, or attitudes.

Survey methods have become so sophisticated that even with a relatively small sample, researchers can infer with accuracy how a larger group would respond. For instance,

In an example of naturalistic observation, researchers observe primates in their natural habitat.
Suzanne Long/Alamy Stock Photo

a sample of just a few thousand voters is typically sufficient to predict within one or two percentage points who will win a presidential election–if the representative sample is chosen with care (Rea & Parker, 2014; Cowles & Nelson, 2018; Doss et al., 2021).

Researchers investigating helping behavior might conduct a survey by asking people to complete a questionnaire in which they indicate their reluctance for giving aid to someone. Similarly, researchers interested in learning about sexual practices have carried out surveys to learn which practices are common and which are not and to chart changing notions of sexual morality historically (Mendoza-Pérez et al., 2019; Griffin et al., 2022).

Surveys also play a role in driving public policy. For example, a recent survey of U.S. teenagers and young adults found that more than 70% believe that climate change will cause a moderate or great deal of harm to people in their generation. Furthermore, a majority are afraid and angry about it, and 1 in 7 have participated in some sort of demonstration or rally, or have written to a public official to discuss their views on global warming. The results of surveys on such topics can influence lawmakers as well as psychological research on the anxieties of people concerned with climate change. Moreover, psychologists may use such survey data to understand how anxieties about climate change are translated into activism. In short, surveys can spur additional research (Hamel et al., 2019; Noth & Tonzer, 2022; Özkula et al., 2022).

However, survey research has several potential pitfalls. For one thing, if the sample of people who are surveyed is not representative of the broader population of interest, the results of the survey will have little meaning. For instance, if a sample of voters in a town includes only Republicans, it would hardly be useful for predicting the results of an election in which both Republicans and Democrats are voting. Consequently, researchers using surveys strive to obtain a *random sample* of the population in question in which every voter in the town has an equal chance of being included in the sample receiving the survey (Davern, 2013; Engel et al., 2015; Nedelec, 2017).

In addition, survey respondents may not want to admit to holding socially undesirable attitudes. For example, a person holding racist attitudes may not want to admit it. Similarly, people who are suspicious of polling or the media may be unwilling to give responses that reflect their true opinions–something that may have led to an underestimation of the extent of support for Donald Trump in polls leading up to the 2016 presidential election (Zitner, 2021).

Furthermore, people may not want to admit they engage in behaviors that they feel are somehow abnormal–a problem that plagues surveys of sexual behavior because people are often reluctant to admit what they really do in private. Finally, in some cases, people may not even be consciously aware of what their true attitudes are or why they hold them (King, 2022).

From the perspective of...

A Marketing Manager How would you design a survey that targets the customers in which you are most interested?

Jack Hollingsworth/Getty Images

ETHNOGRAPHIC RESEARCH

One form of research that is particularly appropriate for studying behavior across and between cultures is known as ethnographic research. First developed by anthropologists,

ethnographic research A type of research that seeks to understand the attitudes, values, and behavior of a culture using in-depth, extended examination of people in their own environment. (Module 3)

ethnographic research seeks to understand the attitudes and values of a culture using in-depth, extended examination of people in their own environment.

Researchers using ethnographic techniques often act as participant observers, embedding themselves in a culture for months or even years. Through in-depth interviews and observation of everyday life, researchers attempt to understand behavior in cultures that may differ significantly from their own. Ethnographic research is also sometimes used to examine subgroups within a culture, such as members of other racial and ethnic groups. For example, a researcher interested in socialization in Latina adolescents might study the practice of holding a *quinceañera*, a celebration of a girl's 15th birthday (Ayón et al., 2020; Graham et al., 2020; Soundy & Heneghan, 2022).

Although an ethnographic study can provide a detailed look at behavior in a particular setting, such studies have several drawbacks. For example, only a relatively small number of people are studied, making it difficult to draw generalizations. Moreover, researchers may not understand or may misinterpret the meaning of behavior in cultures other than their own, thereby invalidating their observations. Still, qualitative studies can offer a good starting point for deeply understanding members of cultures other than one's own (Ruffa & Evangelista, 2021).

THE CASE STUDY

When we hear about the perpetrator of a school shooting, many of us wonder what it is about the shooter's personality or background that leads to such behavior. To answer this question, psychologists might conduct a case study. In contrast to a survey, in which many people are studied, a **case study** is an in-depth, intensive investigation of a single individual or a small group. Case studies might include *psychological testing*, a procedure in which a carefully designed set of questions is used to gain some insight into the personality of the individual or group (Addus et al., 2007; Cowles & Nelson, 2018).

case study An in-depth, intensive investigation of an individual or small group of people. (Module 3)

When case studies are used as a research technique, the goal is to use the insights gained from the study of one or a few individuals to improve our understanding of people in general. Sigmund Freud developed his theories through case studies of individual patients. Similarly, case studies of those who commit school shootings might help identify others who are prone to violence.

The drawback to case studies? If the individuals examined are unique in certain ways or if the sample is too small, it is impossible to make valid generalizations to a larger population. Still, case studies sometimes lead the way to better explanations as well as treatments for psychological disorders.

CORRELATIONAL RESEARCH

In using the descriptive research methods we have discussed, researchers often wish to determine the relationship between two variables. **Variables** are behaviors, events, or other characteristics that can change, or vary, in some way. For example, in a study to determine whether the amount of studying makes a difference in test scores, the variables would be study time and test scores.

variables Behaviors, events, or other characteristics that can change, or vary, in some way. (Module 3)

In **correlational research,** two sets of variables are examined to determine whether they are associated, or "correlated." The strength and direction of the relationship between the two variables are represented by a mathematical statistic known as a *correlation* (or, more formally, a *correlation coefficient*), which can range from +1.0 to −1.0.

correlational research Research in which the relationship between two sets of variables is examined to determine whether they are associated, or "correlated." (Module 3)

A *positive correlation* indicates that as the value of one variable increases, we can predict that the value of the other variable will also increase. For example, if we predict that the more time students spend studying for a test, the higher their grades on the test will be and that the less they study, the lower their test scores will be, we are expecting to find a positive correlation. (Higher values of the variable "amount of study time" would be associated with higher values of the variable "test score," and lower values of "amount of study time" would be associated with lower values of "test score.") The correlation, then, would be indicated by a positive number, and the stronger the association was between studying and test scores, the closer the number would be to +1.0. For example, we might find a correlation of +.85 between test scores and amount of study time, indicating a strong positive association.

In contrast, a *negative correlation* tells us that as the value of one variable increases, the value of the other decreases. For instance, we might predict that as the number of hours spent studying increases, the number of hours spent partying decreases. Here we are expecting a negative correlation, ranging between 0 and −1.0. More studying is associated with less partying, and less studying is associated with more partying. The stronger the association between studying and partying is, the closer the correlation will be to −1.0. For instance, a correlation of −.85 would indicate a strong negative association between partying and studying.

Of course, it's quite possible that little or no relationship exists between two variables. For instance, we would probably not expect to find a relationship between number of study hours and height. Lack of a relationship would be indicated by a correlation close to 0. For example, if we found a correlation of −.02 or +.03, it would indicate that there is virtually no association between the two variables; knowing how much students study does not tell us anything about how tall they are.

When two variables are strongly correlated with each other, it is tempting to assume that one variable causes changes in the other variable. For example, if we find that more study time is associated with higher grades, we might guess that more studying *causes* higher grades. Although this is not a bad guess, it remains just a guess because finding that two variables are correlated does not mean that there is a causal relationship between them. The strong correlation suggests that knowing how much a person studies can help us predict how that person will do on a test, but it does not mean that the studying *causes* the test performance. Instead, for instance, people who are more interested in the subject matter might study more than do those who are less interested, and so the amount of interest, not the number of hours spent studying, would predict test performance. The mere fact that two variables occur together does not mean that one causes the other.

Similarly, suppose you learned that the number of houses of worship in a large sample of cities was positively correlated with the number of people arrested, meaning that the more houses of worship, the more arrests there were in a city. Does this mean that the presence of more houses of worship caused the greater number of arrests? Almost surely not, of course. In this case, the underlying cause is probably the size of the city: In bigger cities, there are both more houses of worship *and* more arrests.

One more example illustrates the critical point that correlations tell us nothing about cause and effect but only provide a measure of the strength of a relationship between two variables. We might find that children who watch a lot of television programs featuring high levels of aggression are likely to demonstrate a relatively high degree of aggressive behavior and that those who watch few television shows that portray aggression are apt to exhibit a relatively low degree of such behavior (see Figure 2). But we cannot say that the aggression is *caused* by the TV viewing because many other explanations are possible.

For instance, children who have an unusually high level of energy may seek out programs with aggressive content *and* are more aggressive. The children's energy level, then, could be the true cause of the children's higher incidence of aggression. Also, people who are already highly aggressive might choose to watch shows with a high aggressive content *because* they are aggressive. Clearly, then, any number of causal sequences are possible–none of which can be ruled out by correlational research.

The inability of correlational research to demonstrate cause-and-effect relationships is a crucial drawback to its use. However, an alternative technique can establish causality: the experiment.

Study Alert

The concept that "correlation does not imply causation" is a key principle.

Many studies show that the observation of violence in the media is associated with aggression in viewers. Can we conclude that the observations of violence cause aggression?
David Grossman/Alamy Stock Photo

FIGURE 2 If we find that frequent viewing of television programs with aggressive content is associated with high levels of aggressive behavior, we might cite several plausible causes, as suggested in this figure. For example, (a) choosing to watch shows with aggressive content could produce aggression; or (b) being a highly aggressive person might cause one to choose to watch televised aggression; or (c) having a high energy level might cause a person to both choose to watch aggressive shows and to act aggressively. Correlational findings, then, do not permit us to determine causality. Can you think of a way to study the effects of televised aggression on aggressive behavior that is not correlational?

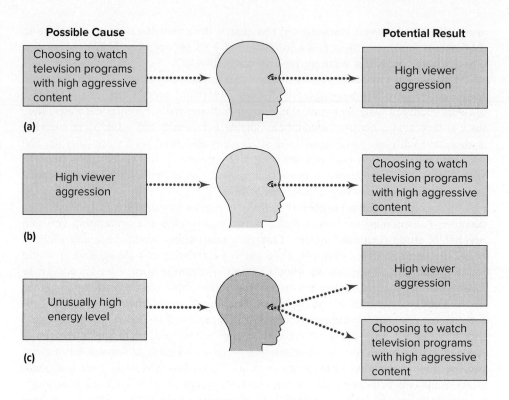

Possible Cause

(a) Choosing to watch television programs with high aggressive content → High viewer aggression — Potential Result

(b) High viewer aggression → Choosing to watch television programs with high aggressive content

(c) Unusually high energy level → High viewer aggression / Choosing to watch television programs with high aggressive content

Experimental Research

Carrying out experiments is the *only* way psychologists can establish cause-and-effect relationships. In a formal **experiment,** the researcher investigates the relationship between two (or more) variables by deliberately changing one variable in a controlled situation and observing the effects of that change on other aspects of the situation. In an experiment, then, the conditions are created and controlled by the researcher, who deliberately makes a change in those conditions in order to observe the effects of that change.

The **experimental manipulation** is the change that a researcher deliberately makes in an experiment. Experimental manipulations are used to detect relationships between different variables (Salazar et al., 2015; Mutz, 2021).

Several steps are involved in carrying out an experiment, but the process typically begins with the development of one or more hypotheses for the experiment to test. For example, Latané and Darley, in testing their theory of the diffusion of responsibility in bystander behavior, developed this hypothesis: The higher the number of people who witness an emergency situation is, the less likely it is that any of them will help the victim. They then designed an experiment to test this hypothesis.

Their first step was to formulate an operational definition of the hypothesis by conceptualizing it in a way that could be tested. Latané and Darley had to take into account the fundamental principle of experimental research mentioned earlier: Experimenters must manipulate at least one variable in order to observe the effects of the manipulation on another variable while keeping other factors in the situation constant. However, the manipulation cannot be viewed by itself, in isolation; if a cause-and-effect relationship is to be established, the effects of the manipulation must be compared with the effects of no manipulation or a different kind of manipulation.

EXPERIMENTAL GROUPS AND CONTROL GROUPS

Experimental research requires, then, that the responses of at least two groups be compared. One group will receive some special **treatment**–the manipulation

experiment The investigation of the relationship between two (or more) variables by deliberately producing a change in one variable in a situation and observing the effects of that change on other aspects of the situation. (Module 3)

experimental manipulation The change that an experimenter deliberately produces in a situation. (Module 3)

treatment The manipulation implemented by the experimenter. (Module 3)

implemented by the experimenter–and another group will receive either no treatment or a different treatment. Any group that receives a treatment is called an **experimental group;** a group that receives no treatment is called a **control group.** (In some experiments, there are multiple experimental and control groups, each of which is compared with another group.)

By employing both experimental and control groups in an experiment, researchers are able to rule out the possibility that something other than the experimental manipulation produced the results observed in the experiment. Without a control group, we couldn't be sure that some other variable, such as the temperature at the time we were running the experiment, the color of the experimenter's hair, or even the mere passage of time, wasn't causing the changes observed.

For example, consider a medical researcher who invents a medicine they think cures the common cold. To test this claim, the researcher gives the medicine one day to a group of 20 people who have colds and finds that 10 days later all of them are cured.

Eureka? Not so fast. An observer viewing this flawed study might reasonably argue that the people would have gotten better even without the medicine. What the researcher obviously needed was a control group consisting of people with colds who *don't* get the medicine and whose health is also checked 10 days later. Only if there is a significant difference between experimental and control groups can the effectiveness of the medicine be assessed. Through the use of control groups, then, researchers can isolate specific causes for their findings–and draw cause-and-effect inferences.

Returning to Latané and Darley's experiment, we see that the researchers needed to translate their hypothesis into something testable. To do this, they decided to create a false emergency situation that would appear to require the aid of a bystander. As their experimental manipulation, they decided to vary the number of bystanders present. They could have had just one experimental group with, say, two people present and a control group for comparison purposes with just one person present. Instead, they settled on a more complex procedure involving the creation of groups of three sizes–consisting of two, three, and six people–that could be compared with one another.

INDEPENDENT AND DEPENDENT VARIABLES

Latané and Darley's experimental design now included an operational definition of what is called the **independent variable.** The independent variable is the condition that is manipulated by an experimenter. (You can think of the independent variable as being independent of the actions of those taking part in an experiment; it is controlled by the experimenter.) In the case of the Latané and Darley experiment, the independent variable was the number of people present, which was manipulated by the experimenters.

The next step was to decide how they were going to determine the effect that varying the number of bystanders had on behavior of those in the experiment. Crucial to every experiment is the **dependent variable.** The dependent variable is the variable that is measured in a study. The dependent variable is expected to change as a result of the experimenter's manipulation of the independent variable. The dependent variable is dependent on the actions of the *participants* or *subjects*–the people taking part in the experiment.

Latané and Darley had several possible choices for their dependent measure. One might have been a simple yes/no measure of the participants' helping behavior. But the investigators also wanted a more precise analysis of helping behavior.

experimental group Any group participating in an experiment that receives a treatment. (Module 3)

control group A group participating in an experiment that receives no treatment. (Module 3)

independent variable The variable that is manipulated by an experimenter. (Module 3)

dependent variable The variable that is measured in an experiment. It is expected to change as a result of the experimenter's manipulation of the independent variable. (Module 3)

In this experiment, the researcher monitors the child's reaction to various types of toys. Can you think of a hypothesis that might be tested in this way?

aquaArts studio/E+/Getty Images

Study Alert

To remember the difference between dependent and independent variables, recall that a hypothesis predicts how a dependent variable *depends* on the manipulation of the independent variable.

Consequently, they also measured the amount of time it took for a participant to provide help.

Latané and Darley now had all the necessary components of an experiment. The independent variable, manipulated by them, was the number of bystanders present in an emergency situation. The dependent variable was the measure of whether bystanders in each of the groups provided help and the amount of time it took them to do so. Consequently, like all experiments, this one had both an independent variable and a dependent variable. *All* true experiments in psychology fit this straightforward model.

RANDOM ASSIGNMENT OF PARTICIPANTS

To make the experiment a valid test of the hypothesis, Latané and Darley needed to add a final step to the design: properly assigning participants to a particular experimental group.

The significance of this step becomes clear when we examine various alternative procedures. For example, the experimenters might have assigned just males to the group with two bystanders, just females to the group with three bystanders, and both males and females to the group with six bystanders. If they had done this, however, any differences they found in helping behavior could not be attributed with any certainty solely to group size because the differences might just as well have been due to the composition of the group. A more reasonable procedure would be to ensure that each group had the same composition in terms of gender; then the researchers would be able to make comparisons across groups with considerably more accuracy.

Participants in each of the experimental groups ought to be comparable, and it is easy enough to create groups that are similar in terms of, for instance, age. The problem becomes a bit more tricky, though, when we consider other participant characteristics. How can we ensure that participants in each experimental group will be equally intelligent, extroverted, cooperative, and so forth, when the list of characteristics–any one of which could be important–is potentially endless?

random assignment to condition A procedure in which participants are assigned to different experimental groups or "conditions" on the basis of chance and chance alone. (Module 3)

The solution is a simple but elegant procedure called **random assignment to condition.** Participants are assigned to different experimental groups, or "conditions," on the basis of chance and chance alone. The experimenter might, for instance, flip a coin for each participant and assign a participant to one group when "heads" came up and to the other group when "tails" came up. The advantage of this technique is that there is an equal chance that participant characteristics will be distributed across the various groups. When a researcher uses random assignment–which in practice is usually carried out using computer-generated random numbers–chances are that each of the groups will have approximately the same proportion of intelligent people, cooperative people, extroverted people of varying genders, and so on.

Figure 3 provides another example of an experiment. Like all experiments, it includes the following set of key elements, which you should keep in mind as you consider whether a research study is truly an experiment:

- An independent variable, the variable that is manipulated by the experimenter
- A dependent variable, the variable that is measured by the experimenter and that is expected to change as a result of the manipulation of the independent variable
- A procedure that randomly assigns participants to different experimental groups, or "conditions," of the independent variable
- A hypothesis that predicts the effect the independent variable will have on the dependent variable

Only if each of these elements is present can a research study be considered a true experiment in which cause-and-effect relationships can be determined. (For a summary of the types of research that we've discussed, see Figure 4.)

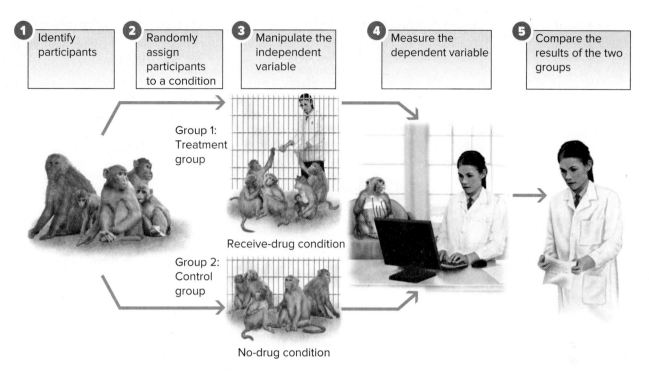

| ① Identify participants | ② Randomly assign participants to a condition | ③ Manipulate the independent variable | ④ Measure the dependent variable | ⑤ Compare the results of the two groups |

Group 1: Treatment group

Receive-drug condition

Group 2: Control group

No-drug condition

FIGURE 3 In this depiction of a study investigating the effects of the pharmaceutical drug propranolol on heart disease, we can see the basic elements of all true experiments. The participants in the experiment were monkeys that were randomly assigned to one of two groups. Monkeys assigned to the treatment group were given propranolol, hypothesized to prevent heart disease, whereas those in the control group were not given the drug. Administration of the drugs, then, was the independent variable.

All the monkeys were given a high-fat diet that was the human equivalent of two eggs with bacon every morning, and they occasionally were reassigned to different cages to increase their stress. To determine the effects of the drug, the monkeys' heart rates and other measures of heart disease were assessed after 26 months. These measures constituted the dependent variable. The results? As hypothesized, monkeys that received the drug showed slower heart rates and fewer symptoms of heart disease than those that did not.
Source: Kaplan & Manuck, 1989.

WERE LATANÉ AND DARLEY RIGHT?

To test their hypothesis that increasing the number of bystanders in an emergency situation would lower the degree of helping behavior, Latané and Darley placed the participants in a room and told them that the purpose of the experiment was to talk about personal problems associated with college. The discussion was to be held over an intercom, supposedly to avoid the potential embarrassment of face-to-face contact. Chatting about personal problems was not, of course, the true purpose of the experiment, but telling the participants that it was provided a way of keeping their expectations from biasing their behavior. (Consider how they would have been affected if they had been told that their helping behavior in emergencies was being tested. The experimenters could never have gotten an accurate assessment of what the participants would actually do in an emergency. By definition, emergencies are rarely announced in advance.)

The sizes of the discussion groups were two, three, and six people, which constituted the manipulation of the independent variable of group size. Participants were randomly assigned to these groups upon their arrival at the laboratory. Each group included one trained confederate of the experimenters. A *confederate* is an actor employed by a researcher who participates in a psychological experiment, pretending to be a participant. The researcher trains the confederate to act in a particular way during the experiment.

As the participants in each group were holding their discussion, they suddenly heard through the intercom one of the other participants–but who in reality was the

Research Method	Description	Advantages	Shortcomings
Descriptive and correlational research	Researcher observes a previously existing situation but does not make a change in the situation.	Offers insight into relationships between variables	Cannot determine causality
Archival research	Examines existing data to confirm hypothesis	Ease of data collection because data already exist	Dependent on availability of data
Naturalistic observation	Observation of naturally occurring behavior, without making a change in the situation	Provides a sample of people in their natural environment	Cannot control the "natural habitat" being observed
Survey research	A sample is chosen to represent a larger population and asked a series of questions.	A small sample can be used to infer attitudes and behavior of a larger population.	Sample may not be representative of the larger population; participants may not provide accurate responses to survey questions.
Ethnographic research	Extended examination of a small group or members of a different culture	Offers a source of hypotheses for more focused and objective research methods	Researchers may misinterpret behavior due to a lack of familiarity with the culture.
Case study	Intensive investigation of an individual or small group	Provides a thorough, in-depth understanding of participants	Results may not be generalizable beyond the sample.
Experimental research	Investigator produces a change in one variable to observe the effects of that change on other variables.	Experiments offer the only way to determine cause-and-effect relationships.	To be valid, experiments require random assignment of participants to conditions, well-conceptualized independent and dependent variables, and other careful controls.

FIGURE 4 Research strategies.

(top): Jim West/Alamy Stock Photo; (bottom): marvent/Shutterstock

confederate–having what sounded like an epileptic seizure. The confederate then called for help.

The actual participants' behavior was now what counted. The dependent variable was the time that elapsed from the start of the "seizure" to the time a participant began trying to help the "victim." If 6 minutes went by without a participant offering help, the experiment was ended.

As predicted by the hypothesis, the size of the group had a significant effect on whether a participant provided help. The more people who were present, the less likely it was that someone would supply help, as you can see in Figure 5 (Latané & Darley, 1970).

Because these results are straightforward, it seems clear that the experiment confirmed the original hypothesis. However, Latané and Darley could not be sure that the results were truly meaningful until they determined whether the results represented what statisticians call a significant outcome.

A **significant outcome** indicates that the findings of a research study are statistically meaningful, making it possible for researchers to feel confident that they have confirmed their hypotheses. Using statistical analysis, researchers can determine whether

significant outcome Meaningful results that make it possible for researchers to feel confident that they have confirmed their hypotheses. (Module 3)

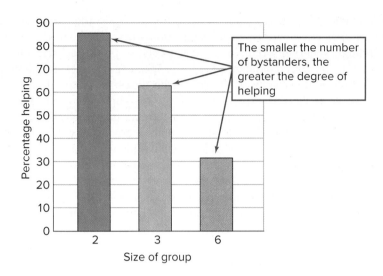

FIGURE 5 The Latané and Darley experiment showed that as the size of the group witnessing an emergency increased, helping behavior decreased. Source: Darley & Latané, 1968.

a numeric difference is a real difference or is due merely to chance. Only when differences between groups are large enough that statistical tests show them to be significant is it possible for researchers to confirm a hypothesis.

MOVING BEYOND THE STUDY

The Latané and Darley study contains all the elements of an experiment: an independent variable, a dependent variable, random assignment to conditions, and multiple experimental groups. Consequently, we can say with some confidence that group size *caused* changes in the degree of helping behavior.

Of course, one experiment alone does not forever resolve the question of bystander intervention in emergencies. Psychologists–like other scientists–require that findings be **replicated,** or repeated, sometimes using other procedures, in other settings, with other groups of participants, before full confidence can be placed in the results of any single experiment. Replication also allows the use of *meta-analysis*, a procedure that permits psychologists to combine the results of many separate studies into one overall conclusion (Harrer et al., 2021).

In terms of studying the bystander effect, psychologists have used a variety of approaches to examine the issue. For example, they have found that college students aren't the only ones who show the bystander effect; young children do as well. In addition, some evidence indicates that even nonhumans are affected by bystander behavior. Rats, which it turns out generally help other rats in distress (such as when they are caught in a trap and struggling to extricate themselves), are influenced by the behavior of other bystander rats in the situation (Plötner et al., 2015; Mason, 2021).

Finally, the work on bystander intervention has led to further research, expanding investigations on how the presence of bystanders may affect social behavior. For example, research on bystander behavior shows that the harm experienced by Black college students who encounter online discrimination on social media is reduced if White college students intervene and publicly express antiracist support (Hurd et al., 2022).

In short, replication is a critical activity, and many researchers believe that psychologists need to increase the number of studies that replicate earlier research in order to have greater confidence in their findings. They point to an influential study that attempted to replicate 100 previous findings but resulted in only 36% of the replications yielding findings that were similarly significant compared with the original studies. Furthermore, systematic and carefully conducted follow-up research attempting to replicate a variety of studies supported these disappointing results (Open Science Collaboration, 2015; Ebersole et al., 2020; Nosek et al., 2022).

replicated research Research that is repeated, sometimes using other procedures, settings, and groups of participants, to increase confidence in prior findings. (Module 3)

In fact, some researchers claim that psychology (and other social sciences) are facing a *replication crisis* because many replication studies have failed to support the original findings. Whether a full-blown crisis exists is open to debate, but it is clear that in order to be fully confident about the meaning of research studies, results need to be replicated (Wiggins & Chrisopherson, 2019; Nosek et al., 2022).

In addition to replicating experimental results, psychologists need to test the limitations of their theories and hypotheses to determine under which specific circumstances they do and do not apply. It seems unlikely, for instance, that increasing the number of bystanders *always* results in less helping. In fact, follow-up research shows that bystander intervention is more likely to occur in situations viewed as clear-cut and dangerous because bystanders are more likely to perceive that the presence of others will provide resources for helping. In short, it is critical to continue carrying out experiments to understand the conditions in which exceptions to this general rule occur and other circumstances in which the rule holds (Garcia-Palacios et al., 2002; Fischer et al., 2011).

Before leaving the Latané and Darley study, note that it represents a good illustration of the basic principles of the scientific method. The two psychologists began with a *question of interest*, in this case stemming from a real-world incident in which bystanders in an emergency did not offer help. They then *formulated an explanation* by specifying a theory of diffusion of responsibility and from that formulated the specific hypothesis that increasing the number of bystanders in an emergency situation would lower the degree of helping behavior. Finally, they *carried out research* to confirm their hypothesis, and they eventually *communicated their findings* by publishing their results. This four-step process embodied in the scientific method underlies all scientific inquiry, allowing us to develop a valid understanding of others'–and our own–behavior.

RECAP/EVALUATE/RETHINK

RECAP

LO 3-1 What is the scientific method?

- The scientific method is the approach psychologists use to understand behavior. It consists of four steps: identifying questions of interest, formulating an explanation, carrying out research that is designed to support or refute the explanation, and communicating the findings.
- To test a hypothesis, researchers must formulate an operational definition, which translates the abstract concepts of the hypothesis into the actual procedures used in the study.

LO 3-2 What role do theories and hypotheses play in psychological research?

- Research in psychology is guided by theories (broad explanations and predictions regarding phenomena of interest) and hypotheses (theory-based predictions stated in a way that allows them to be tested).

LO 3-3 What research methods do psychologists use?

- Archival research uses existing records, such as newspaper articles, online databases, or other documents, to test a hypothesis. In naturalistic observation, the investigator acts mainly as an observer, making no change in a naturally occurring situation. In survey research, people are asked a series of questions about their behavior, thoughts, or attitudes. Ethnographic research is used to conduct descriptive explorations of behavior in other cultures. The case study is an in-depth interview and examination of one person or group.
- These descriptive research methods rely on correlational techniques, which describe associations between variables but cannot determine cause-and-effect relationships.

LO 3-4 How do psychologists establish cause-and-effect relationships in research studies?

- In a formal experiment, the relationship between variables is investigated by deliberately producing a change–called the experimental manipulation–in one variable and observing changes in the other variable.
- In an experiment, at least two groups must be compared to assess cause-and-effect relationships. The group receiving the treatment (the special procedure devised by the experimenter) is the experimental group; the second group (which receives no treatment) is the control group. There also may be multiple experimental groups, each of which is subjected to a different procedure and then compared with the others.

- The variable that experimenters manipulate is the independent variable. The variable that they measure and expect to change as a result of manipulation of the independent variable is called the dependent variable.
- In a formal experiment, participants must be assigned randomly to treatment conditions so that participant characteristics are distributed evenly across the different conditions.
- Psychologists use statistical tests to determine whether research findings are significant.

EVALUATE

1. An explanation for a phenomenon of interest is known as a _____.
2. To test this explanation, a researcher must state it in terms of a testable question known as a _____.
3. An experimenter is interested in studying the relationship between hunger and aggression. The experimenter decides that they will measure aggression by counting the number of times a participant will hit a punching bag. In this case, the experimenter's _____ definition of aggression is the number of times the participant hits the bag.
4. Match the following forms of research to their definitions:
   1. Archival research
   2. Naturalistic observation
   3. Survey research
   4. Case study

   a. Directly asking a sample of people questions about their behavior
   b. Examining existing records to test a hypothesis
   c. Looking at behavior in its true setting without intervening in the setting
   d. Doing an in-depth investigation of a person or small group

5. Match each of the following research methods with its primary disadvantage:
   1. Archival research
   2. Naturalistic observation
   3. Survey research
   4. Case study

   a. The researcher may not be able to generalize to the population at large.
   b. People may lie in order to present a good image.
   c. The data may not exist or may be unusable.
   d. People's behavior can change if they know they are being watched.
6. A psychologist wants to study the effect of attractiveness on willingness to help a person with a math problem. Attractiveness would be the _____ variable, and the amount of helping would be the _____ variable.
7. The group in an experiment that receives no treatment is called the _____ group.

RETHINK

Starting with the theory that diffusion of responsibility causes responsibility for helping to be shared among bystanders, Latané and Darley derived the hypothesis that the more people who witness an emergency situation, the less likely it is that help will be given to a victim. Can you think of other hypotheses that are based on the same theory of diffusion of responsibility?

Answers to Evaluate Questions

1. theory; 2. hypothesis; 3. operational; 4. 1-b, 2-c, 3-a, 4-d; 5. 1-c, 2-d, 3-b, 4-a; 6. Independent, dependent; 7. control

KEY TERMS

scientific method	survey research	experimental	dependent variable
theories	ethnographic research	manipulation	random assignment to
hypothesis	case study	treatment	condition
operational definition	variables	experimental group	significant outcome
archival research	correlational research	control group	replicated research
naturalistic observation	experiment	independent variable	

Module 4
Critical Research Issues

LEARNING OUTCOME

LO 4-1 What major issues confront psychologists conducting research?

! **Study Alert**
Because the protection of experiment participants is essential, remember the key ethical guideline of informed consent.

You probably realize by now that there are few simple formulas for psychological research. Psychologists must make choices about the type of study to conduct, the measures to take, and the most effective way to analyze the results. Even after they have made these essential decisions, they must still consider several critical issues. We turn first to the most fundamental of these issues: ethics.

The Ethics of Research

Put yourself in the place of one of the participants in the experiment conducted by Latané and Darley to examine the helping behavior of bystanders, in which another "bystander" simulating a seizure turned out to be a confederate of the experimenters (Latané & Darley, 1970). How would you feel when you learned that the supposed victim was in reality a paid accomplice?

Although you might at first experience relief that there had been no real emergency, you might also feel some resentment that you had been deceived by the experimenter. You might also experience concern that you had been placed in an embarrassing or compromising situation–one that might have dealt a blow to your self-esteem, depending on how you had behaved.

Most psychologists argue that deception is sometimes necessary to prevent participants from being influenced by what they think a study's true purpose is. (If you knew that Latané and Darley were actually studying your helping behavior, wouldn't you automatically have been tempted to intervene in the emergency?) To avoid such outcomes, a small proportion of research involves deception.

Nonetheless, because research has the potential to violate the rights of participants, psychologists are expected to adhere to a strict set of ethical guidelines aimed at protecting participants (American Psychological Association, 2017; Young, 2017). Those guidelines involve the following safeguards:

- Protection of participants from physical and mental harm
- The right of participants to privacy regarding their behavior
- The assurance that participation in research is completely voluntary
- The necessity of informing participants about the nature of procedures before their participation in the experiment
- All experiments must be reviewed by an independent panel before being conducted (Crano et al., 2015; Lingayat et al., 2022; McNair, 2022).

informed consent A document signed by participants affirming that they have been told the basic outlines of the study and are aware of what their participation will involve. (Module 4)

One of psychologists' key ethical principles is **informed consent.** Before participating in an experiment, the participants must sign a document affirming that they have been told the basic outlines of the study and are aware of what their participation will involve, what risks the experiment may hold, and the fact that their participation is purely voluntary and they may terminate it at any time. Furthermore, after participation in a study, they must be given a debriefing in which they receive an explanation of the study and the procedures that were involved. The only time informed consent and a debriefing can be eliminated is in experiments in which the risks are minimal, as in a purely observational study in a public place (Nagy, 2011; Hetzel-Riggin, 2017; Arigo et al., 2018).

Exploring Diversity

Choosing Participants Who Represent *All* Humans

When Latané and Darley, both college professors, decided who would participate in their experiment, they turned to the people most easily available: college students. Using college students as participants has advantages as well as drawbacks. The big benefit is that because most research occurs in university settings, college students are readily available. Typically, they cost the researcher very little: They participate for either extra course credit or a relatively small payment.

The problem is that college students may not represent the general population adequately. In fact, undergraduate research participants are typically a special group of people: Relative to the general population, college students tend to be from **W**estern, **E**ducated, **I**ndustrialized, **R**ich, and **D**emocratic cultures. That description forms the acronym WEIRD, which led one researcher to apply the nickname to research participants (Schulz et al., 2018; Alper & Yilmaz, 2019; Kupferschmidt, 2019).

Nothing is necessarily wrong with using participants who fit the "WEIRD" characterization. It's just that they may differ from most people who populate the world, and those differences could be psychologically relevant. We certainly know that people in other cultures differ in fundamental ways from those in Western culture, such as in terms of generosity or even in the perception of geometric objects. Yet one review found that most research participants do come from the United States, and most of those are psychology majors (Henrich et al., 2010; Kaiser et al., 2017; Pollet & Saxton, 2019).

In expanding their research beyond "WEIRD" participants, psychologists must be sure to include other types of diversity. For instance, psychologists are increasingly taking into account the way in which people identify in terms of gender and are seeking to include those who identify as transgender or gender-fluid. Moreover, they recognize that in order to be truly representative, their research must consider racial and ethnic identification of participants (Cameron & Stimson, 2019; Dupree & Krauss, 2022).

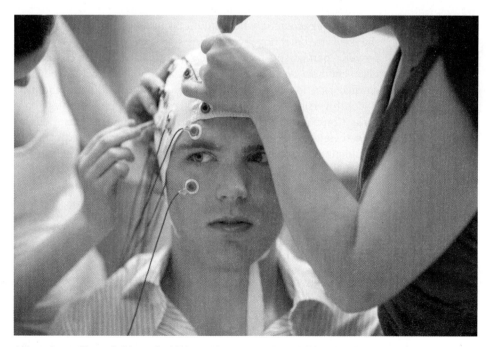

Although readily available and widely used as research participants, college students may not represent the population at large. What are some advantages and drawbacks of using college students as subjects?

annedde/E+/Getty Images

Because psychology is a science whose goal is to explain *all* human behavior generally, its studies must use participants who are fully representative of the general population in terms of gender, age, race, ethnicity, socioeconomic status, and educational level. To encourage a wider range of participants, the National Institute of Mental Health and the National Science Foundation—the primary U.S. funding sources for psychological research—now require that experiments address issues of diverse populations (Hruschka et al., 2018; Sierra-Mercado & Lazaro-Munoz, 2018).

Should Animals Be Used in Research? Like those who work with humans, researchers who use nonhuman animals in experiments have their own set of exacting guidelines to ensure that the animals do not suffer. Specifically, researchers must make every effort to minimize discomfort, illness, and pain. Procedures that subject animals to distress are permitted only when an alternative procedure is unavailable and when the research is justified by its prospective value. Moreover, researchers strive to avoid causing physical discomfort, but they are also required to promote the *psychological* well-being of some species of research animals, such as primates (Herzog, 2017; Díaz et al., 2021; Martin, 2022).

But why should animals be used for research in the first place? Can we really learn about human behavior from the results of research employing rats, gerbils, and pigeons?

The answer is that psychological research that does employ nonhumans is designed to answer questions different from those posed in research with humans and to study those questions in different ways. For example, the shorter life span of animals (rats live an average of 2 years) allows researchers to learn about the effects of aging in a relatively short time frame. Researchers can also provide greater experimental control over nonhumans and carry out procedures that might ethically not be possible with people. For example, some studies require large numbers of participants that share similar backgrounds or have been exposed to particular environments—conditions that could not practically be met with human beings.

Research with animals has provided psychologists with information that has profoundly benefited humans. For instance, it furnished the keys to detecting eye disorders in children early enough to prevent permanent damage, to communicating more effectively with children with severe intellectual disability, and to reducing chronic pain in people. Still, the use of research using nonhumans is controversial, involving complex moral and philosophical concerns. Consequently, all research involving nonhumans must be carefully reviewed beforehand to ensure that it is conducted ethically ("Guidelines for the treatment of animals," 2017; Beauchamp & DeGrazia, 2019; Watts et al., 2019).

Research involving animals can be controversial, but when conducted within ethical guidelines, yields significant benefits for humans.

D-Keine/E+/Getty Images

Threats to Experimental Validity: Avoiding Experimental Bias

experimental bias Factors that distort how the independent variable affects the dependent variable in an experiment. (Module 4)

> **Study Alert**
>
> Learn the main types of potential bias in experiments: experimenter expectations, participant expectations, and placebo effects.

Even the best-laid plans are susceptible to **experimental bias**—meaning factors that distort the way the independent variable affects the dependent variable in an experiment.

In one form of experimenter bias, the researcher unintentionally transmits cues to participants about the way the experimenter expects them to behave, thereby affecting the results. That is, the experimenter's expectations actually produce the expected result (Rosenthal, 2003; Weinstein, 2018; Buetow & Zawaly, 2021).

A related problem is participant expectations. If you have ever been a participant in an experiment, you probably developed *participant expectations*, guesses about what was expected of you. In fact, participants often develop their own hypotheses about what the experimenter hopes to learn from the study. If participants form their own hypotheses and then act on their hunches, it may be their expectations, rather than the experimental manipulation, that produce the results (Rutherford et al., 2009; Scott et al., 2022).

To guard against participant expectations biasing the results of an experiment, the experimenter may try to disguise the true purpose of the experiment. Participants who do not know that helping behavior is being studied, for example, are more apt to act in a "natural" way than they would if they knew.

Sometimes it is impossible to hide the actual purpose of research; when that is the case, other techniques are available to prevent bias. Suppose you were interested in testing the ability of a new pharmaceutical drug to alleviate the symptoms of severe depression. If you simply gave the drug to half your participants and not to the other half, the participants who were given the drug might report feeling less depressed merely because they knew they were getting a drug. Similarly, the participants who got nothing might report feeling no better because they knew that they were in a no-treatment control group.

To solve this problem, psychologists typically use a procedure in which all the participants receive a treatment, but those in the control group receive only a **placebo**—a false treatment, such as a pill, "drug," or other substance that has no significant chemical properties or active ingredient. You may be familiar with the concept of placebo because it was used in the development of COVID-19 vaccines, in which some people received a shot of the real vaccine and others a shot of a placebo that contained no virus-fighting component.

placebo A false treatment, such as a pill, "drug," or other substance, without any significant chemical properties or active ingredient. (Module 4)

Because members of both the actual treatment group and the placebo group are kept in the dark about whether they are getting a real or a false treatment, any differences in outcome can be attributed to the treatment and not to the possible psychological effects of being administered a pill or other substance (Ćurković et al., 2019; WHO Ad Hoc Expert Group, 2021; Tang et al., 2022).

However, a careful researcher must apply one more safeguard in an experiment such as this. To overcome the possibility that *experimenter* expectations will affect the participant, the person who administers the drug shouldn't know whether it is actually the true drug or the placebo. By keeping both the participant and the experimenter who interacts with the participant "blind" to the nature of the drug that is being administered, researchers can more accurately assess the effects of the drug. This method is known as the *double-blind procedure* (Kaptchuk, 2021).

BECOMING AN INFORMED CONSUMER
of Psychology

Thinking Critically About Research

If you were about to purchase an automobile, you would not likely stop at the nearest car dealership and drive off with the first car a salesperson recommended. Instead, you would probably mull over the purchase, read about automobiles, consider the alternatives, talk to others about their experiences, and ultimately put in a fair amount of thought before you made such a major purchase.

In contrast, many of us are considerably less conscientious when we hear about research findings. People often jump to conclusions on the basis of incomplete and inaccurate information, and only rarely do they take the time to critically evaluate the research and data to which they are exposed.

Because the field of psychology is based on an accumulated body of research, we must scrutinize thoroughly the methods, results, and claims of researchers. Several basic questions can help us sort through what is valid and what is not. Among the most important questions to ask are these:

- *What was the purpose of the research?* Research studies should evolve from a clearly specified theory. Furthermore, we must take into account the specific hypothesis that is being tested. Unless we know what hypothesis is being examined, we cannot judge how successful a study has been.
- *Was the study conducted appropriately to answer the questions it was intended to address?* Consider who the participants were, how many were involved, what methods were employed, and what problems the researcher encountered in collecting the data. There are important differences, for example, between a case study that reports the anecdotes of a handful of respondents and a survey that collects data from several thousand people.
- *Are the results presented fairly?* The research findings must be assessed in terms of how closely they relate to the way in which a study was carried out and how they reflect what was found. For instance, suppose a producer of pharmaceutical drugs claims that "no other sleeping pill has been shown to be more effective in helping people get a good night's sleep." This does not mean that theirs is the *best* sleeping pill on the market. It just means that no other sleeping pill has been proved *more* effective; other pills may be just as effective. Expressed in the latter fashion, the finding doesn't seem worth bragging about.

These three basic questions can help you assess the validity of research findings you come across—both within and outside the field of psychology. The more you know how to evaluate research, the better you will be able to assess what the field of psychology has to offer.

RECAP/EVALUATE/RETHINK

RECAP

LO 4-1 What major issues confront psychologists conducting research?

- One of the key ethical principles followed by psychologists is that of informed consent. Participants must be informed, before participation, about the basic outline of the experiment and the risks and potential benefits of their participation.
- Although the use of college students as participants has the advantage of easy availability, there are drawbacks, too. For instance, students do not necessarily represent the population as a whole. The use of nonhuman animals as participants may also have costs in terms of the ability to generalize to humans, although the benefits of using animals in research have been profound.
- Experiments are subject to a number of biases, or threats. Experimenter expectations can produce bias when an experimenter unintentionally transmits cues to participants about their expectations regarding participant behavior in a given experimental condition. Participant expectations can also bias an experiment.

Among the tools experimenters use to help eliminate bias are placebos and double-blind procedures.

EVALUATE

1. Ethical research begins with the concept of informed consent. Before signing up to participate in an experiment, participants should be informed of:
   a. the procedure of the study, stated generally.
   b. the risks that may be involved.
   c. their right to withdraw at any time.
   d. all of these.
2. List three benefits of using animals in psychological research.
3. Deception is one means experimenters can use to try to eliminate participants' expectations. True or false?
4. A false treatment, such as a pill that has no significant chemical properties or active ingredient, is known as a _____.
5. A study has shown that men differ from women in their preference for ice cream flavors. This study was based on a sample of two men and three women. What might be wrong with this study?

RETHINK

A researcher strongly believes that college professors tend to show female students less attention and respect in the classroom than they show male students. The researcher sets up an experimental study involving observations of classrooms in different conditions. In explaining the study to the professors and the students who will participate, what steps should the researcher take to eliminate experimental bias based on both experimenter expectations and participant expectations?

Answers to Evaluate Questions

1. d; 2. (1) We can study some phenomena in animals more easily than we can in people because with animal subjects we have greater control over environmental and genetic factors. (2) Large numbers of similar participants can be easily obtained. (3) We can look at generational effects much more easily in animals, because of their shorter life span; 3. True; 4. placebo; 5. There are far too few participants. Without a larger sample, no valid conclusions can be drawn about ice cream preferences based on gender.

KEY TERMS

informed consent   experimental bias   placebo

LOOKING *Back*

EPILOGUE

The field of psychology, as you have seen, is broad and diverse. It encompasses many subfields and specialties practiced in a variety of settings, with new subfields continually arising. You have also seen that even within the various subfields of the field, it is possible to adopt several approaches, including the neuroscience, psychodynamic, behavioral, cognitive, and humanistic perspectives.

For all its diversity, though, psychology focuses on certain key issues that unify the field along common lines and shared findings. These issues will reappear as themes throughout this course as you learn about the work and accomplishments of psychologists in the many subfields of the discipline.

In light of what you've already learned about the field of psychology, reconsider the consequences of the devastating fire in Hawaii discussed in the prologue to this chapter and answer the following questions:

1. If psychologists were using the biological perspective to explain people's reactions to the fire, what specific factors might they focus on?
2. What types of psychologists might a politician consult in determining how to respond to people's needs following the fire?
3. What aspects of people's reaction to the fire would most interest a psychologist focusing on learning? A clinical psychologist? A social psychologist?
4. What are some ways in which both nature and nurture could contribute to a person's reaction to the fire?

Design Elements: Man with laptop: Dragon Images/Shutterstock; Exclamation point and mobile frame: McGraw Hill; Smartphone: WML Image/Shutterstock; Hands: Stefano Garau/Shutterstock.

VISUAL SUMMARY 1 Introduction to Psychology

MODULE 1 Psychologists at Work

Subfields of Psychology

- Biological foundations
  - Behavioral neuroscience
- Sensing, perceiving, learning, and thinking
  - Experimental and cognitive psychology
- Sources of change and stability
  - Development and personality psychology
- Physical and mental health
  - Health, clinical, and counseling psychology
- Social networks
  - Social and cross-cultural psychology
- Expanding frontiers
  - Evolutionary psychology
  - Behavioral genetics
  - Clinical neuropsychology
  - Diversity science

Working at Psychology

- Where U.S. psychologists work

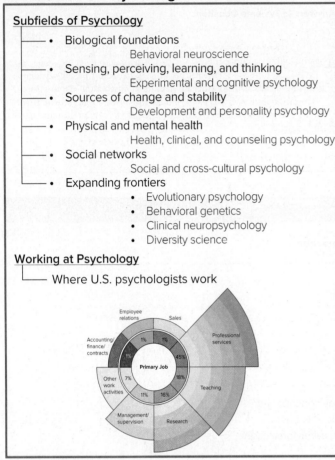

MODULE 2 A Science Evolves

Roots

- Structuralism
- Functionalism

Today's Perspectives: Five major perspectives

Neuroscience
Views behavior from the perspective of biological functioning

Behavioral
Focuses on observable behavior

Psychodynamic
Believes behavior is motivated by inner, unconscious forces over which a person has little control

Cognitive
Examines how people understand and think about the world

Humanistic
Contends that people can control their behavior and that they naturally try to reach their full potential

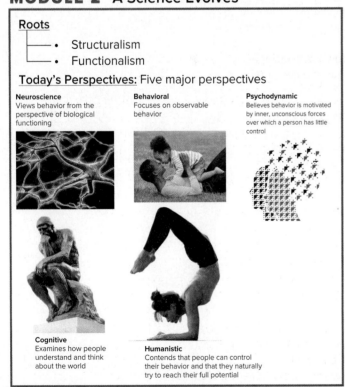

MODULE 3 Research in Psychology

Scientific Method

- Theories: Broad explanations
- Hypotheses: Testable predictions

Descriptive Research: Describes variables and does not explain causality

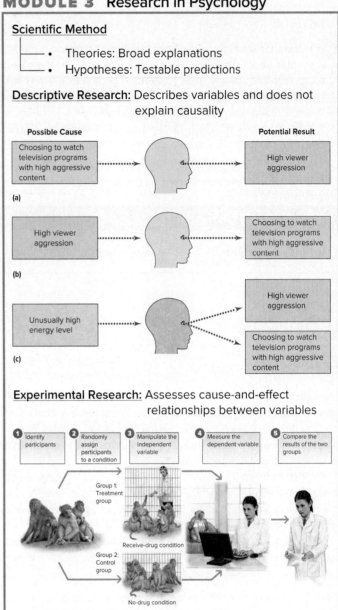

Experimental Research: Assesses cause-and-effect relationships between variables

MODULE 4 Critical Research Issues

Ethics of Research

Informed consent

Animal Research

Has significantly benefited humans

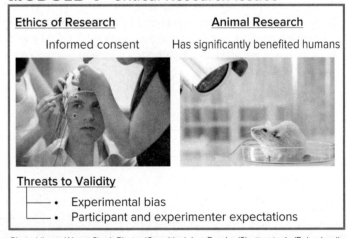

Threats to Validity

- Experimental bias
- Participant and experimenter expectations

(Module 1) Source: Stamm et al., 2016; (Module 2) (Neuroscience): Alfred Pasieka/Science Photo Library/Alamy Stock Photo; (Cognitive): Les Byerley/Shutterstock; (Behavioral): Ariel Skelley/Blend Images LLC; (Humanistic): fizkes/Shutterstock; (Psychodynamic): Athanasia Nomikou/Shutterstock; (Module 3) Source: Based on a study by Kaplan & Manuck, 1989; (Module 4) (EEG): annedde/E+/Getty Images; (Mouse): D-Keine/E+/Getty Images

DGLimages/Shutterstock

CHAPTER 2
Neuroscience and Behavior

LEARNING OUTCOMES FOR CHAPTER 2

PROLOGUE *HEALING HIS BRAIN*

In a single moment, first-year college student Ian Burkhart's life was changed forever. While he was swimming in the ocean waves off the coast of North Carolina, an unpredictable surf slammed him into a hidden sandbar. In a moment, he couldn't feel or move his body.

After Burkhart was rushed to a hospital and underwent emergency surgery, he received a grim diagnosis: His spinal cord was cut, and he would likely never walk again. The range of motion of his arms would be severely limited. His sense of touch would remain compromised.

Despite the severity of his condition, Burkhart was not deterred, and he pursued what would become a lifeline. Four years after the accident, doctors and neuroscientists inserted a tiny computer chip in his brain. The chip responds to signals from his brain and relays them to his body, bypassing the spinal cord entirely.

The results were nothing short of miraculous. Burkhart is now able to move his arm and hand and even play a version of the video game *Guitar Hero*. Scientists are hopeful that future refinements to the computer chip, along with other brain implants, may lead to further improvements in Burkhart's ability to move his body and to ultimately fully regain his sense of touch (Oberhaus, 2020; Help Hope Live, 2022).

LOOKING *Ahead*

It's hard to believe that severe brain injuries like those Burkhart sustained could be reversed. But this is just one example of how a combination of cutting-edge technology, along with the the remarkable capabilities of the nervous system and brain, can be harnessed to improve human life.

An organ roughly half the size of a loaf of bread, the brain controls our physical, emotional, and intellectual behavior through every waking and sleeping moment. Our movements, thoughts, hopes, aspirations, dreams—our very awareness that we are human—all depend on the brain and the nerves that extend throughout the body, constituting the nervous system.

Because of the importance of the nervous system in controlling behavior and because humans at their most basic level are biological beings, many researchers in psychology and other fields as diverse as computer science, zoology, and medicine have made the biological underpinnings of behavior their specialty. These experts collectively are called *neuroscientists* (Vaughan-Graham et al., 2019; Abramson, 2022).

Psychologists who specialize in considering the ways in which the biological structures and functions of the body affect behavior are known as **behavioral neuroscientists** (or *biopsychologists*). They seek to answer several key questions: How does the brain control the voluntary and involuntary functioning of the body? How does the brain communicate with other parts of the body? What is the physical structure of the brain, and how does this structure affect behavior? Are psychological disorders caused by biological factors, and how can such disorders be treated?

As you consider the biological processes that we discuss in this chapter, keep in mind the reason why behavioral neuroscience is an essential part of psychology: Our understanding of human behavior requires knowledge of the brain and other parts of the nervous system. Biological factors are central to our sensory experiences, states of consciousness, motivation and emotion, development throughout the life span, and physical and psychological health. Furthermore, advances in behavioral neuroscience have led to the creation of drugs and other treatments for psychological and physical disorders. In short, we cannot understand behavior without understanding our biological makeup.

behavioral neuroscientists (or biopsychologists) Psychologists who specialize in considering the ways in which the biological structures and functions of the body affect behavior. (Module 5)

Module 5
Neurons: The Basic Elements of Behavior

Watching Serena Williams hit a stinging tennis backhand, Misty Copeland dance a complex ballet routine, or Aaron Judge swing at a baseball, you may have marveled at the complexity—and wondrous abilities—of the human body. But even the most everyday tasks, such as pouring a cup of coffee or humming a tune, depend on a sophisticated sequence of events in the body that is itself truly impressive.

The nervous system is the pathway for the instructions that permit our bodies to carry out such precise activities. Here, we look at the structure and function of neurons, the cells that make up the nervous system, including the brain.

The Structure of the Neuron

Playing the piano, driving a car, or hitting a tennis ball depends, at one level, on exact muscle coordination. But if we consider *how* the muscles can be activated so precisely, we see that more fundamental processes are involved. For the muscles to produce the complex movements that make up any meaningful physical activity, the brain has to provide the right messages to them and coordinate those messages.

Such messages—as well as those that enable us to think, remember, and experience emotion—are passed through specialized cells called neurons. **Neurons,** or nerve cells, are the basic components of the nervous system. Their quantity is staggering: Our bodies have perhaps as many as 1 *trillion* neurons.

Although there are several types of neurons, they all have a similar structure, as illustrated in Figure 1. Like most cells in the body, neurons have a cell body that

LEARNING OUTCOMES

LO 5-1 Why do psychologists study the brain and the nervous system?

LO 5-2 What are the basic elements of the nervous system?

LO 5-3 How does the nervous system communicate electrical and chemical messages from one part to another?

neurons Nerve cells, the basic elements of the nervous system. (Module 5)

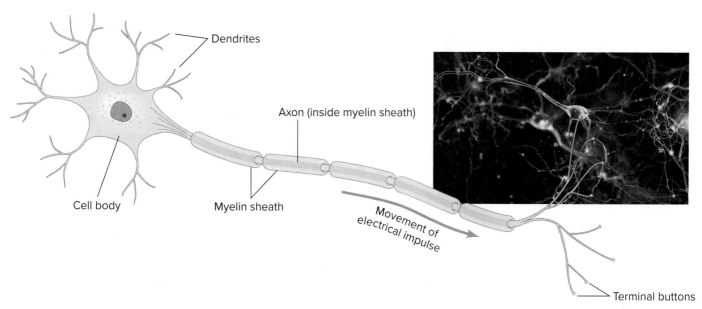

FIGURE 1 The primary components of the neuron, the basic element of the nervous system. A neuron has a cell body and structures that conduct messages: the dendrites, which receive messages from other neurons, and the axon, which carries messages to other neurons or body cells. As with most neurons, this axon is protected by the sausagelike myelin sheath. What advantages does the treelike structure of the neuron provide? (Photo): Whitehoune/Shutterstock

dendrites A cluster of fibers at one end of a neuron that receives messages from other neurons. (Module 5)

axon The part of the neuron that carries messages destined for other neurons. (Module 5)

terminal buttons Small bulges at the end of axons that send messages to other neurons. (Module 5)

 Study Alert

Remember that dendrites detect messages from other neurons; axons carry signals away from the neuron.

myelin sheath A protective coat of fat and protein that wraps around the axon. (Module 5)

all-or-none law The rule that neurons are either on or off. (Module 5)

resting state The state in which there is a negative electrical charge of about −70 millivolts within a neuron. (Module 5)

action potential An electric nerve impulse that travels through a neuron's axon when it is set off by a "trigger," changing the neuron's charge from negative to positive. (Module 5)

contains a nucleus. The nucleus incorporates the hereditary material that determines how a cell will function. Neurons are physically held in place by *glial cells.* Glial cells provide nourishment to neurons, insulate them, help repair damage, and generally support neural functioning (Gould et al., 2019; Schirmer et al., 2021).

In contrast to most other cells, however, neurons have a distinctive feature: They can communicate with other cells and transmit information across relatively long distances. Many of the body's neurons receive signals from outside the body or relay the nervous system's messages to muscles and other target cells, but the vast majority of neurons communicate only with other neurons in the elaborate information system that regulates behavior.

As shown in Figure 1, there's a cluster of fibers at the end of every neuron that are called dendrites. **Dendrites** are the part of the neuron that receives messages from other neurons. They look like the twisted branches of a tree.

On the opposite side of every neuron is a long, slim, tube-like extension called an axon. The **axon** carries messages received by the dendrites to other neurons. The axon is considerably longer than the rest of the neuron. Although most axons are several millimeters in length, some are as long as 3 feet. Axons end in small bulges called terminal buttons. **Terminal buttons** send messages to other neurons.

The messages that travel through a neuron are electrical. Those electrical messages, or *impulses,* generally move across neurons in one direction only, as if they were traveling on a one-way street. Impulses follow a route that begins with the dendrites, continues into the cell body, and leads ultimately along the tube-like extension, the axon, to adjacent neurons.

To prevent messages from short-circuiting one another, axons must be insulated in some fashion (just as electrical wires must be insulated). Most axons are insulated by a **myelin sheath,** a protective coating of fat and protein that wraps around the axon like the casing on links of sausage.

The myelin sheath also serves to increase the velocity with which electrical impulses travel through axons. Those axons that carry the most important and most urgently required information have the greatest concentrations of myelin. If your hand touches a painfully hot stove, for example, the information regarding the pain is passed through axons in the hand and arm that have a relatively thick coating of myelin, speeding the message of pain to the brain so that you can react instantly.

How Neurons Fire

Like a gun, neurons either fire—that is, transmit an electrical impulse along the axon—or don't fire. There is no in-between stage, just as pulling harder on a gun trigger doesn't make the bullet travel faster. Similarly, neurons follow an **all-or-none law:** They are either on or off, with nothing in between the on state and the off state. When there is enough force to pull the trigger, a neuron fires.

Before a neuron is triggered—that is, when it is in a **resting state**—it has a negative electrical charge of about −70 millivolts (a millivolt is one ¹⁄₁,₀₀₀ of a volt). This charge is caused by the presence of more negatively charged ions within the neuron than outside it. (An ion is an atom that is electrically charged.) You might think of the neuron as a miniature battery in which the inside of the neuron represents the negative pole and the outside represents the positive pole.

When a message arrives at a neuron, gates along the cell membrane open briefly to allow positively charged ions to rush in at rates as high as 100 million ions per second. The sudden arrival of these positive ions causes the charge within the nearby part of the cell to change momentarily from negative to positive. When the positive charge reaches a critical level, the "trigger" is pulled, and an electrical impulse, known as an *action potential,* travels along the axon of the neuron (see Figure 2).

The **action potential** moves from one end of the axon to the other like a flame moving along a fuse. As the impulse travels along the axon, the movement of ions causes a change in charge from negative to positive in successive sections of the axon (see Figure 3). After the impulse has passed through a particular section of the axon,

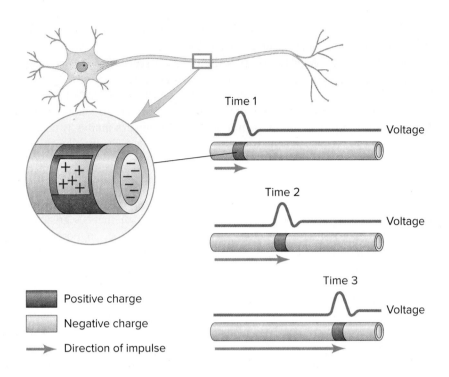

FIGURE 2 Movement of an action potential along an axon. Just before Time 1, positively charged ions enter the cell membrane, changing the charge in the nearby part of the axon from negative to positive and triggering an action potential. The action potential travels along the axon, as illustrated in the changes occurring from Time 1 to Time 3 (from top to bottom in this drawing). Immediately after the action potential has passed through a section of the axon, positive ions are pumped out, restoring the charge in that section to negative. The change in voltage illustrated by the blue line above the axon can be seen in greater detail in Figure 3.

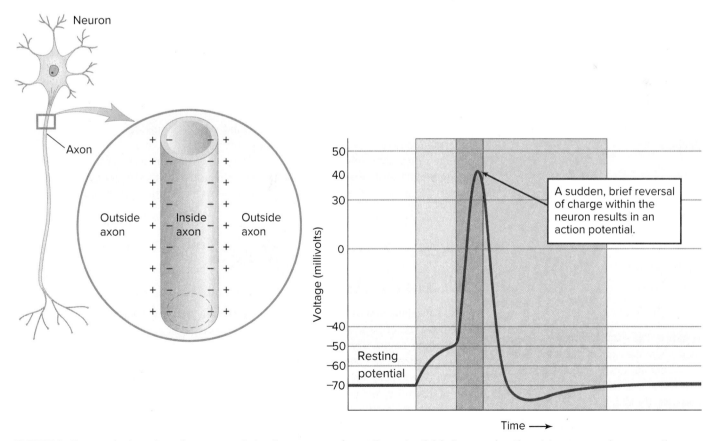

FIGURE 3 Changes in the voltage in a neuron during the passage of an action potential. In its normal resting state, a neuron has a negative charge of about −70 millivolts. When an action potential is triggered, however, the charge becomes positive, increasing from about −70 millivolts to about +40 millivolts. Immediately following the passage of the action potential, the charge becomes even more negative than it is in its typical resting state. After the charge returns to its normal resting state, the neuron will be fully ready to be triggered once again.

positive ions are pumped out of that section, and its charge returns to negative while the action potential continues to move along the axon.

Just after an action potential has passed through a section of the axon, the cell membrane in that region cannot admit positive ions again for a few milliseconds, and so a neuron cannot fire again immediately no matter how much stimulation it receives. It is as if the gun has to be reloaded after each shot. There then follows a period in which, though it is possible for the neuron to fire, a stronger stimulus is needed than would be if the neuron had reached its normal resting state. Eventually, though, the neuron is ready to fire again.

SPEED OF TRANSMISSION

These complex events can occur at dizzying speeds, although there is great variation among different neurons. The particular speed at which an action potential travels along an axon is determined by the axon's size and the thickness of its myelin sheath. Axons with small diameters carry impulses at about 2 miles per hour; longer and thicker ones can average speeds of more than 225 miles per hour.

Neurons differ not only in terms of how quickly an impulse moves along the axon but also in their potential rate of firing. Some neurons are capable of firing as many as 1,000 times per second; others fire at much slower rates. The intensity of a stimulus determines how much of a neuron's potential firing rate is reached. A strong stimulus, such as a bright light or a loud sound, leads to a higher rate of firing than a less intense stimulus does. Thus, even though all impulses move at the same strength or speed through a particular axon–because of the all-or-none law–there is variation in the frequency of impulses, providing a mechanism by which we can distinguish the tickle of a feather from the weight of someone standing on our toes.

MIRROR NEURONS

mirror neurons Specialized neurons that fire not only when a person enacts a particular behavior, but also when a person simply observes *another* individual carrying out the same behavior. (Module 5)

Although all neurons operate through the firing of action potentials, some neurons are specialized. For example, neuroscientists have discovered the existence of **mirror neurons,** neurons that fire not only when a person enacts a particular behavior but also when they simply observe *another* individual carrying out the same behavior (Brucker et al., 2015; Bonini, 2017).

Mirror neurons may help explain how (and why) humans develop the capacity to understand others' intentions. Specifically, mirror neurons may fire when we view someone doing something, leading us to predict what their goals are and what they may do next. The discovery of mirror neurons suggests that the capacity of even young children to imitate others may be an inborn behavior (Krautheim et al., 2019; Heyes & Catmur, 2022).

Where Neurons Meet: Bridging the Gap

synapse The space between two neurons where the axon of a sending neuron communicates with the dendrites of a receiving neuron by using chemical messages. (Module 5)

neurotransmitters Chemicals that carry messages across the synapse to the dendrite (and sometimes the cell body) of a receiver neuron. (Module 5)

If you have looked inside a computer, you've seen that each part is physically connected to another part. In contrast, evolution has produced a neural transmission system that at some points has no need for a structural connection between its components. Instead, a chemical connection bridges the gap, known as a synapse, between two neurons (see Figure 4). The **synapse** is the space between two neurons where the axon of a sending neuron communicates with the dendrites of a receiving neuron by using chemical messages. Adult humans may have as many as 100 *trillion* synapses (Graziano, 2019, 2021).

When a nerve impulse comes to the end of the axon and reaches a terminal button, the terminal button releases a chemical messenger called a neurotransmitter. **Neurotransmitters** carry messages from one neuron to another neuron. Like a boat

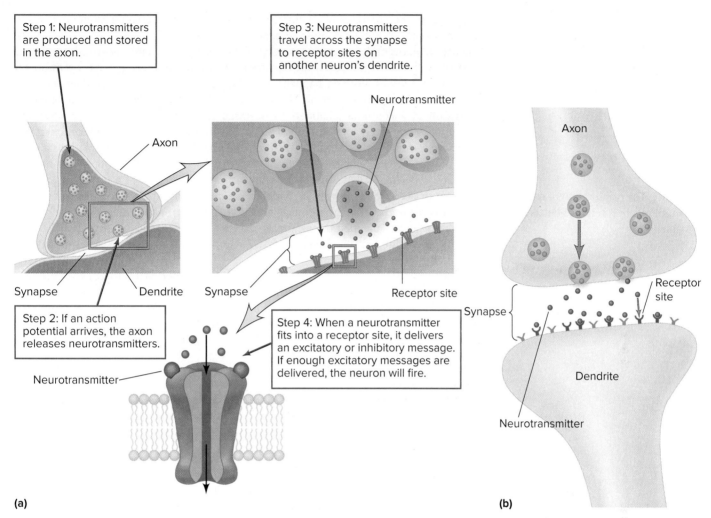

Step 1: Neurotransmitters are produced and stored in the axon.

Step 3: Neurotransmitters travel across the synapse to receptor sites on another neuron's dendrite.

Neurotransmitter

Axon

Synapse   Dendrite   Synapse   Receptor site

Step 2: If an action potential arrives, the axon releases neurotransmitters.

Step 4: When a neurotransmitter fits into a receptor site, it delivers an excitatory or inhibitory message. If enough excitatory messages are delivered, the neuron will fire.

Neurotransmitter

(a)

Axon

Receptor site

Synapse

Dendrite

Neurotransmitter

(b)

FIGURE 4 A synapse is the junction between an axon and a dendrite. Chemical neurotransmitters bridge the synaptic gap between the axon and the dendrite (Mader, 2000). (a) Read Step 1 through Step 4 to follow this chemical process. (b) Just as the pieces of a jigsaw puzzle can fit in only one specific location in a puzzle, each kind of neurotransmitter has a distinctive configuration that allows it to fit into a specific type of receptor cell (Johnson, 2000). Why is it advantageous for axons and dendrites to be linked by temporary chemical bridges rather than by the hard wiring typical of utility cables running along telephone poles?

that ferries passengers across a river, these chemical messengers move from the axon of one neuron to the dendrite of a receiving neurons.

Keep in mind that the chemical mode of message transmission that occurs between neurons differs strikingly from the means by which communication occurs inside neurons: Although messages travel in electrical form *within* a neuron, they move *between* neurons through a chemical transmission system.

Neurotransmitters come in several varieties, and not all neurons are capable of receiving the chemical message carried by a particular neurotransmitter. In the same way that a jigsaw puzzle piece can fit in only one specific location in a puzzle, each kind of neurotransmitter has a distinctive configuration that allows it to fit into a specific type of receptor site on the receiving neuron (see Figure 4b). Only when a neurotransmitter fits precisely into a receptor site can successful chemical communication occur.

If a neurotransmitter does fit into a site on the receiving neuron, the chemical message it delivers is basically one of two types: excitatory or inhibitory. **Excitatory messages** are chemical messages that make it more likely that a receiving neuron will fire and an action potential will travel down its axon. In contrast, inhibitory messages do just the opposite: **Inhibitory messages** provide chemical information that prevents or decreases the likelihood that the receiving neuron will fire.

Study Alert

Remember this key fact: Messages inside neurons are transmitted in electrical form, whereas messages traveling between neurons travel via chemical means.

excitatory message A chemical message that makes it more likely that a receiving neuron will fire and an action potential will travel down its axon. (Module 5)

inhibitory message A chemical message that prevents or decreases the likelihood that a receiving neuron will fire. (Module 5)

Because the dendrites of a neuron receive both excitatory and inhibitory messages simultaneously, the neuron must integrate the messages by using a kind of chemical calculator. Put simply, if the excitatory messages ("Fire!") outnumber the inhibitory ones ("Don't fire!"), the neuron fires. In contrast, if the inhibitory messages outnumber the excitatory ones, nothing happens, and the neuron remains in its resting state.

If neurotransmitters remained at the site of the synapse, receiving neurons would be awash in a continual chemical bath, producing constant stimulation or constant inhibition of the receiving neurons. This would make effective communication across the synapse impossible. To avoid this problem, enzymes deactivate the neurotransmitters, or—more commonly—the terminal button sucks them back up in an example of chemical recycling called reuptake.

reuptake The reabsorption of neurotransmitters by a terminal button. (Module 5)

Reuptake is the process in which a neurotransmitter produced by a terminal button is reabsorbed by the terminal button. Like a vacuum cleaner sucking up dust, neurons reabsorb the neurotransmitters that are now clogging the synapse. All this activity occurs at lightning speed, with the process taking just several milliseconds (Gingrich et al., 2017).

Our understanding of the process of reuptake has permitted the development of a number of drugs used in the treatment of psychological disorders. Some antidepressant drugs, called *SSRIs*, or *selective serotonin reuptake inhibitors*, permit certain neurotransmitters to remain active for a longer period at certain synapses in the brain, thereby reducing the symptoms of depression (Jauhar et al., 2019; Edinoff et al., 2021; Nykamp et al., 2022).

Neurotransmitters: Multitalented Chemical Couriers

Neurotransmitters are a particularly important link between the nervous system and behavior. Not only are they important for maintaining vital brain and body functions, but a deficiency or an excess of a neurotransmitter can produce severe behavior disorders. More than a hundred chemicals have been found to act as neurotransmitters, and neuroscientists believe that more may ultimately be identified. The major neurotransmitters and their effects are described in Figure 5 (Shariatgorji et al., 2019; Hecking et al., 2021).

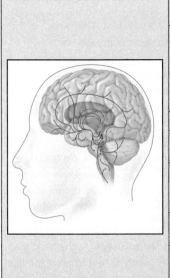

Neurotransmitter Name	Location	Effect	Function
Acetylcholine (ACh)	Brain, spinal cord, peripheral nervous system, especially some organs of the parasympathetic nervous system	Excitatory in brain and autonomic nervous system; inhibitory elsewhere	Muscle movement, cognitive functioning
Glutamate	Brain, spinal cord	Excitatory	Memory
Gamma-amino butyric acid (GABA)	Brain, spinal cord	Main inhibitory neurotransmitter	Eating, aggression, sleeping
Dopamine (DA)	Brain	Inhibitory or excitatory	Movement control, pleasure and reward, attention
Serotonin	Brain, spinal cord	Inhibitory	Sleeping, eating, mood, pain, depression
Endorphins	Brain, spinal cord	Primarily inhibitory, except in hippocampus	Pain suppression, pleasurable feelings, appetites, placebos

FIGURE 5 Major neurotransmitters.

One of the most common neurotransmitters is *acetylcholine* (or *ACh*, its chemical symbol), which is found throughout the nervous system. ACh is involved in our every physical move because–among other things–it transmits messages relating to our skeletal muscles. ACh also aids in memory capabilities. In fact, diminished production of ACh may be related to Alzheimer's disease (Betterton et al., 2017; Chen et al., 2022).

Another common excitatory neurotransmitter, *glutamate*, plays a role in memory. Memories appear to be produced by specific biochemical changes at particular synapses, and glutamate, along with other neurotransmitters, plays an important role in this process (Jelen et al., 2019; Morland & Nordengen, 2022).

Gamma-amino butyric acid (GABA), which is found in both the brain and the spinal cord, appears to be the nervous system's primary inhibitory neurotransmitter. It moderates a variety of behaviors, ranging from eating to aggression. Several common substances, such as the tranquilizer Valium and alcohol, are effective because they permit GABA to operate more efficiently (Luo et al., 2021; Quillin et al., 2021).

Another major neurotransmitter is *dopamine (DA)*, which is involved in movement, attention, and learning. The discovery that certain drugs can have a significant effect on dopamine release has led to the development of effective treatments for a wide variety of physical and mental ailments. For instance, Parkinson's disease is caused by a deficiency of dopamine in the brain. Techniques for increasing the production of dopamine in Parkinson's patients are proving effective (McGuigan et al., 2019; Latif et al., 2021; Pike et al., 2022).

In other instances, overproduction of dopamine produces negative consequences. For example, researchers have hypothesized that schizophrenia and some other severe mental disturbances are affected or perhaps even caused by the presence of unusually high levels of dopamine. Drugs that block the reception of dopamine reduce the symptoms displayed by some people diagnosed with schizophrenia. Other research suggests that obsessive use of online gaming and social media is related to overproduction of dopamine, leading to a kind of addiction (Kimura et al., 2021; Seo et al., 2021; Abi-Dargham et al., 2022).

From the perspective of...

A Health-Care Provider How might your understanding of the nervous system help you explain the symptoms of Parkinson's disease to a patient with the disorder?

Tetra Images/Getty Images

Another neurotransmitter, *serotonin*, is associated with the regulation of sleep, eating, mood, and pain. A growing body of research points toward a broader role for serotonin, suggesting its involvement in such diverse behaviors as alcoholism, depression, suicide, impulsivity, aggression, and coping with stress (Pawluski et al., 2019; Deo & Redpath, 2022).

Endorphins, another class of neurotransmitters, are a family of chemicals produced by the brain that are similar in structure to painkilling drugs such as morphine. The production of endorphins reflects the brain's effort to deal with pain as well as to elevate mood.

Endorphins also may produce the euphoric feelings that runners sometimes experience after long runs. The exertion and perhaps the pain involved in a long run may stimulate the production of endorphins, ultimately resulting in what has been called "runner's high" (Stoll, 2019; Semler, 2021). The use of opioids and heroin also results in the release of endorphins, thereby creating a potent high that can lead very quickly to addiction. The high is so powerful that it makes successful treatment extremely difficult (Herlinger & Lingford-Hughes, 2022).

Many runners experience a "runner's high" after a long, hard run due to the release of endorphins in the brain.

Adam Hester/Getty Images

Endorphin release might also explain other phenomena that have long puzzled psychologists. For example, the act of taking placebos (pills or other substances that contain no actual drugs but that patients *believe* will make them better) may induce the release of endorphins, leading to the reduction of pain (Bruehl et al., 2017; Schoenfeld & Swanson, 2021).

RECAP/EVALUATE/RETHINK

RECAP

LO 5-1 Why do psychologists study the brain and nervous system?

- A full understanding of human behavior requires knowledge of the biological influences underlying that behavior, especially those originating in the nervous system. Psychologists who specialize in studying the effects of biological structures and functions on behavior are known as behavioral neuroscientists.

LO 5-2 What are the basic elements of the nervous system?

- Neurons, the most basic elements of the nervous system, carry nerve impulses from one part of the body to another. Information in a neuron generally follows a route that begins with the dendrites, continues into the cell body, and leads ultimately down the tube-like extension, the axon.

LO 5-3 How does the nervous system communicate electrical and chemical messages from one part to another?

- Most axons are insulated by a coating called the myelin sheath. When a neuron receives a message to fire, it releases an action potential, an electric charge that travels through the axon. Neurons operate according to an all-or-none law: Either they are at rest, or an action potential is moving through them. There is no in-between state.

- When a neuron fires, nerve impulses are carried to other neurons through the production of chemical substances called neurotransmitters that bridge the gaps—known as synapses—between neurons. Neurotransmitters may be either excitatory, telling other neurons to fire, or inhibitory, preventing or decreasing the likelihood of other neurons firing.

- Endorphins, another type of neurotransmitter, are related to the reduction of pain. Endorphins aid in the production of a natural painkiller and are probably responsible for creating the kind of euphoria that joggers sometimes experience after running.

EVALUATE

1. The _____ is the fundamental element of the nervous system.
2. Neurons receive information through their _____ and send messages through their _____.

3. Just as electrical wires have an outer coating, axons are insulated by a coating called the _____.
4. The gap between two neurons is bridged by a chemical connection called a _____.
5. Endorphins are one kind of _____, the chemical "messenger" between neurons.

RETHINK

1. How might psychologists use drugs that mimic the effects of neurotransmitters to treat psychological disorders?

2. In what ways might endorphins help to produce the placebo effect? Is there a difference between *believing* that one's pain is reduced and actually *experiencing* reduced pain? Why or why not?

Answers to Evaluate Questions

1. neuron; 2. dendrites, axons; 3. myelin sheath; 4. synapse; 5. neurotransmitter.

KEY TERMS

behavioral neuroscientists (or biopsychologists)	axon	resting state	neurotransmitters
neurons	terminal buttons	action potential	excitatory message
dendrite	myelin sheath	mirror neurons	inhibitory message
	all-or-none law	synapse	reuptake

Module 6

The Nervous System and the Endocrine System: Communicating Within the Body

LEARNING OUTCOMES

LO 6-1 How are the structures of the nervous system linked?

LO 6-2 How does the endocrine system affect behavior?

In light of the complexity of individual neurons and the neurotransmission process, it should come as no surprise that the connections and structures formed by the neurons are complicated. Because each neuron can be connected to 80,000 other neurons, the total number of possible connections is astonishing. For instance, estimates of the number of neural connections within the brain fall in the neighborhood of 10 quadrillion–a 1 followed by 16 zeros–and some experts put the number even higher. However, connections among neurons are not the only means of communication within the body; as we'll see, the endocrine system, which secretes chemical messages that circulate through the blood, also communicates messages that influence behavior and many aspects of biological functioning (Heintz et al., 2015).

The Nervous System: Linking Neurons

Whatever the actual number of neural connections, the human nervous system has both logic and elegance. We turn now to a discussion of its basic structures.

CENTRAL AND PERIPHERAL NERVOUS SYSTEMS

As you can see from the schematic representation in Figure 1, the nervous system is divided into two main parts: the central nervous system and the peripheral nervous system. The **central nervous system (CNS)** is composed of the brain and spinal cord. The **spinal cord,** which is about the thickness of a pencil, contains a bundle of neurons that leaves the brain and runs down the length of the back (see Figure 2). As you can see in Figure 2, the spinal cord is the primary means for transmitting messages between the brain and the rest of the body.

However, the spinal cord is not just a communication channel. It also controls some simple behaviors on its own, without any help from the brain. An example is the way the knee jerks forward when it is tapped with a rubber hammer. This behavior is a type of **reflex,** an automatic, involuntary response to an incoming stimulus. A reflex is also at work when you touch a hot stove and immediately withdraw your hand. Although the brain eventually analyzes and reacts to the situation ("Ouch–hot stove–pull away!"), the initial withdrawal is directed only by neurons in the spinal cord.

Several kinds of neurons are involved in reflexes. **Sensory (afferent) neurons** transmit information *from* the perimeter of the body *to* the central nervous system and the brain. For example, touching a hot stove sends a message to the brain (hot!) via sensory neurons. **Motor (efferent) neurons** communicate information in the opposite

central nervous system (CNS) The part of the nervous system that includes the brain and spinal cord. (Module 6)

spinal cord A bundle of neurons that leaves the brain and runs down the length of the back and is the main means for transmitting messages between the brain and the body. (Module 6)

reflex An automatic, involuntary response to an incoming stimulus. (Module 6)

sensory (afferent) neurons Neurons that transmit information from the perimeter of the body to the nervous system and brain. (Module 6)

motor (efferent) neurons Neurons that communicate information from the brain and nervous system to muscles and glands. (Module 6)

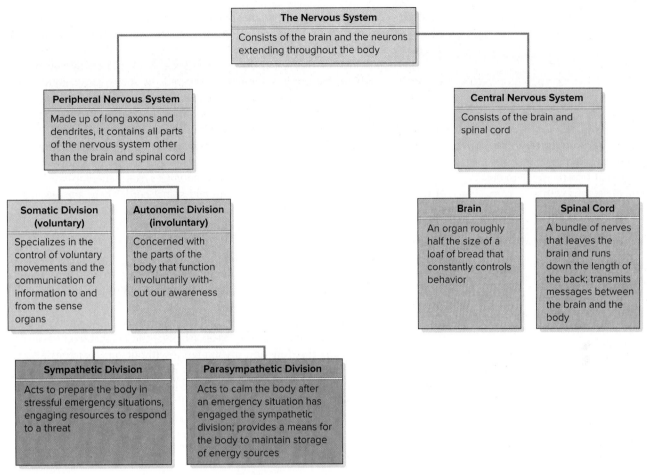

FIGURE 1 A schematic diagram of the relationship of the parts of the nervous system.

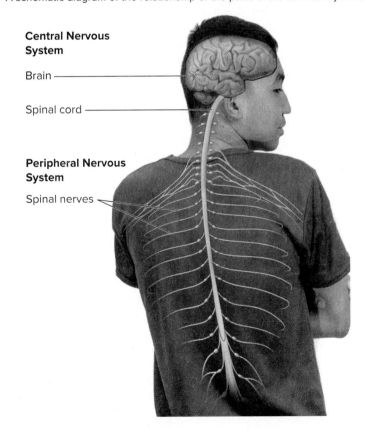

Central Nervous System

Brain

Spinal cord

Peripheral Nervous System

Spinal nerves

FIGURE 2 The central nervous system consists of the brain and spinal cord, and the peripheral nervous system encompasses the network of nerves connecting the brain and spinal cord to other parts of the body.

(Photo): Thiti Sukapan/Alamy Stock Photo

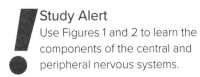

Study Alert

Use Figures 1 and 2 to learn the components of the central and peripheral nervous systems.

direction, sending messages *from* the brain and nervous system *to* the muscles and glands. When the brain sends a message to the muscles of the hand (hot–move away!), the message travels via motor neurons.

The importance of the spinal cord and reflexes is illustrated by the outcome of accidents in which the cord is injured or severed. In some cases, injury results in *quadriplegia*, a condition in which people lose voluntary muscle movement below the neck. In a less severe but still disabling condition, *paraplegia*, people are unable to voluntarily move any muscles in the lower half of the body.

peripheral nervous system The part of the nervous system that includes the autonomic and somatic subdivisions; made up of neurons with long axons and dendrites, it branches out from the spinal cord and brain and reaches the extremities of the body. (Module 6)

As suggested by its name, the **peripheral nervous system** branches out from the spinal cord and brain and reaches the extremities of the body. Made up of neurons with long axons and dendrites, the peripheral nervous system encompasses all the parts of the nervous system other than the brain and spinal cord. There are two major divisions of the peripheral nervous system–the somatic division and the autonomic division–both of which connect the central nervous system with the sense organs, muscles, glands, and other organs.

somatic division The part of the peripheral nervous system that specializes in the control of voluntary movements and the communication of information to and from the sense organs. (Module 6)

The **somatic division** of the peripheral nervous system specializes in the control of voluntary movements, such as the motion of your eyes to read this sentence or those of your hand to scroll down a page. The somatic division also communicates information to and from the sense organs.

autonomic division The part of the peripheral nervous system that controls involuntary movement of the heart, glands, lungs, and other organs. (Module 6)

The **autonomic division** of the peripheral nervous system controls the parts of the body that automatically function to keep us alive–the heart, blood vessels, glands, lungs, and other organs that function involuntarily without our awareness. As you are reading at this moment, the autonomic division of the peripheral nervous system is pumping blood through your body, pushing your lungs in and out, and overseeing the digestion of your last meal.

ACTIVATING THE DIVISIONS OF THE AUTONOMIC NERVOUS SYSTEM

The autonomic division plays a particularly crucial role during emergencies. Suppose that as you are walking down a street and checking your cell phone, you suddenly see the glint of something that might be a knife. As confusion clouds your mind and fear overcomes your attempts to think rationally, what happens to your body? If you are like most people, you react immediately on a biological level. Your heart rate increases, you begin to sweat, and you may develop goose bumps all over your body.

sympathetic division The part of the autonomic division of the nervous system that acts to prepare the body for action in stressful situations, engaging all the organism's resources to respond to a threat. (Module 6)

The biological changes that occur during a crisis result from the activation of the part of the autonomic nervous system called the sympathetic division. The **sympathetic division** prepares the body for action in stressful situations by engaging all the organism's resources to run away or to confront the threat. This is often called the "fight-or-flight" response.

parasympathetic division The part of the autonomic division of the nervous system that acts to calm the body after an emergency has ended. (Module 6)

In contrast, the **parasympathetic division** of the autonomic nervous system acts to calm the body after the emergency has ended. When you find, for instance, that what you thought might be a knife is actually the glint of keys in the stranger's hand, your parasympathetic division begins to take over, lowering your heart rate, stopping your sweating, and returning your body to the state it was in before you became alarmed. The parasympathetic division also directs the body to store energy for use in emergencies.

The sympathetic and parasympathetic divisions work together to regulate many functions of the body (see Figure 3). For instance, sexual arousal is controlled by the parasympathetic division, but sexual orgasm is a function of the sympathetic division. The sympathetic and parasympathetic divisions also are involved in a number of disorders. For example, one explanation of documented examples of "voodoo death"–in which a person is literally scared to death resulting from a voodoo curse–may be produced by overstimulation of the sympathetic division due to extreme fear.

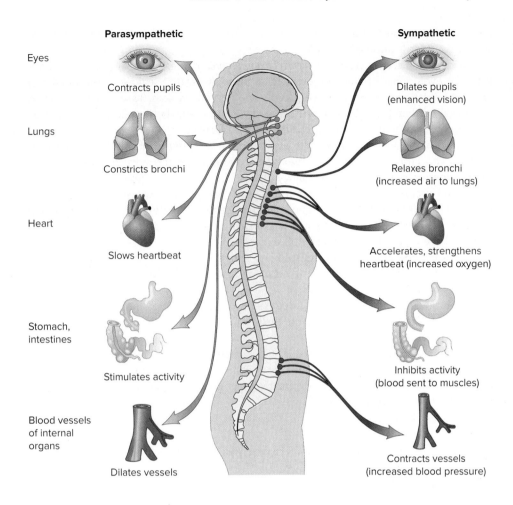

Parasympathetic

Eyes — Contracts pupils

Lungs — Constricts bronchi

Heart — Slows heartbeat

Stomach, intestines — Stimulates activity

Blood vessels of internal organs — Dilates vessels

Sympathetic

Dilates pupils (enhanced vision)

Relaxes bronchi (increased air to lungs)

Accelerates, strengthens heartbeat (increased oxygen)

Inhibits activity (blood sent to muscles)

Contracts vessels (increased blood pressure)

FIGURE 3 The major functions of the autonomic nervous system. The sympathetic division acts to prepare certain organs of the body for stressful situations, and the parasympathetic division acts to calm the body after the emergency has passed. Can you explain why each response of the sympathetic division might be useful in an emergency?

From the perspective of...

A Health-Care Provider How would an understanding of the nervous system be valuable in your job as a medical care provider?

MBI/Shutterstock

The Evolutionary Foundations of the Nervous System

The complexities of the nervous system can be better understood if we take the course of evolution into consideration. The forerunner of the human nervous system is found in the earliest simple organisms to have a spinal cord. Basically, those organisms were simple input-output devices: When the upper side of the spinal cord was stimulated by, for instance, being touched, the organism reacted with a simple response, such as jerking away. Such responses were completely a consequence of the organism's genetic makeup.

Over millions of years, the spinal cord became more specialized, and organisms became capable of distinguishing between different kinds of stimuli and responding appropriately to them. Ultimately, a portion of the spinal cord evolved into what we would consider a primitive brain.

Today, the nervous system is *hierarchically organized,* meaning that relatively newer (from an evolutionary point of view) and more sophisticated regions of the brain regulate the older and more primitive parts of the nervous system. As we move up along the spinal cord and continue upward into the brain then, the functions controlled by the various regions become progressively more advanced.

evolutionary psychology The branch of psychology that seeks to identify behavior patterns that are a result of our genetic inheritance from our ancestors. (Module 6)

Why should we care about the evolutionary background of the human nervous system? The answer comes from researchers working in the area of **evolutionary psychology,** the branch of psychology that seeks to identify how behavior is influenced and produced by our genetic inheritance from our ancestors.

Evolutionary psychologists argue that the course of evolution is reflected in the structure and functioning of the nervous system and that evolutionary factors consequently have a significant influence on our everyday behavior. Their work, in conjunction with the research of scientists studying genetics, biochemistry, and medicine, has led to an understanding of how our behavior is affected by heredity, our genetically determined heritage.

behavioral genetics The study of the effects of heredity on behavior. (Module 6)

Evolutionary psychologists have spawned a new and increasingly influential field: behavioral genetics. As we will discuss further in Chapter 12 on development, **behavioral genetics** is the study of the effects of heredity on behavior. Consistent with the evolutionary perspective, behavioral genetics researchers are finding increasing evidence that cognitive abilities, personality traits, sexual orientation, and psychological disorders are determined to some extent by genetic factors (Barbaro et al., 2017; Wertz et al., 2019; Flint, 2022).

The Endocrine System: Of Chemicals and Glands

endocrine system A chemical communication network that sends messages throughout the body via the bloodstream. (Module 6)

Another of the body's communication systems, the **endocrine system** is a chemical communication network that sends messages throughout the body via the bloodstream. Its job is to secrete **hormones,** chemicals that circulate through the blood and regulate the functioning or growth of the body. It also influences–and is influenced by–the functioning of the nervous system. Although the endocrine system is not part of the brain, it is closely linked to the hypothalamus.

hormones Chemicals that circulate through the blood and regulate the functioning or growth of the body. (Module 6)

As chemical messengers, hormones are like neurotransmitters, although their speed and mode of transmission are quite different. Whereas neural messages are measured in thousandths of a second, hormonal communications may take minutes to reach their destination. Furthermore, neural messages move through neurons in specific lines (like a signal carried by wires strung along telephone poles), whereas hormones travel throughout the body, similar to the way radio waves are transmitted across the entire landscape. Just as radio waves evoke a response only when a radio is tuned to the correct station, hormones flowing through the bloodstream activate only those cells that are receptive and "tuned" to the appropriate hormonal message.

pituitary gland The major component of the endocrine system, or "master gland," which secretes hormones that control growth and other parts of the endocrine system. (Module 6)

A key component of the endocrine system is the tiny **pituitary gland,** which is found near–and regulated by–the hypothalamus in the brain. The pituitary gland plays a significant role because it controls the functioning of the rest of the endocrine system. But the pituitary gland does more than manage other glands; it has important functions in its own right. For instance, hormones secreted by the pituitary gland control growth. Extremely short people and unusually tall ones usually have pituitary gland abnormalities. Other endocrine glands, shown in Figure 4, affect emotional reactions, sexual urges, and energy levels.

Despite its important role in managing other endocrine glands, the pituitary is actually a servant of the brain because the brain is ultimately responsible for the

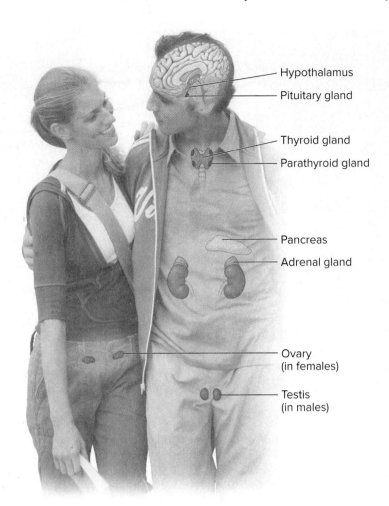

Hypothalamus

Pituitary gland

Thyroid gland

Parathyroid gland

Pancreas

Adrenal gland

Ovary
(in females)

Testis
(in males)

FIGURE 4 Location and function of the major endocrine glands. The pituitary gland controls the functioning of the other endocrine glands and, in turn, is regulated by the hypothalamus.
(Photo): Laurence Mouton/PhotoAlto/Getty Images

endocrine system's functioning. The brain maintains the internal balance of the body through the hypothalamus.

Individual hormones can wear many hats, depending on circumstances. For example, the hormone oxytocin is at the root of many of life's satisfactions and pleasures. In new mothers, oxytocin produces an urge to nurse newborn offspring. The same hormone also seems to stimulate cuddling between species members. And—at least in rats—it encourages sexually active males to seek out females more aggressively and females to be more receptive to males' sexual advances. There's even evidence that oxytocin is related to the development of trust in others, helping to grease the wheels of effective social interaction (de Visser et al., 2017; Berends et al., 2019; Itskovich et al., 2021).

Although hormones are produced naturally by the endocrine system, the ingestion of artificial hormones has proved to be both beneficial and potentially dangerous. For example, before the early 2000s, physicians frequently prescribed hormone replacement therapy to treat symptoms of menopause in older women. However, because more recent research suggested that the treatment had potentially dangerous side effects, health experts now warn that in many cases, the dangers outweigh the benefits (Doty et al., 2015; Gersh & Lavie, 2020; Langer et al., 2021).

The use of testosterone, a male hormone, and drugs known as *steroids*, which act like testosterone, is increasingly common. For athletes and others who want to bulk up their appearance, steroids provide a way to add muscle weight and increase strength. However, these drugs can lead to stunted growth, shrinking of the testicles, heart attacks, strokes, and cancer, making them extremely dangerous. In some cases, steroid use can produce violent behavior toward others (Zahnow et al., 2017; Geniole et al., 2019; Csöndör, 2022).

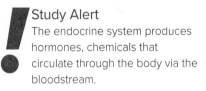

Study Alert

The endocrine system produces hormones, chemicals that circulate through the body via the bloodstream.

Steroids can provide added muscle and strength, but they have dangerous side effects. A number of well-known athletes in a variety of sports, such as baseball player Robinson Cano, pictured here, have been accused of using the drugs illegally. In fact, a number of them have publicly said they have used them.

Rich Schultz/Getty Images

RECAP/EVALUATE/RETHINK

RECAP

LO 6-1 How are the structures of the nervous system linked?

- The nervous system is made up of the central nervous system (the brain and spinal cord) and the peripheral nervous system. The peripheral nervous system is made up of the somatic division, which controls voluntary movements and the communication of information to and from the sense organs, and the autonomic division, which controls involuntary functions such as those of the heart, blood vessels, and lungs.
- The autonomic division of the peripheral nervous system is further subdivided into the sympathetic and parasympathetic divisions. The sympathetic division prepares the body in emergency situations, and the parasympathetic division helps the body return to its typical resting state.
- Evolutionary psychology, the branch of psychology that seeks to identify behavior patterns that are a result of our genetic inheritance, has led to increased understanding of the evolutionary basis of the structure and organization of the human nervous system.

LO 6-2 How does the endocrine system affect behavior?

- The endocrine system secretes hormones, chemicals that regulate the functioning of the body, via the bloodstream. The pituitary gland secretes growth hormones and influences the release of hormones by other endocrine glands and in turn is regulated by the hypothalamus.

EVALUATE

1. If you put your hand on a red-hot piece of metal, the immediate response of pulling it away would be an example of a(n) _____.
2. The central nervous system is composed of the _____ and the _____.
3. In the peripheral nervous system, the _____ division controls voluntary movements, whereas the _____ division controls organs that keep us alive and function without our awareness.
4. Maria saw a young boy run into the street and get hit by a car. When she got to the fallen child, she was in a state of panic. She was sweating, and her heart was racing. Her biological state resulted from the activation of what division of the nervous system?
   a. parasympathetic
   b. central
   c. sympathetic
5. The emerging field of _____ studies ways in which our genetic inheritance predisposes us to behave in certain ways.

RETHINK

1. In what ways is the "fight-or-flight" response helpful to humans in emergency situations?
2. How might communication within the nervous system result in human consciousness?

Answers to Evaluate Questions

1. reflex; 2. brain, spinal cord; 3. somatic, autonomic; 4. c. sympathetic; 5. evolutionary psychology

KEY TERMS

central nervous system (CNS)	sensory (afferent) neurons	autonomic division	behavioral genetics
spinal cord	motor (efferent) neurons	sympathetic division	endocrine system
reflex	peripheral nervous system	parasympathetic division	hormones
	somatic division	evolutionary psychology	pituitary gland

Module 7
The Brain

LEARNING OUTCOMES

LO 7-1 How do researchers identify the major parts and functions of the brain?

LO 7-2 What are the major parts of the brain, and for what behaviors is each part responsible?

LO 7-3 How do the two halves of the brain operate interdependently?

LO 7-4 How can an understanding of the nervous system help us find ways to alleviate disease and pain?

It is not much to look at. Soft, spongy, mottled, and pinkish-gray in color, it hardly can be said to possess much in the way of physical beauty. Despite its physical appearance, however, it ranks as the greatest natural marvel that we know and has a beauty and sophistication all its own.

The object to which this description applies: the brain. The brain is responsible for our loftiest thoughts—and our most primitive urges. It is the overseer of the intricate workings of the human body. If one were to attempt to design a computer to mimic the range of capabilities of the brain, the task would be nearly impossible; in fact, it has proved difficult even to come close. The sheer quantity of nerve cells in the brain is enough to daunt even the most ambitious computer engineer. Many billions of neurons make up a structure weighing just 3 pounds in the average adult. However, it is not the number of cells that is the most astounding thing about the brain but its ability to allow the human intellect to flourish by guiding our behavior and thoughts.

We turn now to a consideration of the particular structures of the brain and the primary functions to which they are related. However, a caution is in order. Although we'll discuss specific areas of the brain in relation to specific behaviors, this approach is an oversimplification. No straightforward, one-to-one correspondence exists between a distinct part of the brain and a particular behavior. Instead, behavior is produced by complex interconnections among sets of neurons in many areas of the brain: Our behavior, emotions, thoughts, hopes, and dreams are produced by a variety of neurons throughout the nervous system working in concert.

Studying the Brain's Structure and Functions: Spying on the Brain

The brain has posed a continual challenge to those who would study it. For most of history, its examination was possible only after an individual had died. Only then could the skull be opened and the brain cut into without serious injury. Although informative, this procedure could hardly tell us much about the functioning of the healthy brain.

Today, however, brain-scanning techniques provide a window into the living brain. Using these techniques, investigators can take a "snapshot" of the internal workings of the brain without having to cut open a person's skull. The most important scanning techniques, illustrated in Figure 1, are the electroencephalogram (EEG), positron emission tomography (PET), functional magnetic resonance imaging (fMRI), and transcranial magnetic stimulation (TMS) imaging.

The *electroencephalogram (EEG)* records electrical activity in the brain through electrodes placed on the outside of the skull. Although traditionally the EEG could produce only a graph of electrical wave patterns, new techniques are now used to transform the brain's electrical activity into a pictorial representation of the brain that allows more precise diagnosis of disorders such as epilepsy and learning disabilities.

Functional magnetic resonance imaging (fMRI) scans provide a detailed, three-dimensional computer-generated image of brain structures and

The brain (shown here in cross section) may not be much to look at, but it represents one of the great marvels of human development. Why do most scientists believe that it will be difficult, if not impossible, to duplicate the brain's abilities with artificial intelligence?

Christine Eckel/McGraw Hill

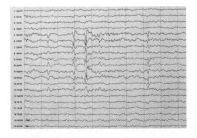

(a) EEG

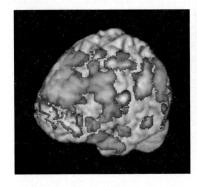

(b) fMRI

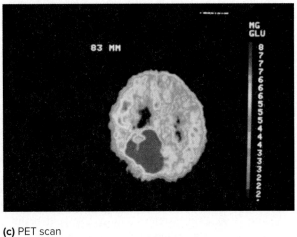

(c) PET scan

(d) TMS apparatus

FIGURE 1 Brain scans produced by different techniques. (a) A computer-produced EEG image. (b) The fMRI scan uses a magnetic field to provide a detailed view of brain activity on a moment-by-moment basis. (c) The PET scan displays the functioning of the brain at a given moment. (d) Transcranial magnetic stimulation (TMS), the newest type of scan, produces a momentary disruption in an area of the brain, allowing researchers to see what activities are controlled by that area. TMS also has the potential to treat some psychological disorders.

(a): Chaikom/Shutterstock; (b): NIH/IMAGE POINT FR/BSIP SA/Alamy Stock Photo; (c): National Institutes of Health; (d): Amelie Benoist/BSIP/Corbis Documentary/Getty Images

activity by aiming a powerful magnetic field at the brain or other parts of the body. With fMRI scanning, it is possible to produce vivid, detailed images of the functioning and structure of the brain.

Using fMRI scans, researchers are able to view features of less than a millimeter in size and changes occurring in intervals of one-tenth of a second. For example, fMRI scans can show the operation of individual bundles of nerves by tracing the flow of blood, opening the way for improved diagnosis of ailments ranging from chronic back pain to nervous system disorders such as strokes, multiple sclerosis, and Alzheimer's disease. Scans using fMRI are routinely used in planning brain surgery because they can help surgeons distinguish areas of the brain involved in normal and disturbed functioning (Hurschler et al., 2015; Sahakian & Gottwald, 2017; Elliott et al., 2021).

Positron emission tomography (PET) scans show biochemical activity within the brain at a given moment. PET scans begin with the injection of a radioactive (but safe) liquid into the bloodstream, which makes its way to the brain. By locating radiation within the brain, a computer can determine which are the more active regions, providing a striking picture of the brain at work. For example, PET scans may be used to diagnose memory problems, seeking to identify the presence of brain tumors. PET scans can even measure blood flow and oxygen use (Konijnenberg et al., 2019; Patel et al., 2020).

Transcranial magnetic stimulation (TMS) uses magnetic fields to produce an understanding of the functioning of the brain. In TMS, a tiny region of the brain is bombarded by a strong magnetic field that causes a momentary interruption of electrical activity. Researchers then are able to note the effects of this interruption on normal brain functioning.

One of the newest procedures used to study the brain, TMS is sometimes called a "virtual lesion" because it produces effects similar to what would occur if areas of the brain were physically cut. The enormous advantage of TMS, of course, is that the virtual cut is only temporary. In addition to identifying areas of the brain that are

Study Alert

Remember how EEG, fMRI, PET, and TMS scans differ in the ways that they produce an image of the brain.

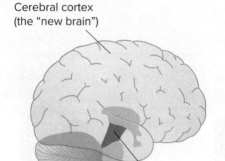

FIGURE 2 The major divisions of the brain: the cerebral cortex and the central core.

central core The "old brain," which controls basic functions such as eating and sleeping and is common to all vertebrates. (Module 7)

responsible for particular functions, TMS has the potential to treat certain kinds of psychological disorders, such as depression and schizophrenia, by shooting brief magnetic pulses through the brain (Prasser et al., 2015; Francis et al., 2019).

Future discoveries may yield even more sophisticated methods of examining the brain. For example, the emerging field of *optogenetics* involves genetic engineering and the use of special types of light to view individual circuits of neurons. In addition, researchers are developing *hydrogel-embedding* methods, which allow observation of individual brain cells and the wiring of brain circuitry. Finally, using nonhumans, researchers have developed *Neuropixels*, miniaturized implanted probes that can be inserted into the brain. Using sophisticated algorithms, neuroscientists can read and record activity in hundreds of neurons in multiple parts of the brain simultaneously (de Sousa et al., 2019; Chen et al., 2021; Steinmetz et al., 2021).

The Central Core: Our "Old Brain"

Although the capabilities of the human brain far exceed those of the brain of any other species, humans share some basic functions, such as breathing, eating, and sleeping, with more primitive animals. Not surprisingly, those activities are directed by a relatively primitive part of the brain. A portion of the brain known as the **central core** (see Figure 2) is quite similar in all vertebrates (species with backbones). The central core is sometimes referred to as the "old brain" because its evolution can be traced back some 500 million years to primitive structures found in nonhuman species.

If we were to move up the spinal cord from the base of the skull to locate the structures of the central core of the brain, the first part we would come to would be the *hindbrain*, which contains the medulla, pons, and cerebellum (see Figure 3). The *medulla* controls a number of critical body functions, the most important of which are breathing and heartbeat. The *pons* is a bridge in the hindbrain. Containing large bundles of nerves, the pons acts as a transmitter of motor information, coordinating muscles

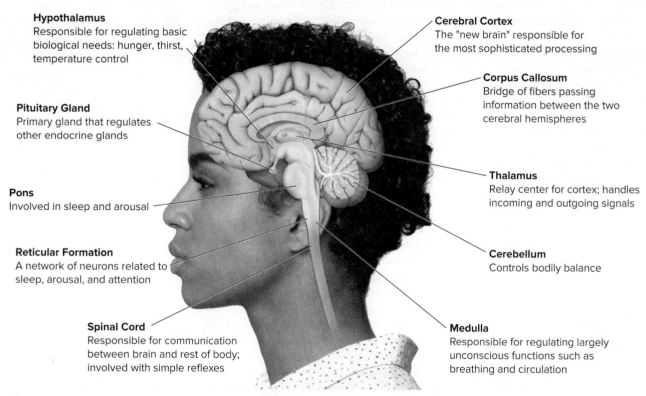

Hypothalamus
Responsible for regulating basic biological needs: hunger, thirst, temperature control

Pituitary Gland
Primary gland that regulates other endocrine glands

Pons
Involved in sleep and arousal

Reticular Formation
A network of neurons related to sleep, arousal, and attention

Spinal Cord
Responsible for communication between brain and rest of body; involved with simple reflexes

Cerebral Cortex
The "new brain" responsible for the most sophisticated processing

Corpus Callosum
Bridge of fibers passing information between the two cerebral hemispheres

Thalamus
Relay center for cortex; handles incoming and outgoing signals

Cerebellum
Controls bodily balance

Medulla
Responsible for regulating largely unconscious functions such as breathing and circulation

FIGURE 3 The major structures in the brain.
(Photo): fizkes/Shutterstock

and integrating movement between the right and left halves of the body. It is also involved in regulating sleep.

The **cerebellum** extends from the rear of the hindbrain. Without the help of the cerebellum, we would be unable to walk a straight line without staggering and lurching forward, for it is the job of the cerebellum to control bodily balance. It constantly monitors feedback from the muscles to coordinate their placement, movement, and tension. In fact, drinking too much alcohol seems to depress the activity of the cerebellum, leading to the unsteady gait and movement characteristic of drunkenness. The cerebellum is also involved in several intellectual functions, ranging from the analysis and coordination of sensory information to problem solving (Swain et al., 2011; Ronconi et al., 2017; Coolidge, 2021).

The **reticular formation** is a nerve network in the brain that extends from the medulla through the pons, passing through the middle section of the brain, called the *midbrain*, and into the front-most part of the brain, called the *forebrain*. Like an ever-vigilant guard, the reticular formation produces general arousal of our body. If, for example, we are startled by a loud noise, the reticular formation can prompt a heightened state of awareness to determine whether a response is necessary. The reticular formation also helps regulate our sleep-wake cycle by filtering out background stimuli to allow us to sleep undisturbed.

The **thalamus,** which is hidden within the forebrain, acts primarily as a relay station for information about the senses. Messages from the eyes, ears, and skin travel to the thalamus to be communicated upward to higher parts of the brain. The thalamus also integrates information from higher parts of the brain, sorting it out so that it can be sent to the cerebellum and medulla.

The **hypothalamus** is located just below the thalamus. Although tiny–about the size of a fingertip–the hypothalamus plays an extremely important role. One of its major functions is to maintain *homeostasis*, a steady internal environment for the body. The hypothalamus helps provide a constant body temperature and monitors the amount of nutrients stored in the cells. A second major function is equally important: the hypothalamus produces and regulates behavior that is critical to the basic survival of the species, such as eating, self-protection, and sex.

The Limbic System: Beyond the Central Core

In an eerie view of the future, science fiction writers have suggested that people someday will routinely have electrodes implanted in their brains. Those electrodes will permit them to receive tiny shocks that will produce the sensation of pleasure by stimulating certain centers of the brain. When they feel upset, people will simply activate their electrodes to achieve an immediate high.

Although far-fetched–and ultimately improbable–such a futuristic fantasy is based on fact. The brain does have pleasure centers in several areas, including some in the **limbic system.** Consisting of a series of doughnut-shaped structures that include the *amygdala* and *hippocampus*, the limbic system borders the top of the central core and has connections with the cerebral cortex (see Figure 4).

The structures of the limbic system jointly control a variety of basic functions relating to emotions and self-preservation, such as eating, aggression, and reproduction. Injury to the limbic system can produce striking changes in behavior. For example, injury to the amygdala, which is involved in fear and aggression, can turn animals that are usually docile and tame into ferocious beasts. Conversely, animals that are usually wild and uncontrollable may become meek and obedient following injury to the amygdala (Smith et al., 2013; Reznikova et al., 2015; Haller, 2018).

cerebellum (ser-uh-BELL-um) The part of the brain that controls bodily balance. (Module 7)

reticular formation The part of the brain extending from the medulla through the pons; it is related to changes in the level of arousal of the body. (Module 7)

thalamus The part of the brain located in the middle of the central core that acts primarily to relay information about the senses. (Module 7)

hypothalamus A tiny part of the brain, located below the thalamus, that maintains homeostasis and produces and regulates vital behavior, such as eating, drinking, and sexual behavior. (Module 7)

limbic system The part of the brain that controls eating, aggression, and reproduction. (Module 7)

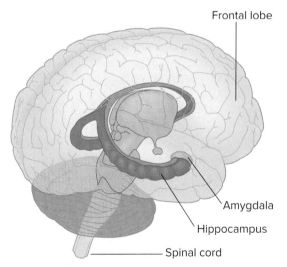

Frontal lobe

Amygdala

Hippocampus

Spinal cord

FIGURE 4 The limbic system is involved in self-preservation, learning, memory, and the experience of pleasure.

Research examining the effects of mild electric shocks to parts of the limbic system and other parts of the brain has produced some thought-provoking findings. In one classic experiment, rats that pressed a bar received mild electric stimulation through an electrode implanted in their brains, which produced pleasurable feelings. Even starving rats on their way to food would stop to press the bar as many times as they could. Some rats would actually stimulate themselves literally thousands of times an hour–until they collapsed with fatigue (Routtenberg & Lindy, 1965; Pieper et al., 2019).

Some humans have also experienced the extraordinarily pleasurable quality of certain kinds of stimulation: As part of the treatment for certain kinds of brain disorders, some people have received electrical stimulation to certain areas of the limbic system. Although at a loss to describe just what it feels like, these people report the experience to be intensely pleasurable, similar in some respects to sexual orgasm.

The limbic system and hippocampus, in particular, play an important role in learning and memory. Their importance is demonstrated in certain patients with epilepsy, who, in an effort to stop their seizures, have had portions of the limbic system removed. One unintended consequence of the surgery is that individuals sometimes have difficulty learning and remembering new information. In one case, a patient who had undergone surgery was unable to remember where he lived, although he had resided at the same address for 8 years. Further, even though the patient was able to carry on animated conversations, he was unable, a few minutes later, to recall what had been discussed (Milner, 1966; de Voogd et al., 2017; Dai et al., 2022).

The limbic system, then, is involved in several important functions, including self-preservation, learning, memory, and the experience of pleasure. These functions are hardly unique to humans; in fact, the limbic system is sometimes referred to as the "animal brain" because its structures and functions are so similar to those of other mammals. To identify the part of the brain that provides the complex and subtle capabilities that are uniquely human, we need to turn to another structure–the cerebral cortex.

The Cerebral Cortex: Our "New Brain"

As we have proceeded up the spinal cord and into the brain, our discussion has centered on areas of the brain that control functions similar to those found in less sophisticated organisms. But where, you may be asking, are the portions of the brain that enable humans to do what they do best and that distinguish humans from all other animals? Those unique features of the human brain–indeed, the very capabilities that allow you to come up with such a question in the first place–are embodied in the ability to think, evaluate, and make complex judgments. The principal location of these abilities, along with many others, is the **cerebral cortex.**

cerebral cortex The "new brain," responsible for the most sophisticated information processing in the brain; contains four lobes. (Module 7)

The cerebral cortex is referred to as the "new brain" because of its relatively recent evolution. It consists of a mass of deeply folded, rippled, convoluted tissue. Although only about one-twelfth of an inch thick, it would, if flattened out, cover an area more than 2 feet square. This configuration allows the surface area of the cortex to be considerably greater than it would be if it were smoother and more uniformly packed into the skull. The uneven shape also permits a high level of integration of neurons, allowing sophisticated information processing.

lobes The four major sections of the cerebral cortex: frontal, parietal, temporal, and occipital. (Module 7)

The cerebral cortex consists of four major sections called **lobes.** Each lobe has specialized areas that relate to particular functions. If we take a side view of the brain, the *frontal lobes* lie at the front center of the cortex and the *parietal lobes* lie behind them. The *temporal lobes* are found in the lower-center portion of the cortex, with the *occipital lobes* lying behind them. These four sets of lobes are physically separated by deep grooves called *sulci.* Figure 5 shows the four areas.

Another way to describe the brain is in terms of the functions associated with a particular area. Figure 5 also shows the specialized regions within the lobes related to specific functions and areas of the body. Three major areas are known: the motor areas, the sensory areas, and the association areas. Although we will discuss these areas as though they were separate and independent, keep in mind that this is an

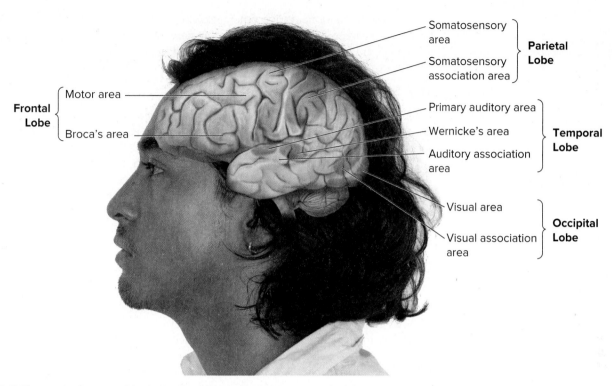

FIGURE 5 The cerebral cortex of the brain. The major physical structures of the cerebral cortex are called lobes. This figure also illustrates the functions associated with particular areas of the cerebral cortex. Are any areas of the cerebral cortex present in nonhuman animals? (Photo): Ranta Images/Shutterstock

oversimplification. In most instances, behavior is influenced simultaneously by several structures and areas within the brain, operating interdependently. To give one example, people use different areas of the brain when they create sentences (a verbal task) compared with when they improvise musical tunes. Furthermore, when people suffer brain injury, uninjured portions of the brain can sometimes take over the functions that were previously handled by the damaged area. In short, the brain is extraordinarily adaptable (Mateos-Aparicio, 2019; Esteves et al., 2021; Meijering & Lettinga, 2022).

THE MOTOR AREA OF THE CORTEX

If you look at the frontal lobe in Figure 5, you will see a shaded portion labeled **motor area.** This part of the cortex is largely responsible for the body's voluntary movement. Every portion of the motor area corresponds to a specific locale within the body. If we were to insert an electrode into a particular part of the motor area of the cortex and apply mild electrical stimulation, there would be involuntary movement in the corresponding part of the body. If we moved to another part of the motor area and stimulated it, a different part of the body would move.

The motor area is so well mapped that researchers have identified the amount and relative location of cortical tissue used to produce movement in specific parts of the human body. For example, the control of movements that are relatively large scale and require little precision, such as the movement of a knee or a hip, is centered in a very small space in the motor area. In contrast, movements that must be precise and delicate, such as facial expressions and finger movements, are controlled by a considerably larger portion of the motor area (Ross et al., 2019).

In short, the motor area of the cortex provides a guide to the degree of complexity and the importance of the motor capabilities of specific parts of the body. In fact, it may do even more: Increasing evidence shows that not only does the motor cortex control different parts of the body, but it may also direct body parts into complex postures, such as the stance of a football center just before the ball is snapped to the quarterback or a swimmer standing at the edge of a diving board (Pool et al., 2013; Massé-Alarie et al., 2017).

motor area The part of the cortex that is largely responsible for the body's voluntary movement. (Module 7)

Ultimately, movement, like other behavior, is produced through the coordinated firing of a complex variety of neurons in the nervous system. The neurons that produce movement are linked in elaborate ways and work closely together.

THE SENSORY AREA OF THE CORTEX

sensory area The site in the brain of the tissue that corresponds to each of the senses, with the degree of sensitivity related to the amount of tissue. (Module 7)

Given the one-to-one correspondence between the motor area and body location, it is not surprising to find a similar relationship between specific portions of the cortex and specific senses. The **sensory area** of the cortex includes three regions: one that corresponds primarily to body sensations (including touch and pressure), one relating to sight, and a third relating to sound.

For instance, the *somatosensory area* in the parietal lobe encompasses specific locations associated with the ability to perceive touch and pressure in a particular area of the body. As with the motor area, the amount of brain tissue related to a particular location on the body determines the degree of sensitivity of that location. Specifically, the greater the area devoted to a specific area of the body within the cortex, the more sensitive is that area of the body.

For example, our fingers are related to a larger portion of the somatosensory area in the brain and are the most sensitive to touch. The weird-looking individual in Figure 6 shows what we would look like if the size of every external part of our body corresponded to the amount of brain tissue related to touch sensitivity.

The senses of sound and sight are also represented in specific areas of the cerebral cortex. The *auditory area* located in the temporal lobe is responsible for the sense of hearing. If your auditory area were to be stimulated electrically, you would hear sounds such as clicks or hums. It also appears that particular locations within the auditory area respond to specific pitches (Anderson et al., 2017; McKetton et al., 2019; Kim et al., 2022).

association areas One of the major regions of the cerebral cortex; the site of the higher mental processes, such as thought, language, memory, and speech. (Module 7)

The *visual area* in the cortex, located in the occipital lobe, responds in an analogous way to electrical stimulation. Stimulation by electrodes produces the experience of flashes of light or colors, suggesting that the raw sensory input of images from the eyes is received in this area of the brain and transformed into meaningful stimuli. The visual area provides another example of how areas of the brain are intimately related to specific areas of the body: Specific structures in the eye are related to a particular part of the cortex—with, as you might guess, more area of the brain given to the most sensitive portions of the retina (Libedinsky & Livingstone, 2011; Smith, 2021).

FIGURE 6 The greater the amount of tissue in the somatosensory area of the brain that is related to a specific body part, the more sensitive is that body part. If the size of our body parts reflected the corresponding amount of brain tissue, we would look like this strange creature.

Natural History Museum, London/Science Source

THE ASSOCIATION AREAS OF THE CORTEX

In a freak accident in 1848, an explosion drove a 3-foot-long iron bar completely through the skull of railroad worker Phineas Gage, where it remained after the accident. Amazingly, Gage survived and, despite the rod lodged through his head, a few minutes later seemed to be fine.

But he wasn't. Before the accident, Gage was hardworking and cautious. Afterward, he became irresponsible, drank heavily, and drifted from one wild scheme to another. In the words of one of his physicians, "He was 'no longer Gage'" (Harlow, 1869).

What had happened to the old Gage? Although we have no way of knowing for sure, we can speculate that the accident injured the region of Gage's cerebral cortex known as the association areas. The **association areas** are the site of higher mental processes such as thinking, language, memory, and speech.

The association areas make up a large portion of the cerebral cortex. The association areas control *executive functions*, which are abilities that are related to planning, goal setting, judgment, and impulse control.

Much of our understanding of the association areas comes from patients who, like Phineas Gage, have suffered some type of brain injury. For example, when parts of the association areas are damaged, people undergo personality changes that affect their ability to make moral judgments and process emotions. At the same time, people with damage in those areas can still be capable of reasoning logically, performing calculations, and recalling information (Beauchamp et al., 2019).

Injuries to the association areas of the brain can produce *aphasia*, problems with language. In *Broca's aphasia*, speech becomes halting, laborious, and often ungrammatical, and a speaker is unable to find the right words. In contrast, *Wernicke's aphasia* produces difficulties both in understanding others' speech and in the production of language. The disorder is characterized by speech that sounds fluent but makes no sense, as in this example from a Wernicke's patient: "Boy, I'm sweating, I'm awful nervous, you know, once in a while I get caught up, I can't mention the tarripoi, a month ago, quite a little . . ." (Ardila, 2015; Nielsen et al., 2019; Bose et al., 2022).

Neuroplasticity and the Brain

> Shortly after he was born, Jacob Stark's arms and legs started jerking every 20 minutes. Weeks later he could not focus his eyes on his mother's face. The diagnosis: uncontrollable epileptic seizures involving his entire brain.
>
> His mother, Sally Stark, recalled: "When Jacob was 2½ months old, they said he would never learn to sit up, would never be able to feed himself . . . They told us to take him home, love him, and find an institution." (Blakeslee, 1992)

Instead, Jacob had brain surgery when he was 5 months old in which physicians removed 20% of his brain. The operation was a complete success. Three years later, Jacob seemed normal in every way, with no sign of seizures.

The surgery that helped Jacob was based on the premise that the diseased part of his brain was producing seizures throughout the brain. Surgeons reasoned that if they removed the misfiring portion, the remaining parts of the brain, which appeared intact in PET scans, would take over. They correctly bet that Jacob could still lead a normal life after surgery, particularly because the surgery was being done at so young an age.

The success of Jacob's surgery illustrates that the brain has the ability to shift functions to different locations after injury to a specific area or in cases of surgery. But equally encouraging are some new findings about the *regenerative* powers of the brain and nervous system.

Scientists have learned in recent years that the brain continually changes, reorganizes itself, and is far more resilient than they once thought. **Neuroplasticity** refers to the brain's ability to change throughout the life span through the addition of new neurons, new interconnections between neurons, and the reorganization of information-processing areas.

Advances in our understanding of neuroplasticity have changed the earlier view that no new brain cells are created after childhood. The reality is very different: Not only do the interconnections between neurons become more complex throughout life, but it now appears that new neurons are also created in certain areas of the brain during adulthood—a process called *neurogenesis*. Each day, thousands of new neurons are created, especially in areas of the brain related to learning and memory. Although the exact number of new neurons is hard to estimate, one study suggested that for adults, 1.75% of neurons are replaced or added each year in the hippocampus alone (Spalding et al., 2013; Apple et al., 2017; Babcock et al., 2021).

The ability of neurons to renew themselves during adulthood has significant implications for the potential treatment of disorders of the nervous system. For example, pharmaceutical drugs that trigger the development of new neurons might be used to counter such diseases as Alzheimer's, which are produced when neurons die (Ekonomou et al., 2015; Dard et al., 2019).

neuroplasticity Changes in the brain that occur throughout the life span relating to the addition of new neurons, new interconnections between neurons, and the reorganization of information-processing areas. (Module 7)

Furthermore, specific experiences can modify the way information is processed. For example, if you learn to read Braille, the amount of tissue in your cortex related to sensation in the fingertips will expand. Similarly, if you take up the violin, the area of the brain that receives messages from your fingers will grow–but only relating to the fingers that actually move across the violin's strings (Makin & Flor, 2020; Bacon & Brinton, 2021).

The future also holds promise for people who suffer from the tremors and loss of motor control produced by Parkinson's disease, although the research is mired in controversy. Because Parkinson's disease is caused by a gradual loss of cells that stimulate the production of dopamine in the brain, many investigators have looked toward a procedure that increases the supply of dopamine. They seem to be on the right track. When *stem cells*–immature cells from human fetuses that have the potential to develop into a variety of specialized cell types, depending on where they are implanted–are injected directly into the brains of Parkinson's sufferers, they take root and stimulate dopamine production. Preliminary results have been promising, with some patients showing great improvement. Furthermore, because many other disabling diseases, ranging from cancer to stroke, result from cell damage, targeted implanting of stem cells might revolutionize medicine (Parmar et al., 2020; Barbuti et al., 2021; Silva et al., 2022).

However, because implanted stem cells typically come from aborted fetuses, their use is controversial. Some critics have argued that the use of stem cells in research and treatment should be prohibited, while supporters argue that the potential benefits are so great that stem cell research should be unrestricted. The issue has been politicized, and the future of stem cell research is unclear (Towns, 2017; Clark et al., 2021; also see the *Neuroscience in Your Life* feature).

NEUROSCIENCE IN YOUR LIFE: THE CULTURAL BRAIN

The interdisciplinary field of *cultural neuroscience* examines how cultural values, beliefs, and practices shape the brain and how the brain in turn affects the ways in which cultural traits develop and spread from person to person. As we discussed in Chapter 1, people in Western cultures tend to hold an *individualistic orientation* that emphasizes personal identity and the uniqueness of individuals, whereas people in Asian countries are more likely to hold a *collectivistic orientation*, the perspective that each of us is part of a larger, interconnected social network.

In support of this distinction, a study by Seishu Nakagawa and colleagues of college students in Japan, which is considered to have a collectivist culture, found an association between collectivism and density of white matter in brain regions related to personality characteristics such as interdependence, cooperativeness, and external locus of control (the belief that external factors determine outcomes in one's life). Of course, we don't know if white matter structure in the brain predisposes people to have a collectivist viewpoint or if collectivist beliefs and practices cause changes in white matter. Either way, the study demonstrates how neuroscience research methods can be integrated with other fields, such as cultural psychology, to identify the brain basis of our behavior and even our thoughts and values (Nakagawa et al., 2019).

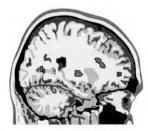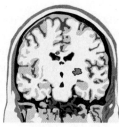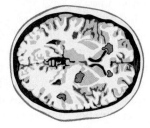

Scores on a collectivism questionnaire were associated with a higher density of white matter in several brain regions, including regions indicated by orange. These regions have been linked to personality characteristics such as interdependence and cooperativeness in other studies.
Source: Nakagawa et al., 2019

The Specialization of the Hemispheres: Two Brains or One?

The most recent development, at least in evolutionary terms, in the organization and operation of the human brain probably occurred in the last several million years: a specialization of the functions controlled by the left and right sides of the brain.

The brain is divided into two roughly mirror-image halves. Just as we have two arms, two legs, and two lungs, we have a left brain and a right brain. Because of the way nerves in the brain are connected to the rest of the body, these symmetrical left and right halves, called **hemispheres,** control motion in–and receive sensation from–the side of the body opposite their location. The left hemisphere of the brain, then, generally controls the right side of the body, and the right hemisphere controls the left side of the body. Thus, damage to the right side of the brain is typically indicated by functional difficulties in the left side of the body.

Despite the appearance of similarity between the two hemispheres of the brain, they are somewhat different in the functions they control and in the ways they control them. Certain behaviors are more likely to reflect activity in one hemisphere than in the other, or are **lateralized.**

For example, for most people, language processing occurs more in the left side of the brain. In general, the left hemisphere concentrates more on tasks that require verbal competence, such as speaking, reading, thinking, and reasoning. In addition, the left hemisphere tends to process information sequentially, one bit at a time (Hines, 2004).

The right hemisphere has different strengths, particularly in nonverbal areas such as the understanding of spatial relationships, recognition of patterns and drawings, music, and expression and understanding of emotions. The right hemisphere tends to process information globally, considering it as a whole (Longo et al., 2015; Gainotti, 2019; Minga et al., 2022).

The degree and nature of lateralization vary from one person to another. If, like most people, you are right-handed, the control of language is probably concentrated more in your left hemisphere. By contrast, if you are among the 10% of people who are left-handed or are ambidextrous (you use both hands interchangeably), it is much more likely that the language centers of your brain are located more in the right hemisphere or are divided equally between the left and right hemispheres.

Keep in mind that despite the different strengths of the two hemispheres, the differences in specialization between the hemispheres are not great. Furthermore, the two hemispheres of the brain function in tandem. It is a mistake to think of particular kinds of information as being processed solely in the right or the left hemisphere. The hemispheres work interdependently in deciphering, interpreting, and reacting to the world.

In addition, people who suffer injury to the left side of the brain and lose linguistic capabilities often recover the ability to speak: The right side of the brain often takes over some of the functions of the left side, especially in young children; the extent of recovery increases the earlier the injury occurs (Chang et al., 2018; Crivelli et al., 2021).

Evidence continues to grow that the differences between processing in the left and right hemispheres are meaningful. For example, researchers have unearthed evidence that there may be subtle differences in brain lateralization patterns between males and females and members of different cultures, as we see in *Exploring Diversity.*

hemispheres Symmetrical left and right halves of the brain that control the side of the body opposite to their location. (Module 7)

lateralization The dominance of one hemisphere of the brain in specific functions, such as language. (Module 7)

! Study Alert

Although the hemispheres of the brain specialize in particular kinds of functions, the degree of specialization is not great, and the two hemispheres work interdependently.

From the perspective of...

An Office Worker Could personal differences in people's specialization of right and left hemispheres be related to occupational success? For example, might a designer who relies on spatial skills have a different pattern of hemispheric specialization than does a lawyer?

Prostock-studio/
Shutterstock

Exploring Diversity

Human Diversity and the Brain

The interplay of biology and environment in behavior is especially clear when we consider evidence suggesting that even in brain structure and function, there are both sex and cultural differences. Some of these differences are apparent from the moment of birth.

Let's consider sex differences first. Accumulating evidence points to intriguing differences in males' and females' brain lateralization, weight, and processing. For instance, the two sexes show differences in the speed at which their brains develop. For example, the frontal lobes, which control aggressiveness and language, develop earlier in girls than boys. On the other hand, boys' brains develop faster in the region that facilitates visual and spatial tasks such as geometry. And even in adulthood, sex differences exist: for example, women's brains seem to age more slowly than those of men (Joel & McCarthy, 2017; Goyal et al., 2019; Kurth et al., 2021).

Furthermore, most males tend to show greater lateralization of language in the left hemisphere. For them, language is clearly relegated largely to the left side of the brain. In contrast, women display less lateralization, with language abilities apt to be more evenly divided between the two hemispheres. Such differences in brain lateralization may account, in part, for the superiority often displayed by females on certain measures of verbal skills, such as the onset and fluency of speech (Etchell et al., 2018; Hirnstein et al., 2019).

Other research suggests that men's brains are somewhat bigger than women's brains, even after taking differences in body size into account. In contrast, part of the *corpus callosum,* a bundle of fibers that connects the hemispheres of the brain, is proportionally larger in women than in men. In addition, research shows differences in brain responses between males and females who are frequent videogame players, particularly in parts of the brain related to the processing of rewards and cravings. These differences might account for sex differences in the use of technology. Finally, evidence shows that compared with men's, women's brains have more interconnections, potentially having implications for greater multitasking capabilities in females (Schmied et al., 2020; Swanson et al., 2020; Carpita et al., 2021).

However, the meaning of such sex differences is far from clear. Consider one possibility related to differences in the proportional size of the corpus callosum: Its greater size in women may permit stronger connections to develop between the parts of the brain that control speech. In turn, this would explain why speech tends to emerge slightly earlier in girls than in boys.

Before we rush to such a conclusion, though, we must consider an alternative hypothesis: The reason verbal abilities emerge earlier in girls may be that infant girls receive greater encouragement to talk than do infant boys. In turn, this greater early experience may foster the growth of certain parts of the brain. Hence, physical brain differences may be a *reflection* of social and environmental influences rather than a *cause* of the differences in men's and women's behavior. At this point, it is impossible to know which of these alternative hypotheses is correct.

Cultural experiences may give rise to differences in brain structure related to sex differences in the use of language.

skaman306/Moment/Getty Images

Culture also gives rise to differences in brain size and lateralization. For example, the volume of gray-matter material in the cortex is greater in higher-income adolescents than in low-income adolescents. Furthermore, brain development is related to differences in academic achievement between students of different income levels. Specifically, the brain's cortex is thicker in higher-income students than in lower-income students, and cortex configuration is related to their academic achievement (Mackey et al., 2015; Dufford et al., 2019; Hair et al., 2022).

One impediment to determining the full extent of brain differences between groups relates to the limitations in the participant pools. For instance, analyses of neuroscience studies of adolescents found that 99% used samples in Western countries. Moreover, most brain studies don't take into account the race or ethnicity of participants, thereby limiting the findings (Qu et al., 2021).

Clearly, our brains reflect a combination of genetically determined structure and functioning. But they also reflect the impact of the social and cultural experiences to which we are exposed.

The Split Brain: Exploring the Two Hemispheres

When Vicki visited her neurologist, she was desperate: Her frequent and severe epileptic seizures weren't just interfering with her day-to-day life–they were putting her in danger. She never knew when she might just collapse suddenly, making many mundane situations such as climbing stairs potentially life-threatening for her.

Vicki's neurologist had a solution, but a radical and potentially dangerous one: surgically severing the bundle of fibers connecting the two hemispheres of her brain. This procedure would stop the firestorms of electrical impulses that were causing Vicki's seizures, but it would also have its own curious effects on her day-to-day functioning.

In the months after the surgery, Vicki was relieved to be free of the seizures that had taken over her life. But she had new challenges to overcome. Simple tasks such as food shopping or even dressing herself became lengthy ordeals–not because she had difficulty moving or thinking but because the two sides of her brain no longer worked in a coordinated way. Each side directed its half of the body to work independently of the other (Wolman, 2012).

People like Vicki, whose corpus collosums have been cut or injured, are called *split-brain patients*. They offer a rare opportunity for researchers investigating the independent functioning of the two hemispheres of the brain. For example, psychologist Roger Sperry–who won the Nobel Prize for his work–developed a number of ingenious techniques for studying how each hemisphere operates (Sperry, 1982; Bagattini et al., 2015; Schechter & Bayne, 2021).

In one experimental procedure, patients who were prevented from seeing an object by a screen touched the object with their right hand and were asked to name it (see Figure 7). Because the right side of the body corresponds to the language-oriented left side of the brain, split-brain patients were able to name it. However, if patients touched the object with their left hand, they were unable to name it aloud, even though the information had registered in their brains. When the screen was removed, patients could identify the object they had touched. Information can be learned and remembered, then, using only the right side of the brain. (By the way, unless you've had split-brain surgery, this experiment won't work with you because the bundle of fibers connecting the two hemispheres of a normal brain immediately transfers the information from one hemisphere to the other.)

It is clear from experiments like this one that the right and left hemispheres of the brain specialize in handling different sorts of information. At the same time, it is important to realize that both hemispheres are capable of understanding, knowing, and being aware of the world, in somewhat different ways. The two hemispheres, then, should be regarded as different in terms of the efficiency with which they process certain kinds of information, rather than as two entirely separate brains. The hemispheres work interdependently to allow the full range and richness of thought of which humans are capable. (Also see the *Applying Psychology in the 21st Century* feature.)

FIGURE 7 Hemispheres of the brain. (a) The corpus callosum connects the cerebral hemispheres of the brain, as shown in this cross section. (b) A split-brain patient is tested by touching objects behind a screen. Patients could name the objects they touched with their right hand but couldn't name them when they touched them with their left hand. If a split-brain patient with her eyes closed was given a pencil to hold and called it a pencil, what hand was the pencil in?

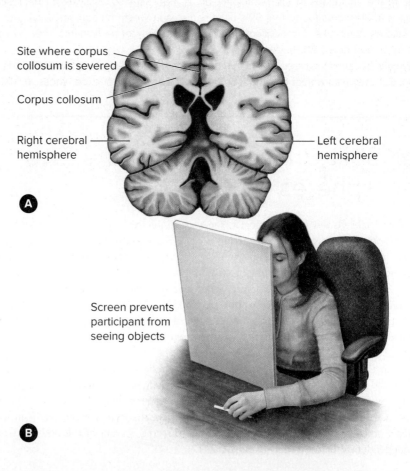

Site where corpus collosum is severed

Corpus collosum

Right cerebral hemisphere

Left cerebral hemisphere

A

Screen prevents participant from seeing objects

B

APPLYING PSYCHOLOGY IN THE 21ST CENTURY

UPLOADING THE BRAIN: WILL THE NEW YOU BE YOU?

This discussion of the brain has given you a good idea of how complex it is. Remember, the adult brain contains around 100 billion neurons, and these neurons are interconnected by about 100 trillion synapses.

But these complexities haven't kept neuroscientists, as well as philosophers, from pondering what the future might hold for brain research. For example, neuroscientist William Graziano suggests that in the future, a supercomputer will be able to scan your brain and copy the pattern of neurons and synapses, making a virtual replica of it that can be preserved after you physically die. It's a process called *mind uploading*, and theoretically, no laws of physics would prevent it from occurring (Graziano, 2019, 2021).

No one knows what such an uploaded mind would be like, or what it would experience. For example, what would the relationship be between your real body and mind and your uploaded mind if you were still alive? And after your actual physical body died, would your virtual mind maintain your relationships--for example, texting and posting on social media? It sounds like science fiction, but it is at least theoretically possible.

Advances in neuroscience already are permitting researchers to reveal, in a very general sense, what people are thinking. Using brain scans, scientists can tell whether a student has mastered a concept by comparing their brain scans to those of an expert or whether someone feels depressed. It's even possible to get a crude sense of the content of someone's dreams from scans of their brains made while they are sleeping (Somers, 2021).

Furthermore, scientists have developed devices that can help people who have prosthetic limbs move them by merely thinking about movement. For example, people who are totally paralyzed can learn to move an artificial limb to lift a bottle of soda to their mouths and drink from it, merely by thinking about the actions and by using a device called a *brain-machine interface*, or BMI (Andersen, 2019; Andersen et al., 2022).

The next challenge is integrating touch feedback with BMI. When you pick up an object, your motor responses are fine-tuned by feedback from your somatosensory receptors. You can feel how your arm and hand are moving through space. You can also feel the shape and texture of the object you're reaching for, and the pressure against your skin tells you how tightly you're grasping the object. Implants in the somatosensory cortex are already able to provide this kind of rich tactile feedback to those who have paralysis, and work is underway to integrate it with BMI output.

Finally, we know that certain kinds of brain implants can successfully end seizures due to Parkinson's disease. For some patients who received implants, though, their personalities changed, and some changed careers, ended their marriages, or became hypersexual. Such results raise the ethical and philosophical issue of whether brain implants can actually change people's identity (Kenneally, 2021).

We don't know yet where advances in neuroscience will ultimately lead nor what their unintended consequences will be. What is clear is that our understanding of the brain and its functioning is rapidly increasing and that the future will produce possibilities we can only dream about now.

> **RETHINK**
>
> 1. How do you think you might interact with your uploaded brain if scientists could create a totally accurate replica of it?
> 2. What are the major ethical issues in uploading a complete replica of someone's brain? Do you think the uploaded brain could represent the entire humanity of the person whose brain was uploaded?

BECOMING AN INFORMED CONSUMER
of Psychology

Learning to Control Your Heart—and Mind—Through Biofeedback

When Tammy DeMichael was involved in a horrific car accident that broke her neck and crushed her spinal cord, experts told her that she was doomed to be a quadriplegic for the rest of her life, unable to move from the neck down. But they were wrong. Not only did she regain the use of her arms, but she also was able to walk 60 feet with a cane.

The key to DeMichael's astounding recovery: biofeedback. **Biofeedback** is a procedure in which a person learns to control through conscious thought internal physiological processes such as blood pressure, heart and respiration rate, skin temperature, sweating, and the constriction of particular muscles. Although it traditionally had been thought that heart rate, respiration rate, blood pressure, and other bodily functions are under the control

biofeedback A procedure in which a person learns to control through conscious thought internal physiological processes such as blood pressure, heart and respiration rate, skin temperature, sweating, and the constriction of particular muscles. (Module 7)

of parts of the brain over which we have no influence, psychologists have discovered that these responses are actually susceptible to voluntary control (Arena & Tankersley, 2018; Lehrer et al., 2021; Vital et al., 2021).

In biofeedback, a person is hooked up to electronic devices that provide continuous feedback relating to the physiological response in question. For instance, someone trying to control headaches through biofeedback might have electronic sensors placed on certain muscles on her head and learn to control the constriction and relaxation of those muscles. Later, when she felt a headache starting, she could relax the relevant muscles and abort the pain (Magis & Schoenen, 2011; Esparham & Dilts, 2019; Campo et al., 2021).

DeMichael's treatment was related to a form of biofeedback called *neurofeedback,* in which brain activity is displayed for a patient. Because not all of her nervous system's connections between the brain and her legs were severed, she was able to learn how to send messages to specific muscles, "ordering" them to move. Although it took more than a year, DeMichael was successful in restoring a large degree of her mobility.

Although the control of physiological processes through the use of biofeedback is not easy to learn, it has been employed with success in a variety of ailments, including emotional problems (such as anxiety, depression, phobias, tension headaches, insomnia, and hyperactivity), physical illnesses with a psychological component (such as asthma, high blood pressure, ulcers, muscle spasms, and migraine headaches), and physical problems (such as DeMichael's injuries, strokes, cerebral palsy, and curvature of the spine) (Nagai, 2019; Alneyadi et al., 2021; Secerbegovic et al., 2021).

RECAP/EVALUATE/RETHINK

RECAP

LO 7-1 How do researchers identify the major parts and functions of the brain?

- Brain scans take a "snapshot" of the internal workings of the brain without having to cut surgically into a person's skull. Major brain-scanning techniques include the electroencephalogram (EEG), positron emission tomography (PET), functional magnetic resonance imaging (fMRI), and transcranial magnetic stimulation imaging (TMS).

LO 7-2 What are the major parts of the brain, and for what behaviors is each part responsible?

- The central core of the brain is made up of the medulla (which controls functions such as breathing and the heartbeat), the pons (which coordinates the muscles and the two sides of the body), the cerebellum (which controls balance), the reticular formation (which acts to heighten arousal and sudden awareness), the thalamus (which communicates sensory messages to and from the brain), and the hypothalamus (which maintains homeostasis, or body equilibrium, and regulates behavior related to basic survival). The functions of the central core structures are similar to those found in other vertebrates. This central core is sometimes referred to as the "old brain."

- The cerebral cortex—the "new brain"—has areas that control voluntary movement (the motor area); the senses (the sensory area); and thinking, reasoning, speech, and memory (the association areas). The limbic system, found on the border of the "old" and "new" brains, is associated with eating, aggression, reproduction, and the experiences of pleasure and pain.

LO 7-3 How do the two halves of the brain operate interdependently?

- The brain is divided into left and right halves, or hemispheres, each of which generally controls the opposite side of the body. Each hemisphere can be thought of as being specialized in the functions it carries out: The left specializes in verbal tasks, such as logical reasoning, speaking, and reading; the right specializes in nonverbal tasks, such as spatial perception, pattern recognition, and emotional expression.

LO 7-4 How can an understanding of the nervous system help us to find ways to alleviate disease and pain?

- Biofeedback is a procedure by which a person learns to control internal physiological processes. By controlling involuntary responses, people are able to relieve anxiety, tension, migraine headaches, and a wide range of other psychological and physical problems.

EVALUATE

1. Match the name of each brain scan with the appropriate description:

   a. EEG
   b. fMRI
   c. PET

   1. By locating radiation within the brain, a computer can provide a striking picture of brain activity.
   2. Electrodes placed around the skull record the electrical signals transmitted through the brain.
   3. This technique provides a three-dimensional view of the brain by aiming a magnetic field at the body.

2. Match the portion of the brain with its function:

   a. Medulla
   b. Pons
   c. Cerebellum
   d. Reticular formation

   1. Maintains breathing and heartbeat
   2. Controls bodily balance
   3. Coordinates and integrates muscle movements
   4. Activates other parts of the brain to produce general bodily arousal

3. A surgeon places an electrode on a portion of your brain and stimulates it. Immediately, your right wrist involuntarily twitches. The doctor has most likely stimulated a portion of the _____ area of your brain.
4. Each hemisphere controls the _____ side of the body.
5. Nonverbal realms, such as emotions and music, are controlled primarily by the _____ hemisphere of the brain, whereas the _____ hemisphere is more responsible for speaking and reading.

RETHINK

1. Before sophisticated brain-scanning techniques were developed, behavioral neuroscientists' understanding of the brain was based largely on the brains of people who had died. What limitations would this pose, and in what ways would current brain-scanning techniques overcome these limitations?
2. Could personal differences in people's specialization of right and left hemispheres be related to occupational success?

Answers to Evaluate Questions

1. a-2, b-3, c-1; 2. a-1, b-3, c-2, d-4; 3. motor; 4. opposite; 5. right, left

KEY TERMS

central core	thalamus	lobes	neuroplasticity
cerebellum (ser-uh-BELL-um)	hypothalamus	motor area	hemispheres
reticular formation	limbic system	sensory area	lateralization
	cerebral cortex	association areas	biofeedback

LOOKING *Back*

EPILOGUE

In our examination of neuroscience, we've traced the ways in which biological structures and functions of the body affect behavior. Starting with neurons, we considered each of the components of the nervous system, culminating in an examination of how the brain permits us to think, reason, speak, recall, and experience emotions—the hallmarks of being human.

Before proceeding, turn back for a moment to the prologue to this chapter about Ian Burkhart, who received a brain implant that helped him to partially recover from the paralysis and loss of his sense of touch following a spinal cord injury while swimming. Consider the following questions:

1. How would you explain Burkhart's ability to recover his lost physical mobility and sense of touch?
2. Do you think that the improvements such as Burkhart experienced would be more or less likely if he had been younger? Older? Why do you think so?
3. How might applications of the technology that has led to improvements in Burkhart's mobility have use for uninjured people? Explain.

Design Elements: Man with laptop: Dragon Images/Shutterstock; Exclamation point and mobile frame: McGraw Hill; Smartphone: WML Image/Shutterstock; Hands: Stefano Garau/Shutterstock.

VISUAL SUMMARY 2 Neuroscience and Behavior

MODULE 5 Neurons: The Basic Elements

Neuron Structure

Neuron Function

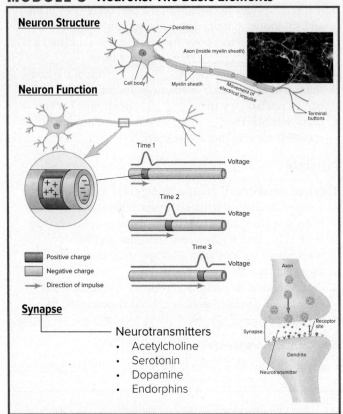

Positive charge
Negative charge
Direction of impulse

Synapse

Neurotransmitters
- Acetylcholine
- Serotonin
- Dopamine
- Endorphins

MODULE 6 Nervous System

Central Nervous System

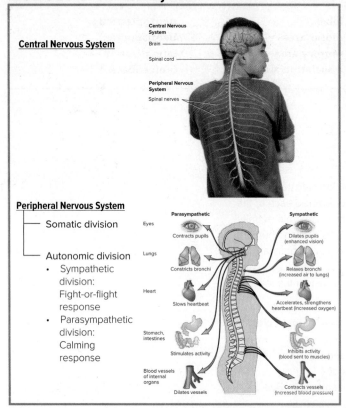

Peripheral Nervous System

- Somatic division

- Autonomic division
  - Sympathetic division: Fight-or-flight response
  - Parasympathetic division: Calming response

MODULE 7 The Brain

Areas of the Brain

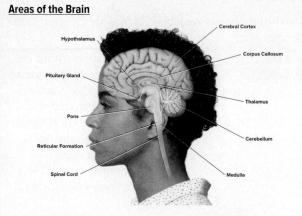

The Central Core: "Old brain"
- Cerebellum
- Reticular formation
- Thalamus
- Hypothalamus

The Cerebral Cortex: "New brain"

- Motor area: Voluntary movement
- Sensory area
  - Somatosensory area
  - Auditory area
  - Visual area
- Association areas
  - Executive functions
  - Personality

The Limbic System
- Emotion
- Self-preservation
- Amygdala
- Hippocampus

Brain Features
- Neuroplasticity
- Lateralization: Two hemispheres with specialized functions
- The split brain: Corpus callosum with independent hemispheric functions

(Module 5) (photo): Whitehoune/Shutterstock; (Module 6) (photo): Thiti Sukapan/Alamy Stock Photo; (Module 7) (photo): fizkes/Shutterstock

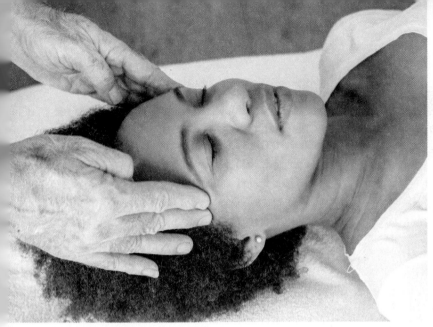

Mladen Zivkovic/Shutterstock

CHAPTER 3
Sensation and Perception

LEARNING OUTCOMES FOR CHAPTER 3

MODULE 8

LO 8-1 What is sensation, and how do psychologists study it?

LO 8-2 What is the relationship between a physical stimulus and the kinds of sensory responses that result from it?

SENSING THE WORLD AROUND US

Absolute Thresholds: Detecting What's Out There

Difference Thresholds: Noticing Distinctions Between Stimuli

Sensory Adaptation: Turning Down Our Responses

MODULE 9

LO 9-1 What basic processes underlie the sense of vision?

LO 9-2 How do we see colors?

VISION: SHEDDING LIGHT ON THE EYE

Illuminating the Structure of the Eye

Color Vision and Color Blindness: The 10-Million-Color Spectrum

MODULE 10

LO 10-1 What role does the ear play in the senses of sound, motion, and balance?

LO 10-2 How do smell and taste function?

LO 10-3 What are the skin senses, and how do they relate to the experience of pain?

HEARING AND THE OTHER SENSES

Sensing Sound

Neuroscience in Your Life: The Neuroscience of Music

Smell and Taste

Applying Psychology in the 21st Century: What Your Smell Tells Others About Who You Are

The Skin Senses: Touch, Pressure, Temperature, and Pain

Becoming an Informed Consumer of Psychology: Managing Pain

How Our Senses Interact

LO 11-1   What principles underlie our organization of the visual world and allow us to make sense of our environment?

LO 11-2   How are we able to perceive the world in three dimensions when our retinas are capable of sensing only two-dimensional images?

LO 11-3   What clues do visual illusions give us about our understanding of general perceptual mechanisms?

PROLOGUE _WHEN THE LOSS OF SMELL LEADS TO A LOSS OF IDENTITY_

Michele Crippa, an Italian chef and food critic, was famous for his sense of smell and taste. He could distinguish between cheeses of various ages and could identify exotic coffee beans from the smell of brewed coffee. And then, he couldn't. One morning, he poured himself a cup of coffee, and all he tasted was hot water.

Crippa had contracted a case of COVID-19, and like many other people during the pandemic, he lost his sense of smell, which is intertwined with the ability to taste. For Crippa, it was a disastrous consequence of the virus, because his professional life was based on his abilities to distinguish subtle differences in smell and taste. In fact, his very identity as a person was tied up with his senses.

Happily, though, Crippa has regained much of what he lost. Through extensive "smell therapy," in which the neural pathways involved with smell are reactivated as the patient recalls instances in which certain smells occurred, Crippa is making progress. He may never reach the same heights of sensory sophistication that he once had, but he has shown considerable improvement (Bubola, 2021).

LOOKING _Ahead_

Crippa's experience illustrates how important, and complicated, our senses can be. Our senses offer a window to the world, not only providing us with an awareness, understanding, and appreciation of the world's beauty but also alerting us to its dangers. Our senses enable us to feel the gentlest of breezes, see flickering lights miles away, and hear the soft murmuring of distant songbirds.

In the upcoming modules, we focus on the field of psychology that is concerned with the ways our bodies take in information through the senses and the ways we interpret that information. We explore both sensation and perception. _Sensation_ encompasses the processes by which our sense organs receive information from the environment. _Perception_ is the brain's and the sense organs' sorting out, interpretation, analysis, and integration of stimuli.

Although perception clearly represents a step beyond sensation, in practice it is sometimes difficult to find the precise boundary between the two. Indeed, psychologists—and philosophers as well—have argued for years over the distinction. The primary difference is that sensation can be thought of as an organism's first encounter with a raw sensory stimulus, whereas perception is the process by which it interprets, analyzes, and integrates that stimulus with other sensory information.

For example, if we were considering sensation, we might ask about the loudness of a ringing fire alarm. If we were considering perception, we might ask whether someone recognizes the ringing sound as an alarm and identifies its meaning.

To a psychologist interested in understanding the causes of behavior, sensation and perception are fundamental topics because so much of our behavior is a reflection of how we react to and interpret stimuli from the world around us. The areas of sensation and perception deal with a wide range of questions—among them, how we respond to the characteristics of physical stimuli; what processes enable us to see, hear, and experience pain; why visual illusions fool us; and how we distinguish one person from another. As we explore these issues, we'll see how the senses work together to provide us with an integrated view and understanding of the world.

Module 8
Sensing the World Around Us

As Isabel sat down to Thanksgiving dinner, her father carried the turkey in on a tray and placed it squarely in the center of the table. The noise level, already high from the talking and laughter of family members, grew louder still. As Isabel picked up her fork, the smell of the turkey reached her, and she felt her stomach growl hungrily. The sight and sound of her family around the table, along with the smells and tastes of the holiday meal, made Isabel feel more relaxed than she had since starting her first year of college in the fall.

Put yourself in this setting and consider how different it might be if any one of your senses were not functioning. What if you had lost your vision and couldn't see the faces of your family members or the welcome shape of the golden-brown turkey? What if you had no sense of hearing and could not listen to the conversations of family members or were unable to feel your stomach growl, smell the dinner, or taste the food? Clearly, you would experience the dinner very differently than someone whose sensory apparatus was intact.

Moreover, the sensations mentioned above barely scratch the surface of sensory experience. Although perhaps you were taught that people have only five senses–sight, sound, taste, smell, and touch–that enumeration is too modest. Human sensory capabilities go well beyond the basic five senses. For example, we are sensitive not merely to touch but to a considerably wider set of stimuli–pain, pressure, temperature, and vibration, to name a few. In addition, vision has two subsystems–relating to day and night vision–and the ear is responsive to information that allows us not only to hear but also to keep our balance.

To consider how psychologists understand the senses and, more broadly, sensation and perception, we first need a basic working vocabulary. In formal terms, **sensation** is the activation of the sense organs by a source of physical energy. **Perception** is the sorting out, interpretation, analysis, and integration of stimuli carried out by the sense organs and brain. A **stimulus** is any passing source of physical energy that produces a response in a sense organ.

Stimuli vary in both type and intensity. Different types of stimuli activate different sense organs. For instance, we can differentiate light stimuli (which activate the sense of sight and allow us to see the colors of the leaves on a tree in autumn) from sound stimuli (which, through the sense of hearing, permit us to hear the sounds of an orchestra). In addition, stimuli differ in intensity, relating to how strong a stimulus needs to be before it can be detected.

Questions of stimulus type and intensity are considered in a branch of psychology known as psychophysics. **Psychophysics** is the study of the relationship between the actual physical aspects of a stimulus and our psychological experience of that stimulus. Psychophysics played a central role in the development of the field of psychology. Many of the first psychologists studied issues related to psychophysics, and there is still an active group of psychophysics researchers (Jack & Schyns, 2017; Vicario et al., 2019; da Pos, 2022).

Absolute Thresholds: Detecting What's Out There

Just when does a stimulus become strong enough to be detected by our sense organs? The answer to this question requires an understanding of the concept of absolute threshold. An **absolute threshold** is the lowest intensity of a stimulus that an organism can detect (Aazh & Moore, 2007; Dey et al., 2022).

LEARNING OUTCOMES

LO 8-1 What is sensation, and how do psychologists study it?

LO 8-2 What is the relationship between a physical stimulus and the kinds of sensory responses that result from it?

! Study Alert
Remember that *sensation* refers to the activation of the sense organs (a physical response), whereas *perception* refers to how stimuli are interpreted (a psychological response).

sensation The activation of the sense organs by a source of physical energy. (Module 8)

perception The sorting out, interpretation, analysis, and integration of stimuli by the sense organs and brain. (Module 8)

stimulus Energy that produces a response in a sense organ. (Module 8)

psychophysics The study of the relationship between the physical aspects of stimuli and our psychological experience of them. (Module 8)

absolute threshold The smallest intensity of a stimulus that must be present for the stimulus to be detected. (Module 8)

How Sensitive Are You?

Take this true/false quiz to test your awareness of the capabilities of your senses:

1. On a clear, dark night, you can see a candle flame from a distance of 30 miles.
   ☐ True   ☐ False

2. A single drop of perfume can be detected over the area of a 3-room apartment.
   ☐ True   ☐ False

3. Under quiet conditions, the ticking of a watch can be heard from 20 feet away.
   ☐ True   ☐ False

4. You would need 2 tablespoons of sugar to detect its taste when dissolved in 2 gallons of water.
   ☐ True   ☐ False

Scoring: For questions 1–3, the answer is **True**. Question 4 is **False**. It takes only 1 teaspoon of sugar for its taste to be detected when dissolved in 2 gallons of water.

FIGURE 1 This test can shed some light on how sensitive the human senses are.
Source: Galanter, 1962.

Despite the "absolute" in absolute threshold, things are not so cut and dried. As the strength of a stimulus increases, the likelihood that it will be detected increases gradually. Technically, then, an absolute threshold is the stimulus intensity that is detected 50% of the time.

It often takes a very small stimulus to produce a response in our senses. For example, the sense of touch is so sensitive that we can feel a bee's wing falling on our cheeks when it is dropped from a distance of 1 centimeter. Test your knowledge of the absolute thresholds of other senses by completing the questionnaire in Figure 1.

In fact, our senses are so fine-tuned that we might have problems if they were any more sensitive. For instance, if our ears were slightly more acute, we would be able to hear the sound of air molecules in our ears knocking into the eardrum—a phenomenon that would surely prove distracting and might even prevent us from hearing sounds outside our bodies.

Of course, the absolute thresholds we have been discussing are measured under ideal conditions. Normally, our senses cannot detect stimulation quite as well because of the presence of noise. *Noise*, as defined by psychophysicists, is background stimulation that interferes with the perception of other stimuli. Hence, *noise* refers not just to auditory stimuli, as the word suggests, but also to unwanted stimuli that interfere with other senses.

For example, picture a talkative group of people crammed into a small, crowded room at a party. The din of the crowd makes it hard to hear individual voices. In this case, the crowded conditions would be considered "noise" because they are preventing sensation at more discriminating levels. Similarly, we have limited ability to concentrate on several stimuli simultaneously.

Crowded conditions, sounds, and sights can all be considered as noise that interferes with sensation. Can you think of other examples of noise that are not auditory in nature?
MikeDotta/Shutterstock

Difference Thresholds: Noticing Distinctions Between Stimuli

Suppose you wanted to choose the six best apples from a supermarket display—the biggest, reddest, and sweetest apples. One approach would be to compare one apple with another systematically until you were left with a few so similar that you could not tell the difference between them. At that point, it wouldn't matter which ones you choose.

Psychologists have discussed this comparison problem in terms of the **difference threshold,** the smallest level of added or reduced stimulation required to sense that a *change* in stimulation has occurred. Thus, the difference threshold is the minimum change in stimulation required to detect the difference between two stimuli, and so it also is called a **just noticeable difference** (Ozana & Ganel, 2019; del Solar Dorrego & Vigeant, 2022).

The size of a stimulus that constitutes a just noticeable difference depends on the initial intensity of the stimulus. The relationship between changes in the original size of a stimulus and the degree to which a change will be noticed forms one of the basic laws of psychophysics: Weber's law, discovered by psychophysicist E. H. Weber (*Weber* is pronounced "VAY-ber"). **Weber's law** states that a just noticeable difference is a *constant proportion* of the intensity of an initial stimulus (rather than a constant amount).

For example, Weber found that the just noticeable difference for weight is 1:50. Consequently, it takes a 1-ounce increase in a 50-ounce weight to produce a noticeable difference, and it would take a 10-ounce increase to produce a noticeable difference if the initial weight were 500 ounces. In both cases, the same proportional increase is necessary to produce a just noticeable difference (1:50 = 10:500). Similarly, the just noticeable difference distinguishing changes in loudness between sounds is larger for sounds that are initially loud than it is for sounds that are initially soft, but the *proportional* increase remains the same.

Weber's law helps explain why a person in a quiet room is more startled by the ringing of a cellphone than is a person in an already noisy room. To produce the same amount of reaction in a noisy room, a cellphone ring would have to be set to a much higher level. Similarly, when the moon is visible during the late afternoon, it appears relatively dim. On the other hand, the moon appears much brighter when it is in the dark night sky.

difference threshold (just noticeable difference) The smallest level of added or reduced stimulation required to sense that a change in stimulation has occurred. (Module 8)

> **Study Alert**
> Remember that Weber's law holds for every type of sensory stimuli: vision, sound, taste, and so on.

Weber's law A basic law of psychophysics stating that a just noticeable difference is a constant proportion to the intensity of an initial stimulus (rather than a constant amount). (Module 8)

From the perspective of...

A Software Designer How might you use principles of psychophysics to direct the attention of a software user to a particular part of the computer screen?

Rubberball/Getty Images

Sensory Adaptation: Turning Down Our Responses

You enter a movie theater, and the smell of popcorn is everywhere. A few minutes later, though, you barely notice the smell. The reason you become accustomed to the odor is sensory adaptation. **Adaptation** is an adjustment in sensory capacity after prolonged exposure to unchanging stimuli. Adaptation occurs as people become accustomed to a stimulus and change their frame of reference. In a sense, our brain mentally turns down the volume of the stimulation that it's experiencing (Erb et al., 2013; Nourouzpour et al., 2015; Shalom-Sperber et al., 2022).

One example of adaptation is the decrease in sensitivity that occurs after repeated exposure to a strong stimulus. If you were to hear a loud tone over and over, eventually it would begin to sound softer. Similarly, although jumping into a cold lake may be temporarily unpleasant, eventually you probably will get used to the temperature.

This apparent decline in sensitivity to sensory stimuli is due to the inability of the sensory nerve receptors to fire off messages to the brain indefinitely. Because these receptor cells are most responsive to *changes* in stimulation, constant stimulation is not effective in producing a sustained reaction (Wark et al., 2007; Summers et al., 2017).

adaptation An adjustment in sensory capacity after prolonged exposure to unchanging stimuli. (Module 8)

Although initially difficult to tolerate, exposure to cold temperatures eventually becomes less unpleasant due to the phenomenon of adaptation.
Michele Ursi/Alamy Stock Photo

Judgments of sensory stimuli are also affected by the context in which the judgments are made. This is the case because judgments are made not in isolation from other stimuli but in terms of preceding sensory experience. You can demonstrate this for yourself by trying a simple experiment: Take two envelopes, one large and one small, and put 15 nickels in each one. Now lift the large envelope, put it down, and lift the small one. Which seems to weigh more? Most people report that the small one is heavier, although, as you know, the weights are nearly identical. The reason for this misconception is that the visual context of the envelope interferes with the sensory experience of weight. Adaptation to the context of one stimulus (the size of the envelope) alters responses to another stimulus (the weight of the envelope) (Coren, 2004; Han et al., 2019).

RECAP/EVALUATE/RETHINK

RECAP

LO 8-1 What is sensation, and how do psychologists study it?

- Sensation is the activation of the sense organs by any source of physical energy. In contrast, perception is the process by which we sort out, interpret, analyze, and integrate stimuli to which our senses are exposed.

LO 8-2 What is the relationship between a physical stimulus and the kinds of sensory responses that result from it?

- Psychophysics studies the relationship between the physical nature of stimuli and the sensory responses they evoke.
- The absolute threshold is the smallest amount of physical intensity at which a stimulus can be detected. Under ideal conditions, absolute thresholds are extraordinarily sensitive, but the presence of noise (background stimuli that interfere with other stimuli) reduces detection capabilities.
- The difference threshold, or just noticeable difference, is the smallest change in the level of stimulation required to sense that a change has occurred. According to Weber's law, a just noticeable difference is a constant proportion of the intensity of an initial stimulus.
- Sensory adaptation occurs when we become accustomed to a constant stimulus and change our evaluation of it. Repeated exposure to a stimulus results in an apparent decline in sensitivity to it.

EVALUATE

1. _____ is the stimulation of the sense organs; _____ is the sorting out, interpretation, analysis, and integration of stimuli by the sense organs and the brain.
2. The term *absolute threshold* refers to the _____ intensity of a stimulus that must be present for the stimulus to be detected.
3. Weber discovered that for a difference between two stimuli to be perceptible, the stimuli must differ by at least a _____ proportion.
4. After completing a very difficult rock climb in the morning, Carmella found the afternoon climb unexpectedly easy. This example illustrates the phenomenon of _____.

RETHINK

1. How might it be possible to have sensation without perception? Conversely, might it be possible to have perception without sensation?
2. How is sensory adaptation essential for everyday psychological functioning?

Answers to Evaluate Questions

1. Sensation, perception; 2. smallest; 3. constant; 4. adaptation

KEY TERMS

sensation	psychophysics	difference threshold	Weber's law
perception	absolute	(just noticeable	adaptation
stimulus	threshold	difference)	

Module 9
Vision: Shedding Light on the Eye

LEARNING OUTCOMES

LO 9-1 What basic processes underlie the sense of vision?

LO 9-2 How do we see colors?

If, as poets say, the eyes provide a window to the soul, they also provide us with a window to the world. Our visual capabilities permit us to admire and to react to scenes ranging from the beauty of a sunset, to the configuration of a lover's face, to the words written on the pages of a book.

Vision starts with *light*, the physical energy that stimulates the eye. Light is a form of electromagnetic radiation waves. Like ocean waves, light is measured in *wavelengths*, the distance between peaks of the lightwaves.

The *visual spectrum* is the range of wavelengths that is visible to the human eye. As shown in Figure 1, the visible spectrum that humans can see includes the wavelengths that make up the colors of a rainbow, from the shortest wavelength of violet blue to the longest wavelength of red. Compared to that of nonhumans, the visual spectrum in humans is relatively restricted. For instance, some reptiles and fish sense energies of longer wavelengths than humans do, and certain insects sense energies of shorter wavelengths than humans do.

Light waves coming from some object outside the body (such as the tree in Figure 2) are sensed by the only organ that is capable of responding to the visible spectrum: the eye. Our eyes convert light to a form that can be used by the neurons that serve as messengers to the brain. The neurons themselves take up a relatively small percentage of the total eye. Most of the eye is a mechanical device that is similar in many respects to an old-fashioned nondigital camera that uses chemical film to capture the image, as you can see in Figure 2.

Despite the similarities between the eye and a camera, vision involves processes that are far more complex and sophisticated than those of any camera. Furthermore, once an image reaches the neuronal receptors of the eye, the eye/camera analogy ends, for the processing of the visual image in the brain is more reflective of a computer than it is of a camera.

Illuminating the Structure of the Eye

The ray of light being reflected off the tree in Figure 2 first travels through the *cornea*, a transparent, protective window at the front of the eye. The cornea, because of its curvature, bends (or *refracts*) light as it passes through, playing a primary role in focusing the light more sharply. After moving through the cornea, the light traverses the

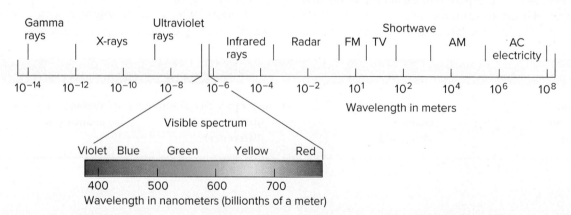

FIGURE 1 The visible spectrum—the range of wavelengths to which people are sensitive—is only a small part of the kinds of wavelengths present in our environment. Is it a benefit or disadvantage to our everyday lives that we aren't more sensitive to a broader range of visual stimuli? Why?

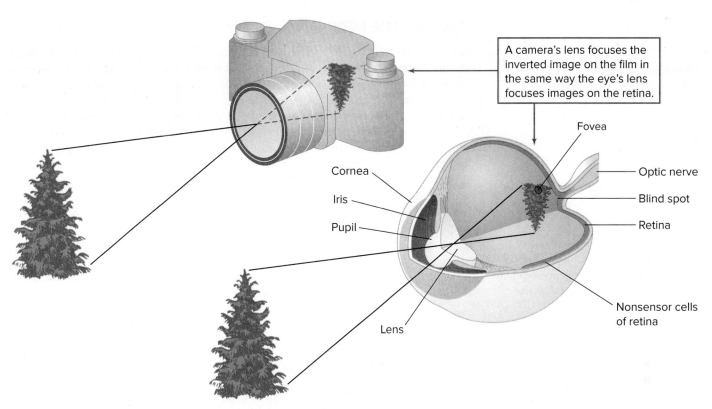

A camera's lens focuses the inverted image on the film in the same way the eye's lens focuses images on the retina.

FIGURE 2 Although human vision is far more complicated than the most sophisticated camera, in some ways basic visual processes are analogous to those used in photography. Like the automatic lighting system of a traditional, nondigital camera, the human eye dilates to let in more light and contracts to block out light.

pupil. The *pupil* is a dark hole in the center of the *iris,* the colored part of the eye, which in humans ranges from a light blue to a dark brown. The size of the pupil opening depends on the amount of light in the environment. The dimmer the surroundings are, the more the pupil opens to allow more light to enter.

Why shouldn't the pupil be open completely all the time, allowing the greatest amount of light into the eye? The answer relates to the basic physics of light. A small pupil greatly increases the range of distances at which objects are in focus. With a wide-open pupil, the range is relatively small, and details are harder to discern. The eye takes advantage of bright light by decreasing the size of the pupil and thereby becoming more discriminating. In dim light, the pupil expands to enable us to view the situation better–but at the expense of visual detail. (Perhaps one reason candlelight dinners are thought of as romantic is that the dim light prevents one from seeing a partner's physical flaws.)

Once light passes through the pupil, it enters the *lens,* which is directly behind the pupil. The lens acts to bend the rays of light so that they are properly focused on the rear of the eye. The lens focuses light by changing its own thickness, a process called *accommodation:* It becomes flatter when viewing distant objects and rounder when looking at closer objects.

Like the automatic lighting system on a camera, the pupil in the human eye expands to let in more light (left) and contracts to block out light (right). Can humans adjust their ears to let in more or less sound in a similar manner?

(Left): Serg Zastavkin/Shutterstock; (Right): Ivan-balvan/iStock/Getty Images

REACHING THE RETINA

retina The part of the eye that converts the electromagnetic energy of light to electrical impulses for transmission to the brain. (Module 9)

rods Thin, cylindrical receptor cells in the retina that are highly sensitive to light. (Module 9)

cones Cone-shaped, light-sensitive receptor cells in the retina that are responsible for sharp focus and color perception, particularly in bright light. (Module 9)

Having traveled through the pupil and lens, the image of the tree finally reaches its ultimate destination in the eye: the retina. The **retina** is the part of the eye that converts the electromagnetic energy of light to electrical impulses for transmission to the brain.

Interestingly, as the image travels through the lens, it has reversed itself. Consequently, the image reaches the retina upside down (relative to its original position). Although it might seem that this reversal would cause difficulties in understanding and moving about the world, this is not the case. The brain automatically interprets the image in terms of its original position.

The retina consists of a thin layer of nerve cells at the back of the eyeball (see Figure 3). There are two kinds of light-sensitive receptor cells in the retina. The names they have been given describe their shapes: rods and cones. **Rods** are thin, cylindrical receptor cells in the retina that are highly sensitive to light. **Cones** are cone-shaped, light-sensitive receptor cells in the retina that are responsible for sharp focus and color perception, particularly in bright light. The rods and cones are distributed unevenly throughout the retina. Cones are concentrated on the part of the retina called the *fovea*. The fovea is a particularly sensitive region of the retina. If you want to focus on

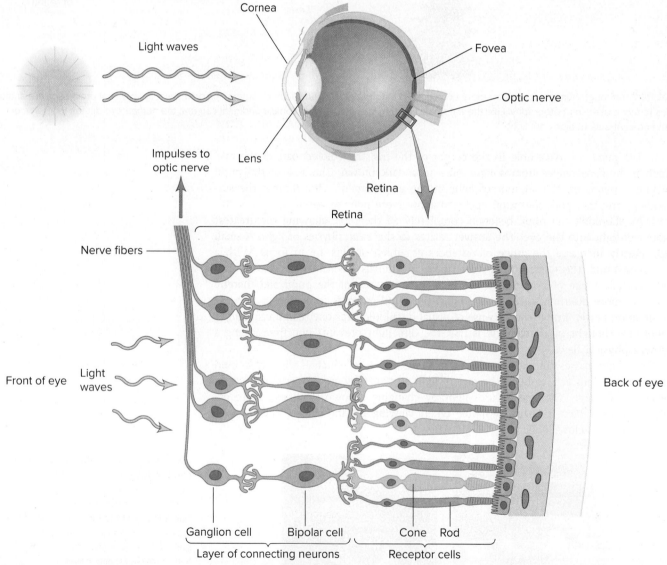

FIGURE 3 The basic cells of the eye. Light entering the eye travels through the ganglion and bipolar cells and strikes the light-sensitive rods and cones located at the back of the eye. The rods and cones then transmit nerve impulses to the brain via the bipolar and ganglion cells.

something of particular interest, you will automatically try to center the image on the fovea to see it more sharply.

The rods and cones not only are structurally dissimilar, but they also play distinctly different roles in vision. Cones are primarily responsible for the sharply focused perception of color, particularly in brightly lit situations; rods are related to vision in dimly lit situations and are largely insensitive to color and to details as sharp as those the cones are capable of recognizing. The rods play a key role in *peripheral vision*–seeing objects that are outside the main center of focus–and in night vision.

Rods and cones also are involved in *dark adaptation*, the phenomenon of adjusting to dim light after being in brighter light. (Think of the experience of walking into a dark movie theater and groping your way to a seat but a few minutes later seeing the seats quite clearly.) The speed at which dark adaptation occurs is a result of the rate of change in the chemical composition of the rods and cones. Although the cones reach their greatest level of adaptation in just a few minutes, the rods take 20 to 30 minutes to reach the maximum level.

An analogous phenomenon describes how we adapt to bright light. *Light adaptation* is the process of adjusting to bright light after being in dim light. Light adaptation occurs much faster than dark adaptation, taking only a minute or so.

SENDING THE MESSAGE FROM THE EYE TO THE BRAIN

When light energy strikes the rods and cones, it starts a chain of events that transforms light into neural impulses that can be communicated to the brain. Even before the neural message reaches the brain, however, some initial coding of the visual information takes place.

What happens when light energy strikes the retina depends in part on whether it encounters a rod or a cone. Rods contain *rhodopsin,* a complex reddish-purple protein whose composition changes chemically when energized by light. The substance in cone receptors is different, but the principles are similar. Stimulation of the rods and cones in the eye triggers a neural response that is transmitted to other nerve cells in the retina called *bipolar cells* and *ganglion cells.*

Bipolar cells receive information directly from the rods and cones and communicate that information to the ganglion cells. The ganglion cells collect and summarize visual information, which is then moved out the back of the eyeball and sent to the brain through a bundle of ganglion axons called the **optic nerve**.

Because the opening for the optic nerve passes through the retina, there are no rods or cones in the area, and that creates a blind spot. Normally, however, this absence of nerve cells does not interfere with vision because you automatically compensate for the missing part of your field of vision. (To find your blind spot, see Figure 4.)

Once beyond the eye itself, the neural impulses relating to the image move through the optic nerve. As the optic nerve leaves the eyeball, its path does not take the most direct route to the part of the brain right behind the eye. Instead, the optic

optic nerve A bundle of ganglion axons that carry visual information to the brain. (Module 9)

> Study Alert
> Remember that **c**ones of the eye relate to **c**olor vision.

FIGURE 4 To find your blind spot, close your right eye and look at the haunted house with your left eye. You will see the ghost on the periphery of your vision. Now, while staring at the house, move the page toward you. When the page is about a foot from your eye, the ghost will disappear. At this moment, the image of the ghost is falling on your blind spot.

But also notice how, when the page is at that distance, not only does the ghost seem to disappear, but the line also seems to run continuously through the area where the ghost used to be. This simple experiment shows how we automatically compensate for missing information by using nearby material to complete what is unseen. That's the reason you never notice the blind spot. What is missing is replaced by what is seen next to the blind spot. Can you think of any advantages that this tendency to provide missing information gives humans as a species?

FIGURE 5 Because the optic nerve coming from the eye splits at the optic chiasm, the image to a person's right eye is sent to the left side of the brain, and the image to the person's left is transmitted to the right side of the brain.

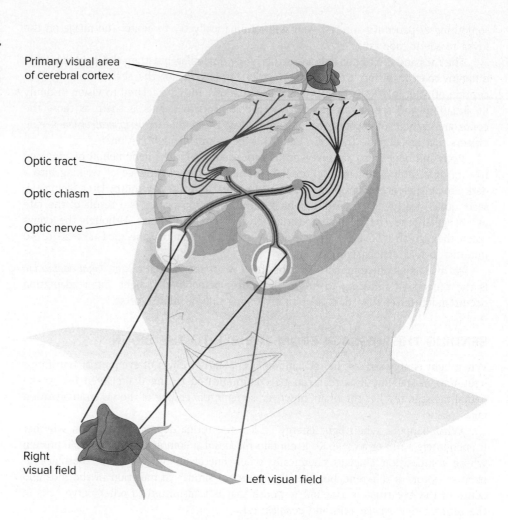

Primary visual area of cerebral cortex

Optic tract

Optic chiasm

Optic nerve

Right visual field

Left visual field

nerves from each eye meet at a point roughly between the two eyes–called the *optic chiasm* (pronounced KI-asm)–where each optic nerve then splits.

When the optic nerves split, the nerve impulses coming from the right half of each retina are sent to the right side of the brain, and the impulses arriving from the left half of each retina are sent to the left side of the brain. Because the image on the retinas is reversed and upside down, however, those images coming from the right half of each retina actually originated in the field of vision to the person's left, and the images coming from the left half of each retina originated in the field of vision to the person's right (see Figure 5).

PROCESSING THE VISUAL MESSAGE

By the time a visual message reaches the brain, it has passed through several stages of processing. One of the initial sites is the ganglion cells. Each ganglion cell gathers information from a group of rods and cones in a particular area of the eye and compares the amount of light entering the center of that area with the amount of light in the area around it. Some ganglion cells are activated by light in the center (and darkness in the surrounding area). Other ganglion cells are activated when there is darkness in the center and light in the surrounding areas. The outcome of this process is to maximize the detection of variations in light and darkness. The image that is passed on to the brain, then, is an enhanced version of the actual visual stimulus outside the body (Sanes & Masland, 2015; Prayag et al., 2019; Paknahad et al., 2021).

The ultimate processing of visual images takes place in the visual cortex of the brain, and it is here that the most complex kinds of processing occur. Psychologists

David Hubel and Torsten Wiesel won a Nobel Prize in 1981 for their discovery of feature detectors. **Feature detectors** are specialized neurons that are activated only by visual stimuli having certain features, such as a particular shape or pattern. For instance, some feature detectors are activated only by lines of a particular width, shape, or orientation. Other feature detectors are activated only by moving, as opposed to stationary, stimuli (Hubel & Wiesel, 2004; Jacoby & Schwartz, 2017; Klapoetke et al., 2022).

Visual information coming from individual neurons is combined and processed in extraordinarily specialized ways, and different parts of the brain jointly process nerve impulses according to the attributes of an image. For instance, one brain system processes shapes, one processes colors, and others process movement, location, and depth. The specialization goes further: specific parts of the brain are involved in the perception of certain *kinds* of stimuli, such as reacting to human faces, nonhuman animal faces, and inanimate stimuli (Zvyagintsev et al., 2013; Stevens, 2015; Ptak & Lazeyras, 2019).

If separate neural systems exist for processing information about specific aspects of the visual world, how are all these data integrated by the brain? The brain makes use of information regarding the frequency, rhythm, and timing of the firing of particular sets of neural cells. Furthermore, the brain's integration of visual information does not occur in any single step or location in the brain but rather is a process that occurs on several levels simultaneously. The ultimate outcome, though, is indisputable: a vision of the world around us.

feature detectors Specialized neurons that are activated only by visual stimuli having specific features, such as a particular shape or pattern. (Module 9)

Color Vision and Color Blindness: The 10-Million-Color Spectrum

Although the range of wavelengths to which humans are sensitive is relatively narrow, at least in comparison with the entire electromagnetic spectrum, the portion to which we are capable of responding allows us great flexibility in sensing the world. Nowhere is this clearer than in terms of the number of colors we can discern. A person with normal color vision is capable of distinguishing as many as 10 million colors (Mukamal, 2017; Witzel & Gegenfurtner, 2018).

Although the variety of colors that people are generally able to distinguish is vast, there are certain individuals whose ability to perceive color is quite limited–the color blind. Interestingly, the condition of these individuals has provided some of the most important clues to understanding how color vision operates (Nijboer et al., 2011; Alfaro et al., 2015; Roostaei & Hamidi, 2022).

Approximately 7% of men and 0.4% of women are color blind. For most people with color-blindness, the world looks dull and lacks contrast (see Figure 6). Red fire

FIGURE 6 Those with color-blindness see a very different view of the world (left) compared to those who have normal vision (right).
(Both): dvande/Shutterstock

engines appear yellow, green grass seems yellow, and the three colors of a traffic light all look yellow. In fact, in the most common form of color-blindness, all red and green objects are seen as yellow. In other forms of color-blindness, people are unable to tell the difference between yellow and blue. In the most extreme cases of color-blindness, which are quite rare, people perceive no color at all. To such individuals, the world looks something like a black-and-white photo.

From the perspective of...

A Graphic Designer How might you market your products to those who are color blind versus those who have normal color vision?

Zoonar GmbH/Alamy Stock Photo

EXPLAINING COLOR VISION

trichromatic theory of color vision The theory that there are three kinds of cones in the retina, each of which responds primarily to a specific range of wavelengths. (Module 9)

To understand why some people are color blind, we need to consider the basics of color vision. Two processes involved. The first process is explained by the **trichromatic theory of color vision,** which was first proposed by Thomas Young and extended by Hermann von Helmholtz in the first half of the 1800s. This theory suggests that there are three kinds of cones in the retina, each of which responds primarily to a specific range of wavelengths. One is most responsive to blue-violet colors, one to green, and the third to yellow-red (Brown & Wald, 1964). According to trichromatic theory, perception of color is influenced by the relative strength with which each of the three kinds of cones is activated. If we see a blue sky, the blue-violet cones are primarily triggered, and the others show less activity.

However, there are aspects of color vision that the trichromatic theory is less successful at explaining. For example, the theory does not explain what happens after you stare at something like the flag shown in Figure 7 for about a minute. Try this yourself and then look at a blank white page: You'll see an image of the traditional red, white, and blue U.S. flag. Where there was yellow, you'll see blue, and where there were green and black, you'll see red and white.

FIGURE 7 Stare at the dot in this flag for about a minute and then look at a piece of plain white paper. What do you see? Most people see an afterimage that converts the colors in the figure into the traditional red, white, and blue U.S. flag. If you have trouble seeing it the first time, blink once and try again.

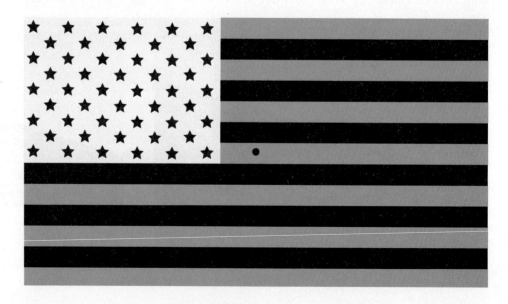

The phenomenon you have just experienced is called an *afterimage*. It occurs because activity in the retina continues even when you are no longer staring at the original picture.

However, the fact that the colors perceived in the afterimage differ from those in the original image calls into question the validity of the trichromatic theory. To explain this failure of the trichromatic theory, alternative explanations for color vision have been developed. One alternative is the opponent-process theory.

According to the **opponent-process theory of color vision,** first proposed by German physiologist Ewald Hering in the 19th century, receptor cells are linked in pairs, working in opposition to each other. Specifically, there are a blue-yellow pairing, a red-green pairing, and a black-white pairing. If an object reflects light that contains more blue than yellow, it will stimulate the firing of the cells sensitive to blue, simultaneously discouraging or inhibiting the firing of receptor cells sensitive to yellow—and the object will appear blue. If, in contrast, a light contains more yellow than blue, the cells that respond to yellow will be stimulated to fire while the blue ones are inhibited, and the object will appear yellow (Robinson, 2007; Grzybowski, & Kupidura-Majewski, 2019).

The opponent-process theory provides a good explanation for afterimages. When we stare at the yellow in the figure, for instance, our receptor cells for the yellow component of the yellow-blue pairing become fatigued and are less able to respond to yellow stimuli. In contrast, the receptor cells for the blue part of the pair are not tired because they are not being stimulated. When we look at a white surface, the light reflected off it would normally stimulate both the yellow and the blue receptors equally. But the fatigue of the yellow receptors prevents this from happening. They temporarily do not respond to the yellow, which makes the white light appear to be blue. Because the other colors in the figure do the same thing relative to their specific opponents, the afterimage produces the opponent colors—for a while. The afterimage lasts only a short time because the fatigue of the yellow receptors is soon overcome, and the white light begins to be perceived more accurately.

We now know that both opponent processes and trichromatic mechanisms are at work in producing the perception of color vision but in different parts of the visual sensing system. Trichromatic processes work within the retina itself, whereas opponent mechanisms operate both in the retina and at later stages of neuronal processing (Horiguchi et al., 2013; Bunce, 2015).

opponent-process theory of color vision The theory that receptor cells for color are linked in pairs, working in opposition to each other. (Module 9)

Study Alert

Keep in mind that there are two explanations for color vision: trichromatic and opponent-process theories.

RECAP/EVALUATE/RETHINK

RECAP

LO 9-1 What basic processes underlie the sense of vision?

- Vision depends on sensitivity to light, electromagnetic waves in the visible part of the spectrum that are either reflected off objects or produced by an energy source. The eye shapes the light into an image that is transformed into nerve impulses and interpreted by the brain.
- As light enters the eye, it passes through the cornea, pupil, and lens and ultimately reaches the retina, where the electromagnetic energy of light is converted to nerve impulses for transmission to the brain. These impulses leave the eye via the optic nerve.
- The visual information gathered by the rods and cones is transferred via bipolar and ganglion cells through the optic nerve, which leads to the optic chiasm—the point where the optic nerve splits.

LO 9-2 How do we see colors?

- Color vision seems to be based on two processes described by the trichromatic theory and the opponent-process theory.
- The trichromatic theory suggests that there are three kinds of cones in the retina, each of which is responsive to a certain range of colors. The opponent-process theory presumes pairs of different types of cells in the eye that work in opposition to each other.

EVALUATE

1. Light entering the eye first passes through the _____, a protective window.
2. The structure that converts light into usable neural messages is called the _____.

3. A person with blue eyes could be described as having blue pigment in their _____.
4. What is the process by which the thickness of the lens is changed in order to focus light properly?
5. The proper sequence of structures that light passes through in the eye is the _____, _____, _____, and _____.
6. Match each type of visual receptor with its function.

   a. rods   **1.** used for dim light, largely insensitive to color

   b. cones   **2.** detect color, good in bright light

7. _____ theory states that there are three types of cones in the retina, each of which responds primarily to a different color.

RETHINK

1. If the eye had a second lens that "unreversed" the image hitting the retina, do you think there would be changes in the way people perceive the world?
2. From an evolutionary standpoint, why might the eye have evolved so that the rods, which we rely on in low light, do not provide sharp images? Are there any advantages to this system?

Answers to Evaluate Questions

1. cornea; 2. retina; 3. iris; 4. accommodation; 5. cornea, pupil, lens, retina; 6. a-1, b-2; 7. Trichromatic

KEY TERMS

retina	optic nerve	trichromatic theory of	opponent-process theory
rods	feature detectors	color vision	of color vision
cones			

Module 10
Hearing and the Other Senses

The blast-off was easy compared with what the astronaut was experiencing now: space sickness. The constant nausea and vomiting were enough to make the astronaut question the hard work to get to this point. Despite the warning of a two-thirds chance of such symptoms the first time in space, the astronaut was unprepared for this terrible sickness.

The astronaut's experience, a major problem for space travelers, is related to a basic sensory process: the sense of motion and balance. This sense allows people to navigate their bodies through the world and keep themselves upright without falling. Along with hearing–the process by which sound waves are translated into understandable and meaningful forms–the sense of motion and balance resides in the ear.

LEARNING OUTCOMES

LO 10-1 What role does the ear play in the senses of sound, motion, and balance?

LO 10-2 How do smell and taste function?

LO 10-3 What are the skin senses, and how do they relate to the experience of pain?

Sensing Sound

Although many of us think primarily of the outer ear when we speak of the ear, that structure is only one simple part of the whole. The outer ear acts as a reverse megaphone, designed to collect and bring sounds into the internal portions of the ear (see Figure 1).

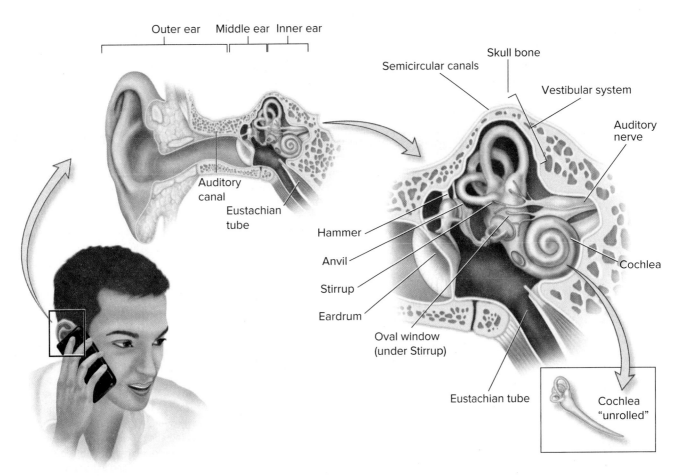

FIGURE 1 The major parts of the ear.

The location of the outer ears on different sides of the head helps with *sound localization,* the process by which we identify the direction from which a sound is coming. Wave patterns in the air enter each ear at a slightly different time, and the brain uses the discrepancy as a clue to the sound's point of origin. In addition, the two outer ears delay or amplify sounds of particular frequencies to different degrees (Tolnai et al., 2017; Sundar et al., 2021).

Sound is the movement of air molecules brought about by a source of vibration. Sounds travel through the air in wave patterns similar in shape to those made in water when a stone is thrown into a still pond. Sounds, arriving at the outer ear in the form of wavelike vibrations, are funneled into the *auditory canal,* a tube-like passage that leads to the eardrum. The **eardrum** is the part of the ear that vibrates when sound waves hit it. The more intense the sound, the more the eardrum vibrates. These vibrations are then transferred into the *middle ear,* a tiny chamber containing three bones (the *hammer,* the *anvil,* and the *stirrup*) that transmit vibrations to the oval window, a thin membrane leading to the inner ear. Because the hammer, anvil, and stirrup act as a set of levers, they not only transmit vibrations but also increase their strength. Moreover, because the opening into the middle ear (the eardrum) is considerably larger than the opening out of it (the *oval window*), the force of sound waves on the oval window becomes amplified. The middle ear, then, acts as a tiny mechanical amplifier.

The *inner ear* is the portion of the ear that changes the sound vibrations into a form in which they can be transmitted to the brain. (As you will see, it also contains the organs that allow us to locate our position and determine how we are moving through space.) When sound enters the inner ear through the oval window, it moves into the **cochlea,** a coiled tube that looks something like a snail and is filled with fluid that vibrates in response to sound. Inside the cochlea is the **basilar membrane,** a structure that runs through the center of the cochlea, dividing it into an upper chamber and a lower chamber. The basilar membrane is covered with **hair cells.** When the hair cells are bent by the vibrations entering the cochlea, the cells send a neural message to the brain (Møller, 2011; Curthoys, 2017; van der Heijden & Vavakou, 2021; also see the *Neuroscience in Your Life* feature).

sound The movement of air molecules brought about by a source of vibration. (Module 10)

eardrum The part of the ear that vibrates when sound waves hit it. (Module 10)

cochlea (KOKE-lee-uh) A coiled tube in the ear filled with fluid that vibrates in response to sound. (Module 10)

basilar membrane A vibrating structure that runs through the center of the cochlea, dividing it into an upper chamber and a lower chamber and containing sense receptors for sound. (Module 10)

hair cells Tiny cells covering the basilar membrane that, when bent by vibrations entering the cochlea, transmit neural messages to the brain. (Module 10)

NEUROSCIENCE IN YOUR LIFE: THE NEUROSCIENCE OF MUSIC

Creating and listening to music are activities that exist across human cultures. And although you may never have reflected on what goes on in your brain when you're listening to your favorite song, neuroscientists are now helping us to understand the complex process that allows us to perceive a series of sounds as music. The fundamental components of music—melody, harmony, and rhythm—involve overlapping but distinct networks in the brain that interact to create the unified perception you experience as a song.

As one example, neuroscience studies show that music perception not only engages the brain's auditory system, but it also involves brain networks related to action, emotion, and learning. According to the predictive coding of music (PCM) model, the experience of music stems from the brain's fundamental capacity for prediction: When we listen to music, we continuously form expectations of what comes next in the song based on prior experience (Vuust et al., 2022).

Also, thanks to advances in neuroscience research methods, scientists are now learning about the social aspect of music. They point out that listening to, creating, and dancing to music with other people involves interpersonal synchronization, improvisation, and communication—all of which require social competencies such as empathy and perspective taking. These social competencies promote interpersonal coordination that allows us to create and enjoy music with others. It follows, then, that understanding the neurobiology of music can offer insights into the therapeutic power of music as well as its role in strengthening social bonds. So the next time you find yourself singing along to a favorite song or stepping out onto the dance floor, you will know that harmony is not just part of the music. Your brain networks are working in harmony, too (Cheever et al., 2018; Speranza et al., 2022).

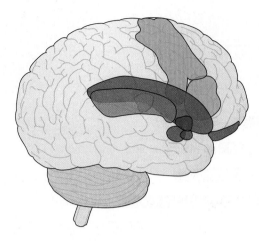

This image shows brain networks involved in music processing. Brain structures related to music perception (in green), action (in blue), and emotion (in orange) are highlighted.
Source: Vuust et al., 2022.

THE PHYSICAL ASPECTS OF SOUND

As we mentioned earlier, what we refer to as sound is actually the physical movement of air molecules in regular, wavelike patterns caused by a vibrating source. Sometimes it is even possible to see these vibrations: If you have ever seen an audio speaker that has no enclosure, you know that, at least when the lowest notes are playing, you can see the speaker moving in and out. Less obvious is what happens next: The speaker pushes air molecules into waves with the same pattern as its movement. Those wave patterns soon reach your ear, although their strength has been weakened considerably during their travels. All other sources that produce sound work in essentially the same fashion, setting off wave patterns that move through the air to the ear. Air—or some other medium, such as water—is necessary to make the vibrations of objects reach us. This explains why there can be no sound in a vacuum.

We are able to see the audio speaker moving when low notes are played because of a primary characteristic of sound called frequency. *Frequency* is the number of wave cycles that occur in a second. At very low frequencies, there are relatively few wave cycles per second (see Figure 2). These cycles are visible to the naked eye as vibrations in the speaker. Low frequencies are translated into a sound that is very low in pitch. (*Pitch* is the characteristic that makes sound seem "high" or "low.") For example, the lowest frequency that humans are capable of hearing is 20 cycles per second. Higher frequencies are heard as sounds of higher pitch. At the upper end of the sound spectrum, people can detect sounds with frequencies as high as 20,000 cycles per second.

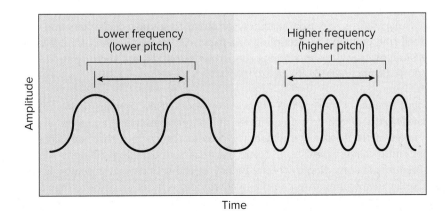

FIGURE 2 The sound waves produced by different stimuli are transmitted—usually through the air—in different patterns, with lower frequencies indicated by fewer peaks and valleys per second.

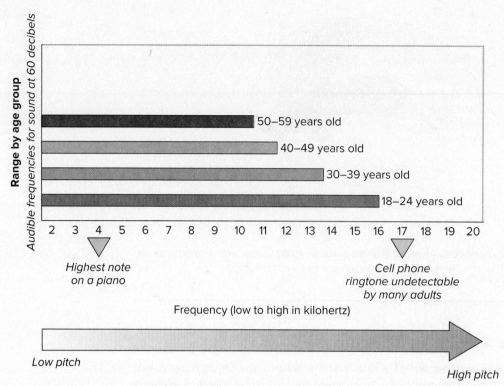

FIGURE 3 Some teenagers set their text-message ring tone to a frequency too high for most adults to hear, allowing them to use cell phones where they are prohibited. Similarly, some organizations use high-frequency sounds to discourage teenage loitering.
Source: Vitello, 2006.

Amplitude is a feature of wave patterns that allows us to distinguish between loud and soft sounds. Amplitude is the spread between the up-and-down peaks and valleys of air pressure in a sound wave as it travels through the air. Waves with small peaks and valleys produce soft sounds; those with relatively large peaks and valleys produce loud sounds.

We are sensitive to broad variations in sound amplitudes. The strongest sounds we are capable of hearing are over a trillion times as intense as the very weakest sound we can hear. This range is measured in *decibels*. When sounds get higher than 120 decibels, they become painful to the human ear.

Our sensitivity to different frequencies changes as we age. For instance, as we get older, the range of frequencies we can detect declines, particularly for high-pitched sounds. This is why high school students sometimes choose high-pitched ring tones for their cell phones in settings where cell phone use is forbidden: The ringing sound goes undetected by teachers who are older (Moreno-Gómez et al., 2017; Winberg, 2019; see Figure 3).

In addition, some individuals are particularly sensitive to sound. In a rare disorder known as *hyperacusis*, a person is acutely sensitive to sounds that others find tolerable. A doorbell ring or even the crumpling of a paper can be extremely painful. Hyperacusis can be brought on by too much exposure to loud sounds, and there is no known cure (Fagelson & Baguley, 2018; Owen, 2019).

Explaining Hearing: Listen to the Theories of Sound How are our brains able to sort out wavelengths of different frequencies and intensities? One important clue comes from studies of the basilar membrane, the area in the cochlea that translates physical vibrations into nerve impulses. It turns out that sounds affect different areas of the basilar membrane according to the frequency of the sound wave reaching it. The part of the basilar membrane nearest to the oval window is most sensitive to high-frequency sounds. In contrast, the part of the basilar membrane nearest to the cochlea's inner end is most sensitive to low-frequency sounds. This finding has led to the **place theory of hearing,** which states that different areas of the basilar membrane are specialized to respond to different sound frequencies.

However, place theory does not tell the full story of hearing because of a significant fact: very low frequency sounds trigger neurons across such a wide area of the basilar membrane that no single site is involved. Consequently, an additional explanation for hearing has been proposed: frequency theory. The **frequency theory of hearing** suggests that the entire basilar membrane acts as a microphone, vibrating as a whole in response to a sound. According to this explanation, the nerve receptors send out signals that are tied directly to the frequency (the number of wave crests per second) of the sounds to which we are exposed, with the number of nerve impulses being a direct function of a sound's frequency. Thus, the higher the pitch of a sound (and therefore the greater the frequency of its wave crests), the greater the number of nerve impulses that are transmitted up the auditory nerve to the brain.

Ultimately, it seems that we need both place theory and frequency theory to understand the process of hearing. Specifically, place theory provides a better explanation for the sensing of high-frequency sounds, whereas frequency theory explains what happens when low-frequency sounds are encountered. Medium-frequency sounds incorporate both processes (Hudspeth, 2013; Vadivel & Ganesh, 2019).

Regardless of whether we employ place theory or frequency theory, we know that after an auditory message leaves the ear, it is transmitted to the auditory cortex of the brain through a complex series of nerve interconnections. And similar to visual nerve cells in the brain that respond to specific kinds of stimuli, auditory neurons respond to specific types of sounds. For example, certain neurons respond selectively to clicks and whistles. Other neurons respond only to a specific sound pattern, such as a steady tone but not an intermittent one. Furthermore, specific neurons transfer information about a sound's location through their particular pattern of firing (Romero-Guevara et al., 2015; Norman-Haignere et al., 2022).

If we were to analyze the configuration of the cells in the auditory cortex, we would find that neighboring cells are responsive to similar frequencies. The auditory cortex, then, provides us with a "map" of sound frequencies, just as the visual cortex furnishes a representation of the visual field. In addition, because of the asymmetry in the two hemispheres of the brain, the left and right ears process sound differently. The right ear reacts more to speech, whereas the left ear responds more to music (McCulloch et al., 2017; Trollinger, 2021).

Speech perception requires that we make fine discriminations among sounds that are quite similar in terms of their physical properties. Furthermore, not only are we able to understand *what* is being said from speech, we also can use vocal cues to determine who is speaking, whether they have an accent and where they may be from, and even their emotional state. Such capabilities illustrate the sophistication of our sense of hearing (Ross et al., 2011; Mattys et al., 2013; Gordon et al., 2019).

Scientists are also beginning to investigate how we use sound to navigate through our environment. *Echolocation* is the use of sound waves and echoes to determine where objects are. It is the navigational technique that bats use, and some people with impaired vision have learned to use echolocation by generating sounds (such as snapping their fingers or making clicking noises) and using the echoes that bounce off objects to navigate. Although psychologists are early in their research on the phenomenon, it may provide a window into sensory processes and ultimately improve the lives of those with sensory impairments (Thaler, 2015; Salles et al., 2019; Susler et al., 2022).

Balance: The Ups and Downs of Life Several structures of the ear are related more to our sense of balance than to our hearing. Collectively, these structures are known as the *vestibular system*, which responds to the pull of gravity and allows us to maintain our balance, even when standing in a bus in stop-and-go traffic.

The main structure of the vestibular system is formed by the **semicircular canals** of the inner ear (refer to Figure 1), which consist of three tubes containing fluid that

place theory of hearing The theory that different areas of the basilar membrane respond to different frequencies. (Module 10)

frequency theory of hearing The theory that the entire basilar membrane acts like a microphone, vibrating as a whole in response to a sound. (Module 10)

Study Alert

Be sure to understand the differences between the place and frequency theories of hearing.

semicircular canals Three tube-like structures of the inner ear containing fluid that sloshes through them when the head moves, signaling rotational or angular movement to the brain. (Module 10)

Zero gravity presents numerous challenges. For example, the weightlessness of the ear's otoliths produces space sickness in most astronauts.

Dusan Petkovic/Shutterstock

sloshes through them when the head moves, signaling rotational or angular movement to the brain. The pull on our bodies caused by the acceleration of forward, backward, or up-and-down motion, as well as the constant pull of gravity, is sensed by the *otoliths*, tiny, motion-sensitive crystals in the semicircular canals. When we move, these crystals shift as sands do on a windy beach, contacting the specialized receptor *hair cells* in the semicircular canals. The brain's inexperience in interpreting messages from the weightless otoliths is the cause of the space sickness commonly experienced by two-thirds of all space travelers, mentioned at the start of this module (Yoder et al., 2015; Macauda et al., 2019).

Smell and Taste

Nothing seemed wrong to Jillian Kobechek until she started chewing a piece of raw cabbage. The cabbage, part of a salad, had a strange taste–almost as though it was burned. Things rapidly spiraled when she took a swallow of a cola, and it tasted like the hottest, spiciest thing she'd ever experienced. After a great deal of trial-and-error testing, her doctors determined that her garbled sense of taste was due to a viral infection.

Even without disruptions in our ability to perceive the world such as those experienced by Jillian Kobechek, we all know the important roles that taste and smell play in our lives. We'll consider these two senses next.

SMELL

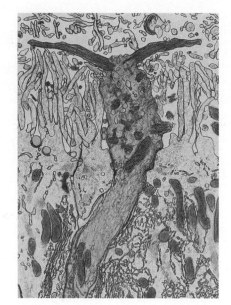

More than 1,000 olfactory receptor cells, like this one in the center of the scan, are spread across the nasal cavity. The cells are specialized to react to particular odors. Do you think it is possible to "train" the nose to pick up a greater number of odors?

Professor Pietro M. Motta/Science Source

Although many animals have keener abilities to detect odors than we do, the human sense of smell (*olfaction*) permits us to detect more than 10,000 separate smells. We also have a good memory for smells, and long-forgotten events and memories–good and bad–can be brought back with the mere whiff of an odor associated with a memory (Arshamian et al., 2013; Glachet et al., 2019; Speed et al., 2021).

Results of "sniff tests" have shown that women generally have a better sense of smell than men do. People also have the ability to distinguish males from females on the basis of smell alone. In one experiment, blindfolded students who were asked to sniff the breath of a female or male volunteer who was hidden from view were able to distinguish the sex of the volunteer at better-than-chance levels. People can also distinguish happy from sad emotions by sniffing underarm smells, and women are able to identify their babies solely on the basis of smell just a few hours after birth (Flohr et al., 2017; Parma et al., 2017; Sorokowski et al., 2019).

The sense of smell is sparked when the molecules of a substance enter the nasal passages and meet *olfactory cells*, the receptor neurons of the nose, which are spread across the nasal cavity. More than 1,000 separate types of receptors have been identified on those cells so far. Each of these receptors is so specialized that it responds only to a small band of different odors. The responses of the separate olfactory cells are then transmitted to the brain, where they are combined into recognition of a particular smell (Lane et al., 2020; Glezer et al., 2021).

Because of their location in the nose, olfactory cells are exposed and vulnerable to a variety of pollutants, viruses, and bacteria that float through the air. Probably because of this vulnerability, olfactory cells (more so than other sensory cells) can regenerate when they are damaged. But because they grow back in different numbers and configurations, people end up with a sense of smell that is different from what it was at earlier stages of their lives, as well as from that of other people. Moreover, by the time they reach the age of 50 or so, most people's smell abilities decline. And by our 80s, three-quarters of us have a significant decline in our sense of smell (Tucker, 2022).

Nevertheless, smell may act as a hidden means of communication for humans. It has long been known that nonhumans release *pheromones*, chemicals they secrete into the environment that produce a social response in other members of the same species. Pheromones transmit messages such as alarm ("danger–predators are close by!") or sexual availability ("I'm interested in sex"). For instance, the vaginal secretions of female monkeys contain pheromones that stimulate the sexual interest of male monkeys (Zizzari et al., 2017; Romero-Lebrón et al., 2019; Voznessenskaya et al., 2022).

The degree to which pheromones are part of the human experience remains an open question. Some psychologists believe that human pheromones affect emotional responses, although the evidence is inconclusive. For one thing, it is not clear what specific sense organ is receptive to pheromones. In nonhumans, it is the *vomeronasal organ* in the nose, but in humans, the organ appears to recede during fetal development (Gelstein et al., 2011; Wyatt, 2020; Voznessenskaya et al., 2020; also see *Applying Psychology in the 21st Century*).

In any case, nonhumans clearly have far more sensitivity to smells than humans. For example, bears have the best sense of smell of all mammals, having the most olfactory receptors. Some bears have reportedly traveled 18 miles to a source of food. Dogs also have an excellent sense of smell. In fact, during the COVID-19 pandemic, scientists found that dogs could detect people who had the virus with great accuracy (Gorman, 2021).

TASTE

The sense of taste (*gustation*) involves receptor cells that respond to four basic stimulus qualities: sweet, sour, salty, and bitter. A fifth category also exists, a flavor called *umami*, although there is controversy about whether it qualifies as a fundamental taste. *Umami* is a hard-to-translate Japanese word, although the English "meaty" or "savory" comes close. Chemically, umami involves food stimuli that contain amino acids (the substances that make up proteins) (Nakamura et al., 2011; Cecchini et al., 2019; Qi et al., 2022).

Although the specialization of the receptor cells leads them to respond most strongly to a particular type of taste, they are capable of responding to other tastes as well. Ultimately, every taste is simply a combination of the basic flavor qualities, in the same way that the primary colors blend into a vast variety of shades and hues (Yeomans et al., 2007; Spence et al., 2015).

APPLYING PSYCHOLOGY IN THE 21ST CENTURY

WHAT YOUR SMELL TELLS OTHERS ABOUT WHO YOU ARE

You smell. And so does everyone else.

Each of us has an odor, and that odor conveys a great deal of information: about a person's age, emotional state, health, and even who they might be likely to marry.

According to a growing number of scientific studies, our bodies constantly emit three levels of information about us via the way we smell. First, our skin emits odors from the soap, perfumes, and deodorants we use. The middle level of odor comes from factors related to the particular culture in which we live, such as our diets or traditions, such as eating foods that are heavily spiced with garlic. Finally, underneath the first two layers, each of us produces a baseline odor known as the *major histocompatibility complex,* or MHC. Genes related to MHC are unique to each person, in much the same way that fingerprints are unique (Herz, 2016; Al Naqbi et al., 2021; Stewart, 2021).

The amount of information provided by MHC genes is extraordinary. For example, mothers and fathers can distinguish, with considerable accuracy, amniotic fluid belonging to their own child from samples of amniotic fluid from other infants. Furthermore, evidence indicates that heterosexuals are attracted to partners whose MHC complex of genes differ from, and complement, their own MHC genes. Moreover, in a study involving sexual orientation and smell, gay men who sniffed a T-shirt were able to identify whether it had been worn by a gay or a straight man. Similarly, lesbian women could distinguish the smell of other lesbian women (Martins et al., 2005; Mahmut & Croy, 2019; Zietsch, 2021).

It's long been believed that particular illnesses are associated with particular smells. For example, in ancient times, healers thought that tuberculosis smelled of stale beer. More recently, researchers have found that people with certain kinds of cancer emit a distinct odor. Even receiving common immunizations can cause a person's body to emit a distinct odor (Kimball et al., 2014; Protoshhak et al., 2019).

In short, the way we smell provides significant information about our personal characteristics. How others interpret that information, though, is an area that needs further research (Stewart, 2021).

RETHINK

- What challenges might researchers have in understanding the ways in which people's unique smells influence their social interaction?
- How might your understanding of the world be different if you had no sense of smell?

The receptor cells for taste are located in roughly 10,000 *taste buds,* which are distributed across the tongue and other parts of the mouth and throat. The taste buds wear out and are replaced every 10 days or so. That's a good thing because if our taste buds weren't constantly reproducing, we'd lose the ability to taste after we'd accidentally burned our tongues.

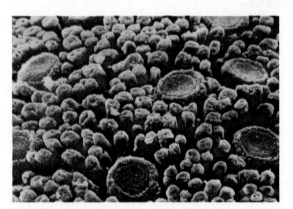

There are 10,000 taste buds on the tongue and on other parts of the mouth. Taste buds wear out and are replaced every 10 days. What would happen if taste buds were not regenerated?

Science History Images/Alamy Stock Photo

The sense of taste differs significantly from one person to another, largely as a result of genetic factors. Some people, dubbed "supertasters," are highly sensitive to taste; they have twice as many taste receptors as "nontasters," who are relatively insensitive to taste. Supertasters (who, for unknown reasons, are more likely to be female than male) find sweets sweeter, cream creamier, and spicy dishes spicier, and weaker concentrations of flavor are enough to satisfy any cravings they may have (Cornelis et al., 2017; Melis et al., 2021).

Supertasters—who make up about 15% of the U.S. population—may even be healthier than nontasters. Because supertasters find fatty foods distasteful, they are thinner than the general population. In contrast, because they aren't so sensitive to taste, nontasters may seek out relatively sweeter and fattier foods in order to maximize the taste. As a consequence, they may be prone to obesity (Reddy, 2013; Harahap & Sihombing, 2022; Spence, 2022).

Are you a supertaster? To find out, complete the questionnaire in Figure 4.

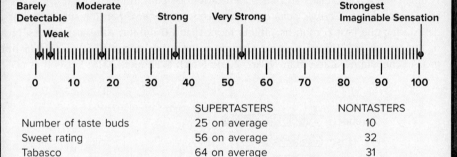

Take a Taste Test

1. **Taste Bud Count**
   Punch a hole with a standard hole punch in a square of wax paper. Paint the front of your tongue with a cotton swab dipped in blue food coloring. Put the wax paper on the tip of your tongue, just to the right of center. With a flashlight and magnifying glass, count the number of pink, unstained circles. They contain taste buds.

2. **Sweet Taste**
   Rinse your mouth with water before tasting each sample. Put a ½ cup of sugar in a measuring cup and then add enough water to make I cup. Mix. Coat the front half of your tongue, including the tip, with a cotton swab dipped in the solution. Wait a few moments. Rate the sweetness according to the scale shown below.

3. **Salt Taste**
   Put 2 teaspoons of salt in a measuring cup and add enough water to make I cup. Repeat the steps listed above, rating how salty the solution is.

4. **Spicy Taste**
   Add I teaspoon of Tabasco sauce to I cup of water. Apply with a cotton swab to the first ½ inch of the tongue, including the tip. Keep your tongue out of your mouth until the burn reaches a peak, then rate the burn according to the scale.

TASTE SCALE

Barely Detectable — Weak — Moderate — Strong — Very Strong — Strongest Imaginable Sensation

0   10   20   30   40   50   60   70   80   90   100

	SUPERTASTERS	NONTASTERS
Number of taste buds	25 on average	10
Sweet rating	56 on average	32
Tabasco	64 on average	31

Average tasters lie in between supertasters and nontasters. Taste researchers Linda Bartoshuk and Laurie Lucchina lack the data at this time to rate salt reliably, but you can compare your results with others taking the test.

FIGURE 4 All tongues are not created equal, according to Bartoshuk and Lucchina. Instead, they suggest that the intensity of a flavor experienced by a given person is determined by that person's genetic background. This taste test can help determine if you are a nontaster, average taster, or supertaster.

Sources: Bartoshuk & Lucchina, 1997; Science Buddies, 2012.

The Skin Senses: Touch, Pressure, Temperature, and Pain

It started innocently when Jennifer Darling hurt her right wrist during gym class. At first, it seemed like a simple sprain. But even though the initial injury healed, the excruciating, burning pain accompanying it did not go away. Instead, it spread to her other arm and then to her legs. The pain, which Jennifer described as similar to "a hot iron on your arm," was unbearable—and never stopped.

The source of Darling's pain turned out to be a rare condition that is now known as *complex regional pain syndrome*, or *CRPS*. CRPS is a disease characterized by constant, intense pain that is out of proportion to any injury. For a victim of CRPS, a stimulus as mild as a gentle breeze or the touch of a feather can produce agony. Even bright sunlight or a loud noise can trigger intense pain (Harden et al., 2013; Edunjobi et al., 2021; Phillips et al., 2022).

Pain such as Darling's can be devastating, yet a lack of pain can be equally bad. If you never experience pain, for instance, you might not notice that your arm had brushed against a hot pan, and you would suffer a severe burn. Similarly, without the warning sign of abdominal pain that typically accompanies an inflamed appendix, your appendix might eventually rupture, spreading a fatal infection throughout your body.

Pain has other benefits, as well. Pain helps us better appreciate pleasurable experiences. It also may lead us to affiliate more closely with others, by arousing their empathy. And pain may lead us to be more vigilant about our surroundings as we seek to avoid or moderate pain we are experiencing (Bastian et al., 2014; Cameron et al., 2017; Liu et al., 2019).

In fact, all our **skin senses**—touch, pressure, temperature, and pain—play a critical role in survival, making us aware of potential danger to our bodies. Most of these senses operate through nerve receptor cells located at various depths throughout the skin, distributed unevenly throughout the body. For example, some areas, such as the fingertips, have many more receptor cells sensitive to touch and as a consequence are notably more sensitive than other areas of the body (Gardner & Kandel, 2000; Macefield, 2022; see Figure 5).

Probably the most extensively researched skin sense is pain, and with good reason: People consult physicians and take medication for pain more than for any other symptom or condition. *Chronic pain*, defined as the presence of pain on most days or every day during the past 6 months, afflicts more than 50 million American adults, or a fifth of the population. Efforts to treat chronic pain cost between $560 and $635 billion a year in the United States alone (Carr, 2019; Smith & Hillner, 2019; Driscoll et al., 2021).

> **!** **Study Alert**
> Remember that there are multiple skin senses, including touch, pressure, temperature, and pain.

skin senses The senses of touch, pressure, temperature, and pain. (Module 10)

FIGURE 5 Skin sensitivity in various areas of the body. The lower the average threshold is, the more sensitive a body part is. The fingers and thumb, lips, nose, cheeks, and big toe are the most sensitive. Why do you think certain areas are more sensitive than others?

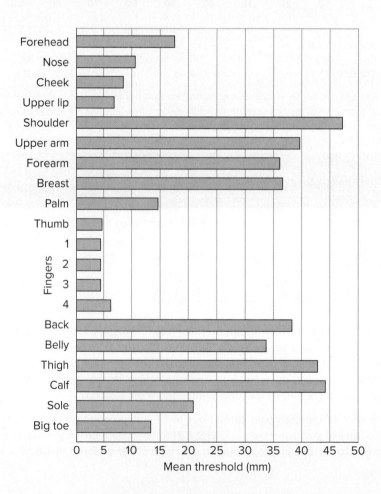

Pain is a response to a great variety of stimuli. A light that is too bright can produce pain, and sound that is too loud can be painful. There are also multiple forms of pain; even itching can be considered a form of pain (Papoiu et al., 2013; Bautista et al., 2014; Sutherland, 2016).

One explanation for pain is that it is an outcome of cell injury; when a cell is damaged, regardless of the source of damage, it releases a chemical called *substance P* that transmits pain messages to the brain.

Some people are more susceptible to pain than others. For example, women experience painful stimuli more intensely than men do. These gender differences are associated with the production of hormones related to menstrual cycles. In addition, certain genes are linked to the experience of pain, so that we may inherit our sensitivity to pain (Park, 2011; Berke et al., 2017; Pester et al., 2022).

But the experience of pain is not determined by biological factors alone. For example, women report that the pain experienced in childbirth is moderated to some degree by the joyful nature of the situation. In contrast, even a minor stimulus can produce the perception of strong pain if it is accompanied by anxiety (for example, during a visit to the dentist). Clearly, then, pain is a perceptual response that depends heavily on our emotions and thoughts (Lang et al., 2006; Kennedy et al., 2011; Jensen & Turk, 2014).

Furthermore, there are racial and ethnic disparities in how medical providers react to their patients' pain. For example, individuals of color seeking treatment for pain are more likely to have their pain minimized or underestimated, compared with White individuals. Moreover, they receive less aggressive treatment for their pain (Driscoll et al., 2021; Mende-Siedlecki et al., 2021).

From the perspective of...

A Medical or Dental Services Provider How would you handle a patient who is anxiously awaiting treatment and complaining that her pain is getting worse?

Trevor Lush/Purestock/SuperStock

gate-control theory of pain The theory that particular nerve receptors in the spinal cord lead to specific areas of the brain related to pain. (Module 10)

According to the **gate-control theory of pain,** particular nerve receptors in the spinal cord lead to specific areas of the brain related to pain. When these receptors are activated because of an injury or problem with a part of the body, a "gate" to the brain is opened, causing us to experience the sensation of pain (Vasudeva et al., 2015; Penlington et al., 2019).

But the gate that produces pain does not necessarily remain open. Specifically, another set of neural receptors can, when stimulated, close the "gate" to the brain, thereby reducing the experience of pain.

The gate can be shut in two ways. First, other impulses can overwhelm the nerve pathways relating to pain, which are spread throughout the brain. In this case, nonpainful stimuli compete with and sometimes displace the neural message of pain, thereby shutting off the painful stimulus. This explains why rubbing the skin around an injury (or even listening to distracting music) helps reduce pain. The competing stimuli can overpower the painful ones (Somers et al., 2011; Lunde et al., 2019).

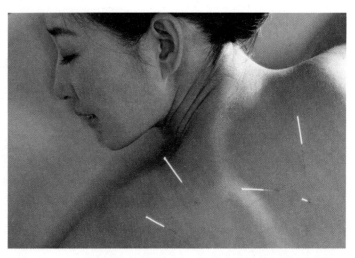

The ancient practice of acupuncture is still used in the 21st century. How does the gate-control theory of pain explain how acupuncture works?
Fuse/Corbis/Getty Images

The gate-control theory of pain suggests that the experience of pain is related to activation of particular nerve receptors in the nervous system and that "gates" in the spinal cord affect the degree to which people experience pain at a given moment.

Stockbakery/Shutterstock

Second, the neural gate producing pain can be shut by psychological factors relating to an individual's current emotions, interpretation of events, and previous experience. Specifically, the brain can close a gate by sending a message down the spinal cord to an injured area, producing a reduction in or relief from pain. Thus, soldiers who are injured in battle may experience no pain—the surprising situation in more than half of all combat injuries. The lack of pain probably occurs because a soldier experiences such relief at still being alive that the brain sends a signal to the injury site to shut down the pain gate (Pincus & Morley, 2001; Bell, 2018).

Gate-control theory also may explain cultural differences in the experience of pain. Some of these variations are astounding. For example, in India, people who participate in the "hook-swinging" ritual to celebrate the power of the gods have steel hooks embedded under the skin and muscles of their backs. During the ritual, they swing from a pole, suspended by the hooks. What would seem likely to induce excruciating pain instead produces a state of celebration and near euphoria. In fact, when the hooks are later removed, the wounds heal quickly, and after 2 weeks, almost no visible marks remain (Krupić et al., 2019; Oddie, 2021).

Gate-control theory suggests that the lack of pain is due to a message from the participant's brain that shuts down the pain pathways. Gate-control theory also may explain the effectiveness of *acupuncture*, an ancient Chinese technique in which sharp needles are inserted into various parts of the body. The sensation from the needles may close the gateway to the brain, reducing the experience of pain. It is also possible that the body's own painkillers—called *endorphins*—as well as positive and negative emotions, play a role in opening and closing the gate (Khedr et al., 2017; Wang et al., 2022).

Although the basic ideas behind gate-control theory have been supported by research, other processes are involved in the perception of pain. For instance, it appears that there are multiple neural pathways involved in the experience of pain. Furthermore, the suppression of pain can occur through the natural release of endorphins and other compounds that produce a reduction of discomfort and a sense of well-being. Finally, cognitive factors—such as people's expectations and their prior learning about pain—play a significant role in the perception of pain (Grahek, 2007; Wiech, 2016).

BECOMING AN INFORMED CONSUMER
of Psychology

Managing Pain

Are you one of the more than 50 million people in the United States who suffers from chronic pain? Psychologists and medical specialists have devised several strategies to fight pain. Among the most important approaches are these:

- *Medication.* Painkilling pharmaceutical drugs are the most popular treatment in fighting pain, despite the dangers of overuse that many see as the source of the current opioid crisis. Medications range from those that directly treat the source of the pain—such as reducing swelling in painful joints—to those that work on the symptoms. Medication can be in the form of pills, patches, injections, or liquids. In a recent innovation, drugs are pumped directly into the spinal cord. Increasing evidence also indicates that medical cannabis (marijuana) can be an effective painkiller (Jain et al., 2019; Wallis, 2019; Harris et al., 2022).

- *Nerve and brain stimulation*. Pain can sometimes be relieved when a low-voltage electric current is passed through the specific part of the body that is in pain. For example, in *peripheral-nerve stimulation,* a tiny battery-operated generator is implanted in the lower back. In even more severe cases, electrodes can be implanted surgically directly into the brain, or a handheld battery pack can stimulate nerve cells to provide direct relief (Landro, 2010; Tan et al., 2011; Conforto et al., 2019).
- *Acupuncture*. Acupuncture is a form of traditional Chinese pain treatment in which thin needles are inserted into the body in precise locations. In some cases, such treatment can produce effective pain relief, though the mechanisms by which it works are not well understood (Lim et al., 2018; Yang et al., 2021).
- *Light therapy*. One of the newest forms of pain reduction involves exposure to specific wavelengths of red or infrared light. Certain kinds of light increase the production of enzymes that may promote healing (Evcik et al., 2007; de Sousa et al., 2019; Chia et al., 2021).
- *Hypnosis*. For people who can be hypnotized—and not everyone is susceptible—hypnosis can greatly relieve pain. In fact, it can affect the brain and spinal-cord functioning in injured people, actually improving their physical functioning (Lee & Raja, 2011; Jensen & Patterson, 2014; Langlois et al., 2022).
- *Biofeedback and relaxation techniques*. Using *biofeedback*, people learn to control what are usually involuntary functions such as heartbeat, respiration, blood pressure, and muscle tension. Through biofeedback, a person can learn to control the stimulus that is causing the pain. For instance, people with tension headaches or back pain can be trained to relax their bodies to bring themselves relief (Sielski et al., 2017; McKenna et al., 2019).
- *Surgery*. In one of the most extreme methods, specific nerve fibers that carry pain messages to the brain can be cut surgically. Still, because of the danger that other bodily functions will be affected, surgery is a treatment of last resort, used most frequently with dying patients (Amid & Chen, 2011; Issa et al., 2013; Beel & Berreovoet, 2021).
- *Cognitive restructuring*. Cognitive treatments are effective for people who continually say to themselves, "This pain will never stop," "The pain is ruining my life," or "I can't take it anymore," and are thereby likely to make their pain even worse. By substituting more positive ways of thinking, people can increase their sense of control—and actually reduce the pain they experience (Ehde et al., 2014; Nowakowski et al., 2019).
- *Mirror pain therapy*. One surprising treatment for people who suffer from phantom-limb pain (where a person with an amputated limb experiences pain where the missing limb used to be) employs mirrors. By using a mirror to make it appear that both limbs are intact, the brain of the amputee stops sending messages perceived as pain (Foell et al., 2014; Xi et al., 2021).
- *Virtual reality therapy*. In one of the newest treatments, pain sufferers wear a headset that creates an entertaining, relaxing, and interactive virtual reality environment. The experience is so rich in stimulation that the brain has no capacity to process pain sensations at the same time (Brody, 2019: Fusaro et al., 2019; Chuan et al., 2021).

How Our Senses Interact

When Matthew Blakeslee shapes hamburger patties with his hands, he experiences a vivid bitter taste in his mouth. Esmerelda Jones (a pseudonym) sees blue when she listens to the note C sharp played on the piano; other notes evoke different hues–so much so that the piano keys are actually color-coded, making it easier for her to remember and play musical scales. (Ramachandran & Hubbard, 2006)

The explanation? Both of these people have an unusual condition known as synesthesia. *Synesthesia* is a perceptual phenomenon in which the stimulation of one

FIGURE 6 (a) At first glance, the figure on the left appears to contain an array of identical number eights, each of which looks like a rectangle with a horizontal slash. However, at closer glance, the array also includes six zeros, appearing as a rectangular "ø" with a slash through it. Most people take several seconds to find the zeros buried among the number eights and to see that the zeros form a triangle. People with certain forms of synesthesia, however, find this easy because they perceive the numbers in contrasting colors, as in (b).

Sources (a and b): Adapted from Ramachandran & Hubbard, 2006; Safran & Sanda, 2015.

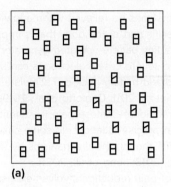
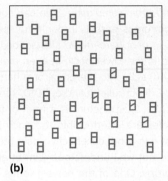

(a) (b)

sensory system (such as hearing) involuntarily leads a person to experience an additional sensory response in a different sensory system (such as vision).

The origins of synesthesia are not totally clear, although some research suggests it is genetically inherited. Also, people with synesthesia may have unusually dense neural linkages between the sensory areas of the brain. Another hypothesis is that they lack the neural controls that usually inhibit connections between sensory areas (Deroy & Spence, 2013; Meier & Rothen, 2015; Jewanski et al., 2019).

Whatever the reason for synesthesia, it is a rare condition. (If you'd like to check out this phenomenon, see Figure 6.) Even so, the senses of all of us do interact and integrate in a variety of ways. For example, the taste of food is influenced by its texture and temperature. We perceive food that is warmer as sweeter (think of the sweetness of steamy hot chocolate compared with cold chocolate milk). Spicy foods stimulate some of the same pain receptors that are also stimulated by heat–making the use of *hot* as a synonym for *spicy* quite accurate (Balaban et al., 2005; Brang et al., 2011; Alfaro et al., 2015).

It's important, then, to think of our senses as interacting with one another. For instance, brain imaging studies show that the senses work in tandem to build our understanding of the world around us. We engage in *multimodal perception*, in which the brain collects the information from the individual sensory systems and integrates and coordinates it (Paulmann et al., 2009; Gruber & Block, 2017; Klein-Soetebier et al., 2021).

Moreover, despite the fact that very different sorts of stimuli activate our individual senses, they all react according to the same basic principles that we discussed at the start of this chapter. For example, our responses to visual, auditory, and taste stimuli all follow Weber's law involving our sensitivity to changes in the strength of stimuli.

In short, in some ways, our senses are more similar to one another than different. Each of them is designed to pick up information from the environment and translate it into usable information. Furthermore, individually and collectively, our senses help us to understand the complexities of the world around us, allowing us to navigate through the world effectively and intelligently.

RECAP/EVALUATE/RETHINK

RECAP

LO 10-1 What role does the ear play in the senses of sound, motion, and balance?

- Sound, motion, and balance are centered in the ear. Sounds, in the form of vibrating air waves, enter through the outer ear and travel through the auditory canal until they reach the eardrum.
- The vibrations of the eardrum are transmitted into the middle ear, which consists of three bones: the hammer, the anvil, and the stirrup. These bones transmit vibrations to the oval window.
- In the inner ear, vibrations move into the cochlea, which encloses the basilar membrane. Hair cells on the basilar membrane change the mechanical energy of sound waves into nerve impulses that are transmitted to the brain. The ear is also involved in the sense of balance and motion.
- Sound has a number of physical characteristics, including frequency and amplitude. The place theory of

hearing and the frequency theory of hearing explain the processes by which we distinguish sounds of varying frequency and intensity.

LO 10-2 How do smell and taste function?

- Smell depends on olfactory cells (the receptor cells of the nose), and taste is centered in the taste buds on the tongue and mouth.

LO 10-3 What are the skin senses, and how do they relate to the experience of pain?

- The skin senses are responsible for the experiences of touch, pressure, temperature, and pain. Gate-control theory suggests that particular nerve receptors, when activated, open a "gate" to specific areas of the brain related to pain and that another set of receptors closes the gate when stimulated.
- Among the techniques used frequently to alleviate pain are medication, hypnosis, biofeedback, relaxation techniques, surgery, nerve and brain stimulation, and cognitive therapy.

EVALUATE

1. The tube-like passage leading from the outer ear to the eardrum is known as the _____ _____.
2. The purpose of the eardrum is to protect the sensitive nerves underneath it. It serves no purpose in actual hearing. True or false?
3. The three middle ear bones transmit their sound to the _____ _____.

4. The _____ theory of hearing states that the entire basilar membrane responds to a sound, vibrating more or less, depending on the nature of the sound.
5. The three fluid-filled tubes in the inner ear that are responsible for our sense of balance are known as the _____ _____.
6. The _____ _____ theory states that when certain skin receptors are activated as a result of an injury, a "pathway" to the brain is opened, allowing pain to be experienced.

RETHINK

1. Much research is being conducted on repairing faulty sensory organs through devices such as personal guidance systems and eyeglasses, among others. Do you think that researchers should attempt to improve normal sensory capabilities beyond their "natural" range (for example, make human visual or audio capabilities more sensitive than normal)? What benefits might this ability bring? What problems might it cause?
2. Why might sensitivity to pheromones have evolved differently in humans than in other species? What cultural factors might have played a role?

Answers to Evaluate Questions

1. auditory canal; 2. False: It vibrates when sound waves hit it and transmits the sound; 3. oval window; 4. frequency; 5. semicircular canals; 6. gate-control

KEY TERMS

sound	basilar membrane	frequency theory of hearing	skin senses
eardrum	hair cells	semicircular canals	gate-control theory of pain
cochlea (KOKE-lee-uh)	place theory of hearing		

Module 11
Perceptual Organization: Constructing Our View of the World

LEARNING OUTCOMES

LO 11-1 What principles underlie our organization of the visual world and allow us to make sense of our environment?

LO 11-2 How are we able to perceive the world in three dimensions when our retinas are capable of sensing only two-dimensional images?

LO 11-3 What clues do visual illusions give us about our understanding of general perceptual mechanisms?

Gestalt (geh-SHTALLT) laws of organization A series of principles that describe how we organize bits and pieces of information into meaningful wholes. (Modules 2, 11)

Consider the vase shown in Figure 1a for a moment. Or is it a vase? Take another look, and instead you may see the profiles of two people.

Now that an alternative interpretation has been pointed out, you will probably shift back and forth between the two interpretations. Similarly, if you examine the shapes in Figure 1b long enough, you will probably experience a shift in what you're seeing. The reason for these reversals is this: Because each figure is two-dimensional, the usual means we employ for distinguishing the figure (the object being perceived) from the *ground* (the background or spaces within the object) do not work.

The fact that we can look at the same figure in more than one way illustrates an important point. We do not just passively respond to visual stimuli that happen to fall on our retinas. Rather, we actively try to organize and make sense of what we see.

We turn now from a focus on the initial response to a stimulus (sensation) to what our minds make of that stimulus (perception). Perception is a constructive process by which we go beyond the stimuli that are presented to us and attempt to construct a meaningful situation.

The Gestalt Laws of Organization

Some of the most basic perceptual processes can be described by a series of principles that focus on the ways we organize bits and pieces of information into meaningful wholes. These principles, known as the **Gestalt laws of organization,** were set forth in the early 1900s by a group of German psychologists who studied patterns, or *gestalts* (Wertheimer, 1923). Those psychologists discovered a number of important principles that are valid for visual (as well as auditory) stimuli, illustrated in Figure 2: closure, proximity, similarity, and simplicity.

Figure 2a illustrates *closure*: We usually group elements to form enclosed or complete figures rather than open ones. We tend to ignore the breaks in Figure 2a and

FIGURE 1 When the usual cues we use to distinguish figure from ground are absent, we may shift back and forth between different views of the same figure. In (a), you can see either a vase or the profiles of two people. In (b), the shaded portion of the figure, called a Necker cube, can appear to be either the front or the back of the cube.

(a)

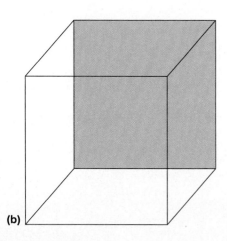

(b)

(a) Closure   **(b)** Proximity   **(c)** Similarity   **(d)** Simplicity

FIGURE 2 Organizing these various bits and pieces of information into meaningful wholes constitutes some of the most basic processes of perception, which are summed up in the Gestalt laws of organization. How might we determine if any other species share this organizational tendency?

concentrate on the overall form. Figure 2b demonstrates the principle of *proximity*: We perceive elements that are closer together as grouped together. As a result, we tend to see pairs of dots rather than a row of single dots in Figure 2b.

Elements that are *similar* in appearance we perceive as grouped together. We see, then, horizontal rows of circles and squares in Figure 2c, rather than vertical mixed columns. Finally, in a general sense, the overriding Gestalt principle is *simplicity*: When we observe a pattern, we perceive it in the most basic, straightforward manner that we can. For example, most of us see Figure 2d as a square with lines on two sides, rather than as the block letter *W* on top of the letter *M*. If we have a choice of interpretations, we generally opt for the simpler one.

Although Gestalt psychology no longer plays a prominent role in contemporary psychology, its legacy endures. One fundamental Gestalt principle that remains influential is that two objects considered together form a whole that differs from the simple combination of individual elements we sense. Consequently, perception represents an active, constructive process carried out within the brain (Wagemans et al., 2012; Chiu et al., 2017; see Figure 3).

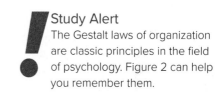

Study Alert

The Gestalt laws of organization are classic principles in the field of psychology. Figure 2 can help you remember them.

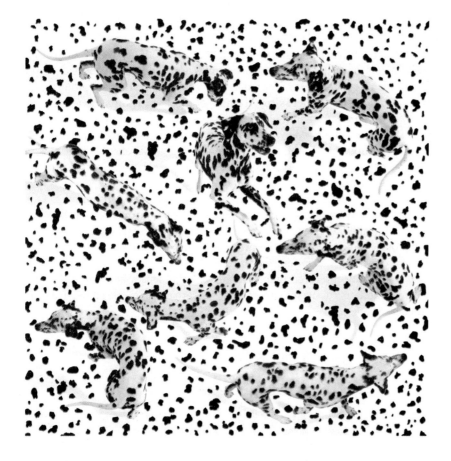

FIGURE 3 Although at first it is difficult to distinguish anything in this drawing, keep looking, and eventually you may see the figure of a dog—or actually, several dogs. Each dog represents a Gestalt, or perceptual, whole, which is something greater than the sum of the individual elements.
Gandee Vasan/Stone/Getty Images

Generally, the organizational principles that drive perception seem to be universal. For example, across cultures, people appear to recognize similar basic constellations of stars. More specifically, in the Southern Hemisphere, multiple cultures perceive the Southern Cross grouping of stars, though they apply a variety of verbal labels to it. For example, the Yolngu peoples of northern Australia see a stingray, the Tainui peoples of New Zealand see an anchor, and others see a cross. In short, basic perceptual principles seem to apply across diverse cultures (Kemp et al., 2022).

Top-Down and Bottom-Up Processing

Ca- yo- re-d t-is -en-en-e, w-ic- ha- ev-ry -hi-d l-tt-r m-ss-ng?

It probably won't take you too long to figure out that it says: "Can you read this sentence, which has every third letter missing?"

If perception were based primarily on breaking down a stimulus into its most basic elements, understanding the sentence, as well as other ambiguous stimuli, would not be possible. The fact that you were probably able to recognize such an imprecise stimulus illustrates that perception proceeds along two different avenues, called top-down processing and bottom-up processing.

top-down processing Perception that is guided by higher-level knowledge, experience, expectations, and motivations. (Module 11)

In **top-down processing**, perception is guided by higher-level knowledge, experience, expectations, and motivations. You were able to figure out the meaning of the sentence with the missing letters because of your prior reading experience and because written English contains redundancies. Not every letter of each word is necessary to decode its meaning. Moreover, your expectations played a role in your being able to read the sentence. You were probably expecting a sentence that had *something* to do with psychology, not the lyrics to a Lady Gaga song.

Top-down processing is illustrated by the importance of context in determining how we perceive objects. Look, for example, at Figure 4. Most of us perceive that the first row consists of the letters *A* through *F*, while the second contains the numbers 9 through 14. But take a more careful look, and you'll see that the B and the 13 are identical. Clearly, our perception is affected by our expectations about the two sequences–even though the two stimuli are exactly the same.

However, top-down processing cannot occur on its own. Even though top-down processing allows us to fill in the gaps in ambiguous and out-of-context stimuli, we would be unable to perceive the meaning of such stimuli without bottom-up processing. **Bottom-up processing** consists of the progression of recognizing and processing information from individual components of a stimuli and moving to the perception of the whole. We would make no headway in our recognition of the sentence without being able to perceive the individual shapes that make up the letters. Some perception, then, occurs at the level of the patterns and features of each of the separate letters.

bottom-up processing Perception that consists of the progression of recognizing and processing information from individual components of a stimuli and moving to the perception of the whole. (Module 11)

Top-down and bottom-up processing occur simultaneously and interact with each other in our perception of the world around us. Bottom-up processing permits us to process the fundamental characteristics of stimuli, whereas top-down processing allows us to bring our experience to bear on perception. As we learn more about the complex processes involved in perception, we are developing a better understanding of how the brain continually interprets information from the senses and permits us to make responses appropriate to the environment (Westerhausen et al., 2009; Falasca et al., 2015; Riener, 2019).

FIGURE 4 The power of context is shown in this figure. Note how the B and the 13 are identical.
Source: Coren & Ward, 1989.

Depth Perception: Translating 2-D to 3-D

As sophisticated as the retina is, the images projected onto it are flat and two-dimensional. Yet the world around us is three-dimensional, and we perceive it that way. How do we make the transformation from 2-D to 3-D?

The ability to view the world in three dimensions and to perceive distance—a skill known as **depth perception**—is due largely to the fact that we have two eyes. Because there is a certain distance between the eyes, a slightly different image reaches each retina. The brain integrates the two images into one view, but it also recognizes the difference in images and uses this difference to estimate the distance of an object from us. The difference in the images seen by the left eye and the right eye is known as *binocular disparity* (Gao et al., 2017; Campagnoli & Domini, 2019; Alvarez et al., 2021).

To get a sense of binocular disparity, hold a pencil at arm's length and look at it first with one eye and then with the other. There is little difference between the two views relative to the background. Now bring the pencil just 6 inches away from your face, and try the same thing. This time you will perceive a greater difference between the two views.

The difference between the images in the two eyes provides us with a way of determining distance. If we view two objects and one is considerably closer to us than the other is, the retinal disparity will be relatively large. That disparity leads us to have a greater sense of depth between the two. However, if two objects are a similar distance from us, the retinal disparity will be minor. Therefore, we will perceive them as being a similar distance from us.

In some cases, certain cues permit us to obtain a sense of depth and distance with just one eye. These cues are known as *monocular cues.*

For example, *motion parallax* is the monocular cue in which a change in position of an object on the retina allows the perception of movement. For example, suppose you are a passenger in a moving car and you focus your eye on a stable object such as a tree. Objects that are closer than the tree will appear to move backward, and the nearer the objects are, the more quickly they will appear to move. In contrast, objects beyond the tree will seem to move at a slower speed but in the same direction as you are. Your brain is able to use these cues to calculate the relative distances of the tree and other objects.

depth perception The ability to view the world in three dimensions and to perceive distance. (Module 11)

Railroad tracks that seem to join together in the distance are an example of linear perspective.
Fuse/Getty Images

Similarly, the monocular cue of *relative size* reflects the assumption that if two objects are the same size, the object that makes a smaller image on the retina is farther away than the one that makes a larger image. But it's not just size of an object that provides information about distance; the quality of the image on the retina helps us judge distance. The monocular cue of *texture gradient* provides information about distance because the details of things that are far away are less distinct (Higashiyama & Yamazaki, 2016; Aguilar-Arguello et al., 2022).

Finally, anyone who has ever seen railroad tracks that seem to come together in the distance knows that distant objects appear to be closer together than are nearer ones, a phenomenon called linear perspective. *Linear perspective* is a type of perspective in which objects in the distance appear to converge. We use linear perspective as a monocular cue in estimating distance, allowing the two-dimensional image on the retina to record the three-dimensional world (Bruggeman et al., 2007; Yildiz et al., 2019).

From the perspective of...

A Computer Game Designer What are some techniques you might use to produce the appearance of three-dimensional terrain on a two-dimensional computer screen? What are some techniques you might use to suggest motion?

Sam Edwards/age fotostock

Perceptual Constancy

Consider what happens as you finish a conversation with a friend and they begin to walk away from you. As you watch your friend walk down the street, the image on your retina becomes smaller and smaller. Do you wonder why your friend is shrinking?

Of course not. Despite the very real change in the size of the retinal image, because of perceptual constancy, you factor into your thinking the knowledge that your friend

Despite the moon appearing very large when it is close to the horizon, perceptual constancy helps us to know that the moon's size has not changed and remains the same.

Don Smith/Stockbyte/Getty Images

is moving farther away from you. **Perceptual constancy** is the recognition that physical objects are consistent and do not vary, even though our sensory input about them changes.

Perceptual constancy allows us to view objects as having an unchanging size, shape, color, and brightness, even if the image on our retina changes. For example, despite the varying size or shape of the images on the retina as an airplane approaches, flies overhead, and then disappears, we do not perceive the airplane as changing shape or size. Experience has taught us that the plane's size remains constant (Garrigan & Kellman, 2008; Sachse et al., 2017; Sato et al., 2019).

In some cases, though, our application of perceptual constancy can mislead us. One good example of this involves the rising moon. When the moon first appears at night, close to the horizon, it seems to be huge—much larger than when it is high in the sky later in the evening. You may have thought that the apparent change in the size of the moon was caused by the moon's being physically closer to the earth when it first appears. In fact, though, this is not the case at all: The actual image of the moon on our retina is the same, whether it is low or high in the sky.

Research offers several explanations for the moon illusion. One suggests that the moon appears to be larger when it is close to the horizon primarily because of perceptual constancy. When the moon is near the horizon, the perceptual cues of intervening terrain and objects such as trees on the horizon produce a misleading sense of distance, leading us to misperceive the moon as relatively large.

In contrast, when the moon is high in the sky, we see it by itself, and we don't try to compensate for its distance from us. In this case, then, perceptual constancy leads us to perceive it as relatively small. To experience perceptual constancy, try looking at the moon when it is relatively low on the horizon through a paper-towel tube; the moon suddenly will appear to "shrink" back to normal size (Rogers & Naumenko, 2015; Francis et al., 2019; Rudrauf et al., 2020).

Perceptual constancy is not the only explanation for the moon illusion, and it remains a puzzle to psychologists. It may be that several different perceptual processes are involved in the illusion (Gregory, 2008; Kim, 2008).

Motion Perception: As the World Turns

In the game of baseball, the most important factor determining a batter's success in hitting a ball pitched to them is the motion of the ball. How is a batter able to judge the speed and location of a pitched ball that is moving at some 90 miles per hour?

The answer rests in part on several cues that provide us with relevant information about the perception of motion. For one thing, the movement of an object across the retina is typically perceived relative to some stable, unmoving background. Moreover, if the stimulus is heading toward us, the image on the retina expands in size, filling more and more of the visual field. In such cases, we assume that the stimulus is approaching—not that it is an expanding stimulus viewed at a constant distance.

It is not, however, just the movement of images across the retina that brings about the perception of motion. If it were, we would perceive the world as moving every time we moved our heads. Instead, one of the critical things we learn about perception is to factor information about our own head and eye movements along with information about changes in the retinal image.

Sometimes we perceive motion when it doesn't occur. Have you ever been on a stationary train that feels as if it is moving because a train on an adjacent track begins to slowly move past? Or have you been in an IMAX movie theater in which you feel as if you were falling as a huge image of a plane moves across the screen? In both cases, the experience of motion is convincing. *Apparent movement* is the perception that a stationary object is moving. It occurs when different areas of the retina are quickly stimulated, leading us to interpret motion (Brandon & Saffran, 2011; Luo et al., 2019; Lin et al., 2021).

perceptual constancy Our understanding that physical objects are unvarying and consistent even though sensory input about them may vary. (Module 11)

Perceptual Illusions:
The Deceptions of Perceptions

If you look carefully at the Parthenon, one of the most famous buildings of ancient Greece, still standing at the top of an Athens hill, you'll see that it was built with a bulge on one side. If it didn't have that bulge–and quite a few other architectural "tricks" like it, such as columns that incline inward–it would look as if it were crooked and about to fall down. Instead, it appears to stand completely straight, at right angles to the ground.

The fact that the Parthenon appears to be completely upright is the result of a series of visual illusions. **Visual illusions** are physical stimuli that consistently produce errors in perception. In the case of the Parthenon, the building appears to be completely square, as illustrated in Figure 5a. However, if it had been built that way, it would look to us as it does in Figure 5b. The reason for this is an illusion that makes right angles placed above a line appear as if they were bent. To offset the illusion, the Parthenon was constructed as in Figure 5c, with a slight upward curvature.

The *Müller-Lyer illusion* (illustrated in Figure 6) has fascinated psychologists for decades. Although the two lines are the same length, the one with the arrow tips pointing outward, away from the vertical line (Figure 6a, left) appears to be shorter than the one with the arrow tips pointing inward (Figure 6a, right).

Although all kinds of explanations for visual illusions have been suggested, most concentrate either on the physical operation of the eye or on our misinterpretation of the visual stimulus. For example, one explanation for the Müller-Lyer illusion is that eye movements are greater when the arrow tips point inward, making us perceive the line as longer than it is when the arrow tips face outward. In contrast, a different explanation for the illusion suggests that we unconsciously attribute particular significance to each of the lines (Gregory, 1978). When we see the left line in Figure 6a, we tend to perceive it as if it were the relatively close outside corner of a rectangular

visual illusions Physical stimuli that consistently produce errors in perception. (Module 11)

Study Alert

The explanation for the Müller-Lyer illusion is complicated. Figure 6 will help you master it.

(a)

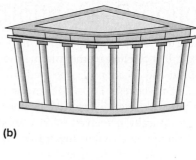

(b)

(c)

FIGURE 5 (a) In building the Parthenon, the Greeks constructed an architectural wonder that looks perfectly straight, with right angles at every corner. (b) However, if it had been built with completely true right angles, it would have looked as it does here. (c) To compensate for this illusion, the Parthenon was designed to have a slight upward curvature, as shown here.

(a): Mlenny Photography/E+/Getty Images; (b and c): Luckiesh, (1921)

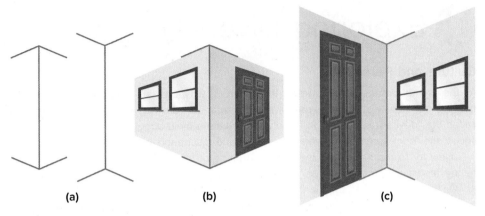

(a)   (b)   (c)

FIGURE 6 In the Müller-Lyer illusion (a), the vertical line on the left appears shorter than the one on the right, even though they are identical in length. One explanation for the Müller-Lyer illusion suggests that the line on the left (with arrow points directed outward) is perceived as the relatively close corner of a rectangular object, such as the building corner in (b), and the line on the right (with the arrow points directed inward) is interpreted as the inside corner of a rectangular object, such as the room extending away from us (c). Our previous experience with distance cues leads us to assume that the outside corner is closer than the inside corner and, consequently, the inside corner must be longer.

object, such as the outside corner of the room illustrated in Figure 6b. In contrast, when we view the line on the right in Figure 6a, we perceive it as the relatively more distant inside corner of a rectangular object, such as the inside room corner in Figure 6c. Because previous experience leads us to assume that the outside corner is closer than the inside corner, we make the further assumption that the inside corner must therefore be longer.

Despite the complexity of the latter explanation, a good deal of evidence supports it. For instance, cross-cultural studies show that people raised in areas where there are few right angles—such as the Zulu in Africa—are much less susceptible to the illusion than are people who grow up where most structures are built using right angles and rectangles (Segall et al., 1966; Fujita et al., 2017).

Optical illusions have been used to slow traffic, as these virtual speed bumps in Iceland illustrate. Although they appear to be hovering aboveground, in fact they are flush to the ground.
Thorir Ingvarsson/Shutterstock

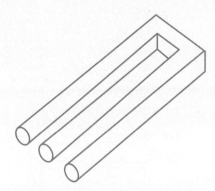

FIGURE 7 The "devil's tuning fork" has three prongs . . . or does it have two?

 # Exploring Diversity

Culture and Perception

As the example of the Zulu indicates, the culture in which we are raised has clear consequences for how we perceive the world. Consider the drawing in Figure 7. Sometimes called the "devil's tuning fork," it is likely to produce a mind-boggling effect, as the center tine of the fork alternates between appearing and disappearing.

Now try to reproduce the drawing on a piece of paper. Chances are that the task is nearly impossible for you—unless you are a member of an African tribe with little exposure to Western cultures. For such individuals, the task is simple; they have no trouble reproducing the figure. The reason is that Westerners automatically interpret the drawing as something that cannot exist in three dimensions, and they therefore are inhibited from reproducing it. The African tribal members, in contrast, do not make the assumption that the figure is "impossible" and instead view it in two dimensions, a perception that enables them to copy the figure with ease (Deregowski, 1973).

Cultural differences are also reflected in depth perception. A Western viewer of Figure 8 would most likely interpret the hunter in the drawing as aiming for the antelope in the foreground, while an elephant stands under the tree in the background. A member of certain isolated Bantu African tribes, however, is more apt to perceive the scene very differently and assume the hunter is aiming at the elephant. Because of their experience, Westerners use the difference in sizes between the two animals as a cue that the elephant is farther away than the antelope (Hudson, 1960; deBruïne et al., 2018).

Does this mean that basic perceptual processes differ among people of different cultures? No. Variations in learning and experience produce cross-cultural differences in perception, and the underlying psychological processes involved in perception are similar (Phillips, 2019).

FIGURE 8 Is the hunter aiming for the elephant or the antelope? Westerners assume that the difference in size between the two animals indicates that the elephant is farther away and, therefore, the man is aiming for the antelope. In contrast, members of certain isolated Bantu African tribes, who may be unfamiliar with depth cues in two-dimensional drawings, assume that the man is aiming for the elephant. Do you think people who view the picture in three dimensions could explain what they see to someone who views the scene in two dimensions and eventually get that person to view it in three dimensions?
Source: Hudson, 1960.

Although visual illusions may seem like mere psychological curiosities, they actually illustrate something fundamental about perception. There is a basic connection between our prior knowledge, needs, motivations, and expectations about how the world is put together and the way we perceive it. Our view of the world is very much an outcome, then, of fundamental psychological factors. Furthermore, each person perceives the environment in a way that is unique and special (Repp & Knoblich, 2007; Phillips, 2019).

SUBLIMINAL PERCEPTION

Can stimuli that we're not consciously aware of change our behavior? In some ways, yes.

Subliminal perception refers to the perception of messages about which we have no awareness. The stimulus could be a written word, a sound, or even a smell that activates the sensory system but that is not intense enough for a person to report having experienced it. For example, in some studies, people are exposed to a descriptive label–called a *prime*–about a person (such as the word *smart* or *happy*) so briefly that they cannot report seeing the label. Later, however, they form impressions that are influenced by the content of the prime. Somehow, they have been influenced by the prime that they say they couldn't see, providing some evidence for subliminal perception (Kawakami & Miura, 2015; Lucini et al., 2019; Railo et al., 2021).

Although subliminal messages (which social psychologists refer to as *priming*) can influence behavior in subtle ways, there's little evidence that they can lead to *major* changes in attitudes or behavior. Most research suggests that they cannot. For example, people who are subliminally exposed to an image of a Coke can and the word *thirst* do later rate themselves as thirstier, and they actually do drink more when given the opportunity. However, they don't particularly care if they drink Coke or some other liquid to quench their thirst (Dijksterhuis et al., 2007; Parkinson et al., 2017).

In short, although we are able to perceive at least some kinds of information of which we are unaware, there's little evidence that subliminal messages can change our attitudes or behavior in substantial ways. At the same time, subliminal perception does have at least some consequences. If our motivation to carry out a behavior is already high and the appropriate stimuli are presented subliminally, subliminal perception may have at least some effect on our behavior (Pratkanis et al., 2007; Randolph-Seng & Nielsen, 2009; Gafner, 2013; Lucini et al., 2019).

EXTRASENSORY PERCEPTION

Psychologists are highly skeptical of reports of *extrasensory perception*, or ESP–perception that does not involve our known senses. Although almost half of the general population of the United States believes it exists, most psychologists reject the existence of ESP, asserting that there is no sound documentation of the phenomenon (Moore, 2005; Branković, 2019).

However, a debate in one of the most prestigious psychology journals, *Psychological Bulletin*, heightened interest in ESP in the early 2000s. According to proponents of ESP, reliable evidence existed for an "anomalous process of information transfer," or *psi* (prounounced "sigh"). These researchers, who painstakingly reviewed considerable evidence, argued that a cumulative body of research shows reliable support for the existence of psi (Parra & Argibay, 2007; Storm & Rock, 2015; Branković, 2019).

Ultimately, their conclusion was challenged and largely discredited for several reasons. For example, critics suggested that the research methodology was inadequate and that the experiments supporting psi are flawed. Furthermore, attempts to replicate their results failed (Kennedy, 2004; Rouder et al., 2013).

Because of questions about the quality of the research, as well as a lack of any credible theoretical explanation for how extrasensory perception might take place, almost no reputable psychologists view it as having any reliable scientific support. Still, the topic continues to inspire research (Wiseman & Greening, 2002; Bem, 2012; Huang, 2019).

RECAP/EVALUATE/RETHINK

RECAP

LO 11-1 What principles underlie our organization of the visual world and allow us to make sense of our environment?

- Perception is a constructive process in which people go beyond the stimuli that are physically present and try to construct a meaningful interpretation.
- The Gestalt laws of organization are used to describe the way in which we organize bits and pieces of information into meaningful wholes, known as Gestalts, through closure, proximity, similarity, and simplicity.
- In top-down processing, perception is guided by higher-level knowledge, experience, expectations, and motivations. In bottom-up processing, perception consists of the progression of recognizing and processing information from individual components of a stimuli and moving to the perception of the whole.

LO 11-2 How are we able to perceive the world in three dimensions when our retinas are capable of sensing only two-dimensional images?

- Depth perception is the ability to perceive distance and view the world in three dimensions, even though the images projected on our retinas are two-dimensional. We are able to judge depth and distance as a result of binocular disparity and monocular cues, such as motion parallax, the relative size of images on the retina, and linear perspective.
- Perceptual constancy permits us to perceive stimuli as unvarying in size, shape, and color despite changes in the environment or the appearance of the objects being perceived.
- Motion perception depends on cues such as the perceived movement of an object across the retina and information about how the head and eyes are moving.

LO 11-3 What clues do visual illusions give us about our understanding of general perceptual mechanisms?

- Visual illusions are physical stimuli that consistently produce errors in perception, causing judgments that do not reflect the physical reality of a stimulus accurately. One of the best-known illusions is the Müller-Lyer illusion.
- Visual illusions are usually the result of errors in the brain's interpretation of visual stimuli. Furthermore, culture clearly affects how we perceive the world.

- Subliminal perception refers to the perception of messages about which we have no awareness. The reality of the phenomenon, as well as of ESP, is open to question and debate.

EVALUATE

1. Match each of the following organizational laws with its meaning:

   a. closure
   b. proximity
   c. similarity
   d. simplicity

   1. Elements close together are grouped together.
   2. Patterns are perceived in the most basic, direct manner possible.
   3. Groupings are made in terms of complete figures.
   4. Elements similar in appearance are grouped together.

2. _____ analysis deals with the way in which we break an object down into its component pieces in order to understand it.
3. Processing that involves higher functions such as expectations and motivations is known as _____, whereas processing that recognizes the individual components of a stimulus is known as _____.
4. When a car passes you on the road and appears to shrink as it gets farther away, the phenomenon of _____ _____ permits you to realize that the car is not in fact getting smaller.
5. _____ _____ is the ability to view the world in three dimensions instead of two.
6. The brain makes use of a phenomenon known as _____ _____, or the difference in the images the two eyes see, to give three dimensions to sight.

RETHINK

1. In what ways do painters represent three-dimensional scenes in two dimensions on a canvas? Do you think artists in non-Western cultures use the same or different principles to represent three-dimensionality? Why?
2. Can you think of examples of the combined use of top-down and bottom-up processing in everyday life? Is one type of processing superior to the other?

Answers to Evaluate Questions

1. a-3, b-1, c-4, d-2; 2. Feature; 3. top-down, bottom-up; 4. perceptual constancy; 5. Depth perception; 6. binocular disparity

KEY TERMS			
Gestalt (geh-SHTALLT) laws of organization	top-down processing bottom-up processing	depth perception perceptual constancy	visual illusions

LOOKING *Back*

EPILOGUE

We have noted the important distinction between sensation and perception, and we have examined the processes that underlie both of them. We've seen how external stimuli evoke sensory responses and how our different senses process the information contained in those responses. We also have focused on the physical structure and internal workings of the individual senses, including vision, hearing, balance, smell, taste, and the skin senses, and we've explored how our brains organize and process sensory information to construct a consistent, integrated picture of the world around us.

Before ending our discussion of sensation and perception, let's reconsider Michele Crippa, whom we met in the prologue of this chapter and who lost his sense of smell and taste due to a COVID-19 infection. Using your knowledge of sensation and perception, answer these questions:

1. COVID caused Crippa to lose his sense of smell entirely. Why did this also affect his sense of taste?
2. Crippa's "smell therapy" involved remembering instances in which he had experienced a particular smell. Why do you think this sort of therapy might be effective?
3. In what ways was Crippa's pre-COVID ability to smell and taste involved with his identity as a person? Might the loss of other senses have a similar impact on a person's identity? How?

Design Elements: Man with laptop: Dragon Images/Shutterstock; Exclamation point and mobile frame: McGraw Hill; Smartphone: WML Image/Shutterstock; Hands: Stefano Garau/Shutterstock.

VISUAL SUMMARY 3 Sensation and Perception

MODULE 8 Sensing the World

<u>Absolute thresholds</u>
<u>Difference thresholds</u>

- Just noticeable difference
- Weber's law

<u>Sensory Adaptation</u>

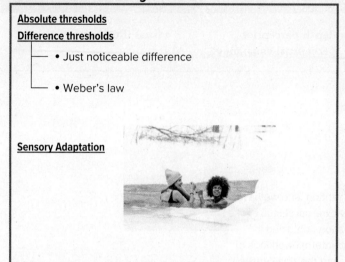

MODULE 9 Vision

<u>Eye Structure</u>

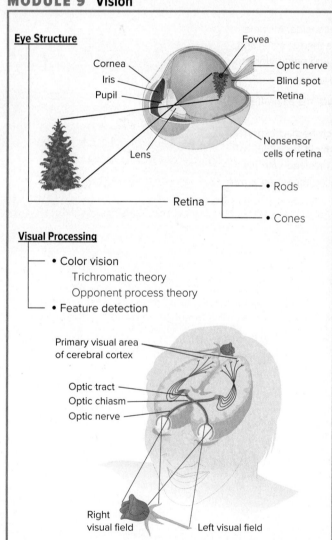

Cornea
Iris
Pupil
Fovea
Optic nerve
Blind spot
Retina
Nonsensor cells of retina
Lens

Retina
- Rods
- Cones

<u>Visual Processing</u>

- Color vision
  Trichromatic theory
  Opponent process theory
- Feature detection

Primary visual area of cerebral cortex
Optic tract
Optic chiasm
Optic nerve
Right visual field
Left visual field

MODULE 10 Hearing and Other Senses

<u>Ear Structure</u>

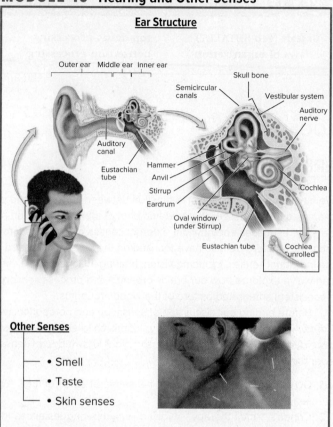

Outer ear Middle ear Inner ear

Skull bone
Semicircular canals
Vestibular system
Auditory nerve
Auditory canal
Eustachian tube
Hammer
Anvil
Stirrup
Eardrum
Cochlea
Oval window (under Stirrup)
Eustachian tube
Cochlea "unrolled"

<u>Other Senses</u>

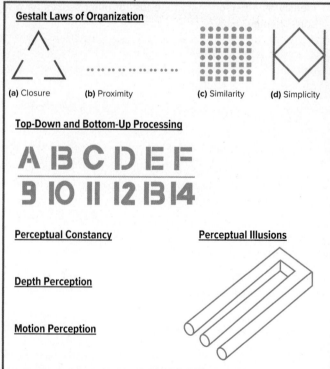

- Smell
- Taste
- Skin senses

MODULE 11 Perception

<u>Gestalt Laws of Organization</u>

(a) Closure **(b)** Proximity **(c)** Similarity **(d)** Simplicity

<u>Top-Down and Bottom-Up Processing</u>

A B C D E F
9 10 11 12 13 14

<u>Perceptual Constancy</u>

<u>Perceptual Illusions</u>

<u>Depth Perception</u>

<u>Motion Perception</u>

(Module 8) (photo): Michele Ursi/Alamy Stock Photo; (Module 10) (photo): Fuse/Corbis/Getty Images; (Module 11) Source: Coren & Ward, 1989.

Odua Images/Shutterstock

CHAPTER 4
States of Consciousness

LEARNING OUTCOMES FOR CHAPTER 4

	MODULE 12

	SLEEP AND DREAMS
LO 12-1 What are the states of consciousness?	The Stages of Sleep
LO 12-2 What happens when we sleep, and what are the meaning and function of dreams?	REM Sleep: The Paradox of Sleep
	Why Do We Sleep, and How Much Sleep Is Necessary?
	The Function and Meaning of Dreaming
LO 12-3 What are the major sleep disorders, and how can they be treated?	**Neuroscience in Your Life:** Brain Microstates During Dreaming
LO 12-4 How much do we daydream?	**Applying Psychology in the 21st Century:** We Interrupt This Dream for a Message from Our Sponsor
	Sleep Disturbances: Slumbering Problems
	Circadian Rhythms: Life Cycles
	Daydreams: Dreams Without Sleep
	Becoming an Informed Consumer of Psychology: Sleeping Better

	MODULE 13

	HYPNOSIS AND MEDITATION
LO 13-1 What is hypnosis, and are hypnotized people in a different state of consciousness?	Hypnosis: A Trance-Forming Experience?
	Meditation: Regulating Our Own State of Consciousness
LO 13-2 What are the effects of meditation?	**Exploring Diversity:** Cross-Cultural Routes to Altered States of Consciousness

LO 14-1 What are the major classifications of drugs, and what are their effects?

PROLOGUE *THE LAST HOPE*

Thirty-five-year-old Gerod Buckhalter had run out of choices. After almost 20 years of addiction to opioids and other drugs, and all that came with it—homelessness, death of friends, overdoses, failed stays at rehab centers—he thought he had tried it all.

Yet one radical option remained: brain surgery. Even though the surgery was experimental and largely untested, Buckhalter felt he had nothing to lose. So he allowed surgeons to drill two small holes in his skull and insert two 5-centimeter electrodes into his brain. The theory was that a brain pacemaker implanted in his chest, combined with electrical stimulation of the brain centers that controlled pleasurable sensations and decision making, could bring his craving for drugs under control.

Although the long-term consequences of the surgery won't be known for decades, the short-term results have been extraordinary—far more successful than even his most optimistic doctors had hoped. Buckhalter has been drug-free for several years following the operation. He says he has no cravings for drugs, his anxiety has been reduced, and his mood has improved.

The experimental surgery that helped rid Buckhalter of his drug addiction is not magical, say his doctors. He still needs other, more conventional treatments such as therapy. But it jumpstarted his ability to feel more in control and allows other treatments to be more effective (Bernstein, 2021).

LOOKING *Ahead*

Although his treatment was unusual, Gerod Buckhalter's addiction was far from unique. The United States is experiencing a full-blown opiate epidemic, with over 100,000 deaths from drug overdoses in 2021 alone. That's an increase of nearly 30% over the prior year and the largest number of deaths from overdoses ever recorded, attributed primarily to the COVID-19 pandemic. The number of deaths from drug overdoses is now higher than the highest yearly death rates from car crashes, gun violence, or the AIDS epidemic (Katz & Sanger-Katz, 2021; Hedegaard et al., 2021).

Opiates such as heroin and fentanyl promise relief from anxiety and stress, as well as physical pain. While we don't know exactly what drove Buckhalter to use narcotics, he clearly had a compelling desire to create an altered state of consciousness.

Why people seek to alter their consciousness, what conscious experience is, and how and why we can alter it are some of the questions we explore in this chapter.

Consciousness is the awareness of the sensations, thoughts, and feelings we are experiencing at a given moment. Consciousness is our subjective understanding of both the environment around us and our private internal world, unobservable to outsiders.

In *waking consciousness*, we are awake and aware of our thoughts, emotions, and perceptions. All other states of consciousness are considered *altered states of consciousness*. Among these, sleeping and dreaming occur naturally; drug use and hypnosis, in contrast, are methods of deliberately altering one's state of consciousness.

In the past, because consciousness is so personal a phenomenon, some psychologists were reluctant to study it. After all, who can say that your consciousness is similar to or, for that matter, different from anyone else's? Although the earliest psychologists, including William James (1890), saw the study of consciousness as central to the field, later psychologists suggested that it was out of bounds for the discipline. They argued that consciousness could be understood only by relying "unscientifically" on what experimental participants said they were experiencing. In this view, it was philosophers—not psychologists—who should speculate on such knotty issues as whether consciousness is separate from the physical body, how people know they exist, and how the body and mind are related to each other (Barresi, 2007; James, 2015; Berger, 2021).

Contemporary psychologists reject the view that the study of consciousness is unsuitable for the field of psychology. Instead, they argue that several approaches permit the scientific study of consciousness. For example, behavioral neuroscientists can measure brain-wave patterns under conditions of consciousness ranging from sleep to waking to hypnotic trances. Furthermore, new understanding of the chemistry of drugs such as marijuana

consciousness The awareness of the sensations, thoughts, and feelings being experienced at a given moment. (Module 12)

and alcohol has provided insights into the way they produce their pleasurable—as well as adverse—effects (Bonin et al., 2021; Halsband & Wolf, 2021).

Moreover, researchers can objectively compare the experience of consciousness across cultures. For example, psychologists have examined the ways in which people in a variety of cultures seek and experience altered states of consciousness by inducing trances or by ingesting drugs, plants, or even substances from the glands of animals. Finally, new cross-species insights about the functioning of the brain are helping scientists explore whether consciousness is a uniquely human quality (Ember & Carolus, 2017; Liechti et al., 2017; Mora et al., 2019).

Yet precisely how humans experience consciousness remains an open question. Some psychologists believe that the experience of consciousness is produced by a quantitative increase in neuronal activity that occurs throughout the brain. For

example, an alarm clock moves us from sleep to waking consciousness by its loud ringing, which stimulates neurons throughout the brain as a whole (Ward, 2011; Blackmore, 2018; Arce & Winkelman, 2021).

In contrast, others believe that states of consciousness are produced by particular sets of neurons and neuronal pathways that are activated in specific ways. In this view, an alarm clock wakes us from sleep into consciousness because specific neurons related to the auditory nerve are activated; the auditory nerve then sends a message to other neurons to release particular neurotransmitters that produce awareness of the alarm (Saper, 2013; Schurger et al., 2015).

Although we don't know yet which of these views is correct, it is clear that whatever state of consciousness we are in—be it waking, sleeping, hypnotic, or drug-induced—the complexities of consciousness are profound.

Module 12
Sleep and Dreams

LEARNING OUTCOMES

LO 12-1 What are the states of consciousness?

LO 12-2 What happens when we sleep, and what are the meaning and function of dreams?

LO 12-3 What are the major sleep disorders, and how can they be treated?

LO 12-4 How much do we daydream?

During a 9-day cross-country bike race, 29-year-old Mike Trevino averaged 1 hour of sleep per day. The first 3 days he didn't sleep at all, and over the next 6, he took completely dream-free naps of at most 90 minutes. His waking thoughts became fuzzy, depicting movielike plots starring himself and his crew. The whole experience was like a serial dream in which he remained conscious, if only barely. He finished in second place.

Trevino's case is unusual–in part because he was able to function with so little sleep for so long–and it raises a host of questions about sleep and dreams. Can we live without sleep? What is the meaning of dreams? More generally, what is sleep?

Although sleeping is a state that we all experience, many unanswered questions about it remain, along with a considerable number of myths. Test your knowledge of sleep and dreams by answering the questionnaire in Figure 1.

Sleep Quiz

Although sleeping is something we all do for a significant part of our lives, myths and misconceptions about the topic abound. Check your knowledge by reading each statement below and check True or False.

1. It is a proven fact that 8 hours of sleep are needed to remain mentally healthy.
☐ True   ☐ False

2. Sleep "turns off" most brain activity to promote brain rest and recovery.
☐ True   ☐ False

3. Sleep deprivation always causes mental imbalance.
☐ True   ☐ False

4. It is impossible to go more than 48 hours without sleep.
☐ True   ☐ False

5. If we lose sleep we can always make it up another night or on the weekend.
☐ True   ☐ False

6. The best long-term cure for sleeplessness is regular use of insomnia medications.
☐ True   ☐ False

7. Dreams are most often the result of stomach distress caused by what and when we eat.
☐ True   ☐ False

8. When we are asleep and dreaming, our muscles are the most relaxed they can get.
☐ True   ☐ False

9. If you can't remember your dreams, it's because you want to forget them.
☐ True   ☐ False

10. Many people never dream.
☐ True   ☐ False

Scoring: It is easy to score this quiz because every statement is false. But don't lose any sleep if you missed a few; these are among the most widely held misconceptions about sleeping and dreaming.

FIGURE 1 Taking this quiz can help you clear up some of the myths that exist around sleep.

Sources: Adapted from Maas, 2016; Palladino & Carducci, 1984.

The Stages of Sleep

Most of us consider sleep a time of tranquility when we set aside the tensions of the day and spend the night in uneventful slumber. However, a closer look at sleep shows that a good deal of activity occurs throughout the night.

Measures of electrical activity show that the brain is quite active during sleep. It produces electrical discharges with systematic, wavelike patterns that change in height (or amplitude) and speed (or frequency) in regular sequences. There is also significant physical activity in the muscles and eyes.

People progress through a series of distinct stages of sleep during a night's rest—known as *stage 1, stage 2, stage 3,* and *REM sleep*—moving through the stages in cycles lasting about 90 minutes. Each of these sleep stages is associated with a unique pattern of brain waves, which you can see in Figure 2.

When people first go to sleep, they move from a waking state in which they are relaxed with their eyes closed into **stage 1 sleep,** which is characterized by relatively rapid, low-amplitude brain waves. This is actually a stage of transition between wakefulness and sleep and lasts only a few minutes. During stage 1, images sometimes appear, as if we were viewing still photos, although this is not true dreaming, which occurs later in the night.

As sleep becomes deeper, people enter **stage 2 sleep,** which makes up about half of the total sleep of those in their early 20s and is characterized by a slower, more regular wave pattern. However, there are also momentary interruptions of sharply pointed, spiky waves that are called, because of their configuration, *sleep spindles.* It becomes increasingly difficult to awaken a person from sleep as stage 2 progresses.

As people drift into **stage 3 sleep,** the deepest stage, the brain waves become slower, with higher peaks and lower valleys in the wave pattern. During stage 3, people are least responsive to outside stimulation.

As you can see in Figure 3, stage 3 sleep is most likely to occur during the early part of the night. In the first half of the night, sleep is dominated by stage 3. The second half is characterized by stages 1 and 2—as well as a fourth stage, REM sleep, during which dreams occur.

stage 1 sleep The state of transition between wakefulness and sleep, characterized by relatively rapid, low-amplitude brain waves. (Module 12)

stage 2 sleep A sleep deeper than that of stage 1, characterized by a slower, more regular wave pattern, along with momentary interruptions of "sleep spindles." (Module 12)

stage 3 sleep The deepest stage of sleep, during which we are least responsive to outside stimulation. (Module 12)

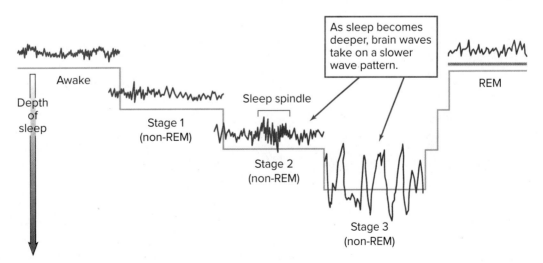

FIGURE 2 Brain-wave patterns (measured by an EEG apparatus) vary significantly during the different stages of sleep. As sleep moves from stage 1 through stage 3, brain waves become slower. During REM sleep, however, the fast wave patterns are similar to relaxed wakefulness.
Sources: Hobson, 2007 and Jawabri & Raja, 2021.

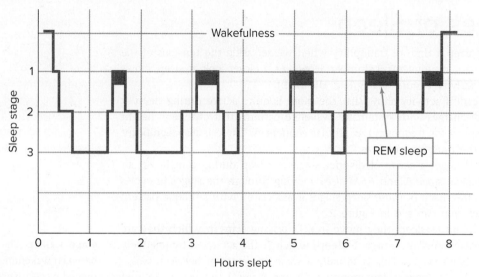

FIGURE 3 During the night, the typical sleeper passes through all three stages of sleep and several REM periods.
Source: Hartmann, 1967.

REM Sleep: The Paradox of Sleep

Several times a night, when sleepers have cycled back to a shallower state of sleep, something curious happens. Their heart rate increases and becomes irregular, their blood pressure rises, and their breathing rate increases. Most characteristic of this period is that their eyes move rapidly, as if they were watching an action-filled movie.

rapid eye movement (REM) sleep
Sleep occupying 20% of an adult's sleeping time, characterized by increased heart rate, blood pressure, and breathing rate; erections; eye movements; and the experience of dreaming. (Module 12)

This stage of sleep is called rapid eye movement sleep. **Rapid eye movement, or REM, sleep,** is characterized by quick, back-and-forth eye movements, and it contrasts with stages 1 through 3, which are collectively labeled *non-REM* (or *NREM*) sleep. REM sleep occupies a little more than 20% of adults' total sleeping time.

While heart rate, blood pressure, and breathing increase during REM sleep, the major muscles of the body appear to be paralyzed. In addition, and most important, REM sleep is usually accompanied by dreams, which–whether or not people remember

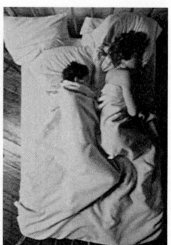

People progress through three distinct stages of sleep during a night's rest spread over cycles lasting about 90 minutes. REM sleep occupies only 20% of adults' sleeping time. These photos, taken at different times of night, show the synchronized patterns of a couple accustomed to sleeping in the same bed.
Ted Spagna/Science Source

them—occur for *everyone* during some part of their night's sleep. Although some dreaming occurs in non-REM stages of sleep, dreams are most likely to occur in the REM period, where they are the most vivid and easily remembered (Blagrove et al., 2019; Malinowski & Horton, 2021; Reinoso-Suárez et al., 2022).

There is good reason to believe that REM sleep plays a critical role in everyday human functioning. People deprived of REM sleep—by being awakened every time they begin to display the physiological signs of that stage—show a *rebound effect* when allowed to rest undisturbed. With this rebound effect, REM-deprived sleepers spend significantly more time in REM sleep than they normally would. In addition, REM sleep may play a role in learning and memory, allowing us to rethink and restore information and emotional experiences that we've had during the day (Nielsen et al., 2015; Karabulut et al., 2019; Eagleman & Vaughn, 2021).

Although the stages of sleep appear to occur universally, in all humans, we know very little about racial, ethnic, or cross-cultural differences in the amount of time spent in the various sleep stages. As in many other areas of investigation, the vast majority of research on the physiology of sleep has been carried out on White research participants living in Western cultures. Still, one study that looked at sleep stages in a sample of White Americans, Black Americans, Mexican Americans, and Asian Americans found some differences between groups. However, the differences did not fall into any clear patterns, and we don't know if they have a practical impact on the experience of sleep (Rao et al., 2009; Ahn et al., 2021).

Study Alert
Differentiate the stages of sleep (stage 1, stage 2, stage 3, and REM sleep), which produce different brain-wave patterns.

From the perspective of...

An Educator How might you use the findings in sleep research to maximize student learning?

Andersen Ross/Blend Images/Getty Images

Why Do We Sleep, and How Much Sleep Is Necessary?

Sleep is a requirement for normal human functioning, although, surprisingly, the reason why has long baffled scientists. It certainly is reasonable to expect that our bodies would require a tranquil "rest and relaxation" period to revitalize themselves, and experiments with rats show that total sleep deprivation results in death. But why?

Although it doesn't directly answer that question, the practices in some cultures highlight the importance they place on getting a good night's sleep. For example, indigenous people of the highlands of Guatemala make "worry dolls" of wood, wire, and cloth. According to cultural legend, by telling the doll one's worries before bedtime and placing it under the pillow, people can sleep soundly, as the dolls take over the worrying (Abrams, 2017).

Today, scientists suggest four reasons why sleep is a requirement for life:

- **Sleep conserves energy for essential daytime activities.** One explanation, based on an evolutionary perspective, suggests that sleep permitted our ancestors to conserve energy at night, a time when food was relatively hard to come by. Consequently, they were better able to forage for food when the sun was up. This reasoning has been supported by new findings that even some organisms that lack brains, such as jellyfish, show signs of sleeping (Pennisi, 2021).

- **Sleep restores and replenishes.** A second explanation for why we sleep is that sleep restores and replenishes our brains and bodies. For instance, the reduced activity of the brain during non-REM sleep may give neurons a chance to repair themselves. That reduced activity may also weaken connections between particular nerve cells to conserve energy, which has the effect of aiding memory. Furthermore, the onset of REM sleep stops the release of neurotransmitters called *monoamines* and so permits receptor cells to get necessary rest and to increase their sensitivity during periods of wakefulness (Tononi & Cirelli, 2013; Menon et al., 2019; Cools & Arnsten, 2022).

- **Sleep helps forgetting.** Another primary purpose of sleep may be to help us forget. In this view, sleep allows the brain to eliminate unnecessary information that accumulates throughout the day so that it doesn't become burdensome or confusing, a process called *reverse learning* (Heller et al., 2014: Feld & Born, 2017).

- **Sleep promotes physical growth and development.** Finally, sleep may assist physical growth and brain development in children. For example, the release of growth hormones is associated with deep sleep (Grigg-Damberger, 2017; Knoop et al., 2021).

Although these explanations are plausible, they remain speculative, and we have no definitive answer as to why sleep is essential. What is increasingly clear is that sleep serves multiple functions and that without sleep, we cannot survive (Stickgold, 2015; Nakada & Sadoshima, 2021).

Yet we still don't know how much is absolutely required. Most people sleep between 7 and 8 hours each night, which is 3 hours a night *less* than people slept a hundred years ago.

In addition, individuals vary widely in how much sleep they report needing, with some people saying they need as little as 3 hours of sleep to feel refreshed. Overall, though, for most people, the more sleep they get, the greater their sense of well-being. However, there are limits to how much sleep is beneficial, and excessive sleep has been linked to health problems such as depression, diabetes, and heart disease (Gariépy et al., 2019; Takeuchi et al., 2020; Antza et al., 2022).

Men and women sleep differently. Women typically fall asleep more quickly, they sleep for longer periods and more deeply than men do, and they get up fewer times in the night. On the other hand, men typically have fewer concerns about the amount of sleep they get than women do, even though they get less sleep. Furthermore, sleep requirements vary over the course of a lifetime: As they age, people generally need less and less sleep (Monk et al., 2011; Petersen, 2011; Jonasdottir et al., 2021; see Figure 4).

Among its many impacts on our lives, the COVID-19 pandemic led to changes in sleeping patterns. For some people, the stress of work disruptions, home-schooling of children, and changes in living arrangements meant they they got less sleep. Other people spent so much time in their homes that they ended up sleeping excessively (as well as eating too much: many people gained weight during the pandemic) (Shillington et al., 2021).

INEQUITIES IN SLEEP DURATION AND DEPTH

Although sleep experts believe that 7 to 9 hours of sleep each night is optimal for adults, many people are unable to get that much sleep because of work and family responsibilities, housing issues, and other environmental factors. Furthermore, research finds significant disparities between racial minorities in terms of how much they report sleeping each night. Overall, people of color take more time to fall asleep, they wake up more frequently during the night, and they spend less time in deep sleep stages (Stern, 2021; see Figure 5).

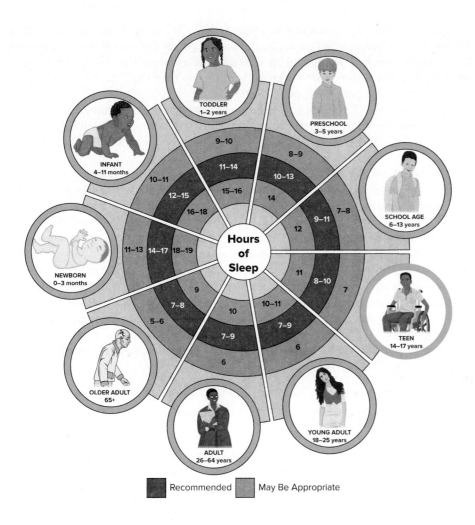

FIGURE 4 Although most adults sleep between 7 and 8 hours each night, the amount that individuals need varies a great deal. Where would you place yourself on this graph, and why do you think you need more or less sleep than others? Source: Suni, 2023.

Moreover, in comparison to Whites, individuals who are Black, Hispanic, or Chinese American report that on average, they are more likely to get extreme levels of sleep, some reporting lower levels and others reporting higher levels. The COVID-19 pandemic has further aggravated these racial disparities in sleep (Ahn et al., 2021; Cheng et al., 2021).

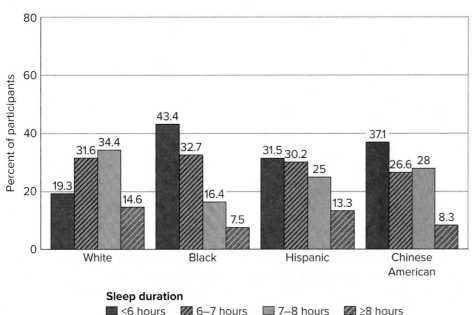

FIGURE 5 **Racial disparities in sleep**. Although sleep experts recommend that 7 to 9 hours of sleep are ideal, people of color are far more likely than White people to sleep less than 6 hours per night. Source: Stern, 2021.

Sleep deprivation is a worldwide phenomenon. The duration and quality of sleep are lower in underdeveloped countries and among poorer individuals in rich countries. For example, research conducted in Chennai, India, found that low-income urban-dwellers averaged 5.58 hours of sleep a night, far less than the 7 to 9 hours per night recommended by experts (Rao et al., 2021).

Extreme levels of sleep matter because, as mentioned earlier, they are associated with negative health and psychological outcomes. For example, sleep helps protect against disease, and it is associated with reduced levels of stress (Kingsbury et al., 2013; Ahn et al., 2021).

On the other hand, short-term sleep deficits are not particularly harmful. People who participate in sleep-deprivation experiments, in which they are kept awake for stretches as long as 200 hours, show no lasting effects. Still, it's no fun. They feel weary and irritable, can't concentrate, and show a loss of creativity, even after only minor deprivation. They also show a decline in logical-reasoning ability. However, after being allowed to sleep normally, they bounce back quickly and are able to perform at predeprivation levels after just a few days (Mograss et al., 2009; Jackson et al., 2013; Maturana et al., 2015).

In short, as far as we know, most people suffer no permanent consequences of such temporary sleep deprivation. But–and this is an important *but*–a lack of sleep can make us feel edgy, slow our reaction time, and lower our performance on academic and physical tasks. In addition, we put ourselves and others at risk when we carry out routine activities, such as driving, when we're very sleepy (Simon et al., 2017; Lewis, 2021).

The Function and Meaning of Dreaming

I was being chased, and I couldn't get away. My attacker, wearing a mask, was carrying a long knife. The attacker was gaining ground on me. I felt it was hopeless; I knew I was about to be killed.

If you have had dreams like this, you know how utterly convincing they can be. *Nightmares* are unusually frightening dreams. Perhaps surprisingly, they occur fairly often. In one survey, almost half of a group of college students who kept records of their dreams over a 2-week period reported having at least one nightmare. Furthermore, nightmares often are associated with negative experiences during the day, including worry and anxiety. For example, during the COVID-19 pandemic, people reported more frequent nightmares. Similarly, when racial protests reached their peak after the murder of George Floyd in 2020, people experienced nightmares that contained more distress and anxiety (Reks et al., 2017; Bulkeley, 2020; Scarpelli et al., 2021).

However, most of the 150,000 dreams the average person experiences by the age of 70 are much less dramatic. They typically encompass everyday events such as going to the supermarket, working at the office, and preparing a meal. Students dream about going to class; professors dream about lecturing. Dental patients dream of getting their teeth drilled; dentists dream of drilling the wrong tooth. The English have tea with the queen in their dreams; in the United States, people hang out at a bar with the president (Taylor & Bryant, 2007; Nosek et al., 2015; Scarpelli et al., 2021).

During the COVID-19 pandemic, some people had more emotional dreams, and the topics of their dreams reflected pandemic-related themes. For example, Brazilian adults who were socially isolated because of the pandemic reported a higher percentage of dreams referring to anger, contamination, and cleanliness (Neilsen, 2020; Pesonen et al., 2020; Schredl & Bulkeley, 2020; see Figure 6, which shows the most common themes found in people's dreams during the pandemic).

But what, if anything, do all these dreams mean? Whether dreams have a specific significance and function is a question that scientists have considered for many years, and they have developed the three alternative theories we discuss below (and summarize in Figure 7).

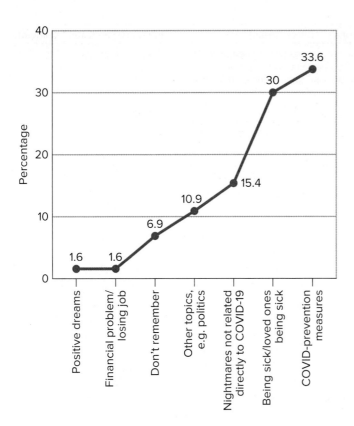

FIGURE 6 Topics of dreams related to COVID-19 during the pandemic.
Source: Schredl & Bulkeley, 2020.

Study Alert
Use Figure 7 to learn the differences between the three main explanations of dreaming.

Theory	Basic Explanation	Meaning of Dreams	Is Meaning of Dream Disguised?
Unconscious wish fulfillment theory (Freud)	Psychoanalytical explanation in which dreams represent unconscious wishes the dreamer wants to fulfill	Latent content reveals unconscious wishes.	Yes, by manifest content of dreams
Dreams-for-survival theory	Evolutionary explanation in which information relevant to daily survival is reconsidered and reprocessed	Clues to everyday concerns about survival	Not necessarily
Activation-synthesis theory	Neuroscience explanation in which dreams are the result of random activation of various memories, which are tied together in a logical story line	Dream scenario that is constructed is related to dreamer's concerns.	Not necessarily

FIGURE 7 Three theories of dreams. As researchers have yet to agree on the fundamental meaning of dreams, several theories about dreaming have emerged.

PSYCHOANALYTIC EXPLANATIONS OF DREAMS: DO THEY REPRESENT UNCONSCIOUS WISH FULFILLMENT?

Using psychoanalytic theory, Sigmund Freud viewed dreams as a guide to the unconscious (Freud, 1900). In his **unconscious wish fulfillment theory,** he proposed that dreams represent unconscious wishes that dreamers desire to see fulfilled. To Freud, the *manifest content* of the dream is what we remember and report about the dream—its story line. The manifest content, however, disguises the *latent content*, which includes the actual, underlying wishes that the dream represents. Because the underlying wishes

unconscious wish fulfillment theory Sigmund Freud's theory that dreams represent unconscious wishes that dreamers desire to see fulfilled. (Module 12)

Symbol (Manifest Content of Dream)	Interpretation (Latent Content)
Climbing up a stairway, crossing a bridge, riding an elevator, flying in an airplane, walking down a long hallway, entering a room, train traveling through a tunnel	Sexual intercourse
Apples, peaches, grapefruits	Breasts
Bullets, fire, snakes, sticks, umbrellas, guns, hoses, knives	Male sex organs
Ovens, boxes, tunnels, closets, caves, bottles, ships	Female sex organs

FIGURE 8 According to Freud, dreams contain common symbols with universal meanings.
Progressman/Shutterstock

(the latent content) are threatening to the dreamer, they are hidden in the dream's story line (the manifest content).

Freud wanted to pierce the armor of a dream's manifest content to understand its true meaning. To do this, he tried to get people to discuss their dreams, associating symbols in the dreams with events in the past. He also suggested that certain common symbols with universal meanings appear in dreams. For example, to Freud, dreams in which a person is flying symbolize a wish for sexual intercourse. (See Figure 8 for other common symbols.)

Most psychologists reject Freud's view that dreams typically represent unconscious wishes and that particular objects and events in a dream are symbolic. Rather, they believe that the direct, overt action of a dream is the focal point of its meaning. For example, a dream in which we are walking down a long hallway to take an exam for which we haven't studied does not relate to unconscious, unacceptable wishes. Instead, it simply may mean that we are concerned about an impending test. Even more complex dreams can often be interpreted in terms of everyday concerns and stress (Cartwright et al., 2006; Boag, 2017).

However, PET brain scan research does lend a degree of support for the wish fulfillment view. For instance, the limbic and paralimbic regions of the brain, which are associated with emotion and motivation, are particularly active during REM sleep. At the same time, the association areas of the prefrontal cortex, which control logical analysis and attention, are inactive during REM sleep. The high activation of emotional and motivational centers of the brain during dreaming makes it more plausible that dreams may reflect unconscious wishes and instinctual needs, as Freud suggested (Occhionero, 2004; Wehrle et al., 2007; Perogamvros & Schwartz, 2015).

EVOLUTIONARY EXPLANATIONS OF DREAMS: DREAMS-FOR-SURVIVAL THEORY

dreams-for-survival theory The theory suggesting that dreams permit information that is critical for our daily survival to be reconsidered and reprocessed during sleep. (Module 12)

According to the **dreams-for-survival theory,** which is based in the evolutionary perspective, dreams permit us to reconsider and reprocess during sleep information that is critical for our daily survival. Dreaming is considered an inheritance from our animal ancestors, whose small brains were unable to sift sufficient information during waking hours. Consequently, dreaming provided a mechanism that permitted the processing of information 24 hours a day.

In the dreams-for-survival theory, dreams represent concerns about our daily lives, illustrating our uncertainties, indecisions, ideas, and desires. Dreams are seen, then, as consistent with everyday living. Rather than being disguised wishes, as Freud suggested, they represent key concerns growing out of our daily experiences (Ross, 2006; Horton, 2011).

Research supports the dreams-for-survival theory, suggesting that certain dreams permit people to focus on and to consolidate memories, particularly dreams that pertain to "how-to-do-it" memories related to motor skills. For example, rats seem to dream about mazes that they learned to run through during the day, at least according to the patterns of brain activity that appear while they are sleeping. Moreover, dreams seem to allow the brain to erase erroneous connections between various pieces of information (such as mistakes made navigating a maze) and to establish new, more accurate connections (Girardeau & Lopes-dos-Santos, 2021; Rosen, 2021; Zadra & Stickgold, 2021).

The relevance of dreaming in the consolidation of memories is also seen in humans. For instance, in one experiment, participants learned a visual memory task late in the day. They were then sent to bed but awakened at certain times during the night. When they were awakened at times that did not interrupt dreaming, their performance on the memory task typically improved the next day. But when they were awakened during rapid eye movement (REM) sleep–the stage of sleep when people dream–their performance declined. The implication is that dreaming, at least when it is uninterrupted, can play a role in helping us remember material to which we have been previously exposed (Marshall & Born, 2007; Nishida et al., 2009; Blechner, 2013; Schoch et al., 2019).

NEUROSCIENCE EXPLANATIONS OF DREAMS: ACTIVATION-SYNTHESIS THEORY

Using the neuroscience perspective, psychiatrist J. Allan Hobson has proposed the activation-synthesis theory of dreams. The **activation-synthesis theory** focuses on the random electrical energy that the brain produces during REM sleep, possibly as a result of changes in the production of particular neurotransmitters. This electrical energy randomly stimulates memories stored in the brain. Because we have a need to make sense of our world even while asleep, the brain takes these chaotic memories and weaves them into a logical story line, filling in the gaps to produce a rational scenario (Hobson, 2005; Hangya et al., 2011).

Activation-synthesis theory has been refined by the *activation information modulation (AIM) theory*. According to AIM theory, dreams are initiated in the brain's pons, which sends random signals to the cortex. Areas of the cortex that are involved in particular waking behaviors are related to the content of dreams. For example, areas of the brain related to vision are involved in the visual aspects of the dream, whereas areas of the brain related to movement are involved in aspects of the dream related to motion (Hobson, 2007).

Activation-synthesis and AIM theories do not entirely reject the view that dreams reflect unconscious wishes. They suggest that the particular scenario a dreamer produces is not random but instead is a clue to the dreamer's fears, emotions, and concerns. Hence, what starts out as a random process culminates in something meaningful. (Also see the *Neuroscience in Your Life* and *Applying Psychology in the 21st Century* features.)

activation-synthesis theory Hobson's theory that the brain produces random electrical energy during REM sleep that stimulates memories stored in the brain. (Module 12)

NEUROSCIENCE IN YOUR LIFE: BRAIN MICROSTATES DURING DREAMING

Since neuroscientists can now measure the brain's electrical activity on the scale of milliseconds, they are learning a great deal about our mental states. And one perhaps surprising discovery is that human consciousness consists of a series of mental states, each one lasting only fractions of seconds—some less than 200 milliseconds—called microstates. Sleep, hypnosis, meditation, and other altered states of consciousness can influence how these microstates fluctuate over time.

A recent study examined whether microstates during non-rapid eye movement (NREM) sleep affect the experience and, later, the recollection of dreams. In the study, researchers measured EEG while participants slept and intentionally woke them periodically. After being awakened, the participants reported whether they had been dreaming, and they also tried to recall the content of any dreams they had. The researchers then compared brain electrical activity during periods when participants had been dreaming versus when they had not been dreaming. The study identified two distinct microstates during NREM sleep. One primarily involved activity in the prefrontal cortex, which was more visible and longer lasting when participants were dreaming. The other microstate consisted of more activity in posterior regions of the brain, and it was less visible when participants were dreaming (Bréchet et al., 2020).

Since the prefrontal cortex plays important roles in cognitive and emotional functioning, the increased prefrontal activity during dreams may explain why some dreams are so vivid. This type of research can give us a deeper understanding of sleep disorders as well as altered states of consciousness, such as meditation.

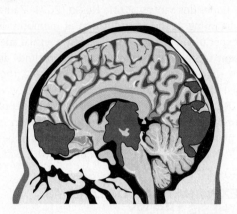

During dreaming, electrical activity in the brain increased in prefrontal brain regions (in red) and decreased in the brainstem and in posterior brain regions (in purple).

APPLYING PSYCHOLOGY IN THE 21ST CENTURY

WE INTERRUPT THIS DREAM FOR A MESSAGE FROM OUR SPONSOR

As far back as the1950s, advertisers began devising tactics to insert their commercial messages into people's minds without their awareness. Whether by playing subaudible message or flashing images on screens too briefly to be consciously perceived, the idea was to influence the target's motivations or consumer behavior by implanting a subliminal marketing message. The public was understandably not too keen on being manipulated in this fashion, but it hardly mattered because subliminal advertising just didn't work (Stanton et al., 2017; Madan et al., 2021; Moutinho, 2021).

But flash forward to the present day, and we find advertisers taking a new approach. Rather than subliminal implantation, marketers are now hoping to erect billboards in our dreams—our literal dreams, that is. And as much as that sounds like the stuff of science fiction, the tactic actually has a basis in research.

It is already fairly easy to infer a person's sleep stage and likelihood of being engaged in a dream from hardware such as a Fitbit or other similar fitness monitors and smart watches. The popularity of these devices is opening

Could advertisers use the time we are sleeping to insert cues that become the subject of dreams?
Emmanuel Faure/The Image Bank/Getty Images

the door to the next step: dream manipulation (Owens & Cribb, 2019).

Researchers have shown that external stimuli, such as specific visual or audio cues presented at just the right time, can trigger specific dream content—a process called *dream incubation*. As a simple analogy, many people have had the experience of incorporating the buzzing of their alarm clock into their dream just

before the alarm clock woke them (Stickgold et al., 2000; Schoeller et al., 2019; Barrett, 2020).

Some researchers are concerned that the technology is already in place for advertisers to implant advertising messages in our dreams. A fitness watch on the sleeper's wrist and a smart speaker in the bedroom, both connected to the web, may be all that's necessary. Specifically, an advertiser could potentially "insert" an external stimuli (such as an audio cue of someone playing an Xbox game or the sound of a can of Coke being opened) at a point in sleep in which the sleeper was already dreaming.

Privacy advocates are quick to point out that such practices would probably run counter to established law, at least in the United States, and dream researchers remain doubtful that any such manipulation could actually alter the dreamers' behavior while awake. Still, at least a few corporations are already looking into dream incubation, though to what end remains to be seen (Moutinho, 2021).

QUESTIONS TO CONSIDER

1. Would you have concerns about marketers incubating people's dreams with advertising messages? Why or why not?
2. If dream incubation can be made to work reliably, what socially beneficial uses might it have?

Sleep Disturbances: Slumbering Problems

At one time or another, almost all of us have difficulty sleeping—a condition known as insomnia. It could be due to a particular situation, such as the breakup of a relationship, concern about a test score, or the loss of a job. Some cases of insomnia, however, have no obvious cause. Some people are simply unable to fall asleep easily, or they go to sleep readily but wake up frequently during the night.

Insomnia is a problem that afflicts as many as one-third of all people. Women and older adults are the most likely to suffer from it, as well as people who are unusually thin or are depressed. In addition, sleep difficulties increased during the COVID-19 pandemic; more people reported having sleep problems than before its start. Moreover, people who suffer from long-term COVID often report sleep difficulties among the symptoms of the disease (Abrams, 2017; Ong, 2017; Hallit et al., 2019; Abrams, 2021).

Research has also found racial disparities in insomnia. For example, the discrimination that racial minorities face appears to be a factor in their higher rates of insomnia. Moreover, research shows that Blacks, Hispanics, and Asian Americans tend to live in areas that have greater noise and light pollution throughout the night, which can clearly affect one's susceptibility to insomnia. Moreover, people of color work night shifts or overtime more frequently than White workers, which can disrupt their sleep cycles and lead to insomnia (Johnson et al., 2016; Cheng et al., 2021).

Some people who *think* they have sleeping problems actually are mistaken. For example, researchers in sleep laboratories have found that some people who report being up all night actually fall asleep in 30 minutes and stay asleep all night. Furthermore, some people with insomnia accurately recall sounds that they heard while they were asleep, which gives them the impression that they were awake during the night (Crönlein et al., 2019; Hermans et al., 2020; Ma et al., 2021).

Many people struggle with insomnia, the most common sleep disorder.
Koldunova Anna/Shutterstock

Other sleep problems are less common than insomnia, although they are still widespread. For instance, some 20 million people suffer from sleep apnea. *Sleep apnea* is a condition in which a person has difficulty breathing while sleeping. The result is disturbed, fitful sleep and a significant loss of REM sleep, as the person is constantly reawakened when the lack of oxygen becomes great enough to trigger a waking response. The incidence of sleep apnea is higher in males than females, and it occurs significantly more in Blacks, and in particular, more in younger adult male Blacks than in Whites (Spilsbury et al., 2015; Ratz et al., 2018).

Some people with apnea wake as many as 500 times during the course of a night, although they may not even be aware that they have wakened. Not surprisingly, such disturbed sleep results in extreme fatigue the next day. Sleep apnea also may play a role in *sudden infant death syndrome (SIDS)*—now sometimes called *sudden unexpected infant death (SUID)*—in which without any obvious cause, seemingly normal infants die while sleeping (Bjornsdottir et al., 2015; Kim et al., 2022).

Night terrors are sudden awakenings from non-REM sleep that are accompanied by extreme fear, panic, and strong physiological arousal. Night terrors may be so frightening that a sleeper awakens screaming. Although night terrors initially produce great agitation, victims usually can get back to sleep fairly quickly. They are far less frequent than nightmares, and, unlike nightmares, they typically occur during stage 3, non-REM sleep. They occur most frequently in children between the ages of 3 and 8 (Lowe et al., 2007; Sasayama et al., 2016).

Narcolepsy is uncontrollable sleeping that occurs for short periods while a person is awake. No matter what the activity—holding a heated conversation, exercising, or driving—a narcoleptic will suddenly fall asleep. People with narcolepsy go directly from wakefulness to REM sleep, skipping the other stages. The causes of narcolepsy are not known, although there could be a genetic component because narcolepsy runs in families (Billiard, 2008; Zamarian et al., 2015; Basseti et al., 2021).

We know relatively little about sleeptalking and sleepwalking, two sleep disturbances that are usually harmless. Both occur during stage 3 sleep and are more common in children than in adults. Sleeptalkers and sleepwalkers usually have a vague consciousness of the world around them, and a sleepwalker may be able to walk with agility around obstructions in a crowded room. Unless a sleepwalker wanders into a dangerous environment, sleepwalking typically poses little risk. And the common idea that it's dangerous to wake a sleepwalker? It's just superstition (Haridi et al., 2017; Drakatos et al., 2019; Mangiaruga et al., 2021).

Circadian Rhythms: Life Cycles

circadian rhythms Biological processes that occur regularly on approximately a 24-hour cycle. (Module 12)

The fact that we cycle back and forth between wakefulness and sleep is one example of the body's circadian rhythms. **Circadian rhythms** (from the Latin *circa diem*, or "about a day") are biological processes that occur regularly on approximately a 24-hour cycle. Sleeping and waking, for instance, occur naturally to the beat of an internal pacemaker that works on a cycle of about 24 hours. Several other bodily functions, such as body temperature, hormone production, and blood pressure, also follow circadian rhythms (Blatter & Cajochen, 2007; Labrecque &Cermakian, 2015; Burns et al., 2021).

Circadian cycles are complex, and they involve a variety of behaviors. For instance, sleepiness occurs not just in the evening but throughout the day in regular patterns, with most of us getting drowsy in mid-afternoon–regardless of whether or not we have eaten a heavy lunch.

By making an afternoon nap part of their everyday habit, people in many cultures take advantage of the body's natural inclination to sleep at this time. The phenomenon of afternoon naps is called a *siesta* in Hispanic cultures, and *siesta* is a term that is sometimes employed by English-speakers to label their afternoon nap. Furthermore, in some cultures, napping is seen as socially desirable. For example, Japan has a practice of *inemuri* (literally, "sleeping while present"), in which people fall asleep in public, such as during a meeting or at a dinner party. The *inemuri* is seen as an indication that the napper must work very hard to be so sleepy, and thus the practice is seen as virtuous (Abrams, 2017; Egan et al., 2017).

Bright lights may counter some of the symptoms of seasonal affective disorder, which occur during the winter.
BSIP SA/Alamy Stock Photo

The brain's *suprachiasmatic nucleus (SCN)* controls our circadian rhythms, but there are a number of circadian "clocks" associated with specific parts of the body. For instance, circadian rhythms speed up the heart before dawn to prepare us for the day's challenges. Similarly, the release and retention of various substances in the kidneys are affected by circadian rhythms. Even the processing of information in various areas of the brain may be affected by circadian rhythms and help shape how we perceive the world (Hickok, 2015; Summa & Turek, 2015; Ono et al., 2021).

Furthermore, the relative amount of light and darkness, which varies with the seasons of the year, also plays a role in regulating circadian rhythms. In fact, some people experience *seasonal affective disorder*, a form of severe depression in which feelings of despair and hopelessness increase during the winter and lift during the rest of the year. The disorder appears to be a result of the brevity and gloom of winter days. Daily exposure to bright lights is sometimes sufficient to improve the mood of those with this disorder (Patten et al., 2017; Rohan et al., 2019; Madsen et al., 2021).

People's moods also follow regular patterns. By examining more than 500 million tweets using publicly available Twitter records, a team of psychologists found that words with positive associations (*fantastic, super*) and negative associations (*afraid, mad*) followed regular patterns. Across the globe and among different cultures, people were happier in the morning and less so during the day, with a rebound in the evening. Moods are also happier on certain days of the week: We're happier on weekends and holidays. Finally, positive emotions increase from late December to late June as the days get longer, and negative emotions increase as days get shorter (Golder & Macy, 2011; see Figure 9).

Furthermore, there seem to be optimal times for carrying out various tasks. Most adults are at their peak for carrying out cognitive tasks in the late morning. In contrast, focus and concentration on academic tasks decline throughout the afternoon. On the other hand, some research findings show that creativity increases in the evening when people are tired. It may be that fatigue decreases inhibitions, allowing for more creative thought (Wieth & Zacks, 2011; Barber, 2019).

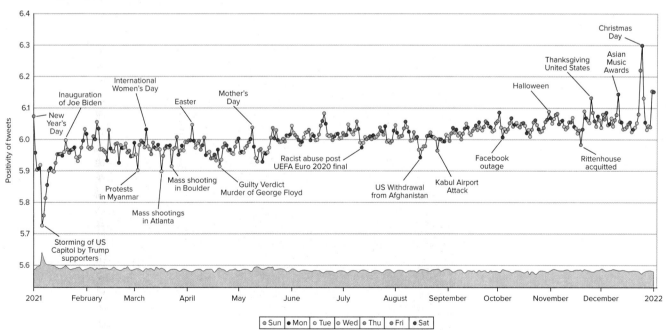

FIGURE 9 A year of tweets shows that Fridays, Saturdays, and Sundays are happier than weekdays. The happiest days are holidays (the highest points on the graph), and the unhappiest days are associated with bad news (the lowest points on the graph).

Average Happiness for Twitter. The MITRE Corporation. Reprinted by permission.

Finally, health issues are more apt to appear at certain times of the day. For instance, heart attacks and strokes occur most frequently and are most severe between 6:00 a.m. and noon. Asthma attacks and heartburn are more common during the evening hours. Furthermore, some researchers believe that medicine for illnesses might be most effective if delivered according to a given person's circadian rhythms. In this view of the future, scientists will be able to identify the optimum time to give a patient a drug, a practice referred to as *personalized circadian medicine* (Beck, 2015; Beker et al., 2017; Tingley, 2022).

Daydreams: Dreams Without Sleep

It is the stuff of magic: Our past mistakes can be wiped out and the future filled with noteworthy accomplishments. Fame, happiness, and wealth can be ours. In the next moment, though, the most horrible tragedies can occur, leaving us devastated, alone, and penniless.

daydreams Fantasies that people construct while awake. (Module 12)

The source of these scenarios is **daydreams,** fantasies people construct while awake. Unlike dreaming that occurs during sleep, daydreams are more under people's control. Therefore, their content is more often related to immediate events in the environment than is the content of the dreams that occur during sleep. Although they may include sexual content, daydreams also pertain to the full gamut of activities or events that are relevant to a person's life. While we are daydreaming, we are still experiencing waking consciousness. However, our awareness of the environment around us declines.

People vary considerably in the amount of daydreaming they do. For example, around 2% to 4% of the population spend at least half their free time fantasizing. Although most people daydream much less frequently, almost everyone fantasizes to some degree. In fact, a study in which experimenters sent texts at random times found that the participants were thinking about something other than what they were doing about half the time (Pisarik et al., 2013; Reddy, 2016; Ostojic-Aitkens et al., 2019).

The brain is surprisingly active during daydreaming. For example, several areas of the brain that are associated with complex problem solving become activated during daydreaming. In fact, daydreaming may be the only time these areas are activated simultaneously, suggesting that daydreaming may lead to insights about problems that we are grappling with. Consistent with that notion, scientists and writers find that

Daydreams are fantasies that people construct while they are awake. What are the similarities and differences between daydreams and night dreams?

Drazen Zigic/Shutterstock

creative ideas routinely arise during periods in which the mind wanders (Carciofo et al., 2017; Gable et al., 2019; Philippi et al., 2021).

In addition, different types of inner mental distraction lead to different brain-wave patterns. For example, when a person is obsessively worrying about something—such as concern over an upcoming test—researchers see wave patterns that differ from those that occur when their mind is wandering. Interestingly, the kind of wave patterns found when the mind is wandering occurs more in highly creative people, suggesting a link between daydreaming and creativity (Kam et al., 2021; Murray et al., 2021). Furthermore, daydreaming may contain elements of *inner speech,* in which people talk to themselves in their heads. Inner speech may help us to plan and regulate our emotions (Alderson-Day et al., 2017; Fernyhough, 2017; Verhaeghen & Mirabito, 2021).

Some scientists see a link between daydreaming and dreams during sleep. The content of daydreams and dreams show many parallels, and the brain areas and processes involved in daydreaming and dreams during sleep are related (Domhoff, 2011).

 ## BECOMING AN INFORMED CONSUMER
# of Psychology

Sleeping Better

Do you have trouble sleeping? If you answered yes, you're not alone; 70 million people in the United States have sleep problems. Half of Americans aged 19 to 29 report they rarely or never get a good night's sleep on weekdays, and nearly a third of working adults say they get less than 6 hours of sleep a night. And the COVID-19 pandemic only made things worse for people across the globe (Bernstein, 2021; Jahrami et al., 2021).

For those of us who spend hours tossing and turning in bed, psychologists studying sleep disturbances have a number of suggestions (Chung et al., 2018; Bernstein, 2021; Petersen, 2022):

- *Don't desperately chase sleep.* Don't go to bed early, and don't sleep late. Set a schedule, and stick to it, 7 days a week. Adhering to a habitual schedule helps your internal timing mechanisms regulate your body.
- *Exercise during the day (but not right before bedtime).* Unsurprisingly, it helps to be tired before going to sleep! Moreover, learning systematic relaxation techniques and biofeedback can help you unwind from the day's stresses and tensions.
- *Avoid long naps—but consider taking short ones.* If you have trouble sleeping at night, it's best to avoid long naps. On the other hand, a short nap lasting 10 to 20 minutes may be ideal to boost energy and increase alertness. In fact, at least in preschool children, midday naps improve recall of material learned earlier in the day—although we don't yet know if that applies to older individuals (Kurdziel et al., 2013; Weir, 2016; Patterson et al., 2021).
- *Avoid screen time before bed.* The blue light emitted by computers and smartphones reduces melatonin production and increases alertness, which is not conducive to sleep. So avoid use of electronic devices for 2 or 3 hours before heading to bed (Twenge et al., 2019).
- *Avoid drinks with caffeine after lunch.* The effects of beverages such as coffee, tea, and some soft drinks can linger for as long as 8 to 12 hours after they are consumed.
- *Turn down the temperature.* Experts suggest keeping the temperature at around 65 degrees in the room where you sleep. If you're too warm or too cold, you're more likely to wake up.
- *Drink a glass of warm milk at bedtime.* Your grandparents were right when they dispensed this advice: Milk contains the chemical tryptophan, which helps people fall asleep.

- *Avoid sleeping pills.* Even though 25% of U.S. adults report having taken medication for sleep in the previous year and some 60 *million* sleeping aid prescriptions are filled annually, in the long run, sleep medications can do more harm than good because they disrupt the normal sleep cycle. Rather than sleeping pills, try behavioral therapy; it's been proven to work better than drugs (DeAngelis, 2016).
- *Try* not *to sleep.* This approach works because people often have difficulty falling asleep because they are trying so hard. A better strategy is to go to bed only when you feel tired. If you don't get to sleep within 10 minutes, leave the bedroom and do something else, returning to bed only when you feel sleepy. Continue this process all night if necessary. But get up at your usual hour in the morning, and don't take any naps during the day. After 3 or 4 weeks, most people become conditioned to associate their beds with sleep—and fall asleep rapidly at night (Smith & Lazarus, 2001; Davidson, 2014).

For long-term problems with sleep, you might consider visiting a sleep disorders center. For information on accredited clinics, consult the American Academy of Sleep Medicine at www.aasm.org.

RECAP/EVALUATE/RETHINK

RECAP

LO 12-1 What are the states of consciousness?

- Consciousness is a person's awareness of the sensations, thoughts, and feelings at a given moment. Waking consciousness can vary from more active to more passive states.
- Altered states of consciousness include naturally occurring sleep and dreaming, as well as hypnotic and drug-induced states.

LO 12-2 What happens when we sleep, and what are the meaning and function of dreams?

- The brain is active throughout the night, and sleep proceeds through stages 1 through 3, which are identified by unique patterns of brain waves.
- REM (rapid eye movement) sleep is characterized by an increase in heart rate, a rise in blood pressure, and an increase in the rate of breathing. Dreams most often occur during this stage.
- According to Freud's psychoanalytic approach, dreams have both a manifest content (an apparent story line) and a latent content (a true meaning). He suggested that the latent content provides a guide to a dreamer's unconscious, revealing unfulfilled wishes or desires.
- The dreams-for-survival theory, grounded in an evolutionary perspective, suggests that information relevant to daily survival is reconsidered and reprocessed in dreams.
- Taking a neuroscience approach, the activation-synthesis theory proposes that dreams are a result of random electrical energy that stimulates different memories, which then are woven into a coherent story line.

LO 12-3 What are the major sleep disorders, and how can they be treated?

- Insomnia is a sleep disorder characterized by difficulty sleeping. Sleep apnea is a condition in which people have difficulty sleeping and breathing at the same time. People with narcolepsy have an uncontrollable urge to sleep. Sleepwalking and sleeptalking are relatively harmless.

LO 12-4 How much do we daydream?

- Wide individual differences exist in the amount of time devoted to daydreaming. Almost everyone daydreams or fantasizes to some degree.

EVALUATE

1. _____ is the term used to describe our understanding of the world external to us, as well as our own internal world.
2. A great deal of neural activity goes on during sleep. True or false?
3. Dreams most often occur in _____ sleep.
4. _____ _____ are internal bodily processes that occur on a daily cycle.
5. Freud's theory of unconscious _____ _____ states that the actual wishes an individual expresses in dreams are disguised because they are threatening to the person's conscious awareness.
6. Match the theory of dreaming with its definition.
   1. activation-synthesis theory
   2. dreams-for-survival theory
   3. dreams as wish fulfillment

a. Dreams permit important information to be reprocessed during sleep.

b. The manifest content of dreams disguises the latent content of the dreams.

c. Electrical energy stimulates random memories, which are woven together to produce dreams.

RETHINK

1. Suppose that a new "miracle pill" allows a person to function with only 1 hour of sleep per night. However, because a night's sleep is so short, a person who takes the pill will never dream again. Knowing what you do about the functions of sleep and dreaming, what would be some advantages and drawbacks of such a pill from a personal standpoint? Would you take such a pill?

2. What solutions can you think of to address racial inequities in sleep duration and depth?

Answers to Evaluate Questions

1. Consciousness; 2. True; 3. REM; 4. Circadian rhythms; 5. wish fulfillment; 6. 1-c, 2-a, 3-b

KEY TERMS

consciousness	stage 3 sleep	unconscious wish	activation-synthesis theory
stage 1 sleep	rapid eye movement	fulfillment theory	circadian rhythms
stage 2 sleep	(REM) sleep	dreams-for-survival theory	daydreams

Module 13
Hypnosis and Meditation

LEARNING OUTCOMES

LO 13-1 What is hypnosis, and are hypnotized people in a different state of consciousness?

LO 13-2 What are the effects of meditation?

You are feeling relaxed and drowsy. You are getting sleepier. Your body is becoming limp. Your eyelids are feeling heavier. Your eyes are closing; you can't keep them open anymore. You are totally relaxed. Now, place your hands above your head. But you will find they are getting heavier and heavier–so heavy you can barely keep them up. In fact, although you are straining as hard as you can, you will be unable to hold them up any longer.

An observer watching this scene would notice a curious phenomenon. Many of the people listening to the voice are dropping their arms to their sides. The reason for this strange behavior? Those people have been hypnotized.

Hypnosis: A Trance-Forming Experience?

hypnosis A trancelike state of heightened susceptibility to the suggestions of others. (Module 13)

People under **hypnosis** are in a trancelike state of heightened susceptibility to the suggestions of others. In some respects, it appears that they are asleep. Yet other aspects of their behavior contradict this notion, for people are attentive to the hypnotist's suggestions and may carry out bizarre or silly suggestions.

How is someone hypnotized? Typically, the process follows a series of four steps. First, a person is made comfortable in a quiet environment. Second, the hypnotist explains what is going to happen, such as telling the person that they will experience a pleasant, relaxed state. Third, the hypnotist tells the person to concentrate on a specific object or image, such as the hypnotist's moving finger or an image of a calm lake. The hypnotist may have the person concentrate on relaxing different parts of the body, such as the arms, legs, and chest. Fourth, once the subject is in a highly relaxed state, the hypnotist may make suggestions that the person interprets as being produced by hypnosis, such as "Your arms are getting heavy" and "Your eyelids are more difficult to open." Because the person begins to experience these sensations, they believe they are caused by the hypnotist and become susceptible to the suggestions of the hypnotist.

Despite their apparent compliance when hypnotized, people do not lose all will of their own. They will not perform antisocial behaviors or self-destructive acts. People will not reveal hidden truths about themselves, and they are capable of lying. Moreover, people cannot be hypnotized against their will–despite popular misconceptions (Raz, 2007; Lynn et al., 2015; Facco et al., 2021).

People vary widely in their susceptibility to hypnosis. About 5% to 20% of the population cannot be hypnotized at all, and some 15% are very easily hypnotized. Most people fall somewhere in between. Moreover, the ease with which a person is hypnotized is related to a number of other characteristics. People who are readily hypnotized are also easily absorbed while reading books or listening to music, becoming unaware of what is happening around them, and they often spend an unusual amount of time daydreaming. In sum, then, they show a high ability to concentrate and to become completely absorbed in what they are doing (Parris, 2017; Gurney et al., 2019; Palfi et al., 2019).

Despite common misconceptions, people cannot be hypnotized against their will, nor do they lose all will of their own when they are hypnotized.
PaulaConnelly/E+/Getty Images

A DIFFERENT STATE OF CONSCIOUSNESS?

The question of whether hypnosis is a state of consciousness that differs qualitatively from normal waking consciousness is controversial. Some psychologists believe hypnosis represents a state of consciousness that differs significantly from other states. In this view, high suggestibility, increased ability to recall and construct images, and acceptance of suggestions that clearly contradict reality characterize it as a different state. Moreover, people who are hypnotized show certain kinds of changes in electrical activity in the brain. Such electrical changes support the position that hypnosis is a state of consciousness different from normal waking (Tart, 2017; Keppler, 2018; Halsband & Wolf, 2021).

In this view, hypnosis represents a state of *divided consciousness*. According to famed hypnosis researcher Ernest Hilgard, hypnosis brings about a *dissociation*, or division, of consciousness into two simultaneous components. In one stream of consciousness, hypnotized people are following the commands of the hypnotist. Yet on another level of consciousness, they are acting as "hidden observers," aware of what is happening to them. For instance, hypnotic subjects may appear to be following the hypnotist's suggestion about feeling no pain, yet in another stream of consciousness, they may be actually aware of the pain.

On the other side of the controversy are psychologists who reject the notion that hypnosis is a state significantly different from normal waking consciousness. They argue that altered brain-wave patterns are not sufficient to demonstrate a qualitative difference because no other specific physiological changes occur when people are in trances. Furthermore, little support exists for the contention that adults can recall memories of childhood events accurately while hypnotized. That lack of evidence suggests that there is nothing qualitatively special about the hypnotic trance (Wagstaff, 2009; Wagstaff et al., 2011).

The controversy over the nature of hypnosis has led to extreme positions on both sides of the issue. In contrast, more recent approaches suggest that the hypnotic state may best be viewed as lying along a continuum. In this view, hypnosis is neither a totally different state of consciousness nor totally similar to normal waking consciousness (Kihlstrom, 2005b; Jamieson, 2007; Ranscombe, 2019).

! Study Alert
The question of whether hypnosis represents a different state of consciousness or is similar to normal waking consciousness is a key issue.

THE VALUE OF HYPNOSIS

As arguments about the true nature of hypnosis continue, though, one thing is clear: Hypnosis has been used successfully to solve practical human problems. In fact, psychologists working in many different areas have found hypnosis to be a reliable, effective tool. It has been applied to a number of areas, including the following:

- *Controlling pain.* Patients have had chronic pain reduced through hypnotic suggestion. In fact, people can be taught to hypnotize themselves to relieve pain or gain a sense of control over their symptoms. Hypnosis has proved to be particularly useful during childbirth and dental procedures. Furthermore, a combination of hypnosis and virtual-reality immersion has been shown to be particularly effective in some cases (Thompson et al., 2019; Moss & Willmarth, 2020; Rousseaux et al., 2020; Rousseaux et al., 2022).

- *Reducing smoking.* Although it hasn't been successful in stopping drug and alcohol abuse, hypnosis more frequently helps people stop smoking through hypnotic suggestions that the taste and smell of cigarettes are unpleasant (Green et al., 2008; Li et al., 2020).

- *Treating psychological disorders.* Hypnosis sometimes is used during treatment for psychological disorders. For example, it may be employed to heighten relaxation, reduce anxiety, increase expectations of success, or modify self-defeating thoughts (Etzrodt, 2013; Valentine et al., 2019; Roberts et al., 2021).

- *Assisting in law enforcement.* Witnesses and victims are sometimes better able to recall the details of a crime when hypnotized. In one case, a witness to the kidnapping of a group of California schoolchildren was placed under hypnosis and was able to recall all but one digit of the license number on the kidnapper's vehicle. On the other hand, hypnotic recollections may also be inaccurate. Consequently, the legal status of hypnosis is unresolved (Knight & Meyer, 2007; Major, 2019).

- *Improving athletic performance.* Athletes sometimes turn to hypnosis to improve their performance. For example, some baseball players have used hypnotism to increase their concentration when batting, with considerable success (Tramontana, 2011; Carlstedt, 2017; Kvitchasty, 2021).

Meditation: Regulating Our Own State of Consciousness

When traditional practitioners of the ancient Eastern religion of Zen Buddhism want to achieve greater spiritual insight, they turn to a technique that has been used for centuries to alter their state of consciousness. This technique is called meditation.

Meditation is a learned technique for refocusing attention that brings about an altered state of consciousness. Meditation typically consists of the repetition of a *mantra*–a sound, word, or syllable–over and over. In some forms of meditation, the focus is on a picture, flame, or specific part of the body. Regardless of the nature of the particular initial stimulus, the key to the procedure is concentrating on it so thoroughly that the meditator becomes unaware of any outside stimulation and reaches a different state of consciousness.

After meditation, people report feeling thoroughly relaxed. They sometimes relate that they have gained new insights into themselves and the problems they are facing. The long-term practice of meditation may even improve health because of the biological changes it produces. For example, during meditation, oxygen usage decreases, heart rate and blood pressure decline, and brain-wave patterns change (Travis et al., 2009; Steinhubl et al., 2015; Goldin et al., 2021).

meditation A learned technique for refocusing attention that brings about an altered state of consciousness. (Module 13)

Meditation leads to short-term changes in a person's physiological state, as well as to longer-term health benefits.
FatCamera/E+/Getty Images

Anyone can meditate by following a few simple procedures. The fundamentals include sitting in a quiet room with the eyes closed, breathing deeply and rhythmically, and repeating a word or sound–such as the word *one*–over and over. Also, a number of phone apps facilitate meditation (Gál et al., 2021; Goldberg et al., 2022).

Practiced regularly, meditation is effective in bringing about greater relaxation not only during meditation but afterward. Evidence even supports long-term positive effects of some kinds of meditation, such as in the reduction of heart disease (Yadav et al., 2017; Voiß et al., 2019; Pauly et al., 2022).

From the perspective of...

A Human Resources Specialist Would you allow (or even encourage) employees to engage in meditation during the workday? Why or why not?

Dex Image/Getty Images

Around 14% of people in the United States have tried meditation at least once, and in some cultures, the use of meditation is far more common. Between 200 and 500 million people meditate worldwide. In the United States, involvement in meditation practices tripled between 2012 and 2017, especially among women, and the use of meditation seems to have increased even more during the pandemic (Laughlin, 2018; Clarke et al., 2018; Priyanka, 2021).

Many cultures use various forms of meditation to alter consciousness, though it can take various forms and serve different purposes, depending on the culture. In fact, one reason psychologists study consciousness is the realization that people in many cultures routinely seek ways to alter their states of consciousness, as we discuss in the *Exploring Diversity* feature.

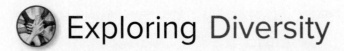

Exploring Diversity

Cross-Cultural Routes to Altered States of Consciousness

A group of Native American Sioux men sit naked in a steaming sweat lodge as a medicine man throws water on sizzling rocks to send billows of scalding steam into the air.

Aztec priests smear themselves with a mixture of crushed poisonous herbs, hairy black worms, scorpions, and lizards. Sometimes they drink the potion.

During the 16th century, a devout Hasidic Jew lies across the tomb of a celebrated scholar. As he murmurs the name of God repeatedly, he seeks attachment to the soul of the dead scholar's spirit. If successful, he will attain a mystical state, and the deceased's words will flow out of his mouth.

Each of these rituals has a common goal: suspension from the bonds of everyday awareness and access to an altered state of consciousness. Although they may seem exotic from the vantage point of many Western cultures, these rituals represent an apparently universal effort to alter consciousness. Moreover, the same efforts to seek altered states of consciousness are found in contemporary Western culture: practices such as meditating, undergoing hypnosis, eating mushrooms containing psilocybin, taking certain unprescribed drugs, and even engaging in extreme exercise all reflect a desire to attain an altered state of consciousness (Bartocci, 2004; Ember & Carolus, 2017; Greene, 2020).

Some scholars suggest that the quest to alter consciousness represents a basic human desire. For instance, one survey of 488 cultures found that in 90% of them, people sought to enter a trance state to attain an altered consciousness (Bourguignon & Evascu, 1977; Keith, 2019).

Whether or not we accept the view that seeking to alter consciousness is a universal human motivation, reports of the experience of altered states of consciousness clearly share some similar characteristics across a variety of cultures. One is an alteration in thinking, which may become shallow, illogical, or otherwise different from normal. In addition, people's sense of time can become disturbed, and their perceptions of the physical world and of themselves may change. They may lose self-control, doing things that they would never otherwise do. Finally, they may feel a sense of *ineffability*—the inability to understand an experience rationally or describe it in words (Amos, 2021; Perry et al., 2021).

Of course, realizing that efforts to produce altered states of consciousness are widespread throughout the world's societies does not answer a fundamental question: Is the experience of unaltered states of consciousness similar across cultures?

Because humans share basic biological commonalities in the ways their brains and bodies are wired, we might assume that the fundamental experience of consciousness is similar across cultures. As a result, we could suppose that consciousness shows some basic similarities across cultures. However, the ways in which certain aspects of consciousness are interpreted and viewed show substantial differences from culture to culture. For example, people in disparate cultures view the passage of time in varying ways. For instance, people from Arabic nations appear to perceive the passage of time more slowly than do people from North America (Alon & Brett, 2007; Agranovich et al., 2021).

In short, researchers find similarities and differences in the ways that people experience both typical consciousness and altered states of consciousness across cultures. But seeking alterations in consciousness seems to be a pervasive human goal.

Study Alert

Remember that although meditation takes various forms, they are all designed to bring about an altered state of consciousness in which attention is refocused.

RECAP/EVALUATE/RETHINK

RECAP

LO 13-1 What is hypnosis, and are hypnotized people in a different state of consciousness?

- Hypnosis produces a state of heightened susceptibility to the suggestions of the hypnotist. Under hypnosis, significant behavioral changes occur, including increased concentration and suggestibility, heightened ability to recall and construct images, lack of initiative, and acceptance of suggestions that clearly contradict reality.

LO 13-2 What are the effects of meditation?

- Meditation is a learned technique for refocusing attention that brings about an altered state of consciousness.
- Different cultures have developed their own unique ways to alter states of consciousness.

EVALUATE

1. _____ is a state of heightened susceptibility to the suggestions of others.

2. A friend tells you, "I once heard of a person who was murdered by being hypnotized and then told to jump from the Golden Gate Bridge!" Could such a thing have happened? Why or why not?
3. _____ is a learned technique for refocusing attention to bring about an altered state of consciousness.
4. Leslie repeats a unique sound, known as a _____, when engaging in meditation.

RETHINK

1. Why do you think people in almost every culture seek ways of altering their states of consciousness?
2. Meditation produces several physical and psychological benefits. Does this suggest that we are physically and mentally burdened in our normal state of waking consciousness? Why?

Answers to Evaluate Questions

1. Hypnosis; 2. No; people who are hypnotized cannot be made to perform self-destructive acts; 3. Meditation; 4. mantra

KEY TERMS

hypnosis   meditation

Module 14
Drug Use: The Highs and Lows of Consciousness

LO 14-1 What are the major classifications of drugs, and what are their effects?

Brittany was desperate. As the rest of her family were grieving over the loss of her grandmother, whose funeral they had just attended, she was searching for cash. She finally found a $5 bill in the purse belonging to her 6-year-old cousin. "How low was it to steal from a 6-year-old to buy drugs?" she wondered. But it didn't matter. Her head was aching, her mouth was dry, and she would do anything to buy the drugs she needed to get high.

Like many others caught up in the opioid crisis facing the United States, Brittany's descent into addiction started with a legal drug, Percocet, that she was prescribed to deal with pain following the removal of her wisdom teeth. She didn't know that it was highly addictive, and even after the pain was gone, Brittany kept on craving the drug. It turned her from an honors student to an addict desperate for drugs (Larsen, 2014; Volkow & Blanco, 2021).

Pharmaceutical drugs of one sort or another are a part of almost everyone's life. From infancy on, most people take vitamins, aspirin, and cold-relief medicine at some point. However, these drugs rarely produce an altered state of consciousness.

In contrast, some substances, known as psychoactive drugs, lead to an altered state of consciousness. **Psychoactive drugs** influence a person's emotions, perceptions, and behavior. Yet even this category of drugs is common in most of our lives. If you have ever had a cup of coffee or sipped a beer, you have taken a psychoactive drug. A large number of individuals have used more potent–and more dangerous–psychoactive drugs than coffee and beer (see Figure 1); for instance, 36.8% of high school seniors have used an illegal drug in the past year. In addition, 36.9% report having been drunk on alcohol in the past year. The figures for the adult population are even higher (Johnston et al., 2021).

Of course, drugs vary widely in the effects they have on users, in part because they affect the nervous system in very different ways. Some drugs alter the limbic system, and others affect the operation of specific neurotransmitters across the synapses of neurons. For example, some drugs block or enhance the release of neurotransmitters, others block the receipt or the removal of a neurotransmitter, and still others mimic the effects of a particular neurotransmitter (see Figure 2).

Addictive drugs produce a biological or psychological dependence (or both) on a drug in the user. When a drug is addictive, its absence leads to a craving for it that may be overpowering and nearly irresistible. In *biological drug dependence*, the body becomes so accustomed to functioning in the presence of a drug that it cannot function without it. In *psychological drug dependence*, people believe that they need the drug to respond to the stresses of daily living. Although we generally associate addiction with drugs such as heroin, everyday sorts of drugs, such as caffeine (found in coffee) and nicotine (found in cigarettes), have addictive aspects as well (Li et al., 2007; Falbe et al., 2019; Khoury et al., 2022).

We know surprisingly little about the underlying causes of addiction. One of the problems in identifying those causes is that different drugs (such as alcohol and cocaine) affect the brain in very different ways–yet they may be equally addicting. Furthermore, it takes longer to become addicted to some drugs than to others, even

psychoactive drugs Drugs that influence a person's emotions, perceptions, and behavior. (Module 14)

addictive drugs Drugs that produce a biological or psychological dependence in the user so that withdrawal from them leads to a craving for the drug that, in some cases, may be nearly irresistible. (Module 14)

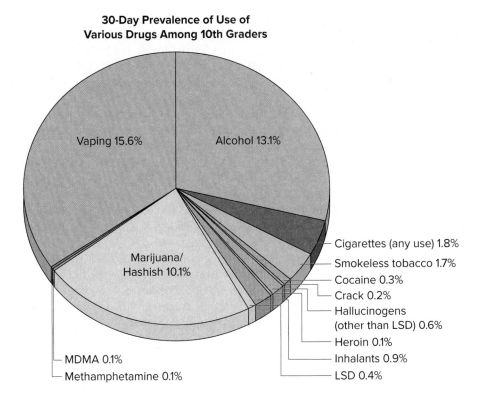

**30-Day Prevalence of Use of
Various Drugs Among 10th Graders**

Vaping 15.6%

Alcohol 13.1%

Marijuana/
Hashish 10.1%

MDMA 0.1%

Methamphetamine 0.1%

Cigarettes (any use) 1.8%

Smokeless tobacco 1.7%

Cocaine 0.3%

Crack 0.2%

Hallucinogens
(other than LSD) 0.6%

Heroin 0.1%

Inhalants 0.9%

LSD 0.4%

FIGURE 1 How many teenagers use drugs? The results of the most recent comprehensive survey of adolescent drug use in the United States show the percentage who have used various substances for nonmedical purposes at least once in their lifetime.
Source: Johnston et al., 2021.

though the ultimate consequences of addiction may be equally grave (Smart, 2007; Holmes, 2017).

Why do people take drugs in the first place? They do so for many reasons, including the perceived pleasure of the experience. In other words, it simply feels good.

In addition, though, a drug-induced high allows people to escape, at least temporarily, from the everyday pressures of life. And in some cases, people use drugs to

! Study Alert
Use Figure 2 to learn how drugs produce their effects on a neurological level.

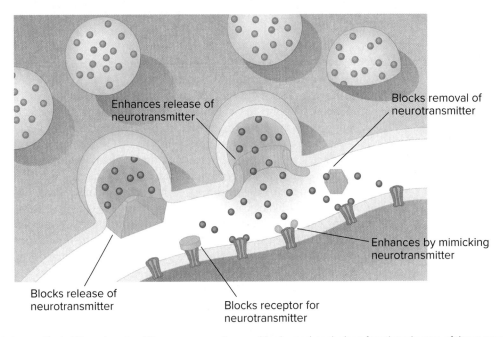

Enhances release of
neurotransmitter

Blocks removal of
neurotransmitter

Enhances by mimicking
neurotransmitter

Blocks release of
neurotransmitter

Blocks receptor for
neurotransmitter

FIGURE 2 Different drugs affect different parts of the nervous system and brain, and each drug functions in one of these specific ways.

attempt to achieve a religious or spiritual state (Korcha et al., 2011; Chapman & Wu, 2015).

People may also be influenced to use drugs by the highly publicized drug use of role models such as movie stars and professional athletes, the easy availability of some illegal drugs, or peer pressure. In some cases, the motive is simply the thrill of trying something new.

Finally, genetic factors may predispose some people to be more susceptible to drugs and to become addicted to them. Regardless of the forces that lead a person to begin using drugs, drug addiction is among the most difficult of all behaviors to modify, even with extensive treatment (Vrieze et al., 2013; Reilly et al., 2017; Thomas et al., 2021).

Because of the difficulty in treating drug problems, most experts believe that the best hope for dealing with the overall societal problem of substance abuse is to prevent or discourage people from becoming involved with addictive drugs in the first place. However, few agree on how to accomplish this goal.

Even widely employed drug reduction programs–such as D.A.R.E. (Drug Abuse Resistance Education)–are of questionable effectiveness. At one time used in more than 80% of school districts in the United States, D.A.R.E. consists of a 10-week series of lessons on the dangers of drugs, alcohol, and gangs taught to 5th- and 6th-graders by a police officer. The program was highly popular with school officials, parents, and politicians.

The problem with D.A.R.E.? Repeated careful evaluations have been unable to demonstrate that the D.A.R.E. program is effective in reducing drug use over the long term. In fact, one study even showed that D.A.R.E. graduates were more likely to use marijuana than was a comparison group of nongraduates. On the other hand, D.A.R.E. has updated its curriculum, and some preliminary evidence suggests it may be more successful than the previous version. But the jury is still out on its effectiveness (Vincus et al., 2010; Singh et al., 2011; Caputi & McLellan, 2017).

Stimulants: Drug Highs

It's 1:00 a.m., and you still haven't finished reading the last chapter of the text on which you will be tested later in the morning. Feeling exhausted, you turn to something that may help you stay awake for the next 2 hours: a cup of strong black coffee.

If you have ever found yourself in such a position, you have resorted to one of the most common stimulants, caffeine, to stay awake. *Caffeine* is one of a number of **stimulants,** drugs whose effect on the central nervous system causes a rise in heart rate, blood pressure, and muscular tension. Caffeine is present not only in coffee; it is an important ingredient in tea, soft drinks, and chocolate as well (see Figure 3).

stimulants Drugs that have an arousal effect on the central nervous system, causing a rise in heart rate, blood pressure, and muscular tension. (Module 14)

Caffeine produces several reactions. The major behavioral effects are an increase in attentiveness and a decrease in reaction time. Caffeine can also bring about an improvement in mood, most likely by mimicking the effects of a natural brain chemical, adenosine. Too much caffeine, however, can result in nervousness and insomnia. People can build up a biological dependence on the drug. Regular users who suddenly stop drinking coffee may experience headaches or depression. Many people who drink large amounts of coffee on weekdays have headaches on weekends because of the sudden drop in the amount of caffeine they are consuming (Kamimori et al., 2015; Sweeney et al., 2019; Aoun et al., 2021).

Nicotine, found in cigarettes, is another common stimulant. The soothing effects of nicotine help explain why cigarette smoking is addictive. Smokers develop a dependence on nicotine, and those who suddenly stop smoking develop a strong craving for the drug. This is not surprising: Nicotine activates neural mechanisms similar to those activated by cocaine, which, as we see in the section on cocaine, is also highly addictive (Wilcox et al., 2017; Picciotto & Kenny, 2021).

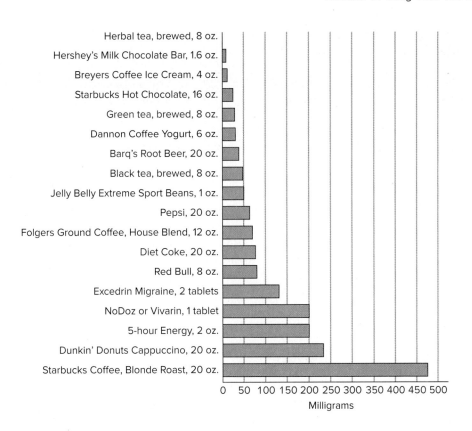

FIGURE 3 How much caffeine do you consume? This chart shows the range of caffeine found in common foods, drinks, and legal drugs.

Source: Center for Science in the Public Interest, n.d.

AMPHETAMINES

Amphetamines such as dexedrine and benzedrine, popularly known as speed, are strong stimulants. In small quantities, amphetamines–which stimulate the central nervous system–bring about a sense of energy and alertness, talkativeness, heightened confidence, and a mood "high." They increase concentration and reduce fatigue.

But not all the effects of amphetamines are positive: They also cause a loss of appetite, increased anxiety, and irritability. When taken over long periods of time, amphetamines can cause feelings of being persecuted by others, as well as a general sense of suspiciousness. People taking amphetamines may lose interest in sex. If taken in too large a quantity, amphetamines overstimulate the central nervous system to such an extent that convulsions and death can occur (Carhart-Harris, 2007; Latronica et al., 2021).

Methamphetamine is a white, crystalline drug that U.S. law enforcement officials now say is the most dangerous street drug. "Meth" is highly addictive and relatively cheap, and it produces a strong, lingering high. It has made addicts of people across the social spectrum, ranging from suburban parents to urban professionals to rural farmers. After becoming addicted, users take it more and more frequently and in increasing doses. Long-term use of the drug can lead to brain damage (Kish et al., 2009; Rindone, 2015; Han et al., 2021).

Approximately 2.6 million people in the United States have used methamphetamine in the past year. Because it can be made from nonprescription cold pills, retailers such as Walmart and Target have removed these medications from the shelves and keep them behind the pharmacy counter. Illicit labs devoted to the manufacture of methamphetamine have sprung up in many locations around the United States.

Adderall is an amphetamine college students often abuse. It was developed to help those who suffer from ADHD, or attention-deficit hyperactivity disorder. However, many college students use the drug illegally, believing that it increases their focus and the ability to study for long hours. Unfortunately, Adderall is addictive, and users need higher and higher doses to achieve the drug's supposed benefits (Diller, 2017; Lueck et al., 2019).

Figure 4 provides a summary of the effects of amphetamines and other illegal drugs.

Drugs	Street Name	Effects	Withdrawal Symptoms	Adverse/Overdose Reactions
Stimulants Amphetamines Benzedrine Dexedrine Cocaine Cathinone	Speed Speed Coke, blow, snow, lady, crack Bath salts	Increased confidence, mood elevation, sense of energy and alertness, decreased appetite, anxiety, irritability, insomnia, transient drowsiness, delayed orgasm	Apathy, general fatigue, prolonged sleep, depression, disorientation, suicidal thoughts, agitated motor activity, irritability, bizarre dreams	Elevated blood pressure, increase in body temperature, face picking, suspiciousness, bizarre and repetitious behavior, vivid hallucinations, convulsions, possible death
Depressants Alcohol Barbiturates Nembutal Seconal Phenobarbital	Booze Yellowjackets Reds	Anxiety reduction, impulsiveness, dramatic mood swings, bizarre thoughts, suicidal behavior, slurred speech, disorientation, slowed mental and physical functioning, limited attention span	Weakness, restlessness, nausea and vomiting, headaches, nightmares, irritability, depression, acute anxiety, hallucinations, seizures, possible death	Confusion, decreased response to pain, shallow respiration, dilated pupils, weak and rapid pulse, coma, possible death
Rohypnol	Roofies, rope, "date-rape" drug	Muscle relaxation, amnesia, sleep	Seizures	Seizures, coma, incapacitation, inability to resist sexual assault
Narcotics Heroin Morphine	H, hombre, junk, smack Drugstore dope, cube, first line, mud	Reduction of anxiety and pain, difficulty in concentration, slowed speech, decreased physical activity, euphoria	Anxiety, vomiting, sneezing, diarrhea, lower back pain, watery eyes, runny nose, yawning, irritability, tremors, panic, chills and sweating, cramps	Depressed levels of consciousness, low blood pressure, rapid heart rate, shallow breathing, convulsions, coma, possible death
Opioids (synthetic drugs such as Vicodin, Percocet, fentanyl, OxyContin)	Oxy, OC, Percs	Pain reduction, shallow breathing, slow heartbeat, seizure (convulsions); cold, clammy skin; confusion	Sweating, chills, abdominal cramps, insomnia, vomiting, diarrhea	Extreme drowsiness, muscle weakness, confusion, cold and clammy skin, pinpoint pupils, shallow breathing, slow heart rate, fainting, or coma
Hallucinogens Cannabis Marijuana Hashish Hash oil	Bhang, kif, ganja, dope, grass, pot, hemp, joint, weed, bone, Mary Jane, reefer	Euphoria, relaxed inhibitions, increased appetite, disoriented behavior	Hyperactivity, insomnia, decreased appetite, anxiety	Severe reactions rare but include panic, paranoia, fatigue, bizarre and dangerous behavior, decreased testosterone over long-term; immune-system effects
MDMA	Ecstasy, Molly	Heightened sense of oneself and insight, feelings of peace, empathy, energy	Depression, anxiety, sleeplessness	Increase in body temperature, memory difficulties
LSD	Acid, quasey, microdot, white lightning	Heightened aesthetic responses; vision and depth distortion; heightened sensitivity to faces and gestures; magnified feelings; paranoia, panic, euphoria	Not reported	Nausea and chills; increased pulse, temperature, and blood pressure; slow, deep breathing; loss of appetite; insomnia; bizarre, dangerous behavior
Steroids	Rhoids, juice	Aggression, depression, acne, mood swings, masculine traits in women and feminine traits in men	Symptoms can mimic other medical problems and include weakness, fatigue, decreased appetite, weight loss; women may note menstrual changes.	Long-term, high-dose effects of steroid use are largely unknown but can lead to swelling and weight gain.

FIGURE 4 Drugs and their effects. A comprehensive breakdown of effects of the most commonly used drugs.

Bath salts (not to be confused with Epsom bath salts) are an amphetamine-like stimulant containing chemicals related to cathinone. They can produce euphoria and a rise in sociability and sex drive, but the side effects can be severe, including paranoia and agitation (Airuehia et al., 2015; Palamar et al., 2019).

COCAINE

The stimulant *cocaine*, and its derivative *crack*, represent a serious concern, although the scope of the problem has declined in recent years. Cocaine is inhaled or "snorted" through the nose, smoked, or injected directly into the bloodstream. It is rapidly absorbed into the body and takes effect almost immediately.

When used in relatively small quantities, cocaine produces feelings of profound psychological well-being, increased confidence, and alertness. Cocaine produces this "high" through the neurotransmitter dopamine. Dopamine is one of the chemicals that transmit messages between neurons that are related to ordinary feelings of pleasure. Normally, when dopamine is released, excess amounts of the neurotransmitter are reabsorbed by the releasing neuron. However, when cocaine enters the brain, it blocks reabsorption of leftover dopamine. As a result, the brain is flooded with dopamine-produced pleasurable sensations (Singer et al., 2017; Canchy et al., 2021).

However, people pay a steep price for the pleasurable effects of cocaine. The brain may become permanently rewired, triggering a psychological and physical addiction in which users grow obsessed with obtaining the drug. Over time, users deteriorate mentally and physically. In extreme cases, cocaine can cause hallucinations—a common one is of insects crawling over one's body. Ultimately, an overdose of cocaine can lead to death (Roncero et al., 2013; Li et al., 2015; Sabe et al., 2021).

Almost 5.5 million people in the United States are occasional cocaine users, and as many as 1.5 million people use the drug regularly. Given the strength of cocaine, withdrawal from the drug is difficult. Although the use of cocaine among high school students has declined in recent years, the drug still represents a major problem (National Institute on Drug Abuse, 2018; National Center for Drug Abuse Statistics, 2022).

> **! Study Alert**
> Figure 4, which summarizes the categories of drugs (stimulants, depressants, narcotics, and hallucinogens), will help you learn the effects of particular drugs.

Depressants: Drug Lows

In contrast to the initial effect of stimulants, which is an increase in arousal of the central nervous system, the effect of **depressants** is to impede the nervous system by causing neurons to fire more slowly. Small doses result in at least temporary feelings of *intoxication*—drunkenness—along with a sense of euphoria and joy. When large amounts are taken, however, speech becomes slurred and muscle control becomes disjointed, making motion difficult. Ultimately, heavy users may lose consciousness entirely.

depressants Drugs that slow down the nervous system. (Module 14)

ALCOHOL

The most common depressant is alcohol, which is used by more people than any other drug. Based on liquor sales, the average person in the United States over the age of 18 drinks 1.94 drinks per day, or 705 drinks a year. Although alcohol consumption has declined steadily over the last decade, surveys show that more than three-fourths of college students indicate that they have had a drink within the last 30 days (May, 2017; Lui, 2019).

One of the more disturbing trends is the high frequency of binge drinking among college students. *Binge drinking* occurs when a person consumes enough alcohol in a single setting to increase the blood alcohol level to .08%. For men, binge drinking corresponds to having five or more drinks in one sitting; for women, who generally weigh less than men and whose bodies absorb alcohol less efficiently, binge drinking corresponds to having four or more drinks at one sitting (Wilsnack et al., 2018; Esser et al., 2021).

In Figure 5, you can see the percentage of people of different ages who reported binge drinking in the past 30 days. Note that the highest percentage of binge drinkers are young adults.

FIGURE 5 Self-reported binge drinking at different ages. For men, binge drinking was defined as consuming five or more drinks in one sitting; for women, the total was four or more.
Source: Bohm et al., 2021.

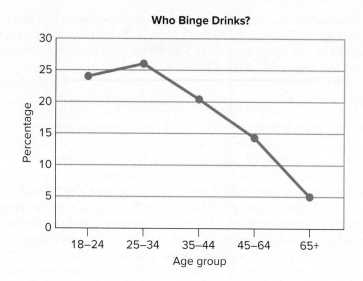

Who Binge Drinks?

Furthermore, in college settings, it turns out that even light drinkers are affected by the high rate of alcohol use by their classmates: Two-thirds of lighter drinkers say they had their studying or sleep disturbed by drunk students, and a quarter of women surveyed say they had been targets of unwanted sexual advances by drunk classmates (Centers for Disease Control and Prevention, 2010; Greene & Maggs, 2017).

Women are typically somewhat lighter drinkers than men at all ages, although the statistics on binge drinking show fairly comparable rates for women and men. Additionally, women are more susceptible to the effects of alcohol, and alcohol abuse may harm the brains of women more than it harms the brains of men (Holzhauer et al., 2017; Centers for Disease Control and Prevention, 2021).

There are also cultural and ethnic differences in alcohol consumption. For example, teenagers in Europe drink more than teenagers in the United States do. Furthermore, people of East Asian backgrounds who live in the United States tend to drink significantly less than do Caucasians and African Americans, and their incidence of alcohol-related problems is lower. It may be that physical reactions to alcohol, which can include sweating, a quickened heartbeat, and facial flushing for some East Asians, are unpleasant enough to discourage alcohol use (McCabe et al., 2019; Harris et al., 2021).

Although alcohol is a depressant, most people believe that it increases their sense of sociability and well-being. This belief is caused because initially alcohol may lead to feelings of happiness, a reduction in tension and stress, and loss of inhibitions.

The effects of alcohol vary significantly, depending on who is drinking it and the setting in which people drink. If alcohol were a newly discovered drug, do you think its sale would be legal?
(Left): Dmytro Sidelnikov/123RF; (Right): bernardbodo/iStock/Getty Images

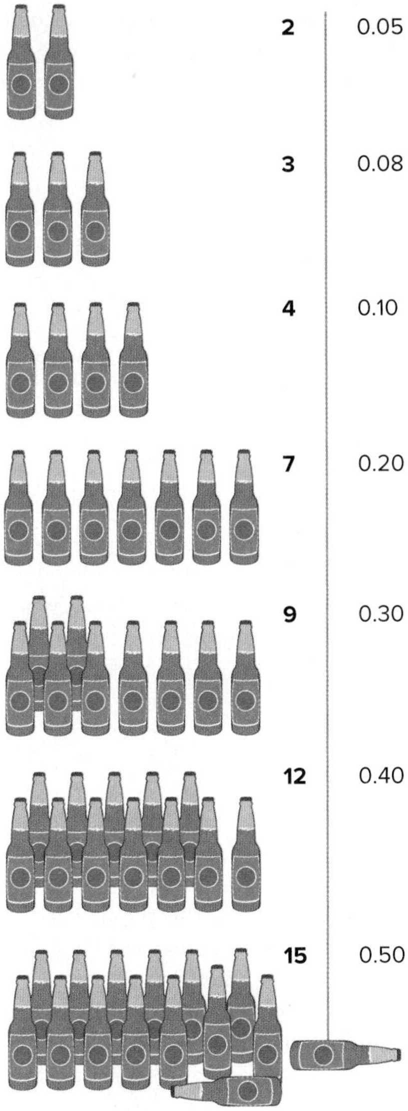

Number of drinks consumed in 2 hours	Alcohol in blood (percentage)	Typical effects
2	0.05	Judgment, thought, and restraint weakened; tension released, giving carefree sensation
3	0.08	Tensions and inhibitions of everyday life lessened; cheerfulness
4	0.10	Voluntary motor action affected, making hand and arm movements, walk, and speech clumsy
7	0.20	Severe impairment—staggering, loud, incoherent, emotionally unstable, 100 times greater traffic risk; exuberance and aggressive inclinations magnified
9	0.30	Deeper areas of brain affected, with stimulus-response and understanding confused; stuporous; blurred vision
12	0.40	Incapable of voluntary action; sleepy, difficult to arouse; equivalent of surgical anesthesia
15	0.50	Comatose; centers controlling breathing and heartbeat anesthetized; death increasingly probable

FIGURE 6 The effects of alcohol. The quantities represent only rough benchmarks; the effects vary significantly depending on an individual's weight, height, recent food intake, genetic factors, and even psychological state.

However, as the dose of alcohol increases, the depressive effects become more pronounced (see Figure 6). People may feel emotionally and physically unstable. They also show poor judgment and may act aggressively. Moreover, memory is impaired, brain processing of spatial information is diminished, and speech becomes slurred and incoherent. Eventually, they may fall into a stupor and pass out. If they drink enough alcohol in a short time, they may die of alcohol poisoning (Wombacher et al., 2019; Baines & Jones, 2021).

Although most people fall into the category of casual users, 14 million people in the United States–1 in every 13 adults–have a drinking problem. *Alcoholics,* people with alcohol-abuse problems, come to rely on alcohol and continue to drink even though it causes serious difficulties. In addition, they become increasingly immune to the effects of alcohol. Consequently, alcoholics must drink progressively more to experience the initial positive feelings that alcohol produces.

In some cases of alcoholism, people must drink constantly in order to feel well enough to function in their daily lives. In other cases, though, people drink inconsistently but occasionally go on binges in which they consume large quantities of alcohol.

It is not clear why certain people become alcoholics and develop a tolerance for alcohol, whereas others do not. There may be a genetic cause, although the question of whether there is a specific inherited gene that produces alcoholism is controversial. What is clear is that the chances of becoming an alcoholic are considerably higher if alcoholics are present in earlier generations of a person's family. However, not all alcoholics have close relatives who are alcoholics. In these cases, environmental stressors are suspected of playing a larger role (Gizer et al., 2011; Buckner & Shah, 2015; Carn et al., 2021).

BARBITURATES

Barbiturates are a form of central nervous system depressant. They include drugs such as Nembutal, Seconal, and phenobarbital. Barbiturates produce a sense of relaxation and are frequently prescribed by physicians to induce sleep or reduce stress. At larger doses, they produce altered thinking, faulty judgment, and sluggishness.

Barbiturates are psychologically and biologically addictive. When combined with alcohol, they can be deadly because such a combination relaxes the muscles of the diaphragm to such an extent that the user stops breathing.

ROHYPNOL

Rohypnol is sometimes called the "date-rape" drug because when it is mixed with alcohol, it can prevent victims from resisting sexual assault. Sometimes people who are unknowingly given the drug are so incapacitated that they have no memory of the assault (Sonone et al., 2021).

Narcotics, Opiates, and Opioids: Relieving Pain and Anxiety

narcotics Drugs that increase relaxation and relieve pain and anxiety. (Module 14)

Narcotics are drugs that increase relaxation and relieve pain and anxiety. Two of the most powerful narcotics, *morphine* and *heroin,* are derived from the poppy seed pod. Although morphine is used medically to control severe pain, heroin is illegal in the United States. This status has not prevented its widespread abuse.

Heroin users usually inject the drug directly into their veins with a hypodermic needle. The immediate effect has been described as a "rush" of positive feeling, similar in some respects to a sexual orgasm–and just as difficult to describe. After the rush, a heroin user experiences a sense of well-being and peacefulness that lasts 3 to 5 hours.

However, when the effects of heroin wear off, users feel extreme anxiety and a desperate desire to repeat the experience. Moreover, larger amounts of heroin are needed each time to produce the same pleasurable effect. These last two properties are all the ingredients necessary for biological and psychological dependence: The user is constantly either shooting up or attempting to obtain ever-increasing amounts of the drug. Eventually, the life of the addict revolves around heroin.

Heroin is part of a class of drugs called opiates. *Opiates* are narcotics that are derived from natural substances, and they include such drugs as morphine and codeine in addition to heroin. In contrast, *opioids* are synthetic narcotics such as Vicodin, Percocet, fentanyl, and OxyContin, all of which are created in laboratories and are often prescribed to alleviate pain. (The terms *opiates* and *opioids* are often used interchangeably, and when people speak of the "opioid crisis," they typically are referring to both categories.)

Opiate and opioid use have reached epidemic proportions. For example, the number of overdose deaths rose to over 107,000 in

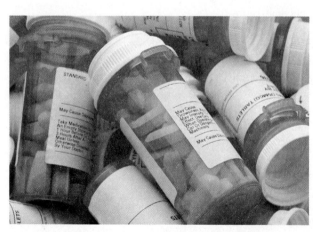

Even drugs that are prescribed legally can lead to addiction when used improperly.

David Smart/Shutterstock

2021. This marked an increase of almost 15% over the prior year, which followed a rise of almost 30% in the previous year. The number of deaths in 2021 was the highest level ever recorded (Levy, 2019; Segers, 2021; Weiland & Sanger-Katz, 2022).

Although the increased use of opioids has reached across racial lines, the rate of overdose deaths has been especially pronounced for Black individuals. One recent study of more than 8 million people living in 67 communities showed that while the rate of opioid overdose deaths stayed about the same for White individuals between 2018 and 2019, the overdose deaths for Black people increased 38% in the same period. The researchers attribute the higher overdose rates in the Black population to systemic challenges involving health care, employment, and other societal impediments (Kamp & Wernau, 2021; Larochelle et al., 2021).

We don't know why overall use of opioids has increased so rapidly, but one reason is that the cost of the drugs has plummeted at the same time the supply has increased substantially. Furthermore, some of the newest opioids are 100 times as potent as natural heroin. And that means drugs bought on the street, which could contain virtually anything, are particularly dangerous and can easily lead to overdoses.

In addition, the COVID-19 pandemic led to increases not only in opioid addiction but also to addiction to alcohol and other drugs, as people sought to deal with the stress of lockdowns and economic insecurity. The increase in isolation and loss of social support also contributed to the increase in addiction (Segers, 2021; Thompson, 2021; Rodrigues et al., 2022).

Because of the powerful positive feelings opioids produce, addiction to them is particularly difficult to cure. In one treatment that has shown some success, users are given alternative drugs that reduce dependence on heroin and other addictive opiates. For example, *methadone* is a synthetic chemical that satisfies a heroin user's biological cravings for the drug without providing the "high" that accompanies heroin. Similarly, *Suboxone* is a painkiller that reduces the withdrawal symptoms from heroin. Suboxone comes in tablet form as well as small film strips, both of which are put under the tongue to dissolve quickly. Another treatment is *Vivitrol*, an injection that lasts about a month. It prevents withdrawal symptoms, and it prevents heroin from producing the positive effects that users crave if heroin is used (Shah et al., 2014; Buck et al., 2021; Chang & Raynor, 2021).

Methadone, Suboxone, and Vivitrol allow heroin users to function relatively normally and without the drug cravings. However, although such drugs remove the psychological dependence on heroin, they replace the biological dependence on heroin with a biological dependence on the alternative drugs. Consequently, researchers are attempting to identify nonaddictive chemical substitutes that do not produce a biological craving. In addition, they are considering experimental treatments such as the brain surgery discussed in the chapter prologue (Prieto et al., 2019; MacDonald et al., 2021).

Hallucinogens: Psychedelic Drugs

Hallucinogens are drugs that alter perceptions, thoughts, and feelings. They can even produce *hallucinations*, the experience of sensing things such as sights, sounds, or smells that seem real but are not.

hallucinogens Drugs that are capable of producing alterations in perception, thoughts, and feelings. (Module 14)

MARIJUANA

The most common hallucinogen in widespread use today is *marijuana*, whose active ingredient—tetrahydrocannabinol (THC)—is found in a common weed, cannabis. Marijuana is typically smoked in cigarettes or pipes, although it can be cooked and eaten. About 30% of high school seniors and around 7% of 8th-graders report having used marijuana in the past year (Johnston et al., 2016; Miech et al., 2021; see Figure 7).

The effects of marijuana vary from person to person, but they typically consist of feelings of euphoria and general well-being. Sensory experiences seem more vivid and

FIGURE 7 The percentage of teenagers who have used marijuana in the past year has remained fairly steady since the mid-2000s.

Source: Miech et al., 2021.

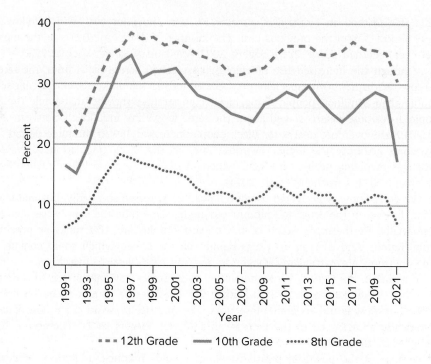

intense, and a person's sense of self-importance seems to grow. Memory may be impaired, causing users to feel pleasantly "spaced out."

Is marijuana safe? The scientific evidence is somewhat mixed. On the one hand, marijuana does not seem to produce addiction except in a small number of heavy users. Furthermore, little scientific evidence supports the belief that users "graduate" from marijuana to more dangerous drugs. Overall, most research suggests its use is less harmful than the use of tobacco and alcohol (Barcott & Scherer, 2015; Śledziński et al., 2019).

On the other hand, some research suggests that there are similarities in the way marijuana and drugs such as cocaine and heroin affect the brain, as well as evidence that heavy use may impact cognitive ability negatively in the long run. Furthermore, heavy use may at least temporarily decrease the production of the male sex hormone testosterone, potentially affecting sexual activity and sperm count (Rossato et al., 2008; Pardini et al., 2015; Berenson, 2019).

In addition, marijuana smoked during pregnancy may have lasting effects on children who are exposed prenatally, although the research results are inconsistent. Heavy use also affects the ability of the immune system to fight off germs and increases stress on the heart, although it is unclear how strong these effects are. Finally, there is one unquestionably negative consequence of smoking marijuana: The smoke damages the lungs much the way cigarette smoke does, producing an increased likelihood of developing cancer and other lung diseases (Reid et al., 2010; Pinky et al., 2019).

Despite the possible dangers of marijuana, its use is increasingly accepted. It clearly has several medical uses: It can prevent nausea from chemotherapy, treat some AIDS symptoms, and relieve muscle spasms for people with spinal cord injuries. Furthermore, it may be helpful in the treatment of Alzheimer's disease (Barcott & Scherer, 2015; Finn, 2015; Saulino et al., 2021).

Many states have made the use of the drug legal if it is prescribed by a health care provider—although it remains illegal under U.S. federal law. And a growing number of states are joining the almost 20 states (and the District of Columbia) in which the use and sale of marijuana are legal, even for recreational use, with no prescription required (Bradford & Bradford, 2017; Sabet, 2021).

MDMA (ECSTASY OR MOLLY) AND LSD

MDMA (*Ecstasy* or *Molly*) and *lysergic acid diethylamide* (*LSD* or *acid*) are hallucinogens. Both drugs affect the operation of the neurotransmitter serotonin in the brain, causing an alteration in brain-cell activity and perception (Aleksander, 2013; van de Blaak & Dumont, 2021).

MDMA produces feelings of increased energy and euphoria, and users report feeling increased empathy and connection with others. Use of forms of MDMA known as *Ecstasy* or *Molly* were initially used primarily at raves and music festivals, but they now affect a broader population. Those who use MDMA may experience declines in memory and performance on intellectual tasks. Such findings suggest that MDMA use may lead to long-term changes in serotonin receptors in the brain (McKinley, 2013; Ebrahimian et al., 2017; Parrott et al., 2017).

LSD, which is structurally similar to serotonin, produces vivid hallucinations and is one of the most powerful mind-altering chemicals. Perceptions of colors, sounds, and shapes are altered so much that even the most mundane experience–such as looking at the knots in a wooden table–can seem moving and exciting. Time perception is distorted, and objects and people may be viewed in a new way, with some users reporting that LSD increases their understanding of the world. For others, however, the experience brought on by LSD can be terrifying, particularly if users have had emotional difficulties in the past. Furthermore, people occasionally experience flash-backs, in which they hallucinate long after they initially used the drug (Yanakieva, 2019; Modak et al., 2019).

Although used illegally and recreationally, LSD and other hallucinogens such as *psilocybin* (a naturally occurring psychoactive ingredient found in some mushrooms) are increasingly being used as part of controlled, legal treatments for certain psycho-logical disorders such as posttraumatic stress disorder and depression. A growing body of research attests to their effectiveness in treating a variety of problems for which other, more conventional treatment techniques have proven ineffective (Fuentes et al., 2020; Ling et al., 2021).

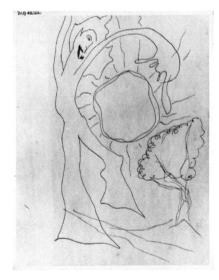

This drawing, made by someone taking LSD, suggests the effects of hallucino-gens on thinking.
Science History Images/Alamy Stock Photo

BECOMING AN INFORMED CONSUMER
of Psychology

Identifying Drug and Alcohol Problems

In a society bombarded with commercials for drugs that are guaranteed to cure everything from restless leg syndrome to erectile dysfunction, it is no wonder that drug-related prob-lems are a major social issue. Yet many people with drug and alcohol problems deny that they have them, and even close friends and family members may fail to realize when occasional social use of drugs or alcohol has turned into abuse.

Certain signs, however, indicate when use becomes abuse (National Institute on Drug Abuse, 2021). Among them are the following:

- Always getting high to have a good time
- Being high more often than not
- Getting high to get oneself going
- Going to work or class while high
- Missing or being unprepared for class or work because you were high
- Feeling bad later about something you said or did while high
- Driving a car while high
- Coming in conflict with the law because of drugs
- Doing something while high that you wouldn't do otherwise

- Being high in nonsocial, solitary situations
- Being unable to stop getting high
- Feeling a need for a drink or a drug to get through the day
- Becoming physically unhealthy due to alcohol or drugs
- Failing at school or on the job related to alcohol or drug use
- Thinking about alcohol or drugs all the time
- Avoiding family or friends while using alcohol or drugs

Any combination of these symptoms should be sufficient to alert you to the potential of a serious drug problem. Because drug and alcohol dependence are almost impossible to cure on one's own, people who suspect that they have a problem should seek immediate attention from a psychologist, physician, or counselor.

You can also get help from national hotlines. For alcohol difficulties, call the National Council on Alcoholism and Drug Dependence at (800) 622-2255. For drug problems, call the U.S. Substance Abuse and Mental Health Services Administration at (800) 662-4357. You can also search the web for a local listing of Alcoholics Anonymous or Narcotics Anonymous. In addition, you can check out the websites of the National Institute on Alcohol Abuse and Alcoholism (www.niaaa.nih.gov) and the National Institute on Drug Abuse (www. nida.nih.gov).

From the perspective of...

A Substance Abuse Counselor How would you explain why people start using drugs to the family members of someone who was addicted? What types of drug prevention programs would you advocate?

AleksandarNakic/E+/Getty Images

RECAP/EVALUATE/RETHINK

RECAP

LO 14-1 What are the major classifications of drugs, and what are their effects?

- Drugs can produce an altered state of consciousness. However, they vary in how dangerous they are and in whether they are addictive.
- Stimulants cause arousal in the central nervous system. Two common stimulants are caffeine and nicotine. More dangerous are cocaine and amphetamines, which in large quantities can lead to convulsions and death.
- Depressants decrease arousal in the central nervous system. They can cause intoxication along with feelings of euphoria. The most common depressants are alcohol and barbiturates.
- Alcohol is the most frequently used depressant. Its initial effects of released tension and positive feelings yield to depressive effects as the dose of alcohol increases. Both heredity and environmental stressors can lead to alcoholism.
- Morphine and heroin are narcotics, drugs that produce relaxation and relieve pain and anxiety. Because of their addictive qualities, morphine and heroin are particularly dangerous.
- Hallucinogens are drugs that produce hallucinations or other changes in perception. The most frequently used hallucinogen is marijuana, which has several long-term risks. Two other hallucinogens are LSD and Ecstasy.
- A number of signals indicate when drug use becomes drug abuse. People who suspect that they have a drug problem should get professional help. People are almost never capable of solving drug problems on their own.

EVALUATE

1. Drugs that affect a person's consciousness are referred to as _____.
2. Match the type of drug to an example of that type.
   1. narcotic–a pain reliever
   2. amphetamine–a strong stimulant
   3. hallucinogen–capable of producing hallucinations
   a. LSD
   b. heroin
   c. dexedrine, or speed
3. Classify each drug listed as a stimulant (S), depressant (D), hallucinogen (H), or narcotic (N).
   1. nicotine
   2. cocaine
   3. alcohol
   4. morphine
   5. marijuana
4. The effects of LSD can recur long after the drug has been taken. True or false?

5. _____ is a drug that has been used to treat people with heroin addiction.

RETHINK

1. Why have drug education campaigns largely been ineffective in stemming the use of illegal drugs? Should the use of certain now-illegal drugs be made legal? Would stressing reduction of drug use be more effective than completely prohibiting drug use?
2. People often use the word *addiction* loosely, speaking of an addiction to candy or a television show. Can you explain the difference between this type of "addiction" and a true biological addiction? Is there a difference between this type of "addiction" and a psychological addiction?

Answers to Evaluate Questions

1. psychoactive; **2.** 1-b, 2-c, 3-a; **3.** 1-S, 2-S, 3-D, 4-N, 5-H; **4.** True; **5.** Methadone

KEY TERMS

psychoactive drugs	stimulants	narcotics
addictive drugs	depressants	hallucinogens

LOOKING *Back*

EPILOGUE

Our examination of states of consciousness has ranged widely. It focuses both on natural factors, such as sleep, dreaming, and daydreaming, and on more intentional modes of altering consciousness, including hypnosis, meditation, and drugs. As we consider why people seek to alter their consciousness, we need to reflect on the uses and abuses of the various consciousness-altering strategies in which people engage.

Return briefly to the prologue of this chapter about Gerod Buckhalter's surgery to end his drug addiction to opioids and other drugs, and answer the following questions in light of your understanding of addictive drugs:

1. Why do you think Buckhalter's surgery was more successful than other kinds of drug treatments he tried? Should surgery be a last resort, or should it become more routinely prescribed for those with addictions?
2. If you wanted to discourage someone from using drugs such as opiates, how would you describe their addictive properties?
3. If you suspected a friend or classmate were addicted to painkillers, what symptoms would you watch for? What actions could you take if you wanted to help?
4. What factors might be responsible for the increasing rate of overdoses on prescription painkillers by young people?

Design Elements: Man with laptop: Dragon Images/Shutterstock; Exclamation point and mobile frame: McGraw Hill; Smartphone: WML Image/Shutterstock; Hands: Stefano Garau/Shutterstock.

VISUAL SUMMARY 4 States of Consciousness

MODULE 12 Sleep and Dreams

Stages of Sleep: Three stages of sleep, plus REM sleep

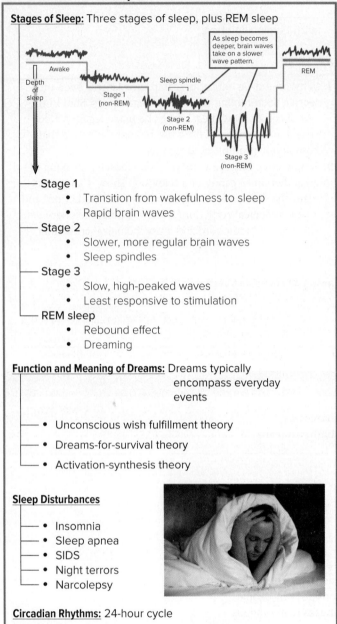

As sleep becomes deeper, brain waves take on a slower wave pattern.

Awake
Depth of sleep
Stage 1 (non-REM)
Sleep spindle
Stage 2 (non-REM)
Stage 3 (non-REM)
REM

- **Stage 1**
  - Transition from wakefulness to sleep
  - Rapid brain waves
- **Stage 2**
  - Slower, more regular brain waves
  - Sleep spindles
- **Stage 3**
  - Slow, high-peaked waves
  - Least responsive to stimulation
- **REM sleep**
  - Rebound effect
  - Dreaming

Function and Meaning of Dreams: Dreams typically encompass everyday events

- Unconscious wish fulfillment theory
- Dreams-for-survival theory
- Activation-synthesis theory

Sleep Disturbances

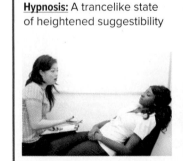

- Insomnia
- Sleep apnea
- SIDS
- Night terrors
- Narcolepsy

Circadian Rhythms: 24-hour cycle

MODULE 13 Hypnosis and Meditation

Hypnosis: A trancelike state of heightened suggestibility

Meditation: Learned technique for refocusing attention

MODULE 14 Drug Use

Stimulants: Increase arousal in the nervous system

- Caffeine
- Cocaine
- Amphetamines

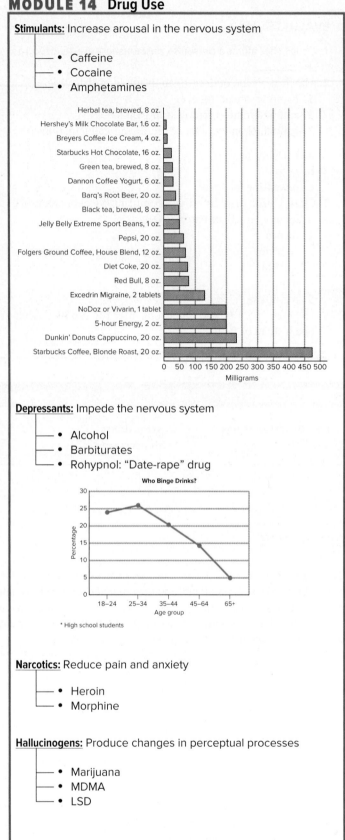

Herbal tea, brewed, 8 oz.
Hershey's Milk Chocolate Bar, 1.6 oz.
Breyers Coffee Ice Cream, 4 oz.
Starbucks Hot Chocolate, 16 oz.
Green tea, brewed, 8 oz.
Dannon Coffee Yogurt, 6 oz.
Barq's Root Beer, 20 oz.
Black tea, brewed, 8 oz.
Jelly Belly Extreme Sport Beans, 1 oz.
Pepsi, 20 oz.
Folgers Ground Coffee, House Blend, 12 oz.
Diet Coke, 20 oz.
Red Bull, 8 oz.
Excedrin Migraine, 2 tablets
NoDoz or Vivarin, 1 tablet
5-hour Energy, 2 oz.
Dunkin' Donuts Cappuccino, 20 oz.
Starbucks Coffee, Blonde Roast, 20 oz.

0 50 100 150 200 250 300 350 400 450 500
Milligrams

Depressants: Impede the nervous system

- Alcohol
- Barbiturates
- Rohypnol: "Date-rape" drug

Who Binge Drinks?

Percentage
30
25
20
15
10
5
0

18–24 25–34 35–44 45–64 65+
Age group

* High school students

Narcotics: Reduce pain and anxiety

- Heroin
- Morphine

Hallucinogens: Produce changes in perceptual processes

- Marijuana
- MDMA
- LSD

(Module 12): Hobson, 2007, Jawabri & Raja, 2021; Koldunova Anna/Shutterstock; (Module 13): (left) Paula Connelly/E+/Getty Images; (right): FatCamera/E+/Getty Images; (Module 14): Center for Science in the Public Interest; Bohm, 2021.

wavebreakmedia/Shutterstock

CHAPTER 5
Learning

LEARNING OUTCOMES FOR CHAPTER 5

PROLOGUE *A HELPING HAND*

Progressive Insurance has a deal for you: If you drive better, you will be rewarded with lower insurance rates.

But Progressive isn't going to take your word for how careful a driver you are. Instead, it will connect a tiny device called Snapshot under your car's dashboard, or you'll be asked to install a Snapshot app on your smartphone. Snapshot will monitor how fast you drive, how quickly you accelerate, how fast you go around corners, how many miles you travel, whether you make any sudden stops—and a lot more. Then, the data are transmitted to the insurance company in real time. The outcome: The better you drive, the more you'll save on your insurance (Geisler & Lobb, 2022; Sham, 2022).

LOOKING *Ahead*

The strategy that Progressive Insurance is using to encourage safe driving is not unique to that industry. For example, power companies use a similar type of device to provide customers with real-time feedback on their moment-to-moment energy use, allowing them to see how certain behaviors, such as turning on an air conditioner or turning off unneeded lights, directly affect their electric bill.

Offering rewards for desired behavior takes advantage of some fundamental principles of learning—the same processes that allow us to learn to read, study for a test, follow the rules of poker, or perform any of the countless activities that make up our daily routine. Each of us must acquire and then refine our skills and abilities through learning.

Learning is a fundamental topic for psychologists and plays a central role in almost every specialty area of psychology. For example, a psychologist studying perception might ask, "How do we learn that people who look small from a distance are far away and not simply tiny?" A developmental psychologist might inquire, "How do babies learn to distinguish their mothers from other people?" A clinical psychologist might wonder, "Why do some people learn to be afraid when they see a spider?" A social psychologist might ask, "How do we learn to believe that we've fallen in love?"

Each of these questions, although drawn from very different branches of psychology, can be answered only through an understanding of basic learning processes. In each case, a skill or a behavior is acquired, altered, or refined through experience.

In this chapter, we will explore several ways in which learning occurs, including through classical and operant conditioning approaches, which focus on outward, behavioral processes, as well as through cognitive approaches, which focus on mental processes. We will discuss cultural differences in learning and individual differences in learning styles that influence learning effectiveness, and we will examine practical learning programs, such as behavior modification, which are based on these learning approaches.

Module 15
Classical Conditioning

Does the mere sight of the golden arches in front of McDonald's make you think about hamburgers and perhaps make you feel pangs of hunger? If it does, you are displaying an elementary form of learning called classical conditioning. *Classical conditioning* helps explain such diverse phenomena as crying at the sight of a bride walking down the aisle, fearing the dark, and falling in love.

Classical conditioning is one of a number of different types of learning that psychologists have identified, but a general definition encompasses them all: **Learning** is a relatively permanent change in behavior that is brought about by experience.

How do we know when a behavior has been influenced by learning–or even is a result of learning? Part of the answer relates to the nature-nurture question, one of the fundamental issues underlying the field of psychology. In the acquisition of behaviors, experience–which is essential to the definition of learning–is the "nurture" part of the nature-nurture question.

However, it's not always easy to identify whether a change in behavior is due to nature or nurture because some changes in behavior or performance come about through maturation alone and don't involve experience. For instance, children become better tennis players as they grow older partly because their strength increases with their size–a maturational phenomenon. To understand when learning has occurred, we must differentiate maturational changes from improvements resulting from practice, which indicate that learning actually has occurred.

Similarly, short-term changes in behavior that are due to factors other than learning, such as declines in performance resulting from fatigue or lack of effort, are different from performance changes that are due to actual learning. If Serena Williams has a bad day on the tennis court because of tension or fatigue, this does not mean that she has not learned to play correctly or has "unlearned" how to play well. Because there is not always a one-to-one correspondence between learning and performance, understanding when true learning has occurred is difficult.

It is clear that we are primed for learning from the beginning of life. Infants exhibit a simple type of learning called habituation. *Habituation* is the decrease in response to a stimulus that occurs after repeated presentations of the same stimulus. For example, young infants may initially show interest in a novel stimulus, such as a brightly colored toy, but they will soon lose interest if they see the same toy over and over. (Adults exhibit habituation, too: Newlyweds soon stop noticing that they are wearing a wedding ring.) Habituation permits us to ignore things that have stopped providing new information.

Most learning is considerably more complex than habituation, and the study of learning has been at the core of the field of psychology. Although philosophers since the time of Aristotle have speculated on the foundations of learning, the first systematic research on learning was done at the beginning of the 20th century, when Ivan Pavlov (does the name ring a bell?) developed the framework for learning called classical conditioning.

The Basics of Classical Conditioning

Ivan Pavlov, a Russian physiologist, never intended to do psychological research. In 1904 he won a Nobel Prize for his work on digestion, testimony to his contribution to that field. Yet Pavlov is remembered not for his physiological research but for his

LEARNING OUTCOMES

LO 15-1 What is learning?

LO 15-2 How do we learn to form associations between stimuli and responses?

learning A relatively permanent change in behavior brought about by experience. (Module 15)

Ivan Pavlov (center) developed the principles of classical conditioning.
Pictorial Press Ltd/Alamy Stock Photo

classical conditioning A type of learning in which a neutral stimulus comes to bring about a response after it is paired with a stimulus that naturally brings about that response. (Module 15)

neutral stimulus A stimulus that, before conditioning, does not naturally bring about the response of interest. (Module 15)

unconditioned stimulus (UCS) A stimulus that naturally brings about a particular response without having been learned. (Module 15)

unconditioned response (UCR) A response that is natural and needs no training (e.g., salivation at the smell of food). (Module 15)

conditioned stimulus (CS) A once-neutral stimulus that has been paired with an unconditioned stimulus to bring about a response formerly caused only by the unconditioned stimulus. (Module 15)

conditioned response (CR) A response that, after conditioning, follows a previously neutral stimulus (e.g., salivation at the ringing of a bell). (Module 15)

experiments on basic learning processes–work that he began quite accidentally (Samoilov & Zayas, 2007; Grant & Wingate, 2011; Todes, 2014).

Pavlov had been studying the secretion of stomach acids and salivation in dogs in response to eating varying amounts and kinds of food. While doing his research, he observed a curious phenomenon: Sometimes salivation would begin in the dogs when they had not yet eaten any food. Just the sight of the experimenter who normally brought the food or even the sound of the experimenter's footsteps was enough to produce salivation in the dogs.

Pavlov's genius lay in his ability to recognize the implications of this discovery. He saw that the dogs were responding not only on the basis of a biological need (hunger) but also as a result of learning–or, as it came to be called, classical conditioning. **Classical conditioning** is a type of learning in which a neutral stimulus (such as the experimenter's footsteps) comes to elicit a response after being paired with a stimulus (such as food) that naturally brings about that response.

To demonstrate classical conditioning, Pavlov (1927) attached a tube to the salivary gland of a dog, allowing him to measure precisely the dog's salivation. He then rang a bell and, just a few seconds later, presented the dog with meat. This pairing occurred repeatedly and was carefully planned so that, each time, exactly the same amount of time elapsed between the presentation of the bell and the meat. At first, the dog would salivate only when the meat was presented, but soon it began to salivate at the sound of the bell. In fact, even when Pavlov stopped presenting the meat, the dog still salivated after hearing the sound. The dog had been classically conditioned to salivate to the bell.

As you can see in Figure 1, the basic processes of classical conditioning that underlie Pavlov's discovery are straightforward. However, the terminology he chose is not simple.

First, consider the diagram in Figure 1a. Before conditioning, there are two unrelated stimuli: the ringing of a bell and meat. We know that typically the sound of a bell does not lead to salivation but instead to some other response, such as pricking up the ears or perhaps a startle reaction. The bell is therefore called the neutral stimulus. A **neutral stimulus** is a stimulus that, before conditioning, does not naturally bring about the response in which we are interested.

Prior to conditioning, we also know that meat naturally causes a dog to salivate. Because food placed in a dog's mouth automatically causes salivation to occur, it is known as an unconditioned stimulus. An **unconditioned stimulus (UCS)** is a stimulus that naturally brings about a particular response without having been learned.

The response that the meat elicits (salivation) is called an unconditioned response. An **unconditioned response (UCR)** is a natural, innate response that occurs automatically and needs no training. Unconditioned responses are always brought about by the presence of unconditioned stimuli.

Figure 1b illustrates what happens during conditioning. The bell is rung just before each presentation of the meat. The goal of conditioning is for the dog to associate the bell with the unconditioned stimulus (meat) and therefore to bring about the same sort of response as the unconditioned stimulus.

After a number of pairings of the bell and meat, the bell alone causes the dog to salivate (as in Figure 1c). When conditioning is complete, the bell has changed from a neutral stimulus to what is called a conditioned stimulus. A **conditioned stimulus (CS)** is a once-neutral stimulus that has been paired with an unconditioned stimulus to bring about a response formerly caused only by the unconditioned stimulus. This time, salivation that occurs as a response to the conditioned stimulus (bell) is called a **conditioned response (CR)**. After conditioning, then, the conditioned stimulus brings about the conditioned response.

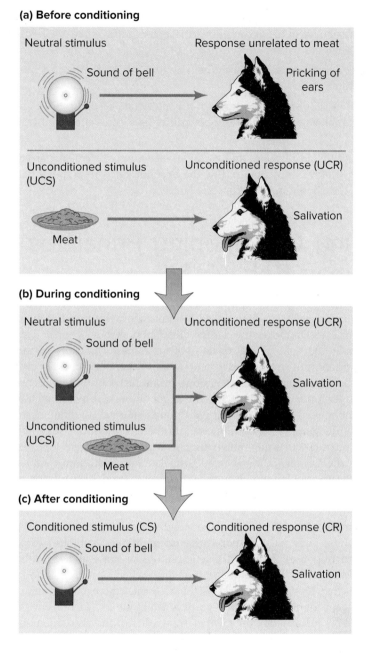

(a) Before conditioning

Neutral stimulus

Sound of bell

Response unrelated to meat

Pricking of ears

Unconditioned stimulus (UCS)

Meat

Unconditioned response (UCR)

Salivation

(b) During conditioning

Neutral stimulus

Sound of bell

Unconditioned response (UCR)

Salivation

Unconditioned stimulus (UCS)

Meat

(c) After conditioning

Conditioned stimulus (CS)

Sound of bell

Conditioned response (CR)

Salivation

FIGURE 1 The basic process of classical conditioning. (a) *Before conditioning:* The sound of a bell does *not* produce salivation, meaning that the bell is a neutral stimulus. In contrast, meat naturally brings about salivation, making the meat an unconditioned stimulus (UCS) and salivation an unconditioned response (UCR). (b) *During conditioning:* The bell rings just before the presentation of the meat. (c) *After conditioning:* Eventually, the sound of the bell alone produces salivation. We now can say that conditioning has been accomplished: The previously neutral stimulus of the bell is now considered a conditioned stimulus (CS) that brings about the conditioned response (CR) of salivation.

The sequence and timing of the presentation of the unconditioned stimulus and the conditioned stimulus are particularly important. Like a malfunctioning warning light at a railroad crossing that goes on after the train has passed by, a neutral stimulus that *follows* an unconditioned stimulus has little chance of becoming a conditioned stimulus. However, just as a warning light works best if it goes on right before a train passes, a neutral stimulus that is presented *just before* the unconditioned stimulus is most apt to result in successful conditioning. More specifically, conditioning is most effective if the neutral stimulus (which will become a conditioned stimulus) precedes the unconditioned stimulus by between a half second and several seconds, depending on what kind of response is being conditioned (Jennings et al., 2013; Harvie et al., 2017; Vandbakk et al., 2019).

Although the terminology Pavlov used to describe classical conditioning may seem confusing, the following summary can help make the relationships between stimuli and responses easier to understand and remember:

- Conditioned = learned
- Unconditioned = not learned

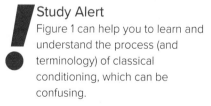

Study Alert

Figure 1 can help you to learn and understand the process (and terminology) of classical conditioning, which can be confusing.

- An *un*conditioned stimulus (UCS) leads to an *un*conditioned response (UCR).
- *Un*conditioned stimulus-*un*conditioned response pairings are *not* learned and *not* trained: They are naturally occurring.
- During conditioning, a previously neutral stimulus is transformed into the conditioned stimulus.
- A conditioned stimulus (CS) leads to a conditioned response (CR), and a conditioned stimulus-conditioned response pairing is a consequence of learning and training.
- An *un*conditioned response and a conditioned response are similar (such as salivation in Pavlov's experiment). But the *un*conditioned response occurs naturally, whereas the conditioned response is learned.

Applying Conditioning Principles to Human Behavior

Although the initial conditioning experiments were carried out with animals, classical conditioning principles were soon found to explain many aspects of everyday human behavior. Recall, for instance, the earlier illustration of how people may experience hunger pangs at the sight of McDonald's golden arches. The cause of this reaction is classical conditioning: The previously neutral arches have become associated with the food inside the restaurant (the unconditioned stimulus), causing the arches to become a conditioned stimulus that brings about the conditioned response of hunger.

Many emotional responses are learned through classical conditioning processes. For instance, how do some of us develop fears of mice, spiders, and other creatures that are typically harmless? In a now infamous case study, psychologist John B. Watson and colleague Rosalie Rayner (1920) showed that classical conditioning was at the root of such fears by conditioning an 11-month-old infant named Albert to be afraid of rats. "Little Albert," like most infants, initially was frightened by loud noises but had no fear of rats.

In the study, the experimenters sounded a loud noise whenever Little Albert touched a white, furry rat. The noise (the unconditioned stimulus) evoked fear (the unconditioned response). After just a few pairings of noise and rat, Albert began to show fear of the rat by itself, bursting into tears when he saw it. The rat, then, had become a CS that brought about the CR, fear. Furthermore, the effects of the conditioning lingered: Five days later, Albert reacted with some degree of fear not only when shown a rat but also when shown objects that looked similar to the white, furry rat, including a white rabbit, a white sealskin coat, and even a white Santa Claus mask.

We should note that we don't know what happened to Little Albert, and his fate remains a source of considerable speculation. Moreover, concerns have been expressed about the extent and strength of the conditioning. In any case, Watson, the experimenter, has been widely condemned for using ethically questionable procedures that could never be conducted today (Digdon, 2017; Fridlund et al., 2020; Powell & Schmaltz, 2021).

Learning by means of classical conditioning clearly also occurs during adulthood. For example, you may not go to a dentist as often as you should because of previous associations of dentists with pain. In more extreme cases, classical conditioning can lead to the development of *phobias*, which are intense, irrational fears. For example, an insect phobia might develop in someone who is stung by a bee. The insect phobia might be so severe that the person refrains from leaving home.

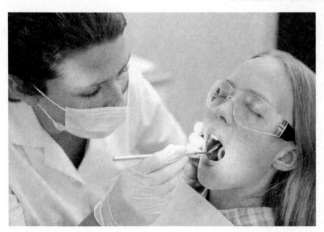

Because of a previous, unpleasant experience, a person may expect a similar occurrence when faced with a comparable situation in the future, a process known as stimulus generalization. Can you think of ways that this process occurs in everyday life?
Robert Daly/OJO Images/age fotostock

Posttraumatic stress disorder (PTSD), suffered by some war veterans and others who have had traumatic experiences, can also be produced by classical conditioning. Even years after their battlefield experiences, veterans may feel a rush of fear and anxiety at a stimulus such as a loud noise (Rosellini et al., 2015; Allen et al., 2019; Ressler et al., 2022).

Classical conditioning also explains why drug addictions are so difficult to treat. Drug addicts learn to associate certain stimuli–for example, drug paraphernalia such as a syringe or a room where they use drugs–with the pleasant feelings produced by the drugs. So simply seeing a syringe or entering a certain room can produce reactions associated with the drug and continued cravings for it (Saunders et al., 2013; Valyear et al., 2017; Baidoo & Leri, 2022).

In addition, racism may be sustained through classical conditioning. Specifically, exposure to certain news stories and social media accounts may lead to misguided expectations that members of certain minority groups are associated with danger, leading to the development of negative attitudes (Dang et al., 2015). On the other hand, classical conditioning also underlies pleasant experiences and emotions. For instance, you may have a particular fondness for the smell of a certain perfume or aftershave lotion because thoughts of an early love come rushing back whenever you encounter it. Or hearing a certain song can bring back happy or bittersweet emotions due to associations you developed in the past.

From the perspective of...

An Advertising Executive How might knowledge of classical conditioning be useful in creating an advertising campaign? What, if any, ethical issues arise from this use?

mentatdgt/Shutterstock

Extinction

What do you think would happen if a dog that had become classically conditioned to salivate at the ringing of a bell never again received food when the bell was rung? The answer lies in one of the basic phenomena of learning: extinction. **Extinction** occurs when a previously conditioned response decreases in frequency and eventually disappears.

To produce extinction, one needs to end the association between conditioned stimuli and unconditioned stimuli. For instance, if we had trained a dog to salivate (the conditioned response) at the ringing of a bell (the conditioned stimulus), we could produce extinction by repeatedly ringing the bell but *not* providing meat (the unconditioned stimulus; see Figure 2). At first, the dog would continue to salivate when it heard the bell, but after a few such instances, the amount of salivation would probably decline, and the dog would eventually stop responding to the bell altogether. At that point, we could say that the response had been extinguished. In sum, extinction occurs when the conditioned stimulus is presented repeatedly without the unconditioned stimulus.

We should keep in mind that extinction can be a helpful phenomenon. Consider, for instance, what it would be like if the fear you experienced while watching the shower murder scene in the classic movie *Psycho* never was extinguished. You might well tremble with fright every time you took a shower.

extinction A basic phenomenon of learning that occurs when a previously conditioned response decreases in frequency and eventually disappears. (Module 15)

FIGURE 2 Acquisition, extinction, and spontaneous recovery of a classically conditioned response. (a) A conditioned response (CR) gradually increases in strength during training. (b) However, if the conditioned stimulus (CS) is presented by itself enough times, the conditioned response gradually fades, and extinction occurs. (c) After a pause (d) in which the conditioned stimulus is not presented, spontaneous recovery can occur. However, extinction typically reoccurs soon after.

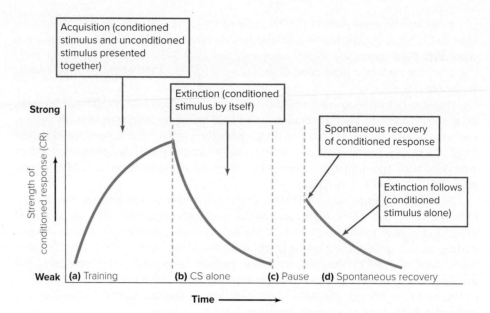

spontaneous recovery The reemergence of an extinguished conditioned response after a period of rest and with no further conditioning. (Module 15)

Once a conditioned response has been extinguished, has it vanished forever? Not necessarily. Pavlov discovered this phenomenon when he returned to his dog a few days after the conditioned behavior had seemingly been extinguished. If he rang a bell, the dog once again salivated—an effect known as spontaneous recovery. **Spontaneous recovery** is the reemergence of an extinguished conditioned response after a period of time and with no further conditioning.

Spontaneous recovery also helps explain why it is so hard to overcome drug addictions. For example, cocaine addicts who are thought to be "cured" can experience an irresistible impulse to use the drug again if they are subsequently confronted by a stimulus with strong connections to the drug, such as a white powder (Tunstall et al., 2013; Santos et al., 2017; Steins-Loeber et al., 2019).

Generalization and Discrimination

> **Study Alert**
>
> Remember that stimulus generalization relates to stimuli that are similar to one another, whereas stimulus discrimination relates to stimuli that are different from one another.

stimulus generalization A process in which, after a stimulus has been conditioned to produce a particular response, stimuli that are similar to the original stimulus produce the same response. (Module 15)

Despite differences in color and shape, to most of us a rose is a rose is a rose. The pleasure we experience at the beauty, smell, and grace of the flower is similar for different types of roses. Pavlov noticed a similar phenomenon. His dogs often salivated not only at the ringing of the bell that was used during their original conditioning but at the sound of a buzzer as well.

Such behavior is the result of stimulus generalization. **Stimulus generalization** is a process in which after a stimulus has been conditioned to produce a particular response, other stimuli that are similar to the original stimulus produce the same response. The greater the similarity between two stimuli, the greater the likelihood of stimulus generalization. Little Albert, who, as we mentioned earlier, was conditioned to be fearful of white rats, grew afraid of other furry white things as well. However, consistent with the principle of stimulus generalization, it is unlikely that Albert would have been afraid of a black dog because its color would have differentiated it sufficiently from the original fear-evoking stimulus.

The conditioned response elicited by the new stimulus is usually not as intense as the original conditioned response, although the more similar the new stimulus is to the old one, the more similar the new response will be. It is unlikely, then, that Little Albert's fear of the Santa Claus mask was as great as his learned fear of a rat. Still, stimulus generalization permits us to know, for example, that we ought to brake at all red lights, even if there are minor variations in size, shape, and shade.

In contrast, **stimulus discrimination** occurs if two stimuli are sufficiently distinct from each other such that one evokes a conditioned response but the other does not. Stimulus discrimination provides the ability to differentiate between stimuli. For example, my dog Cleo comes running into the kitchen when she hears the sound of the electric can opener, which she has learned is used to open her dog food when her dinner is about to be served. She does not bound into the kitchen at the sound of the food processor, although it sounds somewhat similar. In other words, she discriminates between the stimuli of can opener and food processor. Similarly, our ability to discriminate between the behavior of a growling dog and that of one whose tail is wagging can lead to adaptive behavior–avoiding the growling dog and petting the friendly one.

stimulus discrimination The process that occurs if two stimuli are sufficiently distinct from one another that one evokes a conditioned response but the other does not; the ability to differentiate between stimuli. (Module 15)

Beyond Traditional Classical Conditioning: Challenging Basic Assumptions

Although Pavlov hypothesized that all learning is nothing more than long strings of conditioned responses, this notion has not been supported by subsequent research. It turns out that classical conditioning provides us with only a partial explanation of how people and animals learn; indeed, Pavlov was wrong in some of his basic assumptions.

For example, according to Pavlov, the process of linking stimuli and responses occurs in a mechanistic, automatic, and unthinking way. In contrast to this perspective, learning theorists influenced by cognitive psychology have argued that learners actively develop an understanding and expectancy about which particular unconditioned stimuli are matched with specific conditioned stimuli. A ringing bell, for instance, gives a dog something to think about: the impending arrival of food (Kirsch et al., 2004; Giurfa, 2015; Reus-García et al., 2021).

Traditional explanations of how classical conditioning operates have also been challenged by John Garcia, a learning psychologist. He found that some organisms–including humans–were *biologically prepared* to quickly learn to avoid foods that smelled or tasted like something that made them sick. For instance, a dog quickly learns to avoid rotting food that in the past made it sick. Similarly, if every time you ate peanuts you had an upset stomach several hours later, eventually you would learn to avoid peanuts. In fact, you might develop a learned *taste aversion*, when the taste of a particular food is associated with unpleasant symptoms such as nausea or vomiting. If you developed a taste aversion to peanuts, merely tasting (or even smelling or in more extreme cases seeing a peanut) could produce such disagreeable symptoms (Garcia, 2003; Lin et al., 2017; Schier et al., 2019; Han et al., 2022).

The surprising part of Garcia's discovery was his demonstration that conditioning could occur even when the interval between exposure to the conditioned stimulus of tainted food and the response of sickness was as long as 8 hours. Furthermore, the conditioning persisted over very long periods and sometimes occurred after just one exposure.

These findings have had important practical implications. For example, to keep crows from stealing eggs, dairy farmers may lace an egg with a chemical and leave it in a place where crows will find it. The chemical temporarily makes the crows ill, but it does not harm them permanently. After exposure to a chemical-laden egg, crows no longer find the eggs appetizing (Baker et al., 2007; Bouton et al., 2011; Tobajas et al., 2019).

RECAP/EVALUATE/RETHINK

RECAP

LO 15-1 What is learning?

• Learning is a relatively permanent change in behavior resulting from experience.

LO 15-2 How do we learn to form associations between stimuli and responses?

• One major form of learning is classical conditioning, which occurs when a neutral stimulus–one that normally brings about no relevant response–is repeatedly paired with a stimulus (called an unconditioned stimulus) that brings about a natural, untrained response.

• Conditioning occurs when the neutral stimulus is repeatedly presented just before the unconditioned stimulus. After repeated pairings, the neutral stimulus elicits the same response that the unconditioned stimulus brings about. When this occurs, the neutral stimulus has become a conditioned stimulus, and the response a conditioned response.

• Learning is not always permanent. Extinction occurs when a previously learned response decreases in frequency and eventually disappears.

• Stimulus generalization is the tendency for a conditioned response to follow a stimulus that is similar to, but not the same as, the original conditioned stimulus. The opposite phenomenon, stimulus discrimination, occurs when an organism learns to distinguish between stimuli.

EVALUATE

1. _____ involves changes brought about by experience, whereas maturation describes changes resulting from biological development.

2. _____ is the name of the scientist responsible for discovering the learning phenomenon known as _____ conditioning, whereby an organism learns a response to a stimulus to which it normally would not respond.

Refer to the passage below to answer questions 3 through 5:
The last three times little Thandie visited Dr. Lopez for checkups, he administered a painful preventive immunization shot that left her in tears. Today, when her mother takes her for another checkup, Thandie begins to sob as soon as she comes face to face with Dr. Lopez, even before he has had a chance to say hello.

3. The painful shot that Thandie received during each visit was a(n) _____ _____ that elicited the _____ _____, her tears.

4. Dr. Lopez is upset because his presence has become a _____ _____ for Thandie's crying.

5. Fortunately, Dr. Lopez gave Thandie no more shots for quite some time. Over that period, she gradually stopped crying and even came to like him. _____ had occurred.

RETHINK

1. How likely is it that Little Albert, Watson's experimental subject, might have gone through life afraid of Santa Claus? Describe what could have happened to prevent his continual dread of Santa.

2. Can you think of ways that classical conditioning is used by politicians? Advertisers? Filmmakers? Do ethical issues arise from any of these uses?

Answers to Evaluate Questions

1. Learning; 2. Pavlov, classical; 3. unconditioned stimulus, unconditioned response; 4. conditioned stimulus; 5. Extinction

KEY TERMS

learning	unconditioned stimulus (UCS)	conditioned stimulus (CS)	stimulus generalization
classical conditioning	unconditioned response (UCR)	conditioned response (CR) extinction	stimulus discrimination
neutral stimulus		spontaneous recovery	

Module 16
Operant Conditioning

Very good . . . What a clever idea . . . Fantastic . . . I agree . . . Thank you . . . Excellent . . . Super . . . Right on . . . This is the best paper you've ever written; you get an A . . . You are really getting the hang of it . . . I'm impressed . . . You're getting a raise . . . Have a cookie . . . You look great . . . I love you . . . .

Few of us mind being the recipient of any of these comments. But what is especially noteworthy about them is that each of these simple statements can be used, through a process known as operant conditioning, to bring about powerful changes in behavior and to teach the most complex tasks. Operant conditioning is the basis for many of the most important kinds of human and animal learning.

Operant conditioning is learning in which a voluntary response is strengthened or weakened, depending on the response's favorable or unfavorable consequences. When we say that a response has been strengthened or weakened, we mean that it has been made more or less likely to recur regularly.

Unlike classical conditioning, in which the original behaviors are the natural, biological responses to the presence of a stimulus such as food, water, or pain, operant conditioning applies to voluntary responses that an organism performs deliberately to produce a desirable outcome. The term *operant* emphasizes this point: The organism *operates* on its environment to produce a desirable result. Operant conditioning is at work when we learn that toiling industriously can bring about a raise or that studying hard results in good grades.

As with classical conditioning, the basis for understanding operant conditioning was laid by work with animals. We turn now to some of that early research, which began with a simple inquiry into the behavior of cats.

LEARNING OUTCOMES

LO 16-1 What are the roles of reward and punishment in learning?

LO 16-2 What are some practical methods for bringing about behavior change, both in ourselves and in others?

operant conditioning Learning in which a voluntary response is strengthened or weakened, depending on its favorable or unfavorable consequences. (Module 16).

Thorndike's Law of Effect

If you placed a hungry cat in a cage and then put a small piece of food outside the cage, just beyond the cat's reach, chances are that the cat would eagerly search for a way out of the cage. The cat might first claw at the sides or push against an opening. Suppose, though, you had rigged things so that the cat could escape by stepping on a small paddle that released the latch to the door of the cage (see Figure 1). Eventually,

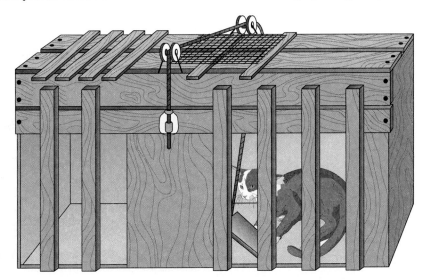

FIGURE 1 Edward L. Thorndike devised this puzzle box to study the process by which a cat learns to press a paddle to escape from the box and receive food. Do you think Thorndike's work has relevance to the question of why people voluntarily work on puzzles and play games, such as sudoku, Angry Birds, and jigsaw puzzles? Do they receive any rewards?

as it moved around the cage, the cat would happen to step on the paddle, the door would open, and the cat would eat the food.

What would happen if you then returned the cat to the box? The next time, it would probably take a little less time for the cat to step on the paddle and escape. After a few trials, the cat would deliberately step on the paddle as soon as it was placed in the cage. What would have occurred, according to Edward L. Thorndike (1932), who studied this situation extensively, was that the cat would have learned that pressing the paddle was associated with the desirable consequence of getting food. To summarize that relationship, Thorndike formulated the *law of effect*, which states that responses that lead to satisfying consequences are more likely to be repeated.

Thorndike believed that the law of effect operates as automatically as leaves fall off a tree in autumn. It was not necessary for an organism to understand that there was a link between a response and a reward. Instead, Thorndike believed, over time and through experience, the organism would make a direct connection between the stimulus and the response without any awareness that the connection existed.

The Basics of Operant Conditioning

Thorndike's early research served as the foundation for the work of one of the 20th century's most influential psychologists, B. F. Skinner (1904–1990). You may have heard of the Skinner box (shown in Figure 2), a chamber with a highly controlled environment that was used to study operant conditioning processes with laboratory animals. Whereas Thorndike's goal was to get his cats to learn to obtain food by leaving the box, animals in a Skinner box learn to obtain food by operating on their environment within the box. Skinner became interested in specifying how behavior varies as a result of alterations in the environment.

Skinner, whose work went far beyond perfecting Thorndike's earlier apparatus, is considered the inspiration for a whole generation of psychologists studying operant conditioning. To illustrate Skinner's contribution, let's consider what happens to a rat in the typical Skinner box (Soorya et al., 2011; Huston et al., 2013; De Meyer et al., 2019).

Suppose you want to teach a hungry rat to press a lever that is in its box. At first, the rat will wander around the box, exploring the environment in a relatively random fashion. At some point, however, it will probably press the lever by chance, and when it does, it will receive a food pellet. The first time this happens, the rat will not learn the connection between pressing a lever and receiving food and will continue to explore the box. Sooner or later, the rat will press the lever again and receive a pellet, and in time, the frequency of the pressing response will increase. Eventually, the rat will press the lever continually until it satisfies its hunger, thereby demonstrating that it has learned that the receipt of food is contingent on pressing the lever.

FIGURE 2 B. F. Skinner with a Skinner box used to study operant conditioning. Laboratory animals such as rats and pigeons could learn to press or peck a lever in order to obtain food.

(right): Science History Images/Alamy Stock Photo

REINFORCEMENT: THE CENTRAL CONCEPT OF OPERANT CONDITIONING

Skinner called the process that leads the rat to continue pressing the key "reinforcement." **Reinforcement** is the process by which a stimulus increases the probability that a preceding behavior will be repeated. In other words, pressing the lever is more likely to occur again because of the stimulus of food.

In a situation such as this one, the food is called a reinforcer. A **reinforcer** is any stimulus that increases the probability that a preceding behavior will occur again. Hence, food is a reinforcer because it increases the probability that the behavior of pressing (formally referred to as the *response* of pressing) will take place.

What kind of stimuli can act as reinforcers? Bonuses, toys, and good grades can serve as reinforcers—if they strengthen the probability of the response that occurred before their introduction. What makes something a reinforcer depends on individual preferences. Although a Hershey's bar can act as a reinforcer for one person, an individual who dislikes chocolate may find $1.00 more desirable. The only way we can know if a stimulus is a reinforcer for a particular organism is to observe whether the frequency of a previously occurring behavior increases after the presentation of the stimulus.

Of course, we are not born knowing that $1.00 can buy us a candy bar. Rather, through experience we learn that money is a valuable commodity because of its association with stimuli, such as food and drink, that are naturally reinforcing. This fact suggests a distinction between primary reinforcers and secondary reinforcers. A *primary reinforcer* satisfies some biological need and works naturally, regardless of a person's previous experience. Examples of primary reinforcers include food for a hungry person, warmth for a cold person, and relief for a person in pain.

In contrast, a *secondary reinforcer* is a stimulus that becomes reinforcing because of its association with a primary reinforcer. For instance, we know that money is valuable because we have learned that it allows us to obtain other desirable objects, including primary reinforcers such as food and shelter. Money thus becomes a secondary reinforcer (Qu et al., 2013; Thrailkill & Bouton, 2017; Rosenthal-von der Pütten et al., 2019).

Secondary reinforcers make up the heart of *token systems* sometimes used in the treatment of some psychological disorders in institutions such as psychiatric hospitals. In a token system, a patient is rewarded for showing desired behavior with a token such as a poker chip. The token—an example of a secondary reinforcer—can then be redeemed for something desirable, such as snacks, games, or money.

Neuroscientists are beginning to explore the biological underpinnings of reinforcers. For example, we now know that the neurotransmitter *dopamine* plays a key role in the reinforcement of behavior. When we are exposed to certain kinds of stimuli, a flood of dopamine cascades through parts of the brain, leading to feelings of pleasure that are reinforcing (Trujillo-Pisanty et al., 2011; Thompson & Wolpaw, 2015; Yang et al., 2021).

POSITIVE REINFORCERS, NEGATIVE REINFORCERS, AND PUNISHMENT

In many respects, reinforcers can be thought of in terms of rewards; both a reinforcer and a reward increase the probability that a preceding response will occur again. But the term *reward* is limited to *positive* occurrences, and this is where it differs from a reinforcer—for it turns out that reinforcers can be positive or negative.

A **positive reinforcer** is a stimulus *added* to the environment that brings about an increase in a preceding response. If food, water, money, or praise is provided after a response, it is more likely that that response will occur again in the future. The paychecks that workers get at the end of the week, for example, increase the likelihood that they will return to their jobs the following week.

In contrast, a **negative reinforcer** refers to an unpleasant stimulus whose removal leads to an increase in the probability that a preceding response will be repeated in

reinforcement The process by which a stimulus increases the probability that a preceding behavior will be repeated. (Module 16)

reinforcer Any stimulus that increases the probability that a preceding behavior will occur again. (Module 16)

Study Alert
Remember that primary reinforcers satisfy a biological need; secondary reinforcers are effective due to previous association with a primary reinforcer.

positive reinforcer A stimulus added to the environment that brings about an increase in a preceding response. (Module 16)

negative reinforcer An unpleasant stimulus whose removal leads to an increase in the probability that a preceding response will be repeated in the future. (Module 16)

the future. For example, if you have an itchy rash (an unpleasant stimulus) that is relieved when you apply a certain brand of ointment, you are more likely to use that ointment the next time you have an itchy rash. Using the ointment, then, is negatively reinforcing because it removes the unpleasant itch. Similarly, if your smartphone's volume is so loud that it hurts your ears when you first turn it on, you are likely to reduce the volume level. Lowering the volume is negatively reinforcing, and you are more apt to repeat the action in the future when you first turn it on. Negative reinforcement, then, teaches the individual that taking an action removes a negative condition that exists in the environment. Like positive reinforcers, negative reinforcers increase the likelihood that preceding behaviors will be repeated (DePaolo et al., 2019; Koob, 2021).

punishment A stimulus that decreases the probability that a previous behavior will occur again. (Module 16)

Note that negative reinforcement is not the same as punishment. **Punishment** refers to a stimulus that *decreases* the probability that a prior behavior will occur again. Unlike negative reinforcement, which produces an *increase* in behavior, punishment reduces the likelihood of a prior response. If we receive a shock that is meant to decrease a certain behavior, then we are receiving punishment, but if we are already receiving a shock and do something to stop that shock, the behavior that stops the shock is considered to be negatively reinforced. In the first case, the specific behavior is apt to decrease because of the punishment; in the second, it is likely to increase because of the negative reinforcement.

There are two types of punishment: positive punishment and negative punishment, just as there are positive reinforcement and negative reinforcement. In both cases, "positive" means adding something, and "negative" means removing something. *Positive punishment* weakens a response by applying an unpleasant stimulus. For instance, spanking a child for misbehaving or sending someone to jail for 10 years for committing a crime are examples of positive punishment. (In both cases, an unpleasant stimulus has been applied.)

In contrast, *negative punishment* consists of the removal of something pleasant. For instance, when a teenager is told they can no longer use their cell phone because they stayed out past curfew or when an employee is informed that they will have a cut in pay because of a poor job evaluation, negative punishment is being administered. (In both cases, something pleasant–cell phone use or pay–is being removed.)

Both positive and negative punishment result in a decrease in the likelihood that a prior behavior will be repeated. So a jail term is meant to lead to a reduction in criminal behavior, and loss of a teenager's cell phone is meant to reduce the likelihood of staying out past curfew.

The following rules (and the summary in Figure 3) can help you distinguish these concepts from one another:

- Reinforcement *increases* the frequency of the behavior preceding it; punishment *decreases* the frequency of the behavior preceding it.

- The *application* of a *positive* stimulus brings about an increase in the frequency of behavior and is referred to as positive reinforcement; the *application* of a *negative* stimulus decreases or reduces the frequency of behavior and is called positive punishment.

- The *removal* of a *negative* stimulus that results in an increase in the frequency of behavior is negative reinforcement; the *removal* of a *positive* stimulus that decreases the frequency of behavior is negative punishment.

Study Alert
The differences between positive reinforcement, negative reinforcement, positive punishment, and negative punishment are tricky, so pay special attention to Figure 3 and the definitions in the text.

THE PROS AND CONS OF PUNISHMENT: WHY REINFORCEMENT BEATS PUNISHMENT

Is punishment an effective way to modify behavior? Punishment often presents the quickest route to changing behavior that, if allowed to continue, might be dangerous to an individual. For instance, a parent may not have a second chance to warn a child not to run into a busy street, and so punishing the first incidence of this behavior

Intended result	When stimulus is added, the result is . . .		When stimulus is removed or terminated, the result is . . .	
Increase in behavior (reinforcement)	**Positive reinforcement** Example: Giving a raise for good performance Result: *Increase* in response of good performance		**Negative reinforcement** Example: Applying ointment that relieves an itchy rash leads to a higher future likelihood of applying the ointment if the rash returns. Result: *Increase* in response of using ointment	
Decrease in behavior (punishment)	**Positive punishment** Example: Yelling at a teenager for stealing a bracelet Result: *Decrease* in frequency of response of stealing		**Negative punishment** Example: Restricting teenager's access to a car due to breaking curfew Result: *Decrease* in response of breaking curfew	

FIGURE 3 Types of reinforcement and punishment.

(Top, Left): fizkes/Shutterstock; (Top, Right): Stockbyte/Getty Images; (Bottom, Left): lightfieldstudios/123RF; (Bottom, Right): WESTOCK PRODUCTIONS/Shutterstock

may prove to be wise. Moreover, the use of punishment to suppress behavior, even temporarily, provides an opportunity to reinforce a person for subsequently behaving in a more desirable way (Bruno, 2016; Wu et al., 2022).

However, punishment has several disadvantages that make its routine use questionable. For one thing, punishment is frequently ineffective, particularly if it is not delivered shortly after the undesired behavior or if the individual is able to leave the setting in which the punishment is being given. An employee who is reprimanded by the boss may quit; a teenager who loses the use of the family car may borrow a friend's car instead. In such instances, the initial behavior that is being punished may be replaced by one that is even less desirable.

Even worse, physical punishment can convey to the recipient the idea that physical aggression is permissible and perhaps even desirable. A father who yells at and hits his son for misbehaving teaches the son that aggression is an appropriate, adult response. The son soon may copy his father's behavior by acting aggressively toward others. In addition, physical punishment is often administered by people who are themselves angry or enraged. It is unlikely that individuals in such an emotional state will be able to think through what they are doing or control carefully the degree of punishment they are inflicting. Ultimately, those who resort to physical punishment run the risk that they will grow to be feared. Punishment can also reduce the self-esteem of recipients unless they can understand the reasons for it (Smith et al., 2011; Alampay et al., 2017; Gonzalez et al., 2019).

Finally, punishment does not convey any information about what an alternative, more appropriate behavior might be. To be useful in bringing about more desirable behavior in the future, punishment must be accompanied by specific information about the behavior that is being punished, along with specific suggestions concerning a more desirable behavior. Punishing a child for staring out the window in school could merely lead the child to stare at the floor instead. Unless we teach the child appropriate ways to respond, we have merely managed to substitute one undesirable behavior for another. If punishment is not followed up with reinforcement for subsequent behavior that is more appropriate, little will be accomplished. That's why the scientific research is clear: Spanking is both ineffective and ultimately harmful to children. Even punishment in the form of yelling is damaging (Wang & Kenny, 2013; Kubanek et al., 2015; Cuartas, 2022).

In short, reinforcing desired behavior is a more appropriate technique for modifying behavior than is using punishment. Both in and out of the scientific arena, then, reinforcement usually beats punishment (Hall et al., 2011; Bruno, 2016; Asadullah et al., 2019).

SCHEDULES OF REINFORCEMENT: TIMING LIFE'S REWARDS

The world would be a different place if poker players never played cards again after the first losing hand, if people who like to fish returned to shore as soon as they missed a catch, or if telemarketers never made another phone call after their first hang-up. The fact that such unreinforced behaviors continue, often with great frequency and persistence, illustrates that reinforcement need not be received continually for behavior to be learned and maintained. In fact, behavior that is reinforced only occasionally can ultimately be learned better than can behavior that is always reinforced.

The pattern of the frequency and timing of reinforcement that follow desired behavior is known as the **schedule of reinforcement**. In a **continuous reinforcement schedule**, behavior is reinforced every time it occurs. In contrast, in a **partial (or intermittent) reinforcement schedule**, behavior is reinforced some but not all the time it occurs. Although learning occurs more rapidly under a continuous reinforcement schedule, behavior lasts longer after reinforcement stops when it was learned under a partial reinforcement schedule (Holtyn & Lattal, 2013; Mullane et al., 2017; Gannon et al., 2021).

Why should intermittent reinforcement result in stronger, longer-lasting learning than with continuous reinforcement? We can answer the question by examining how we might behave when using a candy vending machine compared with a Las Vegas slot machine. When we use a vending machine, previous experience has taught us that every time we put in the appropriate amount of money, the reinforcement, a candy bar, ought to be delivered. In other words, the schedule of reinforcement is continuous. In comparison, a slot machine offers intermittent reinforcement. We have learned that after putting in our cash, most of the time we will not receive anything in return. At the same time, though, we know that we will occasionally win something.

Now suppose that, unknown to us, both the candy vending machine and the slot machine are broken, and so neither one is able to dispense anything. It would not be very long before we stopped depositing coins into the broken candy machine. Probably at most we would try only two or three times before leaving the machine in disgust. But the story would be quite different with the broken slot machine. Here, we would drop in money for a considerably longer time, even though there would be no payoff.

In formal terms, we can see the difference between the two reinforcement schedules: Partial reinforcement schedules (such as those provided by slot machines) maintain performance longer than do continuous reinforcement schedules (such as those established in candy vending machines) before *extinction*–the disappearance of the conditioned response–occurs.

Fixed- and Variable-Ratio Schedules Certain kinds of partial reinforcement schedules produce stronger and lengthier responding before extinction than do others. Some schedules are related to the *number of responses* made before reinforcement is given, and others are related to the *amount of time* that elapses before reinforcement is provided (Miguez et al., 2011; Manzo et al., 2015; Langford et al., 2019).

In a **fixed-ratio schedule**, reinforcement is given only after a specific number of responses. For instance, a rat might receive a food pellet every 10th time it pressed a lever; here, the ratio would be 1:10. Similarly, garment workers are generally paid on fixed-ratio schedules: They receive a specific number of dollars for every blouse they sew. Because a greater rate of production means more reinforcement, people on fixed-ratio schedules are apt to work as quickly as possible (see Figure 4).

In a **variable-ratio schedule**, behaviors are reinforced after an average number of responses, but exactly when reinforcement will occur is unpredictable. A good

---

schedules of reinforcement Different patterns of frequency and timing of reinforcement following desired behavior. (Module 16)

continuous reinforcement schedule A schedule in which behavior is reinforced every time the behavior occurs. (Module 16)

partial (or intermittent) reinforcement schedule Reinforcing of a behavior some but not all of the time. (Module 16)

fixed-ratio schedule A schedule in which reinforcement is given only after a specific number of responses are made. (Module 16)

variable-ratio schedule A schedule by which reinforcement occurs after a varying number of responses rather than after a fixed number. (Module 16)

❗ Study Alert

Remember that the different schedules of reinforcement affect the rapidity with which a response is learned and how long it lasts after reinforcement is no longer provided.

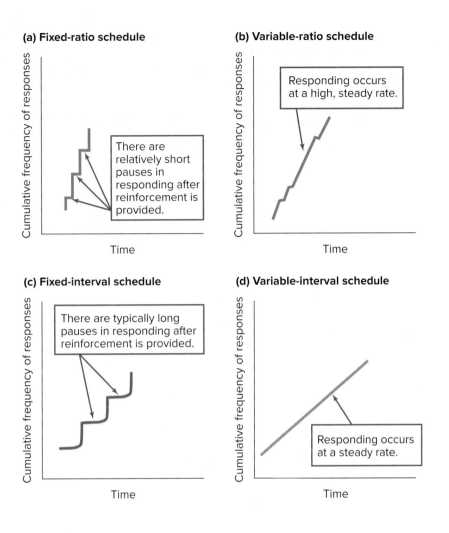

(a) Fixed-ratio schedule

Cumulative frequency of responses

There are relatively short pauses in responding after reinforcement is provided.

Time

(b) Variable-ratio schedule

Cumulative frequency of responses

Responding occurs at a high, steady rate.

Time

(c) Fixed-interval schedule

Cumulative frequency of responses

There are typically long pauses in responding after reinforcement is provided.

Time

(d) Variable-interval schedule

Cumulative frequency of responses

Responding occurs at a steady rate.

Time

FIGURE 4 Typical outcomes of different reinforcement schedules. (a) In a fixed-ratio schedule, reinforcement is provided after a specific number of responses are made. Because more responses lead to more reinforcement, fixed-ratio schedules produce a high rate of responding. (b) In a variable-ratio schedule, responding also occurs at a high rate. (c) A fixed-interval schedule produces lower rates of responding, especially just after reinforcement has been presented, because the organism learns that a specified time period must elapse between reinforcements. (d) A variable-interval schedule produces a fairly steady stream of responses.

example of a variable-ratio schedule is a telephone salesperson's job. The salesperson might make a sale during the 3rd, 8th, 9th, and 20th calls without being successful during any call in between. Although the number of responses they must make before closing a sale varies, it averages out to a 20% success rate. Under these circumstances, you might expect that the salesperson would try to make as many calls as possible in as short a time as possible. This is the case with all variable-ratio schedules, which lead to a high rate of response and resistance to extinction.

Fixed- and Variable-Interval Schedules: The Passage of Time In contrast to fixed- and variable-ratio schedules, in which the crucial factor is the *number* of responses, fixed-interval and variable-interval schedules focus on the *amount of time* that has elapsed since a person or animal was rewarded. One example of a fixed-interval schedule is a weekly paycheck. For people who receive regular, weekly paychecks, it typically makes relatively little difference exactly how much they produce in a given week.

A **fixed-interval schedule** provides reinforcement for a response only if a fixed time period has elapsed. Consequently, overall rates of response are relatively low. This is especially true in the period just after reinforcement, when the time before another reinforcement is relatively great. Students' study habits often exemplify this reality. If the periods between exams are relatively long (meaning that the opportunity for reinforcement for good performance is given fairly infrequently), students often study minimally or not at all until the day of the exam draws near. Just before the exam, however, students begin to cram for it, signaling a rapid increase in the rate of their studying response. As you might expect, immediately after the exam there is a rapid decline in the rate of responding, with few people opening a book the day after a test.

fixed-interval schedule A schedule in which reinforcement is provided for a response only after a fixed time period has elapsed. (Module 16)

Fixed-interval schedules produce the kind of "scalloping" pattern shown in Figure 4 (Daniels & Sanabria, 2017; Belke et al., 2021).

One way to decrease the delay in responding that occurs just after reinforcement and to maintain the desired behavior more consistently throughout an interval is to use a variable-interval schedule. In a **variable-interval schedule,** the time between reinforcements varies around some average rather than being fixed. For example, a professor who gives surprise quizzes that vary from one every 3 days to one every 3 weeks, averaging one every 2 weeks, is using a variable-interval schedule. Compared to the study habits we observed with a fixed-interval schedule, students' study habits under such a variable-interval schedule would most likely be very different. Students would be apt to study more regularly because they would never know when the next surprise quiz was coming. Variable-interval schedules, in general, are more likely to produce relatively steady rates of responding than are fixed-interval schedules, with responses that take longer to extinguish after reinforcement ends.

variable-interval schedule A schedule by which the time between reinforcements varies around some average rather than being fixed. (Module 16)

From the perspective of...

An Educator How would you use your knowledge of operant conditioning to set up a program to increase the likelihood that students will complete their homework more frequently?

Andersen Ross/Blend Images/Getty Images

DISCRIMINATION AND GENERALIZATION IN OPERANT CONDITIONING

It does not take a child long to learn that a red light at an intersection means stop and a green light indicates that it is permissible to continue, in the same way that a pigeon can learn to peck a key when a green light goes on but not when a red light appears. Just as in classical conditioning, then, operant learning involves the phenomena of discrimination and generalization.

The process by which people learn to discriminate stimuli is known as stimulus control training. In *stimulus control training*, a behavior is reinforced in the presence of a specific stimulus but not in its absence. For example, one of the most difficult discriminations many people face is determining when someone's friendliness is not mere friendliness but a signal of romantic interest. People learn to make the discrimination by observing the presence of certain nonverbal cues—such as increased eye contact and touching—that indicate romantic interest. When such cues are absent, people learn that no romantic interest is indicated. In this case, the nonverbal cue acts as a discriminative stimulus, one to which an organism learns to respond during stimulus control training. A *discriminative stimulus* signals the likelihood that reinforcement will follow a response. For example, if you wait until your roommate is in a good mood before you ask to borrow their favorite sweater, your behavior can be said to be under stimulus control because you can discriminate between your roommate's moods.

Just as in classical conditioning, the phenomenon of stimulus generalization, in which an organism learns a response to one stimulus and then exhibits the same response to slightly different stimuli, occurs in operant conditioning. If you have learned that being polite helps you to get your way in a certain situation (reinforcing your politeness), you are likely to generalize your response to other situations. Sometimes, though, generalization can have unfortunate consequences, such as when people behave negatively toward all members of a racial group because they have had an unpleasant experience with one member of that group.

SHAPING: REINFORCING WHAT DOESN'T COME NATURALLY

Consider the difficulty of using operant conditioning to teach people to repair an automobile transmission. If you had to wait until they chanced to fix a transmission perfectly before you provided them with reinforcement, the Model T Ford might be back in style long before they mastered the repair process.

There are many complex behaviors, ranging from auto repair to zoo management, that we would not expect to occur naturally as part of anyone's spontaneous behavior. For such behaviors, for which there might otherwise be no opportunity to provide reinforcement (because the behavior would never occur in the first place), a procedure known as shaping is used. **Shaping** is the process of teaching a complex behavior by rewarding closer and closer approximations of the desired behavior. In shaping, you start by reinforcing any behavior that is at all similar to the behavior you want the person to learn. Later, you reinforce only responses that are closer to the behavior you ultimately want to teach. Finally, you reinforce only the desired response. Each step in shaping, then, moves only slightly beyond the previously learned behavior, permitting the person to link the new step to the behavior learned earlier (Egervari et al., 2017; Sidiropoulos et al., 2021; Wierzbiński et al., 2021).

shaping The process of teaching a complex behavior by rewarding closer and closer approximations of the desired behavior. (Module 16)

Shaping allows even lower animals to learn complex responses that would never occur naturally, ranging from lions jumping through hoops, dolphins rescuing divers lost at sea, rodents finding hidden land mines, or—as we discuss in the *Applying Psychology in the 21st Century* feature—dogs identifying people who have COVID-19.

APPLYING PSYCHOLOGY IN THE 21ST CENTURY

A NOSE FOR DANGER: SNIFFING OUT COVID-19

When the members of the rock band Metallica and a number of other artists went on tour during the COVID-19 pandemic, their entourage contained some vitally important nonhumans: a number of German shepherds, Labrador retrievers, and Belgian malinois. These dogs had been trained to sniff out the presence of the virus on band members, their crews, and families (Browne, 2022).

It turns out that dogs, who have a highly sophisticated sense of smell, can learn to identify the odor of the COVID-19 virus and reliably distinguish it from other smells emanating from human bodies. In fact, dogs may be more accurate than the rapid antigen tests that are widely available, as they can identify even small amounts of the virus (Grandjean et al., 2020),

Using operant conditioning techniques, researchers taught the canine detectors to respond to the smell of COVID-19 face

A dog that can detect COVID-19 via smell visits an elementary school to learn if the virus is present in any students.
Boston Globe/Getty Images

masks from infected patients. In an innovative procedure, they used a scent-detection wheel constructed of cans with masks attached to them. Some masks were from patients with COVID and some from those

testing negative for the disease. The cans had small holes in the lids, and they were attached to the arms of the wheel. The dogs walked around the wheel, sniffing the cans. The results were clear: At high levels of accuracy, the dogs were able to distinguish masks from patients with COVID compared with those without the disease (Mendel et al., 2021).

One concern about the use of COVID-sniffing dogs is that there are no national standards for their appropriate use. In addition, although dogs clearly seem able to identify people with COVID by the smell, researchers have not yet determined the specific chemicals dogs detect (Gorman, 2021; Sakir et al., 2022).

Although we don't know the long-term potential of using dogs to detect disease, the initial results are promising.

Furthermore, classical conditioning might be used to identify other diseases and with animals other than dogs. Finally, the procedure has the potential to be used in other ways, such as finding victims buried during earthquakes. This research highlights the power of classical and operant conditioning.

RETHINK

- Using the terminology of classical conditioning, what is the unconditioned stimulus, the neutral stimulus, and the conditioned stimulus in the process by which dogs learned to associate the smell of COVID?
- What do you think are the advantages, and disadvantages, of using live animals to detect COVID-19 compared to more traditional medical tests using nose swabs?

Shaping also underlies the learning of many complex human skills. For instance, the organization of textbooks (like this one!) is based on the principles of shaping. Typically, information is presented so that new material builds on previously learned concepts or skills. Thus, the concept of shaping could not be presented until we had discussed the more basic principles of operant learning.

BIOLOGICAL CONSTRAINTS ON LEARNING: YOU CAN'T TEACH AN OLD DOG JUST ANY TRICK

Not all behaviors can be trained in all species equally well. Instead, there are *biological constraints,* built-in limitations in the ability of animals to learn particular behaviors. In some cases, an organism has a special predisposition that will aid in its learning a behavior (such as pecking behaviors in pigeons). In other cases, biological constraints act to prevent or inhibit an organism from learning a behavior.

Biological constraints make it nearly impossible for animals to learn certain behaviors. Here, psychologist Marian Breland Bailey attempts to overcome the natural limitations that inhibit the success of conditioning this rooster.

Dr. Marian Breland Bailey

For example, it's impossible to train pigs to pick up a disk because they are genetically programmed to push objects like it along the ground and *not* genetically programmed to pick objects up. Similarly, although a raccoon can be conditioned to drop a single coin into a piggy bank, it will do so only after rubbing the coin against the outside of the bank. The reason? After catching a fish, raccoons instinctively rub them against the ground to remove their outer covering (Breland & Breland, 1966; Vaccarino et al., 2019; Fernandez & Martin, 2021).

The existence of biological constraints is consistent with evolutionary explanations of behavior. Clearly, there are adaptive benefits that promote survival for organisms that quickly learn—or avoid—certain behaviors. For example, our ability to rapidly learn to avoid touching hot surfaces increases our chances of survival. Additional support for the evolutionary interpretation of biological constraints lies in the fact the associations that animals learn most readily involve stimuli that are most relevant to the specific environment in which they live (Davis, 2007; Behrendt, 2011; Mesoudi & Thornton, 2018).

Furthermore, psychologists taking an evolutionary perspective have suggested that we may be genetically predisposed to be fearful of certain stimuli, such as snakes or even threatening faces. For example, people in experiments learn associations relatively quickly between photos of faces with threatening expressions and neutral stimuli (such as an umbrella). In contrast, they are slower to learn associations between faces that have pleasant expressions and neutral stimuli. Stimuli that pose potential threats, such as snakes or people with hostile facial expressions, posed a potential danger to early humans, and there may be an evolved "fear module" in the brain that is sensitized to such threats (DeLoache & LoBue, 2009; Lester et al., 2017; Norrholm & Jovanovic, 2018).

COMPARING CLASSICAL AND OPERANT CONDITIONING

We've considered classical conditioning and operant conditioning as two completely different processes. And, as summarized in Figure 5, there are a number of key distinctions between the two forms of learning. For example, the key concept in classical conditioning is the association between stimuli, whereas in operant conditioning, it is reinforcement. Furthermore, classical conditioning involves an involuntary, natural, innate behavior, but operant conditioning is based on voluntary responses made by an organism.

Some researchers are asking if, in fact, the two types of learning are so different after all. Some learning psychologists have suggested that classical and operant conditioning might share some underlying processes. Arguing from an evolutionary viewpoint, they contend that it is unlikely that two completely separate basic processes would evolve. Instead, one process—albeit with considerable complexity in the way it operates—might better explain behavior. Although it's too early to know if this point of view will be supported, it is clear that there are a number of processes that operate both in classical and operant conditioning, including extinction, stimulus generalization, and stimulus discrimination (Silva et al., 2007; Lattal et al., 2017; Akpan, 2020).

Concept	Classical Conditioning	Operant Conditioning
Basic principle	Building associations between a conditioned stimulus and conditioned response	Reinforcement *increases* the frequency of the behavior preceding it; punishment *decreases* the frequency of the behavior preceding it.
Nature of behavior	Based on involuntary, natural, innate behavior. Behavior is elicited by the unconditioned or conditioned stimulus.	Organism voluntarily operates on its environment to produce a desirable result. After behavior occurs, the likelihood of the behavior occurring again is increased or decreased by the behavior's consequences.
Order of events	Before conditioning, an unconditioned stimulus leads to an unconditioned response. After conditioning, a conditioned stimulus leads to a conditioned response.	Reinforcement leads to an increase in behavior; punishment leads to a decrease in behavior.
Example	After a physician gives a child a series of painful injections (an unconditioned stimulus) that produce an emotional reaction (an unconditioned response), the child develops an emotional reaction (a conditioned response) whenever they see the physician (the conditioned stimulus).	A student who, after studying hard for a test, earns an A (the positive reinforcer), is more likely to study hard in the future. A student who, after going out drinking the night before a test, fails the test (punishment) is less likely to go out drinking the night before the next test.

FIGURE 5 Comparing key concepts in classical conditioning and operant conditioning.
(Left): McGraw Hill; (right): Michaelpuche/Shutterstock

BECOMING AN INFORMED CONSUMER
of Psychology

Using Behavior Analysis and Behavior Modification

A couple who had been living together for 3 years began to fight frequently. The issues of disagreement ranged from who was going to do the dishes to the quality of their love life.

Disturbed, the couple consulted with a *behavior analyst,* a psychologist who specialized in behavior-modification techniques. The behavior analyst asked the couple to keep a detailed written record of their interactions over the next 2 weeks.

When the couple returned with the data, the psychologist carefully reviewed their records. In doing so, the psychologist noticed a pattern: Each of their arguments had occurred just after one or the other had left a household chore undone, such as leaving dirty dishes in the sink or draping clothes on the only chair in the bedroom.

Using the data the couple had collected, the behavior analyst asked the couple to list all the chores that could possibly arise and assign each one a point value depending on how long it took to complete. Then the psychologist had them divide the chores equally and agree in a written contract to fulfill the ones assigned to them. If either failed to carry out one of the assigned chores, they would have to place one dollar per point in a fund for the other to spend. They also agreed to a program of verbal praise, promising to reward each other verbally for completing a chore.

The couple agreed to try it for a month and to keep careful records of the number of arguments they had during that period. To their surprise, the number declined rapidly.

behavior modification A technique whose goal is to increase the frequency of desirable behaviors and decrease the incidence of unwanted ones. (Module 16)

The case just presented provides an illustration of behavior modification. **Behavior modification** is a technique for increasing the frequency of desirable behaviors and decreasing the incidence of unwanted ones.

Using the basic principles of learning theory, behavior-modification techniques have proved to be helpful in a variety of situations. People with severe intellectual disability have been taught to dress and feed themselves for the first time in their lives. Behavior modification has also helped people lose weight, give up smoking, behave more safely, and study more effectively (Etienne, 2013; Warmbold-Brann et al., 2017; Nam & Lee, 2021).

The techniques used by behavior analysts are as varied as the list of processes that modify behavior. They include reinforcement scheduling, shaping, generalization training, discrimination training, and extinction. Participants in a behavior-change program do, however, typically follow a series of similar basic steps that include the following:

- *Identifying goals and target behaviors.* The first step is to define desired behavior. Is it an increase in time spent studying? A decrease in weight? An increase in the use of language? A reduction in the amount of aggression displayed by a child? The goals must be stated in observable terms and must lead to specific targets. For instance, a goal might be "to increase study time," whereas the target behavior would be "to study at least 2 hours per day on weekdays and an hour on Saturdays."
- *Designing a data-recording system and recording preliminary data.* To determine whether behavior has changed, it is necessary to collect data before any changes are made in the situation. This information provides a baseline against which future changes can be measured.
- *Selecting a behavior-change strategy.* The crucial step is to choose an appropriate strategy. Typically, a variety of treatments is used. This might include the systematic use of positive reinforcement for desired behavior (verbal praise or something more tangible, such as food), as well as a program of extinction for undesirable behavior

(ignoring a child who throws a tantrum). Selecting the right reinforcers is critical, and it may be necessary to experiment a bit to find out what is important to a particular individual.

- *Implementing the program.* Probably the most important aspect of program implementation is consistency. It is also important to reinforce the intended behavior. For example, suppose a parent wants their child to spend more time on homework, but as soon as the child sits down to study, they ask for a snack. If the parent gets a snack for them, they are likely to be reinforcing the child's delaying tactic, not their studying.

- *Keeping careful records after the program is implemented.* Another crucial task is record keeping. If the target behaviors are not monitored, there is no way of knowing whether the program has actually been successful.

- *Evaluating and altering the ongoing program.* Finally, the results of the program should be compared with baseline, preimplementation data to determine its effectiveness. If the program has been successful, the procedures employed can be phased out gradually. For instance, if the program called for reinforcing every instance of picking up one's clothes from the bedroom floor, the reinforcement schedule could be modified to a fixed-ratio schedule in which every third instance is reinforced. However, if the program has not been successful in bringing about the desired behavior change, consideration of other approaches might be advisable.

Behavior-change techniques based on these general principles have enjoyed wide success and have proved to be one of the most powerful means of modifying behavior. Clearly, it is possible to employ the basic notions of learning theory to improve our lives.

RECAP/EVALUATE/RETHINK

RECAP

LO 16-1 What are the roles of reward and punishment in learning?

- Operant conditioning is a form of learning in which a voluntary behavior is strengthened or weakened. According to B. F. Skinner, the major mechanism underlying learning is reinforcement, the process by which a stimulus increases the probability that a preceding behavior will be repeated.

- Primary reinforcers are rewards that are naturally effective without previous experience because they satisfy a biological need. Secondary reinforcers begin to act as if they were primary reinforcers through association with a primary reinforcer.

- Positive reinforcers are stimuli that are added to the environment and lead to an increase in a preceding response. Negative reinforcers are stimuli that remove something unpleasant from the environment, also leading to an increase in the preceding response.

- Punishment decreases the probability that a prior behavior will occur. Positive punishment weakens a response through the application of an unpleasant stimulus, whereas negative punishment weakens a response by the removal of something positive. In contrast to reinforcement, in which the goal is to increase the incidence of behavior, punishment is meant to decrease or suppress behavior.

- Schedules and patterns of reinforcement affect the strength and duration of learning. Generally, partial reinforcement schedules—in which reinforcers are not delivered on every trial—produce stronger and longer-lasting learning than do continuous reinforcement schedules.

- Among the major categories of reinforcement schedules are fixed- and variable-ratio schedules, which are based on the number of responses made, and fixed- and variable-interval schedules, which are based on the time interval that elapses before reinforcement is provided.

- Stimulus control training (similar to stimulus discrimination in classical conditioning) is reinforcement of a behavior in the presence of a specific stimulus but not in its absence. In stimulus generalization, an organism learns a response to one stimulus and then exhibits the same response to slightly different stimuli.

- Shaping is a process for teaching complex behaviors by rewarding closer and closer approximations of the desired final behavior.

- There are biological constraints, or built-in limitations, on the ability of an organism to learn: Certain behaviors will be relatively easy for individuals of a species to learn, whereas other behaviors will be either difficult or impossible for them to learn.

LO 16-2 What are some practical methods for bringing about behavior change, both in ourselves and in others?

- Behavior modification is a method for formally using the principles of learning theory to promote the frequency of desired behaviors and to decrease or eliminate unwanted ones.

EVALUATE

1. _____ conditioning describes learning that occurs as a result of reinforcement.
2. Match the type of operant learning with its definition:

    1. An unpleasant stimulus is presented to decrease behavior.
    2. An unpleasant stimulus is removed to increase behavior.
    3. A pleasant stimulus is presented to increase behavior.
    4. A pleasant stimulus is removed to decrease behavior.

    a. positive reinforcement
    b. negative reinforcement
    c. positive punishment
    d. negative punishment

3. Sanjay had had a rough day, and his son's noisemaking was not helping him relax. Not wanting to resort to scolding, Sanjay told his son in a serious manner that he was very tired and would like the boy to play quietly for an hour. This approach worked. For Sanjay, the change in his son's behavior was

    a. positively reinforcing.
    b. negatively reinforcing.

4. In a _____ reinforcement schedule, behavior is reinforced some of the time, whereas in a _____ reinforcement schedule, behavior is reinforced all the time.
5. Match the type of reinforcement schedule with its definition.

    1. Reinforcement occurs after a set time period.
    2. Reinforcement occurs after a set number of responses.
    3. Reinforcement occurs after a varying time period.
    4. Reinforcement occurs after a varying number of responses.

    a. fixed-ratio
    b. variable-interval
    c. fixed-interval
    d. variable-ratio

RETHINK

1. Using the scientific literature as a guide, what would you tell parents who want to know if the routine use of physical punishment is a necessary and acceptable form of child rearing?
2. How might operant conditioning be used to address serious personal concerns, such as smoking and unhealthy eating?

Answers to Evaluate Questions

1. Operant; 2. 1-c, 2-b, 3-a, 4-d; 3. b; 4. partial (or intermittent), continuous; 5. 1-c, 2-a, 3-b, 4-d

KEY TERMS

operant conditioning	punishment	partial (or intermittent) reinforcement schedule	fixed-interval schedule
reinforcement	schedule of reinforcement	fixed-ratio schedule	variable-interval schedule
reinforcer	continuous reinforcement schedule	variable-ratio schedule	shaping
positive reinforcer			behavior modification
negative reinforcer			

Module 17
Cognitive Approaches to Learning

Consider what happens when people learn to drive a car. They don't just get behind the wheel and stumble around until they randomly put the key into the ignition, and later, after many false starts, accidentally manage to get the car to move forward, thereby receiving positive reinforcement. Rather, they already know the basic elements of driving from previous experience as passengers, when they more than likely noticed how the key was inserted into the ignition, the car was put in drive, and the gas pedal was pressed to make the car go forward.

Clearly, not all learning is due to operant and classical conditioning. In fact, such activities as learning to drive a car imply that some kinds of learning must involve higher-order processes in which people's thoughts and memories and the way they process information account for their responses. Such situations argue against regarding learning as the unthinking, mechanical, and automatic acquisition of associations between stimuli and responses, as in classical conditioning, or the presentation of reinforcement, as in operant conditioning.

Some psychologists view learning in terms of the thought processes, or cognitions, that underlie it, an approach known as cognitive learning theory. **Cognitive learning theory** focuses on how people think. Psychologists who use the cognitive learning perspective do not deny the importance of classical and operant conditioning; however, they have developed approaches that focus on the unseen mental processes that occur during learning, rather than concentrating solely on external stimuli, responses, and reinforcements.

In its most basic formulation, cognitive learning theory suggests that it is not enough to say that people make responses because there is an assumed link between a stimulus and a response—a link that is the result of a past history of reinforcement for a response. Instead, according to this point of view, people and even lower animals develop an *expectation* that they will receive a reinforcer after making a response. Two types of learning in which no obvious prior reinforcement is present are latent learning and observational learning.

LEARNING OUTCOME

LO 17-1 What are the roles of cognition and thought in learning?

! Study Alert

Remember that the cognitive learning approach focuses on the *internal* thoughts and expectations of learners, whereas classical and operant conditioning approaches focus on *external* stimuli, responses, and reinforcement.

cognitive learning theory An approach to the study of learning that focuses on the thought processes that underlie learning. (Module 17)

latent learning Learning in which a new behavior is acquired but is not demonstrated until some incentive is provided for displaying it. (Module 17)

Latent Learning

Evidence for the importance of cognitive processes comes from a series of animal experiments that revealed a type of cognitive learning called latent learning. In **latent learning,** a new behavior is learned but not demonstrated until some incentive is provided for displaying it (Tolman & Honzik, 1930). In short, latent learning occurs without reinforcement.

In the studies demonstrating latent learning, psychologists examined the behavior of rats in a maze such as the one shown in Figure 1a. In one experiment, a group of rats was allowed to wander around the maze once a day for 17 days without ever receiving a reward (called the unrewarded group). Understandably, those rats made many errors and spent a relatively long time reaching the end of the maze. A second group, however, was always given food at the end of the maze (the rewarded group). Not surprisingly, those rats learned to run quickly and directly to the food box, making few errors.

Previous experience as an observant passenger in a car helps people learn to drive themselves.
Garnet Photo/Shutterstock

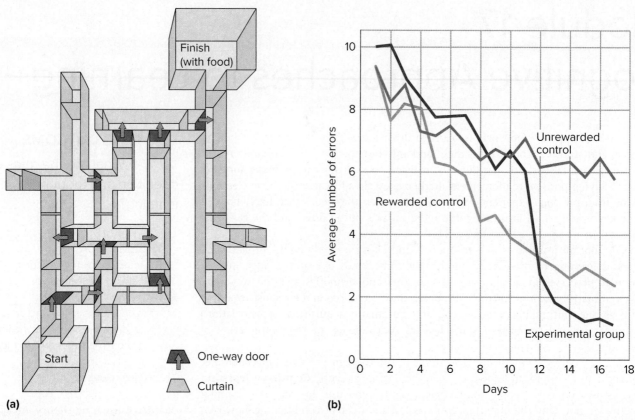

FIGURE 1 Latent learning. (a) Rats were allowed to roam through a maze of this sort once a day for 17 days. (b) The rats that were never rewarded (the unrewarded control condition) consistently made the most errors, whereas those that received food at the finish every day (the rewarded control condition) consistently made far fewer errors. But the results also showed latent learning: Rats that were rewarded only after the 10th day (the experimental group) showed an immediate reduction in errors and soon became similar in error rate to the rats that had been rewarded consistently. According to cognitive learning theorists, the reduction in errors indicates that the rats had developed a cognitive map—a mental representation—of the maze. Can you think of other examples of latent learning?

Source (a and b): Adapted from Tolman & Honzik, 1930.

A third group of rats (the experimental group) started out in the same situation as the unrewarded rats but only for the first 10 days. On the 11th day, a critical experimental manipulation was introduced: From that point on, the rats in this group were given food for completing the maze. The results of this manipulation were dramatic, as you can see from the graph in Figure 1b. The previously unrewarded rats, which had earlier seemed to wander about aimlessly, showed such reductions in running time and declines in error rates that their performance almost immediately matched that of the group that had received rewards from the start.

To cognitive theorists, it seemed clear that the unrewarded rats had learned the layout of the maze early in their explorations; they just never displayed their latent learning until the reinforcement was offered. Instead, those rats seemed to develop a *cognitive map* of the maze—a mental representation of spatial locations and directions.

People, too, develop cognitive maps of their surroundings. For example, latent learning may permit you to know the location of a kitchenware store at a local mall you've frequently visited, even though you've never entered the store and don't even like to cook.

The possibility that we develop our cognitive maps through latent learning presents something of a problem for strict operant conditioning theorists. If we consider the results of the maze-learning experiment, for instance, it is unclear what reinforcement permitted the rats that initially received no reward to learn the layout of the maze because there was no obvious reinforcer present. Instead, the results support a cognitive view of learning, in which changes occurred in unobservable mental processes (Malin et al., 2015; Forbus et al., 2017; Wang & Hayden, 2021).

Observational Learning: Learning Through Imitation

Let's return for a moment to the case of a person learning to drive. How can we account for instances in which an individual with no direct experience in carrying out a particular behavior learns the behavior and then performs it? To answer this question, psychologists have focused on another aspect of cognitive learning: observational learning.

According to psychologist Albert Bandura and colleagues, a major part of human learning consists of **observational learning,** which is learning by watching the behavior of another person, or *model*. Because of its reliance on observation of others–a social phenomenon–the perspective taken by Bandura is often referred to as a *social cognitive* approach to learning (Bandura & Hall, 2018; Carcea & Froemke, 2019; Zhang et al., 2022).

Bandura dramatically demonstrated the ability of models to stimulate learning in a classic experiment. In the study, young children saw a film of an adult wildly hitting a 5-foot-tall inflatable punching toy called a Bobo doll (Bandura et al., 1963a, 1963b). Later, the children were given the opportunity to play with the Bobo doll themselves, and, sure enough, most displayed the same kind of behavior, in some cases mimicking the aggressive behavior almost identically.

Not only negative behaviors are acquired through observational learning. In one experiment, for example, children who were afraid of dogs were exposed to a model–dubbed the Fearless Peer–playing with a dog (Bandura et al., 1967). After exposure, observers were considerably more likely to approach a strange dog than were children who had not viewed the Fearless Peer.

Observational learning is particularly important in acquiring skills in which the operant conditioning technique of shaping is inappropriate. Piloting an airplane and performing brain surgery, for example, are behaviors that could hardly be learned by using trial-and-error methods without grave cost–literally–to those involved in the learning process.

Observational learning may have a genetic basis. For example, we find observational learning at work with mother animals teaching their young such activities as hunting. In addition, the discovery of *mirror neurons* that fire when we observe another person carrying out a behavior suggests that the capacity to imitate others may be innate (Fernald, 2015; Catmur & Heyes, 2019; Maggio et al., 2022; also see the *Neuroscience in Your Life* feature).

Not all behavior that we witness is learned or carried out, of course. One crucial factor that determines whether we later imitate a model is whether the model is rewarded for their behavior. If we observe a friend being rewarded for putting more time into studying by receiving higher grades, we are more likely to imitate that behavior than we would if that behavior resulted only in being stressed and tired. Models who are rewarded for behaving in a particular way are more apt to be mimicked than are models who receive punishment. Observing the punishment of a model, however, does not necessarily stop observers from learning the behavior. Observers can still describe the model's behavior–they are just less apt to perform it (Bandura, 1994).

observational learning Learning by observing the behavior of another person, or model. (Module 17)

! Study Alert

A key point of observational learning approaches: Behavior of models who are rewarded for a given behavior is more likely to be imitated than that of models who are punished for the behavior.

By observing his father sort the laundry, this child may be experiencing observational learning. How might this kind of learning help dispel gender stereotypes?

Art_Photo/Shutterstock

NEUROSCIENCE IN YOUR LIFE: IMAGINE A NEW SKILL AND CHANGE YOUR BRAIN

What would you do if you wanted to learn how to play tennis well? You'd probably repeatedly practice your serve, your backhand stroke, and other key tennis skills. This type of skill acquisition, called motor learning, requires complex processing in a number of brain areas.

But hitting a ball on the tennis court is not the only way to learn a motor skill, and the way a person practices a skill affects the way their brain changes after motor learning. For example, in one study, neuroscientists gave participants five training sessions of a dart-throwing task, with half the participants assigned to physical practice and half to "motor imagery" practice. People in the physical practice group actually carried out the task. But those in the motor imagery practice group were instructed to simply *imagine* throwing a dart at the bullseye. Before and after the training sessions, everyone received a type of magnetic resonance imaging (MRI) scan that measures how parts of the brain synchronize with each other (Kraeutner et al., 2022).

The results of the study showed that both types of training led to changes in synchronized brain activity. But motor imagery practice actually led to more widespread changes compared to physical practice. Moreover, the people who showed the most changes in brain activity also saw the most improvement in their dart throwing. These results provide strong evidence for how incorporating mental imagery enhances the brain's response to motor learning.

Increased Synchronized Activity in Physical Practice Compared to Motor Imagery Practice

Increased Synchronized Activity in Motor Imagery Practice Compared to Physical Practice

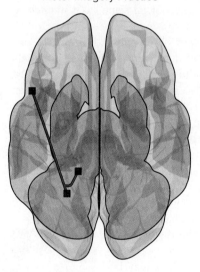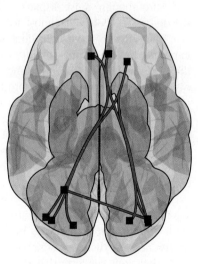

The red lines indicate brain regions that showed more functional connectivity (that is, synchronized activity) after five sessions of dart-throwing training in the physical practice group versus mental imagery practice group. Functional connectivity between a region of the frontal lobes and a region of the cerebellum increased more after physical practice compared to mental imagery practice (left figure). Compared to the physical practice group, the motor imagery group, who imagined throwing a dart rather than physically throwing it, had more widespread increases in functional connectivity between brain regions (right figure).
Source: Kraeutner et al., 2022

Observational learning is central to a number of important issues relating to the extent to which people learn simply by watching the behavior of others. For instance, the degree to which observation of media aggression produces subsequent aggression on the part of viewers is a crucial–and controversial–question, as we discuss next.

VIOLENCE IN TELEVISION AND VIDEO GAMES: DO THE MEDIA'S MESSAGES MATTER?

In an episode of *The Sopranos*, the famous television series, fictional mobster Tony Soprano murdered one of his associates. To make identification of the victim's body difficult, Soprano and one of his henchmen dismembered the body and dumped the body parts.

A few months later, in real life, two half brothers in Riverside, California, strangled their mother and then cut her head and hands from her body. Jason Bautista, 20, and Matthew Montejo, 15, were caught by police after a security guard noticed that the bundle they were attempting to throw in a dumpster had a foot sticking out of it. They told police that the plan to dismember their mother was inspired by *The Sopranos* episode (Martelle et al., 2003; Srisavasdi, 2008).

Like other "media copycat" killings, the brothers' cold-blooded brutality raises a critical issue: Does observing violent, antisocial acts in the media lead viewers to behave in similar ways? Because research on modeling shows that people frequently learn and imitate the aggression that they observe, this question is among the most important issues being addressed by psychologists.

Certainly, the amount of violence in the mass media is enormous. By the age of 18 years, the average young person has viewed some 200,000 acts of violence on television (American Academy of Pediatrics Council on Communication and Media, 2009).

Most psychologists agree that watching high levels of media violence makes viewers more susceptible to acting aggressively. For example, one survey showed that one-fourth of violent young male offenders incarcerated in Florida had attempted to commit a media-inspired copycat crime. A significant proportion of those teenage offenders noted that they paid close attention to the media. In another study, groups that held diverging points of view and that first met online were associated with increased violence when they actually met face-to-face (Boxer et al., 2009; Ferguson, 2015; Gallacher et al., 2021).

Playing violent video games has also been blamed as a source of actual violence. Certainly, after every mass shooting in the United States, some politicians suggest that participation in violent gaming is at the root of the shooter's behavior. Is there any truth to such assertions (Draper, 2019)?

In fact, some evidence supports a link between participating in violent video games and actual aggression. In one of a series of studies by psychologist Craig Anderson and his colleagues, college students who frequently played violent video games were more likely to have been involved in delinquent behavior and aggression. Frequent players also had lower academic achievement (Anderson & Bushman, 2018).

On the other hand, a few contrary research findings exist. For example, one meta-analysis of video game influences finds minimal effects on aggression. Furthermore, some researchers argue that violent video games may produce certain positive results–such as a rise in social networking among players (Ferguson & Beresin, 2017; Ferguson & Wang, 2019; Franceschini et al., 2022).

However, most experts agree that the preponderance of evidence points to at least moderate negative outcomes from viewing violent video games. Further, in light of the research evidence, a task force of the American Psychological Association suggests that violent video game exposure is associated with higher levels of aggressive behavior, increased thoughts about aggression, higher levels of desensitization to violence, and decreased empathy relating to exposure to violence. Based on these findings, the American Pediatric Association has urged parents to minimize their children's exposure to violent media of any sort (American Academy of Pediatrics Council on Communications and Media, 2016; Calvert et al., 2017; Anderson et al., 2017; Mather & vanderWeele, 2019).

From the perspective of...

A Social Worker What advice would you give to families about children's exposure to violent media and video games?

Sam Edwards/OJO Images/age fotostock

Several aspects of media violence may contribute to real-life aggressive behavior. First, viewing violent media may lower inhibitions against behaving aggressively. In other words, watching television portrayals of violence or using violence to win a video game makes aggression seem a legitimate response to particular situations.

Second, exposure to media violence may distort our understanding of the meaning of others' behavior, predisposing us to view even nonaggressive acts by others as aggressive. For example, a teenager who watches considerable media violence may be predisposed to think that a person who accidentally bumps into him as he walks down the street is being purposely aggressive, even if the reality is that it is truly an accident.

Third, a continuous diet of media aggression may leave us desensitized to violence, and what previously would have repelled us now produces little emotional response. Our sense of the pain and suffering brought about by aggression consequently may be diminished (Carnagey et al., 2007; Ramos et al., 2013).

What about real-life exposure to *actual* violence? Does it also lead to increases in aggression? The answer is yes. Exposure to actual firearm violence (being shot or being shot at) doubles the probability that an adolescent will commit serious violence over the next 2 years. In short, whether the violence is real or fictionalized, observing violent behavior leads to increases in aggressive behavior (Quinn et al., 2017; Chesworth et al., 2019).

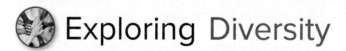

Exploring Diversity

Does Culture Influence How We Learn?

When a member of the Chilcotin Indian nation teaches her daughter to prepare salmon, at first she allows the daughter only to observe the entire process. A little later, she permits her child to try out some basic parts of the task. Her response to questions is noteworthy. For example, when the daughter asks about how to do "the backbone part," the mother's response is to repeat the entire process with another salmon. The reason? The mother feels that one cannot learn the individual parts of the task apart from the context of preparing the whole fish. (Tharp, 1989)

It should not be surprising that children raised in the Chilcotin tradition, which stresses instruction that starts by communicating the entire task, may have difficulty with traditional Western schooling. In the approach to teaching most characteristic of Western culture, tasks are broken down into their component parts. Only after each small step is learned is it thought possible to master the complete task.

Do the differences in teaching approaches between cultures affect how people learn? Some psychologists, taking a cognitive perspective on learning, suggest that people develop particular *learning styles,* characteristic ways of approaching material, based on their cultural background and unique pattern of abilities (Sternberg, 2011; Rogoff et al., 2017).

Relational Style	Analytical Style
• Perceive information as part of total picture	• Focus on detail
• Show intuitive thinking	• Show sequential and structured thinking
• More easily learn materials that have a human, social content	• More easily learn materials that are impersonal
• Have a good memory for verbally presented ideas and information	• Have a good memory for abstract ideas
• Are influenced by others' opinions	• Are not greatly affected by the opinions of others
• Style conflicts with the traditional school environment.	• Style matches traditional school environments.

FIGURE 2 A comparison of relational versus analytical approaches to learning offers one example of how learning styles differ along several dimensions.

Source: Adams et al., 2017.

(Photo): Fuse/Getty Images

Learning styles differ along several dimensions. For example, one central dimension is relational versus analytical approaches to learning. As illustrated in Figure 2, people with a *relational learning style* master material best through understanding the "big picture" about something. They need to understand the complete picture of what they're studying before they understand its component parts. For example, students with a relational learning style might learn about the brain by first focusing on the brain as a whole and how it functions. Only after doing that would they then focus on the specific functions of separate areas of the brain.

In contrast, those with an *analytical learning style* do best when they first analyze the various components underlying an object, phenomenon, or situation. By developing an understanding of the individual parts, they are best able to grasp the full picture. So students with an analytic learning style might learn about the brain most easily by first considering its component parts (neurons, specific areas, lobes) and then by focusing on how they fit together to form the brain.

According to educator Maurianne Adams, certain minority groups in Western societies display particular learning styles. For instance, she argues that Caucasian women and girls and all Black, Native American, and Hispanic Americans are more apt to use a relational style of learning than are Caucasian and Asian American men and boys, who are more likely to employ an analytical style (Adams et al., 2007; Armstrong et al., 2021; Adams, 2022).

The conclusion that members of particular ethnic and gender groups have similar learning styles is controversial. Because there is so much diversity within each particular racial and ethnic group, critics argue that generalizations about learning styles cannot be used to predict the style of any single individual, regardless of group membership.

Still, values about learning, which are communicated through a person's family and cultural background, clearly have an impact on how successful students are in school. One theory suggests that members of minority groups who were voluntary immigrants are more apt to be successful in school than those who were brought into a majority culture against their will. For example, Korean children in the United States—the sons and daughters of voluntary immigrants—perform quite well, as a group, in school. In contrast, Korean children in Japan, who were often the sons and daughters of people who were forced to immigrate during World War II, essentially as forced laborers, do less well in school. The theory suggests that the motivation to succeed is lower for children in forced immigration groups (Ogbu, 2003; Foster, 2005; Klinger et al., 2018).

RECAP/EVALUATE/RETHINK

RECAP

LO 17-1 What are the roles of cognition and thought in learning?

- Cognitive approaches to learning consider learning in terms of thought processes, or cognition. Phenomena such as latent learning–in which a new behavior is learned but not performed until some incentive is provided for its performance–and the apparent development of cognitive maps support cognitive approaches.
- Learning also occurs from observing the behavior of others. The major factor that determines whether an observed behavior will actually be performed is the nature of the reinforcement or punishment a model receives.
- Observation of violence is linked to a greater likelihood of subsequently acting aggressively.
- Learning styles are characteristic ways of approaching learning, based on a person's cultural background and unique pattern of abilities. Whether an individual has an analytical or a relational style of learning, for example, may reflect family background or culture.

EVALUATE

1. Cognitive learning theorists are concerned only with overt behavior, not with its internal causes. True or false?

2. In cognitive learning theory, it is assumed that people develop a(n) _____ about receiving a reinforcer when they behave a certain way.
3. In _____ learning, a new behavior is learned but is not shown until appropriate reinforcement is presented.
4. Bandura's _____ theory of learning states that people learn through watching a(n) _____ (another person displaying the behavior of interest).

RETHINK

1. The relational style of learning sometimes conflicts with the traditional school environment. Could a school be created that takes advantage of the characteristics of the relational style? How? Are there types of learning for which the analytical style is clearly superior?
2. What is the relationship between a model (in Bandura's sense) and a role model (as the term is used popularly)? Celebrities often complain that their actions should not be scrutinized closely because they do not want to be role models. How would you respond?

Answers to Evaluate Questions

1. False: cognitive learning theorists are primarily concerned with mental processes; 2. expectation; 3. latent; 4. observational, model

KEY TERMS

cognitive learning theory   latent learning   observational learning

LOOKING *Back*

EPILOGUE

In this chapter, we discussed several kinds of learning, ranging from classical conditioning, which depends on the existence of natural stimulus/response pairings, to operant conditioning, in which reinforcement is used to increase desired behavior. These approaches to learning focus on outward, behavioral learning processes. Cognitive approaches to learning focus on mental processes that enable learning.

We have also noted that learning is affected by culture and individual differences, with individual learning styles potentially affecting the ways in which people learn most effectively. And we saw some ways in which our learning about learning can be put to practical use through such means as behavior-modification programs designed to decrease negative behaviors and increase positive ones.

Return to the prologue of this chapter and consider the following questions about the use of behavior modification principles to change driving habits:

1. Does the Snapshot device make use of classical conditioning or operant conditioning principles? What are your reasons for your answers?
2. For users of the Snapshot device, what is the reinforcement?
3. Why would a device that provides real-time feedback on energy use (and cost) be a more effective conditioning tool than the electric bill that customers ordinarily get each month?
4. If you were in charge of implementing the Snapshot device program, what additional program features could you include to take advantage of cognitive learning principles?

Design Elements: Man with laptop: Dragon Images/Shutterstock; Exclamation point and mobile frame: McGraw Hill; Smartphone: WML Image/Shutterstock; Hands: Stefano Garau/Shutterstock.

VISUAL SUMMARY 5 Learning

MODULE 15 Classical Conditioning

Ivan Pavlov: Basic principles of classical conditioning

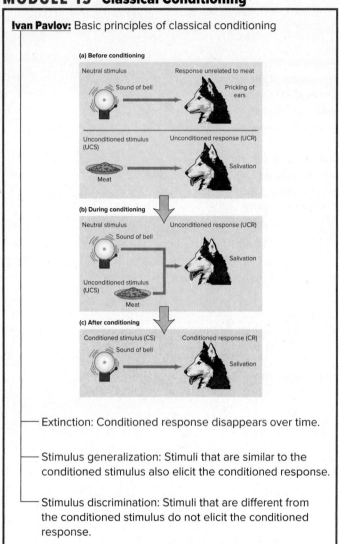

— Extinction: Conditioned response disappears over time.

— Stimulus generalization: Stimuli that are similar to the conditioned stimulus also elicit the conditioned response.

— Stimulus discrimination: Stimuli that are different from the conditioned stimulus do not elicit the conditioned response.

MODULE 16 Operant Conditioning

Basic Principle: Behavior changes in frequency according to its consequences.

— Reinforcement: A stimulus that increases the probability that a preceding behavior will be repeated.

— Positive reinforcement: A pleasant stimulus is presented.

— Negative reinforcement: An unpleasant stimulus is withdrawn.

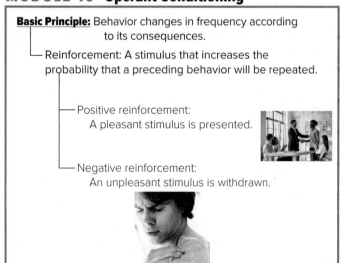

Basic Principle: Behavior changes in frequency according to its consequences (continued).

— Punishment: A stimulus that decreases the probability that a preceding behavior will be repeated.

— Positive punishment: An unpleasant stimulus is presented.

— Negative punishment: A pleasant stimulus is withdrawn.

— Schedules of reinforcement.

(a) Fixed-ratio schedule — There are relatively short pauses in responding after reinforcement is provided.

(b) Variable-ratio schedule — Responding occurs at a high, steady rate.

(c) Fixed-interval schedule — There are typically long pauses in responding after reinforcement is provided.

(d) Variable-interval schedule — Responding occurs at a steady rate.

— Shaping: Reinforcing successive approximations of behavior.

MODULE 17 Cognitive Approaches to Learning

Cognitive Learning Theory: Focuses on the internal thoughts and expectations

— Latent learning: A new behavior is learned but is not demonstrated until it is reinforced.

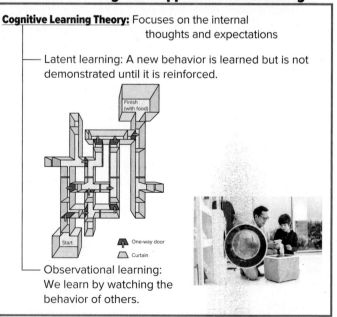

— Observational learning: We learn by watching the behavior of others.

(Module 16): (Executives): fizkes/Shutterstock; (Man): Stockbyte/Getty Images; (Mother): lightfieldstudios/123RF; (Grandfather): WESTOCK PRODUCTIONS/Shutterstock; (Shaping): Dr. Marian Breland Bailey; (Module 17): (Father): Art_Photo/Shutterstock; (Latent learning): Source: Adapted from Tolman & Honzik, 1930).

Photodisc/Getty Images

CHAPTER 6
Memory

LEARNING OUTCOMES FOR CHAPTER 6

PROLOGUE *SHE REMEMBERS IT ALL*

For a lot of her life, Rebecca Sharrock didn't realize that there was anything special about her memory. Sure, she could tell you what happened 5, 10, 20 years earlier on a particular date—such as recalling that her stepfather went to the bookstore on July 21, 2007, to buy a copy of the newest Harry Potter book. Or that she participated in a vocal workshop on October 22, 2003, when she was 13 years old, the same day that she remembers President George Bush, Jr., visiting Australia. Or that she could remember, and actually re-experience, the emotions she felt when asked about what was happening on a specific date a dozen years earlier. Didn't everyone remember things like that?

It wasn't until her mother showed her a news story about people with memories like hers that she realized how special and unusual her memory was. In fact, it's thought fewer than 100 people in the world have the rare ability to remember the details of their day-to-day personal experiences with such great precision—dates, times, locations, events, people they were with, what they wore, and what they felt—years later (Lu, 2022).

LOOKING *Ahead*

Rebecca Sharrock's condition, known as *highly superior autobiographical memory (HSAM)*, affects the part of memory that stores experiences related to life events. Researchers have discovered that people with HSAM process short-term memories the same way most of us do. The difference is that the accuracy and detail of their memories actually *improve* over time (Morris, 2017; Mazzoni et al., 2019; Daviddi et al., 2022).

Sharrock's extraordinary ability illustrates the complexity and the mystery of the phenomenon we call memory. Memory allows us to retrieve a vast amount of information—from the name of a friend we haven't talked with for years to the details of a picture that hung in our childhood bedroom. At the same time, though, memory failures are common. We forget where we left the keys to the car and are unable to answer an exam question about material we studied only a few hours earlier. Why?

We turn now to the nature of memory, considering the ways in which information is stored and retrieved. We examine the problems of retrieving information from memory, the accuracy of memories, and the reasons we sometimes forget information. We also consider the biological foundations of memory and discuss some practical means of increasing memory capacity.

Module 18
The Foundations of Memory

You are playing a game of Trivial Pursuit, and winning the game comes down to one question: On what body of water is Mumbai located? As you rack your brain for the answer, several fundamental processes relating to memory come into play. You may never, for instance, have been exposed to information regarding Mumbai's location. Or if you have been exposed to it, it may simply not have registered in a meaningful way. In other words, the information might not have been recorded properly in your memory. The initial process of recording information in a form usable to memory, a process called *encoding*, is the first stage in remembering something.

Even if you had been exposed to the information and originally knew the name of the body of water, you may still be unable to recall it during the game because of a failure to retain it. Memory specialists speak of *storage*, the maintenance of material saved in memory. If the material is not stored adequately, it cannot be recalled later.

Memory also depends on one last process–*retrieval:* Material in memory storage has to be located and brought into awareness to be useful. Your failure to recall Mumbai's location, then, may rest on your inability to retrieve information that you learned earlier.

In sum, psychologists consider **memory** to be the process by which we encode, store, and retrieve information (see Figure 1). Each of the three parts of this definition–encoding, storage, and retrieval–represents a different process. You can think of these processes as being analogous to a computer's keyboard (encoding), hard drive (storage), and software that accesses the information for display on the screen (retrieval). Only if all three processes have operated will you experience success and be able to recall the body of water on which Mumbai is located: the Arabian Sea.

Recognizing that memory involves encoding, storage, and retrieval gives us a start in understanding the concept. But how does memory actually function? How do we explain what information is initially encoded, what gets stored, and how it is retrieved?

According to the *three-system approach to memory* that dominated memory research for several decades, there are different memory storage systems or stages through which information must travel if it is to be remembered (Atkinson & Shiffrin, 1968; Kesner, 2016). Historically, the approach has been extremely influential in the development of our understanding of memory, and–although new theories have augmented it–it still provides a useful framework for understanding how information is recalled.

The three-system memory theory proposes the existence of the three separate memory stores shown in Figure 2. *Sensory memory* refers to the initial, momentary storage of information that lasts only an instant. Here, an exact replica of the stimulus recorded by a person's sensory system is stored very briefly. In a second stage, *short-term memory* holds information for 15–25 seconds and stores it according to its meaning,

memory The process by which we encode, store, and retrieve information. (Module 18)

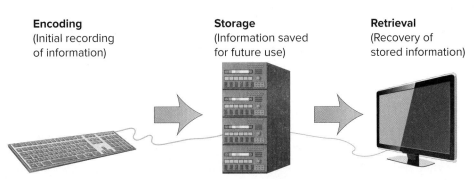

Encoding
(Initial recording of information)

Storage
(Information saved for future use)

Retrieval
(Recovery of stored information)

FIGURE 1 Memory is built on three basic processes—encoding, storage, and retrieval—that are analogous to a computer's keyboard, hard drive, and software to access the information for display on the screen. The analogy is not perfect, however, because human memory is less precise than a computer. How might you modify the analogy to make it more accurate?

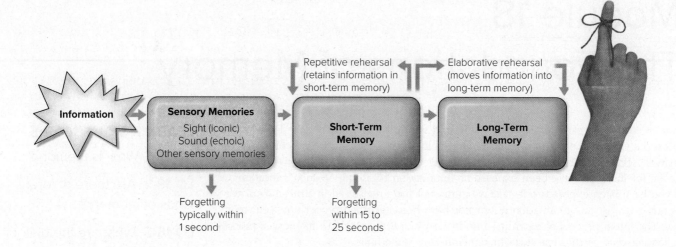

FIGURE 2 In this three-stage model of memory, information initially recorded by the person's sensory system enters sensory memory, which momentarily holds the information. The information then moves to short-term memory, which stores it for 15–25 seconds. Finally, the information can move into long-term memory, which is relatively permanent. Whether the information moves from short-term to long-term memory depends on the kind and amount of rehearsal of the material that is performed.
(Photo): Squared Studios/Getty Images

rather than as mere sensory stimulation. The third type of storage system is *long-term memory*. Information is stored in long-term memory on a relatively permanent basis, although it may be difficult to retrieve.

Sensory Memory

A momentary flash of lightning leaves a sensory visual memory, a fleeting but exact replica of the stimulus, which then fades away.
Steve Allen/Brand X Pictures/Getty Images

sensory memory The initial, momentary storage of information, lasting only an instant. (Module 18)

A momentary flash of lightning, the sound of a twig snapping, and the sting of a pin-prick all represent stimulation of exceedingly brief duration, but they may nonetheless provide important information that can require a response. Such stimuli are initially–and fleetingly–stored in sensory memory.

Sensory memory is the first storehouse of the information the world presents to us. Actually, we have several types of sensory memories, each related to a different kind of sensory information. For instance, *iconic memory* reflects information from the visual system. *Echoic memory* stores auditory information coming from the ears. In addition, there are corresponding memories for each of the other senses.

Sensory memory can store information for only a very short time. If information does not pass into short-term memory, it is lost for good. For instance, iconic memory seems to last less than a second, and echoic memory typically fades within 2 or 3 seconds. However, despite the brief duration of sensory memory, its precision is high: Sensory memory can store an almost exact replica of each stimulus to which it is exposed (Vlassova & Pearson, 2013; Rimmele et al., 2015; Teeuwen et al., 2021).

Psychologist George Sperling (1960) demonstrated the existence of sensory memory in a series of clever and now-classic studies. He briefly exposed people to a series of 12 letters arranged in the following pattern:

F	**T**	**Y**	**C**
K	**D**	**N**	**L**
Y	**W**	**B**	**M**

When exposed to this pattern of letters for just one-twentieth of a second, most people could recall only four or five of the letters accurately. Although they knew that they had seen more, the memory of those letters had faded by the time they reported the first few letters. It was possible, then, that the information had initially been accurately stored in sensory memory. But during the time it took to verbalize the first four or five letters, the memory of the other letters faded.

To test that possibility, Sperling conducted an experiment in which a high, medium, or low tone sounded just after a person had been exposed to the full pattern of letters. People were told to report the letters in the highest line if a high tone was sounded, the middle line if the medium tone occurred, or the lowest line at the sound of the low tone. Because the tone occurred after the exposure, people had to rely on their memories to report the correct row.

The results of the study clearly showed that people had been storing the complete pattern in memory. They accurately recalled the letters in the line that had been indicated by the tone regardless of whether it was the top, middle, or bottom line. Obviously, *all* the lines they had seen had been stored in sensory memory. Despite its rapid loss, then, the information in sensory memory was an accurate representation of what people had seen.

By gradually lengthening the time between the presentation of the visual pattern and the tone, Sperling was able to determine with some accuracy the length of time that information was stored in sensory memory. The ability to recall a particular row of the pattern when a tone was sounded declined progressively as the period between the visual exposure and the tone increased. This decline continued until the period reached about 1 second in duration, at which point the row could not be recalled accurately at all. Sperling concluded that the entire visual image was stored in sensory memory for less than a second.

In sum, sensory memory operates as a kind of snapshot that stores information–which may be of a visual, auditory, or other sensory nature–for a brief moment in time. But it is as if each snapshot, immediately after being taken, is destroyed and replaced with a new one. Unless the information in the snapshot is transferred to some other type of memory, it is lost.

Short-Term Memory

Because the information that is stored briefly in sensory memory consists of representations of raw sensory stimuli, it is not meaningful to us. If we are to make sense of it and possibly retain it, the information must be transferred to the next stage of memory: short-term memory. **Short-term memory** is the memory store in which information first has meaning, although the maximum length of retention there is relatively short (Hamilton & Martin, 2007; Cao et al., 2017; Martin & Becker, 2021).

The specific process by which sensory memories are transformed into short-term memories is not clear. Some theorists suggest that the information is first translated into graphical representations or images, and others hypothesize that the transfer occurs when the sensory stimuli are changed to words (Baddeley & Wilson, 1985). What is clear, however, is that unlike sensory memory, which holds a relatively full and detailed–if short-lived–representation of the world, short-term memory has incomplete representational capabilities.

In fact, researchers have identified the specific amount of information we can hold in short-term memory: seven items, or "chunks," of information, with variations up to plus or minus two chunks (remember it this way: 7 ± 2). A **chunk** is a group of separate pieces of information stored as a single unit in short-term memory. For example, phone numbers are typically depicted in three chunks of information in order to make them easier to remember: (201) 226-4610, rather than a string of the separate numbers 2012264610.

Chunks also may consist of categories as words or other meaningful units. For example, consider the following list of 21 letters:

P B S F O X C N N A B C C B S M T V N B C

Study Alert
Although the three types of memory are discussed as separate memory stores, these are not mini-warehouses located in specific areas of the brain. Instead, they represent three types of memory systems with different characteristics.

short-term memory Memory that holds information for 15 to 25 seconds. (Module 18)

chunk A group of familiar stimuli stored as a single unit in short-term memory. (Module 18)

Because the list of individual letters exceeds seven items, it is difficult to recall the letters after one exposure. But suppose they were presented as follows:

PBS   FOX   CNN   ABC   CBS   MTV   NBC

In this case, even though there are still 21 letters, you'd be able to store them in short-term memory since they represent only seven chunks.

Chunks can vary in size from single letters or numbers to categories that are far more complicated. The specific nature of what constitutes a chunk varies according to one's past experience. You can see this for yourself by trying an experiment that was first carried out as a comparison between expert and inexperienced chess players and is illustrated in Figure 3 (deGroot, 1978; Schneider & Logan, 2015; Tanida et al., 2019; Brady et al., 2021).

The chunks of information in short-term memory do not last very long. Just how brief is short-term memory? If you've ever looked up a phone number, repeated the number to yourself, and then forgotten the number after you've tapped the first three numbers into your phone, you know that information does not remain in short-term memory very long. Most psychologists believe that information in short-term memory is lost after 15 to 25 seconds–unless it is transferred to long-term memory.

REHEARSAL

rehearsal The repetition of information that has entered short-term memory. (Module 18)

The transfer of material from short- to long-term memory proceeds largely on the basis of rehearsal. **Rehearsal** is the repetition of information that has entered short-term memory. Rehearsal accomplishes two things. First, as long as we repeat the information, we lengthen the time it is maintained in short-term memory. More important, however, rehearsal allows us to transfer the information into long-term memory (Jarrold & Tam, 2011; Grenfell-Essam et al., 2013; Festini & Reuter-Lorenz, 2017; Balles et al., 2022).

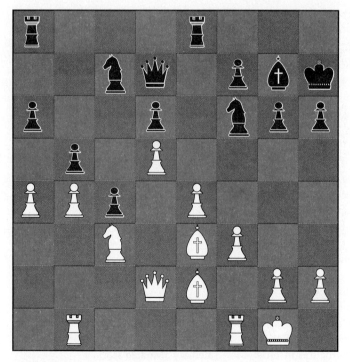 

FIGURE 3 Examine the chessboard on the left for about 5 seconds. Then cover up the board and draw the position of the pieces on the blank chessboard. (You could also use your own chessboard and place the pieces in the same positions.) Unless you are an experienced chess player, you are likely to have great difficulty carrying out such a task. Yet chess masters—those who win tournaments—do this quite well (deGroot, 1966; Villanfaina et al., 2019). They are able to reproduce correctly 90% of the pieces on the board. In comparison, inexperienced chess players are typically able to reproduce only 40% of the board properly. The chess masters generally test normally on other measures of memory. What they can do better than others is see the board in terms of chunks or meaningful units and reproduce the position of the chess pieces by using those units.

Whether the transfer is made from short- to long-term memory seems to depend largely on the kind of rehearsal that is carried out. If the information is simply repeated over and over again—as we might do with a phone number someone tells us as we rush to store it in our phone—it is kept current in short-term memory, but it will not necessarily be placed in long-term memory. Instead, as soon as we stop punching in the phone numbers, the number is likely to be replaced by other information and will be completely forgotten.

In contrast, if the information in short-term memory is rehearsed using a process called elaborative rehearsal, it is much more likely to be transferred into long-term memory. *Elaborative rehearsal* occurs when the information is considered and organized in some fashion. The organization might include expanding the information to make it fit into a logical framework, linking it to another memory, turning it into an image, or transforming it in some other way. For example, a list of vegetables to be purchased at a store could be woven together in memory as items being used to prepare an elaborate salad, could be linked to the items bought on an earlier shopping trip, or could be thought of in terms of the image of a farm with rows of each item.

We can vastly improve our retention of information using such organizational strategies, which are known as mnemonics. *Mnemonics* (pronounced "neh MON ix") are strategies for organizing information in a way that makes the information more likely to be remembered. For instance, when a beginning musician learns that the spaces on the music staff spell the word *FACE* or when we learn the rhyme "Thirty days hath September, April, June, and November . . . ," we are using mnemonics (Stålhammar et al., 2015; Choi et al., 2017; Tullis & Qiu, 2022).

Working Memory

Rather than seeing short-term memory as an independent waystation into which memories arrive, either to fade or to be passed on to long-term memory, most contemporary memory theorists conceive of short-term memory as far more active. In this view, short-term memory is like an information-processing system that manages both new material gathered from sensory memory and older material that has been pulled from long-term storage. In this increasingly influential view, short-term memory is referred to as working memory.

Working memory is the memory system that holds information temporarily while actively manipulating and rehearsing that information. If you use the analogy of a computer, working memory is the processing that occurs in an open window on your desktop, as compared with the long-term storage of information in the computer's hard drive (Vandierendonck & Szmalec, 2011; Adami et al., 2019).

Researchers now assume that working memory is made up of several parts. First, it contains a *central executive* processor that is involved in reasoning, decision making, and planning. The central executive integrates and coordinates information from three distinct subsystems, and it determines what we pay attention to and what we ignore.

The three subsystems of working memory serve as storage-and-rehearsal systems: the visual store, the verbal store, and the episodic buffer. The *visual store* specializes in visual and spatial information. In contrast, the *verbal store* holds and manipulates material relating to language, including speech, words, and numbers. Finally, the *episodic buffer* contains information that represents events and occurrences—things that happen to us (Baddeley et al., 2011; Kuncel & Beatty, 2013; Hilbert et al., 2017; Wiesman et al., 2021; see Figure 4).

Working memory permits us to keep information in an active state briefly so that we can do something with the information. For instance, we use working memory when we're doing a multistep arithmetic problem in our heads, storing the result of one calculation while getting ready to move to the next stage. (I make use of my working memory when I figure a 20% tip in a restaurant by first calculating 10% of the total bill and then doubling it.)

working memory A memory system that holds information temporarily while actively manipulating and rehearsing that information. (Module 18)

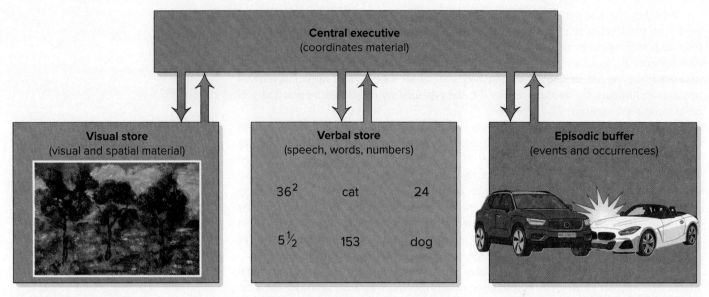

FIGURE 4 Working memory is an active "workspace" in which information is retrieved and manipulated and in which information is held through rehearsal. Working memory includes a central executive processor that coordinates the visual store, verbal store, and episodic buffer.
Source: Adapted from Lexcellent, 2019.

As working memory processes information, it uses a significant amount of cognitive resources during its operation. Furthermore, the amount of information that can be held and processed in working memory seems to be just three to four chunks, depending on the nature of the chunks (Cowan, 2001; Beam, 2014; Heathcoate et al., 2015).

The cognitive effort in the processing of information in working memory also can make us less aware of our surroundings–something that has implications for why it's unsafe to use cell phones while driving. If a phone conversation requires thinking, it will burden working memory and leave drivers less aware of their surroundings, an obviously dangerous state of affairs (Sifrit, 2006; Strayer & Drews, 2007; Turnbull et al., 2021; Wu et al., 2022).

Furthermore, stress can reduce the effectiveness of working memory by reducing its capacity. In fact, one study found that students with the highest working memory capacity and greatest math ability were the ones who were most vulnerable to pressure to perform well. Those who should have performed best, then, were the ones most apt to choke on the test because their working memory capacities were reduced by the stress (Edwards et al., 2015; Banks & Boals, 2017; Bosquet Enlow et al., 2019).

Long-Term Memory

long-term memory Memory that stores information on a relatively permanent basis, although it may be difficult to retrieve. (Module 18)

Material that makes its way from short-term memory enters a storehouse of almost unlimited capacity, called long-term memory. **Long-term memory** stores information on a relatively permanent basis. Like a new file we save on a hard drive, the information in long-term memory is filed and coded so that we can retrieve it when we need it.

Evidence of the existence of long-term memory, as distinct from short-term memory, comes from a number of sources. For example, people with certain kinds of brain damage have no lasting recall of new information received after the damage occurred, although people and events stored in memory before the injury remain intact (Milner, 1966). Because information that was encoded and stored before the injury can be recalled and because short-term memory after the injury appears to be operational–new material can be recalled for a very brief period–we can infer that there are two distinct types of memory: one for short-term and one for long-term storage.

Results from laboratory experiments are also consistent with the notion of separate short-term and long-term memory. For example, in one set of studies, people were asked to recall a relatively small amount of information (such as a set of three letters). Then, to prevent practice of the initial information, participants were required to recite some extraneous material aloud, such as counting backward by threes (Brown, 1958; Peterson & Peterson, 1959). By varying the amount of time between the presentation of the initial material and the need for its recall, investigators found that recall was quite good when the interval was very short, but recall declined rapidly thereafter. After 15 seconds had gone by, recall hovered at around 10% of the material initially presented.

Apparently, the distraction of counting backward prevented almost all the initial material from reaching long-term memory. Initial recall was good because it was coming from short-term memory, but those memories were lost at a rapid rate. Eventually, all that could be recalled was the small amount of material that had made its way into long-term storage despite the distraction of counting backward.

The distinction between short- and long-term memory is also demonstrated by the fact that ability to recall information in a list depends on where in the list an item appears. For instance, in some cases, a *primacy effect* occurs, in which items presented early in a list are remembered better. In other cases, a *recency effect* is seen, in which items presented late in a list are remembered best (Jacoby & Wahlheim, 2013; Tam et al., 2015; Osth & Farrell, 2019; Yeh & Chen, 2021).

LONG-TERM MEMORY MODULES

Just as short-term memory is often conceptualized in terms of working memory, many contemporary researchers now regard long-term memory as having several components, or *memory modules*. Each of these modules represents a separate memory system in the brain.

One major distinction within long-term memory is that between declarative and procedural memory. **Declarative memory** is memory for factual information: names, faces, dates, and facts, such as "a bike has two wheels." The information stored in declarative memory can be verbally communicated to others and is sometimes called *explicit memory*.

In contrast, **procedural memory** (sometimes called *nondeclarative memory* or *implicit memory*) refers to memory for skills and habits, such as how to ride a bike or hit a baseball. For example, procedural memory allows us to ice skate, even if we haven't done it for a long time. (Try to explain how you know how to balance on a bike or catch a ball; it's nearly impossible. Yet you're able to do so because the information is stored in procedural memory.)

You can remember the difference between declarative and procedural memory this way: Information about *things* is stored in declarative memory; information about *how to do things* (procedures) is stored in procedural memory (Freedberg, 2011; Gade et al., 2017; Xie et al., 2019).

Declarative memory can be subdivided into semantic memory and episodic memory. **Semantic memory** is memory for general knowledge and facts about the world, as well as memory for the rules of logic that are used to deduce other facts. Because of semantic memory, we remember that the ZIP code for Beverly Hills is 90210, that Mumbai is on the Arabian Sea, and that *memoree* is the incorrect spelling of *memory*. Thus, semantic memory is somewhat like a mental almanac of facts (McNamara, 2013; Grady et al., 2015; Weidemann et al., 2019; Paplikar et al., 2022).

In contrast, **episodic memory** is memory for events that occur in a particular time, place, or context. For example, recall of learning to hit a baseball, our first kiss, or arranging a surprise 21st birthday party for our brother is based on episodic memories. Episodic memories relate to particular contexts. For example, remembering *when* and *how* we learned that 2 × 2 = 4 would be an episodic memory; the fact itself (that 2 × 2 = 4) is a semantic memory. (Also see Figure 5.)

declarative memory Memory for factual information: names, faces, dates, and the like. (Module 18)

procedural memory Memory for skills and habits, such as riding a bike or hitting a baseball; sometimes referred to as *nondeclarative memory*. (Module 18)

Study Alert
Use Figure 5 to help clarify the distinctions between the different types of long-term memory.

semantic memory Memory for general knowledge and facts about the world, as well as memory for the rules of logic that are used to deduce other facts. (Module 18)

episodic memory Memory for events that occur in a particular time, place, or context. (Module 18)

FIGURE 5 Long-term memory can be subdivided into several types. What type of long-term memory is involved in your recollection of the moment you first arrived on your campus at the start of college? What type of long-term memory is involved in remembering the lyrics to a song, compared with the tune of a song?

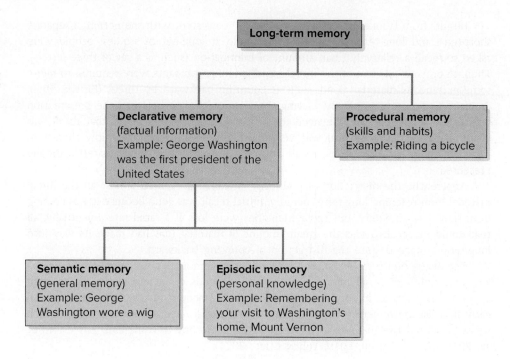

Episodic memories can be surprisingly detailed. Consider, for instance, how you'd respond if you were asked to identify what you were doing on a specific day 2 years ago. Impossible? You may think otherwise as you read the following exchange between a researcher and a participant in a study who was asked, in a memory experiment, what he was doing "on Monday afternoon in the third week of September two years ago."

PARTICIPANT: Come on. How should I know?

EXPERIMENTER: Just try it anyhow.

PARTICIPANT: OK. Let's see: Two years ago . . . I would be in high school in Pittsburgh. . . . That would be my senior year. Third week in September–that's just after summer–that would be the fall term. . . . Let me see. I think I had chemistry lab on Mondays. I don't know. I was probably in chemistry lab. Wait a minute–that would be the second week of school. I remember he started off with the atomic table–a big fancy chart. I thought he was crazy trying to make us memorize that thing. You know, I think I can remember sitting. . . . (Lindsay & Norman, 1977)

Episodic memory, then, can provide information about events that happened long in the past. But semantic memory is no less impressive, permitting us to dredge up tens of thousands of facts ranging from the date of our birthday to the knowledge that $1.00 is less than $5.00.

SEMANTIC NETWORKS

Try to recall, for a moment, as many things as you can think of that are the color red. Now pull from your memory the names of as many fruits as you can recall.

Did the same item appear when you did both tasks? For many people, an apple comes to mind in both cases since it fits equally well in each category. And the fact that you might have thought of an apple when doing the first task makes it even more likely that you'll think of it when doing the second task.

It's actually quite amazing that we're able to retrieve specific material from the vast store of information in our long-term memories. One key organizational tool that allows us to recall detailed information from long-term memory is the associations that

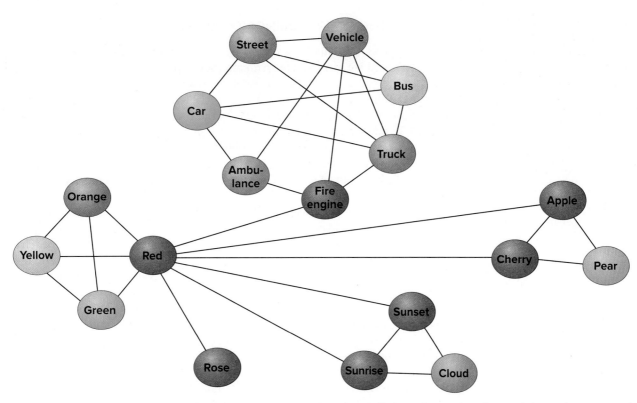

FIGURE 6 Semantic networks in memory consist of relationships between pieces of information, such as those relating to the concept of a fire engine. The lines suggest the connections that indicate how the information is organized within memory. The closer together two concepts are, the greater the strength of the association.

Source: Adapted from Lexcellent, 2019.

we build between pieces of information. In this view, knowledge is stored in **semantic networks,** mental representations of clusters of interconnected information (Cummings et al., 2006; Poirier et al., 2015; Chang et al., 2022).

Consider, for example, Figure 6, which shows some of the relationships in memory relating to fire engines, the color red, and a variety of other semantic concepts. Thinking about a particular concept leads to recall of related concepts. For example, seeing a fire engine may activate our recollections of other kinds of emergency vehicles, such as an ambulance, which in turn may activate recall of the related concept of a vehicle. And thinking of a vehicle may lead us to think about a bus that we've seen in the past. Activating one memory triggers the activation of related memories in a process known as *spreading activation* (Kreher et al., 2008; Nelson et al., 2013; Kenett et al., 2017).

semantic networks Mental representations of clusters of interconnected information. (Module 18)

From the perspective of...

A Marketing Specialist How might advertisers use ways of enhancing memory to promote their products? What ethical principles are involved?

McGraw Hill

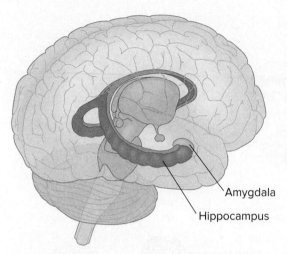

FIGURE 7 The hippocampus and amygdala, parts of the brain's limbic system, play a central role in the consolidation of memories.

Source: Adapted from Van De Graaff, 2000.

THE NEUROSCIENCE OF MEMORY

Can we pinpoint a location in the brain where long-term memories reside? Is there a single site that corresponds to a particular memory, or is memory distributed in different regions across the brain? Do memories leave an actual physical trace that scientists can view?

The *engram* is the term for the physical memory trace in the brain that corresponds to a memory. Locating the engram has proved to be a major challenge to psychologists and neuroscientists interested in memory. But by using advanced brain scanning procedures, investigators have learned that certain brain areas and structures specialize in different types of memory-related activities.

The *hippocampus*, a part of the brain's limbic system (see Figure 7), helps to consolidate memories, stabilizing them after they are initially acquired. The hippocampus acts as a kind of neurological e-mail system. That information is subsequently passed along to the cerebral cortex of the brain, where it is actually stored (Dudai, 2011; Wilmot et al., 2019; Josselyn & Tonegawa, 2020).

The significance of the hippocampus is exemplified by studies of individuals who have particularly good, yet specialized, types of memories. For instance, taxi drivers in London, England, must have accurate, complete recall of the location of the maze of streets and alleys within a 6-mile radius of the center of the city. It takes years of study to memorize the material.

It turns out that MRI brain scans of taxi drivers show differences in the shape of the hippocampus compared to non-taxi drivers. The differences are consistent with the idea that particular areas of the hippocampus are involved in the consolidation of spatial memories (Jiang et al., 2017; Griesbauer et al., 2022).

The *amygdala*, another part of the limbic system, also plays an important role in memory. The amygdala is especially involved with memories involving emotion. For example, if you are frightened by a large, growling pit bull dog, you're likely to remember the event vividly—an outcome related to the functioning of the amygdala. Encountering the pit bull or any large dog in the future is likely to reactivate the amygdala and bring back the unpleasant memory (Kochli et al., 2015; Ressler & Maren, 2019; Morena et al., 2021).

Memory at the Level of Neurons Although it is clear that the hippocampus and amygdala play a central role in memory formation, how is the transformation of information into a memory reflected at the level of neurons?

One answer is *long-term potentiation*, which shows that certain neural pathways become easily excited while a new response is being learned. At the same time, the number of synapses between neurons increases as the dendrites branch out to receive messages. These changes reflect a process called *consolidation*, in which memories become fixed and stable in long-term memory. Long-term memories take some time to stabilize; this explains why events and other stimuli are not suddenly fixed in memory. Instead, consolidation may continue for days and even years (Kawashima et al., 2006; Hwang et al., 2017; Park et al., 2019).

Because a stimulus may contain different sensory aspects, visual, auditory, and other areas of the brain may be simultaneously processing information about that stimulus. Information storage appears to be linked to the sites where this processing occurs, and it is therefore located in the particular areas that initially processed the information in terms of its visual, auditory, and other sensory stimuli. For this reason, memory traces are distributed throughout the brain. For example, when you recall a beautiful beach sunset, your recollection draws on memory stores located in visual areas of the brain (the view of the sunset), auditory areas (the sounds of the ocean), and tactile areas (the feel of the wind) (Squire et al., 2004; Murayama & Kitagami, 2013).

In short, the physical stuff of memory–the engram–is produced by a complex of biochemical and neural processes. Scientists are just beginning to understand how the brain compiles the individual neural components into a single, coherent memory. It may be that the same neurons that fire when we are initially exposed to material are reactivated during efforts to recall that information.

As researchers increasingly understand the biology of memory, they open the door to treatments for people with memory disorders. For example, new research shows that a brain implant that works like a pacemaker helps improve memory. In the research, a method called *transcranial alternating current stimulation (tACS)* stimulates the brain and in turn improves memory in experimental settings (Kucewicz et al., 2018; Grover et al., 2021).

In addition to increasingly understanding the biological basis of how memories are formed and recalled, memory specialists are also beginning to understand how to help people *forget* information through biological treatment. Specifically, they are seeking to understand how to help people forget traumatic events, persistent fears, or even annoying habits. And they are making advances in that direction, learning how to reliably alter memories in mice through a combination of a drug called HDAC inhibitor and training. In humans, such drugs might be used to disrupt the initial encoding of memories, such as treating rape victims soon after the rape to reduce the long-term trauma of the event (Johnson, 2014; Lu, 2015; Takamiya et al., 2019).

Still, although memory researchers have made considerable strides in understanding the neuroscience behind memory, more remains to be learned–and remembered (Gelbard-Sagiv et al., 2008; Brown & Banks, 2015).

RECAP/EVALUATE/RETHINK

RECAP

LO 18-1 What is memory?

- Memory is the process by which we encode, store, and retrieve information.

LO 18-2 Are there different kinds of memory?

- Sensory memory, corresponding to each of the sensory systems, is the first place where information is saved. Sensory memories are very brief, but they are precise, storing a nearly exact replica of a stimulus.
- Roughly seven (plus or minus two) chunks of information can be transferred and held in short-term memory. Information in short-term memory is held 15–25 seconds and then, if not transferred to long-term memory, is lost.
- Memories are transferred into long-term storage through rehearsal. If memories are transferred into long-term memory, they become relatively permanent.
- Some theorists view short-term memory as a working memory in which information is retrieved, manipulated, and held through rehearsal. In this view, it is a central executive processor involved in reasoning and decision making; it coordinates a visual store, a verbal store, and an episodic buffer.
- Long-term memory can be viewed in terms of memory modules, each of which is related to separate memory systems in the brain. For instance, we can distinguish between declarative memory and procedural memory. Declarative memory is further divided into episodic memory and semantic memory.
- Semantic networks suggest that knowledge is stored in long-term memory as mental representations of clusters of interconnected information.

LO 18-3 What are the biological bases of memory?

- The hippocampus and amygdala are especially important in the establishment of memory.
- Memories are distributed across the brain, relating to the different sensory information-processing systems involved during the initial exposure to a stimulus.

EVALUATE

1. Match the type of memory with its definition:
   1. Long-term memory
   2. Short-term memory
   3. Sensory memory

   a. Holds information 15–25 seconds
   b. Stores information on a relatively permanent basis
   c. Direct representation of a stimulus

2. A(n) _____ is a meaningful group of stimuli that can be stored together in short-term memory.

3. There appear to be two types of declarative memory: _____ memory for knowledge and facts and _____ memory for personal experiences.

4. Some memory researchers believe that long-term memory is stored as associations between pieces of information in _____ networks.

RETHINK

1. It is a truism that "you never forget how to ride a bicycle." Why might this be so? In what type of memory is information about bicycle riding stored?

2. The ability to remember specific skills and the order in which they are used is known as procedural memory. Because driving involves procedural memory, why is it so unsafe to use a cell phone while driving?

Answers to Evaluate Questions

1. 1-b, 2-a, 3-c; 2. chunk; 3. semantic, episodic; 4. semantic

KEY TERMS

memory	chunk	long-term memory	semantic memory
sensory memory	rehearsal	declarative memory	episodic memory
short-term memory	working memory	procedural memory	semantic networks

Module 19
Recalling Long-Term Memories

An hour after his job interview, Ricardo was sitting in a coffee shop, telling his friend Laura how well it had gone, when the woman who had interviewed him walked in. "Well, hello, Ricardo. How are you doing?" Trying to make a good impression, Ricardo began to make introductions but suddenly realized he could not remember the interviewer's name. Stammering, he desperately searched his memory but to no avail. "I *know* her name," he thought to himself, "but here I am, looking like a fool. I can kiss this job goodbye."

Have you ever tried to remember someone's name, convinced that you knew it but unable to recall it no matter how hard you tried? This common occurrence exemplifies how difficult it can be to retrieve information stored in long-term memory. The **tip-of-the-tongue phenomenon** is the temporary inability to remember information that one is certain one knows. Although the tip-of-the-tongue phenomenon is often considered a memory failure, it is not a complete failure, given that people do at least remember that they had been able to recall the information in the past (Cleary, 2019; Cleary et al., 2021; Chang et al., 2022).

Retrieval Cues

Perhaps recall of names and other memories is not perfect because there is so much information stored in long-term memory. Because the material that makes its way to long-term memory is relatively permanent, the capacity of long-term memory is vast. For instance, if you are like the average college student, your vocabulary includes some 50,000 words, you know hundreds of mathematical facts, and you are able to conjure up images–such as the way your childhood home looked–with no trouble at all. In fact, simply cataloging all your memories would probably take years of work.

How do we sort through this vast array of material and retrieve specific information at the appropriate time? One way is through retrieval cues. A *retrieval cue* is a stimulus that allows us to recall more easily information that is in long-term memory. It may be a word, an emotion, or a sound; whatever the specific cue, a memory will suddenly come to mind when the retrieval cue is present. For example, the smell of sunscreen may evoke memories of time spent at the beach or a summer vacation.

Retrieval cues guide people through the information stored in long-term memory in much the same way that a search engine such as Google guides people through the Internet. They are particularly important when we are making an effort to *recall* information, as opposed to being asked to *recognize* material stored in memory. In **recall,** a specific piece of information must be retrieved–such as that needed to answer a fill-in-the-blank question or to write an essay on a test. In contrast, **recognition** occurs when people are presented with a stimulus and asked whether they have been exposed to it previously or are asked to identify it from a list of alternatives.

As you might guess, recognition is generally a much easier task than recall (see Figures 1 and 2). Recall is more difficult because it consists of a series of processes: a search through memory, retrieval of potentially relevant information, and then a decision regarding whether the information you have found is accurate. If the information appears to be correct, the search is over, but if it is not, the search must continue. In contrast, recognition is simpler because it involves fewer steps (Moen et al., 2017; O'Brien et al., 2022).

LEARNING OUTCOME

LO 19-1 What causes difficulties and failures in remembering?

tip-of-the-tongue phenomenon The inability to recall information that one realizes one knows–a result of the difficulty of retrieving information from long-term memory. (Module 19)

recall Memory task in which specific information must be retrieved. (Module 19)

recognition Memory task in which individuals are presented with a stimulus and asked whether they have been exposed to it in the past or to identify it from a list of alternatives. (Module 19)

> **! Study Alert**
> Remember the distinction between recall (in which specific information must be retrieved) and recognition (in which information is presented and must be identified or distinguished from other material).

FIGURE 1 Try to recall the names of the seven dwarfs in the Disney movie *Snow White and the Seven Dwarfs*. Because this is a recall task, it is relatively difficult.
Walt Disney Productions/Album/Newscom

FIGURE 2 Naming the characters in Figure 1 (a recall task) is more difficult than solving the recognition problem posed in this list.

Answer this recognition question:	
Which of the following are the names of the seven dwarfs in the Disney movie *Snow White and the Seven Dwarfs*?	
Goofy	Bashful
Sleepy	Meanie
Smarty	Doc
Scaredy	Happy
Dopey	Angry
Grumpy	Sneezy
Wheezy	Crazy

(The correct answers are Bashful, Doc, Dopey, Grumpy, Happy, Sleepy, and Sneezy.)

Levels of Processing

levels-of-processing theory The theory of memory that emphasizes the degree to which new material is mentally analyzed. (Module 19)

One determinant of how well memories are recalled is the way in which material is first perceived, processed, and understood. The **levels-of-processing theory** emphasizes the degree to which new material is mentally analyzed. It suggests that the amount of information processing that occurs when material is initially encountered is central in determining how much of the information is ultimately remembered. According to this approach, the depth of information processing during exposure to material–meaning the degree to which it is analyzed and considered–is critical; the greater the intensity of its initial processing, the more likely we are to remember it (Craik & Lockhart, 2008; Catrysse et al., 2019; Su et al., 2021).

Because we do not pay close attention to much of the information to which we are exposed, very little mental processing typically takes place, and we forget new material almost immediately. However, information to which we pay greater attention is processed more thoroughly. Therefore, it enters memory at a deeper level–and is less apt to be forgotten than is information processed at shallower levels.

The theory goes on to suggest that there are considerable differences in the ways in which information is processed at various levels of memory. At shallow levels, information is processed merely in terms of its physical and sensory aspects. For example, we may pay attention only to the shapes that make up the letters in the word *dog*. At an intermediate level of processing, the shapes are translated into meaningful units–in this case, letters of the alphabet. Those letters are considered in the context of words, and specific phonetic sounds may be attached to the letters.

At the deepest level of processing, information is analyzed in terms of its meaning. We may see it in a wider context and draw associations between the meaning of the information and broader networks of knowledge. For instance, we may think of dogs not merely as animals with four legs and a tail but also in terms of their relationship to cats and other mammals. We may form an image of our own dog, thereby relating the concept to our own lives. According to the levels-of-processing approach, the deeper the initial level of processing of specific information, the longer the information will be retained.

There are considerable practical implications to the notion that recall depends on the degree to which information is initially processed. For example, the depth of information processing is critical when learning and studying course material. Rote memorization of a list of key terms for a test is unlikely to produce long-term recollection of information because processing occurs at a shallow level. In contrast, thinking about the meaning of the terms and reflecting on how they relate to information that one currently knows results in far more effective long-term retention (Albanese & Case, 2015; Badr & Abu-Ayyash, 2019; Belmont et al., 2022).

Explicit and Implicit Memory

If you've ever had surgery, you probably hoped that the surgeons were focused completely on the surgery and gave you their undivided attention while slicing into your body. The reality in most operating rooms is quite different, though. Surgeons may be chatting with nurses about a new restaurant as soon as they sew you up.

If you are like most patients, you are left with no recollection of the conversation that occurred while you were under anesthesia. However, although you had no conscious memories of the discussions about the merits of the restaurant, on some level you probably did recall at least some information. In fact, people who are anesthetized during surgery can sometimes recall snippets of conversations they heard during surgery—even though they have no conscious recollection of the information (Sleigh et al., 2019; Linassi et al., 2021).

The discovery that people have memories about which they are unaware has been an important one. It has led to speculation that two forms of memory, explicit and implicit, may exist side by side. **Explicit memory** refers to intentional or conscious recollection of information. When we try to remember a name or date we have encountered or learned about previously, we are searching our explicit memory.

In contrast, **implicit memory** refers to memories of which people are not consciously aware but that can affect subsequent performance and behavior. Skills that operate automatically and without thinking, such as jumping out of the path of an automobile coming toward us as we walk down the side of a road, are stored in implicit memory. Similarly, a feeling of vague dislike for an acquaintance, without knowing why we have that feeling, may be a reflection of implicit memories. Perhaps the person reminds us of someone else in our past that we didn't like, even though we are not aware of the memory of that other individual (Wu, 2013; Vöhringer et al., 2017; Garcia-Léon et al., 2021).

Implicit memory is closely related to the prejudice and discrimination people exhibit toward members of other ethnic groups. Although people may say and even believe they harbor no prejudice, assessment of their implicit memories may reveal that they have negative associations about members of other ethnic groups. Such associations can influence people's behavior without their being aware of their underlying beliefs (Enge et al., 2015; Lucas et al., 2019; O'Shea et al., 2020).

One way that memory specialists study implicit memory is through experiments that use priming. **Priming** occurs when exposure to a word or concept (called a *prime*) later makes it easier to recall information related to the prime. Priming allows us to

explicit memory Intentional or conscious recollection of information. (Module 19)

implicit memory Memories of which people are not consciously aware but that can affect subsequent performance and behavior. (Module 19)

priming A phenomenon that occurs when exposure to a word or concept (called a prime) later makes it easier to recall information related to the prime. (Module 19)

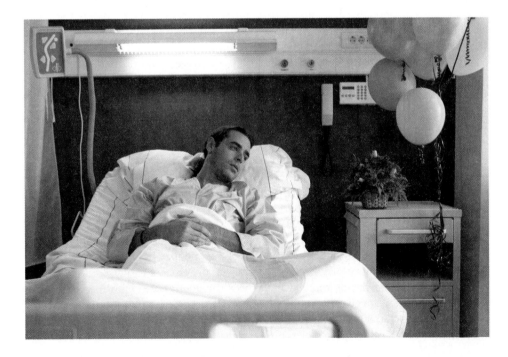

Although patients may have no conscious recollection of conversations that occurred while they were anesthetized during surgery, they still may be able to recall snippets of those conversations.
Pixtal/AGE Fotostock

remember new information better and faster because of material we already have stored in memory. Priming effects occur even when people have no conscious memory of the original word or concept (Geyer et al., 2011; Akhtar & Howe, 2019; Ward, 2022).

The typical experiment designed to illustrate priming helps clarify the phenomenon. In priming experiments, participants are rapidly exposed to a stimulus such as a word, an object, or perhaps a drawing of a face. The second phase of the experiment is done after an interval ranging from several seconds to several months. At that point, participants are exposed to incomplete perceptual information that is related to the first stimulus, and they are asked whether they recognize it. For example, the new material may consist of the first letter of a word that had been presented earlier or a part of a face that had been shown earlier. If participants are able to identify the stimulus more readily than they identify stimuli that have not been presented earlier, priming has taken place. Clearly, the earlier stimulus has been remembered–although the material resides in implicit memory, not explicit memory.

The same thing happens to us in our everyday lives. Suppose several months ago you watched a documentary on the planets, and the narrator described the moons of Mars, focusing on its moon named Phobos. You promptly forget the name of the moon, at least consciously. Then, several months later, you're completing a crossword puzzle that you have partially filled in, and it includes the letters *obos*. As soon as you look at the set of letters, you think of Phobos, and suddenly you recall for the first time since your initial exposure to the information that it is one of the moons of Mars. The sudden recollection occurred because your memory was primed by the letters *obos*.

In short, when information that we are unable to consciously recall affects our behavior, implicit memory is at work. Our behavior may be influenced by experiences of which we are unaware–an example of what has been called "retention without remembering" (White, 2013; Rossi-Arnaud et al., 2017).

Implicit memories also help explain the *other-race effect (ORE)*, which is the phenomenon in which people have more difficulty recognizing and recalling faces of people of other races than people of their own race. The easier recognition and recall of those of one's own race may be due in part to having more experience with same-race individuals, but it can perpetuate prejudice and discrimination against people of other races (Yaros et al., 2019; Marsh, 2021; McKone et al., 2021).

Flashbulb Memories

Ask anyone old enough to recall the day terrorist attacks brought down the Twin Towers in New York City on September 11, 2001. They will likely recall exactly where they were when they heard the news, even though the incident happened years ago.

flashbulb memories Memories of a specific, important, or surprising emotionally significant event that are recalled easily and with vivid imagery. (Module 19)

Their ability to remember details about this fatal event illustrates a phenomenon known as flashbulb memory. **Flashbulb memories** are memories related to a specific, important, or surprising event that are so vivid they represent a virtual snapshot of the event. Several types of flashbulb memories are common among college students. For example, involvement in a car accident, meeting one's roommate for the first time, and the night of high school graduation are all typical flashbulb memories (Lanciano et al., 2013; Talarico et al., 2019; Moreno-Serra et al., 2022; see Figure 3).

Of course, flashbulb memories do not contain every detail of an original scene. I remember vividly that I'd just finished teaching an introductory psych class on September 11, 2001, when I heard about planes flying into the World Trade Center in New York City–later known as 9-11. Although I remember exactly where I was and how others reacted to the news, I do not recollect what I was wearing or what I had for lunch that day. Similarly, although a victim of a crime may hold a flashbulb memory of the crime, the memory may not be accurate in all respects (Curci et al., 2020).

Furthermore, the details recalled in flashbulb memories are often inaccurate, particularly when they involve highly emotional events. For example, research regarding the 9-11 terrorist attacks shows that people typically remember watching television that morning and seeing images of the first plane and then the second plane striking

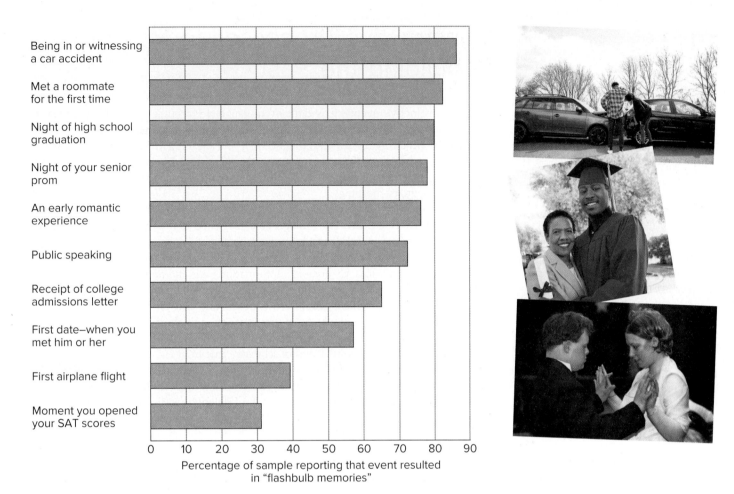

Being in or witnessing a car accident

Met a roommate for the first time

Night of high school graduation

Night of your senior prom

An early romantic experience

Public speaking

Receipt of college admissions letter

First date—when you met him or her

First airplane flight

Moment you opened your SAT scores

Percentage of sample reporting that event resulted in "flashbulb memories"

FIGURE 3 These are the most common flashbulb memory events, based on a survey of college students. What are some of your flashbulb memories?

(first): Southworks/Shutterstock; (second): Digital Vision/SuperStock; (third): DARLENE PFISTER/Star Tribune/Getty Images; (Graph): Source: Adapted from Rubin, 1985.

the towers. However, that recollection is wrong: In fact, television broadcasts showed images only of the second plane on September 11. No video of the first plane was available until early the following morning, September 12, when it was shown on television (Schaefer et al., 2011; Hirst et al., 2015; Muzzulini et al., 2020).

Flashbulb memories illustrate a more general phenomenon about memory: Memories that are exceptional are more easily retrieved (although not necessarily accurately) than are those relating to events that are commonplace. The more distinctive a stimulus is and the more personal relevance the event has, the more likely we are to recall it later (Talarico & Rubin, 2007; Schaefer et al., 2011; Gandolphe & El Haj, 2017).

Even with a distinctive stimulus, however, we may not remember where the information came from. *Source amnesia* occurs when an individual has a memory for some material but cannot recall where they encountered it. For example, source amnesia can explain situations in which you meet someone you know but can't remember where you met that person initially. Moreover, although you may remember particular details about the 2020 coronavirus pandemic vividly, you are less likely to recall when and from whom you learned those details. And that's especially true if you were in quarantine when the memories were formed and each day was so similar to the previous one (Ahmadi Forooshani et al., 2020; Garber, 2020; Green & Naveh-Benjamin, 2020).

Similarly, our motivation to remember material when we are exposed to it initially affects how well we can later recall it. If we know we are going to need to recall material later, we are going to be more attentive to it. In contrast, if we don't expect to need to recall material later, then we are less likely to remember it (Kassam et al., 2009; Phukhachee et al., 2019).

Constructive Processes in Memory: Rebuilding the Past

constructive processes Processes in which memories are influenced by the meaning we give to events. (Module 19)

schemas Organized bodies of information stored in memory that bias the way new information is interpreted, stored, and recalled. (Modules 19, 43)

! Study Alert

A key fact about memory is that it is a constructive process in which memories are influenced by the meaning given to what is being recalled.

As we have seen, although it is clear that we can have detailed recollections of significant and distinctive events, it is difficult to gauge the accuracy of such memories. In fact, it is apparent that our memories reflect, at least in part, **constructive processes,** processes in which memories are influenced by the meaning we give to events. When we retrieve information, then, the memory that is produced is affected not just by the direct prior experience we have had with the stimulus but also by our guesses and inferences about its meaning.

The notion that memory is based on constructive processes was first put forward by Frederic Bartlett, a British psychologist. He suggested that people tend to remember information in terms of **schemas,** organized bodies of information stored in memory that bias the way new information is interpreted, stored, and recalled (Bartlett, 1932). Because we use schemas to organize information, our memories often consist of a reconstruction of previous experience. Consequently, schemas are based not only on the actual material to which people are exposed but also on their understanding of the situation, their expectations about the situation, and their awareness of the motivations underlying the behavior of others.

One of the earliest demonstrations of schemas came from a classic study that involved a procedure similar to the children's game of "telephone," in which information from memory is passed sequentially from one person to another. In the study, a participant viewed a drawing in which a variety of people of differing racial and ethnic backgrounds were on a subway car, one of whom—a White person—was shown with a razor in hand. The first participant was asked to describe the drawing to someone else without looking back at it. Then that person was asked to describe it to another person (without looking at the drawing), and then the process was repeated with still one more participant.

The report of the last person differed in significant, yet systematic, ways from the initial drawing. Specifically, many people described the drawing as depicting a Black person with a knife—an incorrect recollection, given that the drawing showed a razor in the hand of a White person. The transformation of the White person's razor into a Black person's knife clearly indicates that the participants held a schema that included the unwarranted prejudice that Blacks are more violent than Whites and thus more apt to be holding a knife. In short, people's expectations and knowledge—and, in this case, prejudices—affect the reliability of their memories (Allport & Postman, 1958; Brigard et al., 2017; Pelletier & Drozda-Senkowska, 2020).

Although the constructive nature of memory can result in memories that are partially or completely false, they also may be beneficial in some ways. For example, false memories may allow us to keep hold of positive self-images. In addition, they may help us maintain positive relationships with others as we construct overly positive views of them (Howe, 2011; Chew et al., 2020).

Similarly, memory is affected by the emotional meaning of experiences. For example, in one experiment, researchers asked devoted Yankee or Red Sox fans about details of two decisive baseball championship games between the teams, one won by the Yankees and the other won by the Red Sox. Fans recalled details of the game their team won significantly more accurately than the game their team lost (Breslin & Safer, 2011; Guida et al., 2013; Tassone et al., 2019; see Figure 4).

MEMORY IN THE COURTROOM: THE EYEWITNESS ON TRIAL

For Calvin Willis, the inadequate memories of two people cost him more than two decades of his life. Willis was the victim of mistaken identity when a young rape victim picked out his photo as the perpetrator of the rape. On that basis, he was tried, convicted, and sentenced to life in prison. Twenty-one years later, DNA testing showed that Willis was innocent and the victim's identification was wrong.

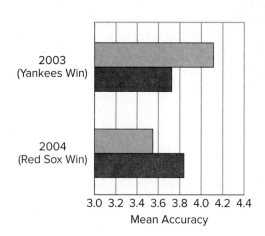

FIGURE 4 Yankee and Red Sox fans were more accurate recalling details of a championship game their team won than they were of a championship game that their team lost.
Source: Adapted from Breslin & Safer, 2011.

Unfortunately, Willis is not the only victim to whom apologies have had to be made; many cases of mistaken identity have led to unjustified legal actions. Research on eyewitness identification of suspects, as well as on memory for other details of crimes, has shown that eyewitnesses are apt to make significant errors when they try to recall details of criminal activity—even if they are highly confident about their recollections. Because more than 75,000 prosecutions a year are totally based on eyewitness recollections, the problem is significant (Lehrer, 2012; McCann et al., 2015; Marr et al., 2021).

One reason eyewitnesses tend to make significant errors is the impact of the weapons used in crimes. When a criminal perpetrator displays a gun or knife, it acts like a perceptual magnet, attracting the eyes of the witnesses. As a consequence, witnesses pay less attention to other details of the crime and are less able to recall what actually occurred (Sheahan et al., 2017; Erickson et al., 2022). Similarly, characteristics of the accused person influence eyewitness memories. For example, race, age, and accent of the accused may affect eyewitness memories (Maeder & Ewanation, 2018; Cantone et al., 2019).

Finally, the specific wording of questions posed to eyewitnesses by police officers or attorneys also can lead to memory errors. For example, in one experiment, the participants were shown a film of two cars crashing into each other. Some were then asked the question, "About how fast were the cars going when they *smashed* into each other?" On average, they estimated the speed to be 40.8 miles per hour. In contrast, when another group of participants was asked, "About how fast were the cars going when they *contacted* each other?" the average estimated speed was only 31.8 miles per hour (Loftus & Palmer, 1974; Dobbins & Kantner, 2019; see Figure 5).

Although eyewitnesses are often confident in their recollections, in many cases, their confidence is misplaced. In fact, the relationship between confidence and accuracy is often small and sometimes even negative; in some cases, the more confident a witness, the less accurate are their recollections. On the other hand, several conditions affect the relationship between eyewitness confidence and better accuracy. Specifically, accuracy improves when witnesses see only one suspect at a time; when the suspects don't look conspicuous in the lineup due to their clothing or ethnicity or race; and when the witness is told the offender is not necessarily in the lineup (Wixted & Wells, 2017; Sauer et al., 2019).

Children's Reliability The problem of memory reliability becomes even more acute when children are witnesses because children's memories are highly vulnerable to the influence of others. For instance, in one experiment, 5- to 7-year-old girls who had just

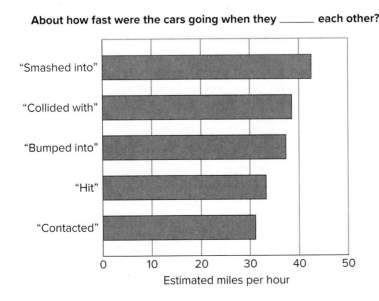

About how fast were the cars going when they _____ each other?

"Smashed into"

"Collided with"

"Bumped into"

"Hit"

"Contacted"

0   10   20   30   40   50
Estimated miles per hour

FIGURE 5 After viewing an accident involving two cars, the participants in a study were asked to estimate the speed of the two cars involved in the collision. Estimates varied substantially, depending on the way the question was worded.
Source: Adapted from Loftus & Palmer, 1974.

Children's memories may show considerable unreliability when they are called as witnesses during trials.

Rob Crandall/SCPhotos/Alamy Stock Photo

had routine physical examinations were shown an anatomically explicit doll. The girls were shown the doll's genital area and asked, "Did the doctor touch you here?" Three of the girls who did not have a vaginal or anal exam said that the doctor had in fact touched them in the genital area, and one of those three made up the detail "The doctor did it with a stick" (Reyna et al., 2017; Irwanda et al., 2022).

Children's memories are especially susceptible to influence when the situation is highly emotional or stressful. For example, in trials in which there is significant pretrial publicity or in which alleged victims are questioned repeatedly, often by untrained interviewers, the memories of the alleged victims may be influenced by the types of questions they are asked. Furthermore, children's less proficient language skills may also hinder the accuracy of their recall (Wright et al., 2015; Saywitz et al., 2019; Perez et al., 2022).

Repressed and False Memories: Separating Truth from Fiction Consider the case of Paul Shanley, a Catholic priest. He was convicted and jailed for sexually abusing a male victim who claimed that for decades, he had not remembered being abused over a 6-year period as a child. However, during adulthood, the victim claimed, his repressed memories gradually moved into consciousness. At that point, he reported clearly recalling his years of abuse, and on the basis of those previously repressed memories, the priest was convicted and sent to jail (Wolf et al., 2010; Otgaar et al., 2017; Goodman et al., 2019).

Repressed memories are apparent recollections of events that are initially so shocking that the mind responds by pushing them into the unconscious. The concept of repressed memory is derived from Freud's psychoanalytic theory. Those who support the concept suggest that traumatic memories may remain hidden, possibly throughout a person's lifetime, unless they are triggered by some current circumstance, such as the probing that occurs during psychological therapy.

Considerable controversy surrounds the legitimacy of repressed memories. Some therapists give great weight to their authenticity, and their views are supported, in part, by research showing that specific regions of the brain help keep unwanted memories out of awareness. However, many therapists, as well as memory researchers, maintain that little evidence supports the phenomenon of repressed memories. They assert that so-called repressed memories may well be inaccurate or even wholly false (Mapelli & Özkurt, 2019; Otgaar et al., 2021).

In fact, many researchers who dispute the existence of repressed memories suggest that they should be considered examples of *false memories,* a phenomenon in which a person remembers events that did not happen or remembers events in an inaccurate way. For example, when recalling an event based on an unclear or ambiguous memory, people may become confused about whether they actually experienced the event or instead imagined it. Ultimately, people come to believe that the event actually occurred (Choi et al., 2013; Lynn et al., 2015).

False memories also may be at work when people embrace what has come to be called "fake news." That is, a person hears or reads news from an unreliable source, such as a biased website or a conversation overheard at the grocery store. Later, they may not recall the source of the erroneous information while eventually coming to believe in its accuracy. Furthermore, they may be predisposed to accept and later recall information that is consistent with those already-existing beliefs (Bronstein et al., 2019; Pennycook & Rand, 2021).

Fake news about vaccines was particularly prevalent during the COVID-19 pandemic. Despite overwhelming scientific evidence supporting their value in reducing the likelihood of contracting the virus, a significant minority of people accepted news to the contrary, coming to believe that the vaccines were ineffective or even harmful (Greene & Murphy, 2020; Scuotto et al., 2021).

Another extreme version of false memories occurs in the case of false confessions. *False confessions* occur when an innocent person, accused of a crime and interrogated extensively by the police, comes to believe and remember that they actually committed the crime and then confess that they are guilty, even though they are, in reality, innocent. Such cases typically occur when innocent people are put under extreme pressure during police interrogation. Deprived of sleep and food, they may come to believe that they actually carried out crimes as extreme as murder and rape, even though they are innocent. About a quarter of defendants who are ultimately exonerated have falsely confessed to a crime they didn't commit (Lackey, 2020; Otgaar et al., 2021; Rizzelli et al., 2021).

In contrast to the controversies about the existence of repressed memories, widespread agreement surrounds the idea that people are susceptible to false memories. Not only do people come to hold memories that are false, but researchers are also developing ways to erase them, as we discuss in the *Applying Psychology in the 21st Century* feature.

Autobiographical Memory: Where Past Meets Present Your memory of experiences in your own past may well be, in part, a fiction–or at least a distortion of what actually occurred. The same constructive processes that make us inaccurately recall the behavior of others also reduce the accuracy of autobiographical memories. **Autobiographical memory** is our recollections of our own life experiences. Autobiographical memories encompass the episodic memories we hold about ourselves (Nalbantian, 2011; Bauer et al., 2019; King et al., 2022).

autobiographical memory Our recollections of our own life experiences. (Module 19)

For example, we tend to forget information about our past that is incompatible with the way in which we currently see ourselves. One study found that adults who were well adjusted but who had been treated for emotional problems during the early years

APPLYING PSYCHOLOGY IN THE 21ST CENTURY

REMEMBERING WHAT NEVER HAPPENED AND THEN FORGETTING IT

Guilty of murder in the first degree.

That was the jury's verdict in the case of George Franklin, Sr., who was charged with murdering his daughter's playmate. But this case was different from most other murder cases: It was based on memories that had been repressed for 20 years. Franklin's daughter claimed that she had forgotten everything about her father's crime until 2 years earlier, when she began to have flashbacks of the event.

Initially, she had only a memory of her friend's look of betrayal. Over the next year, the memories became richer, and she recalled being together with her father and her friend. Then she remembered her father sexually assaulting her friend. She recalled his lifting a rock over his head and then seeing her friend lying on the ground, covered with blood. On the basis of these memories, her father was arrested and convicted–though he ultimately gained his freedom following an appeal of the conviction (Malesevic, 2021).

Although the prosecutor and jury clearly believed Franklin's daughter initially, there were good reasons to question the validity of her recovered memories. According to psychologist Elizabeth Loftus, such recovered memories may well be inaccurate or even wholly false. She notes how easy it is to plant memories that people believe are real (Loftus, 1993; Patihis et al., 2021).

For example, in one classic experiment, a student wrote a totally false story for his younger brother Chris, 14, to read. It described an event in which Chris wandered away from his brother and later was found crying with a tall, oldish man wearing a flannel shirt. Just a few weeks later, after hearing the story, Chris became convinced the event had actually happened. He described the color of the old man's flannel shirt, his bald head, and his feeling of being "really scared." Even when informed that the event never happened, Chris clung to his memory.

Clearly, people are potentially susceptible to false memories. But do they hold on to them forever? Not necessarily, as a recent study suggests. In that study, researchers used interviews to try to convince participants that they had experienced events as children that hadn't actually occurred, such as getting lost or being in a car accident (Oeberst et al., 2021).

Later, the researchers tried to reduce the impact of the false memories. For example, they informed participants that there might have been external sources, such as family narratives, for the memories, or they brought up the possibility that the memories had been inadvertently created during the initial phase of the study. The results showed that these techniques for eradicating the false memories were largely successful. Overall, the study showed that false memories do not necessarily persist. In other words, what one remembers falsely can be forgotten.

RETHINK

- Why do you think people develop false memories?
- What kinds of memories might be more helpful to forget than to retain?

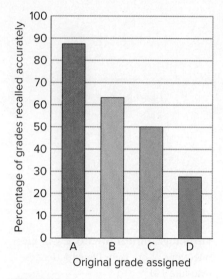

FIGURE 6 We tend to distort memories of unpleasant events. For example, college students are much more likely to accurately recall their good grades while inaccurately recalling their poor ones. Now that you know this, how well do you think you can recall your high school grades?

Source: Adapted from Bahrick et al., 1996.

of their lives tended to forget important but troubling childhood events, such as being in foster care. College students misremember their bad grades–but remember their good ones (Kemps & Tiggemann, 2007; Stanley et al., 2017; Jacobsen, 2021; see Figure 6).

Similarly, when a group of 48-year-olds was asked to recall how they had responded on a questionnaire they had completed in their first year of high school, their accuracy was no better than chance. For example, although 61% of the questionnaire respondents said that playing sports and other physical activities was their favorite pastime, only 23% of the adults recalled it accurately (Offer et al., 2000).

People don't only distort certain kinds of events; they also remember particular periods of life more easily than others. For example, when people reach late adulthood, they remember periods of major transitions, such as attending college and working at their first jobs, better than they remember their middle-age years. Similarly, although most adults' earliest memories of their own lives are of events that occurred when they were toddlers, toddlers show evidence of recall of events that occurred when they were as young as 6 months old. In some cases, then, autobiographical memories can be accurate, particularly for high-impact events (Mace et al., 2015; Wang et al., 2019; also see the *Neuroscience in Your Life* feature).

NEUROSCIENCE IN YOUR LIFE: THE NOSE REMEMBERS

You catch a whiff of something, maybe a perfume or food, and suddenly, a memory floods over you. Does that sound familiar? Scents have a powerful ability to evoke memories that are so vivid, you feel yourself transported back in time. Psychologists have known for decades that smells trigger memory more than any other sense. This is especially true for autobiographical memories, the episodic memories about a person's past. Neuroscience studies shed light on the brain basis of this phenomenon. It turns out that the smell center of the brain—the olfactory bulb—has direct connections to parts of the brain that are important for memory and emotion processing, such as the hippocampus and the amygdala. This three-way connection between smell, memory, and emotion may explain why smells tend to bring back emotional memories.

A part of the frontal lobes in the brain plays a part too, demonstrated by a functional magnetic resonance imaging (fMRI) study of older adults (Masaoka et al., 2021). The researchers tested odors such as baby powder and citrus to see whether they evoked specific memories for the participants, and if so, how vivid and emotional the memories were. Then the participants received an MRI scan while the smells were presented to them again. Odors that evoked the most vivid autobiographical memories activated a portion of the frontal lobes more than odors that were not tied to specific memories. This is meaningful because frontal-lobe activation is important for cognitive function and motivation, but activity in some parts of the frontal lobes declines with age. These results raise the possibility that odor exposure could boost cognitive functioning in older adults and increase positive memories in people with memory disorders such as Alzheimer's disease.

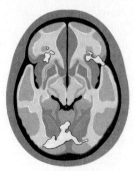
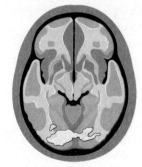

Odors linked to memories   Odors not linked to memories

The brain regions in yellow showed more activation when older adults were presented with odors and less activation when they were presented with unscented air. Also, a portion of the frontal lobes was activated by odors that evoked emotional autobiographical memories (left figure) but not when participants lacked associations between the odors and a specific memory (right figure).

Exploring Diversity

Are There Cross-Cultural Differences in Memory?

Explorers who have visited parts of the world in which there is no written language sometimes return with tales of individuals with phenomenal memories. For instance, storytellers in some preliterate cultures recount long chronicles that include the names and activities of people over multiple generations.

Such feats of memory initially led experts to believe that people in preliterate societies develop a different, and perhaps better, type of memory than do those in cultures that employ a written language. They suggested that in a society that lacks writing, people are motivated to recall information with accuracy, especially information relating to tribal histories and traditions that would be lost if they were not passed down orally from one generation to another (Daftary & Meri, 2002; Berntsen & Rubin, 2004).

Today, however, memory researchers dismiss that view. For one thing, preliterate peoples don't have an exclusive claim to amazing memory feats. Some Hebrew scholars memorize thousands of pages of text and can recall the locations of particular words on the page. Similarly, poetry singers in the Balkans can recall thousands of lines of poetry. Even in cultures in which written language exists, then, astounding feats of memory are possible (Strathern & Stewart, 2003; Rubin et al., 2007; Seamon et al., 2010; Song et al., 2019).

Memory researchers now believe that there are both similarities and differences in memory across cultures. Basic memory processes seem to be similar. For example, short-term memory capacity, working memory, and the structure of long-term memory—the "hardware"—are universal and operate similarly in people in all cultures.

In contrast, the way information is acquired and the degree to which it is rehearsed—the "software" of memory—do differ from culture to culture. Culture determines how people frame information initially, how much they practice learning it, and which strategies they use to recall it (Mack, 2003; Wang & Conway, 2006; Rubin et al., 2007; Goyal et al., 2019).

For example, people in the United States may focus more on important visual details, such as the color of decorations at a birthday party or the kind of icing on the birthday cake. In contrast, East Asians may recall interpersonal details, such as who served the cake. What is recalled, then, reflects what was initially important and significant to the person recalling the information, which is affected by cultural factors (Gutchess & Boduroglu, 2019; Gutchess et al., 2021).

Storytellers in many cultures can recount hundreds of years of history in vivid detail. Research has found that this amazing ability is due less to basic memory processes than to the ways in which they acquire and retain information.
Suthichai Hantrakul/Shutterstock

RECAP/EVALUATE/RETHINK

RECAP

LO 19-1 What causes difficulties and failures in remembering?

- The tip-of-the-tongue phenomenon is the temporary inability to remember information that one is certain one knows. Retrieval cues are a major strategy for recalling information successfully.
- The levels-of-processing approach to memory suggests that the way in which information is initially perceived and analyzed determines the success with which it is recalled. The deeper the initial processing, the greater the recall.
- Explicit memory refers to intentional or conscious recollection of information. In contrast, implicit memory refers to memories of which people are not consciously aware but that can affect subsequent performance and behavior.
- Flashbulb memories are memories centered on a specific, emotionally significant event. The more distinctive a memory is, the more easily it can be retrieved.
- Memory is a constructive process: We relate memories to the meaning, guesses, and expectations we give to events. Specific information is recalled in terms of schemas, organized bodies of information stored in memory that bias the way new information is interpreted, stored, and recalled.
- Eyewitnesses are apt to make substantial errors when they try to recall the details of crimes. The problem of memory reliability becomes even more acute when the witnesses are children.
- Autobiographical memory is influenced by constructive processes.

EVALUATE

1. While with a group of friends at a dance, Eva bumps into a man she dated last month. But when she tries to introduce him to her friends, she cannot remember his name. What is the term for this occurrence?
2. _____ is the process of retrieving a specific item from memory.
3. An aunt says, "I know exactly where I was and what I was doing when I heard about the 9-11 attacks in New York City." What is this type of memory phenomenon called?
4. _____ _____ _____ theory states that the more a person analyzes a statement, the more likely they are to remember it later.

RETHINK

1. Research shows that an eyewitness's memory for details of crimes can contain significant errors. How might a lawyer use this information when evaluating an eyewitness's testimony? Should eyewitness accounts be permissible in a court of law?
2. How do schemas help people process information during encoding, storage, and retrieval? In what ways are they helpful? How can they contribute to inaccurate autobiographical memories?

Answers to Evaluate Questions

1. tip-of-the-tongue phenomenon; 2. Recall; 3. flashbulb memory; 4. Levels-of-processing

KEY TERMS

tip-of-the-tongue phenomenon	recognition	implicit memory	constructive processes
recall	levels-of-processing theory	priming	schemas
	explicit memory	flashbulb memories	autobiographical memory

Module 20
Forgetting: When Memory Fails

LEARNING OUTCOMES

LO 20-1 Why do we forget information?

LO 20-2 What are the major memory impairments?

He could not remember his childhood friends, the house he grew up in, or what he had eaten for breakfast that morning. H. M., as he is referred to in the scientific literature, had lost his ability to remember anything beyond a few minutes, the result of experimental surgery intended to minimize his epileptic seizures. But the removal of his brain's hippocampus and the loss of his temporal lobes quite literally erased H. M.'s past. He had enjoyed a normal memory until he underwent the operation at age 27. After that, H. M. said, every moment felt like waking from a dream. He never knew where he was or the identities of the people around him (Milner, 2005; MacKay, 2019).

As the case of H. M. illustrates, a person without a normal memory faces severe difficulties. All of us who have experienced even routine instances of forgetting–such as not remembering an acquaintance's name or a fact on a test–understand the very real consequences of memory failure.

Of course, memory failure is also essential to remembering important information. The ability to forget inconsequential details about experiences, people, and objects helps us avoid being burdened and distracted by trivial stores of meaningless data. Forgetting helps keep unwanted and unnecessary information from interfering with retrieving information that is wanted and necessary (Schooler & Hertwig, 2012; Anderson & Hulbert, 2021).

Forgetting also permits us to form general impressions and recollections. For example, the reason our friends consistently look familiar to us is because we're able to forget their clothing, facial blemishes, and other transient features that change from one occasion to the next. Instead, our memories are based on a summary of various critical features–a far more economical use of our memory capabilities.

Finally, forgetting provides a practical educational benefit: When we have forgotten something and then are forced to relearn it, we're more likely to remember it better in the future (Bjork, 2015; Boser, 2017).

The first attempts to study forgetting were made by German psychologist Hermann Ebbinghaus about 100 years ago. Using himself as the only participant in his study, Ebbinghaus memorized lists of three-letter nonsense syllables–meaningless sets of two consonants with a vowel in between, such as FIW and BOZ. By measuring how easy it was to relearn a given list of words after varying periods of time had passed since the initial learning, he found that forgetting occurred systematically, as shown in Figure 1. As the figure indicates, the most rapid forgetting occurs in the first 9 hours, particularly in the first hour. After 9 hours, the rate of forgetting slows and declines little, even after the passage of many days.

Despite his primitive methods, Ebbinghaus's study had an important influence on subsequent research, and his basic conclusions have been upheld. There is almost always a strong initial decline in memory, followed by a more gradual drop over time. Furthermore, relearning of previously mastered material is almost always faster than starting from scratch, whether the material is academic information or a motor skill such as serving a tennis ball (Radvansky et al., 2015; Matayoshi et al., 2019; Roe et al., 2021).

Why We Forget

Why do we forget? One reason is that we may not have paid attention to the material in the first place–a failure of *encoding*. For example, if you live in the United States, you probably have been exposed to thousands of pennies during your life. Despite this experience, you probably don't have a clear sense of the details of the coin. (See this

FIGURE 1 In his classic work, Ebbinghaus found that the most rapid forgetting occurs in the first 9 hours after exposure to new material. However, the rate of forgetting then slows down and declines very little even after many days have passed. Check your own memory: What were you doing exactly 2 hours ago? What were you doing last Tuesday at 5 p.m.? Which information is easier to retrieve?

Source: Adapted from Ebbinghaus, 1885/1913.

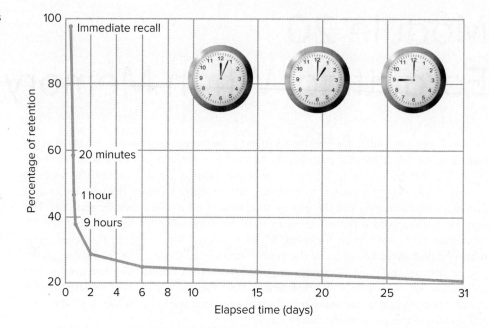

decay The loss of information in memory through its nonuse. (Module 20)

for yourself by looking at Figure 2.) Consequently, the reason for your memory failure is that you probably never encoded the information into long-term memory initially. Obviously, if information was not placed in memory to start with, there is no way the information can be recalled.

But what about material that has been encoded into memory and that can't later be remembered? Several processes account for memory failures, including decay, interference, and cue-dependent forgetting.

Decay is the loss of information in memory through nonuse. This explanation for forgetting assumes that *memory traces*, the physical changes that take place in the brain when new material is learned, simply fade away or disintegrate over time (Ricker et al., 2020; Radvansky et al., 2022).

Although there is evidence that decay does occur, this does not seem to be the complete explanation for forgetting. Often there is no relationship between how long

FIGURE 2 One of these pennies is the real thing. Can you find it? Why is this task harder than it seems at first?

Source: Adapted from Nickerson & Adams, 1979.

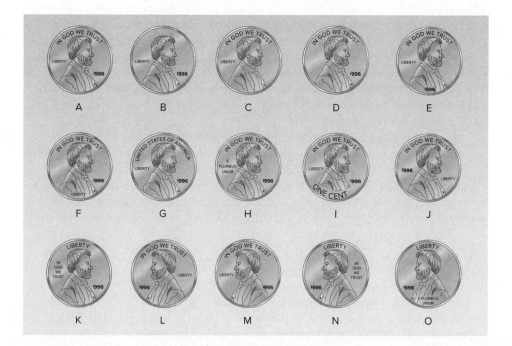

ago a person was exposed to information and how well that information is recalled. If decay explained all forgetting, we would expect that the more time that has elapsed between the initial learning of information and our attempt to recall it, the harder it would be to remember it because there would be more time for the memory trace to decay. Yet people who take several consecutive tests on the same material often recall more of the initial information when taking later tests than they did on earlier tests. If decay were operating, we would expect the opposite to occur (Hardt et al., 2013; Sachser et al., 2017).

Because decay does not fully account for forgetting, memory specialists have proposed an additional mechanism: interference. In **interference**, information stored in memory disrupts the recall of other information stored in memory. For example, if I'm trying to recall my college classmate Jake's name and all I can remember is the name of another classmate, James, interference may be at work (Solesio-Jofre et al., 2011; Ecker et al., 2015; Crawford et al., 2021).

To distinguish between decay and interference, think of the two processes in terms of a row of books on a library shelf. In decay, the old books are constantly crumbling and rotting away, leaving room for new arrivals. Interference processes suggest that new books knock the old ones off the shelf, where they become hard to find or even totally inaccessible.

Finally, forgetting may occur because of **cue-dependent forgetting,** forgetting that occurs when a person has insufficient retrieval cues to rekindle information that is in memory. For example, you may not be able to remember where you lost a set of keys until you mentally walk through your day, thinking of each place you visited. When you think of the place where you lost the keys–say, the library–the retrieval cue of the library may be sufficient to help you recall that you left them on the desk in the library. Without that retrieval cue, you may be unable to recall the location of the keys (Weller et al., 2013; Kluge & Gronau, 2018).

Most research suggests that interference and cue-dependent forgetting are key processes in forgetting. We forget things mainly because new memories interfere with the retrieval of old ones or because appropriate retrieval cues are unavailable, not because the memory trace has decayed (Radvansky, 2010; Caravà, 2021).

Moreover, forgetting serves an important purpose in keeping our thoughts uncluttered and manageable. In a phenomenon known as *retrieval-induced forgetting,* the prefrontal cortex of the brain manages access to information stored in memory, enhancing access to information we use most frequently while also inhibiting access to conflicting information. Rather than remembering everything, the brain prioritizes information, giving more emphasis to the big ideas and less to the inconsequential details. By reducing competing memories, our brains allow us to more easily work with important information so that we can, for example, draw uncomplicated conclusions or detect important underlying patterns (Schlichting & Frankland, 2017; Ryan & Frankland, 2022).

You might think that having access to more, or even all, of the information stored in your brain is better, but that's not true. For one thing, we're constantly being bombarded with information, much of which is not very interesting or important or relevant to our lives. If we didn't forget, we'd constantly be sorting through memories that are not very helpful and that would only impede successful navigation of the world (Josselyn & Tonegawa, 2020; Purtill, 2022).

Furthermore, forgetting reduces the occurrence of other kinds of memory problems, such as interference. You'll be very happy if you can remember where you parked your car on campus last so that you can find it again. But if you had equally accessible memories of where you parked your car for every single time you parked it on campus, you would likely have difficulty pulling up just the one that will lead you to where your car is today. Moreover, forgetting serves another purpose: It disrupts old patterns of responding, clearing the way for new and potentially more creative or more effective ones (Popov et al., 2019; Oberauer & Greve, 2021).

interference The phenomenon by which information in memory disrupts the recall of other information. (Module 20)

Study Alert

Memory loss through decay comes from nonuse of the memory; memory loss through interference is due to the presence of other information in memory.

cue-dependent forgetting Forgetting that occurs when there are insufficient retrieval cues to rekindle information that is in memory. (Module 20)

Proactive and Retroactive Interference: The Before and After of Forgetting

There are actually two sorts of interference that influence forgetting. One is proactive interference, and the other is retroactive interference (Oberauer et al., 2017; Redick et al., 2019; Wixted, 2021).

In **proactive interference,** information learned earlier disrupts the recall of newer material. Suppose, as a student of foreign languages, you first learned French in the 10th grade and then in the 11th grade you took Spanish. When in the 12th grade you take a college subject achievement test in Spanish, you may find you have difficulty recalling the Spanish translation of a word because all you can think of is its French equivalent.

In contrast, **retroactive interference** occurs when material that was learned later disrupts the retrieval of information that was learned earlier. If, for example, you have difficulty on a French subject achievement test because of your more recent exposure to Spanish, retroactive interference is the culprit (see Figure 3). Similarly, retroactive interference can account for the lack of accuracy of eyewitness memories, as newer information about a crime obtained from newspaper accounts may disrupt the initial memory of the observation of the crime.

One way to remember the difference between proactive and retroactive interference is to keep in mind that *pro*active interference progresses in time—the past interferes with the present. In contrast, *retro*active interference retrogresses in time, working backward as the present interferes with the past.

Although the concepts of proactive and retroactive interference illustrate how material may be forgotten, they still do not explain whether forgetting is caused by the actual loss or modification of information or by problems in the retrieval of information. Most research suggests that material that has apparently been lost because of interference can eventually be recalled if appropriate stimuli are presented, but the question has not been fully answered (Haubrich et al., 2020; Radvansky, 2021; Takehara-Nishiuchi, 2021).

proactive interference Interference in which information learned earlier disrupts the recall of material learned later. (Module 20)

retroactive interference Interference in which material that was learned later disrupts the retrieval of information that was learned earlier. (Module 20)

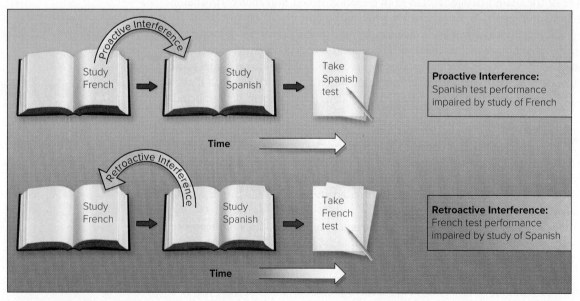

FIGURE 3 Proactive interference occurs when material learned earlier interferes with the recall of newer material. In this example, studying French before studying Spanish interferes with performance on a Spanish test. In contrast, retroactive interference exists when material learned after initial exposure to other material interferes with the recall of the first material. In this case, retroactive interference occurs when recall of French is impaired because of later exposure to Spanish.

Memory Dysfunctions: Afflictions of Forgetting

Memory loss creeps up on its victims. It starts with little things such as misplacing keys or glasses. Then, you forget the names of common household items, and you miss appointments. Next, you can't drive in traffic without becoming confused and anxious. You try to hide what's happening, but others notice. Finally, your lapses become more consequential: You nearly get run over; you have a traffic accident. You no longer can manage the routines of everyday living, such as getting dressed.

These memory problems are symptomatic of **Alzheimer's disease,** a progressive brain disorder that leads to a gradual and irreversible decline in cognitive abilities. Alzheimer's is the sixth-leading cause of death among adults in the United States, affecting an estimated 6.5 million people. Older non-Hispanic Blacks and Hispanic Americans are disproportionately more likely than older Whites to have Alzheimer's disease (Alzheimer's Association, 2022).

In the beginning, Alzheimer's symptoms appear as simple forgetfulness of things such as appointments and birthdays. As the disease progresses, memory loss becomes more profound, and even the simplest tasks—such as using a phone—are forgotten. Ultimately, victims may lose their ability to speak or comprehend language, and physical deterioration sets in, leading to death.

The causes of Alzheimer's disease are not fully understood. Increasing evidence suggests that Alzheimer's results from an inherited susceptibility to a defect in the production of the protein beta amyloid, which is necessary for the maintenance of nerve cell connections. When the synthesis of beta amyloid goes awry, large clumps of cells form, triggering inflammation and the deterioration of nerve cells in the brain (Tan et al., 2015; Reddy et al., 2019; Karran & De Strooper, 2022).

Alzheimer's disease A progressive brain disorder that leads to a gradual and irreversible decline in cognitive abilities. (Modules 20, 30)

From the perspective of...

A Health-Care Provider What sorts of activities might health-care providers offer their patients to help them combat the memory loss of Alzheimer's disease?

Rubberball/Getty Images

Alzheimer's disease is one of a number of memory dysfunctions. Another is **amnesia,** memory loss that occurs without other mental difficulties. The type of amnesia immortalized in countless Hollywood films involves a victim who receives a blow to the head and is unable to remember anything from their past. In reality, amnesia of this type, known as retrograde amnesia, is quite rare. In **retrograde amnesia,** memory is lost for occurrences prior to a certain event but not for new events. Usually, lost memories gradually reappear, although full restoration may take as long as several years. In certain cases, some memories are lost forever. But even in cases of severe memory loss, the loss is generally selective. For example, although people suffering from retrograde amnesia may be unable to recall friends and family members, they still may be able to play complicated card games or knit a sweater quite well (Lee et al., 2019; Lanzoni et al., 2022).

A second type of amnesia is exemplified by people who remember nothing of their current activities. In **anterograde amnesia,** loss of memory occurs for events that follow an injury. Information cannot be transferred from short-term to long-term

amnesia Memory loss that occurs without other mental difficulties. (Module 20)

retrograde amnesia Amnesia in which memory is lost for occurrences prior to a certain event, but not for new events. (Module 20)

anterograde amnesia Amnesia in which memory is lost for events that follow an injury. (Module 20)

Wernicke-Korsakoff syndrome A disease that afflicts long-term alcoholics, leaving some abilities intact but with unusual symptoms including including memory loss, hallucinations ,and a tendency to repeat the same story. (Module 20)

! Study Alert
Except for Alzheimer's disease, memory disorders are relatively rare.

memory, resulting in the inability to remember anything other than what was in long-term storage before the injury (Stöllberger al., 2019; Garland et al., 2021).

Amnesia can also result from **Wernicke-Korsakoff syndrome,** a disease that afflicts long-term alcoholics. Although many of their intellectual abilities may be intact, Wernicke-Korsakoff sufferers display an array of unusual symptoms, including memory loss, hallucinations, and a tendency to repeat the same story over and over (Wester et al., 2013; Scalzo et al., 2015; Segobin & Pitel, 2021).

Fortunately, most of us have intact memory, and the occasional failures we suffer may actually be preferable to having a perfect memory. Consider, for instance, the case of a man who had total recall. After reading passages of Dante's *The Divine Comedy* in Italian–a language he did not speak–he was able to repeat them from memory some 15 years later. He could memorize lists of 50 unrelated words and recall them at will more than a decade later. He could even repeat the same list of words backward, if asked (Luria, 1987; Brandt & Bakker, 2018; Proctor, 2020).

Such a skill at first may seem to be enviable, but it actually presented quite a problem. The man's memory became a jumble of lists of words, numbers, and names; when he tried to relax, his mind was filled with images. Even reading was difficult because every word evoked a flood of thoughts from the past that interfered with his ability to understand the meaning of what he was reading. Partially as a consequence of the man's unusual memory, psychologist A. R. Luria, who studied his case, found him to be a "disorganized and rather dull-witted person" (Luria, 1987). We might be grateful, then, that forgetfulness plays a role in our lives.

 BECOMING AN INFORMED CONSUMER
# of Psychology

Improving Your Memory

Apart from the advantages of forgetting, say, a bad date, most of us would like to find ways to improve our memories. Among the effective strategies for studying and remembering course material are:

- *Rely on organization cues.* Recall material you read in textbooks or online by organizing the material in memory the first time you read it. For example, use cues such as chapter outlines or learning objectives. If you take advantage of these "advance organizers," you can make connections, see relationships among the various facts, and process the material at a deeper level, which in turn will later aid recall (Korur et al., 2016; Lee et al., 2022).
- *Take effective notes.* "Less is more" is perhaps the best advice for taking lecture notes that facilitate recall. Rather than trying to jot down every detail of a lecture, it is better to listen and think about the material, and take down the main points. In effective note taking, thinking about the material when you first hear it is more important than writing it down. This is one reason that borrowing someone else's notes is a bad idea; you will have no framework in memory that you can use to understand them (Feldman, 2017; Colliot et al., 2022).
- *Practice, practice, practice.* Although practice does not necessarily make perfect, it helps. Use *overlearning,* the process of studying and rehearsing material well beyond your initial mastery of it. Lots of research shows that people demonstrate better long-term recall when they overlearn rather than when they stop practicing just after they initially learn the material (Shibata et al., 2017; Zhang et al., 2021).
- *Use the keyword technique.* If you are studying a foreign language, try pairing a foreign word with a common English word that has a similar sound. This is known as the *keyword technique.* For example, to learn the Spanish word for duck (*pato,*

pronounced *pot-o*), you might choose the keyword *pot*. Once you have thought of a keyword, think of an image in which the Spanish word *pato* is interacting with the English keyword. For example, you might envision a duck sitting in an empty pot to remember the word *pato* (Miyatsu & McDaniel, 2019; Al-Faris & Jasmin, 2021).

- *Test yourself.* If you have trouble remembering names of people you have recently met, one way to help yourself is to say their names out loud when you are first introduced. And just a little later, test yourself by trying to recall the name (Shellenbarger, 2019).

- *Be skeptical about claims that certain drugs improve memory.* Advertisements for vitamin supplements with ginkgo biloba or a "Mental Sharpness Product" would have you believe that taking a pharmaceutical drug or supplement can improve your memory. Not so, according to the results of numerous studies. There is no definitive evidence that over-the-counter memory enhancers are effective, and the U.S. Food and Drug Administration has not approved any over-the-counter drug or supplement treatment for this purpose. However, certain prescription drugs do provide a modest degree of memory enhancement for cases of memory impairment due to diseases such as Alzheimer's disease, though they can't stop the progression of the disease (Piton et al., 2018; Liu et al., 2020; Whitehurst & Mednick, 2021).

RECAP/EVALUATE/RETHINK

RECAP

LO 20-1 Why do we forget information?

- Several processes account for memory failure, including decay, interference (both proactive and retroactive), and cue-dependent forgetting.

LO 20-2 What are the major memory impairments?

- Among the memory dysfunctions are Alzheimer's disease, which leads to a progressive loss of memory, and amnesia, a memory loss that occurs without other mental difficulties and can take the forms of retrograde amnesia and anterograde amnesia. Wernicke-Korsakoff syndrome is a disease that afflicts long-term alcoholics, resulting in memory impairment.

- Techniques for improving memory include the keyword technique to memorize foreign language vocabulary; organizing text material and lecture notes; and practice and rehearsal, leading to overlearning.

EVALUATE

1. If, after learning the history of the Middle East for a class 2 years ago, you now find yourself unable to recall what you learned, you are experiencing memory _____, caused by nonuse.
2. Difficulty in accessing a memory because of the presence of other information is known as _____.

3. _____ interference occurs when material is difficult to retrieve because of subsequent exposure to other material; _____ interference refers to difficulty in retrieving material as a result of the interference of previously learned material.
4. Match the following memory disorders with the correct information:

   1. Affects alcoholics; may result in hallucinations
   2. Memory loss occurring without other mental problems
   3. Beta amyloid defect; progressive forgetting and physical deterioration

   a. Alzheimer's disease
   b. Wernicke-Korsakoff syndrome
   c. Amnesia

RETHINK

1. What are the implications of proactive and retroactive interference for learning multiple foreign languages? Would earlier language training in a different language help or hinder learning a new language?
2. Does the phenomenon of interference help to explain the unreliability of autobiographical memory? Why?

Answers to Evaluate Questions

1. decay; 2. interference; 3. Retroactive, proactive; 4. 1-b, 2-c, 3-a

KEY TERMS

decay	proactive interference	amnesia	Wernicke-Korsakoff
interference	retroactive interference	retrograde amnesia	syndrome
cue-dependent forgetting	Alzheimer's disease	anterograde amnesia	

LOOKING *Back*

EPILOGUE

Our examination of memory has highlighted the processes of encoding, storage, and retrieval, and theories about how these processes occur. We also encountered several phenomena relating to memory, including the tip-of-the-tongue phenomenon and flashbulb memories. Above all, we observed that memory is a constructive process by which interpretations, expectations, and guesses contribute to the nature of our memories.

Before moving on to Chapter 7, return to the prologue of this chapter on Rebecca Sharrock's perfect memory of the events in her life. Consider the following questions in light of what you now know about memory.

1. When Sharrock encounters a reminder of a specific date, she automatically goes back to what was happening then. What advantages might this offer her? What burdens might it impose on her ability to live a normal life?
2. Do you think that having highly superior autobiographical memory like Sharrock's is more of a gift or a curse? Why do you think so?
3. What kinds of questions about memory and forgetting might researchers be able to answer by studying people such as Sharrock?

Design Elements: Man with laptop: Dragon Images/Shutterstock; Exclamation point and mobile frame: McGraw Hill; Smartphone: WML Image/ Shutterstock; Hands: Stefano Garau/Shutterstock.

VISUAL SUMMARY 6 Memory

MODULE 18 The Foundations of Memory

Memory: Encoding, storing, and retrieving information

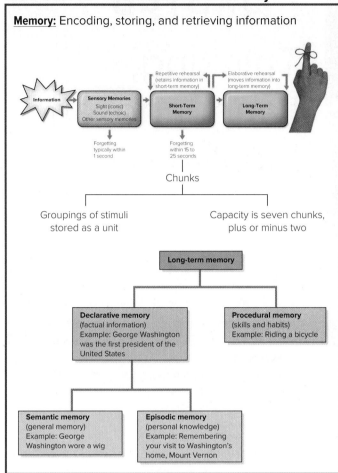

Chunks

Groupings of stimuli stored as a unit

Capacity is seven chunks, plus or minus two

Long-term memory

Declarative memory (factual information)
Example: George Washington was the first president of the United States

Procedural memory (skills and habits)
Example: Riding a bicycle

Semantic memory (general memory)
Example: George Washington wore a wig

Episodic memory (personal knowledge)
Example: Remembering your visit to Washington's home, Mount Vernon

MODULE 19 Recalling Long-Term Memories

Retrieval Cues: Stimuli that allow recall of information stored in long-term memory
- Recall: Remembering specific information
- Recognition: Knowing whether one has been previously exposed to given information

Levels of Processing Theory: Recall depends on how much the information was processed when it was first encountered.

Explicit Memories: Conscious recall of information

Implicit Memories: Memories of which people are not consciously aware

Flashbulb Memories: Memories of a specific, important, or surprising emotionally significant event that are recalled easily and with vivid imagery

Constructive Processes: Processes in which memories are influenced by the meaning we give to events

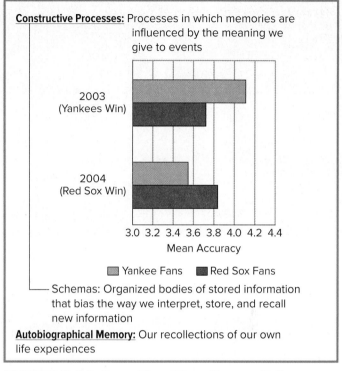

Schemas: Organized bodies of stored information that bias the way we interpret, store, and recall new information

Autobiographical Memory: Our recollections of our own life experiences

MODULE 20 Forgetting: When Memory Fails

Decay: Loss of information through nonuse

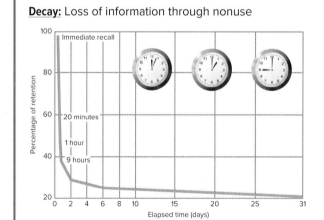

Cue-dependent forgetting: Forgetting that occurs when insufficient retrieval cues are available.

Interference: Information in memory disrupts the recall of other information.

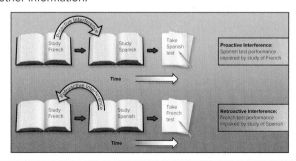

(Module 18) (Photo): Squared Studios/Getty Images; (Module 19) (Photo): Digital Vision/SuperStock; (Graph): Source: Adapted from Breslin & Safer, 2011; (Module 20): (Decay): Source: Adapted from Breslin & Safer, 2011.

Blend Images/Getty Images

CHAPTER 7
Thinking, Language, and Intelligence

LEARNING OUTCOMES FOR CHAPTER 7

MODULE 21

LO 21-1 What is thinking?

LO 21-2 What processes underlie decision making?

LO 21-3 How do people approach and solve problems?

LO 21-4 What are the major obstacles to problem solving?

THINKING

Mental Images: Examining the Mind's Eye

Concepts: Categorizing the World

Algorithms and Heuristics

Solving Problems

Creativity and Problem Solving

Neuroscience in Your Life: You Make Me Laugh!

Becoming an Informed Consumer of Psychology: Thinking Critically and Creatively

MODULE 22

LO 22-1 How do people use language?

LO 22-2 How does language develop?

LANGUAGE

Grammar: Language's Language

Language Development: Developing a Way with Words

Understanding Language Acquisition: Identifying the Roots of Language

The Influence of Language on Thinking: Do the Inuit Have More Words for Snow Than Texans Do?

Applying Psychology in the 21st Century: ¡Hola! Can the Language You Speak Keep You Healthier?

Do Animals Use Language?

Does Speaking Two Languages Make You Smarter?

Exploring Diversity: Teaching with Linguistic Variety: Bilingual Education

LO 23-1 What are the different definitions and conceptions of intelligence?

LO 23-2 What are the major approaches to measuring intelligence, and what do intelligence tests measure?

LO 23-3 How can the extremes of intelligence be characterized?

LO 23-4 Are traditional IQ tests culturally biased?

LO 23-5 To what degree is intelligence influenced by the environment and to what degree by heredity?

PROLOGUE *THOUGHT READING*

For 5 years, the patient had been in what his doctors called a vegetative state following a devastating motorcycle accident. He hadn't said a word and seemed completely unresponsive and oblivious to outside stimuli.

But now a team of researchers were conducting a daring experiment. Using functional magnetic resonance imaging (FMRI), they asked the patient a series of questions and tracked his brain's responses. To answer, he was told to imagine walking around his house to indicate yes and to imagine playing tennis to indicate no.

The researchers knew that the two responses were easy to tell apart using FMRI scanning, at least in healthy people. Thinking about navigating around the house activates spatial areas of the brain, while thinking about playing tennis activates motor areas of the brain.

After explaining the answering system to the apparently unresponsive patient, the researchers presented the questions. Did he have a brother? The motor area of the brain showed activation, so yes. Was his father's name Thomas? The spatial area was activated, so no. At the end of the series of six questions, the patient had answered five correctly—well above chance levels.

Clearly, the patient was, in some way and on some level, conscious and thinking (Monti, 2012; Luppi et al., 2021; Somers, 2021).

LOOKING *Ahead*

Despite the eye-popping results with this patient, researchers have only been able to replicate the findings in a minority of people in vegetative states. But the study proved to be a stepping-stone toward communicating with patients who appear to have no outward signs of consciousness, as well as toward better understanding what is happening inside their brains.

Questions regarding how the brain processes information, as well as how it uses information to solve problems and make decisions, are the topics to which we now turn as we examine cognitive psychology. **Cognitive psychology** is the branch of psychology that focuses on higher mental processes, including thinking, language, memory, problem solving, knowing, reasoning, judging, and decision making.

Although the realm of cognitive psychology is broad, we will focus on three major topics.

We begin by considering the building blocks of thinking. We examine strategies for approaching problems, means of generating solutions, and ways of making judgments about the usefulness and accuracy of solutions.

Next, we turn to the way we communicate with others: language. We consider how people acquire and develop language, its basic characteristics, and the relationship between language and thought.

Finally, we examine intelligence. We consider the challenges involved in defining and measuring intelligence and then examine the two groups displaying extremes of intelligence: people with intellectual disabilities and the gifted. We explore what are probably the two most controversial issues surrounding intelligence: (1) the degree to which intelligence is influenced by heredity and by the environment and (2) whether traditional tests of intelligence are biased toward the dominant cultural groups in society—a difficult issue that has both psychological and social significance.

cognitive psychology The branch of psychology that focuses on the study of higher mental processes, including thinking, language, memory, problem solving, knowing, reasoning, judging, and decision making. (Module 21)

Module 21
Thinking

LEARNING OUTCOMES

LO 21-1 What is thinking?

LO 21-2 What processes underlie decision making?

LO 21-3 How do people approach and solve problems?

LO 21-4 What are the major obstacles to problem solving?

thinking Brain activity in which people mentally manipulate information, including words, visual images, sounds, or other data. (Module 21)

mental images Representations in the mind of an object or event. (Module 21)

Professional musicians often use mental imagery to focus on their performance, a process they call "getting in the zone." What are some other occupations that require the use of strong mental imagery?
SeventyFour/Shutterstock

What are you thinking about at this moment?

The mere ability to pose such a question underscores the distinctive nature of the human ability to think. No other species contemplates, analyzes, recollects, or plans the way humans do. Understanding what thinking is, however, goes beyond knowing that we think. Philosophers, for example, have argued for generations about the meaning of thinking, with some placing it at the core of human beings' understanding of their own existence.

Psychologists define **thinking** as brain activity in which people mentally manipulate information, including words, visual images, sounds, or other data. Thinking transforms information into new and different forms, allowing us to answer questions, make decisions, solve problems, and make plans.

Although a clear sense of what specifically occurs when we think remains elusive, our understanding of the nature of the fundamental elements involved in thinking is growing. We begin by considering our use of mental images and concepts, the building blocks of thought.

Mental Images: Examining the Mind's Eye

Think of your closest friend.

Chances are that you "see" some kind of visual image when asked to think of them, or any other person or object for that matter. To some cognitive psychologists, such mental images constitute a major part of thinking.

Mental images are representations in the mind of an object or event. They are not just visual representations; our ability to "hear" a tune in our heads also relies on a mental image. In fact, every sensory modality may produce corresponding mental images (Senden et al., 2019; Martarelli & Mast, 2022).

Research has found that our mental images have many properties of the actual stimuli they represent. For example, it takes the mind longer to scan mental images of large objects than small ones, just as the eye takes longer to scan an actual large object than to scan an actual small one. Similarly, we are able to manipulate and rotate mental images of objects, just as we are able to manipulate and rotate them in the real world (Reisberg, 2013; Moè, 2021; see Figure 1).

Some experts see the production of mental images as a way to improve various skills. For instance, many athletes use mental imagery in their training. Basketball players may try to produce vivid and detailed images of the court, the basket, the ball, and the noisy crowd. They may visualize themselves taking a foul shot, watching the ball, and hearing the swish as it goes through the net. And it works: The use of mental imagery can lead to improved performance in sports (Velentzas et al., 2011; Lauer et al., 2019; Aikawa & Takai, 2021).

Mental imagery may improve other types of skills as well. For example, piano players who only mentally rehearse an exercise show brain activity that is virtually identical to that of the people who actually practice the exercise manually. Apparently, carrying out the task involved the same network of brain cells as the network used in mentally rehearsing it (Davidson-Kelly et al., 2015; Madeira & dos Santos, 2022).

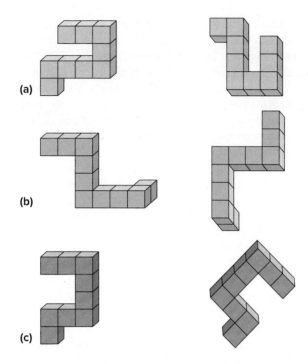

FIGURE 1 Try to mentally rotate one of each pair of patterns to see if it is the same as the other member of that pair. The more you have to mentally rotate a pattern, the longer it will likely take to decide if the patterns match one another. Does this mean that it will take you longer to visualize a map of the world than a map of the United States? Why or why not?

Source: Adapted from Shepard & Metzler, 1971.

From the perspective of...

A Human Resources Specialist How might you use the research on mental imagery to improve employees' performance?

Dex Image/Getty Images

Concepts: Categorizing the World

If someone asks you what is in your kitchen cabinet, you might answer with a detailed list of items (a jar of peanut butter, three boxes of ramen noodles, six dinner plates, and so forth). More likely, though, you would respond by naming some broader categories, such as "food" and "dishes."

Using such categories reflects the operation of concepts. **Concepts** are mental groupings of similar objects, events, or people. Concepts enable us to organize complex phenomena into cognitive categories that are easier to understand and remember (Mack et al., 2016; St. Amant, 2021).

Concepts help us classify newly encountered objects on the basis of our past experience. For example, we can surmise that someone tapping a handheld screen is probably using some kind of phone or tablet, even if we have never encountered that specific model before. Ultimately, concepts influence behavior. We would assume, for instance, that it might be appropriate to pet an animal after determining that it is a dog, whereas we would behave differently after classifying the animal as a wolf.

When cognitive psychologists first studied concepts, they focused on those that were clearly defined by a unique set of properties or features. For example, an equilateral triangle is a closed shape that has three sides of equal length. If an object has these characteristics, it is an equilateral triangle; if it does not, it is not an equilateral triangle.

concept A mental grouping of similar objects, events, or people. (Module 21)

Other concepts–often those with the most relevance to our everyday lives–are more ambiguous and difficult to define. For instance, broader concepts such as "table" and "bird" have a set of general, relatively loose characteristic features rather than unique, clearly defined properties that distinguish an example of the concept from a nonexample.

When we consider these more ambiguous concepts, we usually think of examples called prototypes. **Prototypes** are typical, highly representative examples of a concept that correspond to our mental image or best example of the concept.

For instance, for most people, the prototype of a dog is something like the common beagle rather than the relatively rare Finnish spitz, otterhound, or mudi (breeds you've probably never heard of). Similarly, although a robin and an ostrich are both examples of birds, the robin is an example that comes to most people's minds far more readily. Consequently, robin is a prototype of the concept "bird."

Relatively high agreement exists among people in a particular culture about which examples of a concept are prototypes as well as which examples are not. For instance, most people in Western cultures consider cars and trucks good examples of vehicles, whereas elevators and wheelbarrows are not considered very good examples. Consequently, cars and trucks are prototypes of the concept of a vehicle.

Cultures differ in the specific kinds of prototypes they hold. For example, the prototype of "eating utensil" would be exemplified by forks, knives, and spoons in Western cultures, compared with chopsticks in many Eastern cultures. Or "formal clothing" might be exemplified by a gown in Western cultures compared with a sari in some Asian cultures.

Concepts enable us to think about and understand more readily the complex world in which we live. For example, the suppositions we make about the reasons for other people's behavior are based on the ways in which we classify behavior. Hence, our conclusion about a person who washes their hands 20 times a day could vary, depending on whether we place their behavior within the conceptual framework of a health-care worker or a person with a mental illness. Similarly, physicians make diagnoses by drawing on concepts and prototypes of symptoms that they learned about in medical school.

On the other hand, the use of concepts and prototypes can have negative consequences, as when they perpetuate racial prejudice. For example, store proprietors who hold a prototype of members of minorities as prone to criminality may interpret the behavior of a Black person who is browsing in the store as suspicious, and they thus may behave in an unwelcoming manner (Bastart et al., 2021).

Algorithms and Heuristics

When faced with making a decision, we often turn to various kinds of cognitive short-cuts, known as algorithms and heuristics, to help us. An **algorithm** is a rule that, if applied appropriately, guarantees a solution to a problem. We can use an algorithm even if we cannot understand why it works. For example, you may know that you can find the length of the third side of a right triangle by using the formula $a^2 + b^2 = c^2$, although you may not have the foggiest notion of the mathematical principles behind the formula.

For many problems and decisions, however, no algorithm is available. In those instances, we may be able to use heuristics to help us. A **heuristic** is a thinking strategy that may lead us to a solution to a problem or decision but–unlike algorithms–may sometimes lead to errors. Heuristics increase the likelihood of success in coming to a solution, but unlike algorithms, they cannot ensure it. For example, when I play tic-tac-toe, I follow the heuristic of placing an X in the center square when I start the game. This tactic doesn't guarantee that I will win, but experience has taught me that it will increase my chances of success. Similarly, some students follow the heuristic of preparing for a test by ignoring the assigned textbook reading and only studying their lecture notes–a strategy that may or may not pay off.

prototypes Typical, highly representative examples of a concept. (Module 21)

algorithm A rule that, if applied appropriately, guarantees a solution to a problem. (Module 21)

heuristic A thinking strategy that may lead us to a solution to a problem or decision but–unlike algorithms–may sometimes lead to errors. (Module 21)

Although heuristics often help people solve problems and make decisions, certain kinds of heuristics may lead to inaccurate conclusions. Let's consider some of the major heuristics that bias our thinking:

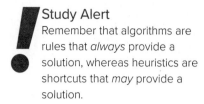

Study Alert
Remember that algorithms are rules that *always* provide a solution, whereas heuristics are shortcuts that *may* provide a solution.

- **Availability heuristic.** When we rely on the *availability heuristic,* we judge the likelihood of an event occurring on the basis of how easily we can bring to mind examples of the event. That is, we assume that events we remember easily are likely to have occurred more frequently in the past–and are more likely to occur in the future–than events that are harder to remember.

  For instance, the availability heuristic makes us more afraid of dying in a plane crash than in an auto accident, despite statistics clearly showing that airplane travel is much safer than auto travel. Similarly, although 10 times as many people die from falling out of bed than from lightning strikes, we're more afraid of being hit by lightning. The reason is that plane crashes and lightning strikes receive far more publicity, and they are therefore more easily remembered (Caruso, 2008; Geurten et al., 2015; Blake & Castel, 2019).

  Similarly, during the COVID pandemic, many parents expressed deep concern over their children's health, fearing their children might become sick and even die from the virus. One reason for the concern can be traced to the availability heuristic, which caused parents to overestimate the risk of the disease, even though the objective reality was that the likelihood of death from COVID for children was much lower than deaths from far more common causes, such as drowning, vehicle accidents, and even homicide (Leonhardt, 2021; see Figure 2).

- **Familiarity heuristic.** The *familiarity heuristic* leads us to prefer familiar objects, people, and things to those that are unfamiliar or strange to us. For example, we might purchase a book written by a familiar author rather than one written by an author we never heard of, even if the topic of the book by the unfamiliar author sounds more appealing.

  The familiarity heuristic typically saves us a great deal of time when we are making decisions, since we often just go with what seems most familiar. On the other hand, it's not so good if you are an emergency room physician susceptible to the familiarity heuristic. If you simply settle on the first, most obvious

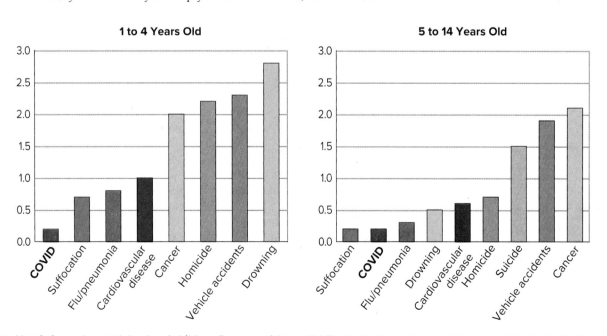

FIGURE 2 Heuristics and annual deaths of children. Because of the availability heuristic, parents tended to overestimate the likelihood of their children dying from COVID. The reality was that children were much more likely to die from other causes. (Note: COVID data are for the 52 weeks ending April 10, 2021. Other data are for 2018).

Source: Leonhart, 2021.

diagnosis for a patient presenting particular symptoms (the ones that are most familiar to you), you may miss making a more accurate diagnosis (Herbert, 2011).

The use of the familiarity heuristic may lead to the *illusion of explanatory depth,* in which we mistakenly believe that if we are familiar with something, we understand it. For example, people typically believe they deeply understand how everyday objects such as bicycles and toilets function, but when asked to describe their operation, they often provide erroneous explanations. The illusion of explanatory depth extends to political beliefs and attitudes, in which people may be unable to logically explain why they hold a particular political position when they are challenged (Fernbach et al., 2013; Vitriol & Marsh, 2018; Gaviria & Corredor, 2021).

- **Present bias.** Another common heuristic is the *present bias*, which is the tendency to more heavily weigh options that are closer to the present than ones further away. For example, suppose you were given the choice between receiving $150 today or $180 a month from now. If you're like most people, you'll probably choose the $150 today. It's actually a bad move: You're giving up a 20% return on investment. But suppose the question you were faced with was to choose between taking $150 in 12 months versus $180 in 13 months. When it's put that way, most people will take the $180, which is definitely the better choice. Bottom line: The present bias is a heuristic that keeps us from thinking logically (Wang & Sloan, 2018: Yagoda, 2018; Laibson et al., 2021).

A real-life example of the present bias relates to the way physicians make decisions about delivering newborns. If a physician encountered complications in their previous vaginal delivery, they are more likely to recommend a cesarean section on their next delivery than if their prior vaginal delivery had no complications. Conversely, if their prior delivery was a cesarean delivery that had complications, they are more likely to recommend a vaginal delivery on the next delivery they perform (Singh, 2021).

Although algorithms and heuristics may be characteristic of human thinking, scientists are now attempting to program computers that optimize problem solving but avoid the biases of human thought. And they are experiencing significant success, as computers are making significant inroads in terms of the ability to solve problems and carry out some forms of intellectual activities. *Artificial intelligence (AI)* is the field that examines how to use technology to imitate human thinking, problem solving, and creative activities.

Initially, attempts to mimic human problem solving with AI proved inadequate because programmers couldn't come up with the full range of possibilities a computer might encounter. Today, AI is built on a process called *machine learning*, in which computers process immense amounts of data and make probabilistic guesses. This permits computers to spot patterns in data that humans are unable to see. Experts argue that current AI programs have the ability to come close to, and may ultimately go beyond, human thinking abilities (Ghahramani, 2015; Hernández-Orallo, 2017; Tariq et al., 2021).

Computers using AI are particularly good at tasks that require speed, persistence, and a huge memory, as you might realize if you've used Apple's Siri or Amazon's Alexa. For example, if you've ever applied for a credit card, it is AI that sifts through vast amounts of information to determine your credit limit and whether the bank should offer you the card in the first place. And this is just the start; thousands of job categories, ranging from radiology to self-driving taxis, are beginning to use AI software. Furthermore, AI applications facilitated the development of vaccines that were used to fight COVID. Still, it remains to be seen whether the quality of thinking produced by AI will match that of humans (Biggi & Stilgoe, 2021; Kabra & Singh, 2021).

Solving Problems

According to an old legend, a group of Vietnamese monks guard three towers on which sit 64 golden rings. The monks believe that if they succeed in moving the rings from the first tower to the third according to a series of rigid rules, the world as we know it will come to an end. (Should you prefer that the world remain in its present state,

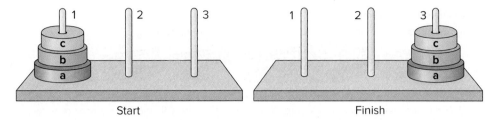

FIGURE 3 The goal of the Tower of Hanoi puzzle is to move all three disks from the first post to the third and still preserve the original order of the disks, using the fewest number of moves possible while following the rules that only one disk at a time can be moved and no disk can cover a smaller one during a move. Try it yourself before you look at the solution, which is listed according to the sequence of moves.
(Solution: Move C to 3, B to 2, C to 2, A to 3, C to 1, B to 3, and C to 3.)

there's no need for immediate concern: The puzzle is so complex that it will take the monks about a trillion years to solve it.)

In the Tower of Hanoi puzzle, a simpler version of the task facing the monks, three disks are placed on three posts in the order shown in Figure 3. The goal of the puzzle is to move all three disks to the third post, arranged in the same order, by using as few moves as possible. There are two restrictions: Only one disk can be moved at a time, and no disk can ever cover a smaller one during a move.

Why are cognitive psychologists interested in the Tower of Hanoi problem? Because the way people go about solving such puzzles helps illuminate how people solve complex, real-life problems. Psychologists have found that problem solving typically involves the three steps illustrated in Figure 4: preparing to create solutions, producing solutions, and evaluating the solutions that have been generated.

PREPARATION: UNDERSTANDING AND DIAGNOSING PROBLEMS

When approaching a problem like the Tower of Hanoi, most people begin by trying to understand the problem thoroughly. If the problem is a novel one, they probably will pay particular attention to any restrictions placed on coming up with a solution—such as the rule for moving only one disk at a time in the Tower of Hanoi problem. If, by contrast, the problem is a familiar one, they are apt to spend considerably less time in this preparation stage.

Problems vary from well-defined to ill-defined. In a *well-defined problem*—such as a mathematical equation or the solution to a jigsaw puzzle—both the nature of the problem itself and the information needed to solve it are available and clear. Thus, we can make straightforward judgments about whether a potential solution is appropriate. With an *ill-defined problem*, such as how to increase morale on an assembly line or to bring peace to the Middle East, not only may the specific nature of the problem be unclear, the information required to solve the problem may be even less obvious (Newman et al., 2011; Mayer, 2013; Tschentscher & Hauk, 2017).

Kinds of Problems Typically, a problem falls into one of the three categories shown in Figure 5: arrangement, inducing structure, and transformation. Solving each type requires somewhat different kinds of psychological skills and knowledge. (See Figure 6 for solutions to these problems.)

Arrangement problems require the problem solver to rearrange or recombine elements of the problem in a way that will satisfy specific criteria. Usually, several arrangements can be made, but only one or a few will produce a solution. Anagrams, games such as Wordle, and jigsaw puzzles are examples of arrangement problems (Reed, 2017; Tillema, 2019; Ammalainen & Moroshkina, 2021).

In *inducing structure problems*, a person must identify the existing relationships among the elements presented in the problem and then construct a new relationship

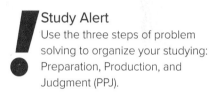

Study Alert
Use the three steps of problem solving to organize your studying: Preparation, Production, and Judgment (PPJ).

Preparation
Understanding and diagnosing problems

Production
Generating solutions

Judgment
Evaluating solutions

FIGURE 4 Steps in problem solving.

FIGURE 5 The three major categories of problems: (a) arrangement, (b) inducing structure, and (c) transformation. Solutions appear in Figure 6.

Source: Adapted from Bourne et al., 1986.

a. Arrangement problems

1. Anagrams: Rearrange the letters in each set to make an English word:

2. Two strings hang from a ceiling but are too far apart to allow a person to hold one and walk to the other. On the floor are a book of matches, a screwdriver, and a few pieces of cotton. How could the strings be tied together?

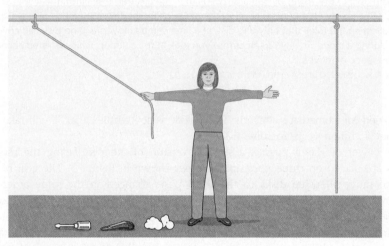

b. Inducing structure problems

1. What number comes next in the series?

1 4 2 4 3 4 4 4 5 4 6 4

2. Complete these analogies:

baseball is to bat as tennis is to _____

merchant is to sell as customer is to _____

c. Transformation problems

1. Water jars: A person has three jars with the following capacities:

Jar A:
28 ounces

Jar B:
7 ounces

Jar C:
5 ounces

How can the person measure exactly 11 ounces of water?

2. Ten coins are arranged in the following way. By moving only *two* of the coins, make two rows that each contains six coins.

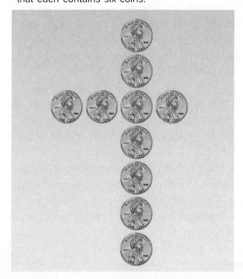

among them. In such a problem, the problem solver must determine not only the relationships among the elements but also the structure and size of the elements involved. In the example shown in Figure 5b, a person must first determine that the solution requires the numbers to be considered in pairs (14-24-34-44-54-64). Only after identifying that part of the problem can a person determine the solution rule (the first number of each pair increases by one, whereas the second number remains the same).

The Tower of Hanoi puzzle represents the third kind of problem—the *transformation problem*—that consists of an initial state, a goal state, and a method for changing the initial state into the goal state. In the Tower of Hanoi problem, the initial state is the original configuration, the goal state is to have the three disks on the third peg, and the method is the rules for moving the disks (Van Belle et al., 2011; Schiff & Vakil, 2015; Yano et al., 2022).

Whether the problem is one of arrangement, inducing structure, or transformation, the preparation stage of understanding and diagnosing is critical in problem solving because it allows us to develop our own cognitive representation of the problem and to place it within a personal framework. We may divide the problem into subparts or ignore some information as we try to simplify the task. Winnowing out nonessential information is often a critical step in the preparation stage of problem solving. The way in which we represent a problem—and the solution we eventually come to—depends on the way a problem is initially framed for us. Imagine that you were a cancer patient having to choose between either the option of surgery or of radiation, as shown in Figure 7, and you were given some statistical information about the options. What would you choose?

It turns out that participants in a study made very different choices depending on how the problem was framed. When their

a. Arrangement problems

1. FACET, DOUBT, THICK, NAIVE, ANVIL

2. The screwdriver is tied to one of the strings. This makes a pendulum that can be swung to reach the other string.

Inducing structure problems

1. 7

2. racket; buy

c. Transformation problems

1. Fill jar A; empty into jar B once and into jar C twice. What remains in jar A is 11 ounces.

2.

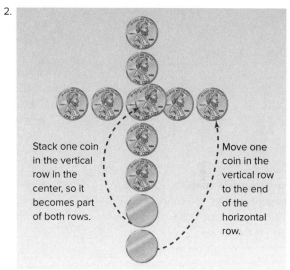

Stack one coin in the vertical row in the center, so it becomes part of both rows.

Move one coin in the vertical row to the end of the horizontal row.

FIGURE 6 Solutions to the problems in Figure 5.
Source: Adapted from Bourne et al., 1986.

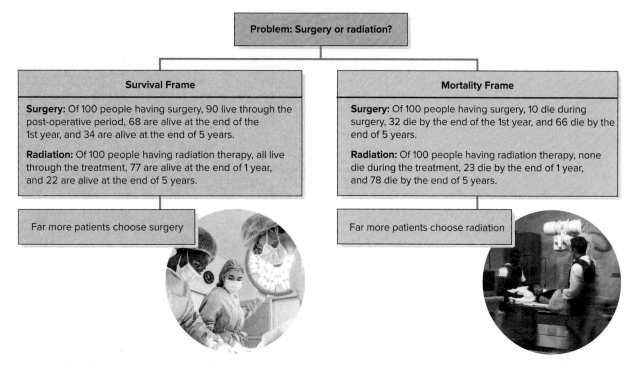

FIGURE 7 A decision often is affected by the way a problem is framed. In this case, most would choose radiation over surgery, despite similar results.

(Left) Photoroyalty/Shutterstock; (Right) Stockbyte/PunchStock/Getty Images

choices were framed in terms of the likelihood of *survival*, only 18% of participants chose radiation over surgery. However, when the choice was framed in terms of the likelihood of *dying*, 44% chose radiation over surgery–even though the outcomes are similar with either treatment option (Tversky & Kahneman, 1987; Krauth-Gruber & Bonnot, 2019).

PRODUCTION: GENERATING SOLUTIONS

After preparation, the next stage in problem solving is the production of possible solutions. If a problem is relatively simple, we may already have a direct solution stored in long-term memory, and all we need to do is retrieve the appropriate information. If we cannot retrieve or do not know the solution, we must generate possible solutions and compare them with information in long- and short-term memory.

At the most basic level, we can solve problems through trial and error. Thomas Edison invented the lightbulb only because he tried thousands of different kinds of materials for a filament before he found one that worked (carbon). The difficulty with trial and error, of course, is that some problems are so complicated that it would take a lifetime to try out every possibility. For example, according to some estimates, there are some 10^{120} possible sequences of chess moves (Fine & Fine, 2003; Gourion, 2021).

means-ends analysis Involves repeated tests for differences between the desired outcome and what currently exists. (Module 21)

In place of trial and error, complex problem solving often involves the use of heuristics, cognitive shortcuts that can generate solutions. Probably the most frequently applied heuristic in problem solving is a **means-ends analysis,** which involves repeated tests for differences between what a desired goal is and where one currently is in terms of reaching it. Consider this simple example (Bieberstein & Roosen, 2015; Abascal, 2019):

> I want to take my child to preschool. What's the difference between what I have and what I want? One of distance. What changes distance? My automobile. My automobile won't work. What is needed to make it work? A new battery. What has new batteries? An auto repair shop. . . .

In a means-end analysis, each step brings the problem solver closer to a resolution. Although this approach is often effective, if the problem requires indirect steps that temporarily *increase* the discrepancy between a current state and the solution, means-ends analysis can be counterproductive. For example, sometimes the fastest route to the summit of a mountain requires a mountain climber to backtrack temporarily; a means-end approach–which implies that the mountain climber should always forge ahead and upward–will be ineffective in such instances.

For other problems, the best approach is to work backward by focusing on the goal, rather than the starting point, of the problem. Consider, for example, the water lily problem:

> Water lilies are growing on Blue Lake. The water lilies grow rapidly, so that the amount of water surface covered by lilies doubles every 24 hours. On the first day of summer, there was just one water lily. On the 90th day of the summer, the lake was entirely covered. On what day was the lake half covered? (Reisberg, 1997)

If you start searching for a solution to the problem by thinking about the initial state on day 1 (one water lily) and move forward from there, you're facing a daunting task of trial-and-error estimation. But try taking a different approach: Start with day 90, when the entire lake was covered with lilies. Given that the lilies double their coverage daily, on the prior day only half the lake was covered. The answer, then, is day 89, a solution found by working backward (Hunt, 1994; Shogren & Wehrmeyer, 2017).

Forming Subgoals: Dividing Problems into Their Parts Another heuristic commonly used to generate solutions is to divide a problem into intermediate steps, or *subgoals,* and solve each of those steps. For instance, in our modified Tower of Hanoi problem, we could choose several obvious subgoals, such as moving the largest disk to the third post.

Insight: Sudden Awareness Some approaches to generating possible solutions focus less on step-by-step heuristics than on the sudden bursts of comprehension that one may experience during efforts to solve a problem. In a classic study, the German psychologist Wolfgang Köhler examined learning and problem-solving processes in chimpanzees (Köhler, 1927). In his studies, Köhler exposed chimps to challenging situations in which the elements of the solution were all present; all the chimps needed to do was put them together.

In one of Köhler's studies, chimps were kept in a cage in which boxes and sticks were strewn about and a bunch of tantalizing bananas hung from the ceiling, out of reach. Initially, the chimps made trial-and-error attempts to get to the bananas: They would throw the sticks at the bananas, jump from one of the boxes, or leap wildly from the ground. Frequently, they would seem to give up in frustration, leaving the bananas dangling temptingly overhead. But then, in what seemed like a sudden revelation, they would stop whatever they were doing and stand on a box to reach the bananas with a stick (see Figure 8). Köhler called the cognitive process underlying the chimps' new behavior **insight,** a sudden awareness of the relationships among various elements that had previously appeared to be unrelated.

Although Köhler emphasized the apparent suddenness of insightful solutions, subsequent research has shown that prior experience and trial-and-error practice in problem solving must precede "insight." Consequently, the chimps' behavior may simply represent the chaining together of previously learned responses, no different from the way a pigeon learns, by trial and error, to peck a key (Wen et al., 2013; Kizilirmak et al., 2015).

Can we help people achieve insight when they are seeking to solve problems? The answer is yes. One way is to directly train them, giving them practice in generating solutions that require out-of-the-box thinking. Another way is to provide cross-cultural experiences that show people that their traditional ways of thinking may be inadequate when applied to the problems faced by those living in other cultures.

For example, people living in *collectivistic cultures*, in which the well-being of the group or society is emphasized more than that of the individual, are often better at solving problems involving interdependence and connection. In contrast, those living in *individualistic cultures*—in which a primary value is personal identity, uniqueness, and

insight A sudden awareness of the relationships among various elements that had previously appeared to be independent of one another. (Module 21)

(a)

(b)

(c)

FIGURE 8 (a) In an impressive display of insight, Sultan, one of the chimpanzees in Köhler's experiments in problem solving, sees a bunch of bananas that is out of reach. (b) He then carries over several crates, stacks them, and (c) stands on them to reach the bananas.

(all): 3LH/SuperStock

freedom—are more proficient at problems involving autonomy (Wen et al., 2013; Arieli & Sagiv, 2018; Sagiv & Schwartz, 2022).

JUDGMENT: EVALUATING SOLUTIONS

The final stage in problem solving is judging the adequacy of a solution. Often this is a simple matter: If the solution is clear—as in the Tower of Hanoi problem—we will know immediately whether we have been successful (Bonomo, 2021).

If the solution is less concrete or if there is no single correct solution, evaluating solutions becomes more difficult. In such instances, we must decide which alternative solution is best. Unfortunately, we often quite inaccurately estimate the quality of our own ideas. For instance, a team of drug researchers working for a particular company may consider their remedy for an illness to be superior to all others, overestimating the likelihood of their success and downplaying the approaches of competing drug companies (Mihalca et al., 2017).

Theoretically, if we rely on appropriate heuristics and valid information, we can make accurate choices among alternative solutions. However, several kinds of obstacles to problem solving act to bias the decisions and judgments we make. In fact, a wide range of behaviors are affected by these biases, ranging from the judgments we form of others to the choices we make about financial investments. Examining biases in decision making has influenced the development of an influential field known as *behavioral economics,* which examines how psychological factors can explain economic decision making (Peters et al., 2017; Jacobsen et al., 2019; Truc, 2021).

IMPEDIMENTS TO SOLUTIONS: WHY IS PROBLEM SOLVING SUCH A PROBLEM?

Consider the following problem-solving test illustrated in Figure 9 (Duncker, 1945):

> You are given a set of push pins, candles, and matches, each in a small box, and told your goal is to place three candles at eye level on a nearby door so that wax will not drip on the floor as the candles burn. How would you approach this challenge?

If you have difficulty solving the problem, you are not alone. Most people cannot solve it when it is presented in the manner illustrated in the figure, in which the objects are *inside* the boxes. However, if the objects were presented *beside* the boxes, just resting on the table, chances are that you would solve the problem much more readily—which, in case you are wondering, requires tacking the boxes to the door and then placing the candles inside them (see Figure 10).

The difficulty you may have encountered in solving this problem stems from its presentation, which misled you at the initial preparation stage. Actually, significant obstacles to problem solving can exist at each of the three major stages. Although cognitive approaches to problem solving suggest that thinking proceeds along fairly rational, logical lines as a person confronts a problem and considers various solutions, several factors can hinder the development of creative, appropriate, and accurate solutions.

FIGURE 9 The problem here is to place three candles at eye level on a nearby door so that the wax will not drip on the floor as the candles burn—using only material in the figure. For a solution, see Figure 10.

Source: Adapted from Duncker, 1945.

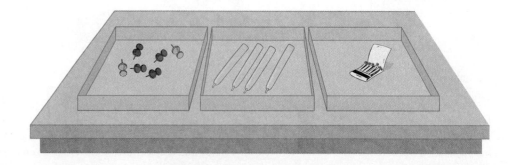

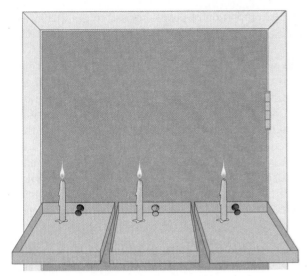

FIGURE 10 A solution to the problem in Figure 9 involves tacking the boxes to the door and placing the candles in the boxes.

Source: Adapted from Duncker, 1945.

Given jars with these capacities (in ounces):

	A	B	C	Obtain:
1.	21	127	3	100
2.	14	163	25	99
3.	18	43	10	5
4.	9	42	6	21
5.	20	59	4	31
6.	28	76	3	25

FIGURE 11 Try this classic demonstration, which illustrates the importance of mental set in problem solving. The object is to use the jars in each row to obtain the designated amount of liquid.

Functional Fixedness The difficulty most people experience with the candle problem is caused by functional fixedness. **Functional fixedness** is the tendency to think of an object only in terms of its typical use. For instance, functional fixedness probably leads you to think of a book as something to read instead of its other potential uses; for example, as a doorstop or as kindling for a fire. In the candle problem, because the objects are first presented inside the boxes, functional fixedness leads most people to see the boxes simply as containers for the objects they hold rather than as a potential part of the solution. They cannot envision another function for the boxes.

A classic experiment (Luchins, 1946) demonstrated functional fixedness. As you can see in Figure 11, the object of the task is to use the jars in each row to measure out the designated amount of liquid. (Try it yourself to get a sense of the power of functional fixedness before moving on.)

If you have tried to solve the problem, you know that the first five rows are all solved in the same way: First fill the largest jar (B) and then from it fill the middle-size jar (A) once and the smallest jar (C) two times. What is left in B is the designated amount. (Stated as a formula, the designated amount is B-A-2C.) The demonstration of mental set comes in the sixth row of the problem, a point at which you probably encountered some difficulty. If you are like most people, you tried the formula and were perplexed when it failed. Chances are, in fact, that you missed the simple (but different) solution to the problem, which involves merely subtracting C from A. Interestingly, people who were given the problem in row 6 *first* had no difficulty with it at all.

Functional fixedness is related to the concept of mental set. **Mental set** is the tendency to solve problems in a certain way, based on past experience, thereby hindering one's ability to come up with other solutions.

Inaccurate Evaluation of Solutions

- "The COVID vaccines were produced too quickly and therefore are unsafe."
- "I'm too young and healthy to need a vaccine. My body can fight it off if I am exposed to COVID."
- The vaccine was produced to make drug companies rich. The pandemic is much less of a problem than the media would have us believe."

functional fixedness The tendency to think of an object only in terms of its typical use. (Module 21)

mental set A framework for thinking about a problem based on our prior experience with similar problems. (Module 21)

confirmation bias The tendency to seek out and weight more heavily information that supports one's initial hypothesis and to ignore contradictory information that supports alternative hypotheses or solutions. (Module 21)

During the pandemic, a substantial proportion of people refused to get vaccinated, citing beliefs like these. And because they found considerable support online, their views were reinforced.

The **confirmation bias** occurs when people are motivated to interpret evidence as supportive of their existing beliefs or theories. They cling to their initial hypotheses and ignore contradictory information that supports alternative hypotheses or solutions. Even when they find evidence that contradicts a solution they have chosen, they are apt to stick with their original hypothesis and to seek information that supports their existing belief.

The confirmation bias occurs for several reasons. For one thing, because rethinking a problem that appears to be solved already takes extra cognitive effort, we are apt to stick with our first solution. For another, we give greater weight to subsequent information that supports our initial position than to information that does not support it (Mercier, 2017; Pearson & Knobloch-Westerwick, 2019; Li et al., 2022).

EVALUATING OTHERS' CONCLUSIONS: THE SCIENCE OF FAKE NEWS

Sometimes we draw erroneous conclusions because others have actively attempted to mislead us. One example is in the rise of *fake news*, fabricated information that is made to look and sound like legitimate news, with the intent of persuading readers to accept false information. The spread of fake news, and claims about it, have provided considerable discussion among politicians and citizens alike, particularly because it's impossible to identify unless people compare several sources of information (Lazer et al., 2018).

Psychologists and other scholars are beginning to understand how fake news is spread and influences us. In one pioneering study, researchers investigated all verified true and false news stories that were distributed on Twitter from 2006 to 2017—some 126,000 of them. They found that false stories (such as rumors of terror attacks) were distributed significantly farther, faster, and more broadly than true news. One reason for this seems to be that the fake news was more novel than true news, thus contributing to its faster distribution (Vosoughi et al., 2018; Grinberg et al., 2019; Edelson et al., 2021).

Other research supports an *illusory truth effect*: That is, simply repeating misinformation may lead people to remember that information—and forget that it might be false. One reason for the illusory truth effect may be "cognitive laziness," in which people don't put in the time and effort it takes to carefully evaluate the truthfulness of news. Moreover, even when people are informed that information is known to be false, many still believe it, including those who deliberately try to avoid being affected by the false information (Fazio et al., 2019; Wu, 2021; Bai, 2022; Ecker et al., 2022).

Additional factors are involved in the acceptance of fake news. For example, people may be unwilling to embrace the validity of scientific information, and instead, they follow their intuitions. At one point during the first year of the pandemic, almost a third of Americans agreed that the virus was purposefully created and spread, even though at that time no credible evidence supported that claim. Even more extreme, some hospital patients suffering from COVID believed it was a hoax even as they were about to die (Romer & Jamieson, 2020; Kinetz, 2021; Naeem et al., 2021).

How do we address fake news? One way is through *cognitive immunization*, in which resistance to fake news, misinformation, and other falsehoods is created by providing accurate information *before* someone is exposed to the false information. When that occurs, people can build up immunity to the falsehoods and become less susceptible to misinformation.

Cognitive immunization has been shown to be effective in producing resistance to fake news. One example relates to the U.S. declassification of information it had acquired about the disinformation Russia planned to circulate before it invaded Ukraine in 2022. That is, to justify the invasion, Russia claimed falsely that Ukraine was a Nazi stronghold. Because people outside Russia were aware of this misinformation before the invasion, they were immunized and did not accept the Russian propaganda campaign (Norman, 2021; Rauch, 2021).

Creativity and Problem Solving

Despite obstacles to problem solving, many people adeptly discover creative solutions to problems. One enduring question that cognitive psychologists have sought to answer is what factors underlie **creativity,** the ability to generate original ideas or solve problems in novel ways.

   Understanding the stages people go through as they approach and solve problems still leaves us with the question: Why are some people better at finding good solutions than other people are? Even the simplest situations reveal a wide range of abilities in problem solving. To explore this for yourself, make a list of all the uses you can think of for a glass jar. When you feel you have run out of possibilities, compare your list to this one compiled by a 12-year-old child:

> You can keep seashells from your vacation in it to decorate your room. You can put sand on the bottom of it and pour melted wax over the sand and stick a wick in it to make a candle. You can use it as a drinking glass. You can keep rubber bands or paper clips or colored marbles in it. You can make a granola mix and store it for months if the jar has a tight lid. You can put water in the bottom and start an avocado tree from a pit. You can store bacon grease in a jar, or fill it with hand soaps and place it by the bathroom sink. You can use it as a flower vase or a "candy dish" for wrapped candies. If you punch holes in the lid, a jar can be a salt or sugar shaker. You can layer pudding and berries and whipped cream in it for a fancy dessert. You can keep your loose change in a jar or use it as a cocktail shaker. You can keep your goldfish in it while you clean the tank. You can organize shelves in the garage or basement by putting small things like nails and screws and bolts with others of the same size, each in their own jar. You can organize your pantry, too: a jar for white rice, one for wild rice, another for black beans, and so on. You can measure rainfall for a month with a jar. Or place it beneath a leaky sink pipe.

   This list shows extraordinary creativity. Unfortunately, it is much easier to identify *examples* of creativity than to determine its causes. Similarly, it's not clear that the kind of creativity shown by highly creative people in the arts, such as playwright, musician, and actor Lin-Manuel Miranda, is the same kind of creativity shown by highly creative people in the sciences, such as Stephen Hawking (Lavazza & Manzotti, 2013; Yi et al., 2015; Simonton, 2022).

Kali Nine LLC/Getty Images

From the perspective of...

A Manufacturer How might you encourage your employees to develop creative ways to improve the products that you produce?

   However, we do know that several characteristics are associated with creativity. For starters, creativity often begins with vision and curiosity. Highly creative people are motivated to solve what has previously been unsolvable and to answer difficult questions in unique ways (Güss et al., 2021).

   In addition, highly creative individuals show divergent thinking. **Divergent thinking** generates multiple and novel, although potentially appropriate, responses to problems or questions. When we use "out-of-the-box" thinking, we're showing divergent thinking.

creativity The ability to generate original ideas or solve problems in novel ways. (Module 21)

divergent thinking Thinking that generates unusual, yet nonetheless appropriate, responses to problems or questions. (Module 21)

Brilliant artists such as Lin-Manuel Miranda, who created the Broadway shows *Hamilton*, and *In the Heights*, as well as the soundtrack for the film *Encanto*, are typically divergent thinkers.
Roy Rochlin/Getty Images

convergent thinking Thinking in which a problem is viewed as having a single answer and which produces responses that are based primarily on knowledge and logic. (Module 21)

Divergent thinking contrasts with convergent thinking. **Convergent thinking** is thinking in which a problem is viewed as having a single answer and which produces a solution that is based primarily on knowledge and logic. For instance, someone relying on convergent thinking would answer "You read it" to the query "What can you do with a newspaper?" In contrast, "You can use it as a dustpan" is a more divergent–and creative–response (Zeng et al., 2011; Hass, 2017; Aga et al., 2021; also see the *Neuroscience in Your Life* feature).

NEUROSCIENCE IN YOUR LIFE: YOU MAKE ME LAUGH!

Has it ever seemed to you that especially creative people—musicians, writers, sculptors—have some kind of special wiring? Well, not surprisingly, they do! The divergent thinking and cognitive complexity that define creativity have a basis in the brain. In neuroimaging studies of creativity, three brain networks show up consistently. One is linked to mind-wandering and spontaneous thinking, and another has a role in focusing and directing thoughts. The third network detects and filters salient stimuli and also funnels information from the other two networks. Neuroscientists hypothesize that creative thinkers are particularly skilled at orchestrating these networks.

Fortunately, we have creative thinkers in a wide range of professions—business, science, literature, the arts, and even comedy. Coming up with a funny joke requires a person to see the world in fresh and unconventional ways, just as other types of creativity do. And evidence indicates that comedians' brains have some of the same characteristics as other creative people. One study compared the brains of professional comedians, amateur comedians, and controls to see whether they differed in surface area, which is one measure of the size of brain regions (Brawer & Amir, 2021).

The neuroscientists found comedic expertise was associated with greater surface area in parts of the brain that previous studies have linked to creative thinking. This brain feature may enable comedians to link concepts and perspectives in new ways that make us laugh.

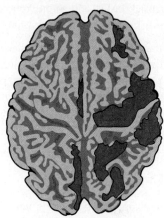

Professional Comedians
vs Amateur Comedians

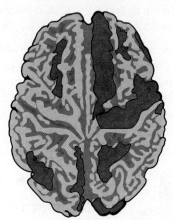

Professional Comedians
vs Controls

The colored areas represent brain regions linked to greater comedic expertise and creativity. Professional comedians had larger surface area in brain regions compared to amateur comedians (left figure) and in even more regions compared to control participants (right figure).

Study Alert
Remember *divergent* thinking produces *different* and *diverse* kinds of responses, whereas *convergent* thinking produces more *commonsense* kinds of responses.

Creative people also show cognitive complexity in their thinking. *Cognitive complexity* is the preference for elaborate, intricate, and complex thoughts and solutions to problems. For instance, creative people often have a wider range of interests and are more independent and more interested in philosophical or abstract problems than are less creative individuals (Kaufman & Plucker, 2011; Gheorghe et al., 2020).

One factor that is *not* closely related to creativity is intelligence. Traditional intelligence tests, which ask focused questions that have only one acceptable answer, tap convergent thinking skills. Highly creative people may therefore find that such tests penalize their divergent thinking. This may explain why researchers consistently find that creativity is only slightly related to school grades and intelligence when intelligence is measured using traditional intelligence tests (Heilman, 2005; Norton et al., 2013; Jung & Chang, 2017).

Women and men don't appear to differ in degree of creativity either, at least when creativity is measured objectively. On the other hand, both women and men tend to assume that men generally are more creative than women, even though objective evidence says otherwise. The belief persists, in part, because creativity is associated with more stereotypic "masculine" traits of boldness, risk-taking, and independence (Proudfoot & Fath, 2021; Taylor & Barbot, 2021; Trapido, 2022).

Does creativity change as we age? Research suggests that we actually become *less* creative the older we get. One reason may be that as we get older, we know more. Although this increased knowledge is generally advantageous, it may hinder creativity because we are more apt to ignore evidence that contradicts what we believe to be true. In a sense, we get stuck in our ways. Furthermore, when we get older, we already have developed a set of solutions to common problems, and we are more likely to turn to them and avoid exploring more creative ideas. In short, getting older is generally not helpful in finding creative solutions to problems (Gopnik et al., 2015; Gopnik & Griffiths, 2017; Hui et al., 2019).

Researchers are increasingly speculating that some kinds of developmental disabilities may help promote creativity. Specifically, people with *autism spectrum disorder*, a severe developmental disability that impairs one's ability to communicate and relate to others, may show enhanced creativity. According to psychologist Simon Baron-Cohen, people with autism spectrum disorder have a special ability to recognize the significance of patterns. To illustrate, he points to the example of a person with autism who can pick out patterns on the surface of ocean waves and tell fishermen where they will catch the most fish. The idea is that these hyperabilities in pattern recognition lead to an unusual degree of creativity. Although still speculative, the relationship between autism spectrum disorder and creativity is intriguing (Baron-Cohen, 2020).

BECOMING AN INFORMED CONSUMER
of Psychology

Thinking Critically and Creatively

Can we learn to be better and more creative thinkers?

Cognitive researchers have found that people can learn the abstract rules of logic and that such knowledge can improve our reasoning about the underlying causes of everyday events in our lives. Research suggests that critical and creative thinkers are made, not born. Consider, for instance, the following suggestions for increasing critical thinking and creativity (Erlam et al., 2018; Mahanal et al., 2019; Bradley & Price, 2021).

- *Redefine problems.* We can modify boundaries and assumptions by rephrasing a problem at either a more abstract or a more concrete level.
- *Use subgoals.* By developing subgoals, we can divide a problem into intermediate steps. This process, known as *fractionation*, allows us to examine each part for new possibilities and approaches, leading to a novel solution for the problem as a whole.
- *Adopt a critical perspective.* Rather than passively accepting assumptions or arguments, we can evaluate material critically, consider its implications, and think about possible exceptions and contradictions.
- *Consider the opposite.* By considering the opposite of a concept we're seeking to understand, we can sometimes make progress. For example, to define "good mental health," it may be useful to consider what "bad mental health" means.
- *Use analogies.* Analogies provide alternative frameworks for the interpretation of facts and help us uncover new understanding. One particularly effective means of

coming up with analogies is to look for examples in the natural world. For instance, architects discovered how to construct the earliest skyscrapers by noting how lily pads on a pond could support the weight of a person (Bearman et al., 2007; Cho et al., 2007).

- *Think divergently.* Instead of the most logical or common use for an object, consider how you might use the object if you were forbidden to use it in the usual way.
- *Think convergently.* Although it sounds counterintuitive, researchers have found that a combination of divergent *and* convergent thinking can lead to greater creativity. Programs that attempt to teach children to be more creative train participants to alternate periods of divergent thinking with intense convergent thinking (Beghetto & Kaufman, 2010).
- *Use heuristics.* Heuristics are cognitive shortcuts that can help bring about a solution to a problem. If the problem has a single correct answer and you can use or construct a heuristic, you can often find the solution more rapidly and effectively.
- *Experiment with various solutions.* Don't be afraid to use different routes to find solutions for problems (verbal, mathematical, graphic, even dramatic). For instance, try to come up with every conceivable idea you can, no matter how wild or bizarre it may seem at first. After you've come up with a list of solutions, review each one and try to think of ways to make what at first appeared impractical seem more feasible.
- *Remember that good enough is good enough.* You may never come up with the perfect solution to a problem. And that's fine. Accept that sometimes an OK solution, even if it's not perfect, is perfectly acceptable (Shain, 2019).
- *Walk away.* Sometimes just taking a step back from a problem you're trying to solve and doing something routine and even thoughtless can help bring about creativity. Watching TV, taking a shower, or having a snack may free our minds to come up with innovative solutions (Wiley & Jarosz, 2012; Shellenbarger, 2013).

RECAP/EVALUATE/RETHINK

RECAP

LO 21-1 What is thinking?

- Cognitive psychology encompasses the higher mental processes, including the way people know and understand the world, process information, make decisions and judgments, and describe their knowledge and understanding to others.
- Thinking is the manipulation of mental representations of information. Thinking transforms such representations into novel and different forms, permitting people to answer questions, solve problems, and reach goals.
- Mental images are representations in the mind of an object or event.
- Concepts are categorizations of objects, events, or people that share common properties.

LO 21-2 What processes underlie decision making?

- Decisions sometimes (but not always) may be improved through the use of algorithms and heuristics. An algorithm is a rule that, if applied appropriately, guarantees a solution; a heuristic is a cognitive shortcut that may lead to a solution but is not guaranteed to do so.

LO 21-3 How do people approach and solve problems?

- Problem solving typically involves three major stages: preparation, production of solutions, and evaluation of solutions that have been generated.
- Preparation involves placing the problem in one of three categories. In arrangement problems, a group of elements must be rearranged or recombined in a way that will satisfy a certain criterion. In inducing structure problems, a person first must identify the existing relationships among the elements presented and then construct a new relationship among them. Finally, transformation problems consist of an initial state, a goal state, and a method for changing the initial state into the goal state.
- In the production stage, people try to generate solutions. They may find solutions to some problems in long-term memory. Alternatively, they may solve some problems through simple trial and error and use algorithms and heuristics to solve more complex problems.
- Using the heuristic of a means-ends analysis, a person will repeatedly test for differences between the desired outcome and what currently exists, trying each time to come closer to the goal.

- Köhler's research with chimpanzees illustrates insight, a sudden awareness of the relationships among elements that had previously seemed unrelated.

LO 21-4 What are the major obstacles to problem solving?

- Several factors hinder effective problem solving. Mental set, of which functional fixedness is an example, is the tendency for old patterns of problem solving to persist. Inappropriate use of algorithms and heuristics can also act as an obstacle to the production of solutions.
- The confirmation bias, in which people are motivated to interpret evidence as supportive of their existing beliefs or theories, can hinder the accurate evaluation of solutions to problems.
- Creativity is the ability to combine responses or ideas in novel ways. Creativity is related to divergent thinking (the ability to generate unusual, but still appropriate, responses to problems or questions) and cognitive complexity.

EVALUATE

1. _____ _____ are representations in the mind of an object or event.
2. _____ are categorizations of objects that share common properties.

3. Solving a problem by trying to reduce the difference between the current state and the goal state is known as a _____ _____.
4. _____ is the term used to describe the sudden "flash" of revelation that often accompanies the solution to a problem.
5. Thinking of an object only in terms of its typical use is known as _____ _____. A broader, related tendency to approach a problem in a certain way because that method worked previously is known as a _____ _____.
6. Generating unusual but appropriate approaches to a question is known as _____ _____.

RETHINK

1. How might the availability heuristic contribute to prejudices based on race, age, and gender? Can awareness of this heuristic prevent this from happening?
2. Why do you think people use algorithms and heuristics? How can we avoid coming to poor solutions based on their use?

Answers to Evaluate Questions

1. Mental images; 2. Concepts; 3. means-end analysis; 4. Insight; 5. functional fixedness; mental set; 6. divergent thinking

---

KEY TERMS

cognitive psychology	prototypes	insight	confirmation bias
thinking	algorithm	functional	creativity
mental images	heuristic	fixedness	divergent thinking
concept	means-ends analysis	mental set	convergent thinking

Module 22
Language

language The communication of information through symbols arranged according to systematic rules. (Module 22)

'Twas brillig, and the slithy toves
Did gyre and gimble in the wabe:
All mimsy were the borogoves,
And the mome raths outgrabe.

Although few of us have ever come face to face with a tove, we have little difficulty in discerning that in Lewis Carroll's (1872) poem "Jabberwocky," the expression *slithy toves* contains an adjective, *slithy*, and the noun it modifies, *toves*.

Our ability to make sense out of nonsense, if the nonsense follows typical rules of language, illustrates the complexity of both human language and the cognitive processes that underlie its development and use. The use of **language**–the communication of information through symbols arranged according to systematic rules–is a central cognitive ability, one that is indispensable for us to communicate with one another. Not only is language central to communication, it is also closely tied to the very way in which we think about and understand the world. Without language, our ability to transmit information, acquire knowledge, and cooperate with others would be tremendously hindered. No wonder psychologists have devoted considerable attention to studying language (Reisberg, 2009; LaPointe, 2013; Carnevale et al., 2017).

Grammar: Language's Language

To understand how language develops and relates to thought, we first need to review some of the formal elements of language. The basic structure of language rests on **grammar,** the system of rules that determines how our thoughts can be expressed.

grammar The system of rules that determine how our thoughts can be expressed. (Module 22)

phonology The study of the smallest units of speech, called phonemes. (Module 22)

phonemes The smallest units of speech. (Module 22)

Grammar deals with three major components of language: phonology, syntax, and semantics. **Phonology** is the study of **phonemes,** the smallest basic units of speech that affect meaning, and of the way we use those sounds to form words and produce meaning. For instance, the *a* sound in *fat* and the *a* sound in *fate* represent two different phonemes in English (Monaghan & Fletcher, 2019).

Linguists have identified more than 800 phonemes among all the world's languages. Although English speakers use just 52 phonemes to produce words, other languages use as few as 15 to as many as 141. Differences in phonemes are one reason people have difficulty learning other languages. For example, to a Japanese speaker, whose native language does not have an *r* phoneme, pronouncing such English words as *roar* presents some difficulty (Redford, 2017; Shinohara & Iverson, 2021).

syntax Ways in which words and phrases can be combined to form sentences. (Module 22)

Syntax refers to the rules that indicate how words and phrases can be combined to form sentences. Every language has intricate rules that guide the order in which words may be strung together to communicate meaning. English speakers have no difficulty recognizing that "TV down the turn" is not a meaningful sequence, whereas "Turn down the TV" is. To understand the effect of syntax in English, consider the changes in meaning caused by the different word orders in the following three utterances: "John kidnapped the boy," "John, the kidnapped boy," and "The boy kidnapped John" (Frank et al., 2013; Hu, 2019; Werfel et al., 2021).

semantics The meaning of words and sentences. (Module 22)

Semantics is the third major component of language. **Semantics** refers to the meaning of words and sentences. Every word has particular semantic features. For example, *foal, filly,* and *mare* share certain semantic features (all refer to female horses), but they also differ semantically (in terms of age).

Semantic rules allow us to use words to convey subtle nuances in meaning. For instance, we can use slightly different wording–semantics–about an event to convey subtle differences in meaning. If we had just seen a girl named Laura get hit by a truck, we might say, "A truck hit Laura." But if we were answering a question about why Laura was not at a party the night before, we might say, "Laura was hit by a truck" (Paciorek & Williams, 2015; Srinivasan et al., 2017).

Despite the complexities of language, most of us acquire the basics of grammar without even being aware that we have learned its rules. Moreover, even though we may have difficulty explicitly stating the rules of grammar, our linguistic abilities are so sophisticated that we can utter an infinite number of statements. How do we acquire such abilities?

Language Development: Developing a Way with Words

To parents, the sounds of their infant babbling and cooing are music to their ears (except, perhaps, at three o'clock in the morning). These sounds also serve an important function. They mark the first step on the road to the development of language.

babble Meaningless speechlike sounds made by children from around the age of 3 months through 1 year. (Module 22)

BABBLING

Children **babble**–make speechlike but meaningless sounds–from around the age of 3 months through 1 year. While babbling, they may produce, at one time or another, any of the sounds found in all languages, not just the language to which they are exposed. Even children with hearing loss display their own form of babbling; infants who are unable to hear yet who are exposed to sign language from birth "babble" with their hands (Shehata-Dieler et al., 2013; Elmlinger et al., 2019; Persson et al., 2021).

An infant's babbling increasingly reflects the specific language being spoken in the infant's environment, initially in terms of pitch and tone and eventually in terms of specific sounds. Young infants can distinguish among all 869 phonemes that have been identified across the world's languages. However, after the age of 6 to 8 months, that ability begins to decline. Infants begin to "specialize" in the language to which they are exposed as neurons in their brains reorganize to respond to the particular phonemes infants routinely hear.

Some theorists argue that a *critical period* exists for language development early in life in which a child is particularly sensitive to language cues and most easily acquires language. In fact, if children are not exposed to language during this critical period, later they will have great difficulty overcoming this deficit. Furthermore, research in the acquisition of second languages suggests that a critical period exists for learning a second language, one that extends until around the age of 17 (Shafer & Garrido-Nag, 2007; Choubsaz & Gheitury, 2017; Hartshorne et al., 2018).

Cases in which abused children have been isolated from contact with others support the theory of critical periods related to language acquisition. In one horrific case, for example, a girl who came to be called Genie, who was abused from an early age, was exposed to virtually no language from the age of 20 months until she was rescued at age 13. She was unable to speak at all. Despite intensive instruction, she learned only some words and was never able to master the complexities of language (Carroll, 2016; Azieb, 2021).

A syllable is shown in sign language, similar to the ones seen in the manual babbling of deaf infants and in the spoken babbling of hearing infants. The similarities in language structure suggest that language has biological roots.
Courtesy, Dr. Laura Ann Petitto @1991. Photo by Robert LaMarche

PRODUCTION OF LANGUAGE

By the time children are approximately 1 year old, they stop producing sounds that are not in the language to which they have been exposed. It is then a short step to the production of actual words. In English, these are typically short words that start with a consonant sound such as *b, d, m, p,* and *t;* this helps explain why *mama* and *dada* are so often among babies' first words. Of course, even before they produce their first words, children can understand a fair amount of the language they hear. Language comprehension precedes language production.

After the age of 1 year, children begin to learn more complicated forms of language. They produce two-word combinations, the building blocks of sentences, and sharply increase the number of different words they are able to use. By age 2, the average child has a vocabulary of more than 50 words. Just 6 months later, that vocabulary has grown to several hundred words.

Also around the age of 2, children begin to produce short, two-word sentences. However, the sentences children first produce are characterized as telegraphic speech. **Telegraphic speech** consists of sentences in which only essential words are used, usually nouns and verbs only. Rather than saying, "I showed you the book," a child using telegraphic speech may say, "I show book," and "I am drawing a dog" may become "Drawing dog." As children get older, of course, they use less telegraphic speech and produce increasingly complex sentences (Pérez-Leroux et al., 2011; Slobin, 2021).

By age 3, children learn to make plurals by adding *-s* to nouns and to form the past tense by adding *-ed* to verbs. This skill also leads to errors, since children tend to apply rules inflexibly. In such **overgeneralization,** children employ language rules they have learned, even when doing so results in errors. Thus, although it is correct to say "he walked" for the past tense of *walk*, the *-ed* rule doesn't work quite so well when children say "he runned" for the past tense of *run* (Kidd & Lum, 2008; Pozzan & Valian, 2017).

By age 5, children have acquired the basic rules of language. However, they do not attain a full vocabulary and the ability to comprehend and use subtle grammatical rules until later. For example, a 5-year-old child who sees a blindfolded doll and is asked, "Is the doll easy or hard to see?" would have great trouble answering the question. In fact, if the child were asked to make the doll easier to see, they would probably try to remove the doll's blindfold. By the time they are 8 years old, however, children have little difficulty understanding this question because they realize that the doll's blindfold has nothing to do with an observer's ability to see the doll (Hoff, 2003; Dockrell & Marshall, 2015).

Understanding Language Acquisition: Identifying the Roots of Language

Anyone who spends even a little time with children will notice the enormous strides that they make in language development throughout childhood. However, the reasons for this rapid growth are far from obvious. Psychologists have offered three major explanations: one based on learning theory, one based on innate processes, and one that involves something of a combination of the two.

LEARNING-THEORY APPROACHES: LANGUAGE AS A LEARNED SKILL

The **learning-theory approach** suggests that language acquisition follows the principles of reinforcement and conditioning discovered by psychologists who study learning. For example, a child who says "mama" receives hugs and praise from their mother, which reinforces the behavior of saying "mama" and makes its repetition more likely. This view suggests that children first learn to speak by being rewarded for making sounds that approximate speech. Ultimately, through a process of *shaping*, in which closer approximations of correct speech are rewarded, language becomes more and more like adult speech (Skinner, 1957; Ornat & Gallo, 2004; Kapur, 2018).

In support of the learning-theory approach to language acquisition, the more that parents speak to their young children, the more proficient the children become in language use. In addition, by the time they are 3 years old, children who hear higher levels of linguistic sophistication in their parents' speech show a greater rate of

---

telegraphic speech Sentences in which only essential words are used. (Module 22)

overgeneralization The phenomenon by which children overapply a language rule, thereby making linguistic errors. (Module 22)

learning-theory approach (to language development) The theory that language acquisition follows the principles of reinforcement and conditioning. (Module 22)

vocabulary growth, vocabulary use, and even general intellectual achievement than do children whose parents' speech is more simple (Hart & Risley, 1997; Ferjan Ramírez et al., 2019).

The learning-theory approach is less successful in explaining how children acquire language rules. Children are reinforced not only when they use language correctly but also when they use it incorrectly. For example, parents answer a child's query of "Why the dog won't eat?" as readily as they do the correctly phrased question, "Why won't the dog eat?" Listeners understand both sentences equally well. Learning theory, then, has difficulty fully explaining language acquisition.

NATIVIST APPROACHES: LANGUAGE AS AN INNATE SKILL

Pointing to such problems with learning-theory approaches to language acquisition, linguist Noam Chomsky (1978, 1991) provided a groundbreaking alternative. He argued that humans are born with an innate linguistic capability that emerges primarily as a function of maturation.

According to Chomsky's **nativist approach,** humans are biologically prewired to learn language at certain periods in their lives and in a particular way. Furthermore, he suggests that all the world's languages share a common underlying structure that is prewired, biologically determined, and universal.

The nativist approach argues that the human brain contains an inherited neural system, which Chomsky calls *universal grammar*, that lets us understand the structure language provides. These inborn capabilities give us strategies and techniques for learning the unique characteristics of our own native language (Yang et al., 2017; Allott et al., 2021).

Some evidence collected by neuroscientists directly supports Chomsky's view. This research suggests that the ability to use language, which was a significant evolutionary advance in human beings, is tied to specific neurological developments. For example, scientists have discovered a gene related to the development of language abilities that may have emerged as recently—in evolutionary terms—as 100,000 years ago.

Furthermore, the brain clearly has specific sites that are closely tied to language, and the shape of the human mouth and throat are clearly tailored to the production of speech. And evidence indicates that features of specific types of languages are tied

nativist approach (to language development) The theory that humans are biologically prewired to learn language at certain times and in particular ways. (Module 22)

According to Chomsky and other proponents of the nativist view, the development of language is genetically wired into the brain.
surachet1969/Shutterstock

to particular genes, such as in "tonal" languages in which pitch is used to convey meaning (Perovic & Radenovic, 2011; Lieberman, 2015; Verhoef et al., 2021).

However, Chomsky's nativist view is contradicted by some researchers. For instance, learning theorists contend that the apparent ability of certain animals, such as chimpanzees, to learn the fundamentals of human language (as we discuss later in this module) contradicts the innate linguistic capability view. Furthermore, some cognitive psychologists believe that what underlies children's language learning is their use of general cognitive abilities, not abilities tied directly to language processing in the brain. Furthermore, language development also seems to reflect skills attained through social interaction with others, such as learning to read others' intentions, in contradiction to Chomsky's view (Ibbotson & Tomasello, 2016; Tomasello, 2019).

INTERACTIONIST APPROACHES

To reconcile the differing views of the learning-theory and nativist approaches, many theorists hold a compromise view, known as the interactionist approach to language development. The **interactionist approach** suggests that language development is determined by both genetic and social factors, produced through a combination of genetically determined predispositions *and* the social world in which one is raised.

Specifically, proponents of the interactionist approach suggest that the brain is hardwired for our acquisition of language, in essence providing the "hardware" that allows us to develop language. However, it is the exposure to language from social interactions with others that allows us to develop the appropriate "software" to understand and produce language.

The interactionist approach has many proponents. Still, the issue of how language is acquired remains hotly contested (Hoff, 2008; Waxman, 2009; Soysal et al., 2021).

interactionist approach (to language development) The view that language development is produced through a combination of genetically determined predispositions and environmental circumstances that help teach language. (Module 22)

! Study Alert

It's important to be able to compare and contrast the major approaches to language development: learning-theory, nativist, and interactionist approaches.

From the perspective of...

A Child-Care Provider How would you encourage children's language abilities at the different stages of development?

Nicole Hill/Rubberball/Getty Images

The Influence of Language on Thinking: Do the Inuit Have More Words for Snow Than Texans Do?

Do the Inuit people, who live in frigid Arctic lands, have a more expansive vocabulary for discussing snow than people living in warmer climates do?

It makes sense, and such arguments have been made since the early 1900s. At that time, linguist Benjamin Lee Whorf contended that because snow is so relevant to the Inuit peoples' lives, their language provides a particularly rich vocabulary to describe it–considerably larger than what we find in other languages, such as English (Pinker, 1994; Cook, 2021).

The contention that the Inuit language (which includes several distinct dialects) is especially abundant in snow-related terms led to the linguistic-relativity hypothesis.

According to the **linguistic-relativity hypothesis,** language shapes and helps determine the way people perceive and understand the world. That is, language provides us with categories we use to construct our view of others and events in the world around us. In this way, language shapes and produces thought (Whorf, 1956; Bylund & Athanasopoulos, 2017; Lowry & Bryant, 2019).

Let's consider another possibility, however. Suppose that instead of language being the *cause* of certain ways of thinking, thought *produces* language. The only reason to expect that the Inuit language might have more words for snow than English is that snow is considerably more relevant to the Inuit people than it is to people in other cultures.

Which view is correct? Most current research refutes the linguistic-relativity hypothesis and suggests, instead, that thinking produces language. In fact, new analyses of the Inuit language suggest that the Inuit have no more words for snow than English speakers do. If one examines the English language closely, one sees that it is hardly impoverished when it comes to describing snow (consider, for example, *sleet, slush, blizzard,* and *dusting).*

Still, the linguistic-relativity hypothesis has not been entirely discarded. A newer version of the hypothesis suggests that speech patterns may influence certain aspects of thinking. For example, English speakers distinguish between nouns that can be counted (such as "five chairs") and nouns that require a measurement unit to be quantified (such as "a liter of water"). However, in some other languages, such as the Mayan language called Yucatec, all nouns require a measurement unit. In such cultures, people appear to think more closely about what things are made of than do people in cultures in which languages such as English are spoken (Tsukasaki & Ishii, 2004; Stam, 2015; Bohnemeyer, 2020).

Similarly, Russian speakers have more words for light and dark blues and are better able to discriminate shades of blue visually than English speakers. The Icelandic language contains 24 words for different types of waves. Furthermore, some tribes say north, south, east, and west instead of left and right, and they have better spatial orientation. And the Piraha language uses terms such as *few* and *many* rather than specific numbers, and speakers are unable to keep track of exact quantities (Boroditsky, 2010; Fuhrman et al., 2011).

Finally, language seems to foster and support certain kinds of reasoning. In essence, language makes us better able to think in more sophisticated ways, helping us to understand such concepts as cause and effect (Gentner, 2016).

In short, although research does not support the linguistic-relativity hypothesis that language *causes* thought, language clearly influences how we think. And, of course, thought certainly influences language, suggesting that language and thinking interact in complex ways (Thorkildsen, 2006; Proudfoot, 2009; Bohnemeyer, 2020; also see the *Applying Psychology in the 21st Century* feature).

linguistic-relativity hypothesis The hypothesis that language shapes and may determine the way people perceive and understand the world. (Module 22)

Study Alert

The linguistic-relativity hypothesis suggests language leads to thought.

APPLYING PSYCHOLOGY IN THE 21ST CENTURY

¡HOLA! CAN THE LANGUAGE YOU SPEAK KEEP YOU HEALTHIER?

Does the specific language someone speaks offer them health benefits?

That's the surprising hypothesis put forward by psychologist María Magadalena Llabre of the University of Miami (Llabre, 2021). And her idea builds on well-established data that Hispanic people who speak Spanish are *less* likely to die from cardiovascular disease than non-Hispanic White individuals and members of other groups who are economically disadvantaged and who speak English.

The finding is contrary to what we'd normally expect because membership in an economically disadvantaged minority group typically makes one more prone to health problems due to the presence of more risk factors for disease. However, that's not true for economically disadvantaged Hispanics, who are at lower risk for cardiovascular disease. This exception to the rule is known as the "Hispanic paradox" (Valencia et al., 2021).

Researchers have never before found a convincing explanation for the "Hispanic paradox." However, Llabre hypothesizes that particular characteristics of the Spanish language affect the way Spanish speakers appraise and experience stress (Llabre, 2021).

According to the hypothesis, the Spanish language has features that provide for emotional expression in ways that promote health. For instance, compared with English, Spanish has a greater range of positive, happy words. Furthermore, Spanish speakers use suffixes that can minimize negative emotions and stress, and that create the potential for the expression of greater optimism. Finally, the Spanish language makes it easier to express negative emotions as transient, meaning that stress can be more easily experienced as a temporary state.

Is the language hypothesis correct? We don't know for sure, and no convincing research has yet determined its accuracy. It's hard to do research on as broad a variable as the language someone speaks, especially because it's essential to tease out the effects of the wider culture associated with the language a group speaks. But the language hypothesis is an important starting point in explaining the cardiovascular advantage that Spanish speakers enjoy (Shaw et al., 2018; Blumer & Rodriguez, 2021).

Does this family's use of Spanish provide them with certain health benefits due to the characteristics of the Spanish language?

Julio Rivalta/Shutterstock

RETHINK

- What other cultural factors beyond language might explain the "Hispanic paradox"?
- Do you think learning Spanish as a second language would provide the same cardiovascular health benefits compared with those whose initial language was Spanish? Why or why not?

Do Animals Use Language?

One question that has long puzzled psychologists is whether language is uniquely human or if other animals are able to acquire it as well. Many animals communicate with one another in rudimentary forms. For instance, fiddler crabs wave their claws to signal, bees dance to indicate the direction in which food will be found, and certain birds call "*zick, zick*" during courtship and "*kia*" when they are about to fly away. Naked mole-rats, nearly blind rodents that live in underground colonies, develop a soft chirp greeting that is specific to their colony and that helps distinguish colony members from intruders. However, researchers have yet to demonstrate conclusively that these animals use true language, which is characterized in part by the ability to produce and communicate new and unique meanings by following a formal grammar (Barker et al., 2021; Muramatsu, 2021).

Psychologists, however, have been able to teach chimps to communicate at surprisingly high levels. For instance, after 4 years of training, a chimp named Washoe learned to make signs for 132 words and combine those signs into simple sentences. Even more impressively, Kanzi, a bonobo (a kind of small chimpanzee), has linguistic skills that some psychologists claim are close to those of a 2-year-old human being. Based on research that is controversial, Kanzi's trainers suggest that Kanzi can create grammatically sophisticated sentences and can even invent new rules of syntax (Dubreuil & Savage-Rumbaugh, 2018; Stern, 2020; Zuberbühler, 2022).

More generally, researchers have found evidence that nonhuman primates use several basic components of human language. For example, they use vocalizations that they modify based on social and other environmental influences, and they take turns communicating about food resources. Furthermore, they have physical structures that allow them to produce vowel sounds similar to human language (Snowdon, 2017; Rendall, 2021).

Despite the language-like capabilities of primates such as Kanzi, critics contend that the language such animals use still lacks the grammar and the complex and novel constructions of human language. Instead, they maintain that the chimps are displaying a skill no different from that of a dog that learns to lie down on command to get a reward. Furthermore, we lack firm evidence that animals can recognize and respond to the mental states of others of their species, an important aspect of human communication. Consequently, the issue of whether other animals can use language in a way that humans do remains controversial (Beran et al., 2013; Crockford et al., 2015; ten Cate, 2017).

As they seek further understanding of language use among nonhuman species, researchers are learning that at the very least, nonhumans have a surprising range of linguistic capabilities. In one intriguing recent example, researchers found that dogs can distinguish between languages as well as between human language and gibberish. In the study, fMRI scans of dogs' brains showed activation of different parts of the brain according to whether dogs were hearing (1) the human language they were raised with, (2) a foreign language with which they weren't familiar, or (3) gibberish that merely "sounded" like a human language. That the dogs distinguished between the three categories suggests that they were aware of the sounds of specific languages and speech rhythms—a considerable achievement (Cuaya et al., 2021).

Psychologist and primatologist Sue Savage-Rumbaugh with a primate friend, Kanzi. Does the use of sign language by primates indicate true mastery of language?

Anna Clopet/The Image Bank Unreleased/Getty Images

Does Speaking Two Languages Make You Smarter?

Does the ability to speak two languages make you smarter? In one sense, of course it does: That you can speak multiple languages shows you know more than someone who can only speak one language. But does it make you more intelligent across other cognitive domains?

The question is not a simple one to answer. In terms of general executive functioning—which refers to a broad range of abilities such as focusing attention, using working memory effectively, and processing spatial stimuli—evidence is mixed. The most recent research seems to suggest that individuals who are bilingual show only minor advantages, if any, in overall executive functioning (Nichols et al., 2020; Lowe et al., 2021; Paap, 2021).

On the other hand, a substantial body of evidence supports the idea that speaking more than one language provides significant cognitive benefits when looking at specific areas of intellectual functioning. For example, bilingual speakers show more cognitive flexibility and may understand concepts more easily than do those who speak only one language. They have more linguistic tools for thinking because of their multiple-language abilities. In turn, this makes them more creative and flexible in solving problems (Christoffels et al., 2015; Hartanto & Yang, 2019; Hartanto et al., 2019).

Furthermore, learning and speaking several languages has discernable effects on the brain. For example, bilingual speakers who learn their second language as adults show different areas of brain activation compared with those who learn their second language in childhood. And those who are immersed in intensive language instruction show growth in the hippocampus. In addition, brain scans show that people who speak multiple languages have distinct patterns of brain activity according to the language they are using, and bilingualism produces more efficient processing on some cognitive tasks (Legault et al., 2019; Voits et al, 2022).

In addition, the advantages of bilingualism start early: By the time bilingual children are 3 or 4 years old, their general cognitive development is superior to that of children who speak only one language. This advantage may last into old age. In fact, bilingualism may provide protection from the cognitive declines that sometimes occur in late adulthood (Bialystok, 2011; Heim et al., 2019; Bialystok et al., 2021).

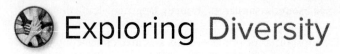 # Exploring Diversity

Teaching with Linguistic Variety: Bilingual Education

In New York City, nearly half of the students speak a language other than English in their homes, with more than 180 languages represented. Furthermore, 1 in 6 of the city's 1.1 million students is enrolled in some form of bilingual or English as a Second Language instruction.

And New York City is far from the only school district with a significant population of nonnative English speakers. From the biggest cities to the most rural areas, the face—and voice—of education in the United States is changing. More and more schoolchildren today have last names such as Kim, Valdez, and Karachnicoff. Overall, almost a quarter of school-aged children in the United States speak a language other than English at home. In six states (California, Texas, New Mexico, New Jersey, New York, and Nevada), more than 1 in 4 residents speaks a language other than English. For some 67 million people in the United States, English is their second language (Shin & Kominski, 2010; Federal Interagency Forum on Child and Family Statistics, 2019; Zeigler & Camarota, 2019; see Figure 1).

How to appropriately and effectively teach the increasing number of children who do not speak English is not always clear. Many educators maintain that *bilingual education* is best. With a bilingual approach, students learn some subjects in their native language while simultaneously learning English. Proponents of bilingualism believe that students must develop a sound footing in basic subject areas and that, initially at least, teaching those subjects in their native language is the only way to provide them with that foundation. During the same period, they learn English, with the eventual goal of shifting all instruction into English.

In contrast, other educators insist that all instruction ought to be in English from the moment students, including those who speak no English at all, enroll in school. In

FIGURE 1 The language of diversity. Almost 22 percent of people in the United States speak a language other than English at home. Spanish is most prevalent; the rest of non-English speakers use an astounding variety of languages.
Source: American Community Survey, 2019.

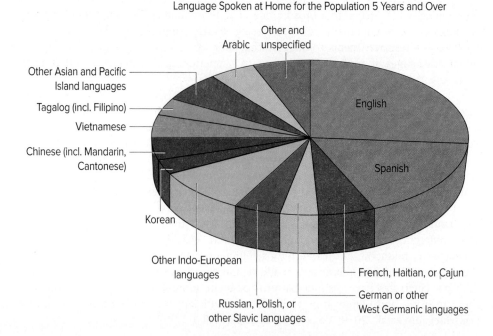

Language Spoken at Home for the Population 5 Years and Over

immersion programs, students are immediately plunged into English instruction in all subjects. The reasoning is that teaching students in a language other than English hinders nonnative English speakers' integration into society and ultimately does them a disservice. Proponents of English-immersion programs point as evidence to improvements in standardized test scores that followed the end of bilingual education programs (Wildavsky, 2000; Grivet et al., 2021).

A broader question about bilingual education is the matter of *biculturalism;* that is, being a member of two cultures and its psychological impact. Some psychologists argue that society should promote an *alternation model* of bicultural competence. Such a model supports members of a culture in their efforts to maintain their original cultural identity as well as in their integration into the adopted culture. In this view, a person can belong to two cultures and have two cultural identities without having to choose between them. In any case, research suggests that a bicultural identity produces mental health benefits and increases feelings of well-being (Tadmor, 2007; Schwartz et al., 2019; MacDonald, 2022).

RECAP/EVALUATE/RETHINK

RECAP

LO 22-1 How do people use language?

- Language is the communication of information through symbols arranged according to systematic rules. All languages have a grammar—a system of rules that determines how thoughts can be expressed—that encompasses the three major components of language: phonology, syntax, and semantics.

LO 22-2 How does language develop?

- Language production, which follows language comprehension, develops out of babbling, which then leads to the production of actual words. After 1 year of age, children use two-word combinations, increase their vocabulary, and use telegraphic speech, which drops words not critical to the message. By age 5, acquisition of language rules is relatively complete.
- Learning theorists suggest that language is acquired through reinforcement and conditioning. In contrast, the nativist approach suggests that an innate language-acquisition device guides the development of language. The interactionist approach argues that language development is produced through a combination of genetically determined predispositions and environmental circumstances that help teach language.
- The linguistic-relativity hypothesis suggests that language shapes and may determine the way people think about the world. Most evidence suggests that although language does not determine thought, it does affect the way people store information in memory and how well they can retrieve it.
- The degree to which language is a uniquely human skill remains an open question. Some psychologists contend that even though certain primates communicate at a high level, those animals do not use language.

Other psychologists suggest that those primates truly understand and produce language in much the same way as humans do.

- People who speak more than one language may have a cognitive advantage over those who speak only one.

EVALUATE

1. Match the component of grammar with its definition:
   1. Syntax
   2. Phonology
   3. Semantics

   a. Rules showing how words can be combined into sentences.
   b. Rules governing the meaning of words and sentences.
   c. The study of the sound units that affect speech.
2. Language production and language comprehension develop in infants about the same time. True or false?
3. _____ _____ refers to the phenomenon in which young children omit nonessential portions of sentences.
4. A child knows that adding *-ed* to certain words puts the words in the past tense. As a result, instead of saying "He came," the child says "He comed." This is an example of _____
5. _____ theory assumes that language acquisition is based on principles of conditioning and shaping.
6. In his theory of language acquisition, Chomsky argues that language acquisition is an innate ability tied to the structure of the brain. True or false?

RETHINK

1. Why might people who speak two languages have cognitive advantages over those who speak only one?

2. Why is overgeneralization seen as an argument against a strict learning-theory approach to explaining language acquisition?

Answers to Evaluate Questions

1. 1-a, 2-c, 3-b; **2.** False; language comprehension precedes language; **3.** Telegraphic speech; **4.** overgeneralization; **5.** Learning; **6.** True

---

KEY TERMS

language	semantics	learning-theory approach (to language development)	interactionist approach (to language development)
grammar	babble		
phonology	telegraphic speech	nativist approach (to language development)	linguistic-relativity hypothesis
phonemes	overgeneralization		
syntax			

Module 23
Intelligence

Native sailors in the Marshall Islands in the South Pacific are capable of traveling 100 miles in open ocean waters. Although their destination may be just a small dot of land less than a mile wide, the sailors are able to navigate precisely toward it without the aid of a compass, chronometer, sextant, or any of the other sailing tools that are used by Western navigators. They are able to sail accurately even when the winds do not allow a direct approach to the island and they must take a zigzag course. (Tingley, 2016)

How do the Marshall Islands sailors navigate so effectively? If you asked them, they could not explain it. They might tell you they use a process that takes into account the rising and setting of the stars and the appearance, sound, and feel of the waves against the side of the boat. But at any given moment as they are sailing along, they could not identify their position or say why they are doing what they are doing. Nor could they explain the navigational theory underlying their sailing technique.

Some people might say that the inability of the Marshall Island sailors to explain in Western terms how their sailing technique works is a sign of primitive or even unintelligent behavior. In fact, if we gave these sailors a Western standardized test of navigational knowledge and theory or, for that matter, a traditional test of intelligence, they might do poorly on it. Yet, as a practical matter, it is not possible to accuse the Marshall Island sailors of being unintelligent: Despite their inability to explain how they do it, they are able to navigate successfully through the open ocean waters.

The navigation used by the natives of the Marshall Islands points out the difficulty in coming to grips with what is meant by intelligence. To a Westerner, traveling in a straight line along the most direct and quickest route by using a sextant and other navigational tools is likely to represent the most "intelligent" kind of behavior; in contrast, a zigzag course, based on the "feel" of the waves, would not seem very reasonable. To the Marshall Islands sailors, who are used to their own system of navigation, however, the use of complicated navigational tools might seem so overly complex and unnecessary that they might think of Western navigators as lacking in intelligence.

It is clear from this example that the term *intelligence* can take on many meanings. If, for instance, you lived in a remote part of the Australian outback, you might differentiate between more intelligent and less intelligent people according to their mastery of hunting skills, whereas to someone living in urban Miami, intelligence might be exemplified by being "streetwise" or achieving success in business.

Each of these conceptions of intelligence is reasonable. Each represents an instance in which more intelligent people are better able to use the resources of their environment than are less intelligent people, a distinction that is presumably basic to any definition of intelligence. Yet it is also clear that these conceptions represent very different views of intelligence.

That two such different sets of behavior can exemplify the same psychological concept has long posed a challenge to psychologists. For years they have grappled with the issue of devising a general definition of intelligence. Ironically, laypeople have fairly clear ideas of what intelligence is, although the nature of their ideas is related to their culture. Westerners

LEARNING OUTCOMES

LO 23-1 What are the different definitions and conceptions of intelligence?

LO 23-2 What are the major approaches to measuring intelligence, and what do intelligence tests measure?

LO 23-3 How can the extremes of intelligence be characterized?

LO 23-4 Are traditional IQ tests culturally biased?

LO 23-5 To what degree is intelligence influenced by the environment and to what degree by heredity?

Some natives of the Marshall Islands can navigate with great accuracy across open seas without the standard navigation tools used by sailors in Western cultures. Their abilities illustrate that people attain their goals in multiple ways and that there is no single route to success.
Peter Essick/Cavan/Getty Images

view intelligence as the ability to establish categories and debate rationally. In contrast, people in some Eastern and African cultures view intelligence more in terms of understanding and relating to one another (Crowne, 2013; Blackwell et al., 2015; Chao et al., 2017).

The definition of intelligence that psychologists employ contains some of the same elements found in the layperson's conception. To psychologists, **intelligence** is the capacity to understand the world, think rationally, and use resources effectively when faced with challenges.

This definition does not lay to rest a key question asked by psychologists: Is intelligence a unitary attribute, or are there different kinds of intelligence? We turn now to various theories of intelligence that address the issue.

Theories of Intelligence: Are There Different Kinds of Intelligence?

Perhaps you see yourself as a good writer but as someone who lacks ability in math. Or maybe you view yourself as a "science person" who easily masters physics but has few strengths in interpreting literature. Perhaps you view yourself as generally fairly smart with intelligence that permits you to excel across domains.

The ways in which people view their own talents mirror a question that psychologists have grappled with. Is intelligence a single, general ability, or is it multifaceted and related to specific abilities? Early psychologists assumed that intelligence could be embodied in a single concept they called *g*. In this view, **g, or the g-factor** was the single, general factor that produced intelligence. This assumption was based on the fact that different measures of intelligence, whether they focused on, say, mathematical expertise, verbal competency, or spatial visualization skills, all ranked test-takers in roughly the same order. People who were good on one test generally were good on others; those who did poorly on one test tended to do poorly on others.

Given this association between performance on different types of tests, the assumption was that a general, global intellectual ability was at work—the *g-factor*. This *g*-factor was assumed to underlie performance in every aspect of intelligence, and it was the *g*-factor that was presumably being measured on tests of intelligence (Major et al., 2011; Das, 2015; Debatin, 2019).

More recent theories explain intelligence in a different light. Rather than viewing intelligence as a unitary entity, some psychologists consider it to be a multidimensional concept that includes different types of intelligence (Downing, 2015; Flanagan & McDonough, 2018; Otero et al., 2022).

FLUID AND CRYSTALLIZED INTELLIGENCE

Some psychologists suggest that there are two kinds of intelligence: fluid intelligence and crystallized intelligence. **Fluid intelligence** is the ability to think logically, reason abstractly, solve problems, and find patterns. We use fluid intelligence when we are solving a personal problem or grappling with a political issue (Euler et al., 2015; Kyllonen & Kell, 2017; Tsukahara & Engle, 2021).

In contrast, **crystallized intelligence** is the accumulation of information, knowledge, and skills that people have learned through experience and education. It reflects the facts that we have learned and the information that resides in our long-term memory. When we learn a new language, we use crystallized intelligence as we acquire new vocabulary words.

intelligence The capacity to understand the world, think rationally, and use resources effectively when faced with challenges. (Module 23)

g or g-factor The single, general factor for mental ability assumed to underlie intelligence in some early theories of intelligence. (Module 23)

fluid intelligence Intelligence that reflects the ability to think logically, reason abstractly, and solve problems. (Module 23)

crystallized intelligence The accumulation of information, knowledge, and skills that people have learned through experience and education. (Module 23)

Piloting a helicopter requires the use of both fluid intelligence and crystallized intelligence. Which of the two kinds of intelligence do you believe is more important for such a task?
ALPA PROD/Shutterstock

The differences between fluid intelligence and crystallized intelligence become especially evident in late adulthood. At that point in the life span, people show declines in fluid, but not crystallized, intelligence (Ackerman, 2011; Pezoulas et al., 2017; Taylor & Bisson, 2019).

GARDNER'S MULTIPLE INTELLIGENCES: THE MANY WAYS OF SHOWING INTELLIGENCE

Psychologist Howard Gardner has taken an approach very different from traditional thinking about intelligence. Gardner argues that rather than asking "How smart are you?" we should be asking a different question: "How are you smart?" In answering the latter question, Gardner has developed a **theory of multiple intelligences** that has become quite influential (Gardner, 2000; Jung & Chang, 2017; Chavarría-Garza et al., 2022).

Gardner argues that we have a minimum eight different forms of intelligence, each relatively independent of the others: musical, bodily kinesthetic, logical-mathematical, linguistic, spatial, interpersonal, intrapersonal, and naturalist. (Figure 1 describes the eight types of intelligence, with examples of people who excel in each type.) In Gardner's view, each of the multiple intelligences is linked to an independent system in the brain. Furthermore, he suggests that there may be even more types of intelligence, such as *existential intelligence*, which involves identifying and thinking about the fundamental questions of human existence. For example, in addition to her intrapersonal intelligence (see Figure 1), the Michelle Obama might exemplify this type of intelligence (Gardner, 1999, 2000).

According to Gardner's theory, all people have the same kinds of intelligence–but in different degrees. Moreover, although the eight basic types of intelligence are presented individually, Gardner suggests that these separate intelligences do not operate in isolation. Normally, any activity encompasses several kinds of intelligence working together.

The concept of multiple intelligences has led to the development of intelligence tests that include questions in which more than one answer can be correct; these provide an opportunity for test-takers to demonstrate creative thinking. In addition, many educators, embracing the concept of multiple intelligences, have designed classroom curricula that are meant to draw on different aspects of intelligence (Davis et al., 2011; Sternberg, 2015; Islam, 2019).

theory of multiple intelligences Gardner's intelligence theory that proposes that there are eight distinct spheres of intelligence. (Module 23)

Study Alert
Remember, Gardner's theory suggests that each individual has every kind of intelligence but in different degrees.

PRACTICAL AND EMOTIONAL INTELLIGENCE: TOWARD A MORE INTELLIGENT VIEW OF INTELLIGENCE

Consider the following situation:

> An employee who reports to one of your subordinates has asked to talk with you about waste, poor management practices, and possible violations of both company policy and the law on the part of your subordinate. You have been in your present position only a year, but in that time you have had no indications of trouble about the subordinate in question. Neither you nor your company has an "open door" policy, so it is expected that employees should take their concerns to their immediate supervisors before bringing a matter to the attention of anyone else. The employee who wishes to meet with you has not discussed this matter with a direct supervisor because of its delicate nature. (Sternberg, 1998)

Your response to this situation has a lot to do with your future success in a business career, according to psychologist Robert Sternberg. The question is one of a series designed to help give an indication of your intelligence. However, it is not traditional intelligence that the question is designed to tap but rather intelligence of a specific kind: practical intelligence. **Practical intelligence** is intelligence related

practical intelligence According to Sternberg, intelligence related to overall success in living. (Module 23)

1. Musical intelligence (skills in tasks involving music). Example: When he was 3, Yehudi Menuhin was smuggled into San Francisco Orchestra concerts by his parents. By the time he was 10 years old, Menuhin was an international performer. 	**5.** Spatial intelligence (skills involving spatial configurations, such as those used by artists and architects). Example: American architect Frank Gehry created architectural masterpieces such as the Guggenheim Museum in Bilbao, Spain, and the Disney Concert Hall in Los Angeles. 
2. Bodily kinesthetic intelligence (skills in using the whole body or various portions of it in the solution of problems or in the construction of products or displays, exemplified by dancers, athletes, actors, and surgeons). Example:  Known for his athleticism, professional basketball star LeBron James played both basketball and football in high school.	**6.** Interpersonal intelligence (skills in interacting with others, such as sensitivity to the moods, temperaments, motivations, and intentions of others). Example:  Rescue workers who provide help following disasters and in emergency situations often demonstrate particularly high levels of interpersonal intelligence in dealing with survivors.
3. Logical-mathematical intelligence (skills in problem solving and scientific thinking). Example: Katherine Johnson was an African-American NASA space scientist, mathematician, and physicist who calculated the orbits of astronauts during the early days of human space exploration. 	**7.** Intrapersonal intelligence (knowledge of the internal aspects of oneself; access to one's own feelings and emotions). Example: Michelle Obama, an accomplished attorney who served as First Lady of the United States, is widely admired for her compassion and her insightful understanding of the challenges that others face. 
4. Linguistic intelligence (skills involved in the production and use of language). Case example:  Writer Toni Morrison, who died in 2019, won Pulitzer and Nobel prizes. She began writing as a college student at Howard University and wrote her first novel while working at a full-time job, raising two children as a single mother, and getting up at 4:00 each morning to work on the book.	**8.** Naturalist intelligence (ability to identify and classify patterns in nature). Case example: Naturalist Sir David Attenborough helped create interest in the natural world through his deep knowledge of plant and animal life and through numerous media broadcasts that sparked the curiosity of millions. 

FIGURE 1 Howard Gardner believes that there are eight major kinds of intelligences, corresponding to abilities in different domains. In what area does your greatest intelligence reside, and why do you think you have particular strengths in that area?

(1): PA Images/Alamy Stock Photo; (2): Li Ying/Xinhua/Alamy Live News; (3): Donaldson Collection/Michael Ochs Archives/Getty Images; (4): John Blanding/The Boston Globe/Getty Images; (5): Peter Horree/Alamy Stock Photo; (6): Ground Picture/Shutterstock; (7): McGraw Hill; (8): Daniel Berehulak/Getty Images

to overall success in living (Wagner, 2011; Baczyńska & Thornton, 2017; Griffith et al., 2019).

Noting that traditional tests were designed to relate to academic success, Sternberg points to evidence showing that most traditional measures of intelligence do not relate especially well to *career* success (McClelland, 1993). Specifically, although successful business executives usually score at least moderately well on intelligence tests, the rate at which they advance and their ultimate business achievements are only minimally associated with traditional measures of their intelligence.

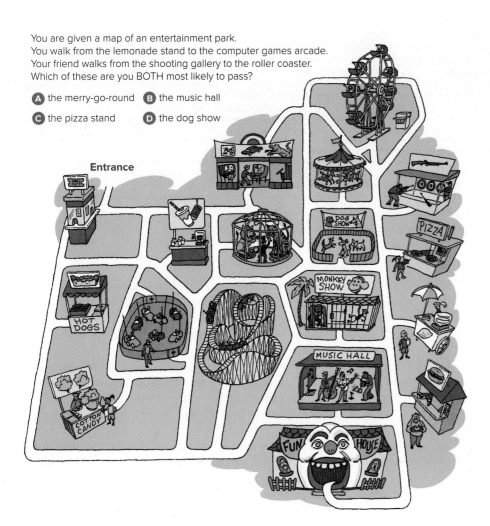

You are given a map of an entertainment park.
You walk from the lemonade stand to the computer games arcade.
Your friend walks from the shooting gallery to the roller coaster.
Which of these are you BOTH most likely to pass?

A the merry-go-round **B** the music hall
C the pizza stand **D** the dog show

FIGURE 2 Most standard tests of intelligence primarily measure analytical skills; more comprehensive tests measure creative and practical abilities as well.
Source: Adapted from Sternberg, 2000.

Sternberg argues that career success requires a very different type of intelligence from that required for academic success. Whereas academic success is based on knowledge of a specific information base obtained from reading and listening, practical intelligence is learned mainly through observation of others' behavior. People who are high in practical intelligence are able to learn general norms and principles and apply them appropriately. Consequently, practical intelligence tests, like the one shown in Figure 2, measure the ability to employ broad principles in solving everyday problems (Stemler & Sternberg, 2006; Stemler et al., 2009; Sternberg, 2013; Sternberg, 2018).

In addition to practical intelligence, Sternberg argues there are two other basic, interrelated types of intelligence related to life success: analytical intelligence and creative intelligence. Analytical intelligence focuses on traditional types of problems measured on IQ tests, whereas creative intelligence involves the generation of novel ideas and products (Sternberg et al., 2005; Sternberg et al., 2019; Sternberg et al., 2021).

Some psychologists broaden the concept of intelligence even further beyond the intellectual realm to include emotions. **Emotional intelligence** is the set of skills that underlie the accurate assessment, evaluation, expression, and regulation of emotions (Anderson et al., 2017; Cabello et al., 2021; Gómez-Leal et al., 2022).

Emotional intelligence is the basis of empathy, self-awareness, and social skills. It encompasses the ability to get along well with others. It provides us with an understanding of what other people are feeling and experiencing, which permits us to respond appropriately to their needs. These abilities may help explain why people with only modest scores on traditional intelligence tests can be quite successful: The basis of their success may be a high emotional intelligence, which allows them to respond appropriately and quickly to others' feelings.

emotional intelligence The set of skills that underlie the accurate assessment, evaluation, expression, and regulation of emotions. (Module 23)

Study Alert
Traditional intelligence relates to academic performance; practical intelligence relates to success in life; emotional intelligence relates to emotional skills.

Major Approaches to Intelligence	
Approach	**Characteristics**
Fluid and crystallized intelligence	Fluid intelligence relates to the ability to think logically, reason abstractly, and solve problems; crystallized intelligence relates to information, skills, and strategies learned through experience
Gardner's multiple intelligences	Eight independent forms of intelligence
Practical intelligence	Intelligence in terms of nonacademic, career, and personal success
Emotional intelligence	Intelligence that provides an understanding of what other people are feeling and experiencing and permits us to respond appropriately to others' needs

FIGURE 3 Just as there are many views of the nature of intelligence, there are also numerous ways to demonstrate intelligent behavior. This summary provides an overview of the various approaches used by psychologists.

Emotional intelligence clearly is an important and useful attribute, both in children and adults. Unfortunately, evidence indicates that emotional intelligence in school-aged children and adults declined during the COVID-19 pandemic as people lost opportunities to learn and use social skills during the prolonged lockdown (Issa & Jaleel, 2021; Martín-Requejo & Santiago-Ramajo, 2021).

Recently, the concept of emotional intelligence has sparked political controversy. Specifically, some politicians and other critics of the concept oppose the view that emotional intelligence is important enough to be taught in school. They suggest that the nurturance of emotional intelligence is best left to students' families (Straus, 2021; Goldstein, 2022).

Still, the notion of emotional intelligence reminds us that people demonstrate intelligent behavior in many ways–just as researchers view the nature of intelligence in multiple ways (Barrett & Salovey, 2002; Parke et al., 2015). Figure 3 presents a summary of the varied approaches used by psychologists.

Assessing Intelligence

Given the variety of approaches to the components of intelligence, it is not surprising that measuring intelligence has proved challenging. Psychologists who study intelligence have focused much of their attention on the development of **intelligence tests** that quantify a person's level of intelligence. These tests have proved to be of great benefit in identifying students in need of special attention in school, diagnosing specific learning difficulties, and helping people make the best educational and vocational choices. At the same time, their use has proved controversial, raising important social and educational issues.

Historically, the first effort at intelligence testing was based on an uncomplicated but completely wrong assumption: that the size and shape of a person's head could be used as an objective measure of intelligence. The idea was put forward by Sir Francis Galton (1822–1911), an eminent English scientist whose ideas in other domains proved to be considerably better than his notions about intelligence.

Galton's motivation to identify people of high intelligence stemmed from personal prejudices. He sought to demonstrate the natural superiority of people of high social class (including himself) by showing that intelligence is inherited. He hypothesized that head configuration, which is genetically determined, is related to brain size and therefore is related to intelligence.

Galton's theories were proved wrong on virtually every count. Head size and shape are not related to intellectual performance. However, Galton's work did have at least one desirable result: He was the first person to suggest that intelligence could be quantified and measured in an objective manner. Furthermore, the advent of advanced brain-scanning techniques has found that brain size–*not* head size–does show some

intelligence tests Tests devised to quantify a person's level of intelligence. (Module 23)

association with intelligence, although the results are preliminary at this point (Lee et al., 2019; Triki et al., 2021).

BINET AND THE DEVELOPMENT OF IQ TESTS

French psychologist Alfred Binet (1857-1911) developed the first real intelligence test. His tests followed from a simple premise: If performance on certain tasks or test items improved with *chronological,* or physical, age, performance could be used to distinguish more intelligent people from less intelligent ones within a particular age group. On the basis of this principle, Binet devised the first formal intelligence test, which was designed to identify the "dullest" students in the Paris school system in order to provide them with remedial aid.

Binet began by presenting tasks to same-age students who had been labeled "bright" or "dull" by their teachers. If a task could be completed by the bright students but not by the dull ones, he retained that task as a proper test item; otherwise, it was discarded. In the end, he came up with a test that distinguished between the bright and dull groups, and–with further work–one that distinguished among children in different age groups (Binet & Simon, 1916; Sternberg & Jarvin, 2003; Wasserman, 2018).

On the basis of the Binet test, children were assigned a score relating to their **mental age,** the age for which a given level of performance is average or typical. For example, if the average 8-year-old answered, say, 45 items correctly on a test, anyone who answered 45 items correctly would be assigned a mental age of 8 years. Consequently, whether the person taking the test was 20 years old or 5 years old, they would have the same mental age of 8 years (Cornell, 2006).

Assigning a mental age to students provided an indication of their general level of performance. However, it did not allow for adequate comparisons among people of different chronological ages. By using mental age alone, for instance, we might assume that an 18-year-old responding at a 20-year-old's level would be demonstrating the same degree of intelligence as a 5-year-old answering at a 7-year-old's level, when actually the 5-year-old would be displaying a much greater *relative* degree of intelligence.

A solution to the problem came in the form of the **intelligence quotient (IQ),** a measure of intelligence that takes into account an individual's mental *and* chronological (physical) age. Historically, the first IQ scores employed the following formula, in which *MA* stands for mental age and *CA* for chronological age:

$$\text{IQ score} = \frac{\text{MA}}{\text{CA}} \times 100$$

Using this formula, we can return to the earlier example of an 18-year-old performing at a mental age of 20 and calculate an IQ score of (20/18) × 100 = 111. In contrast, the 5-year-old performing at a mental age of 7 comes out with a considerably higher IQ score: (7/5) × 100 = 140.

As a bit of trial and error with the formula will show you, anyone who has a mental age equal to their chronological age will have an IQ equal to 100. Moreover, people with a mental age that is lower than their chronological age will have IQs that are lower than 100.

Although the basic principles behind the calculation of an IQ score still hold, today IQ scores are determined in a different manner and are known as *deviation IQ scores.* First, the average test score for everyone of the same age who takes the test is determined, and that average score is assigned an IQ of 100. Then, with the aid of statistical techniques that calculate the differences (or "deviations") between each score and the average, IQ scores are assigned.

As you can see in Figure 4, when IQ scores from large numbers of people are plotted on a graph, they form a *bell-shaped distribution* (called "bell-shaped" because it looks like a bell when plotted). Approximately two-thirds of all individuals fall within 15 IQ points of the average score of 100. As scores increase or fall beyond that range, the percentage of people in a category falls considerably.

Alfred Binet.
Everett Collection Inc/Alamy Stock Photo

mental age The age for which a given level of performance is average or typical. (Module 23)

intelligence quotient (IQ) A score that takes into account an individual's mental and chronological ages. (Module 23)

Study Alert

It's important to know the traditional formula for IQ scores in which IQ is the ratio of mental age divided by chronological age, multiplied by 100. Remember, though, that today, the calculation of IQ scores is done in a more sophisticated manner.

FIGURE 4 The average and most common IQ score is 100, and 68% of all people are within a 30-point range centered on 100. Some 95% of the population have scores that are within 30 points above or below 100, and 99.8% have scores that are between 55 and 145.

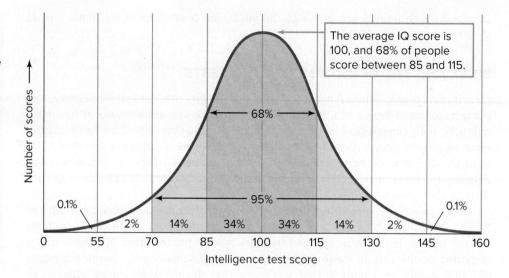

> The average IQ score is 100, and 68% of people score between 85 and 115.

CONTEMPORARY IQ TESTS: GAUGING INTELLIGENCE

Remnants of Binet's original intelligence test are still with us, although the test has been revised in significant ways. Now in its fifth edition and called the *Stanford-Binet Intelligence Scale,* the test consists of a series of items that vary according to the age of the person being tested (Roid et al., 2003; Gibbons & Warne, 2019). For example, young children are asked to copy figures or answer questions about everyday activities. Older people are asked to solve analogies, explain proverbs, and describe similarities that underlie sets of words.

The test is administered orally and includes both verbal and nonverbal assessments. An examiner begins by finding a mental age level at which a person is able to answer all the questions correctly and then moves on to successively more difficult problems. When a mental age level is reached at which no items can be answered, the test is over. By studying the pattern of correct and incorrect responses, the examiner is able to compute an IQ score for the person being tested. In addition, the Stanford-Binet test yields separate subscores that provide clues to a test-taker's particular strengths and weaknesses.

The Stanford-Binet test consists of a series of items that vary in nature according to the age of the person being tested. What can we learn about a person from a test of this type?

Lewis J. Merrim/Science Source

The IQ tests most frequently used in the United States were devised by psychologist David Wechsler and are known as the *Wechsler Adult Intelligence Scale-IV*, or, more commonly, the *WAIS-IV* (for adults) and a children's version, the *Wechsler Intelligence Scale for Children-V*, or *WISC-V*. Both the WAIS-IV and the WISC-V measure verbal comprehension, perceptual reasoning, working memory, and processing speed (see sample WAIS-IV items in Figure 5).

Because the Stanford-Binet, WAIS-IV, and WISC-V all require individualized, one-on-one administration, they are relatively difficult to administer and score on a large-scale basis. Consequently, there are now a number of IQ tests that allow group administration. Rather than having one examiner ask one person at a time to respond to individual items, group IQ tests are strictly paper-and-pencil tests. The primary advantage of group tests is their ease of administration (Danner et al., 2011).

Types of Items on WAIS-IV		
Name	**Goal of Item**	**Example**
Information	Assess general information	Who wrote *Tom Sawyer*?
Comprehension	Assess understanding and evaluation of social norms and past experience	Why is copper often used for electrical wires?
Arithmetic	Assess math reasoning through verbal problems	Three golfers divided 18 golf balls equally among themselves. How many golf balls did each person receive?
Similarities	Test understanding of how objects or concepts are alike, tapping abstract reasoning	In what way are a circle and a triangle alike?
Figure weights	Test perceptual reasoning	Problems require test-taker to determine which possibility balances the final scale. 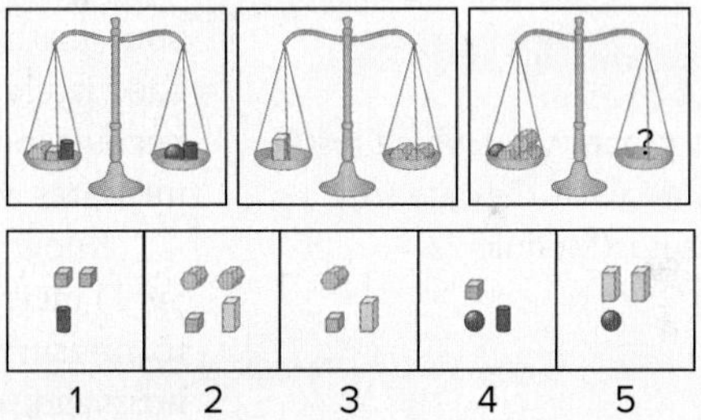
Matrix reasoning	Test spatial reasoning	Test-taker must decide which of the five possibilities replaces the question mark and completes the sequence. 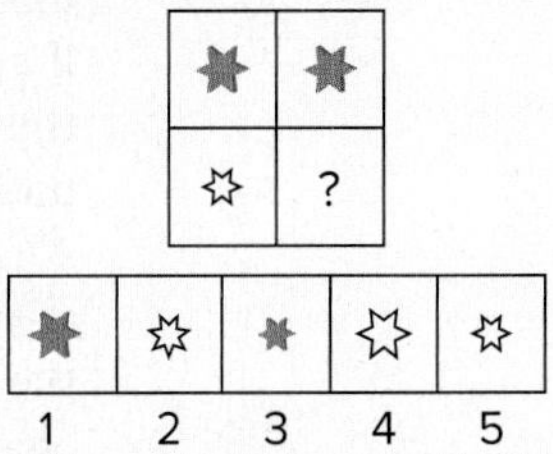
Block design item	Test understanding of relationship of parts to whole	Problems require test-takers to reproduce a design in fixed amount of time. 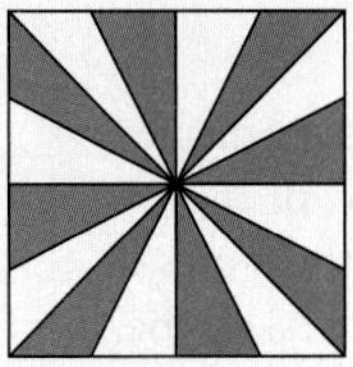

FIGURE 5 These test questions are similar to the types of questions found on the *Wechsler Adult Intelligence Scale (WAIS-IV)*.
Source: Adapted from Wechsler (2008)

However, sacrifices are made in group testing that, in some cases, may outweigh the benefits. For instance, group tests generally offer fewer kinds of questions than do tests administered individually. Furthermore, people may be more motivated to perform at their highest ability level when working on a one-to-one basis with a test administrator than they are in a group. Finally, in some cases, it is simply impossible to employ group tests, particularly with young children or people with unusually low IQs (Brown-Chidsey & Andren, 2015).

RELIABILITY AND VALIDITY: TAKING THE MEASURE OF TESTS

When we use a ruler, we expect to find that it measures an inch in the same way it did the last time we used it. When we weigh ourselves on the bathroom scale, we hope that the variations we see on the scale are due to changes in our weight and not to errors on the part of the scale (unless the change in weight is in an unwanted direction!).

In the same way, we hope that psychological tests have reliability. **Reliability** refers to the consistency of a test in measuring what it is trying to measure. We need to be sure that each time we administer a test, a test-taker will achieve the same or nearly similar results, assuming that nothing about the person has changed relevant to what is being measured.

Suppose, for instance, that when you first took the SAT exams, you scored 400 on the math section of the test. Then, after taking the test again a few months later, you scored 700. Upon receiving your new score, you might well stop celebrating for a moment to question whether the test is reliable because it is unlikely that your abilities could have changed enough to raise your score by 300 points.

But suppose your score changed hardly at all, and both times you received a score of about 400. You couldn't complain about a lack of reliability. However, if you knew your math skills were above average, you might be concerned that the test did not adequately measure what it was supposed to measure. In sum, the question has now become one of validity rather than reliability. A test has **validity** when it actually measures what it is supposed to measure.

Knowing that a test is reliable is no guarantee that it is also valid. For instance, Sir Francis Galton assumed that skull size is related to intelligence, and he was able to measure skull size with great reliability. However, we know that the measure was not valid; that is, we now know that skull size has nothing to do with intelligence. In this case, then, we have reliability without validity.

However, if a test is unreliable, it cannot be valid. Assuming that all other factors—motivation to score well, knowledge of the material, health, and so forth—are similar, if a person scores high the first time they take a specific test and low the second time, the test cannot be measuring what it is supposed to measure. Therefore, the test is both unreliable and not valid.

Test validity and reliability are prerequisites for accurate assessment of intelligence—as well as for any other measurement task carried out by psychologists. Consequently, the measures of personality carried out by personality psychologists, clinical psychologists' assessments of psychological disorders, and social psychologists' measures of attitudes must meet the tests of validity and reliability for the results to be meaningful (Deng & Georgiou, 2015; Gignac et al., 2019; Watkins & Canivez, 2021).

Assuming that a test is both valid and reliable, one further step is necessary in order to interpret the meaning of a particular test-taker's score: the establishment of norms. **Norms** are standards of test performance that permit the comparison of one person's score on a test to the scores of others who have taken the same test. For example, a norm permits test-takers to know that they have scored, say, in the top 15% of those who have taken the test previously. Tests for which norms have been developed are known as *standardized tests*.

Test designers develop norms by calculating the average score achieved by a specific group of people for whom the test has been designed. Then the test designers

reliability The property by which tests measure consistently what they are trying to measure. (Module 23)

validity The property by which tests actually measure what they are supposed to measure. (Module 23)

norms Standards of test performance that permit the comparison of one person's score on a test with the scores of other individuals who have taken the same test. (Module 23)

can determine the extent to which each person's score differs from the scores of the other individuals who have taken the test in the past and provide future test-takers with a qualitative sense of their performance.

Obviously, the samples of test-takers who are employed in the establishment of norms are critical to the norming process. The people used to determine norms must be representative of the individuals to whom the test is directed.

From the perspective of...

A Human Resources Specialist Job interviews are really a kind of test, but they rely on interviewers' judgments and have no formal validity or reliability. Do you think job interviews can be made to have greater validity and reliability?

Dex Image/Getty Images

ADAPTIVE TESTING: USING COMPUTERS TO ASSESS PERFORMANCE

Ensuring that tests are reliable, valid, and based on appropriate norms has become more critical with computer-administered testing. In computer-administered versions of tests such as the digital SAT and GRE General, a test used to determine entrance to graduate school, not only are test questions viewed and answered on a computer, but the test itself is individualized.

That is, with *adaptive testing*, not every test-taker receives identical sets of questions. Instead, the computer first presents a randomly selected question of moderate difficulty. If the test-taker answers it correctly, the computer then presents a randomly chosen item of slightly greater difficulty. If the test-taker answers it incorrectly, the computer presents a slightly easier item. Each question becomes slightly harder or easier than the question preceding it, depending on whether the previous response is correct. Ultimately, the greater the number of difficult questions answered correctly, the higher the score (Liu et al., 2015; Cheng et al., 2017; Jiang et al., 2022).

Variations in Intellectual Ability

More than 7 million people in the United States, including around 11 per 1,000 children, have been identified as far enough below average in intelligence that they can be regarded as having serious deficits. Individuals with low IQs (people with intellectual disabilities) as well as those with unusually high IQs (the intellectually gifted) require special attention if they are to reach their full potential.

INTELLECTUAL DISABILITIES

Although sometimes thought of as a rare phenomenon, intellectual disabilities occur in 1–3% of the population. Worldwide, as many as 200 million people are classified with some form of intellectual disability (Patrick et al., 2021).

There is wide variation among those with intellectual disabilities (formerly known as "mental retardation," an outmoded term that was imprecise and fostered negative stereotypes). **Intellectual disability** is formally defined as disability characterized by significant limitations in both intellectual functioning and adaptive behavior, which covers many everyday social and practical skills, and originates before the age of 22 (Schalock et al., 2021).

intellectual disability A condition characterized by significant limitations both in intellectual functioning and in conceptual, social, and practical adaptive skills. (Module 23)

Although below-average intellectual functioning can be measured in a relatively straightforward manner—using standard IQ tests—it is more difficult to determine how to gauge limitations in adaptive behavior. Consequently, there is a lack of uniformity in how experts apply the term *intellectual disabilities*. People labeled intellectually disabled vary, from those who can be taught to work and function with little special attention to those who cannot be trained and are institutionalized throughout their lives (American Association of Intellectual and Developmental Disabilities, 2022).

Most people with intellectual disabilities have relatively minor deficits and are classified as having *mild intellectual disability*. These individuals, who have IQ scores ranging from 55 to 69, constitute some 90% of all people with intellectual disabilities. Although their development is typically slower than that of their peers, they can function quite independently by adulthood and are able to hold jobs and have families of their own (van Nieuwenhuijzen et al., 2011; Nouwens et al., 2017).

With greater degrees of intellectual deficit, the difficulties are more pronounced. For people with *moderate intellectual disability* (IQs of 40 to 54), deficits are obvious early, with language and motor skills lagging behind those of peers. Although these individuals can hold simple jobs, they need to have some degree of supervision throughout their lives. Individuals with *severe intellectual disability* (IQs of 25 to 39) and *profound intellectual disability* (IQs below 25) are generally unable to function independently and typically require care for their entire lives (Bertelli et al., 2019; Illes & Lou, 2019).

Identifying the Roots of Intellectual Disabilities What produces intellectual disabilities? In nearly one-third of the cases, there is an identifiable cause related to biological or environmental factors. One of the most common, preventable cause of intellectual disabilities is **fetal alcohol spectrum disorder,** produced by a mother's use of alcohol while pregnant. Increasing evidence shows that even small amounts of alcohol intake can produce intellectual deficits. In the United States, as many as 9 children out of 1,000 are born with fetal alcohol spectrum disorder (Lewis et al., 2015; Centers for Disease Control and Prevention, 2022; Lim et al., 2022).

Down syndrome represents another major cause of intellectual disabilities. *Down syndrome* results when a person is born with 47 chromosomes instead of the usual 46. In most cases, the person has an extra copy of the 21st chromosome, which leads to problems in how the brain and body develop (Vicari et al., 2013; Bull, 2020).

In other cases of intellectual disabilities, an abnormality occurs in the structure of particular chromosomes. Birth complications, such as a temporary lack of oxygen, may also cause intellectual disability. In some cases, intellectual disabilities begin after birth following a head injury, a stroke, or infections such as meningitis (Bittles et al., 2007; Fevang et al., 2017).

However, the majority of cases of intellectual disabilities are classified as familial intellectual disability. **Familial intellectual disability** is intellectual disability in which no apparent biological or genetic problems exist, but there is a history of intellectual disability among family members. Whether the family background of intellectual disabilities is caused by environmental factors, such as extreme continuous poverty leading to malnutrition, or by some underlying genetic factor is usually impossible to determine (Franklin & Mansuy, 2011; Lichtenstein et al., 2021).

Integrating Individuals with Intellectual Disabilities Important advances in the care and treatment of those with intellectual disabilities have been made since the Education for All Handicapped Children Act (Public Law 94-142) was passed by Congress in the mid-1970s. In this federal law, Congress stipulated that people with intellectual disabilities are entitled to a full education and that they must be educated and trained in the least restrictive environment—a process known as mainstreaming. *Mainstreaming* is the practice of educating students with intellectual deficits and other special needs in regular classes during specific time periods (Reiner, 2018; De Bruin, 2019).

---

fetal alcohol spectrum disorder
One of the most common cause of intellectual disability in newborns, fetal alcohol spectrum disorder occurs when the mother uses alcohol during pregnancy. (Module 23)

❗ Study Alert
Remember that in most cases of intellectual disability, there is no apparent biological deficiency, but a history of intellectual disability exists in the family.

familial intellectual disability Intellectual disability in which no apparent biological defect exists, but there is a history of intellectual disability in the family. (Module 23)

The philosophy behind mainstreaming suggests that the interaction of students with and without intellectual disabilities in regular classrooms will improve educational opportunities for those with intellectual disabilities, increase their social acceptance, and facilitate their integration into society as a whole. In mainstreaming, special education classes still exist; some individuals with intellectual disabilities function at too low of a level to benefit from placement in regular classrooms. Moreover, children with intellectual disabilities who are mainstreamed into regular classes typically attend special classes for at least part of the day (Benitez et al., 2017; Wiesel et al., 2022).

THE INTELLECTUALLY GIFTED

Another group of people—the intellectually gifted—differ from those with average intelligence as much as individuals with intellectual disability do, although in a different manner. Accounting for 2-4% of the population, the **intellectually gifted** have IQ scores greater than 130.

> **intellectually gifted** The 2-4% segment of the population who have IQ scores greater than 130. (Module 23)

Although stereotypes about the gifted suggests that they are awkward, shy, social misfits who don't get along well with peers, most research indicates just the opposite: The intellectually gifted do well across almost every domain. They are most often outgoing, well-adjusted, healthy, popular people who are able to do most things better than the average person can (Sternberg et al., 2011; Strenze, 2015; Bucaille et al., 2021).

For example, in a famous study by psychologist Lewis Terman that started in the early 1920s, 1,500 children who had IQ scores above 140 were followed for the rest of their lives. From the start, the members of this group were more physically, academically, and socially capable than were their nongifted peers. In addition to doing better in school, they also showed better social adjustment than average. All these advantages paid off in terms of career success: As a group, the gifted received more awards and distinctions, earned higher incomes, and made more contributions in art and literature than did typical individuals. Perhaps most important, they reported greater satisfaction in life than did the nongifted (Warne & Liu, 2017; Warne, 2019; Hodges et al., 2021).

Of course, not every member of the group Terman studied was successful. Furthermore, high intelligence is not a homogeneous quality; a person with a high overall IQ is not necessarily gifted in every academic subject but may excel in just one or two. A high IQ is not a universal guarantee of success (Shurkin, 1992; Holohan, 2021).

Group Differences in Intelligence: Genetic and Environmental Determinants

Kwang is often washed with a pleck tied to a:

a. rundel
b. flink
c. pove
d. quirj

If you found this kind of item on an intelligence test, you would probably complain that the test was totally absurd and had nothing to do with your intelligence or anyone else's—and rightly so. How could anyone be expected to respond to items presented in a language that was so unfamiliar?

Yet to some people, even more reasonable questions may appear just as nonsensical. Consider the example of a child raised in a city who is asked about procedures for milking cows or of someone raised in a rural area who is asked about subway ticketing procedures. Obviously, the previous experience of the test-takers would affect their ability to answer correctly. And if such types of questions were included on an IQ test, a critic could rightly contend that the test had more to do with prior experience than with intelligence.

Although IQ tests do not include questions that are so clearly dependent on prior knowledge as questions about cows and subways, the background and experiences of test-takers do have the potential to affect results. In fact, the issue of devising fair intelligence tests that measure knowledge unrelated to culture and family background and experience is central to explaining an important and persistent finding: Members of certain racial and cultural groups consistently score lower, on average, on traditional intelligence tests than do members of other groups.

For example, as a group, Black individuals tend to attain lower scores on IQ tests than do White individuals. One obvious explanation for this difference is that the questions on the test are biased with regard to the kinds of knowledge they test, rather than reflecting true differences in intelligence. That is, if White individuals perform better because they are more familiar with the kind of information that is being tested, their higher IQ scores do not indicate that they are more intelligent than members of other groups (Suzuki et al., 2011; Loehlin et al., 2015; Rezai-Rashti & Lingard, 2021).

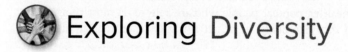 # Exploring Diversity

Can We Develop a Culture-Fair IQ Test?

Consider this question: "What should you do if another child grabs your hat and runs off with it?" Most White middle-class children answer that they would tell an adult, and this response is scored as correct on a common IQ test. However, a reasonable response might be to chase the person and fight to get the hat back, the answer that many urban Black children choose—but one that is scored as incorrect (Reynolds & Ramsay, 2003; Reynolds et al., 2021).

culture-fair IQ test A test trial that does not discriminate against the members of any minority group. (Module 23)

In an attempt to produce a **culture-fair IQ test,** meaning one that does not discriminate against the members of any particular group and that is relatively independent of their background and experiences, psychologists have tried to devise test items that assess experiences common to all cultures or emphasize questions that do not require language usage. However, test makers have found this difficult to do because past experiences, attitudes, and values almost always have an impact on respondents' answers (Fagan & Holland, 2009; Rizzi & Posthuma, 2013).

For example, children raised in Western cultures group things on the basis of what they are (such as putting *dog* and *fish* into the category of *animal*). In contrast, members of the Kpelle tribe in Africa see intelligence demonstrated by grouping things according to what they *do* (grouping *fish* with *swim*). Similarly, when asked to memorize the positions on a chessboard of objects typical to a U.S. household, children in the United States performed better than did children living in remote African villages. But if rocks are used instead of household objects, the African children do better. In short, it is difficult to produce a truly culture-fair test (Valencia & Suzuki, 2003; Barnett et al., 2011).

Finally, tests may include even subtler forms of bias against minority groups. For example, assessments of cognitive ability developed in the United States may favor responses that implicitly reflect North American or European values, customs, or traditions, such as the "rugged individualism" of Western cultures. At the same time, such tests may be biased against African and other cultural value systems that place a greater emphasis on the importance of social groups and embody a more communal worldview.

In short, producing a truly culture-fair test is difficult, but some cross-cultural test comparisons show relatively minor differences in scores regardless of racial and ethnic group membership. Still, creating a truly culture-fair IQ test has remained an elusive goal (Teovanović et al., 2015; Hagmann-von Arx et al., 2018).

IQ AND HERITABILITY: THE RELATIVE INFLUENCE OF GENETICS AND THE ENVIRONMENT

The efforts of psychologists to produce culture-fair measures of intelligence relate to a lingering controversy over whether members of different racial and ethnic groups differ in intelligence. In attempting to identify whether such differences do indeed exist, psychologists have had to confront a broader issue: What is the relative contribution to intelligence of genetic factors (heredity) versus experience (environment)—the nature–nurture issue that is so basic in psychology?

Richard Herrnstein, a psychologist, and Charles Murray, a sociologist, fanned the flames of the debate with the publication of their controversial book *The Bell Curve* in the mid-1990s (Herrnstein & Murray, 1994). They argued that an analysis of IQ differences between Whites and Blacks demonstrated that although environmental factors played a role, basic genetic differences also existed between the two races.

They based their argument on a number of findings. For instance, on average, White individuals score 15 points higher than Black individuals on traditional IQ tests even when socioeconomic status (SES) is taken into account. According to Herrnstein and Murray, middle- and upper-SES Black individuals score lower than middle- and upper-SES Whites, just as lower-SES Black individuals score lower on average than lower-SES Whites. Intelligence differences between Black and White individuals, they concluded, could not be attributed to environmental differences alone.

Intelligence clearly shows high heritability. **Heritability** is the degree to which a characteristic is related to inherited genetic factors. That is, a trait with high heritability is strongly related to genetic factors. In contrast, low-heritability traits are weakly related to genetic factors and thus more influenced by the environment in which a person is raised (Tosto et al., 2017; Toto et al., 2019; Quinn et al., 2022).

heritability The degree to which a characteristic is related to genetic, inherited factors. (Module 23)

As can be seen in Figure 6, the closer the genetic link between two related people, the greater the correspondence of IQ scores. Using data such as these, Herrnstein and Murray argued that differences between races in IQ scores were largely caused by genetically based differences in intelligence.

However, many psychologists reacted strongly against the arguments laid out in *The Bell Curve*, refuting several of the book's basic conclusions. One criticism is that even within similar socioeconomic groups, wide variations in IQ remain among individual households. Furthermore, the living conditions of Black individuals and White individuals are likely different even when their socioeconomic status (SES) is similar due to systemic racism and other factors. In addition, as we discussed earlier, there is

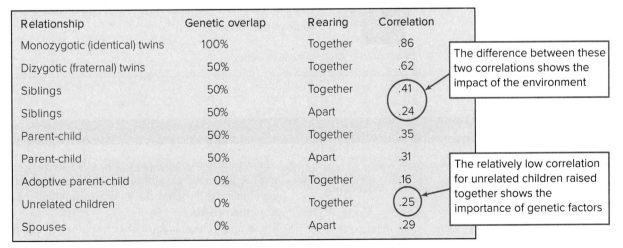

Relationship	Genetic overlap	Rearing	Correlation
Monozygotic (identical) twins	100%	Together	.86
Dizygotic (fraternal) twins	50%	Together	.62
Siblings	50%	Together	.41
Siblings	50%	Apart	.24
Parent-child	50%	Together	.35
Parent-child	50%	Apart	.31
Adoptive parent-child	0%	Together	.16
Unrelated children	0%	Together	.25
Spouses	0%	Apart	.29

The difference between these two correlations shows the impact of the environment

The relatively low correlation for unrelated children raised together shows the importance of genetic factors

FIGURE 6 The relationship between IQ and closeness of genetic relationship. In general, the more similar the genetic and environmental background of two people, the greater the correlation is. Note, for example, that the correlation for spouses, who are genetically unrelated and have been reared apart, is relatively low, whereas the correlation for identical twins reared together is substantial.
Source: Adapted from Henderson, 1982.

reason to believe that traditional IQ tests may discriminate against lower-SES urban Black individuals by asking for information pertaining to experiences they are unlikely to have had (Levine, 2011; Nisbett, 2019; O'Connell & Marks, 2021).

Even more significant, Black individuals who are raised in economically enriched environments have IQ scores similar to White individuals in comparable environments. For example, in a study of Black children who had been adopted at an early age by White middle-class families of above-average intelligence, the IQ scores of those children averaged 106–about 15 points above the average IQ scores of unadopted Black children in the study. Other research shows that the racial gap in IQ narrows considerably after a college education, and cross-cultural data demonstrate that when racial gaps exist in other cultures, the economically disadvantaged groups typically have lower scores. In short, the evidence that genetic factors play the major role in determining racial differences in IQ is not compelling (Fagan & Holland, 2007; Thaler et al., 2015; Nisbett, 2019).

Furthermore, drawing comparisons between races on any dimension, including IQ scores, is an imprecise, potentially misleading, and often fruitless venture. At worst, it may perpetuate stereotypes and discrimination. By far, the greatest discrepancies in IQ scores occur when comparing *individuals,* not when comparing mean IQ scores of different *groups.* Some Black individuals score high on IQ tests, and some White individuals score low, just as some White individuals score high, and some Black individuals score low. For the concept of intelligence to aid in the betterment of society, we must examine how *individuals* perform and not the groups to which they belong.

The more critical question to ask, then, is not whether hereditary or environmental factors primarily underlie intelligence but whether there is anything we can do to maximize the intellectual development of each individual. If we can find ways to do this, we will be able to make changes in the environment–which may take the form of enriched home and school environments–that can lead each person to reach their potential.

> **Study Alert**
> Remember that the differences in IQ scores are much greater when comparing individuals than when comparing groups.

From the perspective of...

A College Admissions Officer Imagine you notice that students who are members of minority groups systematically receive lower scores on standardized college entrance exams. What suggestions do you have for helping these students improve their scores?

Flying Colours Ltd/Digital Vision/Getty Images

RECAP/EVALUATE/RETHINK

RECAP

LO 23-1 What are the different definitions and conceptions of intelligence?

- Because intelligence can take many forms, defining it is challenging. One commonly accepted view is that intelligence is the capacity to understand the world, think rationally, and use resources effectively when faced with challenges.

- The earliest psychologists assumed that there is a general factor for mental ability called *g.* However, later psychologists disputed the view that intelligence is unidimensional.

- Some researchers suggest that intelligence can be broken down into fluid intelligence and crystallized intelligence. Gardner's theory of multiple intelligences proposes that there are eight spheres of intelligence.

- Information-processing approaches examine the processes underlying intelligent behavior rather than focusing on the structure of intelligence.
- Practical intelligence is intelligence related to overall success in living; emotional intelligence is the set of skills that underlie the accurate assessment, evaluation, expression, and regulation of emotions.

LO 23-2 What are the major approaches to measuring intelligence, and what do intelligence tests measure?

- Intelligence tests have traditionally compared a person's mental age and chronological age to yield an IQ, or intelligence quotient, score.
- Specific tests of intelligence include the Stanford-Binet test, the Wechsler Adult Intelligence Scale-IV (WAIS-IV), and the Wechsler Intelligence Scale for Children-V (WISC-V).
- Tests are expected to be both reliable and valid. Reliability refers to the consistency with which a test measures what it is trying to measure. A test has validity when it actually measures what it is supposed to measure.

LO 23-3 How can the extremes of intelligence be characterized?

- The levels of intellectual disability include mild, moderate, severe, and profound intellectual disability.
- About one-third of the cases of intellectual disability have a known biological cause; fetal alcohol spectrum disorder is the most common. Most cases, however, are classified as familial intellectual disability, for which there is no known biological cause.
- The intellectually gifted are people with IQ scores greater than 130. Intellectually gifted people tend to be healthier and more successful than the nongifted.

LO 23-4 Are traditional IQ tests culturally biased?

- Traditional intelligence tests have frequently been criticized for being biased in favor of the White middle-class population. This controversy has led to attempts to devise culture-fair tests, IQ measures that avoid questions that depend on a particular cultural background.

LO 23-5 To what degree is intelligence influenced by the environment and to what degree by heredity?

- Attempting to distinguish environmental from hereditary factors in intelligence is probably futile and certainly misguided. Because individual IQ scores vary far more than do group IQ scores, it is more critical to ask what can be done to maximize the intellectual development of each individual.

EVALUATE

1. _____ is a measure of intelligence that takes into account a person's chronological and mental ages.
2. Some psychologists make the distinction between _____ intelligence, which reflects the ability to think logically, reason abstractly, and solve problems, and _____ intelligence, which is the accumulation of information, knowledge, and skills that people have learned through experience and education.
3. _____ _____ _____ is the most common biological cause of intellectual disability.
4. People with high intelligence are generally shy and socially withdrawn. True or false?
5. A(n) _____ test tries to use only questions appropriate to all the people taking the test.

RETHINK

1. What is the role of emotional intelligence in the classroom? How might emotional intelligence be tested? Should emotional intelligence be a factor in determining academic promotion to the next grade?
2. Why might a test that identifies a disproportionate number of minority group members for special educational services and remedial assistance be considered potentially biased? Isn't the purpose of the test to help persons at risk of falling behind academically? How can a test created for a good purpose be biased?

Answers to Evaluate Questions

1. IQ; 2. fluid; crystallized; 3. fetal alcohol spectrum disorder; 4. False; the gifted are generally more socially adept than those with lower IQs; 5. culture-fair

KEY TERMS

intelligence	practical intelligence	reliability	familial intellectual
g or *g*-factor	emotional intelligence	validity	disability
fluid intelligence	intelligence tests	norms	intellectually
crystallized intelligence	mental age	intellectual disability	gifted
theory of multiple	intelligence	fetal alcohol spectrum	culture-fair IQ test
intelligences	quotient (IQ)	disorder	heritability

LOOKING *Back*

EPILOGUE

The topics in this chapter occupy a central place in the field of psychology, encompassing a variety of areas—including thinking, problem solving, decision making, creativity, language, memory, and intelligence. We first examined thinking and problem solving, focusing on the importance of mental images and concepts and identifying the steps commonly involved in solving problems. We discussed language, describing the components of grammar and tracing language development in children.

Finally, we considered intelligence. Some of the most heated discussions in all of psychology focus on this topic, engaging educators, policymakers, politicians, and psychologists alike. The issues include the very meaning of intelligence, its measurement, individual extremes of intelligence, and finally, the heredity/environment question.

Before proceeding, turn back to the prologue of this chapter about the patient in a vegetative state who was apparently able to respond to simple questions through brain activity. Answer the following questions in light of what you have learned about thinking, problem solving, and creativity:

1. The patient in the vegetative state responded correctly to some, but not all, of the questions he was asked. Why might he have gotten some questions wrong? Do you think it was related to the patient's inabilities, to problems with the experimental procedure, or to both? Why?

2. Why might only a minority of patients in vegetative states show brain activity that suggests they have the capability of thought?

3. Although the patient was instructed to think of "tennis" and "house" when responding to the questions, can we know for sure that he was actually thinking of those words? Why might knowing what the patient was actually thinking be important?

4. How does the research on patients in apparently vegetative states inform our understanding of what consciousness and thinking are?

5. If the ability of scientists to decode thoughts becomes more sophisticated, what are some ethical issues that might be raised?

Design Elements: Man with laptop: Dragon Images/Shutterstock; Exclamation point and mobile frame: McGraw Hill; Smartphone: WML Image/Shutterstock; Hands: Stefano Garau/Shutterstock.

VISUAL SUMMARY 7 Thinking, Language, and Intelligence

MODULE 21 Thinking

Mental images:
Representations in the mind of an object or event

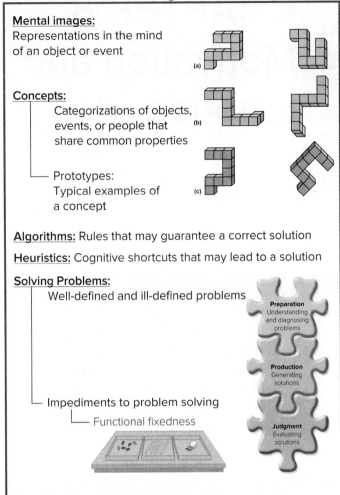

(a)

(b)

(c)

Concepts:
Categorizations of objects, events, or people that share common properties

Prototypes:
Typical examples of a concept

Algorithms: Rules that may guarantee a correct solution

Heuristics: Cognitive shortcuts that may lead to a solution

Solving Problems:
Well-defined and ill-defined problems

Impediments to problem solving
Functional fixedness

Preparation
Understanding and diagnosing problems

Production
Generating solutions

Judgment
Evaluating solutions

MODULE 22 Language

Language Development

Babbling: Speech-like sounds that are meaningless

Telegraphic speech: Sentences in which only essential words are used

Overgeneralization: The phenomenon in which children overapply a language rule, thereby making a linguistic error

Approaches to Learning Language

Learning-theory approach

Nativist approach

Interactionist approach

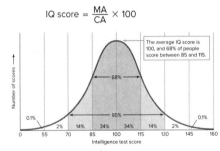

Linguistic-Relativity Hypothesis: The hypothesis that language shapes and may determine the way people perceive and understand the world

MODULE 23 Intelligence

Theories of Intelligence

g-factor: Single factor underlying mental ability

Fluid intelligence: Information-processing capabilities, reasoning, and memory

Crystallized intelligence: Accumulation of information, knowledge, and skills learned through experience and education

Gardner's multiple intelligences

Practical intelligence: Intelligence related to overall success in living

Emotional intelligence: Skills that underlie the accurate assessment, evaluation, expression, and regulation of emotions

Assessing Intelligence: Intelligence tests

Binet developed IQ tests.

- Mental age: the average age of individuals who achieve a particular level of performance on a test

- IQ: a score based on an individual's mental and chronological ages

$$\text{IQ score} = \frac{MA}{CA} \times 100$$

The average IQ score is 100, and 68% of people score between 85 and 115.

68%

95%

0.1% 2% 14% 34% 34% 14% 2% 0.1%

Number of scores

0   55   70   85   100   115   130   145   160
Intelligence test score

Contemporary IQ tests

- Wechsler Adult Intelligence Scale–IV
- Wechsler Intelligence Scale for Children–IV

Variations in Intellectual Ability

Intellectual Disability

- A disability characterized by significant limitations both in intellectual functioning and in conceptual, social, and practical adaptive skills

- Fetal alcohol spectrum disorder and familial retardation

Intellectually Gifted

- IQ scores greater than 130
- Most often outgoing, well adjusted, healthy, popular

(Module 21): (a-c): Source: Adapted from Shepard & Metzler, 1971.; (Bottom): Source: Adapted from Duncker, 1945.; (Module 22): Anna Clopet/The Image Bank Unreleased/Getty Images

wavebreakmedia/Shutterstock

CHAPTER 8
Motivation and Emotion

LEARNING OUTCOMES FOR CHAPTER 8

LO 26-1 What are emotions, and how do we experience them?

LO 26-2 What are the functions of emotions?

LO 26-3 What are the explanations for emotions?

LO 26-4 How does nonverbal behavior relate to the expression of emotions?

PROLOGUE *I AM IRONMAN*

Chris Nikic, born with the chromosomal disorder Down syndrome, didn't learn to walk until he was 4 years old. He didn't try to ride a bike until he was 15, and even then, it took him half a year just to learn to go 100 feet.

But none of that mattered anymore. He had prepared carefully, with 20-mile runs, 100-mile bike rides, and long swims in ocean water. Because Nikic was planning to swim 2.4 miles, bike 112 miles, and then run a marathon—all in less than 17 hours. If he succeeded, he would be the first person with Down syndrome to successfully complete an Ironman triathlon.

The challenges were significant. The ocean waters were particularly choppy that day, but Nikic completed his swim in under 2 hours. On his long bike ride, Nikic was plagued by bugs, coordination problems, and even a crash while racing down a hill. The marathon came close to breaking his will; halfway through, he slowed to a near crawl. But words of encouragement from his dad reminded Nikic of his goal: to finish the challenge, and in so doing, to prove to himself and everyone else that he could accomplish whatever he set his mind to. And with that, he found his pace again and continued jogging, one step after the other, literally chasing down his dream. He found it at the finish line, crossing it triumphantly at the 16-hour, 46-minute, 9-second mark.

With more than 13 minutes to spare, Nikic emerged from his triathlon a victor (Streeter, 2020; Chan, 2021).

LOOKING *Ahead*

How did Chris Nikic find the motivation to become a successful Ironman triathlete?

That's a question psychologists who study the topics of motivation and emotion would like to answer. Psychologists who study motivation seek to discover the particular desired goals—the motives—that underlie behavior. Behaviors as basic as drinking to satisfy thirst and as routine as taking a stroll to get exercise exemplify motives. Psychologists specializing in the study of motivation assume that such underlying motives steer our choices of activities.

Whereas motivation concerns the forces that direct future behavior, emotion pertains to the feelings we experience throughout our lives. The study of emotions focuses on our internal experiences at any given moment. All of us feel a variety of emotions: happiness at succeeding at a difficult task, sadness over the death of a loved one, anger at being treated unfairly. Because emotions not only play a role in motivating our behavior but also act as a reflection of our underlying motivation, they play an important role in our lives.

We begin this set of modules by focusing on the major conceptions of motivation, discussing how motives and needs jointly affect behavior. We consider motives that are biologically based and universal in the animal kingdom, such as hunger and sex, as well as motives that are unique to humans, such as the need for achievement.

We then turn to emotions. We consider the roles and functions that emotions play in people's lives and discuss several approaches that explain how people understand their emotions. Finally, we look at how nonverbal behavior communicates emotions.

Module 24
Explaining Motivation

LEARNING OUTCOME

LO 24-1 How does motivation direct and energize behavior?

motivation The factors that direct and energize the behavior of humans and other organisms. (Module 24)

instincts Inborn patterns of behavior that are biologically determined rather than learned. (Module 24)

instinct approaches to motivation Theories suggesting that motivation stems from the desire to attain external rewards, known as incentives. (Module 24)

What was the motivation behind Aron Ralston's heroic efforts to free himself from the rock that had pinned his arm to the ground?

E Pablo Kosmicki/AP Photo

In just a moment, 27-year-old Aron Ralston's life changed. An 800-pound boulder dislodged where Ralston was hiking in a narrow, isolated Utah canyon, pinning his lower arm to the ground.

For the next five days, Ralston lay trapped, unable to escape. An experienced climber who had search-and-rescue training, he had ample time to consider his options. He tried unsuccessfully to chip away at the rock, and he rigged up ropes and pulleys around the boulder in a vain effort to move it.

Finally, out of water and nearly dehydrated, Ralston reasoned there was only one option left short of dying. In acts of incredible bravery, Ralston broke two bones in his wrist, applied a tourniquet, and used a dull pen knife to amputate his arm beneath the elbow.

Freed from his entrapment, Ralston climbed out from where he had been pinned and then hiked five miles to safety (Fischer, 2018; Clark, 2022).

What factors lay behind Ralston's resolve?

To answer this question, psychologists employ the concept of **motivation,** the factors that direct and energize the behavior of humans and other organisms. Motivation has biological, cognitive, and social aspects, and the complexity of the concept has led psychologists to develop a variety of approaches. All seek to explain the energy that guides people's behavior in specific directions.

Instinct Approaches: Born to Be Motivated

When psychologists first tried to explain motivation, they turned to instincts. **Instincts** are inborn patterns of behavior that are genetically determined rather than learned. According to **instinct approaches to motivation,** people and animals are born preprogrammed with sets of behaviors essential to their survival. Those instincts provide the energy that channels behavior in appropriate directions. Hence, sexual behavior may be a response to an instinct to reproduce, and exploratory behavior may be motivated by an instinct to examine one's territory.

This instinct approach presents several difficulties, however. For one thing, psychologists do not agree on what, or even how many, primary instincts exist. One early psychologist, William McDougall (1908), suggested that there are 18 instincts. Other theorists came up with even more, and one sociologist (Bernard, 1924) claimed there are exactly 5,759 distinct instincts!

Furthermore, instinct approaches are unable to explain why certain patterns of behavior and not others have evolved in a given species. In addition, although it is clear that a great deal of animal behavior is based on instincts, much of the variety and complexity of human behavior is learned and thus cannot be seen as instinctual.

As a result of these shortcomings, newer explanations have replaced conceptions of motivation based on instincts. However, instinct approaches still play a role in certain theories, especially those based on evolutionary approaches that focus on our genetic inheritance. Furthermore, Freud's work suggests that instinctual drives of sex and aggression motivate behavior (Saracho, 2019; Davis & Panskepp, 2018).

Drive-Reduction Approaches: Satisfying Our Needs

After rejecting instinct theory, psychologists first proposed simple drive-reduction theories of motivation to take its place (Hull, 1943). **Drive-reduction approaches to motivation** suggest that a lack of some basic biological need (such as a lack of water) produces a drive to push an organism to satisfy that need (in this case, seeking water).

To understand this approach, we need to understand the concept of drive. A **drive** is motivational tension, or arousal, that energizes behavior to fulfill a need. Many basic drives, such as hunger, thirst, sleep, and sex, are related to biological needs of the body or of the species as a whole. These are called *primary drives*. Primary drives contrast with secondary drives in which behavior fulfills no obvious biological need. In *secondary drives*, prior experience and learning bring about needs. For instance, some people have strong needs to achieve academically and professionally. We can say that their achievement need is reflected in a secondary drive that motivates their behavior (Huang et al., 2017; Tellis et al., 2019; Berto et al., 2021).

We usually try to satisfy a primary drive by reducing the need underlying it. For example, we become hungry after not eating for a few hours and may raid the refrigerator, especially if the next scheduled meal is not imminent. If the weather turns cold, we put on extra clothing or raise the setting on the thermostat to keep warm. If our bodies need liquids to function properly, we experience thirst and seek out water.

drive-reduction approaches to motivation Theories suggesting that a lack of some basic biological need produces a drive to push an organism to satisfy that need. (Module 24)

drive Motivational tension, or arousal, that energizes behavior to fulfill a need. (Module 24)

HOMEOSTASIS

Homeostasis, the body's tendency to maintain a steady internal state, underlies primary drives. Using feedback loops, homeostasis brings deviations in body functioning back to an optimal state, similar to the way a thermostat and a furnace work in a home heating system to maintain a steady temperature. Receptor cells throughout the body constantly monitor factors such as temperature and nutrient levels. When deviations from the ideal state occur, the body adjusts in an effort to return to an optimal state. Many fundamental needs, including the needs for food, water, stable body temperature, and sleep, operate via homeostasis (Betley et al., 2015; Williams et al., 2019; Li & Wang, 2022).

Although drive-reduction theories provide a good explanation of how primary drives motivate behavior, they cannot fully explain a behavior in which the goal is not to reduce a drive but rather to maintain or even increase the level of excitement or arousal. For instance, some behaviors seem to be motivated by nothing more than curiosity or boredom, such as constantly checking our phones. Similarly, many people pursue thrilling activities such as riding a roller coaster or steering a raft down the rapids of a river. Such behaviors certainly don't suggest that people seek to reduce all drives, as drive-reduction approaches would indicate (Wishart et al., 2017; Crone & van Duijvenvoorde, 2021).

Both curiosity and thrill-seeking behavior, then, cast doubt on drive-reduction approaches as a complete explanation for motivation. In both cases, rather than seeking to reduce an underlying drive, people and animals appear to be motivated to increase their overall level of stimulation and activity. To explain this phenomenon, psychologists have devised an alternative: arousal approaches to motivation.

homeostasis The body's tendency to maintain a steady internal state. (Module 24)

Study Alert

To remember the concept of homeostasis, keep in mind the analogy of a thermostat that regulates the temperature in a home.

Arousal Approaches: Beyond Drive Reduction

arousal approaches to motivation
The belief that we try to maintain certain levels of stimulation and activity. (Module 24)

According to **arousal approaches to motivation,** people try to maintain a steady level of stimulation and activity. Similar to drive-reduction explanations of motivation, the arousal approach suggests that if our stimulation and activity levels become uncomfortably high, we try to reduce them. But unlike the drive-reduction perspective, the arousal approach additionally suggests that if levels of stimulation and activity are too *low*, we will try to increase them by seeking stimulation.

People vary widely in the optimal level of arousal they seek out, with some people looking for especially high levels of arousal. For example, people who participate in daredevil sports, high-stakes gamblers, and criminals who pull off high-risk robberies may be exhibiting a particularly high need for arousal (Stevens et al., 2015; Hayes & Wedell, 2019; Kruglanski et al., 2021; see Figure 1).

Incentive Approaches: Motivation's Pull

When a luscious dessert appears on the table after a filling meal, its appeal has little or nothing to do with internal drives or the maintenance of arousal. Rather, if we choose to eat the dessert, such behavior is motivated by the external stimulus of the dessert itself, which acts as an anticipated reward. This reward, in motivational terms, is an *incentive*.

incentive approaches to motivation
Theories suggesting that motivation stems from the desire to attain external rewards, known as incentives. (Module 24)

Incentive approaches to motivation suggest that motivation stems from the desire to attain rewards, known as *incentives*. In this view, the desirable properties of external stimuli–whether grades, money, affection, recognition, food, or sex–account for a person's motivation (Festinger et al., 2009; Bruni et al., 2019; Vilendrer et al., 2021).

Although the theory explains why we may succumb to an incentive (such as a mouth-watering dessert) even though we lack internal cues (such as hunger), it does not provide a complete explanation of motivation because organisms sometimes seek to fulfill needs even when incentives are not apparent. Consequently, many psychologists believe that the internal drives proposed by drive-reduction theory work in tandem with the external incentives of incentive theory to "push" and "pull" behavior, respectively. Thus, at the same time that we seek to satisfy our underlying hunger needs (the push of drive-reduction theory), we are drawn to food that appears very appetizing (the pull of incentive theory). Rather than contradicting each other, then, drives and incentives may work together in motivating behavior (Belasen & Fortunato, 2013; Goswami & Urminsky, 2017).

Cognitive Approaches: The Thoughts Behind Motivation

cognitive approaches to motivation
Theories suggesting that motivation is a result of people's thoughts, beliefs, expectations, and goals. (Module 24)

Cognitive approaches to motivation suggest that motivation is the outcome of people's thoughts, beliefs, expectations, and goals. For instance, the degree to which people are motivated to study for a test is based on their expectation of how well studying will pay off in terms of a good grade.

Cognitive theories of motivation draw a key distinction between intrinsic and extrinsic motivation. *Intrinsic motivation* causes us to participate in an activity for our own enjoyment rather than for any actual or concrete reward that it will bring us. In contrast, *extrinsic motivation* causes us to do something for money, a grade, or some other actual, concrete reward (Hofeditz et al., 2017; Maresh et al., 2019; Fishbach & Woolley, 2022).

Are You a Sensation Seeker?

How much do you crave stimulation in your everyday life? Complete the following questionnaire to find out. Circle either A or B in each pair or statements.

1. A My definition of the good life is to be at peace and comfortable in my skin.
   B My definition of the good life is to grab every experience possible.

2. A When I see an unfamiliar ride at an amusement park, I get right in line.
   B When I see a new ride, I need to watch how it works a few times before trying it.

3. A My ideal job would involve travel and a wealth of new experiences.
   B My ideal job would be to do something I like and keep getting better at it.

4. A I am a big fan of a lazy summer day, a beach or backyard, and a good book.
   B I love summer and outdoor activities such as hiking, running, and bicycling.

5. A I look forward to meeting new people and trying new things.
   B I like hanging out with my friends and doing things we know we enjoy.

6. A I think it's foolish to take unnecessary risks just for a sense of adventure.
   B I am attracted to challenges, even if they're a bit dangerous.

7. A I like movies that are funny or that I know will have a happy ending.
   B I like edgy movies that are unpredictable or explore new ideas.

8. A The best art makes you think or shakes up your old ideas and preconceptions.
   B Good art is beautiful and makes you feel serene.

9. A For vacations I prefer to go places I like and eat at restaurants I know.
   B My ideal vacation is to go somewhere new where I can try different things.

10. A If I lived in frontier days, I would head West to pursue potential opportunities.
    B If I lived in frontier days, I would stay in the East and make a good life there.

11. A The people I'm drawn to are unusual and have kind of wild ideas.
    B I like people who are like me and know who they are.

12. A I would never allow myself to be hypnotized, especially in public.
    B I would probably volunteer to be hypnotized, just to give it a try.

13. A I would love to try things like parachuting, bungee jumping, and hang gliding.
    B It makes no sense to jump out of a perfectly good airplane or off a bridge.

Scoring: Give yourself a point for each of these responses: 1B, 2A, 3A, 4B, 5A, 6B, 7B, 8A, 9B, 10A, 11A, 12B, 13A. Add up the points, and then use the following key to find your sensation-seeking score.

12–13 Very high sensation seeking
10–11 High sensation seeking
 6–9   Average sensation seeking
 4–5   Low sensation seeking
 1–3   Very low sensation seeking

Your results can give you a rough idea of your sensation-seeking tendencies. Understand that this is a short questionnaire based on the responses of a small sample of college students, giving at best an imprecise picture. Understand, too, that as people age, their sensation scores tend to become lower.

FIGURE 1 Some people seek high levels of arousal, whereas others are more easygoing. You can get a sense of your own preferred level of stimulation by completing this questionnaire.
Source: Adapted from Zuckerman, 1978.

For example, when a physician works long hours because she loves medicine, intrinsic motivation is prompting her; if she works hard to make a lot of money, extrinsic motivation underlies her efforts. Similarly, if we study a lot because we love the subject matter, we are being guided by intrinsic motivation. On the other hand, if all we care about is the grade we get in the course, that studying is due to extrinsic motivation (Emmett & McGee, 2013; Good et al., 2022).

We are more apt to persevere, work harder, and produce work of higher quality when motivation for a task is intrinsic rather than extrinsic. In fact, in some cases, providing rewards for desirable behavior (thereby increasing extrinsic motivation) actually may decrease intrinsic motivation (Nishimura et al., 2011; Bolkan, 2015).

From the perspective of...

An Educator Do you think that giving students grades serves as an external reward that may decrease intrinsic motivation for learning about the subject matter? Why or why not?

Andersen Ross/Blend Images/Getty Images

Another example of cognitive approaches comes from research on workplace motivation and particularly on perceptions of workplace stressors. That is, employees perceive some stressors as hindrances and others as challenges, and these perceptions affect motivation. *Hindrance stressors* are those that employees see as outside their control and, thus, as barriers to good performance–for example, when they lack sufficient resources to get a job done. Hindrance stressors are particularly demotivating because no matter how hard people work, they can't succeed. In contrast, *challenge stressors* are those that employees see as something they can overcome, such as learning a new skill that can get the job done more effectively. Challenge stressors motivate employees to work harder (Mazzola & Disselhorst, 2019; LePine, 2022).

During the COVID-19 pandemic, employees tended to perceive stressors more as hindrances than challenges. Many felt that no matter what they did, they couldn't meet the challenges they faced. For instance, many health workers could not get sufficient protective gear during the early part of the pandemic, and they not only felt anxiety that they might become infected with COVID, but they also felt frustrated and unappreciated. In light of these challenges, many found it hard to maintain a positive outlook regarding their work (Sinclair et al., 2020; Pappas, 2021).

Maslow's Hierarchy: Ordering Motivational Needs

What do Eleanor Roosevelt, Abraham Lincoln, and Albert Einstein have in common? The common thread, according to a model of motivation devised by psychologist Abraham Maslow, is that each of them fulfilled the highest levels of motivational needs underlying human behavior.

Maslow's model places motivational needs in a hierarchy and suggests that before more sophisticated, higher-order needs can be met, certain primary needs must be satisfied (Maslow, 1987). A pyramid can represent the model, with the more basic needs at the bottom and the higher-level needs at the top (see Figure 2). To activate a specific higher-order need, thereby guiding behavior, a person must first fulfill the more basic needs in the hierarchy.

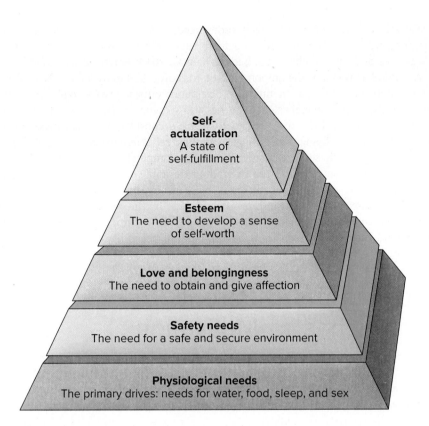

FIGURE 2 Maslow's hierarchy shows how our motivation progresses up the pyramid from the broadest, most fundamental biological needs to higher-order ones. Do you agree that lower-order needs must be satisfied before higher-order needs? Do hermits and monks who attempt to fulfill spiritual needs while denying basic physical needs contradict Maslow's hierarchy?

Source: Adapted from Maslow, 1970.

The basic needs are primary drives: needs for water, food, sleep, sex, and the like. To move up the hierarchy, a person must first meet these basic physiological needs. Safety needs come next in the hierarchy; Maslow suggests that along with basic physiological needs, people need a safe, secure environment in order to function effectively. Physiological and safety needs compose the lower-order needs.

Only after they are secure in the basic two sets of lower-order needs can a person consider fulfilling higher-order needs, such as the needs for love and a sense of belonging, esteem, and self-actualization. Love and belongingness needs include the needs to obtain and give affection and to be a contributing member of some group or society. After fulfilling all the previous levels of needs, a person strives for esteem. Esteem is the recognition that others value your competence and worth, and that they admire you for your qualities.

After these four sets of needs (physiological needs, safety needs, love and belongingness, and esteem) are fulfilled—no easy task—a person is able to strive for the highest-level need, self-actualization. **Self-actualization** is a state of self-fulfillment in which people realize their highest potentials in their own unique way. Although Maslow first suggested that self-actualization occurred in only a few famous individuals, he later expanded the concept to encompass everyday people. For example, a parent with excellent nurturing skills who raises a family, a teacher who year after year creates an environment that maximizes students' opportunities for success, and an artist who realizes their creative potential all may be self-actualized. The important thing is that people feel at ease with themselves and satisfied that they are using their talents to the fullest. In a sense, achieving self-actualization reduces the striving and yearning for greater fulfillment that mark most people's lives and instead provides a sense of satisfaction with their current state of affairs (Ivtzan et al., 2013; Winston et al., 2017; Fabian, 2020).

Although research has been unable to validate the specific ordering of Maslow's stages and it is difficult to measure self-actualization objectively, Maslow's hierarchy of needs is important for two reasons: First, it highlights the complexity of human needs, and it emphasizes the idea that until more basic biological needs are met, people will

self-actualization A state of self-fulfillment in which people realize their highest potential in their own unique way. (Modules 24, 32)

be relatively unconcerned with higher-order needs. For example, if people are hungry, their first interest will be in obtaining food; they will not be concerned with needs such as love and self-esteem (LaLumiere & Kalivas, 2013; Beitel et al., 2015).

A second reason for the importance of Maslow's hierarchy of needs is that not only has it been influential in multiple disciplines outside psychology (among them business, nursing, and several sciences), it has also spawned other theories of motivation. For example, Edward Deci and Richard Ryan have considered human needs in terms of psychological well-being. They suggest in their *self-determination theory* that people have the need for these three basic states: (1) competence, (2) autonomy, and (3) relatedness. Competence is the need to produce desirable outcomes, whereas autonomy is the need to feel control over our own lives. Finally, relatedness is the need to be involved in close, warm relationships with others. In the view of self-determination theory, these three psychological needs are genetically determined and universal across cultures, and they are as essential as basic biological needs (Ryan & Deci, 2017; Bridgman et al., 2019; Howard et al., 2021).

Study Alert

Review the distinctions among the different explanations for motivation (instinct, drive reduction, arousal, incentive, cognitive, and Maslow's hierarchy of needs).

Applying the Different Approaches to Motivation

The various theories of motivation (summarized in Figure 3) give several perspectives on it. Which provides the fullest account of motivation? Actually, many of the approaches are complementary rather than contradictory. In fact, employing more than one approach can help us understand motivation in a particular instance.

Instinct	**Drive reduction**	**Arousal**	**Incentive**	**Cognitive**	**Hierarchy of needs**
People and animals are born with preprogrammed sets of behaviors essential to their survival.	When some basic biological requirement is lacking, a drive is produced.	People seek an optimal level of stimulation. If the level of stimulation is too high, they act to reduce it; if it is too low, they act to increase it.	External rewards direct and energize behavior.	Thoughts, beliefs, expectations, and goals direct motivation.	Needs form a hierarchy; before higher-order needs are met, lower-order needs must be fulfilled.

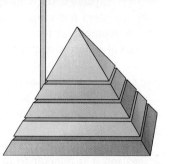

FIGURE 3 The major approaches to motivation.

(Top, Left): Kawee Srital-on/123rf; (Top, Middle): Digital Vision/Getty Images; (Top, Right): wavebreakmedia/Shutterstock; (Bottom, Left): Fabián Ponce/Alamy Stock Photo; (Bottom, Middle): Corbis/VCG/Getty Images

Consider, for example, Aron Ralston's hiking accident, when his arm was pinned under a huge boulder (described at the beginning of this module). His interest in climbing in an isolated and potentially dangerous area may be explained by arousal approaches to motivation. From the perspective of instinct approaches, we realize that Ralston had an overwhelming instinct to preserve his life at all costs. From a cognitive perspective, we see his careful consideration of various strategies to extricate himself from the boulder.

In short, applying multiple approaches to motivation in a given situation provides a broader understanding than we might obtain by employing only a single approach. We'll see this again when we consider specific motives—such as the needs for food, achievement, affiliation, and power—and draw on several of the theories for the fullest account of what motivates our behavior.

RECAP/EVALUATE/RETHINK

RECAP

LO 24-1 How does motivation direct and energize behavior?

- Motivation relates to the factors that direct and energize behavior.
- Drive is the motivational tension that energizes behavior to fulfill a need.
- Homeostasis, the maintenance of a steady internal state, often underlies motivational drives.
- Arousal approaches suggest that we try to maintain a particular level of stimulation and activity.
- Incentive approaches focus on the positive aspects of the environment that direct and energize behavior.
- Cognitive approaches focus on the role of thoughts, expectations, and understanding of the world in producing motivation.
- Maslow's hierarchy suggests that there are five basic needs: physiological, safety, love and belongingness, esteem, and self-actualization. Only after the more basic needs are fulfilled can a person move toward meeting higher-order needs.

EVALUATE

1. _____ are forces that guide a person's behavior in a certain direction.
2. Biologically determined, inborn patterns of behavior are known as _____.
3. Your psychology professor tells you, "Explaining behavior is easy! When we lack something, we are motivated to get it." Which approach to motivation does your professor subscribe to?
4. By drinking water after running a marathon, a runner tries to keep their body at an optimal level of functioning. This process is called _____.
5. I helped my neighbor pull weeds in their yard because doing a good deed makes me feel good. What type of motivation is at work here? What type of motivation would be at work if I were to help my neighbor pull weeds because they paid me $20?
6. According to Maslow, a person with no job, no home, and no friends can become self-actualized. True or false?

RETHINK

1. Which approaches to motivation are more commonly used in the workplace? How might each approach be used to design employment policies that can sustain or increase motivation?
2. A writer who works all day composing copy for an advertising firm has a hard time keeping her mind on her work and continually watches the clock. After work, she turns to a collection of stories she is creating and writes long into the night, completely forgetful of the clock. What ideas from your reading on motivation help to explain this phenomenon?

Answers to Evaluate Questions

1. Motives; 2. instincts; 3. drive reduction; 4. homeostasis; 5. intrinsic; extrinsic; 6. False; lower-order needs must be fulfilled before self-actualization can occur.

KEY TERMS

motivation	drive-reduction approaches to motivation	arousal approaches to motivation	cognitive approaches to motivation
instincts	drive	incentive approaches to motivation	self-actualization
instinct approaches to motivation	homeostasis		

Module 25
Human Needs and Motivation: Eat, Drink, and Be Daring

LEARNING OUTCOMES

LO 25-1 What biological and social factors underlie hunger?

LO 25-2 What are the varieties of sexual behavior?

LO 25-3 How are needs relating to achievement, affiliation, and power motivation exhibited?

For writer Susan Burton, eating was a way to cope with pain or deal with emotional needs that weren't being met. It was about feeling pulled to her kitchen, to opening up the freezer and biting into a cookie, possibly chipping her tooth, but not caring. It was eating granola with chips, string cheese, whatever she could find, eating until she felt uncomfortably sick. It was about afterwards feeling deep distress and self-loathing, about feeling out of control (Burton, 2020; Gross, 2020).

Burton was one of the estimated 28 million people in the United States who suffer from eating disorders at some time in their lives. These disorders, which usually appear during adolescence, can bring about extraordinary changes in weight and other forms of physical deterioration. Extremely dangerous, they sometimes result in death (National Association of Anorexia Nervosa and Associated Disorders, 2021).

Why are some people subject to such disordered eating? Why do some focus on avoiding weight gain at all costs, while others engage in extreme overeating, which can lead to obesity?

To answer these questions, we must consider some of the specific needs that underlie behavior. In this module, we examine several of the most important human needs. We begin with hunger and sex, the primary drives that have received the most attention from researchers. We then turn to secondary drives: those uniquely human endeavors based on learned needs and past experience that help explain why people strive to achieve, to affiliate with others, and to seek power over others.

The Motivation Behind Hunger and Eating

obesity Body weight that is more than 20% above the average weight for a person of a particular height. (Module 25)

More than 40% of adults and 19% of children in the United States suffer from **obesity,** body weight that is more than 20% above the average weight for a person of a particular height. Many others are considered *overweight*, above average weight that doesn't reach the threshold for obesity (Hales et al., 2017, 2020; National Center for Health Statistics, 2021).

And the rest of the world is not far behind: A billion people around the globe are overweight or obese. With average weight rising in most countries, the World Health Organization has said that worldwide obesity has reached epidemic proportions, producing increases in heart disease, diabetes, cancer, and premature deaths. Obesity rates have doubled in 73 countries, and that has led to 4 million premature deaths (Datar, 2017; Jacobs & Richtel, 2017; McConkey et al., 2019).

The most widely used measure of obesity is *body mass index (BMI)*, which is based on a ratio of weight to height. People with a BMI greater than 30 are considered obese, whereas those with a BMI between 25 and 30 are overweight. (Use the formulas in Figure 1 to determine your own BMI.)

Although the definition of obesity is clear from a scientific point of view, people's perceptions of what an ideal body looks like vary significantly across different cultures and within Western cultures from one time period to another. For instance, many contemporary Western cultures stress the importance of slimness in women–a

FIGURE 1 Use this process to find your body mass index.

To calculate your body mass index, follow these steps:

1. Indicate your weight in pounds: _____ pounds

2. Indicate your height in inches: _____ inches

3. Divide your weight (item 1) by your height (item 2), and write the outcome here: _____ .

4. Divide the result above (item 3) by your height (item 2), and write the outcome here: _____ .

5. Multiply the number above by 703, and write the product here: _____ . This is your body mass index.

Example:

For a person who weights 210 pounds and who is 6 feet tall, divide 210 pounds by 72 inches, which equals 2.917. Then divide 2.917 by 72 inches (item 3), which yields .041. Multiplying .041 (from item 4) by 703 yields a BMI of 28.5.

Interpretation:
• Underweight = less than 18.5
• Normal weight = 18.5–24.9
• Overweight = 25–29.9
• Obesity = BMI of 30 or greater

Keep in mind that a BMI greater than 25 may or may not be due to excess body fat. For example, professional athletes may have little fat but weigh more than the average person because they have greater muscle mass.

relatively recent view. In 19th-century Hawaii, the most attractive women were those who were the heaviest. Furthermore, for most of the 20th century–except for periods in the 1920s and the most recent decades–the ideal female figure was relatively full. Even today, weight standards differ among different cultural groups. For instance, in some traditional Arab cultures, obese women are so prized as wives that parents force-feed their female children to make them more desirable (Franko & Roehrig, 2011; Lin et al., 2015).

Regardless of cultural standards for appearance and weight, no one doubts that being overweight represents a major health risk. However, controlling weight is complicated because eating behavior involves a variety of mechanisms. In our discussion of what motivates people to eat, we'll start with the biological aspects of eating.

BIOLOGICAL FACTORS IN THE REGULATION OF HUNGER

In contrast to human beings, other species are unlikely to become obese. Internal mechanisms regulate not only the quantity of food they take in but also the kind of food they desire. For example, rats that have been deprived of particular foods seek out alternatives that contain the specific nutrients their diet is lacking, and many species, given the choice of a wide variety of foods, select a well-balanced diet (Woods et al., 2000; Jones & Corp, 2003; Adler, 2013).

Complex biological mechanisms tell organisms whether they require food or should stop eating. It's not just a matter of an empty stomach causing hunger pangs and a full one alleviating those pangs. (Even individuals who have had their stomachs removed still experience the sensation of hunger.) One important factor is changes in the chemical composition of the blood. For instance, changes in levels of *glucose*, a kind of sugar, regulate feelings of hunger. In addition, the hormone *insulin* leads the body to store excess sugar in the blood as fats and carbohydrates. Finally, the hormone *ghrelin* communicates to the brain feelings of hunger. The production of ghrelin increases according to meal schedules as well as the sight or smell of food, producing the feeling that tells us we're hungry and should eat (Langlois et al., 2011; Massadi et al., 2017; Malhotra & Levitsky, 2021).

The brain's *hypothalamus* monitors glucose levels. Increasing evidence suggests that the hypothalamus carries the primary responsibility for monitoring food intake. Injury to the hypothalamus has radical consequences for eating behavior, depending on the site of the injury. For example, rats whose *lateral hypothalamus* is damaged may literally starve to death. They refuse food when it is offered; unless they are force-fed, they eventually die. On the other hand, rats with an injury to the *ventromedial hypothalamus* display the opposite problem: extreme overeating. Rats with this injury may increase in weight by as much as 400%. Similar phenomena occur in humans who have tumors on the hypothalamus (Nakhate et al., 2019; Arrigoni et al., 2019; Lebedev et al., 2021).

Although the important role the hypothalamus plays in regulating food intake is clear, the exact way this organ operates is still unclear. One hypothesis suggests that injury to the hypothalamus affects the weight set point. The **weight set point** is a particular level of weight that the body strives to maintain. Acting as a kind of internal weight thermostat, the hypothalamus regulates food intake by calling for either greater or lesser food intake (Cornier, 2011; Alboni et al., 2017).

In most cases, the hypothalamus does a good job. Even people who are not deliberately monitoring their weight show only minor weight fluctuations in spite of substantial day-to-day variations in how much they eat and exercise. However, injury to the hypothalamus can alter the weight set point, and a person then struggles to meet the internal goal by increasing or decreasing food consumption. Even temporary exposure to certain drugs can alter the weight set point (Sternson et al., 2013; Palmiter, 2015; Kalra et al., 2022).

Genetic factors determine the weight set point, at least in part. People seem destined, through heredity, to have a particular **metabolism,** the rate at which food is converted to energy and expended by the body. People with a high metabolic rate can eat virtually as much as they want without gaining weight, whereas others with low metabolism may eat literally half as much yet gain weight readily (Westerterp, 2006; Krause et al., 2019).

Although metabolism was previously thought of as remaining relatively constant throughout the life span, new research has found four distinct stages: birth to age 1, when metabolism is at its fastest; age 1 to 20, when metabolism decreases by 3% a year; age 20 to 60, in which metabolism holds relatively steady; and finally, after age 60, when it slowly declines, losing 0.7% a year. The changes in metabolism suggest that eating requirements change as we age (Pontzer et al., 2021; Rhoads & Anderson, 2021).

weight set point The particular level of weight that the body strives to maintain. (Module 25)

metabolism The rate at which food is converted to energy and expended by the body. (Module 25)

SOCIAL FACTORS IN EATING

Study Alert

A key point: Eating and hunger are influenced both by biological and social factors.

You've just finished a full meal and feel completely stuffed. Suddenly your hosts announce with great fanfare that they will be serving their "house specialty" dessert, bananas flambé, and that they have spent the better part of the afternoon preparing it. Even though you are full and don't even like bananas, you accept a serving of dessert and eat it all.

Clearly, internal biological factors do not fully explain our eating behavior. External social factors, based on societal rules and on what we have learned about appropriate eating behavior, also play an important role. Take, for example, the simple fact that people customarily eat breakfast, lunch, and dinner at approximately the same times every day. Because we tend to eat on schedule every day, we feel hungry as the usual hour approaches, sometimes quite independently of what our internal cues are telling us.

Similarly, we put roughly the same amount of food on our plates every day, even though the amount of exercise we may have had (and consequently our need for energy replenishment) varies from day to day. We also tend to prefer particular foods over others. Rats and dogs may be a delicacy in some Asian cultures, but few people in North American cultures find them appealing despite their potentially high nutritional value. Even the amount of food we eat varies according to cultural norms. For instance, people in the United States eat bigger portions than do people in France. In sum, cultural influences and our individual habits play important roles in determining when, what, and how much we eat (Leeman et al., 2011; Gu et al., 2017; Lincoln & Nguyen, 2022).

Other social factors affect our eating behavior as well. Some of us head toward the refrigerator after a difficult day, seeking solace in a pint of Heath Bar Crunch ice cream. Why? Perhaps when we were children, our parents gave us food when we were upset. Eventually, we may have learned through the basic mechanisms of classical and operant conditioning to associate food with comfort and consolation. Similarly, we may learn that eating, which focuses our attention on immediate pleasures, provides an escape from unpleasant thoughts. Consequently, we may eat when we feel distressed (Tsenkova et al., 2013; Higgs, 2015; Lee et al., 2019).

Finally, eating behavior, as well as obesity, are related to systemic racism. Black people, Indigenous people, and other people of color have higher rates of obesity than other groups in the United States, and several factors can account for this. First, facing chronic stress due to racism may lead to obesity, and people of color who are overweight likely also have difficulty getting adequate treatment. Moreover, they may live in poorer urban areas without grocery stores that provide affordable, healthy, and nutritious options, thereby perpetuating poor eating habits and obesity (Aaron & Stanford, 2021; Mackey et al., 2022).

THE ROOTS OF OBESITY

Given that biological as well as social factors influence eating behavior, determining the causes of obesity has proved to be a challenging task. Researchers have followed several paths.

Some psychologists suggest that oversensitivity to external eating cues based on social factors, coupled with insensitivity to internal hunger cues, produce obesity. Others argue that overweight people have higher weight set points than other people do. Because their set points are unusually high, their attempts to lose weight by eating less may make them especially sensitive to external, food-related cues and therefore more apt to overeat and perpetuate their obesity (Kanoski et al., 2011; Müller et al., 2018).

But why may some people's weight set points be higher than those of others? One explanation is genetics: Some people have a clear genetic risk of obesity, and multiple genes appear to be involved (Khera et al., 2019; Bouchard, 2021).

Furthermore, obese individuals have higher levels of the hormone *leptin*, which appears to be designed, from an evolutionary standpoint, to "protect" the body against weight loss. The body's weight-regulation system thus appears to be designed more to protect against losing weight than to protect against gaining it. Therefore, it's easier to gain weight than to lose it (Pontzer, 2017; Clawson et al., 2019; Suriagandhi & Nachiappan, 2022).

Another biologically based explanation for obesity relates to fat cells in the body. Starting at birth, the body stores fat either by increasing the number of fat cells or by increasing the size of existing fat cells. Furthermore, any loss of weight past infancy does not decrease the number of fat cells; it only affects their size. Consequently, people are stuck with the number of fat cells they inherit from an early age, and the rate of weight gain during the first 4 months of life is related to being overweight during later childhood (Moore et al., 2017).

According to the *weight-set-point hypothesis*, the presence of too many fat cells from earlier weight gain may result in the set point's becoming "stuck" at a higher level than desirable. In such circumstances, losing weight becomes a difficult proposition

Although obesity is reaching epidemic proportions in the United States, its exact causes remain unclear.
Anirut Thailand/Shutterstock

because one is constantly at odds with one's own internal set point when dieting (Müller et al., 2010).

Not everyone agrees with the set-point explanation for obesity. For example, it's hard to see how the set-point explanation could explain the rapid rise in obesity that has occurred over the last several decades in the United States. Why would so many people's weight set points simultaneously increase?

Consequently, some researchers argue that the body does not try to maintain a fixed weight set point. Instead, they suggest, the body has a *settling point*, determined by a combination of our genetic heritage and the nature of the environment in which we live. If high-fat foods are prevalent in our environment and we are genetically predisposed to obesity, we settle into an equilibrium that maintains relatively high weight. In contrast, if our environment is nutritionally healthier, a genetic predisposition to obesity will not be triggered, and we will settle into an equilibrium in which our weight is lower (Sullivan et al., 2011).

EATING DISORDERS

anorexia nervosa A severe eating disorder in which people may refuse to eat while denying that their behavior and appearance—which can become skeleton-like—are unusual. (Module 25)

Eating disorders are among the most frequent causes of disability in young women, and they also occur in young men. One devastating weight-related disorder is **anorexia nervosa.** In this severe eating disorder, people may refuse to eat while denying that their behavior and appearance—which can become skeleton-like—are unusual. Some 10% of people with anorexia literally starve themselves to death (Arcelus et al., 2011; Newton, 2019).

Anorexia nervosa most often afflicts females between the ages of 12 and 40, although both men and women of any age may develop it. While the disorder has sometimes been thought of as particularly affecting women who are successful, attractive, and affluent, we now know that it afflicts those at all socioeconomic levels. The disorder often begins after serious dieting, which somehow gets out of control. Life begins to revolve around food: Although people with the disorder eat little, they may cook for others, go shopping for food frequently, or collect cookbooks (Jacobs et al., 2009; Canady, 2019).

bulimia A disorder in which a person binges on large quantities of food, followed by efforts to purge the food through vomiting or other means. (Module 25)

A related problem, **bulimia,** is a disorder in which people binge on large quantities of food. For instance, they may consume an entire gallon of ice cream and a whole pie in a single sitting. After such a binge, sufferers feel guilt and depression and often induce vomiting or take laxatives to rid themselves of the food–behavior known as purging. Constant bingeing-and-purging cycles and the use of drugs to induce vomiting or diarrhea can lead to heart failure. Often, though, the weight of a person with bulimia remains normal (Lampard et al., 2011; Herle & Kahn, 2020).

Eating disorders represent a significant problem: 8.4% of women and 2.2% of men will experience an eating disorder during their lifetime. Furthermore, the incidence of eating disorders grew throughout the world as a result of anxiety due to the COVID-19 pandemic (Douglas et al., 2019; Galmiche et al., 2019; Termorshuizen et al., 2020).

What are the causes of anorexia nervosa and bulimia? Some researchers suspect a biological cause such as a chemical imbalance in the hypothalamus or pituitary gland, perhaps brought on by genetic factors. Furthermore, brain scans of people with eating disorders show that they process information about food differently from healthy individuals (Weir, 2016; de Abreu & Filho, 2017; Murray et al., 2022).

In addition, eating disorders also may have genetic roots; both anorexia and bulemia are highly heritable. For example, people with anorexia nervosa are genetically driven to high levels of physical activity. They are also likely to have other conditions with genetic roots, including depression and anxiety (Huckins et al., 2018; Bulik et al., 2019).

Others believe that the cause has roots in society's valuation of slenderness and the parallel notion that being overweight is undesirable, a social norm that is reinforced through photos and videos on social media such as Instagram and TikTok. In fact, TikTok in particular seems to use algorithms that can inundate teenage users with weight-loss videos even after only a few days of joining the platform (Hobbs et al., 2022).

As a result of exposure to social media, people can become preoccupied with their weight and take to heart the cliché that one can never be too thin. This may explain why eating disorders increase as countries become more developed and Westernized and dieting becomes more popular. Finally, some psychologists suggest that the disorders result from overly demanding parents or other family problems (Milos et al., 2017; Saul et al., 2022).

Complete explanations for anorexia nervosa and bulimia remain elusive. These disorders most likely stem from both biological and social causes, and successful treatment probably encompasses several strategies, including therapy and dietary changes (Cooper & Shafran, 2008; Murray et al., 2019).

If you or a family member needs advice or help with an eating problem, contact the National Eating Disorders Association at www.nationaleatingdisorders.org or call (800) 931-2237. You can get more information at https://medlineplus.gov/eatingdisorders.html.

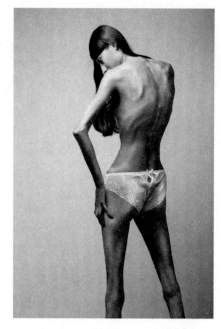

Despite looking skeleton-like to others, people with the eating disorder anorexia nervosa see themselves as overweight.

Denis Putilov/Alamy Stock Photo

BECOMING AN INFORMED CONSUMER
of Psychology

Dieting and Losing Weight Successfully

Although 60% of the people in the United States say they want to lose weight, it's a losing battle for most of them. Most people who diet eventually regain the weight they lost, so they try again and get caught in a seemingly endless cycle of weight loss and gain.

To increase the chances of successfully losing weight, aim to keep several things in mind (Varkevisser et al., 2019; Gholizadeh et al., 2022):

- *Understand that weight control is not easy.* You will have to make permanent changes in your life to lose weight without gaining it back. The most obvious strategy—cutting down on the amount of food you eat—is just the first step toward a lifetime commitment to changing your eating habits.
- *Develop a plan of action.* Set specific goals and develop realistic means of achieving them.

- *Set reasonable goals.* Know how much weight you want to lose before you start to diet. Don't expect to lose too much weight too quickly, or you may doom yourself to failure. Even small changes in behavior—such as walking 15 minutes a day or eating a few less bites at each meal—can lead to weight loss (Spreckley et al., 2021; Spring et al., 2021).
- *Keep track of what you eat and what you weigh.* Unless you keep careful records, you won't really know how much you are eating and whether any diet is working.
- *Eat "big" foods.* Eat fiber and foods that are bulky and heavy but low in calories, such as grapes and soup. Such foods trick your body into thinking you've eaten more and thus decrease hunger.
- *Cut down on screen time.* One reason for the epidemic of obesity is the number of hours people in the United States spend viewing entertainment on their devices. Not only does screen time preclude other activities that burn calories (even walking around the house is helpful), it is also associated with gorging on junk food (Robinson et al., 2017; Nagata et al., 2021).
- *Exercise.* Exercise at least 30 consecutive minutes three times each week. When you exercise, you use up fat stored in your body as fuel for muscles, which is measured in calories. As you use up this fat, you will probably lose weight. Almost any activity helps burn calories.
- *Decrease the influence of external social stimuli on your eating behavior.* Serve yourself smaller portions of food, and leave the table before you see what is being served for dessert. Don't even buy snack foods such as nachos and potato chips; if they're not readily available in the kitchen cupboard, you're not apt to eat them. Wrap refrigerated foods in aluminum foil so that you cannot see the contents and be tempted every time you open the refrigerator.
- *Avoid fad diets and diet pills.* No matter how popular they are at a particular time, extreme diets, including liquid diets, usually don't work in the long run and can be dangerous to your health.
- *Join a support group.* Being part of a group that is working together to lose weight will encourage you to keep to your diet.

Sexual Motivation

Anyone who has seen two dogs mating knows that sexual behavior has a biological basis. Their sexual behavior appears to occur naturally without much prompting on the part of others. A number of genetically controlled factors influence the sexual behavior of nonhuman animals. For instance, animal behavior is affected by the presence of certain hormones in the blood. Moreover, female animals are receptive to sexual advances only during certain relatively limited periods of the year.

Human sexual behavior, by comparison, is more complicated, although the underlying biology is not all that different from that of related species. In males, for example, the *testes* begin to secrete **androgens,** male sex hormones, at puberty. (See Figure 2 for the basic anatomy of the male and female **genitals,** or sex organs.) Not only do androgens produce secondary sex characteristics, such as the growth of body hair and a deepening of the voice, but they also increase the sex drive. Because the level of androgen production by the testes is fairly constant, men are capable of (and interested in) sexual activities without any regard to biological cycles. Given the proper stimuli leading to arousal, male sexual behavior can occur at any time.

Females show a different pattern. When they reach maturity at puberty, the two *ovaries* begin to produce **estrogens,** female sex hormones. However, those hormones are not produced consistently; instead, their production follows a cyclical pattern. The greatest output occurs during **ovulation,** when an egg is released from the ovaries, making the chances of fertilization by a sperm cell highest. Whereas in nonhumans

androgens Male sex hormones secreted by the testes. (Module 25)

genitals The male and female sex organs. (Module 25)

estrogens Class of female sex hormones. (Module 25)

ovulation The point at which an egg is released from the ovaries. (Module 25)

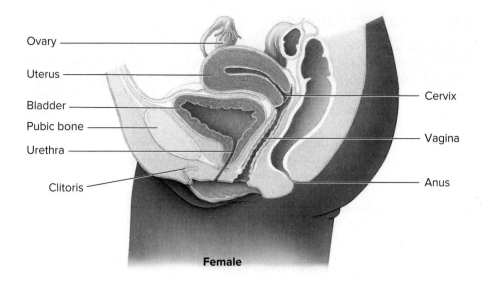

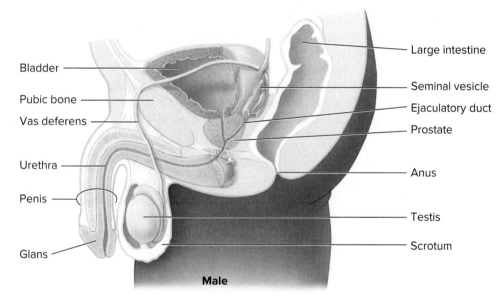

FIGURE 2 Cutaway side views of the female and male sex organs.

the period around ovulation is the only time the female is receptive to sex, people are different. Although there are variations in reported sex drive, women are receptive to sex throughout their cycles (Leiblum & Chivers, 2007; Meston & Stanton, 2019; Laan et al., 2021).

In addition, some evidence suggests that males have a stronger sex drive than females do. For instance, men think about sex more than women do. Specifically, whereas 54% of men report thinking about sex every day, only 19% of women report thinking about it on a daily basis (Baumeister & Stillman, 2006; Carvalho & Nobre, 2011).

Though biological factors "prime" people for sex, it takes more than hormones to motivate and produce sexual behavior. In animals, the presence of a partner who provides arousing stimuli leads to sexual activity. Humans are considerably more versatile; not only other people but nearly any object, sight, smell, sound, or other stimulus can lead to sexual excitement. Because of prior associations, then, people may be turned on sexually by the smell of perfume or the sound of a favorite song hummed softly in their ears. The reaction to a specific, potentially arousing stimulus, as we shall see, is highly individual; what turns one person on may do just the opposite for another (Schäfer et al., 2019; Crosby et al., 2021; Skorska et al., 2022).

MASTURBATION: SOLITARY SEX

masturbation Sexual self-stimulation. (Module 25)

Masturbation, stimulation of one's own genitals with the hand or an object such as a pillow or vibrator, is one of the most frequently practiced sexual activities. Almost all males and the great majority of females masturbate by the time they reach college age; the frequency ranges from "never" to "several times a day." Moreover, the frequency of masturbation increased during the COVID-19 pandemic (Lehmiller et al., 2021; Huang et al., 2022).

Men typically begin to masturbate for the first time at an earlier age than women, and throughout their life spans, men masturbate more often than women do, although frequency varies with age. Male masturbation is most common in the early teens and then declines; females both begin and reach a maximum frequency later (Cooper & Klein, 2018; Barett & Burgess, 2020).

Although masturbation is often considered an activity to engage in only if no other sexual outlets are available, this view bears little relationship to reality. Close to three-fourths of married men age 20 to 40 report masturbating an average of 24 times a year, and 68% of the married women in the same age group masturbate an average of 10 times a year (Das, 2007; Regnerus et al., 2017).

Despite the high incidence of masturbation, attitudes toward it still reflect some of the negative views of yesteryear. For instance, one survey found that around 10% of people who masturbated experienced feelings of guilt. However, most experts on sex view masturbation as a healthy and legitimate–and harmless–sexual activity. In addition, masturbation is seen as providing a means of learning about one's own sexuality and a way of discovering changes in one's body such as the emergence of precancerous lumps (Meiller & Hargons, 2019; Cervilla et al., 2021).

HETEROSEXUALITY

heterosexuality Sexual attraction and behavior directed to the other sex. (Module 25)

For heterosexuals, engaging in sexual intercourse often is perceived as achieving one of life's major milestones. However, **heterosexuality,** sexual attraction and behavior directed to the other sex, consists of far more than male-female intercourse. Kissing, petting, caressing, massaging, and other forms of sex play are all components of heterosexual behavior. Still, sex researchers' focus has been on the act of intercourse, especially in terms of its first occurrence and its frequency.

SEX OUTSIDE OF MARRIAGE

double standard The view that premarital sex is permissible for males but not for females. (Module 25)

Before the 21st century, sexual intercourse outside of heterosexual marriage, at least for women, was considered one of the major taboos in our society. Traditionally, women were warned by society that "nice girls don't do it"; at the same time, men were told that sex outside of marriage was okay for them, but they should marry virgins. This attitude is the basis for what has been called the **double standard**, the view that sex outside of marriage is permissible for males but not for females (Lyons et al., 2011; Penhollow et al., 2017; Guo, 2019).

In fact, 40 years ago, the majority of adult Americans believed that sex outside of marriage was always wrong. But public opinion has shifted dramatically since then, and most people in the United States believe that sex outside of marriage is acceptable. In fact, as you can see in Figure 3, most American adults believe that it is acceptable to live with a partner even if the couple doesn't plan to marry (Horowitz et al., 2019; Manning, 2020).

Actual rates of sexual activity outside marriage have matched changes in attitude. For instance, more than one-half of women between the ages of 15 and 19 have had sexual intercourse before they marry. These figures are close to double the number of women in the same age range who reported having intercourse in 1970. Clearly, the trend over the past 50 years has been toward more women engaging in sexual activity outside marriage (Sprecher et al., 2013; Elias et al., 2015).

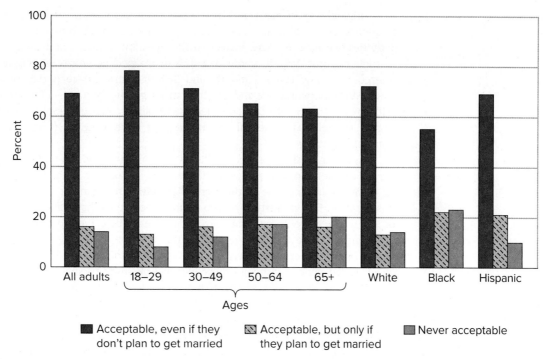

FIGURE 3 Attitudes toward sex outside marriage. About 70% of American adults believe that living together even without plans to marry is acceptable.
Source: Horowitz et al., 2019.

Males, too, have shown an increase in the incidence of incidence of sexual intercourse outside of marriage, although the increase has not been as dramatic as it has been for females–probably because the rates for males were higher to begin with. For instance, the first surveys of premarital intercourse carried out in the 1940s showed an incidence of 84% across males of all ages; recent figures are closer to 95%. Moreover, the average age of males' first sexual experience has been declining steadily. Almost half of males have had sexual intercourse by the age of 18; by the time they reach age 20, 88% have had intercourse. Overall, 70% of all teens have had intercourse by their 19th birthday (Guttmacher Institute, 2012; Lindberg et al., 2019).

What may be most interesting about the patterns of sex outside marriage is that they show a convergence of male and female attitudes and behavior when compared to prior generations. Today, younger individuals, regardless of gender, generally hold more lenient views of sex than in prior generations. Still, the double standard has not disappeared completely: where differing standards remain, the attitudes are typically more lenient toward the male than toward the female (Sprecher & Hatfield, 1996; Thompson et al., 2018).

Furthermore, substantial cultural differences exist regarding the incidence and acceptability of premarital intercourse. For instance, the proportions of male teenagers who have intercourse before their 17th birthday in Jamaica, the United States, and Brazil are about 10 times the level reported in the Philippines. And in some cultures, such as those in sub-Saharan Africa, women become sexually active at an earlier age than men–although this may be due to the fact that they marry at a younger age than men do (Singh et al., 2000; Majumdar, 2018).

MARITAL SEX

To judge by the number of articles about sex in heterosexual marriages, one would think that sexual behavior was the number one standard by which marital bliss is measured. Married couples are often concerned that they are having too little sex, too much sex, or the wrong kind of sex (Wellings et al., 2019; Cox et al., 2021).

Although sex in marriage is measured along many dimensions, one is certainly the frequency of sexual intercourse. What is typical? As with most other types of sexual activities, we have no easy answer to the question because individuals vary so widely in their patterns. We do know that 43% of married heterosexual couples have sexual intercourse a few times a month, and 36% of couples have it two or three times a week. With increasing age and length of marriage, the frequency of intercourse declines. Still, sex continues into late adulthood, with almost half of people reporting that they engage in high-quality sexual activity at least once a month (Grøntvedt et al., 2019; Bond et al., 2022).

According to the most recent trends in sexual activity, the number of adults reporting no sex at all in the past year has reached an all-time high. The numbers seem to be driven by an increase in numbers of people entering older adulthood, when sex is less frequent. But interestingly, even younger people are having less sex: The proportion of 18- to 29-year-olds reporting no sex in the past year more than doubled between 2008 and 2018, to 23%. The reason for this increase in abstinence may be that people in that age group are less likely to have live-in partners or are living with their parents for extended periods, although these explanations remains speculative (Ingraham, 2019).

When it does occur, sexual activity provides benefits beyond the immediate pleasure. It generates a kind of sexual afterglow that cements relationships and increases marital satisfaction. Moreover, the frequency of sexual intercourse may be related to relationship satisfaction (Brody & Costa, 2017; Meltzer et al., 2017; Roels & Janssen, 2020).

extramarital sex Sexual activity between a married person and someone who is not their spouse. (Module 25)

Although early research found **extramarital sex** to be widespread, the current reality appears to be otherwise. According to surveys, 85% of married women and more than 75% of married men report having no sexual partners other than their spouses. Furthermore, the median number of sex partners inside and outside of marriage since the age of 18 was six for men and two for women. Accompanying these numbers is a high, consistent degree of disapproval of extramarital sex, with 9 of 10 people saying that it is "always" or "almost always" wrong (Whisman & Snyder, 2007; DeMaris, 2013; Labrecque & Whisman, 2017).

SEXUAL ORIENTATION

Sexual orientation refers to a person's physical, romantic, and/or emotional attraction to another individual. In addition to heterosexuality (sexual attraction to the other sex), sexual orientations include homosexuality and bisexuality.

homosexuality Sexual attraction to members of one's own sex or gender. (Module 25)

bisexuality Sexual attraction to more than one sex or gender. (Module 25)

Homosexuality is sexual attraction to members of one's own sex or gender, whereas **bisexuality** is sexual attraction to more than one sex or gender. Many people prefer the terms *gay* (for males) and *lesbian* (for females), in part because gay and lesbian refer to a broader array of attitudes and lifestyles than the term *homosexual*, which focuses on the sexual act.

The number of people who choose same-sex sexual partners at one time or another is considerable. Estimates suggest that around 20–25% of males and about 15% of females have had at least one gay or lesbian experience during adulthood. The exact number of people who identify themselves as exclusively gay, lesbian, and bisexual has proved difficult to gauge; some estimates are as low as 1.1% and some as high as 10%. Some experts suggest that around 4.5% of adults in the United States identify as gay, lesbian, or bisexual, and 5–10% of both men and women are exclusively gay, lesbian, or bisexual during extended periods of their lives (Gates, 2017; Newport, 2018; McCarthy, 2019).

Although people often view homosexuality and heterosexuality as two completely distinct sexual orientations, the issue is not that simple. Pioneering sex researcher Alfred Kinsey acknowledged this when he considered sexual orientation along a scale or continuum with "exclusively homosexual" at one end and "exclusively heterosexual" at the other. In the middle were people who showed both homosexual and heterosexual behavior. Kinsey's approach suggests that sexual orientation is dependent on a person's sexual feelings and behaviors and romantic feelings (Jeffery, 2015; Strunk, 2021).

DETERMINING THE CAUSES OF SEXUAL ORIENTATION

What determines people's sexual orientation? Although a number of theories exist, none has proved completely satisfactory.

Considerable research suggests that biological and genetic factors underlie sexual orientation. For example, in one of the largest and most comprehensive studies, a group of researchers examined DNA from almost half a million men and women and found five genes associated with same-sex sexual behavior. These genes don't act alone, but in conjunction with other genes, they may account for as much as a third of the influence in determining whether an individual engages in same-sex behavior (Ganna et al., 2019; Mills, 2019).

Studies of identical twins provide evidence for a genetic cause of sexual orientation. For example, when one twin identified as homosexual, the occurrence of homosexuality in the other twin was higher than it was in the general population. Such results occur even for twins who have been separated early in life and who therefore are not necessarily raised in similar social environments. Furthermore, some research suggests that an area on the X chromosome is associated with homosexuality (Gooren, 2006; LeVay, 2011; Servick, 2014; Sanders et al., 2021).

Hormones also may play a role in determining sexual orientation. For example, some research shows that women exposed before birth to DES (diethylstilbestrol), a pharmaceutical drug their mothers took to avoid miscarriage, were more likely to be gay or bisexual. Other research suggests that variation in exposure to certain hormones before birth may play a greater role in the development of same-sex attraction in women than in men (Reinisch et al., 2017; Bogaert & Skorska, 2020).

Further evidence suggests that differences in brain structures may be related to sexual orientation. For instance, the structure of the anterior hypothalamus, an area of the brain that governs sexual behavior, differs in male homosexuals and heterosexuals. Similarly, other research shows that, compared with heterosexual men or women, gay men have a larger anterior commissure, which is a bundle of neurons connecting the right and left hemispheres of the brain (Rahman & Yusuf, 2015; Niebergall et al., 2019; Swaab et al., 2021).

In short, considerable research suggests the importance of biological and genetic factors at the roots of sexual orientation, but the research is not conclusive in pinpointing a specific cause. Nevertheless, it seems likely that some inherited or biological factor predisposes people toward homosexuality (Burri et al., 2015; Reardon, 2021).

In contrast, little evidence suggests that sexual orientation is brought about by child-rearing practices or family dynamics. Although proponents of psychoanalytic theories once argued that the nature of the parent-child relationship can produce homosexuality (e.g., Freud, 1922/1959), research evidence does not support such explanations (Roughton, 2002; Gundersen, 2021).

Another early explanation for sexual orientation rests on learning theory (Masters & Johnson, 1979). According to this view, sexual orientation is learned through rewards and punishments in much the same way we may learn to prefer swimming over tennis. For example, a young adolescent who had an unpleasant heterosexual experience might develop disagreeable associations with the other sex. If the same person had a rewarding, pleasant gay or lesbian experience, the adolescent might incorporate homosexuality into their sexual fantasies, which might later lead to homosexual behavior.

However, the learning-theory explanation is inadequate as as sole determinant of sexual orientation. Because our society has traditionally held homosexuality in low esteem, one ought to expect that the negative treatment of homosexual behavior would outweigh the rewards attached to it. Furthermore, children growing up with a gay or lesbian parent are statistically unlikely to become gay or lesbian, which thus contradicts the notion that homosexual behavior may be learned from others (Frias-Navarro et al., 2018; Schumm & Crawford, 2019; Dhoest, 2019).

In short, at this point we have no definitive explanation for what determines sexual orientation, and no single factor can likely be viewed as the basis. Instead, a

Extensive research has found that bisexuals and homosexuals enjoy the same overall degree of mental and physical health as heterosexuals do.
wavebreakmedia/Shutterstock

! **Study Alert**
The determinants of sexual orientation have proven difficult to pinpoint. It is important to know the variety of explanations that have been put forward.

transgender An umbrella term for persons whose gender identity, gender expression, or behavior does not conform to that typically associated with the sex to which they were assigned at birth. (Module 25)

combination of biological, genetic, and environmental factors is likely involved (Bailey et al, 2016; Ganna et al., 2019).

Although we don't know exactly why people develop a certain sexual orientation, one thing is clear: Despite increasingly positive attitudes toward homosexuality, many lesbian, gay, and bisexual people still face antigay attitudes and discrimination, and it can take a toll. Lesbian and gay people have higher rates of depression and suicide than do their straight counterparts. Physical health disparities exist as well, due to prejudice that gay, lesbian, and bisexual people may experience. Because of this, the American Psychological Association and other major mental health organizations have endorsed efforts to eliminate discrimination against gay, lesbian, and bisexual people (Moody et al., 2017; Goldhammer et al., 2019; Guz et al., 2021).

TRANSGENDER INDIVIDUALS

Transgender is a general term encompassing people whose gender identity, gender expression, or behavior is not consistent with the sex to which they were assigned at birth.

Transgender people may have male bodies but view their gender identity as female, or they may have female bodies and a male gender identity. In other cases, transgender individuals may view themselves as a third gender (neither male nor female) or as *gender fluid*, in which they don't identify with a single fixed gender. They also may wish to be referred to not as "she" or "he" but rather some other, more neutral pronoun, such as "ze" or "they" (Scelfo, 2015; Darwin, 2020; Sheydaei, 2021).

In the United States, about 1.6 million individuals 13 and up currently identify themselves as transgender, and the number is growing considerably, particularly among youth between the ages of 13 and 25. In fact, the number of young people who identify as transgender almost doubled between 2017 and 2020 (Bazelon, 2022; Ghorayshi, 2022).

In some cases, transgender individuals may seek gender-confirmation surgery in which the goal is to create the physical appearance and functional abilities of the gender that transgender individuals consider themselves to be. Several steps, including intensive counseling, hormone injections, and living as a member of the desired sex for several years, precede surgery, which is, not surprisingly, highly complicated. The outcome, though, can be quite positive (Gorton & Erickson-Schroth, 2017; Akhavan et al., 2021).

Transgender issues have become increasingly prominent and politically charged in recent years, partially because more teenagers are seeking gender-affirming treatments that alter their physical appearance and sexual characteristics to be consistent with their gender identity. In some cases, politicians have sought to prohibit such treatment for minors, labeling parents who seek treatment for their children as child abusers and criminalizing the work of physicians (Turban et al., 2021; Ghorayshi, 2022).

At the college level, campuses have struggled with how to best provide restrooms that address the needs of the transgender community. Do individuals who have the genitals of a male but who identify as females use traditional men's rooms or women's rooms? One solution has been the establishment of unisex or all-gender restrooms (Steinmetz, 2015; Callahan & Zukowski, 2019).

Whereas the term *transgender* centers on gender identity, the term *intersex person* refers to the small number of people who are born with genitals that makes their sexual identity ambiguous. An *intersex person* has an atypical combination of sexual organs or chromosomal or gene patterns, making their sexual identity unclear. In some cases, they are born with both male and female sexual organs, or the organs appear ambiguous in their physical configuration. It is a rare condition, found in 1 in 4,500 births. Intersexism involves a complex mix of physiological and psychological issues (Roen, 2019; Monro et al., 2019).

Smith Collection/Gado Images/Alamy Stock Photo

The Needs for Achievement, Affiliation, and Power

Although hunger and sex are some of the more potent primary drives in our day-to-day lives, powerful secondary drives that have no clear biological basis also motivate us. Among the more prominent of these are the needs for achievement, affiliation, and power.

THE NEED FOR ACHIEVEMENT: STRIVING FOR EXCELLENCE

The **need for achievement** refers to a person's desire to strive for and achieve challenging accomplishments (McClelland et al., 1953). People with a high need for achievement seek out situations in which they can compete against some objective standard–such as grades, money, or winning a game–and prove themselves successful.

But people who have a high need for achievement are selective about their challenges: They tend to avoid situations in which success will come too easily (which would be unchallenging) or situations in which success is highly unlikely. Instead, people high in achievement motivation generally choose tasks that are of intermediate difficulty (Mills, 2011; Staniewski & Awruk, 2019).

In contrast, people with low achievement motivation tend to be motivated primarily by a desire to avoid failure. As a result, they seek out easy tasks so they are sure to avoid failure, or they seek out very difficult tasks for which failure has no negative implications because almost anyone would fail at them. People with a high fear of failure will stay away from tasks of intermediate difficulty because they may fail where others have been successful (Pekrun, 2017; Gupta et al., 2021).

A high need for achievement generally produces positive outcomes, at least in a success-oriented cultures. For instance, people motivated by a high need for achievement are more likely to attend college than are their low-achievement counterparts. And once they are in college, they tend to receive higher grades in classes that are related to their future careers. Furthermore, high achievement motivation is related to future economic and occupational success (McClelland, 1985; Liem, 2015; Akhtar et al., 2020).

How can we measure a person's need for achievement? Most frequently, psychologists employ the *Thematic Apperception Test (TAT)*. In the TAT, participants are

need for achievement A stable, learned characteristic in which a person obtains satisfaction by striving for and achieving challenging goals. (Module 25)

Study Alert

A key feature of people with a high need for achievement is that they prefer tasks of *moderate* difficulty.

FIGURE 4 This ambiguous picture is similar to those used in the Thematic Apperception Test to determine people's underlying motivation. What do you see? Do you think your response is related to your motivation?
Science History Images/Alamy Stock Photo

growth mindset A belief that people can increase their abilities and do better through hard work. (Module 25)

fixed mindset The belief that abilities are fixed and unchangeable. (Module 25)

need for affiliation An interest in establishing and maintaining relationships with other people. (Module 25)

shown a series of ambiguous pictures, such as the one in Figure 4. They are then asked to write a story that describes what is happening, who the people are, what led to the situation, what the people are thinking or wanting, and what will happen next.

Researchers then use a standard scoring system to determine the amount of achievement imagery in people's stories. For example, someone who writes a story in which the main character strives to beat an opponent, studies hard in order to do well at some task, or puts in a lot of effort in order to get a promotion shows clear signs of an achievement orientation.

The inclusion of such achievement-related imagery in participants' stories is assumed to indicate an unusually high degree of concern with—and therefore a relatively strong need for—achievement. Although some critics have called into question the accuracy of TAT testing, the measure has expanded our understanding of achievement motivation in significant ways (McCreadie & Morey, 2019; Joo & Park, 2019; Nissley & DeFreese, 2020).

Growth Mindset and Achievement Do you believe that some people are born smart, talented, and destined to be high achievers, whereas others simply don't have enough intelligence and talent to ever do well in school and life?

If so, consider the work of psychologist Carol Dweck. In her view—and a considerable amount of supportive research—intelligence and other human capabilities are fluid and flexible, and through hard work and effort, people can increase their achievement. In fact, Dweck likens the brain to any muscle: The more you use it, the stronger it becomes (Dweck & Yeager, 2018, 2019).

People who believe in this fluidity and flexibility are said to hold a **growth mindset**, which provides them with grit. *Grit* is the perseverance and passion for long-term goals. They challenge themselves to increase their success, even if at first they fail. They are more persistent in the face of obstacles, and they try harder. They think about the goals they want to accomplish, and they are passionate about achieving them (Duckworth, 2016; Hagger & Hamilton, 2019; Calo et al., 2022).

In contrast, those with a **fixed mindset** inappropriately believe that individual characteristics such as intelligence, talent, and motivation are set at birth and vary little throughout the lifespan. Students with fixed mindsets may label themselves as "not smart" or "incompetent" rather than believing that with effort they can do better. As a result, they do not work as hard as others, which has the self-defeating effect of leading to failure.

Can one develop a growth mindset and avoid a fixed one? The answer seems to be yes. Those who tell themselves that success comes from effort, not from how smart one is, are more likely to succeed. Furthermore, reframing academic setbacks as due to controllable causes (such as insufficient effort or inadequate study strategies) leads to improved academic success (Hamm et al., 2020).

THE NEED FOR AFFILIATION: STRIVING FOR FRIENDSHIP

Few of us choose to lead our lives as hermits. Why?

One main reason is that most people have a **need for affiliation,** an interest in establishing and maintaining relationships with other people. Individuals with a high need for affiliation write TAT stories that emphasize the desire to maintain or reinstate friendships and show concern over being rejected by friends.

People who have higher affiliation needs are particularly sensitive to relationships with others. They desire to be with their friends more of the time and alone less often, compared with people who are lower in the need for affiliation. However, gender is a greater determinant of how much time is actually spent with friends: Regardless of their affiliative orientation, female students spend significantly more time with their friends and less time alone than male students do (Johnson, 2004; Semykina & Linz, 2007; Hofer et al., 2017).

THE NEED FOR POWER: STRIVING FOR IMPACT ON OTHERS

If your fantasies include becoming president of the United States or running Microsoft, your dreams may reflect a high need for power. The **need for power**, a tendency to seek impact, control, or influence over others and to be seen as a powerful individual, is an additional type of motivation (Winter, 2007, 2016; Pratto et al., 2011; Alexander et al., 2021).

need for power A tendency to seek impact, control, or influence over others and to be seen as a powerful individual. (Module 25)

As you might expect, people with strong needs for power are more apt to belong to organizations and seek political office than are those low in the need for power. They also tend to work in professions in which their power needs may be fulfilled, such as business management and–you may or may not be surprised–teaching (Jenkins, 1994). In addition, they seek to display the trappings of power. Even in college, they are more likely to collect prestigious possessions, such as electronic equipment and sports cars.

Some significant gender differences exist in the display of need for power. Men with high power needs tend to show unusually high levels of aggression, drink heavily, act in a sexually exploitative manner, and participate more frequently in competitive sports–behaviors that collectively represent somewhat extravagant, flamboyant behavior. In contrast, women display their power needs with more restraint; this is congruent with traditional societal constraints on women's behavior. Women with high power needs are more apt than men to channel those needs in a socially responsible manner, such as by showing concern for others or displaying highly nurturing behavior (Schultheiss & Schiepe-Tiska, 2013; Sibunruang et al., 2015; Hofer & Busch, 2019).

From the perspective of...

A Human Resources Specialist How might you use characteristics such as need for achievement, need for affiliation, and need for power to select workers for jobs?

Dex Image/Getty Images

RECAP/EVALUATE/RETHINK

RECAP

LO 25-1 What biological and social factors underlie hunger?

- Eating behavior is subject to homeostasis, as most people's weight stays within a relatively stable range. The hypothalamus in the brain is central to the regulation of food intake.
- Social factors, such as mealtimes, cultural food preferences, and other learned habits, also play a role in the regulation of eating by determining when, what, and how much one eats. An oversensitivity to social cues and an insensitivity to internal cues may also be related to obesity. In addition, obesity may be caused by an unusually high weight set point–the weight the body attempts to maintain–and genetic factors.

LO 25-2 What are the varieties of sexual behavior?

- Although biological factors, such as the presence of androgens (male sex hormones) and estrogens (female sex hormones), prime people for sex, almost any kind of stimulus can produce sexual arousal depending on a person's prior sexual experience.
- The frequency of masturbation is high, particularly for males. Although attitudes toward masturbation are increasingly liberal, they have traditionally been negative even though no negative consequences have been detected.
- Sexual orientation refers to a person's physical, romantic, and/or emotional attraction to another individual.

- Heterosexuality, or sexual attraction to members of the other sex, is the most common sexual orientation.
- The double standard by which premarital sex is thought to be more permissible for men than for women has declined, particularly among young people.
- Homosexuals are sexually attracted to members of their own sex; bisexuals are sexually attracted to people of the same sex and the other sex.
- Although a number of theories for the determinants of sexual orientation exist, none has proved completely satisfactory. For example, explanations for homosexuality include genetic or biological factors, childhood and family influences, and prior learning experiences and conditioning. Moreover, no relationship exists between sexual orientation and psychological adjustment.
- *Transgender* is a general term encompassing people whose gender identity, gender expression, or behavior is not consistent with the sex to which they were assigned at birth.

LO 25-3 How are needs relating to achievement, affiliation, and power motivation exhibited?

- Need for achievement refers to the stable, learned characteristic in which a person strives to attain a level of excellence. Need for achievement is usually measured through the Thematic Apperception Test (TAT), a series of pictures about which a person writes a story.
- The need for affiliation is a concern with establishing and maintaining relationships with others, whereas the need for power is a tendency to seek to exert an impact on others.

EVALUATE

1. Match the following terms with their definitions:

   1. Hypothalamus
   2. Lateral hypothalamic damage
   3. Ventromedial hypothalamic damage

   a. Leads to refusal of food and starvation
   b. Responsible for monitoring food intake
   c. Causes extreme overeating

2. The _____ _____ _____ is the specific level of weight the body strives to maintain.
3. _____ is the rate at which the body produces and expends energy.
4. Although the incidence of masturbation among young adults is high, once men and women become involved in intimate relationships, they typically cease masturbating. True or false?
5. The increase in premarital sex in recent years has been greater for women than for men. True or false?
6. Julio is the type of person who constantly strives for excellence. He feels intense satisfaction when he is able to master a new task. Julio most likely has a high need for _____.
7. Riley's Thematic Apperception Test (TAT) story depicts a young girl who is rejected by one of her peers and seeks to regain her friendship. What major type of motivation is Riley displaying in her story?
   a. Need for achievement
   b. Need for motivation
   c. Need for affiliation
   d. Need for power

RETHINK

1. In what ways do societal expectations, expressed by television shows and commercials, contribute to both obesity and excessive concern about weight loss? How could television contribute to better eating habits and attitudes toward weight? Should it be required to do so?
2. Why do discussions of sexual behavior, which is such a necessary part of human life, have so many negative connotations in Western society?

Answers to Evaluate Questions

1. 1-b, 2-a, 3-c; 2. weight set point; 3. Metabolism; 4. False; 5. True; 6. achievement; 7. c

KEY TERMS

obesity	genitals	double standard	need for achievement
weight set point	estrogens	extramarital sex	growth mindset
metabolism	ovulation	homosexuality	fixed mindset
anorexia nervosa	masturbation	bisexuality	need for affiliation
bulimia	heterosexuality	transgender	need for power
androgens			

Module 26
Understanding Emotional Experiences

Karl Nguyen held his fingers over his computer keyboard, knowing that he was about to learn whether he'd receive an offer of admission to his first-choice college. He knew it could go either way. His grades were pretty good, and he had been involved in some extracurricular activities, but his SAT scores had not been terrific. He felt so nervous that his hands shook as he logged into the college's website and added his username and password. "Dear Mr. Nguyen," he read, "The Trustees of the University are pleased to admit you. . . ." That was all he needed to see. With a whoop of excitement, Karl found himself jumping up and down gleefully. A rush of emotion overcame him as it sank in that he had, in fact, been accepted. He was on his way.

At one time or another, all of us have experienced the strong feelings that accompany both very pleasant and very negative experiences. Perhaps we have felt the thrill of getting a sought-after job, the joy of being in love, the sorrow over someone's death, or the anguish of inadvertently hurting someone. Moreover, we experience such reactions on a less intense level throughout our daily lives with such things as the pleasure of a friendship, the enjoyment of a movie, and the embarrassment of breaking a borrowed item.

Despite the varied nature of these feelings, they all represent emotions. Although everyone has an idea of what an emotion is, formally defining the concept has proved to be an elusive task. Here, we'll use a general definition: **Emotions** are feelings that generally have both physiological and cognitive elements and that influence behavior.

Think, for example, about how it feels to be happy. First, we obviously experience a feeling that we can differentiate from other emotions. Most people also experience some identifiable physical changes in their bodies: Perhaps the heart rate increases, or—as in the example of Karl Nguyen—we find ourselves "jumping for joy." Finally, the emotion probably encompasses cognitive elements: Our understanding and evaluation of the meaning of what is happening prompts our feelings of happiness.

However, people also can experience an emotion without the presence of cognitive elements. For instance, we may react with fear to an unusual or novel situation (such as coming into contact with an erratic, unpredictable individual), or we may experience pleasure over sexual excitation without having cognitive awareness or understanding of just what makes the situation exciting.

Some psychologists argue that one system governs emotional responses to a given situation and another governs cognitive reactions to it. Assuming there are two systems, does one predominate over the other? Some theorists suggest that we first respond to a situation with an emotional reaction and later try to make sense of it cognitively. For example, we may enjoy a complex modern symphony without at first understanding it or knowing why we like it. In contrast, other theorists propose that people first develop cognitions about a situation and then react emotionally. This school of thought suggests that we must think about and understand a stimulus or situation, relating it to what we already know, before we can react on an emotional level (Lazarus, 1995; Martin & Kerns, 2011; Zmigrod & Goldenberg, 2021).

Because proponents of both sides of this debate can cite research to support their viewpoints, the question is far from resolved. Perhaps the sequence varies from situation to situation, with emotions predominating in some instances and cognitive processes occurring first in others. Both sides agree that we can experience emotions that involve little or no conscious thought. We may not know why we're afraid of mice because

LEARNING OUTCOMES

LO 26-1 What are emotions, and how do we experience them?

LO 26-2 What are the functions of emotions?

LO 26-3 What are the explanations for emotions?

LO 26-4 How does nonverbal behavior relate to the expression of emotions?

emotions Feelings that generally have both physiological and cognitive elements and that influence behavior. (Module 26)

we understand objectively that they represent no danger, but we may still be frightened when we see them. Neuroimaging studies of the brain may help resolve this debate as well as others about the nature of emotions (Niedenthal, 2007; Karaszewski, 2008; López-Pérez & Ambrona, 2015).

The Functions of Emotions

Imagine what it would be like if we didn't experience emotion. We would have no depths of despair, no depression, and no remorse, but at the same time, we would also have no happiness, joy, or love. Obviously, life would be considerably less satisfying and even dull if we lacked the capacity to sense and express emotion.

But do emotions serve any purpose beyond making life interesting? Indeed they do. Psychologists have identified several important functions that emotions play in our daily lives (Rolls, 2011; Cachero-Martínez & Vázquez-Casielles, 2021). Among the most important of those functions are the following:

- *Preparing us for action.* Emotions act as a link between events in our environment and our responses to them. For example, if you saw an angry dog charging toward you, your emotional reaction (fear) would be associated with physiological arousal of the sympathetic division of the autonomic nervous system, the activation of the "fight-or-flight" response.

- *Shaping our future behavior.* Emotions promote learning that will help us make appropriate responses in the future. For instance, your emotional response to unpleasant events teaches you to avoid similar circumstances in the future.

- *Helping us interact more effectively with others.* We often communicate the emotions we experience through our verbal and nonverbal behaviors, making our emotions obvious to observers. These behaviors can act as signals to observers, allowing them to understand better what we are experiencing and to help them predict our future behavior.

Determining the Range of Emotions: Labeling Our Feelings

If we were to list the words in the English language that have been used to describe emotions, we would end up with at least 500 examples (Averill, 1975). The list would range from such obvious emotions as *happiness* and *fear* to less common ones, such as *adventurousness* and *pensiveness*.

One challenge for psychologists has been to sort through this list to identify the most important, fundamental emotions. Theorists have hotly contested the issue of cataloging emotions and have come up with different lists, depending on how they define the concept of emotion. In fact, some reject the question entirely, saying that *no* set of emotions should be singled out as most basic and that emotions are best understood by breaking them down into their component parts. Other researchers argue for looking at emotions in terms of a hierarchy, dividing them into positive and negative categories and then organizing them into increasingly narrower subcategories (Dillard & Shen, 2007; Livingstone et al., 2011; Cowen & Keltner, 2020; see Figure 1).

Still, most researchers suggest that a list of basic emotions would include, at a minimum, happiness, anger, fear, sadness, and disgust. Other lists are broader, including emotions such as surprise, contempt, guilt, and joy (Tracy & Robins, 2004; Greenberg, 2015).

One difficulty in defining a basic set of emotions is that substantial differences exist in descriptions of emotions among various cultures. For instance, Germans report experiencing *schadenfreude*, a feeling of pleasure over another person's difficulties, and the Japanese experience *hagaii*, a mood of vulnerable heartache colored by frustration. In Tahiti, people experience *musu*, a feeling of reluctance to yield to unreasonable demands made by one's parents.

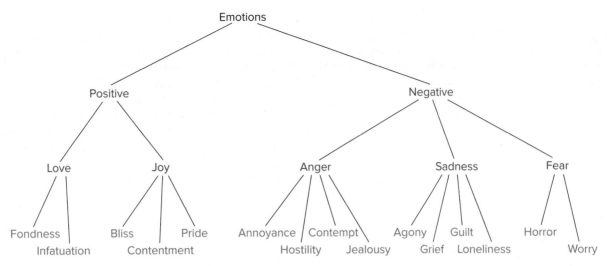

FIGURE 1 One approach to organizing emotions is to use a hierarchy, which divides emotions into increasingly narrow subcategories.
Source: Adapted from Fischer et al., 1990.

Finding *schadenfreude, hagaii,* or *musu* in a particular culture doesn't mean that the members of other cultures are incapable of experiencing such emotions, of course. It suggests, though, that fitting a particular emotion into a linguistic category to describe that emotion may make it easier to discuss, contemplate, and perhaps experience (Dasborough & Harvey, 2017; Lange & Boecker, 2019; Nia & Otto, 2021; also see the *Applying Psychology in the 21st Century* feature).

APPLYING PSYCHOLOGY IN THE 21ST CENTURY

MY COMPUTER SAYS YOU'RE HAPPY

Advances in artificial intelligence are turning what was only recently thought to be the domain of science fiction into modern-day realities. For example, computer-controlled cars can assist drivers in monitoring the road ahead, computer devices at home can respond to spoken commands by recognizing your speech, and airport-security screening devices can scan your face to confirm your identity. These are just some of the applications of *deep learning,* a form of artificial intelligence that mimics how the human brain solves complex and vaguely defined problems, such as driving a car or recognizing a human voice or face.

The latest challenge in artificial intelligence goes well beyond mere facial recognition and attempts to determine people's underlying emotions and even their personalities from their facial expressions. The potential applications are enormous. For example, imagine cameras in airports that

The use of facial recognition software raises important issues, and is controversial.
DedMityay/Shutterstock

can detect subtle emotional indications that a traveler might be concealing illegal goods or a weapon. Such applications of artificial intelligence are already being developed and deployed. But can they actually do what they purport to do (McQuaid, 2021)?

That's the question being posed by some researchers who worry that the technology is getting well ahead of the research. It's one thing, experts point out, to train artificial intelligence to identify stop signs on the road, but what data are technology relying on to assess the emotion underlying a facial expression? Deep learning works by training the software on enormous data sets; for instance, training it to recognize emotions by showing it a great many photos of people exhibiting various known emotions. Programmers have also latched onto the extensive work by early emotion researchers in developing facial-coding rules for emotions, which perfectly fits the machine-learning task. But while these approaches seem to employ sound science, careful examination suggests that they may be deeply flawed (Rosenberg & Ekman, 2020).

The data sets used to train the software can be susceptible to bias in many ways. For example, if one racial group is better represented than another in the data set, the software's accuracy can be substantially compromised for the underrepresented group. Moreover, if human judges are determining the emotions being displayed in the photographs, their own unconscious biases can be encoded right along with their judgments and then inadvertently trained to the software. For example, White judges might unwittingly tend to read anger or hostility into the benign facial expressions of people of color (Rhue, 2019; Schwemmer et al., 2020).

Even if human bias could be minimized or eliminated, researchers still have serious questions about the assumption that facial expressions are reliable indications of emotion. Take, for example, a simple smile. We may assume that a smile indicates happiness, but does it? People smile for many reasons. They may be masking pain, showing sympathy, or just smiling out of politeness. Furthermore, reliance on static snapshots lacking motion and context may make this ambiguity even greater (Barrett et al., 2019).

The conclusion is clear: Before we can teach machines to infer people's emotions from a glance at their faces, we must better learn to do so ourselves, assuming that's even possible.

RETHINK

- Given that you can't know people's internal emotional states directly, can you be sure you are inferring them accurately from their facial expressions? If so, how?
- What potential legal, moral, or ethical problems do you see with using artificial intelligence to infer people's emotions or personalities from their faces?

The Roots of Emotions

> I've never been so angry before; I feel my heart pounding, and I'm trembling all over. . . . I don't know how I'll get through the performance. I feel like my stomach is filled with butterflies. . . . That was quite a mistake I made! My face must be incredibly red. . . . When I heard the footsteps in the night, I was so frightened that I couldn't catch my breath.

English offers multiple ways to describe how we feel when we experience an emotion. However, the language we use to describe emotions is, for the most part, based on the physical symptoms that are associated with a particular emotional experience (Torre & Lieberman, 2018; Sun et al., 2019).

Consider, for instance, the experience of fear. Imagine that it is late on New Year's Eve. You are walking down a dark street, and you hear a stranger approaching behind you. They are clearly not trying to hurry by but are getting closer and closer to you. You think about what you will do if the stranger attempts to hurt you.

While these thoughts are running through your head, something dramatic will be happening to your body. The most likely reactions, which are associated with activation of the autonomic nervous system, include an increase in your rate of breathing, an acceleration of your heart rate, a widening of your pupils (to increase visual sensitivity), and a dryness in your mouth as the functioning of your salivary glands and in fact of your entire digestive system ceases. At the same time, though, your sweat glands probably will increase their activity because increased sweating will help you rid yourself of the excess heat developed by any emergency activity in which you engage.

Of course, all these physiological changes are likely to occur without your awareness. At the same time, though, the emotional experience accompanying them will be obvious to you: You most surely would report being fearful.

Although it is easy to describe the general physical reactions that accompany emotions, defining the specific role that those physiological responses play in the experience of emotions has proved to be a major puzzle for psychologists. As we shall see, some theorists suggest that specific physiological reactions *cause* us to experience a particular emotion. For example, when the heart is pounding and we are breathing deeply, we then experience fear. In contrast, other theorists suggest the opposite sequence; that is, we experience an emotion, and that causes us to have a physiological reaction. In this view, then, as a result of experiencing the emotion of fear, our heart pounds and our breathing deepens.

THE JAMES-LANGE THEORY: DO GUT REACTIONS EQUAL EMOTIONS?

To William James and Carl Lange, who were among the first researchers to explore the nature of emotions, emotional experience is, very simply, a reaction to instinctive bodily events that occur as a result of some situation or event in the environment. This view is summarized in James's statement, "We feel sorry because we cry, angry because we strike, afraid because we tremble" (James, 1890).

James and Lange took the view that the instinctive response of crying at a loss leads us to feel sorrow, that striking out at someone who frustrates us results in our feeling anger, that trembling at a menacing threat causes us to feel fear. They suggested that every major emotion has an accompanying physiological or "gut" reaction of internal organs–called a *visceral experience*, or arousal of the autonomic nervous system. It is this specific pattern of visceral response that leads us to label the emotional experience.

In sum, James and Lange proposed that we experience emotions as a result of physiological changes that produce specific sensations. The brain interprets these sensations as specific kinds of emotional experiences (see Figure 2). This view has come to be called the **James-Lange theory of emotion** (Stolorow & Stolorow, 2013; Šolcová & Lačev, 2017; Retkoceri, 2022).

The James-Lange theory, however, has some serious shortcomings. For the theory to be valid, visceral changes would have to occur rapidly because we experience some emotions–such as fear upon hearing a stranger rapidly approaching on a dark

James-Lange theory of emotion The belief that emotional experience is a reaction to bodily events occurring as a result of an external situation ("I feel sad because I am crying"). (Module 26)

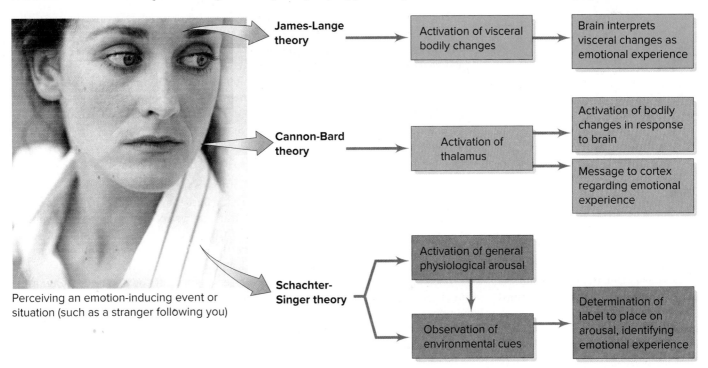

Perceiving an emotion-inducing event or situation (such as a stranger following you)

James-Lange theory → Activation of visceral bodily changes → Brain interprets visceral changes as emotional experience

Cannon-Bard theory → Activation of thalamus → Activation of bodily changes in response to brain / Message to cortex regarding emotional experience

Schachter-Singer theory → Activation of general physiological arousal / Observation of environmental cues → Determination of label to place on arousal, identifying emotional experience

FIGURE 2 A comparison of three models of emotion.
(Photo): Stockbyte/Getty Images

night—almost instantaneously. Yet some visceral changes occur slowly. Therefore, it's hard to see how they could be the source of an immediate emotional experience.

The James-Lange theory poses another difficulty: Physiological arousal does not invariably produce emotional experience. For example, a person who is jogging has an increased heartbeat and respiration rate, as well as many of the other physiological changes associated with certain emotions. Yet joggers typically do not think of such changes in terms of emotion. Thus, visceral changes by themselves are not always sufficient to produce emotion.

Finally, our internal organs produce a relatively limited range of sensations. Although some types of physiological changes are associated with specific emotional experiences, it is difficult to imagine how each of the many emotions that people are capable of experiencing could be the result of a unique visceral change. Many emotions actually are associated with relatively similar sorts of visceral changes, a fact that contradicts the James-Lange theory (Rinaman et al., 2011; Torre & Lieberman, 2018).

THE CANNON-BARD THEORY: PHYSIOLOGICAL REACTIONS AS THE RESULT OF EMOTIONS

In response to the difficulties inherent in the James-Lange theory, Walter Cannon and later Philip Bard suggested an alternative view. In what has come to be known as the **Cannon-Bard theory of emotion,** they proposed the model illustrated in the second part of Figure 2 (Cannon, 1929). This theory rejects the view that physiological arousal alone leads to the perception of emotion. Instead, the theory assumes that both physiological arousal *and* the emotional experience are produced simultaneously by the same nerve stimulus, which Cannon and Bard suggested emanates from the *thalamus* in the brain.

The theory states that after we perceive an emotion-producing stimulus, the thalamus is the initial site of the emotional response. Next, the thalamus sends a signal to the autonomic nervous system, thereby producing a visceral response. At the same time, the thalamus also communicates a message to the cerebral cortex regarding the nature of the emotion being experienced. Hence, it is not necessary for different emotions to have unique physiological patterns associated with them—as long as the message sent to the cerebral cortex differs according to the specific emotion.

The Cannon-Bard theory seems to have been accurate in rejecting the view that physiological arousal alone accounts for emotions. However, more recent research has led to some important modifications of the theory. For one thing, we now understand that the hypothalamus and the limbic system, not the thalamus, play a major role in emotional experience. In addition, the simultaneous occurrence of the physiological and emotional responses, which is a fundamental assumption of the Cannon-Bard theory, has yet to be demonstrated conclusively. This ambiguity has allowed room for yet another theory of emotions: the Schachter-Singer theory.

THE SCHACHTER-SINGER THEORY: EMOTIONS AS LABELS

Suppose that as you are being followed down that dark street on New Year's Eve, you notice a person being followed by another shady figure on the other side of the street. Now assume that instead of reacting with fear, the person being followed begins to laugh and act gleeful. Would the reactions of this other individual be sufficient to lay your fears to rest? Might you, in fact, decide there is nothing to fear and get into the spirit of the evening by beginning to feel happiness and glee yourself?

According to an explanation that focuses on the role of cognition, the **Schachter-Singer theory of emotion,** this might very well happen. This approach to explaining emotions emphasizes that we identify the emotion we are experiencing by observing our environment and comparing ourselves with others (Schachter & Singer, 1962, 2001; Shaked & Clore, 2017).

Schachter and Singer's classic experiment found evidence for this hypothesis. In the study, participants were told that they would receive an injection of a vitamin. In reality, they were given epinephrine, a pharmaceutical drug that causes responses that typically

---

Cannon-Bard theory of emotion
The belief that both physiological arousal and emotional experience are produced simultaneously by the same nerve stimulus. (Module 26)

! **Study Alert**
Use Figure 2 to distinguish the three classic theories of emotion (James-Lange, Cannon-Bard, and Schachter-Singer).

Schachter-Singer theory of emotion
The belief that emotions are determined jointly by a nonspecific kind of physiological arousal and its interpretation, based on environmental cues. (Module 26)

occur during strong emotional reactions, such as an increase in physiological arousal, including higher heart and respiration rates and a reddening of the face. The members of both groups were then placed individually in a situation where a confederate of the experimenter acted in one of two ways. In one condition, the participant acted angry and hostile; in the other condition, the participant behaved with exuberant happiness.

The purpose of the experiment was to determine whether participants' emotions would be influenced by the confederate's behavior. And they were: When participants were asked to describe their own emotional state at the end of the experiment, those participants exposed to the angry confederate reported that they felt angry, whereas those participants exposed to the happy confederate reported feeling happy. In sum, the results suggest that participants used the behavior of the confederate to explain the physiological arousal they were experiencing.

The results of the Schachter-Singer experiment, then, supported a cognitive view of emotions in which emotions are determined jointly by a relatively nonspecific kind of physiological arousal *and* the labeling of that arousal on the basis of cues from the environment (refer to the final line of Figure 2). Although later research has found that arousal is more specific than Schachter and Singer believed, they were right in assuming that when the source of physiological arousal is unclear, we may look to our surroundings to determine what we are experiencing.

From the perspective of...

An Advertising Executive How might you use Schachter and Singer's findings on the labeling of arousal to create interest in a product?

mentatdgt/Shutterstock

CONTEMPORARY PERSPECTIVES ON THE NEUROSCIENCE OF EMOTIONS

When Schachter and Singer carried out their groundbreaking experiment in the early 1960s, the ways in which they could evaluate the physiological changes that accompany emotion were relatively limited. However, advances in the measurement of the nervous system and other parts of the body have allowed researchers to examine more closely the biological responses involved in individual emotions. As a result, evidence is growing that specific patterns of biological arousal are associated with specific emotions. For instance, different emotions produce activation of specific portions of the brain (Christensen et al., 2017; Kanel et al., 2019; Prete et al., 2022).

In addition, research shows that the *amygdala*, in the brain's temporal lobe, plays an important role in the experience of emotions. The amygdala provides a link between the perception of an emotion-producing stimulus and the recall of that stimulus later. For example, if we've once been attacked by a vicious pit bull, the amygdala processes that information and leads us to react with fear when we see a pit bull at future times (Christensen et al., 2017; Ressler & Maren, 2019; Roesler et al., 2021).

Because neural pathways connect the amygdala, the visual cortex, and the *hippocampus* (which plays an important role in the consolidation of memories), some scientists speculate that emotion-related stimuli can be processed and responded to almost instantaneously (see Figure 3). This immediate response occurs so rapidly that higher-order, more rational thinking, which takes more time, seems not to be involved initially. In a slower but more thoughtful response to emotion-evoking stimuli, emotion-related sensory information is first evaluated and then sent on to the amygdala. It

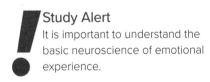

Study Alert
It is important to understand the basic neuroscience of emotional experience.

FIGURE 3 Connections from the amygdala allow it to mediate many of the autonomic expressions of emotional states through the hippocampus and visual cortex.

Sources: (Left) Adapted from Dolan, 2002; (Right) Image Source/Getty Images

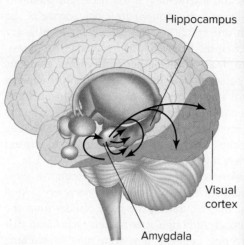

Hippocampus

Visual cortex

Amygdala

appears that the quicker system offers an immediate response to emotion-evoking stimuli, whereas the slower system helps confirm a threat and prepare a more thoughtful response (Šimić et al., 2021; also see the *Neuroscience in Your Life* feature).

NEUROSCIENCE IN YOUR LIFE: LOOKING ON THE BRIGHT SIDE

According to stereotypes, everything goes downhill with age. But research tells us otherwise. Some abilities and experiences actually get better in late life. For example, studies consistently show that older adults are better than their younger counterparts at regulating their emotions. Moreover, during late adulthood, people tend to appreciate and invest more effort in matters that they consider important, so they prioritize positive emotions over negative ones.

Regulating emotions requires the prefrontal cortex to direct the activity of other brain regions that process emotions. Prefrontal cortex activity may also play a role in the moments when we're expecting that something emotional is going to happen. A recent study showed that older adults have a knack for this kind of emotional regulation (Corbett et al., 2020).

In the study, older adults, but not young adults, showed increased activity of the prefrontal cortex when they saw a cue indicating that a negative picture would be shown next. The greater their prefrontal activity during the anticipation phase, the lower the activity in their amygdala, a part of the brain that processes fearful and threatening stimuli, when they actually saw the negative picture. This suggests older adults were better than young adults at using emotion-regulation strategies to dampen their negative emotional responses.

Why does this matter? Emotion-processing problems are common in psychological disorders such as depression, anxiety, and schizophrenia. Understanding strategies that improve emotion regulation and identifying the brain basis of the strategies can help researchers develop treatments for those disorders.

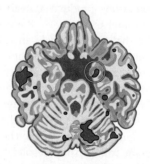

Compared with younger adults, older adults showed greater prefrontal activity when they anticipated viewing a negative picture. This prefrontal activity was associated with lower activity in the regions highlighted in blue when they actually saw the picture. The area in the circle is the amygdala, a brain region that processes fearful and threatening stimuli.

MAKING SENSE OF THE MULTIPLE PERSPECTIVES ON EMOTION

As new approaches to emotion continue to develop, it is reasonable to ask why so many theories of emotion exist and, perhaps more important, which one provides the most complete explanation. Actually, we have only scratched the surface. There are almost as many explanatory theories of emotion as there are individual emotions (e.g., Ford & Gross, 2019; De France & Hollenstein, 2021; Walle et al., 2022).

Why are theories of emotion so plentiful? For one thing, emotions are not a simple phenomenon but are intertwined closely with motivation, cognition, neuroscience, and a host of related branches of psychology. For example, evidence from brain imaging studies shows that even when people come to supposedly rational, nonemotional decisions—such as making moral or philosophical judgments—emotions come into play.

In short, emotions are such complex phenomena, encompassing both biological and cognitive aspects, that no single theory has been able to explain fully all the facets of emotional experience. Furthermore, contradictory evidence of one sort or another challenges each approach. Consequently, no theory has proved invariably accurate in its predictions.

This abundance of perspectives on emotion is not a cause for despair—or unhappiness, fear, or any other negative emotion. It simply reflects the fact that psychology is an evolving, developing science. As we gather more evidence, specific answers to questions about the nature of emotions will become clearer.

 Exploring Diversity

Do People in All Cultures Express Emotion Similarly?

Consider, for a moment, the six photos displayed in Figure 4. Can you identify the emotions being expressed by the person in each of the photos?

If you are a good judge of facial expressions, you will conclude that these expressions display six of the basic emotions: happiness, anger, sadness, surprise, disgust, and fear. Hundreds of studies of nonverbal behavior show that these emotions are consistently distinct and identifiable even by untrained observers (Ekman, 2007).

Interestingly, these six emotions are not unique to members of Western cultures; rather, most research suggests that they constitute the basic emotions expressed universally by members of the human race, regardless of where individuals have been raised and what learning experiences they have had. Psychologist Paul Ekman found support for this view when he studied members of an isolated New Guinea jungle community who had had almost no contact with Westerners (Ekman, 1972). The people of the community did not speak or understand English, had never seen a movie, and had very limited experience with Caucasians before Ekman's arrival. Yet their nonverbal responses to emotion-evoking stories, as well as their ability to identify basic emotions, were quite similar to those of Westerners.

Being so isolated, the New Guineans could not have learned from Westerners to recognize or produce similar facial expressions. Instead, their similar abilities and manner of responding emotionally appear to have been present innately. Although one could argue that similar experiences in both cultures led the members of each one to learn similar types of nonverbal behavior, this appears unlikely because the two cultures are so very different. The results of the Ekman study suggested, then, that the expression of basic emotions was universal (Ekman, 1994; Matsumoto, 2002).

Why might people across cultures express emotions similarly? A hypothesis known as the **facial-affect program** offers one explanation. The facial-affect program—which is assumed to be universally present at birth—is analogous to a computer software program that is activated when a particular emotion is experienced. When set in motion, the "program" produces a set of nerve impulses that make the face display an appropriate expression. Each primary emotion is related to a unique set of muscular movements, forming the

facial-affect program Activation of a set of nerve impulses that make the face display the appropriate expression. (Module 26)

FIGURE 4 These photos demonstrate six of the primary emotions: happiness, sadness, disgust, anger, surprise, and fear.
(top left): fizkes/Shutterstock; (top rightt): Anderson Piza/Alamy Stock Photo; (middle left): Master1305/Shutterstock; (middle right): Rachata Teyparsit/Shutterstock; (bottom left): Daniel Ernst/Alamy Stock Photo; (bottom right): samuel wordley/Alamy Stock Photo

kinds of expressions shown in Figure 4. For example, the emotion of happiness is universally displayed by movement of the zygomatic major, a muscle that raises the corners of the mouth and forms what we would call a smile (Krumhuber & Scherer, 2011; Fernández-Sotos et al., 2021).

However, the link between facial expressions and emotions is not as clear-cut and universal as once thought. According to a comprehensive review of more than 1,000 studies, a group of eminent psychologists found that people communicate the typically expected facial expression—such as smiling when happy—only 20–30% of the time. The remainder of the time, they express emotions in ways that relate to the specific situation, the context, and/or the culture. Personality factors also play a critical role (Barrett et al., 2019; Durán & Fernández-Dols, 2021).

Additional research casts some doubt on the universality of facial expressions. For example, studies done in diverse urban areas and in small hunter-gatherer foraging communities, such as among the Hadza people of Tanzania, suggest considerable heterogeneity in the way people's faces express emotions (Barrett et al., 2019; Gendron et al., 2020; Barrett, 2021).

In any case, facial expressions remain a fundamental way in which we communicate, not only with others but also apparently with ourselves, according to an intriguing notion known as the **facial-feedback hypothesis.** According to this hypothesis, facial expressions not only *reflect* emotional experience, but they also help *determine* how people experience and label emotions. Basically, "wearing" an emotional expression provides muscular feedback to the brain that helps produce an emotion congruent with that expression (Balconi et al., 2013; Damjanovic et al., 2017; Carpenter & Niedenthal, 2020).

For instance, the muscles activated when we smile may send a message to the brain indicating the experience of happiness—even if there is nothing in the environment that would produce that particular emotion. Some theoreticians have gone further by

facial-feedback hypothesis The hypothesis that facial expressions not only reflect emotional experience but also help determine how people experience and label emotions. (Module 26)

suggesting that facial expressions are *necessary* for an emotion to be experienced (Rinn, 1991). In this view, if no facial expression is present, the emotion cannot be felt.

Support for this facial-feedback hypothesis comes from a classic experiment carried out by psychologist Paul Ekman and colleagues (Ekman et al., 1983). In the study, professional actors were asked to follow very explicit instructions regarding the movements of muscles in their faces. You might try this example yourself:

- Raise your brows and pull them together.
- Raise your upper eyelids.
- Now stretch your lips horizontally back toward your ears.

After carrying out these directions—which, as you may have guessed, are meant to produce an expression of fear—the actors' heart rates rose and their body temperatures declined, physiological reactions that characterize fear. Overall, facial expressions representing the primary emotions produced physiological effects similar to those accompanying the genuine emotions in other circumstances (Keillor et al., 2002; Soussignan, 2002).

RECAP/EVALUATE/RETHINK

RECAP

LO 26-1 What are emotions, and how do we experience them?

- Emotions are broadly defined as feelings that may affect behavior and generally have both a physiological component and a cognitive component. Debate continues over whether separate systems govern cognitive and emotional responses and whether one has primacy over the other.

LO 26-2 What are the functions of emotions?

- Emotions prepare us for action, shape future behavior through learning, and help us interact more effectively with others.

LO 26-3 What are the explanations for emotions?

- Several theories explain emotions. The James-Lange theory suggests that emotional experience is a reaction to bodily, or visceral, changes that occur as a response to an environmental event and are interpreted as an emotional response.
- In contrast, the Cannon-Bard theory contends that both physiological arousal and an emotional experience are produced simultaneously by the same nerve stimulus and that the visceral experience does not necessarily differ among differing emotions.
- The Schachter-Singer theory suggests that emotions are determined jointly by a relatively nonspecific physiological arousal and the subsequent labeling of that arousal, using cues from the environment to determine how others are behaving in the same situation.
- The most recent approaches to emotions focus on their biological origins. For instance, it now seems that

specific patterns of biological arousal are associated with individual emotions. Furthermore, new scanning techniques have identified the specific parts of the brain that are activated during the experience of particular emotions.

LO 26-4 How does nonverbal behavior relate to the expression of emotions?

- A person's facial expressions can reveal emotions. In fact, members of different cultures understand others' emotional expressions in similar ways. One explanation for this similarity is that an innate facial-affect program activates a set of muscle movements representing the emotion being experienced.
- The facial-feedback hypothesis suggests that facial expressions not only reflect but also produce emotional experiences.

EVALUATE

1. Emotions are always accompanied by a cognitive response. True or false?
2. The _____ _____ theory of emotion states that emotions are a response to instinctive bodily events.
3. According to the _____ _____ theory of emotion, both an emotional response and physiological arousal are produced simultaneously by the same nerve stimulus.
4. Your friend, a psychology major, tells you, "I was at a party last night. During the course of the evening, my general level of arousal increased. Since I was at a party where people were enjoying themselves, I assume I must have felt happy." What theory of emotion does your friend subscribe to?

5. What are the six primary emotions that can be identified from facial expressions?

RETHINK

1. If researchers learned how to control emotional responses so that targeted emotions could be caused or prevented, what ethical concerns might arise? Under what circumstances, if any, should such techniques be used?

2. Many people enjoy watching movies, sporting events, and music performances in crowded theaters and arenas more than they like watching them at home alone. Which theory of emotions may help explain this? How?

Answers to Evaluate Questions

1. False; emotions may occur without a cognitive response; 2. James-Lange; 3. Cannon-Bard; 4. Schachter-Singer; 5. Surprise, sadness, happiness, anger, disgust, and fear

KEY TERMS

emotions	Cannon-Bard theory of	Schachter-Singer theory of	facial-affect program
James-Lange theory of	emotion	emotion	facial-feedback hypothesis
emotion			

LOOKING *Back*

EPILOGUE

Motivation and emotions are two interrelated aspects of psychology. In these modules, we first considered the topic of motivation, which has spawned a great deal of theory and research examining primary and secondary drives such as hunger, sex, and achievement. We then turned to a discussion of emotions, beginning with their functions and proceeding to a review of three major theories that seek to explain them. Finally, we looked at cultural differences in the expression and display of emotions and discussed the facial-feedback program, which seems to be innate and to regulate the nonverbal expression of the basic emotions.

Return to the prologue of this group of modules, which describes Chris Nikic's desire to be the first person with Down syndrome to finish an Ironman triathalon. Using your knowledge of motivation and emotion, consider the following questions:

1. Why do you think Chris Nikic chose such a difficult challenge?
2. What indicators in Nikic's story suggest that he was highly motivated to accomplish his goal?
3. Which approach to understanding motivation seems to best account for Nikic's triathlon victory?
4. Did Nikic seem to be motivated by a high need for achievement, in your opinion? Why or why not?

Design Elements: Man with laptop: Dragon Images/Shutterstock; Exclamation point and mobile frame: McGraw Hill; Smartphone: WML Image/Shutterstock; Hands: Stefano Garau/Shutterstock.

VISUAL SUMMARY 8 Motivation and Emotion

MODULE 24 Explaining Motivation

Motivation: The factors that direct and energize the behavior of humans and other organisms

└── The major approaches to motivation

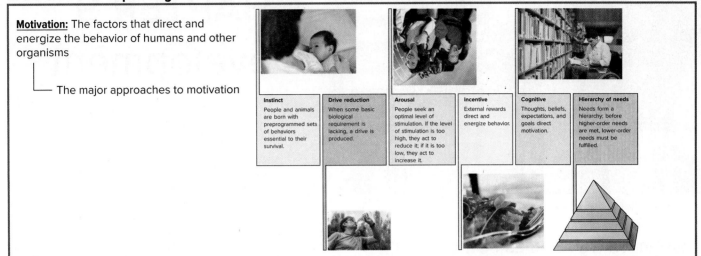

Instinct
People and animals are born with preprogrammed sets of behaviors essential to their survival.

Drive reduction
When some basic biological requirement is lacking, a drive is produced.

Arousal
People seek an optimal level of stimulation. If the level of stimulation is too high, they act to reduce it; if it is too low, they act to increase it.

Incentive
External rewards direct and energize behavior.

Cognitive
Thoughts, beliefs, expectations, and goals direct motivation.

Hierarchy of needs
Needs form a hierarchy; before higher-order needs are met, lower-order needs must be fulfilled.

MODULE 25 Human Needs and Motivation

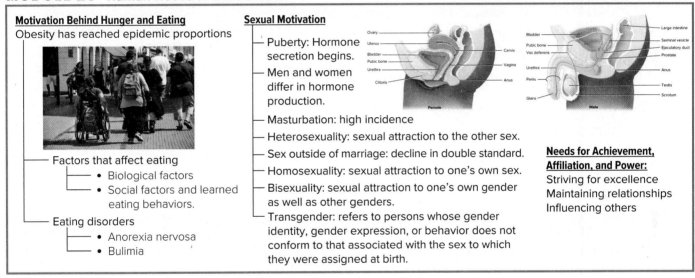

Motivation Behind Hunger and Eating
Obesity has reached epidemic proportions

└── Factors that affect eating
   ├── • Biological factors
   └── • Social factors and learned eating behaviors.
└── Eating disorders
   ├── • Anorexia nervosa
   └── • Bulimia

Sexual Motivation

├── Puberty: Hormone secretion begins.
├── Men and women differ in hormone production.
├── Masturbation: high incidence
├── Heterosexuality: sexual attraction to the other sex.
├── Sex outside of marriage: decline in double standard.
├── Homosexuality: sexual attraction to one's own sex.
├── Bisexuality: sexual attraction to one's own gender as well as other genders.
└── Transgender: refers to persons whose gender identity, gender expression, or behavior does not conform to that associated with the sex to which they were assigned at birth.

Needs for Achievement, Affiliation, and Power:
Striving for excellence
Maintaining relationships
Influencing others

MODULE 26 Understanding Emotional Experiences

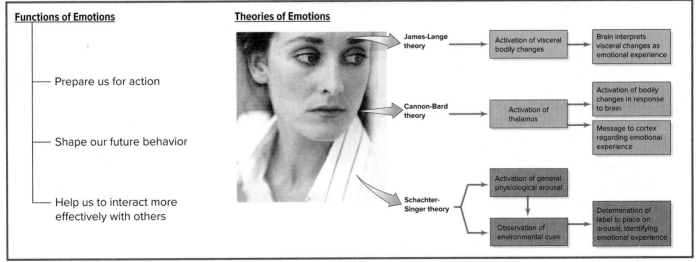

Functions of Emotions

├── Prepare us for action

├── Shape our future behavior

└── Help us to interact more effectively with others

Theories of Emotions

James-Lange theory → Activation of visceral bodily changes → Brain interprets visceral changes as emotional experience

Cannon-Bard theory → Activation of thalamus → Activation of bodily changes in response to brain / Message to cortex regarding emotional experience

Schachter-Singer theory → Activation of general physiological arousal / Observation of environmental cues → Determination of label to place on arousal, identifying emotional experience

(Module 24) (top left): Kawee Srital-on/123rf; (top middle): Digital Vision/Getty Images; (top right): wavebreakmedia/Shutterstock; (bottom left): Fabián Ponce/Alamy Stock Photo; (bottom middle): Corbis/VCG/Getty Images; (Module 25) (photo): Anirut Thailand/Shutterstock; (Module 26) (photo): Stockbyte/Getty Images

FatCamera/E+/Getty Images

CHAPTER 9
Development

LEARNING OUTCOMES FOR CHAPTER 9

MODULE 27

LO 27-1 How do psychologists study the degree to which development is an interaction of hereditary and environmental factors?

LO 27-2 What is the nature of development before birth?

LO 27-3 What factors affect a child during the mother's pregnancy?

NATURE AND NURTURE: THE ENDURING DEVELOPMENTAL ISSUE

Determining the Relative Influence of Nature and Nurture

Developmental Research Techniques

Prenatal Development: Conception to Birth

MODULE 28

LO 28-1 What are the major competencies of newborns?

LO 28-2 What are the milestones of physical and social development during childhood?

LO 28-3 How does cognitive development proceed during childhood?

INFANCY AND CHILDHOOD

The Extraordinary Newborn

The Growing Child: Infancy Through Middle Childhood

MODULE 29

LO 29-1 What major physical, social, and cognitive transitions characterize adolescence?

ADOLESCENCE: BECOMING AN ADULT

Physical Development: The Changing Adolescent

Moral and Cognitive Development: Distinguishing Right from Wrong

Social Development: Finding One's Self in a Social World

Applying Psychology in the 21st Century: Screen Time Is Fine? Hold the Phone

Exploring Diversity: Rites of Passage: Coming of Age Around the World

LO 30-1 What are the principal kinds of physical, social, and intellectual changes that occur in early and middle adulthood, and what are their causes?

LO 30-2 How does the reality of late adulthood differ from the stereotypes about that period?

LO 30-3 How can we adjust to death?

PROLOGUE *STILL DASHING AT 100*

Don Pellmann broke a number of records for his age group at the San Diego Senior Olympics. Five, in fact.

Not bad for a man who was 100 years old.

Pellmann broke records in the 100-meter dash, shot-put, discus, long jump, and high jump. His only disappointment came when he failed to break the pole vault record after three tries. His conclusion? He needs more practice.

Although Pellmann wore a hearing aid, he showed very little bone or muscle degeneration—certainly far less than most of his peer group. A gymnast and high jumper in college, Pellmann cut short his athletic career to take a job during the Depression. When he retired in 1970, one of his children suggested he enter a masters track meet, and from that point on, he ran and pursued his love for competitive athletics. He died at the age of 105 (Crouse, 2015; Stone, 2020).

LOOKING *Ahead*

Many people dread growing older. They imagine themselves slowing down and losing their strength. They fear having their health deteriorate and losing their independence and their memory. But as Don Pellmann proves, later adulthood can be filled with keen focus and new challenges. And although hair thins and grays, regularly exercising the body can sustain and enhance one's genetic inheritance.

Pellmann's continual striving to improve his performance and set new records gets to the heart of one of the broadest and most important areas of psychology: developmental

psychology. Developmental psychology is the branch of psychology that studies the patterns of growth and change that occur throughout life. It deals with issues ranging from new ways of conceiving children, to learning how to raise resilient children, to understanding the milestones of life that we all face.

Developmental psychologists study the interaction between the unfolding of biologically predetermined patterns of behavior and a constantly changing, dynamic environment. They ask how our genetic background affects our behavior throughout our lives and whether heredity limits our potential. Similarly, they seek to understand the ways in which the environment works with—or against—our genetic capabilities, how the world we live in affects our development, and how we can be encouraged to reach our full potential.

We begin by examining the approaches psychologists use to study development change across the life span. Then we consider the very start of development, beginning with conception and the 9 months of life before birth. We look at genetic as well as environmental influences on the developing fetus and the way they can affect behavior throughout the remainder of the life cycle.

Next, we examine development that occurs after birth: the enormous and rapid growth that takes place during the early stages of life and the physical, social, and cognitive changes throughout infancy, toddlerhood, and middle childhood. We then move on to development from adolescence through adulthood and end with a discussion of the ways in which people prepare themselves for death.

Module 27
Nature and Nurture: The Enduring Developmental Issue

LEARNING OUTCOMES

LO 27-1 How do psychologists study the degree to which development is an interaction of hereditary and environmental factors?

LO 27-2 What is the nature of development before birth?

LO 27-3 What factors affect a child during the mother's pregnancy?

developmental psychology The branch of psychology that studies the patterns of growth and change that occur throughout life. (Module 27)

How many bald, 6-foot-6, 250-pound volunteer firefighters in New Jersey wear droopy mustaches, aviator-style eyeglasses, and a key ring on the right side of the belt? The answer is two: Gerald Levey and Mark Newman. They are twins who were separated at birth. Neither twin even knew the other existed until they were reunited—in a fire station—by a fellow firefighter who knew Newman and was startled to see his double, Levey, at a firefighters' convention.

The lives of the twins, although separate, took remarkably similar paths. Levey went to college and studied forestry; Newman planned to study forestry in college but instead took a job trimming trees. Both had jobs in supermarkets. One had a job installing sprinkler systems; the other installed fire alarms.

Both men are unmarried and find the same kind of woman—"tall, slender, long hair"—attractive. They share similar hobbies and enjoy hunting, fishing, going to the beach, and watching old John Wayne movies and professional wrestling. Both like Chinese food and drink the same brand of beer. Their mannerisms are also similar; for example, each one throws his head back when he laughs. And, of course, there is one more thing: They share a passion for fighting fires.

The similarities we see in twins Gerald Levey and Mark Newman vividly raise one of the fundamental questions posed by **developmental psychology,** the study of the patterns of growth and change that occur throughout life. The question is this: How can we distinguish between the *environmental* causes of behavior (the influence of parents, siblings, family, friends, schooling, nutrition, and all the other experiences to which a child is exposed) and *hereditary* causes (those based on an individual's genetic makeup that influence growth and development throughout life)? This question

Identical twins Mark Newman (left) and Gerald Levey (right), who were separated at birth and reunited 31 years later. They are shown with researcher Dr. Nancy Segal, co-director of the Twins Reared Apart study.

AP Images

embodies the **nature-nurture issue.** In this context, nature refers to hereditary factors, and nurture refers to environmental influences.

Although the question was first posed as a nature-*versus*-nurture issue, developmental psychologists today agree that *both* nature and nurture interact to produce specific developmental patterns and outcomes. Consequently, the question has evolved into this: *How and to what degree* do environment and heredity both produce their effects? No one develops free of environmental influences or without being affected by their inherited *genetic makeup.* However, the debate over the comparative influence of the two factors remains active; different approaches and different theories of development emphasize the environment or heredity to a greater or lesser degree (Gruber, 2013; Limberg, 2015; Clinton et al., 2022).

For example, some developmental theories rely on basic psychological principles of learning and stress the role learning plays in producing changes in a developing child's behavior. Such theories emphasize the role of the environment in development. In contrast, other developmental theories emphasize the influence of one's physiological makeup and functioning on development. Such theories stress the role of heredity and *maturation*–the unfolding of biologically predetermined patterns of behavior–in producing developmental change. Maturation can be seen, for instance, in the development of sex characteristics (such as breasts and body hair) that occurs at the start of adolescence.

Furthermore, the work of *behavioral geneticists,* who study the effects of heredity on behavior, and the theories of evolutionary psychologists, who identify behavior patterns that result from our genetic inheritance, have influenced developmental psychologists. Behavioral geneticists are finding increasing evidence that cognitive abilities, personality traits, sexual orientation, and psychological disorders are determined to some extent by genetic factors (Krüger et al., 2017; Burt et al., 2019; Mahjani et al., 2021).

Behavioral genetics lies at the heart of the nature-nurture question. Although no one would argue that our behavior is determined *solely* by inherited factors, evidence collected by behavioral geneticists does suggest that our genetic inheritance predisposes us to respond in particular ways to our environment and even to seek out particular kinds of environments (Barnes & Jacobs, 2013; Marjlesi et al., 2019; Harden, 2021).

Despite their differences over theory, developmental psychologists concur on some points. They agree that genetic factors not only provide the potential for specific behaviors or traits to emerge but also place limitations on the emergence of such behavior or traits. For instance, heredity defines people's general level of intelligence and sets an upper limit that, regardless of the quality of the environment, people cannot exceed. Heredity also places limits on physical abilities; humans simply cannot run at a speed of 60 miles an hour or grow as tall as 10 feet, no matter the quality of their environment (Loehlin et al., 2015; von Stumm & Plomin, 2021).

Figure 1 lists some of the characteristics most affected by heredity. As you consider these items, keep in mind that these characteristics are not *entirely* determined by heredity because environmental factors also play a role.

Developmental psychologists also agree that in most instances environmental factors play a critical role in enabling people to reach the potential capabilities that their genetic background makes possible. If Albert Einstein had received no intellectual stimulation as a child and had not been sent to school, it is unlikely that he would have reached his genetic potential. Similarly, a great athlete such as basketball star Stephen Curry would have been unlikely to display much physical skill if he had not been raised in an environment that nurtured his innate talent and gave him the opportunity to train and perfect his natural abilities.

Clearly, the relationship between heredity and environment is complex. Therefore, developmental psychologists typically take an *interactionist* position on the nature-nurture issue by suggesting that a combination of hereditary and environmental factors influences development. Developmental psychologists face the challenge of identifying the relative strength of each of these influences on the individual as well as that of

nature-nurture issue The issue of the degree to which environment and heredity influence behavior. (Module 27)

Study Alert

The nature–nurture issue is a key question that is pervasive throughout the field of psychology. It explores how and to what degree environment and heredity produce their joint effects.

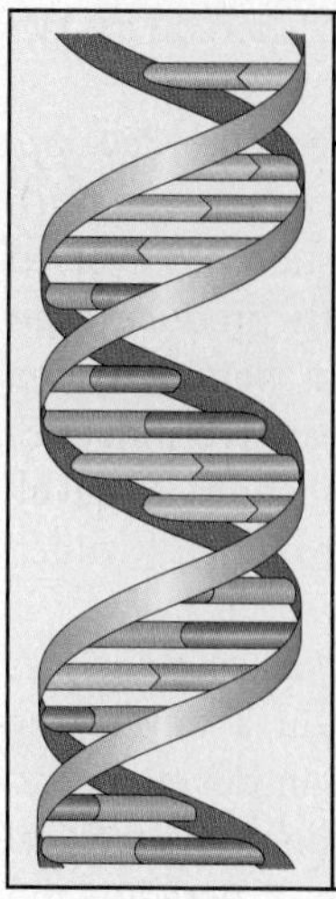

FIGURE 1 Characteristics influenced significantly by genetic factors. Although these characteristics have strong genetic components, they are also affected by environmental factors.

FIGURE 1 Characteristics influenced significantly by genetic factors. Although these characteristics have strong genetic components, they are also affected by environmental factors.

	Physical Characteristics	Intellectual Characteristics	Emotional Characteristics and Disorders
	Height	Memory	Shyness
	Weight	Intelligence	Extraversion
	Obesity	Age of language acquisition	Emotionality
	Tone of voice	Reading disabilities	Neuroticism
	Blood pressure	Intellectual disabilities	Schizophrenia
	Tooth decay		Anxiety
	Athletic ability		Alcoholism
	Age of death		
	Activity level		

identifying the specific changes that occur over the course of development (Steinbeis et al., 2017; Thompson, 2021).

Determining the Relative Influence of Nature and Nurture

Developmental psychologists use several approaches to determine the relative influence of genetic and environmental factors on behavior. In one approach, researchers can experimentally control the genetic makeup of laboratory animals by carefully breeding them for specific traits. For instance, by observing animals with identical genetic backgrounds placed in varied environments, researchers can learn the effects of specific kinds of environmental stimulation. Although researchers must be careful when generalizing the findings of nonhuman research to a human population, findings from animal research provide important information that cannot be obtained for ethical reasons by using human participants.

Human twins serve as another important source of information about the relative effects of genetic and environmental factors. **Identical twins** are genetically identical; they share the same genes and look alike. If they display different patterns of development, those differences have to be attributed to variations in the environment in which the twins were raised. The most useful data come from identical twins (such as Gerald Levey and Mark Newman) who are adopted at birth by different sets of adoptive parents and raised apart in differing environments. Studies of nontwin siblings who are raised in totally different environments also shed some light on the issue. Because they have relatively similar genetic backgrounds, siblings who show similarities as adults provide strong evidence for the importance of heredity (Farnsworth, 2015; Wertz et al., 2019; Gómez-Vallejo et al., 2021).

Researchers can also take the opposite track. Instead of concentrating on people with similar genetic backgrounds who are raised in different environments, they may consider people raised in similar environments who have totally dissimilar genetic backgrounds. For example, if they find similar courses of development in two adopted children who have different genetic backgrounds and have been raised in the same family, they have evidence for the importance of environmental influences on development. Moreover, psychologists can carry out research involving animals with dissimilar genetic backgrounds; by experimentally varying the environment in which the animals are raised, they can determine the influence of environmental factors (independent of heredity) on development (Beam & Turkheimer, 2013; Tosto et al., 2017; Kendler et al., 2021).

identical twins Twins who are genetically identical. (Module 27)

Developmental Research Techniques

Because of the demands of measuring behavioral change across different ages, developmental researchers use several unique methods. The most frequently used, **cross-sectional research,** compares people of different ages at the same point in time. Cross-sectional studies provide information about differences in development between different age groups (Card, 2017; Damian et al., 2019).

Suppose, for instance, we were interested in the development of intellectual ability in adulthood. To carry out a cross-sectional study, we might compare a sample of 25-, 45-, and 65-year-olds who all take the same IQ test. We then can determine whether average IQ test scores differ in each age group.

Cross-sectional research has limitations, however. For instance, we cannot be sure that the differences in IQ scores we might find in our example are due to age differences alone. Instead, the scores may reflect differences in the educational attainment of the cohorts represented. A *cohort* is a group of people who grow up at similar times, in similar places, and in similar conditions. In the case of IQ differences, any age differences we find in a cross-sectional study may reflect educational differences among the cohorts studied: People in the older age group may belong to a cohort that was less likely to attend college than were the people in the younger groups.

A longitudinal study, the second major research strategy developmental psychologists use, provides one way around this problem. **Longitudinal research** traces the behavior of one or more participants as they get older. Longitudinal studies assess *change* in behavior over time, whereas cross-sectional studies assess *differences* among groups of people.

For instance, consider how we might investigate intellectual development during adulthood by using a longitudinal research strategy. First, we might give an IQ test to a group of 25-year-olds. We'd then come back to the same people 20 years later and retest them at age 45. Finally, we'd return to them once more when they were 65 years old and test them again.

By examining changes at several points in time, we can see how individuals develop. Clearly, though, longitudinal research has some drawbacks. First, it requires a significant expenditure of time as the researcher waits for the participants to get older. In addition, participants who begin a study at an early age may drop out, move away, or even die as the research continues. Moreover, participants who take the same test at several points in time may become "test-wise" and perform better each time they take it because they have become more familiar with the test. Still, longitudinal research is an important technique of developmental researchers.

cross-sectional research A research method that compares people of different ages at the same point in time. (Module 27)

longitudinal research A research method that investigates behavior as participants get older. (Module 27)

> **Study Alert**
> Be sure to be able to distinguish the two different types of developmental research: cross-sectional (comparing people of different ages at the same time) and longitudinal (studying participants as they age).

Prenatal Development: Conception to Birth

Leah and John Howard's joy at learning Leah was pregnant turned to anxiety when Leah's doctor discovered that her brother had died from Duchenne muscular dystrophy (DMD) at age 12. The disease, the doctor explained, was an X-linked inherited disorder. If Leah turned out to be a carrier, there was a 50% chance that the baby would inherit the disease if it were male. The doctor advised them to have an ultrasound to determine the baby's sex. It turned out to be a boy.

The Howards faced two options. The doctor could take a chorion villus sampling now or wait a month and perform an amniocentesis. Both carried a very low risk for miscarriage. Leah chose amniocentesis, but the results were inconclusive. The doctor then suggested a fetal muscle biopsy to confirm the presence or lack of the muscle protein dystrophin. The absence of dystrophin would signal DMD. The risk of miscarriage, however, was not inconsiderable.

Four months pregnant at this point and tired of the worries and tears, Leah and John decided to take their chances and look forward to their baby's birth.

The Howards' case shows the difficult choices that parents may encounter due to our increasing understanding of life spent inside a mother's womb.

Yet, our knowledge of the biology of *conception*—when a male's sperm cell penetrates a female's egg cell—and its aftermath makes the start of life no less of a miracle. Let's consider how an individual is created by looking first at the genetic endowment that a child receives at the moment of conception.

THE BASICS OF GENETICS

chromosomes Rod-shaped structures that contain all basic hereditary information. (Module 27)

genes The parts of the chromosomes through which genetic information is transmitted. (Module 27)

! Study Alert

It's important to understand the basic building blocks of genetics: chromosomes, which contain genes, which in turn are composed of sequences of DNA.

The one-cell entity established at conception contains 23 pairs of **chromosomes,** rod-shaped structures that contain all basic hereditary information. One member of each pair is from the mother, and the other is from the father.

Each chromosome contains thousands of **genes**—smaller units through which genetic information is transmitted. Either individually or in combination, genes produce each person's particular characteristics. Composed of sequences of *DNA (deoxyribonucleic acid)* molecules, genes are the biological equivalent of "software" that programs the future development of all parts of the body's hardware. Humans have some 25,000 different genes (see Figure 2).

Some genes control the development of systems common to all members of the human species—the heart, circulatory system, brain, lungs, and so forth; others shape the characteristics that make each human unique, such as facial configuration, height, and eye color. The child's sex is also determined by a particular combination of genes.

Specifically, a child inherits an X chromosome from its mother and either an X or a Y chromosome from its father. When it receives an XX combination, it is a female; with an XY combination, it develops as a male. Male development is triggered by a single gene on the Y chromosome; without the presence of that specific gene, the individual will develop as a female.

As behavioral geneticists have discovered, genes are also at least partially responsible for a wide variety of personal characteristics, including cognitive abilities, personality traits, and psychological disorders. Of course, few of these characteristics are determined by a single gene. Instead, most traits result from a combination of multiple genes that operate together with environmental influences (Armbruster et al., 2011; Kasantseva et al., 2015; Weinschenk et al., 2019; Perlstein & Waller, 2022).

THE HUMAN GENOME PROJECT

Our understanding of genetics took a giant leap forward in 2001, when scientists were able to map the specific location and sequence of every human gene as part of the

 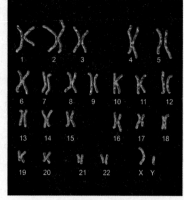  

(a) Conception   (b) 23 pairs of chromosomes   (c) DNA sequence   (d) Genes

FIGURE 2 Every individual's characteristics are determined by the individual's specific genetic information. (a) At the moment of conception, (b) humans receive 23 pairs of chromosomes, half from the mother and half from the father. (c) These chromosomes are made up of coils of DNA. (d) Each chromosome contains thousands of genes that "program" the future development of the body.

(a) MedicalRF.com; (b) BSIP SA/Alamy Stock Photo; (c) Double Brain/Shutterstock; (d) Biophoto Associates/Science Source

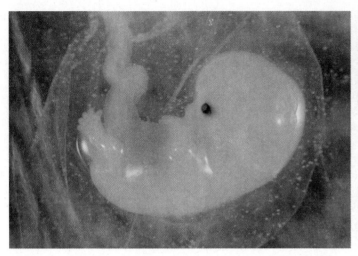 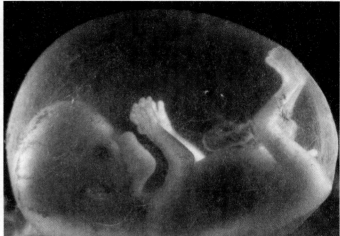

These remarkable photos of live fetuses display the degree of physical development at prenatal ages 4 and 15 weeks.

(Left) Steve Allen/Science Source; (Right) Claude Edelmann/Science Source

massive *Human Genome Project.* The accomplishment was one of the most important in the history of biology (International Human Genome Sequencing Consortium, 2003; Grigorenko & Dozier, 2013; Özdemir et al., 2017; Pennisi, 2022).

The success of the Human Genome Project started a revolution in health care because scientists can identify the particular genes responsible for genetically caused disorders. It is already leading not only to the identification of risk factors in children but also to the development of new treatments for physical and psychological disorders.

THE EARLIEST DEVELOPMENT

When an egg becomes fertilized by the sperm, the resulting one-celled entity, called a **zygote,** immediately begins to develop. The zygote starts out as a microscopic speck. Three days after fertilization, though, the zygote increases to around 32 cells; within a week, it has grown to 100-150 cells. These first 2 weeks are known as the *germinal period.*

Two weeks after conception, the developing cells enter the *embryonic period,* which lasts from week 2 through week 8; the developing zygote is now called an **embryo.** As an embryo develops through an intricate, preprogrammed process of cell division, it grows 10,000 times larger by 4 weeks of age and attains a length of about one-fifth of an inch. At this point, it has developed a rudimentary beating heart, a brain, an intestinal tract, and a number of other organs. Although all these organs are at a primitive stage of development, they are clearly recognizable. Moreover, by week 8, the embryo is about an inch long and has discernible arms, legs, and a face.

From week 8 and continuing until birth, the developing embryo enters the *fetal period* and is called a **fetus.** At the start of this period, it begins to respond to touch; it bends its fingers when touched on the hand. At 16 to 18 weeks, its movements become strong enough for the mother to sense them. At the same time, hair may begin to grow on its head, and the facial features become similar to those the child will display at birth. The major organs begin functioning, although the fetus could not be kept alive outside the mother. In addition, a lifetime's worth of brain neurons are produced—although it is unclear whether the brain is capable of thinking at this early stage.

Within the womb, the fetus continues to develop before birth. It begins to grow fatty deposits under the skin, and it gains weight. The fetus reaches the **age of viability,** the point at which it can survive if born prematurely, at about prenatal age 22 weeks. By week 24, a fetus has many of the characteristics it will display as a newborn. In fact, when an infant is born prematurely at this age, it can open and close its eyes; suck; cry; look up, down, and around; and even grasp objects placed in its hands.

zygote The new cell formed by the union of an egg and sperm. (Module 27)

embryo A developed zygote that has a heart, a brain, and other organs. (Module 27)

fetus A developing individual from 8 weeks after conception until birth. (Module 27)

age of viability The point at which a fetus can survive if born prematurely. (Module 27)

Study Alert

Sensitive (or critical) periods, which can occur before or after birth, are important because they indicate the time that organisms are particularly susceptible to damage that may affect them for the rest of their lives.

At prenatal age 28 weeks, the fetus weighs less than 3 pounds and is about 16 inches long. It may be capable of learning: One study found that the infants of mothers who had repeatedly read aloud *The Cat in the Hat* by Dr. Seuss before the infants' birth preferred the sound of that particular story to other stories after they were born (Spence & DeCasper, 1982; Moon et al., 2013; Cline et al., 2022).

Before birth, a fetus passes through several *sensitive periods*. A sensitive period is the time when organisms are particularly susceptible to certain kinds of stimuli. For example, fetuses are especially affected by their mothers' use of drugs during certain sensitive periods before birth. If they are exposed to a particular drug before or after the sensitive period, it may have relatively little impact; if exposure comes during a sensitive period, the impact will be significant (Sandman, 2015; Röder et al., 2021).

From the perspective of...

An Educator How might awareness of sensitive periods in language development be taken into account to improve students' learning?

Andersen Ross/Blend Images/Getty Images

Sensitive periods can also occur after birth. Some language specialists suggest, for instance, that there is a period in which children are particularly receptive to developing language. If children are not exposed to appropriate linguistic stimuli, their language development may be impaired (Opendak et al., 2017; Dunn et al., 2019; Gee, 2022).

In the final weeks of pregnancy, the fetus continues to gain weight and grow. At the end of the normal 38 weeks of pregnancy, the fetus typically weighs 7 pounds and is about 20 inches in length. However, the story is different for *preterm infants,* who are born before week 38. Because they have not been able to develop fully, they are at higher risk for illness, future problems, and even death. For infants who have been in the womb for more than 30 weeks, the prospects are relatively good. However, for those born before week 30, the story is often less positive. Such newborns, who may weigh as little as 2 pounds at birth, are in grave danger because they have immature organs; they have less than a 50-50 chance of survival. If they do survive–and it takes extraordinarily heroic (and expensive) medical intervention to ensure this–they may later experience significant developmental delays.

GENETIC INFLUENCES ON THE FETUS

The process of fetal growth that we have just described reflects normal development, which occurs in 95-98% of all pregnancies. Some individuals are less fortunate; in the remaining 2-5% of cases, children are born with serious birth defects. A major cause of such defects is faulty genes or chromosomes. Here are some of the more common genetic and chromosomal difficulties.

- *Phenylketonuria (PKU).* A child born with the inherited disease phenylketonuria cannot produce an enzyme that is required for normal development. This deficiency results in an accumulation of poisons that eventually cause profound intellectual disability. The disease is treatable, however, if it is caught early. Most infants today are routinely tested for PKU, and children with the disorder can be placed on a special diet that allows them to develop normally (Widaman, 2009; Romani et al., 2017; Canton et al., 2019).

- *Sickle-cell anemia.* One of a group of diseases know as *sickle cell disease*, sickle-cell anemia gets its name from the abnormally shaped red blood cells that characterize it. About 1 in 13 Black babies is born with the sickle cell trait. They may have episodes of pain, yellowish eyes, stunted growth, and vision problems (Wills, 2013; Pecker & Lanzkron, 2021).

- *Tay-Sachs disease.* Children born with Tay-Sachs disease, a disorder most often found in Jews of Eastern European ancestry, usually die by age 3 or 4 because of the body's inability to break down fat. If both parents carry the genetic defect that produces the fatal illness, their child has a 1 in 4 chance of being born with the disease (McPartland, 2016; Zhang et al., 2019; Flotte et al., 2022).

- *Down syndrome.* Down syndrome, one of the causes of intellectual disability, occurs when the zygote receives an extra chromosome at the moment of conception. Down syndrome is often related to the mother's age; mothers over 35 and younger than 18 stand a higher risk than do other women of having a child with the syndrome (Nærland et al., 2017; Bull, 2020).

PRENATAL ENVIRONMENTAL INFLUENCES

Genetic factors are not the only causes of difficulties in fetal development. Environmental influences–the *nurture* part of the nature–nurture equation–also affect the fetus. Some of the more profound consequences are brought about by **teratogens,** environmental agents such as drugs, chemicals, viruses, or other factors that produce birth defects. Among the major prenatal environmental influences on the fetus are the following:

teratogens Environmental agents such as drugs, chemicals, viruses, or other factors that produce birth defects. (Module 27)

- *Mother's nutrition.* What a mother eats during her pregnancy has important implications for the health of her baby. Seriously undernourished mothers cannot provide adequate nutrition to a growing fetus, and they are likely to give birth to underweight babies. Poorly nourished babies are also more susceptible to disease, and a lack of nourishment may adversely affect their cognitive development. Because some 1 billion people worldwide are vulnerable to undernutrition, the problem is immense. And the COVID-19 pandemic has made the problem worse due to disruptions in the food supply chains in low- and middle-income countries (Carmichael et al., 2019; Littlejohn & Finlay, 2021; Marshall et al., 2022).

- *Mother's illness.* Even minor illnesses that a mother catches during the early months of pregnancy can have devastating consequences for a developing fetus. For example, if pregnant women contract rubella (German measles), syphilis, diabetes, or high blood pressure, each disease may produce permanent, lifelong effects on the fetus (Magoni et al., 2005; Mirambo et al., 2019).

- *Mother's emotional state.* A mother's emotional state affects her baby. Mothers who are anxious and tense during the last months of their pregnancies are more apt to have irritable infants who sleep and eat poorly. The reason? The autonomic nervous system of the fetus becomes especially sensitive as a result of chemical changes produced by the mother's emotional state (Kumari & Joshi, 2013; Craig et al., 2021; Van Den Heuvel et al., 2021).

- *Mother's use of drugs.* Mothers who take illegal, physically addictive drugs such as cocaine run the risk of giving birth to babies who are similarly addicted. Their newborns suffer painful withdrawal symptoms and sometimes show permanent physical and mental impairment. Even legal drugs taken by a pregnant woman (who may not know that she has become pregnant) can have a tragic effect. Moreover, the recent opioid addiction crisis has produced an increase in *neonatal abstinence syndrome,* in which infants born to mothers addicted to codeine, fetanyl, and oxycodon are themselves addicted to the drugs. The syndrome has increased 500% over the past decade to 5.8 per 1,000 hospital births (Nygaard et al., 2017; Patrick et al., 2021; Cestonaro et al., 2022).

FIGURE 3 A variety of environmental factors can play a role in prenatal development.

Environmental Factor	Possible Effect on Prenatal Development
Rubella (German measles)	Blindness, deafness, heart abnormalities, stillbirth
Syphilis	Intellectual disability, physical deformities, maternal miscarriage
Addictive drugs	Low birth weight, addiction of infant to drug, with possible death after birth from withdrawal
Nicotine	Premature birth, low birth weight and length
Alcohol	Intellectual disability, lower-than-average birth weight, small head, limb deformities
Radiation from X-rays	Physical deformities, intellectual disability
Inadequate diet	Reduction in growth of brain, smaller-than-average weight and length at birth
Mother's age—younger than 18 at birth of child	Premature birth, increased incidence of Down syndrome
Mother's age—older than 35 at birth of child	Increased incidence of Down syndrome
DES (diethylstilbestrol)	Reproductive difficulties and increased incidence of genital cancer in children of mothers who were given DES during pregnancy to prevent miscarriage
AIDS	Possible spread of AIDS virus to infant; facial deformities; growth failure
Accutane	Intellectual disability and physical deformities

- *Alcohol.* Alcohol is extremely dangerous to fetal development and may result in *fetal alcohol syndrome disorder (FASD),* a condition resulting in below-average intelligence, growth delays, and facial deformities. Around 1.5 of every 1,000 infants are born with FASD, and for some populations of children (such as those receiving special education services), the incidence is even higher. FASD is now the primary preventable cause of intellectual disability. Even mothers who use small amounts of alcohol during pregnancy place their child at risk (Lewis et al., 2015; Vorgias & Bernstein, 2021; Gosdin et al., 2022).

- *Nicotine use.* Pregnant mothers who smoke put their children at considerable risk. Smoking while pregnant can lead to miscarriage and infant death. For children who do survive, the negative consequences of mother's tobacco use can last a lifetime (Rogers, 2009; Magee et al., 2013; Zambrano-Sánchez et al., 2021; Nagpal et al., 2021).

Several other environmental factors have an impact on the child before and during birth (see Figure 3). Keep in mind, however, that although we have been discussing the influences of genetics and environment separately, neither factor works alone. Furthermore, despite the emphasis here on some of the ways in which development can go wrong, the vast majority of births occur without difficulty. And in most instances, subsequent development also proceeds normally.

RECAP/EVALUATE/RETHINK

RECAP

LO 27-1 How do psychologists study the degree to which development is an interaction of hereditary and environmental factors?

- Developmental psychology studies growth and change throughout life. One fundamental question is how much developmental change is due to heredity and how much is due to environment—the nature-nurture issue. Heredity seems to define the upper limits of our growth and change, whereas the environment affects the degree to which the upper limits are reached.

- Cross-sectional research compares people of different ages with one another at the same point in time. In contrast, longitudinal research traces the behavior of one or more participants as they age. Finally, sequential research combines the two methods by examining several different age groups at several points in time.

LO 27-2 What is the nature of development before birth?

- At the moment of conception, a male's sperm cell and a female's egg cell unite; each contributes to the new entity's genetic makeup. The union of sperm and egg produces a zygote, which contains 23 pairs of chromosomes; one member of each pair comes from the father and the other comes from the mother.

- Each chromosome contains genes through which genetic information is transmitted. Genes, which are composed of DNA sequences, are the "software" that programs the future development of the body's hardware.

- Genes affect not only physical attributes but also a wide array of personal characteristics such as cognitive abilities, personality traits, and psychological disorders.

- After 2 weeks, the zygote becomes an embryo. By week 8, the embryo is called a fetus and is responsive to touch and other stimulation. At about week 22, it reaches the age of viability, which means it may survive if born prematurely. A fetus is normally born after 38 weeks of pregnancy; it weighs around 7 pounds and measures about 20 inches.

LO 27-3 What factors affect a child during the mother's pregnancy?

- Genetic abnormalities produce birth defects such as phenylketonuria (PKU), sickle-cell anemia, Tay-Sachs disease, and Down syndrome.

- Among the environmental influences on fetal growth are the mother's nutrition, illnesses, and drug intake.

EVALUATE

1. Developmental psychologists are interested in the effects of both _____ and _____ on development.

2. Environment and heredity both influence development with genetic potentials generally establishing limits on environmental influences. True or false?

3. By observing genetically similar animals in differing environments, we can increase our understanding of the influences of hereditary and environmental factors in humans. True or false?

4. _____ research studies the same individuals over a period of time, whereas _____ - _____ research studies people of different ages at the same time.

5. Match each of the following terms with its definition:
   1. Zygote
   2. Gene
   3. Chromosome

   a. Smallest unit through which genetic information is passed.
   b. Fertilized egg
   c. Rod-shaped structure containing genetic information

6. Specific kinds of growth must take place during a _____ period if the embryo is to develop normally.

RETHINK

1. When researchers find similarities in development between very different cultures, what implications might such findings have for the nature–nurture issue?

2. Consider the factors that might determine when a child learns to walk. What kinds of environmental influences might be involved? What kinds of genetic influences might be involved?

Answers to Evaluate Questions

1. heredity (or nature), environment (or nurture); 2. True; 3. True; 4. Longitudinal, cross-sectional; 5. 1-b, 2-a, 3-c; 6. sensitive (or critical)

KEY TERMS

developmental psychology	cross-sectional research	genes	fetus
nature–nurture issue	longitudinal research	zygote	age of viability
identical twins	chromosomes	embryo	teratogens

Module 28
Infancy and Childhood

LEARNING OUTCOMES

LO 28-1 What are the major competencies of newborns?

LO 28-2 What are the milestones of physical and social development during childhood?

LO 28-3 How does cognitive development proceed during childhood?

neonate A newborn child. (Module 28)

reflexes Unlearned, involuntary responses that occur automatically in the presence of certain stimuli. (Module 28)

His head was molded into a long melon shape and came to a point at the back. . . . He was covered with a thick greasy white material known as "vernix," which made him slippery to hold and also allowed him to slip easily through the birth canal. In addition to a shock of black hair on his head, his body was covered with dark, fine hair known as "lanugo." His ears, his back, his shoulders, and even his cheeks were furry. . . . His skin was wrinkled and quite loose, ready to scale in creased places such as his feet and hands. . . . His ears were pressed to his head in unusual positions–one ear was matted firmly forward on his cheek. His nose was flattened and pushed to one side by the squeeze as he came through the pelvis. (Brazelton, 1969, p. 3)

What kind of creature is this? Although the description hardly fits that of the adorable babies seen in advertisements for baby food, we are in fact talking about a normal, completely developed child just after the moment of birth. Called a **neonate,** a newborn arrives in the world in a form that hardly meets the standards of beauty against which we typically measure babies. Yet ask any parents: Nothing is more beautiful or exciting than the first glimpse of their newborn.

The Extraordinary Newborn

Several factors cause a neonate's strange appearance. The trip through the mother's birth canal may have squeezed the incompletely formed bones of the skull together and squashed the nose into the head. Also, the skin of a newborn may be slippery because it secretes *vernix*, a white greasy covering, for protection before birth. In addition, the baby may have *lanugo*, a soft fuzz, over the entire body for a similar purpose. And the infant's eyelids may be puffy with an accumulation of fluids because of the upside-down position during birth.

All these features change during the first 2 weeks of life as the neonate takes on a more familiar appearance. Even more impressive are the capabilities a neonate begins to display from the moment of birth–capabilities that grow at an astounding rate over the ensuing months.

REFLEXES

A neonate is born with a number of **reflexes**, unlearned, involuntary responses that occur automatically in the presence of certain stimuli. Critical for survival, many of those reflexes unfold naturally as part of an infant's ongoing maturation. The *rooting reflex*, for instance, causes neonates to turn their heads toward things that touch their cheeks, such as the mother's nipple or a bottle. Similarly, a *sucking reflex* prompts infants to suck at things that touch their lips. Among other reflexes are a *gag reflex* (to clear the throat), the *startle reflex* (a series of movements in which an infant flings out the arms, fans the fingers, and arches the back in response to a sudden noise), and the *Babinski reflex* (a baby's toes fan out when the outer edge of the sole of the foot is stroked).

Infants lose these primitive reflexes after the first few months of life and replace them with more complex and

Many of the reflexes that a neonate is born with are critical for survival and unfold naturally as a part of the infant's ongoing maturation. Do you think humans have more or fewer reflexes than other animals do?
Yoshiwara/E+/Getty Images

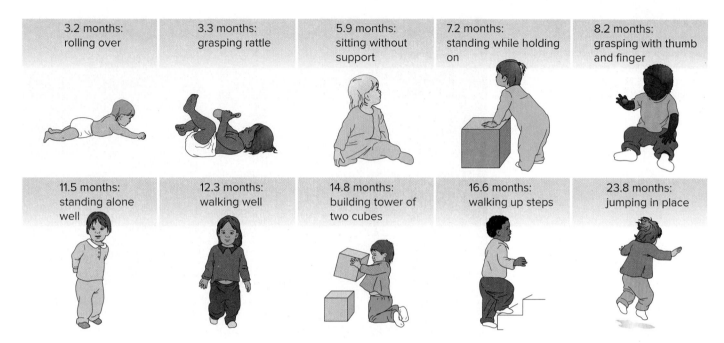

FIGURE 1 Although at birth a neonate can make only jerky, limited voluntary movements, during the first year of life, the ability to move independently grows enormously. The ages shown in this figure indicate the time when 50% of children are able to perform each skill. Remember, however, that the time when each skill appears can vary considerably. For example, 25% of children are able to walk well at age 11 months; by 15 months, 90% of children are walking well.

Source: Adapted from Frankenburg et al., 1992.

organized behaviors. Although at birth a neonate is capable of only jerky, limited voluntary movements, the ability to move independently grows enormously during the first year of life. The typical baby rolls over by the age of about 3 months, sits without support at about 6 months, stands alone at about 11 months, and walks at just over a year old. Not only does the ability to make large-scale movements improve during this time, but fine-muscle movements also become increasingly sophisticated (see Figure 1).

DEVELOPMENT OF THE SENSES: TAKING IN THE WORLD

When proud parents peer into the eyes of their neonate, is the child able to return their gaze? Although it was thought for some time that newborns can only see a hazy blur, most current findings indicate that neonates' capabilities are far more impressive. Newborns can see objects reasonably well that are within 7–8 inches of their eyes, although they have a limited capacity to see beyond that distance, and can follow moving objects within their field of vision. They also show the beginnings of depth perception as they react by raising their hands when an object appears to be moving rapidly toward their face (Craighero et al., 2011; Brown et al., 2018; Capone & Drenser, 2021).

You might think that it would be hard to figure out just how well neonates can see because their lack of both language and reading ability clearly prevents them from saying what direction the E on a vision chart is facing. However, researchers have devised a number of ingenious methods that rely on the newborn's biological responses and innate reflexes to test perceptual skills.

For instance, infants who see a novel stimulus typically pay close attention to it; as a consequence, their heart rates increase. But if they repeatedly see the same stimulus, their attention to it decreases, as indicated by a return to a slower heart rate. This phenomenon is known as **habituation,** the decrease in the response to a stimulus that occurs after repeated presentations of the same stimulus. By studying habituation, developmental psychologists can tell when a child who is too young to speak can detect and discriminate a stimulus (Molina et al., 2015; Friedman, 2018).

Study Alert

The basic reflexes—unlearned, involuntary responses—include the rooting reflex, the sucking reflex, the gag reflex, the startle reflex, and the Babinski reflex.

habituation The decrease in the response to a stimulus that occurs after repeated presentations of the same stimulus. (Module 28)

FIGURE 2 This infant is imitating the expressions of the adult in this photo. How does this ability, which starts at the beginning of infancy, contribute to social development?

Allen Donikowski/Getty Images

Researchers have developed many other methods for measuring neonate and infant perception. One technique, for instance, involves babies sucking on a nipple attached to a computer. A change in the rate and vigor with which the babies suck helps researchers infer that babies can perceive variations in stimuli. Other approaches include examining babies' eye movements and observing which way babies move their heads in response to a visual stimulus (Bulf et al., 2011; Sicard-Cras et al., 2022).

Through the use of such research techniques, we now know that infants' visual perception is remarkably sophisticated from the start of life. At birth, babies prefer patterns with contours and edges over less distinct patterns, indicating that they can respond to the configuration of stimuli. Furthermore, even newborns are aware of size constancy because they are apparently sensitive to the phenomenon by which objects stay the same size even though the image on the retina may change size as the distance between the object and the retina varies (Hadad et al., 2017; Held, 2022).

In fact, neonates can discriminate facial expressions–and even imitate them. As you can see in Figure 2, an infant can produce a good imitation of an adult's expressions. Even very young babies, then, can respond to the emotions and moods that their caregivers' facial expressions reveal. This capability provides the foundation for social interaction skills in children (de Klerk et al., 2019; Onal Ertugrul et al., 2022).

Other visual abilities grow rapidly after birth. By the end of their first month, babies can distinguish some colors from others; after 4 months, they can focus on near or far objects. By the age of 4 or 5 months, they are able to recognize two- and three-dimensional objects, and they can perceive the Gestalt organizing principles discovered by psychologists who study perception. By the age of 7 months, neural systems related to the processing of information about facial expressions are highly sophisticated and cause babies to respond differently to specific facial expressions. Overall, their perceptual abilities rapidly improve: Sensitivity to visual stimuli, for instance, becomes three to four times greater at 1 year of age than it was at birth (Leppänen et al., 2007; Xiao et al., 2015).

In addition to vision, infants display other impressive sensory capabilities. Newborns can distinguish different sounds to the point of being able to recognize their own mothers' voices at the age of 3 days. They can also make the subtle perceptual distinctions that underlie language abilities. For example, at 2 days of age, infants can distinguish between their native tongue and foreign languages, and they can discriminate between such closely related sounds as *ba* and *pa* when they are 4 days old. By

6 months of age, they can discriminate virtually any difference in sound that is relevant to the production of language. Moreover, they can recognize different tastes and smells at a very early age. There even seems to be something of a built-in sweet tooth: Neonates prefer liquids that have been sweetened with sugar over their unsweetened counterparts (Purdy et al., 2013; Smith et al., 2017; Nicklaus & Schwartz, 2019).

The Growing Child: Infancy Through Middle Childhood

Three-year-old Shanthi Subbaswamy always had Cheerios on her breath. Mindy Crowell, Shanthi's day care teacher, thought little of it until she noticed that the classroom Cheerios stash was steadily dwindling.

The Cheerios were stored in a plastic bin in the clothes closet. Keeping an eye on the closet, Mindy soon saw Shanthi enter it, manipulate the fastener of the bin, reach in and withdraw a hand laden with Cheerios, and let the bin refasten itself, as it was designed to do. Mindy was amazed: Somehow, Shanthi, barely able to navigate a crayon, had learned how to undo the supposedly child-proof fastener—a task that Mindy herself found difficult.

Mindy waited to see what would happen next. What she found was that Shanthi was an excellent teacher. In the next few days, Paul, Paloma, and Kelly began to frequent the bin and do exactly what Shanthi had done.

At 3 years old, Shanthi asserted her personality, illustrating the tremendous growth that occurs in a variety of domains during the first year of life. Throughout the remainder of childhood, moving from infancy into middle childhood and the start of adolescence around age 11 or 12, children develop physically, socially, and cognitively in extraordinary ways. In the remainder of this module, we'll consider this development.

PHYSICAL DEVELOPMENT

Children's physical growth provides the most obvious sign of development. During the first year of life, children typically triple their birthweight, and their height increases by about half. This rapid growth slows down as the child gets older; think how gigantic adults would be if that rate of growth were constant. From age 3 to the beginning of adolescence at around age 13, growth averages a gain of about 5 pounds and 3 inches a year (see Figure 3).

The physical changes that occur as children develop are not just a matter of increasing growth; the relationship of the size of the various body parts to one another changes dramatically as children age. As you can see in Figure 4, the head of a fetus (and a newborn) is disproportionately large. However, the head soon becomes more proportional in size to the rest of the body as growth occurs mainly in the trunk and legs (Adolph & Berger, 2011).

DEVELOPMENT OF SOCIAL BEHAVIOR: TAKING ON THE WORLD

As anyone who has seen infants smiling at the sight of their mothers can guess, at the same time that infants grow physically and hone their perceptual abilities, they also develop socially. The nature of a child's early social development provides the foundation for social relationships that will last a lifetime.

Attachment is the positive emotional bond that develops between a child and a particular individual. Attachment is the most important form of social development that occurs during infancy. The earliest studies of attachment were carried out by animal ethologist Konrad Lorenz (1966). Lorenz focused on newborn goslings, which under normal circumstances instinctively follow their mother, the first moving object they perceive after birth. Lorenz found that goslings whose eggs were raised in an

attachment The positive emotional bond that develops between a child and a particular individual. (Module 28)

FIGURE 3 The average heights and weights of males and females in the United States from age 2 through age 20. At what ages are girls typically heavier and taller than boys?

Source: Adapted from National Center for Health Statistics, 2000.

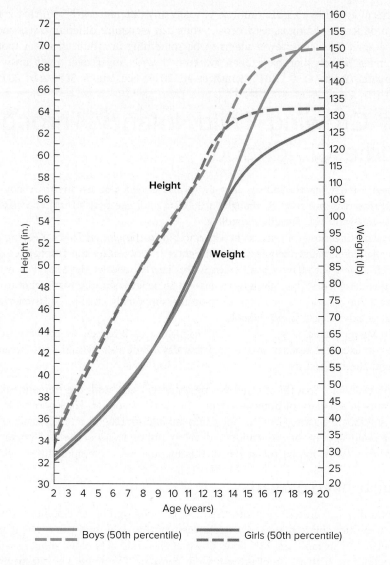

Boys (50th percentile)   Girls (50th percentile)

incubator and that viewed him immediately after hatching would follow his every movement as if he were their mother. He labeled this process *imprinting,* behavior that takes place during a critical period and involves attachment to the first moving object that is observed.

FIGURE 4 As development progresses, the size of the head relative to the rest of the body decreases until the individual reaches adulthood. Why do you think the head starts out so large?

Source: Adapted from Robbins, 1929.

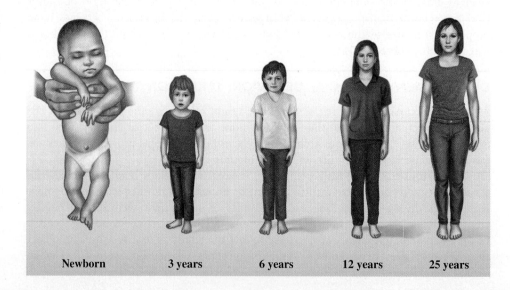

Newborn   **3 years**   **6 years**   **12 years**   **25 years**

Our understanding of attachment progressed when psychologist Harry Harlow, in a classic study, gave infant monkeys the choice of cuddling a wire "monkey" that provided milk or a soft, terry cloth "monkey" that was warm but did not provide milk. Their choice was clear: They spent most of their time clinging to the warm cloth "monkey," although they made occasional forays to the wire monkey to nurse. Obviously, the cloth monkey provided greater comfort to the infants; milk alone was insufficient to create attachment (Harlow & Zimmerman, 1959; Levine & Munsch, 2011; van Rosmalen et al., 2022; see Figure 5).

Building on this pioneering work, developmental psychologists have suggested that human attachment grows through the responsiveness of infants' caregivers to signals such as crying, smiling, reaching, and clinging. The more that caregivers respond to signals that children give off regarding their emotions, the more likely it is that the child will become securely attached to the caregiver. Full attachment eventually develops as a result of the complex series of interactions between caregiver and child. In the course of these interactions, the infant plays as critical and active of a role as the caregiver does in the formation of the bond between them. Infants who respond positively to a caregiver produce more positive behavior on the caregiver's part, which, in turn, produces an even stronger degree of attachment in the child.

FIGURE 5 Although the wire "mother" dispensed milk to the hungry infant monkey, the infant preferred the soft, terry cloth "mother." Do you think human babies would react the same way? What does this experiment tell us about attachment?
Science History Images/Alamy Stock Photo

Study Alert
Attachment—the positive emotional bond that develops between a child and a particular individual—is a key concept in understanding the social development of children.

Assessing Attachment Developmental psychologists have devised a quick and direct way to measure attachment. Developed by Mary Ainsworth, the *Ainsworth strange situation* consists of a sequence of events involving a child and (typically) their mother. Initially, the mother and baby enter an unfamiliar room, and the mother permits the baby to explore while she sits down. An adult stranger then enters the room; after this, the mother leaves. The mother returns, and the stranger leaves. The mother once again leaves the baby alone, and the stranger returns. Finally, the stranger leaves, and the mother returns (Ainsworth et al., 1978; Van Rosmalen et al., 2015; Posada & Trumbell, 2017).

Babies' reactions to the experimental situation vary drastically, depending, according to Ainsworth, on their degree of attachment to the mother:

- *Securely attached children.* Children who are securely attached employ the mother as a kind of home base; they explore independently but return to her occasionally. When she leaves, they exhibit distress, and they go to her when she returns.

- *Avoidant children.* Avoidant children do not cry when the mother leaves, and they seem to avoid her when she returns, as if they were indifferent to her.

- *Ambivalent children.* Ambivalent children display anxiety before they are separated and are upset when the mother leaves, but they may show ambivalent reactions to her return, such as seeking close contact but simultaneously hitting and kicking her.

- *Disorganized-disoriented children.* A fourth reaction is disorganized-disoriented; these children show inconsistent and often contradictory behavior. For example, they may approach their mother but at the same time avoid eye contact or otherwise act in an inappropriate way.

The nature of attachment between children and their mothers has far-reaching consequences for later development. For example, children who are securely attached to their mothers tend to be more socially and emotionally competent than are their less securely attached peers, and others find them more cooperative, capable, and playful. Furthermore, children who are securely attached at age 1 show fewer psychological difficulties when they grow older compared with avoidant and ambivalent youngsters. As adults, children who are securely attached tend to have more successful romantic relationships. On the other hand, being securely attached at an early age does not guarantee good adjustment later; conversely, children who lack secure attachment do not always have difficulties later in life (Redshaw & Martin, 2013; Hennessy & Shair, 2017; Spies & Duchinsky, 2021).

The Father's Role Although early developmental research focused largely on the mother-child relationship, more recent research has highlighted the father's role in parenting—and with good reason: The number of fathers who are primary caregivers for their children has grown significantly, and fathers play an increasingly important role in their children's lives. For example, in almost 13% of families with children, the father is the parent who stays at home to care for preschoolers (Kulik & Sadeh, 2015; Pakaluk & Price, 2020).

When fathers interact with their children, their play often differs from mothers' play. Fathers engage in more physical, rough-and-tumble sorts of activities, whereas mothers play more verbal and traditional games, such as peekaboo. Despite such behavioral differences, the nature of attachment between fathers and children compared with that between mothers and children can be similar. In fact, children can form multiple attachments simultaneously (Bureau et al., 2017; Lin et al., 2019; Amodia-Bidakowska et al., 2020).

Social Relationships with Peers By the time they are 2 years old, children become less dependent on their parents. They are more self-reliant and increasingly prefer to play with friends. Initially, they engage in what is known as *parallel play*—meaning that they play relatively near each other, but they don't try to influence each other's behavior. Thus, even though they may be playing side by side, 2-year-olds pay more attention to their toys than to one another. Later, however, as they play, children actively interact, modify one another's behavior, and exchange roles (Whitney & Green, 2011; Stone, 2015).

Cultural factors also affect children's styles of play. For example, Korean-American children engage in less pretend play than do their Anglo-American counterparts (Drewes, 2005; Rentzou et al., 2019; Hughes, 2021).

As children reach school age, their social interactions become more frequent, and they begin to follow set patterns of behavior. For example, they may engage in elaborate games involving teams and rigid rules. In addition to providing enjoyment, such play allows children to become increasingly competent in their interactions with others. For instance, during play, they learn to take the perspective of other people. Children also learn to infer others' thoughts and feelings, even when those thoughts and feelings are not directly expressed (Yang et al., 2013; Wang & Hofkens, 2020).

In short, social interaction helps children interpret the meaning of others' behavior and develop the capacity to respond appropriately. Furthermore, children learn physical and emotional self-control: They learn to avoid hitting a playmate who beats them at a game. They learn to be polite and to control their emotional displays and facial expressions (e.g., smiling even when receiving a disappointing gift). Situations that provide children with opportunities for social interaction, then, may enhance their social development (Whitebread et al., 2009; Hoffman et al., 2020).

Screen Time: Monitoring Children's Use of Media Another way children learn about their social world is through the media. In many households, children as young as 1 year are exposed to significant amounts of screen time, sometimes from traditional television and sometimes from computers and other devices.

It's very much an open question as to how screen time affects development, but the World Health Organization (WHO) has issued strict guidelines. According to WHO, children in the first year of life should *never* be exposed to screen time, and children ages 2-4 should spend no more than an hour a day watching a screen (World Health Organization, 2019).

The WHO guidelines are roughly consistent with recommendations from the American Academy of Pediatrics. That group recommends that children under 18 months should never get screen time and that those between 2 and 5 should be limited to an hour a day. Moreover, they recommend that any screen time should involve "co-watching" with an engaged adult (American Academy of Pediatrics, 2016).

However, some critics argue that strict screen time guidelines don't take into account *what* children are watching and that research evidence on the issue is slim.

Not all screen time content is the same, and some sorts of screen time may actually be beneficial. In short, although the jury is still out on how or whether screen time affects child development, it does seem reasonable to restrict children's exposure to media and to maximize face-to-face interaction and physical activity. Furthermore, as we'll see when we discuss screen time during later periods of life, the topic remains a pressing one (Przybylski & Weinstein, 2019; Kross et al., 2021).

The Consequences of Child Care Outside the Home Research on the importance of social interaction is corroborated by work that examines the benefits of child care out of the home, which is an important part of many children's lives. For instance, by the age of 6 months, almost two-thirds of infants in the United States are cared for by people other than their parents for part of the day. Furthermore, more than half of 3- to 5-year-olds are enrolled in child-care centers out of the home (Federal Interagency Forum on Child & Family Studies, 2021; see Figure 6).

Do child-care arrangements outside the home benefit children's development? If the programs are of high quality, they can. Children who attend high-quality child-care centers may not only do as well as children who stay at home with their parents, but in some respects, they may actually do better. Children in child care are generally more considerate and sociable than other children, and they interact more positively with teachers. They may also be more compliant and regulate their own behavior more effectively (National Institute of Child Health and Human Development Early Child Care Research Network, 2001; Conger et al., 2019; Davies et al., 2021).

In addition, especially for children from poor or disadvantaged homes, child care in specially enriched environments–those with many toys, books, a variety of children, and high-quality providers–may be more intellectually stimulating than the home environment. Such child care can lead to increased intellectual achievement, demonstrated in higher IQ scores, and better language development. In fact, children in care centers sometimes are found to score higher on tests of cognitive abilities than are those who are cared for by their mothers or by sitters or home day-care providers–effects that last into adulthood (Dearing et al., 2009; Reid et al., 2017; Adair et al., 2021).

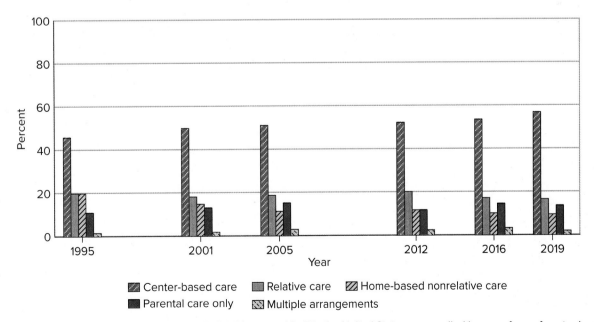

FIGURE 6 Child-care arrangements. More than half of children aged 3–5 in the United States are enrolled in some form of center-based care outside the home, as many parents are employed full time. The amount of center-based care has gradually increased over the past few decades.

Source: U.S. Department of Education, 2021.

However, child care outside the home does not have universally positive outcomes. Children may feel insecure after placement in low-quality child care or in multiple child-care settings. Furthermore, some research suggests that infants who are involved in outside care more than 20 hours a week in the first year show less secure attachment to their mothers than do those who have not been in child care outside the home. Finally, children who spent long hours in child care as infants and preschoolers may have a reduced ability to work independently and to manage their time effectively when they reach elementary school (Pluess & Belsky, 2009; Eckhardt & Egert, 2020).

The key to the success of nonparental child care is its quality. High-quality child care produces benefits; low-quality child care provides little or no gain and may even hinder children's development. In short, significant benefits result from the social interaction and intellectual stimulation provided by high-quality child-care centers—especially for children from impoverished environments (Landry et al., 2013; Araujo et al., 2019).

Parenting Styles and Social Development Parents' child-rearing practices are critical in shaping their children's social competence. According to classic research by developmental psychologist Diana Baumrind, four main categories describe different parenting styles (Baumrind, 2005; Lagacé-Séguin & d'Entremont, 2006; Lewis & Lamb, 2011; see Figure 7):

- **Authoritarian parents** are rigid and punitive, and they value unquestioning obedience from their children. They have strict standards and discourage expressions of disagreement.

- **Permissive parents** give their children relaxed or inconsistent direction and, although they are warm, require little of them.

- **Authoritative parents** are firm and set limits for their children. As the children get older, these parents try to reason and explain things to them. They also set clear goals and encourage their children's independence.

- **Uninvolved parents** show little interest in their children. Emotionally detached, they view parenting as nothing more than providing food, clothing, and shelter for children. At their most extreme, uninvolved parents are guilty of neglect, a form of child abuse.

As you might expect, the four kinds of child-rearing styles seem to produce very different kinds of behavior in children (with many exceptions, of course). Children of authoritarian parents tend to be unsociable, unfriendly, and relatively withdrawn. In

authoritarian parents Parents who are rigid and punitive and value unquestioning obedience from their children. (Module 28)

permissive parents Parents who give their children relaxed or inconsistent direction and, although they are warm, require little of them. (Module 28)

authoritative parents Parents who are firm, set clear limits, reason with their children, and explain things to them. (Module 28)

uninvolved parents Parents who show little interest in their children and are emotionally detached. (Module 28)

! Study Alert

Know the four major types of child-rearing practices—authoritarian, permissive, authoritative, and uninvolved—and their effects.

Parenting Style	Parent Behavior	Type of Behavior Produced in Child
Authoritarian	Rigid, punitive, strict standards (example: "If you don't clean your room, I'm going to take away your iPhone for good and ground you.")	Unsociable, unfriendly, withdrawn
Permissive	Lax, inconsistent, undemanding (example: "It might be good to clean your room, but I guess it can wait.")	Immature, moody, dependent, low self-control
Authoritative	Firm, sets limits and goals, uses reasoning, encourages independence (example: "You'll need to clean your room before we can go out to the restaurant. As soon as you finish, we'll leave.")	Good social skills, likable, self-reliant, independent
Uninvolved	Detached emotionally, sees role only as providing food, clothing, and shelter (example: "I couldn't care less if your room is a pigsty.")	Indifferent, rejecting behavior

FIGURE 7 According to developmental psychologist Diana Baumrind (1971), four main parenting styles characterize child rearing.
Gary John Norman/Digital Vision/Getty Images

contrast, permissive parents' children show immaturity, moodiness, dependence, and low self-control. The children of authoritative parents fare best: With high social skills, they are likable, self-reliant, independent, and cooperative. Worst off are the children of uninvolved parents; they feel unloved and emotionally detached, and their physical development and cognitive development are impeded (Llorca-Mestre et al., 2017; Kuppens & Ceulemans, 2019).

Before we rush to congratulate authoritative parents and condemn authoritarian, permissive, and uninvolved ones, it is important to note that in many cases, nonauthoritative parents also produce perfectly well-adjusted children. Moreover, children are born with a particular **temperament**, a basic, inborn characteristic way of responding and behavioral style. Some children are naturally easygoing and cheerful, whereas others are irritable and fussy or pensive and quiet. The kind of temperament a baby is born with may in part bring about specific kinds of parental child-rearing styles (Costa & Figueiredo, 2011; Wittig & Rodriguez, 2019; Bahtiyar-Saygan & Berument, 2022).

In addition, children vary considerably in their degree of *resilience*, the ability to overcome circumstances that place them at high risk for psychological or even physical harm. Highly resilient children have temperaments that evoke positive responses from caregivers and others in their lives. Such children display unusual social skills: outgoingness, intelligence, and a feeling that they have control over their lives. In a sense, resilient children try to shape their own environment rather than being victimized by it. In fact, as adults, they see their struggles as something from which they drew strength (Naglieri et al., 2013; Jay, 2017; Russell et al., 2022).

We also need to keep in mind that these findings regarding child-rearing styles apply primarily to U.S. society, which highly values children's growing independence and diminishing reliance on their parents. In contrast, Japanese parents encourage dependence to promote the values of cooperation and community life. These differences in cultural values result in very different philosophies of child rearing. For example, Japanese mothers believe it is a punishment to make a young child sleep alone; thus, many children sleep next to their mothers throughout infancy and toddlerhood (Jones, 2007; Pinquart & Kauser, 2017).

Furthermore, those who have come to the United States from other countries and cultures may use child-rearing techniques learned in their original home culture, and these may differ considerably from those found in the typical U.S. home. Still, as parents integrate into U.S. society, children of immigrants generally do quite well, showing levels of adjustment and achievement similar, and sometimes better, than children of nonimmigrant parents (Organisation for Economic Co-operation and Development, 2018; Suárez-Orozco & Suárez-Orozco, 2018).

In sum, a child's upbringing results from the child-rearing philosophy parents hold, the specific practices they use, and the nature of their own and their child's personalities. As is the case with other aspects of development, then, behavior is a function of a complex interaction of environmental and genetic factors.

Erikson's Theory of Psychosocial Development In tracing the course of social development, some theorists have considered how the challenges of society and culture change as an individual matures. Following this path, psychoanalyst Erik Erikson developed one of the more comprehensive theories of social development. Erikson (1963) viewed the developmental changes that occur throughout life as a series of eight stages of psychosocial development; of these, four occur during childhood. **Psychosocial development** involves changes in our interactions and understanding of one another as well as in our knowledge and understanding of ourselves as members of society.

Erikson suggests that passage through each of the stages necessitates the resolution of a crisis or conflict. Accordingly, Erikson represents each stage as a pairing of the most positive and most negative aspects of the crisis of that period. Although each crisis is never resolved entirely–life becomes increasingly complicated as we grow older–it has to be resolved sufficiently to equip us to deal with demands made during the following stage of development.

temperament A basic, inborn characteristic way of responding and behavioral style. (Modules 28, 32)

psychosocial development Development of individuals' interactions and understanding of each other and of their knowledge and understanding of themselves as members of society. (Module 28)

trust-versus-mistrust stage According to Erikson, the first stage of psychosocial development, occurring from birth to age 1½ years, during which time infants develop feelings of trust or lack of trust. (Module 28)

autonomy-versus-shame-and-doubt stage The period during which, according to Erikson, toddlers (ages 1½ to 3 years) develop independence and autonomy if exploration and freedom are encouraged or shame and self-doubt if they are restricted and overprotected. (Module 28)

initiative-versus-guilt stage According to Erikson, the period during which children ages 3 to 6 years experience conflict between independence of action and the sometimes negative results of that action. (Module 28)

industry-versus-inferiority stage According to Erikson, the last stage of childhood, during which children age 6 to 12 years may develop positive social interactions with others or may feel inadequate and become less sociable. (Module 28)

Study Alert
Four of Erikson's stages of psychosocial development occur during childhood: trust-versus-mistrust, autonomy-versus-shame-and-doubt, initiative-versus-guilt, and industry-versus-inferiority.

The first stage of psychosocial development is the **trust-versus-mistrust stage** (ages birth to 1½ years). During this period, infants develop feelings of trust or mistrust, primarily depending on how well their caregivers meet their needs. If their physical requirements and psychological needs for attachment are consistently met and their interactions with the world are generally positive, they will develop a sense of trust. In contrast, inconsistent care and unpleasant interactions with others can lead to mistrust and a view of the world as a harsh and unfriendly place.

In the second stage, the **autonomy-versus-shame-and-doubt stage** (ages 1½–3 years), toddlers develop independence and autonomy if exploration and freedom are encouraged, or they experience shame, self-doubt, and unhappiness if they are overly restricted and protected. According to Erikson, the key to the development of a sense of independence during this period is for the child's caregivers to provide a reasonable amount of control. If parents are overly controlling, children cannot assert themselves and develop their own sense of control over their world; if parents provide too little control, children can become demanding and dictatorial.

Next, children face the crises of the **initiative-versus-guilt stage** (ages 3–6). In this stage, children's desire to act independently conflicts with the guilt that comes from the unintended and unexpected consequences of such behavior. Children in this period come to understand that they are persons in their own right, and they begin to make decisions about their behavior. If parents react positively to children's attempts at independence, their children will develop skills in accomplishing tasks and overcoming challenges.

The fourth and last stage of childhood is the **industry-versus-inferiority stage** (ages 6-12). During this period, increasing competency in all areas, whether social interactions or academic skills, characterizes successful psychosocial development. In contrast, difficulties in this stage lead to feelings of failure and inadequacy.

Erikson's theory suggests that psychosocial development continues throughout life, and he proposes four more crises that are faced after childhood (described in Module 29). Although his theory has been criticized on several grounds—such as the imprecision of the concepts he employs and his greater emphasis on male development than female development—it remains influential and is one of the few theories that encompass the entire life span.

COGNITIVE DEVELOPMENT: CHILDREN'S THINKING ABOUT THE WORLD

Suppose you had two drinking glasses of different shapes, one short and broad and one tall and thin. Now imagine that you filled the short, broad one with soda about halfway and then poured the liquid from that glass into the tall one. The soda would appear to fill about three-quarters of the second glass. If someone asked you whether there was more soda in the second glass than there had been in the first, what would you say?

You might think that such a simple question hardly deserves an answer; of course, there is no difference in the amount of soda in the two glasses. However, most 4-year-olds would be likely to say that there is more soda in the second glass. If you then poured the soda back into the short glass, they would say there is now less soda than there was in the taller glass.

Why are young children confused by this problem? The reason is not immediately obvious. Anyone who has observed preschoolers must be impressed by how far they have progressed from the early stages of development. They speak with ease, know the alphabet, count, play complex games, use computers, tell stories, and communicate ably. Yet despite this seeming sophistication, there are deep gaps in children's understanding of the world. The gaps in children's understanding relate to their level of cognitive development. **Cognitive development** is the process by which children's understanding of the world changes due to their age and experience. In contrast to the theories of physical and social development discussed earlier (such as those of Erikson), theories of cognitive development seek to explain the quantitative and qualitative intellectual advances that occur during development.

cognitive development The process by which a child's understanding of the world changes due to the child's age and experience. (Module 28)

Study Alert
Use Figure 8 to help remember Piaget's stages of cognitive development.

Cognitive Stage	Approximate Age Range	Major Characteristics
Sensorimotor	Birth–2 years	Development of object permanence, development of motor skills, little or no capacity for symbolic representation
Preoperational	2–7 years	Development of language and symbolic thinking, egocentric thinking
Concrete operational	7–12 years	Development of conservation, mastery of the concept of reversibility
Formal operational	12 years–adulthood	Development of logical and abstract thinking

FIGURE 8 According to Piaget, all children pass through four stages of cognitive development.
Gado Images/Alamy Stock Photo

Piaget's Theory of Cognitive Development No theory of cognitive development has had more impact than that of Swiss psychologist Jean Piaget. Piaget (1970) suggested that children around the world proceed through a series of four stages in a fixed order. He maintained that these stages differ not only in the *quantity* of information acquired at each stage but in the *quality* of knowledge and understanding as well. Taking an interactionist point of view, he suggested that movement from one stage to the next occurs when a child reaches an appropriate level of maturation *and* is exposed to relevant types of experiences. Piaget assumed that, without having such experiences, children cannot reach their highest level of cognitive growth.

Piaget's Four Stages of Cognitive Development Piaget proposed four stages: the sensorimotor, preoperational, concrete operational, and formal operational (see Figure 8). Let's examine each of them and the approximate ages that they span.

Sensorimotor Stage: Birth to 2 Years. During the **sensorimotor stage,** children base their understanding of the world primarily on touching, sucking, chewing, shaking, and manipulating objects. In the initial part of the stage, children have relatively little competence in representing the environment by using images, language, or other kinds of symbols. Consequently, infants lack what Piaget calls object permanence. **Object permanence** is the awareness that objects–and people–continue to exist even if they are out of sight.

How can we know that children lack object permanence? Although we cannot ask infants, we can observe their reactions when a toy they are playing with is hidden under a blanket. Until the age of about 9 months, children will make no attempt to locate the hidden toy. However, soon after that age, they will begin an active search for the missing object, indicating that they have developed a mental representation of the toy. Object permanence, then, is a critical development during the sensorimotor stage.

Preoperational Stage: 2–7 Years. During the **preoperational stage,** children develop the use of language. The internal representational systems they develop allow them to describe people, events, and feelings. They even use symbols in play, pretending, for example, that a book pushed across the floor is a car.

Although children use more advanced thinking in this stage than they did in the earlier sensorimotor stage, their thinking is still qualitatively inferior to that of adults. We see this when we observe a preoperational child using **egocentric thought,** a way of thinking in which the child views the world entirely from their own perspective. Preoperational children think that everyone shares their perspective and knowledge. Thus, children's stories and explanations to adults can be frustratingly uninformative because they are delivered without any context. For example, a preoperational child may start a story with, "He wouldn't let me go," neglecting to mention who "he" is

sensorimotor stage According to Piaget, the stage from birth to 2 years, during which a child has little competence in representing the environment by using images, language, or other symbols. (Module 28)

object permanence The awareness that objects–and people–continue to exist even if they are out of sight. (Module 28)

preoperational stage According to Piaget, the period from 2 to 7 years of age that is characterized by language development. (Module 28)

egocentric thought A way of thinking in which a child views the world entirely from their own perspective. (Module 28)

Children who have not mastered the principle of conservation assume that the volume of liquid increases when it is poured from a short, wide container to a tall, thin one. What other tasks might a child under age 7 have difficulty comprehending?
Marmaduke St. John/Alamy Stock Photo

principle of conservation The knowledge that quantity is unrelated to the arrangement and physical appearance of objects. (Module 28)

FIGURE 9 These tests are frequently used to assess whether children have learned the principle of conservation across a variety of dimensions. Do you think children in the preoperational stage can be taught to avoid conservation mistakes before the typical age of mastery?
Source: Adapted from Schickedanz et al., 2001.

or where the storyteller wanted to go. We also see egocentric thinking when children at the preoperational stage play hiding games. For instance, 3-year-olds frequently hide with their faces against a wall and covering their eyes–although they are still in plain view. It seems to them that if *they* cannot see, then no one else will be able to see them because they assume that others share their view.

In addition, preoperational children have not yet developed the ability to comprehend the **principle of conservation,** which is the understanding that quantity is unrelated to the arrangement and physical appearance of objects. Children who can use the principle of conservation have awareness that important attributes of objects (such as amount or volume) do not change despite superficial changes. In contrast, children who have not mastered conservation do not understand that the overall amount or volume of an object does not change when its shape or configuration changes.

The question about the two glasses–one short and broad, and the other tall and thin–with which we began our discussion of cognitive development illustrates this point clearly. Children who do not understand the principle of conservation believe that the amount of liquid changes as it is poured back and forth between glasses of different sizes. They simply are unable to comprehend that a change in appearance does not mean there is a change in amount. Instead, they truly believe that quantity changes as appearance changes (see Figure 9).

Conservation of ...	Modality	Change in physical appearance	Average age at full mastery
Number	Number of elements in a collection	Rearranging or dislocating elements	6–7 years
Substance (mass)	Amount of a malleable substance (e.g., clay or liquid)	Altering shape	7–8 years
Length	Length of a line or object	Altering shape or configuration	7–8 years
Area	Amount of surface covered by a set of plane figures	Rearranging the figures	8–9 years
Weight	Weight of an object	Altering shape	9–10 years
Volume	Volume of an object (in terms of water displacement)	Altering shape	14–15 years

Concrete Operational Stage: 7-12 Years. Mastery of the principle of conservation marks the beginning of the **concrete operational stage.** However, children do not fully understand some aspects of conservation—such as conservation of weight and volume—for a number of years.

During the concrete operational stage, children develop the ability to think in a more logical manner and begin to overcome some of the egocentrism characteristic of the preoperational period. One of the major principles children learn during this stage is reversibility, the idea that some changes can be undone by reversing an earlier action. For example, they can understand that when someone rolls a ball of clay into a long sausage shape, that person can recreate the original ball by reversing the action. Children can even conceptualize this principle in their heads without having to see the action performed before them.

Although children make important advances in their logical capabilities during the concrete operational stage, their thinking still displays one major limitation: They are largely bound to the concrete, physical reality of the world. For the most part, they have difficulty understanding questions of an abstract or hypothetical nature.

Formal Operational Stage: 12 Years to Adulthood. The **formal operational stage** produces a new kind of thinking that is abstract, formal, and logical. Thinking is no longer tied to events that individuals observe in the environment but makes use of logical techniques to resolve problems.

The way in which children approach the "pendulum problem" devised by Piaget (Piaget & Inhelder, 1958) illustrates the emergence of formal operational thinking. The problem solver is asked to figure out what determines how fast a pendulum swings. Is it the length of the string, the weight of the pendulum, or the force with which the pendulum is pushed? (For the record, the answer is the length of the string.)

Children in the concrete operational stage approach the problem haphazardly without a logical or rational plan of action. For example, they may simultaneously change the length of the string, the weight on the string, and the force with which they push the pendulum. Because they are varying all the factors at once, they cannot tell which factor is the critical one. In contrast, people in the formal operational stage approach the problem systematically. Acting as if they were scientists conducting an experiment, they examine the effects of changes in one variable at a time. This ability to rule out competing possibilities characterizes formal operational thought.

Although formal operational thought emerges during the teenage years, some individuals use this type of thinking only infrequently. Moreover, it appears that many individuals never reach this stage at all; most studies show that only 40-60% of college students and adults fully reach it, with some estimates running as low as 25% of the general population. In addition, in certain cultures—particularly those that are less technically oriented than Western societies—almost no one reaches the formal operational stage (Keating & Clark, 1980; Super, 1980; Genovese, 2006).

Evaluating Piaget's Theory No other theorist has given us as comprehensive a theory of cognitive development as Piaget has. Still, many contemporary theorists suggest that a better explanation of how children develop cognitively can be provided by theories that do not involve a stage approach. For instance, children are not always consistent in their performance of tasks that—if Piaget's theory is accurate—ought to be performed equally well at a particular stage (Bjorkland, 2018).

Furthermore, some developmental psychologists suggest that cognitive development proceeds in a more continuous fashion than Piaget's stage theory implies. In other words, rather than moving from one stage to another in a relatively abrupt manner, later findings suggest that cognitive development advances smoothly, in smaller, steadier increments.

Moreover, critics of Piaget propose that cognitive development is primarily quantitative rather than qualitative. They argue that although there are differences in when, how, and to what extent a child can use specific cognitive abilities—reflecting quantitative changes—the underlying cognitive processes change relatively little with age (Gelman & Baillargeon, 1983; Case & Okamoto, 1996; Chen, 2014).

concrete operational stage According to Piaget, the period from 7 to 12 years of age that is characterized by logical thought and a loss of egocentrism. (Module 28)

formal operational stage According to Piaget, the period from age 12 to adulthood that is characterized by abstract thought. (Module 28)

Piaget also underestimated the age at which infants and children can understand specific concepts and principles; in fact, they seem to be more sophisticated in their cognitive abilities than Piaget believed. For instance, some evidence suggests that infants as young as 5 months have rudimentary mathematical skills (McCrink & Wynn, 2007; van Marle & Wynn, 2009; Cheung et al., 2022).

Despite such criticisms, most developmental psychologists agree that although the processes that underlie changes in cognitive abilities may not unfold in the manner Piaget's theory suggests, he has generally provided us with an accurate account of age-related changes in cognitive development. Moreover, his theory has had an enormous influence in education. For example, Piaget suggests that individuals cannot increase their cognitive performance unless both cognitive readiness brought about by maturation and appropriate environmental stimulation are present. This view has inspired the nature and structure of educational curricula and teaching methods. Researchers have also used Piaget's theory and methods to investigate issues surrounding animal cognition, such as whether primates show object permanence (they seem to) (Jablonka, 2017; Veraksa & Samuelsson, 2022).

Information-Processing Approaches: Charting Children's Mental Programs If cognitive development does not proceed as a series of stages as Piaget suggested, what does underlie the enormous growth in children's cognitive abilities that even the most untutored eye can observe? To many developmental psychologists, changes in information-processing capabilities account for cognitive development. **Information processing** refers to the way in which people take in, use, and store information.

information processing The way in which people take in, use, and store information. (Module 28)

According to the information-processing approach, quantitative changes occur in children's ability to organize and manipulate information. From this perspective, children become increasingly adept at information processing, much as a computer program may become more sophisticated as a programmer modifies it on the basis of experience. Information-processing approaches consider the kinds of "mental programs" that children invoke when approaching problems.

Several significant changes occur in children's information-processing capabilities. For one thing, speed of processing increases with age as some abilities become more automatic. The speed at which children can scan, recognize, and compare stimuli increases with age. As they grow older, children can pay attention to stimuli longer and discriminate between different stimuli more readily, and they are less easily distracted (Diaz & Bell, 2011; Marchman et al., 2019).

Memory also improves dramatically with age. Preschoolers can hold only two or three chunks of information in short-term memory, 5-year-olds can hold four, and 7-year-olds can hold five. (Adults are able to keep seven, plus or minus two, chunks in short-term memory.) The size of the chunks also grows with age, as does the sophistication and organization of knowledge stored in memory (see Figure 10). Still, memory capabilities are impressive at a very early age: Even before they can speak, infants can remember for months events in which they actively participated (Ślusarczyk & Niedźwieńska, 2013; Fagan, 2018).

metacognition An awareness and understanding of one's own cognitive processes. (Module 28)

Finally, improvement in information processing relates to advances in **metacognition,** an awareness and understanding of one's own cognitive processes. Metacognition involves the planning, monitoring, and revising of cognitive strategies. Younger children, who lack an awareness of their own cognitive processes, often do not realize their incapabilities. Thus, when they misunderstand others, they may fail to recognize their own errors. It is only later, when metacognitive abilities become more sophisticated, that children are able to know when they *don't* understand. Such increasing sophistication reflects a change in children's *theory of mind*, their knowledge and beliefs about the way the mind operates (Sodian, 2011; O'Leary & Sloutsky, 2017; Pennequin et al., 2020).

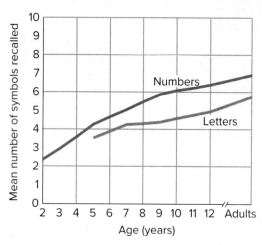

FIGURE 10 Memory span increases with age for both numbers and letters.
Source: Adapted from Dempster, 1981.

Vygotsky's View of Cognitive Development: Considering Culture According to Russian developmental psychologist Lev Vygotsky, the culture in which we are raised significantly affects our cognitive development. In an increasingly influential view, Vygotsky suggests that the focus on individual performance of both Piagetian and information-processing approaches is misplaced. Instead, he holds that we cannot understand cognitive development without taking into account the social and cultural aspects of learning (Vygotsky, 1926/1997; Vasileva & Balyasnikova, 2019; Erbil, 2020).

Vygotsky argues that cognitive development occurs as a consequence of social interactions in which children work with others to jointly solve problems. Through such interactions, children's cognitive skills increase, and they gain the ability to function intellectually on their own. More specifically, he suggests that children's cognitive abilities increase when they encounter information that falls within their zone of proximal development. The **zone of proximal development (ZPD)** is the gap between what children already are able to accomplish on their own and what they are not quite ready to do by themselves. When children receive information that falls within the ZPD, they can increase their understanding or master a new task. In contrast, if the information lies outside children's ZPD, they will not be able to master it.

In short, cognitive development occurs when parents, teachers, or skilled peers assist a child by presenting new information that resides within the child's ZPD, a process Vygotsky calls scaffolding. *Scaffolding* is support for learning and problem solving that encourages independence and growth. Vygotsky claims that scaffolding not only helps children to solve specific problems but also aids in the development of overall cognitive abilities (Coulson & Harvey, 2013; Smagorinsky, 2018).

More than other approaches to cognitive development, Vygotsky's theory considers how an individual's cultural and social background affects intellectual growth. The way in which children understand the world grows out of interactions with parents, peers, and other members of their own, specific culture.

zone of proximal development (ZPD) According to Vygotsky, the gap between what children already are able to accomplish on their own and what they are not quite ready to do by themselves. (Module 28)

RECAP/EVALUATE/RETHINK

RECAP

LO 28-1 What are the major competencies of newborns?

- Newborns, or neonates, have reflexes—unlearned, involuntary responses that occur automatically in the presence of certain stimuli.
- Sensory abilities also develop rapidly; infants can distinguish color, depth, sound, tastes, and smells relatively soon after birth.
- After birth, physical development is rapid; children typically triple their birthweight in a year.

LO 28-2 What are the milestones of physical and social development during childhood?

- Attachment—the positive emotional bond between a child and a particular individual—marks social development in infancy. Measured in the laboratory by means of the Ainsworth strange situation, attachment relates to later social and emotional adjustment.
- As children become older, the nature of their social interactions with peers changes. Initially play occurs relatively independently, but it becomes increasingly cooperative.

- The different child-rearing styles include authoritarian, permissive, authoritative, and uninvolved.
- According to Erikson, eight stages of psychosocial development involve people's changing interactions and understanding of themselves and others. During childhood, the four stages are trust-versus-mistrust (birth to 1½ years), autonomy-versus-shame-and-doubt (1½–3 years), initiative-versus-guilt (3–6 years), and industry-versus-inferiority (6–12 years).

LO 28-3 How does cognitive development proceed during childhood?

- Piaget's theory suggests that cognitive development proceeds through four stages in which qualitative changes occur in thinking: the sensorimotor stage (birth to 2 years), the preoperational stage (2–7 years), the concrete operational stage (7–12 years), and the formal operational stage (12 years to adulthood).
- Information-processing approaches suggest that quantitative changes occur in children's ability to organize and manipulate information about the world, such as significant increases in speed of processing, attention span, and memory. In addition, children advance in

metacognition, the awareness and understanding of one's own cognitive processes.

- Vygotsky argued that children's cognitive development occurs as a consequence of social interactions in which children and others work together to solve problems.

EVALUATE

1. Researchers studying newborns use _____, or the decrease in the response to a stimulus that occurs after repeated presentations of the same stimulus, as an indicator of a baby's interest.

2. The emotional bond that develops between a child and their caregiver is known as _____.

3. Match the parenting style with its definition:
   1. Permissive
   2. Authoritative
   3. Authoritarian
   4. Uninvolved

   a. Rigid; highly punitive; demanding obedience
   b. Gives little direction; lax on obedience
   c. Firm but fair; tries to explain parental decisions
   d. Emotionally detached and unloving

4. Erikson's theory of _____ development involves a series of eight stages, each of which must be resolved for a person to develop optimally.

5. Match the stage of development with the thinking style characteristic of that stage:
   1. Egocentric thought
   2. Object permanence
   3. Abstract reasoning
   4. Conservation

   a. Sensorimotor
   b. Formal operational
   c. Preoperational
   d. Concrete operational

6. _____-_____ theories of development suggest that the way in which a child handles information is critical to their development.

7. According to Vygotsky, information that is within a child's _____ _____ _____ _____ is most likely to result in cognitive development.

RETHINK

1. Do you think the widespread use of IQ testing in the United States contributes to parents' views that their children's academic success is due largely to the children's innate intelligence? Why? Would it be possible (or desirable) to change this view?

2. In what ways might the infant's major reflexes–the rooting, sucking, gagging, and Babinski reflexes–have had survival value from an evolutionary perspective? Does the infant's ability to mimic the facial expressions of adults have a similar value?

Answers to Evaluate Questions

1. habituation; 2. attachment; 3. 1-b, 2-c, 3-a, 4-d; 4. psychosocial; 5. 1-c, 2-a, 3-b, 4-d; 6. Information-processing; 7. zone of proximal development

KEY TERMS

neonate	temperament	industry-versus-inferiority stage	concrete operational stage
reflexes	psychosocial development	cognitive development	formal operational stage
habituation	trust-versus-mistrust stage	sensorimotor stage	information processing
attachment	autonomy-versus-shame-and-doubt stage	object permanence	metacognition
authoritarian parents	initiative-versus-guilt stage	preoperational stage	zone of proximal development (ZPD)
permissive parents		egocentric thought	
authoritative parents		principle of conservation	
uninvolved parents			

Module 29
Adolescence: Becoming an Adult

Vonetta Johnson, age 13: "It's not easy being 13. I feel like I have to be on social media constantly, seeing what my friends are doing and sending photos of myself that make me look, well, perfect. I am so afraid of missing out on something. It can be exhausting."

Elio Gomez, age 15: "I know, I know: my room is a mess. But it's my room, and I just want to keep my parents out. I should have some privacy, and if stuff is all over the floor, what's the big deal? I wish they'd stop hassling me and just leave me alone."

Omar Hassan, age 17: "I got into the National Honors Society, and the school made a big deal about it. But when my parents came to the induction ceremony, they just looked shocked the entire time, wondering how someone like me–with a nose ring and ear studs and hair dyed blue–could have been invited to the ceremony. I half-expected them to go to the teachers and tell them that they'd made some mistake."

Although Vonetta, Elio, and Omar have never met, they share anxieties that are common to adolescence–concerns about friends, parents, appearance, independence, and their futures.

Adolescence is the developmental stage between childhood and adulthood, and it is a crucial period. It is a time of profound changes and, occasionally, turmoil. Considerable biological change occurs as adolescents attain sexual and physical maturity. At the same time and rivaling these physiological changes, important social, emotional, and cognitive changes occur as adolescents strive for independence and move toward adulthood.

Because many years of schooling precede most people's entry into the workforce in most American and European societies, the stage of adolescence is fairly long; it begins just before the teenage years and ends just after them. Adolescents are no longer children, yet society doesn't quite consider them adults. They face a period of rapid physical, cognitive, and social change that affects them for the rest of their lives.

Dramatic changes in society also affect adolescents' development. More than half of all children in the United States will spend all or some of their childhood and adolescence in single-parent families. Furthermore, adolescents spend considerably less time with their parents and more with their peers than they did several decades ago. Finally, the ethnic and cultural diversity of adolescents as a group is increasing dramatically. A third of all adolescents today are of non-European descent; by the year 2045, the number of adolescents who are of Hispanic, Black, Native American, and Asian origin collectively will surpass that of Whites (Frey, 2018).

Physical Development: The Changing Adolescent

If you think back to the start of your own adolescence, the most dramatic changes you probably remember are physical. A spurt in height, the growth of breasts in girls, deepening voices in boys, the development of body hair, and intense sexual feelings cause curiosity, interest, and sometimes embarrassment for individuals entering adolescence.

Not since infancy has development been so dramatic. Beginning around age 10 for girls and age 12 for boys, a growth spurt leads to rapid increases in weight and height. Adolescents may grow as much as 5 inches in 1 year. The physical changes that occur

LEARNING OUTCOME

LO 29-1 What major physical, social, and cognitive transitions characterize adolescence?

adolescence The developmental stage between childhood and adulthood. (Module 29)

puberty The period at which maturation of the sexual organs occurs, beginning at about age 11 or 12 for girls and 13 or 14 for boys. (Module 29)

at the start of adolescence result largely from a surge in levels of growth hormone, and they affect virtually every aspect of an adolescent's life.

Puberty is the period at which maturation of the sexual organs occurs. Over the past century in Western cultures, the average age at which adolescents reach sexual maturity has steadily decreased, most likely as a result of improved nutrition and medical care.

For girls, puberty typically begins at about age 11 or 12, when menstruation starts. However, girls vary widely (see Figure 1). For example, some begin to menstruate as early as age 8 or 9, or in some cases, even earlier. In fact, in the past several decades, puberty has started earlier for a significant minority of girls, who develop breasts as young as age 6 or 7. Although we don't know why this happens, early puberty may be linked to obesity, stress, or exposure to certain chemicals in the environment (Cheng et al., 2022; Ghorayshi, 2022).

In contrast, some girls don't start menstruation until as late as age 16. Furthermore, girls may become sexually attracted to others even before their sexual organs mature at around age 10 (Shanahan et al., 2013; Herting & Sowell, 2017; Huang & Roth, 2021).

For boys, their first ejaculation, formally known as *spermarche,* typically happens at the beginning of puberty. Spermarche usually occurs around the age of 13 (see Figure 1). At first, relatively few sperm are produced during an ejaculation, but the amount increases significantly within a few years.

The age at which puberty begins has significant implications for the way adolescents feel about themselves–as well as the way others treat them. Preadolescents who start puberty considerably earlier than their peers may feel isolated and different, and they are at risk for mental health issues such as depression (Weir, 2016; Park et al., 2017; Sadeh et al., 2019).

FIGURE 1 The range of ages during which major sexual changes occur during adolescence is shown by the colored bars.
Source: Adapted from Tanner, 1978.

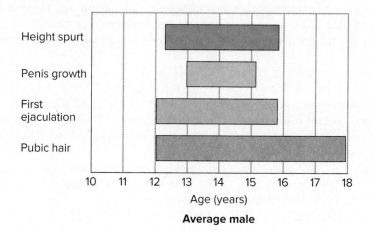

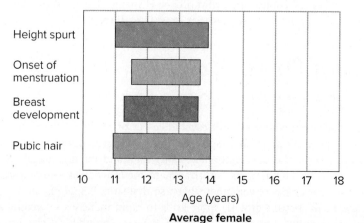

In some cases, early maturation is favorable for boys. For example, early-maturing boys do better in athletics, are generally more popular with peers, and have more positive self-concepts. However, the picture differs for girls. Although early-maturing girls are more sexually desirable and have better self-esteem than do later-maturing girls, some consequences of early physical maturation may be less positive. For example, early breast development may set them apart from their peers and be a source of ridicule, or it may make them the target for sexual attention that they don't know how to handle (Mensah et al., 2013; Natsuaki et al., 2015; Copeland et al., 2019).

Late physical maturation may produce certain psychological difficulties for both boys and girls. Boys who are smaller and less coordinated than their more mature peers tend to feel ridiculed and less attractive. Similarly, late-maturing girls are at a disadvantage in middle school and early high school. They hold relatively lower social status, and it may affect their self-esteem and perceptions of academic success. Moreover, both boys and girls may be delayed in the development of dating and romantic relationships (Mensah et al., 2013; Natsuaki et al., 2015; Copeland et al., 2019).

Although puberty begins around 11 or 12 for girls and 13 or 14 for boys, there are wide variations. What are some of the advantages and disadvantages of early puberty?
Purestock/SuperStock

Clearly, the rate at which physical changes occur during adolescence can affect the way in which people are viewed by others and the way they view themselves. Just as important as physical changes, however, are the psychological and social changes that unfold during adolescence.

Moral and Cognitive Development: Distinguishing Right from Wrong

In a European country, a woman is near death from a special kind of cancer. The one drug that the doctors think might save her is a medicine that a medical researcher has recently discovered. The drug is expensive to make, and the researcher is charging 10 times the cost, or $5,000, for a small dose. The sick woman's husband, Henry, approaches everyone he knows in hope of borrowing money, but he can get together only about $2,500. He tells the researcher that his wife is dying and asks him to lower the price of the drug or let him pay later. The researcher says, "No, I discovered the drug, and I'm going to make money from it." Henry is desperate and considers stealing the drug for his wife.

What would you tell Henry to do?

KOHLBERG'S THEORY OF MORAL DEVELOPMENT

In the view of psychologist Lawrence Kohlberg, the advice you give Henry reflects your level of moral development. According to Kohlberg, people pass through a series of levels in the evolution of their sense of justice and in the kind of reasoning they use to make moral judgments (Kohlberg, 1984).

Specifically, Kohlberg suggests that changes in moral reasoning can be understood best as the three-level sequence described in Figure 2. Because of their cognitive limitations, preadolescent children who reason at Level 1 morality tend to think in terms of concrete, unvarying rules ("It is always wrong to steal" or "I'll be punished if I steal"). At Level 2 morality, older children tend to focus on the broad rules of society ("Good people don't steal" or "What if everyone stole?"). Those at Level 2 consider moral questions in terms of their own position as good and responsible members of society.

	Sample Moral Reasoning	
Level	**In Favor of Stealing the Drug**	**Against Stealing the Drug**
Level 1 Preconventional morality: The main considerations at this level are the avoidance of punishment and the desire for rewards.	"You shouldn't just let your wife die. People will blame you for not doing enough, and they'll blame the scientist for not selling you the drug for less money."	"You can't steal the drug because you'll be arrested and go to jail. Even if you aren't caught, you'll feel guilty, and you'll always worry that the police may figure out what you did."
Level 2 Conventional morality: Membership in society becomes important at this level. People behave in ways that will win the approval of others.	"Who will blame you if you steal a life-saving drug? But if you just let your wife die, you won't be able to hold your head up in front of your family or neighbors."	"If you steal the drug, everyone will treat you like a criminal. They will wonder why you couldn't have found some other way to save your wife."
Level 3 Postconventional morality: People accept that there are certain broad principles of morality that should govern our actions. These principles are more critical than the particular laws in a society.	"If you simply follow the law, you will violate the underlying principle of saving your wife's life. If you do steal the drug, society will understand your actions and respect them. You can't let an inadequate, outdated law prevent you from doing the right thing."	"You can't change your standards of honesty whenever it suits your needs. Others may not blame you for stealing the drug, but your conscience will blame you for betraying your own moral code."

FIGURE 2 Developmental psychologist Lawrence Kohlberg theorized that people move through a three-level sequence of moral reasoning in a fixed order. However, he contended that few people ever reach the highest level of moral reasoning.
Source: Adapted from Kohlberg, 1969.

Adolescents, however, can reason on a higher plane and potentially have the ability to reason at Level 3. At Level 3, adolescents consider moral issues in terms of principles that are broader than the rules of individual societies. Because they can comprehend broad, universal moral principles, they understand that conflict can exist between two sets of socially accepted standards.

Kohlberg's theory assumes that people move through the levels in a fixed order and that they cannot reach the highest level until about age 13–primarily because of limitations in cognitive development before that age. However, many people never reach the highest level of moral reasoning. In fact, research has found that only a relatively small percentage of adults rise above the second level of his model (Gibbs, 2013; Vera-Estay et al., 2015; Ahmeti & Ramadani, 2021).

Although Kohlberg's theory has had a substantial influence on our understanding of moral development, the research support is mixed. One difficulty with the theory is that it pertains to moral *judgments*, not moral *behavior*. Knowing right from wrong does not mean that we will always act in accordance with our judgments. In addition, the theory applies primarily to Western society and its moral code; cross-cultural research conducted in cultures with different moral systems suggests that Kohlberg's theory is not necessarily applicable (Stey et al., 2013; Buon et al., 2017; Mathes, 2019).

MORAL DEVELOPMENT IN WOMEN

One glaring shortcoming of Kohlberg's research is that he primarily used male participants. Furthermore, psychologist Carol Gilligan (1996) argues that because of men's and women's distinctive socialization experiences, a fundamental difference exists in the way each gender views moral behavior. According to Gilligan, men view morality primarily in terms of broad principles, such as justice and fairness. In contrast, women see it in terms of responsibility toward individuals and willingness to make sacrifices to help a specific individual within the context of a particular relationship. Compassion for individuals is a more salient factor in moral behavior for women than it is for men.

Because Kohlberg's model defines moral behavior largely in terms of abstract principles such as justice, Gilligan finds that it inadequately describes females' moral development. She suggests that women's morality centers on individual well-being and social relationships–a morality of *caring*. In her view, compassionate concern for the welfare of others represents the highest level of morality.

! Study Alert
The difference between the Kohlberg and Gilligan approaches to moral development is significant. Kohlberg's theory focuses on stages, and Gilligan's rests on gender differences.

The fact that Gilligan's conception of morality differs greatly from Kohlberg's suggests that gender plays an important role in determining what a person sees as moral. Although the research evidence is not definitive, it seems plausible that their differing conceptions of what constitutes moral behavior may lead men and women to regard the morality of a specific behavior in different ways (Walker & Frimer, 2009; Capraro & Sippel, 2017; Moheghi et al., 2020).

Social Development: Finding One's Self in a Social World

"Who am I?" "How do I fit into the world?" "What is life all about?"

Questions such as these assume special significance during the teenage years, as adolescents seek to find their place in the broader social world. As we will see, this quest takes adolescents along several routes.

ERIKSON'S THEORY OF PSYCHOSOCIAL DEVELOPMENT: THE SEARCH FOR IDENTITY

Erikson's theory of psychosocial development emphasizes the search for identity during the adolescent years. As noted earlier, psychosocial development encompasses the way people's understanding of themselves, one another, and the world around them changes during the course of development (Erikson, 1963).

The fifth stage of Erikson's theory (summarized, with the other stages, in Figure 3), the **identity-versus-role-confusion stage,** encompasses adolescence. During this stage, a time of major testing, people try to determine what is unique about themselves. They attempt to discover who they are, what their strengths are, and what kinds of roles they are best suited to play for the rest of their lives–in short, their **identity.** A person confused about the most appropriate role to play in life may lack a stable identity, adopt an unacceptable role such as that of a social deviant, or have difficulty maintaining close personal relationships later in life (Wicks et al., 2019; Maree, 2021).

identity-versus-role-confusion stage According to Erikson, a time in adolescence of major testing to determine one's unique qualities. (Module 29)

identity The distinguishing character of the individual: who each of us is, what our roles are, and what we are capable of. (Module 29)

Stage	Approximate Age	Positive Outcomes	Negative Outcomes
1. Trust-vs.-mistrust	Birth–1½ years	Feelings of trust from environmental support	Fear and concern regarding others
2. Autonomy-vs.-shame-and-doubt	1½–3 years	Self-sufficiency if exploration is encouraged	Doubts about self, lack of independence
3. Initiative-vs.-guilt	3–6 years	Discovery of ways to initiate actions	Guilt from actions and thoughts
4. Industry-vs.-inferiority	6–12 years	Development of sense of competence	Feelings of inferiority, no sense of mastery
5. Identity-vs.-role-confusion	Adolescence	Awareness of uniqueness of self, knowledge of role to be followed	Inability to identify appropriate roles in life
6. Intimacy-vs.-isolation	Early adulthood	Development of loving, sexual relationships and close friendships	Fear of relationships with others
7. Generativity-vs.-stagnation	Middle adulthood	Sense of contribution to continuity of life	Trivialization of one's activities
8. Ego-integrity-vs.-despair	Late adulthood	Sense of unity in life's accomplishments	Regret over lost opportunities of life

FIGURE 3 Erikson's stages of psychosocial development. According to Erikson, people proceed through eight stages of psychosocial development across their lives. He suggested that each stage requires the resolution of a crisis or conflict and may produce both positive and negative outcomes.

Jon Erikson/Science Source

During the identity-versus-role-confusion period, an adolescent feels pressure to identify what to do with their life. Because these pressures come at a time of major physical changes as well as important changes in what society expects of them, adolescents can find the period an especially difficult one. The identity-versus-role-confusion stage has another important characteristic: declining reliance on adults for information with a shift toward using the peer group as a source of social judgments. The peer group becomes increasingly important, enabling adolescents to form close, adultlike relationships and helping them clarify their personal identities. According to Erikson, the identity-versus-role-confusion stage marks a pivotal point in psychosocial development, paving the way for continued growth and the future development of personal relationships (also see the *Applying Psychology in the 21st Century* feature).

During early adulthood, people enter the **intimacy-versus-isolation stage.** Spanning the period of early adulthood (from postadolescence to the early 30s), this stage focuses on developing close relationships with others. Difficulties during this stage result in feelings of loneliness and a fear of such relationships; successful resolution of the crises of this stage results in the possibility of forming relationships that are intimate on physical, intellectual, and emotional levels.

Development continues during middle adulthood as people enter the **generativity-versus-stagnation stage.** Generativity is the ability to contribute to one's family, community, work, and society and to assist the development of the younger generation. Success in this stage results in a person's feeling positive and optimistic about the continuity of life and their contribution to humanity. On the other hand, difficulties

intimacy-versus-isolation stage According to Erikson, a period during early adulthood that focuses on developing close relationships. (Module 29)

generativity-versus-stagnation stage According to Erikson, a period in middle adulthood during which we take stock of our contributions to family and society. (Module 29)

APPLYING PSYCHOLOGY IN THE 21ST CENTURY

SCREEN TIME IS FINE? HOLD THE PHONE

Have you heard the news? A number of recent popular media articles have boldly declared that children's media consumption, commonly called screen time, is just not that big a deal. It's not exactly good for kids, these articles argue, but they also reassure the reader that the harm it does to kids' mental health is so trivial as to be barely greater than the harm caused by eating potatoes!

The basis for this surprising conclusion comes mainly from one comprehensive study in 2019 in which researchers Amy Orben and Andrew Przybylski ran many analyses on multiple large datasets. They found only a tiny association between digital technology use and adolescent well-being—one so small that it didn't warrant any policy recommendations (Orben & Przybylski, 2019).

However, psychologists Jean Twenge, Jonathan Haidt, and public health researcher Kevin Cummins, raised an important criticism of that research: In the

original study, the researchers defined screen time by lumping together such widely varying activities as using social media, watching television, and even talking with friends on the phone. As Twenge and colleagues point out, this strategy is not unlike lumping candy and soda with oranges and apples and then concluding that consuming a lot of sweet foods isn't actually bad for you (Twenge et al., 2022).

To further study the issue, Twenge and her colleagues submitted the data from the original study to new analyses in which they isolated just the screen time dedicated to social media use. They then examined its relationship with mental health problems using the same statistical analyses as the original researchers.

These researchers found that for girls in particular, the relationship between screen time and mental health problems was 10 times stronger than the original study had reported. Indeed, far from being "small potatoes," the new study found the association between screen time and mental health problems stronger than that between mental health problems and hard drug use, binge drinking, or sexual assault.

Moreover, the researchers make the compelling argument that even a small effect can have an outsized impact when it is widespread over a large population, as is the case with tens of millions of adolescent girls using social media. In short, the consequences of screen time can actually be quite profound (Twenge et al., 2022).

> **RETHINK**
> - In what ways does social media use differ specifically from other screen-based activities such as watching television or playing video games?
> - If various kinds of "screen time" activities differ from one another in important ways, why might researchers pool them all together anyway?

Erikson's theory of psychosocial development argues that psychological change occurs throughout the life span.
Hill Street Studios/Blend Images

in this stage lead people to feel that their activities are trivial and unimportant and that their lives are stagnant. They may feel they have made poor career choices.

Finally, the last stage of psychosocial development, the **ego-integrity-versus-despair stage,** spans later adulthood and continues until death. People in this stage ask themselves if they have lived a meaningful life. If they see their lives positively, they feel a sense of accomplishment; if not, they feel regret over a misspent life.

Notably, Erikson's theory suggests that development does not stop at adolescence but continues throughout adulthood. A substantial amount of research now confirms this view. For instance, a 22-year study by psychologist Susan Whitbourne found considerable support for the fundamentals of Erikson's theory; the study determined that psychosocial development continues through adolescence and adulthood. In sum, adolescence is not an end point but rather a way station on the path of psychosocial development (Whitbourne et al., 1992; Filip et al., 2019; Mitchell et al., 2021).

Although Erikson's theory provides a broad outline of identity development, critics have pointed out that his approach is anchored in male-oriented concepts of individuality and competitiveness. In an alternative conception, psychologist Carol Gilligan suggests that women may develop identity through the establishment of relationships. In her view, a primary component of women's identity is the construction of caring networks among themselves and others (Gilligan, 2004).

STORMY ADOLESCENCE: MYTH OR REALITY?

Does puberty invariably foreshadow a stormy, rebellious period of adolescence?

At one time, psychologists thought that adolescence was a period filled with stress and unhappiness. Today, however, research shows that this characterization is largely a myth. The reality is that most young people pass through adolescence without great turmoil in their lives and that they get along with their parents reasonably well (Granic et al., 2003; Steinberg, 2016).

Not that adolescence is completely calm! In most families with adolescents, the amount of arguing and bickering clearly rises. Most young teenagers, as part of their search for identity, experience tension between their attempts to become independent from their parents and their actual dependence on them. They may experiment with a range of behaviors and flirt with a variety of activities that their parents, and even society as a whole, find objectionable. Happily, though, for most families such tensions

ego-integrity-versus-despair stage
According to Erikson, a period from late adulthood until death during which we review life's accomplishments and failures. (Module 29)

Study Alert
The characterization of adolescence as stormy is a myth for most adolescents.

stabilize during middle adolescence–around age 15 or 16–and eventually decline around age 18 (Hadiwijaya et al., 2017; Santos, 2021).

One reason for the increase in discord during adolescence appears to be the protracted period in which children stay at home with their parents. In prior historical periods–and in some non-Western cultures today–children leave home immediately after puberty and are considered adults. Today, however, sexually mature adolescents may spend as many as 7 or 8 years with their parents.

Current social trends even hint at an extension of the conflicts of adolescence beyond the teenage years because a significant number of young adults–known as *boomerang children*–return to live with their parents, typically for economic reasons, after leaving home for some period. In fact, during the coronavirus pandemic, a majority of 18-29-year-olds lived with their parents–the highest number since the 1930s. Although some parents welcome the return of their children, others are less sympathetic, which opens the way to conflict (Otters & Hollander, 2015; Kreiczer-Levy, 2019).

Another source of strife with parents lies in the way adolescents think. Adolescence fosters *adolescent egocentrism*, a state of self-absorption in which a teenager views the world from their own point of view. Egocentrism leads adolescents to be highly critical of authority figures, unwilling to accept criticism, and quick to fault others. It also makes them believe that they are the center of everyone else's attention, which leads to self-consciousness.

Furthermore, adolescents develop *personal fables*–the belief that one's experience and beliefs are unique, exceptional, and shared by no one else. Such personal fables may make adolescents feel invulnerable to the risks that threaten others (Boeve-de Pauw et al., 2011; Zheng et al., 2019; Fry et al., 2020).

Finally, parent-adolescent discord occurs because adolescents are much more apt to engage in risky behavior than they are later in life. In part, their riskiness is due to the immaturity of brain systems that regulate impulse control, some of which do not fully develop until people are in their mid-20s. Furthermore, adolescents have a greater tolerance for ambiguity and uncertainty, leading them to tolerate risks that adults would be less likely to accept (Steinberg, 2016; Ciranka & van den Bos, 2021).

ADOLESCENT SUICIDE

Although the vast majority of teenagers pass through adolescence without major psychological difficulties, some experience unusually severe psychological problems. Sometimes those problems become so extreme that adolescents take their own lives.

In the United States, *suicide* is the second leading cause of death among individuals between the ages of 10 and 14 and the third leading cause of death for 15- to 24-year-olds. The rate of suicide increased 30% between 2000 and 2018, and decreased in 2019 and 2020. More teenagers and young adults die from suicide than from cancer, heart disease, birth defects, stroke, pneumonia and influenza, and chronic lung disease (National Institute of Mental Health, 2019; Lovett, 2019).

The reported rate may actually be understated because medical personnel hesitate to report suicide as a cause of death. Instead, they frequently label a death as an accident in an effort to protect the survivors. Overall, as many as 200 adolescents may attempt suicide for every one who actually takes their own life. And consistent with the growing number of actual suicides, the occurrence of suicidal thoughts and attempts at suicide by adolescents nearly doubled from 2008 to 2015 (Brausch & Gutierrez, 2009; Martinez-Ales et al., 2020).

Male adolescents are five times more likely to die by suicide than females are, although females *attempt* suicide significantly more often than males do. In 2019, 9% of high school students reported that they attempted suicide during the prior 12 months. In terms of race and ethnicity, non-Hispanic American Indians and Alaskan Natives are particularly at risk for suicide. Furthermore, non-Hispanic Whites have a higher rate of suicide than Blacks and Asians (see Figure 4). In addition, lesbian, gay,

These young people are mourning the death of a peer who died by suicide. The rate of suicide among teenagers has risen significantly over the past few decades. Can you think of any reasons for this phenomenon?

David Silverman/Getty Images

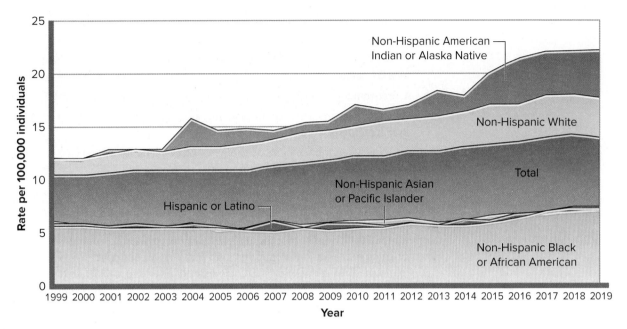

FIGURE 4. Suicide rates, by racial and ethnic group, in youth age 15–24.

Source: Ramchand et al., 2021.

bisexual, and transgender teens are at increased risk of suicide (Yildiz et al., 2019; Ramchand et al., 2021; Centers for Disease Control and Prevention, 2022).

What accounts for the high suicide rate among adolescents? Some psychologists suggest that the sharp rise in stress that teenagers experience–in terms of academic and social pressure, alcoholism, drug abuse, and family difficulties–provokes the most troubled adolescents to take their own lives. Easy access to weapons also tends to increase the chance of suicide (Sood & Linker, 2017; McGinty, 2019).

Although the question of why adolescent suicide rates are so high remains unanswered, several factors put adolescents at risk. One factor is depression, characterized by unhappiness, extreme fatigue, and–a variable that seems especially important–a profound sense of hopelessness. In other cases, adolescents who die by suicide are perfectionists who are inhibited socially and prone to extreme anxiety when they face any social or academic challenge. Furthermore, in some cases, bullying, both in person and cyberbullying, may result in suicide (Barzilay et al., 2015; Young et al., 2017).

Family background and adjustment difficulties are also related to suicide. A long-standing history of conflicts between parents and children may lead to adolescent behavior problems, such as delinquency, dropping out of school, and aggressive tendencies. In addition, teenage alcoholics and abusers of other drugs have a relatively high rate of suicide. Finally, suicides sometimes come in clusters, meaning that the suicide of one adolescent can trigger the suicide of others (Lovett, 2019; Benson et al., 2021; John, 2021).

The COVID-19 pandemic brought about a significant increase in thoughts about suicide, as well as an increase in actual suicide rates in many regions of the United States. These increases reflected a general decline in mental health resulting from the pandemic (Charpignon et al., 2022).

Several warning signs indicate when a teenager's problems may be severe enough to warrant concern about the possibility of a suicide attempt. They include the following:

- School problems, such as missing classes, truancy, and a sudden change in grades

- Frequent incidents of self-destructive behavior, such as careless accidents

- Loss of appetite or excessive eating

- Withdrawal from friends and peers

- Sleeping problems

- Signs of depression, tearfulness, or overt indications of psychological difficulties, such as hallucinations

- A preoccupation with death, an afterlife, or what would happen "if I died"

- Putting affairs in order, such as giving away prized possessions or making arrangements for the care of a pet

- An explicit announcement of thoughts of or plans for suicide. Even jokes about suicide may be a warning sign.

If you know someone who shows signs that they are suicidal, urge that person to seek professional help. Speaking frankly about suicide reduces the risk, according to research. You may need to take assertive action, such as enlisting the assistance of family members, friends, or campus administrators such as Student Affairs personnel. Talk of suicide is a serious signal for help and not a confidence to be kept.

For immediate help with a suicide-related problem, call or text 988, a national hotline staffed with trained counselors, or access www.suicidepreventionlifeline.org.

From the perspective of...

A Social Worker How might you determine if an adolescent is at risk for suicide? What strategies would you use to prevent the teen from dying by suicide? Would you use different strategies depending on the teenager's gender?

Sam Edwards/OJO Images/age fotostock

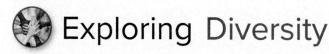

Exploring Diversity

Rites of Passage: Coming of Age Around the World

It is not easy for male members of the Awa tribe in New Guinea to make the transition from childhood to adulthood. First come whippings with sticks and prickly branches, followed by sharpened sticks pushed into the boys' nostrils. Then tribal adults force a 5-foot length of vine into the boys' throats until they gag and vomit. Finally, tribesmen cut the boys' genitals, causing considerable bleeding.

Although the rites that mark the coming of age of boys in the Awa tribe sound alarming to Westerners, they are comparable to those in other cultures. In some, youths must kneel on hot coals without displaying pain. In others, girls must toss wads of burning cotton from hand to hand and allow themselves to be bitten by hundreds of ants (Selsky, 1997; Wiseman, 2019).

Other cultures have less dramatic ceremonies that mark the passage from childhood to adulthood. For instance, when a girl first menstruates in traditional Apache tribes, the event is marked by dawn-to-dusk chanting. Western religions, too, have several types of celebrations, including bar mitzvahs and bat mitzvahs at age 13 for Jewish boys and girls, respectively, and confirmation ceremonies for children in many Christian denominations (Magida, 2006; Forth, 2018).

In most societies, males are the focus of coming-of-age ceremonies. The reason for this gender distinction may be that in most cultures, men traditionally have higher status than women, and therefore, those cultures regard boys' transition into adulthood as more important to celebrate.

However, another fact may explain why most cultures place greater emphasis on male rather than female rites. For females, the transition from childhood is marked by a definite biological event: menstruation. For males, in contrast, no single event can be used to pinpoint entry into adulthood. Thus, men are forced to rely on culturally determined rituals to acknowledge their arrival into adulthood.

RECAP/EVALUATE/RETHINK

RECAP

LO 29-1 What major physical, social, and cognitive transitions characterize adolescence?

- Adolescence, the developmental stage between childhood and adulthood, is marked by the onset of puberty, the point at which sexual maturity occurs. The age at which puberty begins has implications for the way people view themselves and the way others see them.
- Moral judgments during adolescence increase in sophistication, according to Kohlberg's three-level model. Although Kohlberg's levels provide an adequate description of males' moral judgments, Gilligan suggests that women view morality in terms of caring for individuals rather than in terms of broad general principles of justice.
- According to Erikson's model of psychosocial development, adolescence may be accompanied by an identity crisis. Adolescence is followed by three more stages of psychosocial development that cover the remainder of the life span.
- Suicide is the second-leading cause of death among individuals between the ages of 10 and 14 and the third leading cause of death for 15- to 24-year-olds..

EVALUATE

1. _____ is the period during which the sexual organs begin to mature.

2. Delayed maturation typically provides both males and females with a social advantage. True or false?
3. _____ proposed a set of three levels of moral development ranging from reasoning based on rewards and punishments to abstract thinking involving concepts of justice.
4. Erikson believed that during adolescence, people must search for _____, whereas during the early adulthood, the major task is _____.

RETHINK

1. In what ways do school cultures help or hurt teenage students who are going through adolescence? What school policies might benefit early-maturing girls and late-maturing boys? Explain how same-sex schools could help students going through adolescence, as some have argued.
2. Many cultures have rites of passage through which young people are officially recognized as adults. Do you think such rites can be beneficial? Does the United States have any such rites? Would setting up an official designation that one has achieved "adult" status have benefits?

Answers to Evaluate Questions

1. Puberty; 2. False; both male and female adolescents suffer if they mature late; 3. Kohlberg; 4. identity, intimacy

KEY TERMS

adolescence	identity	generativity-versus-	ego-integrity-versus-
puberty	intimacy-versus-isolation	stagnation stage	despair stage
identity-versus-role-	stage		
confusion stage			

Module 30
Adulthood

emerging adulthood The period beginning in the late teenage years and extending into the mid-20s. (Module 30)

As I passed through my 20s into my 30s, I really felt I was getting better in every way–physically stronger, intellectually sharper, just better. That feeling lasted until I moved into my late 30s and 40s, and then I began to have some physical issues. First it was my knees that began to hurt when I played tennis. Then some other kinds of physical things popped up as I moved into my 50s and 60s, culminating with the replacement of one of my hips. And eventually my thinking was not quite the same, as I struggled to find the right word every once and a while. No big deal, but it bothered me a little.

At some point it dawned on me: I wasn't the same person as I was in my 20s. I'm getting old.

It's no surprise that people change as they move through adulthood. Sometimes the changes are dramatic–for example, a major physical event such as a heart attack. But more often the changes are gradual, occurring over many years and decades, accumulating over time. Change and development are part of life, a normal process that affects all people as they move through adulthood.

Psychologists generally agree that early adulthood begins around age 20 and lasts until about age 40-45, when middle adulthood begins and continues until around age 65. Despite the enormous importance of these periods of life in terms of both the accomplishments that occur in them and their overall length (together they span some 44 years), they have been studied less than has any other stage. For one reason, the physical changes that occur during these periods are less apparent and more gradual than those at other times during the life span. In addition, the diverse social changes that arise during this period defy simple categorization.

The variety of changes that occur in early adulthood have led many developmental psychologists to view the start of the period as a transitional phase called emerging adulthood. **Emerging adulthood** is the period beginning in the late teenage years and extending into the mid-20s.

Although the brain is still growing and modifying its neural pathways during emerging adulthood, people are no longer adolescents. And these postadolescents typically face many questions as they approach the responsibilities of adulthood, still engaged in determining who they are and what their life and career paths should be. So this is a time of uncertainty and instability, as well as self-discovery (Wood et al., 2018; Pratt & Matsuba, 2019; Booker et al., 2021).

The view that adulthood is preceded by an extended period of emerging adulthood reflects the new reality of the economies of industrialized countries. These economies have shifted away from manufacturing to a focus on technology and information, thus requiring increasing time spent in educational training. Furthermore, the age at which most people marry and have children has risen significantly (Arnett, 2011; Pessin, 2018).

There's also an increasing ambivalence about reaching adulthood. When people in their late teens and early 20s are asked if they feel they have reached adulthood, most say "yes and no" (see Figure 1). In short, emerging adulthood is an age of identity exploration in which individuals are more self-focused and uncertain than they will be later in early adulthood (Arnett, 2006; Verschueren et al., 2017; Mannerström et al., 2019).

As we discuss the changes that occur through emerging adulthood, early adulthood, middle adulthood, and ultimately late adulthood, keep in mind the demarcations between the periods are fuzzy. However, the changes are certainly no less profound than they were in earlier periods of development.

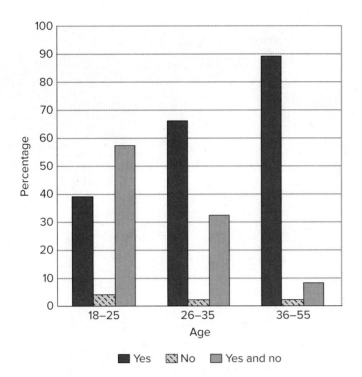

FIGURE 1 Evidence of a period of emerging adulthood is provided by the responses to a questionnaire asking, "Do you feel that you have reached adulthood?" Most people between the ages of 18 and 25 were ambivalent, responding "yes and no." Later, this ambivalence disappeared, with most people ages 26–35 saying "yes."
Source: Adapted from Arnett, 2006.

Physical Development: The Peak of Health

For most people, early adulthood marks the peak of physical health. From about 18-25 years of age, people's strength is greatest, their reflexes are quickest, and their chances of dying from disease are quite slim. Moreover, reproductive capabilities are at their highest level.

Around age 25, the body becomes slightly less efficient and more susceptible to disease. Overall, however, ill health remains the exception; most people stay remarkably healthy during early adulthood. (Can you think of any machine other than the body that can operate without pause for so long a period?)

During middle adulthood, people gradually become aware of changes in their bodies. They often experience weight gain (although they can avoid such increases through diet and exercise). Furthermore, the sense organs gradually become less sensitive, and reactions to stimuli are slower. But generally, the physical declines that occur during middle adulthood are minor and often unnoticeable (Kekäläinen et al., 2019).

The major biological change that does occur during middle adulthood pertains to reproductive capabilities. On average, during their late 40s or early 50s, women begin **menopause,** during which they stop menstruating and are no longer fertile. Because menopause is accompanied by a significant reduction in the production of estrogen, a female hormone, women sometimes experience hot flashes, sudden sensations of heat. Some doctors treat these with *hormone therapy (HT),* in which menopausal women take the hormones estrogen and progesterone.

However, hormone therapy poses several dangers, such as an increase in the risk of breast cancer, blood clots, and coronary heart disease. These uncertainties make the routine use of HT controversial. Currently, the medical consensus seems to be that younger women with severe menopausal symptoms ought to consider HT on a short-term basis. On the other hand, HT is less appropriate for older women after menopause (McCarrey & Resnick, 2015; Shifren et al., 2019).

Menopause was once blamed for a variety of psychological symptoms, including depression and memory loss. However, if such difficulties occur, they may be caused

menopause The period during which women stop menstruating and are no longer fertile. (Module 30)

Women's reactions to menopause vary significantly across cultures. According to one study, the more a society values old age, the less difficulty its women have during menopause. Why do you think this would be the case?
BananaStock/Alamy Stock Photo

by women's expectations about reaching an "old" age in a society that highly values youth. For example, women's reactions to menopause vary significantly across cultures. The more a society values old age, the less difficulty its women have during menopause (Espinola et al., 2017; Bullivant Ngati Pikiao et al., 2021).

For men, the aging process during middle adulthood is more subtle. Men have no physiological signals of increasing age equivalent to the end of menstruation in women; that is, no male menopause exists. In fact, men remain fertile and capable of fathering children until well into late adulthood. However, some gradual physical decline occurs. Men typically become less physically fit, especially after the age of 45. Sperm production decreases, and the frequency of orgasm declines. As is the case for women, though, psychological difficulties associated with these changes are usually brought about more by an aging men's inability to meet the exaggerated standards of youthfulness than by physical deterioration (Jackson et al., 2009; Kuosmanen et al., 2016).

Social Development: Working at Life

Whereas physical changes during adulthood reflect development of a quantitative nature, social developmental transitions are qualitative and more profound. During this period, people typically launch themselves into careers, marriage, and families.

The entry into early adulthood is usually marked by leaving one's childhood home and entering the world of work. People envision life goals and make career choices. Their lives often center on their careers, which form an important part of their identity (Bull et al., 2018; Fadjukoff et al., 2019).

In their early 40s, however, people may begin to question their lives as they enter a period called the *midlife transition*. The idea that life will end at some point can become more influential in their thinking, which leads them to question their past accomplishments (Boylan & Ryff, 2015; Kurther & Burnell, 2019; Soares & Shea, 2021).

Although some psychologists—and popular opinion—suggest that physical aging and dissatisfaction with one's life mark a so-called "midlife crisis," there is little evidence for such a "crisis." In fact, the passage into middle age is relatively calm for most people. Most 40-year-olds view their lives and accomplishments positively enough to proceed relatively smoothly through midlife, and the 40s and 50s are often a particularly rewarding period. Rather than looking to the future, people concentrate on the present; their involvement with their families, friends, and other social groups takes on new importance. A major developmental thrust of this period is coming to terms with one's circumstances (Whitbourne, 2010; Dare, 2011; Wojciechowska, 2017).

Finally, during the last stages of adulthood, people become more accepting of others and of their own lives and are less concerned about issues or problems that once bothered them. They come to accept the fact that death is inevitable, and they try to understand their accomplishments in terms of the broader meaning of life. Although people may begin for the first time to label themselves as "old," many also develop a sense of wisdom and feel freer to enjoy life (Miner-Rubino et al., 2004; Ward-Baker, 2007; Galambos et al., 2015).

Marriage, Children, and Divorce: Family Ties

A mainstay of Western fairy tales has been the handsome, young Prince Charming who finds a beautiful princess to marry, after which they live happily ever after. However, that scenario does not match the realities of love and marriage in the 21st century (if it ever did). Today, couples are just as likely to first live together, then get married and have children, but ultimately get divorced.

The percentage of U.S. households made up of unmarried couples has increased dramatically over the past two decades. At the same time, the average age at which marriage takes place is higher than at any time since the turn of the last century. These changes have been dramatic, and they suggest that the institution of marriage has changed considerably from earlier historical periods.

When people do marry, the possibility of divorce is not trivial. Many marriages end in divorce, though divorce rates have been declining since they peaked in 1979. Today, the rate is 1.6 divorces for every 1,000 marriages, which works out to 39% of first marriages ending in divorce (Luscomb, 2018; McGinty, 2019).

Furthermore, divorce is not only a U.S. phenomenon, and in many countries, such as Russia, the divorce rate is even higher than in the United States. Overall, the divorce rate has accelerated across the globe over the past several decades, particularly in industrialized countries. In some countries, the increase has been enormous (Olson & DeFrain, 2014; Park & Raymo, 2013; Zahl-Olsen et al., 2019).

In addition, 25% of all family households are now headed by one parent, compared with 13% in 1970. The United States has the highest rate of single-parent households in the world. If present trends continue, almost three-fourths of American children will spend some portion of their lives in a single-parent family before they turn 18. For children in minority households, the numbers are even higher. Around 64% of all Black American children and more than 42% of all Hispanic children live in homes with only one parent. Furthermore, in most single-parent families, the children live with the mother rather than the father–a phenomenon that is consistent across racial and ethnic groups throughout the industrialized world (Sarsour et al., 2011; U.S. Census Bureau, 2022).

What are the economic and emotional consequences for children living in homes with only one parent? Single-parent families are often economically less well off, and this economic disadvantage has an impact on children's opportunities. More than a third of single-mother families with children have incomes below the poverty line. In addition, good child care at an affordable price is often hard to find. Furthermore, for children of divorce, the parents' separation is often a painful experience that may result in obstacles to establishing close relationships later in life. Children may blame themselves for the breakup or feel pressure to take sides (Sorek, 2019; Carr et al., 2019).

Most evidence suggests, however, that children from single-parent families are no less well adjusted than are those from two-parent families. In fact, children may be

The number of single-parent families has doubled within the past decade, with the mother usually as head of the household. What are some of the challenges facing children in single-parent families?
Odua Images/Shutterstock

more successful growing up in a harmonious single-parent family than in a two-parent family that engages in continuous conflict (Koh et al., 2017; Chen et al., 2019).

Changing Roles of Men and Women

One of the major changes in family life in the last five decades has been the evolution of men's and women's roles. More women than ever before act simultaneously as wives, mothers, and wage earners—in contrast to women in traditional marriages in which the husband is the sole wage earner and the wife assumes primary responsibility for care of the home and children.

Almost three-fourths of all women with children under the age of 18 are employed outside the home, and 66% of mothers with children under age 6 are working. In the mid-1960s, only 17% of mothers of 1-year-olds worked full-time; now, more than half are in the labor force (U.S. Bureau of Labor Statistics, 2022).

Most married working women are not free of household responsibilities. Even in marriages in which the spouses hold jobs that have similar status and require similar hours, the distribution of household tasks between husbands and wives has not changed substantially. Working wives are still more likely than husbands to feel responsible for traditional homemaking tasks such as cooking and cleaning. In contrast, husbands still view themselves as responsible primarily for household tasks such as repairing broken appliances and doing yardwork (Damaske, 2011; Hwang et al., 2019).

For gay and lesbian couples, household chores are divided more equally—until they have children. At that point, the division of chores becomes less equitable, with one partner concentrating on household chores and child care, and the higher-earning spouse focusing more on career-related activities (Miller, 2018).

WOMEN'S "SECOND SHIFT"

Working mothers can put in a staggering number of hours. One survey, for instance, found that if we add the number of hours worked on the job and in the home, employed mothers of children under 3 years of age put in an average of 90 hours of work per week. Researchers see similar patterns in developing societies throughout the world, with women working at full-time jobs while also having primary responsibilities for child care. Overall, men work 7 hours, 47 minutes a day (most of it paid), whereas women work 8 hours, 39 minutes a day (most of it unpaid). The additional work women perform has been called the *second shift* (Hochschild & Machung, 2012; Brailey & Slatton, 2019; Organisation for Economic Co-operation and Development, 2022).

Consequently, rather than careers being a substitute for what women do at home, they are often an addition to the role of homemaker. It is not surprising that some wives feel resentment toward husbands who spend less time on child care and housework than the wives had expected before the birth of their children (Gerstel, 2005; Fagan & Press, 2008; Brailey & Slatton, 2019).

Later Years of Life: Growing Old

> Joe Handelman runs five days a week for around 30 minutes. He doesn't like to miss a day because it's a way to get out and stay active. It also helps him stay fit, and it allows him to meet people.
>
> Joe is 90 years old. (Dawson, 2021)

If you can't quite picture a 90-year-old running every day, some rethinking of your view of late adulthood may be in order. In spite of the societal stereotype of "old age" as a time of inactivity and physical and mental decline, *gerontologists,* specialists who study aging, are beginning to paint a very different portrait of late adulthood.

By focusing on the period of life that starts at around age 65, gerontologists are making important contributions to clarifying the capabilities of older adults. Their work is demonstrating that significant developmental processes continue even during old age. And as people live longer, the absolute number of people within older adulthood will continue to increase. Consequently, developing an understanding of late adulthood has become a critical priority for psychologists (Moody, 2000; Schaie, 2005b; Jia et al., 2011).

PHYSICAL CHANGES IN LATE ADULTHOOD: THE AGING BODY

The aging process brings many physical changes. The most obvious are those of appearance: hair thinning and turning gray, skin wrinkling and folding, and sometimes a slight loss of height as the thickness of the disks between vertebrae in the spine decreases. But subtler changes also occur in the body's biological functioning. For example, sensory capabilities decrease as a result of aging: Vision, hearing, smell, and taste become less sensitive. Reaction time slows, and physical stamina changes (Schilling & Diehl, 2015; Tucker-Drob et al., 2019).

What are the reasons for these physical declines? **Genetic preprogramming theories of aging** suggest that the DNA genetic code includes a built-in time limit for the reproduction of human cells. These theories suggest that after a certain time cells stop dividing or become harmful to the body–as if a kind of automatic self-destruct button had been pushed. In contrast, **wear-and-tear theories of aging** suggest that the mechanical functions of the body simply work less efficiently as people age. Waste byproducts of energy production eventually accumulate, and mistakes are made when cells divide. Eventually, the body in effect wears out like an old automobile (Hayflick, 2007; Helgeson & Zajdel, 2017).

Evidence supports both the genetic preprogramming and the wear-and-tear views, and it may be that both processes contribute to natural aging. It is clear, however, that physical aging is not a disease but a natural biological process. Many physical functions do not decline with age. For example, sex remains pleasurable well into old age (although the frequency of sexual activity decreases), and some people report that the pleasure they derive from sex increases during late adulthood (Wilkin & Haddock, 2011; Skałacka & Gerymski, 2019).

genetic preprogramming theories of aging Theories that suggest that human cells have a built-in time limit to their reproduction and that they are no longer able to divide after a certain time. (Module 30)

wear-and-tear theories of aging Theories that suggest that the mechanical functions of the body simply stop working efficiently. (Module 30)

 Study Alert

Two major theories of aging—the genetic preprogramming and the wear-and-tear views—explain some of the physical changes that take place in older adults.

COGNITIVE CHANGES: THINKING ABOUT—AND DURING—LATE ADULTHOOD

At one time, many gerontologists would have agreed with the popular view that older adults are forgetful and confused. Today, however, most research indicates that this assessment is far from an accurate one of older people's capabilities.

One reason for the change in view is that more sophisticated research techniques exist for studying the cognitive changes that occur in late adulthood. For example, if we were to give a group of older adults an IQ test, we might find that the average score was lower than the score achieved by a group of younger people. We might conclude that this signifies a decline in intelligence. Yet, if we looked a little more closely at the specific test, we might find that the conclusion was unwarranted. For instance, many IQ tests include portions based on physical performance (such as arranging a group of blocks) or on speed. In such cases, poorer performance on the IQ test may be due to gradual decreases in reaction time–a physical decline that accompanies late adulthood and has little or nothing to do with older adults' intellectual capabilities.

Other difficulties hamper research into cognitive functioning during late adulthood. For example, older people are often less healthy than younger ones; when only *healthy* older adults are compared to healthy younger adults, intellectual differences are far less evident. Furthermore, the average number of years in school is often lower in older adults (for historical reasons) than in younger ones, and older adults may be less motivated to perform well on intelligence tests than younger people are. Finally, traditional IQ tests may be inappropriate measures of intelligence in late adulthood. Older adults sometimes perform better on tests of practical intelligence than younger individuals do (Johnson & Deary, 2011; Tse et al., 2019; Mulas et al., 2021).

Still, some declines in intellectual functioning during late adulthood do occur, although the pattern of age differences is not uniform for different types of cognitive abilities (see Figure 2). In general, skills relating to *fluid intelligence* (which involves information-processing skills such as memory, calculations, and analogy solving) show declines in late adulthood. In contrast, skills relating to *crystallized intelligence* (intelligence based on the accumulation of information, skills, and strategies learned through experience) remain steady and in some cases actually improve (Dixon et al., 2013; Wettstein et al., 2019).

Even when changes in intellectual functioning occur during later adulthood, people often are able to compensate for any decline. They can still learn what they want to learn; it may just take more time. Furthermore, teaching older adults strategies for dealing with new problems can prevent declines in performance (Peters et al., 2007; Finke et al., 2017; Erickson et al., 2022).

Although fluid intelligence declines in late adulthood, skills relating to crystallized intelligence remain steady and may actually improve.

icsnaps/Shutterstock

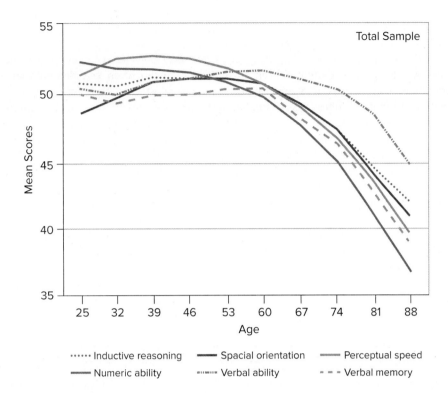

FIGURE 2 Age-related changes in intellectual skills vary according to the specific cognitive ability in question.
Source: Adapted from Schaie, 2005a.

MEMORY CHANGES IN LATE ADULTHOOD: ARE OLDER ADULTS FORGETFUL?

One of the characteristics most frequently attributed to late adulthood is forgetfulness. How accurate is this assumption?

Most evidence suggests that memory change is not an inevitable part of the aging process. For instance, research shows that older people in cultures in which older adults are held in high esteem, such as mainland China, are less likely to show memory losses than do those living in cultures in which the expectation is that memory will decline. Similarly, when older people in Western societies are reminded of the advantages of age (for example, "age brings wisdom"), they tend to do better on tests of memory (Dixon et al., 2007; Pinal et al., 2015).

Even when people show memory declines during late adulthood, their deficits generally are limited to certain types of memory. For instance, losses tend to be limited to episodic memories that relate to specific experiences in people's lives. Other types of memories, such as semantic memories (that refer to general knowledge and facts) and implicit memories (memories of which we are not consciously aware), are largely unaffected by age (Blumen et al., 2013; Gurven et al., 2017; Sejunaite et al., 2019).

Declines in episodic memories can often be traced to changes in older adults' lives. For instance, it is not surprising that a retired person, who may no longer face the same kind of consistent intellectual challenges encountered on the job, may have less practice in using memory or even be less motivated to remember things, which leads to an apparent decline in memory. Even in cases in which long-term memory declines, older adults can profit from training that targets memory skills (West et al., 2007; Morcom & Friston, 2011; Després et al., 2017).

In the past, older adults with severe cases of memory decline accompanied by other cognitive difficulties were said to suffer from *senility*. Now, most gerontologists view senility as an imprecise label that has outlived its usefulness. Instead, gerontologists explain symptoms of mental deterioration using more precise factors.

For example, rather than use senility to describe memory loss in general, gerontologists now recognize **Alzheimer's disease** as a progressive brain disorder that leads to a gradual and irreversible decline in cognitive abilities. More than 5.5 million Americans have the disease, and 1 in 9 people age 65 and older is afflicted. Unless a cure

Alzheimer's disease A progressive brain disorder that leads to a gradual and irreversible decline in cognitive abilities. (Modules 20, 30)

! **Study Alert**

It's important to be able to describe the nature of intellectual changes during late adulthood.

is found, some 12.7 million people are expected to have Alzheimer's in 2050 (Rogers, 2007; Alzheimer's Association, 2022).

Alzheimer's occurs when production of the *beta amyloid precursor protein* goes awry, producing large clumps of cells that trigger inflammation and deterioration of nerve cells. The brain shrinks, neurons die, and several areas of the hippocampus and frontal and temporal lobes deteriorate. So far, there is no effective treatment, although preliminary research suggests that diet, exercise, and an active social life can slow the decline in cognitive capabilities brought on by Alzheimer's (Behrens et al., 2009; Kivipelto & Hakansson, 2017; Milne et al., 2019).

In other cases, cognitive declines may be caused by temporary anxiety and depression, which can be treated successfully, or may even be due to overmedication. The danger is that people with such symptoms may be left untreated, thereby continuing their decline (Sachs-Ericsson et al., 2005; Diniz et al., 2013).

In sum, declines in cognitive functioning in late adulthood are, for the most part, not inevitable. The key to maintaining cognitive skills may lie in intellectual stimulation. Like the rest of us, older adults need a stimulating environment in order to hone and maintain their skills (Glisky, 2007; Hertzog et al., 2008; Hartshorne & Germine, 2015; De Pue et al., 2021; also see the *Neuroscience in Your Life* feature).

NEUROSCIENCE IN YOUR LIFE: HOW TO BE A SUPERAGER

Not everyone ages in the same way. Among other things, some people experience a decline in their memory and cognitive abilities as they grow older, whereas others maintain these abilities well into their 80s and 90s. In fact, some older adults perform just as well or even better than middle-aged and young adults on tests of memory and cognitive functioning. The neurologist Marsel Mesulam labeled this group "SuperAgers" (Maher et al., 2022).

How do SuperAgers maintain their abilities into late life? Neuroscience research gives us some clues. For example, neuroscientists gave brain scans to healthy adults who were age 60 or older. The researchers used a technique called *diffusion tensor imaging* to measure the health of white matter tracts, which are bundles of nerve fibers that connect parts of the brain. SuperAgers, the older adults whose memory scores were as good or better than people in their 40s, had white matter tracts that were more intact—in other words, healthier—than those of the people whose memory scores were in the typical range for their age. And the healthier their white matter tracts, the better were their scores on tests of memory, attention, and mental speed (Kim et al., 2020).

Another distinguishing characteristic of SuperAgers was their physical activity level. Based on Fitbit feedback over 1 week, the SuperAgers were found to be more physically active than the typical agers, and those higher physical activity levels were associated with healthier white matter tracts. These findings suggest that if you want to become a SuperAger and keep your white matter tracts healthy, staying physically active could be one key.

Front of the brain

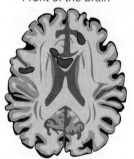

Back of the brain

This image shows a map of white matter tracts in the brain. The red areas indicate tracts that were healthier in SuperAgers compared to typical agers. These tracts connect the left and right hemispheres of the brain, the frontal and parietal lobes of the brain, and different regions within the frontal lobes. The health of these white matter tracts was related to better memory, attention, and mental speed, and to higher levels of physical activity.

THE SOCIAL WORLD OF LATE ADULTHOOD: OLD BUT NOT ALONE

Just as the view that old age predictably means mental decline has proved to be wrong, so has the view that late adulthood inevitably brings loneliness. People in late adulthood most often see themselves as functioning members of society; only a small number report that loneliness is a serious problem. In fact, older people report being less lonely than younger people (Luong et al., 2015; Domènech-Abella et al., 2019; Nguyen et al., 2020).

Certainly, late adulthood brings significant challenges. People who have spent their adult lives working and then enter retirement bring about a major shift in the roles they play. Moreover, many people must face the death of their spouse. Especially if the marriage has been a long and good one, the death of a partner means the loss of a companion, confidante, and lover. It can also bring about changes in economic well-being.

Maintaining interests and activities one had during middle age can contribute to a more successful late adulthood, according to the activity theory of aging.
otnaydur/Shutterstock

There is no single way to age successfully, and several theories have been developed to describe the process. According to the **disengagement theory of aging,** aging is characterized by a gradual withdrawal from the world. In this view, as people get older, they separate themselves from others on physical, psychological, and social levels. In this view, such disengagement is appropriate and even beneficial. The reason is that disengagement serves the purpose of providing an opportunity for increased reflectiveness and decreased emotional investment in others at a time of life when social relationships will inevitably be ended by death (Adams, 2004; Wrosch et al., 2005; Leung et al., 2021).

However, only a little research supports the disengagement theory of aging, and alternative theories have been suggested. The major alternative is the activity theory of aging. According to the **activity theory of aging,** people who age most successfully are those who maintain the interests, activities, and level of social interaction they experienced during their earlier periods of adulthood. Activity theory argues that people who are aging effectively show a continuation of the activities in which they participated during the earlier part of their lives (Crosnoe & Elder, 2002; Nimrod & Kleiber, 2007; Roos & Zaaiman, 2017).

Most research supports the activity theory of aging. On the other hand, not all people in late adulthood need a life filled with activities and social interaction to be happy. As in every stage of life, some older adults are just as satisfied leading a relatively inactive, solitary existence. What may be more important is how people view the aging process: Evidence shows that positive self-perceptions of aging are associated with increased longevity (Levy & Myers, 2004; Amesberger et al., 2019).

Regardless of how people age, most engage in a process of **life review** in which they examine and evaluate their lives. Remembering and reconsidering what has occurred in the past, people in late adulthood often come to a better understanding of themselves. They sometimes resolve lingering problems and conflicts and face their lives with greater wisdom and serenity.

Clearly, people in late adulthood are not just marking time until death. Rather, old age is a time of continued growth and development as important as any other period of life.

disengagement theory of aging The theory that suggests that successful aging is characterized by a gradual withdrawal from the world on physical, psychological, and social levels. (Module 30)

activity theory of aging The theory that suggests that successful aging is characterized by maintaining the interests and activities of earlier stages of life. (Module 30)

life review The process by which people examine and evaluate their lives. (Module 30)

From the perspective of...

A Health-Care Provider What sorts of recommendations would you make to your older patients about how to deal with aging? How would you handle someone who believed that getting older had only negative consequences?

Tetra Images/Getty Images

BECOMING AN INFORMED CONSUMER
of Psychology

Adjusting to Death

At some time in our lives, we all face death—certainly our own as well as the deaths of friends, loved ones, and even strangers. Although death is inevitable, it remains a frightening, emotion-laden topic. Little is more stressful than the death of a loved one or the contemplation of our own imminent death, and preparing for death is one of our most crucial developmental tasks.

A few generations ago, talk of death was taboo. The topic was never mentioned to dying people, and gerontologists had little to say about it. That changed, however, with the pioneering work of Elizabeth Kübler-Ross (1969), who brought the subject of death into the open with her observation that those facing impending death tend to move through five broad stages:

- *Denial.* In this stage, people resist the idea that they are dying. Even if told that their chances for survival are small, they refuse to admit that they are facing death.
- *Anger.* After moving beyond the denial stage, dying people become angry—angry at people around them who are in good health, angry at medical professionals for being ineffective, angry at God.
- *Bargaining.* Anger leads to bargaining in which the dying try to think of ways to postpone death. They may decide to dedicate their lives to religion or service to others if it would save them from death. They may say, "If only I can live to see my son married, I will accept death then."
- *Depression.* When dying people come to feel that bargaining is no use, they move to the next stage: depression. They realize that their lives really are coming to an end, which leads to what Kübler-Ross calls "preparatory grief" for their own deaths.
- *Acceptance.* In this stage, people accept impending death. Usually they are unemotional and uncommunicative; it is as if they have made peace with themselves and are expecting death with no bitterness.

Keep in mind that not everyone experiences each of the stages in the same way, and in fact, researchers have criticized Kübler-Ross's approach. For one thing, her stages are applicable only to people who are fully aware that they are dying and have the time to evaluate their impending death. Furthermore, vast differences occur in the way individuals react to impending death. The specific cause and duration of dying, as well as the person's sex, age, personality, and the type of support received from family and friends, all have an impact on how people respond to death (Clark & Kaufer, 2018; Corr, 2020; Tyrrell et al., 2021).

Few of us enjoy the contemplation of death. Yet awareness of its psychological aspects and consequences can make its inevitable arrival less anxiety producing and perhaps more understandable.

RECAP/EVALUATE/RETHINK

RECAP

LO 30-1 What are the principal kinds of physical, social, and intellectual changes that occur in early and middle adulthood, and what are their causes?

- Early adulthood marks the peak of physical health. Physical changes occur relatively gradually in men and women during adulthood.

- One major physical change occurs at the end of middle adulthood for women: They begin menopause, after which they are no longer fertile.
- During middle adulthood, people typically experience a midlife transition in which the notion that life will end becomes more important. In some cases, this may lead to a midlife crisis, although the passage into middle age is typically relatively calm.

- As aging continues during middle adulthood, people realize in their 50s that their lives and accomplishments are fairly well set, and they try to come to terms with them.
- Among the important developmental milestones during adulthood are marriage, family changes, and divorce. Another important determinant of adult development is work.

LO 30-2 How does the reality of late adulthood differ from the stereotypes about that period?

- Old age may bring marked physical declines caused by genetic preprogramming or physical wear and tear. Although the activities of people in late adulthood are not all that different from those of younger people, older adults experience declines in reaction time, sensory abilities, and physical stamina.
- Intellectual declines are not an inevitable part of aging. Fluid intelligence does decline with age, and long-term memory abilities are sometimes impaired. In contrast, crystallized intelligence shows slight increases with age, and short-term memory remains at about the same level.
- Although disengagement theory sees successful aging as a process of gradual withdrawal from the physical, psychological, and social worlds, there is little research supporting this view. Instead, activity theory, which suggests that the maintenance of interests and activities from earlier years leads to successful aging, is a more accurate explanation.

LO 30-3 How can we adjust to death?

- According to Kübler-Ross, dying people move through five stages as they face death: denial, anger, bargaining, depression, and acceptance.

EVALUATE

1. Rob recently turned 40 and surveyed his goals and accomplishments to date. Although he has accomplished a lot, he realized that many of his goals will not be met in his lifetime. This stage is called a _____ _____.
2. _____ _____ theories suggest that there is a maximum time span in which cells are able to reproduce. This time limit explains the eventual breakdown of the body.
3. Lower IQ test scores during late adulthood do not necessarily mean a decrease in intelligence. True or false?
4. During old age, a person's _____ intelligence continues to increase, whereas _____ intelligence may decline.
5. In Kübler-Ross's _____ stage, people resist the idea of death. In the _____ stage, they attempt to make deals to avoid death, and in the _____ stage, they passively await death.

RETHINK

1. Is the possibility that life may be extended for several decades a mixed blessing? What societal consequences might an extended life span bring about?
2. Does the finding that people in late adulthood require intellectual stimulation have implications for the societies in which older people live? In what way might stereotypes about older individuals contribute to their isolation and lack of intellectual stimulation?

Answers to Evaluate Questions

1. midlife transition; 2. Genetic preprogramming; 3. True; 4. crystallized, fluid; 5. denial, bargaining, acceptance

KEY TERMS

emerging adulthood	wear-and-tear theories of	disengagement theory of	activity theory of aging
menopause	aging	aging	life review
genetic preprogramming	Alzheimer's disease		
theories of aging			

LOOKING *Back*

EPILOGUE

We have traced major events in the development of physical, social, and cognitive growth throughout the life span. Clearly, people change throughout their lives.

As we explored each area of development, we encountered anew the nature–nurture issue, concluding in every significant instance that both nature and nurture contribute to a person's development of skills, personality, and interactions. Specifically, our genetic inheritance—nature—lays down general boundaries within which we can advance and grow; our environment—nurture—helps determine the extent to which we take advantage of our potential.

Before proceeding to the next set of modules, turn once again to the prologue at the beginning of this chapter that discussed Don Pellmann's remarkable athleticism at age 100. Using your knowledge of human development, consider the following questions.

1. How do you think heredity and environment worked hand-in-hand to enable Pell-man to reach 100 in such admirable shape? Is there evidence that his home environment encouraged his innate abilities?
2. If you were a developmental researcher, what questions would you ask Pellman to examine the relative influence of genes and environment on his athletic accomplishments?
3. How would you apply Erikson's theory of psychosocial development to Pellmann's life?

Design Elements: Man with laptop: Dragon Images/Shutterstock; Exclamation point and mobile frame: McGraw Hill; Smartphone: WML Image/Shutterstock; Hands: Stefano Garau/Shutterstock.

VISUAL SUMMARY 9 Development

MODULES 27 Nature and Nurture: The Enduring Developmental Issue

Developmental Research Techniques
- Cross-sectional, longitudinal, sequential

Basics of Genetics: Chromosomes and genes

Earliest Development

- Zygote: A fertilized egg

- Embryo: Between 2 and 8 weeks old after conception

- Fetus: Between 8 weeks and birth

- Age of viability: About 22 weeks from conception

Nature and Nurture
- Nature: Refers to hereditary factors
- Nurture: Refers to environmental influences

MODULE 28 Infancy and Childhood

The Extraordinary Newborn
- Reflexes: Rooting, sucking, gag, Babinski
- Development of the senses

Infancy Through Middle Childhood, about age 12
- Physical development: Rapid growth
- Social development

  - Attachment: Positive emotional bond between child and caregiver
  - Ainsworth strange situation
  - Social relationships with peers
- Child care outside the home
- Four parenting styles
- Erikson's theory of psychosocial development
  - Trust-versus-mistrust stage: Birth to age 1½
  - Autonomy-versus-shame-and-doubt stage: Ages 1½ to 3
  - Initiative-versus-guilt stage: Ages 3 to 6
  - Industry-versus-inferiority stage: Ages 6 to 12
- Cognitive development
  - Piaget's theory of cognitive development

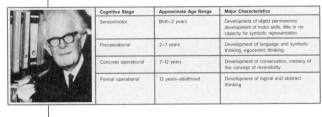

Cognitive Stage	Approximate Age Range	Major Characteristics
Sensorimotor	Birth–2 years	Development of object permanence, development of motor skills, little or no capacity for symbolic representation
Preoperational	2–7 years	Development of language and symbolic thinking, egocentric thinking
Concrete operational	7–12 years	Development of conservation, mastery of the concept of reversibility
Formal operational	12 years–adulthood	Development of logical and abstract thinking

  - Information processing approaches

MODULE 29 Adolescence: Becoming an Adult

Physical Development: Rapid weight and height gains; onset of puberty

Moral Development: Changes in moral reasoning

	Sample Moral Reasoning	
Level	In Favor of Stealing the Drug	Against Stealing the Drug
Level 1 Preconventional morality: The main considerations at this level are the avoidance of punishment and the desire for rewards.	"You shouldn't just let your wife die. People will blame you for not doing enough, and they'll blame the scientist for not selling you the drug for less money."	"You can't steal the drug because you'll be arrested and go to jail. Even if you aren't caught, you'll feel guilty, and you'll always worry that the police may figure out what you did."
Level 2 Conventional morality: Membership in society becomes important at this level. People behave in ways that will win the approval of others.	"Who will blame you if you steal a life-saving drug? But if you just let your wife die, you won't be able to hold your head up in front of your family or neighbors."	"If you steal the drug, everyone will treat you like a criminal. They will wonder why you couldn't have found some other way to save your wife."
Level 3 Postconventional morality: People accept that there are certain broad principles of morality that should govern our actions. These principles are more critical than the particular laws in a society.	"If you simply follow the law, you will violate the underlying principle of saving your wife's life. If you do steal the drug, society will understand your actions and respect them. You can't let an inadequate, outdated law prevent you from doing the right thing."	"You can't change your standards of honesty whenever it suits your needs. Others may not blame you for stealing the drug, but your conscience will blame you for betraying your own moral code."

Social Development: Erikson's theory of psychosocial development

Stage	Approximate Age	Positive Outcomes	Negative Outcomes
1. Trust-vs.-mistrust	Birth–1½ years	Feelings of trust from environmental support	Fear and concern regarding others
2. Autonomy-vs.-shame-and-doubt	1½–3 years	Self-sufficiency if exploration is encouraged	Doubts about self, lack of independence
3. Initiative-vs.-guilt	3–6 years	Discovery of ways to initiate actions	Guilt from actions and thoughts
4. Industry-vs.-inferiority	6–12 years	Development of sense of competence	Feelings of inferiority, no sense of mastery
5. Identity-vs.-role-confusion	Adolescence	Awareness of uniqueness of self, knowledge of role to be followed	Inability to identify appropriate roles in life
6. Intimacy-vs.-isolation	Early adulthood	Development of loving, sexual relationships and close friendships	Fear of relationships with others
7. Generativity-vs.-stagnation	Middle adulthood	Sense of contribution to continuity of life	Trivialization of one's activities
8. Ego-integrity-vs.-despair	Late adulthood	Sense of unity in life's accomplishments	Regret over lost opportunities of life

MODULE 30 Adulthood

Physical Development
- Early adulthood: Peak of health
- Middle adulthood: Menopause for women

Social Development
- Early adulthood: Focus on career, marriage, family
- Midlife transition: Relatively calm, come to terms with one's circumstances
- Late adulthood: Acceptance of others and one's circumstances

Marriage, Children, and Divorce
- People marry later in life than ever before; about half of all first marriages end in divorce
- Many single-parent households

Growing Old: Late adulthood
- Physical changes
  - Genetic preprogramming aging theory
  - Wear-and-tear aging theory
- Cognitive changes
  - Fluid intelligence declines; crystallized intelligence remains steady
  - Memory change not inevitable
    - Alzheimer's disease: Gradual, irreversible brain disorder that leads to a decline in cognitive abilities
- Social world
  - Disengagement theory of aging
  - Activity theory of aging

(Module 27) (fertilization): MedicalRF.com; (human embryo): Steve Allen/Science Source; (Module 28) (baby): Yoshiwara/E+/Getty Images; (monkey): Science History Images/Alamy Stock Photo; (Jean Piaget): Gado Images/Alamy Stock Photo; (Module 29) (Moral Development): Source: Kohlberg, 1969; (Erik Erikson): Jon Erikson/Science Source; (Module 30) (gardening): BananaStock/Alamy Stock Photo; (yoga): otnaydur/Shutterstock

santypan/Shutterstock

CHAPTER 10
Personality

LEARNING OUTCOMES FOR CHAPTER 10

LO 33-1 How can we most accurately assess personality?

LO 33-2 What are the major types of personality measures?

PROLOGUE *WHO IS THE REAL ANNA CHAPMAN?*

To most people, Anna Chapman was a beautiful, wealthy socialite. She owned a successful real estate company, and she had a roster of well-heeled clients who were prominent in New York City society. She made friends with the political elite of the city.

So it came as a shock when Chapman was arrested by federal authorities. She was charged with espionage and accused of being a Russian agent.

Who was the real Anna Chapman: successful entrepreneur, or Russian spy? We may never know for sure because before she could go to trial, she was deported to Russia as part of a prisoner exchange. After arriving in Russia, she achieved Hollywood-like celebrity, appearing on television and hawking a clothing line (Kesslen, 2022).

LOOKING *Ahead*

Many people, like Chapman, have more than one side to their personalities, appearing one way to some people and quite differently to others. Still, you also probably know people who are so consistent in their behavior that you can easily predict what they are going to do, no matter what the situation. Determining who a person truly is falls to a branch of psychology that seeks to understand the characteristic ways people behave: personality psychology.

Personality is the pattern of enduring characteristics that produce consistency and individuality in a given person. Personality encompasses the behaviors that make each of us unique and that differentiate us from others. Personality also leads us to act consistently in different situations and over extended periods of time.

We will consider a number of approaches to personality. For historical reasons, we begin with psychodynamic theories of personality, which emphasize the importance of the unconscious. Next, we consider approaches that concentrate on identifying the most fundamental personality traits; theories that view personality as a set of learned behaviors; biological and evolutionary perspectives on personality; and approaches, known as humanistic theories, that highlight the uniquely human aspects of personality. We end our discussion by focusing on how personality is measured and how personality tests can be used.

personality The pattern of enduring characteristics that produce consistency and individuality in a given person. (Module 31)

Module 31
Psychodynamic Approaches to Personality

LEARNING OUTCOMES

LO 31-1 How do psychologists define and use the concept of personality?

LO 31-2 What do the theories of Freud and his successors tell us about the structure and development of personality?

psychodynamic approaches to personality Approaches that assume that personality is primarily unconscious and motivated by inner forces and conflicts about which people have little awareness. (Module 31)

The college student was intent on making a good first impression on a person he found attractive, who he had spotted across a crowded room at a party. As he walked toward her, he mulled over a line he had heard in an old movie the night before: "I don't believe we've been properly introduced yet." To his horror, what came out was a bit different. After threading his way through the crowded room, he finally reached the person and blurted out, "I don't believe we've been properly seduced yet."

Although this student's error may seem to be merely an embarrassing slip of the tongue, according to some personality theorists, such a mistake is not an error at all (Motley, 1987). Instead, *psychodynamic personality theorists* might argue that the error illustrates one way in which behavior is triggered by inner forces that are beyond our awareness. These hidden drives, shaped by childhood experiences, play an important role in energizing and directing everyday behavior.

Psychodynamic approaches to personality are based on the idea that personality is primarily unconscious and motivated by inner forces and conflicts about which people have little awareness. The most important pioneer of the psychodynamic approach was Sigmund Freud. A number of Freud's followers, including Carl Jung, Karen Horney, and Alfred Adler, refined Freud's theory and developed their own psychodynamic approaches.

Freud's Psychoanalytic Theory: Mapping the Unconscious Mind

psychoanalytic theory Freud's theory that unconscious forces act as determinants of personality. (Module 31)

unconscious A part of the personality that contains the memories, knowledge, beliefs, feelings, urges, drives, and instincts of which the individual is not aware. (Module 31)

Sigmund Freud, an Austrian physician, developed psychoanalytic theory in the early 1900s. **Psychoanalytic theory** assumes that much of our behavior is driven by unconscious determinants. According to Freud's theory, conscious experience is only a small part of our psychological makeup and experience. He argued that much of our behavior is motivated by the **unconscious,** a part of the personality that contains the memories, knowledge, beliefs, feelings, urges, drives, and instincts of which the individual is not aware.

Like the unseen mass of a floating iceberg, the contents of the unconscious far surpass in quantity the information in our conscious awareness. Freud maintained that to understand personality, it is necessary to expose what is in the unconscious. But because the unconscious disguises the meaning of the material it holds, the content of the unconscious cannot be observed directly. It is therefore necessary to interpret clues to the unconscious–slips of the tongue, fantasies, and dreams–to understand the unconscious processes that direct behavior. A slip of the tongue such as the one quoted earlier (sometimes termed a *Freudian slip*) may be interpreted as revealing the speaker's unconscious sexual desires.

To Freud, much of our personality is determined by our unconscious. Some of the unconscious is made up of the *preconscious*, which contains material that is not threatening and is easily brought to mind, such as the knowledge that 2 + 2 = 4. But deeper in the unconscious are instinctual drives: the wishes, desires, demands, and needs that are hidden from conscious awareness because of the conflicts and pain they would cause if they were part of our everyday lives. The unconscious provides a "safe haven" for our recollections of threatening events.

STRUCTURING PERSONALITY: ID, EGO, AND SUPEREGO

To describe the structure of personality, Freud developed a comprehensive theory that held that personality consists of three separate but interacting components: the id, the ego, and the superego. Freud suggested that the three structures can be diagrammed to show how they relate to the conscious and the unconscious (see Figure 1).

Although the three components of personality Freud described may appear to be actual physical structures in the nervous system, they are not. Instead, they represent abstract conceptions of a general *model* of personality that describes the interaction of forces that motivate behavior.

If personality consisted only of primitive, instinctual cravings and longings, it would have just one component: the id. The **id** is the instinctual and unorganized part of personality. From the time of birth, the id attempts to reduce tension created by primitive drives related to hunger, sex, aggression, and irrational impulses. Those drives are fueled by "psychic energy," which we can think of as a limitless energy source constantly putting pressure on the various parts of the personality.

The id operates according to the *pleasure principle* in which the goal is the immediate reduction of tension and the maximization of satisfaction. However, in most cases, reality prevents the fulfillment of the demands of the pleasure principle: We cannot always eat when we are hungry, and we can discharge our sexual drives only when the time and place are appropriate. To account for this fact of life, Freud suggested a second component of personality, which he called the ego.

The **ego** is the rational and logical part of personality. The ego attempts to balance the desires of the id and the realities of the objective, outside world. It starts to develop soon after birth.

In contrast to the pleasure-seeking id, the ego operates according to the *reality principle* in which instinctual energy is restrained to maintain the individual's safety and to help integrate the person into society. In a sense, then, the ego is the "executive" of personality: It makes decisions, controls actions, and allows thinking and problem solving of a higher order than the id's capabilities permit.

The superego is the final personality structure to develop in childhood. According to Freud, the **superego** is the part of personality that harshly judges the morality of

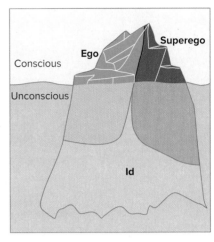

FIGURE 1 In Freud's personality model, there are three major components: the id, the ego, and the superego. As the iceberg analogy shows, only a small portion of personality is conscious. Why do you think that only the ego and superego have conscious components?

id The instinctual and unorganized part of personality whose sole purpose is to reduce tension created by primitive drives related to hunger, sex, aggression, and irrational impulses. (Module 31)

ego The part of personality that attempts to balance the desires of the id and the realities of the objective, outside world. (Module 31)

superego The part of personality that harshly judges the morality of our behavior. (Module 31)

Freud suggests that the superego, the part of the personality that represents the rights and wrongs of society, develops from direct teaching by parents, teachers, and other significant individuals.
Shutterstock

Study Alert

Remember that the three parts of personality in Freud's theory—the id, the ego, and the superego—are abstract conceptions that don't exist as physical structures in the brain.

our behavior. It represents the rights and wrong of society as taught and modeled by a person's parents, teachers, and other significant individuals.

The superego includes the *conscience*, which prevents us from behaving in a morally improper way by making us feel guilty if we do wrong. The superego helps us control impulses coming from the id, making our behavior less selfish and more virtuous.

Neither the id nor superego parts of personality are realistic, practical, or logical in that they do not consider the realities society imposes. For example, the superego, if left to operate by itself and without restraint, would create perfectionists unable to make the moral compromises that life sometimes requires. On the other hand, an unrestrained id would produce primitive, pleasure-seeking, thoughtless individuals on a mission to fulfill every desire without delay. Consequently, the ego must constrain and negotiate between the conflicting demands of the superego and id.

DEVELOPING PERSONALITY: PSYCHOSEXUAL STAGES

Freud also provided us with a view of how personality develops. He suggests personality development proceeds through a series of five **psychosexual stages** during which children encounter conflicts between the demands of society and their own sexual urges (in which sexuality is more about experiencing pleasure and less about lust).

According to Freud, if we are not able to resolve the conflicts that occur at a particular psychosexual stage, we may become locked in that conflict throughout life—something he called fixation. **Fixations** are conflicts or concerns that persist beyond the developmental period in which they first occur. Such conflicts may be due to having needs ignored, such as ending breast feeding too early or being treated too strictly during toilet training. Alternatively, fixation may occur if children are overindulged during an earlier period, such as when parents are overly attentive to a child or provide lavish rewards during toilet training.

The sequence Freud proposed is noteworthy because it explains how experiences and difficulties during a particular childhood stage may predict specific characteristics in the adult personality. This theory is also unique in associating each stage with a major biological function, which Freud assumed to be the focus of pleasure in a given period. (See Figure 2 for a summary of the stages.)

In the first psychosexual stage of development, called the **oral stage,** the baby's mouth is the focal point of pleasure. During the first 12-18 months of life, children suck, eat, mouth, and bite anything they can put into their mouths. To Freud, this behavior suggested that the mouth is the primary site of a kind of sexual pleasure and that weaning (withdrawing the breast or bottle) represents the main conflict during the oral stage. If infants are either overindulged (perhaps by being fed every time they cry) or frustrated in their search for oral gratification, they may become fixated at this stage.

For example, fixation might occur if an infant's oral needs were constantly gratified immediately at the first sign of hunger rather than if the infant learned that feeding

psychosexual stages Developmental periods that children pass through during which they encounter conflicts between the demands of society and their own sexual urges. (Module 31)

fixations Conflicts or concerns that persist beyond the developmental period in which they first occur. (Module 31)

oral stage According to Freud, a stage from birth to age 12 to 18 months, in which an infant's center of pleasure is the mouth. (Module 31)

Study Alert
The five psychosexual stages of personality development in Freud's theory—oral, anal, phallic, latency, and genital—indicate how personality develops as people age.

FIGURE 2 Freud's theory of personality development suggests several distinct stages.

Stage	Age	Major Characteristics
Oral	Birth to 12–18 months	Interest in oral gratification from sucking, eating, mouthing, biting
Anal	12–18 months to 3 years	Gratification from expelling and withholding feces; coming to terms with society's controls relating to toilet training
Phallic	3 to 5–6 years	Interest in the genitals, coming to terms with Oedipal conflict leading to identification with same-sex parent
Latency	5–6 years to adolescence	Sexual concerns largely unimportant
Genital	Adolescence to adulthood	Reemergence of sexual interests and establishment of mature sexual relationships

takes place on a schedule because eating whenever an infant wants to eat is not always realistic. Fixation at the oral stage might produce an adult who was unusually interested in oral activities–eating, talking, smoking–or who showed symbolic sorts of oral interests such as being "bitingly" sarcastic or very gullible ("swallowing" anything).

From around age 12-18 months until 3 years of age–a period in which the emphasis in Western cultures is on toilet training–a child enters the **anal stage.** At this point, the major source of pleasure changes from the mouth to the anal region, and children obtain considerable pleasure from both retention and expulsion of feces. If toilet training is particularly demanding, fixation might occur. Fixation during the anal stage might result in unusual rigidity, orderliness, punctuality–or extreme disorderliness or sloppiness–in adulthood.

At about age 3, the **phallic stage** begins. At this point, there is another major shift in the child's primary source of pleasure. Now interest focuses on the genitals and the pleasures derived from fondling them. During this stage, the child must also negotiate one of the most important hurdles of personality development: the Oedipal conflict.

The **Oedipal conflict** is a child's intense, sexual interest in their opposite-sex parent. According to Freudian theory, the Oedipal conflict plays out as children focus attention on their genitals and the differences between male and female anatomy become more salient.

According to Freud, a male child unconsciously begins to develop a sexual interest in his mother, starts to see his father as a powerful rival, and harbors a wish to replace his father and enjoy the affections of his mother. (The situation mirrors a tragic Greek play in which the son Oedipus kills his father and marries his mother, hence the term *Oedipal conflict*.) But because a son views his father as too powerful, he develops a fear that his father may retaliate drastically by removing the source of the threat: his penis.

Also according to Freud, the fear of losing his penis leads to *castration anxiety*, which ultimately becomes so powerful that the child represses his desires for his mother and identifies with his father. **Identification** is the process of wanting to be like another person as much as possible, imitating that person's behavior and adopting similar beliefs, attitudes, and values. By identifying with his father, a son seeks to obtain a woman like his unattainable mother.

Freud argued that the process is different for girls. He suggested that they experience sexual arousal related to their fathers and begin to have penis envy. They wish they had the anatomical part that seems most clearly "missing" from their bodies; that is, girls realize they lack a penis.

Blaming their mothers for this missing piece of anatomy, girls come to believe that their mothers are responsible for their "castration." Like males, though, they find that they can resolve such unacceptable feelings by identifying with the same-sex parent, behaving like her, and adopting her attitudes and values. In this way, a girl's identification with her mother is completed. (These ideas about the identification process in girls led to considerable criticism that Freud was sexist, favoring males over females.)

Through these complicated–and to many critics, far-fetched–sequences of events, Freud argued that the Oedipal conflict is resolved and that both males and females move on to the next stage of development. If difficulties arise during the resolution of the Oedipal conflict, however, all sorts of problems are thought to occur, including improper sex-role behavior and the failure to develop a conscience.

After the resolution of the Oedipal conflict, typically around age 5 or 6, children move into the **latency period,** which lasts until puberty. During this period, sexual interests become dormant, even in the unconscious. Then, during adolescence, sexual feelings re-emerge, which marks the start of the final period, the **genital stage,** which extends until death. The focus during the genital stage is on mature, adult sexuality, which Freud defined as sexual intercourse.

According to Freud, a child goes through the anal stage from age 12–18 months until 3 years of age. Toilet training is a crucial event at this stage—one that psychoanalytic theory claims directly influences the formation of an individual's personality.
Exactostock/SuperStock

anal stage According to Freud, a stage from age 12 to 18 months to 3 years of age, in which a child's pleasure is centered on the anus. (Module 31)

phallic stage According to Freud, a period beginning around age 3 during which a child's pleasure focuses on the genitals. (Module 31)

Oedipal conflict A child's intense, sexual interest in their opposite-sex parent. (Module 31)

identification The process of wanting to be like another person as much as possible, imitating that person's behavior and adopting similar beliefs and values. (Module 31)

latency period According to Freud, the period between the phallic stage and puberty during which children's sexual concerns are temporarily put aside. (Module 31)

genital stage According to Freud, the period from puberty until death, marked by mature sexual behavior (that is, sexual intercourse). (Module 31)

DEFENSE MECHANISMS

! **Study Alert**
Use Figure 3 to remember the most common defense mechanisms (unconscious strategies used to reduce anxiety by concealing its source from ourselves and others).

defense mechanisms In Freudian theory, unconscious strategies that people use to reduce anxiety by distorting reality and concealing the source of the anxiety from themselves. (Module 31)

repression The defense mechanism in which the ego pushes unacceptable or unpleasant thoughts and impulses out of consciousness but maintains them in the unconscious. (Module 31)

Freud's efforts to describe and theorize about the underlying dynamics of personality and its development were motivated by very practical problems that his patients faced in dealing with *anxiety,* an intense, negative emotional experience. According to Freud, anxiety is a danger signal to the ego. Although anxiety can arise from realistic fears—such as seeing a poisonous snake about to strike—it can also occur in the form of *neurotic anxiety* in which irrational impulses emanating from the id threaten to burst through and become uncontrollable.

Because anxiety is obviously unpleasant, Freud believed that people develop a range of ways to deal with it, which he called defense mechanisms. **Defense mechanisms** are unconscious strategies that people use to reduce anxiety by distorting reality and concealing the source of the anxiety from themselves.

The primary defense mechanism is repression. **Repression** occurs when the ego pushes unacceptable or unpleasant thoughts and impulses out of consciousness but maintains them in the unconscious.

Repression is the most direct method of dealing with anxiety; instead of handling an anxiety-producing impulse on a conscious level, we simply ignore it. For example, a college student who feels hatred for his mother may repress those personally and socially unacceptable feelings. The feelings remain lodged within the unconscious because acknowledging them would provoke anxiety. Similarly, memories of childhood abuse may be repressed. Although such memories may not be consciously recalled, according to Freud, they can affect later behavior, and they may be revealed through dreams or slips of the tongue or symbolically in some other fashion.

If repression is ineffective in keeping anxiety at bay, we might use other defense mechanisms. Freud and later his daughter, Anna Freud (who became a well-known psychoanalyst), formulated an extensive list of potential defense mechanisms. The major defense mechanisms are summarized in Figure 3 (Boag, 2015; Zhang & Guo, 2017; Kupfersmid, 2019).

All of us employ defense mechanisms to some degree, according to Freudian theory, and they can serve a useful purpose by protecting us from unpleasant information. Yet some people fall prey to them to such an extent that they must constantly direct

Freud's Defense Mechanisms		
Defense Mechanism	**Explanation**	**Example**
Repression	Unacceptable or unpleasant impulses are pushed out of awareness and back into the unconscious.	A person is unable to consciously recall they were raped.
Regression	People behave as if they were at an earlier stage of development.	A team leader has a temper tantrum when an employee makes a mistake.
Displacement	The expression of an unwanted feeling or thought is redirected from a more threatening powerful person to a weaker one.	A brother yells at his younger sibling after a teacher gives him a bad grade.
Rationalization	People provide self-justifying explanations in place of the actual, but threatening, reason for their behavior.	A student who goes out drinking the night before a big test rationalizes their behavior by saying the test isn't all that important.
Denial	People refuse to accept or acknowledge an anxiety-producing piece of information.	A student refuses to believe that they have flunked a course.
Projection	People attribute unwanted impulses and feelings to someone else.	A spouse who is unfaithful to their partner and feels guilty suspects that their partner is unfaithful.
Sublimation	People divert unwanted impulses into socially approved thoughts, feelings, or behaviors.	A person with strong feelings of aggression becomes a soldier.
Reaction formation	Unconscious impulses are expressed as their opposite in consciousness.	A parent who unconsciously resents their child acts in an overly loving way toward the child.

FIGURE 3 According to Freud, people use a wide range of defense mechanisms to cope with anxieties.

a large amount of psychic energy toward hiding and rechanneling unacceptable impulses. When this occurs, everyday living becomes difficult. In such cases, the result is a mental disorder produced by anxiety—what Freud called "neurosis." (Psychologists rarely use this term today, although it endures in everyday conversation.)

EVALUATING FREUD'S LEGACY

Freud's theory has had a significant impact on the field of psychology—and even more broadly on Western philosophy and literature. The general ideas that we have unconscious thoughts that influence behavior, that we employ defense mechanisms, and that some adult psychological problems have their roots in childhood difficulties are widely accepted (Boag et al., 2015; Zhang et al., 2016; Rehan et al., 2019).

However, contemporary personality psychologists have leveled significant criticisms against many foundational explanations of personality development in psychoanalytic theory. Among the most important is the lack of compelling scientific data to support the process of personality development that Freud laid out. Although individual case studies *seem* supportive, we lack conclusive evidence that shows the personality is structured and operates along the lines Freud laid out (Tummala-Narra, 2016; Nagel, 2020).

The lack of research evidence is due, in part, to the fact that Freud's conception of personality is built on unobservable abstract concepts. Moreover, the stages of personality Freud laid out may not provide an accurate description of personality development. For example, we know now that important changes in personality can occur in adolescence and adulthood—something that Freud did not believe happened. Instead, he argued that personality largely is set by the time we reach adolescence.

The vague nature of Freud's theory also makes it difficult to predict how an adult will display certain developmental difficulties. For instance, if a person is fixated at the anal stage, according to Freud, they may be unusually messy or unusually neat. Freud's theory offers no way to predict how the difficulty will be exhibited. Furthermore, Freud can be faulted for seeming to view women as inferior to men because he argued that women have weaker superegos than men do and in some ways unconsciously yearn to be men (the concept of penis envy).

Finally, Freud made his observations and derived his theory from a limited population. His theory was based almost entirely on upper-class Austrian women living

Freud developed his theory on observations of upper-class Austrian women, but critics have suggested his conclusions may not apply to people living in cultures that are very different.
Ariel Skelley/Blend Images LLC

in the strict, puritanical era of the early 1900s who had come to him seeking treatment for psychological and physical problems. How far one can generalize beyond this population is a matter of considerable debate. For instance, in some Pacific Island societies, the mother's oldest brother and not the father plays the role of disciplinarian. In such a culture, one cannot reasonably argue that the Oedipal conflict will progress in the same way it did in Austrian society, where the father typically was the major disciplinarian. In short, a cross-cultural perspective raises questions about the universality of Freud's view of personality development (Grünbaum, 2015; Shapira-Berman, 2019).

Still, Freud generated an important method of treating psychological disturbances called *psychoanalysis*. As we will see when we discuss treatment approaches to psychological disorders, psychoanalysis remains in use today (Frosch, 2011; Altman & Stile, 2015; Shulman, 2021).

Moreover, Freud's emphasis on the unconscious has been partially supported by current research on dreams and implicit memory. As first noted when we discussed dreaming, advances in neuroscience are consistent with some of Freud's arguments. For example, the fact that some behavior is motivated by occurrences that apparently have been forgotten, as well as the discovery of neural pathways relating to emotional memories, supports the notion of repression.

Furthermore, cognitive and social psychologists have found increasing evidence that unconscious processes help us think about and evaluate our world, set goals, and choose a course of action. Unconscious processes also help determine how we form attitudes toward others (Teague, 2013; Bargh, 2014; Fayek, 2017).

The Neo-Freudian Psychoanalysts: Building on Freud

Freud laid the foundation for important work done by a series of successors who were trained in traditional Freudian theory but later rejected some of its major points. These theorists are known as **neo-Freudian psychoanalysts**.

The neo-Freudians placed greater emphasis than Freud did on the functions of the ego by suggesting that it has more control than the id does over day-to-day activities. They focused more on the social environment and minimized the importance of sex as a driving force in people's lives. They also paid greater attention to the effects of society and culture on personality development.

JUNG'S COLLECTIVE UNCONSCIOUS

Carl Jung (pronounced "yoong"), one of the most influential neo-Freudians, rejected Freud's view of the primary importance of unconscious sexual urges. Instead, he looked at the primitive urges of the unconscious more positively. He argued that they represented a more general and positive life force that goes back to the dawn of the existence of life, motivating creativity and positive conflict resolution (Cassells, 2007; Wilde, 2011; Addison, 2017).

Jung suggested that we have a universal **collective unconscious**–an inherited set of ideas, feelings, images, and symbols that are shared with all humans because of our common ancestral past. This collective unconscious, which is in the deepest layer of the unconscious, is similar in everyone and is displayed in behavior that is common across diverse cultures–such as love of mother, belief in a supreme being, and even behavior as specific as fear of snakes (Finn, 2011; Jung, 2021).

Jung went on to propose that the collective unconscious contains **archetypes,** universal symbolic representations of particular types of people, objects, ideas, or experiences. For instance, a *mother archetype*, which contains reflections of our ancestors' relationships with mother figures, is suggested by the prevalence of mothers in art,

neo-Freudian psychoanalysts Psychoanalysts who were trained in traditional Freudian theory but who later rejected some of its major points. (Module 31)

collective unconscious According to Jung, an inherited set of ideas, feelings, images, and symbols that are shared with all humans because of our common ancestral past. (Module 31)

archetypes According to Jung, universal symbolic representations of particular types of people, objects, ideas, or experiences. (Module 31)

In terms of Jung's theory, Luke Skywalker and Darth Vader from the *Star Wars* movies represent the archetypes, or universally recognizable symbols, of good and evil.

(left): AF Archive/Alamy Stock Photo; (right): AJ Pics/Alamy Stock Photo

religion, literature, and mythology. (Think of the Virgin Mary, Mother Earth, wicked stepmothers in fairy tales, Mother's Day, and so forth!) Jung also suggested that men possess an unconscious *feminine archetype* that affects how they behave and women have an unconscious *male archetype* that colors their behavior (Potash, 2015; Vaughn Becker & Neuberg, 2019; Roesler & Ulyet, 2021).

To Jung, archetypes play an important role in determining our day-to-day reactions, attitudes, and values. For example, Jung might explain the popularity of the *Star Wars* movies as being due to their use of broad archetypes of good (Luke Skywalker) and evil (Darth Vader).

Although no reliable research evidence confirms the existence of the collective unconscious—and even Jung acknowledged that such evidence would be difficult to produce—Jung's theory has had significant influence in areas beyond psychology. For example, personality types derived from Jung's personality approach form the basis for the Myers-Briggs personality test, which is widely used in business and industry to provide insights into how employees make decisions and perform on the job (Mills, 2013; Wang et al., 2017; Ma et al., 2021).

From the perspective of...

An Advertising Executive How might you use Jung's concept of archetypes in designing your advertisements? Which of the archetypes would you use?

mentatdgt/Shutterstock

HORNEY'S NEO-FREUDIAN PERSPECTIVE

Karen Horney (pronounced "HORN-eye") was one of the earliest psychologists to champion women's issues and is sometimes called the first feminist psychologist. Horney suggested that personality develops in the context of social relationships and depends particularly on the relationship between parents and child and how well the child's needs are met. She rejected Freud's suggestion that women have penis envy; she asserted that what women envy most in men is not their anatomy but the independence, success, and freedom women often are denied (Horney, 1937; Coolidge et al., 2011; Forsythe, 2019).

Horney was also one of the first to stress the importance of cultural factors in the determination of personality. For example, she suggested that society's rigid gender

Psychologist Karen Horney was one of the earliest proponents of women's issues.
Bettmann/Getty Images

roles for women lead them to experience ambivalence about success because they fear they will make enemies if they are too successful. Her conceptualizations, developed in the 1930s and 1940s, laid the groundwork for many of the central ideas of feminism that emerged decades later (Jones, 2006; Horney, 2000).

ADLER AND THE OTHER NEO-FREUDIANS

Alfred Adler, another important neo-Freudian psychoanalyst, also considered Freudian theory's emphasis on sexual needs misplaced. Instead, Adler proposed that the primary human motivation is a striving for superiority, not in terms of superiority over others but in a quest for self-improvement and perfection.

Adler used the term *inferiority complex* to describe adults who have not been able to overcome feelings of inadequacy they developed as children. An *inferiority complex* is a lack of self-worth, a feeling that one is not as good as others. Early social relationships with parents have an important effect on children's ability to outgrow feelings of personal inferiority. If children have positive experiences, they can orient themselves toward attaining socially useful goals.

Other neo-Freudians included Erik Erikson, whose theory of psychosocial development we discussed in other modules, and Freud's daughter, Anna Freud. Like Adler and Horney, they focused less than Freud did on inborn sexual and aggressive drives and more on the social and cultural factors behind personality.

RECAP/EVALUATE/RETHINK

RECAP

LO 31-1 How do psychologists define and use the concept of personality?

- Personality is the pattern of enduring, distinctive characteristics that produce consistency and individuality in a given person.

LO 31-2 What do the theories of Freud and his successors tell us about the structure and development of personality?

- According to psychodynamic approaches to personality, much behavior is caused by parts of personality that are found in the unconscious and of which we are unaware.
- Freud's psychoanalytic theory, one of the psychodynamic approaches, suggests that personality is composed of the id, the ego, and the superego. The id is the unorganized, inborn part of personality whose purpose is to immediately reduce tensions relating to hunger, sex, aggression, and other primitive impulses. The ego restrains instinctual energy to maintain the individual's safety and to help the person be a member of society. The superego represents society's rights and wrongs and includes the conscience.

- Freud's psychoanalytic theory suggests that personality develops through a series of psychosexual stages (oral, anal, phallic, latency, and genital), each of which is associated with a primary biological function.
- Defense mechanisms, according to Freudian theory, are unconscious strategies that people use to reduce anxiety by distorting reality and concealing the true source of the anxiety from themselves.
- Freud's psychoanalytic theory has provoked a number of criticisms, including a lack of supportive scientific data, the theory's inadequacy in making predictions, and its reliance on a highly restricted population. On the other hand, recent neuroscience research has offered some support for the concept of the unconscious.
- Neo-Freudian psychoanalytic theorists built on Freud's work, although they placed greater emphasis on the role of the ego and paid more attention to the role of social factors in determining behavior.

EVALUATE

1. _____ approaches state that behavior is motivated primarily by unconscious forces.

2. Match each section of the personality (according to Freud) with its description:

1. Ego	**a.** Determines right from wrong on the basis of cultural standards
2. Id	
3. Superego	**b.** Operates according to the "reality principle"; energy is redirected to integrate the person into society
	c. Seeks to reduce tension brought on by primitive drives

3. Which of the following represents the proper order of personality development, according to Freud?

a. Oral, phallic, latency, anal, genital

b. Anal, oral, phallic, genital, latency

c. Oral, anal, phallic, latency, genital

d. Latency, phallic, anal, genital, oral

4. _____ _____ is the term Freud used to describe unconscious strategies used to reduce anxiety by distorting reality and concealing the source of the anxiety from themselves.

RETHINK

1. Can you think of ways in which Freud's theories of unconscious motivations are commonly used in popular culture? How accurately do you think such popular uses of Freudian theories reflect Freud's ideas?

2. What are some examples of archetypes in addition to those mentioned in this module? In what ways are archetypes similar to and different from stereotypes?

Answers to Evaluate Questions

1. Psychodynamic; 2. 1-b, 2-c, 3-a; 3. c; 4. Defense mechanisms

---

KEY TERMS

personality	id	anal stage	defense mechanisms
psychodynamic approaches to personality	ego	phallic stage	repression
	superego	Oedipal conflict	neo-Freudian psychoanalysts
psychoanalytic theory	psychosexual stages	identification	
	fixations	latency period	collective unconscious
unconscious	oral stage	genital stage	archetypes

Module 32

Trait, Learning, Biological and Evolutionary, and Humanistic Approaches to Personality

LEARNING OUTCOME

LO 32-1 What are the major aspects of trait, learning, biological and evolutionary, and humanistic approaches to personality?

"Tell me about Nelson," said Johnetta.

"Oh, he's just terrific. He's the friendliest guy I know–goes out of his way to be nice to everyone. He hardly ever gets mad. He's just so even-tempered, no matter what's happening. And he's really smart, too. About the only thing I don't like is that he's always in such a hurry to get things done. He seems to have boundless energy, much more than I have."

"He sounds great to me, especially in comparison to Rico," replied Johnetta. "He is so self-centered and arrogant that it drives me crazy. I sometimes wonder why I ever started going out with him."

Friendly. Even-tempered. Smart. Energetic. Self-centered. Arrogant.

The above exchange is made up of a series of trait characterizations of the speakers' friends. In fact, much of our own understanding of others' behavior is based on the premise that people possess certain traits that are consistent across different situations. For example, we generally assume that if someone is outgoing and sociable in one situation, then they are outgoing and sociable in other situations (Leising et al., 2014; Arvantis & Kalliris, 2020; Atherton et al., 2021).

Dissatisfaction with the emphasis in psychoanalytic theory on unconscious–and difficult-to-demonstrate–processes in explaining a person's behavior led to the development of alternative approaches to personality, including a number of trait-based approaches. Other theories reflect established psychological perspectives, such as learning theory, biological and evolutionary approaches, and the humanistic approach.

traits Consistent, habitual personality characteristics and behaviors that are displayed across different situations. (Module 32)

trait theory A model of personality that seeks to identify the basic traits necessary to describe personality. (Module 32)

Study Alert

All trait theories explain personality in terms of traits (consistent personality characteristics and behaviors), but they differ in terms of which and how many traits are seen as fundamental.

Trait Approaches: Placing Labels on Personality

If someone asked you to characterize another person, as Johnetta did of her friend, you probably would come up with a list of traits. **Traits** are consistent, habitual personality characteristics and behaviors that are displayed across different situations.

Trait theory is the personality approach that seeks to identify the basic traits necessary to describe personality. Trait theorists do not assume that some people have a particular trait while others do not. Instead, they propose that all people possess a set of traits, but the degree to which a particular trait applies to a specific person varies and can be quantified.

For instance, they might assume that all people have the trait of "friendliness" but in different degrees. You may be relatively friendly, whereas I may be relatively unfriendly. But we both have a "friendliness" trait, although your degree of "friendliness" is higher than mine.

The major challenge for trait theorists taking this approach has been to identify the specific basic traits necessary to describe personality. As we shall see, different theorists have come up with surprisingly different sets of traits. (Also see the *Applying Psychology in the 21st Century* feature.)

ALLPORT'S TRAIT THEORY: IDENTIFYING BASIC CHARACTERISTICS

When personality psychologist Gordon Allport systematically pored over an unabridged dictionary in the 1930s, he came up with some 18,000 separate terms that could be used to describe personality. Although he was able to pare down the list to 4,500 descriptors after eliminating words with similar meanings, he was left with a problem crucial to all trait approaches: Which traits are the most important in characterizing personality?

APPLYING PSYCHOLOGY IN THE 21ST CENTURY

IS YOUR PERSONALITY WRITTEN ALL OVER YOUR FACE?

Have you ever seen a self-portrait and wondered whether the artist really looked like that or whether the self-portrait didn't perhaps reflect at least a little bit of wishful thinking?

Personality researchers have wondered the same thing—not just about artists but about all of us. Specifically, they are studying whether the way we see ourselves physically reflects something about how we see ourselves psychologically. That is, if you think of yourself as a shy and meek person, for example, do you imagine those personality characteristics to be apparent from the way you look (Junior et al., 2019; Kachur et al., 2020; Kosinski, 2021)?

To answer this question, researchers used software to generate many hundreds of images of human face shapes with small variations. Then they showed them two at a time to participants and asked them each time to choose which face looked more like their own. Participants then completed questionnaire measures of their personality traits and current self-esteem. The researchers then used software to combine all the facial images that each individual participant chose as more like their own into one composite face for that participant. And, incidentally, software analysis demonstrated that those composite faces did each resemble photographs of the participants' actual faces (Maister et al., 2021).

caia image/Alamy Stock Photo

Then, in a second phase of the study, other participants were randomly shown the composite faces as well as the actual photographs of each of the original participants, and they were asked to rate the personality of each face using the same questionnaire measure of personality the first group used. The researchers found that in relation to participants who had described themselves as more extraverted, raters tended to judge the composite face as looking more extraverted compared with the actual face. The same was true for

personality traits of agreeableness, conscientiousness, neuroticism, and openness to experience. That is, participants in this phase of the study tended to exaggerate the degree to which those personality traits were reflected in their facial appearance.

Interestingly, however, participants whose self-esteem scores were higher with regard to social interactions were less likely to show this exaggerated self-view. The researchers speculated that perhaps people with higher social self-esteem get more frequent and better feedback from others on their actual appearance. Alternatively, people with accurate self-views may be more likely to have satisfying social relationships, and those relationships then bolster their social self-esteem.

Overall, the findings indicate that the beliefs and attitudes people hold about themselves are reflected in how they view their own appearance. These findings consequently suggest that the way in which we view our personality is embodied in how we think we look to others.

> **RETHINK**
>
> - One interpretation of these findings is that people distort their physical self-views to fit their psychological self-views. Do you think it's possible that the opposite happens; that is, that people's personalities develop to match how they look? Why or why not?
> - Why can't the researchers say definitively that accurate self-views enhance social interactions or, alternatively, that better social interactions improve the accuracy of one's self-views?

Extraversion

- Sociable
- Lively
- Active
- Assertive
- Sensation-seeking

Neuroticism

- Anxious
- Depressed
- Guilt feelings
- Low self-esteem
- Tense

Psychoticism

- Aggressive
- Cold
- Egocentric
- Impersonal
- Impulsive

FIGURE 1 Eysenck described personality in terms of three major dimensions: extraversion, neuroticism, and psychoticism. Using these dimensions, he could predict people's behavior in many types of situations.

Source: Ruch et al., 2021.

Allport eventually answered this question by suggesting that there are three fundamental categories of traits: cardinal, central, and secondary (Allport, 1966; Doremus, 2021):

- **Cardinal traits.** A *cardinal trait* is a single, overriding characteristic that motivates most of a person's behavior. For example, a totally selfless person may direct all their energy toward humanitarian activities; an intensely power-hungry person may be driven by an all-consuming need for control.

- **Central traits.** Few people have a single, comprehensive cardinal trait. Instead, they possess 5–10 central traits that make up the core of personality. *Central traits*, such as warmth or honesty, describe an individual's major characteristics. Each central trait is assumed to imply the presence of other traits. For example, people who have a central trait of warmth also are likely to be sociable and friendly.

- **Secondary traits.** Finally, *secondary traits* are characteristics that affect behavior in fewer situations and are less influential than central or cardinal traits. For instance, a reluctance to eat meat and a love of modern art would be considered secondary traits (Kahn et al., 2013; Zhao & Smillie, 2015).

CATTELL AND EYSENCK: FACTORING OUT PERSONALITY

Later attempts to identify primary personality traits centered on a statistical technique known as factor analysis. *Factor analysis* is a statistical method of identifying patterns among a large number of variables and combining them into more fundamental groupings. For example, a personality researcher might ask a large group of people to rate themselves on a number of specific traits. By using factor analysis and statistically computing which traits are associated with one another, a researcher can identify the fundamental patterns of traits–called *factors*–that cluster together in the same person.

Using factor analysis, personality psychologist Raymond Cattell suggested that 16 pairs of *traits* represent the basic dimensions of personality. Using that set of traits, he developed the Sixteen Personality Factor Questionnaire, or 16 PF, a personality scale that is still in use today (Djapo et al., 2011; Wright, 2017; Schermer et al., 2020).

Another trait theorist, psychologist Hans Eysenck (1995), also used factor analysis to identify patterns of traits, but he came to a very different conclusion about the nature of personality. He found that personality could best be described in terms of just three major dimensions: extraversion, neuroticism, and psychoticism. The *extraversion* dimension describes a person's level of sociability, whereas the *neuroticism* dimension encompasses an individual's emotional stability. Finally, *psychoticism* is the degree to which reality is distorted. By evaluating people along these three dimensions, Eysenck was able to predict behavior accurately in a variety of situations. Figure 1 lists specific traits associated with each of the dimensions.

Note that serious questions have been raised about the integrity of Eysenck's research. Still, his work was influential in the field of personality and was a springboard for additional research (Craig et al., 2021).

THE BIG FIVE PERSONALITY TRAITS

For the past two decades, the most influential trait approach contends that five traits or factors–called the "Big Five"–lie at the core of personality. Using factor analytic statistical techniques, a consistent body of research has identified a similar set of five factors that underlie personality. The specific five factors are *openness to experience, conscientiousness, extraversion, agreeableness,* and *neuroticism* (emotional stability). They are described in Figure 2.

The Big Five emerge consistently across a number of domains: for example, factor analyses of major personality inventories, self-report measures made by observers of others' personality traits, and checklists of self-descriptions yield similar factors. In addition, the Big Five emerge consistently in different populations of individuals, including children, college students, older adults, and speakers of different languages. Cross-cultural research conducted in areas ranging from Europe to the Middle East to

Study Alert

You can remember the Big Five set of personality traits by using the acronym OCEAN (*o*penness to experience, *c*onscientiousness, *e*xtraversion, *a*greeableness, and *n*euroticism).

The Big Five Personality Factors and Dimensions of Sample Traits	
Openness to experience	**Agreeableness**
Independent—Conforming Imaginative—Practical Preference for variety—Preference for routine	Sympathetic—Fault-finding Kind—Cold Appreciative—Unfriendly
Conscientiousness	**Neuroticism (Emotional stability)**
Careful—Careless Disciplined—Impulsive Organized—Disorganized	Stable—Tense Calm—Anxious Secure—Insecure
Extraversion	
Talkative—Quiet Fun-loving—Sober Sociable—Retiring	

FIGURE 2 Five broad trait factors, referred to as the "Big Five," are considered to be the core of personality.

Source: Adapted from John, Robins, & Pervin, 2010.

Africa also has been supportive. Finally, studies of brain functioning show that Big Five personality traits are related to the way the brain processes information (Saucier & Srivastava, 2015; Bouvard & Roulin, 2017; Hall et al., 2019; John, 2021).

In short, a growing consensus exists that the Big Five represent the best description of personality traits we have today. Still, the debate over the specific number and kinds of traits–and even the usefulness of trait approaches in general–remains a lively one. (Also see the *Neuroscience in Your Life* feature.)

NEUROSCIENCE IN YOUR LIFE: BOUNCING BACK AFTER DIFFICULT TIMES

How are you at coping with adversity—say, a breakup or the COVID-19 pandemic?

Some people have more of what psychologists call *resilience*, the ability to overcome circumstances that place them at high risk for psychological or physical harm. Research shows that personality characteristics as well as the brain play key roles in resilience.

To demonstrate how resilience is related to the brain, participants in a study received a magnetic resonance imaging scan and completed questionnaires designed to assess their level of resilience and Big Five personality traits. The results of the study showed that participants who scored higher on the resilience questionnaire tended to have lower neuroticism scores and higher extraversion and conscientiousness scores. Higher resilience, extraversion, and conscientiousness scores were also associated with lower activity in the brain's "salience network," which detects and filters information about one's internal state and external stimuli. Researchers interpreted this association as an indication that having higher resilience makes it possible to focus one's mind and avoid distractions (Altinok et al., 2021).

Not only do these findings help us understand the brain mechanisms behind our personality and ability to cope with adversity, but they may also give us a way to identify people who are vulnerable to psychological symptoms and other complications when they go through difficult times. With more research, neuroscientists may be able to develop ways to protect vulnerable people from developing conditions such as posttraumatic stress disorder.

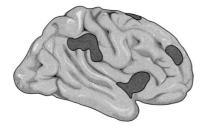

Resilience, extraversion, and conscientiousness were associated with lower activity in brain regions within the salience network, highlighted in red. The salience network has a role in filtering information from our environment, which could mean that lower activity in the salience network indicates an association between better attentional control, better emotion regulation, resilience, and personality traits such as extraversion and conscientiousness.

EVALUATING TRAIT APPROACHES TO PERSONALITY

Trait approaches have several virtues. They provide a clear, straightforward explanation of people's behavioral consistencies. Furthermore, traits allow us to readily compare one person with another. Because of these advantages, trait approaches to personality have had an important influence on the development of several useful personality measures (Cook, 2013; Boyle, 2019; Jayawickreme et al., 2019).

However, trait approaches also have some drawbacks. For example, we have seen that various trait theories describing personality come to different conclusions about which traits are the most fundamental and descriptive. The difficulty in determining which of the theories is the most accurate has led some personality psychologists to question the validity of trait conceptions of personality in general.

Trait approaches suffer from an even more fundamental difficulty: Even if we identify a set of primary traits, all we have done is provide a set of labels for personality. But labeling personality traits is not an *explanation* of how those traits developed in a person nor of how they function to determine behavior. For example, if we say that someone who donates money to charity has the trait of generosity, we still do not know *why* that person became generous in the first place or why the person displays generosity in a specific situation. In the view of some critics, then, traits do not provide explanations for behavior; they merely label it.

Learning Approaches: We Are What We've Learned

The psychodynamic and trait approaches we've been discussing concentrate on the "inner" person—the fury of a powerful id or a critical set of traits that describes the core of an individual. In contrast, learning approaches to personality focus on the external world in which a person lives and how external influences determine and affect personality.

SKINNER'S BEHAVIORIST APPROACH

According to the most influential learning theorist, B. F. Skinner (who carried out pioneering work on operant conditioning), personality is a collection of learned behavior patterns (Skinner, 1975). Similarities in responses across different situations are caused by similar patterns of reinforcement that have been received in such situations in the past. If I am sociable both at parties and at meetings, it is because I have been reinforced for displaying social behaviors—not because I am fulfilling an unconscious wish based on experiences during my childhood or because I have an internal trait of sociability.

Learning theorists such as Skinner are less interested in the consistencies in behavior across situations than in ways of modifying behavior. To a learning theorist who subscribes to Skinner's view, humans are infinitely changeable through the process of learning new behavior patterns. If we are able to control and modify the patterns of reinforcers in a situation, behavior that other theorists would view as stable and unyielding can be changed and ultimately improved. Learning theorists are optimistic in their attitudes about the potential for resolving personal and societal problems through treatment strategies based on learning theory.

SOCIAL COGNITIVE APPROACHES TO PERSONALITY

social cognitive approaches to personality Theories that emphasize the influence of a person's cognitions—thoughts, feelings, expectations, and values—as well as observation of others' behavior, in determining personality. (Module 32)

Not all learning theories of personality take such a rigid view in rejecting the importance of what is "inside" a person by focusing solely on the "outside." Unlike other learning approaches to personality, **social cognitive approaches to personality** emphasize the influence of cognition—thoughts, feelings, expectations, and values—as well as observation of others' behavior on personality. According to Albert Bandura, one of the main proponents of this point of view, people can foresee the possible outcomes of certain behaviors in a specific setting without actually having to carry them out. This understanding comes primarily through *observational learning*–viewing the actions of others and observing the consequences (Bandura, 1999; Rumjaun & Narod, 2020).

For instance, children who view a model behaving in, say, an aggressive manner tend to copy the behavior if the consequences of the model's behavior are seen as positive. If, in contrast, the model's aggressive behavior has resulted in no consequences or negative consequences, children are considerably less likely to act aggressively. According to social cognitive approaches, then, personality develops through repeated observation of others' behavior.

Bandura places particular emphasis on the role played by self-efficacy. **Self-efficacy** is the belief that we can master a situation and produce positive outcomes. Self-efficacy underlies people's faith in their ability to successfully carry out a particular task or to produce a desired outcome. People with high self-efficacy have higher aspirations and greater persistence in working to attain goals than those with lower self-efficacy. Furthermore, they ultimately achieve greater success (Sezgin & Erdogan, 2015; Tazouti & Jarlégan, 2019; Tan et al., 2021).

How do we develop self-efficacy? One way is by paying close attention to our prior successes and failures. If we try snowboarding and experience little success, we'll be less likely to try it again. However, if our initial efforts appear promising, we'll be more likely to attempt it again. Direct reinforcement and encouragement from others also play a role in developing self-efficacy (Artistico et al., 2013; Wright, 2017; Wawrosz & Jurásek, 2021).

Compared with other learning theories of personality, social cognitive approaches are distinctive in their emphasis on the reciprocity between individuals and their environment. Not only is the environment assumed to affect personality, but people's behavior and personalities are also assumed to "feed back" and modify the environment (Bandura, 1999, 2000; Jayawickreme et al., 2019).

Self-efficacy, the belief in one's own capabilities, leads to higher aspirations and greater persistence.
Lars A. Niki

self-efficacy The belief that we can master a situation and produce positive outcomes. (Module 32)

HOW MUCH CONSISTENCY EXISTS IN PERSONALITY?

Another social cognitive theorist, Walter Mischel, takes a different approach to personality from that of Bandura. He rejects the view that personality consists of broad traits that lead to substantial consistencies in behavior across different situations. Instead, he sees personality as considerably more variable from one situation to another (Mischel, 2009).

In this view, particular situations give rise to particular kinds of behavior. Some situations are especially influential (think of a movie theater, where everyone displays pretty much the same behavior by sitting quietly and watching the film). Other situations permit much variability in behavior (such as a party, for example, where some people may be dancing, while others are eating and drinking).

From this perspective, personality cannot be considered without taking the particular context of the situation into account–a view known as *situationism*. In his *cognitive-affective processing system (CAPS)* theory, Mischel argues that people's thoughts and emotions about themselves and the world determine how they view, and then react, in particular situations. Personality is thus seen as a reflection of how people's prior experiences in different situations, as well as the specifics of the situation they are in at the moment, interact and determine their behavior (Mischel & Shoda, 2008; Huprich & Nelson, 2015; Ayduk & Mendoza-Denton, 2021).

SELF-ESTEEM

Our behavior also reflects the view we have of ourselves and the way we value the various parts of our personalities. **Self-esteem** is the component of personality that encompasses our positive and negative evaluations of ourselves. Unlike self-efficacy, which focuses on our views of whether we are able to carry out a task, self-esteem relates to how we feel about ourselves.

self-esteem The component of personality that encompasses our positive and negative self-evaluations. (Module 32)

FIGURE 3 The cycle of low self-esteem begins with an individual already having low self-esteem. As a consequence, the person will have low performance expectations and expect to fail a test, thereby producing anxiety and reduced effort. As a result, the person will actually fail, and failure in turn reinforces low self-esteem.

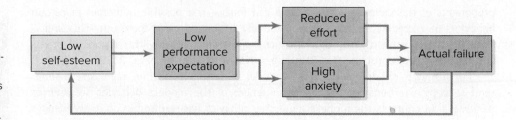

Although people have a general level of self-esteem, it is not unidimensional. We may see ourselves positively in one domain but negatively in others. For example, a good student may have high self-esteem in academic domains but lower self-esteem in athletics (Mirzairad et al., 2017; Musetti & Corsano, 2019; Burger & Bachmann, 2021).

The development of self-esteem is strongly affected by cultural factors. For example, consider the characteristic of *relationship harmony*, which is a sense of success in forming close bonds with others. For people living in Asian cultures, having high relationship harmony is a more important component of self-esteem than it is for those living in more individualistic Western societies (Cheng & Kwan, 2008; Chin, 2015).

Although almost all of us go through periods in which our self-esteem is challenged and temporarily reduced (for instance, after an undeniable failure), some people are chronically low in self-esteem. For them, failure seems to be an inevitable part of life. In fact, low self-esteem may lead to a cycle of failure in which past failure breeds future failure.

For example, consider students with low self-esteem who are studying for a test. Because of their low self-esteem, they expect to do poorly on the test. In turn, this belief raises their anxiety level, which makes it increasingly difficult to study and perhaps even leads them not to work as hard. Because of these attitudes, they do, in fact, perform badly on the test. Ultimately, the failure reinforces their low self-esteem, and the cycle is perpetuated, as illustrated in Figure 3. In short, low self-esteem can lead to a self-destructive cycle of failure.

On the other hand, high levels of self-esteem can also be troublesome if they are unwarranted. According to a growing body of data, an increasing number of college-age students have high levels of *narcissism*, in which people show self-absorption and hold inflated views of themselves. For example, over the past three decades, thousands of American college students participating in a variety of psychological research studies were

Research suggests that narcissism, the degree to which people show self-absorption and hold inflated views of themselves, has increased over the past three decades.

William Perugini/Image Source/Getty Images

asked to take the Narcissism Personality Inventory, a test of narcissistic tendencies. A summary of more than 100 such studies conducted over a 25-year period showed a significant increase in participants' narcissism scores (Twenge & Kasser, 2013; Barry et al., 2017; Demirci et al., 2019).

What might produce the increase in narcissism in young Americans? Research points to social networking media. In recent years, many people self-promote in carefully edited online profiles. The most mundane aspects of their daily lives are viewed as worthy of broadcasting to the world, whether in Twitter tweets, Instagram photos, Facebook postings, or YouTube and TikTok videos. Another explanation is that parents may increasingly be inflating their children's sense of self-importance by shielding them from situations in which they might fail (Kauten et al., 2015; Wang, 2019; Akdeniz et al., 2022).

From the perspective of...

An Educator How might you encourage your students' development of self-esteem and self-efficacy? What steps would you take to ensure that their self-esteem did not become overinflated?

Andersen Ross/Blend Images/Getty Images

EVALUATING LEARNING APPROACHES TO PERSONALITY

Because they ignore the internal processes, such as thoughts and emotions, traditional learning theorists such as Skinner have been accused of oversimplifying personality far too much. Their critics think that reducing behavior to a series of stimuli and responses and excluding thoughts and feelings from the realm of personality leaves behaviorists practicing an unrealistic and inadequate form of science.

Of course, some of these criticisms are blunted by social cognitive approaches, which explicitly consider the role of cognitive processes in personality. Still, learning approaches tend to share a highly *deterministic* view of human behavior, which maintains that behavior is shaped primarily by forces beyond the individual's control. As in psychoanalytic theory (which suggests that personality is determined by the unconscious forces) and trait approaches (which view personality in part as a mixture of genetically determined traits), learning theory's reliance on deterministic principles de-emphasizes people's ability to pilot their own course through life.

Nonetheless, learning approaches have had a major impact on the study of personality. For one thing, they have helped make personality psychology an objective, scientific venture by focusing on observable behavior and the effects of the environments. In addition, they have produced important, successful means of treating a variety of psychological disorders. The degree of success of these treatments is a testimony to the merits of learning theory approaches to personality.

Biological and Evolutionary Approaches: Are We Born with Personality?

Approaching the question of what determines personality from a different direction, **biological and evolutionary approaches to personality** suggest that important components of personality are inherited. Building on the work of behavioral geneticists, researchers using biological and evolutionary approaches argue that personality is determined at least in part by our genes in much the same way that our height is largely

biological and evolutionary approaches to personality Theories that suggest that important components of personality are inherited. (Module 32)

Study Alert

Remember that biological and evolutionary approaches focus on the ways in which people's genetic heritage affects personality.

Biological and evolutionary approaches to personality seek to explain the consistencies in personality that are found in some families.

Photo and Co/The Image Bank/Getty Images

a result of genetic contributions from our ancestors. The evolutionary perspective assumes that personality traits that led to our ancestors' survival and reproductive success are more likely to be preserved and passed on to subsequent generations (Yarkoni, 2015; Mõttus et al., 2019; Workman et al., 2022).

The results of research studies conducted on twins who are genetically identical but raised apart from one another by different caretakers illustrate the importance of genetic factors in personality. Personality tests indicate that in major respects, genetically identical twins raised apart are quite similar in personality, even if they were separated at an early age.

Moreover, certain traits are more heavily influenced by heredity than are others. For example, *social potency* (the degree to which a person assumes mastery and leadership roles in social situations) and *traditionalism* (the tendency to follow authority) had particularly strong genetic components, whereas achievement and social closeness had relatively weak genetic components (Bouchard et al., 2004; Sanchez-Roige et al., 2018; Smederevac et al., 2020; see Figure 4).

temperament A basic, inborn characteristic way of responding and behavioral style. (Modules 28, 32)

Furthermore, it is increasingly clear that the roots of adult personality emerge early in life. Infants are born with a specific **temperament,** an individual's behavioral style and characteristic way of responding. Temperament encompasses several dimensions, including general activity level and mood. For instance, some babies are quite active, whereas others are relatively calm. Similarly, some are relatively easygoing, whereas others are irritable, easily upset, and difficult to soothe. Temperament is quite consistent, with significant stability from infancy well into adolescence (Hori et al., 2011; Bates & Pettit, 2015; Planalp & Goldsmith, 2020).

Some researchers contend that specific genes are related to personality. For example, people with a longer dopamine-4 receptor gene are more likely to be thrill-seekers than are those without such a gene. These thrill-seekers tend to be

Infants are born with particular temperaments—dispositions that are consistent throughout childhood.

Isadora Getty Buyou/Image Source

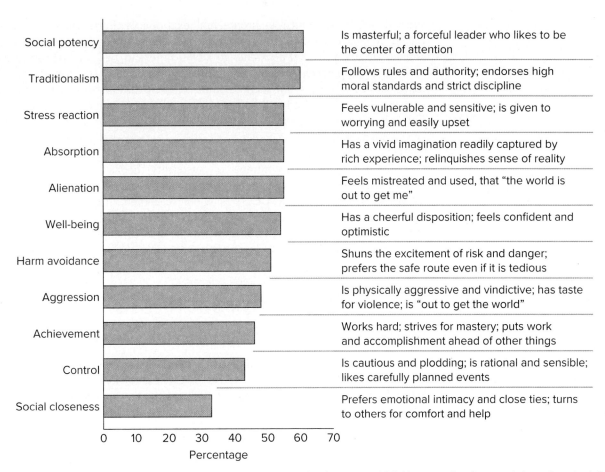

FIGURE 4 The inherited roots of personality. The percentages indicate the degree to which 11 personality characteristics reflect the influence of heredity.
Source: Tellegen et al., 1998.

extroverted, impulsive, quick-tempered, and always in search of excitement and novel situations. Furthermore, the structure of their brains may reflect their thrill-seeking tendencies (Ray et al., 2009; Wishart et al., 2017; Lawal et al., 2021).

Does the identification of specific genes linked to personality, coupled with the existence of temperaments from the time of birth, mean that we are destined to have certain types of personalities? Hardly. First, it is unlikely that any single gene is linked to a specific trait. For instance, the dopamine-4 receptor accounts for only around 10% of the variation in novelty seeking between different individuals. The rest of the variation is attributable to other genes and environmental factors (Lahti et al., 2005; Kandler et al., 2013).

More important, genes interact with the environment. As we see in discussions of the heritability of intelligence and the nature–nurture issue, it is impossible to completely divorce genetic factors from environmental factors. Although studies of identical twins raised in different environments are helpful, they are not definitive because it is impossible to assess and control environmental factors fully. Furthermore, estimates of the influence of genetics are just that–estimates–and apply to groups, not individuals. Consequently, findings such as those shown in Figure 4 must be regarded as approximations.

Finally, even if more genes are found to be linked to specific personality characteristics, genes still cannot be viewed as the sole cause of personality. For one thing, genetically determined characteristics may not be expressed if they are not "turned on" by particular environmental experiences. Furthermore, behaviors produced by genes may help to create a specific environment. For instance, a cheerful, smiley baby may lead the parents to smile more and be more responsive, thereby creating a supportive, pleasant environment. In contrast, the parents of a cranky, fussy baby may be less inclined to smile at the child; in turn, the environment in which that child is raised will be less supportive and pleasant. In a sense, then, genes not only influence a person's behavior; they also help produce the environment in which a person develops (Kendler et al., 2017; Azeredo et al., 2019; Stallings & Neppl, 2021).

Although an increasing number of personality theorists are taking biological and evolutionary factors into account, no comprehensive, unified theory that considers biological and evolutionary factors is widely accepted. Still, it is clear that certain personality traits have substantial genetic components and that heredity and environment interact to determine personality (Bouchard, 2004; South & Krueger, 2008; South et al., 2013).

Humanistic Approaches: The Uniqueness of You

In all the approaches to personality that we have discussed, where is an explanation for the virtuousness of a Mother Teresa or Gandhi, the creativity of a Michelangelo, and the brilliance and perseverance of an Einstein? An understanding of such unique individuals—as well as more ordinary sorts of people who have some of the same attributes—comes from humanistic theory.

According to humanistic theorists, all the approaches to personality we have discussed share a fundamental misperception in their views of human nature. Instead of seeing people as controlled by unconscious, unseen forces (psychodynamic approaches), a set of stable traits (trait approaches), situational reinforcements and punishments (learning theory), or inherited factors (biological and evolutionary approaches), **humanistic approaches to personality** emphasize people's inherent goodness and their tendency to move toward higher levels of functioning. It is this conscious, self-motivated ability to change and improve, along with people's unique creative impulses, that humanistic theorists argue make up the core of personality.

humanistic approaches to personality Theories that emphasize people's innate goodness and desire to achieve higher levels of functioning. (Module 32)

ROGERS AND THE NEED FOR SELF-ACTUALIZATION

The major proponent of the humanistic point of view is Carl Rogers (1971). Along with other humanistic theorists, such as Abraham Maslow, Rogers maintains that all people have a fundamental need for **self-actualization,** a state of self-fulfillment in which people realize their highest potential, each in a unique way. He further suggests that people develop a need for positive regard that reflects the desire to be loved and respected. Because others provide this positive regard, we grow dependent on them. We begin to see and judge ourselves through the eyes of other people, relying on their values and being preoccupied with what they think of us.

self-actualization A state of self-fulfillment in which people realize their highest potential in their own unique way. (Modules 24, 32)

According to Rogers, one outgrowth of placing importance on others' opinions is that a conflict may grow between people's actual life experiences and their self-concept. *Self-concept* is the set of beliefs people hold about their own abilities, behavior, and personality. If the discrepancies between people's self-concepts and what they actually experience in their lives are minor, the consequences are minor. But if the

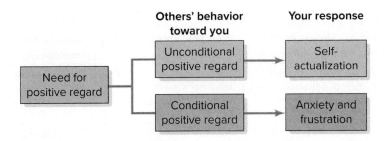

FIGURE 5 According to the humanistic view of Carl Rogers, people have a basic need to be loved and respected. If you receive unconditional positive regard from others, you will develop a more realistic self-concept and ultimately can reach self-actualization. But if the response from others is conditional, it may lead to anxiety and frustration.

discrepancies between one's experience and one's self-concept are great, they will lead to psychological disturbances in daily functioning. For instance, people with large discrepancies may experience frequent anxiety.

Rogers suggests that one way of overcoming the discrepancy between experience and self-concept is through the receipt of unconditional positive regard from another person—a parent, friend, spouse, or even a therapist. **Unconditional positive regard** refers to an attitude of acceptance and respect on the observer's part, no matter what a person says or does. This acceptance, says Rogers, gives people the opportunity to evolve and grow both cognitively and emotionally and to develop more realistic self-concepts. You may have experienced the power of unconditional positive regard when you confided in someone, revealing embarrassing secrets because you knew the listener would still love and respect you even after hearing the worst about you (Patterson & Joseph, 2013; Jayne et al., 2019).

In contrast, *conditional positive regard* depends on your behavior. In such cases, others withdraw their love and acceptance if you do something of which they don't approve. The result is a discrepancy between your true self and what others wish you would be, which leads to anxiety and frustration (see Figure 5).

unconditional positive regard An attitude of acceptance and respect on the part of an observer, no matter what a person says or does. (Module 32)

EVALUATING HUMANISTIC APPROACHES

Although humanistic theories suggest the value of providing unconditional positive regard toward people, unconditional positive regard toward humanistic theories has been less forthcoming. The criticisms have centered on the difficulty of verifying the basic assumptions of the approach as well as on the question of whether unconditional positive regard does, in fact, lead to greater personality adjustment.

Humanistic approaches have also been criticized for making the assumption that people are basically "good"—a notion that is unverifiable—and, equally important, for using nonscientific values to build supposedly scientific theories. Still, humanistic theories have been important in highlighting the uniqueness of human beings and guiding the development of a significant form of therapy designed to alleviate psychological difficulties (Elkins, 2009; Kogstad et al., 2011; Hounkatin et al., 2015).

Comparing Approaches to Personality

In light of the multiple approaches we have discussed, you may be wondering which of the theories provides the most accurate description of personality. That question cannot be answered precisely. Each theory is built on different assumptions and focuses on somewhat different aspects of personality (see Figure 6).

Furthermore, there is no clear way to scientifically test the various approaches and their assumptions against one another. Given the complexity of every individual, it seems reasonable that personality can be viewed from a number of perspectives simultaneously.

Theoretical Approach and Major Theorists	Conscious Versus Unconscious Determinants of Personality	Nature (Hereditary Factors) Versus Nurture (Environmental Factors)	Free Will Versus Determinism	Stability Versus Modifiability
Psychodynamic (Freud, Jung, Horney, Adler)	Emphasizes the unconscious	Stresses innate, inherited structure of personality while emphasizing importance of childhood experience	Stresses determinism, the view that behavior is directed and caused by factors outside one's control	Emphasizes the stability of characteristics throughout a person's life
Trait (Allport, Cattell, Eysenck)	Disregards both conscious and unconscious	Approaches vary	Stresses determinism, the view that behavior is directed and caused by factors outside one's control	Emphasizes the stability of characteristics throughout a person's life
Learning (Skinner, Bandura)	Disregards both conscious and unconscious	Focuses on the environment	Stresses determinism, the view that behavior is directed and caused by factors outside one's control	Stresses that personality remains flexible and resilient throughout one's life
Biological and evolutionary (Tellegen)	Disregards both conscious and unconscious	Stresses the innate, inherited determinants of personality	Stresses determinism, the view that behavior is directed and caused by factors outside one's control	Emphasizes the stability of characteristics throughout a person's life
Humanistic (Rogers, Maslow)	Stresses the conscious more than the unconscious	Stresses the interaction between nature and nurture	Stresses the freedom of individuals to make their own choices	Stresses that personality remains flexible and resilient throughout one's life

FIGURE 6 The multiple perspectives on personality.

RECAP/EVALUATE/RETHINK

RECAP

LO 32-1 What are the major aspects of trait, learning, biological and evolutionary, and humanistic approaches to personality?

- Trait approaches have been used to identify relatively enduring dimensions along which people differ from one another–dimensions known as traits.
- Learning approaches to personality concentrate on observable behavior. To a strict learning theorist, personality is the sum of learned responses to the external environment.
- Social cognitive approaches concentrate on the role of cognition in determining personality. Those approaches pay particular attention to self-efficacy and self-esteem in determining behavior.
- Biological and evolutionary approaches to personality focus on the way in which personality characteristics are inherited.
- Humanistic approaches emphasize people's inherent goodness. They consider the core of personality in terms of a person's ability to change and improve.
- The major personality approaches differ substantially from one another; the differences may reflect both their focus on different aspects of personality and the overall complexity of personality.

EVALUATE

1. Carlos's determination to succeed is the dominant force in all his activities and relationships. According to Allport's theory, this is an example of a _____ trait. In contrast, Taniqa's fondness for old western movies is an example of a _____ trait.
2. Eysenck might describe a person who enjoys activities such as parties and hang gliding as high on what trait?
3. Proponents of which approach to personality would be most likely to agree with the statement, "Personality can be thought of as learned responses to a person's upbringing and environment"?
   a. Humanistic
   b. Biological and evolutionary
   c. Learning
   d. Trait
4. Bandura would rate a person who would make the statement "I know I can't do it" as low on _____ _____.
5. Which approach to personality emphasizes the innate goodness of people and their desire to grow?
   a. Humanistic
   b. Psychodynamic
   c. Learning
   d. Biological and evolutionary

RETHINK

1. If personality traits are merely descriptive and not explanatory, what use are they? Can assigning a trait to a person be harmful–or helpful? Why or why not?
2. In what ways are Cattell's 16 source traits, Eysenck's three dimensions, and the Big Five factors similar, and in what ways are they different? Which traits seem to appear in all three schemes (under one name or another), and which are unique to one scheme? Why is this significant?

Answers to Evaluate Questions

1. cardinal, secondary; 2. extraversion; 3. c; 4. self-efficacy; 5. a

KEY TERMS

traits	self-efficacy	temperament	self-actualization
trait theory	self-esteem	humanistic approaches to personality	unconditional positive regard
social cognitive approaches to personality	biological and evolutionary approaches to personality		

Module 33
Assessing Personality: Determining What Makes Us Distinctive

LEARNING OUTCOMES

LO 33-1 How can we most accurately assess personality?

LO 33-2 What are the major types of personality measures?

You have a need for other people to like and admire you.

You have a tendency to be critical of yourself.

You have a great deal of unused potential that you have not turned to your advantage.

Although you have some personality weaknesses, you generally are able to compensate for them.

Relating to members of the opposite sex has presented problems for you.

Although you appear to be disciplined and self-controlled to others, you tend to be anxious and insecure inside.

At times you have serious doubts about whether you have made the right decision or done the right thing.

You prefer a certain amount of change and variety and become dissatisfied when hemmed in by restrictions and limitations.

You do not accept others' statements without satisfactory proof.

You have found it unwise to be too frank in revealing yourself to others.

If you think these statements provide a surprisingly accurate account of your personality, you are not alone: Most college students think that these descriptions are tailored just to them. In fact, the statements were designed intentionally to be so vague that they apply to just about anyone (Forer, 1949; Russo, 1981; Gaidai, 2021).

The ease with which we can agree with such imprecise statements underscores the difficulty in coming up with accurate and meaningful assessments of people's personalities. Psychologists interested in assessing personality must be able to define the most meaningful ways of discriminating between one person's personality and another's. To do this, they use **psychological tests,** standard measures devised to assess behavior objectively. With the results of such tests, psychologists can help people better understand themselves and make decisions about their lives. Researchers interested in the causes and consequences of personality also employ psychological tests (Miller et al., 2011; Hambleton & Zenisky, 2013; Paulson et al., 2019).

Like the assessments that seek to measure intelligence, all psychological tests must have reliability and validity. *Reliability* refers to a test's measurement consistency. If a test is reliable, it yields the same result each time it is administered to a specific person or group. In contrast, unreliable tests give different results each time they are administered.

For meaningful conclusions to be drawn, tests also must be valid. Tests have *validity* when they actually measure what they are designed to measure. If a test is constructed to measure sociability, for instance, we need to know that it actually measures sociability and not some other trait.

Finally, psychological tests are based on *test norms,* the distribution of test scores for a large sample of individuals who have taken a test. Test norms allow us to compare one person's score on a test with the scores of others who have taken the same test. For example, knowing the norms of a test permits test-takers who have received a certain score to know that they have scored in the top 10% of all those who have taken the test.

psychological tests Standard measures devised to assess behavior objectively; used by psychologists to help people make decisions about their lives and understand more about themselves. (Module 33)

! Study Alert

The distinction between reliability and validity is important. For instance, a test that measures trustfulness is reliable if it yields the same results each time it is administered, whereas it is valid if it measures trustfulness accurately.

Test norms are established by administering a specific test to a large number of people and determining the typical scores. It is then possible to compare a single person's score with the scores of the group, which provides a comparative measure of test performance against the performance of others who have taken the test.

The establishment of appropriate test norms is not a simple endeavor. For instance, the specific group that is employed to determine test norms has a profound effect on the way an individual's performance is evaluated. In fact, as we discuss in *Exploring Diversity*, the process of establishing test norms can take on political overtones.

 # Exploring Diversity

Should Race and Ethnicity Be Used to Establish Test Norms?

The passions of politics may confront the objectivity of science when test norms are established, at least in the realm of standardized tests that are meant to predict future job performance. In fact, a national controversy has developed around the question of whether different test norms should be established for members of various racial and ethnic groups (Pedraza & Mungas, 2008; Nettles, 2019; Payne & Hannay, 2021).

The test that sparked the controversy was the U.S. government's General Aptitude Test Battery, a test that measures a broad range of abilities from eye-hand coordination to reading proficiency. The problem was that Black Americans and Hispanics tend to score lower on the test, on average, than do members of other groups. The lower scores often are due to a lack of prior relevant experience and job opportunities, which in turn has been due to prejudice and discrimination.

To promote the employment of minority racial groups, the government developed a separate set of test norms for Black Americans and Hispanics. Rather than using the pool of all people who took the tests, the scores of Black American and Hispanic applicants were compared only with the scores of other Black Americans and Hispanics. Consequently, a Hispanic who scored in the top 20% of the Hispanics taking the test was considered to have performed equivalently to a White job applicant who scored in the top 20% of the Whites who took the test, even though the absolute score of the Hispanic might be lower than that of the White.

Critics of the adjusted test norming system suggested that such a procedure discriminates in favor of certain racial and ethnic groups at the expense of others, thereby fanning the flames of racial bigotry. The practice was challenged legally; with the passage of the Civil Rights Act in 1991, race-based test norming on the General Aptitude Test Battery was discontinued (Galef, 2001; Starr, 2022).

However, proponents of race-based test norming continued to argue that test norming procedures that take race into account are an affirmative action tool that simply permits minority job-seekers to be placed on an equal footing with White job-seekers. Furthermore, a panel of the National Academy of Sciences supported the practice of adjusting test norms. It suggested that the unadjusted test norms are not very useful in predicting job performance and that they would tend to screen out otherwise qualified minority group members. Ultimately, though, race-based norming in the workplace has largely been discontinued. For example, in 2021, the National Football League ended race-based norming when evaluating concussions and dementia claims of Black athletes (Fleming, 2000; Possin et al., 2021).

Job testing is not the only area in which issues arise regarding test norms and the meaning of test scores. The issue of how to treat racial differences in IQ scores is also controversial and divisive. Clearly, race-based test norming raises profound and intense feelings that may come into conflict with scientific objectivity (Davis, 2009; Hutchinson & Mitchell, 2019; Byrd & Rivera-Mindt, 2022).

The issue of establishing test norms is further complicated by the existence of a wide array of personality measures and approaches to assessment. We next consider some of these measures.

From the perspective of...

A Politician Imagine that you had to vote on a law that would require institutions and organizations to perform race-based test norming procedures on standardized tests. Would you support such a law? Why or why not? In addition to race, should test norming procedures take other factors into account? Which ones and why?

Exactostock/SuperStock

Self-Report Measures of Personality

If someone wanted to assess your personality, one possible approach would be to carry out an extensive interview with you to determine the most important events in your childhood, your social relationships, and your successes and failures. Obviously, though, such a technique would take extraordinary time and effort.

It is also unnecessary. Just as physicians draw only a small sample of your blood to test, psychologists can use self-report measures. In a **self-report measure,** people are asked questions about their own behavior and traits. This sampling of self-report data is then used to infer the presence of particular personality characteristics. For example, a researcher who was interested in assessing a person's orientation to life might administer the questionnaire shown in Figure 1. Although the questionnaire consists of only a few questions, the answers can be used to generalize about personality characteristics. (Try it yourself!)

self-report measure A method of gathering data about people by asking them questions about their own behavior and traits. (Module 33)

MINNESOTA MULTIPHASIC PERSONALITY INVENTORY (MMPI)

One of the best examples of a self-report measure, and one of the most frequently used personality tests, is the **Minnesota Multiphasic Personality Inventory-2-Restructured Form (MMPI-2-RF).** Although the original purpose of this measure was to identify people with specific sorts of psychological difficulties, it has been found to predict a variety of other behaviors. For instance, MMPI-2-RF scores have been shown to be good predictors of whether college students will marry within 10 years of graduating and whether they will get advanced degrees. Police departments use the test to measure whether police officers are likely to use their weapons. Psychologists in Russia administer a modified form of the MMPI-2-RF to the country's astronauts and Olympic athletes (Zahn et al., 2017; Lee et al., 2019; Bryant et al., 2021).

Minnesota Multiphasic Personality Inventory-2-Restructured Form (MMPI-2-RF) A widely used self-report test that identifies people with psychological difficulties and is employed to predict some everyday behaviors. (Module 33)

The test consists of a series of 338 items to which a person responds "true," "false," or "cannot say." The questions cover a variety of issues ranging from mood ("I feel useless at times") to opinions ("People should try to understand their dreams") to physical and psychological health ("I am bothered by an upset stomach several times a week" and "I have strange and peculiar thoughts").

There are no right or wrong answers. Instead, interpretation of the results rests on the pattern of responses. The test yields scores on 51 separate scales, including several scales meant to measure the validity of the respondent's answers. For example, there is a "lie scale" that indicates when people are falsifying their responses in order to present themselves more favorably (through items such as "I can't remember ever having a bad night's sleep") (Stein & Graham, 2005; Bacchiochi, 2006; Anderson et al., 2015).

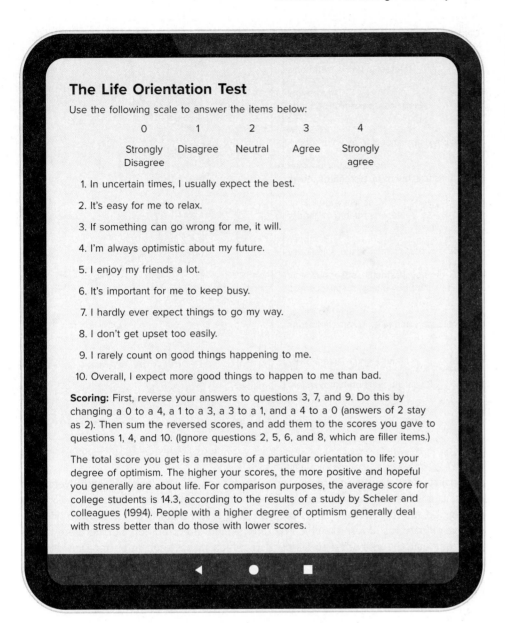

The Life Orientation Test

Use the following scale to answer the items below:

0	1	2	3	4
Strongly Disagree	Disagree	Neutral	Agree	Strongly agree

1. In uncertain times, I usually expect the best.

2. It's easy for me to relax.

3. If something can go wrong for me, it will.

4. I'm always optimistic about my future.

5. I enjoy my friends a lot.

6. It's important for me to keep busy.

7. I hardly ever expect things to go my way.

8. I don't get upset too easily.

9. I rarely count on good things happening to me.

10. Overall, I expect more good things to happen to me than bad.

Scoring: First, reverse your answers to questions 3, 7, and 9. Do this by changing a 0 to a 4, a 1 to a 3, a 3 to a 1, and a 4 to a 0 (answers of 2 stay as 2). Then sum the reversed scores, and add them to the scores you gave to questions 1, 4, and 10. (Ignore questions 2, 5, 6, and 8, which are filler items.)

The total score you get is a measure of a particular orientation to life: your degree of optimism. The higher your scores, the more positive and hopeful you generally are about life. For comparison purposes, the average score for college students is 14.3, according to the results of a study by Scheler and colleagues (1994). People with a higher degree of optimism generally deal with stress better than do those with lower scores.

FIGURE 1 The Life Orientation Test. Complete this test by indicating the degree to which you agree with each of the 10 statements, using the scale from 0 to 4 for each item. Try to be as accurate as possible. There are no right or wrong answers.
Sources: Scheier et al., 1994; Hinz et al., 2022.

How did the authors of the MMPI-2-RF determine what specific patterns of responses indicate? The procedure they used is typical of personality test construction—a process known as test standardization. **Test standardization** is a technique used to validate questions on personality tests by analyzing the responses of people who have completed the same set of questions, under the same circumstances. The responses then can be used to determine an individual's key personality characteristics.

To create and standardize the MMPI-2-RF, the test authors asked groups of psychiatric patients with a specific diagnosis, such as depression or schizophrenia, to complete a large number of items. They then determined which items best differentiated members of those groups from a comparison group of normal participants and included those specific items in the final version of the test. By systematically carrying out this procedure on groups with different diagnoses, the test authors were able to devise a number of subscales that identified forms of abnormal behavior (see Figure 2).

When the MMPI-2-RF is used for the purpose for which it was devised—identification of personality disorders—it does a good job. However, like other

test standardization A technique used to validate questions in personality tests by studying the responses of people with known diagnoses. (Module 33)

FIGURE 2 An MMPI-2-RF profile of a person who suffers from obsessional anxiety, social withdrawal, and delusional thinking.

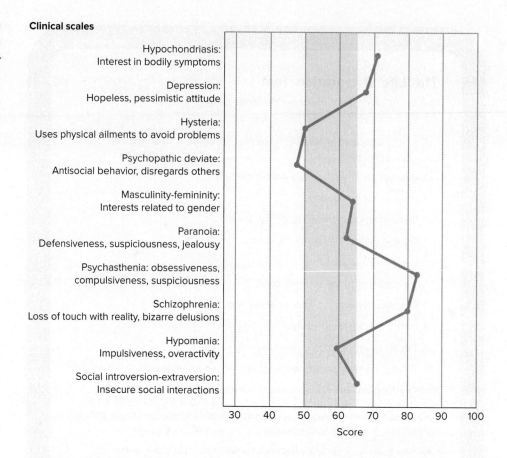

Clinical scales

personality tests, it presents an opportunity for abuse. For instance, employers who use it as a screening tool for job applicants may interpret the results improperly by relying too heavily on the results of individual scales instead of taking into account the overall patterns of results, which requires skilled interpretation. Furthermore, critics point out that the individual scales overlap, which makes their interpretation difficult. In sum, although the MMPI-2-RF remains the most widely used personality test and has been translated into more than 100 languages, it must be used with caution (Williams & Butcher, 2011; Ben-Porath et al., 2017).

OTHER SELF-REPORT MEASURES

The MMPI is not the only self-report questionnaire. For example, a commonly used one is the *Kuder Career Interest Assessment–Likert (KCIA-L)*, which measures the relative level of interest a person has in six broad areas. These results are used to identify career pathways and occupations that match those interests. The Kuder test has been carefully validated, and research has supported its use (Chan et al., 2014; Suen, 2015).

Another self-report measure that is widely used in business settings is the *Myers-Briggs Type Indicator,* which aims to place people along four dimensions: (1) introverts versus extraverts; (2) intuitors versus sensors; (3) thinkers versus feelers; and (4) perceivers versus judgers. Originators of the test argue that employees work best in situations where others share or complement their types and where their personality type is well suited to the tasks on which they must work (Myers and Briggs Foundation, 2019).

Despite its widespread use—some 2 million people a year take the test, at a cost of billions of dollars—many critics believe that objective scientific validation for the test is lacking. They argue that researchers have failed to find that the test predicts much of interest, including professional job-related success. The disconnect between its widespread use and the lack of scientific support is puzzling (Emre, 2019; Lake et al., 2019; Stein & Swan, 2019).

- *Remember that test results are not always accurate.* The results may be in error; the test may be unreliable or invalid. For example, you may have had a "bad day" when you took the test, or the person scoring and interpreting the test may have made a mistake. You should not place too much significance on the results of a single administration of any test.

In sum, keep in mind the complexity of human behavior—particularly your own. No single test, by itself, can evaluate the intricacies of someone's personality.

RECAP/EVALUATE/RETHINK

RECAP

LO 33-1 How can we most accurately assess personality?

- Psychological tests such as the MMPI-2-RF are standard assessment tools that measure behavior objectively. They must be reliable (measuring what they are trying to measure consistently) and valid (measuring what they are supposed to measure).

LO 33-2 What are the major types of personality measures?

- Self-report measures ask people about a sample range of their behaviors. These reports are used to infer the presence of particular personality characteristics.
- Projective personality tests (such as the Rorschach and the TAT) present an ambiguous stimulus; the test administrator infers information about the test-taker from their responses.
- Behavioral assessment is based on the principles of learning theory. It employs direct measurement of an individual's behavior to determine characteristics related to personality.

EVALUATE

1. _____ is the consistency of a personality test; _____ is the ability of a test to actually measure what it is designed to measure.

2. _____ _____ are standards used to compare scores of different people taking the same test.
3. Tests such as the MMPI-2-RF, in which a small sample of behavior is assessed to determine larger patterns, are examples of which of the following?
   a. Cross-sectional tests
   b. Projective tests
   c. Achievement tests
   d. Self-report tests
4. A person shown a picture and asked to make up a story about it would be taking a _____ personality test.

RETHINK

1. Should personality tests be used for personnel decisions? Should they be used for other social purposes, such as identifying individuals at risk for certain types of personality disorders?
2. What do you think are some of the problems that developers and interpreters of self-report personality tests must deal with in their effort to provide useful information about test-takers? Why is a "lie scale" included on such measures?

Answers to Evaluate Questions

1. Reliability, validity; 2. Test norms; 3. d; 4. projective

KEY TERMS

psychological tests	Minnesota Multiphasic	test standardization	Thematic Apperception
self-report measures	Personality Inventory-2-	projective personality test	Test (TAT)
	Restructured Form	Rorschach test	behavioral assessment
	(MMPI-2-RF)		

LOOKING *Back*

EPILOGUE

We have discussed the ways in which psychologists have interpreted the development and structure of personality. The perspectives we examined ranged from Freud's analysis of personality based primarily on internal, unconscious factors to the externally based view championed by learning theorists of personality as a learned set of traits and actions. We also noted that there are many ways to interpret personality; by no means does a consensus exist on a set of key traits central to personality.

Return to the prologue of this chapter and consider the case of Anna Chapman, the Russian spy. Use your understanding of personality to consider the following questions.

1. Which approach to personality do you think best captures a person such as Chapman? Explain.
2. From what you know about her, would you say that Chapman was id-dominated, superego-dominated, or ego-balanced? Why do you think so?
3. Did Chapman seem to have a cardinal trait? If so, what was it?
4. Did Chapman seem to be particularly high or particularly low on any of the Big Five personality traits? If so, which ones, and why do you think so?

Design Elements: Man with laptop: Dragon Images/Shutterstock; Exclamation point and mobile frame: McGraw Hill; Smartphone: WML Image/Shutterstock; Hands: Stefano Garau/Shutterstock.

VISUAL SUMMARY 10 Personality

MODULE 31 Psychodynamic Approaches

Freud's Psychoanalytic Theory

- Conscious experience: Only part of our psychological experience
- Unconscious: Part of the personality of which we are not aware
- Structure of personality
  - Id: Represents the raw, unorganized, inborn part of personality
  - Ego: Strives to balance desires of the id and realities of the outside world
  - Superego: Harshly judges the morality of our behavior

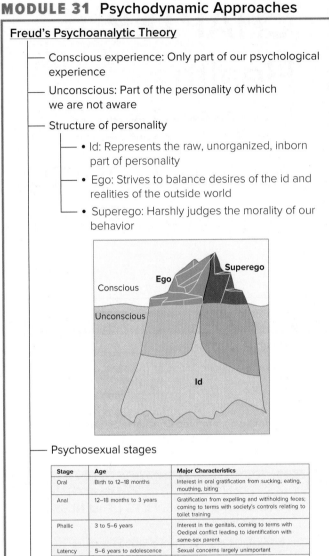

- Psychosexual stages

Stage	Age	Major Characteristics
Oral	Birth to 12–18 months	Interest in oral gratification from sucking, eating, mouthing, biting
Anal	12–18 months to 3 years	Gratification from expelling and withholding feces; coming to terms with society's controls relating to toilet training
Phallic	3 to 5–6 years	Interest in the genitals, coming to terms with Oedipal conflict leading to identification with same-sex parent
Latency	5–6 years to adolescence	Sexual concerns largely unimportant
Genital	Adolescence to adulthood	Reemergence of sexual interests and establishment of mature sexual relationships

- Defense mechanisms: Unconscious strategies people use to reduce anxiety

Neo-Freudian Psychoanalysts: Emphasize the ego more than Freud: Carl Jung, Karen Horney, Alfred Adler

MODULE 32 Trait, Learning, Biological and Evolutionary, and Humanistic Approaches

Trait Approaches: Emphasize consistent personality characteristics and behaviors called traits
- Eysenck: Extraversion, neuroticism, and psychoticism
- The Big Five personality traits: Openness to experience, conscientiousness, extraversion, agreeableness, neuroticism

Learning Approaches: Emphasize that personality is the sum of learned responses to the external environment

- B. F. Skinner: Personality is a collection of learned behavior patterns that are a result of reinforcement.

Learning Approaches (continued)

- Social cognitive approaches: Emphasize the influence of cognition as well as observation of others' behavior on personality
- Self-efficacy and self-esteem

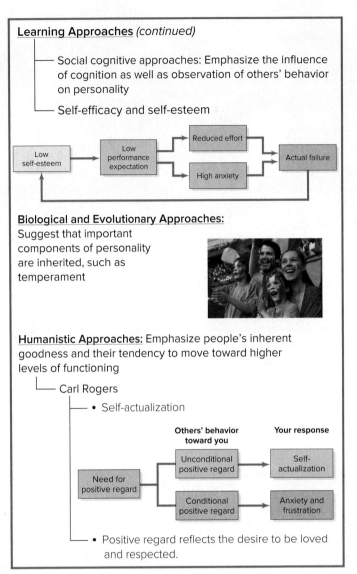

Biological and Evolutionary Approaches: Suggest that important components of personality are inherited, such as temperament

Humanistic Approaches: Emphasize people's inherent goodness and their tendency to move toward higher levels of functioning
- Carl Rogers
  - Self-actualization
  - Positive regard reflects the desire to be loved and respected.

MODULE 33 Assessing Personality

Psychological Tests: Standard measures that assess behavior objectively
- Reliability
- Validity
- Norms

Self-Report Measures: A method of gathering data by asking people questions about their own behavior and traits

Projective Methods: People are shown an ambiguous stimulus and asked to describe it or tell a story about it.
- Rorschach test
- Thematic Apperception Test (TAT)

Behavioral Assessment: Measures of a person's behavior designed to describe characteristics indicative of personality

(Module 32): Photo and Co/The Image Bank/Getty Images; (Module 33): zmeel/E+/Getty Images

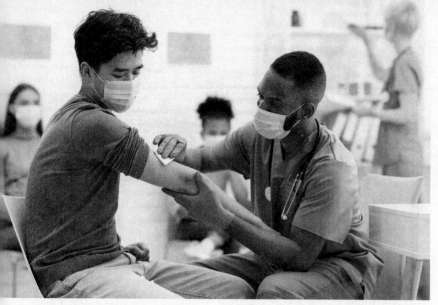

Prostock-studio/Shutterstock

CHAPTER 11

Health Psychology: Stress, Coping, and Well-Being

LEARNING OUTCOMES FOR CHAPTER 11

PROLOGUE *PANDEMIC!*

Arlene Amarosi was very worried when the COVID-19 pandemic began. At 77 years old and with a weak heart, she was at high risk for serious illness and death if she contracted the virus. So she diligently obeyed the lockdown, stopping her regular routine of going out on most days, whether for a walk in the park, lunch with friends, or shopping for necessities. For more than a year, Arlene was instead stuck at home.

At first the isolation wasn't so bad. She watched a lot of TV, but that eventually became boring. Against her physician's advice, she started sleeping in a lot and spent more and more time just sitting in her bedroom feeling sad—sometimes not even bothering to get dressed.

When she finally got vaccinated after a year of isolation, she felt hopeful about resuming her old life. But by then, Arlene was having a lot of difficulty standing and walking. Her mental acuity had declined, too, and she found that she could no longer do many of the things that she had once enjoyed. Despite never actually contracting the virus, she considers herself one of its victims: It didn't take her life, but it did take a lot of the life that was left in her.

LOOKING *Ahead*

The COVID-19 pandemic changed the world starting in 2020, and Arlene Amarosi was but one of millions of its victims. By the third year of the pandemic, more than 7 million people across the globe had died, and millions of others had their lives permanently altered, both physically and psychologically.

The degree to which the pandemic affected people's health and well-being made it particularly of interest to psychologists who belong to a branch of psychology known as health psychology. **Health psychology** investigates the psychological factors related to wellness and illness, including the prevention, diagnosis, and treatment of medical problems. Health psychologists investigate the effects of psychological factors such as stress on illness. They examine the psychological principles underlying treatments for disease and illness.

Health psychologists also study prevention and behavior change. For example, during the coronavirus pandemic, health psychologists helped to craft messages that would lead people to self-quarantine and to socially distance themselves from others.

Health psychologists take a decisive stand on the enduring mind–body issue that philosophers and, later, psychologists have debated since the time of the ancient Greeks. In their view, the mind and the body are clearly linked rather than representing two distinct systems (Grosso, 2015; Ogden, 2022).

Health psychologists recognize that good health and the ability to cope with illness are affected by psychological factors such as thoughts, emotions, and the ability to manage stress. They have paid particular attention to the *immune system,* the complex system of organs, glands, and cells that constitutes our bodies' natural line of defense in fighting disease.

In fact, health psychologists are among the primary investigators in a growing field called **psychoneuroimmunology, or PNI,** the study of the relationship among psychological factors, the immune system, and the brain. PNI has led to discoveries such as the existence of an association between a person's emotional state and the success of the immune system in fighting disease (Sperner-Unterweger & Fuchs, 2015; Ayling et al., 2017; Bower et al., 2022).

In sum, health psychologists view the mind and the body as two parts of a whole human being that cannot be considered independently. This more recent view marks a sharp departure from earlier thinking. Previously, disease was seen as a purely biological phenomenon, and psychological factors were of little interest to most health-care workers. In the early 20th century, the primary causes of death were short-term infections from which one either rapidly recovered—or died. Now, however, the major causes of death, such as heart disease, cancer, and diabetes, are chronic illnesses that pose significant psychological issues because they often cannot be cured and may linger for years (Rotan & Ospina-Kammerer, 2007; Berecki-Gisolf et al., 2013; Chen et al., 2017).

Advances in health psychology have had an impact across a variety of disciplines and professions. For instance, health-care professionals such as physicians and nurses, social workers, dietitians, pharmacists, occupational therapists, as well as clergy, are increasingly likely to receive training in health psychology.

In the following modules, we discuss the ways in which psychological factors affect health. We first focus on the causes and consequences of stress as well as on the means of coping with it. Next, we explore the psychological aspects of several specific health problems, including heart disease, cancer, and COVID-19. Finally, we examine the ways in which patient–physician interactions influence our health and offer suggestions for increasing people's compliance with recommendations about behavior that will improve their well-being.

health psychology The branch of psychology that investigates the psychological factors related to wellness and illness, including the prevention, diagnosis, and treatment of medical problems. (Module 34)

psychoneuroimmunology (PNI) The study of the relationship among psychological factors, the immune system, and the brain. (Module 34)

Module 34
Stress and Coping

LEARNING OUTCOMES

LO 34-1 How is health psychology a union between medicine and psychology?

LO 34-2 What is stress, how does it affect us, and how can we best cope with it?

stress A person's response to events that are threatening or challenging. (Module 34)

Leticia Sanchez remembers the worst moment of her life: The day she heard about the mass shootings at Uvalde Elementary School in her small Texas town. She immediately jumped in the car and drove to the school, which her 7-year-old daughter, Valentina, attended. After a harrowing 3-hour wait, she was reunited with her daughter, who was one of the lucky ones who had not been hurt. "My heart was pounding. I started crying, and I just couldn't stop," Sanchez says. Then and there, she decided that Valentina would never return to Uvalde and that she would instead be homeschooled. Friends could come over, but Sanchez found she couldn't let Valentina out of her sight. "So much can happen when you walk away from your child," Sanchez says. "I was terrified by that loss of control."

Most of us need little introduction to the phenomenon of **stress,** people's response to events that threaten or challenge them. Whether the result of a school shooting or, more likely, a paper deadline, exam, or work or family problem, life is full of circumstances and events known as *stressors* that produce threats to our well-being. Even pleasant events–such as planning a party or beginning a sought-after job–can produce stress, although negative events result in greater detrimental consequences than positive ones do.

Stress: Reacting to Threat and Challenge

! Study Alert

Remember the distinction between stressors and stress, which can be tricky: Stressors (such as an exam) cause stress (the physiological and psychological reaction that comes from the exam).

All of us face stress in our lives. Some health psychologists believe that daily life actually involves a series of repeated sequences of perceiving a threat, considering ways to cope with it, and ultimately adapting to the threat with greater or lesser success. Although adaptation is often minor and occurs without our awareness, adaptation requires a major effort when stress is more severe or long-lasting. Ultimately, our attempts to overcome stress may produce biological and psychological responses that result in health problems (Finan et al., 2011; Dierolf et al., 2017; Furuyashiki & Kitaoka, 2019).

THE NATURE OF STRESSORS: MY STRESS IS YOUR PLEASURE

Stress is a very personal thing. Although certain kinds of events, such as the death of a loved one or participation in military combat, are universally stressful, other situations may or may not be stressful to a specific person.

Consider, for instance, bungee jumping. Some people would find jumping off a bridge while attached to a slender rubber tether extremely stressful. However, others see it as challenging and fun-filled. Whether bungee jumping is stressful depends in part, then, on a person's perception of the activity.

For people to consider an event stressful, they must perceive it as threatening or challenging and must lack all the resources to deal with it effectively. Consequently, the same event may at some times be stressful and at other times provoke no stressful reaction at all. A 25-year-old might experience stress when he is turned down for a date if he attributes the

Even positive events can produce significant stress.
Beijing Eastphoto stockimages Co.,Ltd/Alamy Stock Photo

refusal to his unattractiveness or unworthiness. But if he attributes it to some factor unrelated to his self-esteem, such as a previous commitment of the person he asked, the experience of being refused may create no stress at all. Hence, a person's interpretation of events plays an important role in the determination of what is stressful (Tuckey et al., 2015; Kilby et al., 2021).

CATEGORIZING STRESSORS

What kinds of events tend to be seen as stressful? There are three general types of stressors: cataclysmic events, personal stressors, and background stressors.

Cataclysmic Events **Cataclysmic events** are strong stressors that occur suddenly and typically affect many people simultaneously. Disasters such as wildfires and plane crashes as well as terrorist attacks are examples of cataclysmic events that can affect hundreds or thousands of people simultaneously.

Although you might think that cataclysmic events consistently produce potent, lingering stress, in some cases they do not. In fact, cataclysmic events involving natural disasters may produce less stress in the long run than events that initially are not as devastating. One reason is that natural disasters have a clear start and ending. Once they are over, people can look to the future and work toward recovery. Moreover, others who also experienced the disaster share the stress induced by cataclysmic events. Such sharing permits people to offer one another social support and a firsthand understanding of the difficulties others are going through (Yesilyaprak et al., 2007; Schwarzer & Luszczynska, 2013).

In contrast, cataclysmic events such as the terrorist attacks on the World Trade Center in 2001, the Boston Marathon bombings in 2013, or the 2022 Uvalde, Texas, school shooting produce considerable stress for those involved. Furthermore, exposure to repeated events, whether experienced directly or through the media, may lead to increased sensitivity to stress (Idås et al., 2019; Pakpour et al., 2021; Hadjistavropoulos & Asmundson, 2022).

Personal Stressors The second major category of stressor is the personal stressor. **Personal stressors** include major life events such as the death of a parent, partner, or spouse, the loss of one's job, a major personal failure, or even something positive such as getting married.

Typically, personal stressors produce an immediate major reaction that soon tapers off. For example, stress arising from the death of a loved one tends to be greatest just after the time of death, but people begin to feel less stress and are better able to cope with the loss after the passage of time.

Although both negative and positive events can produce stress, negative events typically have a greater impact. As you might expect, negative events produce more psychological distress and physical symptoms than do positive stressors (Gallagher et al., 2020; Updegraff & Taylor, 2021).

Posttraumatic Stress Disorder Some victims of major catastrophes, cataclysmic events, and severe personal stressors experience **posttraumatic stress disorder, or PTSD,** in which a person has experienced a significantly stressful event that has long-lasting effects that may include re-experiencing the event in vivid flashbacks or dreams. An episode of PTSD may be triggered by an otherwise innocent stimulus, such as the sound of a honking horn, that leads a person to re-experience a past event that produced considerable stress.

Symptoms of posttraumatic stress disorder also include emotional numbing, sleep difficulties, interpersonal problems, alcohol and drug abuse, and in some cases, suicide. Around 12% of soldiers who returned from the Gulf War show symptoms of PTSD, and the United States spends $3 billion a year on treating the disorder in military veterans. The suicide rate for military veterans, many of whom participated in the Gulf and

cataclysmic events Strong stressors that occur suddenly and typically affect many people at once (e.g., natural disasters). (Module 34)

personal stressors Major life events, such as the death of a family member, that have immediate negative consequences that generally fade with time. (Module 34)

posttraumatic stress disorder (PTSD) A phenomenon in which victims of major catastrophes or strong personal stressors feel long-lasting effects that may include re-experiencing the event in vivid flashbacks or dreams. (Module 34)

Afghanistan wars, is more than twice as high as for nonveterans (U.S. Department of Veterans Affairs, 2021; Sokol et al., 2021; Mohatt et al., 2022).

In addition to traditional forms of PTSD, soldiers who have faced multiple tours of duty and who may have actually thrived during years of combat face their own kind of PTSD. After they return home, they may have to unlearn the skills that helped them survive in combat, such as constant vigilance, an intolerance for carelessness, and extreme decisiveness (Carey, 2016).

Furthermore, people who have experienced child abuse or rape, rescue workers facing overwhelming situations, and victims of sudden natural disasters or accidents that produce feelings of helplessness and shock may suffer from PTSD. For example, after a major earthquake in China, 12% of the population still had symptoms of PTSD almost a decade later (Thompson, 2015; Lu et al., 2021; Mahoney et al., 2022).

Terrorist attacks produce high incidences of PTSD. For example, 11% of people in New York City had some form of PTSD in the months after the 9/11 terrorist attacks. But the responses varied significantly with a resident's proximity to the attacks; the closer someone lived to the World Trade Center, the greater the likelihood of PTSD. However, for many people, the effects of PTSD were still evident two decades after the attacks (Neria et al., 2011; Chatterjee, 2021; Rigutto et al., 2021).

The good news is that the most frequent response to negative events is resilience. The majority of people who experience traumas that might be expected to trigger PTSD actually recover on their own (Taitz, 2020; Hiscox et al., 2022). For those who require intervention, PTSD can be treated in a variety of ways. For example, good results can come from various forms of psychological therapy. In addition, some drug treatments have proven effective. Finally, in one experimental treatment approach, the use of MDMA, a drug known by its street names Ecstasy or Molly, in combination with counseling, has shown to be effective in reducing the symptoms of PTSD (Bird et al., 2021; Illingworth et al., 2021).

Gun Violence One personal stressor that became an increasing part of everyday life is the prospect of being injured or killed in a mass shooting. Over 1,500 people in the United States were killed in mass shootings between 2009 and 2020, and the number keeps rising. In the first half of 2022 alone, over 350 mass shootings occurred (Gun Violence Archive, 2021).

But the number of gun deaths that occur goes far beyond mass murders (defined as four or more people killed in a single incident). In fact, mass killings represent less than 1% of all of those killed by guns in the United States, with the most common occurring in households, when a person kills their relatives and then themselves (Duwe, 2020; Berman et al., 2022).

But regardless of the statistics, the stress produced by the fear of being involved in a mass shooting is considerable. Surveys show that one-third of Americans avoid certain places or certain events because they fear being shot. In some urban neighborhoods, the threat of violence is an everyday concern (FBI, 2019; Ellinson et al., 2022).

For those who survive a mass shooting or live close to it, the psychological consequences can be significant and persistent. Survivors, members of victims' families, and even those who simply live near where an incident occurred may experience PTSD, substance abuse problems, and major depression. Even those not directly affected by mass killings may feel stress, anxiety, helplessness, fear, anger, or persistent grief. For example, 75% of young adults between 15 and 21 state that mass shootings were a significant source of stress for them (Novotney, 2018; Canady, 2019; Caron, 2022).

background stressors ("daily hassles") Everyday annoyances, such as being stuck in traffic, that cause minor irritations and may have long-term ill effects if they continue or are compounded by other stressful events. (Module 34)

Background Stressors **Background stressors** or, more informally, *daily hassles*, are the third major category of stressors. Exemplified by standing in a long line at a supermarket checkout and getting stuck in a traffic jam, daily hassles are the minor irritations of life that we all face time and time again. Another type of background stressor is a long-term, chronic problem, such as being dissatisfied with school or a job, being in an unhappy relationship, or living in crowded quarters without privacy (Barke, 2011; Aoued et al., 2019).

By themselves, daily hassles do not require much coping or even a response on the individual's part, although they certainly produce unpleasant emotions and moods. Yet, daily hassles add up, and ultimately, they may take as great of a toll as a single, more stressful incident. In fact, the *number* of daily hassles people face is associated with psychological symptoms and health problems such as flu, sore throat, and backaches.

The flip side of hassles is *uplifts*, the minor positive events that make us feel good–even if only temporarily. Uplifts include relating well to a friend or finding one's surroundings pleasing. What is especially intriguing about uplifts is that they are associated with people's psychological health in just the opposite way that hassles are: The greater the number of uplifts we experience, the fewer the psychological symptoms we report later. Even people who have been diagnosed with major depression report greater well-being if they have experienced a higher level of positive events in their past (Klusmann et al., 2021; Panaite et al., 2021; Eklund et al., 2022).

For these subway riders in Tokyo, the everyday commute was a stressful ordeal.
Rafael Macia/mauritius images GmbH/Alamy Stock Photo

The High Cost of Stress

Stress has both biological and psychological consequences. Some of those consequences begin almost instantaneously, whereas others unfold over time.

Often the most immediate reaction to stress is biological. Specifically, exposure to stressors generates a rise in hormone secretions by the adrenal glands, an increase in heart rate and blood pressure, and changes in how well the skin conducts electrical impulses. On a short-term basis, these responses may be adaptive because they produce an "emergency reaction" in which the body prepares to defend itself through activation of the sympathetic nervous system. Those responses may allow more effective coping with the stressful situation (Berger et al., 2019).

However, continued exposure to stress results in a decline in the body's overall level of biological functioning because of the constant secretion of stress-related hormones. Over time, stressful reactions can promote deterioration of body tissues such as blood vessels and the heart. Ultimately, we become more susceptible to disease as our ability to fight off infection is lowered (Miller et al., 2011; Farrell et al., 2017; Ahmadi et al., 2022).

Furthermore, stress can produce or worsen physical problems. Specifically, **psychophysiological disorders** are medical problems that are influenced by an interaction of psychological, emotional, and physical difficulties. Common psychophysiological disorders include high blood pressure, headaches, backaches, skin rashes, indigestion, fatigue, and constipation. Stress has even been linked to the common cold (Gupta, 2013; Gianaros & Wager, 2015; Tolin et al., 2021).

On a psychological level, high levels of stress prevent people from adequately coping with life. Their view of the environment can become clouded (for example, a minor criticism made by a friend is blown out of proportion). Moreover, at the highest levels of stress, emotional responses may be so extreme that people are unable to act at all. People under a lot of stress also become less able to deal with new stressors.

In short, stress affects us in multiple ways. It may increase the risk that we will become ill, it may directly cause illness, it may make us less able to recover from a disease, and it may reduce our ability to cope with future stress. (See Figure 1 to get a measure of your own level of stress.)

THE GENERAL ADAPTATION SYNDROME MODEL: THE COURSE OF STRESS

The effects of long-term stress are illustrated in a series of stages proposed by Hans Selye (pronounced "sell-yay"), a pioneering stress theorist (Selye, 1993). Selye called this model the general adaptation syndrome. The **general adaptation syndrome (GAS)** suggests that the physiological response to stress follows the same set pattern regardless of the cause of stress.

Study Alert
Remember the three categories of stressors—cataclysmic events, personal stressors, and background stressors—and that they produce different levels of stress.

psychophysiological disorders Medical problems influenced by an interaction of psychological, emotional, and physical difficulties. (Module 34)

general adaptation syndrome (GAS) A theory developed by Selye that suggests that a person's response to a stressor consists of three stages: alarm and mobilization, resistance, and exhaustion. (Module 34)

How Stressed Are You?

Find out how stressed you are by responding to the following statements in terms of the last month only. Add up the score from each box. The rough scoring guide below will help you get a sense of your stress level.

1. I was convinced that the big things in my life were beyond my control.
   - [ ] 0=never, 1=infrequently, 2=sometimes, 3=fairly often, 4=very often

2. I felt that I could at least control the minor irritations in my life.
   - [ ] 4=never, 3=infrequently, 2=sometimes, 1=fairly often, 0=very often

3. I became upset at something that I didn't expect to happen.
   - [ ] 4=never, 3=infrequently, 2=sometimes, 1=fairly often, 0=very often

4. I felt confident that I could handle my personal problems.
   - [ ] 4=never, 3=infrequently, 2=sometimes, 1=fairly often, 0=very often

5. I felt nervous, anxious, and under stress.
   - [ ] 0=never, 1=infrequently, 2=sometimes, 3=fairly often, 4=very often

6. I felt myself to be the master of my life.
   - [ ] 4=never, 3=infrequently, 2=sometimes, 1=fairly often, 0=very often

7. I realized that I simply couldn't manage or cope with everything I had to do.
   - [ ] 0=never, 1=infrequently, 2=sometimes, 3=fairly often, 4=very often

8. I felt that troubles and worries were mounting so high I couldn't get past them.
   - [ ] 0=never, 1=infrequently, 2=sometimes, 3=fairly often, 4=very often

9. I felt that, overall, things were heading in the right direction.
   - [ ] 4=never, 3=infrequently, 2=sometimes, 1=fairly often, 0=very often

10. I lost my temper because of something that I couldn't control.
    - [ ] 0=never, 1=infrequently, 2=sometimes, 3=fairly often, 4=very often

Here's a rough scoring guide:

0–10 low stress
11–20 moderately low stress
21–30 moderately high stress
31–40 high stress

FIGURE 1 To get a sense of the level of stress in your life, complete this questionnaire.
Source: Adapted from Cohen et al., 1983.

As shown in Figure 2, the GAS has three phases. The first stage–*alarm and mobilization*–occurs when people become aware of the presence of a stressor. On a biological level, the sympathetic nervous system becomes energized, which helps a person cope initially with the stressor.

However, if the stressor persists, people move into the second response stage: *resistance*. During this stage, the body is actively fighting the stressor on a biological level. During resistance, people use a variety of means to cope with the stressor–sometimes successfully but at a cost of some degree of physical or psychological well-being. For example, a student who faces the stress of failing several courses might spend long hours studying, seeking to cope with the stress.

If resistance is inadequate, people enter the last stage of the GAS: *exhaustion*. During the exhaustion stage, a person's ability to fight the stressor declines to the point where negative consequences of stress appear: physical illness and psychological symptoms in the form of an inability to concentrate, heightened irritability, or, in severe cases, disorientation and a loss of touch with reality. In a sense, people wear out, and their physiological resources to fight the stressor are used up.

How do people move out of the third stage after they have entered it? In some cases, exhaustion allows people to escape a stressor. For example, people who become ill from overwork may be excused from their duties for a time, which gives them a temporary respite from their responsibilities. At least for a time, then, the immediate stress is reduced.

! Study Alert

Remember the three stages of the general adaptation syndrome with the acronym ARE (*A*larm and mobilization, *R*esistance, and *E*xhaustion).

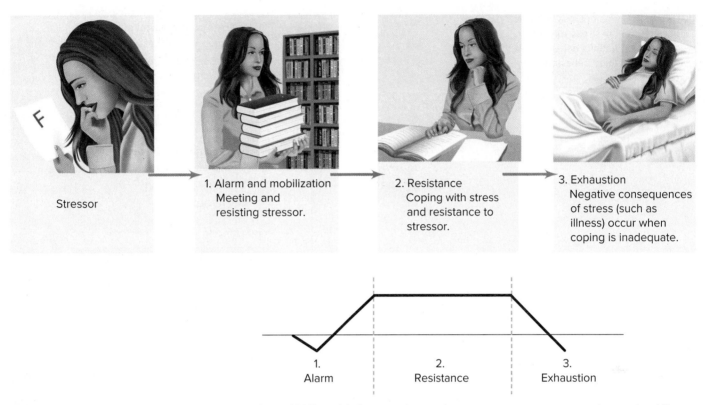

Stressor

1. Alarm and mobilization
Meeting and
resisting stressor.

2. Resistance
Coping with stress
and resistance to
stressor.

3. Exhaustion
Negative consequences
of stress (such as
illness) occur when
coping is inadequate.

1.
Alarm

2.
Resistance

3.
Exhaustion

FIGURE 2 According to the general adaptation syndrome (GAS) model, there are three major stages to stress responses: alarm and mobilization; resistance; and exhaustion. The graph below the illustration shows the degree of effort expended to cope with stressors at each of the three stages.

Although the GAS has had a substantial impact on our understanding of stress, critics have challenged Selye's theory. Specifically, the theory suggests that one's biological reaction to stress is similar regardless of the stressor. However, some health psychologists disagree, asserting instead that people's biological responses are specific to the way they appraise a stressful event. Research supporting this perspective has led to an increased focus on psychoneuroimmunology, as we consider next (Cunanan et al., 2018; Taylor, 2020).

PSYCHONEUROIMMUNOLOGY AND STRESS

Contemporary health psychologists specializing in **psychoneuroimmunology (PNI)** have taken a broader approach to stress. Focusing on the outcomes of stress, they have identified three main consequences of it (see Figure 3).

First, stress has direct physiological results, including an increase in blood pressure, an increase in hormonal activity, and an overall decline in the functioning of the immune system. Second, stress leads people to engage in behaviors that are harmful to their health, including increased nicotine, drug, and alcohol use; poor eating habits; and decreased sleep. Third, stress produces some indirect consequences that ultimately result in declines in health. For example, high levels of stress reduce the likelihood a person will seek health care. In addition, stress may result in less compliance with medical advice when it is sought. Both the reductions in seeking medical care and decreased compliance can indirectly lead to declines in health (Stowell et al., 2013; Douthit & Russotti, 2017).

Why is stress so damaging to the immune system? One reason is that stress likely decreases the ability of the immune system to respond to disease, permitting germs that produce colds to reproduce more easily or allowing cancer cells to spread more rapidly. In normal circumstances, our bodies produce disease-fighting white blood cells

The ability to fight off disease is related to psychological factors. Here a cell from the body's immune system engulfs and destroys disease-producing bacteria.
Science History Images/Alamy Stock Photo

psychoneuroimmunology (PNI)
The study of the relationship among psychological factors, the immune system, and the brain. (Module 34)

FIGURE 3 Three major types of consequences result from stress: direct physiological effects, harmful behaviors, and indirect health-related behaviors.
Source: Adapted from Baum, 1994.

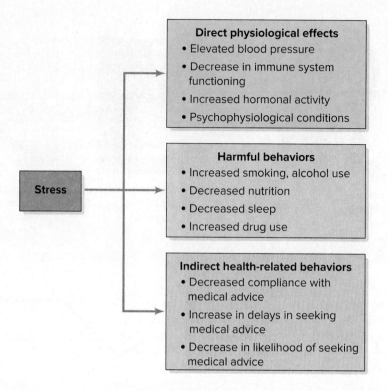

called *lymphocytes*. Our bodies normally produce them at an extraordinary rate—some 10 million every few seconds. Stress may decrease this level of production (Zhou et al., 2017; Jones et al., 2021).

Another way that stress affects the immune system is by overstimulating it. Rather than fighting invading bacteria, viruses, and other foreign invaders, the immune system may begin to attack the body itself and damage healthy tissue. When that happens, it can lead to disorders such as arthritis and allergic reactions (Baum et al., 2011; Marques et al., 2015; Buscemi et al., 2019).

Coping with Stress

Stress is a normal part of life—and not necessarily a completely bad part. For example, without stress, we might not be sufficiently motivated to complete the activities we need to accomplish. Moreover, stress can help us change in positive ways, leading us to align our behavior with values that are important to us (Leibowitz & Crum, 2020; Zion et al., 2022).

However, it is also clear that too much stress can take a toll on physical and psychological health. How do people deal with stress? Is there a way to reduce its negative effects?

coping The efforts to control, reduce, or learn to tolerate the threats that lead to stress. (Module 34)

Efforts to control, reduce, or learn to tolerate the threats that lead to stress are known as **coping.** We habitually use certain coping responses to deal with stress. Most of the time, we're not aware of these responses—just as we may be unaware of the minor stressors of life until they build up to harmful levels (Chao, 2011; Tahara et al., 2021).

We also have other, more direct, and potentially more positive ways of coping with stress, which fall into two main categories (Pow & Cashwell, 2017; Lin, 2022).

- **Emotion-focused coping.** In *emotion-focused coping*, people try to manage their emotions in the face of stress by seeking to change the way they feel about or perceive a problem. Examples of emotion-focused coping include strategies such as accepting sympathy from others and looking at the bright side of a situation.
- **Problem-focused coping.** *Problem-focused coping* attempts to modify the stressful problem or source of stress. Problem-focused strategies lead to changes in behavior or to the development of a plan of action to deal with stress. Starting a study

group to improve poor classroom performance is an example of problem-focused coping. In addition, one might take a time-out from stress by creating positive events. For example, taking a day off from caring for a relative with a serious, chronic illness to go a health club or spa can bring significant relief from stress.

People often employ both emotion-focused and problem-focused coping strategies simultaneously to deal with stress. In other cases, the type of strategy differs according to the situation. For example, they tend to use emotion-focused strategies more frequently when they perceive circumstances as being unchangeable, and they use problem-focused strategies more often in situations they see as relatively modifiable (Tamannaeifar & Shahmirzaei, 2019).

Some forms of coping are less successful. One of the least effective forms of coping is avoidant coping. In *avoidant coping*, a person may use wishful thinking to reduce stress or use more direct escape routes, such as drug use, alcohol use, and overeating. An example of wishful thinking to avoid a test would be to say to oneself, "Maybe it will snow so hard tomorrow that the test will be canceled." Alternatively, a person might get drunk to avoid a problem. Either way, avoidant coping usually results in a postponement of dealing with a stressful situation, and this often makes the problem even worse (Sikkema et al., 2013; Dunkley et al., 2017; Chen et al., 2021).

Another way of dealing with stress occurs unconsciously through the use of defense mechanisms. *Defense mechanisms* are unconscious strategies that people use to reduce anxiety by concealing the source from themselves and others. Defense mechanisms permit people to avoid stress by acting as if the stress were not even there. For example, one study examined California college students who lived in dormitories close to a geological fault (Lehman & Taylor, 1988). Those who lived in dorms that were known to be unlikely to withstand an earthquake were significantly *more* likely to doubt experts' predictions of an impending earthquake than were those who lived in safer structures.

Another defense mechanism used to cope with stress is *emotional insulation* in which a person stops experiencing any emotions at all and thereby remains unaffected and unmoved by both positive and negative experiences. The problem with defense mechanisms, of course, is that they merely hide the problem and do not deal with reality.

LEARNED HELPLESSNESS

Have you ever faced an intolerable situation that you just couldn't resolve, and you finally simply gave up and accepted things the way they were? This example illustrates one of the possible consequences of being in an environment in which control over a situation is not possible–a state that produces learned helplessness. **Learned helplessness** occurs when people conclude that unpleasant or aversive stimuli cannot be controlled. They develop a view of the world that becomes so ingrained that they cease trying to remedy the aversive circumstances even if they actually can exert some influence on the situation. For example, students who decide they are simply "no good in math" may not work very hard in math classes because they believe that no matter how hard they try, they'll never succeed. Their learned helplessness virtually ensures that they won't do well in math classes (Seligman, 2018; Ghasemi, 2021; Raufelder & Kulakow, 2022).

Victims of learned helplessness have concluded that there is no link between the responses they make and the outcomes that occur. People experience more physical symptoms and depression when they perceive that they have little or no control than they do when they feel a sense of control over a situation (Figen, 2011; Trindade et al., 2020).

COPING STYLES: HARDINESS AND RESILIENCE

Most of us characteristically cope with stress by employing a *coping style* that represents our general tendency to deal with stress in a specific way. For example, you may know people who habitually react to even the smallest amount of stress with

learned helplessness A state in which people conclude that unpleasant or aversive stimuli cannot be controlled–a view of the world that becomes so ingrained that they cease trying to remedy the aversive circumstances even if they actually can exert some influence on the situation. (Module 34)

hysteria and others who calmly confront even the greatest stress in an unflappable manner. These kinds of people clearly have very different coping styles.

hardiness A personality trait characterized by a sense of commitment, the perception of problems as challenges, and a sense of control. (Module 34)

Hardiness Among those who cope with stress most successfully are people who exhibit a personality trait known as hardiness. **Hardiness** is a personality trait characterized by a sense of commitment to one's goals, viewing problems as challenges, and having a sense of control over one's life and environment. People with the hardiness trait have a lower rate of stress-related illness (Maddi et al., 2011; Abdollahi et al., 2019; McDonald et al., 2022).

Specifically, the three components of hardiness operate in different ways:

- *Commitment.* People with a strong level of commitment tend to throw themselves into whatever they are doing. They have a sense that their activities are important and meaningful.

- *Challenge.* Hardy people believe that change, rather than stability, is the standard condition of life. To them, the anticipation of change is something positive, rather than change being seen as a threat to their security.

- *Control.* Hardiness is marked by a sense of control–the perception that people can influence the events in their lives.

Hardy individuals approach stress optimistically and take direct action to learn about and deal with stressors; they thereby change stressful events into less threatening ones. As a consequence, hardiness acts as a defense against stress-related illness (Stoppelbein et al., 2017; Gugliandolo et al., 2022).

resilience The ability to withstand, overcome, and actually thrive after profound adversity. (Module 34)

Resilience For those who confront the most profound difficulties, such as the death of a loved one or a permanent injury such as paralysis after an accident, a key ingredient in their psychological recovery is their degree of resilience. **Resilience** is the ability to withstand, overcome, and actually thrive after profound adversity (Jackson, 2006; Schwarz, 2018; Infurna, 2021).

Resilient people are generally optimistic, good-natured, and have good social skills. They are usually independent, and they have a sense of control over their own destiny–even if fate has dealt them a devastating blow. In short, they work with what they have and make the best of whatever situation they find themselves in (Sinclair et al., 2013; Kašpárková et al., 2018).

Resilience may have its origins in a complex series of biological reactions that occur when people confront devastating situations. These reactions involve the release of the hormone cortisol. Although cortisol is helpful in responding to challenges, too much can produce damage. Other chemicals, however, can moderate the effects of cortisol, and it may be that drugs or therapy can stimulate the production of these moderating chemicals. Furthermore, some people may be genetically predisposed to produce these chemicals, making them more resilient (Stix, 2011; Choi et al., 2019; Athota et al., 2020).

From the perspective of...

A Social Worker How would you help people deal with and avoid stress in their everyday lives? How might you encourage people to create social support networks?

Sam Edwards/age fotostock

BECOMING AN INFORMED CONSUMER
of Psychology

Effective Coping Strategies

How can we deal with the stress in our lives? Although there is no universal solution because effective coping depends on the nature of the stressor and the degree to which it can be controlled, here are some general guidelines:

- *Turn a threat into a challenge.* When a stressful situation might be controllable, the best coping strategy is to treat the situation as a challenge and focus on ways to control it. For instance, if you experience stress because your car is always breaking down, you might take a course in auto mechanics and learn to deal directly with the car's problems.
- *Make a threatening situation less threatening.* When a stressful situation seems to be uncontrollable, you need to take a different approach. It is possible to change your appraisal of the situation, view it in a different light, and modify your attitude toward it. Research supports the old truism "Look for the silver lining in every cloud" (Pathak & Lata, 2018; Liu et al., 2019).
- *Change your goals.* If you are faced with an uncontrollable situation, a reasonable strategy is to adopt new goals that are practical in view of the particular situation. For example, a dancer who has been in an automobile accident and has lost full use of her legs may no longer aspire to a career in dance but might modify her goals and try to become a choreographer.
- *Modify your physiological reactions to stress.* Many people don't know that they can directly change their physiological reactions to stress, which can help with coping. For example, biofeedback (in which a person learns to control internal physiological processes through conscious thought) can alter basic physiological reactions to stress and permit the person to reduce blood pressure, heart rate, and other consequences of heightened stress. Exercise can also be effective in reducing stress (Langreth, 2000; Spencer et al., 2003; Hamer et al., 2006).
- *Change the situations that are likely to cause stress.* In *proactive coping,* you anticipate and try to head off stress *before* you encounter it. For example, if you know your upcoming week is going to be grueling because you must take a number of major tests, rearrange your schedule so you have more time to study or take direct steps to improve your chances for success by attending test review sessions (Neubauer et al., 2019; Tuan, 2022).

RECAP/EVALUATE/RETHINK

RECAP

LO 34-1 How is health psychology a union between medicine and psychology?

- The field of health psychology considers how psychology can be applied to the prevention, diagnosis, and treatment of medical problems.

LO 34-2 What is stress, how does it affect us, and how can we best cope with it?

- Stress is a response to threatening or challenging environmental conditions. People encounter stressors—the

circumstances that produce stress—of both a positive and a negative nature.
- The way an environmental circumstance is interpreted affects whether it will be considered stressful. Still, there are general classes of events that provoke stress: cataclysmic events, personal stressors, and background stressors (daily hassles).
- Stress produces immediate physiological reactions. In the short term, those reactions may be adaptive, but in the long term, they may have negative consequences, including the development of psychophysiological disorders.

- The consequences of stress can be explained in part by Selye's general adaptation syndrome (GAS), which suggests that there are three stages in stress responses: alarm and mobilization, resistance, and exhaustion.
- Coping with stress can take a number of forms, including the unconscious use of defense mechanisms and the use of emotion-focused or problem-focused coping strategies.
- Stress can be reduced by developing a sense of control over one's circumstances. In some cases, however, people develop a state of learned helplessness.

EVALUATE

1. _____ is defined as a response to challenging or threatening events.
2. Match each portion of the GAS with its definition.

1. Alarm and mobilization	**a.** Ability to adapt to stress diminishes; symptoms appear
2. Exhaustion	**b.** Activation of sympathetic nervous system
3. Resistance	**c.** Use of various strategies to cope with a stressor

3. Stressors that affect a single person and produce an immediate major reaction are known as
   a. Personal stressors
   b. Psychic stressors
   c. Cataclysmic stressors
   d. Daily stressors
4. People with the personality characteristic of _____ seem to be better able to successfully combat stressors.

RETHINK

1. Why are cataclysmic stressors less stressful in the long run than other types of stressors?
2. Given what you know about coping strategies, how would you train people to avoid stress in their everyday lives? How would you use this information with a group of veterans suffering from posttraumatic stress disorder?

Answers to Evaluate Questions

1. Stress; 2. 1-b, 2-a, 3-c; 3. a; 4. hardiness

KEY TERMS

health psychology	background stressors	general adaptation	coping
stress	("daily hassles")	syndrome (GAS)	learned helplessness
cataclysmic events	psychophysiological	psychoneuroimmunology	hardiness
personal stressors	disorders	(PNI)	resilience
posttraumatic stress disorder (PTSD)			

Module 35
Psychological Aspects of Illness and Well-Being

Can simply talking with others about your experiences as a patient fighting cancer extend your life?

As recently as three decades ago, most psychologists and health-care providers would have scoffed at the notion that participating in a discussion group could improve a cancer patient's chances of survival. Today, however, such methods have gained increasing acceptance.

Growing evidence suggests that psychological factors have a substantial impact both on major health problems that were once seen in purely physiological terms and on our everyday sense of health, well-being, and happiness. We'll consider the psychological components of three major health problems: heart disease, cancer, and smoking.

The As, Bs, and Ds of Coronary Heart Disease

Kim knew it wasn't going to be her day when she got stuck in traffic behind a slow-moving farm truck. How could the driver dawdle like that? Didn't they have anything of any importance to do?

Things didn't get any better when Kim arrived on campus and discovered the library didn't have the books she needed, even though she'd checked online earlier to make sure the books would be there. She could literally feel the tension rising.

Kim knew that meant she wouldn't be able to get her paper done early, and that meant she wouldn't have the time she wanted to revise the paper. She wanted it to be a first-class paper. This time, she wanted to get a better grade than her roommate, Lola. Although Lola didn't know it, Kim felt that they were in competition and that Lola was always trying to better her, whether academically or socially.

"In fact," Kim mused to herself, "I feel like I'm in competition with everyone, no matter what I'm doing."

Have you, like Kim, ever seethed impatiently at being caught behind a slow-moving vehicle, felt anger and frustration at not finding material you needed at the library, or experienced a sense of competitiveness with your classmates?

Many of us experience these sorts of feelings at one time or another, but for some people, they represent a pervasive, characteristic set of personality traits known as the Type A behavior pattern. The **Type A behavior pattern** is a cluster of behaviors involving hostility, competitiveness, time urgency, and feeling driven. In contrast, the **Type B behavior pattern** is characterized by a patient, cooperative, noncompetitive, and nonaggressive manner. It's important to keep in mind that Type A and Type B represent the ends of a continuum and most people fall somewhere in between the two endpoints. Few people are purely a Type A or a Type B.

The importance of the Type A behavior pattern lies in its links to coronary heart disease. Men who display the Type A pattern develop coronary heart disease twice as

LEARNING OUTCOMES

LO 35-1 How do psychological factors affect health-related problems such as coronary heart disease, cancer, and smoking?

LO 35-2 What are the psychological impacts of the COVID-19 pandemic?

Type A behavior pattern A cluster of behaviors involving hostility, competitiveness, time urgency, and feeling driven. (Module 35)

Type B behavior pattern A cluster of behaviors characterized by a patient, cooperative, noncompetitive, and nonaggressive manner. (Module 35)

often and suffer significantly more fatal heart attacks than do those classified as having the Type B pattern. Moreover, the Type A pattern predicts who is going to develop heart disease at least as well as–and independently of–any other single factor, including age, blood pressure, smoking habits, and cholesterol levels in the body (Korotkov et al., 2011; Schneiderman et al., 2019; Heine & Weiss, 2021).

Hostility is the key component of the Type A behavior pattern that is related to heart disease. Although competition, time urgency, and feelings of being driven may produce stress and potentially other health and emotional problems, they aren't linked to coronary heart disease the way that hostility is (Lin et al., 2018; Mishra & Srivastava, 2018).

Why is hostility so toxic? The key reason is that hostility produces excessive physiological arousal in stressful situations. That arousal, in turn, results in increased production of the hormones epinephrine and norepinephrine as well as increases in heart rate and blood pressure. Such an exaggerated physiological response ultimately produces an increased incidence of coronary heart disease (Sadeghi et al., 2020; Vella, 2020).

Keep in mind that not everyone who displays Type A behaviors is destined to have coronary heart disease. For one thing, a firm association between Type A behaviors and coronary heart disease has not been established for women; most findings pertain to males partly because, until recently, most research was done on men. In addition, other types of negative emotions besides the hostility found in Type A behavior appear to be related to heart attacks. For example, psychologist Johan Denollet has found evidence that what he calls *Type D*–for "distressed"–behavior is linked to coronary heart disease. In this view, insecurity, anxiety, and the negative outlook Type Ds display put them at risk for repeated heart attacks (Lin et al., 2017; Aluja et al., 2019; Abdollahi et al., 2021).

! Study Alert

It's important to distinguish among Type A (hostility, competitiveness), Type B (patience, cooperativeness), and Type D (distressed) behaviors.

From the perspective of...

A Health-Care Provider What advice would you give to your patients about the connections between personality and disease? For example, would you encourage Type A people to become "less Type A" to decrease their risk of heart disease?

Rubberball/Getty Images

Psychological Aspects of Cancer

Hardly any disease is feared more than cancer. Most people think of cancer in terms of lingering pain, and being diagnosed with the disease is typically viewed as receiving a death sentence.

Although a diagnosis of cancer is not as grim as it once was–several kinds of cancer have a high cure rate if detected early enough–cancer remains the second-leading cause of death after coronary heart disease. The precise trigger for the disease is not well understood, but the process by which cancer spreads is straightforward. Certain cells in the body become altered and multiply rapidly in an uncontrolled fashion. As those cells grow, they form tumors; if left unchecked, the tumors suck nutrients from healthy cells and body tissue and ultimately destroy the body's ability to function properly.

Although the processes involved in the spread of cancer are basically physiological, some research suggests that the emotional responses of cancer patients to their disease may affect its course. For example, some findings show that a "fighting spirit" leads to better coping. On the other hand, there is little evidence that long-term survival rates are better than for patients with less-positive attitudes (Heitzmann et al., 2011; Brandao et al., 2015; Forte et al., 2021).

Despite conflicting evidence, health psychologists believe that patients' emotions may at least partially determine the course of their disease. In the case of cancer, it is possible that positive emotional responses may help generate specialized "killer" cells that help control the size and spread of cancerous tumors. Conversely, negative emotions may suppress the ability of those cells to fight tumors (Mosher et al., 2015; Lutgendorf & Andersen, 2015; Cheng et al., 2019).

Is a particular personality type linked to cancer? Some researchers suggest that cancer patients are less emotionally reactive, suppress anger, and lack outlets for emotional release. However, the data are too tentative and inconsistent to suggest firm conclusions about a link between personality characteristics and cancer. Certainly no conclusive evidence suggests that people who develop cancer would not have done so if their personality had been of a different sort or if their attitudes had been more positive (Porcerelli et al., 2015; Jagielski et al., 2020).

What is increasingly clear, however, is that certain types of psychological therapy have the potential for improving quality of life and even extending the lives of cancer patients by slowing the progression of the disease. For example, the results of one study showed that women with breast cancer who received psychological treatment lived at least a year and a half longer and experienced less anxiety and pain than did women who did not participate in therapy. Research on patients with other health problems, such as heart disease, also has found that therapy can be both psychologically and medically beneficial (Lemogne et al., 2013; Spiegel, 2014; Perrier & Ginis, 2017).

Smoking

Would you walk into a convenience store and buy an item with a label warning you that its use could kill you? Although most people would probably answer no, millions make such a purchase everyday: a pack of cigarettes. Furthermore, they do this despite clear, well-publicized evidence that smoking is linked to cancer, heart attacks, strokes, bronchitis, emphysema, and a host of other serious illnesses. Smoking is the leading preventable cause of death in the United States; worldwide, 8 million people die each year from the effects of smoking (World Health Organization, 2022).

WHY PEOPLE SMOKE

Why do people smoke despite all the evidence showing that it is bad for their health? It is not that they are somehow unaware of the link between smoking and disease; surveys show that most *smokers* agree with the statement "Cigarette smoking frequently causes disease and death." And almost three-quarters of the nearly 40 million cigarette smokers in the United States say they would like to quit (Price, 2008; Centers for Disease Control and Prevention, 2013, 2019).

Although smoking is prohibited in an increasing number of places, it remains a substantial social problem.

Jack Holtel/McGraw Hill

Genetics seems to determine, in part, whether people will become smokers, how much they will smoke, and how easily they can quit. Genetics also influence how susceptible people are to the harmful effects of smoking. For instance, although Black Americans smoke at slightly lower rates (13%) than White Americans (14%), they are more likely to die from smoking-related illnesses than White people. This difference may be due to genetically produced variations in how efficiently enzymes can reduce the effects of the cancer-causing chemicals in tobacco smoke. Another explanation is that Blacks receive lower-quality health care if they do get sick from smoking (Minică, 2017; Kamimura et al., 2018; Erzurumluoglu et al., 2019).

Although genetics plays a role in smoking, social factors are the primary cause of the habit. Smoking at first may be seen as "cool" or sophisticated, as a rebellious act, or as facilitating calm performance in stressful situations. Exposure to smoking in media such as film also leads to a higher risk of becoming an established smoker. In addition, smoking is sometimes viewed as a "rite of passage" for adolescents, undertaken at the urging of friends and seen as a sign of growing up (Dono et al., 2020; Wailoo, 2021; Wu et al., 2022).

Ultimately, smoking becomes a habit. And it's an easy habit to pick up: Smoking even a single cigarette can lead to a smoker finding that *not* smoking requires an effort or involves discomfort. Subsequently, people begin to label themselves smokers, and smoking becomes part of how they view themselves. Moreover, they become dependent physiologically because nicotine, a primary ingredient of tobacco, is highly addictive.

When people become addicted to smoking, a complex relationship develops among smoking, nicotine levels, and a smoker's emotions. When this happens, a certain nicotine level becomes associated with a positive emotional state brought about by smoking. As a result, people smoke in an effort to regulate *both* their emotional states and the nicotine levels in the blood (Dennis, 2011; Martin & Savette, 2018; Poormahdy et al., 2022).

Vaping and E-cigarettes The newest trend in smoking is *vaping*, the inhalation of vapors created by electronic cigarettes. *Electronic cigarettes*, or *e-cigarettes*, are battery-powered, cigarette-shaped devices that deliver nicotine that is vaporized to form a mist. Some e-cigarettes, such as those manufactured by Juul, contain replaceable pods, while some newer versions of vaping products consist of one-time use disposables. All provide the experience of smoking tobacco.

The popularity of e-cigarettes grew exponentially at first, though recently use has begun to decline. Still, the habit is increasingly concerning to medical experts. For example, the use among high school students is considerable: More than a third have tried e-cigarettes at least once, and the numbers continue to rise. Data from the Centers for Disease Control and Prevention show that e-cigarette use among middle- and high-school age youth rose 900% between 2011 and 2015, surpassing use of every other form of tobacco among those age groups. About 20% of 12th-grade students report using e-cigarettes in the prior month (Miech et al., 2021; Johnston et al., 2022; see Figure 1).

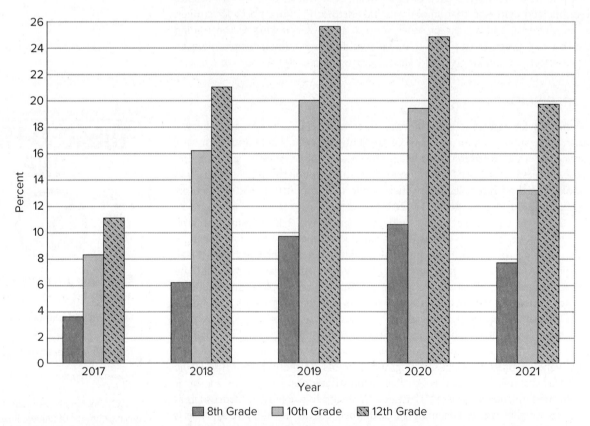

FIGURE 1 The percentage of teenagers who reported using nicotine vaping products in the past month soared from 2017 to 2019, but more recently, it has begun to decline.

Source: Johnston et al., 2022.

The trend is worrisome for several reasons. Although e-cigarettes do not contain the tar and other toxic chemicals found in cigarette smoke, the nicotine itself is harmful to developing adolescent brains. Also, in an increasing number of cases, contaminants in e-cigarettes have led to serious health consequences, lung damage, and, in some cases, even the deaths of users. Some municipalities have banned the sale of vaping equipment, and in 2022, the U.S. Food and Drug Administration considered banning vaping and e-cigarette products sold by the manufacturer Juul (Sun, 2019; Jewett, 2022).

This is because the nicotine in e-cigarettes such as Juul is an addictive substance that can become a long-term habit. Furthermore, some research suggests that young users may be more prone to smoke regular cigarettes in the future, although the research findings are mixed on this point. Such concerns have led to laws restricting advertising targeted at teenagers and banning flavor additives (Centers for Disease Control and Prevention, 2015, 2019; Struik et al., 2020; Kostygina et al., 2021).

The risks of vaping are becoming more apparent as increasing research shows its dangers.
pixinoo/Shutterstock

Because they are so new, little is known about the long-term effects of using e-cigarettes. Teenagers who have a clear understanding of the risks of cigarette smoking are often unsure about the risks of using e-cigarettes, and instead, they point to benefits such as looking cool and being trendy, as well as enjoying the flavorings of the e-cigarettes.

Not surprisingly, teens who perceive e-cigarettes as being less harmful than are other forms of tobacco are more likely to use them, even if they have never tried any form of tobacco before. Although some research finds that e-cigarette use may make it easier to give up smoking of regular cigarettes, the rise in e-cigarette use remains of deep concern (Giovenco & Delnevo, 2018).

QUITTING SMOKING

Because smoking has both psychological and biological components, few habits are as difficult to break. Long-term successful treatment typically occurs in just 15% of those who try to stop smoking; once smoking becomes a habit, it is as hard to stop as an addiction to cocaine or heroin. In fact, some of the biochemical reactions to nicotine are similar to those to cocaine, amphetamines, and morphine. Furthermore, changes in brain chemistry brought about by smoking may make smokers more resistant to anti-smoking messages (Ostroumov et al., 2020; Mahajan et al., 2021; So, 2021).

Many people try to quit smoking but fail. The average smoker tries to quit 8–10 times before being successful, and many smokers try 30 times before they succeed. And even then, many relapse. Even long-time quitters can fall off the wagon: About 10% relapse after more than a year of avoiding cigarettes (U.S. Department of Health and Human Services, 2020; Gravely et al., 2022).

Among the most effective tools for ending the smoking habit are drugs that replace the nicotine found in cigarettes. Whether in the form of gum, patches, nasal sprays, or inhalers, these products provide a dose of nicotine that reduces dependence on cigarettes. In addition, e-cigarettes containing nicotine are more effective than other nicotine substitutes in helping smokers quit, although for some people, the risk of vaping may outweigh the benefits of smoking cessation (Hajek et al., 2019; Chan et al., 2021; Hajek et al., 2022).

Another approach is exemplified by the medications Zyban and Chantix. Rather than replacing nicotine, they reduce the pleasure from smoking and suppress withdrawal symptoms that smokers experience when they try to stop (Dawkins et al., 2019; Rosen et al., 2021).

Behavioral strategies, which view smoking as a learned habit and concentrate on changing the smoking response, can also be effective. Initial "cure" rates of 60% have been reported, and 1 year after treatment, more than half of those who quit have not resumed smoking. Individual or group counseling also increases the rate of success in breaking the habit. The best treatment seems to be a combination of nicotine

FIGURE 2 Teenage smoking. Although smoking among teenagers has declined considerably over the past several decades, a significant number still report smoking regularly. What factors might account for the continued high use of tobacco by teenagers despite the increase in antismoking advertising?
Source: Johnston et al., 2022.

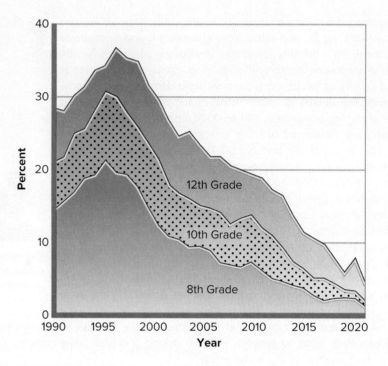

replacement and counseling. What doesn't work? Going it alone: Only 5% of smokers who quit cold turkey on their own are successful (Woodruff et al., 2007; Green & Lynn, 2019; World Health Organization, 2019b).

In the long term, the most effective means of reducing smoking may be changes in societal norms and attitudes toward the habit. For instance, many cities and towns in the United States have made smoking in public places illegal; legislation based on strong popular sentiment that bans smoking in places such as college classrooms and buildings is being passed with increasing frequency. In addition, smokers are more likely to quit when their friends are quitting, so the social support of others quitting is helpful (Christakis & Fowler, 2008; McDermott et al., 2013; Mollen et al., 2017).

The long-term effect of the barrage of information regarding the negative consequences of smoking on people's health has been substantial; overall, smoking has declined over the last two decades, particularly among males. Still, more than one-fourth of students enrolled in high school are active smokers by the time they graduate, and there is evidence that the decline in smoking is leveling off. Among these students, around 10% become active smokers as early as the 8th grade (Fichtenberg & Glantz, 2006; Johnston et al., 2017; see Figure 2).

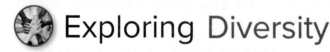 # Exploring Diversity

Reducing Health Disparities to Attain Health Equity

Consider these stark health disparities that exist in the United States today (Caratala & Maxwell, 2020; Nafiu et al., 2020; Centers for Disease Control and Prevention, 2022; Kelly, 2022; Sun et al., 2022):

- Black women are three times more likely to die from a pregnancy-related cause than are White women.
- Among Black Americans, 11 infant deaths occur per 1,000 live births—about twice the national average.
- Compared with only 8% of non-Hispanic Whites, 17% of American Indians and Alaska Natives, 14% of African Americans, and 10% of Hispanics report being in fair or poor health.

- In counties with high segregation, Black children experience greater poverty and higher infant mortality than those living in counties with less segregation.
- Black children suffer more postsurgery problems than White children, even when controlling for degree of healthfulness.
- Black patients are 2.5 times more likely to be labeled as uncooperative than are White patients, according to notes in their medical records

These are just a few of many health disparities that characterize health care and health outcomes in the United States. And health disparities are the norm around the world: In every country, the lower the socioeconomic status of an individual, the poorer the health outcomes. Ultimately, these health disparities are associated with higher rates of death and with life expectancy in low-income countries being 18 years lower than in high-income countries (Population & Public Health, 2020; Kelly, 2022).

Clearly, poorer health outcomes are tied to poorer economic and environmental conditions. But they are also linked to racial, ethnic, and cultural discrimination, and the sources of the disparities are complex, involving characteristics of the individual and the health-care providers.

Consider the research on differences in the treatment of pain as it relates to racial and ethnic identity. Psychologist Jennifer Kelly, who has written extensively on such health disparities, points out that African Americans tend to be undertreated for pain, in part because some health-care providers believe that the bodies of Black individuals are biologically different from those of White individuals, with Black patients being less susceptible to pain than are White patients—a belief that is not supported by any research. Providers who endorse this false belief rate the pain experienced by their Black patients as lower, and they are more likely to make inaccurate treatment recommendations. In short, some Black patients are receiving inadequate pain relief because of the stereotyped beliefs held by their health-care providers (Hoffman et al., 2016; Kelly, 2022).

Moreover, existing health disparities became even more pronounced during the COVID pandemic. Not only were people of color more likely to become infected with COVID, vaccines were less available to them, and they received less adequate treatment, both for physical and mental health issues (Gollust et al., 2022; Thomeer et al., 2022; Willems et al., 2022).

Health disparities do not only take a toll on physical and mental health. They have a significant economic cost as well. For example, the Center for Medicare Advocacy argues that the U.S. health system would save many billions of dollars in direct and indirect health-care costs each year if health disparities were eliminated (Center for Medicare Advocacy, 2022).

In short, psychological, social, economic, and moral needs underlie the goal of working to eliminate health-care inequities. Psychologists are seeking to address the problems, along with practitioners in other disciplines. Although achieving health equity is a daunting challenge, the goal is essential.

The Psychological Impacts of the COVID-19 Pandemic

For Noe Rodriguez, Jr., the symptoms started with stomach issues, but they soon became more severe–like a terrible case of flu, along with breathing problems. After testing positive for COVID, Noe's symptoms worsened. He stopped making sense, and his oxygen levels plummeted. He was rushed to the hospital, and his two children, 16-year-old Izzy and 11-year-old Sonny, were never able to speak to him again. After falling into a coma, he died just over 3 weeks later. He was unvaccinated for COVID, sharing with family that he was waiting until the vaccine was FDA-approved to get his shot. When he died, the vaccine had already been approved, months earlier (Griswald, 2022).

By 2022, over a million people in the United States died due to the COVID pandemic; worldwide, more than 6 million people lost their lives. Life expectancy in the United States dropped by 3 years in 2020 and 2021, the greatest 2-year decline in a century. Like Izzy and Sonny, an estimated 200,000 children in the United States lost a parent. And many children lost both parents and additional relatives to a pandemic that relentlessly turned the world upside down (Rabin, 2022; World Health Organization, 2022).

But the COVID-19 pandemic did not only produce physical illness and death. The psychological toll has been significant. In fact, in some ways, the pandemic was as much a psychological phenomenon as a medical event (Rosenfeld et al., 2022).

Health psychologists, along with psychologists specializing in nearly every area of the field, have brought their expertise to better understanding COVID and helping those affected by it. Here, we'll look at some ways in which the pandemic affected people's behavior, examining topics ranging from stress and the importance of social support, to vaccination hesitancy and learning loss.

STRESS AND THE PANDEMIC

Virtually no one was immune to the stress produced by the pandemic. Although it played out differently for each individual, during the height of the pandemic, people were forced to engage in constant risk assessment based on ever-changing conditions. Was the transmission rate of the virus going up or down? How risky was public transportation? Would schools be open or closed next week? Do I really need to follow the current mask mandate? Should I disinfect my groceries after I bring them home? Can I hang out with my friends? Can I have sex with my partner?

People were weighing and evaluating such questions for themselves at the same time that scientists were refining their understanding of the disease and how it was transmitted. In fact, the scale of stressors was considerable, ranging from simply figuring out how to live in a world with COVID, how to keep oneself and others safe, how to manage when a close relation became ill, and of course, what to do when and if you contracted it. And beyond the fear of COVID itself were the challenges of everyday life: dealing with job issues, child care, home schooling, and a host of others. In the face of all this, many people experienced stress, along with several other emotion-laden problems (Pakpour et al., 2021; Aknin et al., 2022; Hadjistavropoulos & Asmundson, 2022; see Figure 3).

Even after treatments for the virus became widely available and the overall death rates from the pandemic began to decline, many people still experienced unusually high levels of stress. This was particularly true for members of racial and ethnic minority groups. While people of color had to contend with all the objective threats to health, safety, and financial insecurity, the pandemic also highlighted instances of systemic racism as well as discrimination and prejudice. For example, the number of hate crimes grew to historically high levels during the pandemic, including a spike in anti-Asian and anti-Semitic crimes (American Psychological Association, 2020; Lee, 2022; Jones, 2022).

FIGURE 3 Reactions to COVID. The coronavirus pandemic caused considerable stress and anxiety while also disrupting many other areas of life among college students.
Source: Active Minds, 2020.

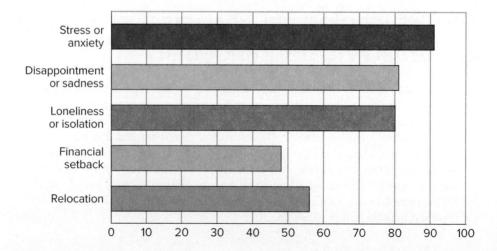

Moreover, data showed that Blacks and Hispanics were hospitalized and died from the virus at disproportionately high levels. In fact, at one point early in the pandemic, the COVID death rate was almost 10 times higher in urban areas, where the population was largely made up of people of color, than in predominantly White counties, even in areas with similar income levels (Aubrey, 2020; Moyer, 2021).

In addition, groups that have traditionally been discriminated against suffered disproportionally from the pandemic in other ways. For example, they had relatively less access to computers and the Internet, making it harder to deal with work and school disruptions (Atske & Perrin, 2021).

Overall, during the pandemic, Hispanic, Black, and Asian adults experienced higher levels of stress than non-Hispanic White adults (see Figure 4). The higher levels of stress among Hispanic individuals can be explained in part by the findings that they were considerably more likely to know someone who had been sick with or died of COVID. Moreover, compared with other groups, Hispanic individuals were more likely to say that they were struggling with the pandemic and felt less able to manage the stress they felt (American Psychological Association, 2021).

In other demographic groups, parents were especially affected by stress due to the pandemic. In addition to the usual challenges of parenting, those who were able to stay home had to mentor their children academically as they struggled with online classes, many times balancing their own remote jobs with their children's schooling. Also, because schools were physically closed, parents who were front-line workers had to find places for children to learn while they went to work. The toll was great: Almost half of parents reported struggling to make even simple decisions such as what to wear or eat. Three-quarters of parents said that family responsibilities were a significant source of stress (American Psychological Association, 2021).

Although those who experience unusually high levels of stressors typically tend to return to their original baseline levels once the stressor ends, this pattern didn't hold during the pandemic. Given that the pandemic had no clear endpoint, the related stress often lingered. And that, as we consider next, has led to considerable declines in mental health.

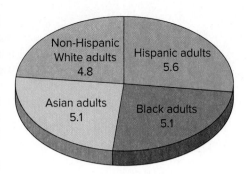

FIGURE 4 During the pandemic, Hispanic, Black, and Asian people in the United States reported higher levels of stress than non-Hispanic Whites.

Source: American Psychological Association, 2021.

THE PANDEMIC AND MENTAL HEALTH

According to the World Health Organization, the pandemic brought about a 25% increase in the prevalence of anxiety and depression across the globe. Although mental health declines were reported across all populations, younger people, women, and those with preexisting health conditions were particularly vulnerable to these problems (World Health Organization, 2022).

Data from the United States are consistent with findings from around the globe. For instance, studies revealed that by the end of 2020, the year the pandemic began, more than 4 in 10 U.S. individuals had experienced anxiety or depressive symptoms. This level of anxiety was significantly higher than what had been observed the previous year. Moreover, the American Academy of Pediatrics declared a state of emergency regarding child and adolescent mental health, in part because so many children and adolescents had been affected by the deaths of their primary caregivers (American Academy of Pediatrics, 2021; Drexler, 2021).

Among college students, levels of psychological distress reached new heights during the pandemic. For example, 41% of students reported feeling depressed, and 34% experienced clinical levels of anxiety. Although these are the highest levels since data began being collected in 2007, they have been gradually rising for years. Still, the pandemic likely exacerbated the trend, and in fact, these results are consistent with increases in depression and anxiety seen in younger adolescents during the pandemic (De France et al., 2021; Lipson et al., 2022).

The day-to-day logistical and emotional challenges that life presented during the pandemic were not the only reason mental health deteriorated. Contracting COVID itself had the potential to instigate psychological disorders. For instance, in one study, researchers recruited people who had no mental health diagnoses or treatment for

2 years before the pandemic. They then compared the mental health of those who had contracted COVID with those who had not. The finding was that those who had contracted COVID were 38% more likely to display stress and adjustment disorders than those who had not. Similarly, those with COVID were 80% more likely to develop cognitive problems such as brain fog, confusion, and forgetfulness than those who hadn't become ill (Xie et al., 2022).

Why would having COVID increase the risk of psychological disorders? The answer probably lies in the intersection of psychology and biology. For example, COVID can produce inflammation or tiny clots in the brain and can cause small strokes. Also, the immune response that is activated in the body to fight off COVID may remain effectively stuck in the "on" position and similarly produce lingering brain inflammation. In turn, these bodily responses can produce stress that leads to psychological symptoms (Belluck, 2022; also see the *Neuroscience and Your Life* feature).

NEUROSCIENCE IN YOUR LIFE: MENTAL HEALTH AND THE BRAIN AFTER COVID

Physical health and mental health are closely intertwined, partly because they both relate to brain health. COVID-19 gives a great example of these interrelationships. About 30% of COVID survivors have experienced depression, posttraumatic distress, and other psychological symptoms for weeks or even months after recovering from the virus. Neuroscience studies show how these symptoms are linked to the structure and function of the brain. One study of COVID survivors found that greater levels of depressive symptoms and distress 2–3 months after COVID were associated with smaller brain volumes and unhealthy white matter tracts (bundles of nerve fibers that connect parts of the brain) in regions linked to mood and anxiety disorders in other studies (Benedetti et al., 2021).

These psychological symptoms may have been directly caused by the body's response to COVID-19. This is because infections and illnesses such as COVID-19 can cause systematic inflammation—an overactivation of the immune system that puts the body at risk for complications such as damage to the brain. In fact, research shows that COVID survivors who had the most systemic inflammation while they had the virus also had the most damage to their brain months later, demonstrating how a medical condition can affect the brain, which in turn increases the risk for emotional symptoms.

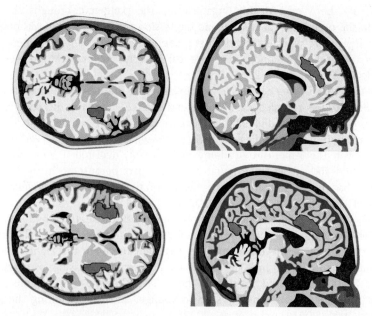

The brain regions shown in orange have been linked to depression, posttraumatic stress disorders, and other mental health conditions. In COVID survivors, higher symptoms of depression (top row) and distress (bottom row) were associated with smaller volumes in those brain regions.

Note that not all psychological disturbances increased in frequency as a result of the pandemic. For example, suicide rates for most populations did not increase. Furthermore, people reported that even during the pandemic, they experienced improved mental health on days in which they engaged in certain activities that generally reduce stress, including exercising, spending time in nature, reading, or volunteering (Aknin et al., 2022).

In addition, some people who had relatively higher levels of anxiety before the pandemic actually found that their anxiety level declined during the pandemic. The reason for this counterintuitive phenomenon was that those with high levels of anxiety often fear that they will do something wrong in everyday social situations. When their social lives became restricted and they had fewer interactions with others, highly anxious people felt relieved. And ironically, their anxiety may increase the more that life returns to normal (Özmete & Pak, 2020; Drexler, 2021).

LONELINESS, SOCIAL ISOLATION, AND THE IMPORTANCE OF SOCIAL SUPPORT

Consider the measures that public health officials urged people to follow during the height of the pandemic:

- Physical social distancing
- Sheltering in place
- Travel bans
- Remote learning, which kept students out of physical classrooms and schools
- Office closures, resulting in fewer opportunities to work with and socialize with coworkers

All these practices led to increases in **social isolation**; that is, the number of social interactions declined and the size of social networks diminished. However, social isolation is not the same as loneliness. Loneliness is a subjective state. **Loneliness** occurs when people cannot experience the level of connection with others that they desire. In short, a person can be totally physically alone and not feel lonely, or someone can be in the midst of a crowd and feel lonely (Dahlberg, 2021; Rumas et al., 2021; Kung et al., 2022).

Several carefully crafted research studies showed the experience of loneliness generally increased during the pandemic. On the other hand, for some people, loneliness was not an issue. For example, some less-outgoing individuals were content to be socially isolated, and their isolation was actually a plus for them (Buecker & Horstmann, 2021; Holt-Lunstad, 2021; Ernst et al., 2022).

But for those who did experience loneliness during the pandemic, it was in part because they lost the social support of others. It turns out, as we discuss next, that social support typically has a protective effect, which allows people to cope with stress more effectively (Li et al., 2021).

The Importance of Social Support During the Pandemic In general, our relationships with others help us cope with stress. Researchers have found that having **social support**—that is, being part of a mutual network of caring, interested others—enables us to experience lower levels of stress, better cope with the stress we do undergo, and experience better health in general (García-Herrero et al., 2013; Pietromonaco & Collins, 2017; Braasch et al., 2019).

During the coronavirus pandemic, the importance of social support was embodied in the frequently repeated phrase "We're all in this together." Even while isolated, many people craved the company of others, and many sought social engagement through Zoom calls and other social media. These online connections made the negative, socially isolating aspects of the pandemic more tolerable (Pfefferbaum & North, 2020; Szkody et al., 2021).

social isolation The experience in which the objective number of social interactions are reduced and the size of a person's social networks is diminished. (Module 44)

loneliness The lack of experiencing the level of connection with others that a person seeks. (Module 44)

social support A mutual network of caring, interested others. (Module 34)

The social and emotional support people provide each other helps in dealing with stress in several ways. For instance, such support demonstrates that a person is an important and valued member of a social network. Similarly, connections with other people are sources for information and advice about appropriate ways of dealing with stress (Day & Livingstone, 2003; Lindorff, 2005; Li et al., 2015).

Finally, people who are part of a social support network can provide actual, physical aid to others in stressful situations. For instance, they might supply temporary living quarters to a person whose roommate tested positive for COVID, or they might offer study help to a student who is experiencing stress because of poor academic performance (Takizawa et al., 2007).

Even casual acquaintances who are part of one's social networks might have helped reduce stress and provide health benefits during COVID: for example, people you knew from the gym who you arranged to work out with over Zoom, the person you regularly saw behind the counter at the dining commons and checked in with through Facebook, even strangers who you repeatedly said hello to while waiting for a bus and then ran into by chance while out on a daily walk. The greater one's social integration, the greater the benefits (Cohen et al., 2019; Kinkade & Fuller, 2021).

Recent research is also beginning to identify ways in which social support affects brain processing. For instance, one experiment found that activation in the brain areas reflecting stress was reduced when social support–simply being able to hold the hand of another person–was available (Coan et al., 2006; Graff et al., 2019; also see the *Applying Psychology in the 21st Century* feature).

Refusing to vaccinate one's children can have deadly consequences for that child and the many others they may encounter.
CHBD/E+/Getty Images

VACCINE HESITANCY AND THE COVID-19 VACCINE

One of the greatest public health success stories of the past hundred years has been the development and widespread use of vaccines. Vaccines drastically reduced the spread of COVID and reduced the consequences of the disease for those who became infected. Other vaccines have totally eradicated smallpox, largely eliminated polio in most of the world, and prevented countless millions of cases of other potentially crippling or deadly diseases such as measles, mumps, rubella, tetanus, and influenza. Through systematic research, vaccines have been thoroughly established as both safe and effective (Dudley et al., 2020; Sonawane et al., 2021; Gesualdo et al., 2022).

Yet, none of these facts has stopped laypersons and politicians from challenging the scientific consensus on vaccine safety. During the pandemic, a significant minority of people refused to get vaccinated, saying the vaccines were developed too quickly, weren't safe, had life-threatening side effects, were a scheme by "Big Pharma" to make a quick profit, or represented a government plot to subjugate the American citizenry. Others claimed that the vaccines caused organ damage, harmed pregnant women, or were themselves responsible for spreading COVID. Although they had no scientific evidence for any of these objections, many people came to believe them, and such antivaccine misinformation still exists across social media and the internet (Aw et al., 2021; Wallis, 2021; Peterson et al., 2022).

As a result, many people–even some health-care workers–became reluctant to get vaccinated. In fact, some people refused to believe that COVID itself existed. Some deniers maintained these extreme beliefs even as they were being treated for severe cases and even as they were close to death due to the disease (Abbasi, 2021; Lavorgna & Myles, 2021; Wang et al., 2022).

Vaccine hesitancy is hardly new, however. For decades, some parents have refused to vaccinate their children, based on religious or philosophical grounds. These parents claim, without scientific evidence, that vaccines are dangerous or deadly, often based on a single study that purported to show a link between the measles, mumps, and rubella (MMR) vaccine and autism---a study that was discredited and retracted.

APPLYING PSYCHOLOGY IN THE 21ST CENTURY

RELIEVING THE ISOLATION OF THE PANDEMIC: TALK TO A STRANGER

For many people, the COVID pandemic brought an unprecedented degree of social isolation, and it caused a variety of negative consequences for their mental health and quality of life. Considerable research evidence shows that maintaining strong social connectedness supports both emotional well-being and physical health, including the risk of dying. But are these protective benefits limited to social contact with close others, or can they be derived even from contact with strangers?

One recent study suggests that they can. The researchers argued that although we tend to think otherwise, the reality is that most interactions with strangers are basically positive, that most people show kindness to strangers, and that the majority of interactions with strangers actually enhance well-being (Holt-Lunstad, 2021; Van Lange & Columbus, 2021).

For example, research finds that people are much less willing to take the last remaining food item from a buffet table when they believe that other diners may come along after them; the concern that "someone else may want this" leads them to put even unknown others before themselves. And kindness to strangers isn't limited to low-stakes situations; in another study, researchers dropped thousands of wallets in various locales around the world,

Diners at a buffet are unwilling to take the last bit of food if they think other people may come along after them, showing a form of kindness to strangers.
luckybusiness/123rf

and while there was geographic variability in the likelihood that strangers would return the found wallets, almost universally, the strangers were more likely to do so when the wallet contained money than when it did not (Van Doesum et al., 2018; Cohn et al., 2019).

Most tellingly, research evidence suggests that interactions with strangers can enhance well-being. Examples abound: People who have more casual acquaintances tend to be happier than those who have

fewer. Most job-seekers find employment through casual acquaintances–often from people they seldom even see. Feeling ignored or excluded, even by total strangers, tends to make people feel bad. People who greet others frequently, even if briefly, report greater feelings of belongingness and well-being. And in experimental studies in which people are directed to initiate a single brief pleasant encounter with a stranger (such as a bus driver, a fellow commuter, or a coffee vendor), they subsequently show an increase in reported happiness. Even the person who was randomly greeted feels happier (Epley & Schroeder, 2014; Sandstrom & Dunn, 2014a)!

Moreover, interactions with strangers may even offer some benefits that are not experienced in interactions with closer connections. These include low likelihood of any shared information spreading beyond that one interaction, benefiting from new perspectives, and exposure to new opportunities.

The conclusion? Talking to strangers is a bit like taking a daily multivitamin: It's unlikely to hurt, and it might help!

RETHINK

- Based on these research findings, would you predict that people whose jobs involve considerable interaction with the public would tend to be happier than those who work in relative solitude? Why or why not?
- Do you think that having many shallow acquaintances (such as social media connections) can compensate for having fewer close relationships? Why or why not?

Furthermore, social media has enabled widespread conspiracy theories and other misinformation to influence public discourse on vaccine safety, despite the fact that absolutely no scientific evidence supports a link between vaccines and autism (Eggertson, 2010; Hviid et al., 2019).

This all might not be a concern if vaccine-deniers were putting only their own health at risk by refusing vaccines. But in many cases, they are risking the health of their children, who have no voice in the decision. Moreover, their refusal increases the number of unvaccinated children in schools and in the community, thus increasing the number of children who can potentially contract and spread diseases. In turn, then, these parents are also risking the health of other people who cannot be vaccinated for medical reasons or because they are still too young (Kluger, 2019).

Psychologists have sought to understand the source of the disconnect between the clear messages from the scientific community on the safety of vaccines and the persistent skepticism from those involved in the antivaccine ("antivax") movement. Past research on a phenomenon known as the *Dunning-Kruger effect* shows that people can be so ignorant about a body of knowledge that they lack even the understanding necessary to appreciate the depth of their own ignorance; as a result, they tend to overestimate and express overconfidence in their understanding (Motta et al., 2018; Canady & Larzo, 2022).

In the case of the antivaccine movement, the Dunning-Kruger effect may cause antivax supporters to value their own opinions over those of scientists. In short, people who think they know better than medical experts about the causes of a disease tend to overestimate their knowledge and to support information and public policy decisions that align with their limited, but overly certain, understanding of the issue (Light et al., 2022).

RECAP/EVALUATE/RETHINK

RECAP

LO 35-1 How do psychological factors affect health-related problems such as coronary heart disease, cancer, and smoking?

- Hostility, a key component of the Type A behavior pattern, is linked to coronary heart disease. The Type A behavior pattern is a cluster of behaviors involving hostility, competitiveness, time urgency, and feeling driven.
- People's attitudes and emotional responses may affect the course of cancer through links to the immune system.
- Smoking, the leading preventable cause of health problems, has proved to be difficult to quit, even though most smokers are aware of the dangerous consequences of the behavior.

LO 35-2 What are the psychological impacts of the COVID-19 pandemic?

- The COVID pandemic produced unusually high levels of stress, particularly among the most vulnerable populations.
- Mental health declined considerably as a result of the pandemic. For example, anxiety and depression increased by 25% across the globe during the start of the pandemic. Younger people, women, parents, and those with preexisting health conditions were particularly vulnerable.
- Although loneliness increased for many people due to the social isolation of the pandemic, social support helped people cope with stress.

EVALUATE

1. Type _____ behavior is characterized by cooperativeness and being easygoing; Type _____ behavior is characterized by hostility and competitiveness.

2. The Type A behavior pattern is known to directly cause heart attacks. True or false?
3. Smoking is used to regulate both nicotine levels and emotional states in smokers. True or false?
4. Social _____ helped people cope with the stress of the pandemic, as it does in other circumstances.
5. Despite the lack of scientific support for their view, a significant minority of parents believe that childhood vaccines pose a danger and should be avoided. True or false?

RETHINK

1. Is there a danger of "blaming the victim" when we argue that the course of cancer can be improved if a person with the disease holds positive attitudes or beliefs, particularly when we consider people with cancer who are not recovering? Explain your answer.
2. What were the unique qualities of the COVID pandemic that made people particularly vulnerable to stress and declines in mental health?
3. How can people prepare themselves psychologically for future pandemics?

Answers to Evaluate Questions

1. B, A; 2. False; Type A behavior is related to a higher incidence of coronary heart disease but does not necessarily cause it directly; 3. True; 4. support; 5. False. The level of stress due to the pandemic was high, and the stress led to a higher level of psychological disorders.

KEY TERMS

Type A behavior pattern	social isolation	social support
Type B behavior pattern	loneliness	

Module 36
Promoting Health and Wellness

When Rishi Patel first noticed the small lump in his arm, he assumed it was just a bruise from the touch football game he had played the previous week. But as he thought about it more, he considered more serious possibilities and decided that he'd better get it checked out at the university health service. But the visit was less than satisfactory. A shy person, Rishi felt embarrassed talking about his medical condition. Even worse, after answering a string of questions, he couldn't even understand the physician's diagnosis and was too embarrassed to ask for clarification.

Many of us share Rishi Patel's attitudes toward health care. We approach physicians the same way we approach auto mechanics. When something goes wrong with the car, we want the mechanic to figure out the problem and then fix it. In the same way, when something isn't working right with our bodies, we want a diagnosis of the problem and then a (we hope, quick) repair.

Yet such an approach ignores the fact that–unlike auto repair–good health care requires taking psychological factors into account. Health psychologists have sought to determine the factors involved in the promotion of good health and, more broadly, a sense of well-being and happiness. Let's take a closer look at two areas they have tackled: increasing compliance with health-related advice and identifying the determinants of well-being and happiness.

LEARNING OUTCOMES

LO 36-1 How do our interactions with physicians affect our health and compliance with medical treatment?

LO 36-2 How does a sense of well-being develop?

Complying with Medical Advice

We're not very good at following medical advice. As many as 85% of patients do not fully comply with their physician's recommendations, sometimes because of misunderstandings or simply forgetting to follow a particular regimen. People may use medications incorrectly, or they may inadvertently take others' medications. Twenty to 30% of medication prescriptions are never filled. In some cases, these errors are deliberate: Patients sometimes practice *creative nonadherence*, in which they alter a prescribed treatment by substituting their own medical judgment. Not surprisingly, patients' lack of medical knowledge may be harmful (Viswanthanan et al., 2012; Brody, 2017; Schönenberg et al., 2022).

As mentioned, noncompliance can result from misunderstanding medical directions. For example, patients with low literacy skills may find complex instructions difficult to understand. In one study, only a third of patients were able to understand that the direction "take two tablets by mouth twice daily" meant that they should take a total of 4 pills a day. Noncompliance can also be caused by emotional factors: Some patients are emotionally unable to accept bad medical news and consequently distort the information to make it less threatening (Landro, 2011; Amorim et al., 2021).

Whatever their causes, noncompliance and medical errors committed by patients and health-care providers are the third-leading cause of death in the United States. More than 250,000 Americans die annually from medical mistakes (DeAngelis, 2016; Sunshine et al., 2019).

COMMUNICATING EFFECTIVELY WITH HEALTH-CARE PROVIDERS

Raquel Barrior lay in the surgical ward as a her doctor drew incision lines on her chest with a felt-tipped pen. The operation would be grueling: 6 hours of surgery to use muscle tissue from her back to reconstruct her breasts, which had been removed months earlier to combat her cancer.

Raquel knew the operation wasn't the worst part; the extended recovery time would be even more grueling. She dreaded the damper it would put on her life as the mother of three young children and a serious runner and swimmer. As the doctor decorated her chest with marker ink, her husband asked a question that no one had asked before. "Is this operation really necessary?"

The answer was mind-blowing: No, it wasn't. If she left her chest as it was, she would recover in half the time with less pain and no adverse effects. The doctor had simply assumed that Raquel would want the reconstructive surgery for cosmetic reasons. Raquel and her husband looked at each other and reached a simultaneous decision. "Get me up off this gurney, please," said Raquel.

Lack of communication between medical care providers and patients can be a major obstacle to good medical care. Such communication failures occur for several reasons. One is that physicians make assumptions about what patients prefer, or they push a specific treatment that they prefer without consulting patients.

Furthermore, the relatively high prestige of physicians may intimidate patients. Patients may also be reluctant to volunteer information that might cast them in a bad light, and physicians may have difficulties encouraging their patients to provide information. In many cases, physicians dominate an interview with questions of a technical nature, whereas patients attempt to communicate a personal sense of their illness and the impact it is having on their lives (Wallace et al., 2013; Xiang & Stanley, 2017; Houwen et al., 2019).

Furthermore, the view many patients hold that physicians are "all-knowing" can result in serious communication problems. Many patients do not understand their treatments yet fail to ask their physicians for clear explanations of a prescribed course of action. About half of all patients are unable to report accurately how long they are to continue taking a medication prescribed for them, and about a quarter do not even know the purpose of the drug. In fact, some patients are not even sure, as they are about to be rolled into the operating room, why they are having surgery (Pugliese et al., 2014; Sheikh et al., 2018; Convie et al., 2020)!

Sometimes patient–physician communication difficulties occur because the material that must be communicated is too technical for patients, who may lack fundamental knowledge about the body and basic medical practices. In an overreaction to this problem, some health-care providers use baby talk (calling patients "honey" or telling them to go "night-night") and assume that patients cannot understand even simple information. In other cases, physicians are uncomfortable breaking bad news to patients, so they use medical jargon to avoid being direct (Mika et al., 2007; Feng et al., 2011; Links et al., 2019).

To address such problems, medical schools increasingly include training to improve the communication skills of health-care providers. For example, they teach physicians to allow patients to speak first and ask questions, and how to convey empathy and honesty through their speech (Reddy, 2015).

The amount and quality of physician–patient communication also are related to the gender of a physician and patient. Overall, female primary-care physicians provide more patient-centered communications than do male primary-care physicians. Furthermore, patients often prefer same-sex physicians (Bertakis et al., 2009; Shin et al., 2015).

Cultural values and expectations also contribute to communication barriers between patients and their physicians. Providing medical advice to a patient whose native language is not English may be problematic. Furthermore, medical practices differ between cultures, and medical practitioners need to be familiar with a patient's culture in order to produce compliance with medical recommendations (Brooks et al., 2019; Al Shamsi et al., 2020).

Finally, the newest approaches to improving communication between health-care providers and patients is *telehealth*, which uses technology to convey information. For example, patients may be virtually reminded using smartphone texting technology to take their prescribed medicines. Similarly, some health-care providers offer virtual office hours in which patients can communicate with them via Zoom or FaceTime (Celi et al., 2017; Chang et al., 2019; Snoswell et al., 2021).

What can patients do to improve communication with health-care providers? Here are some tips (National Institutes of Health, 2022):

- Make a list of your medical questions and concerns before your visit.
- To prepare for a visit, write down the names and dosages of every drug you currently take.
- Take notes during your visit so you can remember what your health-care provider tells you.
- Ask how to access your medical records online and whether you can communicate with your health-care provider via e-mail and phone.
- Consider bringing a friend or relative with you. They can ask questions and in general advocate for you.

INCREASING COMPLIANCE WITH MEDICAL ADVICE

Although compliance with medical advice does not guarantee that a patient's medical problems will go away, it does optimize the possibility that the patient's condition will improve. What, then, can health-care providers do to produce greater compliance on the part of their patients? One strategy is to provide clear instructions to patients regarding drug regimens. Maintaining good, warm relations with patients also leads to increased compliance (Arbuthnott & Sharpe, 2009; Spencer, 2018).

In addition, honesty helps. Patients generally prefer to be well informed–even if the news is bad; their degree of satisfaction with their medical care is linked to how well and how accurately physicians are able to convey the nature of their medical problems and treatments (MacLaine et al., 2021; Artioli et al., 2022).

The way in which a message is framed also can result in more positive responses to health-related information. *Positively framed messages* suggest that a change in behavior will lead to a gain and thus emphasize the benefits of carrying out a health-related behavior. For instance, suggesting that skin cancer is curable if it is detected early and that you can reduce your chances of getting the disease by using a sunscreen places information in a positive frame. In contrast, *negatively framed messages* highlight what you can lose by not performing a behavior. For instance, a physician might say that if

Positively framed messages suggest that a change in behavior will lead to a health-related gain.
UpperCut Images/SuperStock

you don't use sunscreen, you're more likely to get skin cancer, which can kill you if it's not detected early.

What type of message is more effective? It depends on the type of health behavior the health-care provider is trying to bring about. Positively framed messages are best for motivating *preventive* behavior. However, negatively framed messages are most effective in producing behavior that will lead to the detection of a disease (Brookes & Harvey, 2015; Ort et al., 2021).

From the perspective of...

A Health-Care Provider How would you try to better communicate with your patients? How might your techniques vary depending on the patient's background, gender, age, and culture?

Tetra Images/Getty Images

Well-Being and Happiness

What makes for a good life?

This is a question that philosophers and theologians have pondered for centuries. Now health psychologists are turning their spotlight on the question by investigating **subjective well-being,** people's sense of their happiness and satisfaction with their lives (Giannopoulos & Vella-Brodrick, 2011; Vally & D'Souza, 2019).

subjective well-being People's sense of their happiness and satisfaction with their lives. (Module 36)

WHAT ARE THE CHARACTERISTICS OF HAPPY PEOPLE?

Research on the subject of well-being shows that happy people share several characteristics (Nisbet et al., 2011; Burns, 2017; Orúzar et al., 2019):

- *Happy people have high self-esteem.* People who are happy like themselves. This is particularly true in Western cultures, which emphasize the importance of individuality. Furthermore, people who are happy see themselves as more intelligent and better able to get along with others than the average person is. In fact, they may hold *positive illusions* in which they hold moderately inflated views of themselves, believing that they are good, competent, and desirable (McLeod, 2015).

- *Happy people have a strong sense of control over their environment and themselves.* They feel more in control of events in their lives, unlike those who feel they are the pawns of others and who experience learned helplessness.

- *Happy individuals are optimistic.* Their optimism permits them to persevere at tasks and ultimately to achieve more. In addition, their health is better (Efklides & Moraitou, 2013; Fortier & Morgan, 2021).

- *Happy people like to be around other people.* They tend to be extroverted and have a supportive network of close relationships.

- *Happy people don't always feel good.* Happy people feel a range of emotions, both positive and negative, but the key to their happiness is that they can manage their emotions effectively (Ekman & Simon-Thomas, 2021).

Perhaps most important, most people living in a wide variety of circumstances report being at least moderately happy most of the time. Furthermore, life-altering events that one might expect would produce long-term spikes in happiness, such as winning the lottery, probably won't make you much happier than you already are, as we discuss next.

DOES MONEY BUY HAPPINESS?

If you were to win the lottery, would you be happier?

Probably not, at least in the long run. That's the implication of health psychologists' research on subjective well-being. That research shows that although winning the lottery brings an initial surge in happiness, a year later, winners' level of happiness returns to what it was before they won.

A similar pattern, although in reverse, occurs for people who have had extremely serious injuries in accidents, such as losing a limb or becoming paralyzed: Initially, they decline in happiness after the accident. But in the long run, most victims return to their prior levels of happiness after the passage of time (Priester & Petty, 2011; Weimann et al., 2015; Wang et al., 2017).

Why is the level of subjective well-being so stable? One explanation is that people have a general *set point* for happiness, a marker that establishes the tone for one's life. Although specific events may temporarily elevate or depress one's mood (a surprise promotion or a job loss, for example), people ultimately return to their general level of happiness.

Although it is not certain how people's happiness set points are initially established, some evidence suggests that the set point is determined at least in part by genetic factors. Specifically, identical twins who grow up in widely different circumstances turn out to have very similar levels of happiness (Sheldon & Lucas, 2014; Bartells, 2022).

Most people's well-being set point is relatively high. For example, some 30% of people in the United States rate themselves as "very happy," and only 10% rate themselves "not too happy." Most people declare themselves to be "pretty happy." Such feelings are graphically confirmed by people who are asked to place themselves on the measure of happiness illustrated in Figure 1. The scale clearly illustrates that most people view their lives quite positively.

Similar results are found when people are asked to compare themselves with others. For example, when asked "Who of the following people do you think is the happiest?" survey respondents answered "Oprah Winfrey" (23%), "Bill Gates" (7%), "the Pope" (12%), and "yourself" (49%), with 6% saying they didn't know (Black & McCafferty, 1998; Rosenthal, 2003).

Few differences exist between members of different demographic groups. Men and women report being equally happy, and Black Americans are only slightly less likely than White Americans to rate themselves as "very happy." Furthermore, happiness is hardly unique to U.S. culture. Even countries that are not economically prosperous have, on the whole, happy residents (Cummings, 2019; Eternod, 2021).

The bottom line: Money does *not* automatically bring about happiness. It certainly doesn't hurt; one needs some minimal level of income to be happy. For example, research shows that people living in extreme poverty are sadder than those with higher incomes. And the more you earn, the more likely you are to be happy. But a law of

> **Study Alert**
>
> Remember the concept that individuals have a set point (a general, consistent level) relating to subjective well-being.

Faces Scale: "Which face comes closest to expressing how you feel about your life as a whole?"

| 20% | 46% | 27% | 4% | 2% | 1% | 0% |

FIGURE 1 Most people in the United States rate themselves as happy, whereas only a small minority indicate they are "not too happy."
Source: Andrews & Withey, 1976.

diminishing returns comes into play, and increasing amounts of income are related to smaller and smaller amounts of increased happiness (Whillans et al., 2017; Whillians & Dunn, 2019; Killingsworth, 2021; Tauseef, 2022).

Despite the ups and downs of life, then, most people tend to be reasonably happy, and they adapt to the trials and tribulations—and joys and delights—of life by returning to a steady-state level of happiness. In fact, habitual level of happiness can have profound—and even life-prolonging—consequences: Research suggests that happiness may improve one's health (Grover & Helliwell, 2019; Kushlev et al., 2020; Vela & Kamsickas, 2022).

RECAP/EVALUATE/RETHINK

RECAP

LO 36-1 How do our interactions with physicians affect our health and compliance with medical treatment?

- Although patients would often like physicians to base a diagnosis only on a physical examination, communicating one's problem to the physician is equally important.
- Patients may find it difficult to communicate openly with their physicians because of physicians' high social prestige and the technical nature of medical information.

LO 36-2 How does a sense of well-being develop?

- Subjective well-being, the measure of how happy people are, is highest in people with high self-esteem, a sense of control, optimism, and a supportive network of close relationships.

EVALUATE

1. Health psychologists are most likely to focus on which of the following problems with health care?
   a. Incompetent health-care providers
   b. Rising health-care costs
   c. Ineffective communication between physician and patient
   d. Scarcity of medical research funding

2. If you want people to floss more to prevent gum disease, the best approach is to
   a. Use a negatively framed message.
   b. Use a positively framed message.
   c. Have a dentist deliver an encouraging message on the pleasures of flossing.
   d. Provide people with free dental floss.

3. Winning the lottery is likely to
   a. Produce an immediate and long-term increase in the level of well-being.
   b. Produce an immediate but not lingering increase in the level of well-being.
   c. Produce a decline in well-being over the long run.
   d. Lead to an increase in greed over the long run.

RETHINK

1. Do you think stress plays a role in making communication between physicians and patients difficult? Why?
2. If money doesn't buy happiness, what *can* you do to make yourself happier? As you answer, consider the research findings on stress and coping, as well as on emotions.

Answers to Evaluate Questions

1. c; 2. b; 3. b

KEY TERM

subjective well-being

EPILOGUE

In this set of modules, we have explored the intersection of psychology and biology. We have seen how the emotional and psychological experience of stress can lead to physical symptoms of illness, how personality factors may be related to major health problems, and how psychological factors can interfere with effective communication between physician and patient. We have also looked at the other side of the coin, noting that some relatively simple strategies can help us control stress, affect illness, and improve our interactions with physicians.

Turn back to the prologue of this set of modules, about Arlene Amarosi's experience during the pandemic.

1. Why do you think Amarosi's physical and psychological health took a turn for the worse during the COVID-19 pandemic?

2. In a general sense, why would being isolated at home, even with entertainment and access to the Internet, be stressful?

3. What strategies did Amarosi use to cope with the stress of her isolation? What might have been some better strategies? Why do you think she didn't use those better strategies?

4. What might be some reasons why Amarosi did not comply with the advice of her physician? What strategies might her physician have tried to improve Arlene's compliance?

Design Elements: Man with laptop: Dragon Images/Shutterstock; Exclamation point and mobile frame: McGraw Hill; Smartphone: WML Image/Shutterstock; Hands: Stefano Garau/Shutterstock.

VISUAL SUMMARY 11 Health Psychology

MODULE 34 Stress and Coping

Stress: People's response to events that threaten or challenge them

— Interpretation of events is important in determining what is stressful.
  - • Cataclysmic events
  - • Personal stressors
  - • Background stressors (daily stressors)
— Posttraumatic stress disorder (PTSD)

The Cost of Stress

— Psychophysiological disorders: An interaction of psychological, emotional, and physical difficulties

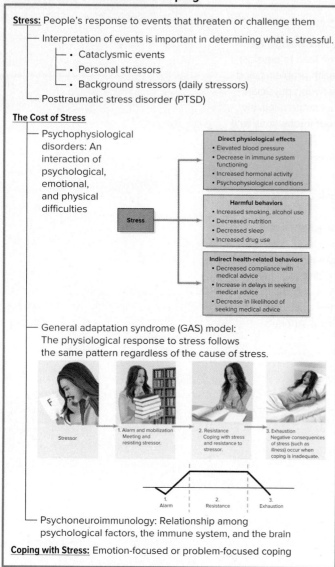

Direct physiological effects
• Elevated blood pressure
• Decrease in immune system functioning
• Increased hormonal activity
• Psychophysiological conditions

Harmful behaviors
• Increased smoking, alcohol use
• Decreased nutrition
• Decreased sleep
• Increased drug use

Indirect health-related behaviors
• Decreased compliance with medical advice
• Increase in delays in seeking medical advice
• Decrease in likelihood of seeking medical advice

— General adaptation syndrome (GAS) model: The physiological response to stress follows the same pattern regardless of the cause of stress.

Stressor

1. Alarm and mobilization Meeting and resisting stressor.

2. Resistance Coping with stress and resistance to stressor.

3. Exhaustion Negative consequences of stress (such as illness) occur when coping is inadequate.

1. Alarm   2. Resistance   3. Exhaustion

— Psychoneuroimmunology: Relationship among psychological factors, the immune system, and the brain

Coping with Stress: Emotion-focused or problem-focused coping

MODULE 35 Psychological Aspects of Illness and Well-Being

Coronary Heart Disease

— Type A behavior: A cluster of behaviors involving hostility, competitiveness, time urgency, and feeling driven
— Type B behavior: Characterized by a patient, cooperative, noncompetitive and nonaggressive manner
— Type D behavior: Insecure, anxious, and negative outlook

Cancer: Psychological therapy may improve quality of life.

Smoking

— Over 5 million people die each year from smoking.
— Heredity, in part, determines whether people will become smokers and are susceptible to harmful effects of smoking.
— Few habits are as difficult to break.

COVID Impacted Indivisuals in a Number of Ways, Particularly Leading to Increases in Stress

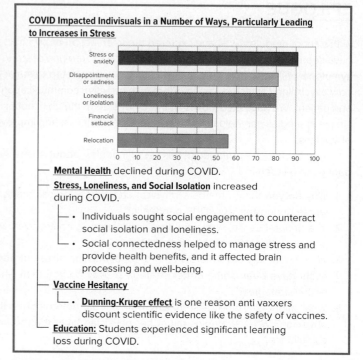

— **Mental Health** declined during COVID.
— **Stress, Loneliness, and Social Isolation** increased during COVID.

  - • Individuals sought social engagement to counteract social isolation and loneliness.
  - • Social connectedness helped to manage stress and provide health benefits, and it affected brain processing and well-being.

— **Vaccine Hesitancy**
  - • **Dunning-Kruger effect** is one reason anti vaxxers discount scientific evidence like the safety of vaccines.
— **Education:** Students experienced significant learning loss during COVID.

MODULE 36 Promoting Health and Wellness

Following Medical Advice: Noncompliance with medical advice takes many forms.

— Communicating with health-care providers.
  - • Lack of communication can be a major obstacle.
— Increasing compliance with medical advice.
  - • Patients prefer to be well informed even if the news is bad.
  - • Positively framed messages: Most likely to motivate preventive behavior.

  - • Negatively framed messages: Most likely to lead to the detection of a disease.

Well-Being and Happiness

— Subjective well-being: People's own evaluation of their lives in terms of their thoughts and their emotions.
— Characteristics of happy people: High self-esteem, sense of control, optimism, enjoy being with others.
— Most people are moderately happy most of the time.

Faces Scale: "Which face comes closest to expressing how you feel about your life as a whole?"

20%   46%   27%   4%   2%   1%   0%

(Module 34): (top): Source: Adapted from Baum, 1994.(Module 35) (photo): pixinoo/Shutterstock; Source: Active Minds, 2020. (Module 36) (photo): UpperCut Images/SuperStock; Source: Andrews & Withey, 1976.

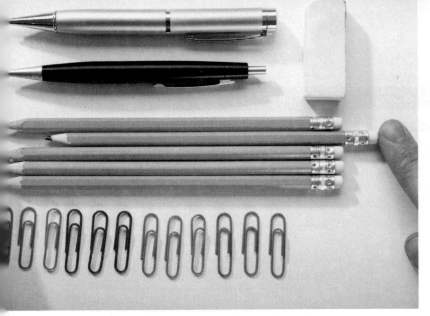

Andrey_Popov/Shutterstock

CHAPTER 12
Psychological Disorders

LEARNING OUTCOMES FOR CHAPTER 12

LO 39-1 How prevalent are psychological disorders?

LO 39-2 What indicators signal a need for the help of a mental health practitioner?

PROLOGUE *HEARING VOICES AND SEEING VISIONS*

For Caroline Mazel-Carlton, the voices in her head started while she was in preschool. By the time she began middle school, the voices had moved from inside her head to outside. Beings that she couldn't see spoke and yelled at her from space around her body. They warned her of catastrophes that would strike her family. They told her that her clothes smelled and that she shouldn't raise her hand in class, even if she was sure of an answer to a question her teacher asked. Another voice followed her around, describing every move she made in a teasing manner. When she was older, a voice told her that it would remove her fingers "one by one by one." In distress, she considered suicide (Bergner, 2022).

LOOKING *Ahead*

Caroline Mazel-Carlton, a victim of a severe psychological disturbance, was losing her grip on reality. Happily, though, today she leads a more typical life due to a variety of treatment approaches. But her experience raises many questions. What caused her disorder? Were genetic factors to blame, or were external events in her life responsible? Could her symptoms have been prevented? And, more generally, how do we identify and classify abnormal behavior?

We address the issues raised by Mazel-Carlton's case in this chapter. We begin by discussing the difference between normal and abnormal behavior, which can be surprisingly indistinct. We then turn to a consideration of the most significant kinds of psychological disorders. Finally, we'll consider ways of evaluating behavior—one's own and that of others—to determine whether seeking help from a mental health professional is warranted.

Module 37
Normal Versus Abnormal: Making the Distinction

Universally that person's acumen is esteemed very little perceptive concerning whatsoever matters are being held as most profitable by mortals with sapience endowed to be studied who is ignorant of that which the most in doctrine erudite and certainly by reason of that in them high mind's ornament deserving of veneration constantly maintain when by general consent they affirm that other circumstances being equal by no exterior splendour is the prosperity of a nation. . . .

You might quickly conclude that these are the musings of someone with serious psychological disabilities; to most of us, the passage does not seem to make any sense at all. But literary scholars disagree. Actually, this passage is from James Joyce's classic *Ulysses,* hailed as one of the major works of 20th-century literature (Joyce, 1934).

As this example illustrates, casually examining a person's writing is insufficient to determine the degree to which that person is "normal." But even when we consider more extensive samples of a person's behavior, we may find only a fine line between behavior that is considered normal and behavior that is considered abnormal.

LEARNING OUTCOMES

LO 37-1 How can we distinguish normal from abnormal behavior?

LO 37-2 What are the major perspectives on psychological disorders used by mental health professionals?

LO 37-3 What are the major categories of psychological disorders?

Defining Abnormality

Because of the difficulty in distinguishing normal from abnormal behavior, psychologists have struggled to devise a precise, scientific definition of "abnormal behavior." For instance, consider the following definitions, each of which has advantages and disadvantages:

- *Abnormality as a deviation from average behavior.* According to this definition, behaviors that are unusual or rare in a society or culture are considered abnormal. It is basically a statistical definition: If most people behave in a certain way, it is viewed as normal; if only a few people do it, it is considered abnormal.

  The difficulty with this definition is that some statistically unusual behaviors hardly seem abnormal. If most people eat meat but you are a vegetarian, this deviation from the average hardly makes your behavior abnormal. Similarly, a concept of abnormality that depends on what is unusual would unreasonably label a person who has an unusually high IQ as abnormal simply because a high IQ is statistically rare. In short, a definition of abnormality that rests on deviation from the average is insufficient.

- *Abnormality as a deviation from an ideal.* An alternative definition of abnormality considers behavior in relation to some kind of ideal or morally appropriate standard toward which most people are striving.

  This sort of definition considers behavior abnormal if it is different from what society considers ideal behavior or from some moral standard. However, society has few ideals on which people universally agree. (For example, it would be hard to find agreement on whether the New Testament, the Koran, the Talmud, or the Book of Mormon provides the most appropriate ideal behavior.) Furthermore, standards that do arise change over time and vary across cultures. Thus, the deviation-from-the-ideal approach is also inadequate.

- *Abnormality as producing a sense of personal discomfort.* A more useful definition concentrates on the psychological consequences of behavior for the individual. In this approach, behavior is considered abnormal if it produces a sense of

Study Alert
Remember the definitions of abnormality: deviation from average behavior, deviation from ideal behavior, a sense of personal discomfort, an inability to function effectively, and abnormality as a legal concept.

Andrea Yates, who initially was found sane by a jury despite having drowned her five children in a bathtub, was later found innocent due to insanity.

Brett Coomer/Pool Houston Chronicle/AP Images

personal distress, anxiety, or guilt in an individual—or if it is harmful to others in some way.

However, even a definition that relies on personal discomfort has drawbacks. For example, in some especially severe forms of mental disturbance, people report feeling wonderful, even though their behavior seems bizarre to others. Similarly, most of us would think that a person who says they hear uplifting messages from Martians would be displaying abnormal behavior even though they may say that the messages bring them great satisfaction.

- *Abnormality as the inability to function effectively.* Most people are able to feed themselves, hold a job, get along with others, and in general live as productive members of society. Yet some are unable to adjust to the demands of society or function effectively.

  According to this view, people who cannot function effectively and adapt to the demands of society are considered abnormal. For example, an unemployed, homeless person living on the street may be considered unable to function effectively. Therefore, the homeless person's behavior can be viewed as abnormal even if they have chosen to live this way. Their inability to adapt to the requirements of society is what makes this person "abnormal," according to this approach.

- *Abnormality as a legal concept.* According to the jury that first heard her case, Andrea Yates, a woman who drowned her five children in a bathtub, was sane. She was sentenced to life in prison for her act (Chan, 2016).

  Although you might question this view (and an appeals court jury overturned the conviction), the initial verdict reflected the way in which the law defines abnormal behavior. To the judicial system, the distinction between normal and abnormal behavior rests on the definition of *insanity*, which is a legal but not a psychological term.

  In fact, the definition of *insanity* varies from one jurisdiction to another. In some states, *insanity* simply means that defendants cannot understand the difference between right and wrong at the time they commit a criminal act. Other states consider whether defendants are substantially incapable of understanding the criminality of their behavior or unable to control themselves. And in some jurisdictions, pleas of insanity are not allowed at all (Yelderman & Miller, 2017; Gilligan, 2019; Appelbaum, 2022).

Clearly, none of the previous definitions is broad enough to cover all instances of abnormal behavior, and the distinction between normal and abnormal behavior often remains ambiguous even to trained professionals. Furthermore, to a large extent, cultural expectations for "normal" behavior in a particular society influence the understanding of "abnormal behavior."

Given the difficulties in precisely defining the construct, psychologists typically use a broad definition of abnormal behavior. Specifically, **abnormal behavior** is generally defined as behavior that causes people to experience distress and hinders them from functioning in their daily lives (Bassett & Baker, 2015; Sue et al., 2021).

abnormal behavior Behavior that causes people to experience distress and prevents them from functioning in their daily lives. (Module 37)

From the perspective of…

An Employer Imagine that you learned that a well-paid employee was arrested for shoplifting a sweater that cost only $24. Would you fire the employee if you thought the behavior was caused by a psychological disorder?

Sam Edwards/OJO Images/age fotostock

Because this definition is imprecise, it's best to view abnormal behavior and normal behavior as marking two ends of a continuum rather than as absolute, precise conditions. Behavior should be evaluated in terms of gradations that range from fully normal functioning to extremely abnormal behavior. Behavior typically falls somewhere between those extremes.

Perspectives on Abnormality: From Superstition to Science

Throughout much of human history, people linked abnormal behavior to superstition, magic, and spells. Individuals who displayed abnormal behavior were accused of being possessed by the devil or some sort of demonic god. Authorities felt justified in "treating" abnormal behavior by attempting to drive out the source of the problem. This often involved whipping, immersion in hot water, starvation, or other forms of torture in which the cure was worse than the affliction (Starkey, 2018).

Contemporary approaches take a more enlightened view. Today, six major perspectives are used to understand psychological disorders. These perspectives, which are discussed next, suggest not only different causes of abnormal behavior but different treatment approaches as well. Furthermore, some perspectives are more applicable to specific disorders than are others.

MEDICAL PERSPECTIVE

When people display the symptoms of tuberculosis, medical professionals can generally find tubercular bacteria in their body tissue. Similarly, the **medical perspective** suggests that when an individual displays symptoms of a psychological disorder, the fundamental cause will be found through a physical examination of the individual, which may reveal a hormonal imbalance, a chemical deficiency, or a brain injury. Indeed, when we speak of mental "illness," "symptoms" of psychological disorders, and mental "hospitals," we are using terminology associated with the medical perspective.

Because a growing body of research shows that many forms of abnormal behavior are linked to biological causes, the medical perspective provides at least part of the explanation for psychological disorders. Yet serious criticisms have been leveled against it. For one thing, some types of abnormal behavior have no apparent biological cause. In addition, some critics have argued that the use of the term *mental illness* implies that people who display abnormal behavior have no responsibility for or control over their actions (Yang et al., 2013; Prior & Bond, 2017).

Still, recent advances in our understanding of the neurological bases of behavior underscore the importance of considering physiological factors in abnormal behavior. For instance, some of the more severe forms of psychological disorders, such as major depression and schizophrenia spectrum disorder, clearly are influenced in important ways by genetic factors and malfunctions in neurotransmitter signals (Pillai et al., 2018; Borgmann-Winter et al., 2019; Tiwari et al., 2022).

PSYCHOANALYTIC PERSPECTIVE

Whereas the medical perspective suggests that biological causes are at the root of abnormal behavior, the **psychoanalytic perspective** holds that abnormal behavior stems from childhood conflicts over opposing wishes regarding sex and aggression. According to Freud, children pass through a series of stages in which sexual and aggressive impulses take different forms and produce conflicts that require resolution. If these childhood conflicts are not dealt with successfully, they remain unresolved in the unconscious and eventually bring about abnormal behavior during adulthood.

To uncover the roots of people's disordered behavior, the psychoanalytic perspective scrutinizes their early life history. However, there is no sure way to link what

medical perspective The perspective that suggests that when an individual displays symptoms of abnormal behavior, the root cause will be found in a physical examination of the individual, which may reveal a hormonal imbalance, a chemical deficiency, or a brain injury. (Module 37)

psychoanalytic perspective The perspective that suggests that abnormal behavior stems from childhood conflicts over opposing wishes regarding sex and aggression. (Module 37)

happens to people during childhood to abnormal behavior that they display as adults. Consequently, we can never be sure that specific childhood experiences can be linked to specific adult abnormal behaviors.

In addition, psychoanalytic theory paints a picture of people as having relatively little control over their behavior. Instead, the theory assumes that behavior is largely guided by unconscious impulses over which people have neither control nor awareness. Consequently, in the eyes of some critics, this perspective suggests that people have little responsibility for their own behavior.

On the other hand, the contributions of psychoanalytic theory have been significant. More than any other approach to abnormal behavior, this perspective highlights the fact that people can have a rich, involved inner life. Furthermore, it underscores that experiences that occurred long ago in the past can have a profound effect on current psychological functioning (Rangell, 2007; Zhang et al., 2022).

BEHAVIORAL PERSPECTIVE

behavioral perspective The approach that suggests that observable, external behavior, which can be objectively measured, should be the focus of study. (Modules 2, 37)

Both the medical and psychoanalytic perspectives look at abnormal behaviors as *symptoms* of an underlying problem. In contrast, the **behavioral perspective** looks at the rewards and punishments in the environment that determine abnormal behavior. It views the disordered behavior itself as the problem. Using the basic principles of learning, behavioral theorists see both normal and abnormal behaviors as responses to various stimuli–responses that have been learned through past experience and are guided in the present by stimuli in the individual's environment. To explain why abnormal behavior occurs, we must analyze how an individual has learned it and observe the circumstances in which it is displayed.

The emphasis on observable behavior represents both the greatest strength and the greatest weakness of the behavioral approach to abnormal behavior. This perspective provides the most precise and objective approach for examining behavioral symptoms of specific disorders, such as attention-deficit hyperactivity disorder (ADHD), which we discuss in Module 38. At the same time, though, critics charge that the perspective ignores the rich inner world of thoughts, attitudes, and emotions that may contribute to abnormal behavior.

COGNITIVE PERSPECTIVE

cognitive perspective The approach that focuses on how people think, understand, and know about the world. (Modules 2, 37)

The medical, psychoanalytic, and behavioral perspectives view people's behavior as the result of factors largely beyond their control. To many critics of these views, however, people's thoughts cannot be ignored.

In response to such concerns, some psychologists employ a **cognitive perspective.** Rather than considering only external behavior, as in traditional behavioral approaches, the cognitive approach assumes that *cognitions* (people's thoughts and beliefs) are central to a person's abnormal behavior. A primary goal of treatment using the cognitive perspective is to explicitly teach new, more adaptive ways of thinking.

For instance, suppose that you develop the erroneous belief that "doing well on this exam is crucial to my entire future" whenever you take an exam. Through therapy, you might learn to hold the more realistic and less anxiety-producing thought, "my entire future is not dependent on this one exam." By changing cognitions in this way, psychologists working within a cognitive framework help people free themselves from thoughts and behaviors that are potentially maladaptive (Ray et al., 2015; Robbins et al., 2019; Ciharova et al., 2021).

The cognitive perspective has its critics. For example, they argue that rather than maladaptive cognitions being the *cause* of a psychological disorder, they could be just another *symptom* of the disorder. Furthermore, under certain circumstances, negative beliefs may not be irrational at all but simply reflect accurately the realities of people's lives. (For example, feeling depressed because you've been found guilty of a crime may be entirely rational because you are, in fact, likely to go to jail.) Still, cognitive theorists would argue that there are adaptive ways of framing beliefs even in the most negative circumstances.

HUMANISTIC PERSPECTIVE

The **humanistic perspective** emphasizes the responsibility people have for their own behavior, even when such behavior is abnormal. The humanistic perspective–growing out of the work of Carl Rogers and Abraham Maslow–concentrates on what is uniquely human; that is, it views people as basically rational, oriented toward a social world, and motivated to seek self-actualization (Rogers, 1995; DeRobertis & Bland, 2019).

Humanistic approaches focus on the relationship of the individual to society; they consider the ways in which people view themselves in relation to others and see their place in the world. The humanistic perspective views people as having an awareness of life and of themselves that leads them to search for meaning and self-worth. Rather than assuming that individuals require a "cure," the humanistic perspective suggests that they can, by and large, set their own limits of what is acceptable behavior. As long as they are not hurting others and do not feel personal distress, people should be free to choose the behaviors in which they engage.

Although the humanistic perspective has been criticized for its reliance on unscientific, unverifiable information and its vague, almost philosophical formulations, it offers a distinctive view of abnormal behavior. It stresses the unique aspects of being human and provides a number of important suggestions for helping those with psychological problems.

humanistic perspective The approach that suggests that all individuals naturally strive to grow, develop, and be in control of their lives and behavior. (Modules 2, 37)

SOCIOCULTURAL PERSPECTIVE

The **sociocultural perspective** assumes that society and culture shape abnormal behavior. According to this view, societal and cultural factors such as poverty and prejudice may be at the root of abnormal behavior. Specifically, the kinds of stresses and conflicts people experience in their daily lives can promote and maintain abnormal behavior.

Consistent with the sociocultural perspective, some kinds of psychological disorders are far more prevalent among particular social classes, races, and ethnicities than they are in others. For instance, diagnoses of schizophrenia spectrum disorder tend to be higher among members of less affluent socioeconomic groups than among members of more affluent groups. Proportionally more Black Americans are hospitalized involuntarily for psychological disorders than are White Americans. In a given geographical region, people with the lowest incomes are 1.5 to 3 times more likely than more affluent people to suffer from depression or anxiety (Ridley et al., 2020).

Furthermore, poor economic times seem to be linked to general declines in psychological functioning, and social problems such as homelessness are associated with psychological disorders and deeply intertwined with socioeconomic factors. Homelessness, in particular, is linked with high levels of psychological disorder: Approximately 30% of homeless people in the United States suffer from serious psychological disorders. In some areas, psychological disorders are even more prevalent among the homeless: Fifty percent of the homeless in Los Angeles are estimated to have a psychological disorder (Treatment Advocacy Center, 2016; Novasky & Rosales, 2020).

Also consistent with the sociocultural perspective, the coronavirus pandemic, which massively disrupted people's daily lives, including their health and economic security, led to a significant increase in reports of psychological disorders. For example, one poll 2 months into the pandemic found that almost half the people surveyed said that the pandemic was harming their mental health (see Figure 1). Moreover, an emergency hotline run by the U.S. federal government showed a 1,000% increase in calls

sociocultural perspective The perspective that assumes that people's behavior–both normal and abnormal–is shaped by the kind of family group, society, and culture in which they live. (Module 37)

FIGURE 1 The impact of the coronavirus pandemic on perceptions of mental health. The graph shows the percentage of people who said they felt that worry or stress related to coronavirus had a negative impact on their mental health.

Source: Kirzinger et al., 2020.

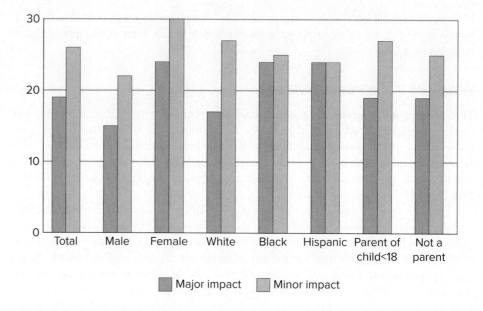

and texts over the previous year (Solomon, 2020; Proto & Quintana-Domeque, 2021; Cost et al., 2022).

Of course, social factors alone do not account for cases of psychological disorder, and there are plausible alternative explanations for the association between psychological difficulties and social factors. For example, people from lower socioeconomic levels may be less likely than those from higher levels to seek help or to have access to it. Similarly, in the case of the pandemic, it may be that the unprecedented disruption and isolation of quarantine intensified problems from which people already suffered. Still, the sociocultural perspective provides important insights into our understanding of the causes of psychological disorders (White et al., 2017).

Figure 2 summarizes the main perspectives on psychological disorders. In addition, it applies each of them to the case of Caroline Mazel-Carlton, discussed in the chapter prologue.

Study Alert

Use Figure 2 to review the six major perspectives on abnormality and consider how they relate to the major perspectives on the field of psychology.

Perspectives on Psychological Disorders		
Perspective	**Description**	**Application of Perspective to Caroline Mazel-Carlton's Case, Discussed in Chapter Prologue**
Medical	Assumes that physiological causes are at the root of psychological disorders	Examine Mazel-Carlton for medical problems, such as brain tumor, chemical imbalance in the brain, or disease.
Psychoanalytic	Argues that psychological disorders stem from childhood conflicts	Seek out information about Mazel-Carlton's past, considering possible childhood conflicts.
Behavioral	Assumes that abnormal behaviors are learned responses	Concentrate on rewards and punishments for Mazel-Carlton's behavior, and identify environmental stimuli that reinforce her behavior.
Cognitive	Assumes that cognitions (people's thoughts and beliefs) are central to psychological disorders	Focus on Mazel-Carlton's perceptions of herself and her environment.
Humanistic	Emphasizes people's responsibility for their own behavior and the need to self-actualize	Consider Mazel-Carlton's behavior in terms of her choices and efforts to reach her potential.
Sociocultural	Assumes that behavior is shaped by family, society, and culture	Focus on how societal demands contributed to Mazel-Carlton's disorder.

FIGURE 2 In considering the case of Caroline Mazel-Carlton, discussed in the prologue, we can employ each of the perspectives on abnormal behavior. Note that because of the nature of her psychological disorder, some of the perspectives are more applicable than others.

Classifying Abnormal Behavior: The ABCs of DSM

Crazy. Nuts. Mental. Loony. Insane. Neurotic. Psycho. Strange. Demented. Odd. Possessed.

Society has long placed labels on people who display abnormal behavior. Unfortunately, most of the time, these labels have reflected intolerance and have been used with little thought as to what each signifies.

Providing appropriate and specific names and classifications for abnormal behavior has presented a major challenge to psychologists. It is not hard to understand why, given the difficulties discussed earlier in simply distinguishing normal from abnormal behavior. Yet psychologists and other care providers need to classify abnormal behavior in order to diagnose it and ultimately treat it.

DSM-5-TR: DETERMINING DIAGNOSTIC DISTINCTIONS

The ***Diagnostic and Statistical Manual of Mental Disorders,*** **Fifth Edition–Text Revision (DSM-5-TR)** is the most widely used system to classify and define psychological disorders (American Psychiatric Association, 2022).

The DSM-5-TR, most recently revised in 2022, provides comprehensive and relatively precise definitions for more than 200 disorders. By following the criteria presented in the DSM-5-TR classification system, diagnosticians use clients' reported symptoms to identify the specific problem the clients are experiencing. Figure 3 provides a brief outline of the major diagnostic categories (American Psychiatric Association, 2013, 2022).

The authors of the newest update of the DSM suggest that the manual should be viewed as a work in progress. In fact, the DSM has been consistently revised since it

Diagnostic and Statistical Manual of Mental Disorders, **Fifth Edition-Text Revision (DSM-5-TR)** A system, devised by the American Psychiatric Association, used by most professionals to classify and define psychological disorders. (Module 46)

Categories of Disorders	Examples
Anxiety (problems in which anxiety impedes daily functioning)	Generalized anxiety disorder, panic disorder, phobic disorder
Somatic symptom and related disorders (psychological difficulties displayed through physical problems)	Illness anxiety disorder, functional neurologic disorder (conversion disorder)
Dissociative (the splitting apart of crucial parts of personality that are usually integrated)	Dissociative identity disorder (multiple personality), dissociative amnesia, dissociative fugue
Mood (emotions of depression or euphoria that are so strong they intrude on everyday living)	Major depressive disorders, bipolar disorder
Schizophrenia spectrum and other psychotic disorders (declines in functioning, thought and language disturbances, perception disorders, emotional disturbances, and withdrawal from others)	Delusional disorder
Personality (problems that create little personal distress but that lead to an inability to function as a normal member of society)	Antisocial (sociopathic) personality disorder, narcissistic personality disorder
Sexual (problems related to sexual arousal from unusual objects or problems related to functioning)	Paraphilic disorders, sexual dysfunction
Substance-related (problems related to drug dependence and abuse)	Alcohol, cocaine, hallucinogens, marijuana
Neurocognitive disorders	Alzheimer's

American Psychiatric Association

FIGURE 3 This list of disorders represents the major categories from the DSM-5-TR. It is only a partial list of the scores of disorders included in the diagnostic manual.

Source: American Psychiatric Association, 2022.

first appeared in 1952, based on user feedback, societal changes, and scientific advances (Horwitz, 2021).

The DSM takes an *atheoretical* approach to identifying psychological disorders, meaning it does not rely on any particular theoretical perspective. Consequently, it is primarily descriptive and attempts to avoid suggesting an underlying cause for an individual's behavior and problems. Instead, it seeks to paint a picture of the behavior that is being displayed.

For example, the DSM does not use the term *neurotic*–a label commonly used by people in their everyday descriptions of abnormal behavior–as a category. Because the term *neurosis* refers to problems associated with a specific cause based in Freud's theory of personality, it is not included in DSM-5-TR.

Why is this atheoretical, descriptive approach be important? For one thing, it allows communication between mental health professionals of diverse backgrounds and theoretical approaches. In addition, precise classification enables researchers to explore the causes of a problem. Without reliable descriptions of abnormal behavior, researchers would be hard pressed to find ways to investigate the disorder. Finally, DSM-5-TR provides a kind of conceptual shorthand through which professionals can describe the behaviors that tend to occur together in an individual (Widiger, 2015; Busch et al., 2017).

CONNING THE CLASSIFIERS: THE SHORTCOMINGS OF DSM

When clinical psychologist David Rosenhan and eight colleagues sought admission to separate mental hospitals across the United States in the 1970s, each stated that they were hearing voices–"unclear voices" that said "empty," "hollow," and "thud"–and each was immediately admitted to the hospital. However, the truth was that they actually were conducting a study, and none of them was really hearing voices. Aside from these misrepresentations, *everything* else they did and said represented their true behavior, including the responses they gave during extensive admission interviews and their answers to the battery of tests they were asked to complete. In fact, as soon as they were admitted, they said they no longer heard any voices. In short, each of the pseudo-patients acted in a "normal" way (Rosenhan, 1973).

We might assume that Rosenhan and his colleagues would have been quickly discovered as the impostors they were, but this was not the case. Instead, each of them was diagnosed as severely abnormal on the basis of observed behavior. Mental health professionals labeled most as suffering from schizophrenia and kept them in the hospital 3 to 52 days, with the average stay of 19 days. Even when they were discharged, most of the "patients" left with the label *schizophrenia–in remission*, implying that the abnormal behavior had only temporarily subsided and could recur at any time. Most disturbing, no one on the hospital staff identified any of the pseudo-patients as impostors–although some of the actual patients figured out the ruse.

Rosenhan's study has been criticized on both ethical and methodological grounds. The (real) patients never gave their consent to participate in an experiment, and even the staff at the hospital were kept in the dark that an experiment was occurring. Furthermore, doubts have been raised about the accuracy with which Rosenhan, who died in 2012, reported the results. Still, the study was influential, and it led to greater scrutiny of how labeling individuals with a diagnosis could affect their future lives (Pols, 2019; Cahalan, 2020).

THE STIGMA OF LABELING

Determining a psychological diagnosis is not always a clear-cut or even necessarily an accurate process. Moreover, placing labels on individuals powerfully influences the way mental health workers, as well as laypersons, perceive and interpret their future behavior. Therefore, labeling a person with a diagnosis raises multiple concerns.

Gender dysphoria (in which one's gender identity is in conflict with one's biological sex) provides a contemporary illustration of the dilemma between the pros of a formal diagnosis and the cons of patient labeling. For example, most medical insurance providers require a formal, specific diagnosis in order to provide health-care coverage for procedures such as a sex change operation. Many individuals who experience a conflict between their gender identity and their biological sex object theoretically to the idea that their desire to be the other sex should be labeled a "disorder." Yet without a formal diagnosis, those same individuals may be forced to pay out of pocket for an expensive medical procedure.

This diagnosis-based system of insurance coverage often creates a Catch-22 for mental health-care professionals: They must decide between potentially stigmatizing their clients by providing a formal diagnosis, implying some type of disorder, or leaving patients undiagnosed and potentially without the financial support necessary to receive important procedures that will significantly improve the clients' quality of life (Kamens, 2011; Kleinplatz et al., 2013).

Critics of the DSM argue that labeling an individual as abnormal provides a dehumanizing, lifelong stigma. Furthermore, after an initial diagnosis has been made, mental health professionals, who may concentrate on the initial diagnostic category, could overlook other diagnostic possibilities (Frances, 2013; Kim et al., 2017; Parrish et al., 2019).

Although the DSM-5-TR was developed to provide more accurate and consistent diagnoses of psychological disorders, it isn't always successful. For instance, critics charge that because it was drawn up by psychiatrists, who are trained as physicians, psychologically disordered behavior is viewed as a symptom of an underlying medical problem. Moreover, critics suggest that the DSM compartmentalizes people into inflexible, all-or-none categories rather than considering the degree to which a person displays psychologically disordered behavior (Ferranti, 2015; Lasalvia, 2015; Mond & Gorrell, 2021).

Still, despite the drawbacks inherent in any labeling system, the DSM has had an important influence on the way in which mental health professionals view psychological disorders. It has increased both the reliability and the validity of diagnostic categorization. In addition, it offers a logical way to organize examination of the major types of mental disturbances.

Study Alert

It is important to understand the advantages and weaknesses of the DSM classification system.

RECAP/EVALUATE/RETHINK

RECAP

LO 37-1 How can we distinguish normal from abnormal behavior?

- Definitions of abnormality include deviation from average behavior, deviation from ideal behavior, a sense of personal discomfort, the inability to function effectively, and legal conceptions.
- Although no single definition is adequate, abnormal behavior can be considered to be behavior that causes people to experience distress and prevents them from functioning in their daily lives. Most psychologists believe that abnormal and normal behavior should be considered in terms of a continuum.

LO 37-2 What are the major perspectives on psychological disorders used by mental health professionals?

- The medical perspective views abnormality as a symptom of an underlying disease.
- Psychoanalytic perspectives suggest that abnormal behavior stems from childhood conflicts in the unconscious.

- Behavioral approaches focus on the rewards and punishments in the environment that determine abnormal behavior.
- The cognitive approach suggests that abnormal behavior is the result of faulty cognitions (thoughts and beliefs). In this view, abnormal behavior can be remedied by changing one's flawed thoughts and beliefs.
- Humanistic approaches emphasize the responsibility people have for their own behavior even when such behavior is seen as abnormal.
- Sociocultural approaches view abnormal behavior in terms of difficulties arising from family and other social relationships.

LO 37-3 What are the major categories of psychological disorders?

- The most widely used system for classifying psychological disorders is DSM-5-TR–*Diagnostic and Statistical Manual of Mental Disorders*, Fifth Edition–Text Revision.

EVALUATE

1. One problem in defining abnormal behavior is that
   a. Statistically rare behavior may not be abnormal.
   b. Not all abnormalities are accompanied by feelings of discomfort.
   c. Cultural standards are too general to use as a measuring tool.
   d. All of the above are correct.
2. If abnormality is defined as behavior that causes personal discomfort or harms others, which of the following people is most likely to need treatment?
   a. An executive is afraid to accept a promotion because it would require moving from their ground-floor office to the top floor of a tall office building.
   b. A friend decides to quit her job and chooses to live on the street in order to live a "simpler life."
   c. A neighbor believes that friendly spacemen visit his house every Thursday.
   d. A photographer lives with 19 cats in a small apartment, lovingly caring for them.
3. Virginia's mother thinks that her daughter's behavior is clearly abnormal because, despite being offered admission to medical school, Virginia decides to become a server. What approach is Virginia's mother using to define abnormal behavior?
4. Which of the following is a strong argument against the medical perspective on abnormality?
   a. Physiological abnormalities are almost always impossible to identify.
   b. There is no conclusive way to link past experience and behavior.
   c. The medical perspective rests too heavily on the effects of nutrition.
   d. Assigning behavior to a physical problem takes responsibility away from the individual for changing their behavior.
5. Rae is painfully shy. According to the behavioral perspective, the best way to deal with Rae's "abnormal" behavior is to
   a. treat the underlying physical problem.
   b. use the principles of learning theory to modify the shy behavior.
   c. express a great deal of caring.
   d. uncover her negative past experiences through hypnosis.

RETHINK

1. Do you agree or disagree that DSM should be updated every several years? Why? What makes abnormal behavior so variable?
2. Imagine that an acquaintance of yours was recently arrested for shoplifting a $15 necktie. Write an explanation for this behavior from *each* perspective on abnormality: the medical perspective, the psychoanalytic perspective, the behavioral perspective, the cognitive perspective, the humanistic perspective, and the sociocultural perspective.

Answers to Evaluate Questions

1. d; 2. a; 3. deviation from the ideal; 4. d; 5. b

KEY TERMS

abnormal behavior	behavioral	humanistic	*Diagnostic and Statistical*
medical perspective	perspective	perspective	*Manual of Mental*
psychoanalytic	cognitive	sociocultural	*Disorders,* Fifth Edition–
perspective	perspective	perspective	Text Revision (DSM-5-TR)

Module 38
The Major Psychological Disorders

Ayisha's first panic attack was a surprise. Visiting her parents after college, she suddenly felt dizzy, broke into a cold sweat, and began hyperventilating. Her father clocked her pulse at 180 and rushed her to the hospital, where all symptoms vanished. She laughed it off and returned to her apartment.

But the panic attacks continued. At the gym, at work, in restaurants and movie theaters, Ayisha was never safe from them. Not just frightening, they were downright embarrassing. She quit her job to work at home. She avoided crowds and turned down invitations to dinners, parties, and movies. The only way to escape humiliation was to wall herself inside her apartment with a blanket and a pillow.

Ayisha suffered from panic disorder, one of the specific psychological disorders we'll consider in this module. Keep in mind that although we'll be discussing these disorders objectively, each represents a very human set of difficulties that influence and, in some cases, considerably disrupt people's lives.

LEARNING OUTCOME

LO 38-1 What are the major psychological disorders?

Anxiety Disorders

All of us at one time or another experience *anxiety,* a feeling of apprehension or tension, in reaction to stressful situations. There is nothing "wrong" with such anxiety. It is a normal reaction to stress that often helps rather than hinders our daily functioning. Without some anxiety, for instance, most of us probably would not have much motivation to study hard, undergo physical exams, or spend long hours at our jobs.

But some people experience anxiety in situations in which there is no apparent reason or cause for such distress. **Anxiety disorders** occur when anxiety arises without external justification and begins to affect people's daily functioning. We'll discuss three major types of anxiety disorders: phobic disorder, panic disorder, and generalized anxiety disorder.

anxiety disorder The occurrence of anxiety without an obvious external cause that affects daily functioning. (Module 38)

PHOBIC DISORDER

Forty-five-year-old Jackson is terrified of electricity. He's unable to change a lightbulb for fear of getting electrocuted. The thought of static electricity on clothing sends him into a panic. He can't even open a refrigerator door without being terrified a short circuit will send electricity through his body. And thunderstorms? Forget it: He is beside himself with fear of getting electrocuted by lightning (Kluger, 2001).

Jackson suffers from a **specific phobia,** an intense, irrational fear of a specific object or situation. For example, claustrophobia is a fear of enclosed places, acrophobia is a fear of high places, xenophobia is a fear of strangers or foreigners, social phobia is the fear of being judged or embarrassed by others, and–as in Jackson's case–electrophobia is a fear of electricity.

specific phobia Intense, irrational fears of specific objects or situations. (Module 38)

The actual danger posed by an anxiety-producing stimulus (which can be just about anything, as you can see in Figure 1) is typically small or nonexistent. However, to someone suffering from the phobia, the danger is great, and a full-blown panic attack may follow exposure to the stimulus. Phobic disorders differ from generalized anxiety disorders and panic disorders in that there is a specific, identifiable stimulus that sets off the anxiety reaction.

Phobias may have only a minor impact on people's lives if those who suffer from them can avoid the stimuli that trigger fear. For example, a fear of heights may have

Phobic Disorder	Description	Example
Agoraphobia	Fear of places, such as unfamiliar or crowded spaces, where help might not be available in case of emergency	Person becomes housebound because any place other than the person's home arouses extreme anxiety symptoms.
Specific phobias	Fear of specific objects, places, or situations	
Animal type	Specific animals or insects	Person has extreme fear of dogs, cats, or spiders.
Natural environment type	Events or situations in the natural environment	Person has extreme fear of storms, heights, or water.
Situational type	Public transportation, tunnels, bridges, elevators, flying, driving	Person becomes extremely claustrophobic in elevators.
Blood injection injury type	Blood, injury, injections	Person panics when viewing a child's scraped knee.
Social phobia	Fear of being judged or embarrassed by others	Person avoids all social situations and becomes a recluse for fear of encountering others' judgment.

FIGURE 1 Phobic disorders differ from generalized anxiety and panic disorders because with phobic disorders, a specific stimulus can be identified. Listed here are a number of types of phobias and their triggers.
Source: Nolen-Hoeksema, 2023.

(spider) Pets in Frames/Shutterstock; (needle) Stockbyte/Photodisc Collection/Getty Images; (woman) Maridav/123RF; (businessman) JohnnyGreig/E+/Getty Images

little impact on people's everyday lives (although it may prevent them from living in an apartment on a high floor). On the other hand, a *social phobia,* or a fear of strangers, presents a more serious problem. For example, in one extreme case, a Washington woman left her home just three times in 30 years–once to visit her family, once for an operation, and once to purchase ice cream for a dying companion (Wong et al., 2011; Stopa et al., 2013; Lau et al., 2021).

PANIC DISORDER

panic disorder Anxiety disorder that takes the form of panic attacks lasting from a few seconds to several hours. (Module 38)

In another type of anxiety disorder, **panic disorder,** *panic attacks* occur that last from a few seconds to several hours. Panic disorders do not have any identifiable, specific triggers (unlike phobias, which are triggered by specific objects or situations). Instead, during an attack such as those Ayisha experienced in the case described earlier, anxiety suddenly–and often without warning–rises, and an individual feels a sense of impending, unavoidable doom.

Although the physical symptoms of a panic attack differ from person to person, they may include heart palpitations, shortness of breath, unusual amounts of sweating, faintness and dizziness, gastric sensations, and sometimes a sense of imminent death. After such an attack, it is no wonder that people tend to feel exhausted (Montgomery, 2011; Carleton et al., 2014; Hewitt et al., 2021).

Panic attacks seemingly come out of nowhere and are unconnected to any specific stimulus. Because they don't know what triggers their feelings of panic, victims of panic attacks may become fearful of going places. In fact, some people with panic disorder develop a complication called *agoraphobia,* the fear of being in a situation in which escape is difficult and in which help for a possible panic attack would not be available. In extreme cases, people with agoraphobia never leave their homes (Kim & Yoon, 2017; Stech et al., 2019; Preti et al., 2021).

In addition to the physical symptoms, panic disorder affects how the brain processes information. For instance, people with panic disorder have reduced reactions in the anterior cingulate cortex to stimuli (such as viewing a fearful face) that normally produce a strong reaction in those without the disorder. It may be that recurring high levels of emotional arousal that patients with panic disorder experience desensitize them to emotional stimuli (Maddock et al., 2013; Lai, 2019).

GENERALIZED ANXIETY DISORDER

People with **generalized anxiety disorder** experience long-term, persistent anxiety and uncontrollable worry. Sometimes their concerns are about identifiable issues involving family, money, work, or health. In other cases, though, people with the disorder feel that something dreadful is about to happen but can't identify the reason and thus experience "free-floating" anxiety.

Because of persistent anxiety, people with generalized anxiety disorder cannot concentrate or set their worry and fears aside; their lives become centered on their worry. Furthermore, their anxiety is often accompanied by physiological symptoms, such as muscle tension, headaches, dizziness, heart palpitations, or insomnia (Starcevic et al., 2007). Figure 2 shows the most common symptoms of generalized anxiety disorder.

Acrophobia, the fear of heights, is not an uncommon phobia. What sort of behavior-modification approaches might be used to deal with acrophobia?
Imagine China/Newscom

generalized anxiety disorder The experience of long-term, persistent anxiety and worry. (Module 38)

Obsessive-Compulsive Disorder

In **obsessive-compulsive disorder (OCD),** people are plagued by unwanted thoughts, called *obsessions,* or feel that they must carry out behaviors, termed *compulsions,* that they feel driven to perform.

An **obsession** is a persistent, unwanted thought or idea that keeps recurring. For example, a student may be unable to stop thinking that she has neglected to put her name on a test and may think about it constantly for the 2 weeks it takes to get the paper back. A man may go on vacation and wonder the whole time whether he locked his house. A woman may hear the same tune running through her head over and over. In each case, the thought or idea is unwanted and difficult to put out of mind. Of course, many people suffer from mild obsessions from time to time, but usually such thoughts persist only for a short period. For people with serious obsessions, however, the thoughts persist for days or months and may consist of bizarre, troubling images (Rassin & Muris, 2007; Wenzel, 2011; Iliceto et al., 2017; Llorens-Aguilar et al., 2022).

As the name suggests, as part of an obsessive-compulsive disorder, people may also experience compulsions. **Compulsions** are irresistible urges to repeatedly carry out some behavior that seems strange and unreasonable even to them. Whatever the compulsive behavior is, people experience extreme anxiety if they cannot do it, even if it is something they want to stop. The acts may be relatively trivial, such as repeatedly checking the stove to make sure all the burners are turned off, or more unusual, such as washing one's hands so much that they bleed (Moretz & McKay, 2009; Gillan & Sahakian, 2015; Robbins et al., 2019).

For example, consider this passage from the autobiography of a person with obsessive-compulsive disorder:

> I thought my parents would die if I didn't do everything in exactly the right way. When I took my glasses off at night I'd have to place them on the dresser at a particular angle. Sometimes I'd turn on the light and get out of bed seven times until I

obsessive-compulsive disorder (OCD) A disorder characterized by obsessions or compulsions. (Module 38)

obsession A persistent, unwanted thought or idea that keeps recurring. (Module 38)

compulsion An irresistible urge to repeatedly carry out some act that seems strange and unreasonable. (Module 38)

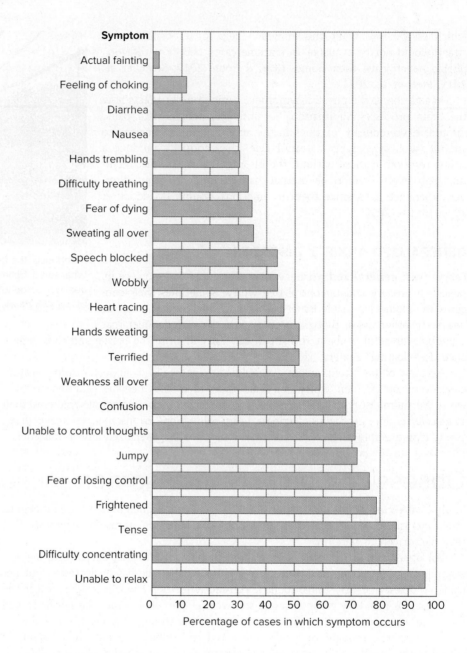

FIGURE 2 Frequency of symptoms in cases of generalized anxiety disorder. Source: Beck & Emery, 2005.

felt comfortable with the angle. If the angle wasn't right, I felt that my parents would die. The feeling ate up my insides.

If I didn't grab the molding on the wall just the right way as I entered or exited my room; if I didn't hang a shirt in the closet perfectly; if I didn't read a paragraph a certain way; if my hands and nails weren't perfectly clean, I thought my incorrect behavior would kill my parents. (Summers, 2000)

Although carrying out compulsive rituals may lead to some immediate reduction of anxiety, in the long run the anxiety returns. In fact, people with severe cases lead lives filled with unrelenting tension (Dittrich et al., 2011; Kalanthroff et al., 2013).

THE CAUSES OF ANXIETY DISORDERS AND OBSESSIVE-COMPULSIVE DISORDER

We've considered several of the major types of anxiety disorders and obsessive-compulsive disorder, but there are many other related disorders. The variety of anxiety disorders means that no single explanation fits all cases.

remember where he grew up and received training, he may still be able to prepare gourmet meals.

In some cases of dissociative amnesia, the memory loss is profound. For example, in one dramatic case, Raymond Power Jr., an attorney, husband, father of two, and a Boy Scout leader, left home to go to work one morning. Two days later, he was homeless, living a new life a thousand miles away, and had no memory of who he was or how he got there. He was found 6 months later but still had no recollection of his previous life, including any knowledge of his wife of 30 years or even that he had children (Dell, 2013).

Dissociative fugue is a form of amnesia in which a person leaves home suddenly and assumes a new identity. In this unusual and rare state, people take sudden, impulsive trips and adopt a new identity. After a period of time–days, months, or sometimes even years–they suddenly realize that they are in a strange place and completely forget the time they have spent wandering. Their last memories are those from the time just before they entered the fugue state (Agenagnew et al., 2020; Libdeh et al., 2022).

> **dissociative fugue** A form of amnesia in which a person leaves home and assumes a new identity. (Module 38)

The common thread among dissociative disorders is that they allow people to escape from some anxiety-producing situation. Either the person produces a new personality to deal with stress, or the individual forgets or leaves behind the situation that caused the stress as they journey to some new–and perhaps less anxiety-ridden–environment (Lynn et al., 2019).

Mood Disorders

> From the time I woke up in the morning until the time I went to bed at night, I was unbearably miserable and seemingly incapable of any kind of joy or enthusiasm. Everything–every thought, word, movement–was an effort. Everything that once was sparkling now was flat. I seemed to myself to be dull, boring, inadequate, thick brained, unlit, unresponsive, chill skinned, bloodless, and sparrow drab. I doubted, completely, my ability to do anything well. It seemed as though my mind had slowed down and burned out to the point of being virtually useless. (Jamison, 1995)

We all experience mood swings. Sometimes we are happy, perhaps even euphoric; at other times, we feel upset, saddened, or depressed. Such changes in mood are a normal part of everyday life.

In some people, however, moods are so pronounced and lingering–like the feelings described above by writer (and psychiatrist) Kay Jamison–that they interfere with the ability to function effectively. **Mood disorders** are disturbances in emotional experience that are strong enough to interfere with everyday living. In extreme cases, a mood may become life threatening; in other cases, it may cause the person to lose touch with reality.

> **mood disorder** A disturbance in emotional experience that is strong enough to intrude on everyday living. (Module 38)

MAJOR DEPRESSIVE DISORDER

President Abraham Lincoln. Queen Victoria. Demi Lovato.

The common link among these people? Each suffered from periodic attacks of major depressive disorder. **Major depressive disorder** is a severe form of depression that interferes with concentration, decision making, and sociability.

Major depressive disorder is one of the more common forms of mood disorders. Nearly 18 million people in the United States suffer from major depression, and at any one time, 6-10% of the U.S. population is clinically depressed. Almost 1 in 5 people in the United States experiences major depression at some point in life, and 15% of college students have received a diagnosis of depression. The cost of depression is more than $236 billion a year in lost productivity and other costs (Substance Abuse and Mental Health Services Administration, 2021; Greenberg et al., 2021).

> **major depressive disorder** A severe form of depression that interferes with concentration, decision making, and sociability. (Module 38)

Women are twice as likely to experience major depression as men are, with one-fourth of all females apt to encounter it at some point during their lives. Furthermore, although no one is sure why, the rate of depression is going up throughout the world, a trend that started before the onset of the COVID pandemic, which itself led to significant rises in depression (Santomauro et al., 2021).

Results of in-depth interviews conducted in the United States, Puerto Rico, Taiwan, Lebanon, Canada, Italy, Germany, and France indicate that the incidence of depression has increased significantly over previous rates in every area. In fact, in some countries, the likelihood that individuals will have major depression at some point in their lives is three times higher than it was for earlier generations. Worldwide, over 280 million people suffer from major depressive disorder (Sarubin et al., 2017; Ojagbemi et al., 2018; Santomauro et al., 2021).

When psychologists speak of major depressive disorder, they do not mean the sadness that accompanies one of life's disappointments, which we all have experienced. Some depression is normal after the breakup of a long-term relationship, the death of a loved one, or the loss of a job. It is normal even after less serious problems, such as doing badly on a test or having a romantic partner forget one's birthday.

People who suffer from major depressive disorder experience similar feelings, but the severity tends to be considerably greater. They may feel useless, worthless, and lonely, and they may think the future is hopeless and no one can help them. They may lose their appetite and have no energy. Moreover, they may experience such feelings for months or even years. They may cry uncontrollably, have sleep disturbances, and be at risk for suicide. The depth and duration of such behavior are the hallmarks of major depressive disorder. (Figure 4 provides a self-assessment of depression.)

! Study Alert

Major depression differs from the normal depression that occasionally occurs during most people's lives; major depression is more intense, lasts longer, and may have no clear trigger.

FIGURE 4 This test is based on the list of signs and symptoms of depression found on the National Institute of Mental Health website at https://www.nimh.nih.gov/health/topics/depression.

Source: National Institutes of Health, n.d.

A Test for Major Depression

To complete the questionnaire, count the number of statements with which you agree:

1. I feel sad, anxious, or empty.
2. I feel hopeless or pessimistic.
3. I feel guilty, worthless, or helpless.
4. I feel irritable or restless.
5. I have lost interest in activities or hobbies that were once pleasurable, including sex.
6. I feel tired and have decreased energy.
7. I have difficulty concentrating, remembering details, and making decisions.
8. I have insomnia, early-morning wakefulness, or sleep too much.
9. I overeat or have appetite loss.
10. I have thoughts of suicide or have attempted suicide.
11. I have aches or pains, headaches, cramps, or digestive problems that do not ease even with treatment.

Scoring: If you agree with at least five of the statements, including either 1 or 2, and if you have had these symptoms for at least 2 weeks, help from a professional is strongly recommended. If you answer yes to number 10, seek immediate help. And remember: These are only general guidelines. If you feel you may need help, seek it.

MANIA AND BIPOLAR DISORDER

While depression leads to the depths of despair, mania leads to emotional heights. **Mania** is an extended state of intense, wild elation. People experiencing mania feel intense happiness, power, invulnerability, and energy. Believing they will succeed at anything they attempt, they may become involved in wild schemes. Consider, for example, the following description of an individual who experienced a manic episode:

> Mr. O'Reilly took a leave of absence from his civil service job. He purchased a large number of cuckoo clocks and then an expensive car, which he planned to use as a mobile showroom for his wares, anticipating that he would make a great deal of money. He proceeded to "tear around town" buying and selling clocks and other merchandise, and when he was not out, he was continuously on the phone making "deals." . . . He was $3,000 in debt and had driven his family to exhaustion with his excessive activity and talkativeness. He said, however, that he felt "on top of the world." (Spitzer et al., 1983)

Some people sequentially experience periods of mania and depression. This alternation of mania and depression is called **bipolar disorder** (a condition previously known as *manic-depressive disorder*). The swings between highs and lows may occur a few days apart or may alternate over a period of years. In addition, in bipolar disorder, periods of depression are usually longer than periods of mania.

Ironically, some of society's most creative individuals may have suffered from bipolar disorder. The imagination, drive, excitement, and energy that they display during manic stages allow them to make unusually creative contributions. For instance, historical analysis of the composer Robert Schumann's music shows that he was most prolific during periods of mania. In contrast, his output dropped off drastically during periods of depression (see Figure 5). On the other hand, the high output associated with mania does not necessarily lead to higher quality: Some of Schumann's greatest works were created outside his periods of mania (Kyaga et al., 2013; Cruz et al., 2021; Andreasen, 2022).

Although creativity may be increased when someone is experiencing mania, persons who experience this disorder often show a recklessness that produces emotional and sometimes physical self-injury. They may alienate people with their talkativeness, inflated self-esteem, and indifference to the needs of others (Simonton, 2014; Miller et al., 2019).

mania An extended state of intense, wild elation. (Module 38)

bipolar disorder A disorder in which a person alternates between periods of euphoric feelings of mania and periods of depression. (Module 38)

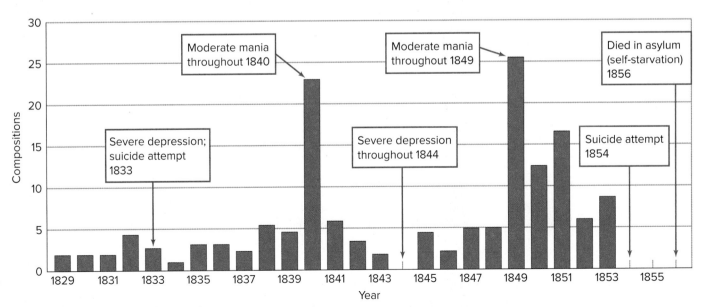

FIGURE 5 The number of pieces written by composer Robert Schumann in a given year was related to his periods of depression and mania. Why do you think mania might be associated with creative productivity in some people?
Source: Slater & Meyer, 1959.

CAUSES OF MOOD DISORDERS

Because they represent a major mental health problem, mood disorders–and, in particular, depression–have received a good deal of study. Several approaches have been used to explain the disorders.

Genetic and biological causes of mood disorders. Some mood disorders have clear genetic and biological roots. In fact, most evidence suggests that bipolar disorders are caused primarily by biological factors. For instance, bipolar disorder (and some forms of major depression) clearly runs in some families, pointing to a genetic cause. Furthermore, researchers have found that several neurotransmitters play a role in depression. For example, alterations in the functioning of serotonin and norepinephrine in the brain are related to the disorder.

In addition, research on neuroimaging suggests that a brain structure called *area 25* is related to depression: When area 25 is smaller than normal, it is associated with a higher risk of depression. Furthermore, the right anterior insula, a region of the brain related to self-awareness and interpersonal experience, also appears to be related to depression (Cisler et al., 2013; Serretti, 2017; Coenen et al., 2019; Pizzagalli & Roberts, 2022).

Internal, unconscious conflicts as causes of mood disorders. Supporters of psychoanalytic perspectives see depression as the result of feelings of loss (real or potential) or of anger directed inwardly at oneself. However, little research supports this explanation (Vanheule et al., 2006; Sa, 2015; Kernberg, 2021).

Environmental causes of mood disorders. Some explanations of depression take a behavioral approach, looking to influences outside the person. For example, behavioral theories of depression argue that the stresses of life produce a reduction in positive reinforcers. As a result, people begin to withdraw, which only reduces positive reinforcers further. In addition, people receive attention for their depressive behavior, which further reinforces the depression (Lewinsohn et al., 2003; Domschke, 2013; Kwong et al., 2019).

Cognitive and emotional causes of mood disorders. Some explanations for mood disorders attribute them to cognitive factors. For example, psychologist Martin Seligman suggests that depression is largely a response to learned helplessness. *Learned helplessness* is a learned expectation that events in one's life are uncontrollable and that one cannot escape from the situation. As a consequence, people simply give up fighting aversive events and submit to them, which thereby produces depression. Other theorists go a step further and suggest that depression results from hopelessness, a combination of learned helplessness and an expectation that negative outcomes in one's life are inevitable (Bjornstad, 2006; Li et al., 2011; Shirayama & Hashimoto, 2017; Song & Vilares, 2021).

Clinical psychologist Aaron Beck has proposed that faulty cognitions underlie people's depressed feelings. Specifically, his cognitive theory of depression suggests that depressed individuals typically view themselves as life's losers and blame themselves whenever anything goes wrong. By focusing on the negative side of situations, they feel inept and unable to act constructively to change their environment. In sum, their negative cognitions lead to feelings of depression (Newman et al., 2002; Bockting et al., 2015; Beck, 2019).

Brain imaging studies suggest that people with depression experience a general blunting of emotional reactions. For example, one study found that the brains of people with depression showed significantly less activation when they viewed photos of human faces displaying strong emotions than did those without the disorder (Gotlib et al., 2004; Kajanoja et al., 2018; Ma et al., 2021; Christensen et al., 2022).

DEPRESSION IN WOMEN

The various theories of depression have not provided a complete answer to an elusive question that has dogged researchers: Why does depression occur in approximately twice as many women as men—a pattern that is similar across a variety of cultures?

One explanation suggests that the stress women experience may be greater than the stress men experience at certain points in their lives—such as when a woman must simultaneously earn a living and be the primary caregiver for her children. In addition, women have a higher risk for physical and sexual abuse, typically earn lower wages than men, report greater unhappiness with their marriages, and generally experience chronic negative circumstances. Furthermore, women and men may respond to stress with different coping mechanisms. For instance, men may abuse drugs, whereas women respond with depression (Hyde et al., 2008; Komarovskaya et al., 2011; Sun et al., 2017; Buckman et al., 2021).

Biological factors may also explain some women's depression. For example, the rate of female depression begins to rise during puberty, so some psychologists believe that hormones make women more vulnerable to the disorder. In addition, 25-50% of women who take oral contraceptives report symptoms of depression, and depression that occurs after the birth of a child, known as *postpartum depression,* is linked to hormonal changes. Finally, structural differences in men's and women's brains may be related to gender differences in depression (Jones et al., 2017; Yang et al., 2017; Post & Leuner, 2019; de Wit et al., 2020).

Ultimately, researchers have discovered no definitive solutions to the puzzle of depression, and they offer many alternative explanations. Most likely, a complex interaction of several factors causes mood disorders.

Schizophrenia Spectrum Disorder

Things that relate, the town of Antelope, Oregon, Jonestown, Charlie Manson, the Hillside Strangler, the Zodiac Killer, Watergate, King's trial in L.A., and many more. In the last 7 years alone, over 23 Star Wars scientists committed suicide for no apparent reason. The AIDS cover-up, the conference in South America in 87 had over 1,000 doctors claim that insects can transmit it. To be able to read one's thoughts and place thoughts in one's mind without the person knowing it's being done. Realization is a reality of bioelectromagnetic control, which is thought transfer and emotional control, recording individual brainwave frequencies of thought, sensation, and emotions. (Nolen-Hoeksema, 2023)

This excerpt illustrates the efforts of a person with schizophrenia spectrum disorder, one of the more severe forms of mental disturbance, to communicate. People with schizophrenia spectrum disorder account for by far the largest percentage of those hospitalized for psychological disorders. They are also in many respects the least likely to recover from their difficulties.

Schizophrenia spectrum disorder refers to a class of disorders in which severe distortion of reality occurs. Thinking, perception, and emotion may deteriorate; the individual may withdraw from social interaction; and the person may display bizarre behavior. The symptoms displayed by persons with schizophrenia spectrum disorder may vary considerably over time. Nonetheless, a number of characteristics reliably distinguish schizophrenia spectrum disorder from other disorders. They include the following:

- *Decline from a previous level of functioning.* An individual can no longer carry out activities they were once able to do.

- *Disturbances of thought and speech.* People with schizophrenia spectrum disorder use logic and language in a peculiar way. Their thinking often does not make sense, and their logic is frequently faulty, which is referred to as a *formal thought disorder.* They also do not follow conventional linguistic rules (Penn et al., 1997). Consider, for example, the following response to the question "Why do you think people believe in God?"

schizophrenia spectrum disorder A class of disorders in which severe distortion of reality occurs. (Module 47)

Uh, let's, I don't know why, let's see, balloon travel. He holds it up for you, the balloon. He don't let you fall out, your little legs sticking down through the clouds. He's down to the smokestack, looking through the smoke trying to get the balloon gassed up you know. Way they're flying on top that way, legs sticking out. I don't know, looking down on the ground, heck, that'd make you so dizzy you just stay and sleep you know, hold down and sleep there. I used to be sleep outdoors, you know, sleep outdoors instead of going home. (Chapman & Chapman, 1973)

As this selection illustrates, although the basic grammatical structure may be intact, the substance of thinking that is characteristic of schizophrenia spectrum disorder is often illogical, garbled, and lacking in meaningful content (Cavelti et al., 2018; Oeztuerk et al., 2022).

- *Delusions.* People with schizophrenia spectrum disorder often have delusions—firmly held, unshakable beliefs with no basis in reality. Among the common delusions people with schizophrenia spectrum disorder experience are the beliefs that they are being controlled by someone else, they are being persecuted by others, and their thoughts are being broadcast so that others know what they are thinking (Phalen et al., 2017; Fouladirad et al., 2022).

- *Hallucinations and perceptual problems.* People with schizophrenia spectrum disorder sometimes do not perceive the world as most other people do. For example, they may have *hallucinations,* the experience of perceiving things that do not actually exist. Furthermore, they may see, hear, or smell things differently from others (see Figure 6). In fact, they may not even have a sense of their bodies in the way that others do, having difficulty determining where their bodies stop and the rest of the world begins (Phadke et al., 2015; Siemerkus et al., 2019; Barber et al., 2021).

- *Inappropriate emotions.* People with schizophrenia spectrum disorder sometimes show a lack of emotion, with even the most dramatic events producing little or no emotional response. Alternately, they may display strong bursts of emotion that are inappropriate to a situation. For example, a person with schizophrenia spectrum disorder may laugh uproariously at a funeral or react with rage when being helped by someone.

- *Withdrawal.* People with schizophrenia spectrum disorder tend to have little interest in others. They tend not to socialize or hold real conversations with others, although they may talk at another person. In the most extreme cases, they do not even acknowledge the presence of other people and appear to be in their own isolated worlds.

Usually, the onset of schizophrenia spectrum disorder occurs in early adulthood, and the symptoms follow one of two primary courses. In *process schizophrenia,* the symptoms develop slowly and subtly. There may be a gradual withdrawal from the world, excessive daydreaming, and a blunting of emotion until eventually the disorder reaches the point where others cannot overlook it. In other cases, known as *reactive schizophrenia,* the onset of symptoms is sudden and conspicuous. The treatment outlook for reactive schizophrenia is relatively favorable, but process schizophrenia has proved more difficult to treat.

DSM-5-TR classifies the symptoms of schizophrenia spectrum disorder into two types. *Positive-symptom schizophrenia* is indicated by the presence of disordered behavior such as hallucinations, delusions, and emotional extremes. Those with positive-symptom schizophrenia clearly lose touch with reality.

In contrast, those with *negative-symptom schizophrenia* show disruptions to normal emotions and behaviors. For example, there may be an absence or loss of normal functioning, such as social withdrawal or blunted emotions (Tandon et al., 2013; Lauriello & Rahman, 2015; Ahmed et al., 2022).

FIGURE 6 This unusual art was created by an individual suffering from a severe psychological disorder.

Wellcome Images/Science Source

The distinction between positive and negative symptoms of schizophrenia is important because it suggests that two different kinds of causes might trigger schizophrenia. Furthermore, it has implications for predicting treatment outcomes.

SOLVING THE PUZZLE OF SCHIZOPHRENIA SPECTRUM DISORDER: BIOLOGICAL CAUSES

Although schizophrenic behavior clearly departs radically from normal behavior, its causes are less apparent. It does appear, however, that schizophrenia spectrum disorder has both biological and environmental origins (Pavão et al., 2015; Torrey & Yolken, 2019).

Let's first consider the evidence pointing to a biological cause. Because schizophrenia spectrum disorder is more common in some families than in others, genetic factors seem to be involved in producing at least a susceptibility to or readiness for developing schizophrenia spectrum disorder. For example, the closer the genetic link between a person with schizophrenia spectrum disorder and another individual, the greater the likelihood that the other person will experience the disorder (Rodrigues-Amorim et al., 2017; Tiwari et al., 2022; see Figure 7).

However, if genetics alone were responsible for schizophrenia spectrum disorder, the chance of both of two identical twins having this disorder would be 100% instead of just under 50% because identical twins have the same genetic makeup. Moreover, attempts to find a link between schizophrenia spectrum disorder and a particular gene have been only partly successful. Apparently, genetic factors alone do not produce this disorder (Abel & Nickl-Jochschat, 2016).

Some researchers suggest that epigenetics are involved. *Epigenetics* looks at the way in which genes are expressed and influenced by the environment. In this view, genes by themselves do not invariably lead a person to display schizophrenia spectrum disorder. Instead, they are affected by the environment. Furthermore, genes can be altered in a way that then passes on the behavior to future generations. An epigenetic explanation of schizophrenia spectrum disorder, then, suggests that changes in gene expression may produce the disorder and that subsequently it can be passed on genetically (Alelú-Paz et al., 2016; Föcking et al., 2019; Srivastava et al., 2021).

Despite advances in our understanding of genetic and epigenetic causes, most researchers agree that no single gene is responsible for this disorder. Consequently, scientists have looked to other possible biological causes (Balter, 2017).

Another biological explanation suggests that the brains of people with schizophrenia spectrum disorder may have a biochemical imbalance. For example, the *dopamine*

Risk of Developing Schizophrenia Spectrum Disorder, Based on Genetic Relatedness to a Person with Schizophrenia Spectrum Disorder		
Relationship	**Genetic Relatedness, %**	**Risk of Developing Schizophrenia Spectrum Disorder, %**
Identical twin	100	48
Child of two parents with schizophrenia spectrum disorder	100	46
Fraternal twin	50	17
Offspring of one parent with schizophrenia spectrum disorder	50	17
Sibling	50	9
Nephew or niece	25	4
Spouse	0	2
Unrelated person	0	1

FIGURE 7 The closer the genetic links between two people, the greater the likelihood that if one experiences schizophrenia spectrum disorder, so will the other sometime during their lifetime. However, genetics is not the full story; if it were, the risk of identical twins having schizophrenia spectrum disorder would be 100% and not the 48% shown in this figure.
Source: Gottesman, 1991.

hypothesis suggests that this disorder results from excess activity in the areas of the brain that use dopamine as a neurotransmitter. This explanation came to light after the discovery that drugs that block dopamine action in brain pathways can be effective in reducing the symptoms of schizophrenia spectrum disorder. Other research suggests that glutamate, another neurotransmitter, may contribute to the disorder, and drugs that reduce the release of glutamate in the brain also show promise in alleviating symptoms (Howes et al., 2017; Seeman, 2021; Howes & Shatalina, 2022).

Another biological explanation relates to structural abnormalities in the brains of people with this disorder. For example, researchers have found abnormalities in the neural circuits of the cortex and limbic systems, as well as reduced amounts of gray matter, in the brains of those with schizophrenia spectrum disorder. Furthermore, differences exist in the way the brain functions (Reichenberg & Harvey, 2007; Reichenberg et al., 2009; Bustillo et al., 2017).

Further evidence for the importance of biological factors shows that when people with schizophrenia spectrum disorder hear voices during hallucinations, the parts of the brain responsible for hearing and language processing become active. When they have visual hallucinations, the parts of the brain involved in movement and color are active. At the same time, people with this disorder often have unusually low activity in the brain's frontal lobes—the parts of the brain involved with emotional regulation, insight, and the evaluation of sensory stimuli (Lavigne et al., 2015; Gill et al., 2021).

SITUATIONAL CAUSES OF SCHIZOPHRENIA SPECTRUM DISORDER

Biological factors provide important pieces of the puzzle of schizophrenia spectrum disorder. However, we also need to consider past and current experiences of people who develop the disturbance.

For instance, psychoanalytic explanations suggest that this disorder occurs when people experience regression to earlier stages of life. Specifically, Freud believed that people with schizophrenia lack egos that are strong enough to cope with their unacceptable impulses. They regress to the oral stage—a time when the id and ego are not yet separated. Therefore, individuals with schizophrenia essentially are presumed to act out impulses without concern for reality.

However, little research evidence supports psychoanalytic explanations. More plausible theories suggest that the emotional and communication patterns of the families of people with schizophrenia spectrum disorder are to blame for the disorder. For instance, some researchers suggest that the disorder is related to a family interaction style known as expressed emotion.

Expressed emotion is an interaction style characterized by high levels of criticism, hostility, and emotional intrusiveness within a family. Other researchers suggest that faulty communication patterns lie at the heart of schizophrenia spectrum disorder (Nader et al., 2013; Ma et al., 2021).

Psychologists who take a cognitive perspective on this disorder suggest that the problems in thinking that people experience point to a cognitive cause. Some suggest that this disorder results from *overattention* to stimuli in the environment. Rather than being able to screen out unimportant or inconsequential stimuli and focus on the most important things in the environment, people with the disorder may be excessively receptive to virtually everything in their environment. As a consequence of their inability to screen out noncritical information, their information-processing capabilities become overloaded and eventually break down.

Other cognitive experts argue that this disorder results from *underattention* to certain stimuli. According to this explanation, people with schizophrenia spectrum disorder fail to focus sufficiently on important stimuli and pay attention to other, less important information in their surroundings (Remington et al., 2014; Catalano et al., 2021).

Although overattention and underattention may be related to different forms of this disorder, these phenomena do not explain the origins of such information-processing disorders. Consequently, cognitive approaches—like other environmental explanations—do not provide a full explanation of the disorder.

THE MULTIPLE CAUSES OF SCHIZOPHRENIA SPECTRUM DISORDER: THE PREDISPOSITION EXPLANATION

Most scientists now believe that schizophrenia spectrum disorder is caused by a combination of biological and situational factors. Specifically, *predisposition explanations of schizophrenia spectrum disorder* suggest that individuals may inherit a predisposition or an inborn sensitivity to developing this disorder. This genetic predisposition makes them particularly vulnerable to stressors in their lives, such as social rejection, dysfunctional family communication patterns, or severe economic stress.

The stressors in people's lives may vary, but if they are strong enough and are coupled with a genetic predisposition, they result in the appearance of schizophrenia spectrum disorder. Furthermore, a strong genetic predisposition may lead to the onset of this disorder even when the environmental stressors are relatively weak. On the other hand, someone with a genetic predisposition may avoid developing the disorder if that person experiences relatively few life stressors.

In short, schizophrenia spectrum disorder is related to several kinds of biological and situational factors. Increasingly, it has become clear that no single factor but rather a combination of interrelated variables produces this disorder (Balter, 2017; Aas et al., 2018; Lysaker et al., 2018).

> **Study Alert**
>
> Remember that the multiple causes of schizophrenia spectrum disorder include biological and environmental factors.

Personality Disorders

I had always wanted lots of things; as a child I can remember wanting a bullet that a friend of mine had brought in to show the class. I took it and put it into my school bag and when my friend noticed it was missing, I was the one who stayed after school with him and searched the room, and I was the one who sat with him and bitched about the other kids and how one of them took his bullet. I even went home with him to help him break the news to his uncle, who had brought it home from the war for him.

But that was petty compared with the stuff I did later. I wanted a Ph.D. very badly, but I didn't want to work very hard—just enough to get by. I never did the experiments I reported; hell, I was smart enough to make up the results. I knew enough about statistics to make anything look plausible. I got my master's degree without even spending one hour in a laboratory. I mean, the professors believed anything. I'd stay out all night drinking and being with my friends, and the next day I'd get in just before them and tell 'em I'd been in the lab all night. They'd actually feel sorry for me. (Duke & Nowicki, 1979)

This excerpt provides a graphic first-person account of a person with a personality disorder. A **personality disorder** is characterized by a set of inflexible, maladaptive behavior patterns that keep a person from functioning appropriately in society.

Unlike the other disorders we have discussed, people with personality disorders typically have little sense of personal distress. Moreover, people with personality disorders frequently lead seemingly normal lives. However, just below the surface lies a set of inflexible, maladaptive personality traits that prevent them from functioning effectively as members of society (Anderson et al., 2015; Sharp & Wall, 2021).

The best-known type of personality disorder, illustrated by the case above, is the **antisocial personality disorder** (sometimes referred to as a sociopathic personality). Individuals with this disturbance show no regard for the moral and ethical rules of society or the rights of others. Although they can appear quite intelligent and likable (at least at first), upon closer examination they turn out to be manipulative and deceptive. Moreover, they lack any guilt or anxiety about their wrongdoing. When those with antisocial personality disorder behave in a way that injures someone else, they understand intellectually that they have caused harm but feel no remorse (Rosenström et al., 2017; Velotti et al., 2019; Anderson & Kelley, 2022).

personality disorder A disorder characterized by a set of inflexible, maladaptive behavior patterns that keep a person from functioning appropriately in society. (Module 38)

antisocial personality disorder A disorder in which individuals show no regard for the moral and ethical rules of society or the rights of others. (Module 38)

> **Study Alert**
>
> Unlike most psychological disorders, personality disorders produce little or no personal distress.

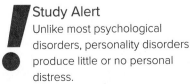

People with antisocial personality disorder are often impulsive and lack the ability to withstand frustration. They can be extremely manipulative. They also may have excellent social skills; they can be charming, engaging, and highly persuasive. Some of the best con artists have antisocial personalities.

What causes such an unusual constellation of problem behaviors? A variety of factors have been suggested ranging from an inability to experience emotions appropriately to problems in family relationships. For example, in many cases of antisocial behavior, the individual has come from a home in which a parent has died or left or one in which there is a lack of affection, a lack of consistency in discipline, or outright rejection. Other explanations concentrate on sociocultural factors because an unusually high proportion of people with antisocial personalities come from lower socioeconomic groups. Still, no one has been able to pinpoint the specific causes of antisocial personalities, and it is likely that some combination of factors is responsible (Chen et al., 2011; Singh, 2022).

borderline personality disorder A disorder characterized by problems regulating emotions and thoughts, displaying impulsive and reckless behavior, and having unstable relationships with others. (Module 38)

People with **borderline personality disorder** have problems regulating emotions and thoughts, display impulsive and reckless behavior, and have unstable relationships with others. They also have difficulty in developing a clear understanding of who they are. As a consequence, they tend to rely on relationships with others to define their identity. The problem with this strategy is that even minor rejection by others is devastating to those with borderline personality disorder. Furthermore, they generally distrust others and have difficulty controlling their anger. Their emotional volatility leads to impulsive and self-destructive behavior.

Individuals with borderline personality disorder often feel empty and alone, and they have difficulty cooperating with others. They may form intense, sudden, one-sided relationships in which they demand the attention of another person and then feel angry when they don't receive it. One reason for this behavior is that they may have a background in which others discounted or criticized their emotional reactions, and they may not have learned to regulate their emotions effectively. In other cases, people with borderline personality disorder have suffered severe emotional trauma during childhood (Samuel et al., 2013; Herzog et al., 2022; Kwon, 2022).

narcissistic personality disorder A personality disturbance characterized by an exaggerated sense of self-importance. (Module 38)

The narcissistic personality disorder is another type of personality disorder. The **narcissistic personality disorder** is characterized by an exaggerated sense of self-importance. Those with the disorder expect special treatment from others while also disregarding others' feelings, showing little or no sense of empathy for them.

There are several other categories of personality disorder that range in severity from individuals who may simply be regarded by others as eccentric, obnoxious, or difficult to people who act in a manner that is criminal and dangerous to others. Although they are not out of touch with reality like people with schizophrenia spectrum disorder, people with personality disorders often lead lives that put them on the fringes of society (Wright et al., 2016; Sharp & Wall, 2021).

Sam Edwards/age fotostock

From the perspective of...

A Social Worker Because people with personality disorders often appear from the outside to function well in society, should you try to address their problems?

Disorders That Affect Childhood

We typically view childhood as a time of innocence and relative freedom from stress. In reality, though, almost 20% of children and 40% of adolescents experience significant emotional or behavioral disorders (Kafali et al., 2019; Nolen-Hoeksema, 2020; Perrotta & Fabiano, 2021).

For example, although major depression is more prevalent in adults, around 2.5% of children and more than 8% of adolescents suffer from the disorder. In fact, by the time they reach age 20, 15–20% of children and adolescents will experience an episode of major depression. Among adolescents aged 12–17, 17% will have had an episode of major depression in the previous year. Other disorders change in prevalence with increasing age (Frodl et al., 2017; Substance Abuse and Mental Health Services Administration, 2019; see Figure 8).

Children do not always display depression in the same way adults do. Rather than showing the expression of profound sadness or hopelessness, childhood depression may produce the expression of exaggerated fears, clinginess, or avoidance of everyday activities. In older children, the symptoms may be sulking, school problems, and even acts of delinquency (Blain-Arcaro & Vaillancourt, 2019; Racine et al., 2021).

A considerably more common childhood disorder is **attention-deficit hyperactivity disorder, *or* ADHD,** a disorder marked by inattention, impulsiveness, a low tolerance for frustration, and generally a great deal of inappropriate activity. Although all children show such behavior some of the time, it is so common in children diagnosed with ADHD that it interferes with their everyday functioning (Barkley et al., 2011; Walton et al., 2017).

ADHD is surprisingly widespread, with estimates ranging between 3 and 9% of the school-age population–or some 3.3 million children under the age of 18 in the United States. Children diagnosed with the disorder are often exhausting to parents and teachers, and even their peers find them difficult to deal with (Centers for Disease Control and Prevention, 2022).

The cause of ADHD is not known, although most experts feel that it is produced by dysfunctions in the nervous system. For example, one theory suggests that unusually low levels of arousal in the central nervous system cause ADHD. To compensate, children with ADHD seek out stimulation to increase arousal. Still, such theories are

attention-deficit hyperactivity disorder (ADHD) A disorder marked by inattention, impulsiveness, a low tolerance for frustration, and a great deal of inappropriate activity. (Module 38)

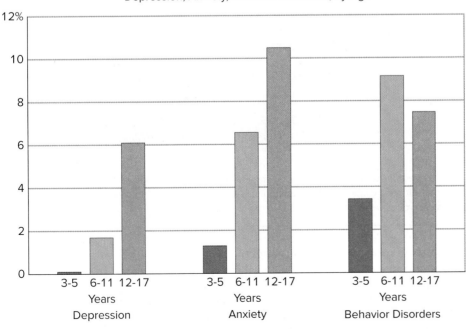

Depression, Anxiety, Behavior Disorders, by Age

FIGURE 8 Children's mental health. The prevalence of disorders changes with increasing age.

Sources: Centers for Disease Control and Prevention, 2019; U.S. Department of Health and Human Services, 2019.

speculative. Furthermore, because many children occasionally show behaviors characteristic of ADHD, it often is misdiagnosed or in some cases overdiagnosed. Only the frequency and persistence of the symptoms of ADHD allow for a correct diagnosis, which only a trained professional can do (Barkley, 2000; Sciutto & Eisenberg, 2007; Ketisch & Jones, 2013; Rocco et al., 2021; also see the *Neuroscience in Your Life* feature).

NEUROSCIENCE IN YOUR LIFE: DIFFERENT DISORDERS, COMMON BRAIN FEATURES

Thanks to advances in functional magnetic resonance imaging (fMRI) and other neuroimaging techniques, we have learned a great deal over the past several decades about how psychological disorders look in the brain. Most neuroimaging studies focus on a single psychological disorder. However, recent studies are attempting to identify brain abnormalities, such as changes in brain volume or in blood-flow patterns, that look similar in different disorders. For example, one recent study looked at children with attention-deficit/hyperactivity disorder, conduct or oppositional defiant disorder, anxiety disorders, and major depressive disorders to see how their brains differed from those of children without psychological disorders (Dugre et al., 2022).

Combining the results of 147 fMRI experiments, the researchers found that different disorders shared common features in the brain, such as reduced activation in regions important for controlling emotions and for storing, processing, and using information about other people. The finding that children with a range of psychological disorders shared particular brain features explains why particular kinds of psychological disorders tend to occur together in children. This finding also raises the possibility that medical or psychotherapeutic interventions that help to remedy dysfunction in certain brain regions could be effective in treating more than one psychological disorder.

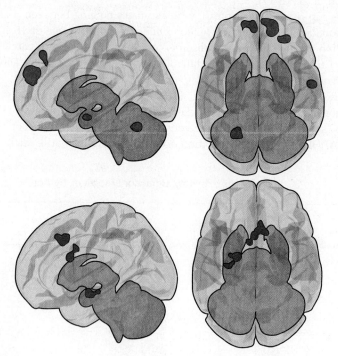

The brain regions associated with social cognition (in red) and emotional control (in blue) had lower activation in children with psychological disorders compared to children without a psychological disorder.

autism spectrum disorder A severe developmental disability that impairs children's ability to communicate and relate to others. (Module 38)

Autism spectrum disorder, a severe developmental disability that impairs one's ability to communicate and relate to others, is another disorder that usually appears in the first 3 years and typically continues throughout life. Children with autism have difficulties in both verbal and nonverbal communication, and they may avoid social contact. About 1 in 44 children is now thought to have the disorder, with boys four times more likely to be diagnosed with autism spectrum disorder than girls (Chiarotti & Venerosi, 2020; Zeidan et al., 2022).

The prevalence of the disorder has risen significantly in the past decade. Whether the increase is the result of an actual rise in the incidence of autism or is due to better reporting is a question of intense debate among researchers (Neal et al., 2013; Maenner et al., 2021).

Other Disorders

It's important to keep in mind that the various forms of psychological disorders described in DSM-5-TR cover much more ground than we have been able to discuss in this module. Some relate to topics considered in other chapters. For example, *psychoactive substance use disorder* relates to problems that arise from the use and abuse of drugs. Furthermore, *alcohol use disorders* are among the most serious and widespread problems. Both psychoactive substance use disorder and alcohol use disorder co-occur with many other psychological disorders, such as mood disorders, trauma- and stress-or-related disorders, and schizophrenia spectrum disorder, which complicate treatment considerably.

Another widespread problem is *eating disorders*. They include such disorders as *anorexia nervosa* and *bulimia*, which we considered in the chapter on motivation and emotion, as well as *binge-eating disorder*, characterized by binge eating without behaviors designed to prevent weight gain. Finally, *sexual disorders*, in which one's sexual activity is unsatisfactory, are another important class of problems. They include *sexual desire disorders, sexual arousal disorders*, and *paraphilic disorders*, atypical sexual activities that may include nonhuman objects or nonconsenting partners.

Another important class of disorders is *neurocognitive disorders*, problems with a biological cause that affect thinking and behavior. We considered some of them earlier, such as Alzheimer's disease and some types of developmental disabilities that are fully the consequence of biological issues.

The latest revision of the DSM included a new disorder, prolonged grief disorder. *Prolonged grief disorder* is characterized by distressing symptoms of grief that continue for at least 12 months after the loss of a close contact. The latest edition also included revised criteria for 70 existing disorders. Furthermore, we have not mentioned many other disorders at all. And each of the categories of disorder we have discussed can be divided into several subcategories. In short, the DSM seeks to provide a comprehensive, yet ever-changing, set of disorders, helping to catalog and understand the array that can affect us (First et al., 2022).

Autism spectrum disorder is a developmental disability that impairs communication and relationships with others. It affects four times as many boys as girls.
BSIP SA/Alamy Stock Photo

RECAP/EVALUATE/RETHINK

RECAP

LO 38-1 What are the major psychological disorders?

- Anxiety disorders are present when a person experiences so much anxiety that it affects daily functioning. Specific types of anxiety disorders include phobic disorder, panic disorder, and generalized anxiety disorder. Also related is obsessive-compulsive disorder.
- Somatic symptom disorders are psychological difficulties that take a physical (somatic) form but for which there is no medical cause. Examples are illness anxiety disorder and functional neurologic disorder (conversion disorder).
- Dissociative disorders are marked by the separation, or dissociation, of different facets of a person's personality that are usually integrated. Major kinds of dissociative disorders include dissociative identity disorder, dissociative amnesia, and dissociative fugue.
- Mood disorders are characterized by emotional states of depression or euphoria so strong that they intrude on everyday living. They include major depression and bipolar disorder.
- Schizophrenia spectrum disorder is one of the more severe forms of mental illness. Symptoms include declines in functioning, thought and language disturbances, perceptual disorders, emotional disturbance, and withdrawal from others.
- Strong evidence links schizophrenia spectrum disorder to genetic, biochemical, and environmental factors.

According to the predisposition explanation, an interaction between various factors produces the disorder.

- People with personality disorders experience little or no personal distress, but they do suffer from an inability to function as normal members of society. These disorders include antisocial personality disorder, borderline personality disorder, and narcissistic personality disorder.
- Childhood disorders include major depression, attention-deficit hyperactivity disorder (ADHD), and autism spectrum disorder.

EVALUATE

1. Xavier is terrified of elevators. He could be suffering from a(n)
   a. Obsessive-compulsive disorder
   b. Phobic disorder
   c. Panic disorder
   d. Generalized anxiety disorder
2. Carmen described an incident in which her anxiety suddenly rose to a peak and she felt a sense of impending doom. Carmen experienced a(n) _____ _____
3. Troubling thoughts that persist for weeks or months are known as
   a. Obsessions
   b. Compulsions
   c. Rituals
   d. Panic attacks
4. An overpowering urge to carry out a strange ritual is called a(n) _____

5. The separation of the personality, which provides escape from stressful situations, is the key factor in _____ disorders.
6. States of extreme euphoria and energy paired with severe depression characterize _____ disorder.
7. _____ schizophrenia spectrum disorder is characterized by symptoms that are sudden and of easily identifiable onset; _____ schizophrenia spectrum disorder develops gradually over a person's life span.
8. The _____ _____ states that schizophrenia spectrum disorder may be caused by an excess of certain neurotransmitters in the brain.

RETHINK

1. What cultural factors might contribute to the rate of anxiety disorders found in a culture? How might the experience of anxiety differ among people of different cultures?
2. Personality disorders are often not apparent to others, and many people with these problems seem to live basically normal lives and are not a threat to others. Because these people can function well in society, why should they be considered psychologically disordered?

Answers to Evaluate Questions

1. b; 2. panic attack; 3. a; 4. compulsion; 5. dissociative; 6. bipolar; 7. Reactive, process; 8. dopamine hypothesis

KEY TERMS

anxiety disorder
specific phobia
panic disorder
generalized anxiety disorder
obsessive-compulsive disorder (OCD)
obsession
compulsion
somatic symptom disorders

illness anxiety disorder
functional neurologic disorder (conversion disorder)
dissociative disorders
dissociative identity disorder (DID)
dissociative amnesia
dissociative fugue
mood disorder

major depressive disorder
mania
bipolar disorder
schizophrenia spectrum disorder
personality disorder
antisocial personality disorder
borderline personality disorder

narcissistic personality disorder
attention-deficit hyperactivity disorder (ADHD)
autism spectrum disorder

Module 39
Psychological Disorders in Perspective

How common are the kinds of psychological disorders we've been discussing? Here's one answer: One out of 2 people in the United States is likely to experience a psychological disorder at some point in their lives.

That's the conclusion drawn from the most comprehensive study on the prevalence of psychological disorders conducted. In that study, researchers conducted face-to-face interviews with more than 8,000 men and women between the ages of 15 and 54. The sample was designed to be representative of the population of the United States.

According to results of the study, 48% of those interviewed had experienced a disorder at some point in their lives. In addition, 30% experienced a disorder in any particular year. Furthermore, many people experience comorbidity. *Cormorbidity* is the appearance of multiple, simultaneous psychological disorders in the same person (Hansen et al., 2018; Jenkins et al., 2021).

The most common disorder reported in the study was depression. Some 17% of those surveyed reported at least one major episode. Ten percent had suffered from depression during the current year. The next most common disorder was alcohol dependence, which occurred at a lifetime incidence rate of 14%. In addition, 7% of those interviewed had experienced alcohol dependence in the previous year. Other frequently occurring psychological disorders were drug dependence, disorders involving panic (such as an overwhelming fear of talking to strangers or terror of heights), and posttraumatic stress disorder.

The national findings are consistent with studies of college students and their psychological difficulties. For example, in one study of the students who visited college mental health centers, almost a quarter had anxiety, and around 20% were depressed (see Figure 1) (Center for Collegiate Mental Health, 2019; also see the *Applying Psychology in the 21st Century* feature).

Because of the high prevalence of anxiety and depression, in 2022, a federal Preventive Services Task Force panel suggested that all adults under the age of 65 should be routinely screened for anxiety and all adults should be screened for depression. The panel viewed these screenings as particularly critical due to the COVID pandemic (Abbott, 2022).

LEARNING OUTCOMES

LO 39-1 How prevalent are psychological disorders?

LO 39-2 What indicators signal a need for the help of a mental health practitioner?

Study Alert

Remember that the incidence of various psychological disorders in the general population is surprisingly high, particularly in terms of depression and alcohol dependence.

From the perspective of...

A College Counselor What indicators might be most important in determining whether a college student is experiencing a psychological disorder?

Blend

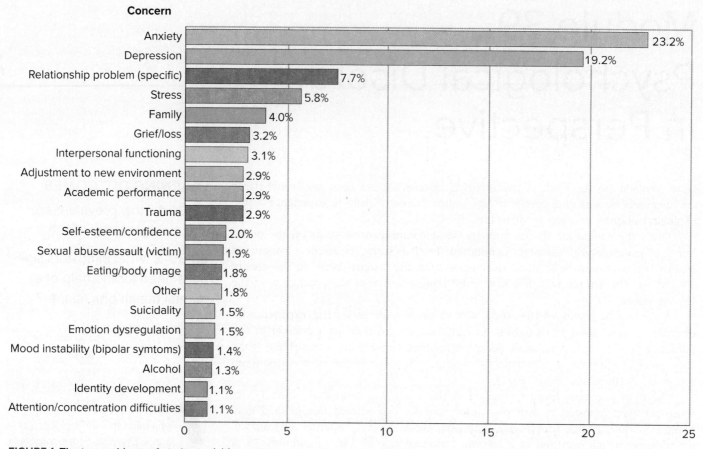

Concern

FIGURE 1 The top problems of students visiting college counseling centers. Would you have predicted this pattern of psychological difficulties?

Source: Adapted from Center for Collegiate Mental Health, 2019.

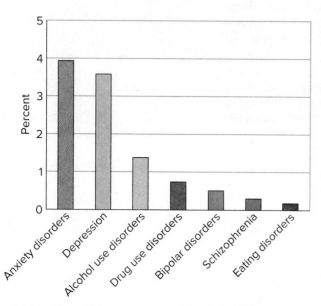

FIGURE 2 Global disorders. This summary shows the prevalence of psychological and substance-use disorders in people across the globe.

Source: Ritchie & Roser, 2021.

The significant level of psychological disorders is a problem not only in the United States; according to the World Health Organization, mental health difficulties are a global concern. Globally, 970 million people have some sort of psychological or substance use disorder, which amounts to 13% of the world's population (Ritchie & Roser, 2018; see Figure 2).

Furthermore, economic disparities affect treatment; more affluent people with mild disorders receive more and better treatment than do less fortunate people who have more severe disorders. In fact, psychological disorders make up 14% of global illness, but 90% of people in developing countries receive no care at all for their disorders (Scott et al., 2018).

Also, keep in mind that the incidence of specific disorders varies significantly in other cultures. For instance, cross-cultural surveys show that the incidence of major depression varies significantly from one culture to another. The probability of having at least one episode of depression is only 1.5% in Taiwan, 2.3% in Japan, 2.9% in Korea, and 6.4% in Greenland, compared with 11.6% in New Zealand and 16.4% in France. Such notable differences underscore the importance of considering the cultural context of psychological disorders (Arifin et al., 2018; De Los Reyes et al., 2019).

APPLYING PSYCHOLOGY IN THE 21ST CENTURY

A TEENAGE MENTAL HEALTH CRISIS

Are you feeling stressed out, perhaps more than some of the adults around you? How did the coronavirus pandemic affect your level of stress?

If you answered something along the lines of "significantly," you're not alone. Many others of the current generation of college students report feeling the same way, and the stress is taking a toll on their mental health.

Teenagers in the United States also are experiencing a mental health crisis, and experts aren't sure why that is. By many indicators, they should actually be doing pretty well: Teens today are better educated and less likely to smoke, to use drugs or alcohol, or to get pregnant than they were a generation ago. But the data are clear: As their physical health got better over the past two decades, their mental health got worse. Mood disorders, anxiety, and self-injurious behaviors are all soaring. For young people between the ages of 10 and 24, depression and suicide are up 60% since 2007 (Richtel, 2022).

The pandemic is not the only reason. For example, one popular explanation for this crisis is the rise in use of social media. Part of the thinking is that social media apps present a sanitized and idealized portrayal of users' lives and that teens are constantly comparing themselves to these unrealistic standards and coming up short. For example, in one study, teens whose responses to a questionnaire showed them as being particularly concerned with social standing were more likely to use social media, and they experienced a dip in self-esteem and a rise in anxiety after

Many people experience significant amounts of stress in their lives, potentially impacting their mental health.
g-stockstudio/Shutterstock

viewing their peers' positive social media profiles (Vogel et al., 2015).

Researcher Tracy Dennis-Tiwary (2022) suggests that social media apps aren't so much the cause of the problem as they are another symptom of it: Anxious teens may use social media as a way to avoid their anxiety rather than confront it, and that avoidance may be the real problem. She argues that anxiety serves important protective functions, such as alerting us to threats and motivating us to prepare for the future, and that avoiding or suppressing anxiety may therefore be counterproductive to our mental health. For example, when Dennis-Tiwary and colleagues induced anxiety in a group of young adult research participants, those participants subsequently showed greater attention and

focus than a comparison group induced to feel happy—evidence that anxiety is helpful in responding to threats or emergences. Other research showed that people produce more creative solutions to a problem when they are induced to feel anxiety (Birk et al., 2011; Barendse et al., 2022; Findley et al., 2022).

Dennis-Tiwary suggests that anxiety can be managed better by changing how we think about it—that is, by seeing it as an advantage rather than a liability. Research supports her argument. In one study, adults with an anxiety disorder were put in a stressful situation; those who had been taught that anxiety prepares people to respond better to threats and to think of their anxious feelings as indicators of being ready to face the challenge ahead responded to that challenge with greater confidence, focus, and engagement than those who hadn't been taught to reframe their anxiety that way. Another study showed that when parents were taught to help their clinically anxious children face their anxiety rather than avoid it, 87% of those children showed improvement in their symptoms of anxiety (Jamieson et al., 2013; Lebowitz et al., 2020; Barendse et al., 2021).

One thing is clear: The crisis in teen mental health will require continued study into its causes as well as development of new and innovative treatment approaches.

QUESTIONS TO CONSIDER

- Besides the pandemic and social media use, what might be some other reasons for the recent sudden rise in mental health disorders in young people?
- Do you think you would you be able to handle anxiety better if you thought of it as excitement instead? Why or why not?

The Social and Cultural Context of Psychological Disorders

In considering the nature of the psychological disorders described in DSM-5-TR, it's important to keep in mind that the disorders that were included in the manual are a reflection of Western culture at the start of the 21st century. The classification system provides a snapshot of how its authors viewed mental disorder when it was published.

In fact, the development of the most recent version of the DSM was a source of great debate, which in part reflects issues that divide society.

One specific, newly classified disorder that was added to DSM-5-TR and that has caused controversy is known as disruptive mood dysregulation disorder. This particular diagnosis is characterized by temperamental outbursts grossly out of proportion to the situation, both verbally and physically, in children between the ages of 6 and 18. Some practitioners argue these symptoms simply define a child having a temper tantrum rather than a disorder (Bruno et al., 2019; Moore et al., 2019; Mürner-Lavanchy et al., 2021).

Similarly, someone who overeats 12 times in 3 months can be considered to be suffering from the new classification of binge-eating disorder, which seems to some critics to be overly inclusive. Finally, hoarding behavior is now placed in its own category of psychological disorder. Some critics, however, suggest that the inclusion of hoarding as a category is more a reflection of the rise of reality television shows focusing on hoarding rather than a distinct category of psychological disturbance (Hudson et al., 2012; Racine et al., 2017; Moulding et al., 2017).

The social and cultural environment may also play a role in the mass shootings that plague the United States. According to some politicians, mass murderers are severely psychologically disordered, whereas others believe the easy availability of guns and weapons is the cause.

The scientific data are clear, though: While a small percentage of mass murderers do have some diagnosable disorder, the majority have no such history. Obviously, they are not emotionally stable or in good mental health, and many have experienced violence as children or have drug- and alcohol-abuse issues. However, the impetus to commit murder typically stems less from mental illness and more from feelings of disgruntlement, grievance, humiliation, or anger about what perpetrators see as difficult circumstances in their lives. They ultimately turn to violence when triggered by some threatening event rather than by a mental disorder, and, often, easy access to weapons permits a violent response (Brucato et al., 2021; Pan, 2022).

In support of this reasoning, we can look to the rates of psychological disturbance across the world and the rates of gun violence. What we find is that although rates of psychological disturbance are similar globally, in countries where access to guns is more restricted, we don't find the same level of violence as we do in the United States. Such conclusions are politically controversial, however, and debates about the source of mass violence will likely continue (Budenz et al., 2018; Leander et al., 2019; Yelderman et al., 2019).

Such controversies underline the fact that our understanding of psychological disorders reflects the society and culture in which we live. Future revisions of DSM may include a different catalog of disorders. Even now, other cultures might include a list of disorders that differ significantly from the list that appears in the current DSM, as we discuss next.

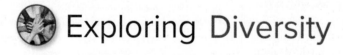 Exploring Diversity

DSM and Culture—and the Culture of DSM

To most people raised in the United States, a person who hears voices of the recently deceased is probably a victim of a psychological disturbance. Yet some Plains Indians routinely hear the voices of the dead calling to them from the afterlife, and in their culture, that's considered perfectly normal.

The voices Plains Indians hear are only one example of the role of culture in determining what behavior should be labeled as "abnormal." In fact, among all the major adult disorders included in the DSM categorization, just a minority are found across all cultures of the world. Most others only are prevalent in North America and Western Europe (Jacob, 2014; Allen & Becker, 2019; Langa & Gone, 2019).

Study Alert

It is important to understand that the DSM is a living document that presents a view of disorders that reflects the culture and historical context of its authors.

For instance, take anorexia nervosa, the disorder in which people become obsessed with their weight and sometimes stop eating, ultimately starving to death in the process. It turns out that anorexia nervosa occurs most frequently in cultures that hold the societal standard that slender female bodies are the most desirable. In most of the world, where such a standard does not exist, anorexia nervosa is rare. Furthermore, the disorder may appear in specific ways in a particular culture. For instance, in Hong Kong, symptoms of one form of anorexia relate to complaints of bloated stomachs, rather than fears of becoming overweight (Watters, 2010; Munro et al., 2017; Fadus et al., 2019).

Similarly, dissociative identity (multiple personality) disorder makes sense as a problem only in societies in which a sense of self is fairly concrete. In certain parts of India, the sense of self is based on external factors that are relatively independent of the person. In those places, when an individual displays symptoms of what people in a Western society would call dissociative identity disorder, people in these parts of India assume that the person is possessed either by demons (which they view as a malady) or by gods (which does not require treatment).

Furthermore, even though disorders such as schizophrenia spectrum disorder are found throughout the world, cultural factors influence the specific symptoms of the disorder. Hence, catatonic schizophrenia, in which unmoving patients appear to be frozen in the same position (sometimes for days), is rare in North America and Western Europe. In contrast, in India, 80% of those with schizophrenia spectrum disorders are catatonic.

Other cultures have disorders that do not appear in the West. For example, in Malaysia, a behavior called *amok* is characterized by a wild outburst in which a usually quiet and withdrawn person kills or severely injures another. *Koro* is a condition found in Southeast Asian males who develop an intense panic that their penis is about to withdraw irretrievably into their abdomens. Finally, *ataque de nervios* is a disorder found most often among Latinos from the Caribbean. It is characterized by trembling, crying, uncontrollable screams, and incidents of verbal or physical aggression (Cohen et al., 1999; Adams & Dzokoto, 2007; Ebigbo et al., 2015; Ustun, 2022).

Explanations for and experiences of psychological disorders also differ among cultures. For example, in China, psychological disorders are commonly viewed as weaknesses of the heart, a concept that derives from thousands of years of traditional Chinese medicine. Chinese people are more likely than people in Western cultures to express their emotional anguish in terms of physical symptoms such as heart pain, "heart panic," or "heart vexed." Similarly, Nigerians' acute anxiety may be accompanied by the sensation of insects crawling under their skin, a condition known as *odi ori* (Lee et al., 2007; Watters, 2010; McRobbie, 2018).

In sum, we should not assume that the DSM provides the final word on psychological disorders. The disorders it includes are very much a creation and function of Western cultures at a particular moment in time, and its categories should not be seen as universally applicable (Tseng, 2003; Haroz et al., 2017; Frisby, 2020).

BECOMING AN INFORMED CONSUMER
of Psychology

Deciding When You Need Help

After you've considered the range and variety of psychological disturbances that can afflict people, you may begin to feel that you suffer from one (or more) of the problems we have discussed. In fact, this perception has a name: *medical student's disease*. Although in this case it might more aptly be labeled *psychology student's disease*, the basic symptoms are the same: feeling that you suffer from the same sorts of problems you are studying.

Most often, of course, your concerns will be unwarranted. As we have discussed, the differences between normal and abnormal behavior are often so fuzzy that it is easy to jump to the conclusion that you might have the same symptoms that are involved in serious forms of mental disturbance.

Before coming to such a conclusion, though, keep in mind that from time to time, we all experience a wide range of emotions, and it is not unusual to feel deeply unhappy, fantasize about bizarre situations, or feel anxiety about life's circumstances. It is the persistence, depth, and consistency of such behavior that set normal reactions apart from abnormal ones. If you have not previously had serious doubts about the normality of your behavior, it is unlikely that reading about others' psychological disorders will prompt you to reevaluate your earlier conclusion.

On the other hand, many people do have problems that merit concern, and in such cases, it is important to consider the possibility that professional help is warranted. The following list of symptoms can serve as a guideline to help you determine whether outside intervention might be useful (American Psychiatric Association, 2018; American Psychological Association, 2019).

- Long-term feelings of distress that interfere with your sense of well-being, competence, and ability to function effectively in daily activities
- Occasions in which you experience overwhelmingly high stress accompanied by feelings of inability to cope with the situation
- Prolonged depression or feelings of hopelessness, especially when they do not have any clear cause
- Withdrawal from others
- Thoughts of inflicting harm on oneself or suicide
- A chronic physical problem for which no physical cause can be determined
- A fear or phobia that prevents you from engaging in everyday activities
- Feelings that other people are out to get you or are talking about and plotting against you
- Inability to interact effectively with others, preventing the development of friendships and loving relationships
- Alcohol or drug abuse
- Changes in sleeping, eating, and personal hygiene habits

This list offers a rough set of guidelines for determining when the normal problems of everyday living have escalated beyond your ability to deal with them by yourself. In such situations, the *least* reasonable approach would be to pore over the psychological disorders we have discussed in an attempt at self-diagnosis. A more reasonable strategy is to consider seeking professional help. Also, remember that if you are in severe psychological stress and feel you may harm yourself, you can call the U.S. national hotline at 988, 24 hours a day, and speak to a trained counselor.

RECAP/EVALUATE/RETHINK

RECAP

LO 39-1 How prevalent are psychological disorders?

- About half the people in the United States are likely to experience a psychological disorder at some point in their lives; 30% experience a disorder in any specific year.

LO 39-2 What indicators signal a need for the help of a mental health practitioner?

- The signals that indicate a need for professional help include long-term feelings of psychological distress,

feelings of inability to cope with stress, withdrawal from other people, thoughts of inflicting harm on oneself or suicide, prolonged feelings of hopelessness, chronic physical problems with no apparent causes, phobias and compulsions, paranoia, and an inability to interact with others.

EVALUATE

1. The latest version of DSM is considered to be the definitive guide to defining psychological disorders. True or false?

2. Match the disorder with the culture in which it is most common:

1. *Amok*
2. Anorexia nervosa
3. *Ataque de nervios*
4. Catatonic schizophrenia

a. India
b. Malaysia
c. United States
d. Caribbean

RETHINK

1. Why is inclusion in DSM-5-TR of disorders such as hoarding behavior so controversial and political? What disadvantages does inclusion bring? Does inclusion bring any benefits?

2. What societal changes would have to occur for psychological disorders to be regarded as the equivalent of appendicitis or another treatable physical disorder? Do you think a person who has been treated for a psychological disorder could become president of the United States? Should such a person become president?

Answers to Evaluate Questions

1. False; the development of the latest version of DSM was a source of great controversy, in part reflecting issues that divide society; 2. 1-b, 2-c, 3-d, 4-a

LOOKING *Back*

EPILOGUE

We've discussed some of the many types of psychological disorders to which people are prone, noted the difficulty psychologists and physicians have in clearly differentiating normal from abnormal behavior, and looked at some of the approaches mental health professionals have taken to explain and treat psychological disorders. We considered today's most commonly used classification scheme, categorized in DSM-5-TR, and examined some of the more prevalent forms of psychological disorders. To gain a perspective on the topic of psychological disorders, we discussed the surprisingly broad incidence of psychological disorders in U.S. society and the cultural nature of such disorders.

Turn back to the prologue, which described the case of Caroline Mazel-Carlton. Using the knowledge you've gained about psychological disorders, consider the following questions.

1. How can we tell that Mazel-Carlton's behavior is abnormal?
2. In what ways does her behavior fit the definition of a particular disorder? Why?
3. How would each perspective on abnormality explain Mazel-Carlton's condition?
4. Which perspective on abnormality do you think gives the best insight into the origin of Mazel-Carlton's condition? Why do you think so?

Design Elements: Man with laptop: Dragon Images/Shutterstock; Exclamation point and mobile frame: McGraw Hill; Smartphone: WML Image/Shutterstock; Hands: Stefano Garau/Shutterstock.

VISUAL SUMMARY 12 Psychological Disorders

MODULE 37 Normal Versus Abnormal: Making the Distinction

Defining Abnormality

- Deviation from average behavior
- Deviation from ideal behavior
- Sense of personal discomfort
- Inability to function effectively
- Legal concept

Perspectives on Abnormality

Perspectives on Psychological Disorders

Perspective	Description	Application of Perspective to Caroline Mazel-Carlton's Case, Discussed in Chapter Prologue
Medical	Assumes that physiological causes are at the root of psychological disorders	Examine Mazel-Carlton for medical problems, such as brain tumor, chemical imbalance in the brain, or disease.
Psychoanalytic	Argues that psychological disorders stem from childhood conflicts	Seek out information about Mazel-Carlton's past, considering possible childhood conflicts.
Behavioral	Assumes that abnormal behaviors are learned responses	Concentrate on rewards and punishments for Mazel-Carlton's behavior, and identify environmental stimuli that reinforce her behavior.
Cognitive	Assumes that cognitions (people's thoughts and beliefs) are central to psychological disorders	Focus on Mazel-Carlton's perceptions of herself and her environment.
Humanistic	Emphasizes people's responsibility for their own behavior and the need to self-actualize	Consider Mazel-Carlton's behavior in terms of her choices and efforts to reach her potential.
Sociocultural	Assumes that behavior is shaped by family, society, and culture	Focus on how societal demands contributed to Mazel-Carlton's disorder.

Classifying Abnormal Behavior: DSM-5-TR attempts to provide comprehensive and relatively precise definitions for more than 200 disorders.

MODULE 38 Major Psychological Disorders

Anxiety Disorders: Anxiety without external justification

- Phobic disorder
- Panic disorder
- Generalized anxiety disorder
- Causes of anxiety disorders

Obsessive-Compulsive Disorder

Somatic Symptom Disorders: Psychological difficulties that take on a physical form with no medical cause

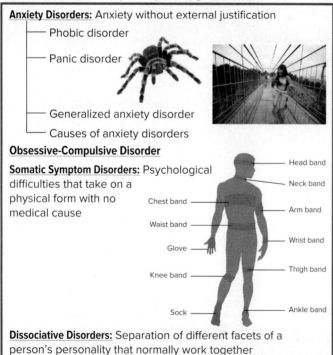

Head band
Neck band
Chest band
Arm band
Waist band
Glove
Wrist band
Knee band
Thigh band
Sock
Ankle band

Dissociative Disorders: Separation of different facets of a person's personality that normally work together

Mood Disorders: Disturbances in emotional experience

- Major depressive disorder
- Mania and bipolar disorder
- Causes of mood disorders
  - Genetics
  - Psychological: feelings of loss or anger
  - Behavioral: stress
  - Cognitive: learned helplessness and no hope

Schizophrenia Spectrum Disorder: A class of disorders in which distortion of reality occurs

- Decline from a previous level of functioning
- Disturbances of thought and language
- Delusions
- Hallucinations and perceptual disorders
- Emotional disturbances

Personality Disorders: A set of inflexible, maladaptive behavior patterns

- Antisocial personality disorder
- Borderline personality disorder
- Narcissistic personality disorder

Childhood Disorders: Start during childhood or adolescence

- Attention-deficit hyperactivity disorder
- Autism spectrum disorder

MODULE 39 Psychological Disorders in Perspective

Social and Cultural Context: The significant level of psychological disorders is a problem not only in the United States; according to the World Health Organization, mental health difficulties are a global concern.

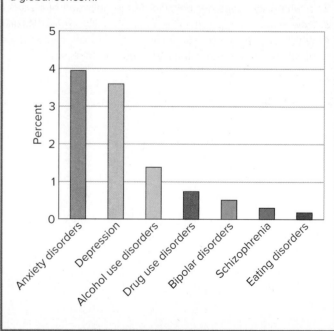

(Module 37): (top): Brett Coomer/Pool Houston Chronicle/AP Images; (bottom): American Psychiatric Association; (Module 38) (top left): Pets in Frames/Shutterstock; (top right): Imagine China/Newscom (Module 39) Ritchie & Roser, 2021.

bernardbodo/Getty Images

CHAPTER 13
Treatment of Psychological Disorders

LEARNING OUTCOMES FOR CHAPTER 13

	MODULE 40
LO 40-1 What are the goals of psychologically based and biologically based treatment approaches?	**PSYCHOTHERAPY: PSYCHODYNAMIC, BEHAVIORAL, AND COGNITIVE APPROACHES TO TREATMENT**
LO 40-2 What are the psychodynamic, behavioral, and cognitive approaches to treatment?	Psychodynamic Approaches to Therapy
	Behavioral Approaches to Therapy
	Cognitive Approaches to Therapy
	MODULE 41
LO 41-1 What are the humanistic approaches to treatment?	**PSYCHOTHERAPY: HUMANISTIC, INTERPERSONAL, GROUP AND ONLINE APPROACHES TO TREATMENT**
LO 41-2 What is interpersonal therapy?	Humanistic Therapy
LO 41-3 How does group therapy differ from individual types of therapy?	Interpersonal Therapy
	Group Therapies
LO 41-4 Is online therapy effective?	**Applying Psychology in the 21st Century:** Online Therapy
LO 41-5 How effective is psychotherapy, and which kind of psychotherapy works best in a given situation?	Evaluating Psychotherapy: Does Therapy Work?
	Exploring Diversity: Racial and Ethnic Factors in Treatment: Should Therapists Be Color-Blind?

LO 42-1 How are pharmaceutical drugs, electroconvulsive therapies, and psychosurgical techniques used today in the treatment of psychological disorders?

PROLOGUE *PUTTING LIFE ON HOLD*

Five years ago, Sarah was so overwhelmed with depression that she couldn't stop crying or thinking about ending her life. She was so unable to function that she had to quit her job, and her doctors insisted that she move back home with her parents for her own safety. She tried many therapies, including dozens of antidepressant drugs, hospitalizations, and electroconvulsive therapy, but nothing worked for her.

Then Sarah was recruited to be the first person to try a new experimental therapy: what researchers call *deep brain stimulation,* or—more informally—a "pacemaker for the brain." A small battery-powered device was surgically implanted in her brain, in a region that was identified as related to her particular manifestation of depression. When the device sensed a pattern of neural activity consistent with a depressive episode, it stimulated the specific regions of Sarah's brain to disrupt it. It therefore was a form of treatment personalized to Sarah, matched to her brain.

Within weeks, Sarah felt much better. While her depression hasn't gone away, it has become much more manageable. She lives on her own again, take classes, and participate in hobbies that she enjoys. Enjoyment is a feeling that evaded Sarah for many years, and the moments when she experiences it again give her new hope for her future (Belluck, 2021).

LOOKING *Ahead*

Deep brain stimulation designed to match a particular individual's brain is among the newest ways to treat people experiencing psychological disorders. Although such personalized treatment is particularly innovative, such new approaches share a common objective with more traditional forms of therapy: to enable individuals to achieve richer, more meaningful, and more fulfilling lives.

Approaches to treating psychological disorders fall into two main categories: psychologically based and biologically based therapies. **Psychotherapy** is psychologically based treatment in

which a trained professional—a therapist—uses psychological techniques to help someone overcome psychological difficulties and disorders, resolve problems in living, or bring about personal growth. The goal of psychotherapy is to produce lasting psychological change in a person (called a *client* or *patient*) through discussions and interactions with the therapist. In contrast, **biomedical therapy** is biologically based and relies on drugs and medical procedures to improve psychological functioning.

As we describe the various approaches to therapy, keep in mind that although the distinctions may seem clear-cut, the classifications and procedures overlap a good deal. In fact, many therapists today take an *eclectic approach* to therapy, which means they use a variety of methods with an individual patient. Assuming that psychological as well as biological processes often produce psychological disorders, eclectic therapists may draw from several perspectives simultaneously to address the psychological as well as the biological aspects of a person's problems.

Regardless of the specific form of therapy, treatment of psychological disorders has become commonplace. Nearly 1 in 4 adults aged 18 to 44 in the United States reports receiving treatment for their mental health in the prior 12 months. Although those seeking treatment have a variety of reasons for doing so, they share the goals of improving their quality of their life and achieving positive psychological and behavioral change (Terlizzi & Schiller, 2022).

psychotherapy Treatment in which a trained professional—a therapist—uses psychological techniques to help a person overcome psychological difficulties and disorders, resolve problems in living, or bring about personal growth. (Module 40)

biomedical therapy Therapy that relies on drugs and other medical procedures to improve psychological functioning. (Module 40)

Module 40

Psychotherapy: Psychodynamic, Behavioral, and Cognitive Approaches to Treatment

Hundreds of varieties of psychotherapy exist. They range from the truly experimental (such as the guided use of psychedelic drugs or the use of personalized deep brain stimulation described in the prologue) to more conventional, tried-and-true methods that have a long and proven history of use and effectiveness.

Although the methods are diverse, all psychological approaches have a common perspective: They seek to solve psychological problems by modifying people's behavior and helping them obtain a better understanding of themselves and their past, present, and future.

In light of the variety of psychological approaches, it is not surprising that the people who provide therapy vary considerably in educational background and training (see Figure 1). Many have doctoral degrees in psychology, having attended graduate school, learned clinical and research techniques, and held an internship in a facility that treats people with psychological disorders. But therapy is also provided by people in fields allied with psychology, such as psychiatrists (who have a medical degree with a specialization in psychological disorders) and social workers (who have a master's degree and have specialized in psychological disorders).

Depending on the kind of problem a person is experiencing, certain types of therapists may be more appropriate than others. For example, a person who is suffering from a severe disturbance and who has lost touch with reality may typically require some sort of biologically based drug therapy. In that case, a psychiatrist–who has

LEARNING OUTCOMES

LO 40-1 What are the goals of psychologically based and biologically based treatment approaches?

LO 40-2 What are the psychodynamic, behavioral, and cognitive approaches to treatment?

Getting Help from the Right Person

Clinical Psychologists
Psychologists with a PhD or PsyD with about 5 years of training and who have also completed a postgraduate internship. They specialize in assessment and treatment of psychological difficulties, providing psychotherapy and, in some U.S. states, can prescribe drugs.

Counseling Psychologists
Psychologists with a PhD or EdD who typically treat day-to-day adjustment problems, often in a university mental health clinic

Psychiatrists
MDs with postgraduate training in psychological disorders. Because they can prescribe medication, they often treat the most severe disorders.

Psychoanalysts
Either MDs or psychologists who specialize in psychoanalysis, the treatment technique first developed by Freud

Licensed Professional Counselors or Clinical Mental Health Counselors
Professionals with a master's degree who provide therapy to individuals, couples, and families and who hold a national or state certification

Clinical or Psychiatric Social Workers
Professionals with a master's degree and specialized training who may provide therapy, usually regarding common family and personal problems

FIGURE 1 A variety of professionals provide therapy and counseling. Each could be expected to give helpful advice and direction. However, the nature of the problem a person is experiencing may make one or another therapist more appropriate.

trained as a physician–might be the professional of choice. In contrast, those suffering from milder disorders, such as difficulty adjusting to the death of a family member, have a broader array of choices, including other types listed in Figure 1.

Regardless of their specific training, all psychotherapists employ one of four major approaches to therapy that we'll consider next: psychodynamic, behavioral, cognitive, and humanistic treatment approaches. These approaches grow out of the perspectives of personality and psychological disorders developed by psychologists.

Psychodynamic Approaches to Therapy

psychodynamic therapy Therapy that seeks to bring unresolved past conflicts and unacceptable impulses from the unconscious into the conscious, where patients may deal with the problems more effectively. (Module 40)

Psychodynamic therapy seeks to bring unresolved past conflicts and unacceptable impulses from the unconscious into the conscious, where patients may deal with the problems more effectively. Although psychodynamic approaches originally derived from Freud's psychoanalytic theories of personality, today they encompass a wider range of therapies. The common assumptions behind psychodynamic therapies are that unconscious forces affect our behavior and that the goal of therapy is to try to identify and control them.

Psychodynamic approaches hold that people employ *defense mechanisms*, psychological strategies to protect themselves from unacceptable unconscious impulses. The most common defense mechanism is *repression*, which pushes threatening and unpleasant thoughts and impulses back into the unconscious. However, because people cannot completely bury their unacceptable thoughts and impulses, anxiety associated with them can produce abnormal behavior.

How do we rid ourselves of the anxiety produced by unconscious, unwanted thoughts and impulses? To Freud, the answer was to confront the conflicts and impulses by bringing them out of the unconscious part of the mind and into the conscious part. Freud assumed that this technique would reduce anxiety stemming from past conflicts and that the patient could then participate in their daily life more effectively.

A psychodynamic therapist, then, faces the challenge of finding a way to assist patients' attempts to explore and understand the unconscious. The technique that has evolved has a number of components, but basically it consists of guiding patients to consider and discuss their past experiences in explicit detail from the time of their first memories. This process assumes that patients will eventually stumble upon long-hidden crises, traumas, and conflicts that are producing anxiety in their adult lives. They will then be able to "work through"–understand and rectify–those difficulties.

PSYCHOANALYSIS: FREUD'S THERAPY

psychoanalysis Freud's psychotherapy in which the goal is to release hidden thoughts and feelings from the unconscious part of our minds in order to reduce their power in controlling behavior. (Module 40)

Psychoanalysis is Freud's specific version of psychodynamic therapy. The goal of psychoanalysis is to release hidden thoughts and feelings from the unconscious part of our mind in order to reduce their power in controlling behavior.

In traditional psychoanalysis, which tends to be a lengthy and expensive process, patients may meet with a therapist with considerable frequency, sometimes as much as 50 minutes a session, 4-5 days a week, for several years. In their sessions, therapists and patients typically use a technique developed by Freud called *free association*. Patients using free association say aloud whatever comes to mind, regardless of its apparent irrelevance or senselessness. The psychoanalyst then attempts to recognize and label the connections between what a patient says and the patient's unconscious.

Therapists also use *dream interpretation*, examining dreams to find clues to unconscious conflicts and problems. Moving beyond the surface description of a dream (called the *manifest content*), therapists seek its underlying meaning (the *latent content*), which supposedly reveals the true unconscious meaning of the dream (Hill et al., 2013; Sandford, 2017; Mahon, 2021).

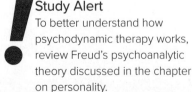

Study Alert

To better understand how psychodynamic therapy works, review Freud's psychoanalytic theory discussed in the chapter on personality.

The processes of free association and dream interpretation do not always move forward easily. The same unconscious forces that initially produced repression may keep past difficulties out of the conscious mind, which produces resistance. *Resistance* is an inability or unwillingness to discuss or reveal particular memories, thoughts, or motivations.

Patients can show resistance in many ways. For instance, they may be discussing a childhood memory and suddenly forget what they were saying, or they may abruptly change the subject completely. It is the therapist's job to discern instances of resistance and interpret their meaning. The therapists also need to try to make patients return to the subject they are trying to avoid–which is likely to hold difficult or painful memories for the patients.

Because of the close, almost intimate interaction between patient and psychoanalyst, the relationship between the two often becomes emotionally charged and takes on a complexity unlike most other relationships. Patients may eventually think of the analyst as a symbol of a significant other in their past, perhaps a parent or a lover, and apply some of their feelings for that person to the analyst–a phenomenon known as transference. **Transference** is the transfer of feelings to a psychoanalyst of love or anger that had been originally directed to a patient's parents or other authority figures (Turri, 2015; McCluskey & O'Toole, 2019; Hersh, 2021).

A therapist can use transference to help a patient recreate past relationships that were psychologically difficult. For instance, if a patient undergoing transference views her therapist as a symbol of her father with whom she had a difficult relationship, the patient and therapist may "redo" an earlier interaction, this time including more positive aspects. Through this process, the patient may resolve conflicts regarding her real father–something that is beginning to happen in the following therapy session:

> SANDY: My father . . . never took any interest in any of us. . . . It was my mother–rest her soul–who loved us, not our father. He worked her to death. Lord, I miss her. . . . I must sound angry at my father. Don't you think I have a right to be angry?
>
> THERAPIST: Do you think you have a right to be angry?
>
> SANDY: Of course, I do! Why are you questioning me? You don't believe me, do you?
>
> THERAPIST: You want me to believe you.
>
> SANDY: I don't care whether you believe me or not. . . . I know what you're thinking–you think I'm crazy–you must be laughing at me–I'll probably be a case in your next book! You're just sitting there–smirking–making me feel like a bad person–thinking I'm wrong for being mad, that I have no right to be mad.
>
> THERAPIST: Just like your father.
>
> SANDY: Yes, you're just like my father.–Oh my God! Just now–I–I–thought I was talking to him. (Sue & Sue, 1990)

CONTEMPORARY PSYCHODYNAMIC APPROACHES

Few people have the time, money, or patience to participate in years of traditional psychoanalysis. Even more important, no conclusive evidence shows that psychoanalysis, as Freud originally conceived it in the 19th century, works better than other, more recent forms of psychodynamic therapy.

Today, psychodynamic therapy tends to be of shorter duration, usually lasting no longer than 3 months or 20 sessions. Psychodynamic therapists take a more active role than Freud would have prescribed, and they prod and advise the patient with considerable directness. Finally, contemporary psychodynamic therapists put less emphasis on a patient's past history and childhood. Instead, they concentrate on an individual's current relationships and specific concerns (Brafman, 2011; Dreissen et al., 2017).

The close and intense relationship between therapist and patient often becomes highly complex.
SDI Productions/Getty Images

transference The transfer of feelings to a psychoanalyst of love or anger that had been originally directed to a patient's parents or other authority figures. (Module 40)

EVALUATING PSYCHODYNAMIC THERAPY

Even with its current modifications, psychodynamic therapy has its critics. In its longer versions, it can be time-consuming and expensive, especially in comparison with other forms of psychotherapy, such as behavioral and cognitive approaches. Furthermore, less articulate patients may not do as well as more articulate ones.

Ultimately, the most important concern about psychodynamic treatment is whether it actually works, and there is no simple answer to this question. Psychodynamic treatment techniques have been controversial since Freud introduced them. Part of the problem is the difficulty in establishing whether patients have improved after psychodynamic therapy. Determining effectiveness depends on reports from the therapist or the patients themselves–reports that are obviously open to bias and subjective interpretation.

Furthermore, critics have questioned the entire theoretical basis of psychodynamic theory; they maintain that constructs such as the unconscious have not been scientifically confirmed. Despite the criticism, though, the psychodynamic treatment approach has remained viable. For some people, it provides solutions to difficult psychological issues, provides effective treatment for psychological disturbance, and permits the potential development of an unusual degree of insight into their life (Thase, 2013; Sell et al., 2017; Berzoff et al., 2021).

behavioral treatment approaches
Treatment approaches that make use of the basic processes of learning, such as reinforcement and extinction, to reduce or eliminate maladaptive behavior. (Module 40)

Behavioral Approaches to Therapy

Perhaps, when you were a child, your parents rewarded you with an ice cream cone when you were especially good . . . or sent you to your room if you misbehaved. Sound principles back up such a child-rearing strategy: Good behavior is maintained by reinforcement, and unwanted behavior can be eliminated by punishment.

These principles represent the basic underpinnings of behavioral treatment approaches. **Behavioral treatment approaches** use the principles of learning, such as reinforcement and extinction, to reduce or eliminate maladaptive behavior. These approaches are built on a fundamental assumption: Both abnormal behavior and normal behavior are *learned*.

In this view, people who act abnormally either have failed to learn the skills they need to cope with problems of living, or they have acquired faulty skills and patterns that are being maintained through some form of reinforcement. To modify abnormal behavior, then, proponents of these approaches propose that people must learn new behavior to replace the faulty skills they have developed, and they need to unlearn their maladaptive behavior patterns (Kowalik et al., 2011; Kivlighan et al., 2015; Brown et al., 2021).

Behavioral psychologists do not need to delve into people's pasts or their psyches. Rather than viewing abnormal behavior as a symptom of an underlying problem, they consider the abnormal behavior as the problem in need of modification. The goal of therapy is to change people's behavior to allow them to function more effectively. In this view, then, there is no problem other than the maladaptive behavior itself; if you can change that behavior, treatment is successful.

CLASSICAL CONDITIONING TREATMENTS

Suppose you bite into your favorite candy bar and find that not only is it infested with ants, but you've also swallowed a bunch of them. You immediately become sick to your stomach and throw up. Your long-term reaction? You never eat that kind of candy bar again, and it may be months before you eat any type of candy. You have learned through the basic process of classical conditioning to avoid candy so that you will not get sick and throw up.

Behavioral approaches to treatment would seek to modify the behavior of this couple rather than to focus on the underlying causes of the behavior.
metinkiyak/Getty Images

Aversive Conditioning This simple example illustrates how a person can be classically conditioned to modify behavior. Behavior therapists use this principle in **aversive conditioning,** which aims to reduce the frequency of undesired behavior by pairing an unpleasant stimulus with undesired behavior. For example, behavior therapists might use aversive conditioning by pairing alcohol with a medication that causes severe nausea and vomiting. After the two have been paired a few times, the person associates the alcohol alone with vomiting and finds alcohol less appealing.

aversive conditioning A form of therapy that reduces the frequency of undesired behavior by pairing an aversive, unpleasant stimulus with undesired behavior. (Module 40)

Aversion therapy works reasonably well with some specific kinds of disorders, including substance-abuse problems such as alcoholism and certain kinds of sexual disorders. On the other hand, critics question the long-term effectiveness of aversion therapy because rates of relapse are significant (Waters et al., 2017; Jaqua & Jaqua, 2019).

In addition, important ethical concerns surround aversion techniques such as electric shock, even though therapists use such potent stimuli only in the most extreme cases, such as with patients who harm themselves. Clearly, though, aversion therapy offers an important procedure for eliminating maladaptive responses for some period of time—a respite that provides, even if only temporarily, an opportunity to encourage more adaptive behavior patterns (Twining et al., 2015; Surya et al., 2019; Spandler & Carr, 2022).

Systematic Desensitization Another treatment that grew out of the classical conditioning is systematic desensitization. **Systematic desensitization** is a behavioral technique in which exposure to an anxiety-producing stimulus is paired with deep relaxation in order to reduce an anxiety response. The idea is to learn to associate relaxation with a stimulus that previously produced anxiety (Ijeoma & Oladipo, 2019; Ha & Yoo, 2022).

systematic desensitization A behavioral technique based on classical conditioning in which exposure to an anxiety-producing stimulus is paired with deep relaxation to extinguish the response of anxiety. (Module 40)

Suppose, for instance, you were extremely afraid of flying. The very thought of being in an airplane would make you begin to sweat and shake, and you couldn't get yourself near enough to an airport to know how you'd react if you actually had to fly somewhere. Using systematic desensitization to treat your problem, you would first be trained in relaxation techniques by a behavior therapist and learn to relax your body fully—a highly pleasant state, as you might imagine (see Figure 2).

Dragana Gordic/Shutterstock

To achieve a state of relaxation, follow these steps once or twice a day.

Step 1. Choose a word or phrase that you can repeat to achieve calm. This might be a yoga mantra (*Om* or *Om Mani Padme Hum*, for instance), a word such as *peace, shanti,* or *shalom,* or any word or phrase that sounds soft and resonant to you (such as *Peace to my heart*).

Step 2. Find a quiet and comfortable place and sit down.

Step 3. Close your eyes and try to see and feel the darkness.

Step 4. Relax your muscles one by one, starting from your toes and moving slowly up to your scalp.

Step 5. Keep your breathing steady and natural, neither deep nor shallow, and repeat your word or phrase continuously.

Step 6. Do not monitor yourself, but become passive and accepting. If outside thoughts arrive, dismiss them lightly with a smile and return to your repeated word or phrase.

Step 7. Keep this up for 15 minutes. Do not set an alarm; just open your eyes when you feel it is right. If you fall asleep, that is fine.

Step 8. When you have finished, sit quietly, eyes closed, for a minute or two, then stand up.

FIGURE 2 Following these basic steps will help you achieve a sense of calmness by employing the relaxation response.
Source: Adapted from Benson et al., 1993.

The next step would involve constructing a *hierarchy of fears*—a list in order of increasing severity of the things you associate with your fears. For instance, your hierarchy might resemble this one:

1. Watching a plane fly overhead
2. Going to an airport
3. Buying a ticket
4. Stepping into the plane
5. Seeing the plane door close
6. Having the plane taxi down the runway
7. Taking off
8. Being in the air

From the perspective of...

A Child-Care Provider How might you use systematic desensitization to help children overcome their fears?

Nicole Hill/Rubberball/Getty Images

Study Alert
To help remember the concept of hierarchy of fears, think of something that you are afraid of and construct your own hierarchy of fears.

flooding A behavioral treatment for anxiety in which people are suddenly confronted with a stimulus that they fear. (Module 40)

Once you had developed this hierarchy and learned relaxation techniques, you would learn to associate the two sets of responses. To do this, your therapist might ask you to put yourself into a relaxed state and then imagine yourself in the first situation identified in your hierarchy. Once you could consider that first step while remaining relaxed, you would move on to the next situation. Eventually, you would move up the hierarchy in gradual stages until you could imagine yourself being in the air without experiencing anxiety. Ultimately, you would be asked to make a visit to an airport and later to take a flight.

The newest form of exposure therapy makes use of virtual reality technology. In *virtual reality exposure therapy,* clients wear virtual reality goggles that provide highly realistic depictions of stimuli that trigger anxiety. For example, someone who fears heights might be taken virtually to the top of a skyscraper. Or a person who has developed anxiety about driving after a car crash could be taken virtually to the intersection where the crash occurred. Once at the (virtual) site of the source of their anxiety, clients can be treated with traditional systematic desensitization techniques.

The extreme realism of virtual reality ensures that clients face their fears in a highly impactful manner, yet one that can be controlled more precisely than traditional means permit. The treatment is promising, although it is so new that the long-term effectiveness is not yet clear (Metz, 2017; McClay et al., 2017; North & North, 2017; Peebles et al., 2022).

Virtual reality exposure therapy immerses clients in highly realistic depictions of stimuli that trigger anxiety.

Monika Wisniewska/Alamy Stock Photo

Flooding Treatments Although systematic desensitization has proven to be a successful treatment, today it is often replaced with a less-complicated form of therapy called flooding. **Flooding** is a behavioral treatment for anxiety in which people are suddenly confronted with a stimulus that they fear. However, unlike systematic desensitization, relaxation training is not included. The goal behind flooding is to allow the maladaptive response of anxiety or avoidance to become extinct (Miles-Novelo & Anderson, 2020; Chavan et al., 2022).

For example, a patient who has a deep fear of germs may be made to soil their hands in dirt and to keep them dirty for hours. For a person with a fear of germs, initially this is a highly anxiety-producing situation. After a few hours, however, the anxiety will decline, leading to extinction of the anxiety.

Flooding has proved to be an effective treatment for a number of problems, including phobias, anxiety disorders, and even impotence and fear of sexual contact. Through this technique, people can learn to enjoy the things they once feared (Tuerk et al., 2011; de Jong et al., 2019; Chavin et al., 2022).

OPERANT CONDITIONING TECHNIQUES

Some behavioral approaches make use of the operant conditioning principles that we discussed in the chapter on learning. These approaches are based on the notion that we should reward people for carrying out desirable behavior and extinguish undesirable behavior by either ignoring it or punishing it.

One example of the systematic application of operant conditioning principles is the *token system*, which rewards a person for desired behavior with a token such as a poker chip or some kind of play money. The person can later exchange the chip or play money for an actual reward, such as real money or food.

Token systems are most frequently used in institutions for people with relatively serious problems and sometimes with children as a classroom-management technique. The system resembles what parents do when they give children money for being well behaved—money that the children can later exchange for something they want. The desired behavior may range from simple things such as keeping one's room neat to personal grooming and interacting with other people. In institutions, patients can exchange tokens for some object or activity, such as snacks, new clothes, or, in extreme cases, sleeping in one's own bed rather than in a sleeping bag on the floor.

Contingency contracting is a variant of the token system that has proved quite effective in modifying behavior. In *contingency contracting*, the therapist and client prepare a written agreement, known as a contract. The contract states a series of behavioral goals the client hopes to achieve. It also specifies positive consequences for the client if they reach those goals—usually an explicit reward such as money or privileges.

Contingency contracts also may state negative consequences if clients do not meet their goals. For example, clients who are trying to quit smoking might write out a check to a cause they have no interest in supporting (for instance, the National Rifle Association if they are strong supporters of gun control). If the client smokes on a given day, the therapist will mail the check.

Behavior therapists also use observational learning to systematically teach people new skills and ways of handling their fears and anxieties. *Observational learning* occurs through observing the behavior of others. For example, for clients who are socially fearful, a therapist may model and teach basic social skills, such as maintaining eye contact during conversation and acting assertively. Similarly, children with dog phobias have been able to overcome their fears by watching another child—called the "Fearless Peer"—repeatedly walk up to a dog, touch it, pet it, and finally play with it. Observational learning, then, can play a role in resolving some kinds of behavior difficulties, especially if the person being observed receives a reward for their behavior (Bandura et al., 1967; Waismeyer & Meltzoff, 2017; Bruton et al., 2019).

EVALUATING BEHAVIOR THERAPY

Behavior therapy works especially well for eliminating anxiety disorders, treating phobias and compulsions, establishing control over impulses, and learning complex social skills to replace maladaptive behavior. More than any of the other therapeutic techniques, it provides methods that nonprofessionals can use to change their own behavior.

Moreover, it is efficient because it focuses on solving carefully defined problems (Kertz et al., 2015; Wright et al., 2019; Barlow, 2020).

Critics of behavior therapy believe that because it emphasizes changing external behavior, it ignores people's inner life–their thoughts and anxieties. Consequently, people do not necessarily gain insight into thoughts and expectations that may be fostering their maladaptive behavior.

On the other hand, neuroscientific evidence shows that behavioral treatments can produce actual changes in brain functioning, which suggests that behavioral treatments can produce changes beyond external behavior. For example, one experiment looked at the neurological reactions of patients with borderline personality disorder who participated in a 12-week behavioral therapy program. Compared with a control group composed of people who did not have the disorder, the patients showed significant changes in their reactions to highly arousing, emotion-evoking stimuli. Following therapy, the patients' neurological functioning was more similar to those without the disorder than it was prior to therapy (Schnell & Herpertz, 2007).

Cognitive Approaches to Therapy

If you assumed that illogical thoughts and beliefs lie at the heart of psychological disorders, wouldn't the most direct treatment route be to teach people new, more adaptive modes of thinking? The answer is yes, according to psychologists who take a cognitive approach to treatment.

cognitive treatment approaches
Treatment approaches that teach people to think in more adaptive ways by changing their dysfunctional cognitions about the world and themselves. (Module 40)

Cognitive treatment approaches teach people to think in more adaptive ways by changing their dysfunctional cognitions about the world and themselves. In contrast to behavior therapists, who primarily focus on modifying external behavior, cognitive therapists focus on changing the way people think. Because they often use basic principles of learning, the methods they employ are sometimes referred to as the **cognitive-behavioral approach** (Sivec et al., 2017; Gros et al., 2019; Moritz et al., 2022).

cognitive-behavioral approach A treatment approach that incorporates basic principles of learning to change the way people think. (Module 40)

Although cognitive treatment approaches take many forms, they all share the assumption that anxiety, depression, and negative emotions develop from maladaptive thinking. Accordingly, cognitive treatments seek to change the thought patterns that lead to getting "stuck" in dysfunctional ways of thinking. Therapists systematically teach clients to challenge their assumptions and adopt new approaches to old problems.

Cognitive therapy is relatively short-term and usually lasts a maximum of 20 sessions. Therapy tends to be highly structured and focused on concrete problems. Therapists often begin by teaching the theory behind the approach and then continue to take an active role throughout the course of therapy by acting as a combination of teacher, coach, and partner.

One example of cognitive therapy is rational-emotive behavior therapy. **Rational-emotive behavior therapy** attempts to restructure a person's belief system into a more realistic, rational, and logical set of views. By adopting more accurate thought patterns, it is assumed that people will lead more psychologically healthy lives.

rational-emotive behavior therapy A form of therapy that attempts to re-structure a person's belief system into a more realistic, rational, and logical set of views by challenging dysfunctional beliefs that maintain irrational behavior. (Module 40)

Building on these views, psychologist Albert Ellis (2004) suggests that many people lead unhappy lives and suffer from psychological disorders because they harbor irrational, unrealistic ideas such as these:

- We need the love or approval of virtually every significant other person for everything we do.
- We should be thoroughly competent, adequate, and successful in all possible respects in order to consider ourselves worthwhile.
- It is horrible when things don't turn out the way we want them to.

Such irrational beliefs trigger negative emotions, which in turn support the irrational beliefs and lead to a self-defeating cycle. Ellis calls it the A-B-C model in which negative activating conditions (A) lead to the activation of an irrational belief system

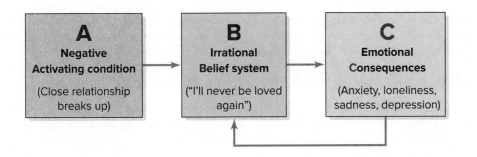

FIGURE 3 In the A-B-C model of rational-emotive behavior therapy, negative activating conditions (A) lead to the activation of an irrational belief system (B), which leads to emotional consequences (C). Those emotional consequences then feed back and support the belief system. At what steps in the model could change occur as a result of rational-emotive behavior therapy?
Source: Ellis, 1974.

(B), which in turn leads to emotional consequences (C). For example, if a person experiences the breakup of a close relationship (A) and holds the irrational belief (B) that "I'll never be loved again," this triggers negative emotions (C) that in turn feed back into support of the irrational belief (see Figure 3).

The goal of rational-emotive therapy is to help clients eliminate maladaptive thoughts and beliefs and adopt more effective thinking. To accomplish this goal, therapists take an active, directive role during therapy and openly challenge patterns of thought that appear to be dysfunctional. Consider this example:

> MARTHA: The basic problem is that I'm worried about my family. I'm worried about money. And I never seem to be able to relax.
>
> THERAPIST: Why are you worried about your family? . . . . What's to be concerned about? They have certain demands which you don't want to adhere to.
>
> MARTHA: I was brought up to think that I mustn't be selfish.
>
> THERAPIST: Oh, we'll have to knock that out of your head!
>
> MARTHA: My mother feels that I shouldn't have left home–that my place is with them. There are nagging doubts about what I should–
>
> THERAPIST: Why are there doubts? Why should you?
>
> MARTHA: I think it's a feeling I was brought up with that you always have to give of yourself. If you think of yourself, you're wrong.
>
> THERAPIST: That's a belief. Why do you have to keep believing that–at your age? You believed a lot of superstitions when you were younger. Why do you have to retain them? Your parents indoctrinated you with this nonsense, because that's their belief. . . . Who needs that philosophy? All it's gotten you, so far, is guilt. (Ellis, 1974)

By poking holes in Martha's reasoning, the therapist is attempting to help her adopt a more realistic view of herself and her circumstances (Ellis, 2002; Dryden & David, 2008; Ellis, 2021).

Another influential form of therapy that builds on a cognitive perspective is that of Aaron Beck (Beck et al., 2015). Like rational-emotive behavior therapy, Beck's *cognitive behavior therapy* aims to change people's illogical thoughts about themselves and the world.

However, cognitive behavior therapy is considerably less confrontational and challenging than rational-emotive behavior therapy is. Instead of the therapist actively arguing with clients about their dysfunctional cognitions, cognitive behavior therapists more often play the role of teacher. Therapists urge clients to obtain information on their own that will lead them to discard their inaccurate thinking through a process of cognitive appraisal.

In *cognitive appraisal*, clients are asked to evaluate situations, themselves, and others in terms of their memories, values, beliefs, thoughts, and expectations. During the course of treatment, therapists help clients discover ways of thinking more appropriately about themselves and others (Leaper et al., 2013; Simães et al., 2019).

Cognitive appraisal can also be used to help change students' attributions about the causes of their academic success or failure. For example, rather than attributing academic failure to a lack of intelligence, students can be helped to see that their performance is related to the amount of hard work and perseverance they invest in academic tasks (Elliot et al., 2017; Forsblom et al., 2022).

EVALUATING COGNITIVE APPROACHES TO THERAPY

Cognitive approaches to therapy have proved successful in dealing with a broad range of disorders, including anxiety disorders, depression, substance abuse, and eating disorders. Furthermore, the willingness of cognitive therapists to incorporate additional treatment approaches (e.g., combining cognitive and behavioral techniques in cognitive behavior therapy) has made this approach a particularly effective form of treatment (Goldberg et al., 2019; Schmidt et al., 2019).

At the same time, critics have pointed out that the focus on helping people to think more rationally ignores the fact that life is in reality sometimes irrational. Changing one's assumptions to make them more reasonable and logical thus may not always be helpful—even assuming it is possible to bring about true cognitive change. Still, the success of cognitive approaches has made them some of the most frequently employed therapies (Fresco, 2013; Lindner, 2021).

RECAP/EVALUATE/RETHINK

RECAP

LO 40-1 What are the goals of psychologically based and biologically based treatment approaches?

- Psychotherapy (psychologically based therapy) and biomedical therapy (biologically based therapy) share the goal of resolving psychological problems by modifying people's thoughts, feelings, expectations, evaluations, and ultimately behavior.

LO 40-2 What are the psychodynamic, behavioral, and cognitive approaches to treatment?

- Psychoanalytic approaches seek to bring unresolved past conflicts and unacceptable impulses from the unconscious into the conscious, where patients may deal with the problems more effectively. To do this, therapists use techniques such as free association and dream interpretation.
- Behavioral approaches to treatment view abnormal behavior as the problem rather than viewing that behavior as a symptom of some underlying cause. To bring about a "cure," this view suggests that the outward behavior must be changed by using methods such as aversive conditioning, systematic desensitization, observational learning, token systems, and contingency contracting.
- Cognitive approaches to treatment consider that the goal of therapy is to help a person restructure their faulty belief system into a more realistic, rational, and logical view of the world. Two examples of cognitive treatments are the rational-emotive behavior therapy and cognitive behavior therapy.

EVALUATE

1. Match the following mental health practitioners with the appropriate description.

   1. Psychiatrist
   2. Clinical psychologist
   3. Counseling psychologist
   4. Psychoanalyst

   a. PhD specializing in the treatment of psychological disorders
   b. Professional specializing in Freudian therapy techniques
   c. MD trained in abnormal behavior
   d. PhD specializing in the adjustment of day-to-day problems

2. According to Freud, people use _____ _____ as a means of preventing unwanted impulses from intruding on conscious thought.

3. In dream interpretation, a psychoanalyst must learn to distinguish between the _____ content of a dream, which is what appears on the surface, and the _____ content, its underlying meaning.

4. Which of the following treatments deals with phobias by gradual exposure to the item producing the fear?
   a. Systematic desensitization
   b. Partial reinforcement
   c. Behavioral self-management
   d. Aversion therapy

RETHINK

1. In what ways are psychoanalysis and cognitive therapy similar, and how do they differ?
2. How might you examine the reliability of dream interpretation?

Answers to Evaluate Questions

1. 1-c, 2-a, 3-d, 4-b; 2. defense mechanisms; 3. manifest, latent; 4. a

KEY TERMS

psychotherapy
biomedical therapy
psychodynamic therapy
psychoanalysis

transference
behavioral treatment
 approaches
aversive conditioning

systematic desensitization
flooding
cognitive treatment
 approaches

cognitive-behavioral
 approach
rational-emotive behavior
 therapy

Module 41

Psychotherapy: Humanistic, Interpersonal, Group, and Online Approaches to Treatment

humanistic therapy Therapy in which the underlying rationale is that people have control of their behavior, can make choices about their lives, and are essentially responsible for solving their own problems. (Module 41)

Humanistic Therapy

As you know from your own experience, a student cannot master the material covered in a course without some hard work, no matter how good the teacher and the textbook are. *You must* take the time to study, memorize the vocabulary, and learn the concepts. Nobody else can do it for you. If you choose to put in the effort, you'll succeed; if you don't, you'll fail. The responsibility is primarily yours.

Humanistic therapy reflects this philosophy. **Humanistic therapy** is the approach that assumes people have control of their behavior, can make choices about their lives, and are essentially responsible for solving their own problems.

Humanistic therapists believe that people naturally are motivated to strive for self-actualization. As we discussed in the chapter on motivation, *self-actualization* is the term that clinical psychologist Abraham Maslow used to describe the state of self-fulfillment in which people realize their highest potentials in their own unique way.

Instead of acting in the more directive manner of some psychodynamic and behavioral approaches, humanistic therapists view themselves as guides or facilitators. Therapists using humanistic techniques seek to help people understand themselves and find ways to come closer to the ideal they hold for themselves. In this view, psychological disorders result from the inability to find meaning in life, from feelings of loneliness, and from a lack of connection to others (Lewis & Umbreit, 2015; Van Deurzen et al., 2019; Hoffman, 2021).

Humanistic approaches have produced many therapeutic techniques. Among the most important is person-centered therapy.

PERSON-CENTERED THERAPY

Consider the following therapy session excerpt:

> SAGAR: I'm in a tough, competitive business, and I'm trying to stand out. But I have this habit of trying to smooth out situations and make everybody happy, and it doesn't really help me in terms of the business.
>
> THERAPIST: In other words, what you do is try to keep others happy and make them feel better.
>
> SAGAR: Yes. I think that's what it is. I can't even make myself stop, and I feel like others don't respect me much because of it. So it actually harms my chances for getting ahead at my workplace.
>
> THERAPIST: So as you try to make others feel better, you're actually feeling that it makes you less effective at your job?
>
> SAGAR: Right.
>
> THERAPIST: So you feel you're holding yourself back.

The therapist does not interpret or answer the questions the client has raised. Instead, the therapist clarifies or reflects back what the client has said, using phrases like "In other words, what you do. . . ."; "So you feel that. . . ."; "Is that it?" This therapeutic technique, known as *nondirective counseling,* is at the heart of person-centered therapy, which was first practiced by Carl Rogers in the mid-20th century (Raskin & Rogers, 1989; Joseph, 2019; Chańska, 2022).

Person-centered therapy (also called *client-centered therapy*) aims to enable people to reach their potential for self-actualization. By providing a warm and accepting environment, therapists hope to motivate clients to air their problems and feelings. In turn, this enables clients to make realistic and constructive choices and decisions about the things that bother them in their current lives (McLean et al., 2017; Knutson & Koch, 2019; Tudor, 2022).

Instead of directing the choices clients make, therapists provide what Rogers calls unconditional positive regard. *Unconditional positive regard* involves providing wholehearted acceptance, support, and understanding, and no disapproval, no matter what feelings and attitudes a client expresses. By doing this, therapists hope to create an atmosphere that enables clients to come to decisions that can improve their lives (Patterson & Joseph, 2013; Proctor et al., 2021; Ort et al., 2022).

Furnishing unconditional positive regard does not mean that therapists must approve of everything their clients say or do. Rather, therapists need to communicate that they are caring, nonjudgmental, and *empathetic;* that is, understanding of a client's emotional experiences.

Today, therapists using person-centered therapy techniques are more directive with their clients. Rather than merely reflecting back their clients' statements, therapists actively nudge clients toward insights. However, therapists still view their clients' insights as central to the therapeutic process (Tudor, 2022).

person-centered therapy Therapy in which the goal is to reach one's potential for self-actualization. (Module 41)

> **! Study Alert**
> To better remember the concept of unconditional positive regard, try offering it to a friend during a conversation by showing your support, acceptance, and understanding no matter what thought or attitude your friend expresses.

EVALUATING HUMANISTIC APPROACHES TO THERAPY

The notion that psychological disorders result from restricted growth potential appeals philosophically to many people. Furthermore, when humanistic therapists acknowledge that the freedom we possess can lead to psychological difficulties, clients find an unusually supportive environment for therapy. In turn, this atmosphere can help clients discover solutions to difficult psychological problems.

However, humanistic treatments lack specificity, a problem that has troubled their critics. Humanistic approaches are not very precise and are probably the least scientifically and theoretically developed type of treatment. Moreover, this form of treatment works best for the same type of highly verbal client who profits most from psychoanalytic treatment (Wiryosutomo et al., 2019; Renger & Macaskill, 2021).

Interpersonal Therapy

Interpersonal therapy (IPT) is short-term therapy designed to help patients control their moods and emotions by focusing on the context of their current social relationships. Although its roots stem from psychodynamic approaches, interpersonal therapy concentrates more on the here and now with the goal of improving a client's existing relationships. It typically focuses on interpersonal issues such as conflicts with others, social skills issues, role transitions (such as divorce), or grief (Stangier et al., 2011; Dimaggio et al., 2015; Chakraborty & Roy, 2022).

Interpersonal therapy is more active and directive than are traditional psychodynamic approaches, and sessions are more structured. The approach makes no assumptions about the underlying causes of psychological disorders but focuses on the interpersonal context in which a disorder is developed and maintained. It also tends to be shorter than traditional psychodynamic approaches and typically lasts only 12-16 weeks. During those sessions, therapists make concrete suggestions on improving relations with others and actively offer recommendations and advice.

Considerable research supports the effectiveness of interpersonal therapy. It is especially effective in dealing with depression, anxiety, addictions, and eating disorders (Dimaggio et al., 2017; Lee & Mason, 2019; Lal et al., 2021).

interpersonal therapy (IPT) Short-term therapy that focuses on the context of current social relationships, helping patients to control their moods and emotions. (Module 41)

Group Therapies

group therapy Therapy in which people meet in a group with a therapist to discuss problems. (Module 41)

Although most treatment takes place between a single individual and a therapist, some forms of therapy involve groups of people seeking treatment. In **group therapy,** several unrelated people meet with a therapist to discuss some aspect of their psychological functioning.

People typically discuss with the group their problems, which often center on a common difficulty, such as alcoholism or a lack of social skills. The other members of the group provide emotional support and dispense advice on ways they have coped effectively with similar problems (Schachter, 2011; Burlingame et al., 2018; Tasca et al., 2021).

Groups vary greatly in terms of the particular model they employ; there are psychoanalytic groups, humanistic groups, and groups corresponding to the other therapeutic approaches. In one of the newest, and still experimental, uses of group therapy, people with posttraumatic stress disorder (PTSD) together process the experience of taking therapeutic doses of psychedelic drugs under the guidance of therapists (Trope et al., 2019; Gasser, 2022).

Furthermore, groups also differ with regard to the degree of guidance the therapist provides. In some, the therapist is quite directive; in others, the members of the group set their own agenda and determine how the group will proceed (Arlo, 2017; Burlingame et al., 2018).

Because several people are treated simultaneously in group therapy, it is a much more economical means of treatment than individual psychotherapy is. On the other hand, critics argue that group settings lack the individual attention inherent in one-to-one therapy and that especially shy and withdrawn individuals may not receive the attention they need in a group setting.

FAMILY THERAPY

family therapy An approach that focuses on the family and its dynamics. (Module 41)

One specialized form of group therapy is family therapy. As the name implies, **family therapy** involves two or more family members, one (or more) of whose problems led to treatment. But rather than focusing simply on the members of the family who present the initial problem, family therapists consider the family as a unit to which each member contributes. By meeting with the entire family simultaneously, family therapists try to understand how the family members interact with one another (Bischoff et al., 2011; McLean et al., 2021).

Family therapists view the family as a system, and they assume that individuals cannot improve without understanding the conflicts that exist among family members. Thus, therapists expect each member of a family to contribute to the resolution of the problem being addressed (Wretman, 2016; Scarborough, 2019).

Family therapists believe that family members often fall into rigid roles or patterns of behavior. For example, one person may act as the victim, another as a bully, and so forth. In their view, that system of roles supports and perpetuates family disturbances. One goal of family therapy, then, is to get family members to adopt new, more constructive patterns of behavior and to get members of the family to view others in new ways (Conoley et al., 2015; Lebow, 2019; Szapocznik & Hervis, 2020).

In family therapy, multiple members of a family meet with a therapist to discuss psychological problems that involve one or more members of the family.
bluecinema/Getty Images

SELF-HELP THERAPY

In self-help therapy, people with similar problems get together to discuss their shared feelings and experiences, sometimes without any formal therapist participating. For example, people who have recently experienced the death of a spouse might meet in a *bereavement support group,* or college students may get together to discuss their adjustment to college.

One of the best-known self-help groups is Alcoholics Anonymous (AA), a type of treatment program designed to help members deal with alcohol-related problems. AA prescribes 12 steps that alcoholics must pass through on their road to recovery. Alcoholics begin by admitting that they are alcoholics and powerless over alcohol and move through additional steps in the process of recovery by attending frequent AA meetings. Proponents of AA believe that no one is fully cured of alcoholism and that members should permanently think of themselves as recovering alcoholics (Best, 2017; Williams & Mee-Lee, 2019; Breuninger et al., 2020).

Alcoholics Anonymous does not work for everyone. For one thing, the program has a strong spiritual component, and it emphasizes the need for a higher power, which does not appeal to some people. More important, some critics say that AA's requirement of total abstinence from alcohol may not be an effective or realistic approach. Finally, despite its popularity, the scientific evidence about the effectiveness of AA is mixed, with some studies showing it is effective (and in fact more effective than other treatments) and others finding less support for the program (Dodes, 2015; Glaser, 2015; Kelly et al., 2020).

Still, AA provides more treatment for alcoholics than does any other therapy. Furthermore, research studies show that AA and other 12-step programs (such as Narcotics Anonymous) can be as successful in treating alcohol and other substance-abuse problems as traditional types of therapy (Pagano et al., 2013; Galanter, 2018; Kelly et al., 2020; also see the accompanying *Applying Psychology in the 21st Century* feature on online therapy to learn about this increasingly prevalent form of therapy).

APPLYING PSYCHOLOGY IN THE 21ST CENTURY

ONLINE THERAPY

At the height of the coronavirus pandemic, almost 45% of those polled said that their mental health had been affected by the global health and economic crisis. For them, and for most quarantined people, online therapy, whether via Zoom, FaceTime, or some other medium, was the only way of getting access to psychotherapy. And postpandemic, online therapy remains a popular, and effective, alternative to face-to-face therapy (Hoffman, 2020; Meraji & Hodges, 2020; Barker & Barker, 2022).

Actually, online psychotherapy was available even before the onset of the pandemic because its potential benefits were and are considerable. First, online sessions can be scheduled with ease for convenient times, and transportation isn't an issue. Furthermore, some clients may lack the emotional strength to get themselves to a real-world therapy session, in which case online therapy brings the therapist to them. Furthermore, sessions can be conducted in real-time teleconferencing style, by text-based chat, or even asynchronously; that is, not in real time, but more like an exchange of e-mails (American Psychological Association, 2019; Kecmanovic, 2020; Lin et al., 2022).

Another advantage of online therapy is that it normalizes mental health care by

Online therapy is an increasingly popular means of receiving treatment for psychological disorders.
milkos/123rf

removing many of the traditional barriers and integrating it into people's daily lives. Indeed, online therapy can even act as a gateway to broader mental health services: Some research shows that when clients see that therapy can be a force for positive change in their lives, they are more likely to seek out further mental health care if they need it (Jones et al., 2014).

On the other hand, online therapy has some significant limitations. For one thing, it's not the best channel for treating clients with serious mental disorders, who may have difficulty adequately connecting with a therapist. Furthermore, some clients find it cold and impersonal, and therapists may find it difficult to assess clients accurately without direct face-to-face contact. Finally, conducting therapy online may not be in full compliance with licensing requirements and privacy law regulations (Novotney, 2017; Barker & Barker, 2022).

Still, most research suggests that online therapy remains an effective and popular means of receiving treatment. It can be effective not only for adults but for younger individuals as well. Moreover, some therapists also have expanded their use of virtual treatments, including the use of apps, texting, and online self-help courses (Rolles-Abraham, 2020; Petersen, 2021; Venturo-Conerly et al., 2022).

RETHINK

- How might the lack of face-to-face contact between therapist and client impede the success of therapy?
- What might therapists do to increase the sense of connection with clients when using online therapy?

Evaluating Psychotherapy: Does Therapy Work?

Your best friend, Myhala, comes to you because she just hasn't been feeling right about things lately. She's upset because she and her partner aren't getting along, but her difficulties go beyond that. She can't concentrate on her studies, has a lot of trouble getting to sleep, and–this is what really bothers her–has begun to think that people are ganging up on her. She feels that no one really cares about or understands her.

Myhala knows that she ought to get *some* kind of help, but she is not sure where to turn. She knows that many types of therapy are available, but she doesn't have a clue about which would be best for her. She turns to you for advice because she knows you are taking a psychology course, asking, "Which kind of therapy works best?"

Myhala is asking a reasonable question that is difficult to answer. To address it, we'll first consider the evidence of whether psychotherapy, in general, is effective, and then turn to which of the many types of therapies work best.

IS THERAPY EFFECTIVE?

The question of whether therapy is effective requires a complex response. In fact, identifying the single most appropriate form of treatment is a controversial and still unresolved task for psychologists specializing in psychological disorders. Even before considering whether one form of therapy works better than another, we need to determine whether therapy in any form effectively alleviates psychological disturbances.

Until the 1950s, most people simply assumed that therapy was effective. But in 1952, psychologist Hans Eysenck published an historically important study challenging that assumption. He claimed that people who received psychodynamic treatment and related therapies were no better off at the end of treatment than were people who were placed on a waiting list for treatment but never received it. Eysenck concluded that people would go into **spontaneous remission,** recovery without formal treatment, if they were simply left alone–certainly a cheaper and simpler process.

Although other psychologists quickly challenged Eysenck's conclusions–and in fact, the scientific integrity of his research has been questioned–his review stimulated a continuing stream of better controlled, more carefully crafted studies on the effectiveness of psychotherapy. Today most psychologists agree: Therapy does work. Several comprehensive reviews indicate that therapy brings about greater improvement than no treatment at all, with the rate of spontaneous remission being fairly low. In most cases, then, the symptoms of abnormal behavior do not go away by themselves if left untreated–although the issue continues to be hotly debated (Gaudiano & Miller, 2013; Abbass et al., 2017; Cuijpers et al., 2019).

WHICH KIND OF THERAPY WORKS BEST?

Almost all psychologists agree that psychotherapeutic treatment *in general* is more effective than no treatment at all. However, the question of what specific *kind* of treatment is superior to others has not been answered definitively (Tryer et al., 2015; Norcross & Lambert, 2019; Howley, 2022).

For instance, one classic study comparing the effectiveness of various approaches found that although success rates vary somewhat by treatment form, most treatments show fairly equal success rates. As Figure 1 indicates, the rates ranged from about 75-80% greater success for treated individuals compared with untreated individuals. Behavioral and cognitive approaches tended to be slightly more successful, but that result may have been due to differences in the severity of the cases treated (Smith et al., 1980; Orwin & Condray, 1984).

Study Alert

Pay special attention to the discussion of (1) whether therapy is effective in general and (2) what specific types of therapy are effective because these are key issues for therapists.

spontaneous remission Recovery without formal treatment. (Module 41)

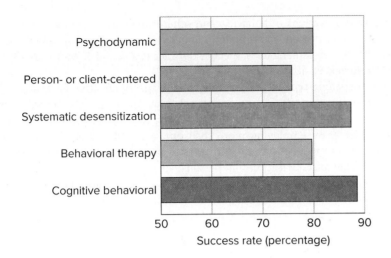

Other research, which relies on *meta-analysis* in which data from a large number of studies are statistically combined, yields similar general conclusions. For instance, a large survey of 186,000 individuals found that respondents felt they had benefited substantially from psychotherapy. However, there was little difference in "consumer satisfaction" on the basis of the specific type of treatment they had received (Seligman, 1995; Dakin & Areán, 2013; Lee et al., 2018).

In short, converging evidence allows us to draw several conclusions about the effectiveness of psychotherapy:

- *For most people, psychotherapy is effective.* This conclusion holds over different lengths of treatment, specific kinds of psychological disorders, and various types of treatment. Thus, the question, "Does psychotherapy work?" appears to have been answered convincingly: It does (Gaudiano & Miller, 2013; Leszcz et al., 2015; Norcross & Lambert, 2019).

- *On the other hand, psychotherapy doesn't work for everyone.* As many as 10% of people treated show no improvement—or actually deteriorated (Wendt et al., 2015; Duffy et al., 2019; Price et al., 2021).

- *No single form of therapy works best for every problem, and certain specific types of treatment are better, although not invariably, for specific types of problems.* For example, cognitive therapy works especially well for panic disorders, and flooding therapy relieves specific phobias effectively. However, there are exceptions to these generalizations, and often the differences in success rates for different types of treatment are not substantial (McAleavey et al., 2019; Duffy et al., 2019; Munder et al., 2019).

- *Most therapies share several basic similar elements.* Despite the fact that the specific methods used in different therapies are very different from one another, there are several common themes that lead them to be effective. These elements include the opportunity for a client to develop a positive relationship with a therapist, an explanation or interpretation of a client's symptoms, and confrontation of negative emotions. The fact that these common elements exist in most therapies makes it difficult to compare one treatment against another (David et al., 2018; Wampold, 2019).

Consequently, we can offer no single, definitive answer to the broad question, "Which therapy works best?" because of the complexity in sorting out the various factors that enter into successful therapy. Recently, however, clinicians and researchers have reframed the question by focusing on evidence-based psychotherapy practice. *Evidence-based psychotherapy practice* seeks to use research findings to determine the best practices for treating a specific disorder. To determine best practices, researchers use clinical interviews, client self-reports of improvement in quality of life, reductions in symptoms, observations of behavior, and other outcomes to compare different therapies. By using objective research findings, clinicians are increasingly able to determine the most effective treatment for a specific disorder (Gaudiano & Miller, 2013; Maguen et al., 2019; Rozek et al., 2022).

Because no single type of psychotherapy is invariably effective for every individual, some therapists use an eclectic approach to therapy. In an *eclectic approach to therapy*, therapists use a variety of techniques, thus integrating several perspectives, to treat a person's problems. By employing more than one approach, therapists can choose the appropriate mix of evidence-based treatments to match the individual's specific needs. Furthermore, therapists with certain personal characteristics may work better with particular individuals and types of treatments, and—as we consider next—even racial and ethnic factors may be related to the success of treatment (Kertz et al., 2015; Wampold, 2019; Vasile, 2021).

Exploring Diversity

Racial and Ethnic Factors in Treatment: Should Therapists Be Color-Blind?

Consider the following case report written by a school counselor about Alejandro Cruz, a 12-year-old student who was referred to a counselor because of his lack of interest in schoolwork:

> Alejandro does not pay attention and frequently falls asleep during class. There is a strong possibility that Alejandro is harboring repressed rage that needs to be dealt with. His inability to directly express his anger had led him to adopt passive-aggressive ways of expressing it, i.e., inattentiveness, daydreaming, falling asleep. It is recommended that Alejandro receive intensive counseling to discover the basis of the anger. (Based on Sue & Sue, 1990)

The counselor was wrong, however. Rather than suffering from "repressed rage," Alejandro lived in a poverty-stricken and disorganized home. Because of overcrowding at his house, he did not get enough sleep and consequently was tired the next day. Frequently, he was also hungry. In short, the stresses arising from his environment and not any deep-seated psychological disturbances caused his problems.

This incident underscores the importance of taking people's environmental and cultural backgrounds into account during treatment for psychological disorders. In particular, members of racial and ethnic minority groups, especially those who are also economically challenged, may behave in ways that help them deal with a society that discriminates against them. As a consequence, behavior that may signal psychological disorder in middle-class and upper-class White people may simply be adaptive in people from other racial and socioeconomic groups. For instance, characteristically suspicious and distrustful people may be displaying a survival strategy to protect themselves from psychological and physical injury rather than suffering from a psychological disturbance (Pottick et al., 2007; Hillier, 2018; Ameen & Kahn, 2020).

In fact, therapists must question some basic assumptions of psychotherapy when dealing with racial, ethnic, and cultural minority group members. For example, compared with the dominant culture, Asian and Latino cultures typically place much greater emphasis on the group, family, and society. In many Asian or Latino families, when someone faces a critical decision, the family helps make it—a cultural practice suggesting that family members should also play a role in psychological treatment.

Therapists' interpretation of their clients' behavior is influenced by racial, ethnic, cultural, and social class backgrounds of the clients. For example, this student could be seen as lazy, drunk, or merely exhausted, depending on the context.

Arts Illustrated Studios/Shutterstock

Similarly, the traditional Chinese recommendation for dealing with depression or anxiety is for the person to avoid thinking about whatever is upsetting them. Consider how this advice contrasts with treatment approaches that emphasize the value of insight (McCarthy, 2005; Tanaka-Matsumi, 2019; Ameen & Kahn, 2020).

Clearly, therapists must take into account the racial, ethnic, cultural, and economic backgrounds of their clients in determining the nature of a psychological disorder and the course of treatment (Hays, 2008; Moodley et al., 2013; Lee et al., 2021).

From the perspective of...

A Social Worker How might the types of therapies you employ vary depending on a client's cultural and socioeconomic background?

Sam Edwards/age fotostock

RECAP/EVALUATE/RETHINK

RECAP

LO 41-1 What are humanistic approaches to treatment?

- Humanistic therapy is based on the premise that people have control of their behavior, that they can make choices about their lives, and that it is up to them to solve their own problems. Humanistic therapies, which take a nondirective approach, include person-centered therapy.

LO 41-2 What is interpersonal therapy?

- Interpersonal therapy focuses on interpersonal relationships and strives for immediate improvement during short-term therapy.

LO 41-3 How does group therapy differ from individual types of therapy?

- In group therapy, several unrelated people meet with a therapist to discuss some aspect of their psychological functioning and often center on a common problem.

LO 41-4 Is online therapy effective?

- Research shows that online therapy can be an effective treatment modality, although it has limitations.

LO 41-5 How effective is psychotherapy, and which kind of psychotherapy works best in a given situation?

- Most research suggests that, in general, therapy is more effective than no therapy, although how much more effective is not known.

- The more difficult question of which therapy works best is harder to answer, but it is clear particular kinds of therapy are more appropriate for some problems than for others.
- Because no single type of psychotherapy is invariably effective, eclectic approaches in which a therapist uses a variety of techniques and thus integrates several perspectives are sometimes used.

EVALUATE

1. Match each of the following treatment strategies with the statement you might expect to hear from a therapist using that strategy.

   1. Group therapy
   2. Unconditional positive regard
   3. Behavioral therapy
   4. Nondirective counseling

   a. "In other words, you don't get along with your mother because she hates your partner, is that right?"
   b. "I want you all to take turns talking about why you decided to come and what you hope to gain from therapy."
   c. "I can understand why you wanted to wreck your friend's car after he hurt your feelings. Now tell me more about the accident."
   d. "That's not appropriate behavior. Let's work on replacing it with something else."

2. _____ therapies assume that people should take responsibility for their lives and the decisions they make.

3. One of the major criticisms of humanistic therapies is that
   a. They are too imprecise and unstructured.
   b. They treat only the symptom of the problem.
   c. The therapist dominates the patient-therapist interaction.
   d. They work well only on clients of lower socioeconomic status.

4. In a controversial study, Eysenck found that some people go into _____ _____, or recovery without treatment, if they are simply left alone instead of treated.

RETHINK

1. How can people be successfully treated in group therapy when individuals with the "same" problem are so different? What advantages might group therapy offer over individual therapy?

2. List some examples of behavior that might be considered abnormal among members of one cultural or economic group and normal by members of a different cultural or economic group. Suppose that most therapies had been developed by psychologists from minority culture groups or people who grew up homeless; how might they differ from current therapies?

Answers to Evaluate Questions

1. 1-b, 2-c, 3-d, 4-a; 2. Humanistic; 3. a; 4. spontaneous remission

KEY TERMS

humanistic therapy	interpersonal therapy (IPT)	family therapy
person-centered therapy	group therapy	spontaneous remission

Module 42
Biomedical Therapy: Biological Approaches to Treatment

If you get a kidney infection, your doctor gives you an antibiotic; with luck, your kidneys should be as good as new about a week later. If your appendix becomes inflamed, a surgeon removes it, and your body functions normally once more. Could a comparable approach that focuses on the body's physiology be effective for psychological disturbances?

According to biological approaches to treatment, the answer is yes. Therapists routinely use biomedical therapies that rely on drugs and medical procedures to improve psychological functioning.

The biomedical approach focuses treatment directly on altering brain chemistry or other neurological factors rather than concentrating on a patient's psychological conflicts, past traumas, or other issues of daily life that may produce psychological disorder. To do this, therapists provide treatment with drugs, electric shock, or surgery, as we will discuss.

LEARNING OUTCOME

LO 42-1 How are pharmaceutical drugs, electroconvulsive therapies, and psychosurgical techniques used today in the treatment of psychological disorders?

Drug Therapy

Drug therapy is the treatment of psychological disorders using medication. Drug therapy works by altering the operation of neurons and neurotransmitters in the brain.

Some drugs operate by *inhibiting* neurotransmitters or receptor neurons, which reduces activity at particular synapses. (Recall from our discussion of neurons in the neuroscience chapter that synapses are the gaps where nerve impulses travel from one neuron to another.) Thus, particular neurons are inhibited from firing.

Other drugs do just the opposite: They *increase* the activity of certain neurotransmitters or neurons, which allows particular neurons to fire more frequently (see Figure 1).

drug therapy Treatment of psychological disorders through the use of drugs. (Module 42)

Drug Treatments			
Class of Drug	**Effects of Drug**	**Primary Action of Drug**	**Examples**
Antipsychotic Drugs	Reduction in loss of touch with reality, agitation	Block dopamine receptors	Antipsychotic: chlorpromazine (Thorazine), clozapine (Clozaril), haloperidol (Haldol) Atypical antipsychotic: risperidone, olanzapine
Antidepressant Drugs			
Tricyclic antidepressants	Reduction in depression	Permit rise in neurotransmitters such as norepinepherine	Trazodone (Desyrel), amitriptyline (Elavil), desipramine (Norpamin)
MAO inhibitors	Reduction in depression	Prevent MAO from breaking down neurotransmitters	Phenelzine (Nardil), tranylcypromine (Parnate)
Selective serotonin reuptake inhibitors (SSRIs)	Reduction in depression	Inhibit reuptake of serotonin	Fluoxetine (Prozac), Luvox, Paxil, Celexa, Zoloft, nefazodone (Serzone)
Mood Stabilizers			
Lithium	Mood stabilization	Can alter transmission of impulses within neurons	Lithium (Lithonate), Depakote, Tegretol
Antianxiety Drugs	Reduction in anxiety	Increase activity of neurotransmitter GABA	Benzodiazepines (Valium, Xanax)

FIGURE 1 The major classes of drugs used to treat psychological disorders have different effects on the brain and nervous system.

antipsychotic drugs Drugs that temporarily reduce psychotic symptoms such as agitation, hallucinations, and delusions. (Module 42)

antidepressant drugs Medications that improve a severely depressed patient's mood and feeling of well-being. (Module 42)

> **Study Alert**
>
> To help organize your study of different drugs used in therapy, review Figure 1, which classifies them according to the categories of antipsychotic, antidepressant, mood-stabilizing, and antianxiety drugs.

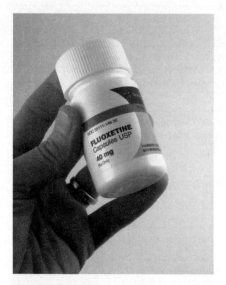

The drug fluoxetine, commonly known as Prozac, is a widely prescribed antidepressant.
Jill Braaten/McGraw Hill

ANTIPSYCHOTIC DRUGS

Probably no greater change has occurred in mental hospitals than the successful introduction in the mid-1950s of **antipsychotic drugs**–drugs used to reduce severe symptoms of disturbance, such as loss of touch with reality and agitation. Previously, the typical mental hospital wasn't very different from the stereotypical 19th-century insane asylum; it gave mainly custodial care to screaming, moaning, clawing patients who displayed bizarre behaviors. However, in just a matter of days after hospital staff members administered antipsychotic drugs, the wards became considerably calmer environments in which professionals could do more than just try to get patients through the day without causing serious harm to themselves or others.

This dramatic change came about through the introduction of the drug *chlorpromazine*. Along with other similar drugs, chlorpromazine rapidly became the most popular and successful treatment for schizophrenia. Today, drug therapy is typically the preferred treatment for most cases of severely abnormal behavior and is used for most patients hospitalized with psychological disorders. The newest generation of antipsychotics, referred to as *atypical antipsychotics*, have fewer side effects; they include *risperidone, olanzapine,* and *paliperidone* (Hattori et al., 2017; Henshall et al., 2019; Tendilla-Beltrán et al., 2021).

How do antipsychotic drugs work? Most block dopamine receptors at the brain's synapses, the space between pairs of neurons that communicate via chemical messengers. Atypical antipsychotics affect both serotonin and dopamine levels in the brain, particularly those related to planning and goal-directed activity (Fantegrossi et al., 2018; Seeman, 2021; Stroup et al., 2022).

Despite the effectiveness of antipsychotic drugs, they do not produce a "cure" in the same way that, say, penicillin cures an infection. Most of the time, the symptoms reappear when the drug is withdrawn. Furthermore, such drugs can have long-term side effects, such as dryness of the mouth and throat, dizziness, and sometimes tremors and loss of muscle control, which may continue after drug treatments are stopped (Pijnenborg et al., 2015; Ali et al., 2021).

ANTIDEPRESSANT DRUGS

As their name suggests, **antidepressant drugs** are a class of medications used in cases of severe depression to improve a patient's mood and feeling of well-being. They are also sometimes used for other disorders, such as anxiety disorders and bulimia (Hedges et al., 2007; Deacon & Spielmans, 2017; McElroy et al., 2019).

Most antidepressant drugs work by changing the concentration of specific neurotransmitters in the brain. For example, *tricyclic drugs* increase the availability of norepinephrine at the synapses of neurons, whereas *MAO inhibitors* prevent the enzyme monoamine oxidase (MAO) from breaking down neurotransmitters. Newer antidepressants–such as Lexapro–are *selective serotonin reuptake inhibitors (SSRIs)*. SSRIs target the neurotransmitter serotonin and permit it to linger at the synapse. Some antidepressants produce a combination of effects. For instance, nefazodone (Serzone) blocks serotonin at some receptor sites but not others, whereas bupropion (Wellbutrin and Zyban) affects the norepinephrine and dopamine systems (Harmer et al., 2017; Jarończyk & Walory, 2022; see Figure 2).

Overall, the success rates of antidepressant drugs are quite good. In fact, antidepressants can produce lasting, long-term recovery from depression. In many cases, even after patients stop taking the drugs, their depression does not return. On the other hand, antidepressant drugs may produce side effects such as drowsiness and cognitive deficits such as memory loss. Evidence also suggests that SSRI antidepressants can increase the risk of suicide in children and adolescents–clearly a significant concern (Shehab et al., 2016; Forsman et al., 2019; Chen et al., 2021).

Consumers spend billions of dollars each year on antidepressant drugs. More than 13% of Americans have taken them in the past 30 days, and for women over 60 years old, the figure is 24%. In particular, the antidepressant *fluoxetine*, sold under the trade name *Prozac*, has been highlighted on magazine covers and has been the topic of best-selling books (Rabin, 2013; Brody & Gu, 2020).

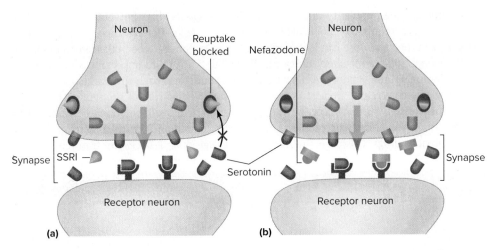

FIGURE 2 In (a), selective serotonin reuptake inhibitors (SSRIs) reduce depression by permitting the neurotransmitter serotonin to remain in the synapse. In (b), a newer antidepressant, nefazodone (Serzone), operates more selectively to block serotonin at some sites but not others, which helps to reduce the side effects of the drug.

Does Prozac deserve its acclaim? In some respects, yes. It is effective and has relatively few side effects. Furthermore, many people who do not respond to other types of antidepressants do well on Prozac. On the other hand, 20-30% of users report experiencing nausea and diarrhea, and a smaller number report sexual dysfunctions (Jha et al., 2018; Sadowsky, 2021).

Another substance that has received considerable publicity is *St. John's wort*, an herb that some have called a "natural" antidepressant. Although it is widely used in Europe for the treatment of depression, the U.S. Food and Drug Administration considers it a dietary supplement, and therefore, the substance is available here without a prescription.

Despite the popularity of St. John's wort, definitive clinical tests have found that the herb is ineffective in the treatment of depression. However, because some research shows that the herb successfully reduces certain psychological symptoms, some proponents argue that using it is reasonable. In any case, people should not use St. John's wort to medicate themselves without consulting a mental health-care professional (Ng et al., 2017; Forsdike & Pirotta, 2019).

MOOD STABILIZERS

Mood stabilizers are used to treat mood disorders characterized by intense mood swings, especially manic episodes in bipolar disorder. For example, the drug *lithium*, a form of mineral salts, has been used very successfully in patients with bipolar disorders. Although no one knows definitely why, lithium and other mood stabilizers such as divalproex sodium (*Depakote*) and carbamazepine (*Tegretol*) effectively reduce manic episodes. However, they do not effectively treat depressive phases of bipolar disorder, so antidepressants are usually prescribed during those phases (Inoue et al., 2011; Baritoli et al., 2018; Kishi et al., 2021).

Lithium and similar drugs have a quality that sets them apart from other drug treatments: They can be a *preventive* treatment that blocks future episodes of manic depression. Often, people who have had episodes of bipolar disorder can take a daily dose of lithium to prevent a recurrence of their symptoms. Most other drugs are useful only when symptoms of psychological disturbance occur.

mood stabilizers Drugs used to treat mood disorders characterized by intense mood swings, especially manic episodes in bipolar disorder. (Module 42)

ANTIANXIETY DRUGS

As the name implies, **antianxiety drugs** reduce the level of anxiety a person experiences and increase feelings of well-being. They are prescribed not only to reduce general tension in people who are experiencing temporary difficulties but also to aid in the treatment of more serious anxiety disorders.

Antianxiety drugs such as alprazolam and Valium are among the medications physicians most frequently prescribe. In fact, more than half of all U.S. families have someone who has taken such a drug at one time or another.

antianxiety drugs Drugs that reduce the level of anxiety a person experiences essentially by reducing excitability and increasing feelings of well-being. (Module 42)

Although the popularity of antianxiety drugs suggests that they hold few risks, they can produce a number of potentially serious side effects. For instance, they can cause fatigue, and long-term use can lead to dependence. Moreover, when taken in combination with alcohol, some antianxiety drugs can be lethal. But a more important issue concerns their use to suppress anxiety. Almost every therapeutic approach to psychological disturbance views continuing anxiety as a signal of some other sort of problem. Thus, drugs that mask anxiety may simply be hiding other difficulties. Consequently, rather than confronting their underlying problems, people may be hiding from them through the use of antianxiety drugs. (Also see the *Applying Psychology in the 21st Century* feature.)

APPLYING PSYCHOLOGY IN THE 21ST CENTURY

WILL PSYCHEDELIC THERAPY RESHAPE TREATMENT FOR PSYCHOLOGICAL DISORDERS?

It's been a difficult decade for mental health in the United States. We've seen opioid and suicide crises, steadily growing numbers of mental health issues among teens and young adults, and widespread mental health declines as a result of the pandemic—all underscoring an urgent need for new therapies to treat psychological disorders. But a long-abandoned form of drug research now seems to hold great promise for treating many otherwise difficult-to-treat psychological disorders: *psychedelic drugs*, which are drugs that trigger unusual states of consciousness, such as hallucinations. They include such drugs as MDMA, psilocybin, and ketamine.

You may be surprised to learn that researchers are taking a serious look at drugs that have long been considered illicit and dangerous—and they are dangerous, in large doses and when taken in uncontrolled settings. But research shows that they are neither addictive nor harmful at low, carefully controlled doses. Moreover, recent changes in attitudes toward recreational drugs, spurred by the widespread legalization of marijuana for medical and recreational use, has opened the door to a resurgence in the study of therapeutic uses of psychedelic drugs (O'Leary, 2021).

Ongoing studies are looking at whether psychedelic drugs can help people suffering from a variety of difficult-to-treat psychological disorders. These include severe depression, anxiety disorders such as PTSD and OCD, social anxiety in people with

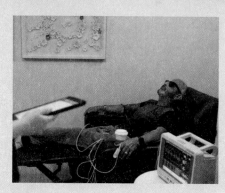

Increasing evidence indicates that some psychedelic drugs have therapeutic value in treating psychological disorders.
Julia Rendleman for The Washington Post/Getty Images

autism, substance abuse, and eating disorders (Doblin et al., 2019; Nutt, 2022).

One of the first drugs to come under new investigation was *ketamine*, which can be used as a recreational drug for its ability to induce hallucinations. It has also shown the potential for treating depression and PTSD.

More recently, researchers have been turning their attention to *psilocybin* as a treatment for depression. Psilocybin is the compound found in what have been called "magic mushrooms." One recent study shows that psilocybin works by creating new neural pathways in depressed people's brains, freeing them from rigid self-defeating thought patterns and allowing newer and healthier perspectives to emerge. Further research is needed to determine how long-lasting these

beneficial effects are, but brain scans clearly show that psilocybin works differently in the brain compared with other antidepressant drugs, offering new hope to patients whose depression hasn't responded well to existing therapies. In a similar fashion, MDMA—a drug commonly known as Ecstasy or Molly—combined with psychotherapy has been shown to help people with PTSD by enabling them to work through and resolve painful memories (Mitchell et al., 2021; Nutt & de Wit, 2021; Dai et al., 2022).

Of course, psychedelic drugs are not do-it-yourself treatments. They must be part of a therapeutic process that includes supervised use under the care of a therapist who guides the patient to have a positive experience and in a carefully controlled environment that facilitates the same goal.

Efforts are underway to create shorter-acting versions of these psychedelic drugs to minimize the duration and cost of the therapy sessions. And of course, progress has to be undertaken very carefully. Legalization that facilitates widespread misuse of these drugs, or even hasty therapeutic applications that end up exacerbating the conditions they are trying to treat, could quickly produce a backlash in public opinion and in legislative movement. However, if these new psychedelic therapies are researched thoroughly, the result could be a revolution in treatment options for a variety of mental illnesses (Jacobs, 2021).

RETHINK

- What other drugs have a potential for abuse but are legal to possess in the United States? Why do you think psychedelic drugs were treated differently?
- Why do you think the therapeutic value of psychedelic drugs wasn't considered when their use was made illegal in the United States?

Electroconvulsive Therapy and Newer Brain Stimulation Techniques

First introduced in the 1930s, **electroconvulsive therapy (ECT)** is a procedure in which a weak electric current of around 0.8 amperes at 120 volts is briefly administered to a patient's head. It is used most frequently to treat severe major depression that has not responded to other treatments.

Typically, health-care professionals place patients under general anesthesia before administering the current; such preparations help reduce the intensity of muscle contractions produced during ECT. The typical patient receives about 10 ECT treatments in the course of a month, but some patients continue with maintenance treatments for months afterward (Glass et al., 2017; Martin et al., 2019; Wilkinson et al., 2021).

ECT is a controversial technique. Apart from the obvious distastefulness of a treatment that evokes images of electrocution, side effects occur frequently. For instance, after treatment, patients often experience disorientation, confusion, and sometimes memory loss that may remain for months. Furthermore, ECT often does not produce long-term improvement; one study found that without follow-up medication, depression returned in most patients who had undergone ECT treatments. Finally, even when ECT does work, we do not know why, and some critics believe it may cause permanent brain damage (Weiner & Falcone, 2011; Ousdal et al., 2021).

Despite the drawbacks to ECT, it remains widely used, primarily because it offers the only quickly effective treatment in many severe cases of major depression. For instance, it may prevent depressed, suicidal individuals from taking their own lives, and it can act more quickly than antidepressive medications (Gergel et al., 2021).

The use of ECT has increased in the past decade, with more than 100,000 people undergoing it each year. Advances in the procedure have reduced its side effects, and practitioners are trying to reduce the stigma that surrounds it. In fact, research shows that ECT may be useful in reducing the symptoms of dementia. Still, ECT tends to be used only when other treatments have proved ineffective, and researchers continue to search for alternative treatments (Tokutsu et al., 2013; Izuhara et al., 2020; Reddy, 2019).

One new and promising alternative to ECT is **transcranial magnetic stimulation (TMS)**. TMS creates a precise magnetic pulse in a specific area of the brain. By activating particular neurons, TMS has been effective in relieving the symptoms of major depression in a number of controlled experiments. However, the therapy can produce side effects, such as seizures and convulsions, and it is still considered experimental (Bentwich et al., 2011; Sabbagh et al., 2019).

Another promising therapy, still in the early stages of development, is the use of implants placed deep inside the brain to provide short jolts of electricity, a method called *deep brain stimulation (DBS)*. Unlike ECT, which affects the entire brain, DBS pinpoints specific, tiny regions of the brain. It has been shown to provide relief from major depression. And in its newest version, discussed in this chapter's prologue, DBS has the potential to be personalized to the specific brain areas and neuronal configuration associated with a patient's depressive disorder (Sun et al., 2015; Ng et al., 2019; Krauss et al., 2021).

Because DBS treatment is so new, researchers are still trying the stimulation in different regions of the brain and fine-tuning the exact placement within given regions to get the best results. The location may vary depending on the specific symptoms the patient is experiencing. Furthermore, the optimal level, frequency, and duration of stimulation are also being explored, as are the long-term effects. Still, initial results are promising (deGusmao et al., 2017; Belluck, 2021).

electroconvulsive therapy (ECT) A procedure used in the treatment of severe depression in which an electric current of 70-150 volts is briefly administered to a patient's head. (Module 42)

transcranial magnetic stimulation (TMS) A depression treatment in which a precise magnetic pulse is directed to a specific area of the brain. (Module 42)

Psychosurgery

psychosurgery Brain surgery once used to reduce the symptoms of mental disorder but rarely used today. (Module 42)

If ECT strikes you as a questionable procedure, the use of **psychosurgery**–brain surgery in which the object is to reduce symptoms of mental disorder–probably appears even more dubious. A technique used exceedingly rarely today, psychosurgery was introduced as a "treatment of last resort" in the 1930s.

The first form of psychosurgery to be developed was the prefrontal lobotomy. *Prefrontal lobotomy* consists of surgically destroying or removing parts of a patient's frontal brain lobes, which surgeons thought controlled emotionality. In the 1930s and 1940s, surgeons performed the procedure on thousands of patients, often with little precision. For example, in one common technique, surgeons jabbed an ice pick under a patient's eyeball and swiveled it back and forth; in other cases, they drilled into the patient's skull (Chodakiewitz et al., 2015; Carroll, 2017; Terrier et al., 2019).

Psychosurgery sometimes did improve a patient's behavior–but not without drastic side effects. Along with remission of the symptoms of the mental disorder, patients sometimes experienced personality changes and became bland, colorless, and unemotional. In other cases, patients became aggressive and unable to control their impulses. In the worst cases, treatment resulted in the patient's death.

With the introduction of effective drug treatments–and the obvious ethical questions regarding the appropriateness of forever altering someone's personality–psychosurgery became nearly obsolete. However, it is still used in very rare cases when all other procedures have failed and the patient's behavior presents a high risk to the patient and others. For example, surgeons sometimes use a more precise form of psychosurgery called a *cingulotomy* in rare cases of obsessive-compulsive disorder in which they destroy tissue in the *anterior cingulate* area of the brain. In another technique, *gamma knife surgery,* beams of radiation are used to destroy areas of the brain related to obsessive-compulsive disorder (Wilkinson, 2009; Eljamel, 2015; Staudt et al., 2019).

Occasionally, dying patients with severe, uncontrollable pain also receive psychosurgery. Still, even these cases raise important ethical issues, and psychosurgery remains a highly controversial treatment (Garfield, 2014; Licthterman, 2022.). (Also see the *Neuroscience in Your Life* box.).

From the perspective of...

A Politician How would you go about regulating the use of electroconvulsive therapy and psychosurgery?

Exactostock/SuperStock

NEUROSCIENCE IN YOUR LIFE: MENTAL HEALTH IS BRAIN HEALTH

In many ways, the field of neuroscience revolutionized the field of mental health by revealing the brain basis of psychological disorders. Combined with experimental research methods, neuroscience research is shedding light on the brain-changing power of combining psychotherapy with biomedical treatments. The clear message is that to change the mind, you must change the brain.

Not only does the brain change in response to mental health treatment, but the brain also provides clues about who is most likely to get better with treatment. Advanced research techniques allow scientists to scan the brain of participants before and after treatment and then see if patterns of brain activity before the treatment relate to improvement in their psychological symptoms after treatment. This approach has been applied to a variety of psychological disorders, including posttraumatic stress disorder (PTSD). Studies have shown that brain activity in regions involved in fear and emotion, such as the prefrontal cortex and amygdala, predict the effectiveness of PTSD treatment (van Rooij et al., 2021).

Other studies show that the degree of brain-activity changes in those regions positively correlates with the amount of PTSD symptom improvement after treatment. These findings are important because they suggest that psychological treatment can be personalized based on a person's brain-activity patterns before they start treatment. Since different treatments affect the brain in different ways, people might be matched to treatments that are best suited to their patterns of brain activity. This exciting prospect could lead to greater symptom improvement in people with mental health disorders (Fenster et al., 2018; Monsour et al., 2022).

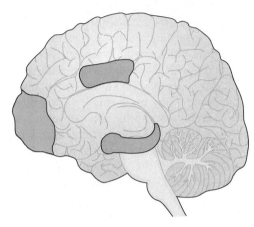

Pretreatment activity patterns in the highlighted brain regions correlate with symptom improvement after posttraumatic stress disorder treatment. These regions include the amygdala and portions of the prefrontal cortex, which are involved in fear learning, threat detection, and emotion regulation.

Biomedical Therapies in Perspective

In some respects, no greater revolution has occurred in the field of mental health than biological approaches to treatment. As previously violent, uncontrollable patients have been calmed by the use of drugs, mental hospitals have been able to concentrate more on actually helping patients and less on custodial functions. Similarly, patients whose lives have been disrupted by depression or bipolar episodes have been able to function normally, and other forms of drug therapy have also shown remarkable results.

Furthermore, new forms of biomedical therapy are promising. For example, the newest treatment possibility—which remains experimental at this point—is gene therapy. Specific genes may be introduced to particular regions of the brain. These genes then have the potential to reverse or even prevent biochemical events that give rise to psychological disorders (Valenzuela et al., 2016; Anguela & High, 2019).

Another new treatment, now in its infancy, addresses disorders such as depression and anxiety using brain scan neurofeedback. In *brain scan neurofeedback*, patients are exposed to real-time brain scans showing brain activity as they recall emotion-laden memories or triggers for anxiety. By attempting to modify their brain activity, they seem to better cope with their symptoms (McDonald et al., 2017; Young et al., 2017; Kerr et al., 2022).

Despite their current usefulness and future promise, biomedical therapies do not represent a complete and lasting cure for psychological disorders. For example, biomedical therapies typically provide only temporary relief of symptoms, and in most cases, symptoms return as soon as the drugs are withdrawn. Consequently, biomedical treatment may not solve the underlying problems that led a patient to therapy in the first place.

Study Alert
Remember that biomedical treatments have benefits as well as drawbacks.

Second, critics note that drugs may produce side effects that range from minor to serious physical reactions. In the worst case, biomedical therapies may lead to the development of new symptoms of a psychological disorder.

Finally, an overreliance on biomedical therapies may lead therapists to overlook alternative forms of treatment, such as psychotherapy, that may be helpful. In fact, new research demonstrates that adding psychotherapy involving talk sessions with a therapist to drug treatments is preferable in even severe psychological disorders such as schizophrenia (Carey, 2015; Kane et al., 2016; Browne et al., 2017).

Thus, biomedical therapies—sometimes alone and more often in conjunction with psychotherapy—have permitted millions of people to function more effectively. Furthermore, although biomedical therapy and psychotherapy appear distinct, research shows that biomedical therapies ultimately may not be as different from talk therapies as one might imagine, at least in terms of their consequences.

Specifically, measures of brain functioning as a result of drug therapy compared with psychotherapy show little difference in outcomes. For example, one study compared the reactions of patients with major depression who received either an antidepressant drug or psychotherapy. After 6 weeks of either therapy, activity in the portion of the brain related to the disorder—the basal ganglia—had changed in similar ways, and that area appeared to function more normally. Although such research is not definitive, it does suggest that at least for some disorders, psychotherapy may be just as effective as biomedical interventions—and vice versa. Research also makes it clear that no single treatment is effective universally and that each type of treatment has advantages as well as disadvantages (Greenberg & Goldman, 2009; Gaudiano & Miller, 2013).

community psychology A branch of psychology that focuses on the prevention and minimization of psychological disorders in the community. (Module 42)

deinstitutionalization The transfer of former mental patients from institutions to the community. (Module 42)

Community Psychology: Focus on Prevention

Each of the treatments we have reviewed has a common element: It is a "restorative" treatment aimed at alleviating psychological difficulties that already exist. However, an approach known as **community psychology** has a different aim: to prevent or minimize the incidence of psychological disorders.

Community psychology came of age in the 1960s, when mental health professionals developed plans for a nationwide network of community mental health centers. The hope was that those centers would provide low-cost mental health services, including short-term therapy and community educational programs. In another development, the population of mental hospitals has plunged as drug treatments made physical restraint of patients unnecessary.

The community psychology movement encouraged deinstitutionalization. **Deinstitutionalization** is the process of transferring patients who have been hospitalized for long periods into less-isolated community mental health settings. Proponents of deinstitutionalization wanted to ensure not only that deinstitutionalized patients received proper treatment but also that their civil rights were maintained (Pow et al., 2015; Hudson, 2019; Brown, 2022).

Unfortunately, the promise of deinstitutionalization has not been met. One important reason is that deinstitutionalized patients rarely receive sufficient resources. What started as a worthy attempt to move people out of mental institutions ended, in many cases, with former patients being dumped into the community without any real support. Many became homeless—as many as 75% of homeless adults are estimated to have a psychological disorder of some sort, and around 25% are thought to have a major psychological disorder—and some became involved in illegal acts caused by their disorders (Searight, 2013; Durbin et al., 2019; Gutwinski et al., 2021).

In short, many people who need treatment do not get it, and in some cases, care for people with psychological disorders has simply shifted from one type of treatment site to another. In fact, for many people, the only form of mental health treatment

While deinstitutionalization has had many successes, it has also contributed to the release of mental patients into the community with little or no support. As a result, many have become homeless.

Gary He/McGraw Hill

comes in emergency rooms of hospitals, with little or no follow-up care (Tsemberis & Macnaughton, 2017).

The lack of adequate mental health care is a worldwide problem. For example, in low- and middle-income countries, less than 5% of the population receives treatment for major depression. Even in higher-income countries, only around 20% of the people receive adequate care for depression. Treatment for psychological disorders remains out of reach for most of the world's population (Thornicroft et al., 2017; Keynejad et al., 2021; Singla, 2021).

Why is treatment so hard to receive? Cost is only part of the problem. Some places, including poverty-stricken areas, have few well-trained providers. In other cases, a cultural stigma discourages people from seeking out support for mental health treatment (Lu et al., 2021; Wijeratne et al., 2021).

Still, the community psychology movement has had some positive outcomes. Its emphasis on prevention has led to new approaches to psychological disorders. Furthermore, hotlines, available through phone calls or texts, are now common. At any time of the day or night, people experiencing acute stress can call a trained, sympathetic listener who can provide immediate–although obviously limited–treatment (Nelson & MaCleod, 2017; Ramchand et al., 2017).

College and high school crisis centers are another innovation that grew out of the community psychology movement. Modeled after suicide prevention hotline centers, crisis centers give callers an opportunity to discuss life crises with a sympathetic listener, who is often a volunteer.

BECOMING AN INFORMED CONSUMER
of Psychology

Choosing the Right Therapist

If you decide to seek therapy, you're faced with a daunting task. Choosing a therapist is not a simple matter. One place to begin the process of identifying a therapist is at the "Help Center" of the American Psychological Association at http://www.apa.org/helpcenter. And if you start therapy, several general guidelines can help you determine whether you've made the right choice:

You and your therapist should agree on the goals for treatment. They should be clear, specific, and attainable.

- *You should feel comfortable with your therapist.* You should not be intimidated by or in awe of a therapist. Rather, you should trust the therapist and feel free to discuss the most personal issues without fearing a negative reaction. In sum, the "personal chemistry" should be right.
- *Therapists should have appropriate training and credentials and should be licensed by appropriate state and local agencies.* Check therapists' membership in national and state professional associations. In addition, the cost of therapy, billing practices, and other business matters should be clear. It is not a breach of etiquette to put these matters on the table during an initial consultation.
- *You should feel that you are making progress after therapy has begun, despite occasional setbacks.* If you have no sense of improvement after repeated visits, you and your therapist should discuss this issue frankly. Although there is no set timetable, the most obvious changes resulting from therapy tend to occur relatively early in the course of treatment (Taibbi, 2018; De Shazer et al., 2021; Franklin et al., 2022).

Be aware that you will have to put in a great deal of effort in therapy. Although our culture tends to promise quick cures for any problem, in reality, solving difficult problems is not easy. You must be committed to making therapy work and should know that it is you, not the therapist, who must do most of the work to resolve your problems. The effort has the potential to pay off handsomely—as you experience a more positive, fulfilling, and meaningful life.

RECAP/EVALUATE/RETHINK

RECAP

LO 42-1 How are pharmaceutical drugs, electroconvulsive therapies, and psychosurgical techniques used today in the treatment of psychological disorders?

- Biomedical treatment approaches suggest that therapy should focus on the physiological causes of abnormal behavior rather than considering psychological factors. Drug therapy, the best example of biomedical treatments, has brought about dramatic reductions in the symptoms of mental disturbance.
- Antipsychotic drugs such as chlorpromazine very effectively reduce psychotic symptoms. Antidepressant drugs such as Prozac reduce depression so successfully that they are used very widely. Antianxiety drugs, or minor tranquilizers, are among the most frequently prescribed medications of any sort.
- In electroconvulsive therapy (ECT), used in severe cases of depression, a patient receives a brief electric current of 70–150 volts.
- Psychosurgery typically consists of surgically destroying or removing certain parts of a patient's brain.
- The community psychology approach encouraged deinstitutionalization in which previously hospitalized mental patients were released into the community.

EVALUATE

1. Antipsychotic drugs have provided effective, long-term, and complete cures for spectrum disorder. True or false?

2. One highly effective biomedical treatment for a psychological disorder that is used mainly to arrest and prevent manic-depressive episodes is
   a. Chlorpromazine
   b. Lithium
   c. Librium
   d. Valium
3. Psychosurgery has grown in popularity as a method of treatment as surgical techniques have become more precise. True or false?
4. The trend toward releasing more patients from mental hospitals and into the community is known as_____.

RETHINK

1. One of the main criticisms of biological therapies is that they treat the symptoms of mental disorder without uncovering and treating the underlying problems from which people are suffering. Do you agree with this criticism? Why?
2. If a dangerously violent person could be "cured" of violence through a new psychosurgical technique, would you approve the use of this technique? Suppose the person agreed to–or requested–the technique? What sort of policy would you develop for the use of psychosurgery?

Answers to Evaluate Questions

1. False: spectrum disorder can be controlled but not cured by medication; 2. b; 3. False: psychosurgery is now used only as a treatment of last resort; 4. deinstitutionalization

KEY TERMS

drug therapy	antianxiety drugs	transcranial magnetic	community psychology
antipsychotic drugs	electroconvulsive therapy	stimulation (TMS)	deinstitutionalization
antidepressant drugs	(ECT)	psychosurgery	
mood stabilizers			

LOOKING *Back*

EPILOGUE

We have examined how psychological professionals treat people with psychological disorders. We have considered a range of approaches that include both psychologically based and biologically based therapies. Clearly, the field has made substantial progress in recent years both in treating the symptoms of mental disorders and in understanding their underlying causes.

Before we leave the topic of treating psychological disorders, turn back to the prologue describing the implantation of a device that provided deep brain stimulation that was personalized and targeted to treat Sarah's particular form of depression. On the basis of your understanding of the treatment of psychological disorders, consider the following questions.

1. Which broad approach to treatment does the personalized deep brain stimulation seem to most closely fall under? Why do you think so?
2. What do you think the researchers studying the personalized deep brain stimulation should consider as indicators that the treatment is successful? If it helps with some symptoms but doesn't result in total remission, do you think it's still a useful therapeutic option? Why or why not?
3. How does the implanting of devices that provide brain stimulation differ from older forms of psychosurgery?
4. What are the ethical considerations in experimenting on humans with neurosurgical procedures such as targeted deep brain stimulation?

Design Elements: Man with laptop: Dragon Images/Shutterstock; Exclamation point and mobile frame: McGraw Hill; Smartphone: WML Image/Shutterstock; Hands: Stefano Garau/Shutterstock.

VISUAL SUMMARY 13 Treatment of Psychological Disorders

MODULE 40 Psychotherapy: Psychodynamic, Behavioral, and Cognitive Approaches

<u>Psychodynamic Therapy</u>

- Psychoanalysis
  - Free association: say aloud whatever comes to mind
  - Dream interpretation: looking for clues to unconscious conflicts and problems in dreams.
  - Frequent sessions for a long time
- Contemporary psychodynamic approaches
  - Sessions are of shorter duration
  - Therapist takes more active role: focus is more in the present.

<u>Behavioral Treatment Approaches:</u> Help modify behavior rather than find underlying causes

- Classical conditioning treatments
  - Aversive conditioning
  - Systematic desensitization
  - Flooding
- Operant conditioning techniques
  - Token system
  - Contingency contracting
  - Observational learning

<u>Cognitive Approaches:</u> Teach people to think in adaptive ways

- Rational-emotive behavior therapy

A	B	C
Negative Activating condition	**Irrational Belief system**	**Emotional Consequences**
(Close relationship breaks up)	("I'll never be loved again")	(Anxiety, loneliness, sadness, depression)

MODULE 41 Psychotherapy: Humanistic, Interpersonal, Group, and Online Approaches

<u>Humanistic Therapy:</u> Focuses on self-responsibility in treatment techniques

- Person-centered therapy: helps people to reach their potential for self-actualization using unconditional positive regard.

<u>Interpersonal Therapy:</u> Focuses on interpersonal relationships and improvement through short-term therapy.

<u>Group Therapy:</u> Several people meet with a therapist to discuss psychological functioning.

- Family therapy
- Self-help therapy

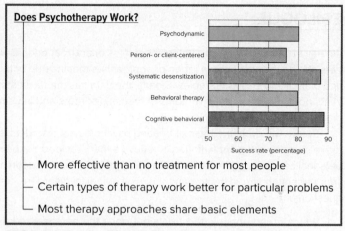

<u>Does Psychotherapy Work?</u>

Success rate (percentage) — Psychodynamic, Person- or client-centered, Systematic desensitization, Behavioral therapy, Cognitive behavioral (50 60 70 80 90)

- More effective than no treatment for most people
- Certain types of therapy work better for particular problems
- Most therapy approaches share basic elements

MODULE 42 Biomedical Therapy: Biological Approaches to Treatment

<u>Drug Therapy:</u> Controlling psychological disorders with drugs

Drug Treatments			
Class of Drug	**Effects of Drug**	**Primary Action of Drug**	**Examples**
Antipsychotic Drugs	Reduction in loss of touch with reality, agitation	Block dopamine receptors	Antipsychotic: chlorpromazine (Thorazine), clozapine (Clozaril), haloperidol (Haldol) Atypical antipsychotic: risperidone, olanzapine
Antidepressant Drugs			
Tricyclic antidepressants	Reduction in depression	Permit rise in neurotransmitters such as norepinepherine	Trazodone (Desyrel), amitriptyline (Elavil), desipramine (Norpamin)
MAO inhibitors	Reduction in depression	Prevent MAO from breaking down neurotransmitters	Phenelzine (Nardil), tranylcypromine (Parnate)
Selective serotonin reuptake inhibitors (SSRIs)	Reduction in depression	Inhibit reuptake of serotonin	Fluoxetine (Prozac), Luvox, Paxil, Celexa, Zoloft, nefazodone (Serzone)
Mood Stabilizers			
Lithium	Mood stabilization	Can alter transmission of impulses within neurons	Lithium (Lithonate), Depakote, Tegretol
Antianxiety Drugs	Reduction in anxiety	Increase activity of neurotransmitter GABA	Benzodiazepines (Valium, Xanax)

<u>Electroconvulsive Therapy:</u> Used as the only quickly effective treatment for severe depression

<u>Psychosurgery:</u> Brain surgery to reduce symptoms of mental disorders

<u>Community Psychology:</u> Prevention of the incidence of psychological disorders

- Deinstitutionalization: transfer of mental patients into the community where they may not receive necessary treatment

(Module 40): Source: Ellis, 1974; (Module 41) (photo): bluecinema/Getty Images; Source: Smith et al., 1980; (Module 42) (photo): Gary He/McGraw Hill

Agencja Fotograficzna Caro/Alamy Stock Photo

CHAPTER 14
Social Psychology

LEARNING OUTCOMES FOR CHAPTER 14

PROLOGUE *PUTTING LIFE ON HOLD*

When war broke out in Ukraine in early 2022, Teresa Gray, a nurse who lived 4,500 miles away in Anchorage, Alaska, watched the unfolding refugee crisis and knew she had to act. As dangerous as it is to enter an area wracked by war, she and a small team of volunteers deployed to the Ukrainian border prepared for anything—including chemical warfare attacks.

Gray and her team set up a 24-hour clinic in Romania that attended to the medical needs of Ukrainians who were exiled from their home country, in need of medicine and treatment, and unable to function normally in their host country with its unfamiliar language and culture. At great personal risk, Gray's team distributed supplies, rendered medical aid, and reached out to suffering people near and far.

"It isn't just about fixing the broken arm or giving you medicine. It's making that human connection," Teresa told a CNN reporter. "Human suffering has no borders. People are people, and love is love" (Toner, 2022).

LOOKING *Ahead*

What drove Teresa Gray and her small team of volunteers to leave their homes and travel across the globe to help total strangers overcome the adversity they faced?

We can answer this and similar questions only by taking into account findings from the field of social psychology, the branch that focuses on the aspects of human behavior that unite—and separate—us from one another. **Social psychology** is the scientific study of how people's thoughts, feelings, and actions are affected by others. Social psychologists consider the kinds and causes of the individual's behavior in social situations. They examine how the nature of situations in which we find ourselves influences our behavior in important ways.

social psychology The scientific study of how people's thoughts, feelings, and actions are affected by others. (Module 43)

The broad scope of social psychology is conveyed by the kinds of questions social psychologists ask: How can we convince people to change their attitudes or adopt new ideas and values? In what ways do we come to understand what others are like? How are we influenced by what others do and think? Why do some people display so much violence, aggression, and cruelty toward others that people throughout the world live in fear of annihilation at their hands? And why, in comparison, do some people place their own lives at risk to help others? In exploring these and other questions, we also discuss strategies for confronting and solving a variety of problems and issues that all of us face, ranging from achieving a better understanding of persuasive tactics to forming more accurate impressions of others.

We begin with a look at how our attitudes shape our behavior and how we form judgments about others. We'll discuss how we are influenced by others, and we will consider prejudice and discrimination by focusing on their roots and the ways we can reduce them. After examining what social psychologists have learned about the ways people form friendships and relationships, we'll look at the determinants of aggression and helping. Finally, we'll focus on the influence culture has on our behavior as well as the experience of living in a diverse society.

Module 43
Attitudes and Social Cognition

attitudes Evaluations of people, objects, ideas, and behavior. (Module 43)

Do celebrities such as Awkwafina influence attitudes? Advertisers certainly believe this is true, investing millions of dollars in endorsement fees.

ZUMA Press, Inc./Alamy Stock Photo

What do Tom Brady, Awkwafina, and SpongeBob SquarePants have in common?

Each has appeared in television advertisements designed to mold or change our attitudes. Such commercials are part of the barrage of messages we receive each day from sources as varied as politicians, social media influencers, and celebrities—all of which are meant to influence us.

Persuasion: Changing Attitudes

The concept of attitudes is central in social psychology. **Attitudes** are evaluations of people, objects, ideas, and behavior. We have all sorts of attitudes, ranging from those about others ("I think the president is great"), to attitudes about behavior ("I hate it when people are late for appointments"), to attitudes toward more abstract concepts ("I support affirmative action") (Verplanken & Orbell, 2022).

Persuasion involves changing attitudes. The ease with which attitudes can be changed depends on a number of factors, including:

- *Message source.* The characteristics of a person who delivers a persuasive message, known as an *attitude communicator,* have a major impact on the effectiveness of that message. For example, we tend to trust sources that we perceive as being more like us than those that we see as different. Moreover, communicators who are physically and socially attractive produce greater attitude change than do those who are less attractive. And although authority figures can be influential, research conducted during the COVID pandemic found that personal stories were often more influential in persuading people to get vaccinated than were those from government experts. Finally, we are more likely to be persuaded by people who are, in a sense, one of us—that is, those with whom we share a personal or social identity (Ooms et al., 2019; Eberhardt, 2022; Hastall et al., 2022).

- *Characteristics of the message.* It is not just *who* delivers a message but what the message is like that affects attitudes. Generally, two-sided messages—which include both the communicator's position and the one they are arguing against—are more effective than one-sided messages, at least if the assumption that the arguments for the other side can be effectively refuted and the audience is knowledgeable about the topic. In addition, fear-producing messages ("If you don't practice safer sex, you might get a sexually transmitted infection") are generally effective when they provide the audience with a means for reducing the fear. However, if the fear that is aroused is too strong, messages may evoke people's defense mechanisms and be ignored. Similarly, messages that push too hard may produce *reactance*, a negative response that causes people to dig in their heels and resist change (Cornelis et al., 2020; Berger, 2022; Xu & Petty, 2022).

- *Characteristics of the target.* Once a communicator has delivered a message, characteristics of the *target* of the message may determine whether the message will be accepted. For example, people with higher intelligence (as measured by IQ scores) generally are more resistant to persuasion than are those with lower intelligence, although it depends on the type of persuasive message (Shang et al., 2019).

ROUTES TO PERSUASION

Recipients' receptiveness to persuasive messages relates to the type of information-processing they use. Social psychologists have discovered two primary information-processing routes to persuasion: central route and peripheral route processing. **Central route processing** occurs when the recipient thoughtfully considers the issues and arguments involved in persuasion. In central route processing, people are swayed in their judgments by the logic, merit, and strength of arguments.

In contrast, **peripheral route processing** occurs when people are persuaded on the basis of factors unrelated to the nature or quality of the content of a persuasive message. Instead, factors that are irrelevant or extraneous to the issue, such as who is providing the message, how long the arguments are, or the emotional appeal of the arguments, influence them (Xie & Johnson, 2015; Manca et al., 2020; Short et al., 2022).

In general, people who are highly involved and motivated use central route processing to comprehend a message. However, if a person is disinterested, unmotivated, bored, or distracted, the characteristics of the message become less important, and peripheral factors become more influential (see Figure 1). Although both central route and peripheral route processing lead to attitude change, central route processing generally leads to stronger, more lasting attitude change.

Are some people more likely than others to habitually use central route processing rather than peripheral route processing? The answer is yes. *Need for cognition* is someone's typical level of thoughtfulness and cognitive activity. People who have a high need for cognition are more likely to employ central route processing. In contrast, people with a low need for cognition are more likely to use peripheral route processing. See Figure 2 to get a sense of your own need for cognition (Hill et al., 2013; Luttrell et al., 2017; Ingendahl et al., 2021).

People who have a high need for cognition enjoy thinking, philosophizing, and reflecting on the world. Because they are more likely to reflect on persuasive messages by using central route processing, they are persuaded by complex, logical, and detailed messages. In contrast, those who have a low need for cognition become impatient when forced to spend too much time thinking about an issue. Consequently, they usually use peripheral route processing and are persuaded by factors other than the quality and detail of messages (Sohlberg, 2019; Turner et al., 2021).

central route processing The type of mental processing that occurs when a persuasive message is evaluated by thoughtful consideration of the issues and arguments used to persuade. (Module 43)

peripheral route processing The type of mental processing that occurs when a persuasive message is evaluated on the basis of irrelevant or extraneous factors. (Module 43)

! Study Alert

Central route processing involves the content of the message; peripheral route processing involves how the message is provided.

From the perspective of...

A Sales Specialist Suppose you wanted to sell an automobile to a customer who has just walked in the door. What strategies might you use to be persuasive?

fizkes/Shutterstock

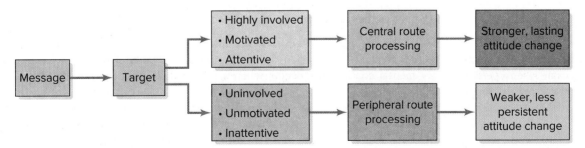

FIGURE 1 Routes to persuasion. Targets who are highly involved, motivated, and attentive use central route processing when they consider a persuasive message, which leads to a more lasting attitude change. In contrast, uninvolved, unmotivated, and inattentive targets are more likely to use peripheral route processing, and attitude change is likely to be less enduring. Can you think of specific advertisements that try to produce central route processing?

FIGURE 2 This simple questionnaire will give you a general idea of the level of your need for cognition.

Sources: Adapted from Cacioppo et al., 1996, and Coelho et al., 2020.

The Need for Cognition

Which of the following statements apply to you?

1. I really enjoy a task that involves coming up with new solutions to problems.
2. I would prefer a task that is intellectual, difficult, and important to one that is somewhat important but does not require much thought.
3. I prefer simple problems rather than complex ones.
4. The idea of relying on thought to make my way to the top does not appeal to me.
5. I think only as hard as I have to.
6. I like tasks that require little thought once I've learned them.
7. I prefer to think about small, daily projects rather than long-term ones.
8. I would rather do something that requires little thought than something that is sure to challenge my thinking abilities.
9. I don't find much satisfaction in deliberating hard and for long hours.
10. I don't like to be responsible for a situation that requires a lot of thinking.

Scoring: The more you agree with statements 1 and 2, and disagree with the rest, the greater the likelihood that you have a high need for cognition.

THE LINK BETWEEN ATTITUDES AND BEHAVIOR

Attitudes influence behavior. The strength of the link between particular attitudes and behavior varies, of course, but generally, people strive for consistency between their attitudes and their behavior. Furthermore, people hold fairly consistent attitudes. For instance, you would probably not hold the attitude that eating meat is immoral and still have a positive attitude toward hamburgers (Elen et al., 2013; Rodrigues & Girandola, 2017).

Ironically, the consistency that leads attitudes to influence behavior sometimes works the other way around; in some cases, our behavior shapes our attitudes. Consider, for instance, the following incident:

> You've just spent what you feel is the most boring hour of your life turning pegs for a psychology experiment. Just as you finally finish and are about to leave, the experimenter tells you they need a helper for future experimental sessions to introduce participants to the peg-turning task. Your specific job will be to tell them that turning the pegs is an interesting, fascinating experience. Each time you tell this tale to another participant, you'll be paid $1.

If you agree to help the experimenter, you may be setting yourself up for a state of psychological tension called cognitive dissonance. **Cognitive dissonance** is the mental conflict that occurs when a person holds two contradictory thoughts, beliefs, or attitudes (Festinger, 1957).

If you participate in the situation just described, you are likely to experience two contradictory thoughts: (1) I believe the task is boring, but (2) I said it was interesting with little justification ($1). Given the contradiction between them, these two thoughts should arouse cognitive dissonance.

How can you reduce the cognitive dissonance? You cannot deny having said that the task is interesting because you just said it. On the other hand, it is relatively easy to change your attitude toward the task–and thus, the theory predicts that participants

cognitive dissonance The mental conflict that occurs when a person holds two contradictory attitudes or thoughts (referred to as cognitions). (Module 43)

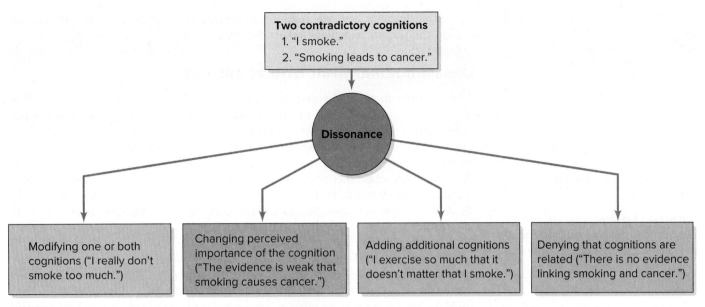

FIGURE 3 Cognitive dissonance. The simultaneous presence of two contradictory cognitions ("I smoke." and "Smoking leads to cancer.") produces dissonance, which can be reduced through several methods. What are additional ways in which dissonance can be reduced?

will reduce dissonance by adopting more positive attitudes toward the task (Harmon-Jones et al., 2015; Cooper, 2019; Edenbrandt et al., 2021).

A classic experiment (Festinger & Carlsmith, 1959) confirmed this prediction. The experiment followed essentially the same procedure outlined earlier in which a participant was offered $1 to describe a boring task as interesting. In addition, in a comparison condition, some participants were offered $20 to say that the task was interesting. The reasoning behind this condition was that $20 was so much money that participants in this condition had a good reason to be conveying incorrect information; dissonance would not be aroused, and less attitude change would be expected. The results supported this notion. More of the participants who were paid $1 changed their attitudes (becoming more positive toward the peg-turning task) than did participants who were paid $20.

Cognitive dissonance explains many everyday events involving attitudes and behavior. For example, smokers who know that smoking leads to lung cancer hold contradictory cognitions: (1) I smoke, and (2) smoking leads to lung cancer. The theory predicts that these two thoughts will lead to a state of cognitive dissonance. More important, it predicts that smokers will be motivated to reduce their dissonance.

There are four ways to reduce the dissonance in this case:

- Modifying one or both of the cognitions (e.g., "I really don't smoke that much.")
- Changing the perceived importance of one cognition ("The link between cancer and smoking is weak.")
- Adding cognitions ("I exercise so much that I'm really a healthy person.")
- Denying that the two cognitions are related to each other ("There's no compelling evidence linking smoking and cancer.")

Whichever strategy the smoker uses results in reduced dissonance (see Figure 3).

Social Cognition: Understanding Others

Regardless of Donald Trump's personal transgressions and impeachment trials, millions of Americans continued to find him admirable and likable throughout his presidency and afterward. Cases like this illustrate the power of our lingering impressions and attest to the importance of determining how people develop an understanding of others. One of the dominant areas in social psychology during the last few years has focused on learning how we come to understand what others are like and how we explain the reasons underlying others' behavior.

UNDERSTANDING WHAT OTHERS ARE LIKE

Consider for a moment the enormous amount of information about other people to which we are exposed. How can we decide what is important and what is not and make judgments about the characteristics of others? Social psychologists interested in this question study **social cognition**—the way people understand and make sense of others and themselves. Those psychologists have learned that individuals have highly developed **schemas,** sets of cognitions about people and social experiences. Those schemas organize information stored in memory; represent in our minds the way the social world operates; and give us a framework to recognize, categorize, and recall information relating to social stimuli such as people and groups (Amodio & Ratner, 2011; Leahy, 2015; Kitayama, 2017).

We typically hold schemas for specific types of people. Our schema for "teacher," for instance, generally consists of a number of characteristics: knowledge of the subject matter they are teaching, a desire to impart that knowledge, and an awareness of the student's need to understand what is being said. Or we may hold a schema for "mother" that includes the characteristics of warmth, nurturance, and caring. Regardless of their accuracy, schemas are important because they organize the way in which we recall, recognize, and categorize information about others. Moreover, they help us predict what others are like on the basis of relatively little information because we tend to fit people into schemas even when we do not have much concrete evidence to go on (Yamada & Itsukushima, 2013; McArthur et al., 2019).

FORMING IMPRESSIONS OF OTHERS

How do we decide that Sayreeta is a flirt, Rae is obnoxious, and Travon is a really nice person? The earliest work on social cognition examined *impression formation,* the process by which an individual organizes information about another person to form an overall impression of that person. In a classic study, for instance, students learned that they were about to hear a guest lecturer (Kelley, 1950). Researchers told one group of students that the lecturer was "a rather warm person, industrious, critical, practical, and determined" and told a second group that he was "a rather cold person, industrious, critical, practical, and determined."

The simple substitution of "cold" for "warm" caused drastic differences in the way the students in each group perceived the lecturer even though he gave the same talk in the same style in each condition. Students who had been told he was "warm" rated him considerably more positively overall than did students who had been told he was "cold."

The findings from this experiment led to additional research on impression formation that focused on the way in which people pay particular attention to certain unusually important traits—known as **central traits**—to help them form an overall impression of others. According to this work, the presence of a central trait alters the meaning of other traits. Hence, the description of the lecturer as "industrious" presumably meant something different when it was associated with the central trait "warm" than it meant when it was associated with "cold" (McCarthy & Skowronski, 2011; Huang et al., 2017; Di Pierro et al., 2019).

Some researchers have used information-processing approaches to develop mathematical models of how we combine individual personality traits to develop an overall impression of others. Generally, we calculate a kind of psychological "average" of the individual traits we see in a person to form an overall judgment, just as we would find the mathematical average of several numbers (Ivcevic & Ambady, 2012; Hehman et al., 2019).

We also form impressions remarkably quickly. In just a few seconds, using what have been called "thin slices of behavior," we are able to make judgments of people. Interestingly, these quick impressions are surprisingly accurate and typically match those of people who make judgments based on longer samples of behavior. The process

social cognition The cognitive processes by which people understand and make sense of others and themselves. (Module 43)

schemas Organized bodies of information stored in memory that bias the way new information is interpreted, stored, and recalled. (Modules 19, 43)

central traits The major traits considered in forming impressions of others. (Module 43)

is also remarkably similar across cultures (Pretsch et al., 2013; Murphy et al., 2019; Murphy & Hall, 2021; Hester et al., 2021).

Of course, as we gain more experience with people and see them exhibiting behavior in a variety of situations, our impressions of them become more complex. However, because our knowledge of others usually has gaps, we still tend to fit individuals into personality schemas that represent particular "types" of people. For instance, we may hold a "gregarious person" schema made up of the traits of friendliness, aggressiveness, and openness. The presence of just one or two of those traits may be sufficient to make us assign a person to a particular schema.

However, our schemas are susceptible to error. For example, mood affects how we perceive others. Happy people form more favorable impressions and make more positive judgments than do people who are in a bad mood (Human & Biesanz, 2011; Vanlessen et al., 2016; Forgas, 2022).

Even when schemas are not entirely accurate, they serve an important function: They allow us to develop expectations about how others will behave. Those expectations permit us to plan our interactions with others more easily and serve to simplify a complex social world.

ATTRIBUTION PROCESSES: UNDERSTANDING THE CAUSES OF BEHAVIOR

> When Nia Washington, a new employee at the Ablex Computer Company, completed a major staffing project 2 weeks early, her boss, Yolanda, was delighted. At the next staff meeting, she announced how pleased she was with Nia and explained that *this* was an example of the kind of performance she was looking for in her staff. The other staff members looked on resentfully, trying to figure out why Nia had worked night and day to finish the project not just on time but 2 weeks early. She must be an awfully compulsive person, they decided.

At one time or another, most of us have puzzled over the reasons behind someone's behavior. Perhaps it was in a situation similar to the one above, or it may have been in more formal circumstances, such as being a judge on a student judiciary board in a cheating case. **Attribution theory** considers how we decide, on the basis of samples of a person's behavior, what the specific causes of that behavior are. Unlike impression formation, which focuses on how people develop an overall impression of others' personality traits, attribution theory asks the "why" question: Why is someone acting in a particular way?

In seeking an explanation for behavior, we must answer one central question: Is the cause situational or dispositional? **Situational causes** are causes of behavior that are external to a person. For instance, someone who knocks over a quart of milk and then cleans it up probably does the cleaning not because they are necessarily a neat person but because the *situation* requires it. In contrast, a person who spends hours shining the kitchen floor probably does so because they are an unusually neat person. Hence, the behavior has a dispositional cause. **Dispositional causes** are causes of behavior brought about by a person's traits or personality characteristics.

In our example involving Nia Washington, her fellow employees attributed her behavior to her disposition rather than to the situation. But from a logical standpoint, it is equally plausible that something about the situation caused the behavior. If asked, Nia might attribute her accomplishment to situational factors and explain that she had so much other work to do she just had to get the project out of the way or that the project was not all that difficult and was easy to complete ahead of schedule. To her, then, the reason for her behavior might not be dispositional at all; it could be situational.

ATTRIBUTION BIASES: TO ERR IS HUMAN

If we always processed information in the rational manner that attribution theory suggests, the world might run a lot more smoothly. Unfortunately, although attribution

attribution theory The theory that considers how we decide, on the basis of samples of a person's behavior, what the specific causes of that behavior are. (Module 43)

situational causes (of behavior) Causes of behavior that are external to a person. (Module 43)

dispositional causes (of behavior) Perceived causes of behavior brought about by a person's traits or personality characteristics. (Module 43)

! Study Alert
The central question in making an attribution is whether the cause of behavior is due to situational or dispositional factors.

theory generally makes accurate predictions, people do not always process information about others as logically as the theory seems to suggest. In fact, research reveals consistent biases in the ways people make attributions. Typical biases include the following:

- *The halo effect.* Riley is intelligent, kind, and loving. Is Riley also conscientious? If you were to guess, your most likely response probably would be yes. Your guess reflects the **halo effect,** a phenomenon in which an initial understanding that a person has positive traits is used to infer other uniformly positive characteristics. The opposite would also hold true. Learning that Riley was unsociable and argumentative would probably lead you to assume that he was lazy as well. However, few people have either uniformly positive or uniformly negative traits, so the halo effect leads to misperceptions of others (Forgas & Laham, 2017; Austin & Halvorson, 2019; Lokhorst & Reich, 2022).

- *Assumed-similarity bias.* How similar to you–in terms of attitudes, opinions, likes, and dislikes–are your friends and acquaintances? Most people believe that their friends and acquaintances are fairly similar to themselves. This belief exemplifies the **assumed-similarity bias,** which is the tendency to think of people as being similar to oneself. Given the diversity of people in the world, this assumption often impairs our ability to make accurate judgments (Kouros & Papp, 2019; Carson & Kouros, 2022).

- *The self-serving bias.* When their teams win, coaches usually feel that the success is due to their coaching. But when their teams lose, coaches may think it's due to their players' poor skills. Similarly, if you get an A on a test, you may think it's due to your hard work, but if you get a poor grade, it's due to the professor's inadequacies. The reason is the **self-serving bias,** the tendency to attribute success to personal factors (skill, ability, or effort) and attribute failure to factors outside oneself (Ferring et al., 2015; Warach et al., 2019; Li et al., 2022).

- *The fundamental attribution error.* One of the more common attribution biases is the **fundamental attribution error,** which is the tendency to overattribute others' behavior to dispositional causes and the corresponding failure to recognize the importance of situational causes. The fundamental attribution error is prevalent in Western cultures. We tend to exaggerate the importance of personality characteristics (dispositional causes) in producing others' behavior and minimize the influence of the environment (situational factors). For example, we are

halo effect A phenomenon in which an initial understanding that a person has positive or negative traits is used to infer other uniformly positive or negative characteristics. (Module 43)

assumed-similarity bias The tendency to think of people as being similar to oneself even when meeting them for the first time. (Module 43)

self-serving bias The tendency to attribute personal success to personal factors (skill, ability, or effort) and to attribute failure to factors outside oneself. (Module 43)

fundamental attribution error A tendency to overattribute others' behavior to dispositional causes and minimize the importance of situational causes. (Module 43)

The assumed-similarity bias leads us to believe that others hold similar attitudes, opinions, and likes and dislikes.
James Hardy/PhotoAlto/SuperStock

more likely to jump to the conclusion that someone who is often late to work is lazy or a routinely tardy person (dispositional causes) than to assume that, perhaps, the subway they take to work frequently runs behind schedule, causing them to be late (a situational cause).

Why is the fundamental attribution error so common? One reason pertains to the nature of information available to the people making an attribution. When we view another person's behavior in a particular setting, the most conspicuous information is the person's behavior. Because the individual's immediate surroundings remain relatively unchanged and less attention grabbing, we center our attention on the person whose behavior we're considering. Consequently, we are more likely to make attributions based on personal dispositional factors and less likely to make attributions relating to the situation (Weber, 2019; Flick & Schweitzer, 2021).

Social psychologists' awareness of attribution biases has led, in part, to the development of a new branch of economics called behavioral economics. *Behavioral economics* is concerned with how economic conditions are affected by individuals' biases and irrationality. Rather than viewing people as rational, thoughtful decision makers who are impartially weighing choices to draw conclusions, behavioral economists focus on the irrationality of judgments (Kamenica, 2012; Corr & Plagnol, 2018; Littman et al., 2022).

RECAP/EVALUATE/RETHINK

RECAP

LO 43-1 What are attitudes, and how are they formed, maintained, and changed?

- Social psychology is the scientific study of the ways in which people's thoughts, feelings, and actions are affected by others and the nature and causes of individual behavior in social situations.
- Attitudes are evaluations of a particular person, behavior, belief, or concept.
- Cognitive dissonance occurs when an individual simultaneously holds two cognitions–attitudes or thoughts–that contradict each other. To resolve the contradiction, the person may modify one cognition, change its importance, add a cognition, or deny a link between the two cognitions–thus bringing about a reduction in dissonance.

LO 43-2 How do people form impressions of what others are like and the causes of their behavior?

- Social cognition involves the way people understand and make sense of others and themselves. People develop schemas that organize information about people and social experiences in memory and allow them to interpret and categorize information about others.
- People form impressions of others in part through the use of central traits–personality characteristics that receive unusually heavy emphasis when we form an impression.
- Information-processing approaches have found that we tend to average together sets of traits to form an overall impression.

- Attribution theory tries to explain how we understand the causes of behavior, particularly with respect to situational or dispositional factors.

LO 43-3 What are the biases that influence the ways in which people view others' behavior?

- Even though logical processes are involved, attribution is prone to error. For instance, people are susceptible to the halo effect, assumed-similarity bias, self-serving bias, and fundamental attribution error (the tendency to overattribute others' behavior to dispositional causes and the corresponding failure to recognize the importance of situational causes).

EVALUATE

1. An evaluation of a particular person, behavior, belief, or concept is called a(n) _____.
2. One brand of peanut butter advertises its product by describing its taste and nutritional value. It is hoping to persuade customers through _____ route processing. In ads for a competing brand, a popular actor happily eats the product–but does not describe it. This approach hopes to persuade customers through _____ route processing.
3. Cognitive dissonance theory suggests that we commonly change our behavior to keep it consistent with our attitudes. True or false?
4. Sopan was happy to lend a textbook to a fellow student who seemed bright and friendly. Sopan was surprised when the classmate did not return it. Sopan's assumption

that the bright and friendly student would also be responsible reflects the _____ effect.

RETHINK

1. Jada sees Devin, a new coworker, acting in a way that seems abrupt and curt. Jada concludes that Devin is unkind and unsociable. The next day, Jada sees Devin acting kindly toward another worker. Is Jada likely to change their impression of Devin? Why or why not? Jada then sees several of their friends laughing and joking with Devin, treating Devin in a very friendly fashion. Is Jada likely to change their impression of Devin? Why or why not?

2. Suppose you were assigned to develop a full advertising campaign for a product, including television, print ads, and social media. How might the theories in this chapter guide your strategy to suit the different media?

Answers to Evaluate Questions

1. attitude; 2. central, peripheral; 3. False; we typically change our attitudes and not our behavior to reduce cognitive dissonance; 4. halo

KEY TERMS

social psychology	cognitive dissonance	situational causes (of behavior)	assumed-similarity bias
attitudes	social cognition		self-serving bias
central route processing	schemas	dispositional causes (of behavior)	fundamental attribution error
peripheral route processing	central traits	halo effect	
	attribution theory		

Module 44
Social Influence and Groups

You have just transferred to a new college and are attending your first class. When the professor enters, your fellow classmates instantly rise, bow to the professor, and then stand quietly with their hands behind their backs. You've never encountered such behavior, and it makes no sense to you. Is it more likely that you will (1) jump up to join the rest of the class or (2) remain seated?

Most people would probably choose the first option. As you undoubtedly know from your own experience, pressures to conform to others' behavior can be painfully strong and can bring about changes in behavior that otherwise never would have occurred.

Conformity pressures are just one type of social influence. **Social influence** is the process by which social groups and individuals exert pressure on an individual, either deliberately or unintentionally.

Social influence is so powerful in part because groups and other people generally play a central role in our lives. As defined by social psychologists, **groups** consist of two or more people who (1) interact with one another; (2) perceive themselves as part of a group; and (3) are interdependent; that is, the events that affect one group member affect other members, and the behavior of members has significant consequences for the success of the group in meeting its goals.

Groups develop and hold *norms*: informal beliefs, expectations, and standards about what is appropriate behavior for group members. Norms not only tell us how people in a group should behave ("wearing pink is fashionable this year") but also what members shouldn't do ("under no circumstances wear black"). Group members understand that not adhering to group norms can result in retaliation from other group members, ranging from being ignored to being overtly derided or even being rejected or excluded by the group. Thus, people conform to meet the beliefs and expectations of the group (Miles et al., 2011; Becker et al., 2017; Molina et al., 2022).

Groups exert considerable social pressure over individuals. We'll consider three types of social pressure: conformity, compliance, and obedience.

Conformity: Following What Others Do

Conformity is a change in behavior or attitudes brought about by a desire to follow the beliefs or standards of other people. Subtle or even unspoken social pressure results in conformity.

The classic demonstration of pressure to conform comes from a series of studies carried out in the 1950s by Solomon Asch (1951). In the experiments, the participants thought they were taking part in a test of perceptual skills with six other people. The experimenter showed the participants one card with three lines of varying length and a second card that had a fourth line that matched one of the first three (see Figure 1). The task was seemingly straightforward: Each of the participants had to announce aloud which of the first three lines was identical in length to the "standard" line on the second card. Because the correct answer was always obvious, the task seemed easy to the participants.

Indeed, because the participants all agreed on the first few trials, the procedure appeared to be simple. But then something odd began to happen. From the perspective

LEARNING OUTCOME

LO 44-1 What are the major sources and tactics of social influence?

social influence The process by which social groups and individuals exert pressure on an individual, either deliberately or unintentionally. (Module 44)

group Two or more people who interact with one another, perceive themselves as part of a group, and are interdependent. (Module 44)

conformity A change in behavior or attitudes brought about by a desire to follow the beliefs or standards of other people. (Module 44)

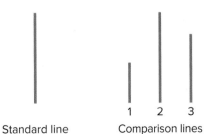

Standard line   Comparison lines

FIGURE 1 Which of the three comparison lines is the same length as the "standard" line?

of the participant in the group who answered last on each trial, all the answers of the first six participants seemed to be wrong—in fact, unanimously wrong. And this pattern persisted. Over and over again, the first six participants provided answers that contradicted what the last participant believed to be correct. The last participant faced the dilemma of whether to follow their own perceptions or follow the group by repeating the answer everyone else was giving.

As you might have guessed, there was more to this experiment than it first appeared. The first six participants were actually confederates (paid employees of the experimenter) who had been instructed to give unanimously erroneous answers on many of the trials. And the study had nothing to do with perceptual skills. Instead, the issue under investigation was conformity.

Asch found that in about one-third of the trials, the participants conformed to the erroneous group answer; about 75% of all participants conformed at least once. However, he found strong individual differences. Some participants conformed nearly all the time, whereas others never did.

CONFORMITY CONCLUSIONS

Since Asch's pioneering work, literally hundreds of studies have examined conformity, and we now know a great deal about the phenomenon. Significant findings focus on:

status The social standing of someone in a group. (Module 44)

- *The characteristics of the group.* The more attractive a group appears to its members, the greater its ability to produce conformity. Furthermore, a person's relative **status,** the social standing of someone within a group, is critical: The lower a person's status in the group, the greater groups' power over that person's behavior (Abrams & Hogg, 2017; Laursen & Faur, 2022).

- *The situation in which the individual is responding.* Conformity is considerably higher when people must respond publicly than it is when they can do so privately, as the founders of the United States noted when they authorized secret ballots in voting.

- *The kind of task.* People working on ambiguous tasks and questions (those with no clear answer) are more susceptible to social pressure. When asked to give an opinion on something, such as what type of clothing is fashionable, a person will more likely yield to conformist pressures than they will if asked a question of fact. In addition, tasks at which an individual is less competent than others in the group make conformity more likely. For example, a person who is an infrequent computer user may feel pressure to conform to an opinion about computer brands when in a group of experienced computer users.

social supporter A group member whose dissenting views make nonconformity to the group easier. (Module 44)

- *Unanimity of the group.* Groups that unanimously support a position show the most pronounced conformity pressures. But what about the case in which people with dissenting views have an ally in the group, known as a **social supporter,** who agrees with them? Having just one person present who shares the minority point of view is sufficient to reduce conformity pressures (Levitan & Verhulst, 2016; Ouyang & Xu, 2022).

GROUPTHINK: CAVING IN TO CONFORMITY

Although we usually think of conformity in terms of our individual relations with others, in some instances, conformity pressures in organizations can lead to disastrous effects with long-term consequences. One classic example concerns the space shuttle *Columbia* and the engineers who had to consider whether insulation that slammed into the space shuttle during takeoff would pose danger during landing. In fact, despite misgivings on the part of some engineers, a strong consensus emerged among them that the insulation would not impair the landing. Ultimately, that consensus proved wrong: The shuttle came apart as it attempted to land, killing all the astronauts on board (Mintz & Wayne, 2014; Wang & Wagner, 2018; Murata, 2022). How could they have made such a poor decision?

Groupthink may explain the poor decision making of NASA engineers that led to the destruction of the space shuttle *Columbia* in 2003.

NASA/Getty Images

A phenomenon known as groupthink may provide an explanation. **Groupthink** is a type of thinking in which group members share such a strong motivation to achieve consensus that they lose the ability to critically evaluate alternative points of view. Groupthink is most likely to occur when a popular or powerful leader is surrounded by people of lower status–which is obviously the case with any U.S. president and advisers but is also true for leaders in a variety of other organizations.

Groupthink may have been a partial cause of numerous questionable decisions and conclusions in the political and business worlds. For example, the United States invading Iraq or the consensus among media experts that Hillary Clinton would beat Donald Trump in the 2016 presidential election can be seen at least in part as a result of groupthink (Baumeister et al., 2015; Levine, 2019).

Groupthink typically leads to poor decisions. Groups limit the list of possible solutions to just a few, and they spend relatively little time considering any alternatives once the leader seems to be leaning toward a particular solution. In addition, groups may fall prey to *entrapment*, a circumstance in which commitments to a failing point of view or course of action are increased to justify investments in time and energy that have already been made (Willis, 2017; Plank & Bergmann, 2021).

Ultimately, group members may completely ignore information that challenges a developing consensus. Because historical research suggests that many disastrous decisions reflect groupthink, it is important for groups to be on guard (Burnette et al., 2011; Lee, 2020; DiPierro et al., 2022).

groupthink A type of thinking in which group members share such a strong motivation to achieve consensus that they lose the ability to critically evaluate alternative points of view. (Module 44)

Compliance: Submitting to Direct Social Pressure

When we refer to conformity, we usually mean a phenomenon in which the social pressure is subtle or indirect. But in some situations, social pressure is much more obvious with direct, explicit pressure to endorse a particular point of view or behave in a certain way. **Compliance** is behavior that occurs in response to direct social pressure.

compliance Behavior that occurs in response to direct social pressure. (Module 44)

Several specific techniques, including the following, represent attempts to gain compliance.

- *Foot-in-the-door technique.* The use of the *foot-in-the-door technique* begins when someone asks a target to comply with a small, trivial request. Because such a request is easy to fulfill, the likelihood that the target of the request will comply is high. Later, though, the target is asked to comply with a significantly larger request related to the first one. It turns out that compliance with the second request increases substantially when the target has first agreed to the initial, smaller request.

  Researchers first demonstrated the foot-in-the-door phenomenon in a study in which experimenters went door to door asking residents to sign a petition in favor of safe driving (Freedman & Fraser, 1966). Almost everyone complied with that small, easy-to-agree-to request. However, a few weeks later, different experimenters contacted the residents and made a request that took considerably more effort, asking residents to erect a huge sign on their front lawns that read, "Drive Carefully." The results were clear: Fifty-five percent of those who had initially signed the petition agreed to the request to put up a sign, whereas only 17% of those in a control group who initially had not been asked to sign the petition agreed to put up a sign.

  Why does the foot-in-the-door technique work? For one reason, consideration of the small request may lead to an interest in the topic of the request or issue; taking an action—any action—makes the individual more committed to the issue, thereby increasing the likelihood of future compliance. Another explanation revolves around people's self-perceptions. By complying with the initial request, individuals may come to see themselves as people who provide help when asked. Then, when confronted with the larger request, they agree in order to maintain the kind of consistency in attitudes and behavior that we described earlier. Although we don't know which of these two explanations is more accurate, it is clear that the foot-in-the-door strategy is effective (Guéguen et al., 2008; Lee & Liang, 2019; Batzella, 2021).

- *Door-in-the-face technique.* A fund-raiser asks for a $1,000 contribution. You laughingly refuse and tell her that the amount is way out of your league. She then asks for a $10 contribution. How would you react? If you are like most people, you'll probably be a lot more generous than you would be if she hadn't asked for the huge contribution first. In this tactic, called the *door-in-the-face technique,* someone makes a large request, expects it to be refused, and follows it with a smaller one. This strategy, which is the opposite of the foot-in-the-door

A variety of techniques have been proven to increase compliance to requests from others.
SDI Productions/Getty Images

approach, has proven to be effective (Cantarero et al., 2017; Howard, 2019; Genschow et al., 2021).

In a research study that demonstrates the success of this approach, experimenters stopped college students on the street and asked them to agree to a substantial favor: acting as unpaid counselors for juvenile delinquents 2 hours a week for 2 years (Cialdini et al., 1975). Unsurprisingly, no one agreed to make such an enormous commitment. But when they were later asked the considerably smaller favor of taking a group of delinquents on a 2-hour trip to the zoo, 50% of the people complied. In comparison, only 17% of a control group of participants who had not first received the larger request agreed.

The use of this technique is widespread and is easily implemented. You may have tried it at some point yourself by asking a parent for a large increase in your allowance and later settling for less. Similarly, television writers, by sometimes sprinkling their scripts with obscenities that they know network censors will cut out, hope to keep other key phrases intact. Finally, although asking people first to donate blood over a period of a year results in a high rate of refusal, afterward people are much more likely to give a one-time blood donation (Cialdini, 2021; Mauny et al., 2022).

- *That's-not-all technique.* In this technique, a salesperson offers you a deal at an inflated price. But immediately after the initial offer, the salesperson offers an incentive, discount, or bonus to clinch the deal.

  Although it sounds transparent, this practice can be quite effective. In one study, the experimenters set up a booth and sold cupcakes for 75¢ each. In one condition, the experimenters directly told customers that the price was 75¢. In another condition, they told customers that the price was originally $1 but had been reduced to 75¢. As we might predict, more people bought cupcakes at the "reduced" price–even though it was identical to the price in the other experimental condition (Pratkanis, 2007; Lee et al., 2019).

- *Not-so-free sample.* If you ever receive a free sample, keep in mind that it comes with a psychological cost. Although they may not couch it in these terms, salespeople who provide samples to potential customers do so to bring the norm of reciprocity into play. The *norm of reciprocity* is the social standard that we should treat other people as they treat us. (It's a variant of the Golden Rule we learn as kids: "Do unto others as they will do unto you.") It's a strong cultural standard: When someone does something nice for us, we tend to feel obligated to return the favor. In the case of the *not-so-free sample*, receiving a free sample activates the norm of reciprocity and makes us feel that we should return the favor–in the form of a purchase (Burger, 2009; Chernyak et al., 2019; Adams & Miller, 2022).

Companies seeking to sell their products to consumers often use the techniques identified by social psychologists for promoting compliance. Employers also use them to bring about compliance and raise employees' productivity in the workplace. In fact, **industrial-organizational (I/O) psychology**, a close cousin to social psychology, considers issues such as worker motivation, satisfaction, safety, and productivity. I/O psychologists also focus on the operation and design of organizations; they ask questions such as how decision making can be improved in large organizations and how the fit between workers and their jobs can be maximized.

industrial-organizational (I/O) psychology The branch of psychology focusing on work- and job-related issues, including worker motivation, satisfaction, safety, and productivity. (Module 44)

Obedience: Following Direct Orders

The compliance techniques that we've been discussing share a common thread: They are used to gently lead people toward agreement with a request. In some cases, however, requests are made in a strong manner. In fact, they're hardly requests at all but rather commands, aimed at producing obedience. **Obedience** is a change in behavior in response to the commands of others. Although obedience is considerably less

obedience A change in behavior in response to the commands of others. (Module 44)

Study Alert

The distinction between the three types of social pressure—conformity, compliance, and obedience—depends on the nature and strength of the social pressure brought to bear on a person.

common than conformity and compliance, it does occur in several specific kinds of relationships. For example, we may show obedience to our bosses, teachers, or parents merely because of the power they hold to reward or punish us.

To acquire an understanding of obedience, consider for a moment how you might respond if a stranger said to you:

> I've devised a new way of improving memory. All I need is for you to teach people a list of words and then give them a test. The test procedure requires only that you give learners a shock each time they make a mistake on the test. To administer the shocks, you will use a "shock generator" that gives shocks ranging from 15 to 450 volts. You can see that the switches are labeled from "slight shock" through "danger: severe shock" at the top level, where there are three red Xs. But don't worry; although the shocks may be painful, they will cause no permanent damage.

Presented with this situation, you would be likely to think that neither you nor anyone else would go along with the stranger's unusual request. Clearly, it lies outside the bounds of what we consider good sense.

Or does it? Suppose the stranger asking for your help was a psychologist conducting an experiment. Or suppose the request came from your teacher, your employer, or your military commander—all people in authority with a seemingly legitimate reason for the request.

If you still believe you would not comply, think again. The situation presented above describes a classic experiment conducted by social psychologist Stanley Milgram in the 1960s. In the study, an experimenter told participants to give increasingly stronger shocks to another person as part of a study on learning (see Figure 2). In reality, the experiment had nothing to do with learning; the real issue under consideration was the degree to which participants would comply with the experimenter's requests. In fact, the "learner" supposedly receiving the shocks was a confederate who never really received any punishment (Milgram, 2005; Maher, 2015; Griggs, 2017).

Most people who hear a description of Milgram's experiment feel it is unlikely that *any* participant would give the maximum level of shock—or, for that matter, any shock at all. Even a group of psychiatrists to whom the situation was described predicted that fewer than 2% of the participants would fully comply and administer the strongest shocks.

However, the results contradicted both experts' and nonexperts' predictions. Some 65% of the participants eventually used the highest setting on the shock generator—450 volts—to shock the learner. This obedience occurred even though the learner, who had

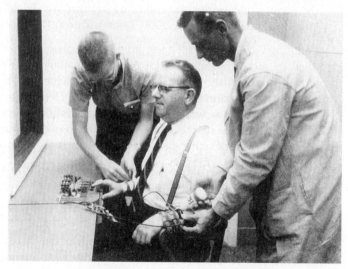

FIGURE 2 This fearsome "shock generator" led participants to believe they were administering electric shocks to another person, who was connected to the generator by electrodes attached to the skin.

(Both): From the film OBEDIENCE © 1968 by Stanley Milgram, © renewed 1993 by Alexandra Milgram. Permission granted by Alexandra Milgram

mentioned at the start of the experiment that he had a heart condition, demanded to be released, screaming, "Let me out of here! Let me out of here! My heart's bothering me. Let me out of here!" Despite the learner's pleas, most participants continued to administer the shocks.

Why did so many individuals comply with the experimenter's demands? The participants, who were extensively interviewed after the experiment, said they obeyed primarily because they believed that the experimenter would be responsible for any potential ill effects that befell the learner. The participants accepted the experimenter's orders, then, because they thought that they personally could not be held accountable for their actions; they could always blame the experimenter (Blass, 2004; Kaposi, 2017).

From the perspective of...

An Educator Student obedience in the elementary and secondary classroom is a major issue for many teachers. How might you promote student obedience in the classroom?

insta_photos/Getty Images

Most participants in the Milgram experiment said later they felt the knowledge gained from the study outweighed the discomfort they may have felt. However, the experiment has been criticized for creating an extremely trying set of circumstances for the participants, thereby raising serious ethical concerns. Undoubtedly, the same experiment could not be conducted today because of ethical considerations (Perry, 2013; Kaposi, 2022).

Other critics have suggested that Milgram's methods were ineffective in creating a situation that actually mirrored real-world obedience. For example, how often are people placed in a situation in which someone orders them to continue hurting a victim while the victim's protests are ignored (Werhane et al., 2013)?

Despite these concerns, Milgram's research remains the strongest laboratory demonstration of obedience. And partial replications of Milgram's work, conducted in an ethically defensible way, find similar results, which adds credence to the original work (Burger, 2009; Gibson, 2013; Kaposi, 2022).

Furthermore, we need only consider actual instances of obedience to authority to witness some frightening real-life parallels. For instance, after World War II, the major defense that Nazi officers gave to excuse their participation in atrocities during the war was that they were "only following orders." Milgram's experiment, which was motivated in part by his desire to explain the behavior of everyday Germans during World War II, forces us to ask ourselves this question: Would we be able to withstand the intense power of authority?

 Study Alert
Because of its graphic demonstration of obedience to authority, the Milgram experiment is one of the most famous and influential studies in social psychology.

RECAP/EVALUATE/RETHINK

RECAP

LO 44-1 What are the major sources and tactics of social influence?

- Social influence is the area of social psychology concerned with situations in which the actions of an individual or group affect the behavior of others.

- Conformity refers to changes in behavior or attitudes that result from a desire to follow the beliefs or standards of others.
- Compliance is behavior that results from direct social pressure. Among the ways of eliciting compliance are the foot-in-the-door, door-in-the-face, that's-not-all, and not-so-free sample techniques.

- Obedience is a change in behavior in response to the commands of others.

EVALUATE

1. A _____ _____, or person who agrees with the dissenting viewpoint, is likely to reduce conformity.
2. Who pioneered the study of conformity?
   a. Skinner
   b. Asch
   c. Milgram
   d. Fiala
3. Which of the following techniques asks a person to comply with a small initial request to enhance the likelihood that the person will later comply with a larger request?
   a. Door-in-the-face
   b. Foot-in-the-door
   c. That's-not-all
   d. Not-so-free sample
4. The _____ _____ _____ _____ technique begins with an outrageous request that makes a subsequent, smaller request seem reasonable.

5. _____ is a change in behavior that is due to another person's orders.

RETHINK

1. Why do you think the Milgram experiment is so controversial? What sorts of effects might the experiment have had on participants? Do you think the experiment would have had similar results if it had not been conducted in a laboratory setting but among members of a social group (such as a fraternity or sorority) with strong pressures to conform?
2. Imagine that you have been trained to use the various compliance techniques described in this section. Because these compliance techniques are so powerful, should the use of certain such techniques be forbidden? Should consumers be taught defenses against such techniques? Is the use of such techniques ethically and morally defensible? Why?

Answers to Evaluate Questions

1. social supporter; 2. b; 3. b; 4. door-in-the-face; 5. Obedience

KEY TERMS

social influence	status	compliance	obedience
group	social supporter	industrial-organizational	
conformity	groupthink	(I/O) psychology	

Module 45
Prejudice and Discrimination

If you're like most people, you probably quickly (without even realizing it) form some sort of impression of what others are like. Most likely your impression is based on a **stereotype,** a set of generalized beliefs and expectations about a specific group and its members. Stereotypes grow out of our tendency to categorize and organize the vast amount of information we encounter in our everyday lives. All stereotypes share the common feature of oversimplifying the world: We view individuals not in terms of their unique, personal characteristics but also in terms of characteristics we attribute to all the members of a particular group.

Stereotypes can lead to **prejudice,** a negative (or positive) evaluation of a group and its members. For instance, racial prejudice, also called *racism*, occurs when a member of a racial group is evaluated in terms of race and not because of their own characteristics or abilities. Although prejudice can be positive, social psychologists have focused on understanding the roots of negative prejudice.

Common stereotypes and forms of prejudice involve race, religion, ethnicity, and gender. Over the years, members of various groups have been called "lazy" or "shrewd" or "cruel" with varying degrees of regularity by those who are not members of that group. Even today, despite major progress toward reducing legally sanctioned forms of prejudice, such as school segregation, stereotypes remain (Devos, 2011; Bhatia, 2017; Master, 2021).

Even people who may think of themselves unprejudiced may harbor hidden prejudice. For example, when White participants in experiments are shown faces on a computer screen so rapidly that they cannot consciously perceive the faces, they react more negatively to Black than to White faces–an example of what has been called *modern racism* (Pearson et al., 2007; Blanton et al., 2015; Yu & Hyun, 2021).

Stereotypes can have harmful consequences because acting on stereotypes results in discrimination. **Discrimination** is behavior directed toward individuals on the basis of their membership in a particular group. Discrimination can lead to exclusion from jobs, neighborhoods, and educational opportunities, and it may result in lower salaries and benefits for members of specific groups. Discrimination can also result in more favorable treatment to favored groups; for example, when an employer hires a job applicant of their own racial group because of the applicant's race (Pager & Shepherd, 2008; Leskinen et al., 2015; Waite, 2021).

Stereotyping not only leads to overt discrimination but also can cause members of stereotyped groups to behave in ways that reflect the stereotype through a phenomenon known as the *self-fulfilling prophecy*. Self-fulfilling prophecies are expectations about the occurrence of a future event or behavior that act to increase the likelihood the event or behavior will occur. For example, if people think that members of a specific group lack ambition, they may treat them in a way that actually brings about a lack of ambition (Tappin et al., 2017; Peters et al., 2019; Jeffries & Reed, 2021).

Ultimately, the consequences of prejudice and discrimination can be profound, not only in terms of lost opportunities for victims but also in regard to their psychological functioning. Thus, discrimination may lead targets to feel hurt, inadequate, and anxious, and it can even negatively affect their cognitive functioning, such as their planning, decision-making, and problem-solving capabilities (Ozier et al., 2019; Torres et al., 2022).

LEARNING OUTCOMES

LO 45-1 How do stereotypes, prejudice, and discrimination differ?

LO 45-2 How can we reduce prejudice and discrimination?

stereotype A set of generalized beliefs and expectations about a particular group and its members. (Module 45)

prejudice A negative (or positive) evaluation of a particular group and its members. (Module 45)

discrimination Behavior directed toward individuals on the basis of their membership in a particular group. (Module 45)

Study Alert

Remember that *prejudice* relates to *attitudes* about a group and its members, whereas *discrimination* relates to *behavior* directed to a group and its members.

Members of racial and ethnic groups that have long faced discrimination suffered disproportionately from the coronavirus pandemic. Here, people line up for testing during the early stages of the pandemic.
Timothy A. Clary/Getty Images

The Foundations of Prejudice

No one is born disliking a specific racial, religious, or ethnic group. People learn to hate in much the same way that they learn the alphabet.

According to *observational learning approaches* to stereotyping and prejudice, the behavior of parents, other adults, and peers shapes children's feelings about members of various groups. For instance, bigoted parents may commend their children for expressing prejudiced attitudes. Likewise, young children learn prejudice by imitating the behavior of adult models. Such learning starts at an early age: Infants as young as 3 months old who have been exposed primarily to faces of their own race prefer same-race faces to faces of those of other races (Quinn et al., 2018; Matsuda et al., 2020; Waxman, 2021).

Moreover, the bias people encounter does not need to be overt. Even subtle and ambiguous forms of discriminatory behavior, such as someone avoiding sitting next to a person of color on a bus or providing poor service at a restaurant, can send a message of discrimination (Ozier et al., 2019; Ozturk & Berber, 2022).

Mass media also transmit information about stereotypes, not just for children but for adults as well. Even today, media portrayals can be found that depict Italians as Mafia-like mobsters, Jews as greedy bankers, and Black Americans as promiscuous or lazy. Newspaper articles overrepresent Black and Hispanic individuals as associated with low-skills jobs, crime, and poverty. When people's primary source of information about minority groups comes from such inaccurate portrayals, they can develop and maintain unfavorable stereotypes (Scharrer & Ramasubramanian, 2015; Jin et al., 2019; Ash et al., 2022).

Other explanations of prejudice and discrimination focus on how being a member of a specific group helps to magnify one's sense of self-esteem. According to *social identity theory*, we use group membership as a source of pride and self-worth. Social identity theory suggests that people tend to be ethnocentric, viewing the world from their own perspective and judging others in terms of their group membership. Slogans such as "gay pride" and "Black is beautiful" illustrate that the groups to which we belong give us a sense of self-respect (Hogg, 2006; Kahn et al., 2017; Edwards et al., 2019; Steffens et al., 2021).

However, the use of group membership to provide social respect produces an unfortunate outcome. In an effort to maximize our sense of self-esteem, we may come to think that our own group (our *ingroup*) is better than groups to which we don't belong (our *outgroups*). Consequently, we inflate the positive aspects of our ingroup— and, at the same time, devalue outgroups. Ultimately, we come to view members of outgroups as inferior to members of our ingroup (Tajfel & Turner, 2004; Ratner et al., 2014; Berry et al., 2021; Kawakami et al., 2022). The end result is prejudice toward members of groups of which we are not a part.

Neither the observational learning approach nor the social identity approach provides a full explanation for stereotyping and prejudice. For instance, some psychologists argue that prejudice results when there is perceived competition for scarce societal resources. Thus, when competition exists for jobs or housing, members of majority groups may believe (however unjustly or inaccurately) that minority group members are hindering their efforts to attain their goals; this belief can lead to prejudice. In addition, other explanations for prejudice emphasize human cognitive limitations that lead us to categorize people on the basis of visually conspicuous physical features such as race, sex, and ethnic group. Such categorization can lead to the development of stereotypes and, ultimately, to discriminatory behavior (Weeks & Lupfer, 2004; Hugenberg & Sacco, 2008; Yoo & Pituc, 2013).

The most recent approach to understanding prejudice comes from an increasingly important area in social psychology: social neuroscience. **Social neuroscience** seeks to identify the neurological basis of social behavior. It looks at how we can illuminate our understanding of groups, interpersonal relations, and emotions by understanding their neuroscientific underpinnings (Todorov et al., 2011; Kasemsap, 2017; Kavaliers et al., 2019; Ford & Young, 2021).

In one example of the value of social neuroscience approaches, researchers examined activation of the *amygdala*, the structure in the brain that relates to emotion-evoking stimuli and situations, while people viewed White and Black faces. Because the amygdala is especially responsive to threatening, unusual, or highly arousing stimuli, the researchers hypothesized greater activation of the amygdala during exposure to Black faces, which would be due to negative cultural associations with racial minorities, a hypothesis that was confirmed: The amygdala showed more activation when participants saw a Black face than when they saw a White one, suggesting that culturally learned societal messages about race led to the brain activation (Lieberman, 2007; Nelson, 2013; Singh et al., 2022). Research also indicates that being the target of racial discrimination can have damaging effects on the brain, and in turn, on one's health. See the *Neuroscience in Your Life* feature.

Social learning approaches to stereotyping and prejudice suggest that attitudes and behaviors toward members of minority groups are learned through the observation of parents and other individuals. How can this cycle be broken?

Mark Peterson/Corbis/Getty Images

social neuroscience The subfield of social psychology that seeks to identify the neurological basis of social behavior. (Module 45)

NEUROSCIENCE IN YOUR LIFE: EFFECTS OF DISCRIMINATION ON BRAIN CONNECTIVITY

Experiencing discrimination has many negative effects on a person's health and well-being. A recent study of Black older adults demonstrated how discrimination affects functional connectivity, the ways in which activity in two or more brain regions correlate with each other. Participants received a brain scan and completed a questionnaire that assessed how frequently they had experienced mistreatment in everyday life. Those who reported more experiences of discrimination showed particular patterns in how activity in one region of their brains—the insula—correlated with activity in other parts of the brain (Han et al., 2021).

Why might this be? The insula plays a major role in emotional regulation. Other studies have linked the insula to "gut" reactions to situations or stimuli and to the assessment of how trustworthy another person is.

It's not surprising that experiencing discrimination would affect a person's emotional processes and sense of trust. However, this might be especially salient for Black older adults, who have lived through decades of racial injustices, including racial terror related to lynchings, Jim Crow laws that legalized racial segregation, redlining that prohibited Black Americans from buying homes and building equity, and continual racial disparities in the criminal justice and healthcare systems. Since people with irregular connectivity patterns in the brain tend to have a poorer response to treatment for disorders such as depression (Geugies et al., 2019), the study results highlight one way that discrimination perpetuates race-based health disparities.

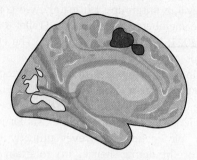

The amount of connection between activity in the insula and other regions of the brain was related to self-reports of having experienced discrimination (Han et al., 2021). The greater the experience of discrimination, the higher the correlation between activity in the insula and regions of the brain (shown in purple) and the lower the correlation between activity in the insula and other regions of the brain (shown in yellow).

Measuring Prejudice and Discrimination: The Implicit Association Test

Could you be prejudiced and not even know it? Probably yes, according to the researchers who developed a test that reveals hidden prejudice.

The *Implicit Association Test*, or *IAT*, is an ingenious measure of prejudice that permits a more accurate assessment of people's discrimination between members of different groups.

The IAT uses the fact that people's automatic, instant reactions often provide the most valid indicator of what they actually believe. The test asks people questions that assess the degree to which they associate members of target groups (say, Black Americans versus Whites) with positive stimuli (such as a puppy) versus negative stimuli (such as a funeral). The test is based on the fact that growing up in a particular culture teaches us to unconsciously associate members of particular groups with positive or negative qualities, and we tend to absorb associations about those groups that reflect the culture without even being aware of it (Blanton et al., 2015; Roberts et al., 2017; McConnell & Rydell, 2019; Schimmack, 2021).

The results of the IAT show that almost 90% of test-takers have an implicit pro-White bias, and more than two-thirds of non-Arab, non-Muslim volunteers display implicit biases against Arab Muslims (Westgate et al., 2015; Axt et al., 2021; Hong et al., 2022).

So, of course, having an implicit bias does not mean that people will overtly discriminate, which is a criticism that has been made of the test. Yet it does mean that the cultural lessons to which we are exposed have a considerable unconscious influence on us. (If you would like to try a version of the IAT yourself, there is a sample test at https://implicit.harvard.edu/implicit. You may well be surprised at the results.)

The good news is that certain types of implicit bias declined over the 10-year period from 2007 to 2017. Using responses from 4.4 million online implicit-bias test-takers, researchers found a decline in several domains, including a reduction in preferences for White, straight, and light-skinned individuals (see Figure 1). On the other hand, implicit bias regarding older people and those with disabilities remained fairly stable during that period, and it actually increased for overweight people.

Study Alert

Remember that the IAT allows measurement of attitudes about which people might not be consciously aware as well as attitudes they wish to keep hidden from others.

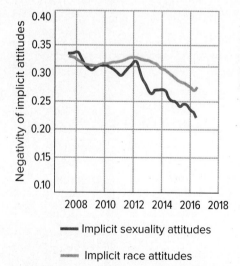

— Implicit sexuality attitudes

--- Implicit race attitudes

FIGURE 1 Implicit bias on the decline? Implicit bias favoring straight and White people declined from 2007 to 2016.

Source: Charlesworth & Banaji, 2019.

The reductions in implicit bias in some domains suggest that societal changes regarding prejudices may be reflected in individuals' attitudes in a positive way. Still, it remains to be seen how changes in U.S. society as a result of the Black Lives Matter movement and the killing of George Floyd may have affected attitudes in the racial domain more recently (Charlesworth & Banaji, 2019).

Reducing the Consequences of Prejudice and Discrimination

How can we diminish the effects of prejudice and discrimination? Psychologists have developed several strategies that have proved effective.

- *Increasing contact between the target of stereotyping and the holder of the stereotype.* Research consistently shows that increasing the amount of interaction between people can reduce negative stereotyping. But only certain kinds of contact are likely to reduce prejudice and discrimination. Situations in which contact is relatively intimate, the individuals are of equal status, or participants must cooperate with one another or are dependent on one another are more likely to reduce stereotyping. On the other hand, even virtual contact via social media may be sufficient to improve intergroup relations (White et al., 2015; Stone et al., 2019; White et al., 2021).

- *Making values and norms against prejudice more conspicuous.* Sometimes just reminding people about the values they already hold regarding equality and fair treatment of others is enough to reduce discrimination. Similarly, people who hear others making strong, vehement antiracist statements are subsequently more likely to strongly condemn racism. Furthermore, one study found that even a short, 10-minute conversation with voters asking them to recall a time when they were judged negatively and unfairly was sufficient to reduce prejudice toward transgender people that lasted 3 months (Rutland & Killen, 2015; Broockman & Kalla, 2016; Kalla et al., 2021).

- *Providing information about the targets of stereotyping.* Probably the most direct means of changing stereotypical and discriminatory attitudes is education: teaching people to be more aware of the positive characteristics of targets of stereotyping. For instance, when the meaning of puzzling behavior is explained to people who hold stereotypes, they may come to appreciate the actual significance of the behavior (Sukhera et al., 2017; Cook, 2021; Lee et al., 2022).

- *Reducing stereotype threat.* Social psychologist Claude Steele suggests that many Black Americans suffer from *stereotype vulnerability,* obstacles to performance that stem from their awareness of society's stereotypes regarding minority group members. He argues that Black American students too often receive instruction from teachers who doubt their students' abilities and who set up remedial programs to assist their students. As a result of their teachers' (as well as society's) low expectations for their performance, Black American students may come to accept society's stereotypes and come to believe that they are likely to fail (Aronson & Dee, 2012; Zhao et al., 2019; Petzel & Casad, 2022).

    Such beliefs can have devastating effects. When confronted with an academic task, Black American students may fear that their performance will simply confirm society's negative stereotypes. The immediate consequence of this fear is anxiety that hampers performance. But the long-term consequences may be even worse: Doubting their ability to perform successfully in academic environments, Black Americans may decide that the risks of failure are so great it is not worth the effort even to attempt to do well. Ultimately, they may "disidentify" with academic success by minimizing the importance of academic endeavors (Lombaard & Naudé, 2017; Simms et al., 2023).

However, Steele's analysis suggests that Black Americans may be able to overcome their predicament. Specifically, schools can design intervention programs to train minority group members about their vulnerability to stereotypes and provide them with self-affirmation that reinforces their confidence in their abilities and thereby inoculates them against the fear and doubt triggered by negative stereotypes (Shnabel et al., 2013; Borman et al., 2021; Petzel & Casad, 2022).

- *Increasing the sense of social belonging of ethnic minority students.* Although almost every college student faces feelings of inadequacy and uncertainty about belonging at the start of college, such feelings are especially strong for members of groups who are underrepresented and have been the targets of prejudice and discrimination. However, research shows that a simple intervention in which members of minority groups are made to understand that feelings of inadequacy are not unique to them—and that such feelings usually diminish with time—can help minority students increase their sense of social belonging (Walton & Cohen, 2011; Mullangi & Jagsi, 2019; Naidoo et al., 2021).

From the perspective of...

A Corrections Officer How might overt forms of prejudice and discrimination toward disadvantaged groups be reduced in a state or federal prison?

Hill Street Studios/
Blend Images

RECAP/EVALUATE/RETHINK

RECAP

LO 45-1 How do stereotypes, prejudice, and discrimination differ?

- Stereotypes are generalized beliefs and expectations about a specific group and its members. Stereotyping can lead to prejudice and self-fulfilling prophecies.
- Prejudice is the negative (or positive) evaluation of a particular group and its members.
- Stereotyping and prejudice can lead to discrimination, behavior directed toward individuals on the basis of their membership in a particular group.
- According to observational learning approaches, children learn stereotyping and prejudice by observing the behavior of parents, other adults, and peers. Social identity theory suggests that group membership is used as a source of pride and self-worth, and this may lead people to think of their own group as better than others.
- Social neuroscientific approaches to prejudice examine the functioning of the brain and nervous system to understand the basis of prejudice.

LO 45-2 How can we reduce prejudice and discrimination?

- Among the ways of reducing prejudice and discrimination are increasing contact, demonstrating positive values against prejudice, and education.

EVALUATE

1. Any expectation—positive or negative—about an individual solely on the basis of that person's membership in a group can be a stereotype. True or false?
2. The negative (or positive) evaluation of a group and its members is called
   a. Stereotyping
   b. Prejudice
   c. Self-fulfilling prophecy
   d. Discrimination
3. Paul is a store manager who does not expect women to succeed in business. He therefore offers important, high-profile responsibilities only to men. If the female employees fail to move up in the company, it could be an example of a _____ _____ prophecy.

RETHINK

1. Do you think women can be victims of stereotype vulnerability? In what topical areas might this occur? Can men be victims of stereotype vulnerability? Why?

2. How are stereotypes, prejudice, and discrimination related? In a society committed to equality, which of the three should be changed first? Why?

Answers to Evaluate Questions

1. True; 2. b; 3. self-fulfilling

KEY TERMS

stereotype   prejudice   discrimination   social neuroscience

Module 46
Positive and Negative Social Behavior

LEARNING OUTCOMES

LO 46-1 Why are we attracted to certain people, and what progression do social relationships follow?

LO 46-2 What factors underlie aggression and prosocial behavior?

interpersonal attraction (or close relationship) Positive feelings for others; liking and loving. (Module 46)

Like philosophers and theologians, social psychologists have pondered the basic nature of humanity. Is it represented mainly by the violence and cruelty we see throughout the world, or does something special about human nature permit loving, considerate, unselfish, and even noble behavior as well?

We turn to two routes that social psychologists have followed in seeking answers to these questions. We first consider what they have learned about the sources of our attraction to others; we end with a look at two opposite sides of human behavior: aggression and helping.

Liking and Loving: Interpersonal Attraction and the Development of Relationships

Nothing is more important in most people's lives than their feelings for others. Consequently, it is not surprising that liking and loving have become a major focus of interest for social psychologists. Known more formally as the study of **interpersonal attraction or close relationships,** this area addresses the factors that lead to positive feelings for others.

HOW DO I LIKE THEE? LET ME COUNT THE WAYS

By far, the greatest amount of research has focused on liking, probably because it is easier for investigators conducting short-term experiments to produce states of liking in strangers who have just met than to instigate and observe loving relationships over long periods. Consequently, research has given us a good deal of knowledge about the factors that initially attract two people to each other. The important factors social psychologists consider are the following:

- *Proximity.* If you live in a residence hall or an apartment, consider the friends you made when you first moved in. Chances are that you became friendliest with those who lived geographically nearest to you. In fact, this is one of the more firmly established findings in the research on interpersonal attraction: Proximity leads to liking (Smith & Weber, 2005; Semin & Garrido, 2013; Shin et al., 2019; Faur & Laursen, 2022).

- *Mere exposure.* Repeated exposure to a person is often sufficient to produce attraction. Interestingly, repeated exposure to *any* stimulus–a person, picture, tweet, or virtually anything–usually makes us like the stimulus more. Becoming familiar with a person can evoke positive feelings; we then transfer the positive feelings stemming from familiarity to the person. Of course, there are exceptions: In cases of strongly negative initial encounters, repeated exposure is unlikely to cause us to like a person more. Instead, the more we are exposed to the person, the more we are likely to dislike the individual (Zajonc, 2001; Butler & Berry, 2004; Van Dessel et al., 2017; Chow et al., 2022).

- *Similarity.* Folk wisdom tells us that birds of a feather flock together. However, folk wisdom also maintains that opposites attract. Which is right? Social psychologists have come up with a clear verdict regarding which of the two statements is correct: We tend to like those who are similar to us. Discovering that others have similar attitudes, values, or traits promotes our liking for them. Furthermore, the more similar others are, the more we like them. One reason similarity increases the likelihood of interpersonal attraction is that we assume people with similar attitudes will evaluate us positively. Because we experience a strong **reciprocity-of-liking effect**, a tendency to like those who like us, knowing that someone evaluates us positively promotes our attraction to that person. In addition, if *we* like someone else, we tend to assume that person likes us in return (Heffernan & Fraley, 2015; Wróbel & Królewiak, 2017).

- *Physical attractiveness.* For most people, the equation *beautiful = good* is quite true. As a result, physically attractive people are more popular than are physically unattractive ones, if all other factors are equal. This finding, which contradicts the values that most people say they hold, is apparent even in childhood (preschoolers' popularity is related to their attractiveness) and continues into adulthood. Indeed, physical attractiveness may be the single most important element promoting initial liking in college dating situations, although its influence eventually decreases when people get to know each other better (Luo & Zhang, 2009; Zhang et al., 2019).

These factors alone, of course, do not account for liking. For example, in one experiment that examined what people desired from a same-sex friendship, the top-rated qualities included sense of humor, warmth and kindness, expressiveness and openness, an exciting personality, and similarity of interests and leisure activities. But men and women differed. Men placed more value on having same-sex friends who were physically strong, had high status, and were relatively wealthy. In comparison, women were more likely to seek out friends who provided emotional support, intimacy, and useful information about social networks (Sprecher & Regan, 2002; Williams et al., 2022).

Friendship and Social Networking The newest forms of friendship are found on social network sites. Many college students spend substantial amounts of time each day switching between TikTok, Twitter, Instagram, YouTube, SnapChat, and Facebook. Not only do these social media sites allow for social-networking opportunities, they also offer a means for self-documentation and self-expression. Furthermore, students may use them for academic purposes, such as interacting with instructors and other students in their classes. Many people also get their understanding of what is happening in the news from social media sites (Elder, 2022; Healy, 2021; Tafesse, 2022).

In addition, college students may use social media sites to explore their developing identities. Because users can control how they present themselves to the world on a social network profile, they can easily "try on" identities by posting selected photos of themselves, revealing specific tastes and interests, or otherwise shaping their images in new and different ways. The feedback they get from others may help them decide which identities and forms of self-presentation suit them best (Phua et al., 2017; Cauberghe et al., 2021).

But how do social network sites affect users' nonvirtual social lives? Maintaining social connections with people you can't see in person seems like a good thing. But it may be detrimental to those who spend so much time engaged in online distant or superficial friendships that they devote little to intimate, face-to-face interactions (Sharifian & Zahodne, 2019; Yuen et al., 2019).

Furthermore, use of social media has other potential downsides. For example, because posts of others tend to be skewed to positive events, social media often presents a sanitized version of others' lives. Constant exposure to others' apparently positive lives can lead observers to feel that their lives, in comparison, are deficient.

reciprocity-of-liking effect A tendency to like those who like us. (Module 46)

APPLYING PSYCHOLOGY IN THE 21ST CENTURY

DO YOU HAVE GOOD CHEMISTRY?

Chances are very good that you've described yourself or someone else as having really good "chemistry" with another person or perhaps with an entire group of people, such as a sports team that has good "chemistry" together. This notion of people having chemistry is common, and we all have a strong intuitive sense of what we mean by that. But what exactly is chemistry? How would you define it?

If you're having a hard time answering that question, don't feel bad. Psychologists haven't been very good at wrapping their heads around it either. Perhaps that's why the experience of chemistry has been rarely studied in psychological research, despite perceptions that it can explain the quality of romantic relationships, both at their start and as they progress, as well as nonromantic friendships and relationships between team members, musicians, and even coworkers. When it has been studied, it has generally been defined loosely to refer to "individuals who seem to mesh well together, who exhibit rapport, and whose coordinated actions appear seamless and effective" (Reis et al., 2022, p. 531).

Social psychologist Harry Reis and colleagues have laid out a more precise model of interpersonal chemistry that seeks to

The warm relationship that formed between iconic singers Tony Bennett and Lady Gaga is an example of cross-generational interpersonal chemistry.
BBC/Album/Alamy Stock Photo

explain what it is, how it arises, and what it does. They suggest that chemistry entails both subjective experience and behavior. The subjective piece has three parts. First, it has a cognitive piece, or a sense of having a shared identity. Second, it has an emotional piece, which involves feeling good about the other person. Finally, it has a behavioral piece, or the perception that two people are working effectively toward mutual goals. The actual behavior—what

chemistry "looks like"–includes interacting in a synchronous way that supports and facilitates achieving each other's goals.

Reid and colleagues acknowledge in their model that other factors influence chemistry, such as the traits and goals and expectations of the interacting persons. They also emphasize that chemistry doesn't come from any one interacting person; it only arises out of an interaction between or among the people involved. This observation would explain why chemistry is notoriously difficult to predict: You have to meet and interact to see if it happens (Reis et al., 2022).

Reis and colleagues point to existing bodies of research that touch on one or more components of their model of chemistry, such as attraction, similarity, complementarity, rapport, and charisma. And they hope that their model will facilitate further research and theorizing on chemistry, especially given the potential it has to help us better understand some of our deepest and most important kinds of interpersonal relationships.

RETHINK

- Why do you think chemistry has gotten so little research attention despite its apparent importance?
- If chemistry is truly impossible to predict before people meet, is it still useful to study and understand? Why or why not?

Unsurprisingly, then, some research shows that high users of social media experience greater anxiety, loneliness, depression, and even body image problems (Shakya & Christakis, 2017; Hogue & Mills, 2019; Huang, 2022; also see the *Applying Psychology in the 21st Century* feature).

HOW DO I LOVE THEE? LET ME COUNT THE WAYS

Whereas our knowledge of what makes people like one another is extensive, our understanding of love is more limited in scope and recently acquired. For some time, many social psychologists believed that love was too difficult to observe and study in a controlled, scientific way. However, love is such a central issue in most people's lives that eventually social psychologists could not resist its allure.

As a first step, researchers tried to identify the characteristics that distinguish between mere liking and full-blown love. They discovered that love is not simply a greater quantity of liking but a qualitatively different psychological state. For instance, at least in its early stages, love includes relatively intense physiological arousal, an all-encompassing interest in the other individual, fantasizing about the other, and relatively rapid swings of emotion. Similarly, love, unlike liking, includes elements of passion, closeness, fascination, exclusiveness, sexual desire, and intense caring. We idealize partners by exaggerating their good qualities and minimizing their imperfections (Tamini et al., 2011; Gignac & Zajenkowski, 2019).

Other researchers have theorized that there are two main types of love: passionate love and companionate love. **Passionate (or romantic) love** represents a state of intense absorption in someone. It includes intense physiological arousal, psychological interest, and caring for the needs of another. In contrast, **companionate love** is the strong affection we have for those with whom our lives are deeply involved. The love we feel for parents, other family members, and even some close friends falls into the category of companionate love (Loving et al., 2009; Yildirim & Barnett, 2017; Cannas Aghedu et al., 2019).

Psychologist Robert Sternberg makes an even finer differentiation between types of love. He proposes that love consists of three parts (see Figure 1):

- *Decision/commitment,* the initial thoughts that one loves someone and the longer-term feelings of commitment to maintain love
- *Intimacy component,* feelings of closeness and connectedness
- *Passion component,* the motivational drives relating to sex, physical closeness, and romance

According to Sternberg, these three components combine to produce the different types of love. He suggests that different combinations of the three components vary over the course of relationships. For example, in strong, loving relationships, the level of commitment peaks and then remains stable. Passion, on the other hand, peaks quickly and then declines and levels off relatively early in most relationships. In addition, relationships are happiest in which the strength of the various components are similar between the two partners (Sternberg & Sternberg, 2018; Sorokowski et al., 2021).

What are people seeking in a mate? Across the world, differences between the sexes tend to be remarkably consistent. In a massive study involving people living in 45 countries, men, more than women, preferred physically attractive, relatively younger mates, whereas women, more than men, preferred older mates with good financial prospects (Walter et al., 2020).

How we meet our romantic partners and spouses has changed drastically over the years. In the 1940s, heterosexual Americans met their future partners most often through family and friends. Now the Internet is by far the most frequent matchmaker

passionate (or romantic) love A state of intense absorption in someone that includes intense physiological arousal, psychological interest, and caring for the needs of another. (Module 46)

companionate love The strong affection we have for those with whom our lives are deeply involved. (Module 46)

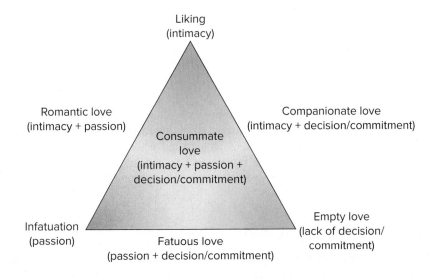

FIGURE 1 According to Sternberg, love has three main components: intimacy, passion, and decision/commitment. Different combinations of these components can create other types of love. Nonlove contains none of the three components.
Source: Adapted from Sternberg, 1986.

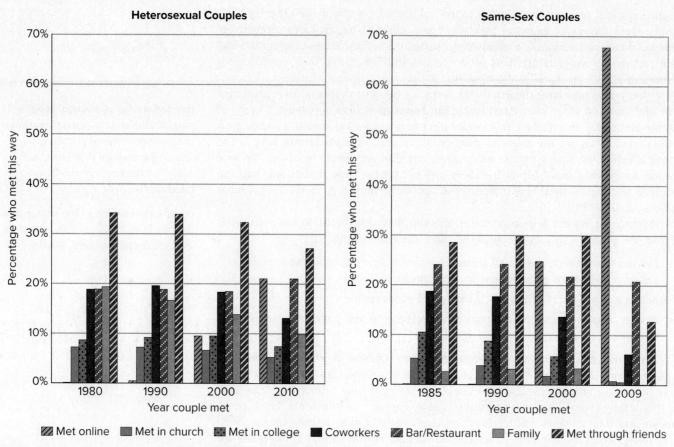

FIGURE 2 For both heterosexual couples (left graph) and same-sex couples (right graph), the trend is clear: over time, more couples report meeting online.

Sources: Rosenfeld & Thomas, 2012 (graph on left); Rosenfeld et al., 2019 (graph on right).

(see Figure 2). The likelihood of meeting online is even greater for same-sex couples; some 70% of gay couples report meeting online (Rosenfeld & Thomas, 2012; Rosenfeld et al., 2019).

Liking and loving clearly show a positive side of human social behavior. Now we turn to behaviors that are just as much a part of social behavior: aggression and helping behavior.

Aggression and Prosocial Behavior: Hurting and Helping Others

Mass shootings, carjackings, and abductions are just a few examples of the violence that seems all too common today. Yet we also find examples of generous, unselfish, thoughtful behavior that suggest a more optimistic view of humankind. Consider, for instance, people who minister to war refugees or to those living in extremes of poverty. Or contemplate the simple kindnesses of life: sharing class notes, stopping to help a child who has fallen off a bicycle, or merely sharing a candy bar with a friend. Such instances of helping are no less characteristic of human behavior than are the distasteful examples of aggression.

HURTING OTHERS: AGGRESSION

We need look no further than the daily news cycle to be bombarded with examples of aggression on both a societal level (war, invasion, assassination) and an individual level (crime, child abuse, and the many petty cruelties humans are capable of inflicting on one another). Is such aggression an inevitable part of the human condition? Or is aggression primarily a product of particular circumstances that, if changed, could lead to its reduction?

The difficulty of answering such knotty questions becomes apparent as soon as we consider how best to define the term *aggression*. Depending on the way we define the word, many examples of inflicted pain or injury may or may not qualify as aggression (see Figure 3). For instance, a rapist is clearly acting with aggression toward a chosen victim. On the other hand, a physician carrying out an emergency medical procedure without an anesthetic, thereby causing incredible pain to the patient, should not necessarily be considered aggressive.

Most social psychologists define aggression in terms of the *intent* and the *purpose* behind the behavior. **Aggression** is intentional injury of or harm to another person. By this definition, the rapist is clearly acting aggressively, whereas the physician causing pain during a medical procedure is not (Berkowitz, 2001).

aggression The intentional injury of, or harm to, another person. (Module 46)

Also, the aggression we encounter in our daily lives can take many forms. Not only do we hurt others through direct physical or verbal attacks, but we also can hurt people indirectly by doing such things as spreading rumors or purposely ignoring someone. In fact, some research finds that *microaggressions*—small, daily slights, put-downs, and insults, often perpetrated against members of marginalized groups based on race, gender, and sexual orientation—may be more harmful in the long run than are highly visible acts of aggression.

Many microaggressions are unintentional, sometimes couched as compliments or questions. "Your English is very good" or "What do lesbians think about same-sex marriage?" are examples. For members of marginalized groups, responding can be

FIGURE 3 What is aggression? It depends on how the word is defined and in what context it is used.
Source: Adapted from Benjamin, 1985.

Is This Aggression?

Defining aggression can be difficult. To see the challenges it raises, read each of the following scenarios and consider whether it describes an aggressive act—according to your own definition of aggressive behavior.

1. A dog chases a rabbit and kills it. Yes _____ No _____

2. A person places a live lobster into boiling water to prepare it for dinner. Yes _____ No _____

3. A war pilot bombs a village, killing both enemy soldiers and civilians. Yes _____ No _____

4. A carpenter repairing a roof accidentally drops a hammer. The hammer hits a child in the yard below, causing permanent brain damage. Yes _____ No _____

5. A child repeatedly yanks the leash sharply when walking a dog, ignoring the dog's cries of pain. Yes _____ No _____

6. An angry parent, hoping to get her child's teacher fired, spreads nasty rumors online about the teacher to other parents. Yes _____ No _____

7. A parent continually threatens to spank their toddler for "acting up" while they are shopping for groceries. Yes _____ No _____

8. A person does nothing to help a drowning person at the beach, even though they are an excellent swimmer. Yes _____ No _____

9. A rock star trashes a hotel room while celebrating the success of their latest CD. Yes _____ No _____

10. A person throws herself under a train. Yes _____ No _____

exhausting at best and harmful to psychological and physical well-being at worst. Moreover, the number of microaggressions that members of some groups experience is substantial. For example, in one study, Black adolescents in Washington, D.C., reported being watched closely or followed around by security guards or a clerk at a store or mall an an average of seven times in the prior 2 weeks (Williams, 2019; Harmon, 2020; Abrams, 2021; Smith & Griffiths, 2022).

Although the negative impact of microaggressions seems obvious, the degree and extent to which they influence recipients' behavior, emotions, and physical health are not fully understood. Clearly, more research needs to be done to understand their impact (Sue, 2017; Lilienfeld, 2019; Williams, 2021).

We turn now to several approaches to understanding aggressive behavior developed by social psychologists.

INSTINCT APPROACHES: AGGRESSION AS A RELEASE

If you have ever punched an adversary in the nose, you may have experienced a certain satisfaction despite your better judgment. Instinct theories, which note the prevalence of aggression not only in humans but in animals as well, propose that aggression is primarily the outcome of innate—or inborn—urges.

Sigmund Freud was one of the first to suggest, as part of his theory of personality, that aggression is a primary instinctual drive. Konrad Lorenz, an ethologist (a scientist who studies animal behavior), expanded Freud's notions by arguing that humans, along with members of other species, have a fighting instinct, which in earlier times ensured protection of food supplies and weeded out the weaker of the species (Lorenz, 1974). Lorenz's instinct approach led to the controversial notion that aggressive energy constantly builds up in an individual until the person finally discharges it in a process called **catharsis.** The longer the energy builds up, said Lorenz, the greater the amount of the aggression displayed when it is discharged.

catharsis The process of discharging built-up aggressive energy. (Module 46)

Lorenz believed that society should offer people acceptable ways of experiencing catharsis. For example, he suggested that participation in aggressive sports and games would prevent the discharge of aggression in less socially desirable ways. However, little research has found evidence for the existence of a pent-up reservoir of aggression that needs to be released. In fact, some studies flatly contradict the notion of catharsis, which leads psychologists to look for other explanations for aggression (Richardson & Hammock, 2011; Tonnaer et al., 2019; Bing & Kim, 2021).

Although little research supports Lorenz's ideas about the need to release pent-up aggression, work on the neural circuitry of the brain does suggest that particular parts of the brain may be involved in aggressive behavior. For example, the amygdala responds to emotionally charged occurrences and is related to threat detection and fear (Fields, 2016; daCunha-Bang et al., 2019).

FRUSTRATION-AGGRESSION APPROACHES: AGGRESSION AS A REACTION TO FRUSTRATION

Suppose you've been working on a paper that is due for a class early the next morning and your computer printer runs out of ink just before you can print out the paper. You rush to the store to buy more ink only to find the sales clerk locking the door for the day. Even though the clerk can see you gesturing and begging him to open the door, he refuses, shrugs his shoulders, and points to a sign that indicates when the store will open the next day. At that moment, the feelings you experience toward the sales clerk probably place you on the verge of real aggression, and you are undoubtedly seething inside.

Frustration-aggression approaches explain how the frustration one might feel standing at that closed door could lead to aggression. According to these approaches, frustration (the experience of having one's goals thwarted or blocked) produces anger, which in turn produces a readiness to act aggressively.

But anger doesn't always lead to aggression. Whether actual aggression occurs depends on the presence of aggressive cues. *Aggressive cues* are stimuli that have been associated in the past with actual aggression or violence and that may trigger aggression again (Burton et al., 2013; Kersten & Greitemeyer, 2022).

What kinds of stimuli act as aggressive cues? They can range from the most explicit, such as the presence of weapons, to more subtle cues, such as the mere mention of the name of an individual who behaved violently in the past. For example, angered participants in experiments behave significantly more aggressively when in the presence of a gun than in a comparable situation in which no guns are present. Similarly, frustrated participants who view a violent movie are more physically aggressive toward a confederate with the same name as the star of the movie than they are toward a confederate with a different name (Jovanović et al., 2011; Wang & Zhong, 2015; Turner & Leyens, 2019).

It appears, then, that frustration does lead to aggression—at least when aggressive cues are present. However, psychologists have come to realize that frustration is not the only trigger of aggression. For example, physical pain, verbal insults, and unpleasant experiences in general can also lead to aggression. Similarly, violent behavior increases when the temperature rises—suggesting that one consequence of global warming may be an increase in aggression and intergroup conflict (Plante & Anderson, 2017; Bradshaw, 2019; Gallucci et al., 2020).

Is road rage a result of frustration? According to frustration-aggression approaches, frustration is a likely cause.

Chris Ryan/OJO Images/age fotostock

OBSERVATIONAL LEARNING APPROACHES: LEARNING TO HURT OTHERS

Do we learn to be aggressive? The *observational learning* (sometimes called *social learning*) approach to aggression says that we do. Taking an almost opposite view from instinct theories, which focus on innate explanations of aggression, observational learning theory emphasizes that social and environmental conditions can teach individuals to be aggressive. The theory sees aggression not as inevitable but rather as a learned response that can be understood in terms of rewards and punishments.

Observational learning theory pays attention to the direct rewards and punishments that people receive for acting aggressively. For example, a father may tell his son how glad he was that he "stood up for himself" after getting into a fight, thereby rewarding aggressive behavior.

More frequently, though, people learn aggression through watching others' behavior. According to the *observational learning approach*, we learn to be aggressive by viewing the rewards and punishments that models provide. *Models* are individuals who provide a guide to appropriate behavior through their own behavior. According to observational learning theory, people observe the behavior of models and the subsequent consequences of that behavior. If the consequences are positive, the behavior is likely to be imitated when observers find themselves in a similar situation.

Suppose, for instance, a child hits their younger sibling when the sibling damages a new toy. Whereas instinct theory would suggest that the aggression had been pent up and was now being discharged, and frustration-aggression theory would examine the child's frustration at no longer being able to use their new toy, observational learning theory would look to previous situations in which the child had viewed others being rewarded for their aggression. For example, perhaps the child had watched a friend get to play with a toy after they painfully twisted it out of the hand of another child.

Observational learning theory has received wide research support. For example, children of nursery school age who have watched an adult model behave aggressively and then receive reinforcement for it later display similar behavior themselves if they have been angered, insulted, or frustrated after exposure. Furthermore, a significant amount of research links watching television shows and other media displays containing violence with subsequent viewer aggression (Carnagey et al., 2007; Ma et al., 2018; Zografova et al., 2019).

> **! Study Alert**
> Understand the distinction between the instinctual, frustration-aggression, and observational learning approaches to aggression.

From the perspective of...

A Criminal Justice Worker How would proponents of the three main approaches to the study of aggression—instinct approaches, frustration-aggression approaches, and observational learning approaches—interpret the aggression of the killer in the Uvalde, Texas, school shooting, in which 21 children and adults were killed?

DMITRI MARUTA/
Deposit Photos/
Glow Images

Helping Others: The Brighter Side of Human Nature

prosocial behavior Helping behavior. (Module 46)

Turning away from aggression, we move now to the opposite–and brighter–side of human nature: how we provide aid to others. **Prosocial behavior,** which is the term that psychologists use for helping behavior, has been considered under many different conditions.

Those who engage in acts of prosocial behavior enjoy a number of benefits that go beyond the satisfaction of being helpful. For instance, acts of kindness and expressions of empathy bolster mental health and a sense of well-being. Such acts even produce physical benefits, with some research suggesting that those who practice kindness may have longer lifespans. At the very least, kindness and empathy foster a sense of connection with others (Curry et al., 2018; Gherghel et al., 2021; Hui, 2022).

One question that psychologists have looked at most closely relates to bystander intervention in emergency situations. What are the factors that lead someone to help a person in need?

One critical factor related to helping in emergency situations is the number of other individuals present. When multiple people witness an emergency situation, a sense of diffusion of responsibility can arise among the bystanders. **Diffusion of responsibility** is the belief that responsibility for taking action is shared, or diffused, among those present. The more people present in an emergency, the less personally responsible each individual feels–and therefore the less help they provide (Martin & North, 2015; Christensen, 2019; Liu et al., 2022).

diffusion of responsibility The belief that responsibility for intervening is shared, or diffused, among those present. (Module 46)

For example, think back to the classic case of Kitty Genovese that we described when discussing the topic of research. Genovese was stabbed multiple times, and–according to some accounts of the event–no one offered help, despite the fact that allegedly close to 40 people who lived in nearby apartments heard her screams for help. The lack of help has been attributed to diffusion of responsibility: The fact that there were so many potential helpers led each individual to feel diminished personal responsibility (Gallo, 2015; Griggs, 2015; Scott et al., 2021).

Although most research on helping behavior supports the diffusion-of-responsibility explanation, other factors are clearly involved in helping behavior. The decision to give aid involves four basic steps (see Figure 4; Latané & Darley, 1970; Garcia et al., 2002; López-Pérez et al., 2019):

- *Noticing a person, event, or situation that may require help.* If we are to provide help, we first have to perceive that a situation is one that potentially requires our help and intervention.

- *Interpreting the event as one that requires help.* Even if we notice an event, it may be sufficiently ambiguous for us to interpret it as a nonemergency situation that requires no help. Thus, we make an interpretation as to whether or not the event requires help.

- *Assuming responsibility for helping.* It is at this key point that diffusion of responsibility is likely to occur if others are present. Moreover, a bystander's particular expertise is likely to play a role in determining whether they help. For instance, if people with training in medical aid or lifesaving techniques are present, untrained bystanders are less likely to intervene because they feel they have less expertise.

- *Deciding on and implementing the form of helping.* After we assume responsibility for helping, we must decide how to provide assistance. Helping can range from very indirect forms of intervention, such as calling the police, to more direct forms, such as giving first aid or taking the victim to a hospital. Most social psychologists use a *rewards-costs approach* for helping to predict the nature of the assistance a bystander will choose to provide. The general notion is that the bystander's perceived rewards for helping must outweigh the costs if helping is to occur, and most research tends to support this notion (Hu et al., 2021; Liang & Park, 2022).

After determining the nature of the assistance needed, the actual help must be implemented. A rewards-costs analysis suggests that we are most likely to use the least costly form of implementation. However, this is not always the case: In some situations, the help that is provided shows altruism. **Altruism** is behavior meant to help another without regard for self-interest. It is putting the welfare of others above oneself. For example, we can see altruism in soldiers who risk their own lives to save another soldier who is wounded or in a person who jumps into an icy pond to save a drowning stranger (Xi et al., 2017; Sparrow et al., 2021; Pfattheicher et al., 2022).

People who intervene in emergency situations tend to possess certain personality characteristics that differentiate them from nonhelpers. For example, helpers are more self-assured, sympathetic, emotionally understanding, and empathetic (empathy is a personality trait in which someone observing another person experiences the emotions of that person) than are nonhelpers (Batson, 2011; Li et al., 2019).

Still, most social psychologists agree that no single set of attributes differentiates helpers from nonhelpers. For the most part, temporary situational factors (such as the mood we're in) determine whether we will intervene in a situation requiring aid (Snyder & Dwyer, 2013; Berry et al., 2021).

More generally, what leads people to make moral decisions? Clearly, situational factors make a difference. For example, one study asked people to judge the morality of plane crash survivors cannibalizing an injured boy to avoid starvation. Participants in the study were more likely to condemn the behavior if they were placed in an emotional state than if they were less emotional (Broeders et al., 2011; Driver, 2022).

Other psychologists, using a neuroscience perspective, believe that there's a kind of tug-of-war between emotion and rational thinking in the brain. If the rational side wins out, we're more likely to take a logical view of moral situations (if you're at risk for starving, go ahead and eat the injured boy). On the other hand, if the emotional side prevails, we're more likely to condemn the cannibalism, even if it means we may be harmed. In support of such reasoning, researchers have found that different areas of the brain are involved in moral decisions (Greene & Paxton, 2009; Beauchamp et al., 2019).

Evidence also exists that our brains are hardwired to help us feel empathy for others. In this view, helping others in some ways is just as natural as other, more

Noticing a person, event, or situation that may require help

↓

Interpreting the event as one that requires help

↓

Assuming responsibility for helping

↓

Deciding on and implementing the form of helping

FIGURE 4 The basic steps of helping.
Source: Latané & Darley, 1970.

altruism Behavior meant to help another person without regard for self-interest. (Module 46)

Study Alert

The distinction between *prosocial behavior* and *altruism* is important. Prosocial behavior does not need to have a self-sacrificing component; altruism, by definition, contains an element of self-sacrifice.

Altruism is often the only bright side of a natural disaster.

Victor J. Blue/Bloomberg/Getty Images

negative behaviors. The question becomes, then, how we balance the positive and negative behaviors that are equally the result of the functioning of the brain (Pfaff, 2014; de Waal, 2014; Fedyk, 2017).

BECOMING AN INFORMED CONSUMER
of Psychology

Dealing Effectively with Anger

At one time or another, almost everyone feels angry. The anger may result from a frustrating situation, or it may be due to another individual's behavior. The way we deal with anger may determine the difference between a promotion and a lost job or a broken relationship and one that mends itself.

Social psychologists who have studied the topic suggest several good strategies to deal with anger that maximize the potential for positive consequences (Nelson & Finch, 2000; Bernstein, 2011; Faupel et al., 2018). Among the most useful strategies are the following:

- *Calm down.* Take a walk or engage in some other physical activity in order to cool down your emotional arousal.
- *Look again at the anger-provoking situation from the perspective of others.* By taking others' points of view, you may be able to understand the situation better, and with increased understanding, you may become more tolerant of the apparent shortcomings of others.
- *Minimize the importance of the situation.* Does it really matter that someone is driving too slowly and that you'll be late to an appointment as a result? Reinterpret the situation in a way that is less bothersome.
- *Use language effectively by saying "I," not "you."* Don't say *"You did _____ wrong."* Instead, say *"I felt hurt when you did _____."* When you accuse people of being wrong, they are likely to feel the need to fight back.
- *Fantasize about getting even—but don't act on it.* Fantasy provides a safety valve. In your fantasies, you can yell at that unfair professor all you want and suffer no consequences at all. However, don't spend too much time brooding: Fantasize, but then move on.
- *Relax.* By teaching yourself the relaxation techniques used in systematic desensitization (discussed in the chapter on treatment of psychological disorders), you can help reduce your reactions to anger. In turn, your anger may dissipate.

No matter which of these strategies you try, above all, don't ignore your anger. People who always try to suppress their anger may experience a variety of consequences, such as self-condemnation, frustration, and even physical illness (Rice et al., 2020; Conrad et al., 2021).

RECAP/EVALUATE/RETHINK

RECAP

LO 46-1 Why are we attracted to certain people, and what progression do social relationships follow?

- The primary determinants of liking include proximity, exposure, similarity, and physical attractiveness.

- Loving is distinguished from liking by the presence of intense physiological arousal, an all-encompassing interest in another, fantasies about the other, rapid swings of emotion, fascination, sexual desire, exclusiveness, and strong feelings of caring.

- Love can be categorized as passionate or companionate. In addition, love has several components: intimacy, passion, and decision/commitment.

LO 46-2 What factors underlie aggression and prosocial behavior?

- Aggression is intentional injury of or harm to another person.
- Explanations of aggression include instinct approaches, frustration-aggression theory, and observational learning.
- Helping behavior in emergencies is determined in part by the phenomenon of diffusion of responsibility, which results in a lower likelihood of helping when more people are present.
- Deciding to help is the outcome of a four-stage process that consists of noticing a possible need for help, interpreting the situation as requiring aid, assuming responsibility for taking action, and deciding on and implementing a form of assistance.

EVALUATE

1. We tend to like people who are similar to us. True or false?
2. Which of the following sets are the three components of love proposed by Sternberg?
   a. Passion, closeness, sexuality
   b. Attraction, desire, complementarity
   c. Passion, intimacy, decision/commitment
   d. Commitment, caring, sexuality

3. Based on research evidence, which of the following might be the best way to reduce the amount of fighting a young boy does?
   a. Take them to the gym to work out on the boxing equipment.
   b. Make them repeatedly watch violent scenes from the film *The Matrix Resurrections* in the hope that it will provide catharsis.
   c. Reward them if they don't fight for a certain length of time.
   d. Ignore the fighting and let it die out naturally.
4. If a person in a crowd does not help in an apparent emergency situation because many other people are present, that person is falling victim to the phenomenon of

_____ _____ _____.

RETHINK

1. Can love be studied scientifically? Is there an elusive quality to love that makes it at least partially unknowable? How would you define "falling in love"? How would you study it?
2. How would the aggression of the Boston Marathon bombers be interpreted by the three main approaches to the study of aggression: instinct approaches, frustration-aggression approaches, and observational learning approaches? Do you think one of these approaches fits the bombers' case more closely than the others?

Answers to Evaluate Questions

1. true; 2. c; 3. c; 4. diffusion of responsibility

KEY TERMS

interpersonal attraction (or close relationship)	passionate (or romantic) love	aggression	diffusion of responsibility
reciprocity-of-liking effect	companionate love	catharsis	altruism
		prosocial behavior	

Module 47
Diversity, Equity, Inclusion, and Culture

LEARNING OUTCOME

LO 47-1 What are the basic elements of diversity and culture?

Diversity and Culture

No matter where we live, we are increasingly likely to encounter people who differ from us racially, ethnically, and culturally. Technology is bringing people from across the globe into our homes, as close to us as the phone in our hand. Businesses now operate globally, so the coworkers we find ourselves interacting with on Zoom are likely to come from many countries and cultures. Being comfortable with people whose backgrounds and beliefs differ from one's own is not only a social necessity but also a requirement for career success.

Moreover, by the mid-21st century, the percentage of people in the United States of African, Latin American, Asian, and Arabic ancestry will be greater than the percentage of those of Western European ancestry–a profound statistical and social shift. College enrollments will mirror these changes, as populations that were minority become the majority (Cohn & Caumont, 2016; Pappano, 2019; Velez & Jessup-Anger, 2022).

More specifically, consider the following population trends (Cohn & Caumont, 2016; U.S. Census Bureau, 2017, 2019; Esterline & Batalova, 2022).

- By 2055, the United States will not have any single racial or ethnic majority. Put another way, we will all be members of minority groups.

- Almost 60 million immigrants have come to the United States since 1970.

- Most population growth in the United States is projected to be related to Hispanic and Asian immigration.

Increasingly, many workplaces include staff from a wide variety of countries and cultures, and with a wide range of customs and beliefs. What are your experiences with people who differ from you culturally?

fizkes/Shutterstock

- Around 14% of the U.S. population is foreign-born.
- Nearly 22% of U.S. residents speak a language other than English at home.

Furthermore, diversity is not only based in racial, ethnic, and cultural characteristics. The world's population is also diverse in terms of sex, gender identity, sexual orientation, age, and mental and physical abilities. Then, layer on factors such as level and type of education, religion, and level of income, and you can see that each person is a complex mix of identities. The way those diverse identities overlap or interact is known as *intersectionality*. One can be, for instance, a lesbian Black American woman with hearing impairments and evoke responses from others that reflect any, all, or none of those identities (DeBlaere et al., 2018; Mays & Ghavami, 2018; Else-Quest et al., 2022).

The Language of Diversity

The language we use to describe others and their diverse identities is important, and social-cultural norms often determine what labels are appropriate. For example, should one use the term African American or Black American or Black? Caucasian, White, or Euro-American? Hispanic or Latino? American Indian or Native American? Gay, lesbian, straight, or queer? Transgender, cisgender, male, or female? Physically challenged, differently abled, or disabled? The choice of labels matters. The subtleties of language affect how people think about members of particular groups and how they think about themselves (Forson, 2018; Murphy, 2022).

One difficulty is that many of the terms we use to describe these identities are ill-defined and often overlapping. For example, the term **race** generally refers to

race Generally refers to obvious physical differences that set one group apart from others. (Module 47)

The term *race* is generally used to refer to obvious physical differences between groups of people. However, as you can see from these images, skin tone, hair texture, and facial features come in many varieties and combinations, so the lines between groups can't be clearly drawn.
Rawpixel.com/Shutterstock

obvious physical differences that set one group apart from others. As we first discussed in Chapter 1, however, depending on how race is defined, there are between 3 and 300 races, with no race genetically distinct. And the reality is that 99.9% of our genetic makeup is similar across all human beings. Because of this, race is generally thought of as a *social construction*, something that is defined by people's attitudes and beliefs (Zuberi et al., 2015; Gross & Weiss, 2018; Bryant et al., 2022).

Ethnicity refers to shared national origins or cultural patterns. In the United States, for example, the terms *Puerto Rican*, *Irish*, and *Italian American* typically are considered ethnicities. However, ethnicity–like race–is very much in the eye of the beholder. For instance, a Cuban American who is a third-generation citizen of the United States may feel few ties or associations with Cuba or Cuban culture. Yet White Americans may view this person as "Hispanic," and Black Americans may view them as "White."

ethnicity Shared national origins or cultural patterns. (Module 47)

Race and ethnicity shape each of us to an enormous degree, profoundly influencing our view of others as well as ourselves. They affect how others treat us and how we treat them in turn. They can also determine a broad range of behaviors, ranging from whether we look people in the eye when we meet them (in some cultures, direct eye contact is viewed as disrespectful, so it is avoided) or how much food we eat when we're invited to dinner at a friend's house (in some cultures, leaving food on one's plate is considered impolite) (Mannarini et al., 2017; Park et al., 2018; Helou et al., 2022).

Even the words we use to describe others reflect our beliefs and values. For instance, the term *African American* is a label that has historical, geographical, and sociological implications. On the other hand, *Black* focuses primarily on skin color (Aspinall, 2020, 2021).

Similarly, we do not yet have clear rules about the language to use for the varieties of gender identities and sexualities individuals may hold. For example, *transgender* refers to individuals whose sense of whether they are male or female (their *gender identity*) does not match the sex they were assigned at birth. Transgender people may refer to themselves as trans, transexual, agender, demigender, or genderqueer, and some prefer the use of gender-neutral pronouns, such as *ze*, *zir*, or *they*.

Furthermore, gender identity is not the same as *sexual orientation*, which describes a person's physical and emotional attraction to another person. For example, people may consider themselves straight, lesbian, gay, bisexual–or something else–depending on who they are attracted to sexually.

Culture

As a graduate student from Korea, Jung felt she was adjusting to her psychology program in the United States. She got along well with her professors, and her office-mates seemed cordial and friendly. But she felt uneasy in one area. Every Friday afternoon, other graduate students would gather at a local bar for what they called "Happy Hour," which–although Jung didn't know it–was a long-standing tradition among students in the psychology program. No one extended a personal invitation to Jung, and although she wished she could go with the other students, she felt it would be presumptuous to attend without an invitation. Since they never invited her to go along, she wondered if she had somehow insulted them.

How would you respond to Jung about her concerns? Most people familiar with the social customs of the United States would probably tell her that she needs no invitation to join her fellow students at the bar. Such gatherings are informal, and most U.S. natives would neither expect nor routinely offer personal invitations to them.

Jung's confusion over the customs of public gatherings is just one example of the ways in which cultural assumptions differ. Although this problem appears to be relatively trivial, variations in such everyday behaviors indicate fundamental differences between people of diverse cultures. Furthermore, such misunderstandings may lead to stereotyping and prejudice. For example, Jung's classmates might think she is standoffish or unfriendly, and they might generalize such a view to something about Koreans. Learning about culture is essential to understanding the differences between people.

Culture comprises the learned behaviors, beliefs, and attitudes that are characteristic of a society. Culture is transmitted from one generation to another in both written and spoken form. Culture also encompasses people's creations, such as art, music, literature, and architecture. In sum, culture both shapes and reflects a society's behavior, understanding of the world, attitudes, and values (Han & Ma, 2015; Bornstein & Lansford, 2019; Arshad & Chung, 2022).

Despite their broad impact on people, cultural factors have traditionally received little attention from psychologists. One reason is that many psychologists have instead focused on broad universal principles of human behavior. Presumably, the thinking went, such principles should apply to all people, regardless of their culture.

Today, however, psychologists increasingly appreciate the importance of culture. Rather than considering it an obstacle to finding universal psychological principles, psychologists now view culture as a major factor in shaping behavior. In fact, explanations for many central aspects of behavior remain elusive without an understanding of the consequences of culture. Indeed, psychologists can identify broad, universal principles of behavior only by determining which ones apply across cultures and which are specific to particular cultures. For example, a psychologist studying grief as a universal emotion would want to determine what a festive New Orleans jazz funeral has in common with a more conventional funeral at a graveside (Rosenblatt, 2013; Gercama & Jones, 2020).

Understanding the role of culture has also become increasingly important due to the growing diversity of U.S. society. The fabric of society is changing to reflect the contributions of people of diverse ethnic, racial, and religious backgrounds. We can understand the similarities and differences around us only when we consider culture. Furthermore, when we are aware of the effects of cultural differences, we may overcome our prejudices and better understand the roots of discrimination, allowing us to feel more comfortable reaching out to others.

Furthering interest in culture is the concept of multiculturalism, which has both psychological and political implications for how members of racial, ethnic, religious, and other demographic groups are perceived. **Multiculturalism** is the view that

culture The learned behaviors, beliefs, and attitudes that characterize an individual society or population. (Module 47)

multiculturalism The view that members of all cultures deserve equal respect and that their contributions to society should be recognized (Module 47).

Cultures vary in multiple ways, including their funeral ceremonies. In this traditional New Orleans funeral procession, jazz musicians provide a send-off to a loved one on the way to the cemetery. What is the funeral tradition in your culture or religion?
RSBPhoto/Alamy Stock Photo

members of all cultures deserve equal respect and that their contributions to society should be recognized. This concept not only acknowledges differences among subcultural groups, it also furthers the argument that society is stronger due to the presence of multiple groups and cultures.

Let's examine some primary psychological considerations related to culture, including differing cultural orientations and how people in different cultures vary in their view of themselves.

Collectivism and Individualism: The Group Versus the Individual

Do you think teenagers should take their parents' views into account when choosing a career? Do you think you ought to help a neighbor who is in financial distress? Do you have an obligation to lend your class notes to a fellow student who missed a class?

If you answer yes to these questions, your responses represent values similar to those found in many Eastern cultures. On the other hand, if you reply no to these questions, your value orientation is more like that fostered in Western cultures.

These two orientations are known as *collectivism* and *individualism.* Cultures that support **collectivism** promote the idea that the well-being of the group or society is more important than that of the individual. People in collectivistic societies place the welfare of the group above their own personal well-being (Arpaci et al., 2018; Xiao, 2021).

In contrast, societies that encourage **individualism** hold as a primary value the personal identity, uniqueness, freedom, and worth of the individual person. In individualistic cultures, personal goals are viewed as more important than goals relating to society in general.

The individualistic and collectivistic tendencies of these cultures influence the way people interpret and understand behavior. For example, students and teachers in the United States tend to attribute their scholastic success to stable, internal characteristics. Consequently, a student who does well is seen as being smart, which is a stable, internal trait and is an outgrowth of an individualistic view of the world. In contrast, in China and Japan, both countries that have a more collectivistic culture than the United States, people see scholastic performance in terms of temporary,

collectivism The concept that the well-being of the group or society is more important than that of the individual. (Module 47)

individualism The concept that holds as a primary value the personal identity, uniqueness, freedom, and worth of the individual person. (Module 47)

In Eastern collectivist cultures, students are more likely to view academic achievement as tied to situational factors, such as how hard they work. In contrast, those in Western individualistic cultures tie achievement to more stable characteristics, such as how smart they think they are. How do you view academic success?
Paul Burns/Blend Images

situational factors, such as how hard a student works (Dean & Koenig, 2019; Brossoie et al., 2022).

The varying cultural perceptions that underlie academic success lead to different levels of scholastic motivation. Because Chinese and Japanese students are more apt to assume that academic success results from hard work, they are likely to put greater effort into their studies. U.S. students may exert less effort because they believe that their stable, unvarying level of ability underlies their school performance. After all, students who assume that their internal ability is the primary cause of their performance may not understand that studying harder may bring better results. In other words, they may feel they can't do much to change the outcome (Fetvadjiev et al., 2018; Wu et al., 2018; Lam & Zhou, 2022).

Whether a culture is collectivistic or individualistic also influences people's willingness to share scarce resources with others. For instance, people living in collectivistic cultures primarily employ the *norm of equality* to determine how rewards should be granted. The norm of equality suggests that all people ought to be rewarded equally, regardless of who they are or how competent or successful they are. In this case, an equality norm would mean that all students working on a project together as a group would receive the same grade.

In contrast, people living in individualistic societies tend to distribute resources according to a *norm of equity*, in which rewards are based on the size of the contribution people make or the quality of their performance. Those who receive the most are the ones seen as having made the greatest contribution, whereas those who receive the least are the ones seen as having made the smallest contribution. In an individualistic society, then, workers are paid according to their perceived merit. As a consequence, great discrepancies exist in the rewards people receive (Okely et al., 2018; Voulgarides, 2021).

Our View of Ourselves: Looking Inward

In Western cultures, "the squeaky wheel gets the grease." In Asian cultures, "the nail that stands out gets pounded down."

The differences in these two sayings reflect profound cultural variations between the West and East in how people see themselves. In the Western perspective, people tend to differentiate themselves, making their voices heard and letting others know what their individual needs are in a situation. The Asian perspective suggests that the best approach is to blend in, to avoid being noticed (Krassner et al., 2017; Amir & McAuliffe, 2020).

These divergent points of view exemplify how people in Eastern and Western cultures view the **self**, the way in which we look inward and define ourselves as individuals. Research suggests that people raised in Asian societies have an **interdependent** view of themselves, in part reflective of their collectivistic orientation. They think of themselves as members of a larger society, working together with others to achieve social harmony. In this view, people strive to fit in, to behave in a way that coincides with how others think, feel, and act (Levine et al., 2016; Fan et al., 2021; Kitayama et al., 2022).

People in Western societies, however, see themselves as **independent** of others, reflecting in part their individualistic orientation. Rather than striving to fit in, they may compete rather than cooperate with others. In many cases, they pride themselves on their uniqueness, distinctiveness, and above all, individuality.

These distinct views of the self are revealed on many levels and in all aspects of individualistic cultures. Even the languages people speak reflect the differences. For instance, the English language has more words for emotions focused on oneself, such as jealousy and anger, than the Japanese language. In contrast, the Japanese language contains many more terms for emotions involving others, such as sympathy, than the

self A person's essential being distinguishing themselves from others; how we define ourselves as individuals. (Module 47)

interdependent (view of self) To view oneself as a member of a larger society, working together with others to achieve social harmony. (Module 47)

independent (view of self) To view oneself as behaving independently, competing rather than cooperating with others. (Module 47)

English language. In fact, the Japanese language contains words for some emotions that do not have similar words in English. *Oime,* for instance, refers to being indebted to another individual–a word for which English has nothing comparable (Markus & Kitayama, 2010; Andersen, 2017; Lingis, 2022).

People in Eastern cultures also view achievement very differently than people in Western cultures. For example, Westerners assess achievement in terms of personal gains. They look at how well they are doing relative to others, comparing whether they are better or worse off. Grades, salaries, and the size of one's home or office are things that people may use to compare and measure achievements. Thus, the value they place on their success is relative to what others achieve.

In contrast, people in interdependent societies tend to measure success in terms of group achievement. Rewards are thought to be appropriate in terms of how well one's group does, rather than how one does as an individual. For example, a student's success on a group project would be measured in terms of how well the overall project turns out, rather than in terms of each student's individual contribution. Similarly, salary raises in a business might be based on the performance of the company as a whole.

The degree of interdependence and independence of a culture has real consequences. For example, the United States, with its independent cultural values, had per capita more deaths due to the COVID pandemic than any other country in the world during the first year of the pandemic, and the country continued to lag in its response to the pandemic. An analysis of what went wrong showed that many Americans were resistant to collective mask and vaccine mandates and refused to follow what they saw was politicized advice from experts (Kitayama et al., 2022).

Most aspects of a culture, such as the degree of its individualism and collectivism, are neither inherently good nor bad. In an absolute sense, neither individualism nor collectivism is preferable to the other. But elements in some cultures are clearly harmful. One such element is the aggressiveness of a given society, which we consider next.

A Culture of Violence?

Violence is as American as apple pie.

At least that's the grim conclusion of some observers of society in the United States, who point to the quantity of violence that occurs. For example, the homicide rate in the United States is four times greater than in comparable countries such as the United Kingdom. The number of mass shootings–defined as incidents in which four or more people, not including the shooter, were hurt or killed–exceeded 600 in 2022. Moreover, within the United States, certain segments of the population are especially at risk: Black Americans make up 54% of all murder victims, yet they make up only about 14% of the population (Rosenfeld et al., 2017; Grawert & Kim, 2022; Ledur & Rabinowitz, 2022).

The United States is also an outlier when it comes to the magnitude of school violence. Since 1970, over 600 students and teachers have have been killed in shootings in 217 schools. In the 2020-21 school year, the U.S. Department of Education reported 93 school shootings–a rate of just about two per week (Cox et al., 2018; Wolfe & Walker, 2019; Cox et al., 2023).

Do these figures imply that U.S. society is uniquely violent compared to other societies? Before we can answer such a question, we need to consider several factors because comparing levels of aggression across cultures is no easy matter.

Take, for instance, the difficulty in defining the term *aggression.* Most researchers suggest that for an act to be considered aggressive, it must involve intentional injury or harm to another person; others use broader definitions. The particular definition of aggression becomes critical when comparing statistics collected from a variety of settings in very different cultures.

In addition, cultures are not homogeneous. For example, regions differ within the United States: The rate of murder in the Texas panhandle is four times higher than the murder rate in Nebraska. Generalizing across an entire country or culture, then, may obscure important differences among subgroups (Nisbett & Cohen, 1996; Anwar et al., 2018; Hornsveld et al., 2018).

Despite such critical difficulties in comparing rates of violence across cultures, several researchers have attempted to identify differences between cultures in the levels of aggression. As a result, several findings have emerged.

One finding is that cultures have very different views of aggression. For instance, people in some cultures hold extremely positive attitudes about aggression. Among the Simbu of New Guinea, the most admired people are the most aggressive. The more violent a male is, the more followers he is likely to have and the higher his status. These higher-status males often seek fights and urge others to join in fighting. As a consequence, warfare is frequent (Brown, 1986; Dernbach & Marshall, 2001; Richardson et al., 2021).

In contrast, some cultures are notably nonviolent. For instance, the Semai, who live in the Malaysian rain forest, traditionally hold negative attitudes about aggression. They tend to deride people who are violent and hold nurturance in high esteem. Perhaps because they live in an area rich in natural resources, they generally see less practical value in antagonistic or adversarial behavior (Dentan, 2000; Anwar et al., 2018; Tavangar, 2022).

Other studies have focused on more direct comparisons. In one classic study, cross-cultural psychologist William Lambert (1971) examined aggression in Kenya, India, Mexico, Okinawa, the Philippines, and the United States. He looked at how mothers, the primary child-care providers in each of the cultures, reacted to their own children's aggression toward other children. The results showed that Mexican mothers were the strictest, whereas mothers in the United States showed the greatest leniency toward aggressive behavior. A different set of results occurred when mothers witnessed acts of aggression by their children toward adults. Children who were aggressive toward adults received the greatest punishment in Kenya, the Philippines, and Mexico and the least punishment in India. U.S. children received a relatively moderate degree of punishment (Stacks et al., 2009; Lansford et al., 2014; Lansford et al., 2018).

How mothers react to aggression is ultimately reflected in overall rates of societal aggression, though the display of aggression depends on the children's activity level and opportunities for social interaction. For instance, active children who frequently interact with other children seem to learn their culture's lessons about aggression most readily. Thus, active Mexican children are relatively less aggressive than U.S. children because mothers in Mexico tend to react strongly against displays of aggressive behavior. In contrast, active children in the United States show more aggression since their aggression typically earns only a mild rebuke from their mothers.

These findings demonstrate that culture plays a role in providing children with experiences that ultimately result in different levels of social aggression. How a culture trains its children, then, affects their degree of aggressiveness.

Although people in various cultures differ in levels of aggression, at least one common factor bridges across cultures: Males are more aggressive than females. In no culture do females commit more aggressive acts than males, a finding that holds for adults as well as children (Slotboom et al., 2011; Bass et al., 2018; Kim et al., 2022).

Why should this be true? Although we might attribute the finding to heredity—the idea that males are born with a predisposition to be more aggressive than females—this is not the only possibility. For instance, across cultures, societies may hold similar expectations about the behaviors boys and girls are taught, and these expectations lead to the differences in aggression. In many cultures, boys are explicitly taught to be aggressive, whereas aggression in girls is discouraged. Related explanations suggest that boys act aggressively to accentuate their masculine identity, most likely because their societies value "strong," aggressive males (Pellegrini et al., 2010; Bosson & Vandello, 2011; Aimé et al., 2018).

Although the universal differences in male and female aggression levels are striking, the fact that psychologists find substantial differences in levels of aggression from

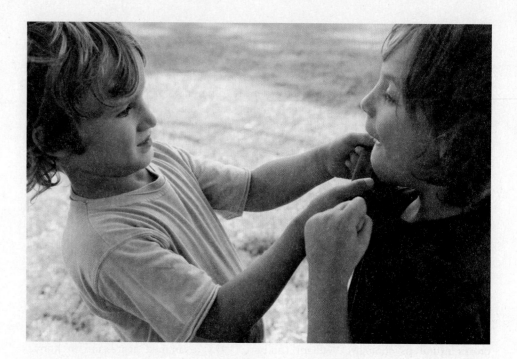

Across cultures, males tend to be more aggressive than females. Why might this be true?

Odilon Dimier/PhotoAlto/Getty Images

culture to culture is also noteworthy. It suggests that aggression is not an inevitable aspect of human behavior, and it implies that people may be able to learn to control and reduce violence in the world. In turn, it may be possible to diminish global aggression and enhance the potential for peace in our time.

Immigrants and Immigration

Much anti-immigrant rhetoric in the United States today describes these newcomers as rapists, murderers, and worse who are straining the prison system, stealing jobs, living on welfare, and contributing little to society. However, the reality, as embodied by statistical evidence, is quite different. For instance, consider the following points (Lazear, 2017; Nowrasteh, 2021; Tong & Fong, 2022):

- The majority of legal and illegal immigrants ultimately become financially successful. Although initially they have higher rates of poverty than native-born Americans, most immigrants eventually have higher average family incomes than native-born citizens. They have a higher rate of business startups.

- Most of the projected increase in immigration comes from increases in legal immigration, not illegal immigration.

- Few immigrants come to the United States to receive welfare. Instead, most say they come because of opportunities to work and prosper in the United States. Many come to escape political oppression, violence, and crippling poverty, and their goal is to work and earn a living. In fact, the unemployment rate for immigrants is about 10% lower than for the native-born population. Immigrants use significantly less welfare than native-born Americans.

- Although they are initially more costly to the government, immigrants become increasingly productive as they get older, paying taxes that outweigh their cost to government.

Why do immigrants so often end up financially successful? One hypothesis is that those immigrants who voluntarily leave their native countries are unusually motivated to become successful, more so than immigrants who choose not to immigrate. Whatever the reason, the evidence suggests that most immigrants eventually become part of the fabric of U.S. life (Houri & Sullivan, 2019; Radford, 2019; Nowrasteh, 2021).

BECOMING AN INFORMED CONSUMER
of Psychology

Reducing War, Promoting Peace, and Creating a Just World

As the violence in Ukraine, Somalia, Gaza, and many other spots shows, the world is a dangerous place. Although the threat of a major, all-out nuclear war has diminished, the danger remains high for smaller, more limited wars. Furthermore, other problems of the world continue unabated, such as environmental degradation, overpopulation, disease, and famine.

Yet, the world's citizens are not powerless. Several strategies, developed as a result of work conducted by psychologists, can create a world that is safer and more just in the future. Here are some of the most promising possibilities:

- *Increase cross-cutting relations between people.* **Cross-cutting relations** are the links between groups in the areas of work, education, and recreation. By arranging opportunities for people to interact with one another, cross-cutting relations can allow people to understand the underlying similarities among all the world's peoples. Ultimately, such relationships can lead to feelings of connectedness and the awareness that we all share basic needs and aspirations (Nowak et al., 2010; Adler & Aycan, 2018; Gill, 2022).

- *Use education to overcome attitudes that devalue outgroups.* One method to reduce violence against members of minority groups and other outgroups is to extend the boundaries that delineate the people who are considered "us" to include those who are considered "them." When people become more accepting of other cultures and better understand their own, they learn that their own culture may not be the standard against which to judge all others (Staub et al., 2010; Staub, 2011, 2018; Adelman et al., 2022).

- *Create a robust multicultural society.* Demographic trends show that the White majority in the United States is shrinking. Over the coming decades, the rise in the Hispanic population will be particularly dramatic. Experts estimate that by 2050, nearly 1 in every 3 Americans will be Hispanic. Whether or not the United States is prepared, it is about to become an even more deeply multicultural society with direct links to countries throughout the world. Indeed, as international travel becomes increasingly affordable and social networking tools such as TikTok, Instagram, Facebook, and Twitter become steadily more prominent, people all over the globe will have increasing opportunities to interact (Shrestha & Heisler, 2011; Herskovits, 2018; Matassi & Boczkowski, 2021).

Increased intercultural interaction can bring several benefits. For one thing, it can reduce ingroup–outgroup bias, in which people hold more favorable opinions about members of ingroups and less favorable opinions about outgroups. By reducing this bias, people can become more flexible in their thinking and better understand the subtleties of others' behavior (Brewer, 2007; Giannakakis, & Fritsche, 2011; Jacoby-Senghor et al., 2015; Yau & Ross, 2022).

Perhaps more important, direct interaction with people from varied racial, cultural, ethnic, and religious backgrounds, and of various sexual orientations, gender identities, and physical abilities may allow us to see the basic similarities that underlie all human behavior. Throughout this book, we have discussed the broad principles that psychologists use to explain behavior. The understanding provided by this knowledge can encourage citizens to become keenly interested in the prospects for a more peaceful, equitable, and just world for all the globe's inhabitants.

cross-cutting relations The links between groups in the areas of work, education, and recreation. (Module 47)

RECAP/EVALUATE/RETHINK

RECAP

LO 47-1 What are the basic elements of diversity and culture?

- Culture includes the learned behaviors, beliefs, and attitudes that are characteristic of an individual society or population. Culture both shapes and reflects a society's behavior, understanding of the world, attitudes, and values.
- Societies that encourage individualism hold as a primary value the personal identity, uniqueness, freedom, and worth of the individual. In contrast, cultures that support collectivism promote the idea that the well-being of the group or society is more important than that of the individual.
- Culture has an impact on people's view of themselves, meaning the way in which they look inward and define themselves as individuals. People in Eastern societies tend to have an interdependent view, perceiving themselves as members of a larger society and working together with others to achieve social harmony. In comparison, people in Western societies generally see themselves as independent. The emphasis in such societies is on competing rather than cooperating with others.
- Societies and cultures vary significantly in the degree of aggression their members display. However, at least one universal principle crosses cultures: Males are more aggressive than females.

- Despite political rhetoric to the contrary, research shows that most immigrants to the United States are productive and ultimately successful.

EVALUATE

1. _____ comprises the learned behaviors, beliefs, and attitudes that are characteristic of a society.
2. In _____ cultures, personal goals are viewed as more important than goals relating to society in general.
3. Studies have shown that males are universally more aggressive than females. True or false?
4. Immigrants, as a group, typically become financially successful in the United States, despite initially having higher rates of poverty. True or false?

RETHINK

1. What culture(s) do you consider yourself a member of? How does being part of a culture affect your everyday behavior?
2. Do you consider yourself an aggressive person? Are you more or less aggressive than other members of your family? Do you think you learned to be more or less aggressive from your family or the broader culture, or do you believe you were born more or less aggressive?

Answers to Evaluate Questions

1. Culture; 2. individualistic; 3. True; 4. True

KEY TERMS

race	multiculturalism	self	independent
ethnicity	collectivism	interdependent	(view of self)
culture	individualism	(view of self)	cross-cutting relations

LOOKING *Back*

EPILOGUE

We have touched on some of the major ideas, research topics, and experimental findings of social psychology. We examined how people form, maintain, and change attitudes and how they form impressions of others and assign attributions to them. We also saw how groups, through conformity and tactics of compliance, can influence individuals' actions and attitudes. We also discussed interpersonal relationships, including both liking and loving, and looked at aggression and prosocial behavior, the two sides of a coin that represent the extremes of social behavior. Finally, we examined diversity and culture and the ways they affect behavior.

Turn back to the prologue to this set of modules, which describes how Teresa Gray left her home in the United States and volunteered to directly aid Ukrainian refugees. Use your understanding of social psychology to consider the following questions.

1. What do you think motivated Teresa Gray and her team to help strangers at great personal risk?
2. What kinds of social challenges might refugees encounter when they are forced to leave their homes and live as foreigners in a foreign land?
3. What strategies might be employed to assist refugees in adjusting to their new home?
4. In what ways might local natives be misperceiving the refugees living among them? How might their perceptions of those refugees be biased? How might they be changed to be more positive?

Design Elements: Man with laptop: Dragon Images/Shutterstock; Exclamation point and mobile frame: McGraw Hill; Smartphone: WML Image/Shutterstock; Hands: Stefano Garau/Shutterstock.

VISUAL SUMMARY 14 Social Psychology

MODULE 43 Attitudes and Social Cognition

Persuasion and Attitudes

Attitudes: Evaluations of a particular person, behavior, belief, or concept

— Routes to persuasion

— Attitude-behavior link

Social Cognition: How people understand what others and themselves are like

— Forming impressions of others: Central traits help us form impressions of others

— Attribution theory: How we decide the specific causes of a person's behavior

- Situational causes: of behavior that are external to a person

- Dispositional causes: of behavior brought about by a person's traits or internal personality characteristics

- Attribution biases

MODULE 44 Social Influence and Groups

Conformity: A desire to follow the beliefs or standards of other people

— Groupthink: Group members want to achieve consensus and lose the ability to evaluate alternative points of view.

— Social roles: Behaviors associated with people in a given position

Compliance: Social pressure to behave in a certain way

— Foot-in-the-door technique

— Door-in-the-face technique

— That's-not-all technique

— Not-so-free sample

Obedience: Behavior change in response to the commands of others

MODULE 45 Prejudice and Discrimination

Prejudice: A negative or positive evaluation of a group

Discrimination: Behavior directed toward individuals on the basis of their membership in a particular group

Stereotype: Generalized beliefs and expectations about a specific group that arise when we categorize information

Reducing Prejudice and Discrimination

— Increase contact between the target of stereotyping and the holder of the stereotype

— Make values and norms against prejudice more conspicuous

— Provide information about the targets of stereotyping

— Reduce stereotype threat

— Increase a sense of belonging

MODULE 46 Positive and Negative Social Behavior

Liking and Loving

— Determinants of liking
- Proximity
- Mere exposure
- Similarity
- Physical attractiveness

— What is love?
- Qualitatively different from liking
- Three components of love

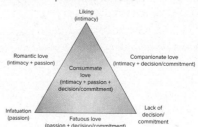

Aggression: Intentional injury of or harm to another person

— Instinct approaches

— Frustration-aggression approach

— Observational learning approaches

Helping (Prosocial) Behavior: Actions intended to provide aid to others

MODULE 47 Diversity, Equity, Inclusion, and Culture

Language of Diversity

— Culture
— Collectivism and individualism
— Our view of ourselves
— A culture of violence?
— Immigrants

(Module 44) (photo top): NASA/Getty Images; (photo bottom): From the film OBEDIENCE © 1968 by Stanley Milgram, © renewed 1993 by Alexandra Milgram. Permission granted by Alexandra Milgram; (Module 45) (photo): Mark Peterson/Corbis/Getty Images; (Module 46): Source: Adapted from Sternberg, 1986.; (Module 47): Rawpixel.com/Shutterstock

Glossary

abnormal behavior Behavior that causes people to experience distress and prevents them from functioning in their daily lives. (Module 37)

absolute threshold The smallest intensity of a stimulus that must be present for the stimulus to be detected. (Module 8)

action potential An electric nerve impulse that travels through a neuron's axon when it is set off by a "trigger," changing the neuron's charge from negative to positive. (Module 5)

activation-synthesis theory Hobson's theory that the brain produces random electrical energy during REM sleep that stimulates memories stored in the brain. (Module 12)

activity theory of aging The theory that suggests that successful aging is characterized by maintaining the interests and activities of earlier stages of life. (Module 30)

adaptation An adjustment in sensory capacity after prolonged exposure to unchanging stimuli. (Module 8)

addictive drugs Drugs that produce a biological or psychological dependence in the user so that withdrawal from them leads to a craving for the drug that, in some cases, may be nearly irresistible. (Module 14)

adolescence The developmental stage between childhood and adulthood. (Module 29)

age of viability The point at which a fetus can survive if born prematurely. (Module 27)

aggression The intentional injury of, or harm to, another person. (Module 46)

algorithm A rule that, if applied appropriately, guarantees a solution to a problem. (Module 21)

all-or-none law The rule that neurons are either on or off. (Module 5)

altruism Behavior meant to help another person without regard for self-interest. (Module 46)

Alzheimer's disease A progressive brain disorder that leads to a gradual and irreversible decline in cognitive abilities. (Modules 20, 30)

amnesia Memory loss that occurs without other mental difficulties. (Module 20)

anal stage According to Freud, a stage from age 12 to 18 months to 3 years of age, in which a child's pleasure is centered on the anus. (Module 31)

androgens Male sex hormones secreted by the testes. (Module 25)

anorexia nervosa A severe eating disorder in which people may refuse to eat while denying that their behavior and appearance—which can become skeleton-like—are unusual. (Module 25)

anterograde amnesia Amnesia in which memory is lost for events that follow an injury. (Module 20)

antianxiety drugs Drugs that reduce the level of anxiety a person experiences essentially by reducing excitability and increasing feelings of well-being. (Module 42)

antidepressant drugs Medications that improve a severely depressed patient's mood and feeling of well-being. (Module 42)

antipsychotic drugs Drugs that temporarily reduce psychotic symptoms such as agitation, hallucinations, and delusions. (Module 42)

antisocial personality disorder A disorder in which individuals show no regard for the moral and ethical rules of society or the rights of others. (Module 38)

anxiety disorder The occurrence of anxiety without an obvious external cause that affects daily functioning. (Module 38)

archetypes According to Jung, universal symbolic representations of particular types of people, objects, ideas, or experiences. (Module 31)

archival research Research in which existing data, such as census documents, college records, and newspaper articles, are examined to test a hypothesis. (Module 3)

arousal approaches to motivation The belief that we try to maintain certain levels of stimulation and activity. (Module 24)

association areas One of the major regions of the cerebral cortex; the site of the higher mental processes, such as thought, language, memory, and speech. (Module 7)

assumed-similarity bias The tendency to think of people as being similar to oneself even when meeting them for the first time. (Module 43)

attachment The positive emotional bond that develops between a child and a particular individual. (Module 28)

attention-deficit hyperactivity disorder (ADHD) A disorder marked by inattention, impulsiveness, a low tolerance for frustration, and a great deal of inappropriate activity. (Module 38)

attitudes Evaluations of people, objects, ideas, and behavior. (Module 43)

attribution theory The theory that considers how we decide, on the basis of samples of a person's behavior, what the specific causes of that behavior are. (Module 43)

authoritarian parents Parents who are rigid and punitive and value unquestioning obedience from their children. (Module 28)

authoritative parents Parents who are firm, set clear limits, reason with their children, and explain things to them. (Module 28)

autism spectrum disorder A severe developmental disability that impairs children's ability to communicate and relate to others. (Module 38)

autobiographical memory Our recollections of our own life experiences. (Module 19)

autonomic division The part of the peripheral nervous system that controls involuntary movement of the heart, glands, lungs, and other organs. (Module 6)

autonomy-versus-shame-and-doubt stage The period during which, according to Erikson, toddlers (ages 1½ to 3 years) develop independence and autonomy if exploration and freedom are encouraged or shame and self-doubt if they are restricted and overprotected. (Module 28)

aversive conditioning A form of therapy that reduces the frequency of undesired behavior by pairing an aversive, unpleasant stimulus with undesired behavior. (Module 40)

axon The part of the neuron that carries messages destined for other neurons. (Module 5)

babble Meaningless speechlike sounds made by children from around the age of 3 months through 1 year. (Module 22)

background stressors ("daily hassles") Everyday annoyances, such as being stuck in traffic, that cause minor irritations and may have long-term ill effects if they continue or are compounded by other stressful events. (Module 34)

basilar membrane A vibrating structure that runs through the center of the cochlea, dividing it into an upper chamber and a lower chamber and containing sense receptors for sound. (Module 10)

behavior modification A technique whose goal is to increase the frequency of desirable behaviors and decrease the incidence of unwanted ones. (Module 16)

behavioral assessment Direct measures of an individual's behavior used to describe personality characteristics. (Module 33)

behavioral genetics The study of the effects of heredity on behavior. (Module 6)

behavioral neuroscientists (or biopsychologists) Psychologists who specialize in considering the ways in which the biological structures and functions of the body affect behavior. (Module 5)

behavioral perspective The approach that suggests that observable, external behavior, which can be objectively measured, should be the focus of study. (Module 2, 37)

behavioral treatment approaches Treatment approaches that make use of the basic processes of learning, such as reinforcement and extinction, to reduce or eliminate maladaptive behavior. (Module 40)

biofeedback A procedure in which a person learns to control through conscious thought internal physiological processes such as blood pressure, heart and respiration rate, skin temperature, sweating, and the constriction of particular muscles. (Module 7)

biological and evolutionary approaches to personality Theories that suggest that important components of personality are inherited. (Module 32)

biomedical therapy Therapy that relies on drugs and other medical procedures to improve psychological functioning. (Module 40)

bipolar disorder A disorder in which a person alternates between periods of euphoric feelings of mania and periods of depression. (Module 38)

bisexuals Sexual attraction to more than one sex or gender. (Module 25)

borderline personality disorder A disorder characterized by problems regulating emotions and thoughts, displaying impulsive and reckless behavior, and having unstable relationships with others. (Module 38)

bottom-up processing Perception that consists of the progression of recognizing and processing information from individual components of a stimuli and moving to the perception of the whole. (Module 11)

bulimia A disorder in which a person binges on large quantities of food, followed by efforts to purge the food through vomiting or other means. (Module 25)

Cannon-Bard theory of emotion The belief that both physiological arousal and emotional experience are produced simultaneously by the same nerve stimulus. (Module 26)

case study An in-depth, intensive investigation of an individual or small group of people. (Module 3)

cataclysmic events Strong stressors that occur suddenly and typically affect many people at once (e.g., natural disasters). (Module 34)

catharsis The process of discharging built-up aggressive energy. (Module 46)

central core The "old brain," which controls basic functions such as eating and sleeping and is common to all vertebrates. (Module 7)

central nervous system (CNS) The part of the nervous system that includes the brain and spinal cord. (Module 6)

central route processing The type of mental processing that occurs when a persuasive message is evaluated by thoughtful consideration of the issues and arguments used to persuade. (Module 43)

central traits The major traits considered in forming impressions of others. (Module 43)

cerebellum (ser-uh-BELL-um) The part of the brain that controls bodily balance. (Module 7)

cerebral cortex The "new brain," responsible for the most sophisticated information processing in the brain; contains four lobes. (Module 7)

chromosomes Rod-shaped structures that contain all basic hereditary information. (Module 27)

chunk A group of familiar stimuli stored as a single unit in short-term memory. (Module 18)

circadian rhythms Biological processes that occur regularly on approximately a 24-hour cycle. (Module 12)

classical conditioning A type of learning in which a neutral stimulus comes to bring about a response after it is paired with a stimulus that naturally brings about that response. (Module 15)

cochlea (KOKE-lee-uh) A coiled tube in the ear filled with fluid that vibrates in response to sound. (Module 10)

cognitive approaches to motivation Theories suggesting that motivation is a result of people's thoughts, beliefs, expectations, and goals. (Module 24)

cognitive-behavioral approach A treatment approach that incorporates basic principles of learning to change the way people think. (Module 40)

cognitive development The process by which a child's understanding of the world changes due to the child's age and experience. (Module 28)

cognitive dissonance The mental conflict that occurs when a person holds two contradictory attitudes or thoughts (referred to as cognitions). (Module 43)

cognitive learning theory An approach to the study of learning that focuses on the thought processes that underlie learning. (Module 17)

fetus A developing individual from 8 weeks after conception until birth. (Module 27)

fixations Conflicts or concerns that persist beyond the developmental period in which they first occur. (Module 31)

fixed-interval schedule A schedule in which reinforcement is provided for a response only after a fixed time period has elapsed. (Module 16)

fixed mindset The belief that abilities are fixed and unchangeable. (Module 25)

fixed-ratio schedule A schedule in which reinforcement is given only after a specific number of responses are made. (Module 16)

flashbulb memories Memories of a specific, important, or surprising emotionally significant event that are recalled easily and with vivid imagery. (Module 19)

flooding A behavioral treatment for anxiety in which people are suddenly confronted with a stimulus that they fear. (Module 40)

fluid intelligence Intelligence that reflects the ability to think logically, reason abstractly, and solve problems. (Module 23)

formal operational stage According to Piaget, the period from age 12 to adulthood that is characterized by abstract thought. (Module 28)

free will The idea that behavior is caused primarily by choices that are made freely by the individual. (Module 2)

frequency theory of hearing The theory that the entire basilar membrane acts like a microphone, vibrating as a whole in response to a sound. (Module 10)

functional neurologic disorder (conversion disorder) A major somatic symptom disorder that involves an actual physical disturbance, such as the inability to use a sensory organ or the complete or partial inability to move an arm or leg. (Module 38)

functional fixedness The tendency to think of an object only in terms of its typical use. (Module 21)

functionalism An early approach to psychology that concentrated on what the mind does–the functions of mental activity–and the role of behavior in allowing people to adapt to their environments. (Module 2)

fundamental attribution error A tendency to overattribute others' behavior to dispositional causes and minimize the importance of situational causes. (Module 43)

g or g-factor The single, general factor for mental ability assumed to underlie intelligence in some early theories of intelligence. (Module 23)

gate-control theory of pain The theory that particular nerve receptors in the spinal cord lead to specific areas of the brain related to pain. (Module 10)

general adaptation syndrome (GAS) A theory developed by Selye that suggests that a person's response to a stressor consists of three stages: alarm and mobilization, resistance, and exhaustion. (Module 34)

generalized anxiety disorder The experience of long-term, persistent anxiety and worry. (Module 38)

generativity-versus-stagnation stage According to Erikson, a period in middle adulthood during which we take stock of our contributions to family and society. (Module 29)

genes The parts of the chromosomes through which genetic information is transmitted. (Module 27)

genetic preprogramming theories of aging Theories that suggest that human cells have a built-in time limit to their reproduction and that they are no longer able to divide after a certain time. (Module 30)

genital stage According to Freud, the period from puberty until death, marked by mature sexual behavior (that is, sexual intercourse). (Module 31)

genitals The male and female sex organs. (Module 25)

Gestalt (geh-SHTALLT) laws of organization A series of principles that describe how we organize bits and pieces of information into meaningful wholes. (Modules 2, 11)

grammar The system of rules that determine how our thoughts can be expressed. (Module 22)

group Two or more people who interact with one another, perceive themselves as part of a group, and are interdependent. (Module 44)

group therapy Therapy in which people meet in a group with a therapist to discuss problems. (Module 41)

groupthink A type of thinking in which group members share such a strong motivation to achieve consensus that they lose the ability to critically evaluate alternative points of view. (Module 44)

growth mindset A belief that people can increase their abilities and do better through hard work. (Module 25)

habituation The decrease in the response to a stimulus that occurs after repeated presentations of the same stimulus. (Module 28)

hair cells Tiny cells covering the basilar membrane that, when bent by vibrations entering the cochlea, transmit neural messages to the brain. (Module 10)

hallucinogens Drugs that are capable of producing alterations in perception, thoughts, and feelings. (Module 14)

halo effect A phenomenon in which an initial understanding that a person has positive or negative traits is used to infer other uniformly positive or negative characteristics. (Module 43)

hardiness A personality trait characterized by a sense of commitment, the perception of problems as challenges, and a sense of control. (Module 34)

health psychology The branch of psychology that investigates the psychological factors related to wellness and illness, including the prevention, diagnosis, and treatment of medical problems. (Module 34)

hemispheres Symmetrical left and right halves of the brain that control the side of the body opposite to their location. (Module 7)

heritability The degree to which a characteristic is related to genetic, inherited factors. (Module 23)

heterosexuality Sexual attraction and behavior directed to the other sex. (Module 25)

heuristic A thinking strategy that may lead us to a solution to a problem or decision but–unlike algorithms–may sometimes lead to errors. (Module 21)

homeostasis The body's tendency to maintain a steady internal state. (Module 24)

homosexuality Sexual attraction to members of one's own sex or gender. (Module 25)

hormones Chemicals that circulate through the blood and regulate the functioning or growth of the body. (Module 6)

humanistic approaches to personality Theories that emphasize people's innate goodness and desire to achieve higher levels of functioning. (Module 32)

humanistic perspective The approach that suggests that all individuals naturally strive to grow, develop, and be in control of their lives and behavior. (Modules 2, 37)

humanistic therapy Therapy in which the underlying rationale is that people have control of their behavior, can make choices about their lives, and are essentially responsible for solving their own problems. (Module 41)

hypnosis A trancelike state of heightened susceptibility to the suggestions of others. (Module 13)

hypothalamus A tiny part of the brain, located below the thalamus, that maintains homeostasis and produces and regulates vital behavior, such as eating, drinking, and sexual behavior. (Module 7)

hypothesis A prediction, stemming from a theory, stated in a way that allows it to be tested. (Module 3)

id The instinctual and unorganized part of personality whose sole purpose is to reduce tension created by primitive drives related to hunger, sex, aggression, and irrational impulses. (Module 31)

identical twins Twins who are genetically identical. (Module 27)

identification The process of wanting to be like another person as much as possible, imitating that person's behavior and adopting similar beliefs and values. (Module 31)

identity The distinguishing character of the individual: who each of us is, what our roles are, and what we are capable of. (Module 29)

identity-versus-role-confusion stage According to Erikson, a time in adolescence of major testing to determine one's unique qualities. (Module 29)

illness anxiety disorder A disorder in which people have a constant fear of illness and a preoccupation with their health. (Module 38)

implicit memory Memories of which people are not consciously aware but that can affect subsequent performance and behavior. (Module 19)

incentive approaches to motivation Theories suggesting that motivation stems from the desire to attain external rewards, known as incentives. (Module 24)

independent variable The variable that is manipulated by an experimenter. (Module 3)

independent (view of self) To view oneself as behaving independently, competing rather than cooperating with others (Module 47).

individualism The concept that holds as a primary value the personal identity, uniqueness, freedom, and worth of the individual person (Module 47).

industrial-organizational (I/O) psychology The branch of psychology focusing on work- and job-related issues, including worker motivation, satisfaction, safety, and productivity. (Module 44)

industry-versus-inferiority stage According to Erikson, the last stage of childhood, during which children age 6 to 12 years may develop positive social interactions with others or may feel inadequate and become less sociable. (Module 28)

information processing The way in which people take in, use, and store information. (Module 28)

informed consent A document signed by participants affirming that they have been told the basic outlines of the study and are aware of what their participation will involve. (Module 4)

inhibitory message A chemical message that prevents or decreases the likelihood that a receiving neuron will fire. (Module 5)

initiative-versus-guilt stage According to Erikson, the period during which children ages 3 to 6 years experience conflict between independence of action and the sometimes negative results of that action. (Module 28)

insight A sudden awareness of the relationships among various elements that had previously appeared to be independent of one another. (Module 21)

instinct approaches to motivation Theories suggesting that motivation stems from the desire to attain external rewards, known as incentives. (Module 24)

instincts Inborn patterns of behavior that are biologically determined rather than learned. (Module 24)

intellectual disability A condition characterized by significant limitations both in intellectual functioning and in conceptual, social, and practical adaptive skills. (Module 23)

intellectually gifted The 2-4% segment of the population who have IQ scores greater than 130. (Module 23)

intelligence The capacity to understand the world, think rationally, and use resources effectively when faced with challenges. (Module 23)

intelligence quotient (IQ) A score that takes into account an individual's mental and chronological ages. (Module 23)

intelligence tests Tests devised to quantify a person's level of intelligence. (Module 23)

interactionist approach (to language development) The view that language development is produced through a combination of genetically determined predispositions and environmental circumstances that help teach language. (Module 22)

interdependent (view of self) To view oneself as a member of a larger society, working together with others to achieve social harmony (Module 47).

interference The phenomenon by which information in memory disrupts the recall of other information. (Module 20)

interpersonal attraction (or close relationship) Positive feelings for others; liking and loving. (Module 46)

interpersonal therapy (IPT) Short-term therapy that focuses on the context of current social relationships, helping patients to control their moods and emotions. (Module 41)

intimacy-versus-isolation stage According to Erikson, a period during early adulthood that focuses on developing close relationships. (Module 29)

introspection A procedure in which people are presented with a stimulus—such as an image or sentence—and asked to describe, in their own words and in as much detail as they can, what they were experiencing. (Module 2)

James-Lange theory of emotion The belief that emotional experience is a reaction to bodily events occurring as a result of an external situation ("I feel sad because I am crying"). (Module 26)

language The communication of information through symbols arranged according to systematic rules. (Module 22)

latency period According to Freud, the period between the phallic stage and puberty during which children's sexual concerns are temporarily put aside. (Module 31)

latent learning Learning in which a new behavior is acquired but is not demonstrated until some incentive is provided for displaying it. (Module 17)

lateralization The dominance of one hemisphere of the brain in specific functions, such as language. (Module 7)

learned helplessness A state in which people conclude that unpleasant or aversive stimuli cannot be controlled–a view of the world that becomes so ingrained that they cease trying to remedy the aversive circumstances even if they actually can exert some influence on the situation. (Module 34)

learning A relatively permanent change in behavior brought about by experience. (Module 15)

learning-theory approach (to language development) The theory that language acquisition follows the principles of reinforcement and conditioning. (Module 22)

levels-of-processing theory The theory of memory that emphasizes the degree to which new material is mentally analyzed. (Module 19)

life review The process by which people examine and evaluate their lives. (Module 30)

limbic system The part of the brain that controls eating, aggression, and reproduction. (Module 7)

linguistic-relativity hypothesis The hypothesis that language shapes and may determine the way people perceive and understand the world. (Module 22)

lobes The four major sections of the cerebral cortex: frontal, parietal, temporal, and occipital. (Module 7)

loneliness The lack of experiencing the level of connection with others that a person seeks. (Module 44)

longitudinal research A research method that investigates behavior as participants get older. (Module 27)

long-term memory Memory that stores information on a relatively permanent basis, although it may be difficult to retrieve. (Module 18)

major depressive disorder A severe form of depression that interferes with concentration, decision making, and sociability. (Module 38)

mania An extended state of intense, wild elation. (Module 38)

masturbation Sexual self-stimulation. (Module 25)

means-ends analysis Involves repeated tests for differences between the desired outcome and what currently exists. (Module 21)

medical perspective The perspective that suggests that when an individual displays symptoms of abnormal behavior, the root cause will be found in a physical examination of the individual, which may reveal a hormonal imbalance, a chemical deficiency, or a brain injury. (Module 37)

meditation A learned technique for refocusing attention that brings about an altered state of consciousness. (Module 13)

memory The process by which we encode, store, and retrieve information. (Module 18)

menopause The period during which women stop menstruating and are no longer fertile. (Module 30)

mental age The age for which a given level of performance is average or typical. (Module 23)

mental images Representations in the mind of an object or event. (Module 21)

mental set A framework for thinking about a problem based on our prior experience with similar problems. (Module 21)

metabolism The rate at which food is converted to energy and expended by the body. (Module 25)

metacognition An awareness and understanding of one's own cognitive processes. (Module 28)

Minnesota Multiphasic Personality Inventory-2-Restructured Form (MMPI-2-RF) A widely used self-report test that identifies people with psychological difficulties and is employed to predict some everyday behaviors. (Module 33)

mirror neurons Specialized neurons that fire not only when a person enacts a particular behavior, but also when a person simply observes *another* individual carrying out the same behavior. (Module 5)

mood disorder A disturbance in emotional experience that is strong enough to intrude on everyday living. (Module 38)

mood stabilizers Drugs used to treat mood disorders characterized by intense mood swings, especially manic episodes in bipolar disorder. (Module 42)

motivation The factors that direct and energize the behavior of humans and other organisms. (Module 24)

motor area The part of the cortex that is largely responsible for the body's voluntary movement. (Module 7)

motor (efferent) neurons Neurons that communicate information from the brain and nervous system to muscles and glands. (Module 6)

multiculturalism The view that members of all cultures deserve equal respect and that their contributions to society should be recognized. (Module 47)

myelin sheath A protective coat of fat and protein that wraps around the axon. (Module 5)

narcissistic personality disorder A personality disturbance characterized by an exaggerated sense of self-importance. (Module 38)

narcotics Drugs that increase relaxation and relieve pain and anxiety. (Module 14)

nativist approach (to language development) The theory that humans are biologically prewired to learn language at certain times and in particular ways. (Module 22)

naturalistic observation Research in which an investigator simply observes some naturally occurring behavior and does not make a change in the situation. (Module 3)

nature-nurture issue The issue of the degree to which environment and heredity influence behavior. (Module 27)

need for achievement A stable, learned characteristic in which a person obtains satisfaction by striving for and achieving challenging goals. (Module 25)

need for affiliation An interest in establishing and maintaining relationships with other people. (Module 25)

need for power A tendency to seek impact, control, or influence over others and to be seen as a powerful individual. (Module 25)

negative reinforcer An unpleasant stimulus whose removal leads to an increase in the probability that a preceding response will be repeated in the future. (Module 16)

neo-Freudian psychoanalysts Psychoanalysts who were trained in traditional Freudian theory but who later rejected some of its major points. (Module 31)

neonate A newborn child. (Module 28)

neurons Nerve cells, the basic elements of the nervous system. (Module 5)

neuroplasticity Changes in the brain that occur throughout the life span relating to the addition of new neurons, new interconnections between neurons, and the reorganization of information- processing areas. (Module 7)

neuroscience perspective The approach that views behavior from the perspective of the brain, the nervous system, and other biological functions. (Module 2)

neurotransmitters Chemicals that carry messages across the synapse to the dendrite (and sometimes the cell body) of a receiver neuron. (Module 5)

neutral stimulus A stimulus that, before conditioning, does not naturally bring about the response of interest. (Module 15)

norms Standards of test performance that permit the comparison of one person's score on a test with the scores of other individuals who have taken the same test. (Module 23)

obedience A change in behavior in response to the commands of others. (Module 44)

obesity Body weight that is more than 20% above the average weight for a person of a particular height. (Module 25)

object permanence The awareness that objects–and people–continue to exist even if they are out of sight. (Module 28)

observational learning Learning by observing the behavior of another person, or model. (Module 17)

obsession A persistent, unwanted thought or idea that keeps recurring. (Module 38)

obsessive-compulsive disorder (OCD) A disorder characterized by obsessions or compulsions. (Module 38)

Oedipal conflict A child's intense, sexual interest in his or her opposite-sex parent. (Module 31)

operant conditioning Learning in which a voluntary response is strengthened or weakened, depending on its favorable or unfavorable consequences. (Module 16).

operational definition The translation of a hypothesis into specific, testable procedures that can be measured and observed. (Module 3)

opponent-process theory of color vision The theory that receptor cells for color are linked in pairs, working in opposition to each other. (Module 9)

optic nerve A bundle of ganglion axons that carry visual information to the brain. (Module 9)

oral stage According to Freud, a stage from birth to age 12 to 18 months, in which an infant's center of pleasure is the mouth. (Module 31)

overgeneralization The phenomenon by which children overapply a language rule, thereby making linguistic errors. (Module 22)

ovulation The point at which an egg is released from the ovaries. (Module 25)

panic disorder Anxiety disorder that takes the form of panic attacks lasting from a few seconds to several hours. (Module 38)

parasympathetic division The part of the autonomic division of the nervous system that acts to calm the body after an emergency has ended. (Module 6)

partial (or intermittent) reinforcement schedule Reinforcing of a behavior some but not all of the time. (Module 16)

passionate (or romantic) love A state of intense absorption in someone that includes intense physiological arousal, psychological interest, and caring for the needs of another. (Module 46)

perception The sorting out, interpretation, analysis, and integration of stimuli by the sense organs and brain. (Module 8)

perceptual constancy Our understanding that physical objects are unvarying and consistent even though sensory input about them may vary. (Module 11)

peripheral nervous system The part of the nervous system that includes the autonomic and somatic subdivisions; made up of neurons with long axons and dendrites, it branches out from the spinal cord and brain and reaches the extremities of the body. (Module 6)

peripheral route processing The type of mental processing that occurs when a persuasive message is evaluated on the basis of irrelevant or extraneous factors. (Module 43)

permissive parents Parents who give their children relaxed or inconsistent direction and, although they are warm, require little of them. (Module 28)

person-centered therapy Therapy in which the goal is to reach one's potential for self-actualization. (Module 41)

personal stressors Major life events, such as the death of a family member, that have immediate negative consequences that generally fade with time. (Module 34)

personality The pattern of enduring characteristics that produce consistency and individuality in a given person. (Module 31)

personality disorder A disorder characterized by a set of inflexible, maladaptive behavior patterns that keep a person from functioning appropriately in society. (Module 38)

phallic stage According to Freud, a period beginning around age 3 during which a child's pleasure focuses on the genitals. (Module 31)

phonemes The smallest units of speech. (Module 22)

phonology The study of the smallest units of speech, called phonemes. (Module 22)

pituitary gland The major component of the endocrine system, or "master gland," which secretes hormones that control growth and other parts of the endocrine system. (Module 6)

placebo A false treatment, such as a pill, "drug," or other substance, without any significant chemical properties or active ingredient. (Module 4)

place theory of hearing The theory that different areas of the basilar membrane respond to different frequencies. (Module 10)

positive reinforcer A stimulus added to the environment that brings about an increase in a preceding response. (Module 16)

posttraumatic stress disorder (PTSD) A phenomenon in which victims of major catastrophes or strong personal stressors feel long-lasting effects that may include re-experiencing the event in vivid flashbacks or dreams. (Module 34)

practical intelligence According to Sternberg, intelligence related to overall success in living. (Module 23)

prejudice A negative (or positive) evaluation of a particular group and its members. (Module 45)

preoperational stage According to Piaget, the period from 2 to 7 years of age that is characterized by language development. (Module 28)

priming A phenomenon that occurs when exposure to a word or concept (called a prime) later makes it easier to recall information related to the prime. (Module 19)

principle of conservation The knowledge that quantity is unrelated to the arrangement and physical appearance of objects. (Module 28)

proactive interference Interference in which information learned earlier disrupts the recall of material learned later. (Module 20)

procedural memory Memory for skills and habits, such as riding a bike or hitting a baseball; sometimes referred to as *nondeclarative memory*. (Module 18)

projective personality test A test in which a person is shown an ambiguous stimulus and asked to describe it or tell a story about it. (Module 33)

prosocial behavior Helping behavior. (Module 46)

prototypes Typical, highly representative examples of a concept. (Module 21)

psychoactive drugs Drugs that influence a person's emotions, perceptions, and behavior. (Module 14)

psychoanalysis Freud's psychotherapy in which the goal is to release hidden thoughts and feelings from the unconscious part of our minds in order to reduce their power in controlling behavior. (Module 40)

psychoanalytic perspective The perspective that suggests that abnormal behavior stems from childhood conflicts over opposing wishes regarding sex and aggression. (Module 37)

psychoanalytic theory Freud's theory that unconscious forces act as determinants of personality. (Module 31)

psychodynamic approaches to personality Approaches that assume that personality is primarily unconscious and motivated by inner forces and conflicts about which people have little awareness. (Module 31)

psychodynamic perspective The approach based on the view that behavior is motivated by unconscious inner forces over which the individual has little control. (Module 2)

psychodynamic therapy Therapy that seeks to bring unresolved past conflicts and unacceptable impulses from the unconscious into the conscious, where patients may deal with the problems more effectively. (Module 40)

psychological tests Standard measures devised to assess behavior objectively; used by psychologists to help people make decisions about their lives and understand more about themselves. (Module 33)

psychology The scientific study of behavior and mental processes. (Module 1)

psychoneuroimmunology (PNI) The study of the relationship among psychological factors, the immune system, and the brain. (Module 34)

psychophysics The study of the relationship between the physical aspects of stimuli and our psychological experience of them. (Module 8)

psychophysiological disorders Medical problems influenced by an interaction of psychological, emotional, and physical difficulties. (Module 34)

psychosexual stages Developmental periods that children pass through during which they encounter conflicts between the demands of society and their own sexual urges. (Module 31)

psychosocial development Development of individuals' interactions and understanding of each other and of their knowledge and understanding of themselves as members of society. (Module 28)

psychosurgery Brain surgery once used to reduce the symptoms of mental disorder but rarely used today. (Module 42)

psychotherapy Treatment in which a trained professional–a therapist–uses psychological techniques to help a person overcome psychological difficulties and disorders, resolve problems in living, or bring about personal growth. (Module 40)

puberty The period at which maturation of the sexual organs occurs, beginning at about age 11 or 12 for girls and 13 or 14 for boys. (Module 29)

punishment A stimulus that decreases the probability that a previous behavior will occur again. (Module 16)

race Generally refers to obvious physical differences that set one group apart from others (Module 47).

random assignment to condition A procedure in which participants are assigned to different experimental groups or "conditions" on the basis of chance and chance alone. (Module 3)

rapid eye movement (REM) sleep Sleep occupying 20% of an adult's sleeping time, characterized by increased heart rate, blood pressure, and breathing rate; erections; eye movements; and the experience of dreaming. (Module 12)

rational-emotive behavior therapy A form of therapy that attempts to restructure a person's belief system into a more realistic, rational, and logical set of views by challenging dysfunctional beliefs that maintain irrational behavior. (Module 40)

recall Memory task in which specific information must be retrieved. (Module 19)

reciprocity-of-liking effect A tendency to like those who like us. (Module 46)

recognition Memory task in which individuals are presented with a stimulus and asked whether they have been exposed to it in the past or to identify it from a list of alternatives. (Module 19)

reflex An automatic, involuntary response to an incoming stimulus. (Module 6)

reflexes Unlearned, involuntary responses that occur automatically in the presence of certain stimuli. (Module 28)

rehearsal The repetition of information that has entered short-term memory. (Module 18)

reinforcement The process by which a stimulus increases the probability that a preceding behavior will be repeated. (Module 16)

reinforcer Any stimulus that increases the probability that a preceding behavior will occur again. (Module 16)

reliability The property by which tests measure consistently what they are trying to measure. (Module 23)

replicated research Research that is repeated, sometimes using other procedures, settings, and groups of participants, to increase confidence in prior findings. (Module 3)

repression The defense mechanism in which the ego pushes unacceptable or unpleasant thoughts and impulses out of consciousness but maintains them in the unconscious. (Module 31)

resilience The ability to withstand, overcome, and actually thrive after profound adversity. (Module 34)

resting state The state in which there is a negative electrical charge of about −70 millivolts within a neuron. (Module 5)

reticular formation The part of the brain extending from the medulla through the pons; it is related to changes in the level of arousal of the body. (Module 7)

retina The part of the eye that converts the electromagnetic energy of light to electrical impulses for transmission to the brain. (Module 9)

retroactive interference Interference in which material that was learned later disrupts the retrieval of information that was learned earlier. (Module 20)

retrograde amnesia Amnesia in which memory is lost for occurrences prior to a certain event, but not for new events. (Module 20)

reuptake The reabsorption of neurotransmitters by a terminal button. (Module 5)

rods Thin, cylindrical receptor cells in the retina that are highly sensitive to light. (Module 9)

Rorschach test A test that involves showing a series of symmetrical visual stimuli to people who then are asked what the figures represent to them. (Module 33)

Schachter-Singer theory of emotion The belief that emotions are determined jointly by a nonspecific kind of physiological arousal and its interpretation, based on environmental cues. (Module 26)

schedules of reinforcement Different patterns of frequency and timing of reinforcement following desired behavior. (Module 16)

schemas Organized bodies of information stored in memory that bias the way new information is interpreted, stored, and recalled. (Modules 19, 43)

schizophrenia spectrum disorder A class of disorders in which severe distortion of reality occurs. (Module 47)

scientific method The approach through which psychologists systematically acquire knowledge and understanding about behavior and other phenomena of interest. (Module 3)

self-actualization A state of self-fulfillment in which people realize their highest potential in their own unique way. (Modules 24, 32)

self A person's essential being distinguishing themselves from others; how we define ourselves as individuals (Module 47).

self-efficacy The belief that we can master a situation and produce positive outcomes. (Module 32)

self-esteem The component of personality that encompasses our positive and negative self-evaluations. (Module 32)

self-report measure A method of gathering data about people by asking them questions about their own behavior and traits. (Module 33)

self-serving bias The tendency to attribute personal success to personal factors (skill, ability, or effort) and to attribute failure to factors outside oneself. (Module 43)

semantic memory Memory for general knowledge and facts about the world, as well as memory for the rules of logic that are used to deduce other facts. (Module 18)

semantic networks Mental representations of clusters of interconnected information. (Module 18)

semantics The meaning of words and sentences. (Module 22)

semicircular canals Three tube-like structures of the inner ear containing fluid that sloshes through them when the head moves, signaling rotational or angular movement to the brain. (Module 10)

sensation The activation of the sense organs by a source of physical energy. (Module 8)

sensorimotor stage According to Piaget, the stage from birth to 2 years, during which a child has little competence in representing the environment by using images, language, or other symbols. (Module 28)

sensory (afferent) neurons Neurons that transmit information from the perimeter of the body to the nervous system and brain. (Module 6)

sensory area The site in the brain of the tissue that corresponds to each of the senses, with the degree of sensitivity related to the amount of tissue. (Module 7)

sensory memory The initial, momentary storage of information, lasting only an instant. (Module 18)

shaping The process of teaching a complex behavior by rewarding closer and closer approximations of the desired behavior. (Module 16)

short-term memory Memory that holds information for 15 to 25 seconds. (Module 18)

significant outcome Meaningful results that make it possible for researchers to feel confident that they have confirmed their hypotheses. (Module 3)

situational causes (of behavior) Causes of behavior that are external to a person. (Module 43)

skin senses The senses of touch, pressure, temperature, and pain. (Module 10)

social cognition The cognitive processes by which people understand and make sense of others and themselves. (Module 43)

social cognitive approaches to personality Theories that emphasize the influence of a person's cognitions–thoughts, feelings, expectations, and values–as well as observation of others' behavior, in determining personality. (Module 32)

social influence The process by which social groups and individuals exert pressure on an individual, either deliberately or unintentionally. (Module 44)

social isolation The experience in which the objective number of social interactions are reduced and the size of a person's social networks is diminished. (Module 44)

social neuroscience The subfield of social psychology that seeks to identify the neurological basis of social behavior. (Module 45)

social psychology The scientific study of how people's thoughts, feelings, and actions are affected by others. (Module 43)

social support A mutual network of caring, interested others. (Module 34)

social supporter A group member whose dissenting views make nonconformity to the group easier. (Module 44)

sociocultural perspective The perspective that assumes that people's behavior—both normal and abnormal—is shaped by the kind of family group, society, and culture in which they live. (Module 37)

somatic division The part of the peripheral nervous system that specializes in the control of voluntary movements and the communication of information to and from the sense organs. (Module 6)

somatic symptom disorders Psychological difficulties that take on a physical (somatic) form, but for which there is no medical cause. (Module 38)

sound The movement of air molecules brought about by a source of vibration. (Module 10)

specific phobia Intense, irrational fears of specific objects or situations. (Module 38)

spinal cord A bundle of neurons that leaves the brain and runs down the length of the back and is the main means for transmitting messages between the brain and the body. (Module 6)

spontaneous recovery The reemergence of an extinguished conditioned response after a period of rest and with no further conditioning. (Module 15)

spontaneous remission Recovery without formal treatment. (Module 41)

stage 1 sleep The state of transition between wakefulness and sleep, characterized by relatively rapid, low-amplitude brain waves. (Module 12)

stage 2 sleep A sleep deeper than that of stage 1, characterized by a slower, more regular wave pattern, along with momentary interruptions of "sleep spindles." (Module 12)

stage 3 sleep The deepest stage of sleep, during which we are least responsive to outside stimulation. (Module 12)

status The social standing of someone in a group. (Module 44)

stereotype A set of generalized beliefs and expectations about a particular group and its members. (Module 45)

stimulants Drugs that have an arousal effect on the central nervous system, causing a rise in heart rate, blood pressure, and muscular tension. (Module 14)

stimulus Energy that produces a response in a sense organ. (Module 8)

stimulus discrimination The process that occurs if two stimuli are sufficiently distinct from one another that one evokes a conditioned response but the other does not; the ability to differentiate between stimuli. (Module 15)

stimulus generalization A process in which, after a stimulus has been conditioned to produce a particular response, stimuli that are similar to the original stimulus produce the same response. (Module 15)

stress A person's response to events that are threatening or challenging. (Module 34)

structuralism Wundt's approach, which focuses on uncovering the fundamental mental components of consciousness, thinking, and other kinds of mental states and activities. (Module 2)

subjective well-being People's sense of their happiness and satisfaction with their lives. (Module 36)

superego The part of personality that harshly judges the morality of our behavior. (Module 31)

survey research Research in which people chosen to represent a larger population are asked a series of questions about their behavior, thoughts, or attitudes. (Module 3)

sympathetic division The part of the autonomic division of the nervous system that acts to prepare the body for action in stressful situations, engaging all the organism's resources to respond to a threat. (Module 6)

synapse The space between two neurons where the axon of a sending neuron communicates with the dendrites of a receiving neuron by using chemical messages. (Module 5)

syntax Ways in which words and phrases can be combined to form sentences. (Module 22)

systematic desensitization A behavioral technique based on classical conditioning in which exposure to an anxiety-producing stimulus is paired with deep relaxation to extinguish the response of anxiety. (Module 40)

telegraphic speech Sentences in which only essential words are used. (Module 22)

temperament A basic, inborn characteristic way of responding and behavioral style. (Modules 28, 32)

teratogens Environmental agents such as drugs, chemicals, viruses, or other factors that produce birth defects. (Module 27)

terminal buttons Small bulges at the end of axons that send messages to other neurons. (Module 5)

test standardization A technique used to validate questions in personality tests by studying the responses of people with known diagnoses. (Module 33)

thalamus The part of the brain located in the middle of the central core that acts primarily to relay information about the senses. (Module 7)

Thematic Apperception Test (TAT) A test consisting of a series of pictures about which a person is asked to write a story. (Module 33)

theories Broad explanations and predictions concerning observations of interest. (Module 3)

theory of multiple intelligences Gardner's intelligence theory that proposes that there are eight distinct spheres of intelligence. (Module 23)

thinking Brain activity in which people mentally manipulate information, including words, visual images, sounds, or other data. (Module 21)

tip-of-the-tongue phenomenon The inability to recall information that one realizes one knows—a result of the difficulty of retrieving information from long-term memory. (Module 19)

top-down processing Perception that is guided by higher-level knowledge, experience, expectations, and motivations. (Module 11)

traits Consistent, habitual personality characteristics and behaviors that are displayed across different situations. (Module 32)

trait theory A model of personality that seeks to identify the basic traits necessary to describe personality. (Module 32)

transcranial magnetic stimulation (TMS) A depression treatment in which a precise magnetic pulse is directed to a specific area of the brain. (Module 42)

transference The transfer of feelings to a psychoanalyst of love or anger that had been originally directed to a patient's parents or other authority figures. (Module 40)

transgender An umbrella term for persons whose gender identity, gender expression, or behavior does not conform to that typically associated with the sex to which they were assigned at birth. (Module 25)

treatment The manipulation implemented by the experimenter. (Module 3)

trichromatic theory of color vision The theory that there are three kinds of cones in the retina, each of which responds primarily to a specific range of wavelengths. (Module 9)

trust-versus-mistrust stage According to Erikson, the first stage of psychosocial development, occurring from birth to age 1½ years, during which time infants develop feelings of trust or lack of trust. (Module 28)

Type A behavior pattern A cluster of behaviors involving hostility, competitiveness, time urgency, and feeling driven. (Module 35)

Type B behavior pattern A cluster of behaviors characterized by a patient, cooperative, noncompetitive, and nonaggressive manner. (Module 35)

unconditional positive regard An attitude of acceptance and respect on the part of an observer, no matter what a person says or does. (Module 32)

unconditioned response (UCR) A response that is natural and needs no training (e.g., salivation at the smell of food). (Module 15)

unconditioned stimulus (UCS) A stimulus that naturally brings about a particular response without having been learned. (Module 15)

unconscious A part of the personality that contains the memories, knowledge, beliefs, feelings, urges, drives, and instincts of which the individual is not aware. (Module 31)

unconscious wish fulfillment theory Sigmund Freud's theory that dreams represent unconscious wishes that dreamers desire to see fulfilled. (Module 12)

uninvolved parents Parents who show little interest in their children and are emotionally detached. (Module 28)

validity The property by which tests actually measure what they are supposed to measure. (Module 23)

variable-interval schedule A schedule by which the time between reinforcements varies around some average rather than being fixed. (Module 16)

variable-ratio schedule A schedule by which reinforcement occurs after a varying number of responses rather than after a fixed number. (Module 16)

variables Behaviors, events, or other characteristics that can change, or vary, in some way. (Module 3)

visual illusions Physical stimuli that consistently produce errors in perception. (Module 11)

wear-and-tear theories of aging Theories that suggest that the mechanical functions of the body simply stop working efficiently. (Module 30)

Weber's law A basic law of psychophysics stating that a just noticeable difference is a constant proportion to the intensity of an initial stimulus (rather than a constant amount). (Module 8)

weight set point The particular level of weight that the body strives to maintain. (Module 25)

Wernicke-Korsakoff syndrome A disease that afflicts long-term alcoholics, leaving some abilities intact but with unusual symptoms including including memory loss, hallucinations, and a tendency to repeat the same story. (Module 20)

working memory A memory system that holds information temporarily while actively manipulating and rehearsing that information. (Module 18)

zone of proximal development (ZPD) According to Vygotsky, the gap between what children already are able to accomplish on their own and what they are not quite ready to do by themselves. (Module 28)

zygote The new cell formed by the union of an egg and sperm. (Module 27)

References

Aaron, D. G., & Stanford, F. C. (2021). Is obesity a manifestation of systemic racism? A ten-point strategy for study and intervention. *Journal of Internal Medicine, 290*(2), 416-420.

Aas, M., Melle, I., Bettella, F., Djurovic, S., Le Hellard, S., Bjella, T., Ringen, P. A., Lagerberg, T. V., Smeland, O. B., Agartz, I., Andreassen, O. A., & Tesli, M. (2018). Psychotic patients who used cannabis frequently before illness onset have higher genetic predisposition to schizophrenia than those who did not. *Psychological Medicine, 48*(1), 43-49.

Aazh, H., & Moore, B. C. J. (2007). Dead regions in the cochlea at 4 kHz in elderly adults: Relation to absolute threshold, steepness of audiogram, and pure-tone average. *Journal of the American Academy of Audiology, 18*, 97-106.

Abascal, T. E. (2019). Indigenous tourism in Australia: Understanding the link between cultural heritage and intention to participate using the means-end chain theory. *Journal of Heritage Tourism, 14*(3), 263-281.

Abbasi, J. (2021). COVID-19 conspiracies and beyond: How physicians can deal with patients' misinformation. *JAMA, 325*(3), 208-210.

Abbass, A., Town, J., Ogrodniczuk, J., Joffres, M., & Lilliengren, P. (2017). Intensive short-term dynamic psychotherapy trial therapy: Effectiveness and role of "unlocking the unconscious." *Journal of Nervous and Mental Disease, 205*, 453-457.

Abbott, B. (2022, September 20). Most adults should be screened for anxiety, U.S. panel recommends. *Wall Street Journal.* https://www.wsj.com/articles/most-adults-should-be-screened-for-anxiety-u-s-panel-recommends-11663686000?mod=djemalertNEWS

Abdollahi, A., Panahipour, H., Hosseinian, S., & Allen, K. A. (2019). The effects of perceived stress on hope in women with breast cancer and the role of psychological hardiness. *Psycho-Oncology.* https://doi.org/10.1002/pon.5102.

Abdollahi, E., Eskandari, N., Hosseinpour, M. R., & Tork, A. (2021). Personality Type A or personality Type D, which is a strong predictor of coronary heart disease? *Trends Journal of Sciences Research, 5*(1), 34-39.

Abeles, A. T., Howe, L. C., Krosnick, J. A., & MacInnis, B. (2019). Perception of public opinion on global warming and the role of opinion deviance. *Journal of Environmental Psychology, 63*, 118-129.

Abel, T., & Nickl-Jockschat, T. (2016). *The neurobiology of schizophrenia.* Elsevier Academic Press.

Abi-Dargham, A., Javitch, J. A., Slifstein, M., Anticevic, A., Calkins, M. E., Cho, Y. T., Fonteneau, C., Gil, R., Girgios, R., Gur, R. C., Gur, R. C., Grinband, J., Kantrowitz, J., Kohler, C., Krystal, J., Murray, J., Ranganathan, M., Santamauro, N., Van Snellenberg, J., . . . Lieberman, J. (2022). Dopamine D1R receptor stimulation as a mechanistic pro-cognitive target for schizophrenia. *Schizophrenia Bulletin, 48*(1), 199-210.

Abrams, A. (2017, April 27). 9 sleep habits from around the world. *Time.* https://time.com/4713813/sleep-habits-napping-siesta/, downloaded January 10, 2022.

Abrams, D., & Hogg, M. A. (2017). Twenty years of group processes and intergroup relations research: A review of past progress and future prospects. *Group Processes & Intergroup Relations, 20*(5), 561-569.

Abramson, A. (2022). New frontiers in neuroscience. *Monitor on Psychology. 53*(1), 62. https://www.apa.org/monitor/2022/01/special-frontiers-neuroscience

Abrams, Z. (2021, June). Growing concerns about sleep. *Monitor on Psychology,* p. 30-34.

Abrams, Z. (2021, September.). How bystanders can shut down microaggressions. *Monitor on Psychology,* pp. 54-60.

Ackerman, P. L. (2011). Intelligence and expertise. In R. J. Sternberg & S. Kaufman (Eds.), *The Cambridge handbook of intelligence.* Cambridge University Press.

Active Minds. (2020). Mental Health Amid the COVID-19 Pandemic. Downloaded from https://www.activeminds.org/about-mental-health/be-there/coronavirus/

Adair, L. S., Carba, D. B., Lee, N. R., & Borja, J. B. (2021). Stunting, IQ, and final school attainment in the Cebu Longitudinal Health and Nutrition Survey birth cohort. *Economics & Human Biology, 42*, 100999.

Adami, Z., Alilou, M. M., & Nazari, M. A. (2019). The comparison of emotional working memory capacity in patients with social anxiety disorder and normal subjects. *Advances in Cognitive Science, 20*(4), 35-45.

Adams, G., & Dzokoto, V. A. (2007). Genital-shrinking panic in Ghana: A cultural psychological analysis. *Culture & Psychology, 13*, 83-104.

Adams, K. B. (2004). Changing investment in activities and interests in elders' lives: Theory and measurement. *International Journal of Aging and Human Development, 58*, 87-108.

Adams, M. (2022). Frameworks for social justice education practice. In T. K. Chapman & N. Hobbel (Eds.), *Social justice pedagogy across the curriculum: The practice of freedom.* Routledge.

Adams, M., Bell, L. A., & Griffin, P. (2007). *Teaching for diversity and social justice* (2nd ed.). Routledge/Taylor & Francis Group.

Adams, M., Bell, L. A., & Griffin, P. (2017). *Teaching for diversity and social justice* (2nd ed.). Routledge/Taylor & Francis Group.

Adams, M. M., & Miller, J. G. (2022). The flexible nature of everyday reciprocity: Reciprocity, helping, and relationship closeness. *Motivation and Emotion, 46*, 461-475.

Addison, A. (2017). Jung's psychoid concept: An hermeneutic understanding. *International Journal of Jungian Studies, 9*, 1-16.

Addus, A. A., Chen, D., & Khan, A. S. (2007). Academic performance and advisement of university students: A case study. *College Student Journal, 41*, 316-326.

Adler, M. (2013). Hunger and longing: A developmental regulation model for exploring core relational needs. In S. P. Gantt & B. Badenoch (Eds.), *The interpersonal neurobiology of group psychotherapy and group process.* Karnac Books.

Adolph, K. E., & Berger, S. E. (2011). Physical and motor development. In M. H. Bornstein & M. E. Lamb (Eds.), *Cognitive development: An advanced textbook.* Psychology Press.

Aga, K., Inamura, M., Chen, C., Hagiwara, K., Yamashita, R., Hirotsu, M., Seki, T., Takao, A., Fujii, Y., Matsubara, T., & Nakagawa, S. (2021). The effect of acute aerobic exercise on divergent and convergent thinking and its influence by mood. *Brain Sciences, 11*(5), 546.

Agenagnew, L., Tesfaye, E., Alemayehu, S., Masane, M., Bete, T., & Tadessa, J. (2020). Dissociative amnesia with dissociative fugue and psychosis: A case report from a 25-year-old Ethiopian woman. *Case Reports in Psychiatry, 2020.* https://doi.org/10.1155/2020/3281487

Agranovich, A. V., Melikyan, Z. A., & Panter, A. T. (2021). The culture of time inventory: Comparison of time attitudes pertaining to timed testing in Russian and American adults. *Cross-Cultural Research, 55*(2-3), 179-208.

Aguilar-Arguello, S., Taylor, A. H., & Nelson, X. J. (2022). Jumping spiders do not seem fooled by texture gradient illusions. *Behavioural Processes, 196*, 104603.

Ahmadi, N., Sasangohar, F., Nisar, T., Danesh, V., Larsen, E., Sultana, I., & Bosetti, R. (2022). Quantifying occupational stress in intensive care unit nurses: An applied naturalistic study of correlations among stress, heart rate, electrodermal activity, and skin temperature. *Human Factors, 64*(1), 159-172.

Ahmadi Forooshani, S., Murray, K., Izadikhah, Z., & Khawaja, N. (2020). Identifying the most effective strategies for improving autobiographical memory specificity and its implications for mental health problems: A meta-analysis. *Cognitive Therapy and Research, 44*(2), 258-274.

Ahmed, A. O., Kirkpatrick, B., Granholm, E., Rowland, L. M., Barker, P. B., Gold, J. M., Buchanan, R. W., Outram, T., Bernardo, M., García-Portilla, M. P., Mane, A., Fernandez-Egea, E., & Strauss, G. P. (2022). Two factors, five factors, or both? External validation studies of negative symptom dimensions in schizophrenia. *Schizophrenia Bulletin, 48*(3), 620-630.

Ahmeti, K., & Ramadani, N. (2021). Determination of Kohlberg's moral development stages and chronological age. *International Journal of Social and Human Sciences, 8*(15-16), 37-48.

Ahn, S., Lobo, J. M., Logan, J. G., Kang, H., Kwon, Y., & Sohn, M. W. (2021). A scoping review of racial/ethnic disparities in sleep. *Sleep Medicine, 81*, 169-179.

Aikawa, S., & Takai, H. (2021). Relationship Between Imagery Ability, Performance, and Variables Related to Performance. *The Sport Psychologist, 35*(2), 123-130.

Ainsworth, M. D. S., Blehar, M. C., Waters, E., & Wall, S. (1978). *Patterns of attachment: A psychological study of the strange situation.* Erlbaum.

Airuehia, E., Walker, L. Y., & Nittler, J. (2015). A review of "bath salts": Evolving designer drugs of abuse. *Journal of Child & Adolescent Substance Abuse, 24*, 186-190.

Akdeniz, S., Budak, H., & Ahçi, Z. G. (2022). Development of a scale of narcissism in social media and investigation of its psychometric characteristics. *International Education Studies, 15*(1), 200-209.

Akhavan, A. A., Sandhu, S., Ndem, I., & Ogunleye, A. A. (2021). A review of gender affirmation surgery: What we know, and what we need to know. *Surgery, 170*(1), 336-340.

Akhtar, S., Hongyuan, T., Iqbal, S., & Ankomah, F. Y. N. (2020). Impact of need for achievement on entrepreneurial intentions; Mediating role of self-efficacy. *Journal of Asian Business Strategy, 10*(1), 114-121.

Akhtar, S., & Howe, M. L. (2019). Priming older adults and people with Alzheimer's disease analogical problem-solving with true and false memories. *Journal of Clinical and Experimental Neuropsychology, 41*(7), 704-714.

Aknin, L. B., De Neve, J. E., Dunn, E. W., Fancourt, D. E., Goldberg, E., Helliwell, J. F., Jones, S. P., Karam, E., Layard, R., Lyubomirsky, S., Rzepa, A., Saxena, S., Thornton, E. M., VanderWeele, T. J., Whillans, A. V., Zaki, J., Karadag, O., & Ben Amor, Y. (2022). Mental health during the first year of the COVID-19 pandemic: A review and recommendations for moving forward. *Perspectives on Psychological Science, 17*(4), 915-936.

Akpan, B. (2020). Classical and Operant Conditioning– Ivan Pavlov; Burrhus Skinner. In *Science Education in Theory and Practice* (pp. 71-84). Springer, Cham.

Alampay, L. P., Godwin, J., Lansford, J. E., Bombi, A. S., Bornstein, M. H., Chang, L., Deater-Deckard, K., Di Giunta, L., Dodge, K. A., Malone, P. S., Oburu, P., Pastorelli, C., Skinner, A. T., Sorbring, E., Tapanya, S., Uribe Tirado, L. M., Zelli, A., Al-Hassan, S., & Bacchini, D. (2017). Severity and justness do not moderate the relation between corporal punishment and negative child outcomes: A multicultural and longitudinal study. *International Journal of Behavioral Development, 41,* 491-502.

Albanese, M., & Case, S. M. (2015). Progress testing: Critical analysis and suggested practices. *Advances in Health Sciences Education, 21,* 221-234.

Alboni, S., Di Bonaventura, M. M., Benatti, C., Giusepponi, M. E., Brunello, N., & Cifani, C. (2017). Hypothalamic expression of inflammatory mediators in an animal model of binge eating. *Behavioural Brain Research, 320,* 420-430.

Alderson-Day, B., Weis, S., McCarthy-Jones, S., Moseley, P., Smailes, D., & Fernyhough, C. (2016). The brain's conversation with itself: Neural substrates of dialogic inner speech. *Social Cognitive and Affective Neuroscience, 11*(1), 110-120.

Aleksander, I. (2013, June 23). Molly: Pure, but not so simple. *The New York Times,* p. ST1.

Alelú-Paz, R., Carmona, F. J., Sanchez-Mut, J. V., Cariaga-Martínez, A., González-Corpas, A., Ashour, N., Orea, M. J., Escanilla, A., Monje, A., Márquez, C. G., Saiz-Ruiz, J., Esteller, M., & Ropero, S. (2016). Epigenetics in schizophrenia: A pilot study of global DNA methylation in different brain regions associated with higher cognitive functions. *Frontiers In Psychology, 7,* 1496.

Alexander, M. B., Gore, J., & Estep, C. (2021). How need for power explains why narcissists are antisocial. *Psychological Reports, 124*(3), 1335-1352.

Al-Faris, S., & Jasim, B. Y. (2021). Memory strategies and vocabulary learning strategies: Implications on teaching and learning vocabulary. *Journal of Humanities and Social Sciences Studies, 3*(10), 11-21.

Alfaro, A., Bernabeu, Á., Agulló, C., Parra, J., & Fernández, E. (2015). Hearing colors: An example of brain plasticity. *Frontiers In Systems Neuroscience, 9,* 42-50.

Ali, T., Sisay, M., Tariku, M., Mekuria, A. N., & Desalew, A. (2021). Antipsychotic-induced extrapyramidal side effects: A systematic review and meta-analysis of observational studies. *PLOS ONE, 16*(9), e0257129.

Allakhverdov, V. M. (2019). Consciousness and the problem of free will. *Neuroscience and Behavioral Physiology.* doi:10.1007/s11055-019-00780-6.

Allen, D. N., & Becker, M. L. (2019). Clinical interviewing. In G. Goldstein, D. N. Allen, & J. DeLuca (Eds.), *Handbook of psychological assessment* (4th ed.). Elsevier Academic Press.

Allen, M. T., Handy, J. D., Miller, D. P., & Servatius, R. J. (2019). Avoidance learning and classical eyeblink conditioning as model systems to explore a learning diathesis model of PTSD. *Neuroscience & Biobehavioral Reviews, 100,* 370-386.

Allott, N., Lohndal, T., & Rey, G. (Eds.). (2021). *A companion to Chomsky.* John Wiley & Sons.

Allport, G. W. (1966). Traits revisited. *American Psychologist, 21,* 1-10.

Allport, G. W., & Postman, L. J. (1958). The basic psychology of rumor. In E. D. Maccoby, T. M. Newcomb, & E. L. Hartley (Eds.), *Readings in social psychology* (3rd ed.). New York: Holt, Rinehart and Winston.

Al Naqbi, H., Mawart, A., Alshamsi, J., Al Safar, H., & Tay, G. K. (2021). Major histocompatibility complex (MHC) associations with diseases in ethnic groups of the Arabian Peninsula. *Immunogenetics, 73*(2), 131-152.

Alneyadi, M., Drissi, N., Almeqbaali, M., & Ouhbi, S. (2021). Biofeedback-based connected mental health interventions for anxiety: Systematic literature review. *JMIR mHealth and uHealth, 9*(4), e26038.

Alon, I., & Brett, J. M. (2007). Perceptions of time and their impact on negotiations in the Arabic-speaking Islamic world. *Negotiation Journal, 23,* 55-73.

Al Shamsi, H., Almutairi, A. G., Al Mashrafi, S., & Al Kalbani, T. (2020). Implications of language barriers for healthcare: A systematic review. *Oman Medical Journal, 35*(2), e122.

Al-Shawaf, L., Lewis, D. M. G., & Buss, D. M. (2018). Sex differences in disgust: Why are women more easily disgusted than men? *Emotion Review, 10*(2), 149-160.

Altinok, D. C. A., Rajkumar, R., Niessen, D., Sbaihat, H., Kersey, M., Shah, N. J., Veselinovic, T., & Neuner, I. (2021). Common neurobiological correlates of resilience and personality traits within the triple resting-state brain networks assessed by 7-Tesla ultra-high field MRI. *Scientific Reports, 11*(1), 11564. https://doi.org/10.1038/s41598-021-91056-y

Aluja, A., Malas, O., Lucas, I., Worner, F., & Bascompte, R. (2019). Assessment of the Type D personality distress in coronary heart disease patients and healthy subjects in Spain. *Personality and Individual Differences, 142,* 301-309.

Altman, N., & Stile, J. (2015). Staying alive: Freud for a new generation. *PsycCRITIQUES, 60,* 25-32.

Alvarez, I., Hurley, S. A., Parker, A. J., & Bridge, H. (2021). Human primary visual cortex shows larger population receptive fields for binocular disparity-defined stimuli. *Brain Structure and Function, 226*(9), 2819-2838.

Alzheimer's Association. (2022). *2017 Alzheimer's disease: Facts and figures.* https://www.alz.org/alzheimers-dementia/facts-figures

Alzheimer's Association. (2022). Alzheimer's disease facts and figures. https://www.alz.org/alzheimers-dementia/facts-figures

Ameen, M., & Khan, P. M. A. (2020). Effect of counselling on social adjustment of underachievers. *International Journal of Psychosocial Rehabilitation, 24*(06), 13766-13778.

American Academy of Pediatrics. (2016). Media and young minds. *Pediatrics, 138,* 1-6.

American Academy of Pediatrics, American Academy of Child and Adolescent Psychiatry, & Children's Hospital Association. (2021). AAP-AACAP-CHA declaration of a national emergency in child and adolescent mental health. https://www.aap.org/en/advocacy/child-and-adolescent-healthy-mental-development/aap-aacap-cha-declaration-of-a-national-emergency-in-child-and-adolescent-mental-health/

American Academy of Pediatrics Council on Communication and Media. (2009). Media violence. *Pediatrics, 124,* 1495-1503.

American Academy of Pediatrics Council on Communications and Media. (2016). Virtual violence. *Pediatrics. 138,* e20161298.

American Association of Intellectual and Developmental Disabilities. (2022). FAQs on intellectual disability. https://www.aaidd.org/intellectual-disability/faqs-on-intellectual-disability

American Community Survey. (2019). Language spoken at home for the population 5 years and over. U. S. Census Bureau. https://data.census.gov/

American Psychiatric Association. (2013). *Diagnostic and statistical manual of mental disorders* (5th ed.). Author.

American Psychiatric Association. (2018). Warning signs of mental illness. https://www.psychiatry.org/patients-families/warning-signs-of-mental-illness

American Psychiatric Association. (2022). *Diagnostic and statistical manual of mental disorders* (5th ed., text rev.). Author.

American Psychological Association. (2011). *Careers in psychology.* Washington DC: Author.

American Psychological Association. (2016, June). What do people do with their psychology degrees? *Monitor on Psychology,* p. 12.

American Psychological Association. (2018). Demographics of the U.S. psychology workforce: Findings from the 2007-16 American Community Survey. Washington, DC: Author.

American Psychological Association. (2019). Guidelines for the practice of telepsychology. https://www.apa.org/practice/guidelines/telepsychology

American Psychological Association. (2019). Supporting a family member with serious mental illness. https://www.apa.org/helpcenter/improving-care

American Psychological Association. (2020). Demographics of U.S. Psychology Workforce. https://www.apa.org/workforce/data-tools/demographics

American Psychological Association. (2020). Psychology's workforce is becoming more diverse. *Monitor on Psychology, 51*(8). https://www.apa.org/monitor/2020/11/datapoint-diverse

American Psychological Association. (2020). Stress in America™ 2020: A national mental health crisis. https://www.apa.org/news/press/releases/stress/2020/sia-mental-health-crisis.pdf

American Psychological Association. (2021). Careers in Psychology [interactive data tool]. https://www.apa.org/workforce/data-tools/careers-psychology

American Psychological Association. (2021). Ethnicity and Health in America Series: Featured Psychologists. https://www.apa.org/pi/oema/resources/ethnicity-health/psychologists

American Psychological Association. (2021). Stress in America™ 2021: Stress and decision-making during the pandemic. https://www.apa.org/news/press/releases/stress/2021/decision-making-october-2021.pdf

Amid, P. K., & Chen, D. C. (2011). Surgical treatment of chronic groin and testicular pain after laparoscopic and open preperitoneal inguinal hernia repair. *Journal of the American College of Surgeons, 213,* 531-536.

Ammalainen, A., & Moroshkina, N. (2021). The effect of true and false unreportable hints on anagram problem solving, restructuring, and the Aha!-experience. *Journal of Cognitive Psychology, 33*(6-7), 644-658.

Amodia-Bidakowska, A., Laverty, C., & Ramchandani, P. G. (2020). Father-child play: A systematic review of its frequency, characteristics and potential impact on children's development. *Developmental Review, 57,* 100924.

Amodio, D. M., & Ratner, K. G. (2011). A memory systems model of implicit social cognition. *Current Directions In Psychological Science, 20,* 143-148.

Amorim, W. W., Passos, L. C., Gama, R. S., Souza, R. M., & Oliveira, M. G. (2021). Factors associated with older patients' misunderstandings of medication dosage regimen instructions after consultation in primary care in Brazil. *Journal of Evaluation in Clinical Practice, 27*(4), 817-825.

Amos, I. A. (2021). Attempting to capture the ineffable quality: An interpretative phenomenological analysis of the experience of an epiphany. *Transpersonal Psychology Review, 23*(1), 32-44.

Andersen, R. (2019, April). The intention machine. *Scientific American,* 25-31.

Andersen, R. A., Aflalo, T., Bashford, L., Bjånes, D., & Kellis, S. (2022). Exploring cognition with brain-machine interfaces. *Annual Review of Psychology, 73,* 131-158.

Anderson, C. A., & Bushman, B. J. (2018). Media violence and the general aggression model. *Journal of Social Issues, 74*(2), 386-413.

Anderson, C. A., Bushman, B. J., Bartholow, B. D., Cantor, J., Christakis, D., Coyne, S. M., Donnerstein, E., Funk Brockmyer, J., Gentile, D. A., Green, C. S., Huesmann, R., Hummer, T., Krahé, B., Strasburger, V. C., Warburton, W., Wilson, B. J., & Ybarra, M. (2017). Screen violence and youth behavior. *Pediatrics, 140*(5, Supp 2), S142-S147.

Anderson, C. A., Lazard, D. S., & Hartley, D. H. (2017). Plasticity in bilateral superior temporal cortex: Effects of deafness and cochlear implantation on auditory and visual speech processing. *Hearing Research, 343,* 138-149.

Anderson, J. L., & Kelley, S. E. (2022). Antisocial personality disorder and psychopathy: The AMPD in review. *Personality Disorders: Theory, Research, and Treatment, 13*(4), 397-401. https://doi.org/10.1037/per0000525

Anderson, J. L., Sellbom, M., Pymont, C., Smid, W., De Saeger, H., & Kamphuis, J. H. (2015). Measurement of DSM-5 section II personality disorder constructs using the MMPI-2-RF in clinical and forensic samples. *Psychological Assessment, 27*, 786-800.

Anderson, L. B., Paul, L. K., & Brown, W. S. (2017). Emotional intelligence in agenesis of the corpus callosum. *Archives of Clinical Neuropsychology, 32*, 267-279.

Anderson, M. C., & Hulbert, J. C. (2021). Active forgetting: Adaptation of memory by prefrontal control. *Annual Review of Psychology, 72*, 1-36.

Andoh, E. (2021). Psychology's urgent need to dismantle racism. *Monitor on Psychology, 52*(3). https://www.apa.org/monitor/2021/04/cover-dismantle-racism

Andreasen, N. C. (2022). The relationship between creativity and mood disorders. *Dialogues in Clinical Neuroscience, 10*(2), 251-255.

Andrews, F. M., & Withey, S. B. (1976). *Social indicators of well-being: Americans' perceptions of life quality.* Plenum.

Anguela, X. M., & High, K. A. (2019). Entering the modern era of gene therapy. *Annual Review of Medicine, 70*, 273-288.

Antza, C., Kostopoulos, G., Mostafa, S., Nirantharakumar, K., & Tahrani, A. (2022). The links between sleep duration, obesity and type 2 diabetes mellitus. *Journal of Endocrinology, 252*(2), 125-141.

Aoued, H. S., Sannigrahi, S., Doshi, N., Morrison, F. G., Linsenbaum, H., Hunter, S. C., Walum, H., Baman, J., Yao, B. Jin, P., Ressler, K. J., & Dias, B. G. (2019). Reversing behavioral, neuroanatomical, and germline influences of intergenerational stress. *Biological Psychiatry, 85*(3), 248-256.

Aoun, M. H., Hilal, N., Beaini, C., Sleilaty, G., Hajal, J., Boueri, C., & Chelala, D. (2021). Effects of Caffeinated and Decaffeinated Coffee on Hemodialysis-Related Headache (CoffeeHD): A Randomized Multicenter Clinical Trial. *Journal of Renal Nutrition, 31*(6), 648-660.

APA. (2021a). Apology to People of Color for APA's Role in Promoting, Perpetuating, and Failing to Challenge Racism, Racial Discrimination, and Human Hierarchy in U.S. Resolution adopted by the APA Council of Representatives on October 29, 2021. https://www.apa.org/about/policy/racism-apology.

APA. (2021b). Equity, diversity and inclusion framework. Washington, DC: APA. https://www.apa.org/about/apa/equity-diversity-inclusion/equity-division-inclusion-framework.pdf

Apple, D. M., Fonseca, R. S., & Kokovay, E. (2017). The role of adult neurogenesis in psychiatric and cognitive disorders. *Brain Research, 1655*, 270-276.

Appelbaum, P. S. (2022). Settled insanity: Substance use meets the insanity defense. *Psychiatric Services, 73*(1), 105-107.

Araujo, M. C., Dormal, M., & Schady, N. (2019). Childcare quality and child development. *Journal of Human Resources, 54*(3), 656-682.

Arbuthnott, A., & Sharpe, D. (2009). The effect of physician-patient collaboration on patient adherence in non-psychiatric medicine. *Patient Education and Counseling, 77*, 60-67.

Arce, J. M. R., & Winkelman, M. J. (2021). Psychedelics, sociality, and human evolution. *Frontiers in Psychology, 12*.

Arcelus, J., Mitchell, A. J., Wales, J., & Nielsen, S. (2011). Mortality rates in patients with anorexia nervosa and other eating disorders: A meta-analysis of 36 studies. *Archives of General Psychiatry, 68*, 724-731.

Ardila, A. (2015). A proposed neurological inter-pretation of language evolution. *Behavioural Neurology, 20*, 15-22.

Arena, J. G., & Tankersley, J. D. (2018). Introduction to biofeedback training for chronic pain disorders. In D. C. Turk & R. J. Gatchel (Eds.), *Psychological approaches to pain management: A practitioner's handbook* (3rd ed.), (pp. 138-159). The Guilford Press.

Arieli, S., & Sagiv, L. (2018). Culture and problem-solving: Congruency between the cultural mindset of individualism versus collectivism and problem type. *Journal of Experimental Psychology: General, 147*(6), 789-814. https://doi.org/10.1037/xge0000444

Arifin, S. R. M., Cheyne, H., & Maxwell, M. (2018). Review of the prevalence of postnatal depression across cultures. *AIMS Public Health, 5*(3), 260.

Armbruster, D., Mueller, A., Strobel, A., Lesch, K., Kirschbaum, C., & Brocke, B. (2011). Variation in genes involved in dopamine clearance influence the startle response in older adults. *Journal of Neural Transmission, 118*, 1281-1292.

Armstrong, V. O., Tudor, T. R., & Hughes, G. D. (2021). Course retention in community colleges: Demographics, motivation, learning style, and locus of control. *American Journal of Distance Education, 35*(1), 32-47.

Arnáez, S., García-Soriano, G., López-Santiago, J., & Belloch, A. (2021). Illness-related intrusive thoughts and illness anxiety disorder. *Psychology and Psychotherapy: Theory, Research and Practice, 94*(1), 63-80.

Arnett, J. J. (2006). *Emerging adulthood: The winding road from the late teens through the twenties.* Oxford University Press.

Aronson, J., & Dee, T. (2012). Stereotype threat in the real world. In M. Inzlicht & T. Schmader (Eds.), *Stereotype threat: Theory, process, and application.* Oxford University Press.

Arrigoni, E., Chee, M. J. S., & Fuller, P. M. (2019). To eat or to sleep: That is a lateral hypothalamic question. *Neuropharmacology, 154*, 34-49.

Arshamian, A., Iannilli, E., Gerber, J. C., Willander, J., Persson, J., Seo, H., Hummel, T., & Larsson, M. (2013). The functional neuroanatomy of odor evoked auto-biographical memories cued by odors and words. *Neuropsychologia, 51*(1), 123-131.

Artioli, G., Ghirotto, L., Alquati, S., & Tanzi, S. (2022). Behavioral patterns in breaking bad news communication: An ethnographic study with hematologists. *International Journal of Environmental Research and Public Health, 19*(5), 2585.

Artistico, D., Pinto, A., Douek, J., Black, J., & Pezzuti, L. (2013). The value of removing daily obstacles via everyday problem-solving theory: Developing an applied novel procedure to increase self-efficacy for exercise. *Frontiers in Psychology, 4*.

Arvanitis, A., & Kalliris, K. (2020). Consistency and moral integrity: A self-determination theory perspective. *Journal of Moral Education, 49*(3), 316-329.

Asadullah, A. B. M., Juhdi, N. B., Islam, M. N., Ahmed, A. A. A., & Abdullah, A. B. M. (2019). The effect of reinforcement and punishment on employee performance. *ABC Journal of Advanced Research, 8*(2), 47-58.

Aschieri, F., & Pascarella, G. (2021). A systematic narrative review of evaluating change in psychotherapy with the Rorschach test. *Rorschachiana, 42*(2), 232-257. https://doi.org/10.1027/1192-5604/a000142

Asch, S. E. (1951). Effects of group pressure upon the modification and distortion of judgments. In H. Guetzkow (Ed.), *Groups, leadership, and men.* Carnegie Press.

Ash, E., Durante, R., Grebenshchikova, M., & Schwarz, C. (2022). Visual representation and stereotypes in news media. The Centre for Economic Policy Research. Press Discussion Paper No. 16624. https://cepr.org/publications/dp16624.

Atherton, O. E., Grijalva, E., Roberts, B. W., & Robins, R. W. (2021). Stability and change in personality traits and major life goals from college to midlife. *Personality and Social Psychology Bulletin, 47*(5), 841-858.

Athota, V. S., Budhwar, P., & Malik, A. (2020). Influence of personality traits and moral values on employee well-being, resilience and performance: A cross-national study. *Applied Psychology, 69*(3), 653-685.

Atkinson, R. C., & Shiffrin, R. M. (1968). Human memory: A proposed system and its control processes. In K. W. Spence & J. T. Spence (Eds.), *The psychology of learning and motivation: Advances in research and theory* (Vol. 2). Academic Press.

Atske, S., & Perrin, A. (2021, July 16). Home broadband adoption, computer ownership vary by race, ethnicity in the U.S. PEW Research Center. https://www.pewresearch.org/fact-tank/2021/07/16/home-broadband-adoption-computer-ownership-vary-by-race-ethnicity-in-the-u-s/

Aubrey, A. (2020, April 18). Who's hit hardest by COVID-19? Why obesity, stress and race all matter. *National Public Radio.* https://www.npr.org/sections/health-shots/2020/04/18/835563340/whos-hit-hardest-by-covid-19-why-obesity-stress-and-race-all-matter

Austin, J. P., & Halvorson, S. A. (2019). Reducing the expert halo effect on pharmacy and therapeutics committees. *Journal of the American Medical Association, 321*(5), 453-454.

Averill, J. R. (1975). A semantic atlas of emotional concepts. *Catalog of Selected Documents in Psychology, 5*, 330.

Aw, J., Seng, J. J. B., Seah, S. S. Y., & Low, L. L. (2021). COVID-19 vaccine hesitancy—A scoping review of literature in high-income countries. *Vaccines, 9*(8), 900.

Axt, J. R., Feng, T. Y., & Bar-Anan, Y. (2021). The good and the bad: Are some attribute words better than others in the Implicit Association Test? *Behavior Research Methods, 53*(6), 2512-2527.

Ayduk, Ö., & Mendoza-Denton, R. (2021). A cognitive-affective processing system approach to personality dispositions: Rejection sensitivity as an illustrative case study. In O. P. John & R. W. Robins (Eds.), *Handbook of personality: Theory and research.* Guilford Press.

Ayling, K., Bowden, T., Tighe, P., Todd, I., Dilnot, E. M., Negm, O. H., et al. (2017). The application of protein microarray assays in psychoneuroimmunology. *Brain, Behavior, and Immunity, 59*, 62-66.

Azeredo, A., Moreira, D., Figueiredo, P., & Barbosa, F. (2019). Delinquent behavior: Systematic review of genetic and environmental risk factors. *Clinical Child and Family Psychology Review.* https://doi.org/10.1007/s10567-019-00298-w.

Azieb, S. (2021). The critical period hypothesis in second language acquisition: A review of the literature. *International Journal of Research in Humanities and Social Studies, 8*(4), 20-26.

Babcock, K. R., Page, J. S., Fallon, J., & Webb, A. E. (2021). Adult hippocampal neurogenesis in aging and Alzheimer's disease. *Stem Cell Reports, 16*(4), 681-693.

Bacchiochi, J. R. (2006). Development and validation of the Malingering Discriminant Function Index (M-DFI) for the Minnesota Multiphasic Personality Inventory-2 (MMPI-2). *Dissertation Abstracts International: Section B: The Sciences and Engineering, 66*(10-B), 5673.

Bacon, E. R., & Brinton, R. D. (2021). Epigenetics of the developing and aging brain: Mechanisms that regulate onset and outcomes of brain reorganization. *Neuroscience & Biobehavioral Reviews, 125*, 503-516.

Baczyńska, A., & Thornton, G. C. (2017). Relationships of analytical, practical, and emotional intelligence with behavioral dimensions of performance of top managers. *International Journal of Selection and Assessment, 25*, 171-182.

Baddeley, A., & Wilson, B. (1985). Phonological coding and short-term memory in patients without speech. *Journal of Memory and Language, 24*, 490-502.

Baddeley, A. D., Allen, R. J., & Hitch, G. J. (2011). Binding in visual working memory: The role of the episodic buffer. *Neuropsychologia, 49*, 1393-1400.

Badr, H. M., & Abu-Ayyash, E. A. (2019). Semantic mapping or rote memorisation: Which strategy is more effective for students' acquisition and memorization of L2 vocabulary? *Journal of Education and Learning, 8*(3), 158-174.

Bagattini, C., Mele, S., Brignani, D., & Savazzi, S. (2015). No causal effect of left hemisphere hyperactivity in the genesis of neglect-like behavior. *Neuropsychologia, 72*, 12-21.

Bahrick, H. P., Hall, L. K., & Berger, S. A. (1996). Accuracy and distortion in memory for high school grades. *Psychological Science, 7*, 265-269.

Bahtiyar-Saygan, B., & Berument, S. K. (2022). The role of temperament and parenting on anxiety problems among toddlers: Moderating role of parenting and mediating role of attachment. *Infant Mental Health Journal.* Advanced online publication. https://doi.org/10.1002/imhj.21988

Bai, M. H. (2022, May). Fake news known as fake still enduringly changes beliefs. Talk presented at the annual meeting of the Association for Psychological Science.

Baidoo, N., & Leri, F. (2022). Extended amygdala, conditioned withdrawal and memory consolidation. *Progress in Neuro-Psychopharmacology and Biological Psychiatry, 113*, 110435.

Bailey, J. M., Vasey, P. L., Diamond, L. M., Breedlove, S. M., Vilain, E., & Epprecht, M. (2016). Sexual orientation, controversy, and science. *Psychological Science in the Public Interest, 17*(2), 45-101.

Baines, L., & Jones, A. (2021). The Associations Between Proactive Slowing, Working Memory, Alcohol Sensitivity, and Alcohol Use. *Journal of Studies on Alcohol and Drugs, 82*(1), 142-151.

Baker, S. E., Johnson, P. J., & Slater, D. (2007). Learned food aversion with and without an odour cue for protecting untreated baits from wild mammal foraging [Special issue: Conservation, enrichment, and animal behavior]. *Applied Animal Behaviour Science, 102*, 410-428.

Balaban, C. D., McBurney, D. H., & Affeltranger, M. A. (2005). Three distinct categories of time course of pain produced by oral capsaicin. *The Journal of Pain, 6*, 315-322.

Balconi, M., Bortolotti, A., & Crivelli, D. (2013). Self-report measures, facial feedback, and personality differences (BEES) in cooperative vs. noncooperative situations: Contribution of the mimic system to the sense of empathy. *International Journal of Psychology, 48*, 631-640.

Balles, L., Zappella, G., & Archambeau, C. (2022). Gradient-matching coresets for rehearsal-based continual learning. *arXiv preprint. arXiv:2203.14544.*

Balter, M. (2017). Schizophrenia's unyielding mysteries. *Scientific American, 316*(5), 54-61.

Bandura, A. (1994). Social cognitive theory of mass communication. In J. Bryant & D. Zillmann (Eds.), *Media effects: Advances in theory and research: LEA's communication series.* Erlbaum.

Bandura, A. (1999). Social cognitive theory of personality. In D. Cervone & Y. Shod (Eds.), *The coherence of personality.* Guilford.

Bandura, A. (2000). Self-efficacy: The foundation of agency. In W. J. Perrig & A. Grob (Eds.), *Control of human behavior, mental processes, and consciousness: Essays in honor of the 60th birthday of August Flammer.* Erlbaum.

Bandura, A., Grusec, J. E., & Menlove, F. L. (1967). Vicarious extinction of avoidance behavior. *Journal of Personality and Social Psychology, 5*, 16-23.

Bandura, A., & Hall, P. (2018). Albert bandura and social learning theory. *Learning theories for early years practice, 63.*

Bandura, A., Ross, D., & Ross, S. (1963a). Imitation of film-mediated aggressive models. *Journal of Abnormal and Social Psychology, 66*, 3-11.

Bandura, A., Ross, D., & Ross, S. (1963b). Vicarious reinforcement and imitative learning. *Journal of Abnormal and Social Psychology, 67*, 601-607.

Banks, J. B., & Boals, A. (2017). Understanding the role of mind wandering in stress-related working memory impairments. *Cognition and Emotion, 31*, 1023-1030.

Barbaro, N., Boutwell, B. B., Barnes, J. C., & Shackelford, T. K. (2017). Rethinking the transmission gap: What behavioral genetics and evolutionary psychology mean for attachment theory: A comment on Verhage et al. (2016). *Psychological Bulletin, 143*, 107-113.

Barber, L., Reniers, R., & Upthegrove, R. (2021). A review of functional and structural neuroimaging studies to investigate the inner speech model of auditory verbal hallucinations in schizophrenia. *Translational Psychiatry, 11*(1), 1-12.

Barber, N. (2019). The most creative time of day. *Psychology Today.* Retrieved from https://www.psychologytoday.com/us/blog/the-human-beast/201906/the-most-creative-time-day.

Barbuti, P. A., Barker, R. A., Brundin, P., Przedborski, S., Papa, S. M., Kalia, L. V., Mochizuki, H., & MDS Scientific Issues Committee. (2021). Recent advances in the development of stem-cell-derived dopaminergic neuronal transplant therapies for Parkinson's disease. *Movement Disorders, 36*(8), 1772-1780.

Barcott, B., & Scherer, M. (2015, May 25). The great pot experiment. *Time,* pp. 38-44.

Barendse, M. E., Flannery, J., Cavanagh, C., Aristizabal, M., Becker, S. P., Berger, E.,Breaux, R., Campione-Barr, N., Church, J. A., Crone, E. A., Dahl, R. E., Dennis-Tiwary, T. A., Dvorsky, M. R., Dziura, S. L., van de Groep, S., Ho, T. C., Killoren, S. E., Langberg, J. M., Larguinho, T. L., Magis-Weinberg, L., et al. (2021). Longitudinal change in adolescent depression and anxiety symptoms from before to during the COVID-19 pandemic: A collaborative of 12 samples from 3 countries. https://doi.org/10.1111/jora.12781.

Barendse, M. E., Flannery, J., Cavanagh, C., Aristizabal, M., Becker, S. P., Berger, E.,Breaux, R., Campione-Barr, N., Church, J. A., Crone, E. A., Dahl, R. E., Dennis-Tiwary, T. A., Dvorsky, M. R., Dziura, S. L., van de Groep, S., Ho, T. C., Killoren, S. E., Langberg, J. M., Larguinho, T. L., Magis-Weinberg, L., et al. (2022). Longitudinal change in adolescent depression and anxiety symptoms from before to during the COVID-19 pandemic. *Journal of Research on Adolescence, 33*(1), 74-91.

Bargh, J. A. (2014). Our unconscious mind. *Scientific American, 310*, 30-37.

Barisano, G., Sepehrband, F., Collins, H. R., Jillings, S., Jeurissen, B., Taylor, J. A., Schoenmaekers, C., De Laet, C., Rukavishnikov, I., Nosikova, I., Litvinova, L., Rumshiskaya, A., Annen, J., Sijbers, J., Laureys, S., Van Ombergen, A., Petrovichev, V., Sinitsyn, V., Pechenkova, E., . . . Wuyts, F. L. (2022). The effect of prolonged spaceflight on cerebrospinal fluid and perivascular spaces of astronauts and cosmonauts. *Proceedings of the National Academy of Sciences of the United States of America, 119*(17), e2120439119. https://doi.org/10.1073/pnas.2120439119

Barke, D. B. (2011). Self-selection for stressful experiences. *Stress and Health: Journal of the International Society for the Investigation of Stress, 27*, 194-205.

Barker, A. J., Veviurko, G., Bennett, N. C., Hart, D. W., Mograby, L., & Lewin, G. R. (2021). Cultural transmission of vocal dialect in the naked mole-rat. *Science, 371*(6528), 503-507.

Barker, G. G., & Barker, E. E. (2022). Online therapy: lessons learned from the COVID-19 health crisis. *British Journal of Guidance & Counselling, 50*(1), 66-81.

Barkley, R. (2000). *Taking charge of ADHD* (rev. ed.). Guilford Press.

Barkley, R. A., Knouse, L. E., & Murphy, K. R. (2011). Correspondence and disparity in the self- and other ratings of current and childhood ADHD symptoms and impairment in adults with ADHD. *Psychological Assessment, 23*, 437-446.

Barlow, D. H. (2020). Behavior therapy: The next decade. In *The Neurotic Paradox* (Vol. 1). Routledge.

Barnes, J. C., & Jacobs, B. A. (2013). Genetic risk for violent behavior and environmental exposure to disadvantage and violent crime: The case for gene-environment interaction. *Journal ofInterpersonal Violence, 28*, 92-120.

Barnett, S. M., Rindermann, H., Williams, W. M., & Ceci, S. J. (2011). Society and intelligence. In R. J. Sternberg & S. Kaufman (Eds.), *The Cambridge handbook of intelligence.* Cambridge University Press.

Baron-Cohen, S. (2020). *The pattern seekers: How autism drives human invention.* Basic Books.

Barresi, J. (2007). Consciousness and intentionality. *Journal of Consciousness Studies, 14, Special issue: Concepts of Consciousness: Integrating an Emerging Science,* 77-93.

Barrett. D. (2020, July-August). When the answer comes in a dream. *American Scientist, 108*, 200.

Barrett, L. (2011). *Beyond the brain: How body and environment shape animal and human minds.* Princeton, NJ: Princeton University Press.

Barrett, L. F. (2021). AI weighs in on debate about universal facial expressions. *Nature, 589*(7841), 202-204.

Barrett, L. F., Adolphs, R., Marsella, S., Martinez, A. M., & Pollak, S. D. (2019). Emotional expressions reconsidered: Challenges to inferring emotion from human facial movements. *Psychological Science in the Public Interest, 20*(1), 1-68.

Barrett, L. F., & Salovey, P. (Eds.). (2002). *The wisdom in feeling: Psychological processes in emotional intelligence.* Guilford Press.

Barrett, P., & Burgess, E. (2020). Who masturbates? It depends: Predictors of masturbation by gender and partnership of older adults. *Innovation in Aging, 4*(Suppl. 1), 314-314.

Barry, C. T., Doucette, H., Loflin, D. C., Rivera-Hudson, N., & Herrington, L. L. (2017). "Let me take a selfie": Associations between self-photography, narcissism, and self-esteem. *Psychology of Popular Media Culture, 6*, 48-60.

Bartells, M. (2022). Genetics of happiness and wellbeing. *Biological Psychiatry, 91*(9). https://doi.org/10.1016/j.biopsych.2022.02.020

Bartlett, F. (1932). *Remembering: A study in experimental and social psychology.* Cambridge University Press.

Bartocci, G. (2004). Transcendence techniques and psychobiological mechanisms underlying religious experience. *Mental Health, Religion and Culture, 7*, 171-181.

Bartoli, F., Clerici, M., Di Brita, C., Riboldi, I., Crocamo, C., & Carra, G. (2018). Effect of clinical response to active drugs and placebo on antipsychotics and mood stabilizers relative efficacy for bipolar depression and mania: A meta-regression analysis. *Journal of Psychopharmacology, 32*(4), 416-422.

Bartoshuk, L., & Lucchina, L. (1997, January 13). Are you a supertaster? *U.S. News & World Report,* 58-59.

Barzilay, S., Feldman, D., Snir, A., Apter, A., Carli, V., Hoven, C. W., Wasserman, C., Sarchiapone, M., & Wasserman, D. (2015). The interpersonal theory of suicide and adolescent suicidal behavior. *Journal of Affective Disorders, 183*, 68-74.

Bassett, A. M., & Baker, C. (2015). Normal or abnormal? 'Normative uncertainty' in psychiatric practice. *Journal of Medical Humanities, 36*, 89-111.

Bassetti, C. L., Kallweit, U., Vignatelli, L., Plazzi, G., Lecendreux, M., Baldin, E., . . . & Lammers, G. J. (2021). European guideline and expert statements on the management of narcolepsy in adults and children. *European journal of neurology, 28*(9), 2815-2830.

Bastart, J., Branscombe, N. R., Sarda, E., & Delmas, F. (2021). Sexism and racism perceptions: It depends on who does it and why. *European Journal of Social Psychology, 51*(1), 54-67.

Bastian, B., Jetten, J, Hornsey, M. J., & Leknes, S. (2014). The positive consequences of pain: A biopsychosocial approach. *Personality and Social Psychology Review, 18*, 256-279.

Bates, J. E., & Pettit, G. S. (2015). Temperament, parenting, and social development. In J. E. Grusec & P. D. Hastings (Eds.), *Handbook of socialization: Theory and research (2nd ed.).* New York: Guilford Press.

Batson, C. (2011). *Altruism in humans.* Oxford University Press.

Batzella, F. (2021). The role of the Commission in Intergovernmental Agreements in the field of energy. A foot in the door technique? *JCMS: Journal of Common Market Studies, 59*(4), 745-761.

Bauer, P. J., Larkina, M., Güler, E., & Burch, M. (2019). Long-term autobiographical memory across middle childhood: Patterns, predictors, and implications for conceptualizations of childhood amnesia. *Memory, 27*(9), 1175-1193.

Baum, A. (1994). Behavioral, biological, and environmental interactions in disease processes. In S. Blumenthal, K. Matthews, & S. Weiss (Eds.), *New research frontiers in behavioral medicine: Proceedings of the National Conference*. NIH Publications.

Baum, A., Lorduy, K., & Jenkins, F. J. (2011). The molecular biology of stress: Cellular defense, immune response, and aging. In R. J. Contrada & A. Baum (Eds.), *The handbook of stress science: Biology, psychology, and health*. Springer Publishing.

Baumeister, R. F., Ainsworth, S. E., & Vohs, K. D. (2015). Are groups more or less than the sum of their members? The moderating role of individual identification. *Behavioral and Brain Sciences, 39*, e137. https://doi.org/10.1017/S0140525X15000618

Baumeister, R. F., & Stillman, T. (2006). Erotic plasticity: Nature, culture, gender, and sexuality. In R. D. McAnulty & M. M. Burnette (Eds.), *Sex and sexuality, Vol 1: Sexuality today: Trends and controversies*. Praeger Publishers/Greenwood Publishing.

Baumrind, D. (1971). Current patterns of parental authority. *Developmental Psychology, 4*, 1-104.

Baumrind, D. (2005). Patterns of parental authority and adolescent autonomy. *New Directions for Child and Adolescent Development, 108*, 61-69.

Bautista, D. M., Wilson, S. R., & Hoon, M. A. (2014). Why we scratch an itch: The molecules, cells and circuits of itch. *Nature Neuroscience, 17*(2), 175-182.

Bazelon, E. (2022, June 19). The battle over gender therapy. *The New York Times Magazine*, pp. 29-35.

Beam, A. (2014, August 21). Four-bit recall. *Boston Globe*, p. 1.

Beam, C. R., & Turkheimer, E. (2013). Phenotype-environment correlations in longitudinal twin models. *Development and Psychopathology, 25*, 7-16.

Bearman, C. R., Ball, L. J., & Ormerod, T. C. (2007). The structure and function of spontaneous analogising in domain-based problem solving. *Thinking & Reasoning, 13*, 273-294.

Beauchamp, M. H., Vera-Estay, E., Morasse, F., Anderson, V., & Dooley, J. (2019). Moral reasoning and decision-making in adolescents who sustain traumatic brain injury. *Brain Injury, 33*(1), 32-39.

Beck, A. T. (2019). Cognitive therapy: Reflections. In J. K. Zeig (Ed.), *The evolution of psychotherapy*. Routledge.

Beck, A. T., & Emery, G., with Greenberg, R. L. (2005). *Anxiety disorders and phobias: A cognitive perspective*. Basic Books.

Beck, A. T., Davis, D. D., & Freeman, A. (2015). *Cognitive therapy of personality disorders* (3rd ed.). Guilford Press.

Beck, M. (2015, June 2). Your body's witching hours. *Wall Street Journal*, pp. D1-D2.

Becker, J., Brackbill, D., & Centola, D. (2017). Network dynamics of social influence in the wisdom of crowds. *PNAS Proceedings of the National Academy of Sciences of the United States of America, 114*, 70-76.

Beel, E., & Berrevoet, F. (2021). Surgical treatment for chronic pain after inguinal hernia repair: A systematic literature review. *Langenbeck's Archives of Surgery, 407*, 541-548.

Beghetto, R. A., & Kaufman, J. C. (Eds.). (2010). *Nurturing creativity in the classroom*. Cambridge University Press.

Behrendt, R. (2011). *Neuroanatomy of social behaviour: An evolutionary and psychoanalytic perspective*. London England: Karnac Books.

Behrens, M., Lendon, C., & Roe, C. (2009). A common biological mechanism in cancer and Alzheimer's disease? *Current Alzheimer Research, 6*, 196-204.

Beitel, M., Wald, L. M., Midgett, A., Green, D., Cecero, J. J., Kishon, R., & Barry, D. T. (2015). Humanistic experience and psychodynamic understanding: Empirical associations among facets of self-actualization and psychological mindedness. *Person-Centered and Experiential Psychotherapies, 14*, 137-148.

Beker, M. C., Caglayan, B., Yalcin, E., Caglayan, A. B., Turkseven, S., Gurel, B., . . . & Kilic, E. (2017). Time-of-day dependent neuronal injury after ischemic stroke: implication of circadian clock transcriptional

factor bmal1 and survival kinase AKT. *Molecular neurobiology, 55*(3), 2565-2576.

Belasen, A. T., & Fortunato, M. V. (2013). Situational motivation: Challenge the binary. In M. A. Paludi (Ed.), *Psychology for business success, Vol 1: Juggling, balancing, and integrating work and family roles and responsibilities, Vol 2: Institutional equity and compliance, Vol 3: Managing, leading, and developing employees, Vol 4: Implementing best practices in human resources*. Praeger/ABC-CLIO.

Belke, T. W., Pierce, W. D., & Sexton, C. A. (2021). Effects of pre-operant running and sucrose concentration on operant wheel running on a fixed interval schedule of reinforcement. *Journal of the Experimental Analysis of Behavior, 115*(2), 510-539.

Bell, A. (2018). The neurobiology of acute pain. *The Veterinary Journal, 237*, 55-62.

Belluck, P. (2022, February 17). Covid patients more likely to develop mental health issues, study finds. *The New York Times*, p. A15.

Belluck, S. (2021, October 5). A brain implant fights depression. *The New York Times*, p. D1.

Belmont, R., Knudson, D., Costa, P. H. L. D., & Lemos, E. D. S. (2022). Meaningful learning of biomechanical concepts: An experience with physical education teachers in continuing education. *Journal of Physical Education, 32*.

Bem, D. (2012). ESP is not a psychological anomaly. *PsychCRITIQUES, 57*, 2012.

Benedetti, F., Palladini, M., Paolini, M., Melloni, E., Vai, B., De Lorenzo, R., Furlan, R., Rovere-Querini, P., Falini, A., & Mazza, M. G. (2021). Brain correlates of depression, post-traumatic distress, and inflammatory biomarkers in COVID-19 survivors: A multimodal magnetic resonance imaging study. *Brain, Behavior, and Immunity-Health, 18*, 100387. https://doi.org/10.1016/j.bbih.2021.100387

Benitez, P., de CarvalhoGomes, M. L., Bondioli, R., & Domeniconi, C. (2017). Mapping of inclusive strategies for students with intellectual disabilities and autism. *Psicologia Em Estudo, 22*, 81-93.

Benjamin, L. T., Jr. (1985). Defining aggression: An exercise for classroom discussion. *Teaching of Psychology, 12*(1), 40-42.

Ben-Porath, Y. S., Corey, D. M., & Tarescavage, A. M. (2017). Using the MMPI-2-RF in preemployment evaluations of police officer candidates. In C. L. Mitchell & E. H. Dorian (Eds.), *Police psychology and its growing impact on modern law enforcement*. Information Science Reference/IGI Global.

Benson, H., Kornhaber, A., Kornhaber, C., & LeChanu, M. N. (1993). Increases in positive psychological characteristics with a new relaxation-response curriculum in high school students. *Journal of Research and Development in Education, 27*, 226-231.

Benson, R., McTernan, N., Ryan, F., & Arensman, E. (2021). Suicide clustering and contagion: The role of the media. *Suicidologi, 26*(2).

Bentwich, J., Dobronevsky, E., Aichenbaum, S., Shorer, R., Peretz, R., Khaigrekht, M., Maron, R. G., & Rabey, J. M. (2011). Beneficial effect of repetitive transcranial magnetic stimulation combined with cognitive training for the treatment of Alzheimer's disease: A proof of concept study. *Journal of Neural Transmission, 118*, 463-471.

Beran, M. J., Smith, J., & Perdue, B. M. (2013). Language-trained chimpanzees (Pan troglodytes) name what they have seen but look first at what they have not seen. *Psychological Science, 24*, 660-666.

Berecki-Gisolf, J., McKenzie, S. J., Dobson, A. J., McFarlane, A., & McLaughlin, D. (2013). A history of comorbid depression and anxiety predicts new onset of heart disease. *Journal of Behavioral Medicine, 36*, 347-353.

Berends, Y. R., Tulen, J. H. M., Wierdsma, A. I., van Pelt, J., Kushner, S. A., & van Marle, H. J. C. (2019). Oxytocin, vasopressin and trust: Associations with aggressive behavior in healthy young males. *Physiology & Behavior, 204*, 180-185.

Berenson, A. (2019, January 5-6). Marijuana is more dangerous than you think. *Wall Street Journal*, p. 5.

Berger, D. L. (2021). *Indian and intercultural philosophy: Personhood, consciousness, and causality*. Bloomsbury Publishing.

Berger, I., Werdermann, M., Bornstein, S. R., & Steenblock, C. (2019). The adrenal gland in stress-adaptation on a cellular level. *The Journal of Steroid Biochemistry and Molecular Biology, 190*, 198-206.

Berger, J. (2022). *The catalyst: How to change anyone's mind*. Simon and Schuster.

Bergner, D. (2022, May 17). Open minds. *The New York Times Sunday Magazine*, p. 44.

Berke, D. S., Reidy, D. E., Miller, J. D., & Zeichner, A. (2017). Take it like a man: Gender-threatened men's experience of gender role discrepancy, emotion activation, and pain tolerance. *Psychology of Men & Masculinity, 18*, 62-69.

Berkowitz, L. (2001). On the formation and regulation of anger and aggression: A cognitive-neoassociationistic analysis. In W. G. Parrott (Ed.), *Emotions in social psychology: Essential readings*. Psychology Press.

Berman, M., Bernstein, L., Keating, D., Tran, A.B., & Galocha, A. (2022, July 8). The staggering scope of U.S. gun deaths goes far beyond mass shootings. *Washington Post*. https://www.washingtonpost.com/nation/interactive/2022/gun-deaths-per-year-usa/

Bernard, L. L. (1924). *Instinct: A study in social psychology*. Holt.

Bernstein, E. (2011, April 19). Friendly fight: A smarter way to say "I'm angry." *Wall Street Journal*, pp. D1, D4.

Bernstein, E. (2021, March 24). Can't sleep? Here are strategies that work. *Wall Street Journal*, P. A12.

Bernstein, L. (2021, June 18). Addiction treatment had failed. Could brain surgery save him? *Washington Post*. https://www.washingtonpost.com/health/2021/06/18/deep-brain-stimulation-addiction/

Berntsen, D., & Rubin, D. C. (2004). Cultural life scripts structure recall from autobiographical memory. *Memory and Cognition, 32*, 427-442.

Berry, D. R., Wall, C. S., Tubbs, J. D., Zeidan, F., & Brown, K. W. (2021). Short-term training in mindfulness predicts helping behavior toward racial ingroup and outgroup members. *Social Psychological and Personality Science*, 19485506211053095.

Bertakis, K., Franks, P., & Epstein, R. (2009). Patient-centered communication in primary care: Physician and patient gender and gender concordance. *Journal of Women's Health, 18*, 539-545.

Bertelli, M. O., Bianco, A., Rossi, A., Mancini, M., La Malfa, G., & Brown, I. (2019). Impact of severe intellectual disability on proxy instrumental assessment of quality of life. *Journal of Intellectual and Developmental Disability, 44*(3), 272-281.

Berto, L. M., Costa, P. D., Simoes, A. S., Gudwin, R. R., & Colombini, E. L. (2021, August). An Iowa Gambling Task-based experiment applied to robots: A study on long-term decision making. In *2021 IEEE International Conference on Development and Learning*. Institute of Electrical and Electronics Engineers.

Berzoff, J., Flanagan, L. M., & Hertz, P. (Eds.). (2021). *Inside out and outside in: Psychodynamic clinical theory and psychopathology in contemporary multicultural contexts*. Rowman & Littlefield.

Best, D. (2017). Why the mechanisms of 12-step behaviour change should matter to clinicians. *Addiction, 112*, 938-939.

Betley, J. N., Xu, S., Cao, Z. H., Gong, R., Magnus, C. J., Yu, Y., & Sternson, S. M. (2015). Neurons for hunger and thirst transmit a negative-valence teaching signal. *Nature, 521*, 180-185.

Betterton, R. T., Broad, L. M., Tsaneva-Atanasova, K., & Mellor, J. R. (2017). Acetylcholine modulates gamma frequency oscillations in the hippocampus by activation of muscarinic M1 receptors. *European Journal of Neuroscience, 45*, 1570-1585.

Bhatia, S. (2017). The semantic representation of prejudice and stereotypes. *Cognition, 164*, 46-60.

Bhogal, M. S., Farrelly, D., & Galbraith, N. (2019). The role of prosocial behaviors in mate choice: A critical review of the literature. *Current Psychology: A Journal for Diverse Perspectives on Diverse Psychological*. Advance online publication. https://doi.org/10.1007/s12144-019-00308-8.

Bialystok, E. (2011). Reshaping the mind: The benefits of bilingualism. *Canadian Journal of Experimental Psychology, 65*, 229-235.

Bialystok, E., Anderson, J. A., & Grundy, J. G. (2021). Interpreting cognitive decline in the face of cognitive reserve: Does bilingualism affect cognitive aging? *Linguistic Approaches to Bilingualism, 11*(4), 484-504.

Bieberstein, A., & Roosen, J. (2015). Gender differences in the meanings associated with food hazards: A means-end chain analysis. *Food Quality and Preference, 42*, 165-176.

Biggi, G., & Stilgoe, J. (2021). Artificial intelligence in self-driving cars research and innovation: A scientometric and bibliometric analysis. *Available at SSRN 3829897.*

Billiard, M. (2008). Narcolepsy: Current treatment options and future approaches. *Neuropsychiatric Disease and Treatment, 4*, 557-566.

Binet, A., & Simon, T. (1916). *The development of intelligence in children (The Binet-Simon Scale).* Williams & Wilkins.

Bing, W. C., & Kim, S. J. (2021). A phenomenological study of mental health enhancement in taekwondo training: Application of catharsis theory. *International Journal of Environmental Research and Public Health, 18*(8), 4082.

Bird, C. I., Modlin, N. L., & Rucker, J. J. (2021). Psilocybin and MDMA for the treatment of trauma-related psychopathology. *International Review of Psychiatry, 33*(3), 229-249.

Birk, J. L., Dennis, T. A., Shin, L. M., & Urry, H. L. (2011). Threat facilitates subsequent executive control during anxious mood. *Emotion, 11*(6), 1291-1304.

Bischoff, R. J., Springer, P. R., Felix, D. S., & Hollist, C. S. (2011). Finding the heart of medical family therapy: A content analysis of medical family therapy casebook articles. *Families, Systems, & Health, 29*, 184-196.

Bittles, A. H., Bower, C., & Hussain, R. (2007). The four ages of Down syndrome. *European Journal of Public Health, 17*, 121-225.

Bjork, R. A. (2015). Forgetting as a friend of learning. In D. S. Lindsay, A. P. Yonelinas, H. I. Roediger, D. S. Lindsay, A. P. Yonelinas, & H. I. Roediger (Eds.), *Remembering: Attributions, processes, and control in human memory: Essays in honor of Larry Jacoby.* Psychology Press.

Bjorklund, D. F. (2018). A metatheory for cognitive development (or "Piaget is dead" revisited). *Child Development, 89*(6), 2288-2302.

Bjornsdottir, E., Keenan, B. T., Eysteinsdottir, B., Arnardottir, E. S., Janson, C., Gislason, T., et al. (2015). Quality of life among untreated sleep apnea patients compared with the general population and changes after treatment with positive airway pressure. *Journal of Sleep Research, 24*, 328-338.

Bjornstad, R. (2006). Learned helplessness, discouraged workers, and multiple unemployment equilibria. *Journal of Socio-Economics, 35*, 458-475.

Black, A. L., & McCafferty, D. (1998, July 3-5). The age of contentment. *USA Weekend*, pp. 4-6.

Blackmore, S. (2018, September). Decoding the puzzle of human consciousness. *Scientific American,* pp. 49-53.

Blackwell, L. S., Rodriguez, S., & Guerra-Carrillo, B. (2015). Intelligence as a malleable construct. In S. Goldstein, D. Princiotta, & J. A. Naglieri (Eds.), *Handbook of intelligence: Evolutionary theory, historical perspective, and current concepts.* New York: Springer Science + Business Media.

Blagrove, M., Edwards, C., van Rijn, E., Reid, A., Malinowski, J., Bennett, P., et al. (2019). Insight from the consideration of REM dreams, non-REM dreams, and daydreams. *Psychology of Consciousness: Theory, Research, and Practice, 6*(2), 138-162.

Blain-Arcaro, C., & Vaillancourt, T. (2019). Longitudinal associations between externalizing problems and symptoms of depression in children and adolescents. *Journal of Clinical Child & Adolescent Psychology, 48*(1), 108-119.

Blake, A. B., & Castel, A. D. (2019). Memory and availability-biased metacognitive illusions for flags of varying familiarity. *Memory & Cognition, 47*(2), 365-382.

Blakeslee, (1992, September 29). Radical brain surgery, the earlier the better, offers epileptics hope. *The New York Times*, p. C3.

Blanton, H., Jaccard, J., & Burrows, C. N. (2015). Implications of the Implicit Association Test D-transformation for psychological assessment. *Assessment, 22*, 429-440.

Blass, T. (2004). *The man who shocked the world: The life and legacy of Stanley Milgram.* Basic Books.

Blatter, K., & Cajochen, C. (2007). Circadian rhythms in cognitive performance: Methodological constraints, protocols, theoretical underpinnings. *Physiology & Behavior, 90*, 196-208.

Blechner, M. J. (2013). New ways of conceptualizing and working with dreams. *Contemporary Psychoanalysis, 49*, 259-275.

Blumer, V., & Rodriguez, F. (2021). Heterogeneity, nativity, and disaggregation of cardiovascular risk and outcomes in Hispanic Americans. In K. C. Ferdinand, H. A. Taylor Jr., & C. J. Rodriguez (Eds.), *Cardiovascular disease in racial and ethnic minority populations.* Springer.

Boag, S. (2015). Repression, defence, and the psychology of science. In S. Boag, L. W. Brakel, & V. Talvitie (Eds.), *Philosophy, science, and psychoanalysis: A critical meeting.* Karnac Books.

Boag, S. (2017). On dreams and motivation: Comparison of Freud's and Hobson's views. *Frontiers in Psychology, 8*, 1-13.

Boag, S., Brakel, L. W., & Talvitie, V. (2015). *Philosophy, science, and psychoanalysis: A critical meeting.* Karnac Books.

Bockting, C. L., Smid, N. H., Koeter, M. W., Spinhoven, P., Beck, A. T., & Schene, A. H. (2015). Enduring effects of preventive cognitive therapy in adults remitted from recurrent depression: a 10 year follow-up of a randomized controlled trial. *Journal of Affective Disorders, 185*, 188-194.

Boeve-de Pauw, J., Donche, V., & Van Petegem, P. (2011). Adolescents' environmental worldview and personality: An explorative study. *Journal of Environmental Psychology, 31*, 109-117.

Bogaert, A. F., & Skorska, M. N. (2020). A short review of biological research on the development of sexual orientation. *Hormones and Behavior, 119*, 104659.

Bohm, M. K., Liu, Y., Esser, M. B., Mesnick, J. B., Lu, H., Pan, Y., & Greenlund, K. J. (2021). Binge drinking among adults, by select characteristics and state—United States, 2018. *Morbidity and Mortality Weekly Report, 70*, 1441-1446.

Bohnemeyer, J. (2020). Linguistic relativity: From Whorf to now. In D. Gutzmann, L. Matthewson, C. Meier, H. Rullmann, & T. E. Zimmerman (Eds.), *The Wiley Blackwell companion to semantics.* Wiley.

Bolkan, S. (2015). Intellectually stimulating students' intrinsic motivation: The mediating influence of affective learning and student engagement. *Communication Reports, 28*, 80-91.

Bond, J. C., Geller, R. J., White, K. O., Hatch, E. E., Rothman, K. J., & Wise, L. A. (2022). Concordance of self-reported sexual intercourse frequency between members of mixed-sex couples attempting conception. *The Canadian Journal of Human Sexuality,* (aop), e20210059.

Bonin, E. A., Martens, G., Cassol, H., Chatelle, C., Laureys, S., & Thibaut, A. (2021). PET imaging in altered states of consciousness: Coma, sleep, and hypnosis. In R. A. J. O. Dierckx, A. Otte, E. F. J. Vries, A. Waarde, & K. L. Leenders (Eds.), *PET and SPECT in Neurology* (pp. 1149-1176). Springer.

Bonini, L. (2017). The extended mirror neuron network: Anatomy, origin, and functions. *The Neuroscientist, 23*, 56-67.

Bonomo, J. P. (2021). Back to the tower. *The College Mathematics Journal, 52*(4), 265-273.

Booker, J. A., Dunsmore, J. C., & Fivush, R. (2021). Adjustment factors of attachment, hope, and motivation in emerging adult well-being. *Journal of Happiness Studies, 22*(7), 3259-3284.

Borgmann-Winter, K. E., Wang, K., Bandyopadhyay, S., Torshizi, A. D., Blair, I. A., & Hahn, C.-G. (2019). The proteome and its dynamics: A missing piece for integrative multi-omics in schizophrenia. *Schizophrenia Research.* https://doi.org/10.1016/j.schres.2019.07.025.

Borman, G. D., Choi, Y., & Hall, G. J. (2021). The impacts of a brief middle-school self-affirmation intervention help propel African American and Latino students through high school. *Journal of Educational Psychology, 113*(3), 605-620. https://doi.org/10.1037/edu0000570

Boroditsky, L. (2010, July 24-25). Lost in translation. *Wall Street Journal*, p. W3.

Bose, A., Patra, A., Antoniou, G. E., Stickland, R. C., & Belke, E. (2022). Verbal fluency difficulties in aphasia: A combination of lexical and executive control deficits. *International Journal of Language & Communication Disorders.* Advance online publication. https://doi.org/10.1111/1460-6984.12710

Boser, U. (2017). *Learn better: Mastering the skills for success in life, business, and school, or, how to become an expert in just about anything.* Rodale Books.

Bouchard, C. (2021). Genetics of obesity: What we have learned over decades of research. *Obesity, 29*(5), 802-820.

Bouchard, T. J., Jr. (2004). Genetic influence on human psychological traits: A survey. *Current Directions in Psychological Science, 13*, 148-151.

Bouchard, T. J., Jr., Segal, N. L., Tellegen, A., McGue, M., Keyes, M., & Krueger, R. (2004). Genetic influence on social attitudes: Another challenge to psychology from behavior genetics. In L. F. DiLalla (Ed.), *Behavior genetics principles: Perspectives in development, personality, and psychopathology.* Washington, DC: American Psychological Association.

Boulet, C., Lopez-Castroman, J., Mouchabac, S., Olié, E., Courtet, P., Thouvenot, E., Abbar, M., & Conejero, I. (2022). Stress response in dissociation and conversion disorders: A systematic review. *Neuroscience & Biobehavioral Reviews, 132*, 957-967.

Bourguignon, E., & Evascu, T. L. (1977). Altered states of consciousness within a general evolutionary perspective: A holocultural analysis. *Behavior Science Research, 12*(3), 197-216.

Bourne, L. E., Dominowski, R. L., Loftus, E. F., & Healy, A. F. (1986). *Cognitive processes* (2nd ed.). Prentice Hall.

Bouton, M. E., Todd, T. P., Vurbic, D., & Winterbauer, N. E. (2011). Renewal after the extinction of free operant behavior. *Learning & Behavior, 39*, 57-67.

Bouvard, M., Fournet, N., Denis, A., Sixdenier, A., & Clark, D. (2017). Intrusive thoughts in patients with obsessive compulsive disorder and non-clinical participants: A comparison using the International Intrusive Thought Interview Schedule. *Cognitive Behaviour Therapy, 46*, 287-299.

Bouvard, M., & Roulin, J. (2017). Exploratory factor analysis of the French version of the Big Five Questionnaire for Children (BFQ-C). *Swiss Journal of Psychology, 76*, 125-130.

Bower, J. E., Radin, A., & Kuhlman, K. R. (2022). Psychoneuroimmunology in the time of COVID-19: Why neuro-immune interactions matter for mental and physical health. *Behaviour Research and Therapy, 104104.*

Boxer, P., Huesmann, L., Bushman, B., O'Brien, M., & Moceri, D. (2009). The role of violent media preference in cumulative developmental risk for violence and general aggression. *Journal of Youth and Adolescence, 38*, 417-428.

Boylan, J. M., & Ryff, C. D. (2015). Psychological well-being and metabolic syndrome: Findings from the Midlife in the United States national sample. *Psychosomatic Medicine, 77*, 548-558.

Boyle, G. J. (2019). Overarching personality paradigm: A neo-Cattellian psychometric model. *Personality and Individual Differences, 147*, 317-325.

Braasch, M., Buchwald, P., & Hobfoll, S. (2019). Commerce and crossover of resources in Facebook groups—A qualitative study. *Computers in Human Behavior, 99*, 101-108.

Bradford, A. C., & Bradford, W. D. (2017). Factors driving the diffusion of medical marijuana legalisation in the United States. *Drugs: Education, Prevention & Policy, 24*, 75-84.

Bradley, S., & Price, N. (2021). *Critical thinking: Proven strategies to improve decision making skills, increase intuition and think smarter.* Createspace Independent Publishing.

Bradshaw, A. (2019). Temperature and civil conflict. *Nature Human Behaviour, 3*(6), 548.

Brady, T., Allen, M., & DeStefano, I. (2021). Chunking is not all-or-none: Hierarchical representations preserve perceptual detail within chunks. *Journal of Vision, 21*(9), 2312-2312.

Brafman, A. H. (2011). *Fostering independence: Helping and caring in psychodynamic therapies.* Karnac Books.

Brailey, C. D., & Slatton, B. C. (2019). Women, work, and inequality in the US: Revising the second shift. *Journal of Sociology, 7*(1), 29-35.

Brandao, T., Tavares, R., Schulz, M. S., & Matos, P. M. (2015). Measuring emotion regulation and emotional expression in breast cancer patients: A systematic review. *Clinical Psychology Review, 43*, 114-127.

Brandon, M., & Saffran, J. R. (2011). Apparent motion enhances visual rhythm discrimination in infancy. *Attention, Perception, & Psychophysics, 73*, 1016-1020.

Brandt, J., & Bakker, A. (2018). Neuropsychological investigation of "the Amazing Memory Man." *Neuropsychology, 32*(3), 304.

Brang, D., Rouw, R., Ramachandran, V. S., & Coulson, S. (2011). Similarly shaped letters evoke similar colors in grapheme-color synesthesia. *Neuropsychologia, 49*, 1355-1358.

Branković, M. (2019). Who believes in ESP: Cognitive and motivational determinants of the belief in extrasensory perception. *Europe's Journal of Psychology, 15*(1), 120.

Brausch, A. M., & Gutierrez, P. M. (2009). Differences in non-suicidal self-injury and suicide attempts in adolescents. *Journal of Youth and Adolescence, 21*, 46-51.

Brawer, J., & Amir, O. (2021). Mapping the 'funny bone': Neuroanatomical correlates of humor creativity in professional comedians. *Social Cognitive and Affective Neuroscience, 16*(9), 915-925.

Brazelton, T. B. (1969). *Infants and mothers: Differences in development.* Dell.

Breland, K., & Breland, M. (1966). *Animal behavior.* New York: Macmillan.

Breslin, C. W., & Safer, M. A. (2011). Effects of event valence on long-term memory for two baseball championship games. *Psychological Science, 20*, 1-5.

Breuninger, M. M., Grosso, J. A., Hunter, W., & Dolan, S. L. (2020). Treatment of alcohol use disorder: Integration of Alcoholics Anonymous and cognitive behavioral therapy. *Training and Education in Professional Psychology, 14*(1), 19-26. https://doi. org/10.1037/tep0000265

Bridgman, T., Cummings, S., & Ballard, J. (2019). Who built Maslow's pyramid? A history of the creation of management studies' most famous symbol and its implications for management education. *Academy of Management Learning & Education, 18.*

Brody, D. J., & Gu, Q. (2020). Antidepressant use among adults: United States, 2015-2018. NCHS Data Brief, 377. https://www.cdc.gov/nchs/products/ databriefs/db377.htm

Brody, J. (2017, April 17). The case of not taking your medicine. *The New York Times.* https://www. nytimes.com/2017/04/17/well/the-cost-of-not-taking-your-medicine.html

Brody, J. (2019, April 30). Virtual reality as therapy for pain. *The New York Times*, p. D7.

Brody, S., & Costa, R. M. (2017). Vaginal orgasm is associated with indices of women's better psychological, intimate relationship, and psychophysiological function. *Canadian Journal of Human Sexuality, 26*, 1-4.

Broeders, R., van den Bos, K., Müller, P. A., & Ham, J. (2011). Should I save or should I not kill? How people solve moral dilemmas depends on which rule is most accessible. *Journal of Experimental Social Psychology, 47*, 923-934.

Bronstein, M. V., Pennycook, G., Bear, A., Rand, D. G., & Cannon, T. D. (2019). Belief in fake news is associated with delusionality, dogmatism, religious fundamentalism, and reduced analytic thinking. *Journal of Applied Research in Memory and Cognition, 8*(1), 108-117.

Broockman, D., & Kalla, J. (2016). Durably reducing transphobia: A field experiment on door-to-door canvassing. *Science, 352*, 220-224.

Brookes, G., & Harvey, K. (2015). Peddling a semiotics of fear: A critical examination of scare tactics and commercial strategies in public health promotion. *Social Semiotics, 25*(1), 57-80.

Brooks, L. A., Bloomer, M. J., & Manias, E. (2019). Culturally sensitive communication at the end-of-life in the intensive care unit: A systematic review. *Australian Critical Care, 32*(6), 516-523.

Brown, A. M., Opoku, F. O., & Stenger, M. R. (2018). Neonatal contrast sensitivity and visual acuity: basic psychophysics. *Translational Vision Science & Technology, 7*(3), 18-18.

Brown, M. W., & Banks, P. J. (2015). In search of a recognition memory engram. *Neuroscience and Biobehavioral Reviews, 50*, 12-28.

Brown, P. (Ed.). (2022). *The transfer of care: Psychiatric deinstitutionalization and its aftermath* (Vol. 7). Routledge.

Brown, P. K., & Wald, G. (1964). Visual pigments in single rod and cones of the human retina. *Science, 144*, 45-52.

Brown, R. (1958). How shall a thing be called? *Psychological Review, 65*, 14-21.

Brown, T. R., Xu, K. Y., & Glowinski, A. L. (2021). Cognitive behavioral therapy and the implementation of antiracism. *JAMA Psychiatry, 78*(8), 819-820.

Brown-Chidsey, R., & Andren, K. J. (Eds.). (2015). *Assessment for intervention: A problem-solving approach* (2nd ed). The Guilford Press.

Browne, D. (2022, January 7). Who let the dogs in? Covid-sniffing canines are helping keep Metallica, Eric Church on the road. *Rolling Stone.* https://www. rollingstone.com/music/music-news/ covid-sniffing-dogs-concert-tours-1280953

Browne, J., Penn, D. L., Meyer-Kalos, P. S., Mueser, K. T., Estroff, S. E., Brunette, M. F., Correll, C. U., Robinson, J., Rosenheck, R. A., Schooler, N., Robinson, D. G., Addington, J., Marcy, P., & Kane, J. M. (2017). Psychological well-being and mental health recovery in the NIMH RAISE early treatment program. *Schizophrenia Research, 185*, 167-172.

Brucato, G., Appelbaum, P. S., Hesson, H., Shea, E. A., Dishy, G., Lee, K., Pia, T., Syed, F., Villalobos, A., Wall, M. M., Lieberman, J. A., & Girgis, R. R. (2021). Psychotic symptoms in mass shootings v. mass murders not involving firearms: Findings from the Columbia mass murder database. *Psychological Medicine, 17*, 1-9.

Brucker, B., Ehlis, A., Häußinger, F. B., Fallgatter, A. J., & Gerjets, P. (2015). Watching corresponding gestures facilitates learning with animations by activating human mirror-neurons: An fNIRS study. *Learning and Instruction, 36*, 27-37.

Bruehl, S., Burns, J. W., Gupta, R., Buvanendran, A., Chont, M., Orlowska, D., Schuster, E., & France, C. R. (2017). Do resting plasma β-endorphin levels predict responses to opioid analgesics? *Clinical Journal of Pain, 33*, 12-20.

Bruggeman, H., Yonas, A., & Konczak, J. (2007). The processing of linear perspective and binocular information for action and perception. *Neuropsychologia, 45*, 1420-1426.

Bruni, L., Pelligra, V., Reggiani, T., & Rizzolli, M. (2019). The pied piper: Prizes, incentives, and motivation crowding-in. *Journal of Business Ethics*, 1-16.

Bruno, A., Celebre, L., Torre, G., Pandolfo, G., Mento, C., Cedro, C., Zoccali, R. A., & Muscatello, M. R. A. (2019). Focus on disruptive mood dysregulation disorder: A review of the literature. *Psychiatry Research, 279*, 323-330.

Bruno, D. (2016, November 23). An electric shock therapy stops self-harm among the autistic, but at what cost? *Washington Post Magazine.* https://www.

washingtonpost.com/lifestyle/magazine/an-electric-shock-therapy-stops-self-harm-among-the-autistic-but-at-what-cost/2016/11/21/b9b06c64-8f2c-11e6-9c85-ac42097b8cc0.story.html

Bruton, A. M., Shearer, D. A., & Mellalieu, S. D. (2019). Who said "there is no 'I' in team"? The effects of observational learning content level on efficacy beliefs in groups. *Psychology of Sport and Exercise, 45*, 101563.

Bryant, W. T., Livingston, N. A., McNulty, J. L., Choate, K. T., & Brummel, B. J. (2021). Examining Minnesota Multiphasic Personality Inventory-2-Restructured Form (MMPI-2-RF) scale scores in a transgender and gender diverse sample. *Psychological Assessment, 33*(12), 1239-1246. https://doi.org/10.1037/pas0001087

Bubola, E. (2021, August 21). Losing a perfect palate, and desperate to reclaim it. *The New York Times*, p. A9.

Bucaille, A., Jarry, C., Allard, J., Brochard, S., Peudenier, S., & Roy, A. (2021). Neuropsychological profile of intellectually gifted children: A systematic review. *Journal of the International Neuropsychological Society, 28*(4), 424-440.

Buck, M. C., McCormick, A. N., Meagher, M. M., Kauppila, G., & Witt, T. J. (2021). Fulfilling a Need: A Residency-Based Program to Preserve a Suboxone Treatment Program in a Rural Community. *Annals of family medicine, 19*(6), 561-562.

Buckman, J., Saunders, R., Stott, J., Arundell, L., O'Driscoll, C., Davies, M., Eley, T. C., Hollon, S. D., Kendrick, T., Ambler, G., Cohen, Z. D., Watkins, E., Gilbody, S., Wiles, N., Kessler, D., Richards, D., Brabyn, S., Littlewood, E., DeRubeis, R. J., Lewis, G., et al. (2021). Role of age, gender and marital status in prognosis for adults with depression: An individual patient data meta-analysis. *Epidemiology and Psychiatric Sciences, 30*, E42. https://doi. org/10.1017/S2045796021000342

Buckner, J. D., & Shah, S. M. (2015). Fitting in and feeling fine: Conformity and coping motives differentially mediate the relationship between social anxiety and drinking problems for men and women. *Addiction Research & Theory, 23*, 231-237.

Budenz, A., Purtle, J., Klassen, A., Yom-Tov, E., Yudell, M., & Massey, P. (2018). The case of a mass shooting and violence-related mental illness stigma on twitter. *Stigma and Health.* https://doi-org.silk.library. umass.edu/10.1037/sah0000155.

Buecker, S., & Horstmann, K. T. (2021). Loneliness and social isolation during the COVID-19 pandemic: A systematic review enriched with empirical evidence from a large-scale diary study. *European Psychologist, 26*(4), 272.

Buhl, H. M., Noack, P., & Kracke, B. (2018). The role of parents and peers in the transition from university to work life. *Journal of Career Development, 45*(6), 523-535.

Bulf, H., Johnson, S. P., & Valenza, E. (2011). Visual statistical learning in the newborn infant. *Cognition, 121*, 127-132.

Bulik, C. M., Blake, L., & Austin, J. (2019). Genetics of eating disorders: What the clinician needs to know. *Psychiatric Clinics, 42*(1), 59-73.

Bulkeley, K. (2020, June 25). Dreams about recent protests about racial injustice. *Psychology Today.* Downloaded from https://www.psychologytoday. com/us/blog/dreaming-in-the-digital-age/202006/ dreams-about-recent-protests-against-racial-injustice, January 10, 2022.

Bull, M. J. (2020). Down syndrome. *New England Journal of Medicine, 382*(24), 2344-2352.

Bullivant Ngati Pikiao, K., McClunie-Trust, P., & Syminton Te Atiawa, K. (2021). A meta ethnography of the cultural constructs of menopause in indigenous women and the context of Aotearoa/ New Zealand. *Health Care for Women International*, 1-21. Advance online publication. https://doi.org/1 0.1080/07399332.2021.1923717

Bunce, J. A. (2015). Incorporating ecology and social system into formal hypotheses to guide field studies of color vision in primates. *American Journal of Primatology, 77*, 516-526.

Buon, M., Habib, M., & Frey, D. (2017). Moral development: Conflicts and compromises. In J. A.

Sommerville & J. Decety (Eds.), *Social cognition: Development across the life span*. Routledge/Taylor & Francis Group.

Bureau of Labor Statistics, U.S. Department of Labor, Occupational Outlook Handbook, Psychologists, at https://www.bls.gov/ooh/life-physical-and-social-science/psychologists.htm (visited February 13, 2022).

Bureau, J., Martin, J., Yurkowski, K., Schmiedel, S., Quan, J., Moss, E., Deneault, A-A., & Pallanca, D. (2017). Correlates of child-father and child-mother attachment in the preschool years. *Attachment & Human Development*, 19, 130-150.

Burger, C., & Bachmann, L. (2021). Perpetration and victimization in offline and cyber contexts: A variable-and person-oriented examination of associations and differences regarding domain-specific self-esteem and school adjustment. *International Journal of Environmental Research and Public Health*, 18(19), 10429.

Burger, J. M. (2009). Replicating Milgram: Would people still obey today? *American Psychologist*, 64, 1-11.

Burlingame, G. M., McClendon, D. T., & Yang, C. (2018). Cohesion in group therapy: A meta-analysis. *Psychotherapy*, 55(4), 384-398. https://doi.org/10.1037/pst0000173

Burnette, J. L., Pollack, J. M., & Forsyth, D. R. (2011). Leadership in extreme contexts: A groupthink analysis of the May 1996 Mount Everest disaster. *Journal of Leadership Studies*, 4(4), 29-40.

Burns, A. C., Saxena, R., Vetter, C., Phillips, A. J., Lane, J. M., & Cain, S. W. (2021). Time spent in outdoor light is associated with mood, sleep, and circadian rhythm-related outcomes: A cross-sectional and longitudinal study in over 400,000 UK Biobank participants. *Journal of Affective Disorders*, 295, 347-352.

Burns, G. W. (2017). *101 stories for enhancing happiness and well-being: Using metaphors in positive psychology and therapy*. Routledge/Taylor & Francis Group.

Burri, A., Spector, T., & Qazi, R. (2015). Common genetic factors among sexual orientation, gender nonconformity, and number of sex partners in female twins: Implications for the evolution of homosexuality. *Journal of Sexual Medicine*, 12, 1004-1011.

Burton, L., Bensimon, E., Allimant, J., Kinsman, R., Levin, A., Kovacs, L., Koskorelos, E., & Bahrami, J. (2013). Relationship of prosody perception to personality and aggression. *Current Psychology: A Journal for Diverse Perspectives on Diverse Psychological Issues*, 32, 275-280.

Burton, L. (2020). *Empty: A memoir*. Random House.

Burt, S. A., Plaisance, K. S., & Hambrick, D. Z. (2019). Understanding "what could be:" A call for "experimental behavioral genetics." *Behavior Genetics*, 49(2), 235-243.

Buscemi, V., Chang, W.-J., Liston, M. B., McAuley, J. H., & Schabrun, S. M. (2019). The role of perceived stress and life stressors in the development of chronic musculoskeletal pain disorders: A systematic review. *The Journal of Pain*. https://doi.org/10.1016/j.jpain.2019.02.008.

Busch, A. J., Morey, L. C., & Hopwood, C. J. (2017). Exploring the assessment of the DSM-5 alternative model for personality disorders with the personality assessment inventory. *Journal of Personality Assessment*, 99, 211-218.

Bustillo, J. R., Jones, T., Chen, H., Lemke, N., Abbott, C., Qualls, C., Stromberg, S., Canive, J., & Gasparovic, C. (2017). Glutamatergic and neuronal dysfunction in gray and white matter: A spectroscopic imaging study in a large schizophrenia sample. *Schizophrenia Bulletin*, 43, 611-619.

Butler, L. T., & Berry, D. C. (2004). Understanding the relationship between repetition priming and mere exposure. *British Journal of Psychology*, 95, 467-487.

Butler, S. (2009). Mamie Katherine Phipps Clark (1917-1983). The Encyclopedia of Arkansas History & Culture. Retrieved March 2, 2022.

Bylund, E., & Athanasopoulos, P. (2017). The Whorfian time warp: Representing duration through the language hourglass. *Journal of Experimental Psychology: General*, 146, 911-916.

Byrd, D. A., & Rivera-Mindt, M. G. (2022). Neuropsychology's race problem does not begin or end with demographically adjusted norms. *Nature Reviews Neurology*, 18(3), 125-126.

Cabello, R., Gómez-Leal, R., Gutiérrez-Cobo, M. J., Megías-Robles, A., Salovey, P., & Fernández-Berrocal, P. (2021). Ability emotional intelligence in parents and their offspring. *Current Psychology*, 1-7.

Cachero-Martínez, S., & Vázquez-Casielles, R. (2021). Building consumer loyalty through e-shopping experiences: The mediating role of emotions. *Journal of Retailing and Consumer Services*, 60, 102481.

Cacioppo, J. T., Berntson, G. G., & Crites, S. L., Jr. (1996). Social neuroscience: Principles of psychophysiological arousal and response. In E. T. Higgins & A. W. Kruglanski (Eds.), *Social psychology: Handbook of basic principles*. Guilford.

Cacioppo, J. T., & Decety, J. (2009). What are the brain mechanisms on which psychological processes are based? *Perspectives on Psychological Science*, 4, 10-18.

Cahalan, S. (2020). Insane places. *New Scientist*, 245(3268), 38-40.

Callahan, M. P., & Zukowski, K. T. (2019). Reactions to transgender women and men in public restrooms: Correlates and gender differences. *Journal of Homosexuality*, 66(1), 117-138.

Calo, M., Judd, B., Chipchase, L., Blackstock, F., & Peiris, C. L. (2022). Grit, resilience, mindset, and academic success in physical therapist students: A cross-sectional, multicenter study. *Physical Therapy*. Advance online publication. https://doi.org/10.1093/ptj/pzac038

Calvert, S. L., Appelbaum, M., Dodge, K. A., Graham, S., Nagayama Hall, G. C., Hamby, S., Fasig-Caldwell, L. G., Citkowicz, M., Galloway, D. P., & Hedges, L. V. (2017). The American Psychological Association Task Force assessment of violent video games: Science in the service of public interest. *American Psychologist*, 72, 126-143.

Cameron, C. D., Spring, V. L., & Todd, A. R. (2017). The empathy impulse: A multinomial model of intentional and unintentional empathy for pain. *Emotion*, 17, 395-411.

Campagnoli, C., & Domini, F. (2019). Does depth-cue combination yield identical biases in perception and grasping? *Journal of Experimental Psychology: Human Perception and Performance*, 45(5), 659-680.

Campo, M., Zadro, J. R., Pappas, E., Monticone, M., Secci, C., Scalzitti, D., Lucas Findley, J., & Graham, P. L. (2021). The effectiveness of biofeedback for improving pain, disability and work ability in adults with neck pain: A systematic review and meta-analysis. *Musculoskeletal Science and Practice*, 52, 102317.

Campos, R. C. (2011). "It might be what I am": Looking at the use of Rorschach in psychological assessment. *Journal of Projective Psychology & Mental Health*, 18, 28-38.

Canady, B. E., & Larzo, M. (2022). Overconfidence in managing health concerns: The Dunning-Kruger effect and health literacy. *Journal of Clinical Psychology in Medical Settings*, 1-9.

Canady, V. A. (2019). Anorexia nervosa may have both metabolic, psychiatric origins. *Mental Health Weekly*, 29(30), 4-6.

Canady, V. A. (2019). APA annual stress survey finds 2020 election one major cause. *Mental Health Weekly*, 29(43), 6-7.

Canchy, L., Girardeau, P., Durand, A., Vouillac-Mendoza, C., & Ahmed, S. H. (2021). Pharmacokinetics trumps pharmacodynamics during cocaine choice: a reconciliation with the dopamine hypothesis of addiction. *Neuropsychopharmacology*, 46(2), 288-296.

Cannas Aghedu, F., Veneziani, C. A., Manari, T., Feybesse, C., & Bisiacchi, P. S. (2019). Assessing passionate love: Italian validation of the PLS (reduced version). *Sexual and Relationship Therapy*, 1-12.

Cannon, W. B. (1929). Organization for physiological homeostatics. *Physiological Review*, 9, 280-289.

Cantarero, K., Gamian-Wilk, M., & Dolinski, D. (2017). Being inconsistent and compliant: The moderating role of the preference for consistency in the door-in-the-face technique. *Personality and Individual Differences*, 115, 54-57.

Cantone, J. A., Martinez, L. N., Willis-Esqueda, C., & Miller, T. (2019). Sounding guilty: How accent bias affects juror judgments of culpability. *Journal of Ethnicity in Criminal Justice*, 17(3), 228-253.

Canton, M., Gall, D. L., Feillet, F., Bonnemains, C., & Roy, A. (2019). Neuropsychological profile of children with early and continuously treated phenylketonuria: Systematic review and future approaches. *Journal of the International Neuropsychological Society*, 25(6), 624-643.

Cao, R., Nosofsky, R. M., & Shiffrin, R. M. (2017). The development of automaticity in short-term memory search: Item-response learning and category learning. *Journal of Experimental Psychology: Learning, Memory, and Cognition*, 43, 669-679.

Capone Jr, A., & Drenser, K. A. (2021). Teleophthalmology for the newborn eye: Telemedicine for an overlooked patient population. *Ophthalmic Surgery, Lasers and Imaging Retina*, 52(S2), S4-S5.

Capraro, V., & Sippel, J. (2017). Gender differences in moral judgment and the evaluation of gender-specified moral agents. *Cognitive Processing*, 18(4), 399-405.

Caputi, T. L., & McLellan, A. T. (2017). Truth and DARE: Is DARE's new Keepin' IT REAL curriculum suitable for American nationwide implementation? *Drugs: Education, Prevention & Policy*, 24(1), 49-57.

Caratala, S., & Maxwell, C. (2020, May 7). Health disparities by race and ethnicity. Center for American Progress. https://www.americanprogress.org/article/health-disparities-race-ethnicity/

Caravà, M. (2021). An exploration into enactive forms of forgetting. *Phenomenology and the Cognitive Sciences*, 20(4), 703-722.

Carcea, I., & Froemke, R. C. (2019). Biological mechanisms for observational learning. *Current Opinion in Neurobiology*, 54, 178-185.

Carciofo, R., Song, N., Du, F., Wang, M. M., & Zhang, K. (2017). Metacognitive beliefs mediate the relationship between mind wandering and negative affect. *Personality and Individual Differences*, 107, 78-87.

Card, N. A. (2017). Developmental methodology: I. Developmental methodology as a central subdiscipline of developmental science. *Monographs of the Society for Research in Child Development*, 82, 7-12.

Carey, B. (2015, October 20). New approach may alleviate schizophrenia. *The New York Times*, p. A1.

Carey, B. (2016, May 30). After thriving in combat tours, veterans are struggling at home. *The New York Times*, pp. A1, A3.

Carhart-Harris, R. (2007). Speed > Ecstasy > Ritalin: The science of amphetamines. *Journal of Psychopharmacology*, 21, 225.

Carleton, R. N., Duranceau, S., Freeston, M. H., Boelen, P. A., McCabe, R. E., & Antony, M. M. (2014). "But it might be a heart attack": Intolerance of uncertainty and panic disorder symptoms. *Journal of Anxiety Disorders*, 28, 463-470.

Carlstedt, R. A. (2017). Sports performance. In G. R. Elkins (Ed.), *Handbook of medical and psychological hypnosis: Foundations, applications, and professional issues*. Springer.

Carmichael, S. L., Ma, C., Feldkamp, M. L., Shaw, G. M., & National Birth Defects Prevention Study. (2019). Comparing usual dietary intakes among subgroups of mothers in the year before pregnancy. *Public Health Reports*, 134(2), 155-163.

Carn, D., Lanaspa, M. A., Benner, S. A., Andrews, P., Dudley, R., Andres-Hernando, A., . . . & Johnson, R. J. (2021). The role of thrifty genes in the origin of alcoholism: A narrative review and hypothesis. *Alcoholism: Clinical and Experimental Research*. Advance online publication. https://doi.org/10.1111/acer.14655

Carnagey, N., Anderson, C., & Bartholow, B. (2007). Media violence and social neuroscience: New questions and new opportunities. *Current Directions in Psychological Science*, 16, 178-182.

Carnagey, N., Anderson, C. A., & Bushman, B. J. (2007). The effect of video game violence on physiological desensitization to real-life violence. *Journal of Experimental Social Psychology, 43,* 489-496.

Carnevale, M., Luna, D., & Lerman, D. (2017). Brand linguistics: A theory-driven framework for the study of language in branding. *International Journal of Research in Marketing, 34*(2), 572-591.

Caron, C. (2022, May 31). What gun violence does to our mental health. *The New York Times,* p. D7.

Carpenter, S. M., & Niedenthal, P. M. (2020). Disrupting facial action increases risk taking. *Emotion.* http://dx.doi.org/10.1037/emo0000597

Carpita, B., Muti, D., Nardi, B., Benedetti, F., Cappelli, A., Cremone, I. M., Carmassi, C., & Dell'Osso, L. (2021). Biochemical correlates of video game use: From physiology to pathology. A narrative review. *Life, 11*(8), 775.

Carr, C. M., Wolchik, S. A., Tein, J. Y., & Sandler, I. (2019). Mother-adolescent and father-adolescent relationships after divorce: Relations with emerging adults' romantic attachment. *Journal of Divorce & Remarriage, 60*(3), 194-210.

Carr, T. (2019, June). Real pain relief, now! *Consumer Reports,* pp. 24-33.

Carroll, D. W. (2017). The ethics of memory research. *PsycCRITIQUES, 62,* 15-22.

Carroll, R. (2016, July 14). Starved, tortured, forgotten: Genie, the feral child who left a mark on researchers. *The Guardian.* https://www.theguardian.com/society/2016/jul/14/genie-feral-child-los-angeles-researchers

Carson, C. N., & Kouros, C. D. (2022). Couples' perceptions of each other's depressive symptoms: Empathic accuracy and assumed similarity bias. *Journal of Social and Personal Relationships, 39*(2), 285-302.

Cartwright, R., Agargum, M. Y., & Kirkby, J. (2006). Relation of dreams to waking concerns. *Psychiatry Research, 141,* 261-270.

Caruso, E. (2008). Use of experienced retrieval ease in self and social judgments. *Journal of Experimental Social Psychology, 44,* 148-155.

Carvalho, J., & Nobre, P. (2011). Biopsychosocial determinants of men's sexual desire: Testing an integrative model. *Journal of Sexual Medicine, 8,* 754-763.

Case, R., & Okamoto, Y. (1996). The role of central conceptual structures in the development of children's thought. *Monographs of the Society for Research in Child Development, 61,* v-265.

Cassells, J. V. S. (2007). The virtuous roles of truth and justice in integral dialogue: Research, theory, and model practice of the evolution of collective consciousness. *Dissertation Abstracts International Section A: Humanities and Social Sciences, 67*(10-A), 4005.

Catalano, L. T., Wynn, J. K., Lee, J., & Green, M. F. (2021). A comparison of stages of attention for social and nonsocial stimuli in schizophrenia: An ERP study. *Schizophrenia Research, 238,* 128-136.

Catmur, C., & Heyes, C. (2019). Mirroring "meaningful" actions: Sensorimotor learning modulates imitation of goal-directed actions. *The Quarterly Journal of Experimental Psychology, 72*(2), 322-334.

Catrysse, L., Gijbels, D., & Donche, V. (2019). A systematic review on the conceptualization and operationalization of students' levels of processing in functional magnetic resonance imaging studies. *Mind, Brain, and Education, 13*(3), 198-210.

Cauberghe, V., Van Wesenbeeck, I., De Jans, S., Hudders, L., & Ponnet, K. (2021). How adolescents use social media to cope with feelings of loneliness and anxiety during COVID-19 lockdown. *Cyberpsychology, Behavior, and Social Networking, 24*(4), 250-257.

Cavelti, M., Kircher, T., Nagels, A., Strik, W., & Homan, P. (2018). Is formal thought disorder in schizophrenia related to structural and functional aberrations in the language network? A systematic review of neuroimaging findings. *Schizophrenia Research, 199,* 2-16.

Cavicchioli, M., Ferrucci, R., Guidetti, M., Canevini, M. P., Pravettoni, G., & Galli, F. (2021, January). What will be the impact of the Covid-19 quarantine on psychological distress? Considerations based on a systematic review of pandemic outbreaks. In Healthcare (Vol. 9, No. 1, p. 101). MDPI.

Cecchini, M. P., Knaapila, A., Hoffmann, E., Boschi, F., Hummel, T., & Iannilli, E. (2019). A cross-cultural survey of umami familiarity in European countries. *Food Quality and Preference, 74,* 172-178.

Celi, L. A. G., Fraser, H. S. F., Nikore, V., Osorio, J. S., & Paik, K. (2017). *Global health informatics: Principles of eHealth and mHealth to improve quality of care.* MIT Press.

Center for Collegiate Mental Health. (2019, January). *2018 annual report* (Publication no. STA 19-180), p. 17.

Center for Medicare Advocacy. (2022). Racial and ethnic health care disparities. https://medicareadvocacy.org/medicare-info/health-care-disparities/

Center for Science in the Public Interest. (nd). Caffeine chart. https://cspinet.org/eating-healthy/ingredients-of-concern/caffeine-chart

Centers for Disease Control and Prevention. (2010, October 5). Binge drinking. *Vital Signs.*

Centers for Disease Control and Prevention. (2013). Adult cigarette smoking in the United States: Current estimate. http://www.cdc.gov/tobacco/data_statistics/fact_sheets/adult_data/cig_smoking/

Centers for Disease Control and Prevention. (2015, April 16). E-cigarette use triples among middle and high school students in just one year. Press release. http://www.cdc.gov/media/releases/2015/p0416-e-cigarette-use.html

Centers for Disease Control and Prevention. (2019). Current cigarette smoking among adults in the United States. http://www.cdc.gov/tobacco/data_statistics/fact_sheets/adult_data/cig_smoking/

Centers for Disease Control and Prevention. (2019). Facts about mental disorders in U.S. children. https://www.cdc.gov/childrensmentalhealth/data.html

Centers for Disease Control and Prevention. (2021). High School Youth Behavior Risk Survey. United States 2017-2019 results. https://nccd.cdc.gov/Youthonline/App/Results.aspx?TT=L&OUT=0&SID=HS&QID=H42&LID=XX&YID=YY&LID2=&YID2=&COL=S&ROW1=N&ROW2=N&HT=QQ&LCT=LL&FS=S1&FR=R1&FG=G1&FA=A1&FI=I1&FP=P1&FSL=S1&FRL=R1&FGL=G1&FAL=A1&FIL=I1&FPL=P1&PV=&TST=False&C1=&C2=&QP=G&DP=1&VA=CI&CS=Y&SYID=2017&EYID=2019&SC=DEFAULT&SO=ASC

Centers for Disease Control and Prevention. (2022, April 6). Working together to reduce Black maternal mortality. https://www.cdc.gov/healthequity/features/maternal-mortality/index.html

Centers for Disease Control and Prevention. (2022). Data and statistics about ADHD. https://www.cdc.gov/ncbddd/adhd/data.html

Centers for Disease Control and Prevention. (2022). Fetal alcohol spectrum disorders (FASDs): Data and statistics. https://www.cdc.gov/ncbddd/fasd/data.html

Centers for Disease Control and Prevention. (2022). Suicide disparities. https://www.cdc.gov/suicide/facts/disparities-in-suicide.html#age

Cervilla, O., Vallejo-Medina, P., Gómez-Berrocal, C., & Sierra, J. C. (2021). Development of the Spanish short version of Negative Attitudes Toward Masturbation Inventory. *International Journal of Clinical and Health Psychology, 21*(2), 100222.

Cestonaro, C., Menozzi, L., & Terranova, C. (2022). Infants of mothers with cocaine use: Review of clinical and medico-legal aspects. *Children, 9*(1), 67.

Chakraborty, S., & Roy, P. K. (2022). Interpersonal therapy in primary infertility, life-cycle transitions, and dysthymia: A single case study. *Clinical Case Studies, 21*(2), 87-99.

Chan, J. M. (2021, October 11). The first Ironman with Down syndrome turns his winning moment into a growing movement for inclusion. *CNN.* https://www.cnn.com/2021/10/11/us/iyw-chris-nikic-ironman-down-syndrome-special-olympics/index.html

Chan, M. (2016, June 20). Revisiting Andrea Yates 15 years after she drowned her children. *Time.* https://time.com/4375398/andrea-yates-15-years-drown-children/

Chan, E. K., Munro, D. W., Huang, A. H., Zumbo, B. D., Vojdanijahromi, R., & Ark, N. (2014). Validation practices in counseling: Major journals, mattering instruments, and the Kuder Occupational Interest Survey (KOIS). In B. D. Zumbo & E. K. H. Chan (Eds.), *Validity and validation in social, behavioral, and health sciences.* Springer.

Chan, G. C., Stjepanović, D., Lim, C., Sun, T., Anandan, A. S., Connor, J. P., Gartner, C., Hall, W. D., & Leung, J. (2021). A systematic review of randomized controlled trials and network meta-analysis of e-cigarettes for smoking cessation. *Addictive Behaviors, 119,* 106912.

Chang, H. T., Chiu, M-J., Chen, T-F., Liu, M-Y., Fan, W-C., Cheng, T-W., Lai, Y-M., & Hua, M-S. (2022). Deterioration and predictive values of semantic networks in mild cognitive impairment. *Journal of Neurolinguistics, 61,* 101025.

Chang, K. L., Hu, P., & Abrams, L. (2022). The tip-of-the-Mandarin tongue: Phonological and orthographic priming of TOT resolution in Mandarin speakers. *Language, Cognition and Neuroscience,* 1-14.

Chang, Y. P., & Raynor, T. (2021). Factors associated with relapse in individuals with opioid use disorder receiving suboxone in rural areas. *Journal of addictions nursing, 32*(1), 20-26.

Chang, Y.-W., Hsu, P.-Y., Wang, Y., & Chang, P.-Y. (2019). Integration of online and offline health services: The role of doctor-patient online interaction. *Patient Education and Counseling.* https://doi.org/10.1016/j.pec.2019.04.018.

Chang, Y.-T., Lin, S., Meng, L., & Fan, Y.-T. (2018). Atypical temporal activation pattern and central-right brain compensation during semantic judgment task in children with early left brain damage. *Brain and Language, 177-178,* 37-43.

Chańska, W. (2022). The principle of nondirectiveness in genetic counseling. Different meanings and various postulates of normative nature. *Medicine, Health Care and Philosophy,* 1-11. https://doi.org/10.1007/s11019-022-10085-0

Chao, M. M., Takeuchi, R., & Farh, J. (2017). Enhancing cultural intelligence: The roles of implicit culture beliefs and adjustment. *Personnel Psychology, 70,* 257-292.

Chao, R. (2011). Managing stress and maintaining well-being: Social support, problem-focused coping, and avoidant coping. *Journal of Counseling & Development, 89,* 338-348.

Chapman, L. J., & Chapman, J. P. (1973). *Disordered thought in schizophrenia.* Appleton-Century-Crofts.

Chapman, S. C., & Wu, L. (2015). Epidemiology and demography of illicit drug use and drug use disorders among adults aged 50 and older. In I. Crome, L. Wu, R. Rao, & P. Crome, (Eds.), *Substance use and older people.* New York: Wiley-Blackwell.

Charlesworth, T. E., & Banaji, M. R. (2019). Patterns of implicit and explicit attitudes: I. Long-term change and stability from 2007 to 2016. *Psychological science, 30*(2), 174-192.

Charpignon, M. L., Ontiveros, J., Sundaresan, S., Puri, A., Chandra, J., Mandl, K. D., & Majumder, M. S. (2022). Evaluation of suicides among US adolescents during the COVID-19 pandemic. *JAMA Pediatrics, 176*(7), 724-726.

Chaterjee, R. (2021). For many who were present, the 9/11 attacks have had a lasting mental health impact. *All Things Considered.* National Public Radio. https://www.npr.org/sections/health-shots/2021/09/08/1035224815/for-many-there-that-day-the-attacks-on-9-11-have-had-lasting-mental-health-impact

Chavan, B. S., Domun, I., & Machal, V. (2022). Brief flooding with exposure and response prevention In vivo in OCD. *Indian Journal of Social Psychiatry, 38*(2), 201.

Chavarría-Garza, W. X., Santos-Guevara, A., Morones-Ibarra, J. R., & Aquines-Gutiérrez, O. (2022).

Assessment of multiple intelligences in first-year engineering students in northeast Mexico. *Sustainability, 14*(8), 4631.

Cheever, T., Taylor, A., Finkelstein, R., Edwards, E., Thomas, L., Bradt, J., Holochwost, S. J., Johnson, J. K., Limb, C., Patel, A. d., Tottenham, N., Iyengar, S., Rutter, D., Fleming, R., & Collins, F. S. (2018). NIH/Kennedy center workshop on music and the brain: Finding harmony. *Neuron, 97*(6), 1214–1218.

Chen, I. J., Zhang, H., Wei, B., & Guo, Z. (2019). The model of children's social adjustment under the gender-roles absence in single-parent families. *International Journal of Psychology, 54*(3), 316–324.

Chen, Q. H., Li, Y. L., Hu, Y. R., Liang, W. Y., & Zhang, B. (2021). Observing time effect of SSRIs on suicide risk and suicide-related behaviour: A network meta-analysis protocol. *BMJ Open, 11*(12), e054479.

Chen, R. (2014). *Cognitive development: Theories, stages and processes and challenges.* (R. Chen, Ed.). Nova Science Publishers.

Chen, R., Gore, F., Nguyen, Q-A., Ramakrishnan, C., Patel, S., Kim, S. H., Raffiee, M., Kim, Y. S., Hsueh, B., Krook-Magnusson, E., Soltesz, I., & Deisseroth, K. (2021). Deep brain optogenetics without intracranial surgery. *Nature Biotechnology, 39*(2), 161–164.

Chen, T., Yue, G. H., Tian, Y., & Jiang, C. (2017). Baduanjin mind-body intervention improves the executive control function. *Frontiers in Psychology, 7,* 72–81.

Chen, Y., Li, X., Chen, C., An, Y., Shi, J., Huang, J., & Zhao, Y. (2021). Influence of avoidant coping on posttraumatic stress symptoms and job burnout among firefighters: The mediating role of perceived social support. *Disaster Medicine and Public Health Preparedness,* 1–6.

Chen, Z., Fu, L., Peng, Y., Cai, R., & Zhou, S. (2011). The relationship among childhood abuse, parenting styles, and antisocial personality disorder tendency. *Chinese Journal of Clinical Psychology, 19,* 212–214.

Chen, Z. R., Huang, J. B., Yang, S. L., & Hong, F. F. (2022). Role of cholinergic signaling in Alzheimer's disease. *Molecules, 27*(6), 1816.

Cheng, C. T., Ho, S. M., Liu, W. K., Hou, Y. C., Lim, L. C., Gao, S. Y., Chang, W. Y., & Wang, G. L. (2019). Cancer-coping profile predicts long-term psychological functions and quality of life in cancer survivors. *Supportive Care in Cancer, 27*(3), 933–941.

Cheng, P., Casement, M. D., Cuellar, R., Johnson, D. A., Kalmbach, D. A., Cuamatzi-Castelan, A., & Drake, C. L. (2021). Sleepless in COVID-19: racial disparities during the pandemic as a consequence of structural inequity. *Sleep.*

Cheng, S., & Kwan, K. (2008). Attachment dimensions and contingencies of self-worth: The moderating role of culture. *Personality and Individual Differences, 45,* 509–514.

Cheng, T. S., Ong, K. K., & Biro, F. M. (2022). Trends towards earlier puberty timing in girls and its likely mechanisms. *Journal of Pediatric and Adolescent Gynecology, 25*(5), 527–531.

Cheng, Y., Diao, Q., & Behrens, J. T. (2017). A simplified version of the maximum information per time unit method in computerized adaptive testing. *Behavior Research Methods, 49,* 502–512.

Chernyak, N., Leimgruber, K. L., Dunham, Y. C., Hu, J., & Blake, P. R. (2019). Paying back people who harmed us but not people who helped us: Direct negative reciprocity precedes direct positive reciprocity in early development. *Psychological Science, 30*(9), 1273–1286.

Chesworth, B., Lanier, P., & Rizo, C. F. (2019). The association between exposure to intimate partner violence and child bullying behaviors. *Journal of Child and Family Studies, 28,* 2220–2231.

Cheung, S. K., Siu, T. S. C., & Caldwell, M. P. (2022). Mathematical ability at a very young age: The contributions of relationship quality with parents and teachers via children's language and literacy abilities. *Early Childhood Education Journal,* 1–11.

Chew, S. H., Huang, W., & Zhao, X. (2020). Motivated false memory. *Journal of Political Economy, 128*(10), 3913–3939.

Chia, W. C., Chang, C. H., & Hou, W. H. (2021). Effects of laser therapy on rheumatoid arthritis: A systematic review and meta-analysis. *American Journal of Physical Medicine & Rehabilitation, 100*(11), 1078–1086.

Chiarotti, F., & Venerosi, A. (2020). Epidemiology of autism spectrum disorders: A review of worldwide prevalence estimates since 2014. *Brain Sciences, 10*(5), 274.

Chin, T. (2015). Harmony and organizational citizenship behavior in Chinese organizations. *International Journal of Human Resource Management, 26,* 1110–1129.

Chiu, Y., Lo, S., & Hsieh, A. (2017). How colour similarity can make banner advertising effective: Insights from Gestalt theory. *Behaviour & Information Technology, 36,* 606–619.

Cho, S., Holyoak, K. J., & Cannon, T. D. (2007). Analogical reasoning in working memory: Resources shared among relational integration, interference resolution, and maintenance. *Memory & Cognition, 35,* 1445–1455.

Chodakiewitz, Y., Williams, J., Chodakiewitz, J., & Cosgrove, G. R. (2015). Ablative surgery for neuropsychiatric disorders: Past, present, future. In B. Sun & A. De Salles (Eds.), *Neurosurgical treatments for psychiatric disorders.* Springer Science + Business Media.

Choi, H., Kensinger, E. A., & Rajaram, S. (2013). Emotional content enhances true but not false memory for categorized stimuli. *Memory & Cognition, 41,* 403–415.

Choi, H., Kensinger, E. A., & Rajaram, S. (2017). Mnemonic transmission, social contagion, and emergence of collective memory: Influence of emotional valence, group structure, and information distribution. *Journal of Experimental Psychology: General, 146,* 1247–1265.

Choi, K. W., Stein, M. B., Dunn, E. C., Koenen, K. C., & Smoller, J. W. (2019). Genomics and psychological resilience: A research agenda. *Molecular Psychiatry.* https://doi.org/10.1038/s41380-019-0457-6.

Choma, B. L., Jagayat, A., Hodson, G., & Turner, R. (2018). Prejudice in the wake of terrorism: The role of temporal distance, ideology, and intergroup emotions. *Personality and Individual Differences, 123,* 65–75.

Chomsky, N. (1978). On the biological basis of language capacities. In G. A. Miller & E. Lennenberg (Eds.), *Psychology and biology of language and thought.* Academic Press.

Chomsky, N. (1991). Linguistics and cognitive science: Problems and mysteries. In A. Kasher (Ed.), *The Chomskyan turn.* Blackwell.

Choubsaz, Y., & Gheitury, A. (2017). Is semantics affected by missing a critical period? Evidence from the Persian deaf. *Journal of Psycholinguistic Research, 46,* 77–88.

Chow, J. K., Rhodes, S., Rule, N. O., Buchsbaum, B. R., & Hasher, L. (2022). Absence of a mere-exposure effect in older and younger adults. *Psychology and Aging.* Advance online publication. https://doi.org/10.1037/pag0000702

Christakis, N. A., & Fowler, J. H. (2008). The collective dynamics of smoking in a large social network. *The New England Journal of Medicine, 358,* 2249–2258.

Christensen, K. A., Aldao, A., Sheridan, M. A., & McLaughlin, K. A. (2017). Habitual reappraisal in context: Peer victimisation moderates its association with physiological reactivity to social stress. *Cognition and Emotion, 31,* 384–394.

Christensen, M. C., Ren, H., & Fagiolini, A. (2022). Emotional blunting in patients with depression. Part I: Clinical characteristics. *Annals of General Psychiatry, 21*(1), 1–8.

Christensen, S. S. (2019). Escape from the diffusion of responsibility: A review and guide for nurses. *Journal of Nursing Management, 27*(2), 264–270.

Christoffels, I. K., de Haan, A. M., Steenbergen, L., van den Wildenberg, W. M., & Colzato, L. S. (2015). Two is better than one: Bilingual education promotes the flexible mind. *Psychological Research, 79,* 371–379.

Chuan, A., Zhou, J. J., Hou, R. M., Stevens, C. J., & Bogdanovych, A. (2021). Virtual reality for acute and chronic pain management in adult patients: a narrative review. *Anaesthesia, 76*(5), 695–704.

Chung, K.-F., Lee, C.-T., Yeung, W.-F., Chan, M.-S., Chung, E. W.-Y., & Lin, W.-L. (2018). Sleep hygiene education as a treatment of insomnia: A systematic review and meta-analysis. *Family Practice, 35*(4), 365–375.

Cialdini, R. (2021). *Influence, new and expanded: The psychology of persuasion.* Harper Business.

Cialdini, R. B., Schaller, M., Houlihan, D., Arps, K., Fultz, J., & Beaman, A. L. (1975). Reciprocal concessions procedure for inducing compliance: The door-in-the-face technique. *Journal of Personality and Social Psychology, 31,* 206–215.

Ciharova, M., Furukawa, T. A., Efthimiou, O., Karyotaki, E., Miguel, C., Noma, H., Cipriani, A., Riper, H., & Cuijpers, P. (2021). Cognitive restructuring, behavioral activation and cognitive-behavioral therapy in the treatment of adult depression: A network meta-analysis. *Journal of Consulting and Clinical Psychology, 89*(6), 563–574. https://doi.org/10.1037/ccp0000654

Ciranka, S., & van den Bos, W. (2021). Adolescent risk-taking in the context of exploration and social influence. *Developmental Review, 61,* 100979.

Cisler, J. M., James, G. A., Tripathi, S., Mletzko, T., Heim, C., Hu, X. P., Mayberg, H. S., Nemeroff, C. B., & Kilts, C. D. (2013). Differential functional connectivity within an emotion regulation neural network among individuals resilient and susceptible to the depressogenic effects of early life stress. *Psychological Medicine, 43,* 507–518.

Clark, A. T., Brivanlou, A., Fu, J., Kato, K., Mathews, D., Niakan, K. K., Rivron, N., Saitou, M., Surani, A., Tang, F., & Rossant, J. (2021). Human embryo research, stem cell-derived embryo models and in vitro gametogenesis: Considerations leading to the revised ISSCR guidelines. *Stem Cell Reports, 16*(6), 1416–1424.

Clark, E. J., & Kaufer, S. D. (2018). The profession of social work and the legacy of Kübler-Ross. *Families in Society, 99*(4), 369–377.

Clark, O. (2022). Aron Ralston, climber and subject of film *127 Hours. Climbing.* https://www.climbing.com/people/aron-ralston-climber-speaker-subject-film-127-hours/

Clarke, T. C., Barnes, P.M., Black, L. I., Stussman, B. J., & Nahin, R. L. (2018, November). Use of yoga, meditation, and chiropractors among U.S. adults aged 18 and over. NCHS Data Brief No. 325. National Center for Health Statistics.

Clawson, R. C., dela Cruz, L. N., Allen, S., Wolgemuth, T., Maner, A., Dorsett, A., & l'Anson, H. (2019). Continuous access to snacks from weaning onwards in female rats causes weight gain, insulin insensitivity, and sustained leptin resistance in adulthood. *Physiology & Behavior, 201,* 165–174.

Clay, R.A. (2017, July/August). Women outnumber men in psychology, but not in the field's top echelons. *Monitor on Psychology,* pp. 18–19.

Cleary, A. M. (2019). The biasing nature of the tip-of-the-tongue experience: When decisions bask in the glow of the tip-of-the-tongue state. *Journal of Experimental Psychology, 148*(7), 1178–1191.

Cleary, A. M., McNeely-White, K. L., Russell, S. A., Huebert, A. M., & Hausman, H. (2021). The tip-of-the-tongue state as a form of access to information: Use of tip-of-the-tongue states for strategic adaptive test-taking. *Journal of Applied Research in Memory and Cognition, 10*(1), 131–142.

Cline, K. D., Dimmitt, E., & Gann, M. (2022). Books before birth: A qualitative multiple case study of mothers reading to babies in utero. *Journal of Reproductive and Infant Psychology,* 1–14. Advance online publication. https://doi.org/10.1080/0264683 8.2022.2077222

Clinton, S. M., Unroe, K. A., Shupe, E. A., McCoy, C. R., & Glover, M. E. (2022). Resilience to stress: Lessons from rodents about nature versus nurture. *The Neuroscientist, 28*(3), 283–298.

Coan, J. A., Schaefer, H. S., & Davidson, R. J. (2006). Lending a hand: Social regulation of the neural response to threat. *Psychological Science, 17*(12), 1032-1039.

Coelho, G. L. D. H., Hanel, P. H. P., & Wolf, L. J. (2020). The very efficient assessment of need for cognition: Developing a six-item version. *Assessment, 27*(8), 1879-1885.

Coenen, V. A., Bewernick, B. H., Kayser, S., Kilian, H., Boström, J., Greschus, S., Hurlemann, R., Klein, M. E., Spanier, S., Sajonz, B., Urbach, H., & Schlaepfer, T. E. (2019). Superolateral medial forebrain bundle deep brain stimulation in major depression: A gateway trial. *Neuropsychopharmacology, 44*(7), 1224-1232.

Cohen, P., Slomkowski, C., & Robins, L. N. (Eds.). (1999). *Historical and geographical influences on psychopathology.* Erlbaum.

Cohen, S., Kamarck, T., & Mermelstein, R. (1983). A global measure of perceived stress. *Journal of Health and Social Behavior, 24,* 385-396.

Cohen, S., Murphy, M. L. M., & Prather, A. A. (2019). Ten surprising facts about stressful life events and disease risk. *Annual Review of Psychology, 70,* 577-597.

Cohn, A., Maréchal, M. A., Tannenbaum, D., & Zünd, C. L. (2019). Civic honesty around the globe. *Science, 365*(6448), 70-73.

Colliot, T., Kiewra, K. A., Luo, L., Flanigan, A. E., Lu, J., Kennedy, C., & Black, S. (2022). The effects of graphic organizer completeness and note-taking medium on computer-based learning. *Education and Information Technologies, 27*(2), 2435-2456.

Conforto, A. B., Luccas, R., Menezes, I. S., Machado, A. G., Mello, E. A., Assis, P. S., Freitas, P. F., Pires, D. S., Peckham, P. H., & Cohen, L. G. (2019). Peripheral nerve stimulation to enhance upper limb motor function in stroke. *Stroke, 50*(Suppl 1), A120-A120.

Conger, D., Gibbs, C. R., Uchikoshi, Y., & Winsler, A. (2019). New benefits of public school pre-kindergarten programs: Early school stability, grade promotion, and exit from ELL services. *Early Childhood Research Quarterly, 48,* 26-35.

Conoley, C. W., Plumb, E. W., Hawley, K. J., Spaventa-Vancil, K. Z., & Hernández, R. J. (2015). Integrating positive psychology into family therapy: Positive family therapy. *The Counseling Psychologist, 43,* 703-733.

Conrad, R., Forstner, A. J., Chung, M. L., Mücke, M., Geiser, F., Schumacher, J., & Carnehl, F. (2021). Significance of anger suppression and preoccupied attachment in social anxiety disorder: A cross-sectional study. *BMC Psychiatry, 21*(1), 1-9.

Conroy, J., Lin, L., & Christidis, P. (2019). How satisfied are psychology-degree holders with their job? *Monitor on Psychology,50,* 19.

Conroy, J., Lin, L., & Stamm, K. (2021, July/August). A psychology major opens doors. *Monitor on Psychology,* p. 21.

Convie, L. J., Carson, E., McCusker, D., McCain, R. S., McKinley, N., Campbell, W. J., Kirk, S. J., & Clarke, M. (2020). The patient and clinician experience of informed consent for surgery: A systematic review of the qualitative evidence. *BMC Medical Ethics, 21*(1), 1-17.

Cook, L. (2021). HIV stigma reduction and health literacy education program with a cross-generational populaton [sic] in an African American faith-based church. *Journal of Public Health, 29*(5), 1089-1106.

Cook, M. (2013). *Levels of personality* (3rd ed.). Cambridge University Press.

Cook, V. (2021). The language in language and thinking. *Vigo International Journal of Applied Linguistics,* (18), 35-58.

Coolidge, F. L. (2021). The role of the cerebellum in creativity and expert stone knapping. *Adaptive Behavior, 29*(2), 217-229.

Coolidge, F. L., Segal, D. L., Estey, A. J., & Neuzil, P. J. (2011). Preliminary psychometric properties of a measure of Karen Horney's Tridimensional Theory in children and adolescents. *Journal of Clinical Psychology, 67,* 383-390.

Cools, R., & Arnsten, A. F. (2022). Neuromodulation of prefrontal cortex cognitive function in primates: the powerful roles of monoamines and acetylcholine. *Neuropsychopharmacology, 47*(1), 309-328.

Cooper, D. T., & Klein, J. L. (2018). College students' online pornography use: Contrasting general and specific structural variables with social learning variables. *American Journal of Criminal Justice, 43*(3), 551-569.

Cooper, J. (2019). Cognitive dissonance: Where we've been and where we're going. *International Review of Social Psychology, 32*(1).

Cooper, Z., & Shafran, R. (2008). Cognitive behaviour therapy for eating disorders. *Behavioural and Cognitive Psychotherapy, 36,* 713-722.

Copeland, W. E., Worthman, C., Shanahan, L., Costello, E. J., & Angold, A. (2019). Early pubertal timing and testosterone associated with higher levels of adolescent depression in girls. *Journal of the American Academy of Child & Adolescent Psychiatry, 58*(12), 1197-1206.

Corbett, B., Rajah, M. N., & Duarte, A. (2020). Preparing for the worst: Evidence that older adults proactively downregulate negative affect. *Cerebral Cortex, 30*(3), 1291-1306. https://doi.org/10.1093/cercor/bhz166

Coren, S. (2004). Sensation and perception. In I. B. Weiner (Ed.), *Handbook of Psychology* (Vol. 1). John Wiley & Sons.

Coren, S., & Ward, L. M. (1989). *Sensation and perception* (3rd ed.). Harcourt Brace Jovanovich.

Cornelis, E., Heuvinck, N., & Majmundar, A. (2020). The ambivalence story: Using refutation to counter the negative effects of ambivalence in two-sided messages. *International Journal of Advertising, 39*(3), 410-432.

Cornelis, M. C., Tordoff, M. G., El-Sohemy, A., & van Dam, R. M. (2017). Recalled taste intensity, liking and habitual intake of commonly consumed foods. *Appetite, 109,* 182-189.

Cornell, C. B. (2006). A graduated scale for determining mental age. *Dissertation Abstracts International: Section B: The Sciences and Engineering,66*(9-B), 5121.

Cornier, M. (2011). Is your brain to blame for weight regain? *Physiology & Behavior, 104,* 608-612.

Corr, C. A. (2020). Elisabeth Kübler-Ross and the "five stages" model in a sampling of recent American textbooks. *OMEGA–Journal of Death and Dying, 82*(2), 294-322.

Corr, P., & Plagnol, A. (2018). *Behavioral economics: The basics.* Routledge.

Cost, K. T., Crosbie, J., Anagnostou, E., Birken, C. S., Charach, A., Monga, S., Kelley, E., Nicolson, R., Maguire, J. L., Burton, C. L., Schachar, R. J., Arnold, P. D., & Korczak, D. J. (2022). Mostly worse, occasionally better: Impact of COVID-19 pandemic on the mental health of Canadian children and adolescents. *European Child & Adolescent Psychiatry, 31*(4), 671-684.

Costa, R., & Figueiredo, B. (2011). Infant's psychophysiological profile and temperament at 3 and 12 months. *Infant Behavior & Development, 34,* 270-279.

Coulson, D., & Harvey, M. (2013). Scaffolding student reflection for experience-based learning: A framework. *Teaching in Higher Education, 18,* 401-413.

Cowan, N. (2001). The magical number 4 in short-term memory: A reconsideration of mental storage capacity. *Behavioral and Brain Sciences, 24,* 97-185.

Cowen, A. S., & Keltner, D. (2020). What the face displays: Mapping 28 emotions conveyed by naturalistic expression. *American Psychologist, 75*(3), 349-364.

Cowles, E. L., & Nelson, E. (2018). *An introduction to survey research, Volume I: The basics of survey research.* Business Expert Press.

Cox, D. W., Fleckenstein, J. R., & Sims-Cox, L. R. (2021). Comparing the self-reported health, happiness, and marital happiness of a multinational sample of consensually non-monogamous adults with those of the US general population: Additional comparisons by gender, number of sexual partners, frequency of sex, and marital status. *Archives of Sexual Behavior, 50*(4), 1287-1309.

Craig, F., Gioia, M. C., Muggeo, V., Cajiao, J., Aloi, A., Martino, I., Tenuta, F., Cerasa, A., & Costabile, A. (2021). Effects of maternal psychological distress and perception of COVID-19 on prenatal attachment in a large sample of Italian pregnant women. *Journal of Affective Disorders, 295,* 665-672.

Craig, P. L. (2017). Clinical neuropsychologists. In R. J. Sternberg (Ed.), *Career paths in psychology: Where your degree can take you.* American Psychological Association.

Craig, R., Pelosi, A., & Tourish, D. (2021). Research misconduct complaints and institutional logics: The case of Hans Eysenck and the British Psychological Society. *Journal of Health Psychology, 26*(2), 296-311.

Craighero, L., Leo, I., Umilta, C., & Simion, F. (2011). Newborns' preference for goal-directed actions. *Cognition, 120,* 26-32.

Craik, F., & Lockhart, R. (2008). Levels of processing and Zinchenko's approach to memory research. *Journal of Russian & East European Psychology, 46,* 52-60.

Crawford, L. K., Caplan, J. B., & Loprinzi, P. D. (2021). The impact of acute exercise timing on memory interference. *Perceptual and Motor Skills, 128*(3), 1215-1234.

Crespo, R. F., & Mesurado, B. (2015). Happiness economics, eudaimonia and positive psychology: From happiness economics to flourishing economics. *Journal of Happiness Studies, 16*(4), 931-946.

Crivelli, D., Spinosa, C., Angelillo, M. T., & Balconi, M. (2021). The influence of language comprehension proficiency on assessment of global cognitive impairment following acquired brain injury: A comparison between MMSE, MoCA and CASP batteries. *Applied Neuropsychology: Adult,* 1-6.

Crockford, C., Wittig, R. M., & Zuberbühler, K. (2015). An intentional vocalization draws others' attention: A playback experiment with wild chimpanzees. *Animal Cognition, 18,* 581-591.

Crone, E. A., & van Duijvenvoorde, A. C. (2021). Multiple pathways of risk taking in adolescence. *Developmental Review, 62,* 100996.

Crönlein, T., Lehner, A., Schüssler, P., Geisler, P., Rupprecht, R., & Wetter, T. C. (2019). Changes in subjective-objective sleep discrepancy following inpatient cognitive behavior therapy for insomnia. *Behavior Therapy.* http://dx.doi.org/10.1016/j.beth.2019.03.002.

Crosby, C. L., Buss, D. M., Cormack, L. K., & Meston, C. M. (2021). Sex, sexual arousal, and sexual decision making: An evolutionary perspective. *Personality and Individual Differences, 177,* 110826.

Crosnoe, R., & Elder, G. H., Jr. (2002). Successful adaptation in the later years: A life course approach to aging. *Social Psychology Quarterly, 65,* 309-328.

Crouse, K. (2015, September 22). 100 Years Old. 5 World Records. *New York Times,* P. A1.

Crowne, K. (2013). Cultural exposure, emotional intelligence, and cultural intelligence: An exploratory study. *International Journal of Cross-Cultural Management, 13*(1), 5-22.

Cruz, T. N. D., Camelo, E. M., Nardi, A. E., & Cheniaux, E. (2021). Creativity in bipolar disorder: A systematic review. *Trends in Psychiatry and Psychotherapy.* Advance online publication. https://doi.org/10.47626/2237-6089-2021-0196

Csöndör, É., Karvaly, G., Ligetvári, R., Kovács, K., Komka, Z., Móra, Á., Stromájer-Rácz, T., Oláh, A., Tóth, M., & Ács, P. (2022). Adrenal, gonadal and peripherally steroid changes in response to extreme physical stress for characterizing load capacity in athletes. *Metabolites, 12*(2), 91.

Cuartas, J. (2022). The effect of spanking on early social-emotional skills. *Child Development, 93*(1), 180-193.

Cuaya, L. V., Hernández-Pérez, R., Boros, M., Deme, A., & Andics, A. (2021). Speech naturalness detection and language representation in the dog brain. *NeuroImage,* 118811.

Cuijpers, P., Karyotaki, E., Reijnders, M., & Ebert, D. D. (2019). Was Eysenck right after all? A reassessment of the effects of psychotherapy for adult depression. *Epidemiology and Psychiatric Sciences, 28*(1), 21-30.

Cuijpers, P., van Straten, A., Andersson, G., & van Oppen, P. (2008). Psychotherapy for depression in adults: A meta-analysis of comparative outcome studies. *Journal of Consulting and Clinical Psychology, 76*, 909-922.

Cummings, A., Ceponiene, R., & Koyama, A. (2006). Auditory semantic networks for words and natural sounds. *Brain Research, 1115*, 92-107.

Cummings Center for the History of Psychology. (2021). Historical Chronology; Examining psychology's contributions to the belief in racial hierarchy and perpetuation of inequality for people of color in U.S. Downloaded from https://www.apa.org/about/apa/addressing-racism/historical-chronology. April 21, 2022.

Cummings, J. L. (2019). Assessing US racial and gender differences in happiness, 1972-2016: An intersectional approach. *Journal of Happiness Studies, 21*(2), 709-732.

Cunanan, A. J., DeWeese, B. H., Wagle, J. P., Carroll, K. M., Sausaman, R., Hornsby, W. G., Haff, G. G., Triplett, N. T., Pierce, K. C., & Stone, M. H. (2018). The general adaptation syndrome: a foundation for the concept of periodization. *Sports Medicine, 48*(4), 787-797.

Curci, A., Lanciano, T., Curtotti, D., & Sartori, G. (2020). Lessons for the courtroom from the study of flashbulb memory: An integrative review. *Memory, 28*(3), 441-449.

Curry, O. S., Rowland, L. A., Van Lissa, C. J., Zlotowitz, S., McAlaney, J., & Whitehouse, H. (2018). Happy to help? A systematic review and meta-analysis of the effects of performing acts of kindness on the well-being of the actor. *Journal of Experimental Social Psychology, 76*, 320-329.

Curthoys, I. S. (2017). The new vestibular stimuli: Sound and vibration–anatomical, physiological and clinical evidence. *Experimental Brain Research, 235*, 957-972.

da Cunha-Bang, S., Fisher, P. M., Hjordt, L. V., Holst, K., & Knudsen, G. M. (2019). Amygdala reactivity to fearful faces correlates positively with impulsive aggression. *Social Neuroscience, 14*(2), 162-172.

Daftary, F., & Meri, J. W. (2002). *Culture and memory in medieval Islam.* I. B. Tauris.

Dahlberg, L. (2021). Loneliness during the COVID-19 pandemic. *Aging & Mental Health, 25*(7), 1161-1164.

Dai, D., Miller, C., Valdivia, V., Boyle, B., Bolton, P., Li, S., Seiner, S., & Meisner, R. (2022). Neurocognitive effects of repeated ketamine infusion treatments in patients with treatment resistant depression: A retrospective chart review. *BMC Psychiatry, 22*.

Dai, Z. H., Xu, X., Chen, W. Q., Nie, L. N., Liu, Y., Sui, N., & Liang, J. (2022). The role of hippocampus in memory reactivation: An implication for a therapeutic target against opioid use disorder. *Current Addiction Reports, 9*(2), 67-79.

Dakin, E. K., & Areán, P. (2013). Patient perspectives on the benefits of psychotherapy for late-life depression. *American Journal of Geriatric Psychiatry, 21*, 155-163.

Damaske, S. (2011). A "major career woman"? How women develop early expectations about work. *Gender & Society, 25*, 409-430.

Damian, R. I., Spengler, M., Sutu, A., & Roberts, B. W. (2019). Sixteen going on sixty-six: A longitudinal study of personality stability and change across 50 years. *Journal of Personality and Social Psychology, 117*(3), 674-695.

Damjanovic, L., Meyer, M., & Sepulveda, F. (2017). Raising the alarm: Individual differences in the perceptual awareness of masked facial expressions. *Brain and Cognition, 114*, 1-10.

Dang, J., Xiao, S., & Mao, L. (2015). A new account of the conditioning bias to out-groups. *Frontiers in Psychology, 6*, 197.

Daniels, C. W., & Sanabria, F. (2017). Interval timing under a behavioral microscope: Dissociating motivational and timing processes in fixed-interval performance. *Learning & Behavior, 45*, 29-48.

Danner, D., Hagemann, D., Schankin, A., Hager, M., & Funke, J. (2011). Beyond IQ: A latent state-trait analysis of general intelligence, dynamic decision making, and implicit learning. *Intelligence, 39*, 323-334.

da Pos, O. (2022). Psychophysics and phenomenology of perceptual transparency. *Psychology of Consciousness: Theory, Research, and Practice.* Advance online publication. https://doi.org/10.1037/cns0000318

Dard, R. F., Dahan, L., & Rampon, C. (2019). Targeting hippocampal adult neurogenesis using transcription factors to reduce Alzheimer's disease-associated memory impairments. *Hippocampus, 29*(7), 579-586.

Dare, J. S. (2011). Transitions in midlife women's lives: Contemporary experiences. *Health Care for Women International, 32*, 111-133.

Darwin, H. (2020). Challenging the cisgender/transgender binary: Nonbinary people and the transgender label. *Gender & Society, 34*(3), 357-380.

Das, A. (2007). Masturbation in the United States. *Journal of Sex & Marital Therapy, 33*, 301-317.

Das, J. P. (2015). Search for intelligence by PASSing g. *Canadian Psychology/Psychologie Canadienne, 56*, 39-45.

Dasborough, M., & Harvey, P. (2017). Schadenfreude: The (not so) secret joy of another's misfortune. *Journal of Business Ethics, 141*, 693-707.

Datar, A. (2017). The more the heavier? Family size and childhood obesity in the U.S. *Social Science & Medicine, 180*, 143-151.

David, D., Lynn, S. J., & Montgomery, G. H. (Eds.). (2018). *Evidence-based psychotherapy: The state of the science and practice.* Wiley Blackwell.

David, E. R., & Derthick, A. O. (2018). *The psychology of oppression.* New York: Springer Publishing Co.

Daviddi, S., Pedale, T., Serra, L., Macri, S., Campolongo, P., & Santangelo, V. (2022). Altered hippocampal resting-state functional connectivity in highly superior autobiographical memory. *Neuroscience, 480*, 1-8.

Davidson, J. (2014). Want to sleep better? Stop trying so hard. *Globe and Mail.* Downloaded from https://www.theglobeandmail.com/life/health-and-fitness/health-advisor/want-to-sleep-better-stop-trying-so-hard/article18111346/, January 12, 2021.

Davidson-Kelly, K., Schaefer, R. S., Moran, N., & Overy, K. (2015). "Total inner memory": Deliberate uses of multimodal musical imagery during performance preparation. *Psychomusicology: Music, Mind, and Brain, 25*, 83-92.

Davies, C., Hendry, A., Gibson, S. P., Gliga, T., McGillion, M., & Gonzalez-Gomez, N. (2021). Early childhood education and care (ECEC) during COVID-19 boosts growth in language and executive function. *Infant and Child Development, 30*(4), e2241.

Davis, K., Christodoulou, J., Seider, S., & Gardner, H. (2011). The theory of multiple intelligences. In R. J. Sternberg & S. Kaufman (Eds.), *The Cambridge handbook of intelligence.* Cambridge University Press.

Davis, K. L., & Panksepp, J. (2018). *The emotional foundations of personality: A neurobiological and evolutionary approach.* W. W. Norton & Company.

Davis, L. J. (2009, June 15). Sotomayor and the New Haven firefighters case: More myths than facts. *Washington Times*, p. A04.

Davis, S. R. (2007). The nose knows best. *PsycCRITIQUES, 52*, 22-31.

Dawkins, L., Ford, A., Bauld, L., Balaban, S., Tyler, A., & Cox, S. (2019). A cross sectional survey of smoking characteristics and quitting behaviour from a sample of homeless adults in Great Britain. *Addictive Behaviors, 95*, 35-40.

Dawson, A. (2021, February 16). Meet the 90-Year-old runner who still hHits the track five days a week. *Runner's World.* https://www.runnersworld.com/runners-stories/a35511452/joe-handelman-90-year-old-runner/

Day, A. L., & Livingstone, H. A. (2003). Gender differences in perceptions of stressors and utilization of social support among university students. *Canadian Journal of Behavioural Science, 35*, 73-83.

de Abreu, C. N., & Filho, R. C. (2017). Anorexia nervosa and bulimia nervosa–A psychotherapeutic cognitive-constructivist approach. *International Review of Psychiatry, 29*, 248-253.

Deacon, B. J., & Spielmans, G. I. (2017). Is the efficacy of "antidepressant" medications overrated? In S. O. Lilienfeld & I. D. Waldman (Eds.), *Psychological science under scrutiny: Recent challenges and proposed solutions.* Wiley Blackwell.

DeAngelis, T. (2016). Behavioral therapy works best for insomnia. *Monitor on Psychology, 47*, 18-19.

DeAngelis, T. (2016, September). Preventing medical errors. *Monitor on Psychology*, pp. 48-52.

Dearing, E., McCartney, K., & Taylor, B. (2009). Does higher quality early child care promote low-income children's math and reading achievement in middle childhood? *Child Development, 80*, 1329-1349.

Debatin, T. (2019). A revised mental energy hypothesis of the *g*factor in light of recent neuroscience. *Review of General Psychology, 23*(2), 201-210.

De Brigard, F., Brady, T. F., Ruzic, L., & Schacter, D. L. (2017). Tracking the emergence of memories: A category-learning paradigm to explore schema-driven recognition. *Memory & Cognition, 45*, 105-120.

De Bruin, K. (2019). The impact of inclusive education reforms on students with disability: An international comparison. *International Journal of Inclusive Education, 23*(7-8), 1-16.

de Bruïne, G., Vredeveldt, A., & van Koppen, P. J. (2018). Cross-cultural differences in object recognition: Comparing asylum seekers from Sub-Saharan Africa and a matched Western European control group. *Applied Cognitive Psychology, 32*(4), 463-473.

De France, K., Hancock, G. R., Stack, D. M., Serbin, L. A., & Hollenstein, T. (2021). The mental health implications of COVID-19 for adolescents: Follow-up of a four-wave longitudinal study during the pandemic. *American Psychologist, 77*(1), 85-99.

De France, K., & Hollenstein, T. (2021). Implicit theories of emotion and mental health during adolescence: The mediating role of emotion regulation. *Cognition and Emotion, 35*(2), 367-374.

deGroot, A. (1978). *Thought and choice in chess.* Mouton de Gruyter.

deGroot, A. D. (1966). Perception and memory versus thought: Some old ideas and recent findings. In B. Kleinmuntz (Ed.), *Problem solving: Research, method, and theory.* Wiley.

de Gusmao, C. M., Pollak, L. E., & Sharma, N. (2017). Neuropsychological and psychiatric outcome of GPi-deep brain stimulation in dystonia. *Brain Stimulation, 10*, 994-996.

de Jong, R., Lommen, M. J., de Jong, P. J., & Nauta, M. H. (2019). Using multiple contexts and retrieval cues in exposure-based therapy to prevent relapse in anxiety disorders. *Cognitive and Behavioral Practice, 26*(1), 154-165.

de Klerk, C. C., Bulgarelli, C., Hamilton, A., & Southgate, V. (2019). Selective facial mimicry of native over foreign speakers in preverbal infants. *Journal of Experimental Child Psychology, 183*, 33-47.

Dell, P. F. (2013). Three dimensions of dissociative amnesia. *Journal of Trauma & Dissociation, 14*, 25-39.

DeLoache, J., & LoBue, V. (2009). The narrow fellow in the grass: Human infants associate snakes and fear. *Developmental Science, 12*, 201-207.

De Los Reyes, A., Lerner, M. D., Keeley, L. M., Weber, R. J., Drabick, D. A., Rabinowitz, J., & Goodman, K. L. (2019). Improving interpretability of subjective assessments about psychological phenomena: A review and cross-cultural meta-analysis. *Review of General Psychology, 23*(3), 293-319.

del Solar Dorrego, F., & Vigeant, M. C. (2022). A study of the just noticeable difference of early decay time for symphonic halls. *The Journal of the Acoustical Society of America, 151*(1), 80-94.

DeMaris, A. (2013). Burning the candle at both ends: Extramarital sex as a precursor of marital disruption. *Journal of Family Issues, 34*, 1474-1499.

De Meyer, H., Beckers, T., Tripp, G., & van der Oord, S. (2019). Reinforcement contingency learning in children with ADHD: Back to the basics of behavior therapy. *Journal of Abnormal Child Psychology.* https://doi.org/10.1007/s10802-019-00572-z.

Demirci, I., Halil, E. K. S. I., & Fusun, E. K. S. I. (2019). Narcissism, life satisfaction, and harmony: The mediating role of self-esteem and self-compassion.

Eurasian Journal of Educational Research, 19(84), 159-178.

Dempster, F. N. (1981). Memory span: Sources for individual and developmental differences. *Psychological Bulletin, 89*, 63-100.

Deng, C., & Georgiou, G. K. (2015). Establishing measurement invariance of the cognitive assessment system across cultures. In T. C. Papadopoulos, R. K. Parrila, & J. R. Kirby (Eds.), *Cognition, intelligence, and achievement: A tribute to J. P. Das.* Elsevier Academic Press.

Denmark, G. L., & Fernandez, L. C. (1993). Historical development of the psychology of women. In F. L. Denmark & M. A. Paludi (Eds.), *A handbook of issues and theories.* Westport, CT: Greenwood Press.

Dennis, S. (2011). Smoking causes creative responses: On state antismoking policy and resilient habits. *Critical Public Health, 21*, 25-35.

Dennis-Tiwary, T. (2022). *Future Tense: Why Anxiety Is Good for You Even Though It Feels Bad.* Harper Wave.

Deo, N., & Redpath, G. (2022). Serotonin receptor and transporter endocytosis is an important factor in the cellular basis of depression and anxiety. *Frontiers in Cellular Neuroscience, 24.*

DePaolo, J., Gravina, N. E., & Harvey, C. (2019). Using a behavioral intervention to improve performance of a women's college lacrosse team. *Behavior Analysis in Practice, 12*(2), 407-411.

De Pue, S., Gillebert, C., Dierckx, E., Vanderhasselt, M. A., De Raedt, R., & Van den Bussche, E. (2021). The impact of the COVID-19 pandemic on wellbeing and cognitive functioning of older adults. *Scientific Reports, 11*(1), 1-11.

Deregowski, J. B. (1973). Illusion and culture. In R. L. Gregory & G. H. Combrich (Eds.), *Illusion in nature and art.* Scribner.

DeRobertis, E. M. (2021). The humanistic revolution in psychology: Its inaugural vision. *Journal of Humanistic Psychology, 61*(1), 8-32.

DeRobertis, E. M., & Bland, A. M. (2019). Lifespan human development and "the humanistic perspective": A contribution toward inclusion. *The Humanistic Psychologist.* http://dx.doi.org/10.1037/hum0000141.

Deroy, O., & Spence, C. (2013). Are we all born synaesthetic? Examining the neonatal synaesthesia hypothesis. *Neuroscience and Biobehavioral Reviews, 37,* 1240-1253.

De Shazer, S., Dolan, Y., Korman, H., Trepper, T., McCollum, E., & Berg, I. K. (2021). *More than miracles: The state of the art of solution-focused brief therapy.* Routledge.

de Sousa, A. F., Cowansage, K. K., Zutshi, I., Cardozo, L. M., Yoo, E. J., Leutgeb, S., & Mayford, M. (2019). Optogenetic reactivation of memory ensembles in the retrosplenial cortex induces systems consolidation. *Proceedings of the National Academy of Sciences of the United States of America, 116*(17), 8576-8581.

de Sousa, D. F. M., Gonçalves, M. L. L., Politti, F., de Paula Lovisetto, R. D., Fernandes, K. P. S., Bussadori, S. K., & Mesquita-Ferrari, R. A. (2019). Photo-biomodulation with simultaneous use of red and infrared light emitting diodes in the treatment of temporomandibular disorder: Study protocol for a randomized, controlled and double-blind clinical trial. *Medicine, 98*(6), e14391.

Després, O., Lithfous, S., Tromp, D., Pebayle, T., & Dufour, A. (2017). Gamma oscillatory activity is impaired in episodic memory encoding with age. *Neurobiology of Aging, 52*, 53-65.

de Visser, E. J., Monfort, S. S., Goodyear, K., Lu, L., O'Hara, M., Lee, M. R., Parasuraman, R., & Krueger, F. (2017). A little anthropomorphism goes a long way: Effects of oxytocin on trust, compliance, and team performance with automated agents. *Human Factors, 59*, 116-133.

de Voogd, L. D., Klumpers, F., Fernández, G., & Hermans, E. J. (2017). Intrinsic functional connectivity between amygdala and hippocampus during rest predicts enhanced memory under stress. *Psychoneuroendocrinology, 75*, 192-202.

Devos, T. (2011). The role of race in American politics: Lessons learned from the 2008 presidential election.

In G. S. Parks & M. W. Hughey (Eds.), *The Obamas and a (post) racial America?* Oxford University Press.

de Waal, F. B. M. (2014). Hard-wired for good? *Science, 347,* 379.

de Wit, A. E., Booij, S. H., Giltay, E. J., Joffe, H., Schoevers, R. A., & Oldehinkel, A. J. (2020). Association of use of oral contraceptives with depressive symptoms among adolescents and young women. *JAMA Psychiatry, 77*(1), 52-59.

Dey, A., Zele, A. J., Feigl, B., & Adhikari, P. (2021). Threshold vision under full-field stimulation: Revisiting the minimum number of quanta necessary to evoke a visual sensation. *Vision Research, 180,* 1-10.

Dhoest, A. (2019). Learning to be gay: LGBTQ forced migrant identities and narratives in Belgium. *Journal of Ethnic and Migration Studies, 45*(7), 1075-1089.

Diaz, A., & Bell, M. (2011). Information processing efficiency and regulation at five months. *Infant Behavior & Development, 34,* 239-247.

Dierolf, A. M., Fechtner, J., Böhnke, R., Wolf, O. T., & Naumann, E. (2017). Influence of acute stress on response inhibition in healthy men: An ERP study. *Psychophysiology, 54,* 684-695.

Digdon, N. (2017). The Little Albert controversy: Intuition, confirmation bias, and logic. *History of Psychology.* Accessed from https://www.ncbi.nlm.nih.gov/pubmed/28125246.

Di Ieva, A., Esteban, F. J., Grizzi, F., Klonowski, W., & Martin-Landrove, M. (2015). Fractals in the neurosciences, part II: Clinical applications and future perspectives. *The Neuroscientist, 21,* 30-43.

Dijksterhuis, A., Chartrand, T. L., & Aarts, H. (2007). Effects of Priming and Perception on Social Behavior and Goal Pursuit. *Frontiers of Social Psychology, 17,* 33-40.

Dillard, J. P., & Shen, L. (2007). Self-report measures of discrete emotions. In R. A. Reynolds, R. Woods, & J. D. Baker (Eds.), *Handbook of research on electronic surveys and measurements.* Idea Group Reference/IGI Global.

Diller, L. (2017, January 17). The United States of Adderall. *Huffington Post.* Accessed from http://www.huffingtonpost.com/larry-diller/the-united-states-of-adderall_b_8914480.html.

Dimaggio, G., D'Urzo, M., Pasinetti, M., Salvatore, G., Lysaker, P. H., Catania, D., & Popolo, R. (2015). Metacognitive interpersonal therapy for co-occurrent avoidant personality disorder and substance abuse. *Journal of Clinical Psychology, 71,* 157-166.

Dimaggio, G., Salvatore, G., MacBeth, A., Ottavi, P., Buonocore, L., & Popolo, R. (2017). Metacognitive interpersonal therapy for personality disorders: A case study series. *Journal of Contemporary Psychotherapy, 47,* 11-21.

Diniz, B. S., Butters, M. A., Albert, S. M., Dew, M., & Reynolds, C. (2013). Late-life depression and risk of vascular dementia and Alzheimer's disease: Systematic review and meta-analysis of community-based cohort studies. *British Journal of Psychiatry, 202,* 329-335.

DiPierro, K., Lee, H., Pain, K. J., Durning, S. J., & Choi, J. J. (2022). Groupthink among health professional teams in patient care: A scoping review. *Medical Teacher, 44*(3), 309-318.

Di Pierro, R., Costantini, G., Benzi, I. M. A., Madeddu, F., & Preti, E. (2019). Grandiose and entitled, but still fragile: A network analysis of pathological narcissistic traits. *Personality and Individual Differences, 140,* 15-20.

Dittrich, W. H., Johansen, T., & Fineberg, N. A. (2011). Cognitive Assessment Instrument of Obsessions and Compulsions (CAIOV-13)—A new 13-item scale for evaluating functional impairment associated with OCD. *Psychiatry Research, 187,* 283-290.

Dixon, R. A., McFall, G., Whitehead, B. P., & Dolcos, S. (2013). Cognitive development in adulthood and aging. In R. M. Lerner, M. Easterbrooks, J. Mistry, & I. B. Weiner (Eds.), *Handbook of psychology, Vol. 6: Developmental psychology* (2nd ed.). John Wiley & Sons.

Dixon, R. A., Rust, T. B., & Feltmate, S. E. (2007). Memory and aging: Selected research directions and

application issues. *Canadian Psychology Psychologie Canadienne, 48,* 67-76.

Djapo, N., Kolenovic-Djapo, J., Djokic, R., & Fako, I. (2011). Relationship between Cattell's 16PF and fluid and crystallized intelligence. *Personality and Individual Differences, 51,* 63-67.

Dobbins, I. G., & Kantner, J. (2019). The language of accurate recognition memory. *Cognition, 192,* 103988.

Doblin, R. E., Christiansen, M., Jerome, L., & Burge, B. (2019). The past and future of psychedelic science: An introduction to this issue. *Journal of Psychoactive Drugs, 51*(2), 93-97.

Dockrell, J. E., & Marshall, C. R. (2015). Measurement issues: Assessing language skills in young children. *Child and Adolescent Mental Health, 20,* 116-125.

Dodes, L. (2015). *The sober truth: Debunking the bad science behind 12-step programs and the rehab industry.* Beacon Press.

Dolan, R. J. (2002). Emotion, cognition, and behavior. *Science, 298,* 1191-1194.

Domhoff, G. W. (2011). The neural substrate for dreaming: Is it a subsystem of the default network? *Consciousness and Cognition, 20,* 1163-1174.

Domschke, K. (2013). Clinical and molecular genetics of psychotic depression. *Schizophrenia Bulletin, 39,* 766-775.

Domènech-Abella, J., Mundó, J., Haro, J. M., & Rubio-Valera, M. (2019). Anxiety, depression, loneliness and social network in the elderly: Longitudinal associations from the Irish Longitudinal Study on Ageing (TILDA). *Journal of Affective Disorders, 246,* 82-88.

Dono, J., Miller, C., Ettridge, K., & Wilson, C. (2020). The role of social norms in the relationship between anti-smoking advertising campaigns and smoking cessation: A scoping review. *Health Education Research, 35*(3), 179-194.

Doremus, C. F. (2021). Trait theory of Allport. In B. J. Carducci & C. S. Nave (Eds.), *The Wiley Encyclopedia of Personality and Individual Differences, Vol. 1, Models and Theories.* Wiley.

Doty, R. L., Tourbier, I., Ng, V., Neff, J., Armstrong, D., Battistini, M., Sammel, M. D., Gettes, D., Evans, D. L., Mirza, N., Moberg, P. J., Connolly, T., & Sondheimer, S. J. (2015). Influences of hormone replacement therapy on olfactory and cognitive function in post-menopausal women. *Neurobiology of Aging, 36,* 2053-2059.

Douglas, V. J., Kwan, M. Y., Minnich, A. M., & Gordon, K. H. (2019). The interaction of sociocultural attitudes and gender on disordered eating. *Journal of Clinical Psychology.* https://doi.org/10.1002/jclp.22835.

Douthit, K. Z., & Russotti, J. (2017). Biology of marginality: A neurophysiological exploration of the social and cultural foundations of psychological health. In T. A. Field, L. K. Jones, L. A. Russell-Chapin, T. A. Field, L. K. Jones, & L. A. Russell-Chapin (Eds.), *Neurocounseling: Brain-based clinical approaches.* American Counseling Association.

Downing, K. L. (2015). *Intelligence emerging.* MIT Press.

Drakatos, P., Marples, L., Muza, R., Higgins, S., Nesbitt, A., Dongol, E. M., et al. (2019). Video polysomnographic findings in non-rapid eye movement parasomnia. *Journal of Sleep Research, 28*(2), 1-8.

Draper, K. (2019, August 6). Video games get blame, despite lack of evidence. *The New York Times,* p. 13.

Dresler, T., Guhn, A., Tupak, S. V., Ehlis, A., Herrmann, M. J., Fallgatter, A. J., Deckert, J., & Domschke, K. (2013). Revise the revised? New dimensions of the neuroanatomical hypothesis of panic disorder. *Journal of Neural Transmission, 120,* 3-29.

Drewes, A. A. (2005). Play in selected cultures: Diversity and universality. In E. Gil & A. A. Drewes (Eds.), *Cultural issues in play therapy.* Guilford Press.

Drexler, P. (2021, April 3-4). When the pandemic's end means the return of anxiety. *Wall Street Journal,* p. C3.

Driessen, E., Van, H. L., Peen, J., Don, F. J., Twisk, J. R., Cuijpers, P., & Dekker, J. J. M. (2017). Cognitive-behavioral versus psychodynamic therapy for major depression: Secondary outcomes of a randomized clinical trial. *Journal of Consulting and Clinical Psychology, 85,* 653-663.

Driscoll, M. A., Edwards, R. R., Becker, W. C., Kaptchuk, T. J., & Kerns, R. D. (2021). Psychological interventions for the treatment of chronic pain in adults. *Psychological Science in the Public Interest, 22*(2), 52-95.

Driver, M. Y. (2022). Switching codes and shifting morals: How code-switching and emotion affect moral judgment. *International Journal of Bilingual Education and Bilingualism, 25*(3), 905-921.

Dryden, W., & David, D. (2008). Rational emotive behavior therapy: Current status. *Journal of Cognitive Psychotherapy, 22,* 195-209.

Dubreuil, L., & Savage-Rumbaugh, S. (2018). *Dialogues on the human ape.* University of Minnesota Press.

Duckworth, A. (2016). *Grit: The power of passion and perseverance.* Scribner/Simon & Schuster.

Dudai, Y. (2011). The engram revisited: On the elusive permanence of memory. In S. Nalbantian, P. M. Matthews, & J. L. McClelland (Eds.), *The memory process: Neuroscientific and humanistic perspectives.* Cambridge, MA: MIT Press.

Dudley, M. Z., Halsey, N. A., Omer, S. B., Orenstein, W. A., T O'Leary, S., Limaye, R. J., & Salmon, D. A. (2020). The state of vaccine safety science: Systematic reviews of the evidence. *The Lancet Infectious Diseases, 20*(5), e80-e89.

Dufford, A. J., Bianco, H., & Kim, P. (2019). Socioeconomic disadvantage, brain morphometry, and attentional bias to threat in middle childhood. *Cognitive, Affective & Behavioral Neuroscience, 19*(2), 309-326.

Duffy, F., Sharpe, H., & Schwannauer, M. (2019). Review: The effectiveness of interpersonal psychotherapy for adolescents with depression-a systematic review and meta-analysis. *Child and Adolescent Mental Health, 24*(4), 307-317.

Dugre, J. R., Eickhoff, S. B., & Potvin, S. (2022). Meta-analytical transdiagnostic neural correlates in common pediatric psychiatric disorders. *Scientific Reports, 12*(1), 4909. https://doi.org/10.1038/s41598-022-08909-3

Duke, M., & Nowicki, S., Jr. (1979). *Abnormal psychology: Perspectives on being different.* Brooks/Cole.

Duncker, K. (1945). On problem solving. (L S. Lees, Trans). *Psychological Monographs, 58* (5), i-113.

Dunkley, D. M., Lewkowski, M., Lee, I. A., Preacher, K. J., Zuroff, D. C., Berg, J., Foley, J. E., Myhr, G., & Westreich, R. (2017). Daily stress, coping, and negative and positive affect in depression: Complex trigger and maintenance patterns. *Behavior Therapy, 48,* 349-365.

Dunn, E. C., Soare, T. W., Zhu, Y., Simpkin, A. J., Suderman, M. J., Klengel, T., Smith, A. D. A. C., Ressler, K. J., & Relton, C. L. (2019). Sensitive periods for the effect of childhood adversity on DNA methylation: Results from a prospective, longitudinal study. *Biological Psychiatry, 85*(10), 838-849.

Durán, J. I., & Fernández-Dols, J.-M. (2021). Do emotions result in their predicted facial expressions? A meta-analysis of studies on the co-occurrence of expression and emotion. *Emotion, 21*(7), 1550-1569. https://doi.org/10.1037/emo0001015

Durbin, A., Nisenbaum, R., Kopp, B., O'Campo, P., Hwang, S. W., & Stergiopoulos, V. (2019). Are resilience and perceived stress related to social support and housing stability among homeless adults with mental illness? *Health & Social Care in the Community, 27*(4), 1053-1062.

Duwe, G. (2020). Patterns and prevalence of lethal mass violence. *Criminology & Public Policy, 19*(1), 17-35.

Dweck, C. S. (2017). Is psychology headed in the right direction? Yes, no, and maybe. *Perspectives on Psychological Science, 12,* 656-659.

Dweck, C. S., & Yeager, D. S. (2018). Mindsets change the imagined and actual future. In G. Oettingen, A. T. Sevincer, & P. Gollwitzer (Eds.), *The psychology of thinking about the future.* Guilford Press.

Dweck, C. S., & Yeager, D. S. (2019). Mindsets: A view from two eras. *Perspectives on Psychological Science, 14*(3), 481-496.

Eagleman, D. M., & Vaughn, D. A. (2021). The Defensive Activation Theory: REM Sleep as a Mechanism to Prevent Takeover of the Visual Cortex. *Frontiers in neuroscience, 15,* 632853. https://doi.org/10.3389/fnins.2021.632853

Ebbinghaus, H. (1885/1913). *Memory: A contribution to experimental psychology* (H. A. Roger & C. E. Bussenius, Trans.). Columbia University Press.

Eberhardt, J. L. (2022, March/April). Presidential column: Robert B. Cialdini and Jennifer L. Eberhardt on the 7 principles of influence. *Observer.*

Ebigbo, P. O., Lekwas, E. C., & Chukwunenyem, N. F. (2015). Brain fag: New perspectives from case observations. *Transcultural Psychiatry, 52,* 311-330.

Ebrahimian, Z., Karimi, Z., Khoshnoud, M. J., Namavar, M. R., Daraei, B., & Haidari, M. R. (2017). Behavioral and stereological analysis of the effects of intermittent feeding diet on the orally administered MDMA ("ecstasy") in mice. *Innovations in Clinical Neuroscience, 14,* 40-52.

Ecker, U. H., Tay, J., & Brown, G. A. (2015). Effects of prestudy and poststudy rest on memory: Support for temporal interference accounts of forgetting. *Psychonomic Bulletin & Review, 22,* 772-778.

Ecker, U. K., Lewandowsky, S., Cook, J., Schmid, P., Fazio, L. K., Brashier, N., Brashier, N., Kendeou, P., Vraga, E. K., & Amazeen, M. A. (2022). The psychological drivers of misinformation belief and its resistance to correction. *Nature Reviews Psychology, 1*(1), 13-29.

Eckhardt, A. G., & Egert, F. (2020). Predictors for the quality of family child care: A meta-analysis. *Children and Youth Services Review, 116,* 105205.

Edelson, L., Nguyen, M. K., Goldstein, I., Goga, O., McCoy, D., & Lauinger, T. (2021, November). Understanding engagement with US (mis) information news sources on Facebook. In *Proceedings of the 21st ACM Internet Measurement Conference.*

Edenbrandt, A. K., Lagerkvist, C. J., & Nordström, J. (2021). Interested, indifferent or active information avoiders of carbon labels: Cognitive dissonance and ascription of responsibility as motivating factors. *Food Policy, 101,* 102036.

Edinoff, A. N., Akuly, H. A., Hanna, T. A., Ochoa, C. O., Patti, S. J., Ghaffar, Y. A., Kaye, A. D., Viswanath, O., Urits, I., Boyer, A. G., Cornett, E. M., & Kaye, A. M. (2021). Selective serotonin reuptake inhibitors and adverse effects: A narrative review. *Neurology International, 13*(3), 387-401.

Edunjobi, A. S., Adelowo, O. O., Oguntona, S. A., & Olatunde, O. A. (2021). Reflex sympathetic dystrophy syndrome (Complex Regional Pain Syndrome type 1) in a Nigerian woman-a case report. *African Journal of Medicine and Medical Sciences, 50*(1), 151-154.

Edwards, C., Edwards, A., Stoll, B., Lin, X., & Massey, N. (2019). Evaluations of an artificial intelligence instructor's voice: Social identity theory in human-robot interactions. *Computers in Human Behavior, 90,* 357-362.

Edwards, M. S., Moore, P., Champion, J. C., & Edwards, E. J. (2015). Effects of trait anxiety and situational stress on attentional shifting are buffered by working memory capacity. *Anxiety, Stress & Coping: An International Journal, 28,* 1-16.

Efklides, A., & Moraitou, D. (2013). *A positive psychology perspective on quality of life.* Springer Science + Business Media.

Egan, K. J., Knutson, K. L., Pereira, A. C., & von Schantz, M. (2017). The role of race and ethnicity in sleep, circadian rhythms and cardiovascular health. *Sleep Medicine Reviews, 33,* 70-78.

Egervari, G., Ciccocioppo, R., Jentsch, J. D., & Hurd, Y. L. (2017). Shaping vulnerability to addiction-the contribution of behavior, neural circuits and molecular mechanisms. *Neuroscience and Biobehavioral Reviews.* http://www.sciencedirect.com/science/article/pii/S0149763417300866

Eggertson L. (2010). Lancet retracts 12-year-old article linking autism to MMR vaccines. *CMAJ: Canadian Medical Association Journal = Journal de l'Association Medicale Canadienne, 182*(4), E199-E200.

Ehde, D. M., Dillworth, T. M., & Turner, J. A. (2014). Cognitive-behavioral therapy for individuals with chronic pain: Efficacy, innovations, and directions for research. *American Psychologist, 69,* 153-177.

Eklund, R., Bondjers, K., Hensler, I., Bragesjö, M., Johannesson, K. B., Arnberg, F. K., & Sveen, J. (2022). Daily uplifts during the COVID-19 pandemic: What is considered helpful in everyday life? *BMC Public Health, 22*(1), 1-10.

Ekman, E., & Simon-Thomas, E. (2021). Teaching the science of human flourishing, unlocking connection, positivity, and resilience for the greater good. *Global Advances in Health and Medicine, 10,* 2164956121102307.

Ekman, P. (1972). Universals and cultural differences in facial expressions of emotion. In J. Cole (Ed.), *Darwin and facial expression: A century of research in review.* Academic Press.

Ekman, P. (1994). Strong evidence for universals in facial expressions: A reply to Russell's mistaken critique. *Psychological Bulletin, 115,* 268-287.

Ekman, P. (2007). *Emotions revealed* (2nd ed.). Holt.

Ekman, P., Levenson, R. W., & Friesen, W. V. (1983). Autonomic nervous system activity distinguishes among emotions. *Science, 223,* 1208-1210.

Ekonomou, A., Savva, G. M., Brayne, C., Forster, G., Francis, P. T., Johnson, M., Perry, E. K., Attems, J., Somani, A., Minger, S. L., Ballard, C. G., & Medical Research Council Cognitive Function and Ageing Neuropathy Study. (2015). Stage-specific changes in neurogenic and glial markers in Alzheimer's disease. *Biological Psychiatry, 77,* 711-719.

Elder, A. (2022). Friendship and social media. In D. Jeske (Ed.), *The Routledge Handbook of Philosophy of Friendship.* Routledge.

Elen, M., D'Heer, E., Geuens, M., & Vermeir, I. (2013). The influence of mood on attitude-behavior consistency. *Journal of Business Research, 66,* 917-923.

Elias, V. L., Fullerton, A. S., & Simpson, J. M. (2015). Long-term changes in attitudes toward premarital sex in the United States: Reexamining the role of cohort replacement. *Journal of Sex Research, 52,* 129-139.

Eljamel, S. (2015). Ablative surgery for depression. In B. Sun & A. De Salles (Eds.), *Neurosurgical treatments for psychiatric disorders.* Springer Science + Business Media.

Elkins, D. (2009). Why humanistic psychology lost its power and influence in American psychology: Implications for advancing humanistic psychology. *Journal of Humanistic Psychology, 49,* 267-291.

Ellinson, Z., Campo-Flores, A., McWhirter, C., & Frosch, D. (2022, June 3). The altered lives of America's school-shooting survivors. *Wall Street Journal,* pp. A1, A9.

Elliot, A. J., Dweck, C. S., & Yeager, D. S. (2017). *Handbook of competence and motivation: Theory and application* (2nd ed.). Guilford Press.

Elliott, M. L., Knodt, A. R., & Hariri, A. R. (2021). Striving toward translation: Strategies for reliable fMRI measurement. *Trends in Cognitive Sciences, 25*(9), 776-787.

Ellis, A. (1974). *Growth through reason.* Wilshire Books.

Ellis, A. (2002). *Overcoming resistance: A rational emotive behavior therapy integrated approach* (2nd ed.). Springer.

Ellis, A. (2004). Expanding the ABCs of rational emotive behavior therapy. In A. Freeman, M. J. Mahoney, P. Devito, & D. Martin (Eds.), *Cognition and psychotherapy* (2nd ed.). Springer Publishing.

Ellis, D. J. (2021). Rational emotive behavior therapy. In A. Wenzel (Ed.), *Handbook of cognitive behavioral therapy: Overview and approaches.* American Psychological Association. https://doi.org/10.1037/0000218-015

Elmlinger, S. L., Schwade, J. A., & Goldstein, M. H. (2019). The ecology of prelinguistic vocal learning: Parents simplify the structure of their speech in response to babbling. *Journal of Child Language,* 1-14. https://doi.org/10.1017/S0305000919000291

Ember, C. R., & Carolus, C. (2017). Altered states of consciousness. *Explaining human culture.* https://hraf.yale.edu/ehc/summaries/altered-states-of-consciousness

Emmett, J., & McGee, D. (2013). Extrinsic motivation for large-scale assessments: A case study of a student achievement program at one urban high school. *High School Journal, 96*, 116-137.

Emre, M. (2019). *The personality brokers.* Doubleday.

Enge, L. R., Lupo, A. K., & Zárate, M. A. (2015). Neurocognitive mechanisms of prejudice formation: The role of time-dependent memory consolidation. *Psychological Science, 26*, 964-971.

Epley, N., & Schroeder, J. (2014). Mistakenly seeking solitude. *Journal of Experimental Psychology: General, 143(5)*, 1980-1999.

Erb, J., Henry, M. J., Eisner, F., & Obleser, J. (2013). The brain dynamics of rapid perceptual adaptation to adverse listening conditions. *Journal of Neuroscience, 33*, 10688-10697.

Erbil, D. G. (2020). A review of flipped classroom and cooperative learning method within the context of Vygotsky theory. *Frontiers in Psychology, 11*, 1157.

Erickson, K. I., Gildengers, A. G., & Butters, M. A. (2022). Physical activity and brain plasticity in late adulthood. *Dialogues in Clinical Neuroscience, 15(1)*, 99-108.

Erickson, W. B., Wright, A., & Naveh-Benjamin, M. (2022). "He was the one with the gun!" Associative memory for white and black faces seen with weapons. *Cognitive research: principles and implications, 7(1)*, 1-18.

Erikson, E. H. (1963). *Childhood and society.* Norton.

Erlam, G., Smythe, L., & Wright-St Clair, V. (2018). Action research and millennials: Improving pedagogical approaches to encourage critical thinking. *Nurse Education Today, 61*, 140-145.

Ernst, M., Niederer, D., Werner, A. M., Czaja, S. J., Mikton, C., Ong, A. D., Rosen, T., Brähler, E., & Beutel, M. E. (2022). Loneliness before and during the COVID-19 pandemic: A systematic review with meta-analysis. *American Psychologist, 77(5)*, 660-677.

Erzurumluoglu, A. M., Liu, M., Jackson, V. E., Barnes, D. R., Datta, G., Melbourne, C. A., Young, R., Batini, C., Surendran, P., Jiang, T., Adnan, S. D., Afaq, S., Agrawal, A., Altmaier, E., Antoniou, A., C., Asselbergs, F. W., Baumbach, C., Bierut, L., Bertelsen, S., Boehnke, M., et al. (2019). Meta-analysis of up to 622,409 individuals identifies 40 novel smoking behaviours associated genetic loci. *Molecular Psychiatry, 25(10)*, 2392-2409. https://doi.org/10.1038/s41380-018-0313-0

Esparham, A. E., & Dilts, J. J. (2019). Integrative management of pediatric primary headaches. *Pediatric Annals, 48(6)*, e231-e235.

Espinola, M., DeVinney, H., & Steinberg, A. (2017). Women at midlife. In K. A. Kendall-Tackett & L. M. Ruglass (Eds.), *Women's mental health across the lifespan: Challenges, vulnerabilities, and strengths.* Routledge/Taylor & Francis Group.

Esser, M. B., Pickens, C. M., Guy Jr, G. P., & Evans, M. E. (2021). Binge drinking, other substance use, and concurrent use in the US, 2016-2018. *American journal of preventive medicine, 60(2)*, 169-178.

Esteves, M., Ganz, E., Sousa, N., & Leite-Almeida, H. (2021). Asymmetrical brain plasticity: Physiology and pathology. *Neuroscience, 454*, 3-14.

Etchell, A., Adhikari, A., Weinberg, L. S., Choo, A. L., Garnett, E. O., Chow, H. M., & Chang, S. E. (2018). A systematic literature review of sex differences in childhood language and brain development. *Neuropsychologia, 114*, 19-31.

Eternod, V. (2021). The cultural perspective: Are some societies happier than others? In T. Dutta & M. K. Mandal (Eds.), *Consumer happiness: Multiple perspectives.* Springer.

Etienne, J. (2013). Thoughts on how to regulate behaviours: An overview of the current debate. *British Journal of Guidance & Counselling, 41*, 36-45.

Etxeberria, I., Etxebarria, I., & Urdaneta, E. (2019). Subjective well-being among the oldest old: The role of personality traits. *Personality and Individual Differences, 146*, 209-216.

Etzrodt, C. M. (2013). Ethical considerations of therapeutic hypnosis and children. *American Journal of Clinical Hypnosis, 55*, 370-377.

Euler, M. J., Weisend, M. P., Jung, R. E., Thoma, R. J., & Yeo, R. A. (2015). Reliable activation to novel stimuli predicts higher fluid intelligence. *Neuroimage, 114*, 311-319.

Evcik, D., Kavuncu, V., Cakir, T., Subasi, V., & Yaman, M. (2007). Laser therapy in the treatment of carpal tunnel syndrome: A randomized controlled trial. *Photomedical Laser Surgery, 25*, 34-39.

Eysenck, H. J. (1995). *Eysenck on extraversion.* Wiley.

Fabian, M. (2019). The coalescence of being: A model of the self-actualisation process. *Journal of Happiness Studies: An Interdisciplinary Forum on Subjective Well-Being.* https://doi.org/10.1007/s10902-019-00141-7.

Facco, E., Bacci, C., Casiglia, E., & Zanette, G. (2021). Preserved critical ability and free will in deep hypnosis during oral surgery. *American Journal of Clinical Hypnosis, 63(3)*, 229-241.

Fadjukoff, P., Feldt, T., Kokko, K., & Pulkkinen, L. (2019). Identity status change within personal style clusters: A longitudinal perspective from early adulthood to midlife. *Identity, 19(1)*, 1-17.

Fadus, M., Odunsi, O. T., & Squeglia, L. M. (2019). Race, ethnicity, and culture in the medical record: Implicit bias or patient advocacy? *Academic Psychiatry*, 1-5.

Fagan III, J. F. (2018). Infant recognition memory as a present and future index of cognitive abilities. In N. R. Ellis (Ed.), *Aberrant development in infancy.* Routledge.

Fagan, J., & Press, J. (2008). Father influences on employed mothers' work-family balance. *Journal of Family Issues, 29*, 1136-1160.

Fagan, J. F., & Holland, C. R. (2007). Racial equality in intelligence: Predictions from a theory of intelligence as processing. *Intelligence, 35*, 319-334.

Fagan, J. F., & Holland, C. R. (2009). Culture-fair prediction of academic achievement. *Intelligence, 37*, 62-67.

Fagelson, M., & Baguley, D. M. (2018). Hyperacusis: Past, present, and future. In M. Fagelson & D. M. Baguley (Eds.), *Hyperacusis and disorders of sound intolerance: Clinical and research perspectives.* Plural Publishing.

Falasca, N. W., D'Ascenzo, S., Di Domenico, A., Onofrj, M., Tommasi, L., Laeng, B., & Franciotti, R. (2015). Hemispheric lateralization in top-down attention during spatial relation processing: A Granger causal model approach. *European Journal of Neuroscience, 41*, 912-922.

Falbe, J., Thompson, H. R., Patel, A., & Madsen, K. A. (2019). Potentially addictive properties of sugar-sweetened beverages among adolescents. *Appetite, 133*, 130-137.

Fantegrossi, W. E., Wilson, C. D., & Berquist, M. D. (2018). Pro-psychotic effects of synthetic cannabinoids: Interactions with central dopamine, serotonin, and glutamate systems. *Drug Metabolism Reviews, 50(1)*, 65-73.

Farnsworth, D. L. (2015). Identical twins raised apart. *Teaching Statistics, 37*, 1-6.

Farrell, A. K., Simpson, J. A., Carlson, E. A., Englund, M. M., & Sung, S. (2017). The impact of stress at different life stages on physical health and the buffering effects of maternal sensitivity. *Health Psychology, 36*, 35-44.

Faupel, A., Herrick, E., & Sharp, P. M. (2018). *Anger management: A practical guide for teachers* (3rd ed.). Routledge/Taylor & Francis Group.

Faur, S., & Laursen, B. (2022). Classroom seat proximity predicts friendship formation. *Frontiers in Psychology*, 2183. https://doi.org/10.3389/fpsyg.2022.796002

Favreau, M., Hillert, A., Osen, B., Gärtner, T., Hunatschek, S., Riese, M., . . . & Voderholzer, U. (2021). Psychological consequences and differential impact of the COVID-19 pandemic in patients with mental disorders. *Psychiatry research, 302*, 114045.

Fayek, A. (2017). *Understanding classical psychoanalysis: Freudian concepts in contemporary practice.* Routledge/Taylor & Francis Group.

Fazio, L. K., Rand, D. G., & Pennycook, G. (2019). Repetition increases perceived truth equally for plausible and implausible statements. *Psychonomic Bulletin & Review, 26(5)*, 1705-1710.

Federal Bureau of Investigation. (2019, September 30). FBI releases 2018 crime statistics. News release. https://www.fbi.gov/news/pressrel/press-releases/fbi-releases-2018-crime-statistics

Federal Interagency Forum on Child and Family Statistics. (2019). Fam5 language spoken at home and difficulty speaking English: Number of children ages 5-17 who speak a language other than English at home by language spoken and ability to speak English, and the percentages of those speaking a language other than English at home and those with difficulty speaking English by selected characteristics, selected years 1979-2019. https://www.childstats.gov/americaschildren/tables/fam5.asp

Federal Interagency Forum on Child, & Family Studies (Eds.). (2021). *America's Children: Key National Indicators of Well-Being, 2017.* Government Printing Office.

Fedyk, M. (2017). *The social turn in moral psychology.* MIT Press.

Feld, G. B., & Born, J. (2017). Sculpting memory during sleep: Concurrent consolidation and forgetting. *Current Opinion in Neurobiology, 44*, 20-27.

Feldman, R. S. (2017). *P.O.W.E.R. Learning: Strategies for success in college and life.* McGraw Hill.

Feng, B., Bell, R. A., Jerant, A. F., & Kravitz, R. L. (2011). What do doctors say when prescribing medications? An examination of medical recommendations from a communication perspective. *Health Communication, 26*, 286-296.

Fenster, R. J., Lebois, L. A., Ressler, K. J., & Suh, J. (2018). Brain circuit dysfunction in post-traumatic stress disorder: From mouse to man. *Nature Reviews Neuroscience, 19(9)*, 535-551.

Ferguson, C. J. (2015). "Everybody knows psychology is not a real science": Public perceptions of psychology and how we can improve our relationship with policymakers, the scientific community, and the general public. *American Psychologist, 70*, 527-542.

Ferguson, C. J., & Beresin, E. (2017). Social science's curious war with pop culture and how it was lost: The media violence debate and the risks it holds for social science. *Preventive Medicine: An International Journal Devoted to Practice and Theory, 99*, 69-76.

Ferguson, C. J., & Wang, J. C. K. (2019). Aggressive video games are not a risk factor for future aggression in youth: A longitudinal study. *Journal of Youth and Adolescence, 48(8)*, 1439-1451.

Ferjan Ramirez, N., Lytle, S. R., Fish, M., & Kuhl, P. K. (2019). Parent coaching at 6 and 10 months improves language outcomes at 14 months: A randomized controlled trial. *Developmental Science, 22(3)*, e12762.

Fernald, R. D. (2015). Social behaviour: Can it change the brain? *Animal Behaviour, 103*, 259-265.

Fernandez, E. J., & Martin, A. L. (2021). Animal Training, Environmental Enrichment, and Animal Welfare: A History of Behavior Analysis in Zoos. *Journal of Zoological and Botanical Gardens, 2(4)*, 531-543.

Fernbach, P. M., Rogers, T., Fox, C. R., & Sloman, S. A. (2013). Political extremism is supported by an illusion of understanding. *Psychological Science, 24(6)*, 939-946.

Fernyhough, C. (2017). Talking to ourselves. *Scientific American, 317*, 74-79.

Fernández-Sotos, P., García, A. S., Vicente-Querol, M. A., Lahera, G., Rodriguez-Jimenez, R., & Fernández-Caballero, A. (2021). Validation of dynamic virtual faces for facial affect recognition. *PLOS ONE, 16(1)*, e0246001.

Ferranti, J. (2015). DSM-5: Development and implementation. In C. Scott (Ed.), *DSM-5® and the law: Changes and challenges.* Oxford University Press.

Ferring, D., Tournier, I., & Mancini, D. (2015). "The closer you get . . .": Age, attitudes and self-serving evaluations about older drivers. *European Journal of Ageing, 12(3)*, 229-238.

Festinger, D., Marlowe, D., Croft, J., Dugosh, K., Arabia, P., & Benasutti, K. (2009). Monetary incentives improve recall of research consent information: It pays to remember. *Experimental and Clinical Psychopharmacology, 17*, 99-104.

Festinger, L. (1957). *A theory of cognitive dissonance.* Stanford University Press.

Festinger, L., & Carlsmith, J. M. (1959). Cognitive consequences of forced compliance. *Journal of Abnormal and Social Psychology, 58,* 203-210.

Festini, S. B., & Reuter-Lorenz, P. A. (2017). Rehearsal of to-be-remembered items is unnecessary to perform directed forgetting within working memory: Support for an active control mechanism. *Journal of Experimental Psychology: Learning, Memory, and Cognition, 43,* 94-108.

Fevang, S. E., Hysing, M., Sommerfelt, K., & Elgen, I. (2017). Mental health assessed by the strengths and difficulties questionnaire for children born extremely preterm without severe disabilities at 11 years of age: A Norwegian, national population-based study. *European Child & Adolescent Psychiatry, 26*(12), 1523-1531.

Fichtenberg, C. M., & Glantz, S. A. (2006). Association of the California tobacco control program with declines in cigarette consumption and mortality from heart disease. In K. E. Warner (Ed.), *Tobacco control policy.* Jossey-Bass.

Fields, R.D. (2016). *Why we snap: Understanding the rage circuit in your brain.* Penguin.

Figen, A. (2011). The relationship between test anxiety and learned helplessness. *Social Behavior and Personality, 39,* 101-112.

Filip, M., Lukavská, K., & Šolcová, I. P. (2019). Dialogical and integrated self in late adulthood: Examining two adaptive ways of growing old. *The International Journal of Aging and Human Development.* https://doi.org/10.1177/0091415019831445.

Finan, P. H., Zautra, A. J., & Wershba, R. (2011). The dynamics of emotion in adaptation to stress. In R. J. Contrada & A. Baum (Eds.), *The handbook of stress science: Biology, psychology, and health.* Springer.

Findley, A. M., de Rutte, J. L., & Dennis-Tiwary, T. A. (2022). The Impact of Social Media Use on Youth and Adolescent Health. Routledge.

Fine, R., & Fine, L. (2003). *Basic chess endings.* Random House.

Fink, S. (2017, July 28). Two C.I.A. psychologists can face trial, judge rules. *The New York Times,* p. A18.

Finke, M. S., Howe, J. S., & Huston, S. J. (2017). Old age and the decline in financial literacy. *Management Science, 63,* 213-230.

Finn, A. (2011). Jungian analytical theory. In D. Capuzzi & D. R. Gross (Eds.), *Counseling and psychotherapy* (5th ed.). American Counseling Association.

Finn, K. (2015). Sequelae of cannabis as medicine. *Pain Medicine, 16,* 1447-1449.

First, M. B., Yousif, L. H., Clarke, D. E., Wang, P. S., Gogtay, N., & Appelbaum, P. S. (2022). DSM-5-TR: Overview of what's new and what's changed. *World Psychiatry, 21*(2), 218.

Fischer, K. W., Shaver, P. R., & Carnochan, P. (1990). How emotions develop and how they organize development. *Cognition and Emotion, 4,* 81-127.

Fischer, M. C. (2018, October 29). It's been 15 years since Aron Ralston amputated his arm in Blue John Canyon. *5280.* https://www.5280.com/2018/10/its-been-15-years-since-aron-ralston-amputated-his-arm-in-blue-john-canyon/

Fishbach, A., & Woolley, K. (2022). The structure of intrinsic motivation. *Annual Review of Organizational Psychology and Organizational Behavior, 9*(1), 339-363.

Fisher, A. K., Moore, D. J., Simmons, C., & Allen, S. C. (2017). Teaching social workers about microaggressions to enhance understanding of subtle racism. *Journal of Human Behavior in the Social Environment, 27*(4), 346-355.

Fisher, G. G., & Barnes-Farrell, J. L. (2013). Use of archival data in occupational health psychology research. In R. R. Sinclair, M. Wang, & L. E. Tetrick (Eds.), *Research methods in occupational health psychology: Measurement, design, and data analysis.* Routledge/Taylor & Francis Group.

Fiske, S. T. (2017). Going in many right directions, all at once. *Perspectives on Psychology, 12,* 652-655.

Flanagan, D. P., & McDonough, E. M. (Eds.). (2018). *Contemporary intellectual assessment: Theories, tests, andissues* (4th ed.). The Guilford Press.

Flannelly, K. J. (2017). *Religious beliefs, evolutionary psychiatry, and mental health in America: Evolutionary threat assessment systems theory.* Cham, Switzerland: Springer International Publishing.

Fleming, J. (2000). Affirmative action and standardized test scores. *Journal of Negro Education, 69,* 27-37.

Flick, C., & Schweitzer, K. (2021). Influence of the fundamental attribution error on perceptions of blame and negligence. *Experimental Psychology, 68*(4), 175-188. https://doi.org/10.1027/1618-3169/a000526

Flint, J. (2022). Behavioral genetics in the 21st century. *Current Biology, 32*(5), R202-R203.

Flohr, E. R., Erwin, E., Croy, I., & Hummel, T. (2017). Sad man's nose: Emotion induction and olfactory perception. *Emotion, 17,* 369-378.

Flotte, T. R., Cataltepe, O., Puri, A., Batista, A. R., Moser, R., McKenna-Yasek, D., Douthwright, C., Gernoux, G., Blackwood, M., Mueller, C., Tai, P. W. L., Jiang, X., Bateman, S., Spanakis, S. G., Parzych, J. Keeler, A. M., Abayazeed, A., Rohatgi, S., Gibson, L., Finberg, R., et al. (2022). AAV gene therapy for Tay-Sachs disease. *Nature Medicine, 28*(2), 251-259.

Föcking, M., Doyle, B., Munawar, N., Dillon, E. T., Cotter, D., & Cagney, G. (2019). Epigenetic factors in schizophrenia: Mechanisms and experimental approaches. *Molecular Neuropsychiatry, 5*(1), 6-12.

Foell, J., Bekrater-Bodmann, R., Diers, M., & Flor, H. (2014). Mirror therapy for phantom limb pain: Brain changes and the role of body representation. *European Journal of Pain, 18*(5), 729-739.

Forbus, K. D., Liang, C., & Rabkina, I. (2017). Representation and computation in cognitive models. *Topics in Cognitive Science, 9*(3), 694-718.

Ford, B. Q., & Gross, J. J. (2019). Why beliefs about emotion matter: An emotion-regulation perspective. *Current Directions in Psychological Science, 28*(1), 74-81.

Ford, C. L., & Young, L. J. (2021). Translational opportunities for circuit-based social neuroscience: Advancing 21st century psychiatry. *Current Opinion in Neurobiology, 68,* 1-8.

Forer, B. (1949). The fallacy of personal validation: A classroom demonstration of gullibility. *Journal of Abnormal and Social Psychology, 44,* 118-123.

Forgas, J. P. (2022). Mood effects on sociability: How affect regulates relationship behaviors. In J. P. Forgas, W. Crano, & K. Fiedler (Eds.), *The psychology of sociability.* Routledge.

Forgas, J. P., & Laham, S. M. (2017). Halo effects. In R. F. Pohl (Ed.), *Cognitive illusions: Intriguing phenomena in thinking, judgment and memory.* Routledge/Taylor & Francis Group.

Forsblom, L., Pekrun, R., Loderer, K., & Peixoto, F. (2022). Cognitive appraisals, achievement emotions, and students' math achievement: A longitudinal analysis. *Journal of Educational Psychology, 114*(2), 346-367. https://doi.org/10.1037/edu0000671

Forsdike, K., & Pirotta, M. (2019). St John's wort for depression: Scoping review about perceptions and use by general practitioners in clinical practice. *Journal of Pharmacy and Pharmacology, 71*(1), 117-128.

Forsman, J., Masterman, T., Ahlner, J., Isacsson, G., & Hedström, A. K. (2019). Selective serotonin reuptake inhibitors and the risk of violent suicide: A nationwide postmortem study. *European Journal of Clinical Pharmacology, 75*(3), 393-400.

Forsythe, A. (2019). *Key thinkers in individual differences: Ideas on personality and intelligence.* Routledge.

Forte, A. J., Guliyeva, G., McLeod, H., Salinas, M., Avila, F. R., & Perlman, A. (2021). The impact of optimism on cancer-related and postsurgical cancer pain: A systematic review. *Journal of Pain and Symptom Management, 63*(2), e203-e211.

Forth, G. (2018). Rites of passage. In H. Callan & S. Coleman (Eds.), *The International Encyclopedia of Anthropology.* Wiley.

Fortier, M. S., & Morgan, T. L. (2021). How optimism and physical activity interplay to promote happiness. *Current Psychology,* 1-9.

Foster, K. M. (2005). Introduction: John Uzo Ogbu (1939-2003): How do you ensure the fair consideration of a complex ancestor? Multiple approaches to assessing the work and legacy of John Uzo Ogbu. *International Journal of Qualitative Studies in Education, 18,* 559-564.

Fouladirad, S., Chen, L. V., Roes, M., Chinchani, A., Percival, C., Khangura, J., Zahid, H., Moscovitz, A., Arreaza, L., Wun, C., Sanford, N., Balzan, R., Moritz, S., Menon, M., & Woodward, T. S. (2022). Functional brain networks underlying probabilistic reasoning and delusions in schizophrenia. *Psychiatry Research: Neuroimaging, 323,* 111472.

Frances, A. (2013). *Saving normal: An insider's revolt against out-of-control psychiatric diagnosis, DSM-5, Big Pharma, and the medicalization of ordinary life.* Morrow.

Franceschini, S., Bertoni, S., Lulli, M., Pievani, T., & Facoetti, A. (2022). Short-term effects of videogames on cognitive enhancement: The role of positive emotions. *Journal of Cognitive Enhancement, 6*(1), 29-46.

Francis, G., Cummins, B., Kim, J., Grzeczkowski, L., & Thunell, E. (2019). The moon size illusion does not improve perceptual judgments. *Consciousness and Cognition, 73,* 102754.

Francis, M. M., Hummer, T. A., Vohs, J. L., Yung, M. G., Visco, A. C., Mehdiyoun, N. F., Kulig, T. C., Um, M., Yang, Z., Motamed, M., Liffick, E., Zhang, Y., & Breier, A. (2019). Cognitive effects of bilateral high frequency repetitive transcranial magnetic stimulation in early phase psychosis: A pilot study. *Brain Imaging and Behavior, 13*(3), 852-861.

Frankenburg, W. K., Dodds, J., Archer, P., Shapiro, H., & Bresnick, B. (1992). The Denver II: A major revision and restandardization of the Denver developmental screening test. *Pediatrics, 89,* 91-97.

Franklin, C., Guz, S., Zhang, A., Kim, J., Zheng, H., Hai, A. H., Cho, Y., & Shen, L. (2022). Solution-focused brief therapy for students in schools: A comparative meta-Analysis of the English and Chinese Literature. *Journal of the Society for Social Work and Research, 13*(2).

Franklin, T. B., & Mansuy, I. M. (2011). The involvement of epigenetic defects in mental retardation. *Neurobiology of Learning and Memory, 96,* 61-67.

Frank, S., Goldwater, S., & Keller, F. (2013). Adding sentence types to a model of syntactic ca tegory acquisition. *Topics in Cognitive Science, 5,* 495-521.

Franko, D. L., & Roehrig, J. P. (2011). African American body images. In T. F. Cash & L. Smolak (Eds.), *Body image: A handbook of science, practice, and prevention* (2nd ed.). Guilford Press.

Frantzidis, C. A., Kontana, E., Karkala, A., Nigdelis, V., Karagianni, M., Nday, C. M., . . . & Kourtidou-Papadeli, C. (2019). Current trends and future perspectives of space neuroscience towards preparation for interplanetary missions. *Neurology India, 67*(8), 182.

Freedberg, D. (2011). Memory in art: History and the neuroscience of response. In S. Nalbantian, P. M. Matthews, & J. L. McClelland (Eds.), *The memory process: Neuroscientific and humanistic perspectives.* MIT Press.

Freedman, J. L., & Fraser, S. C. (1966). Compliance without pressure: The foot-in-the-door technique. *Journal of Personality and Social Psychology, 4,* 195-202.

Fresco, D. M. (2013). Tending the garden and harvesting the fruits of behavior therapy. *Behavior Therapy, 44,* 177-179.

Freud, S. (1900). *Group psychology and the analysis of the ego.* London: Hogarth.

Freud, S. (1922/1959). *Group psychology and the analysis of the ego.* Hogarth.

Frey, W. H. (2018). The US will become "minority white" in 2045, Census projects. Brookings Institute. https://www.brookings.edu/blog/the-avenue/2018/03/14/the-us-will-become-minority-white-in-2045-census-projects/

Frias-Navarro, D., Garcia, L., Garcia-Banda, G., Pascual-Soler, M., & Badenes-Ribera, L. (2018). Attitudinal change toward same-sex parents: The effect of the explanation of the etiology of the homosexual sexual orientation. *Sexuality Research and Social Policy, 15*(4), 516-529.

Fridlund, A. J., Beck, H. P., Goldie, W. D., & Irons, G. (2020). The case for Douglas Merritte: Should we bury what is alive and well? *History of Psychology, 23*(2), 132–148. https://doi.org/10.1037/hop0000142

Friedman, S. (2018). Infant habituation: Process, problems and possibilities. In N. R. Ellis (Ed.), *Aberrant development in infancy*. Routledge.

Frisby, C. L. (2020). DSM revisions and the "Western Conundrum". In L. T. Benuto, M. P. Duckworth, A. Masuda, & W. O'Donohue (Eds.), *Prejudice, Stigma, and Oppression*. Springer.

Frodl, T., Janowitz, D., Schmaal, L., Tozzi, L., Dobrowolny, H., Stein, D. J., Veltman, D. J., Wittfeld, K., van Erp, T. G. M., Jahanshad, N., Block, A., Hegenscheid, K., Völzke, H., Lagopoulos, J., Hatton, S., N., Hickie, I. B., Frey, E. M., Carbelledo, A., Brooks, S. J., Vuletic, D., et al. (2017). Childhood adversity impacts on brain subcortical structures relevant to depression. *Journal of Psychiatric Research, 86,* 58–65.

Frosch, A. (2011). The effect of frequency and duration on psychoanalytic outcome: A moment in time. *Psychoanalytic Review, 98,* 11–38.

Frost, J. C., Molinari, V., Dobbs, D., Edgar, V. B., Jones, K. S., Pietz, C., et al. (2019). Who gets certified by the American Board of Professional Psychology and why: A diversity survey. *Journal of Clinical Psychology, 75*(10), 1820–1837.

Fry, R., Passel, J.S., & Cohn, D. (2020, September 4). A majority of young adults in the U.S. live with their parents for the first time since the Great Depression. Pew Research Center. https://www.pewresearch.org/fact-tank/2020/09/04/a-majority-of-young-adults-in-the-u-s-live-with-their-parents-for-the-first-time-since-the-great-depression/

Fryling, M. J. (2017). The functional independence of Skinner's verbal operants: Conceptual and applied implications. *Behavioral Interventions, 32,* 70–78.

Fuentes J J, Fonseca F, Elices M, Farré M, Torrens M. (2020) Therapeutic Use of LSD in Psychiatry: A Systematic Review of Randomized-Controlled Clinical Trials. Front Psychiatry. 10:943.

Fuhrman, O., McCormick, K., Chen, E., Jiang, H., Shu, D., Mao, S., & Boroditsky, L. (2011). How linguistic and cultural forces shape conceptions of time: English and Mandarin time in 3D. *Cognitive Science: A Multidisciplinary Journal, 7,* 1305–1328.

Fujita, K., Nakamura, N., Watanabe, S., & Ushitani, T. (2017). Comparative visual illusions: Evolutionary, cross-cultural, and developmental perspectives. In J. Call, G. M. Burghardt, I. M. Pepperberg, C. T. Snowdon, & T. Zentall (Eds.), *APA handbook of comparative psychology: Perception, learning, and cognition*. American Psychological Association.

Furumoto, L., & Scarborough, E. (2002). Placing women in the history of psychology: The first American women psychologists. In W. E. Pickren (Ed.), *Evolving perspectives on the history of psychology*. Washington, DC: American Psychological Association.

Furuyashiki, T., & Kitaoka, S. (2019). Neural mechanisms underlying adaptive and maladaptive consequences of stress: Roles of dopaminergic and inflammatory responses. *Psychiatry and Clinical Neurosciences.* https://doi.org/10.1111/pcn.12901.

Fusaro, M., Tieri, G., & Aglioti, S. M. (2019). Influence of cognitive stance and physical perspective on subjective and autonomic reactivity to observed pain and pleasure: An immersive virtual reality study. *Consciousness and Cognition: An International Journal, 67,* 86–97.

Gable, S.L., Hopper, E.A., Schooler, J.W. (2019). When the muses strike: Creative ideas of physicists and writers routinely occur during mind wandering. *Psychological Science,* 1–9.

Gade, M., Souza, A. S., Druey, M. D., & Oberauer, K. (2017). Analogous selection processes in declarative and procedural working memory: N-2 list-repetition and task-repetition costs. *Memory & Cognition, 45,* 26–39.

Gafner, G. (2013). Review of Subliminal: How your unconscious mind rules your behavior. *American Journal of Clinical Hypnosis, 56,* 192–193.

Gaidai, A. (2021). Factors of the Barnum effect: Analysis and prospects. *Psikhologicheskii Zhurnal, 42*(2), 61–70.

Gainotti, G. (2019). Emotions and the right hemisphere: Can new data clarify old models? *The Neuroscientist, 25*(3), 258–270.

Gál, É., Ștefan, S., & Cristea, I. A. (2021). The efficacy of mindfulness meditation apps in enhancing users' well-being and mental health related outcomes: A meta-analysis of randomized controlled trials. *Journal of Affective Disorders, 279,* 131–142.

Galambos, N. L., Fang, S., Krahn, H. J., Johnson, M. D., & Lachman, M. E. (2015). Up, not down: The age curve in happiness from early adulthood to midlife in two longitudinal studies. *Developmental Psychology, 51*(11), 1664–1671.

Galanter, M., III. (2018). Combining medically assisted treatment and twelve-step programming: A perspective and review. *The American Journal of Drug and Alcohol Abuse, 44*(2), 151–159.

Galdi, G. (2015). Celebrating the 75th anniversary of the *American Journal of Psychoanalysis*. *American Journal of Psychoanalysis, 75,* 1–2.

Galef, D. (2001). The information you provide is anonymous, but what was your name again? *Chronicle of Higher Education, 47,* p. B5.

Gallacher, J. D., Heerdink, M. W., & Hewstone, M. (2021). Online engagement between opposing political protest groups via social media is linked to physical violence of offline encounters. *Social Media+ Society, 7*(1), 2056305120984445.

Gallagher, M. W., Long, L. J., & Phillips, C. A. (2020). Hope, optimism, self-efficacy, and posttraumatic stress disorder: A meta-analytic review of the protective effects of positive expectancies. *Journal of Clinical Psychology, 76*(3), 329–355.

Gallo, M. M. (2015). *"No one helped": Kitty Genovese, New York City, and the myth of urban apathy*. Cornell University Press.

Gallucci, A., Riva, P., Lauro, L. J. R., & Bushman, B. J. (2020). Stimulating the ventrolateral prefrontal cortex (VLPFC) modulates frustration-induced aggression: A tDCS experiment. *Brain Stimulation, 13*(2), 302–309.

Galmiche, M., Déchelotte, P., Lambert, G., & Tavolacci, M. P. (2019). Prevalence of eating disorders over the 2000–2018 period: A systematic literature review. *The American Journal of Clinical Nutrition, 109*(5), 1402–1413.

Gandolphe, M., & El Haj, M. (2017). Flashbulb memories of the Paris attacks. *Scandinavian Journal of Psychology, 58,* 199–204.

Ganna, A., Verweij, K. J. H., Nivard, M. G., Maier, R., Wedow, R., Busch, A. S., Abdellaoui, A., Guo, S., Sathirapongsasuti, J. F., 23andMe Research Team, Lichtenstein, P., Lundström, S., Långström, N., Auton, A., Harris, K. M., Beecham, G. W., Martin, E. R., Sanders, A. R., Perry, J. R. B., Neale, B. M., et al. (2019). Large-scale GWAS reveals insights into the genetic architecture of same-sex sexual behavior. *Science, 365.*

Gannon, B. M., Rice, K. C., & Murnane, K. S. (2021). MDPV "high-responder" rats also self-administer more oxycodone than their "low-responder" counterparts under a fixed ratio schedule of reinforcement. *Psychopharmacology, 238*(4), 1183–1192.

Gao, Y., Schneider, B., & Li, L. (2017). The effects of the binocular disparity differences between targets and maskers on visual search. *Attention, Perception, & Psychophysics, 79,* 459–472.

Garber, M. (2020, April 30). *Groundhog Day* was a horror movie all along. *The Atlantic.* https://www.theatlantic.com/culture/archive/2020/04/groundhog-day-horror-movie-quarantine/610867

Garcia, J. (2003). Psychology is not an enclave. In R. J. Sternberg (Ed.), *Psychologists defying the crowd: Stories of those who battled the establishment and won.* American Psychological Association.

Garcia, S. M., Weaver, K., Moskowitz, G. B., & Darley, J. M. (2002). Crowded minds: The implicit bystander effect. *Journal of Personality and Social Psychology, 83,* 843–853.

García-Herrero, S., Mariscal, M. A., Gutiérrez, J. M., & Ritzel, D. O. (2013). Using Bayesian networks to analyze occupational stress caused by work demands: Preventing stress through social support. *Accident Analysis and Prevention, 57,* 114–123.

García-León, I. A., Beltrán, N. P., Alanis, A., & Moreno, J. S. (2021). Intelligent system for the evaluation of implicit memory with semantic emotional stimuli (is-eimses). In *Agents and Multi-Agent Systems: Technologies and Applications 2021* (pp. 337–347). Springer.

Garcia-Palacios, A., Hoffman, H., & Carlin, A. (2002). Virtual reality in the treatment of spider phobia: A controlled study. *Behavior Research & Therapy, 40,* 983–993.

Gardner, E. P., & Kandel, E. R. (2000). Touch. In E. R. Kandel, J. H. Schwartz, & T. M. Jessell (Eds.), *Principles of neural science* (4th ed.). McGraw Hill.

Gardner, H. (1999). *Intelligence reframed: Multiple intelligences for the 21st century*. New York: Basic Books.

Gardner, H. (2000). The giftedness matrix: A developmental perspective. In R. C. Friedman & B. M. Shore (Eds.), *Talents unfolding: Cognition and development.* American Psychological Association.

Garfield, J. (2014). Sad psychosurgery. *Brain: A Journal of Neurology, 137,* 1262–1265.

Gariépy, G., Riehm, K. E., Whitehead, R. D., Doré, I., & Elgar, F. J. (2019). Teenage night owls or early birds? Chronotype and the mental health of adolescents. *Journal of Sleep Research, 28*(3), 1–8.

Garland, M. M., Vaidya, J. G., Tranel, D., Watson, D., & Feinstein, J. S. (2021). Who are you? The study of personality in patients with anterograde amnesia. *Psychological Science, 32*(10), 1649–1661.

Garrigan, P., & Kellman, P. (2008). Perceptual learning depends on perceptual constancy. *PNAS Proceedings of the National Academy of Sciences of the United States of America, 105,* 2248–2253.

Gasser, P. (2022). *Psychedelic group therapy*. Springer.

Gates, G. J. (2017, January 11). In U.S., more adults identifying as LGBT. Gallup Social & Policy Issues. http://news.gallup.com/poll/201731/lgbt-identification-rises.aspx

Gaudiano, B. A., & Miller, I. W. (2013). The evidence-based practice of psychotherapy. *Clinical Psychology Review, 33,* 813–824.

Gaviria, C., & Corredor, J. (2021). Illusion of explanatory depth and social desirability of historical knowledge. *Metacognition and Learning, 16*(3), 801–832.

Gee, D. G. (2022). When do sensitive periods emerge later in development? *Trends in Cognitive Sciences, 26*(2), 97–98.

Geher, G. (2019). *Own your psychology major! A guide to student success*. Washington, DC: American Psychological Association.

Geisler, K.H., & Lobb, J. (2022, March 9). How do those car insurance tracking devices work? *U.S. News & World Report.* Downloaded from https://www.usnews.com/insurance/auto/how-do-those-car-insurance-tracking-devices-work. April 12, 2022.

Gelbard-Sagiv, H., Mukamel, R., Harel, M., Malach, R., & Fried, I. (2008). Internally generated reactivation of single neurons in human hippocampus during free recall. *Science, 322,* 96–101.

Gelman, R., & Baillargeon, R. (1983). A review of some Piagetian concepts. In J. H. Flavell & E. M. Markman (Eds.), *Handbook of child psychology, Vol. 3: Cognitive development* (4th ed.). Wiley.

Gelstein, S., Yeshurun, Y., Rozenkrantz, L., Shusha, S., Frumin, I., Roth, Y., & Sobel, N. (2011). Human tears contain a chemosignal. *Science, 331,* 226–230.

Gendron, M., Hoemann, K., Crittenden, A. N., Mangola, S. M., Ruark, G. A., & Barrett, L. F. (2020). Emotion perception in Hadza hunter-gatherers. *Scientific Reports, 10*(1), 1–17.

Geniole, S. N., Procyshyn, T. L., Marley, N., Ortiz, T. L., Bird, B. M., Marcellus, A. L., Welker, K. M., Bonin, P. L., Goldfarb, B., Watson, N. V., & Carré, J. M. (2019). Using a psychopharmacogenetic approach to identify the pathways through which—and the people for whom—testosterone promotes aggression. *Psychological Science, 30*(4), 481–494.

Genovese, J. E. C. (2006). Piaget, pedagogy, and evolutionary psychology. *Evolutionary Psychology,4*, 2127-2137.

Genschow, O., Westfal, M., Crusius, J., Bartosch, L., Feikes, K. I., Pallasch, N., & Wozniak, M. (2021). Does social psychology persist over half a century? A direct replication of Cialdini et al.'s (1975) classic door-in-the-face technique. *Journal of Personality and Social Psychology, 120*(2), e1-e7. https://doi.org/10.1037/pspa0000261

Gentner, D. (2016). Language as cognitive tool kit: How language supports relational thought. *American psychologist, 71*(8), 650.

Gergel, T., Howard, R., Lawrence, R., & Seneviratne, T. (2021). Time to acknowledge good electroconvulsive therapy research. *The Lancet Psychiatry, 8*(12), 1032-1033.

Gersh, F. L., & Lavie, C. J. (2020). Menopause and hormone replacement therapy in the 21st century. *Heart, 106*(7), 479-481.

Gerstel, N. (2005). In search of time. *Science, 308*, 204-205.

Gesualdo, F., Bucci, L. M., Rizzo, C., & Tozzi, A. E. (2022). Digital tools, multidisciplinarity and innovation for communicating vaccine safety in the COVID-19 era. *Human Vaccines & Immunotherapeutics, 18*(1), 1865048.

Geugies, H., Opmeer, E. M., Marsman, J. B. C., Figueroa, C. A., van Tol, M. J., Schmaal, L., van der Wee, N. J. A., Aleman, A., Penninx, B. W. J. H., Veltman, D. J., Schoevers, R. A., & Ruhé, H. G. (2019). Decreased functional connectivity of the insula within the salience network as an indicator for prospective insufficient response to antidepressants. *NeuroImage: Clinical, 24*, 102064.

Geurten, M., Willems, S., Germain, S., & Meulemans, T. (2015). Less is more: The availability heuristic in early childhood. *British Journal of Developmental Psychology,12*, 503-505.

Geyer, T., Gokce, A., & Müller, H. J. (2011). Reinforcement of inhibitory positional priming by spatial working memory contents. *Acta Psychologica, 137*, 235-242.

Ghahramani, Z. (2015). Probabilistic machine learning and artificial intelligence. *Nature, 521*(7553), 452-459.

Ghasemi, F. (2021). A motivational response to the inefficiency of teachers' practices towards students with learned helplessness. *Learning and Motivation, 73*, 101705.

Gheorghe, A., Fodor, O., & Pavelea, A. (2020). Ups and downs on the roller coaster of task conflict: The role of group cognitive complexity, collective emotional intelligence and team creativity. *Psihologia Resurselor Umane, 18*(1), 23-37.

Gherghel, C., Nastas, D., Hashimoto, T., & Takai, J. (2021). The relationship between frequency of performing acts of kindness and subjective well-being: A mediation model in three cultures. *Current Psychology, 40*(9), 4446-4459.

Gholizadeh, A., Solhi, M., Amiri, F. S., Hoseini, A. F., & Lotfizadeh, M. (2022). Determinants of weight loss and obesity control behaviors among women based on the Pender's Health Promotion Model. *Journal of Education and Community Health, 9*(1), 3-10.

Ghorayshi, A. (2022, May 24). An earlier start to puberty. *The New York Times*, p. D1.

Ghorayshi, A. (2022, June 11). Number of youths who identify as transgender doubles in U.S. *The New York Times*, pp. A1, A15.

Gianaros, P. J., & Wager, T. D. (2015). Brain-body pathways linking psychological stress and physical health. *Current Directions In Psychological Science, 24*, 313-321.

Giannopoulos, V. L., & Vella-Brodrick, D. A. (2011). Effects of positive interventions and orientations to happiness on subjective well-being. *Journal of Positive Psychology, 6*, 95-105.

Gibbons, A., & Warne, R. T. (2019). First publication of subtests in the Stanford-Binet 5, WAIS-IV, WISC-V, and WPPSI-IV. *Intelligence, 75*, 9-18.

Gibbs, J. C. (2013). *Moral development and reality: Beyond the theories of Kohlberg, Hoffman, and Haidt* (3rd ed.). Oxford University Press.

Gibson, S. (2013). Milgram's obedience experiments: A rhetorical analysis. *British Journal of Social Psychology, 52*, 290-309.

Gignac, G. E., Bartulovich, A., & Salleo, E. (2019). Maximum effort may not be required for valid intelligence test score interpretations. *Intelligence, 75*, 73-84.

Gignac, G. E., & Zajenkowski, M. (2019). People tend to overestimate their romantic partner's intelligence even more than their own. *Intelligence, 73*, 41-51.

Gill, K., Percival, C., Roes, M., Arreaza, L., Chinchani, A., Sanford, N., Sena, W., Mohammadsadeghi, H., Menon, M., Hughes, M., Carruthers, S., Sumner, P., Woods, W., Jardri, R., Sommer, I. E., Rossell, S. L., & Woodward, T. S. (2021). Brain networks detectable by fMRI during on-line self report of hallucinations in schizophrenia. *bioRxiv*. https://doi.org/10.1101/2021.11.06.467564

Gillan, C. M., & Sahakian, B. J. (2015). Which is the driver, the obsessions or the compulsions, in OCD? *Neuropsychopharmacology, 40*, 247-248.

Gilligan, C. (1996). The centrality of relationships in psychological development: A puzzle, some evidence, and a theory. In G. G. Noam & K. W. Fischer (Eds.), *Development and vulnerability in close relationships*. Erlbaum.

Gilligan, C. (2004). Recovering psyche: Reflections on life-history and history. *Annual of Psychoanalysis, 32*, 131-147.

Gilligan, J. (2019). Why we should universalize the insanity defense and replace punishment with therapy and education. *Aggression and Violent Behavior, 46*, 225-231.

Gingrich, J.A., Malm, H., Ansorge, M.S., Brown, A., Sourander, A., Suri, D., Teixeira, C. M., Caffrey Cagliostro, M. K., Mahadevia, D., & Weissman, M. M. (2017). New insights into how serotonin selective reuptake inhibitors shape the developing brain. *Brain Defects Research, 109*, 924-932.

Giovenco, D. P., & Delnevo, C. D. (2018). Prevalence of population smoking cessation by electronic cigarette use status in a national sample of recent smokers. *Addictive Behaviors, 76*, 129-134.

Girardeau, G., & Lopes-dos-Santos, V. (2021). Brain neural patterns and the memory function of sleep. *Science, 374*(6567), 560-564.

Giurfa, M. (2015). Learning and cognition in insects. *Wiley Interdisciplinary Reviews: Cognitive Science, 6*(4), 383-395.

Gizer, I. R., Ehlers, C. L., Vieten, C., Seaton-Smith, K. L., Feiler, H. S., Lee, J. V., et al. (2011). Linkage scan of alcohol dependence in the UCSF Family Alcoholism Study. *Drug and Alcohol Dependence, 113*, 125-132.

Glachet, O., Moustafa, A. A., Gallouj, K., & El Haj, M. (2019). Smell your memories: Positive effect of odor exposure on recent and remote autobiographical memories in Alzheimer's disease. *Journal of Clinical and Experimental Neuropsychology, 41*(6), 555-564.

Glaser, G. (2015, April.) The irrationality of Alcoholics Anonymous. *The Atlantic*. https://www.theatlantic.com/magazine/archive/2015/04/the-irrationality-of-alcoholics-anonymous/386255/

Glass, O. M., Forester, B. P., & Hermida, A. P. (2017). Electroconvulsive therapy (ECT) for treating agitation in dementia (major neurocognitive disorder)—A promising option. *International Psychogeriatrics, 29*, 717-726.

Glezer, L., Bruni-Cardoso, A., Schechtman, D., & Malnic, B. (2021). Viral infection and smell loss: The case of COVID-19. *Journal of Neurochemistry, 157*(4), 930-943.

Glisky, E. L. (2007). Changes in cognitive function in human aging. In D. R. Riddle (Ed.), *Brain aging: Models, methods, and mechanisms*. CRC Press.

Goldberg, S. B., Lam, S. U., Simonsson, O., Torous, J., & Sun, S. (2022). Mobile phone-based interventions for mental health: A systematic meta-review of 14 meta-analyses of randomized controlled trials. *PLOS Digital Health, 1*(1), e0000002.

Goldberg, S. B., Tucker, R. P., Greene, P. A., Davidson, R. J., Kearney, D. J., & Simpson, T. L. (2019). Mindfulness-based cognitive therapy for the treatment of current depressive symptoms: A meta-analysis. *Cognitive Behaviour Therapy, 48*(6), 445-462.

Golder, S. A., & Macy, M. W. (2011). Diurnal and seasonal mood vary with work, sleep, and day length across diverse cultures. *Science, 333*, 1878-1881.

Goldhammer, H., Krinsky, L., & Keuroghlian, A. S. (2019). Meeting the behavioral health needs of LGBT older adults. *Journal of the American Geriatrics Society*. https://doi.org/10.1111/jgs.15974.

Goldin, P. R., Thurston, M., Allende, S., Moodie, C., Dixon, M. L., Heimberg, R. G., & Gross, J. J. (2021). Evaluation of cognitive behavioral therapy vs. mindfulness meditation in brain changes during reappraisal and acceptance among patients with social anxiety disorder: A randomized clinical trial. *JAMA Psychiatry, 78*(10), 1134-1142.

Goldstein, D. (2022, April 19). Florida rejects math textbooks, citing "prohibited topics." *The New York Times*, p. A14.

Goldstein, J., Ross, D. A., & Moreno De Luca, D. (2019). Found in translation: Autism genetics and the quest for its Rosetta stone. *Biological Psychiatry, 85*(7), e29-e30.

Gollust, S. E., Fowler, E. F., Vogel, R. I., Rothman, A. J., Yzer, M., & Nagler, R. H. (2022). Americans' perceptions of health disparities over the first year of the COVID-19 pandemic: Results from three nationally-representative surveys. *Preventive Medicine, 162*, 107135.

Gómez-Leal, R., Holzer, A. A., Bradley, C., Fernández-Berrocal, P., & Patti, J. (2022). The relationship between emotional intelligence and leadership in school leaders: A systematic review. *Cambridge Journal of Education, 52*(1), 1-21.

Gómez-Vallejo, S., Leoni, M., Ronald, A., Colvert, E., Happé, F., & Bolton, P. (2021). Autism spectrum disorder and obstetric optimality: A twin study and meta-analysis of sibling studies. *Journal of Child Psychology and Psychiatry, 62*(11), 1353-1362.

Gonzalez, M., Ateah, C. A., Durrant, J. E., & Feldgaier, S. (2019). The impact of the Triple P Seminar Series on Canadian parents' use of physical punishment, non-physical punishment and non-punitive responses. *Behaviour Change, 36*(2), 102-120.

Good, V., Hughes, D. E., Kirca, A. H., & McGrath, S. (2022). A self-determination theory-based meta-analysis on the differential effects of intrinsic and extrinsic motivation on salesperson performance. *Journal of the Academy of Marketing Science, 50*(3), 586-614.

Goodman, G. S., Gonzalves, L., & Wolpe, S. (2019). False memories and true memories of childhood trauma: Balancing the risks. *Clinical Psychological Science, 7*(1), 29-31.

Gooren, L. (2006). The biology of human psychosexual differentiation. *Hormones and Behavior,50*, 589-601.

Gopnik, A., & Griffiths, T. (2017, August 20). What happens to creativity as we age? *The New York Times*, p. SR9.

Gopnik, A., Griffiths, T. L., & Lucas, C. G. (2015). When younger learners can be better (or at least more open-minded) than older ones. *Current Directions in Psychological Science, 24*(2), 87-92.

Gordon, J. K., Andersen, K., Perez, G., & Finnegan, E. (2019). How old do you think I am? Speech-language predictors of perceived age and communicative competence. *Journal of Speech, Language, and Hearing Research, 62*(7), 2455-2472.

Gorman, J. (2021, June 13). Covid-sniffing dogs are accurate but face hurdles for widespread use. *The New York Times*, p. A23.

Gorton, R. N., & Erickson-Schroth, L. (2017). Hormonal and surgical treatment options for transgender men (female-to-male). *Psychiatric Clinics of North America, 40*, 79-97.

Gosdin, L. K., Deputy, N. P., Kim, S. Y., Dang, E. P., & Denny, C. H. (2022). Alcohol consumption and binge drinking during pregnancy among adults aged 18-49 years–United States, 2018-2020. *Morbidity and Mortality Weekly Report, 71*(1), 10-13. https://doi.org/10.15585/mmwr.mm7101a2

Gosmann, N. P., Costa, M. D. A., Jaeger, M. D. B., Motta, L. S., Frozi, J., Spanemberg, L., Manfro, G. G., Cuijpers. P., Pine, D. S., & Salum, G. A. (2021). Selective serotonin reuptake inhibitors, and serotonin and norepinephrine reuptake inhibitors for anxiety, obsessive-compulsive, and stress disorders: A 3-level network meta-analysis. *PLOS Medicine, 18*(6), e1003664.

Goswami, I., & Urminsky, O. (2017). The dynamic effect of incentives on postreward task engagement. *Journal of Experimental Psychology: General, 146,* 1–19.

Gotlib, I. H., Krasnoperova, E., Yue, D. N., & Joorman, J. (2004). Attentional biases for negative interpersonal stimuli in clinical depression. *Journal of Abnormal Psychology, 113,* 127–135.

Goto, T., Ishibashi, Y., Kajimura, S., Oka, R., & Kusumi, T. (2015). Development of free will and determinism scale in Japanese. *Japanese Journal of Psychology, 86,* 32–41.

Gottesman, I. I. (1991). *Schizophrenia genesis: The origins of madness.* Freeman.

Gould, T. W., Dominguez, B., de Winter, F., Yeo, G. W., Liu, P., Sundararaman, B., Stark, T., Vu, A., Degen, J., Weichun, L., & Kuo-Fen, L. (2019). Glial cells maintain synapses by inhibiting an activity-dependent retrograde protease signal. *PLOS Genetics, 15*(3), e1007948.

Gourion, D. (2021). An upper bound for the number of chess diagrams without promotion. *arXiv preprint.* arXiv:2112.09386.

Goyal, M. S., Blazey, T. M., Su, Y., Couture, L. E., Durbin, T. J., Bateman, R. J., Benzinger, T. L-S., Morris, J. C., Raichle, M. E., & Vlassenko, A. G. (2019). Persistent metabolic youth in the aging female brain. *Proceedings of the National Academy of Sciences , 116*(8), 3251–3255.

Goyal, N., Adams, M., Cyr, T. G., Maass, A., & Miller, J. G. (2019). Norm-based spontaneous categorization: Cultural norms shape meaning and memory. *Journal of Personality and Social Psychology.* http://dx.doi.org/10.1037/pspi0000188.

Grady, C. L., St-Laurent, M., & Burianová, H. (2015). Age differences in brain activity related to unsuccessful declarative memory retrieval. *Brain Research, 161,* 230–47.

Graff, T. C., Luke, S. G., & Birmingham, W. C. (2019). Supportive hand-holding attenuates pupillary responses to stress in adult couples. *PLOS One, 14*(2), e0212703.

Grahek, N. (2007). *Feeling pain and being in pain* (2nd ed.). MIT Press.

Grandjean, D., Sarkis, R., Tourtier, J. P., Julien-Lecocq, C., Benard, A., Roger, V., Levesque, E., Bernes-Luciani, E., Maestracci, B., Morvan, P., Gully, E., Berceau-Falancourt, D., Pesce, J-L., Lecomte, B., Haufstater, P., Herin, G., Cabrera, J., Muzzine, Q., Gallet, C., . . . Desquilbet, L. (2020). Detection dogs as a help in the detection of COVID-19. Can the dog alert on COVID-19 positive persons by sniffing axillary sweat samples? Proof-of-concept study. *bioRxiv.* https://doi.org/10.1101/2020.06.03.132134

Granic, I., Hollenstein, T., & Dishion, T. (2003). Longitudinal analysis of flexibility and reorganization in early adolescence: A dynamic systems study of family interactions. *Developmental Psychology, 39,* 606–617.

Grant, D. M., & Wingate, L. R. (2011). Cognitive-behavioral therapy. In C. Silverstein (Ed.), *The initial psychotherapy interview: A gay man seeks treatment.* Elsevier.

Gravely, S., Meng, G., Hammond, D., Hyland, A., Cummings, K. M., Borland, R., Kasza, K., Yong, H. H., Thompson, M. E., Quah, A. C. K., Ouimet, J., Martin, N., O'Connor, R. J., East, K. A., McNeill, A., Boudreau, C., Levy, D. T., Sweanor, D. T., & Fong, G. T. (2022). Differences in cigarette smoking quit attempts and cessation between adults who did and did not take up nicotine vaping: Findings from the ITC four country smoking and vaping surveys. *Addictive Behaviors, 132,* 107339.

Graziano, M. S. (2019). *Rethinking consciousness: a scientific theory of subjective experience.* W. W. Norton & Company.

Graziano, M. S. (2021). Understanding consciousness. *Brain, 144*(5), 1281–1283.

Green, J., Lynn, S., & Montgomery, G. (2008). Gender-related differences in hypnosis-based treatments for smoking: A follow-up meta-analysis. *American Journal of Clinical Hypnosis, 50,* 259–271.

Green, J. P., & Lynn, S. J. (2019). *Cognitive-behavioral therapy, mindfulness, and hypnosis for smoking cessation: A scientifically informed intervention.* Wiley-Blackwell.

Greenberg, L. S. (2015). Working with primary emotions. In *Emotion-focused therapy: Coaching clients to work through their feelings* (2nd ed.). American Psychological Association.

Greenberg, P. E., Fournier, A. A., Sisitsky, T., Simes, M., Berman, R., Koenigsberg, S. H., & Kessler, R. C. (2021). The economic burden of adults with major depressive disorder in the United States (2010 and 2018). *Pharmacoeconomics, 39*(6), 653–665.

Greenberg, R., & Goldman, E. (2009). Antidepressants, psychotherapy or their combination: Weighing options for depression treatments. *Journal of Contemporary Psychotherapy, 39,* 83–91.

Greene, C. M., & Murphy, G. (2020). Individual differences in susceptibility to false memories for COVID-19 fake news. *Cognitive Research: Principles and Implications, 5*(1), 1–8.

Greene, J. D., & Paxton, J. M. (2009). Patterns of neural activity associated with honest and dishonest moral decisions. *PNAS Proceedings of the National Academy of Sciences of the United States of America, 106*(30), 12506–12511.

Greene, J. O. (2020). Mutually driven ideation and occasions of interpersonal transcendence. *Atlantic Journal of Communication, 28*(1), 37–53.

Greene, K. M., & Maggs, J. L. (2017). Academic time during college: Associations with mood, tiredness, and binge drinking across days and semesters. *Journal of Adolescence, 56,* 24–33.

Greene, N. R., & Naveh-Benjamin, M. (2020). A specificity principle of memory: Evidence from aging and associative memory. *Psychological Science, 31*(3), 316–331.

Gregory, R. L. (2008). Emmert's Law and the moon illusion. *Spatial Vision, 21,* 407–720.

Grenfell-Essam, R., Ward, G., & Tan, L. (2013). The role of rehearsal on the output order of immediate free recall of short and long lists. *Journal of Experimental Psychology: Learning, Memory, and Cognition, 39,* 317–347.

Griesbauer, E. M., Manley, E., Wiener, J. M., & Spiers, H. J. (2022). London taxi drivers: A review of neuro-cognitive studies and an exploration of how they build their cognitive map of London. *Hippocampus, 32*(1), 3–20.

Griffith, T. L., Sawyer, J. E., & Poole, M. S. (2019). Systems savvy: Practical intelligence for transformation of sociotechnical systems. *Group Decision and Negotiation.* https://doi.org/10.1007/s10726-019-09619-4.

Grigg-Damberger, M. M. (2017). Ontogeny of sleep and its functions in infancy, childhood, and adolescence. In S. Nevšímalová, O. Bruni, S. Nevšímalová, & O. Bruni (Eds.), *Sleep disorders in children.* Cham, Switzerland: Springer International Publishing.

Griggs, R. A. (2015b). The Kitty Genovese story in introductory psychology textbooks: Fifty years later. *Teaching of Psychology, 42,* 149–152.

Griggs, R. A. (2017). Milgram's obedience study: A contentious classic reinterpreted. *Teaching of Psychology, 44,* 32–37.

Grigorenko, E. L., & Dozier, M. (2013). Introduction to the special section on genomics. *Child Development, 84,* 6–16.

Grinberg, N., Joseph, K., Friedland, L., Swire-Thompson, B., & Lazer, D. (2019). Fake news on Twitter during the 2016 US presidential election. *Science, 363*(6425), 374–378.

Griswald, E. (2022, July 13). The kids who lost parent to Covid. *New Yorker.* https://www.newyorker.com/news/dispatch/the-kids-who-lost-parents-to-covid

Grivet, C. S., Haj-Broussard, M., & Broomé, R. (2021). School administrators' perspectives of French immersion programs. *Foreign Language Annals, 54*(1), 114–138.

Grøntvedt, T. V., Kennair, L. E. O., & Bendixen, M. (2019). How intercourse frequency is affected by relationship length, relationship quality, and sexual strategies using couple data. *Evolutionary Behavioral Sciences,* http://dx.doi.org/10.1037/ebs0000173.

Gros, D. F., Merrifield, C., Rowa, K., Szafranski, D. D., Young, L., & McCabe, R. E. (2019). A naturalistic comparison of group transdiagnostic behaviour therapy (TBT) and disorder-specific cognitive behavioural therapy groups for the affective disorders. *Behavioural and Cognitive Psychotherapy, 47*(1), 39–51.

Gross, T. (2020, June 23). From "empty" to "satisfied": Author traces a hunger that food can't fix. *Fresh Air.* www.npr.org/sections/health-shots/2020/06/23/882045262/from-empty-to-satisfied-author-traces-a-hunger-that-food-cant-fix

Grosso, M. (2015). The "transmission" model of mind and body: A brief history. In E. F. Kelly, A. Crabtree, & P. Marshall (Eds.), *Beyond physicalism: Toward reconciliation of science and spirituality.* Lanham, MD: Rowman & Littlefield.

Grover, S., & Helliwell, J. F. (2019). How's life at home? New evidence on marriage and the set point for happiness. *Journal of Happiness Studies: An Interdisciplinary Forum on Subjective Well-Being, 20,* 373–390.

Grover, S., Nguyen, J. A., & Reinhart, R. M. (2021). Synchronizing brain rhythms to improve cognition. *Annual Review of Medicine, 72,* 29–43.

Gruber, J., Mendle, J., Lindquist, K. A., Schmader, T., Clark, L. A., Bliss-Moreau, E., Akinla, M., et al. (2021). The future of women in psychological science. *Perspectives on Psychological Science, 16*(3), 483–516.

Gruber, R. P., & Block, R. A. (2017). Perception of scenes in different sensory modalities: A result of modal completion. *American Journal of Psychology, 130,* 23–34.

Gruber, T. R. (2013). Nature, nurture, and knowledge acquisition. *International Journal of Human-Computer Studies, 71,* 191–194.

Grueschow, M., Stenz, N., Thörn, H., Ehlert, U., Breckwoldt, J., Brodmann Maeder, M., Exadaktylos, A. K., Bingisser, R., Ruff, C. C., & Kleim, B. (2021). Real-world stress resilience is associated with the responsivity of the locus coeruleus. *Nature Communications, 12*(1), 1–17.

Grünbaum, A. (2015). Critique of psychoanalysis. In S. Boag, L. W. Brakel, & V. Talvitie (Eds.), *Philosophy, science, and psychoanalysis: A critical meeting.* Karnac Books.

Grzybowski, A., & Kupidura-Majewski, K. (2019). What is color and how it is perceived? *Clinics in Dermatology, 37*(5), 392–401.

Gu, C., Warkentin, S., Mais, L. A., & Carnell, S. (2017). Ethnic differences in parental feeding behaviors in UK parents of preschoolers. *Appetite, 113,* 398–404.

Guéguen, N., Marchand, M., Pascual, A., & Lourel, M. (2008). Foot-in-the-door technique using a courtship request: A field experiment. *Psychological Reports, 103,* 529–534.

Gugliandolo, M. C., Liga, F., Larcan, R., & Cuzzocrea, F. (2022). Parents of children with developmental disorders: Family hardiness and resilience. *Journal of Intellectual & Developmental Disability,* 1–6. Advance online publication. https://doi.org/10.3109/136682 50.2022.2079056

Guida, A., Tardieu, H., Le Bohec, O., & Nicolas, S. (2013). Are schemas sufficient to interpret the personalization effect? Only if long-term working memory backs up. *European Review of Applied Psychology/Revue Européenne De Psychologie Appliquée, 63,* 99–107.

Gundersen, S. (2021). The structure of neuropsychoanalytic explanations. *Neuropsychoanalysis, 23*(1), 15–26.

Gun Violence Archive. (2021). GVA seven year review. https://www.gunviolencearchive.org/

Guo, Y. (2019). Sexual double standards in white and Asian Americans: Ethnicity, gender, and acculturation. *Sexuality & Culture, 23*(1), 57–95.

Gupta, D., Gupta, M., Tiwari, S., & Singh, N. (2021). Motivation due to fear of failure is a key contributor in maximising workers' productivity in today's competitive arena. *International Journal of Indian Culture and Business Management, 23*(2), 193–217.

Gupta, M. A. (2013). Review of somatic symptoms in post-traumatic stress disorder. *International Review of Psychiatry, 25*, 86-99.

Gurney, A., Dienes, Z., & Scott, R. B. (2019). Hypnotic suggestibility is unaffected by a challenging inhibitory task or mental exhaustion. *Psychology of Consciousness: Theory, Research, and Practice.* http://dx.doi.org/10.1037/cns0000186.

Gurven, M., Fuerstenberg, E., Trumble, B., Stieglitz, J., Beheim, B., Davis, H., & Kaplan, H. (2017). Cognitive performance across the life course of Bolivian forager-farmers with limited schooling. *Developmental Psychology, 53*(1), 160-176.

Güss, C. D., Ahmed, S., & Dörner, D. (2021). From da Vinci's flying machines to a theory of the creative process. *Perspectives on Psychological Science, 16*(6), 1184-1197.

Gutchess, A., & Boduroglu, A. (2019). Cultural differences in categorical memory errors persist with age. *Aging & Mental Health, 23*(7), 851-854.

Gutchess, A., Mukadam, N., Zhang, W., & Zhang, X. (2021). Influence of aging on memory across cultures. In J. Y. Chiao, S.C. Li, R. Turner, S. Y. Lee-Tauler, & B. Pringle (Eds.) *The Oxford handbook of cultural neuroscience and global mental health* (pp. 262-287). Oxford University Press.

Guttmacher Institute (2012). Facts on American teens' sources of Information about sex. http://www.guttmacher.org/pubs/FB-Teen-Sex-Ed.html

Gutwinski, S., Schreiter, S., Deutscher, K., & Fazel, S. (2021). The prevalence of mental disorders among homeless people in high-income countries: An updated systematic review and meta-regression analysis. *PLOS Medicine, 18*(8), e1003750.

Guz, S., Kattari, S. K., Atteberry-Ash, B., Klemmer, C. L., Call, J., & Kattari, L. (2021). Depression and suicide risk at the cross-section of sexual orientation and gender identity for youth. *Journal of Adolescent Health, 68*(2), 317-323.

Ha, Y. N., & Yoo, E. (2022). Food Exposure Interventions to Improve Food Selectivity Among Children With Autism Spectrum Disorder: A Systematic Review. *The American Journal of Occupational Therapy, 76*(Supplement_1), 7610510209p1-7610510209p1.

Hadad, B., Maurer, D., & Lewis, T. L. (2017). The role of early visual input in the development of contour interpolation: The case of subjective contours. *Developmental Science, 20*, 25-32.

Hadiwijaya, H., Klimstra, T. A., Vermunt, J. K., Branje, S. T., & Meeus, W. J. (2017). On the development of harmony, turbulence, and independence in parent-adolescent relationships: A five-wave longitudinal study. *Journal of Youth and Adolescence, 46*, 1772-1788.

Hadjistavropoulos, T., & Asmundson, G. J. (2022). COVID stress in older adults: Considerations during the Omicron wave and beyond. *Journal of Anxiety Disorders, 86*, 102535.

Hagger, M. S., & Hamilton, K. (2019). Grit and self-discipline as predictors of effort and academic attainment. *British Journal of Educational Psychology, 89*(2), 324-342.

Hagmann-von Arx, P., Lemola, S., & Grob, A. (2018). Does IQ= IQ? Comparability of intelligence test scores in typically developing children. *Assessment, 25*(6), 691-701.

Hair, N. L., Hanson, J. L., Wolfe, B. L., & Pollak, S. D. (2022). Low household income and neuro-development from infancy through adolescence. *PLOS One, 17*(1), e0262607.

Hajek, P., Phillips-Waller, A., Przulj, D. , Pesola, F., Smith, K. M., Bisal, N., Li, J., Parrott, S., Sasieni, P., Dawkins, L., Ross, L., Goniewicz, M., Wu, Q., & McRobbie, H. J. (2019). A randomized trial of e-cigarettes versus nicotine-replacement therapy. *New England Journal of Medicine, 380*, 629-637.

Hajek, P., Przulj, D., Pesola, F., Griffiths, C., Walton, R., McRobbie, H., Coleman, T., Lewis, S., Whitemore, R., Clark, M., Ussher, M., Sinclair, L., Seager, E., Cooper, S., Bauld, L., Naughton, F., Sasieni, P., Manyonda, I., & Myers Smith, K. (2022). Electronic cigarettes versus nicotine patches for smoking cessation in pregnancy: A randomized controlled trial. *Nature Medicine, 28*(5), 958-964.

Hales, C. M., Carroll, M. D., Fryar, C. D., & Ogden, C. L. (2017). Prevalence of obesity among adults and youth: United States, 2015-2016. *NCHS Data Brief, 288.* https://www.cdc.gov/nchs/data/databriefs/db288.pdf

Hales, C. M., Carroll, M. D., Fryar, C. D., & Ogden, C. L. (2020). Prevalence of obesity and severe obesity among adults: United States, 2017-2018. *NCHS Data Brief, 360.* https://www.cdc.gov/nchs/data/databriefs/db360-h.pdf

Haller, J. (2018). The role of central and medial amygdala in normal and abnormal aggression: a review of classical approaches. *Neuroscience & Biobehavioral Reviews, 85*, 34-43.

Hallit, S., Hajj, A., Sacre, H., Al Karaki, G., Malaeb, D., Kheir, N., et al. (2019). Impact of sleep disorders and other factors on the quality of life in general population: A cross-sectional study. *Journal of Nervous and Mental Disease, 207*(5), 333-339.

Hall, J. A., Schlegel, K., Castro, V. L., & Back, M. (2019). What laypeople think the Big Five trait labels mean. *Journal of Research in Personality, 78*, 268-285.

Hall, P. J., Chong, C., McNaughton, N., & Corr, P. J. (2011). An economic perspective on the reinforcement sensitivity theory of personality. *Personality and Individual Differences, 51*, 242-247.

Halsband, U., & Wolf, T. G. (2021). Current neuro-scientific research database findings of brain activity changes after hypnosis. *American Journal of Clinical Hypnosis, 63*(4), 372-388.

Hambleton, R. K., & Zenisky, A. L. (2013). Reporting test scores in more meaningful ways: A research-based approach to score report design. In K. F. Geisinger, B. A. Bracken, J. F. Carlson, J. C. Hansen, N. R. Kuncel, S. P. Reise, & M. C. Rodriguez (Eds.), *APA handbook of testing and assessment in psychology, Vol. 3: Testing and assessment in school psychology and education.* American Psychological Association.

Hamer, M., Taylor, A., & Steptoe, A. (2006). The effect of acute aerobic exercise on stress related blood pressure responses: A systematic review and meta-analysis. *Bi Psychology, 71*, 183-190.

Hamilton, A. C., & Martin, R. C. (2007). Semantic short-term memory deficits and resolution of interference: A case for inhibition? In D. S. Gorfein & C. M. Macleod (Eds.), *Inhibition in cognition.* American Psychological Association.

Hamm, J. M., Perry, R. P., Chipperfield, J. G., Hladkyj, S., Parker, P. C., & Weiner, B. (2020). Reframing achievement setbacks: A motivation intervention to improve 8-year graduation rates for students in science, technology, engineering, and mathematics (STEM) fields. *Psychological Science, 31*(6), 623-633.

Han, B., Compton, W. M., Jones, C. M., Einstein, E. B., & Volkow, N. D. (2021). Methamphetamine use, methamphetamine use disorder, and associated overdose deaths among US adults. *JAMA psychiatry, 78*(12), 1329-1342.

Han, F., Xu, F., Zhu, Q., Sun, P., Zhou, Y., & Yu, M. (2022). Virus-mediated GHS-R1a expression in the basolateral amygdala blocks extinction of conditioned taste aversion memory in rats. *Biochemical and Biophysical Research Communications, 602*, 57-62.

Han, P., Fark, T., de Wijk, R. A., Roudnitzky, N., Iannilli, E., Seo, H.-S., & Hummel, T. (2019). Modulation of sensory perception of cheese attributes intensity and texture liking via ortho- and retro-nasal odors. *Food Quality and Preference, 73*, 1-7.

Han, S. D., Lamar, M., Fleischman, D., Kim, N., Bennett, D. A., Lewis, T. T., Arfanakis, K., & Barnes, L. L. (2021). Self-reported experiences of discrimination in older black adults are associated with insula functional connectivity. *Brain Imaging and Behavior, 15*(4), 1718-1727.

Hangya, B., Tihanyi, B. T., Entz, L., Fabo, D., Eross, L., Wittner, L., et al. (2011). Complex propagation patterns characterize human cortical activity during slow-wave sleep. *Journal of Neuroscience, 31*, 8770-8779.

Hansen, B. H., Oerbeck, B., Skirbekk, B., Petrovski, B. É., & Kristensen, H. (2018). Neurodevelopmental disorders: Prevalence and comorbidity in children

referred to mental health services. *Nordic Journal of Psychiatry, 72*(4), 285-291.

Harahap, A. A., & Sihombing, E. E. (2022, March). The association between taste perception with caries experience and body mass index of 12-13 years old Children in the 2 sub-districts in Medan. In *2nd Aceh International Dental Meeting 2021 (AIDEM 2021)* (pp. 115-121). Atlantis Press.

Harden, K. P. (2021). "Reports of my death were greatly exaggerated": Behavior genetics in the postgenomic era. *Annual Review of Psychology, 72*, 37-60.

Harden, R., Oaklander, A., Burton, A. W., Perez, R. M., Richardson, K., Swan, M., Barthel, J., Costa, B., Graciosa, J. R., Bruehl, S., & Reflex Sympathetic Dystrophy Syndrome Association. (2013). Complex regional pain syndrome: Practical diagnostic and treatment guidelines, 4th edition. *Pain Medicine, 14*, 180-229.

Hardt, O., Nader, K., & Nadel, L. (2013). Decay happens: The role of active forgetting in memory. *Trends in Cognitive Sciences, 17*, 111-120.

Haridi, M., Weyn Banningh, S., Clé, M., Leu-Semenescu, S., Vidailhet, M., & Arnulf, I. (2017). Is there a common motor dysregulation in sleepwalking and REM sleep behaviour disorder? *Journal of Sleep Research. 26*(5), 614-622.

Harlow, H. F., & Zimmerman, R. R. (1959). Affectional responses in the infant monkey. *Science,130*, 421-432.

Harlow, J. M. (1869). Recovery from the passage of an iron bar through the head. *Massachusetts Medical Society Publication, 2*, 329-347.

Harmer, C. J., Duman, R. S., & Cowen, P. J. (2017). How do antidepressants work? New perspectives for refining future treatment approaches. *The Lancet Psychiatry, 4*, 409-418.

Harmon, A. (2020, January 20). How much racism do you face every day? *The New York Times.*https://www.nytimes.com/interactive/2020/us/racism-african-americans-quiz.html

Harmon-Jones, E., Harmon-Jones, C., & Levy, N. (2015). An action-based model of cognitive-dissonance processes. *Current Directions In Psychological Science, 24*, 184-189.

Haroz, E. E., Ritchey, M., Bass, J. K., Kohrt, B. A., Augustinavicius, J., Michalopoulos, L., Burkey, M. D., & Bolton, P. (2017). How is depression experienced around the world? A systematic review of qualitative literature. *Social Science & Medicine, 183*, 151-162.

Harris, J. C., Mereish, E. H., Faulkner, M. L., Assari, S., Choi, K., Leggio, L., & Farokhnia, M. (2021). Racial Differences in the Association Between Alcohol Drinking and Cigarette Smoking: Preliminary Findings From an Alcohol Research Program. *Alcohol and Alcoholism.* Advance online publication. DOI: 10.1093/alcalc/agab038

Harris, M., Erridge, S., Ergisi, M., Nimalan, D., Kawka, M., Salazar, O., Ali, R., Loupasaki, K., Holvey, C., Coomber, R., Usmani, A., Sajad, M., Hoare, J., Rucker, J. J., Platt, M., & Sodergren, M. H. (2022). UK Medical Cannabis registry: An analysis of clinical outcomes of medicinal cannabis therapy for chronic pain conditions. *Expert Review of Clinical Pharmacology, 15*(4), 1-13. https://doi.org/10.1080/17512433.2022.2017771

Hartanto, A., Toh, W. X., & Yang, H. (2019). Bilingualism narrows socioeconomic disparities in executive functions and self-regulatory behaviors during early childhood: Evidence from the early childhood longitudinal study. *Child Development, 90*(4), 1215-1235.

Hartanto, A., & Yang, H. (2019). Does early active bilingualism enhance inhibitory control and monitoring? A propensity-matching analysis. *Journal of Experimental Psychology: Learning, Memory, and Cognition, 45*(2), 360-378.

Hart, B., & Risley, T. R. (1997). Use of language by three-year-old children. Courtesy of Drs. Betty Hart and Todd Risley, University of Kansas.

Hartmann, E., & Benum, K. (2019). Rorschach assessment of two distinctive personality states of a person with dissociative identity disorder. *Journal of Personality Assessment, 101*(2), 213-228.

Hartmann, E. (1967). *The biology of dreaming.* Charles C. Thomas Publisher.

Hartshorne, J., & Germine, L. (2015). When does cognitive functioning peak? The asynchronous rise and fall of different cognitive abilities across the life span. *Psychological Science, 26,* 433-443.

Hartshorne, J. K., Tenenbaum, J. B., & Pinker, S. (2018). A critical period for second language acquisition: Evidence from 2/3 million English speakers. *Cognition, 177,* 263-277.

Harvie, D. S., Moseley, G. L., Hillier, S. L., & Meulders, A. (2017). Classical conditioning differences associated with chronic pain: A systematic review. *The Journal of Pain, 18*(8), 889-898.

Hass, R. W. (2017). Tracking the dynamics of divergent thinking via semantic distance: Analytic methods and theoretical implications. *Memory & Cognition, 45,* 233-244.

Hastall, M. R., Koinig, I., Kunze, U., Meixner, O., Sachse, K., & Würzner, R. (2022). Multidisciplinary expert group: Communication measures to increase vaccine compliance in adults. *Wiener Medizinische Wochenschrift,* 1-4.

Hattori, S., Kishida, I., Suda, A., Miyauchi, M., Shiraishi, Y., Fujibayashi, M., Tsujita, N., Ishii, C., Ishii, N., Moritani, T., Taguri, M., & Hirayasu, Y. (2017). Effects of four atypical antipsychotics on autonomic nervous system activity in schizophrenia. *Schizophrenia Research, 193,* 134-138.

Haubrich, J., Bernabo, M., Baker, A. G., & Nader, K. (2020). Impairments to consolidation, reconsolidation, and long-term memory maintenance lead to memory erasure. *Annual Review of Neuroscience, 43,* 297-314.

Hayes, S. C. (2015). Humanistic psychology and contextual behavioral perspectives. In K. J. Schneider, J. F. Pierson, J. T. Bugental (Eds.), *The handbook of humanistic psychology: Theory, research, and practice* (2nd ed.). Thousand Oaks, CA: Sage Publications, Inc.

Hayes, W. M., & Wedell, D. H. (2019). Modeling the role of feelings in the Iowa Gambling Task. *Decision, 7*(1), 67-89.

Hayflick, L. (2007). Biological aging is no longer an unsolved problem. *Annals of the New York Academy of Sciences, 1100,* 1-13.

Hays, P. A. (2008). *Addressing cultural complexities in practice: Assessment, diagnosis, and therapy* (2nd ed.). American Psychological Association.

Healy, M. (2021). Keeping company: Educating for online friendship. *British Educational Research Journal, 47*(2), 484-499.

Heathcote, A., Coleman, J. R., Eidels, A., Watson, J. M., Houpt, J., & Strayer, D. L. (2015). Working memory's workload capacity. *Memory & Cognition, 43,* 973-989.

Hecking, J., Davoudian, P. A., & Wilkinson, S. T. (2021). Emerging therapeutics based on the amino acid neurotransmitter system: An update on the pharmaceutical pipeline for mood disorders. *Chronic Stress, 5,* 24705470211020446.

Hedegaard, H., Miniño, A. M., Spencer, M. R., & Warner, M. (2021). Drug overdose deaths in the United States, 1999-2020. *NCHS Data Brief,* (426), 1-8. https://www.cdc.gov/nchs/products/databriefs/db428.htm

Hedges, D. W., Brown, B. L., Shwalk, D. A., Godfrey, K., & Larcher, A. M. (2007). The efficacy of selective serotonin reuptake inhibitors in adult social anxiety disorder: A meta-analysis of double-blind, placebo-controlled trials. *Journal of Psychopharmacology, 21,* 102-111.

Heffernan, M. E., & Fraley, R. C. (2015). How early experiences shape attraction, partner preferences, and attachment dynamics. In V. Zayas & C. Hazan (Eds.), *Bases of adult attachment: Linking brain, mind and behavior.* Springer Science + Business Media.

Hehman, E., Stolier, R. M., Freeman, J. B., Flake, J. K., & Xie, S. Y. (2019). Toward a comprehensive model of face impressions: What we know, what we do not, and paths forward. *Social and Personality Psychology Compass, 13*(2), e12431.

Heilman, K. M. (2005). *Creativity and the brain.* Psychology Press.

Heim, S., Stumme, J., Bittner, N., Jockwitz, C., Amunts, K., & Caspers, S. (2019). Bilingualism and "brain reserve": A matter of age. *Neurobiology of Aging, 81,* 157-165.

Heine, H., & Weiss, M. (2021). Behavioral and Psychosocial Characteristics in Coronary Heart Disease. *Perspectives on Research in Emotional Stress,* 303-312.

Heintz, M. M., Brander, S. M., & White, J. W. (2015). Endocrine disrupting compounds alter risk-taking behavior in guppies (Poecilia reticulata). *Ethology, 121,* 480-491.

Heitzmann, C. A., Merluzzi, T. V., Jean-Pierre, P., Roscoe, J. A., Kirsh, K. L., & Passik, S. D. (2011). Assessing self-efficacy for coping with cancer: Development and psychometric analysis of the brief version of the Cancer Behavior Inventory (CBI-B). *Psycho-Oncology, 20,* 302-312.

Held, R. (2022). Neonate Cognition Symposium. In J. Anderson (Ed.), *12th Annual Conference.* CSS Pod. Psychology Press.

Helgeson, V. S., & Zajdel, M. (2017). Adjusting to chronic health conditions. *Annual Review of Psychology, 68,* 545-571.

Heller, H. C., Ruby, N. F., Rolls, A., Makam, M., & Colas, D. (2014). Adaptive and pathological inhibition of neuroplasticity associated with circadian rhythms and sleep. *Behavioral Neuroscience, 128,* 273-282.

Help Hope Live. (2022). Ian Burkhart, Spinal Cord Injury Ambassador (Ohio). https://helphopelive.org/about/team/. Downloaded March 28, 2022.

Henderson, N. D. (1982). Correlations in IQ for pairs of people with varying degrees of genetic relatedness and shared environment. *Annual Review of Psychology, 33,* 219-243.

Hennessy, M. B., & Shair, H. N. (2017). Filial attachment: Development, mechanisms, and consequences. In J. Call, G. M. Burghardt, I. M. Pepperberg, C. T. Snowdon, & T. Zentall (Eds.), *APA handbook of comparative psychology: Basic concepts, methods, neural substrate, and behavior.* American Psychological Association.

Henshall, C., Cipriani, A., Ruvolo, D., Macdonald, O., Wolters, L., & Koychev, I. (2019). Implementing a digital clinical decision support tool for side effects of antipsychotics: a focus group study. *Evidence-Based Mental Health, 22*(2), 56-60.

Herbert, W. (2011). *On second thought: Outsmarting your mind's hard-wired habits.* Broadway.

Herle, M., & Kahn, C. (2020). Longitudinal analyses suggest genomic and psychological origins of disordered eating and comorbidities. *JAMA Network Open, 3*(12), e2027188-e2027188.

Herlinger, K., & Lingford-Hughes, A. (2022). Opioid use disorder and the brain: A clinical perspective. *Addiction, 117*(2), 495-505.

Hermans, L. W., Nano, M. M., Leufkens, T. R., van Gilst, M. M., & Overeem, S. (2020). Sleep onset (mis)perception in relation to sleep fragmentation, time estimation and pre-sleep arousal. *Sleep medicine: X, 2,* 100014.

Hernández-Orallo, J. (2017). Evaluation in artificial intelligence: from task-oriented to ability-oriented measurement. *Artificial Intelligence Review, 48,* 397-447.

Herrnstein, R. J., & Murray, D. (1994). *The bell curve.* Free Press.

Hersh, R. G. (2021). Applied transference-focused psychotherapy: An overview and update. *Psychodynamic Psychiatry, 49*(2), 273-295.

Herting, M. M., & Sowell, E. R. (2017). Puberty and structural brain development in humans. *Frontiers in Neuroendocrinology, 44,* 122-137.

Hertzog, C., Kramer, A., Wilson, R., & Lindenberger, U. (2008). Enrichment effects on adult cognitive development: Can the functional capacity of older adults be preserved and enhanced? *Psychological Science in the Public Interest, 9,* 1-65.

Herz, R. (2016). The role of odor-evoked memory in psychological and physiological health. *Brain Sciences, 6*(3), 22.

Herzog, P., Kube, T., & Fassbinder, E. (2022). How childhood maltreatment alters perception and cognition–the predictive processing account of borderline personality disorder. *Psychological Medicine, 52,* 1-18.

Hester, N., Xie, S. Y., & Hehman, E. (2021). Little between-region and between-country variance when people form impressions of others. *Psychological Science, 32*(12), 1907-1917.

Hewitt, O. M., Tomlin, A., & Waite, P. (2021). The experience of panic attacks in adolescents: An interpretative phenomenological analysis study. *Emotional and Behavioural Difficulties, 26*(3), 240-253.

Heyes, C., & Catmur, C. (2022). What happened to mirror neurons? *Perspectives on Psychological Science, 17,* 153-168.

Hickok, G. (2015, May 10). Rhythms of the brain. *The New York Times,* p. SR 9.

Higashiyama, A., & Yamazaki, T. (2016). Anisotropic perception of slant from texture gradient: Size contrast hypothesis. *Attention, Perception, & Psychophysics, 78*(2), 647-662.

Higgs, S. (2015). Social norms and their influence on eating behaviours. *Appetite, 86,* 38-44.

Highhouse, S., Nye, C. D., & Zhang, D. C. (2019). Dark motives and elective use of brainteaser interview questions. *Applied Psychology, 68*(2), 311-340.

Hilbert, S., Schwaighofer, M., Zech, A., Sarubin, N., Arendasy, M., & Bühner, M. (2017). Working memory tasks train working memory but not reasoning: A material- and operation-specific investigation of transfer from working memory practice. *Intelligence, 61,* 102-114.

Hill, B. D., Foster, J. D., Elliott, E. M., Shelton, J., McCain, J., & Gouvier, W. (2013). Need for cognition is related to higher general intelligence, fluid intelligence, and crystallized intelligence, but not working memory. *Journal of Research in Personality, 47,* 22-25.

Hillier, K. M. (2018). Counselling diverse groups: Addressing counsellor bias toward the BDSM and D/S Subculture. *Canadian Journal of Counselling and Psychotherapy, 52*(1).

Hinz, A., Schulte, T., Finck, C., Gómez, Y., Brähler, E., Zenger, M., Körner, A., & Tibubos, A. N. (2022). Psychometric evaluations of the Life Orientation Test-Revised (LOT-R), based on nine samples. *Psychology & Health, 37*(6), 767-779.

Hirnstein, M., Hugdahl, K., & Hausmann, M. (2019). Cognitive sex differences and hemispheric asymmetry: A critical review of 40 years of research. *Laterality: Asymmetries of Body, Brain and Cognition, 24*(2), 204-252.

Hirst, W., Phelps, E. A., Meksin, R., Vaidya, C. J., Johnson, M. K., Mitchell, K. J., Buckner, R. L., Budson, A. E. Gabrieli, J. D. E., Lustic, C., Mather, M., Ochsner, K. N., Schacter, D., Simons, J. S. Lyle, K. B., Cuc, A. F., & Olsson, A. (2015). A ten-year follow-up of a study of memory for the attack of September 11, 2001: Flashbulb memories and memories for flashbulb events. *Journal of Experimental Psychology: General, 144,* 604-623.

Hiscox, L. V., Bray, S., Fraser, A., Meiser-Stedman, R., Seedat, S., & Halligan, S. L. (2022). Sex differences in the severity and natural recovery of child PTSD symptoms: A longitudinal analysis of children exposed to acute trauma. *Psychological Medicine,* 1-7.

Hobbs, T. D., Barry, R., & Koh, Y. (2022, January 9). How TikTok innundates teens with eating-disorder videos. *Wall Street Journal.* pp. A1, A 15.

Hobson, J. A. (2005). In bed with Mark Solms? What a nightmare! A reply to Domhoff (2005). *Dreaming, 15,* 21-29.

Hobson, J. A. (2007). States of conciseness: Normal and abnormal variation. In P. D. Zelazo, M. Moscovitch, & E. Thompson (Eds.), The Cambridge Handbook of Consciousness. London: Cambridge University Press.

Hochschild, A., & Machung, A. (2012). *The second shift: Working families and the revolution at home.* Penguin.

Hodges, J., Mun, R. U., & Johnson, R. (2021). Lewis Terman in context: An analysis of citations of genetic studies of genius inside and outside the field of gifted education. *Journal for the Education of the Gifted, 44*(3), 227-259.

Hofeditz, M., Nienaber, A., Dysvik, A., & Schewe, G. (2017). "Want to" versus "have to": Intrinsic and extrinsic motivators as predictors of compliance behavior intention. *Human Resource Management, 56,* 25-49.

Hofer, J., & Busch, H. (2019). Women in power-themed tasks: Need for power predicts task enjoyment and power stress. *Motivation and Emotion.* https://doi.org/10.1007/s11031-019-09782-w

Hofer, J., Busch, H., Raihala, C., Šolcová, I. P., & Tavel, P. (2017). The higher your implicit affiliation-intimacy motive, the more loneliness can turn you into a social cynic: A cross-cultural study. *Journal of Personality, 85,* 179–191.

Hoff, E. (2003). Language development in childhood. In I. Weiner, R. M. Lerner, M. A. Easterbrooks, & J. Mistry (Eds.), *Handbook of psychology: Developmental psychology* (Vol. 6). Wiley.

Hoff, E. (2008). *Language development.* Wadsworth.

Hoffman, J. (2020, April 2). Here to help: Online resources for help with sobriety. *The New York Times,* p. A3.

Hoffman, K. M., Trawalter, S., Axt, J. R., & Oliver, M. N. (2016). Racial bias in pain assessment and treatment recommendations, and false beliefs about biological differences between blacks and whites. *Proceedings of the National Academy of Sciences, 113*(16), 4296-4301.

Hoffman, L. (2021). Existential-humanistic therapy and disaster response: Lessons from the COVID-19 pandemic. *Journal of Humanistic Psychology, 61*(1), 33-54.

Hoffmann, J. D., Brackett, M. A., Bailey, C. S., & Willner, C. J. (2020). Teaching emotion regulation in schools: Translating research into practice with the RULER approach to social and emotional learning. *Emotion, 20*(1), 105.

Hogg, M. A. (2006). Social identity theory. In P. J. Burke (Ed.), *Contemporary social psychological theories.* Stanford University Press.

Hogue, J. V. & Mills, J.S. (2019). The effects of active social media engagement with peers on body image in young women. *Body Image, 28,* 1-5.

Holahan, C. K. (2021). Achievement across the life span: Perspectives from the Terman study of the gifted. *Gifted Child Quarterly, 65*(2), 185-195.

Hollingworth, H. L. (1943/1990). *Leta Stetter Hollingworth: A biography.* Boston: Anker.

Holmes, A. (2017). Drug addictions: New insight into causes, comorbidity and potential treatments. *Genes, Brain & Behavior, 16,* 5-7.

Holt-Lunstad, J. (2021). The major health implications of social connection. *Current Directions in Psychological Science, 30*(3), 251-259.

Holtyn, A. F., & Lattal, K. A. (2013). Briefly delayed reinforcement effects on variable "ratio and yoked" interval schedule performance. *Journal of the Experimental Analysis of Behavior, 100,* 198-210.

Holt-Lunstad, J. (2021). A pandemic of social isolation? *World Psychiatry, 20*(1), 55.

Holzhauer, C. G., Wemm, S., & Wulfert, E. (2017). Distress tolerance and physiological reactivity to stress predict women's problematic alcohol use. *Experimental and Clinical Psychopharmacology, 25,* 156-165.

Hong, L., He, X., Xue, L., Guo, L., & Liu, W. (2022). Comprehensive sexuality education improves primary students' explicit and implicit attitudes toward homosexuality. *International Journal of Sexual Health,* 1-18.

Horiguchi, H., Winawer, J., Dougherty, R. F., & Wandell, B. A. (2013). Human trichromacy revisited. *Proceedings of the National Academy of Sciences, 110,* 199-106.

Hori, H., Teraishi, T., Sasayama, D., Matsuo, J., Kawamoto, Y., Kinoshita, Y., & Kunugi, H. (2011). Relationships between season of birth, schizotypy, temperament, character and neurocognition in a non-clinical population. *Psychiatry Research, 189,* 388-397.

Horney, K. (1937). *Neurotic personality of our times.* Norton.

Horney, K. (2000). The unknown Karen Horney. In B. J. Paris (Ed.), *The Unknown Karen Horney.* Yale University Press.

Horowitz, J. M., Graf, N., & Livingston, G. (2019). Marriage and cohabitation in the U.S. Pew Research Center. https://www.pewresearch.org/social-trends/2019/11/06/marriage-and-cohabitation-in-the-u-s/

Horton, C. L. (2011). Recall and recognition of dreams and waking events: A diary paradigm. *International Journal of Dream Research, 4,* 8-16.

Horwitz, A. V. (2021). *DSM: A history of psychiatry's bible.* Johns Hopkins University Press.

Hounkpatin, H. O., Wood, A. M., Boyce, C. J., & Dunn, G. (2015). An existential-humanistic view of personality change: Co-occurring changes with psychological well-being in a 10 year cohort study. *Social Indicators Research, 121,* 455-470.

Houwen, J., Moorthaemer, B. J. E., Lucassen, P. L. B. J., Akkermans, R. P., Assendelft, W. J. J., olde Hartman, T. C., & van Dulmen, S. (2019). The association between patients' expectations and experiences of task-, affect- and therapy-oriented communication and their anxiety in medically unexplained symptoms consultations. *Health Expectations: An International Journal of Public Participation in Health Care & Health Policy, 22*(3), 338-347.

Howard, D. J. (2019). A dual process theory explanation for door-in-the-face effectiveness. *Basic and Applied Social Psychology, 41,* 1-14.

Howard, J. L., Bureau, J., Guay, F., Chong, J. X., & Ryan, R. M. (2021). Student motivation and associated outcomes: A meta-analysis from self-determination theory. *Perspectives on Psychological Science, 16*(6), 1300-1323.

Howe, M. L. (2011). The adaptive nature of memory and its illusions. *Psychological Science, 20,* 312-315.

Howell, E. F. (2011). *Understanding and treating dissociative identity disorder: A relational approach.* Routledge/Taylor & Francis Group.

Howes, O. D., & Shatalina, E. (2022). Integrating the neurodevelopmental and dopamine hypotheses of schizophrenia and the role of cortical excitation-inhibition balance. *Biological Psychiatry.* Advanced online publication. https://doi.org/10.1016/j.biopsych.2022.06.017

Howes, O. D., McCutcheon, R., Owen, M. J., & Murray, R. M. (2017). The role of genes, stress, and dopamine in the development of schizophrenia. *Biological Psychiatry, 81*(1), 9-20.

Howley, E.K. (2022, July 25). Types of therapy: Choosing the right one for you. *U.S. News & World Report.* https://health.usnews.com/health-care/patient-advice/articles/types-of-therapy

Hu, J. (2019). *Prominence and locality in grammar: The syntax and semantics of wh-questions and reflexives.* Routledge.

Hu, J., Hu, Y., Li, Y., & Zhou, X. (2021). Computational and neurobiological substrates of cost-benefit integration in altruistic helping decision. *Journal of Neuroscience, 41*(15), 3545-3561.

Huang, A., & Roth, C. L. (2021). The link between obesity and puberty: what is new? *Current Opinion in Pediatrics, 33*(4), 449-457.

Huang, C. (2022). A meta-analysis of the problematic social media use and mental health. *International Journal of Social Psychiatry, 68*(1), 12-33.

Huang, L. M., Sacchi, D. M., & Sherman, J. W. (2017). On the formation of context-based person impressions. *Journal of Experimental Social Psychology, 68,* 146-156.

Huang, S., Etkin, J., & Jin, L. (2017). How winning changes motivation in multiphase competitions. *Journal of Personality and Social Psychology, 112,* 813-837.

Huang, S., Niu, C., & Santtila, P. (2022). Masturbation frequency and sexual function in individuals with and without sexual partners. *Sexes, 3*(2), 229-243.

Huang, W. (2019). A psychological perspective on extrasensory perception. In N. Rezaei & A. Saghazadeh, (Eds). *Biophysics and neurophysiology of the sixth sense.* Springer.

Hubel, D. H., & Wiesel, T. N. (2004). *Brain and visual perception: The story of a 25-year collaboration.* Oxford University Press.

Huckins, L. M., Hatzikotoulas, K., Southam, L., Thornton, L. M., Steinberg, J., Aguilera-McKay, F., Treasure, J., Schmidt, U., Gunasinghe, C., Romero, A., Curtis, C., Rhodes, D., Moens, J., Kalsi, G., Dempster, D., Leung, R., Koehane, A., Burghardt, R., Ehrlich, S., Hebebrand, J., et al. (2018). Investigation of common, low-frequency and rare genome-wide variation in anorexia nervosa. *Molecular Psychiatry, 23*(5), 1169-1180.

Hudson, C. G. (2019). Deinstitutionalization of mental hospitals and rates of psychiatric disability: An international study. *Health & Place, 56,* 70-79.

Hudson, J. I., Coit, C. E., Lalonde, J. K., & Pope, H. G. (2012). By how much will the proposed new DSM-5 criteria increase the prevalence of binge eating disorder? *International Journal of Easting Disorders, 45,* 139-141.

Hudson, W. (1960). Pictorial depth perception in subcultural groups in Africa. *Journal of Social Psychology, 52,* 183-208.

Hudspeth, A. J. (2013). The inner ear. In E. R. Kandel, J. H. Schwartz, & T. M. Jessell (Eds.), *Principles of neural science* (5th ed.). McGraw-Hill.

Hugenberg, K., & Sacco, D. (2008). Social categorization and stereotyping: How social categorization biases person perception and face memory. *Social and Personality Psychology Compass, 2,* 1052-1072.

Hughes, F. P. (2021). *Children, play, and development.* SAGE publications.

Hui, A., He, M., & Wong, W. (2019). Understanding the development of creativity across the life span. In J. Kaufman & R. Sternberg (Eds.), *The Cambridge Handbook of Creativity* (2nd ed.) (Cambridge: Cambridge University Press.

Hui, B. P. (2022). Prosocial behavior and well-being: Shifting from the "chicken and egg" to positive feedback loop. *Current Opinion in Psychology, 44,* 231-236.

Hull, C. L. (1943). *Principles of behavior.* Appleton-Century-Crofts.

Human, L. J., & Biesanz, J. C. (2011). Through the looking glass clearly: Accuracy and assumed similarity in well-adjusted individuals' first impressions. *Journal of Personality and Social Psychology, 100,* 349-364.

Hunt, E. (1994). Problem solving. In R. J. Sternberg (Ed.), *Thinking and problem solving: Handbook of perception and cognition* (2nd ed.). Academic Press.

Huprich, S. K., & Nelson, S. M. (2015). Advancing the assessment of personality pathology with the Cognitive-Affective Processing System. *Journal of Personality Assessment, 97,* 467-477.

Hurschler, M. A., Liem, F., Oechslin, M., Stämpfli, P., & Meyer, M. (2015). fMRI reveals lateralized pattern of brain activity modulated by the metrics of stimuli during auditory rhyme processing. *Brain and Language, 14,* 741-750.

Husain, O. (2015). From persecution to depression: A case of chronic depression–Associating the Rorschach, the TAT, and Winnicott. *Journal of Personality Assessment, 97,* 230-240.

Huston, J. P., Silva, M., Komorowski, M., Schulz, D., & Topic, B. (2013). Animal models of extinction-induced depression: Loss of reward and its consequences. *Neuroscience and Biobehavioral Reviews, 37*(9A), 2059-2070.

Hutchinson, B., & Mitchell, M. (2019, January). 50 years of test (un)fairness: Lessons for machine learning. In *Proceedings of the Conference on Fairness, Accountability, and Transparency* (pp. 49-58). ACM.

Hviid, A., Hansen, J. V., Frisch, M., & Melbye, M. (2019). Measles, mumps, Rubella vaccination and autism: A nationwide cohort. *Annals of Internal Medicine, 170*(8): 513-520. doi: 10.7326/M18-0101.

Hwang, E-S., Kim, H-B., Lee, S., Kim, M-J., Lee, S-O., Han, S-M., Maeng, S., & Park, J-H. (2017). Loganin enhances long-term potentiation and recovers scopolamine-induced learning and memory impairments. *Physiology & Behavior, 171,* 243-248.

Hwang, J., Lee, C., & Lee, E. (2019). Gender norms and housework time allocation among dual-earner couples. *Labour Economics, 57,* 102-116.

Hyde, J., Mezulis, A. H., & Abramson, L. Y. (2008). The ABCs of depression: Integrating affective, biological, and cognitive models to explain the emergence of the gender difference in depression. *Psychological Review, 115,* 291-313.

Ibbotson, P., & Tomasello, M. (2016). Language in a new key. *Scientific American, 315,* 70-75.

Idås, T., Backholm, K., & Korhonen, J. (2019). Trauma in the newsroom: Social support, post-traumatic stress and post-traumatic growth among journalists working with terror. *European Journal of Psychotraumatology, 10*(1).

Ijeoma, O. B., & Oladipo, A. I. (2019). Efficacy of systematic desensitization Therapy on academic boredom among adolescents in Edo state secondary schools. *Journal of Educational and Social Research, 9*(2), 83-89.

IJzerman, H., Dutra, N., Silan, M., Adetula, A., Brown, D. M. B., & Forscher, P. (2021). Psychological science needs the entire globe. *APS Observer, 34*(5).

Iliceto, P., D'Antuono, L., Cassarà, L., Giacolini, T., Sabatello, U., & Candilera, G. (2017). Obsessive-compulsive tendencies, self/other perception, personality, and suicidal ideation in a non-clinical sample. *Psychiatric Quarterly, 88,* 411-422.

Illes, J., & Lou, H. (2019). A cross-cultural neuroethics view on the language of disability. *AJOB Neuroscience, 10*(2), 75-84.

Illingworth, B. J., Lewis, D. J., Lambarth, A. T., Stocking, K., Duffy, J. M., Jelen, L. A., & Rucker, J. J. (2021). A comparison of MDMA-assisted psychotherapy to non-assisted psychotherapy in treatment-resistant PTSD: A systematic review and meta-analysis. *Journal of Psychopharmacology, 35*(5), 501-511.

Infurna, F. J. (2021). Utilizing principles of life-span developmental psychology to study the complexities of resilience across the adult life span. *The Gerontologist, 61*(6), 807-818.

Ingendahl, M., Hummel, D., Maedche, A., & Vogel, T. (2021). Who can be nudged? Examining nudging effectiveness in the context of need for cognition and need for uniqueness. *Journal of Consumer Behaviour, 20*(2), 324-336.

Ingraham, C. (2019, March 29). The share of Americans not having sex has reached a record high. *Washington Post.*

Inoue, T., Abekawa, T., Nakagawa, S., Suzuki, K., Tanaka, T., Kitaichi, Y., Boku, S., Nakato, Y., Toda, H., & Koyama, T. (2011). Long-term naturalistic follow-up of lithium augmentation: Relevance to bipolarity. *Journal of Affective Disorders, 129,* 64-67.

International Human Genome Sequencing Consortium. (2003). *International Consortium completes Human Genome Project.* National Human Genome Research Institute.

Irwanda, D. Y., Maulina, D., Sekarmewangi, T. H., Putri, K. M. H., Otgaar, H., & Bücken, C. (2022). The effect of different delivery modes of misinformation on false memories in adolescents and adults. *Journal of Cognitive Psychology, 34*(2), 208-216.

Islam, R. F. (2019). Revisiting the universality of multiple intelligences theory in English writing classroom: Putting theory Into practice. *ELS Journal on Interdisciplinary Studies in Humanities, 2*(1), 148-155.

Issa, H., & Jaleel, E. (2021). Social isolation and psychological wellbeing: Lessons from Covid-19. *Management Science Letters, 11*(2), 609-618.

Issa, Y., Van Santvoort, H. C., van Goor, H., Cahen, D. L., Bruno, M. J., & Boermeester, M. A. (2013). Surgical and endoscopic treatment of pain in chronic pancreatitis: A multidisciplinary update. *Digestive Surgery, 30*(1), 35-50.

Itskovich, E., Bowling, D. L., Garner, J. P., & Parker, K. J. (2022). Oxytocin and the social facilitation of placebo effects. *Molecular Psychiatry, 1*-10.

Ivcevic, Z., & Ambady, N. (2012). Personality impressions from identity claims on Facebook. *Psychology of Popular Media Culture, 1*(1), 38-45. https://doi.org/10.1037/a0027329

Ivtzan, I., Gardner, H. E., Bernard, I., Sekhon, M., & Hart, R. (2013). Well-being through self-fulfilment: Examining developmental aspects of self-actualization. *Humanistic Psychologist, 41,* 119-132.

Izuhara, M., Hashioka, S., Sato, T., Nishikoori, H., Koike, M., Matsuda, H., Kanayama, M., Miura, S., Yamashita, S., Nagahama, M., Otsuki, K., Hayashida, M., Wake, R., Miyaoka, T., Inagaki, M., & Horiguchi, J. (2020). The effectiveness of electroconvulsive therapy for

psychiatric symptoms and cognitive fluctuations similar to dementia with Lewy bodies: A case report. *Psychogeriatrics : The official journal of the Japanese Psychogeriatric Society, 20*(2), 229-231. https://doi.org/10.1111/psyg.12465

Jablonka, E. (2017). The evolution of linguistic communication: Piagetian insights. In N. Budwig, E. Turiel, & P. D. Zelazo (Eds.), *New perspectives on human development.* Cambridge University Press.

Jack, R. E., & Schyns, P. G. (2017). Toward a social psychophysics of face communication. *Annual Review of Psychology, 68,* 269-297.

Jackson, A. S., Sui, X., Hébert, J. R., Church, T. S., & Blair, S. N. (2009). Role of lifestyle and aging on the longitudinal change in cardiorespiratory fitness. *Archives of Internal Medicine, 169*(19), 1781-1787. https://doi.org/10.1001/archinternmed.2009.312

Jackson, J. D. (2006). Trauma, attachment, and coping: Pathways to resilience. *Dissertation Abstracts International: Section B: The Sciences and Engineering, 67*(1-B), 547.

Jackson, M. L., Gunzelmann, G., Whitney, P., Hinson, J. M., Belenky, G., Rabat, A., et al. (2013). Deconstructing and reconstructing cognitive performance in sleep deprivation. *Sleep Medicine Reviews, 17,* 215-225.

Jacob, K. S. (2014). DSM-5 and culture: The need to move towards a shared model of care within a more equal patient-physician partnership. *Asian Journal of Psychiatry, 7,* 89-91.

Jacobs, A. (2021, May 10). Psychedelics are poised to reshape psychiatry. *The New York Times,* pp. A1, A16-A17.

Jacobs, A., & Richtel, M. (2017, September 18). How big business got Brazil hooked on junk foods. *The New York Times.* https://www.nytimes.com/interactive/2017/09/16/health/brazil-obesity-nestle.html

Jacobs, M., Roesch, S., Wonderlich, S., Crosby, R., Thornton, L., Wilfley, D., Berrettini, W. H., Brandt, H., Crawford, S., Fichter, M. M., Halmi, K. A., Johnson, C., Kaplan, A. S., Lavia, M., Mitchell, J. E., Rotondo, A., Strober, M., Woodside, D. B., Kaye, W. H., & Bulik, C. M. (2009). Anorexia nervosa trios: Behavioral profiles of individuals with anorexia nervosa and their parents. *Psychological Medicine, 39,* 451-461.

Jacobsen, B. N. (2021). Sculpting digital voids: The politics of forgetting on Facebook. *Convergence, 27*(2), 357-370.

Jacobsen, P. B., Prasad, R., Villani, J., Lee, C.-M., Rochlin, D., Scheuter, C., Kaplan, R. M., Freedland, K. E., Manber, R., Kanaan, J., & Wilson, D. K. (2019). The role of economic analyses in promoting adoption of behavioral and psychosocial interventions in clinical settings. *Health Psychology, 38*(8), 680-688.

Jacoby, J., & Schwartz, G. W. (2017). Three small-receptive-field ganglion cells in the mouse retina are distinctly tuned to size, speed, and object motion. *Journal of Neuroscience, 37,* 610-625.

Jacoby, L. L., & Wahlheim, C. N. (2013). On the importance of looking back: The role of recursive remindings in recency judgments and cued recall. *Memory & Cognition, 41,* 625-637.

Jagielski, C. H., Tucker, D. C., Dalton, S. O., Mrug, S., Würtzen, H., & Johansen, C. (2020). Personality as a predictor of well-being in a randomized trial of a mindfulness-based stress reduction of Danish women with breast cancer. *Journal of Psychosocial Oncology, 38*(1), 4-19.

Jahrami, H., BaHammam, A. S., Bragazzi, N. L., Saif, Z., Faris, M., & Vitiello, M. V. (2021). Sleep problems during the COVID-19 pandemic by population: a systematic review and meta-analysis. *Journal of Clinical Sleep Medicine, 17*(2), 299-313.

Jain, S., Malinowski, M., Chopra, P., Varshney, V., & Deer, T. R. (2019). Intrathecal drug delivery for pain management: Recent advances and future developments. *Expert Opinion on Drug Delivery, 16*(8), 815-822.

James, W. (1890). *The principles of psychology.* Holt.

James, W. (2015). The principles of psychology (excerpt). In T. Alter & Y. Nagasawa (Eds.),

Consciousness in the physical world: Perspectives on Russellian monism. Oxford University Press.

Jamieson, G. A. (2007). *Hypnosis and conscious states: The cognitive neuroscience perspective.* Oxford University Press.

Jamieson, J. P., Nock, M. K., & Mendes, W. B. (2013). Changing the conceptualization of stress in social anxiety disorder: Affective and physiological consequences. *Clinical Psychological Science, 1*(4), 363-374.

Jamison, K. R. (1995). *An unquiet mind: A memoir of moods and madness.* Knopf.

Jaqua, T., & Jaqua, E. (2019). Classical conditioning: Aversion therapy. *Global Journal of Addiction & Rehabilitation Medicine, 6*(3), 37-39.

Jarończyk, M., & Walory, J. (2022). Novel molecular targets of antidepressants. *Molecules, 27*(2), 533.

Jarrold, C., & Tam, H. (2011). Rehearsal and the development of working memory. In P. Barrouillet & V. Gaillard (Eds.), *Cognitive development and working memory: A dialogue between neo-Piagetian theories and cognitive approaches.* Psychology Press.

Jauhar, S., Hayes, J., Goodwin, G. M., Baldwin, D. S., Cowen, P. J., & Nutt, D. J. (2019). Antidepressants, withdrawal, and addiction; where are we now? *Journal of Psychopharmacology, 33*(6), 655-659.

Jawabri, K. H., & Raja, A. (2021). Physiology, sleep patterns. In StatPearls. https://pubmed.ncbi.nlm.nih.gov/31869144/

Jay, M. (2017). *Supernormal: The untold story of adversity and resilience.* Twelve.

Jayawickreme, E., Zachry, C. E., & Fleeson, W. (2019). Whole trait theory: An integrative approach to examining personality structure and process. *Personality and Individual Differences, 136,* 2-11.

Jayne, K. M., Purswell, K. E., & Stulmaker, H. L. (2019). Facilitating congruence, empathy, and unconditional positive regard through therapeutic limit-setting: Attitudinal conditions limit-setting model (ACLM). *International Journal of Play Therapy, 28*(4), 238.

Jeffery, A. J. (2015). Two behavioral hypotheses for the evolution of male homosexuality in humans. In T. K. Shackelford & R. D. Hansen (Eds.), *The evolution of sexuality.* Springer International Publishing.

Jeffries, R., & Reed, H. (2021). The self-fulfilling prophecy of teacher perception on low achievers. In *Research Anthology on Instilling Social Justice in the Classroom.* IGI Global.

Jelen, L. A., King, S., Horne, C. M., Lythgoe, D. J., Young, A. H., & Stone, J. M. (2019). Functional magnetic resonance spectroscopy in patients with schizophrenia and bipolar affective disorder: Glutamate dynamics in the anterior cingulate cortex during a working memory task. *European Neuropsychopharmacology, 29*(2), 222-234.

Jenkins, P. E., Ducker, I., Gooding, R., James, M., & Rutter-Eley, E. (2021). Anxiety and depression in a sample of UK college students: A study of prevalence, comorbidity, and quality of life. *Journal of American College Health, 69*(8), 813-819.

Jenkins, S. R. (1994). Need for power and women's careers over 14 years: Structural power, job satisfaction, and motive change. *Journal of Personality and Social Psychology, 66,* 155-165.

Jennings, D. J., Alonso, E., Mondragón, E., Franssen, M., & Bonardi, C. (2013). The effect of stimulus distribution form on the acquisition and rate of conditioned responding: Implications for theory. *Journal of Experimental Psychology: Animal Behavior Processes, 39,* 233-248.

Jensen, M. P., & Patterson, D. R. (2014). Hypnotic approaches for chronic pain management: Clinical implications of recent research findings. *American Psychologist, 69,* 167-177.

Jensen, M. P., & Turk, D. C. (2014). Contributions of psychology to the understanding and treatment of people with chronic pain: Why it matters to ALL psychologists. *American Psychologist, 69,* 105-118.

Jewanski, J., Simner, J., Day, S. A., Rothen, N., & Ward, J. (2019). The "golden age" of synesthesia inquiry in the late nineteenth century (1876-1895). *Journal of the History of the Neurosciences, 1*-28.

Jewett, C. (2022, July 7). Ban of Juul vaping products is put on hold as the F.D.A. reviews its ruling. *The New York Times*, p. A17.

Jha, M. K., Rush, A. J., & Trivedi, M. H. (2018). When discontinuing SSRI antidepressants is a challenge: Management tips. *American Journal of Psychiatry, 175*(12), 1176-1184.

Jia, H., Zack, M. M., & Thompson, W. W. (2011). State quality-adjusted life expectancy for U.S. adults from 1993 to 2008. *Quality of Life Research: An International Journal of Quality of Life Aspects of Treatment, Care & Rehabilitation,20*, 853-863.

Jiang, S., Miao, B., & Chen, Y. (2017). Prolonged duration of isoflurane anesthesia impairs spatial recognition memory through the activation of JNK1/2 in the hippocampus of mice. *Neuroreport: For Rapid Communication of Neuroscience Research, 28*, 386-390.

Jiang, Z., Ma, W., Flory, K., Zhang, D., Zhou, W., Shi, D., Hua, X., & Liu, R. (2022). Development of a computerized adaptive testing for ADHD using Bayesian networks: An attempt at classification. *Current Psychology*, 1-11. Advance online publication. https://doi.org/10.1007/s12144-022-03056-4

Jin, B., & Kim, J. (2017). Grit, basic needs satisfaction, and subjective well-being. *Journal of Individual Differences, 38*(1), 29-35.

Jin, J., Pei, G., & Ma, Q. (2019). They are what you hear in media reports: The racial stereotypes toward Uyghurs activated by media. *Frontiers in Neuroscience, 13*, 168.

Joel, D., & McCarthy, M.M. (2017). Incorporating sex as a biological variable in neuropsychiatric research: Where are we now and where should we be? *Neuropsychopharmacology, 42*, 379-385.

John, A. (2021). Suicide clusters and contagion in the HE and FE student population. In S. Mallon & J. Smith (Eds.), *Preventing and responding to student suicide: A practical guide for FE and HE settings*. Jessica Kingsley Publishers.

John, O. P. (2021). History, measurement, and conceptual elaboration of the Big-Five trait taxonomy: The paradigm matures. In O. P. John & R. W. Robins (Eds.), *Handbook of personality: Theory and research*. Guilford Press.

John, O. P., Robins, R. W., & Pervin, L. A. (2010). *Handbook of personality*. (3rd ed.). Guilford Press.

Johnson, C. Y. (2014, January 17). Finding a way to erase harmful memories. *Boston Globe*, p. 1.

Johnson, D. A., Lisabeth, L., Lewis, T. T., Sims, M., Hickson, D. A., Samdarshi, T., . . . & Roux, A. V. D. (2016). The contribution of psychosocial stressors to sleep among African Americans in the Jackson Heart Study. *Sleep, 39*(7), 1411-1419.

Johnson, G. B. (2000). *The living world* (p. 600). McGraw Hill.

Johnson, H. D. (2004). Gender, grade and relationship differences in emotional closeness within adolescent friendships. *Adolescence, 39*, 243-255.

Johnson, W., & Deary, I. J. (2011). Placing inspection time, reaction time, and perceptual speed in the broader context of cognitive ability: The VPR model in the Lothian Birth Cohort 1936. *Intelligence, 39*, 405-417.

Johnston, L. D., Miech, R. A., O'Malley, P. M., Bachman, J. G., & Schulenberg, J. E. (2016, December 13). Teen use of any illicit drug other than marijuana at new low, same true for alcohol. Ann Arbor, MI: University of Michigan News Service. Accessed from http://www.monitoringthefuture.org.

Johnston, L. D., Miech, R. A., O'Malley, P. M., Bachman, J. G., Schulenberg, J. E., & Patrick, M. E. (2021). *Monitoring the Future national survey results on drug use, 1975-2020: Overview, key findings on adolescent drug use*. Ann Arbor: Institute for Social Research, The University of Michigan.

Johnston, L. D., Miech, R. A., O'Malley, P. M., Bachman, J. G., Schulenberg, J. E., & Patrick, M. E. (2022). *Monitoring the Future national survey results on drug use, 1975-2021: Overview, key findings on adolescent drug use*. Institute for Social Research. https://monitoringthefuture.org/data/

Johnston, L. D., O'Malley, P. M., Miech, R. A., Bachman, J. G., & Schulenberg, J. E. (2017). *Monitoring the Future national survey results on drug use, 1975-2016: Overview, key findings on adolescent drug use*. Institute for Social Research.

Jonasdottir, S. S., Minor, K., & Lehmann, S. (2021). Gender differences in nighttime sleep patterns and variability across the adult lifespan: a global-scale wearables study. *Sleep, 44*(2), zsaa169.

Jones, A. L. (2006). The contemporary psychoanalyst: Karen Horney's theory applied in today's culture. *PsycCRITIQUES, 51*, 127-134.

Jones, D., Wang, Z., Chen, I. X., Zhang, S., Banerji, R., Lei, P. J., . . . & Padera, T. P. (2021). Solid stress impairs lymphocyte infiltration into lymph-node metastases. *Nature Biomedical Engineering, 5*(12), 1426-1436.

Jones, J. E., & Corp, E. S. (2003). Effect of naltrexone on food intake and body weight in Syrian hamsters depends on metabolic status. *Physiology and Behavior, 78*, 67-72.

Jones, J. M. (2007). Exposure to chronic community violence: Resilience in African American children. *Journal of Black Psychology, 33*, 125-149.

Jones, M., Kass, A. E., Trockel, M., Glass, A. I., Wilfley, D. E., & Taylor, C. B. (2014). A population-wide screening and tailored intervention platform for eating disorders on college campuses: The Healthy Body Image program. *Journal of American College Health, 62*, 351-356.

Jones, S. W., Weitlauf, J., Danhauer, S. C., Qi, L., Zaslavsky, O., Wassertheil-Smoller, S., Brenes, G. A., & LaCroix, A. Z. (2017). Prospective data from the Women's Health Initiative on depressive symptoms, stress, and inflammation. *Journal of Health Psychology, 22*, 457-464.

Jones, Z. C. (2022, April 26). Antisemitic incidents hit record while jumping 34% in 2021, report says. *CBS News*. https://www.cbsnews.com/news/antisemitic-incidents-increased-34-percent-in-2021-anti-defamation-league-report/

Joo, M., & Park, S. W. (2019). Depression is associated with negativity in TAT narratives: The mediating role of agency. *Current Psychology: A Journal for Diverse Perspectives on Diverse Psychological Issues*. https://doi.org/10.1007/s12144-019-00245-6

Joseph, S. (2019). Why we need a more humanistic positive organizational scholarship: Carl Rogers' person-centered approach as a challenge to neoliberalism. *The Humanistic Psychologist*. http://dx.doi.org/10.1037/hum0000151

Josselyn, S. A., & Tonegawa, S. (2020). Memory engrams: Recalling the past and imagining the future. *Science, 367*(6473), 4325.

Jovanović, D., Stanojević, P., & Stanojević, D. (2011). Motives for, and attitudes about, driving-related anger and aggressive driving. *Social Behavior and Personality, 39*, 755-764.

Joyce, J. (1934). *Ulysses*. Random House.

Jung, C. G. (2021). The personal and the collective unconscious. In *The Basic Writings of C. G. Jung*. Princeton University Press.

Jung, J., & Chang, D. (2017). Types of creativity–Fostering multiple intelligences in design convergence talents. *Thinking Skills and Creativity, 23*, 101-111.

Junior, J. C. S. J., Güçlütürk, Y., Pérez, M., Güçlü, U., Andujar, C., Baró, X., Escalante, H. J., Guyon, I., Van Gerven, M. A. J., Van Lier, R., & Escalera, S. (2019). First impressions: A survey on vision-based apparent personality trait analysis. *IEEE Transactions on Affective Computing*.

Kabra, R., & Singh, S. (2021). Evolutionary artificial intelligence based peptide discoveries for effective Covid-19 therapeutics. *Biochimica et Biophysica Acta (BBA)-Molecular Basis of Disease, 1867*(1), 165978.

Kachur, A., Osin, E., Davydov, D., Shutilov, K., & Novokshonov, A. (2020). Assessing the Big Five personality traits using real-life static facial images. *Scientific Reports, 10*(1), 1-11.

Kafali, H. Y., Bildik, T., Bora, E., Yuncu, Z., & Erermis, H. S. (2019). Distinguishing prodromal stage of bipolar disorder and early onset schizophrenia spectrum disorders during adolescence. *Psychiatry Research, 275*, 315-325.

Kahn, K. B., Lee, J. K., Renauer, B., Henning, K. R., & Stewart, G. (2017). The effects of perceived phenotypic racial stereotypicality and social identity threat on racial minorities' attitudes about police. *Journal of Social Psychology, 157*, 416-428.

Kahn, R. E., Frick, P. J., Youngstrom, E. A., Kogos Youngstrom, J., Feeny, N. C., & Findling, R. L. (2013). Distinguishing primary and secondary variants of callous-unemotional traits among adolescents in a clinic-referred sample. *Psychological Assessment, 25*, 966-978.

Kajanoja, J., Scheinin, N. M., Karukivi, M., Karlsson, L., & Karlsson, H. (2018). Is antidepressant use associated with difficulty identifying feelings? A brief report. *Experimental and Clinical Psychopharmacology, 26*(1), 2-5. https://doi.org/10.1037/pha0000165

Kalanthroff, E., Anholt, G. E., Keren, R., & Henik, A. (2013). What should I (not) do? Control over irrelevant tasks in obsessive-compulsive disorder patients. *Clinical Neuropsychiatry: Journal of Treatment Evaluation, 10*, (Suppl. 1), 61-64.

Kalla, J. L., Broockman, D. E., & Sekhon, J. S. (2021). Field experiments with survey outcomes. *Advances in Experimental Political Science*, 56.

Kalra, S., Arora, S., & Kapoor, N. (2022). How to reset metabolic setpoint in obesity management. *Journal of the Pakistan Medical Association, 72*(2), 375-376.

Kamenica, E. (2012). Behavioral economics and psychology of incentives. *Annual Review of Economics, 4*(1), 427-452.

Kamens, S. R. (2011). On the proposed sexual and gender identity diagnoses for DSM-5: History and controversies. *Humanistic Psychologist, 39*, 37-59.

Kamimori, G. H., McLellan, T. M., Tate, C. M., Voss, D. M., Niro, P., & Lieberman, H. R. (2015). Caffeine improves reaction time, vigilance and logical reasoning during extended periods with restricted opportunities for sleep. *Psychopharmacology, 232*, 2031-2042.

Kamimura, D., Cain, L. R., Mentz, R. J., White, W. B., Blaha, M. J., DeFilippis, A. P., Fox, E. R., Rodriguez, C. J., Keith, R. J., Benjamin, E. J., Butler, J., Bhatnagar, A., Robertson, R. M., Winniford, M. D., Correa, A., & Hall, M. E. (2018). Cigarette smoking and incident heart failure: Insights from the Jackson Heart Study. *Circulation, 137*(24), 2572-2582.

Kam, J. W., Irving, Z. C., Mills, C., Patel, S., Gopnik, A., & Knight, R. T. (2021). Distinct electrophysiological signatures of task-unrelated and dynamic thoughts. *Proceedings of the National Academy of Sciences, 118*(4). Chicago

Kamp, J., & Wernau, J. (2021, December 21). Fentanyl spreads in illicit drugs. *Wall Street Journal*, p. A8.

Kandler, C., Riemann, R., & Angleitner, A. (2013). Patterns and sources of continuity and change of energetic and temporal aspects of temperament in adulthood: A longitudinal twin study of self- and peer reports. *Developmental Psychology, 49*, 1739-1753.

Kane, J. M., Robinson, D. G., Schooler, N. R., Mueser, K. T., Penn, D. L., Rosenheck, R. A., Addington, J., Brunette, M. F., Correll, C. U., Estroff, S. E., Marcy, P., Robinson, J., Meyer-Kalos, P. S., Gottlieb, J. D., Glynn, S., M., Lynde, D. W., Pipes, R., Kurian, B. T., Miller, A. L., Azrin, S. T., et al. (2016). Comprehensive versus usual community care for first-episode psychosis: 2-year outcomes from the NIMH RAISE Early Treatment Program. *American Journal of Psychiatry, 173*, 362-372.

Kanel, D., Al-Wasity, S., Stefanov, K., & Pollick, F. E. (2019). Empathy to emotional voices and the use of real-time fMRI to enhance activation of the anterior insula. *NeuroImage, 198*, 53-62.

Kanoski, S. E., Hayes, M. R., Greenwald, H. S., Fortin, S. M., Gianessi, C. A., Gilbert, J. R., & Grill, H. J. (2011). Hippocampal leptin signaling reduces food intake and modulates food-related memory processing. *Neuropsychopharmacology, 36*, 1859-1870.

Kaposi, D. (2017). The resistance experiments: Morality, authority and obedience in Stanley Milgram's account. *Journal for the Theory of Social Behaviour, 47*(4), 382-401.

Kaposi, D. (2022). The second wave of critical engagement with Stanley Milgram's "obedience to authority" experiments: What did we learn? *Social and Personality Psychology Compass, 16*, e12667.

Kaptchuk, T. J. (2001). The double-blind, randomized, placebo-controlled trial: gold standard or golden calf? *Journal of Clinical Epidemiology, 54*(6), 541-549.

Kapur, S. (2018). Some applications of formal learning theory results to natural language acquisition. In B. Lust & G. Herman (Eds.), *Binding, dependencies, and learnability.* Psychology Press.

Karabulut, S., Korkmaz Bayramov, K., Bayramov, R., Ozdemir, F., Topaloglu, T., Ergen, E., et al. (2019). Effects of post-learning REM sleep deprivation on hippocampal plasticity-related genes and microRNA in mice. *Behavioural Brain Research, 361*, 7-13.

Karaszewski, B. (2008). Sub-neocortical brain: A mechanical tool for creative generation? *Trends in Cognitive Sciences, 12*, 171-172.

Karran, E., & De Strooper, B. (2022). The amyloid hypothesis in Alzheimer disease: New insights from new therapeutics. *Nature Reviews Drug Discovery,* 1-13.

Kasemsap, K. (2017). Mastering cognitive neuroscience and social neuroscience perspectives in the information age. In M. A. Dos Santos (Ed.), *Applying neuroscience to business practice.* Business Science Reference/IGI Global.

Kašpárková, L., Vaculík, M., Procházka, J., & Schaufeli, W. B. (2018). Why resilient workers perform better: The roles of job satisfaction and work engagement. *Journal of Workplace Behavioral Health, 33*(1), 43-62.

Kassam, K. S., Gilbert, D. T., Swencionis, J. K., & Wilson, T. D. (2009). Misconceptions of memory: The Scooter Libby effect. *Psychological Science, 20*, 551-552.

Kasten, E., Barbosa, F., Kosmidis, M. H., Persson, B. A., Constantinou, M., Baker, G. A., Lettner, S., Hokkanen, L., Ponchel, A., Mondini, S., Jonsdottir, M. K., Varako, N., Nikolai, T., Pranckeviciene, A., Harper, L., & Hessen, E. (2021). European clinical neuropsychology: Role in healthcare and access to neuropsychological services. *Healthcare, 9*(6), 734.

Katz, J., & Sanger-Katz, M. (2021, July 14). Drug deaths surged to record as pandemic ravaged country. *The New York Times,* pp. A1, A18.

Kaufman, J. C., & Plucker, J. A. (2011). Intelligence and creativity. In R. J. Sternberg & S. Kaufman (Eds.), *The Cambridge handbook of intelligence.* Cambridge University Press.

Kauten, R. L., Lui, J. L., Stary, A. K., & Barry, C. T. (2015). 'Purging my friends list. Good luck making the cut': Perceptions of narcissism on Facebook. *Computers In Human Behavior, 51*, 244-254.

Kavaliers, M., Ossenkopp, K. P., & Choleris, E. (2019). Social neuroscience of disgust. *Genes, Brain and Behavior, 18*(1), e12508.

Kawakami, K., Friesen, J. P., & Fang, X. (2022). Perceiving ingroup and outgroup faces within and across nations. *British Journal of Psychology, 113*(3), 551-574.

Kawakami, N., & Miura, E. (2015). Image or real? Altering the mental imagery of subliminal stimuli differentiates explicit and implicit attitudes. *Imagination, Cognition and Personality, 34*, 259-269.

Kawashima, H., Izaki, Y., & Grace, A. A. (2006). Cooperativity between hippocampal-pre-frontal short-term plasticity through associative long-term potentiation. *Brain Research, 1109*, 37-44.

Kazantseva, A., Gaysina, D., Kutlumbetova, Y., Kanzafarova, R., Malykh, S., Lobaskova, M., & Khusnutdinova, E. (2015). Brain derived neurotrophic factor gene (BDNF) and personality traits: The modifying effect of season of birth and sex. *Progress in Neuro-Psychopharmacology & Biological Psychiatry, 56*, 58-65.

Keating, D. P., & Clark, L. V. (1980). Development of physical and social reasoning in adolescence. *Developmental Psychology, 16*, 23-30.

Kecmanovic, J. (2020, April 27). Could therapy ease your coronavirus stress? How to decide, what to expect and where to find it. *Washington Post.*

https://www.washingtonpost.com/lifestyle/wellness/finding-therapy-coronavirus-stress-anxiety-anger/2020/04/25/4c00dd3c-866d-11ea-a3eb-e9fc93160703_story.html

Keillor, J. M., Barrett, A. M., Crucian, G. P., Kortenkamp, S., & Heilman, K. M. (2002). Emotional experience and perception in the absence of facial feedback. *Journal of the International Neuropsychological Society, 8*, 130-135.

Keith, K. D. (2019). Consciousness and culture. *Cross-Cultural Psychology: Contemporary Themes and Perspectives,* 342-353.

Kekäläinen, T., Freund, A. M., Sipilä, S., & Kokko, K. (2019). Cross-sectional and longitudinal associations between leisure time physical activity, mental well-being and subjective health in middle adulthood. *Applied Research in Quality of Life,* 1-18.

Kelley, H. (1950). The warm-cold variable in first impressions of persons. *Journal of Personality and Social Psychology, 18*, 431-439.

Kelly, J. F. (2022). Building a more equitable society: Psychology's role in achieving health equity. *American Psychologist, 77*(5), 633-645.

Kelly, J. F., Humphreys, K., & Ferri, M. (2020). Alcoholics Anonymous and other 12-step programs for alcohol use disorder. *Cochrane Database of Systematic Reviews,* (3). https://doi.org/10.1002/14651858.CD012880.pub2

Kemp, C., Hamacher, D. W., Little, D. R., & Cropper, S. J. (2022). Perceptual grouping explains similarities in constellations across cultures. *Psychological Science, 33*(3), 354-363.

Kemps, E., & Tiggemann, M. (2007). Reducing the vividness and emotional impact of distressing autobiographical memories: The importance of modality-specific interference. *Memory, 15*, 412-422.

Kendler, K. S., Aggen, S. H., Gillespie, N., Neale, M. C., Knudsen, G. P., Krueger, R. F., Czajkowski, N., Ystrom, E., & Reichborn-Kjennerud, T. (2017). The genetic and environmental sources of resemblance between normative personality and personality disorder traits. *Journal of Personality Disorders, 31*, 193-207.

Kendler, K. S., Ohlsson, H., Sundquist, J., & Sundquist, K. (2021). The rearing environment and the risk for alcohol use disorder: A Swedish national high-risk home-reared v. adopted co-sibling control study. *Psychological Medicine, 51*(14), 2370-2377.

Kenett, Y. N., Levi, E., Anaki, D., & Faust, M. (2017). The semantic distance task: Quantifying semantic distance with semantic network path length. *Journal of Experimental Psychology: Learning, Memory, and Cognition, 43*, 1470-1489.

Kenneally, C. (2021, April 19). Do brain implants change your identity? *New Yorker.* https://www.newyorker.com/magazine/2021/04/26/do-brain-implants-change-your-identity

Kennedy, C. E., Moore, P. J., Peterson, R. A., Katzman, M. A., Vermani, M., & Charmak, W. D. (2011). What makes people anxious about pain? How personality and perception combine to determine pain anxiety responses in clinical and non-clinical populations. *Anxiety, Stress & Coping: An International Journal, 24*, 179-200.

Kennedy, J. E. (2004). A proposal and challenge for proponents and skeptics of psi. *Journal of Parapsychology, 68*, 157-167.

Keppler, J. (2018). Shedding light on the fundamental mechanism underlying hypnotic analgesia. *Annals of Palliative Medicine, 7*(1), 170-176.

Kernberg, O. F. (2021). Challenges for the future of psychoanalysis. *The American Journal of Psychoanalysis, 81*(3), 281-300.

Kerr, K. L., Ratliff, E. L., Cohen, Z. P., Fuller, S., Cosgrove, K. T., DeVille, D. C., Misaki, M., Morris, A. S., & Bodurka, J. (2022). Real-time functional magnetic resonance imaging dyadic neurofeedback for emotion regulation: A proof-of-concept study. *Frontiers in Human Neuroscience, 16.*

Kersten, R., & Greitemeyer, T. (2022). Why do habitual violent video game players believe in the

cathartic effects of violent video games? A misinterpretation of mood improvement as a reduction in aggressive feelings. *Aggressive Behavior, 48*(2), 219-231.

Kertz, S. J., Koran, J., Stevens, K. T., & Björgvinsson, T. (2015). Repetitive negative thinking predicts depression and anxiety symptom improvement during brief cognitive behavioral therapy. *Behaviour Research and Therapy, 68*, 54-63.

Kesner, R. P. (2016). Exploration of the neurobiological basis for a three-system, multiattribute model of memory. *Behavioral Neuroscience of Learning and Memory, 37*, 325-359.

Ketisch, T., & Jones, R. A. (2013). Review of "ADHD diagnosis & management." *American Journal of Family Therapy, 41*, 272-274.

Keynejad, R., Spagnolo, J., & Thornicroft, G. (2021). WHO mental health gap action programme (mhGAP) intervention guide: Updated systematic review on evidence and impact. *Evidence-Based Mental Health, 24*(3), 124-130.

Khedr, E. M., Omran, E. A., Ismail, N. M., El-Hammady, D. H., Goma, S. H., Kotb, H., Galal, H., Osman, A. M., Faghaly, H. S. M., Karim, A. A., & Ahmed, G. A. (2017). Effects of transcranial direct current stimulation on pain, mood and serum endorphin level in the treatment of fibromyalgia: A double blinded, randomized clinical trial. *Brain Stimulation, 10*(5), 893-90.

Khera, A. V., Chaffin, M., Wade, K. H., Zahid, S., Brancale, J., Xia, R., Distefano, M., Senol-Cosar, O., Haas, M. E., Bick, A., Aragam, K. G., Lander, E. S., Smith, G. D., Mason-Suares, H., Fornage, M., Lebo, M., Timpson, N. J., Kaplan, L. M., & Kathiresan, S. (2019). Polygenic prediction of weight and obesity trajectories from birth to adulthood. *Cell, 177*(3), 587-596.

Khoury, R., Grossberg, G. T., Maldonado, G. F., Brown, D., Hoffman, H., Kahlon, C., & Grossberg, G. (2022). Alcohol and Substance Abuse in Older Adults. *Clinics in Geriatric Medicine, 38*(1), https://doi.org/10.1016/S0749-0690(21)00095-1

Kidd, E., & Lum, J. (2008). Sex differences in past tense overregularization. *Developmental Science,11*, 882-889.

Kihlstrom, J. F. (2005b). Is hypnosis an altered state of consciousness or what? Comment. *Contemporary Hypnosis, 22*, 34-38.

Kilby, C. J., Sherman, K. A., & Wuthrich, V. (2021). How do you think about stress? A qualitative analysis of beliefs about stress. *Journal of Health Psychology, 26*(14), 2756-2767.

Killingsworth, M. A. (2021). Experienced well-being rises with income, even above $75,000 per year. *Proceedings of the National Academy of Sciences, 118*(4), e2016976118.

Kim, B. R., Kwon, H., Chun, M. Y., Park, K. D., Lim, S. M., Jeong, J. H., & Kim, G. H. (2020). White matter integrity is associated with the amount of physical activity in older adults with super-aging. *Frontiers in Aging Neuroscience, 12*, 549983.

Kim, N. (2008). The moon illusion and the size-distance paradox. In S. Cummins-Sebree, M. A. Riley, & K. Shockley (Eds.), *Studies in perception and action IX: Fourteenth International Conference on Perception and Action.* Lawrence Erlbaum Associates.

Kim, R. E. Y., Abbott, R. D., Kim, S., Thomas, R. J., Yun, C. H., Kim, H., . . . & Shin, C. (2022). Sleep duration, sleep apnea, and gray matter volume. *Journal of geriatric psychiatry and neurology, 35*(1), 47-56.

Kim, S., Polari, A., Melville, F., Moller, B., Kim, J., Amminger, P., Herrman, H., McGorry, P., & Nelson, B. (2017). Are current labeling terms suitable for people who are at risk of psychosis? *Schizophrenia Research, 188*, 172-177.

Kim, S. G., Overath, T., Sedley, W., Kumar, S., Teki, S., Kikuchi, Y., Patterson, R., & Griffiths, T. D. (2022). MEG correlates of temporal regularity relevant to pitch perception in human auditory cortex. *NeuroImage, 249*, 118879.

Kim, Y., & Yoon, H. (2017). Common and distinct brain networks underlying panic and social anxiety disorders. *Progress in Neuro-Psychopharmacology & Biological Psychiatry.* https://www.ncbi.nlm.nih.gov/pubmed/28642079

Kimball, B. A., Opiekun, M., Yamazaki, K., & Beauchamp, G. K. (2014). Immunization alters body odor. *Physiology & Behavior, 128*, 80-85.

Kimura, H., Kanahara, N., & Iyo, M. (2021). Rationale and neurobiological effects of treatment with antipsychotics in patients with chronic schizophrenia considering dopamine supersensitivity. *Behavioural Brain Research, 403*, 113126.

Kinetz, E. (2021, February 15). Anatomy of a conspiracy: With COVID, China took a leading role. *Associated Press.* https://apnews.com/article/pandemics-beijing-only-on-ap-epidemics-media-122b73e134b780919cc1808f3f6f16e8

King, C. I., Romero, A. S., Schacter, D. L., & St. Jacques, P. L. (2022). The influence of shifting perspective on episodic and semantic details during autobiographical memory recall. *Memory*, 1-13.

Kingsbury, J. H., Buxton, O. M., Emmons, K. M., & Redline, S. (2013). Sleep and its relationship to racial and ethnic disparities in cardiovascular disease. *Current cardiovascular risk reports, 7*(5), 387-394.

Kinkade, E., & Fuller, H. (2021). Stress-buffering factors of social integration on depressive symptoms over time in late-life. *Innovation in Aging, 5*(Suppl 1), 927-927.

Kirsch, I., Lynn, S. J., Vigorito, M., & Miller, R. R. (2004). The role of cognition in classical and operant conditioning. *Journal of Clinical Psychology, 60*, 369-392.

Kirzinger, A, Kearney, A., Hamel, L., & Brodie, M. (2020, April 2). KFF Health tracking poll—early April 2020: The impact of coronavirus on life in America. Kaiser Family Foundation.

Kish, S., Fitzmaurice, P., Boileau, I., Schmunk, G., Ang, L., Furukawa, Y., et al. (2009). Brain serotonin transporter in human methamphetamine users. *Psychopharmacology, 202*, 649-661.

Kishi, T., Ikuta, T., Matsuda, Y., Sakuma, K., Okuya, M., Mishima, K., & Iwata, N. (2021). Mood stabilizers and/or antipsychotics for bipolar disorder in the maintenance phase: A systematic review and network meta-analysis of randomized controlled trials. *Molecular Psychiatry, 26*(8), 4146-4157.

Kitayama, S. (2017). Journal of Personality and Social Psychology: Attitudes and social cognition. *Journal of Personality and Social Psychology, 112*, 357-360.

Kivipelto, M. & Hakansson, K. (2017). A rare success against Alzheimer's. *Scientific American, 316*, 32-37.

Kivlighan, D. M., Goldberg, S. B., Abbas, M., Pace, B. T., Yulish, N. E., Thomas, J. G., Cullen, M. M., Flückiger, C., & Wampold, B. E. (2015). The enduring effects of psychodynamic treatments vis-à-vis alternative treatments: A multilevel longitudinal meta-analysis. *Clinical Psychology Review, 40*, 1-14.

Kizilirmak, J. M., Galvao Gomes da Silva, J., Imamoglu, F., & Richardson-Klavehn, A. (2015). Generation and the subjective feeling of "aha!" are independently related to learning from insight. *Psychological Research, 80*(6), 1059-1074.

Klapoetke, N. C., Nern, A., Rogers, E. M., Rubin, G. M., Reiser, M. B., & Card, G. M. (2022). A functionally ordered visual feature map in the Drosophila brain. *Neuron.* Advance online publication. https://doi.org/10.1016/j.neuron.2022.02.013

Kleinplatz, P. J., Moser, C., & Lev, A. (2013). Sex and gender identity disorders. In G. Stricker, T. A. Widiger, & I. B. Weiner (Eds.), *Handbook of psychology, Vol. 8: Clinical psychology* (2nd ed.). John Wiley & Sons.

Klein-Soetebier, T., Noël, B., & Klatt, S. (2021). Multimodal perception in table tennis: The effect of auditory and visual information on anticipation and planning of action. *International Journal of Sport and Exercise Psychology, 19*(5), 834-847.

Klinger, D., Volante, L., & Bilgili, O. (2018). Cross-cultural approaches to mitigating the immigrant student performance disadvantage. In *Immigrant Student Achievement and Education Policy* (pp. 197-206). Springer.

Kluge, A., & Gronau, N. (2018). Intentional forgetting in organizations: The importance of eliminating retrieval cues for implementing new routines. *Frontiers in Psychology, 9*, 51. https://doi.org/10.3389/fpsyg.2018.00051

Kluger, J. (2019, June 24). The vaccine battlegrounds. *Time*, pp. 38-43.

Klusmann, U., Aldrup, K., Schmidt, J., & Lüdtke, O. (2021). Is emotional exhaustion only the result of work experiences? A diary study on daily hassles and uplifts in different life domains. *Anxiety, Stress, & Coping, 34*(2), 173-190.

Knight, S. C., & Meyer, R. G. (2007). Forensic hypnosis. In A. M. Goldstein (Ed.), *Forensic psychology: Emerging topics and expanding roles.* John Wiley & Sons.

Knoop, M. S., de Groot, E. R., & Dudink, J. (2021). Current ideas about the roles of rapid eye movement and non-rapid eye movement sleep in brain development. *Acta Paediatrica, 110*(1), 36-44.

Knutson, D., & Koch, J. M. (2019). Person-centered therapy as applied to work with transgender and gender diverse clients. *Journal of Humanistic Psychology*, 0022167818791082.

Kochli, D. E., Thompson, E. C., Fricke, E. A., Postle, A. F., & Quinn, J. J. (2015). The amygdala is critical for trace, delay, and contextual fear conditioning. *Learning & Memory, 22*, 92-100.

Kogstad, R. E., Ekeland, T. J., & Hummelvoll, J. K. (2011). In defence of a humanistic approach to mental health care: Recovery processes investigated with the help of clients' narratives on turning points and processes of gradual change. *Journal of Psychiatric and Mental Health Nursing, 18*, 479-486.

Kohlberg, L. (1969). Stage and sequence: The cognitive-developmental approach to socialization. In D. Goslin (Ed.), *Handbook of socialization theory and research.* Rand McNally.

Kohlberg, L. (1984). *The psychology of moral development: Essays on moral development* (Vol. 2). Harper & Row.

Koh, E., Stauss, K., Coustaut, C., & Forrest, C. (2017). Generational impact of single-parent scholarships: Educational achievement of children in single-parent families. *Journal of Family Issues, 38*, 607-632.

Komarovskaya, I., Loper, A., Warren, J., & Jackson, S. (2011). Exploring gender differences in trauma exposure and the emergence of symptoms of PTSD among incarcerated men and women. *Journal of Forensic Psychiatry & Psychology, 22*, 395-410.

Konijnenberg, E., den Braber, A., Ten Kate, M., Tomassen, J., Mulder, S. D., Yaqub, M., Teunissen, C. E., Lammertsma, A. A., van Berckel, B. N. M., Scheltens, P., Boonsma, D. I., & Jelle Visser, P. (2019). Association of amyloid pathology with memory performance and cognitive complaints in cognitively normal older adults: A monozygotic twin study. *Neurobiology of Aging, 77*, 58-65.

Koob, G. F. (2021). Drug addiction: Hyperkatifeia/negative reinforcement as a framework for medications development. *Pharmacological Reviews, 73*(1), 163-201.

Korcha, R. A., Polcin, D. L., Bond, J. C., Lapp, W. M., & Galloway, G. (2011). Substance use and motivation: A longitudinal perspective. *American Journal of Drug and Alcohol Abuse, 37*, 48-53.

Korotkov, D., Perunovic, M., Claybourn, M., Fraser, I., Houlihan, M., Macdonald, M., & Korotkov, K. (2011). The Type B behavior pattern as a moderating variable of the relationship between stressor chronicity and health behavior. *Journal of Health Psychology, 16*, 397-409.

Korur, F., Toker, S., & Eryilmaz, A. (2016). Effects of the integrated online advance organizer teaching materials on students' science achievement and attitude. *Journal of Science Education and Technology* [serial online], *25*(4), 628-640.

Kosinski, M. (2021). Facial recognition technology can expose political orientation from naturalistic facial images. *Scientific Reports, 11*(1), 1-7.

Kostygina, G., Szczypka, G., Czaplicki, L., Borowiecki, M., Ahn, R., Schillo, B., & Emery, S. L. (2021). Promoting corporate image or preventing underage use? Analysis of the advertising strategy and expenditures of the JUUL parent education for youth vaping prevention campaign. *Tobacco Control.* Advance online publication. https://doi.org/10.1136/tobaccocontrol-2020-056355

Kouros, C. D., & Papp, L. M. (2019). Couples' perceptions of each other's daily affect: Empathic accuracy, assumed similarity, and indirect accuracy. *Family Process, 58*(1), 179-196.

Kowalik, J., Weller, J., Venter, J., & Drachman, D. (2011). Cognitive behavioral therapy for the treatment of pediatric posttraumatic stress disorder: A review and meta-analysis. *Journal of Behavior Therapy and Experimental Psychiatry, 42*, 405-413.

Kraeutner, S. N., Cui, A. X., Boyd, L. A., & Boe, S. G. (2022). Modality of practice modulates resting state connectivity during motor learning. *Neuroscience Letters, 781*, 136659. https://doi.org/10.1016/j.neulet.2022.136659

Krause, M., Civelek, M., Romanoski, C., & Fang, Y. (2019). Human genetics in vascular mechanotransduction and metabolism. *Arteriosclerosis, Thrombosis, and Vascular Biology, 39*(Suppl. 1), A162-A162.

Krauss, J. K., Lipsman, N., Aziz, T., Boutet, A., Brown, P., Chang, J. W., Davidson, B., Grill, W. M., Hariz, M. I., Horn, A., Schulder, M., Mammis, A., Tass, P. A., Volkmann, J., & Lozano, A. M. (2021). Technology of deep brain stimulation: Current status and future directions. *Nature Reviews Neurology, 17*(2), 75-87.

Krautheim, J. T., Dannlowski, U., Steines, M., Neziroğlu, G., Acosta, H., Sommer, J., Straube, B., & Kircher, T. (2019). Intergroup empathy: Enhanced neural resonance for ingroup facial emotion in a shared neural production-perception network. *NeuroImage, 194*, 182-190.

Krauth-Gruber, S., & Bonnot, V. (2019). Collective guilt, moral outrage, and support for helping the poor: A matter of system versus in-group responsibility framing. *Journal of Community & Applied Social Psychology, 30*(1), 59-72.

Kreher, D., Holcomb, P., Goff, D., & Kuperberg, G. (2008). Neural evidence for faster and further automatic spreading activation in schizophrenic thought disorder. *Schizophrenia Bulletin, 34*, 473-482.

Kreiczer-Levy, S. (2019). Parents and adult children: The elusive boundaries of the legal family. *Law and Social Inquiry,44*(2), 519-525.

Kross, E., Verduyn, P., Sheppes, G., Costello, C. K., Jonides, J., & Ybarra, O. (2021). Social media and well-being: Pitfalls, progress, and next steps. *Trends in Cognitive Sciences, 25*(1), 55-66.

Krüger, O., Korsten, P., & Hoffman, J. I. (2017). The rise of behavioral genetics and the transition to behavioral genomics and beyond. In J. Call, G. M. Burghardt, I. M. Pepperberg, C. T. Snowdon, & T. Zentall (Eds.), *APA handbook of comparative psychology: Basic concepts, methods, neural substrate, and behavior.* Washington, DC: American Psychological Association.

Kruglanski, A. W., Szumowska, E., & Kopetz, C. (2021). The call of the wild: How extremism happens. *Current Directions in Psychological Science, 30*(2), 181-185.

Krumhuber, E. G., & Scherer, K. R. (2011). Affect bursts: Dynamic patterns of facial expression. *Emotion, 11*, 825-841.

Kubanek, J., Snyder, L. H., & Abrams, R. A. (2015). Reward and punishment act as distinct factors in guiding behavior. *Cognition, 139*, 154-167.

Kucewicz, M. T., Berry, B. M., Miller, L. R., Khadjevand, F., Ezzyat, Y., Stein, J. M., Kremen, V., Brinkmann, B. H., Wanda, P., Sperling, M. R., Gorniak, R., Davis, K. A., Jobst, B. C., Gross, R. E., Lega, B., Van Gompel, J., Stead, S. M., Rizzuto, D. S., Kahana, M. J., & Worrell, G. A. (2018). Evidence for verbal memory enhancement with electrical brain stimulation in the lateral temporal cortex. *Brain: A Journal of Neurology, 141*(4), 971-978.

Kulik, L., & Sadeh, I. (2015). Explaining fathers' involvement in childcare: An ecological approach. *Community, Work & Family, 18*, 19-40.

Kumari, S., & Joshi, S. (2013). Neonatal outcomes in women with depression during pregnancy. *Journal of Projective Psychology & Mental Health,20*, 141-145.

Kuncel, N. R., & Beatty, A. S. (2013). Thinking at work: Intelligence, critical thinking, job knowledge, and reasoning. In K. F. Geisinger, B. A. Bracken, J. F. Carlson, J. C. Hansen, N. R. Kuncel, S. P. Reise, & M. C. Rodriguez (Eds.), *APA handbook of testing and* assessment in psychology, Vol. 1: Test theory and testing and assessment in industrial and organizational psychology. American Psychological Association.

Kung, C. S., Pudney, S. E., & Shields, M. A. (2022). Economic gradients in loneliness, social isolation and social support: Evidence from the UK Biobank. Social Science & Medicine, 115122.

Kuosmanen, K., Rovio, S., Kivipelto, M., Tuomilehto, J., Nissinen, A., & Kulmala, J. (2016). Determinants of self-rated health and self-rated physical fitness in middle and old age. European Journal of Mental Health, 11(1–2), 128–143.

Kupfersmid, J. (2019). Freud's clinical theories then and now. Psychodynamic Psychiatry, 47(1), 81–97.

Kuppens, S., & Ceulemans, E. (2019). Parenting styles: A closer look at a well-known concept. Journal of Child and Family Studies, 28(1), 168–181.

Kurdziel, L., Duclos, K., & Spencer, R. M. C. (2013). Sleep spindles in midday naps enhance learning in preschool children. PNAS Early Edition, 1–6.

Kurth, F., Gaser, C., & Luders, E. (2021). Development of sex differences in the human brain. Cognitive Neuroscience, 12(3-4), 155–162.

Kushlev, K., Heintzelman, S. J., Lutes, L. D., Wirtz, D., Kanippayoor, J. M., Leitner, D., & Diener, E. (2020). Does happiness improve health? Evidence from a randomized controlled trial. Psychological Science, 31(7), 807–821.

Kuther, T. L. (2003). Your career in psychology: Psychology and the law. Wadsworth.

Kuther, T. L., & Burnell, K. (2019). A life span developmental perspective on psychosocial development in midlife. Adultspan Journal, 18(1), 27–39.

Kvitchasty, A. V. (2021). Altered states of consciousness in sports psychology: Hypnosis, suggestion and auto-suggestion. Journal of Modern Foreign Psychology, 10(3), 92–102.

Kwon, D. (2022, January). The long shadow of trauma. Scientific American, pp. 49–55.

Kwong, A. S., López-López, J. A., Hammerton, G., Manley, D., Timpson, N. J., Leckie, G., & Pearson, R. M. (2019). Genetic and environmental risk factors associated with trajectories of depression symptoms from adolescence to young adulthood. JAMA Network Open, 2(6), e196587-e196587.

Kyaga, S., Landén, M., Boman, M., Hultman, C. M., Långström, N., & Lichtenstein, P. (2013). Mental illness, suicide and creativity: 40-year prospective total population study. Journal of Psychiatric Research, 47, 83–90.

Kyllonen, P., & Kell, H. (2017). What is fluid intelligence? Can it be improved? In M. Rosén, K. Yang Hansen, & U. Wolff (Eds.), Cognitive abilities and educational outcomes: A festschrift in honour of Jan-Eric Gustafsson. Springer International Publishing.

Köhler, W. (1927). The mentality of apes. Routledge & Kegan Paul.

Kübler-Ross, E. (1969). On death and dying. Macmillan.

Laan, E. T., Klein, V., Werner, M. A., van Lunsen, R. H., & Janssen, E. (2021). In pursuit of pleasure: A biopsychosocial perspective on sexual pleasure and gender. International Journal of Sexual Health, 33(4), 516–536.

Labrecque, L. T., & Whisman, M. A. (2017). Attitudes toward and prevalence of extramarital sex and descriptions of extramarital partners in the 21st century. Journal of Family Psychology, 31(7), 952–957.

Labrecque, N., & Cermakian, N. (2015). Circadian clocks in the immune system. Journal of Biological Rhythms, 30, 277–290.

Lackey, J. (2020). False confessions and testimonial injustice. Journal of Criminal Law & Criminology, 110, 43.

Laddis, A., Dell, P. F., & Korzekwa, M. (2017). Comparing the symptoms and mechanisms of "dissociation" in dissociative identity disorder and borderline personality disorder. Journal of Trauma & Dissociation, 18, 139–173.

Lagacé-Séguin, D. G., & d'Entremont, M. L. (2006). The role of child negative affect in the relations between parenting styles and play. Early Child Development and Care, 176, 461–477.

Lahti, J., Räikkönen, K., Ekelund, J., Peltonen, L., Raitakari, O. T., & Keltikangas-Järvinen, L. (2005). Novelty seeking: Interaction between parental alcohol use and dopamine D4 receptor gene exon III polymorphism over 17 years. Psychiatric Genetics, 15, 133–139.

Lai, C. H. (2019). The neural markers of MRI to differentiate depression and panic disorder. Progress in Neuro-Psychopharmacology and Biological Psychiatry, 91, 72–78.

Laibson, D., Maxted, P., & Moll, B. (2021). Present bias amplifies the household balance-sheet channels of macroeconomic policy (No. w29094). National Bureau of Economic Research. https://www.nber.org/papers/w29094

Lake, C. J., Carlson, J., Rose, A., & Chlevin-Thiele, C. (2019). Trust in name brand assessments: The case of the Myers-Briggs Type Indicator. The Psychologist-Manager Journal, 22(2), 91–107.

Lal, A., Le, L. K. D., Engel, L., Lee, Y. Y., & Mihalopoulos, C. (2021). Modelled cost-effectiveness of interpersonal therapy and exercise classes for the prevention of postnatal depression. Mental Health & Prevention, 24, 200214.

Lal, S. (2002). Giving children security: Mamie Phipps Clark and the racialization of child psychology. American Psychologist, 57, 20–28.

LaLumiere, R. T., & Kalivas, P. W. (2013). Motivational systems: Rewards and incentive value. In R. J. Nelson, S. Y. Mizumori, & I. B. Weiner (Eds.), Handbook of psychology, Vol. 3: Behavioral neuroscience (2nd ed.). John Wiley & Sons.

Lampard, A. M., Byrne, S. M., McLean, N., & Fursland, A. (2011). An evaluation of the enhanced cognitive-behavioural model of bulimia nervosa. Behaviour Research and Therapy, 49, 529–535.

Lanciano, T., Curci, A., Mastandrea, S., & Sartori, G. (2013). Do automatic mental associations detect a flashbulb memory? Memory, 21, 482–493.

Landro, L. (2010, May 11). New ways to treat pain. Wall Street Journal, p. D1–D2.

Landro, L. (2011, April 26). "Use only as directed" isn't easy. Wall Street Journal, pp. D1–D2.

Landry, S. H., Zucker, T. A., Taylor, H. B., Swank, P. R., Williams, J. M., Assel, M., Crawford, M., Huang, W., Clancy-Menchettie, J., Lonigan, C. J., Phillips, B. M., Eisenberg, N., Spinrad, T. L., de Villiers, J., de Villiers, P., Barnes, M., Starkey, P., Klein, A., & School Readiness Research Consortium. (2013). Enhancing early child care quality and learning for toddlers at risk: The responsive early childhood program. Developmental Psychology, 50(2), 526–541.

Lane, G., Zhou, G., Noto, T., & Zelano, C. (2020). Assessment of direct knowledge of the human olfactory system. Experimental Neurology, 329, 113304.

Lang, A. J., Sorrell, J. T., & Rodgers, C. S. (2006). Anxiety sensitivity as a predictor of labor pain. European Journal of Pain, 10, 263–270.

Langa, M. E., & Gone, J. P. (2020). Cultural context in DSM diagnosis: An American Indian case illustration of contradictory trends. Transcultural Psychiatry, 57(4), 567–580.

Lange, J., & Boecker, L. (2019). Schadenfreude as social-functional dominance regulator. Emotion, 19(3), 489–502.

Langer, R. D., Hodis, H. N., Lobo, R. A., & Allison, M. A. (2021). Hormone replacement therapy–where are we now? Climacteric, 24(1), 3–10.

Langford, J. S., Pitts, R. C., & Hughes, C. E. (2019). Assessing functions of stimuli associated with rich-to-lean transitions using a choice procedure. Journal of the Experimental Analysis of Behavior. https://doi.org/10.1002/jeab.540.

Langlois, F., Langlois, M., Carpentier, A. C., Brown, C., Lemieux, S., & Hivert, M. (2011). Ghrelin levels are associated with hunger as measured by the Three-Factor Eating Questionnaire in healthy young adults. Physiology & Behavior, 104, 373–377.

Langlois, P., Perrochon, A., David, R., Rainville, P., Wood, C., Vanhaudenhuyse, A., Pageaux, B., Ounajim, A., Lavalliere, M., Debarnot, U., Luque-Moreno, C., Roulaud, M., Simoneau, M., Goudman,

L., Moens, M., Rigoard, P., & Billot, M. (2022). Hypnosis to manage musculoskeletal and neuropathic chronic pain: A systematic review and meta-analysis. Neuroscience & Biobehavioral Reviews, 104591.

Langreth, R. (2000, May 1). Every little bit helps: How even moderate exercise can have a big impact on your health. Wall Street Journal, p. R5.

Lanzoni, D., Vitali, A., Regazzoni, D., & Rizzi, C. (2022). Design of customized virtual reality serious games for the cognitive rehabilitation of retrograde amnesia after brain stroke. Journal of Computing and Information Science in Engineering, 22(3), 031009 .

LaPointe, L. L. (2013). Paul Broca and the origins of language in the brain. Plural Publishing.

Larochelle, M. R., Slavova, S., Root, E. D., Feaster, D. J., Ward, P. J., Selk, S. C., . . . & Samet, J. H. (2021). Disparities in opioid overdose death trends by race/ethnicity, 2018-2019, from the healing communities study. American journal of public health, 111(10), 1851–1854.

Larsen, E. F. (2014). Good teens turned addicts. Choices. Accessed from http://www.huffingtonpost.com/2014/09/24/teens-turned-drug-addicts n 5877306.html.

Lasalvia, A. (2015). DSM-5 two years later: Facts, myths and some key open issues. Epidemiology and Psychiatric Sciences, 24, 185–187.

Latané, B., & Darley, J. M. (1970). The unresponsive bystander: Why doesn't he help? Appleton-Century-Crofts.

Latif, S., Jahangeer, M., Razia, D. M., Ashiq, M., Ghaffar, A., Akram, M., El Allam, A., Bouyahya, A., Garipova, L., Ali Shariati, M., Thiruvengadam, M., & Ansari, M. A. (2021). Dopamine in Parkinson's disease. Clinica Chimica Acta, 522, 114–126.

Latronica, J. R., Clegg, T. J., Tuan, W. J., & Bone, C. (2021). Are amphetamines associated with adverse cardiovascular events among elderly individuals?. The Journal of the American Board of Family Medicine, 34(6), 1074–1081.

Lattal, K. A., Cançado, C. X., Cook, J. E., Kincaid, S. L., Nighbor, T. D., & Oliver, A. C. (2017). On defining resurgence. Behavioural Processes, 141(Part 1), 85–91.

Lau, H. M., Sim, K. S., Chew, Q. H., & Sim, K. (2021). Quality of life and clinical correlates in adults with social phobia: A scoping review. Clinical Practice and Epidemiology in Mental Health: CP & EMH, 17, 224.

Lauer, E. E., Martin, S. B., & Zakrajsek, R. A. (2019). iSCORE: Using technology and imagery to enhance performance of closed motor skills. Strategies, 32(3), 19–24.

Laughlin, C. D. (2018). Meditation across cultures: A neuroanthropological approach. Time and Mind, 11(3), 221–257.

Lauriello, J., & Rahman, T. (2015). Schizophrenia spectrum and other psychotic disorders. In L. W. Roberts & A. K. Louie (Eds.), Study Guide to DSM-5®. American Psychiatric Publishing.

Laursen, B., & Faur, S. (2022). What does it mean to be susceptible to influence? A brief primer on peer conformity and developmental changes that affect it. International Journal of Behavioral Development, 46(3), 222–237.

Lavazza, A., & Manzotti, R. (2013). An externalist approach to creativity: Discovery versus recombination. Mind & Society, 12, 61–72.

Lavigne, K. M., Rapin, L. A., Metzak, P. D., Whitman, J. C., Jung, K., Dohen, M., Loevenbruck, H., & Woodward, T. S. (2015). Left-dominant temporal-frontal hypercoupling in schizophrenia patients with hallucinations during speech perception. Schizophrenia Bulletin, 41, 259–267.

Lavorgna, A., & Myles, H. (2021). Science denial and medical misinformation in pandemic times: A psycho-criminological analysis. European Journal of Criminology, 1477370820988832.

Lawal, I., Vorster, M., Nyakale, N., & Sathekge, M. (2021). Impulsivity imaging. In R. A. J. O. Dierckx, A. Otte, E. J. F. de Vries, & A. van Waarde (Eds.), PET and SPECT in psychiatry. Springer.

Lazarus, R. S. (1995). Emotions express a social relationship, but it is an individual mind that creates them. Psychological Inquiry, 6, 253–265.

Lazer, D. M. J., Baum, M. A., Benkler, Y., Berinsky, A., Greehill, K., Menczer, F., Metzger, M. J., Nyhan, B., Pennycook, G., Rothschild, D., Schudson, M., Sloman, S. A., Sunstein, C. R., Thorson, E. A., Watts, D. J., & Zittrain, J. L. (2018). The science of fake news. *Science, 359*, 1094-1096.

Leahy, R. L. (2015). Emotional schema therapy. In N. C. Thoma & D. McKay (Eds.), *Working with emotion in cognitive-behavioral therapy: Techniques for clinical practice.* Guilford Press.

Leander, N. P., Stroebe, W., Kreienkamp, J., Agostini, M., Gordijn, E., & Kruglanski, A. W. (2019). Mass shootings and the salience of guns as means of compensation for thwarted goals. *Journal of Personality and Social Psychology, 116*(5), 704-723.

Leaper, C., Brown, C., & Ayres, M. M. (2013). Adolescent girls' cognitive appraisals of coping responses to sexual harassment. *Psychology in the Schools, 50,* 969-986.

Lebedev, A. A., Bessolova, Y. N., Efimov, N. S., Bychkov, E. R., Karpova, I. V., Tissen, I. Y., . . . & Shabanov, P. D. (2021). Lateral hypothalamic self-stimulation with threshold current intensity induces emotional over-eating in self-deprivation paradigm in well-fed rats: Role of orexin and dopaminergic systems of the brain. *Reviews on Clinical Pharmacology and Drug Therapy, 19*(4), 421-429.

Lebow, J. L. (2019). Current issues in the practice of integrative couple and family therapy. *Family Process, 58*(3), 610-628.

Lebowitz, E. R., Marin, C., Martino, A., Shimshoni, Y., & Silverman, W. K. (2020). Parent-based treatment as efficacious as cognitive-behavioral therapy for childhood anxiety: A randomized noninferiority study of supportive parenting for anxious childhood emotions. *Journal of the American Academy of Child & Adolescent Psychiatry, 59*(3), 362-372.

Leder, J., Schlegel, R., & Schütz, A. (2021). Understanding the Motives for Terrorism–Does it Have an Effect on Psychological Reactions? A Replication and Extension. *Journal of interpersonal violence,* 08862605211025045.

Lee, A. Y., Reynolds, K. D., Stacy, A., Niu, Z., & Xie, B. (2019). Family functioning, moods, and binge eating among urban adolescents. *Journal of Behavioral Medicine, 42*(3), 511-521.

Lee, D., Kleinman, J., & Kleinman, A. (2007). Rethinking depression: An ethnographic study of the experiences of depression among Chinese. *Harvard Review of Psychiatry, 15,* 1-8.

Lee, E., Greenblatt, A., & Hu, R. (2021). A knowledge synthesis of cross-cultural psychotherapy research: A critical review. *Journal of Cross-Cultural Psychology, 52*(6), 511-532.

Lee, F. H., & Raja, S. N. (2011). Complementary and alternative medicine in chronic pain. *Pain, 152,* 28-30.

Lee, J. (2022, May 18.) Confronting the invisibility of anti-Asian racism. Brookings Institution. https://www.brookings.edu/blog/how-we-rise/2022/05/18/confronting-the-invisibility-of-anti-asian-racism/

Lee, J., Lee, H. J., & Bong, M. (2022). Boosting children's math self-efficacy by enriching their growth mindsets and gender-fair beliefs. *Theory Into Practice, 61*(1), 35-48.

Lee, J. J., McGue, M., Iacono, W. G., Michael, A. M., & Chabris, C. F. (2019). The causal influence of brain size on human intelligence: Evidence from within-family phenotypic associations and GWAS modeling. *Intelligence, 75,* 48-58.

Lee, J. Q., McDonald, R. J., & Sutherland, R. J. (2019). Hippocampal damage causes retrograde amnesia and slower acquisition of a cue-place discrimination in a concurrent cue-place water task in rats. *Neuroscience, 412,* 131-143.

Leeman, R. F., Fischler, C., & Rozin, P. (2011). Medical doctors' attitudes and beliefs about diet and health are more like those of their lay countrymen (France, Germany, Italy, UK and USA) than those of doctors in other countries. *Appetite, 56,* 558-563.

Lee, S., & Mason, M. (2019). Effectiveness of brief DBT-informed group therapy on psychological resilience: A preliminary naturalistic study. *Journal of College Student Psychotherapy, 33*(1), 25-37.

Lee, S., Moon, S. I., & Feeley, T. H. (2019). The "that's-not-all" compliance-gaining technique: when does it work? *Social Influence,* 1-15.

Lee, S. A., & Liang, Y. J. (2019). Robotic foot-in-the-door: Using sequential-request persuasive strategies in human-robot interaction. *Computers in Human Behavior, 90,* 351-356.

Lee, S. W. Y., Hsu, Y. T., & Cheng, K. H. (2022). Do curious students learn more science in an immersive virtual reality environment? Exploring the impact of advance organizers and curiosity. *Computers & Education,* 104456.

Lee, T. C. (2020). Groupthink, qualitative comparative analysis, and the 1989 Tiananmen Square disaster. *Small Group Research, 51*(4), 435-463.

Lee, T. T., Taylor, A. M., Holbert, A. M., & Graham, J. R. (2019). MMPI-2-RF predictors of interpersonal relationship characteristics in committed couples. *Psychological Assessment, 31*(9), 1118.

Lee, Y., Ragguett, R. M., Mansur, R. B., Boutilier, J. J., Rosenblat, J. D., Trevizol, A., Brietzke, E., Lin, K., Pan, Z., Subramaniapillai, M., Chan, T. C. Y., Fus, D., Park, C., Musial, N., Zuckerman, H., Chen, V. C., Ho, R., Rong, C., & McIntyre, R. S. (2018). Applications of machine learning algorithms to predict therapeutic outcomes in depression: A meta-analysis and systematic review. *Journal of Affective Disorders, 241,* 519-532.

Legault, I., Fang, S. Y., Lan, Y. J., & Li, P. (2019). Structural brain changes as a function of second language vocabulary training: Effects of learning context. *Brain and Cognition, 134,* 90-102.

Lehman, D. R., & Taylor, S. E. (1988). Date with an earthquake: Coping with a probable, unpredictable disaster. *Personality and Social Psychology Bulletin, 13,* 546-555.

Lehmiller, J. J., Garcia, J. R., Gesselman, A. N., & Mark, K. P. (2021). Less sex, but more sexual diversity: Changes in sexual behavior during the COVID-19 coronavirus pandemic. *Leisure Sciences, 43*(1-2), 295-304.

Lehrer, J. (2012, April 13). When memory commits an injustice. *Wall Street Journal,* p. C18.

Lehrer, P., Kaur, K., Sharma, A., Shah, K., Huseby, R., Bhavsar, J., Sgobba, P., & Zhang, Y. (2020). Heart rate variability biofeedback improves emotional and physical health and performance: A systematic review and meta analysis. *Applied Psychophysiology and Biofeedback, 45*(3), 109-129.

Leiblum, S. R., & Chivers, M. L. (2007). Normal and persistent genital arousal in women: New perspectives. *Journal of Sex & Marital Therapy, 33,* 357-373.

Leibowitz, K., & Crum, A. (2020, April 7). Stress can be your friend. *The New York Times,* p. D6.

Leising, D., Scharloth, J., Lohse, O., & Wood, D. (2014). What types of terms do people use when describing an individual's personality? *Psychological Science, 25,* 1787-1794.

Lemogne, C., Consoli, S. M., Geoffroy-Perez, B., Coeuret-Pellicer, M., Nabi, H., Melchior, M., Limosin, F., Zins, M., Ducimetier, P., Goldberg, M., & Cordier, S. (2013). Personality and the risk of cancer: A 16-year follow-up study of the GAZEL cohort. *Psychosomatic Medicine, 75,* 262-271.

Leonhart, D. (2021, June 18). Kids, Covid, and Delta. *The New York Times.* https://www.nytimes.com/2021/06/18/briefing/kids-covid-and-delta.html

LePine, M. A. (2022). The challenge-hindrance stressor framework: An integrative conceptual review and path forward. *Group & Organization Management, 47*(2), 223-254.

Leppänen, J. M., Moulson, M. C., Vogel-Farley, V. K., & Nelson, C. A. (2007). An ERP study of emotional face processing in the adult and infant brain. *Child Development, 78,* 232-245.

Leskinen, E. A., Rabelo, V. C., & Cortina, L. M. (2015). Gender stereotyping and harassment: A "catch-22" for women in the workplace. *Psychology, Public Policy, and Law, 21,* 192-204.

Lester, K. J., Coleman, J. I., Roberts, S., Keers, R., Breen, G., Bögels, S., et al. (2017). Genetic variation in the endocannabinoid system and response to cognitive behavior therapy for child anxiety disorders. *American Journal of Medical Genetics Part B: Neuropsychiatric Genetics, 174,* 144-155.

Leszcz, M., Pain, C., Hunter, J., Maunder, R., & Ravitz, P. (2015). *Achieving psychotherapy effectiveness.* W. W. Norton & Co.

Leung, A. Y., Molassiotis, A., & Carino, D. A. (2021). A challenge to healthy aging: Limited social participation in old age. *Aging and Disease, 12*(7), 1536-1538.

LeVay, S. (2011). *Gay, straight, and the reason why: The science of sexual orientation.* Oxford University Press.

Levine, L. E., & Munsch, J. (2011). *Child development: An active learning approach.* Sage Publications.

Levine, R. (2019). A group analyst's perspective on the Trump-Clinton election and aftermath. *International Journal of Group Psychotherapy, 69*(2), 192-220.

Levine, S. Z. (2011). Elaboration on the association between IQ and parental SES with subsequent crime. *Personality and Individual Differences, 50,* 1233-1237.

Levitan, L. C., & Verhulst, B. (2016). Conformity in groups: The effects of others' views on expressed attitudes and attitude change. *Political Behavior, 38*(2), 277-315.

Levy, B. R., & Myers, L. M. (2004). Preventive health behaviors influenced by self-perceptions of aging. *Preventive Medicine: An International Journal Devoted to Practice and Theory, 39,* 625-629.

Levy, S. (2019). Youth and the opioid epidemic. *Pediatrics, 143*(2), e20182752.

Lewinsohn, P. M., Petit, J. W., Joiner, T. E., Jr., & Seeley, J. R. (2003). The symptomatic expression of major depressive disorder in adolescents and young adults. *Journal of Abnormal Psychology, 112,* 244-252.

Lewis, C., & Lamb, M. (2011). The role of parent-child relationships in child development. In M. E. Lamb & M. H. Bornstein (Eds.), *Social and personality development: An advanced textbook.* Psychology Press.

Lewis, C. E., Thomas, K. F., Dodge, N. C., Molteno, C. D., Meintjes, E. M., Jacobson, J. L., & Jacobson, S. W. (2015). Verbal learning and memory impairment in children with fetal alcohol spectrum disorders. *Alcoholism: Clinical and Experimental Research, 39,* 724-732.

Lewis, D. G., Al-Shawaf, L., Conroy-Beam, D., Asao, K., & Buss, D. M. (2017). Evolutionary psychology: A how-to guide. *American Psychologist, 72*(4), 353-373.

Lewis, L. D. (2021). The interconnected causes and consequences of sleep in the brain. *Science, 374*(6567), 564-568.

Lewis, T., & Umbreit, M. (2015). A humanistic approach to mediation and dialogue: An evolving transformative practice. *Conflict Resolution Quarterly, 33*(1), 3-17.

Lexcellent, C. (2019). *Human memory and material memory.* Springer Nature.

Lexcellent, Christian. *Human memory and material memory.* Cham, Switzerland: Springer Nature, 2019.

Li, B., Piriz, J., Mirrione, M., Chung, C., Proulx, C. D., Schulz, D., Henn, F., & Malinow, R. (2011). Synaptic potentiation onto habenula neurons in learned helplessness model of depression. *Nature, 470,* 535-539.

Li, C., Tang, H., Zhang, W., Wang, X., Zheng, L., & Guo, X. (2022). Individuals with higher economic insecurity manifest greater self-serving bias. *Analyses of Social Issues and Public Policy, 22*(1), 304-314.

Li, F., Luo, S., Mu, W., Li, Y., Ye, L., Zheng, X., Xu, B., Ding, Y., Ling, P., Zhou, M., & Chen, X. (2021). Effects of sources of social support and resilience on the mental health of different age groups during the COVID-19 pandemic. *BMC Psychiatry, 21*(1), 1-14.

Li, J., & Wang, Y. (2022). Golgi metal ion homeostasis in human health and diseases. *Cells, 11*(2), 289.

Li, J., Tao, X., Gong, T., & Li, X. (2022). How confirmation bias influences risk and contingency management: Lessons from global leaders' responses to the 2020 pandemic. *International Journal of Risk and Contingency Management, 11*(1), 1-12.

Li, T. K., Volkow, N. D., & Baler, R. D. (2007). The biological bases of nicotine and alcohol co-addiction. *Biological Psychiatry, 61,* 1-3.

Li, X., Chen, L., Ma, R., Wang, H., Wan, L., Bu, J., Hong, W., Lv, W., Yang, Y., Rao, H., & Zhang, X. (2020). The neural mechanisms of immediate and follow-up of the treatment effect of hypnosis on smoking craving. *Brain Imaging and Behavior, 14*(5), 1487–1497.

Li, Y., Hofstetter, C. R., Wahlgren, D., Irvin, V., Chhay, D., & Hovell, M. F. (2015). Social networks and immigration stress among first-generation Mandarin-speaking Chinese immigrants in Los Angeles. *International Journal of Social Welfare, 24,* 170–181.

Li, Y., Zuo, Y., Yu, P., Ping, X., & Cui, C. (2015). Role of basolateral amygdala dopamine D2 receptors in impulsive choice in acute cocaine-treated rats. *Behavioural Brain Research, 287,* 187–195.

Li, Z., Yu, J., Yang, X., & Zhu, L. (2019). Associations between empathy and altruistic sharing behavior in Chinese adults. *The Journal of General Psychology, 146*(1), 1–16.

Liang, Y., & Park, Y. (2022). Understanding bystander intervention: A cost-reward perspective. In *Academy of Management Proceedings* (Vol. 2022, No. 1). Academy of Management.

Libdeh, A. A., Brenner, L., & Quigg, M. (2022). Recurrent dissociative fugue episodes in a child with autism spectrum disorder. *Clinical Pediatrics, 61*(3), 253–255.

Libedinsky, C., & Livingstone, M. (2011). Role of prefrontal cortex in conscious visual perception. *Journal of Neuroscience, 31,* 64–69.

Lichtenstein, P., Tideman, M., Sullivan, P. F., Serlachius, E., Larsson, H., Kuja-Halkola, R., & Butwicka, A. (2021). Familial risk and heritability of intellectual disability: A population-based cohort study in Sweden. *Journal of Child Psychology and Psychiatry, 63*(9), 1092–1102. https://doi.org/10.1111/jcpp.13560

Lichterman, B. L. (2022). Ethics in psychosurgery. *Progress in Brain Research, 272*(1), 191–199.

Lieberman, M. D. (2007). Social cognitive neuro-science: A review of core processes. *Annual Review of Psychology, 58,* 259–289.

Lieberman, P. (2015). A tangled tale of circuits, evolution, and language. *PsycCRITIQUES, 60,* 88–97.

Liechti, M. E., Dolder, P. C., & Schmid, Y. (2017). Alterations of consciousness and mystical-type experiences after acute LSD in humans. *Psychopharmacology, 234,* 1499–1510.

Liem, G. D. (2015). Academic and social achievement goals: Their additive, interactive, and specialized effects on school functioning. *British Journal of Educational Psychology, 86*(1), 37–56.

Light, N., Fernbach, P. M., Rabb, N., Geana, M. V., & Sloman, S. A. (2022). Knowledge overconfidence is associated with anti-consensus views on controversial scientific issues. *Science Advances, 8*(29), eabo0038.

Lilienfeld, S. O. (2012). Further sources of our field's embattled public reputation. *American Psychologist,* 808–809.

Lilienfeld, S. O. (2020). Microaggression Research and Application: Clarifications, Corrections, and Common Ground. *Perspectives on Psychological Science, 15*(1), 27–37.

Lim, T. K., Ma, Y., Berger, F., & Litscher, G. (2018). Acupuncture and neural mechanism in the management of low back pain–an update. *Medicines, 5*(3), 63.

Lim, Y. H., Watkins, R. E., Jones, H., Kippin, N. R., & Finlay-Jones, A. (2022). Fetal alcohol spectrum disorders screening tools: A systematic review. *Research in Developmental Disabilities, 122,* 104168.

Linassi, F., Obert, D. P., Maran, E., Tellaroli, P., Kreuzer, M., Sanders, R. D., & Carron, M. (2021). Implicit memory and anesthesia: A systematic review and meta-analysis. *Life, 11*(8), 850.

Lincoln, K. D., & Nguyen, A. W. (2022). Race, ethnicity, and age differences in social relationships and obesity: Findings From the National Survey of American Life. *Journal of Aging and Health,* 08982643221085900.

Lin, C. W., Huang, L. L., Liao, C. M., & Fan, H. (2021, July). Measuring the apparent movement perception thresholds of kinetic forms with surface lines and forms of various color combinations. In *International Conference on Human-Computer Interaction* (pp. 127–132). Springer.

Lindberg, L. D., Maddow-Zimet, I., & Marcell, A. V. (2019). Prevalence of sexual initiation before age 13 years among male adolescents and young adults in the United States. *JAMA Pediatrics, 173*(6), 553–560.

Lindner, P. (2021). Better, virtually: the past, present, and future of virtual reality cognitive behavior therapy. *International Journal of Cognitive Therapy, 14*(1), 23–46.

Lindorff, M. (2005). Determinants of received social support: Who gives what to managers? *Journal of Social and Personal Relationships, 22,* 323–337.

Lindsay, P. H., & Norman, D. A. (1977). *Human information processing* (2nd ed.). New York: Academic Press.

Ling, S., Ceban, F., Lui, L. M., Lee, Y., Teopiz, K. M., Rodrigues, N. B., . . . & McIntyre, R. S. (2021). Molecular mechanisms of psilocybin and implications for the treatment of depression. *CNS drugs,* 1–14.

Lin, I., Wang, S., Chu, I., Lu, Y., Lee, C., Lin, T., & Fan, S. (2017). The association of Type D personality with heart rate variability and lipid profiles among patients with coronary artery disease. *International Journal of Behavioral Medicine, 24,* 101–109.

Lin, J., Arthurs, J., & Reilly, S. (2017). Conditioned taste aversions: From poisons to pain to drugs of abuse. *Psychonomic Bulletin & Review, 24,* 335–351.

Links, A. R., Callon, W., Wasserman, C., Walsh, J., Beach, M. C., & Boss, E. F. (2019). Surgeon use of medical jargon with parents in the outpatient setting. *Patient Education and Counseling, 102*(6), 1111–1118.

Lin, L., Conroy, J., & Ghaness, A. (2020, November/December). Psychology's workforce is becoming more diverse. *Monitor on Psychology,* p. 19.

Linley, P. (2013). Human strengths and well-being: Finding the best within us at the intersection of eudaimonic philosophy, humanistic psychology, and positive psychology. In A. S. Waterman (Ed.), *The best within us: Positive psychology perspectives on eudaimonia.* Washington, DC: American Psychological Association.

Lin, L., McCormack, H., Kruczkowski, L., & Berg, M. B. (2015). How women's perceptions of peer weight preferences are related to drive for thinness. *Sex Roles, 72,* 117–126.

Lin, L., Stamm, K., & Christidis, P. (2018, February). How diverse is the psychology workforce? *Monitor on Psychology,* p. 19.

Lin, L. West, C., Ghaness, A., Fowler, G. A., Stamm, K., & Conroy, J. (2021). Bridging education and career: Nonlinear career pathways in psychology. https://www.apa.org/workforce/publications/psycpathways/nonlinear-career.pdf

Lin, M. P. (2022). Avoidance/emotion-focused coping mediates the relationship between distress tolerance and problematic Internet use in a representative sample of adolescents in Taiwan: One-year follow-up. *Journal of Adolescence, 94*(4), 600–610

Lin, P., Li, L., Wang, Y., Zhao, Z., Liu, G., Chen, W., Tao, H., & Gao, X. (2018). Type D personality, but not Type A behavior pattern, is associated with coronary plaque vulnerability. *Psychology, Health & Medicine, 23*(2), 216–223.

Lin, T., Heckman, T. G., & Anderson, T. (2022). The efficacy of synchronous teletherapy versus in-person therapy: A meta-analysis of randomized clinical trials. *Clinical Psychology: Science and Practice, 29*(2), 167–178. https://doi.org/10.1037/cps0000056

Lin, X., Xie, S., & Li, H. (2019). Chinese mothers' and fathers' involvement in toddler play activity: Type variations and gender differences. *Early Child Development and Care, 189*(2), 179–190.

Lipson, S. K., Zhou, S., Abelson, S., Heinze, J., Jirsa, M., Morigney, J., Patterson, A., Singh, M., & Eisenberg, D. (2022). Trends in college student mental health and help-seeking by race/ethnicity: Findings from the national healthy minds study, 2013–2021. *Journal of Affective Disorders, 306,* 138–147.

Littlejohn, P., & Finlay, B. B. (2021). When a pandemic and an epidemic collide: COVID-19, gut microbiota, and the double burden of malnutrition. *BMC Medicine, 19*(1), 1–8.

Littman, D., Sherman, S. E., Troxel, A. B., & Stevens, E. R. (2022). Behavioral economics and tobacco control: Current practices and future opportunities. *International Journal of Environmental Research and Public Health, 19*(13), 8174.

Liu, D., Liu, X., & Wu, S. (2022, June). A literature review of diffusion of responsibility phenomenon. In *2022 8th International Conference on Humanities and Social Science Research.* Atlantis Press.

Liu, H., Ye, M., & Guo, H. (2020). An updated review of randomized clinical trials testing the improvement of cognitive function of Ginkgo biloba extract in healthy people and Alzheimer's patients. *Frontiers in Pharmacology, 10,* 1688.

Liu, J., Ying, Z., & Zhang, S. (2015). A rate function approach to computerized adaptive testing for cognitive diagnosis. *Psychometrika, 80,* 468–490

Liu, J. J. W., Reed, M., & Vickers, K. (2019). Reframing the individual stress response: Balancing our knowledge of stress to improve responsivity to stressors. *Stress and Health, 35*(5), 607–616.

Liu, Y., Meng, J., Yao, M., Ye, Q., Fan, B., & Peng, W. (2019). Hearing other's pain is associated with sensitivity to physical pain: An ERP study. *Biological psychology, 145,* 150–158.

Livingstone, A. G., Spears, R., Manstead, A. R., Bruder, M., & Shepherd, L. (2011). We feel, therefore we are: Emotion as a basis for self-categorization and social action. *Emotion,11,* 754–767.

Llabre, M. M. (2021). Insight into the Hispanic paradox: The language hypothesis. *Perspectives on Psychological Science, 16*(6), 1324–1336.

Llorens-Aguilar, S., Arnáez, S., Aardema, F., & García-Soriano, G. (2022). The relationship between obsessions and the self: Feared and actual self-descriptions in a clinical obsessive–compulsive disorder sample. *Clinical Psychology & Psychotherapy, 29*(2), 642–651.

Llorca-Mestre, A., Samper-García, P., Malonda-Vidal, E., & Cortés-Tomás, M. T. (2017). Parenting style and peer attachment as predictors of emotional instability in children. *Social Behavior and Personality, 45,* 677–694.

Loehlin, J. C., Bartels, M., Boomsma, D. I., Bratko, D., Martin, N. G., Nichols, R. C., & Wright, M. J. (2015). Is there a genetic correlation between general factors of intelligence and personality? *Twin Research and Human Genetics, 18,* 234–242.

Loftus, E. F. (1993) The reality of repressed memories. *American Psychologist, 48,* 518–537.

Loftus, E. F., & Palmer, J. C. (1974). Reconstruction of automobile destruction: An example of the interface between language and memory. *Journal of Verbal Learning and Verbal Behavior, 13,* 585–589.

Lokhorst, S. L., & Reich, C. M. (2022). The alliance-outcome correlation: Is there a halo effect? *Journal of Psychotherapy Integration.* Advance online publication. https://doi.org/10.1037/int0000285

Lombaard, N., & Naudé, L. (2017). "Breaking the cycle": Black adolescents' experiences of being stereotyped during identity development. *Journal of Psychology in Africa, 27,* 185–190.

Longo, M. R., Trippier, S., Vagnoni, E., & Lourenco, S. F. (2015). Right hemisphere control of visuospatial attention in near space. *Neuropsychologia, 70,* 350–357.

López-Pérez, B., & Ambrona, T. (2015). The role of cognitive emotion regulation on the vicarious emotional response. *Motivation and Emotion, 39,* 299–308.

López-Pérez, B., Carrera, P., Oceja, L., Ambrona, T., & Stocks, E. (2019). Sympathy and tenderness as components of dispositional empathic concern: Predicting helping and caring behaviors. *Current Psychology: A Journal for Diverse Perspectives on Diverse Psychological Issues, 38*92), 458–468.

Lorenz, K. (1966). *On aggression.* Harcourt Brace Jovanovich.

Lorenz, K. (1974). *Civilized man's eight deadly sins.* New York: Harcourt Brace Jovanovich.

Loriedo, C., & Di Leone, F. G. (2017). Conversion disorder. In G. R. Elkins (Ed.), *Handbook of medical and psychological hypnosis: Foundations, applications, and professional issues.* Springer Publishing.

Lovett, I. (2019, April 13-14). One teenager killed himself, then six more followed. *Wall Street Journal,* pp. A1, A12.

Loving, T., Crockett, E., & Paxson, A. (2009). Passionate love and relationship thinkers: Experimental evidence for acute cortisol elevations in women. *Psychoneuroendocrinology, 34,* 939-946.

Lowe, C. J., Cho, I., Goldsmith, S. F., & Morton, J. B. (2021). The bilingual advantage in children's executive functioning is not related to language status: A meta-analytic review. *Psychological Science, 32*(7), 1115-1146.

Lowe, P., Humphreys, C., & Williams, S. J. (2007). Night terrors: Women's experiences of (not) sleeping where there is domestic violence. *Violence against Women, 13,* 549-561.

Lowry, M., & Bryant, J. (2019). Blue is in the eye of the beholder: A cross-linguistic study on color perception and memory. *Journal of Psycholinguistic Research, 48*(1), 163-179.

Lu, B., Zeng, W., Li, Z., & Wen, J. (2021). Risk factors of post-traumatic stress disorder 10 years after Wenchuan earthquake: A population-based case-control study. *Epidemiology and Psychiatric Sciences, 30.*

Lucas, H. D., Creery, J. D., Hu, X., & Paller, K. A. (2019). Grappling with implicit social bias: A perspective from memory research. *Neuroscience, 406,* 684-697.

Luchins, A. S. (1946). Classroom experiments on mental set. *American Journal of Psychology, 59,* 295-298.

Lucini, F. A., Del Ferraro, G., Sigman, M., & Makse, H. A. (2019). How the brain transitions from conscious to subliminal perception. *Neuroscience, 411,* 280-290.

Lu, D. (2022, January 18). 'It's awful to be a medical exception': the woman who cannot forget. *The Guardian.* Downloaded from https://www.theguardian.com/society/2022/jan/19/its-awful-to-be-a-medical-exception-the-woman-who-cannot-forget, April 25, 2022.

Lu, S. (2015, February.) Erasing bad memories. Monitor on Psychology, pp. 41-45.

Lu, W., Todhunter-Reid, A., Mitsdarffer, M. L., Muñoz-Laboy, M., Yoon, A. S., & Xu, L. (2021). Barriers and facilitators for mental health service use among racial/ethnic minority adolescents: A systematic review of literature. *Frontiers in Public Health, 9,* 641605.

Lueck, J. A., Costantini, R., & Knobloch, M. (2019). The making of an addiction: Examining psychological determinants of prescription stimulant abuse among college students. *Health Communication.* Advance online publication. https://doi.org/10.1080/104102 36.2019.1598743

Lui, P. P. (2019). College alcohol beliefs: Measurement invariance, mean differences, and correlations with alcohol use outcomes across sociodemographic groups. *Journal of Counseling Psychology, 66*(4), 487-495.

Lunde, S. J., Vuust, P., Garza-Villarreal, E. A., & Vase, L. (2019). Music-induced analgesia: How does music relieve pain? *Pain, 160*(5), 989-993.

Lundgren, H., Kroon, B., & Poell, R. F. (2019). Pigeonholing or learning instrument? Test takers' reactions to personality testing in management development. *European Journal of Training and Development, 43*(3/4), 354-374.

Luo, H., Liu, Z., Xie, F., Bilal, M., Liu, L., Yang, R., & Wang, Z. (2021). Microbial production of gamma-aminobutyric acid: Applications, state-of-the-art achievements, and future perspectives. *Critical Reviews in Biotechnology, 41*(4), 491-512.

Luo, J., He, K., Andolina, I. M., Li, X., Yin, J., Chen, Z., et al. (2019). Going with the flow: The neural mechanisms underlying illusions of complex-flow motion. *The Journal of Neuroscience, 39*(14), 2664-2685.

Luo, S., & Zhang, G. (2009). What leads to romantic attraction: Similarity, reciprocity, security, or beauty? Evidence from a speed-dating study. *Journal of Personality, 77,* 933-964.

Luong, G., Rauers, A., & Fingerman, K. L. (2015). The multifaceted nature of late-life socialization: Older

adults as agents and targets of socialization. In J. E. Grusec & P. D. Hastings (Eds.), *Handbook of socialization: Theory and research* (2nd ed.). Guilford Press.

Luppi, A. I., Cain, J., Spindler, L. R., Górska, U. J., Toker, D., Hudson, A. E., Brown, E. N., Diringer, M. N., Stevens, R. D., Massimini, M., Monti, M. M., Stamatakis, E. A. Boly, M., & the Curing Coma Campaign and Its Contributing Collaborators. (2021). Mechanisms underlying disorders of consciousness: Bridging gaps to move toward an integrated translational science. *Neurocritical Care, 35*(1), 37-54.

Luria, A. R. (1987). *The mind of a mnemonist: A little book about a vast memory, with a new foreword by Jerome S. Bruner.* Harvard University Press.

Luria, A. R. (1987). *The mind of a mnemonist.* Cambridge, MA: Basic Books.

Luscomb, B. (2018, November 26). The divorce rate is dropping. That may not actually be good news. *Time.* https://time.com/5434949/divorce-rate-children-marriage-benefits/

Lutgendorf, S. K., & Andersen, B. L. (2015). Biobehavioral approaches to cancer progression and survival: Mechanisms and interventions. *American Psychologist, 70,* 186-197.

Luttrell, A., Petty, R. E., & Xu, M. (2017). Replicating and fixing failed replications: The case of need for cognition and argument quality. *Journal of Experimental Social Psychology, 69,* 178-183.

Lynn, S. J., Krackow, E., Loftus, E. F., Locke, T. G., & Lilienfeld, S. O. (2015). Constructing the past: Problematic memory recovery techniques in psychotherapy. In S. O. Lilienfeld, S. J. Lynn & J. M. Lohr (Eds.), *Science and pseudoscience in clinical psychology* (2nd ed.). Guilford Press.

Lynn, S. J., Laurence, J., & Kirsch, I. (2015). Hypnosis, suggestion, and suggestibility: An integrative model. *American Journal of Clinical Hypnosis, 57,* 314-329.

Lynn, S. J., Maxwell, R., Merckelbach, H., Lilienfeld, S. O., van Heugten-van der Kloet, D., & Miskovic, V. (2019). Dissociation and its disorders: Competing models, future directions, and a way forward. *Clinical Psychology Review, 73,* 101755.

Lyons, H., Giordano, P. C., Manning, W. D., & Longmore, M. A. (2011). Identity, peer relationships, and adolescent girls' sexual behavior: An exploration of the contemporary double standard. *Journal of Sex Research, 48,* 437-449.

Lysaker, P. H., Pattison, M. L., Leonhardt, B. L., Phelps, S., & Vohs, J. L. (2018). Insight in schizophrenia spectrum disorders: Relationship with behavior, mood and perceived quality of life, underlying causes and emerging treatments. *World Psychiatry, 17*(1), 12-23.

Ma, C. F., Chan, S. K. W., Chung, Y. L., Ng, S. M., Hui, C. L. M., Suen, Y. N., & Chen, E. Y. H. (2021). The predictive power of expressed emotion and its components in relapse of schizophrenia: A meta-analysis and meta-regression. *Psychological Medicine, 51*(3), 365-375.

Ma, F., Heyman, G. D., Jing, C., Fu, Y., Compton, B. J., Xu, F., & Lee, K. (2018). Promoting honesty in young children through observational learning. *Journal of Experimental Child Psychology, 167,* 234-245.

Ma, H., Cai, M., & Wang, H. (2021). Emotional blunting in patients with major depressive disorder: a brief non-systematic review of current research. *Frontiers in Psychiatry, 12.*

Ma, L., Guo, H., & Fang, Y. (2021). Analysis of construction workers' safety behavior based on Myers-Briggs Type Indicator Personality Test in a bridge construction project. *Journal of Construction Engineering and Management, 147*(1), 04020149.

Ma, Y., Goldstein, M. R., Davis, R. B., & Yeh, G. Y. (2021). Profile of subjective-objective sleep discrepancy in patients with insomnia and sleep apnea. *Journal of Clinical Sleep Medicine,* jcsm-9348.

Maas, J. (2016). Sleep myths–true or false? American Sleep Association. https://www.sleepassociation.org/blog-post/sleep-myths-true-false

Macauda, G., Ellis, A. W., Grabherr, L., Francesco, R. B., & Mast, F. W. (2019). Canal-otolith interactions alter the perception of self-motion direction. *Attention, Perception, & Psychophysics, 81*(5), 1698-1714.

MacDonald, L. (2022). Whose story counts? Staking a claim for diverse bicultural narratives in New Zealand secondary schools. *Race Ethnicity and Education, 25*(1), 55-72.

MacDonald, S. F., Russell, C., Beauchamp, T., Derkzen, D., & Fischer, B. (2022). Comparing characteristics and outcomes of different opioid agonist treatment modalities among opioid-dependent federal men correctional populations in Canada. *International Journal of Drug Policy, 100,* 103480.

Mace, J. H., Bernas, R. S., & Clevinger, A. (2015). Individual differences in recognising involuntary autobiographical memories: Impact on the reporting of abstract cues. *Memory, 23,* 445-452.

Macefield, V. G. (2022). Why is our sense of touch so good at our fingertips? *The Journal of Physiology, 600*(7), 1539-1540.

Mack, J. (2003). *The museum of the mind.* British Museum Publications.

Mack, M. L., Love, B. C., & Preston, A. R. (2016). Dynamic updating of hippocampal object representations reflects new conceptual knowledge. *PNAS Proceedings of the National Academy of Sciences of the United States of America, 113,* 13203-13208.

MacKay, D. M. (2019). The earthquake that reshaped the intellectual landscape of memory, mind and brain: Case H. M. In MacPherson, S. E. & Sala, S. D. (Eds). *Cases of amnesia: Contributions to understanding memory and the brain.* Routledge.

Mackey, A. P., Finn, A. S., Leonard, J. A., Jacoby-Senghor, D. S., West, M. R., Gabrieli, C. F. O., et al. (2015). Neuroanatomical correlates of the income-achievement gap. *Psychological Science, 26*(6), 1-9.

Mackey, E. R., Burton, E. T., Cadieux, A., Getzoff, E., Santos, M., Ward, W., & Beck, A. R. (2022). Addressing structural racism is critical for ameliorating the childhood obesity epidemic in black youth. *Childhood Obesity, 18*(2), 75-83.

MacLaine, T. D., Lowe, N., & Dale, J. (2021). The use of simulation in medical student education on the topic of breaking bad news: A systematic review. *Patient Education and Counseling, 104*(11), 2670-2681.

Madan, A., Rosca, M. I., & Bucovicean, M. (2021). Theoretical Approach of Subliminal Advertising. In *Eurasian Business and Economics Perspectives* (pp. 293-302). Springer, Cham.

Maddi, S. R., Khoshaba, D. M., Harvey, R. H., Fazel, M., & Resurreccion, N. (2011). The personality construct of hardiness, V: Relationships with the construction of existential meaning in life. *Journal of Humanistic Psychology, 51,* 369-388.

Maddock, R. J., Buonocore, M. H., Miller, A. R., Yoon, J. H., Soosman, S. K., & Unruh, A. M. (2013). Abnormal activity-dependent brain lactate and glutamate + glutamine responses in panic disorder. *Biological Psychiatry, 73,* 1111-1119.

Madeira, R. M., & dos Santos, R. A. T. (2022). The effects of sensory deprivations during the initial practice of short piano pieces: An experiment with four students at different academic levels. *Psychology of Music, 50*(1), 280-297.

Mader, S. S. (2000). *Biology* (6th ed.). McGraw Hill.

Madsen, H. Ø., Ba-Ali, S., Hageman, I., Lund-Andersen, H., & Martiny, K. (2021). Light therapy for seasonal affective disorder in visual impairment and blindness-a pilot study. *Acta Neuropsychiatrica,* 1-9.

Maeder, E. M., & Ewanation, L. (2018). What makes race salient? Juror decision-making in same-race versus cross-race identification scenarios and the influence of expert testimony. *Criminal Justice and Behavior, 45*(8), 1234-1251.

Maenner, M. J., Shaw, K. A., Bakian, A. V., Bilder, D. A., Durkin, M. S., Esler, A., Furnier, S. M., Hallas, L., Hall-Lande, J., Hudson, A., Hughes, M. M., Patrick, M., Pierce, K., Poynter, J. N., Salinas, A., Shenouda, J., Vehorn, A., Warren, Z., Constantino, J. N., DiRienzo, M., et al. (2021). Prevalence and characteristics of autism spectrum disorder among children aged 8 years–autism and developmental disabilities monitoring network, 11 sites, United States, 2018. *MMWR Surveillance Summaries, 70*(11), 1-16.

Magee, S. R., Bublitz, M. H., Orazine, C., Brush, B., Salisbury, A., Niaura, R., & Stroud, L. R. (2013). The relationship between maternal-fetal attachment and cigarette smoking over pregnancy. *Maternal and Child Health Journal, 18*(4), 1017–1022.

Maggio, M. G., Piazzitta, D., Andaloro, A., Latella, D., Sciarrone, F., Casella, C., Naro, A., Manuli, A., & Calabrò, R. S. (2022). Embodied cognition in neurodegenerative disorders: What do we know so far? A narrative review focusing on the mirror neuron system and clinical applications. *Journal of Clinical Neuroscience, 98*, 66–72.

Magida, A. J. (2006). *Opening the doors of wonder: Reflections on religious rites of passage.* University of California Press.

Magis, D., & Schoenen, J. (2011). Treatment of migraine: Update on new therapies. *Current Opinions in Neurology, 24*, 203–210.

Magoni, M., Bassani, L., Okong, P., Kituuka, P., Germinario, E. P., Giuliano, M., & Vella, S. (2005). Mode of infant feeding and HIV infection in children in a program for prevention of mother-to-child transmission in Uganda. *AIDS, 19*, 433–437.

Maguen, S., Li, Y., Madden, E., Seal, K. H., Neylan, T. C., Patterson, O. V., DuVall, S. L., Lujan, C., & Shiner, B. (2019). Factors associated with completing evidence-based psychotherapy for PTSD among veterans in a national healthcare system. *Psychiatry Research, 274*, 112–128.

Mahajan, S. D., Homish, G. G., & Quisenberry, A. (2021). Multifactorial etiology of adolescent nicotine addiction: A review of the neurobiology of nicotine addiction and its implications for smoking cessation pharmacotherapy. *Frontiers in Public Health, 9*, 664748.

Mahanal, S., Zubaidah, S., Sumiati, I. D., Sari, T. M., & Ismirawati, N. (2019). RICOSRE: A learning model to develop critical thinking skills for students with different academic abilities. *International Journal of Instruction, 12*(2), 417–434.

Maher, A. C., Makowski-Woidan, B., Kuang, A., Zhang, H., Weintraub, S., Mesulam, M. M., & Rogalski, E. (2022). Neuropsychological profiles of older adults with superior versus average episodic memory: The Northwestern "SuperAger" Cohort. *Journal of the International Neuropsychological Society, 28*(6), 563–573.

Maher, B. (2015). The anatomy of obedience. *Nature, 523*, 408–409.

Mahjani, B., Bey, K., Boberg, J., & Burton, C. (2021). Genetics of obsessive-compulsive disorder. *Psychological Medicine, 51*(13), 2247–2259. https://doi.org/10.1017/S0033291721001744

Mahmut, M. K., & Croy, I. (2019). The role of body odors and olfactory ability in the initiation, maintenance and breakdown of romantic relationships-A review. *Physiology & behavior, 207*, 179–184.

Mahon, E. (2021). The evolution of dreams: A fifty year follow-up. *The Psychoanalytic Quarterly, 90*(2), 203–234.

Mahoney, C. T., Cestodio, V., Porter, K. J., & Marchant, K. M. (2022). The moderating roles of emotion regulation and coping self-efficacy on the association between PTSD symptom severity and drug use among female sexual assault survivors. *Psychological Trauma: Theory, Research, Practice, and Policy.* Advance online publication. https://doi.org/10.1037/tra0001194

Maister, L., De Beukelaer, S., Longo, M. R., & Tsakiris, M. (2021). The self in the mind's eye: Revealing how we truly see ourselves through reverse correlation. *Psychological Science, 32*(12), 1965–1978.

Majlesi, K., Lundborg, P., Black, S., & Devereux, P. (2019). Poor little rich kids? The role of nature versus nurture in wealth and other economic outcomes and behaviors. *Review of Economic Studies.* https://doi.org/10.1093/restud/rdz038.

Major, J. S. (2019). *Anti-terrorism, forensic science, psychology in police investigations.* Routledge.

Major, J. T., Johnson, W., & Bouchard, T. J. (2011). The dependability of the general factor of intelligence: Why small, single-factor models do not adequately represent g. *Intelligence, 39*, 418–433.

Majumdar, C. (2018). Attitudes towards premarital sex in India: Traditionalism and cultural change. *Sexuality & Culture, 22*(2), 614–631.

Makin, T. R., & Flor, H. (2020). Brain (re) organisation following amputation: Implications for phantom limb pain. *NeuroImage, 218*, 116943.

Malesevic, D. S. (2021, October 15). A house of hell: New docuseries examines the trial of man who was accused by his daughter of molesting and murdering her best friend, 8, in 1969–a crime she remembered 20 years later after suppressing the memory. *Daily Mail.* https://www.dailymail.co.uk/news/article-10085171/Buried-looks-George-Franklins-conviction-based-repressed-memories-daughter-Eileen.html

Malhotra, S., & Levitsky, L. L. (2021). Ghrelin: Growth hormone release to hunger hormone to glucose regulation: Lessons from a rare genetic disorder. *The Journal of Clinical Endocrinology & Metabolism, 106*(1), e375–e376.

Malin, D. H., Schaar, K. L., Izygon, J. J., Nghiem, D. M., Jabitta, S. Y., Henceroth, M. M., Chang, Y-H., Daggett, J. M., & Ward, C. P. (2015). Validation and scopolamine-reversal of latent learning in the water maze utilizing a revised direct platform placement procedure. *Pharmacology, Biochemistry and Behavior, 13*, 590–596.

Malinowski, J. E., & Horton, C. L. (2021). Dreams reflect nocturnal cognitive processes: Early-night dreams are more continuous with waking life, and late-night dreams are more emotional and hyperassociative. *Consciousness and Cognition, 88*, 103071.

Manca, S., Altoè, G., Schultz, P. W., & Fornara, F. (2020). The persuasive route to sustainable mobility: elaboration likelihood model and emotions predict implicit attitudes. *Environment and Behavior, 52*(8), 830–860.

Mangiaruga, A., D'Atri, A., Scarpelli, S., Alfonsi, V., Camaioni, M., Annarumma, L., . . . & De Gennaro, L. (2021). Sleep talking vs. sleep moaning: electrophysiological patterns preceding linguistic vocalizations during sleep. *Sleep.* Advance online publication https://doi.org/10.1093/sleep/zsab284

Mannerström, R., Muotka, J., & Salmela-Aro, K. (2019). Associations between identity processes and success in developmental tasks during the transition from emerging to young adulthood. *Journal of Youth Studies.* https://doi.org/10.1080/13676261.2019.1571179.

Manning, W. D. (2020). Young adulthood relationships in an era of uncertainty: A case for cohabitation. *Demography, 57*(3), 799–819.

Manzo, L., Gómez, M. J., Callejas-Aguilera, J. E., Fernández-Teruel, A., Papini, M. R., & Torres, C. (2015). Partial reinforcement reduces vulnerability to anti-anxiety self-medication during appetitive extinction. *International Journal of Comparative Psychology, 28*, 22–30.

Manjhi, A., & Purty, S. (2017). Response to the blank card of Thematic Apperception Test (TAT) and its correlation with personality factors. *Journal of Projective Psychology & Mental Health, 24*, 52–56.

Mapelli, I., & Özkurt, T. E. (2019). Brain oscillatory correlates of visual short-term memory errors. *Frontiers in Human Neuroscience, 13*, 33.

Marchman, V. A., Ashland, M. D., Loi, E. C., Adams, K. A., Fernald, A., & Feldman, H. M. (2019). Predictors of early vocabulary growth in children born preterm and full term: A study of processing speed and medical complications. *Child Neuropsychology*, 1–21.

Maree, J. G. (2021). The psychosocial development theory of Erik Erikson: Critical overview. *Early Child Development and Care, 191*(7–8), 1107–1121.

Maresh, E. L., Stim, J. J., Voorhis, A. C., Kang, S. S., Luciana, M., Sponheim, S. R., & Urošević, S. (2019). Neurophysiological correlates of cognitive control and approach motivation abnormalities in adolescent bipolar disorders. *Cognitive, Affective & Behavioral Neuroscience, 19*(3), 677–691.

Marques, A. H., Bjørke-Monsen, A., Teixeira, A. L., & Silverman, M. N. (2015). Maternal stress, nutrition and physical activity: Impact on immune function, CNS development and psychopathology. *Brain Research, 161*, 728–746.

Marr, C., Sauerland, M., Otgaar, H., Quaedflieg, C. W., & Hope, L. (2021). The effects of acute stress on eyewitness memory: an integrative review for eyewitness researchers. *Memory, 29*(8), 1091–1100.

Marsh, B. U. (2021). The cost of racial salience on face memory: How the cross-race effect is moderated by racial ambiguity and the race of the perceiver and the perceived. *Journal of Applied Research in Memory and Cognition, 10*(1), 13–23.

Marshall, L., & Born, J. (2007). The contribution of sleep to hippocampus-dependent memory consolidation. *Trends in Cognitive Sciences, 11*(10), 442–450.

Marshall, N. E., Abrams, B., Barbour, L. A., Catalano, P., Christian, P., Friedman, J. E., Hay, W. W. Jr., Hernandez, T. L., Krebs, N. F., Oken, E., Purnell, J. Q., Roberts, J. M., Soltani, H., Wallace, J., & Thornburg, K. L. (2022). The importance of nutrition in pregnancy and lactation: Lifelong consequences. *American Journal of Obstetrics and Gynecology, 225*(5), 607–632.

Martarelli, C. S., & Mast, F. W. (2022). Pictorial low-level features in mental images: evidence from eye fixations. *Psychological Research, 86*(2), 350–363.

Martelle, S., Hanley, C., & Yoshino K. (2003, January 28). "Sopranos" scenario in slaying? *Los Angeles Times*, p. B1.

Martin, A., & Becker, S. I. (2021). A relational account of visual short-term memory (VSTM). *Cortex, 144*, 151–167.

Martin, D., Katalinic, N., Hadzi-Pavlovic, D., Ingram, A., Ingram, N., Simpson, B., McGoldrick, J., Dowling, N., & Loo, C. (2019). Cognitive effects of brief and ultra-brief pulse bitemporal electroconvulsive therapy: A randomised controlled proof-of-concept trial. *Psychological Medicine*, 1–8.

Martin, E. A., & Kerns, J. G. (2011). The influence of positive mood on different aspects of cognitive control. *Cognition and Emotion, 25*, 265–279.

Martin, K. K., & North, A. C. (2015). Diffusion of responsibility on social networking sites. *Computers In Human Behavior, 44*, 124–131.

Martin, L. M., & Sayette, M. A. (2018). A review of the effects of nicotine on social functioning. *Experimental and Clinical Psychopharmacology, 26*(5), 425.

Martinez-Ales, G., Hernandez-Calle, D., Khauli, N., & Keyes, K. M. (2020). Why are suicide rates increasing in the United States? Towards a multilevel reimagination of suicide prevention. *Current Topics in Behavioral Neurosciences, 46*, 1–23.

Martins, Y., Preti, G., Crabtree, C. R., Runyan, T., Vainius, A. A., & Wysocki, C. J. (2005). Preference for human body odors is influenced by gender and sexual orientation. *Psychological Science, 16*(9), 694–701.

Martín-Requejo, K., & Santiago-Ramajo, S. (2021). Reduced emotional intelligence in children aged 9-10 caused by the COVID-19 pandemic lockdown. *Mind, Brain, and Education, 15*(4), 269–272.

Marulanda, D., & Radtke, H. L. (2019). Men pursuing an undergraduate psychology degree: What's masculinity got to do with it? *Sex Roles: A Journal of Research,81*(5–6), 338–354.

Masaoka, Y., Sugiyama, H., Yoshida, M., Yoshikawa, A., Honma, M., Koiwa, N., Kamijo, S., Watanabe, K., Kubota, S., Iizuka, N., Ida, M., Ono, K., & Izumizaki, M. (2021). Odors associated with autobiographical memory induce visual imagination of emotional scenes as well as orbitofrontal-fusiform activation. *Frontiers in Neuroscience, 15*, 709050. https://doi.org/10.3389/fnins.2021.709050

Maslow, A. H. (1970). *Motivation and personality.* Harper & Row.

Maslow, A. H. (1987). *Motivation and personality* (3rd ed.). New York: Harper & Row.

Massadi, O. A., López, M., Tschöp, M., Diéguez, C., & Nogueiras, R. (2017). Current understanding of the hypothalamic ghrelin pathways inducing appetite and adiposity. *Trends In Neurosciences, 40*, 167–180.

Massé-Alarie, H., Beaulieu, L., Preuss, R., & Schneider, C. (2017). The side of chronic low back pain matters: Evidence from the primary motor cortex excitability and the postural adjustments of multifidi muscles. *Experimental Brain Research, 235*, 647–659.

Master, A. (2021). Gender stereotypes influence children's STEM motivation. *Child Development Perspectives, 15*(3), 203-210.

Masters, W. H., & Johnson, V. E. (1979). *Homosexuality in perspective.* Little, Brown.

Matayoshi, J., Uzun, H., & Cosyn, E. (2019, June). Deep (un) learning: Using neural networks to model retention and forgetting in an adaptive learning system. In *International Conference on Artificial Intelligence in Education* (pp. 258-269). Springer.

Mateos-Aparicio, P., & Rodríguez-Moreno, A. (2019). The impact of studying brain plasticity. *Frontiers in Cellular Neuroscience, 13,* 66.

Mather, M. B., & vanderWeele, T. J. (2019). Finding common ground in meta-analysis "wars" on violent video games. *Perspectives on Psychological Science, 14,* 705-708.

Mathes, E. W. (2019). An evolutionary perspective on Kohlberg's theory of moral development. *Current Psychology,* 1-14.

Matsuda, K., Garcia, Y., Catagnus, R., & Brandt, J. A. (2020). Can behavior analysis help us understand and reduce racism? A review of the current literature. *Behavior Analysis in Practice, 13*(2), 336-347.

Matsumoto, D. (2002). Methodological requirements to test a possible in-group advantage in judging emotions across cultures: Comment on Elfenbein and Ambady (2002) and evidence. *Psychological Bulletin, 128,* 236-242.

Mattan, B. D., Kubota, J. T., & Cloutier, J. (2017). How social status shapes person perception and evaluation: A social neuroscience perspective. *Perspectives on Psychological Science, 12,* 468-507.

Mattys, S. L., Seymour, F. F., Attwood, A. S., & Munafò, M. R. (2013). Effects of acute anxiety induction on speech perception: Are anxious listeners distracted listeners? *Psychological Science, 24,* 1606-1608.

Maturana, M. J., Pudell, C., Targa, A. S., Rodrigues, L. S., Noseda, A. D., Fortes, et al. (2015). REM sleep deprivation reverses neurochemical and other depressive-like alterations induced by olfactory bulbectomy. *Molecular Neurobiology, 51,* 349-360.

Mauny, N., Mange, J., Mortier, A., Somat, A., & Sénémeaud, C. (2022). When a refusal turns into donation: The moderating effect of the initial position toward blood donation in the door-in-the-face effectiveness. *The Journal of Social Psychology,* 1-18.

Maxson, S. C. (2013). Behavioral genetics. In R. J. Nelson, S. Y. Mizumori, & I. B. Weiner (Eds.), *Handbook of psychology, Vol. 3: Behavioral neuroscience* (2nd ed.). New York: John Wiley & Sons Ltd.

May, A. (2017, December 28). How many alcoholic drinks are too many per week? *U.S.A. Today,* downloaded from https://www.usatoday.com/story/news/nation-now/2017/12/28/how-many-alcoholic-drinks-too-many-per-week/822604001/, January 10, 2021.

Mayer, R. E. (2013). Problem solving. In D. Reisberg (Ed.), *The Oxford handbook of cognitive psychology.* Oxford University Press.

Mazzola, J. J., & Disselhorst, R. (2019). Should we be "challenging" employees? A critical review and meta-analysis of the challenge-hindrance model of stress. *Journal of Organizational Behavior, 40*(8), 949-961.

Mazzoni, G., Clark, A., De Bartolo, A., Guerrini, C., Nahouli, Z., Duzzi, D., De Marco, M., McGeown, W., & Venneri, A. (2019). Brain activation in highly superior autobiographical memory: The role of the precuneus in the autobiographical memory retrieval network. *Cortex: A Journal Devoted to the Study of the Nervous System and Behavior, 120,* 588-602.

McAleavey, A. A., Youn, S. J., Xiao, H., Castonguay, L. G., Hayes, J. A., & Locke, B. D. (2019). Effectiveness of routine psychotherapy: Method matters. *Psychotherapy Research, 29*(2), 139-156.

McArthur, B. A., Burke, T. A., Connolly, S. L., Olino, T. M., Lumley, M. N., Abramson, L. Y., & Alloy, L. B. (2019). A longitudinal investigation of cognitive self-schemas across adolescent development. *Journal of Youth and Adolescence, 48*(3), 635-647.

McCabe, B. E., Lee, D. L., & Viray, T. (2019). Does Ethnicity Moderate the Link Between Drinking Norms and Binge Drinking in College Students?. *International journal of mental health and addiction, 17*(3), 493-501.

McCann, J. T., Lynn, S. J., Lilienfeld, S. O., Shindler, K. L., & Hammond Natof, T. R. (2015). The science and pseudoscience of expert testimony. In S. O. Lilienfeld, S. J. Lynn, & J. M. Lohr (Eds.), *Science and pseudoscience in clinical psychology (2nd ed.).* New York: Guilford Press.

McCarrey, A. C., & Resnick, S. M. (2015). Postmenopausal hormone therapy and cognition. *Hormones and Behavior, 74,* 167-172.

McCarthy, J. (2005). Individualism and collectivism: What do they have to do with counseling? *Journal of Multicultural Counseling and Development, 33,* 108-117.

McCarthy, J. (2019). Americans still greatly overestimate U.S. gay population. *Gallup.* https://news.gallup.com/poll/259571/americans-greatly-overestimate-gay-population.aspx

McCarthy, R. J., & Skowronski, J. J. (2011). You're getting warmer: Level of construal affects the impact of central traits on impression formation. *Journal of Experimental Social Psychology, 47,* 1304-1307.

McCauley, T. G., Billingsley, J., & McCullough, M. E. (2022). An evolutionary psychology view of forgiveness: individuals, groups, and culture. *Current Opinion in Psychology, 44,* 275-280.

McClelland, D. C. (1985). How motives, skills, and values determine what people do. *American Psychologist, 40,* 812-825.

McClelland, D. C. (1993). Intelligence is not the best predictor of job performance. *Current Directions in Psychological Research,2,* 5-8.

McClelland, D. C., Atkinson, J. W., Clark, R. A., & Lowell, E. L. (1953). *The achievement motive.* Appleton-Century-Crofts.

McCluskey, U., & O'Toole, M. (2019). *Transference and countertransference from an attachment perspective: A guide to clinical practice.* Routledge.

McConkey, R., Sadowsky, M., & Shellard, A. (2019). An international survey of obesity and underweight in youth and adults with intellectual disabilities. *Journal of Intellectual and Developmental Disability, 44*(3), 374-382.

McConnell, A. R., & Rydell, R. J. (2019). The Implicit Association Test: Implications for understanding consumer behavior. In F. R. Kardes, P. M. Herr, & N. Schwarz (Eds.), *Handbook of research methods in consumer psychology.* Routledge.

McCredie, M. N., & Morey, L. C. (2019). Convergence between Thematic Apperception Test and self-report: Another look at some old questions. *Journal of Clinical Psychology.* https://doi-org.silk.library.umass.edu/10.1002/jclp.22826.

McCrink, K., & Wynn, K. (2007). Ratio abstraction by 6-month-old infants. *Psychological Science,18,* 740-745.

McCulloch, K., Lachner Bass, N., Dial, H., Hiscock, M., & Jansen, B. (2017). Interaction of attention and acoustic factors in dichotic listening for fused words. *Laterality: Asymmetries of Body, Brain and Cognition, 22,* 473-494.

McDermott, M. S., Beard, E., Brose, L. S., West, R., & McEwen, A. (2013). Factors associated with differences in quit rates between "specialist" and "community" stop-smoking practitioners in the English stop-smoking services. *Nicotine & Tobacco Research, 15,* 1239-1247.

McDonald, A. R., Muraskin, J., Van Dam, N. T., Froehlich, C., Puccio, B., Pellman, J., Bauer, C. C. C., Akeyson, A., Breland, M. M., Calhoun, V. D., Carter, S., Chang, T. P., Gessner, C., Gianonne, A., Giavasis, S., Glass, J., Homann, S., King, M., Kramer, M., Landis, D., et al. (2017). The real-time fMRI neurofeedback based stratification of Default Network Regulation Neuroimaging data repository. *Neuroimage, 146,* 157-170.

McDonald, S. E., Murphy, J. L., Tomlinson, C. A., Matijczak, A., Applebaum, J. W., Wike, T. L., & Kattari, S. K. (2022). Relations between sexual and gender minority stress, personal hardiness, and psychological stress in emerging adulthood: Examining indirect effects via human-animal interaction. *Youth & Society, 54*(2), 240-261.

McDougall, W. (1908). *Introduction to social psychology.* Methuen.

McElroy, S. L., Guerdjikova, A. I., Mori, N., & Romo-Nava, F. (2019). Progress in developing pharmacologic agents to treat bulimia nervosa. *CNS drugs, 33*(1), 31-46.

McGinn, D. (2003, June 9). Testing, testing: The new job search. *Time,* pp. 36-38.

McGinty, J. C. (2019, June 22-23). Divorces are down, unless you're 55 or older. *Wall Street Journal,* p. A2.

McGinty, J. C. (2019, September 14-15). To lower suicides methods matter. *Wall Street Journal,* p. A2.

McGuigan, S., Zhou, S. H., Brosnan, M. B., Thyagarajan, D., Bellgrove, M. A., & Chong, T. T. (2019). Dopamine restores cognitive motivation in Parkinson's disease. *Brain, 142*(3), 719-732.

McKenna, K., Goodrich, L., Forbes, P. W., & Ibeziako, P. (2019). Pilot study to examine the clinical utility of biofeedback in solid organ transplant. *Clinical Practice in Pediatric Psychology, 7*(2), 127-139.

McKetton, L., DeSimone, K., & Schneider, K. A. (2019). Larger auditory cortical area and broader frequency tuning underlie absolute pitch. *The Journal of Neuroscience, 39*(15), 2930-2937.

McKinley, J. C. Jr. (2013, September 12). Overdoses of "Molly" led to Electric Zoo deaths. *The New York Times.* Accessed from http://artsbeat.blogs.nytimes.com/2013/09/12/overdoses-of-molly-led-to-electric-zoo-deaths/.

McKone, E., Dawel, A., Robbins, R. A., Shou, Y., Chen, N., & Crookes, K. (2021). Why the other-race effect matters: Poor recognition of other-race faces impacts everyday social interactions. *British Journal of Psychology.*

McLay, R. N., Baird, A., Webb-Murphy, J., Deal, W., Tran, L., Anson, H., Klam, W., & Johnston, S. (2017). A randomized, head-to-head study of virtual reality exposure therapy for posttraumatic stress disorder. *Cyberpsychology, Behavior, and Social Networking, 20,* 218-224.

McLean, C. P., Su, Y., Carpenter, J. K., & Foa, E. B. (2017). Changes in PTSD and depression during prolonged exposure and client-centered therapy for PTSD in adolescents. *Journal of Clinical Child and Adolescent Psychology, 46,* 500-510.

McLean, S. A., Booth, A. T., Schnabel, A., Wright, B. J., Painter, F. L., & McIntosh, J. E. (2021). Exploring the efficacy of telehealth for family therapy through systematic, meta-analytic, and qualitative evidence. *Clinical Child and Family Psychology Review, 24*(2), 244-266.

McLeod, J. (2015). Happiness, wellbeing and self-esteem: Public feelings and educational projects. In K. Wright & J. McLeod (Eds.), *Rethinking youth wellbeing: Critical perspectives.* Springer Science + Business Media.

McNamara, T. P. (2013). Semantic memory and priming. In A. F. Healy, R. W. Proctor, & I. B. Weiner (Eds.), *Handbook of psychology, Vol. 4: Experimental psychology* (2nd ed.). Hoboken, NJ: John Wiley & Sons Inc.

McPartland, R. (2016). *Tay-Sachs disease.* Cavendish Square.

McQuaid, J. (December, 2021). Spying on your emotions. *Scientific American,* 41-47.

McRobbie, L.R. (2018, November 28). How culture shapes your mind–and your mental illness *Boston Globe.* https://www.bostonglobe.com/ideas/2018/11/28/how-culture-shapes-your-mind-and-your-mental-illness/sMlhWP5LGSOvQAFd83I3qN/story.html

Meier, B., & Rothen, N. (2015). Developing synaesthesia: A primer. *Frontiers in Human Neuroscience, 9,* 211.

Meijering, L., & Lettinga, A. (2022). Hopeful adaptation after acquired brain injury: The case of late referrals in the Netherlands. *Social Science & Medicine, 293,* 114651.

Meiller, C., & Hargons, C. N. (2019). "It's happiness and relief and release": Exploring masturbation among bisexual and queer women. *Journal of Counseling Sexology & Sexual Wellness: Research, Practice, and Education, 1*(1), 3.

Melis, M., Mastinu, M., Pintus, S., Cabras, T., Crnjar, R., & Tommasini Barbarossa, I. (2021). Differences in salivary proteins as a function of PROP taster status and gender in normal weight and obese subjects. *Molecules, 26*(8), 2244.

Meltzer, A. L., Makhanova, A., Hicks, L. L., French, J. E., McNulty, J. K., & Bradbury, T. N. (2017). Quantifying the sexual afterglow: The lingering benefits of sex and their implications for pair-bonded relationships. *Psychological Science, 28*(5), 587-598.

Mendel, J., Frank, K., Edlin, L., Hall, K., Webb, D., Mills, J., . . . & Mills, D. (2021). Preliminary accuracy of COVID-19 odor detection by canines and HS-SPME-GC-MS using exhaled breath samples. *Forensic Science International: Synergy, 3,* 100155.

Mende-Siedlecki, P., Lin, J., Ferron, S., Gibbons, C., Drain, A., & Goharzad, A. (2021). Seeing no pain: Assessing the generalizability of racial bias in pain perception. *Emotion, 21*(5), 932.

Menon, J. M. L., Nolten, C., Achterberg, E. J. M., Joosten, R. N. J. M. A., Dematteis, M., Feenstra, M. G. P., et al. (2019). Brain microdialysate monoamines in relation to circadian rhythms, sleep, and sleep deprivation–a systematic review, network meta-analysis, and new primary data. *Journal of Circadian Rhythms, 17(1),* 1. DOI: http://doi.org/10.5334/jcr.174.

Mensah, F. K., Bayer, J. K., Wake, M., Carlin, J. B., Allen, N. B., & Patton, G. C. (2013). Early puberty and childhood social and behavioral adjustment. *Journal of Adolescent Health, 53,* 118-124.

Meraji, S. M., & Hodges, L. (2020, April 6). How to get therapy when you can't leave the house. *National Public Radio.* https://www.npr.org/2020/04/03/826726628/how-to-get-therapy-when-you-cant-leave-the-house

Mercier, H. (2017). Confirmation bias–myside bias. In R. F. Pohl (Ed.), *Cognitive illusions: Intriguing phenomena in thinking, judgment and memory.* Routledge/Taylor & Francis Group.

Mesoudi, A., & Thornton, A. (2018). What is cumulative cultural evolution?. *Proceedings of the Royal Society B, 285*(1880), 20180712.

Mesoudi, A. (2011). Evolutionary psychology meets cultural psychology. *Journal of Evolutionary Psychology, 9,* 83-87.

Meston, C. M., & Stanton, A. M. (2019). Understanding sexual arousal and subjective-genital arousal desynchrony in women. *Nature Reviews Urology, 16*(2), 107-120.

Metz, C. (2017, July 31). Therapy in a dose of illusion. *The New York Times,* pp. B1, B4.

Miech, R. A., Johnston, L. D., O'Malley, P. M., Bachman, J. G., Schulenberg, J. E., & Patrick, M. E. (2021). *Monitoring the Future national survey results on drug use, 1975-2020: Volume I, Secondary school students.* Institute for Social Research, University of Michigan. http://monitoringthefuture.org/data/21data/MJ/MJjsFigures.htm

Miech, R., Leventhal, A., Johnston, L., O'Malley, P. M., Patrick, M. E., & Barrington-Trimis, J. (2021). Trends in use and perceptions of nicotine vaping among US youth from 2017 to 2020. *JAMA Pediatrics, 175*(2), 185-190.

Miech, R. A., Johnston, L. D., O'Malley, P. M., Bachman, J. G., Schulenberg, J. E., & Patrick, M. E. (2021). *Monitoring the Future national survey results on drug use, 1975-2020: Volume I, Secondary school students.* Institute for Social Research, University of Michigan.

Miguez, G., Witnauer, J. E., & Miller, R. R. (2011). The role of contextual associations in producing the partial reinforcement acquisition deficit. *Journal of Experimental Psychology: Animal Behavior Processes, 37,* 88-97.

Mihalca, L., Mengelkamp, C., & Schnotz, W. (2017). Accuracy of metacognitive judgments as a moderator of learner control effectiveness in problem-solving tasks. *Metacognition and Learning,12*(3), 357-379.

Mihura, J. L., Bombel, G., Dumitrascu, N., Roy, M., & Meadows, E. A. (2019). Why we need a formal systematic approach to validating psychological tests: The case of the Rorschach Comprehensive System. *Journal of Personality Assessment, 101*(4), 374-392.

Mika, V. S., Wood, P. R., Weiss, B. D., & Trevino, L. (2007). Ask Me 3: Improving communication in a Hispanic pediatric outpatient practice. *American Journal of Behavioral Health, 31,* S115-S121.

Miles, P., Schaufeli, W. B., & van den Bos, K. (2011). When weak groups are strong: How low cohesion groups allow individuals to act according to their personal absence tolerance norms. *Social Justice Research, 24,* 207-230.

Miles-Novelo, A., & Anderson, C. A. (2020). Desensitization. In J. Van Den Bulck (Ed.), *The International Encyclopedia of Media Psychology.* John Wiley & Sons.

Milgram, S. (2005). *Obedience to authority.* Pinter & Martin.

Miller, C. C. (2018, May 17). What same-sex couples reveal about modern parenting. *The New York Times,* p. A12.

Miller, G. E., Chen, E., & Parker, K. J. (2011). Psychological stress in childhood and susceptibility to the chronic diseases of aging: Moving toward a model of behavioral and biological mechanisms. *Psychological Bulletin, 137,* 959-997.

Miller, J. A., & Leffard, S. A. (2007). Behavioral assessment. In S. R. Smith & L. Handler (Eds.), *The clinical assessment of children and adolescents: A practitioner's handbook.* Lawrence Erlbaum Associates.

Miller, L. A., McIntire, S. A., & Lovler, R. L. (2011). *Foundations of psychological testing: A practical problem* (3rd ed.). Sage Publications.

Miller, N., Perich, T., & Meade, T. (2019). Depression, mania and self-reported creativity in bipolar disorder. *Psychiatry Research, 276,* 129-133.

Mills, J. (2013). Jung's metaphysics. *International Journal of Jungian Studies, 5,* 19-43.

Mills, M. C. (2019). How do genes affect same-sex behavior? *Science, 365,* 869-870.

Mills, M. J. (2011). Associations among achievement measures and their collective prediction of work involvement. *Personality and Individual Differences, 50,* 360-364.

Milne, M. R., Qian, L., Turnbull, M. T., Kinna, G., Collins, B. M., Teasdale, R. D., et al. (2019). Downregulation of SNX27 expression does not exacerbate amyloidogenesis in the APP/PS1 Alzheimer's disease mouse model. *Neurobiology of Aging, 77,* 144-153.

Milner, B. (1966). Amnesia following operation on temporal lobes. In C. W. M. Whitty & P. Zangwill (Eds.), *Amnesia.* Butterworth.

Milner, B. (2005). The medial temporal-lobe amnesic syndrome. *Psychiatric Clinics of North America, 28,* 599-611.

Milos, G., Baur, V., Schumacher, S., Kuenzli, C., Schnyder, U., Mueller-Pfeiffer, C., & Martin-Soelch, C. (2017). How fat will it make me? Estimation of weight gain in anorexia nervosa. *Appetite, 114,* 368-373.

Miner-Rubino, K., Winter, D. G., & Stewart, A. J. (2004). Gender, social class, and the subjective experience of aging: Self-perceived personality change from early adulthood to late midlife. *Personality and Social Psychology Bulletin, 30,* 1599-1610.

Minga, J., Fromm, D., Jacks, A., Stockbridge, M. D., Nelthropp, J., & MacWhinney, B. (2022). The effects of right hemisphere brain damage on question-asking in conversation. *Journal of Speech, Language, and Hearing Research, 65*(2), 727-737.

Minică, C. C., Mbarek, H., Pool, R., Dolan, C. V., Boomsma, D. I., & Vink, J. M. (2017). Pathways to smoking behaviours: Biological insights from the Tobacco and Genetics Consortium meta-analysis. *Molecular Psychiatry, 22,* 82-88.

Mintz, A., & Wayne, C. (2014). Group decision making in conflict: From groupthink to polythink in the war in Iraq. In P. T. Coleman, M. Deutsch, & E. C. Marcus (Eds.), *The handbook of conflict resolution: Theory and practice* (3rd ed.). Jossey-Bass.

Mirambo, M. M., Aboud, S., Majigo, M., Groß, U., & Mshana, S. E. (2019). Adverse pregnancy outcomes among pregnant women with acute rubella infections in Mwanza city, Tanzania. *International Journal of Infectious Diseases, 78,* 72-77

Mirzairad, R., Haydari, A., Pasha, R., Ehteshamzadeh, P., & Makvandi, B. (2017). The relationship between perfectionism and psychological distress with the mediation of coping styles and self-esteem. *International Journal of Mental Health and Addiction, 15,* 614-620.

Mischel, W. (2009). From Personality and Assessment (1968) to Personality Science, 2009. *Journal of Research in Personality, 43,* 282-290.

Mischel, W., & Shoda, Y. (2008). Toward a unified theory of personality: Integrating dispositions and processing dynamics within the cognitive-affective processing system. In O. P. Oliver, R. W. Robins, & L. A. Pervin (Eds.), *Handbook of personality psychology: Theory and research* (3rd ed.). Guilford Press.

Mishra, P., & Srivastava, A. K. (2018). The association of impatience, hostility and hypertension: A review. *IAHRW International Journal of Social Sciences Review, 6*(4), 721-723.

Mitchell, J., Bogenschutz, M., Lilienstein, A., Harrison, C., Kleiman, S., Parker-Guilbert, K., Ot'alora G, M., Garas, W., Paleos, C., Gorman, I., Nicholas, C., Mithoefer, M., Carlin, S., Poulter, B., Mihoefer, A., Quevedo, S., Wells, G., Klaire, S. S., van der Kolk, B., Tzarfaty, K., et al. (2021). MDMA-assisted therapy for severe PTSD: A randomized, double-blind, placebo-controlled phase 3 study. *Nature Medicine, 27,* 1025-1033.

Mitchell, L. L., Lodi-Smith, J., Baranski, E. N., & Whitbourne, S. K. (2021). Implications of identity resolution in emerging adulthood for intimacy, generativity, and integrity across the adult lifespan. *Psychology and Aging, 36*(5), 545-556. https://doi.org/10.1037/pag0000537

Miyatsu, T., & McDaniel, M. A. (2019). Adding the keyword mnemonic to retrieval practice: A potent combination for foreign language vocabulary learning? *Memory & Cognition, 47*(4), 1-16.

Modak, T., Bhad, R., & Rao, R. (2019). A rare case of physical dependence with psychedelic LSD–A case report. *Journal of Substance Use, 24*(4), 347-349.

Moen, K. C., Miller, J. K., & Lloyd, M. E. (2017). Selective attention meets spontaneous recognition memory: Evidence for effects at retrieval. *Consciousness and Cognition: An International Journal, 49,* 181-189.

Moffitt, T. E., Caspi, A., & Rutter, M. (2006). Measured gene-environment interactions in psychopathology: Concepts, research strategies, and implications for research, intervention, and public understanding of genetics. *Perspectives on Psychological Science, 1,* 5-27.

Mograss, M., Guillem, F., Brazzini-Poisson, V., & Godbout, R. (2009). The effects of total sleep deprivation on recognition memory processes: A study of event-related potential. *Neurobiology of Learning and Memory, 91,* 343-352.

Mohatt, N. V., Hoffmire, C. A., Schneider, A. L., Goss, C. W., Shore, J. H., Spark, T. L., & Kaufman, C. E. (2022). Suicide among American Indian and Alaska Native veterans who use Veterans Health Administration care: 2004-2018. *Medical Care, 60*(4), 275.

Moheghi, M., Ghorbanzadeh, M., & Abedi, J. (2020). The investigation and criticism moral development ideas of Kohlberg, Piaget and Gilligan. *International Journal of Multicultural and Multireligious Understanding, 7*(2), 362-374.

Molina, M., Nee, V., & Holm, H. (2022). Cooperation with strangers: Spillover of community norms. *Organization Science.* https://doi.org/10.1287/orsc.2021.1521

Molina, M., Sann, C., David, M., Touré, Y., Guillois, B., & Jouen, F. (2015). Active touch in late-preterm and early-term neonates. *Developmental Psychobiology, 57,* 322-335.

Mollen, S., Engelen, S., Kessels, L. E., & van den Putte, B. (2017). Short and sweet: The persuasive effects of message framing and temporal context in anti-smoking warning labels. *Journal of Health Communication, 22,* 20-28.

Møller, A. R. (2011). Anatomy and physiology of the auditory system. In A. R. Møller, B. Langguth, D. De-Ridder, & T. Kleinjung (Eds.), *Textbook of tinnitus.* Springer Science + Business Media.

Monaghan, P., & Fletcher, M. (2019). Do sound symbolism effects for written words relate to individual phonemes or to phoneme features? *Language and Cognition, 11*(2), 235-255.

Mond, J., & Gorrell, S. (2021). "Excessive exercise" in eating disorders research: Problems of definition and perspective. *Eating and Weight Disorders-Studies on Anorexia, Bulimia and Obesity, 26*(4), 1017–1020.

Monk, T. H., Buysse, D. J., Billy, B. D., Fletcher, M. E., Kennedy, K. S., Schlarb, et al. (2011). Circadian type and bed-timing regularity in 654 retired seniors: Correlations with subjective sleep measures. *Sleep, 34*, 235–239.

Monro, S., Crocetti, D., & Yeadon-Lee, T. (2019). Intersex/variations of sex characteristics and DSD citizenship in the UK, Italy and Switzerland. *Citizenship Studies, 23*(8), 780–797.

Monsour, M., Ebedes, D., & Borlongan, C. V. (2022). A review of the pathology and treatment of TBI and PTSD. *Experimental Neurology,* 114009.

Montgomery, K. L. (2011). Living with panic, worry, and fear: Anxiety disorders. In C. Franklin & R. Fong (Eds.), *The church leader's counseling resource book: A guide to mental health and social problems.* Oxford University Press.

Monti, M. M. (2012). Cognition in the vegetative state. *Annual Review of Clinical Psychology, 8*, 431–454.

Moodley, R., Gielen, U. P., & Wu, R. (2013). *Handbook of counseling and psychotherapy in an international context.* Routledge/Taylor & Francis Group.

Moody, H. R. (2000). *Aging: Concepts and controversies.* Sage.

Moody, R. L., Starks, T. J., Grov, C., & Parsons, J. T. (2017). Internalized homophobia and drug use in a national cohort of gay and bisexual men: Examining depression, sexual anxiety, and gay community attachment as mediating factors. *Archives of Sexual Behavior, 47.*

Moon, C., Lagercrantz, H., & Kuhl, P. (2013). Language experienced in utero affects vowel perception after birth: A two-country study. *Acta Paediatrica,102*, 156–160.

Moore, A. A., Lapato, D. M., Brotman, M. A., Leibenluft, E., Aggen, S. H., Hettema, J. M., York, T. P., Silberg, J. L., & Roberson-Nay, R. (2019). Heritability, stability, and prevalence of tonic and phasic irritability as indicators of disruptive mood dysregulation disorder. *Journal of Child Psychology and Psychiatry, 60*(9), 1032–1041.

Moore, D. W. (2005, June 16). Three in four Americans believe in paranormal. Gallup News Service.

Moore, E. S., Wilkie, W. L., & Desrochers, D. M. (2017). All in the family? Parental roles in the epidemic of childhood obesity. *Journal of Consumer Research, 43*, 824–859.

Mora, M., Urdaneta, E., & Chaya, C. (2019). Effect of personality on the emotional response elicited by wines. *Food Quality and Preference, 76*, 39–46.

Morcom, A. M., & Friston, K. J. (2011). Decoding episodic memory in ageing: A Bayesian analysis of activity patterns predicting memory. *Neuroimage, 33*, 88–91.

Moè, A. (2021). Doubling mental rotation scores in high school students: Effects of motivational and strategic trainings. *Learning and Instruction, 74*, 101461.

Morena, M., Colucci, P., Mancini, G. F., De Castro, V., Peloso, A., Schelling, G., & Campolongo, P. (2021). Ketamine anesthesia enhances fear memory consolidation via noradrenergic activation in the basolateral amygdala. *Neurobiology of Learning and Memory, 178*, 107362.

Moreno-Gómez, F. N., Véliz, G., Rojas, M., Martínez, C., Olmedo, R., Panussis, F., Dagnino-Subiabre, A., Delgado, C., & Delano, P. H. (2017). Music training and education slow the deterioration of music perception produced by presbycusis in the elderly. *Frontiers in Aging Neuroscience, 9*, 1–10.

Moreno-Serra, R., Anaya-Montes, M., León-Giraldo, S., & Bernal, O. (2022). Addressing recall bias in (post-) conflict data collection and analysis: lessons from a large-scale health survey in Colombia. *Conflict and Health, 16*(1), 1–14.

Moretz, M., & McKay, D. (2009). The role of perfectionism in obsessive-compulsive symptoms: "Not just right" experiences and checking compulsions. *Journal of Anxiety Disorders, 23*, 640–644.

Moritz, S., Klein, J. P., Lysaker, P. H., & Mehl, S. (2022). Metacognitive and cognitive-behavioral interventions for psychosis: New developments. *Dialogues in Clinical Neuroscience, 3*, 309–317.

Morland, C., & Nordengen, K. (2022). N-acetyl-aspartyl-glutamate in brain health and disease. *International Journal of Molecular Sciences, 23*(3), 1268.

Morris, S. Y. (2017, May 25). What does it mean to have hyperthymesia or highly superior autobiographical memory (HSAM)? *HealthLine.* http://www.healthline.com/health/ hyperthymesia#overview1

Moscoso, S. C., Chaves, S. S., & Argilaga, M. T. A. (2013). Reporting a program evaluation: Needs, program plan, intervention, and decisions. *International Journal of Clinical and Health Psychology, 13*, 58–66.

Mosher, C. E., Winger, J. G., Given, B. A., Helft, P. R., & O'Neil, B. H. (2015). Mental health outcomes during colorectal cancer survivorship: A review of the literature. *Psycho-Oncology, 25*(11), 1261–1270.

Moss, D., & Willmarth, E. (2019). Hypnosis, anesthesia, pain management, and preparation for medical procedures. *Annals of Palliative Medicine, 8*(4), 498–503.

Motta, M., Callaghan, T., & Sylvester, S. (2018). Knowing less but presuming more: Dunning-Kruger effects and the endorsement of anti-vaccine policy attitudes. *Social Science & Medicine, 211*, 274–281.

Môttus, R., Briley, D. A., Zheng, A., Mann, F. D., Engelhardt, L. E., Tackett, J. L., et al. (2019). Kids becoming less alike: A behavioral genetic analysis of developmental increases in personality variance from childhood to adolescence. *Journal of Personality and Social Psychology, 117*(3), 635–658.

Moulding, R., Nedeljkovic, M., Kyrios, M., Osborne, D., & Mogan, C. (2017). Short-term cognitive-behavioural group treatment for hoarding disorder: A naturalistic treatment outcome study. *Clinical Psychology & Psychotherapy, 24*, 235–244.

Moutinho, S. (2021, June 25). Advertisers could come for your dreams, researchers warn. *Science, 372*(6549), 1380.

Moyer, M. W. (2021, March). Coping with pandemic stress. *Scientific American,* pp. 46–51.

Moynihan, A. B., Igou, E. R., & van Tilburg, W. P. (2017). Free, connected, and meaningful: Free will beliefs promote meaningfulness through belongingness. *Personality and Individual Differences, 107*, 54–65.

Mukamal, R. (2017). How humans see in color. American Academy of Ophthalmology. https://www.aao.org/ eye-health/tips-prevention/how-humans-see-in-color

Mulas, I., Ruiu, M., & Fastame, M. C. (2021). The role of cognitive reserve as mediator for addition and multiplication skills in late adulthood. *Aging Clinical and Experimental Research, 33*(5), 1377–1382.

Mullane, M. P., Martens, B. K., Baxter, E. L., & Steeg, D. V. (2017). Children's preference for mixed- versus fixed-ratio schedules of reinforcement: A translational study of risky choice. *Journal of the Experimental Analysis of Behavior, 107*, 161–175.

Mullangi, S., & Jagsi, R. (2019). Imposter syndrome: Treat the cause, not the symptom. *JAMA, 322*(5), 403–404.

Müller, M., Bosy-Wesphal, A., & Heymsfield, S. B. (2010). Is there evidence for a set point that regulates human body weight? *F1000Medicine Reports, 2*, 59.

Müller, M. J., Geisler, C., Heymsfield, S. B., & Bosy-Westphal, A. (2018). Recent advances in understanding body weight homeostasis in humans. *F1000Research, 7.*

Munder, T., Flückiger, C., Leichsenring, F., Abbass, A. A., Hilsenroth, M. J., Luyten, P., Rabung, S., Stgeinert, C., & Wampold, B. E. (2019). Is psychotherapy effective? A re-analysis of treatments for depression. *Epidemiology and Psychiatric Sciences, 28*(3), 268–274.

Munro, C., Randell, L., & Lawrie, S. M. (2017). An integrative bio-psycho-social theory of anorexia nervosa. *Clinical Psychology & Psychotherapy, 24*, 1–21.

Muramatsu, D. (2021). Sand-bubbler crabs distinguish fiddler crab signals to predict intruders. *Behavioral Ecology and Sociobiology, 75*(9), 1–11.

Murata, A. (2022). Implications for risk taking behavior leading to crashes or disasters–Effects of perceived risk on risk taking decision. *IEEE Access, 10*, 34960–34969.

Mürner-Lavanchy, I., Kaess, M., & Koenig, J. (2021). Diagnostic instruments for the assessment of disruptive mood dysregulation disorder: A systematic

review of the literature. *European Child & Adolescent Psychiatry, 32*, 1–23. https://doi.org/10.1007/ s00787-021-01840-4

Murayama, K., & Kitagami, S. (2013). Consolidation power of extrinsic rewards: Reward cues enhance long-term memory for irrelevant past events. *Journal of Experimental Psychology: General, 143*, 15–20.

Murphy, N. A., Hall, J. A., Ruben, M. A., Frauendorfer, D., Schmid Mast, M., Johnson, K. E., & Nguyen, L. (2019). Predictive validity of thin-slice nonverbal behavior from social interactions. *Personality and Social Psychology Bulletin, 45*(7), 983–993.

Murray, S., Liang, N., Brosowsky, N., & Seli, P. (2021). What are the benefits of mind wandering to creativity? *Psychology of Aesthetics, Creativity, and the Arts.*

Murray, S. B., Duval, C. J., Balkchyan, A. A., Cabeen, R. P., Nagata, J. M., Toga, A. W., Siegel, S. J., & Jann, K. (2022). Regional gray matter abnormalities in pre-adolescent binge eating disorder: A voxel-based morphometry study. *Psychiatry Research, 310*, 114473.

Murray, S. B., Quintana, D. S., Loeb, K. L., Griffiths, S., & Le Grange, D. (2019). Treatment outcomes for anorexia nervosa: A systematic review and meta-analysis of randomized controlled trials. *Psychological Medicine, 49*(4), 535–544.

Musetti, A., & Corsano, P. (2021). Multidimensional self-esteem and secrecy from friends during adolescence: The mediating role of loneliness. *Current Psychology, 40*(5), 2381–2389.

Muzzulini, B., Tinti, C., Conway, M. A., Testa, S., & Schmidt, S. (2020). Flashbulb memory: Referring back to Brown and Kulik's definition. *Memory, 28*(6), 766–782.

Myers and Briggs Foundation. (2019). MBTI basics. https://www.myersbriggs.org/my-mbti-personality-type/mbti-basics/home.htm?bhcp=1

Nader, E. G., Kleinman, A., Gomes, B., Bruscagin, C., Santos, B., Nicoletti, M., Soares, J. C., Lafer, B., & Caetano, S. C. (2013). Negative expressed emotion best discriminates families with bipolar disorder children. *Journal of Affective Disorders, 148*, 418–423.

Naeem, S. B., Bhatti, R., & Khan, A. (2021). An exploration of how fake news is taking over social media and putting public health at risk. *Health Information & Libraries Journal, 38*(2), 143–149.

Nærland, T., Bakke, K. A., Storvik, S., Warner, G., & Howlin, P. (2017). Age and gender-related differences in emotional and behavioural problems and autistic features in children and adolescents with Down syndrome: A survey-based study of 674 individuals. *Journal of Intellectual Disability Research, 61*, 594–603.

Nafiu, O. O., Mpody, C., Kim, S. S., Uffman, J. C., & Tobias, J. D. (2020). Race, postoperative complications, and death in apparently healthy children. *Pediatrics, 146*(2).

Nagai, Y. (2019). Autonomic biofeedback therapy in epilepsy. *Epilepsy Research, 153*, 76–78.

Nagata, J. M., Iyer, P., Chu, J., Baker, F. C., Pettee Gabriel, K., Garber, A. K., Murray, S. B., Bibbins-Domingo, K., & Ganson, K. T. (2021). Contemporary screen time modalities among children 9–10 years old and binge-eating disorder at one-year follow-up: A prospective cohort study. *International Journal of Eating Disorders, 54*(5), 887–892.

Nagel, E. (2020). Methodological issues in psychoanalytic theory. In *Psychoanalysis, scientific method, and philosophy.* Routledge.

Naglieri, J. A., LeBuffe, P. A., & Ross, K. M. (2013). Measuring resilience in children: From theory to practice. In S. Goldstein & R. B. Brooks (Eds.), *Handbook of resilience in children* (2nd ed.). Springer Science + Business Media.

Nagpal, T. S., Green, C. R., & Cook, J. L. (2021). Vaping during pregnancy: What are the potential health outcomes and perceptions pregnant women have? *Journal of Obstetrics and Gynaecology Canada, 43*(2), 219–226.

Nai, A., & Otto, L. P. (2021). When they go low, we gloat: How trait and state Schadenfreude moderate the perception and effect of negative political messages. *Journal of Media Psychology: Theories, Methods, and Applications, 33*(2), 82-93. https://doi. org/10.1027/1864-1105/a000283

Naidoo, K., Yuhaniak, H., Borkoski, C., Levangie, P., & Abel, Y. (2021). Networked mentoring to promote social belonging among minority physical therapist students and develop faculty cross-cultural psychological capital. *Mentoring & Tutoring: Partnership in Learning, 29*(5), 586-606.

Nakada, Y., & Sadoshima, J. (2021). Sleep deficiency and mortality: is the solution in the gut?. *Cardiovascular Research, 117*(2), e26-e28.

Nakagawa, S., Takeuchi, H., Taki, Y., Nouchi, R., Kotozaki, Y., Shinada, T., Maruyama, T., Sekiguchi, A., Iizuka, K., Yokoyama, R., Yamamoto, Y., Hanawa, S., Araki, T., Miyauchi, C. M., Magistro, D., Sakaki, K., Jeong, H., Sasaki, Y., & Kawashima, R. (2019). Mean diffusivity related to collectivism among university students in Japan. *Scientific Reports, 9*(1), 1338. https://doi.org/10.1038/s41598-018-37995-5

Nakamura, Y., Goto, T. K., Tokumori, K., Yoshiura, T., Kobayashi, K., Nakamura, Y., Honda, H., Ninomiya, Y., & Yoshiura, K. (2011). Localization of brain activation by umami taste in humans. *Brain Research, 1406,* 18-29.

Nakhate, K. T., Subhedar, N. K., & Kokare, D. M. (2019). Involvement of neuropeptide CART in the central effects of insulin on feeding and body weight. *Pharmacology, Biochemistry and Behavior, 181,* 101-109.

Nalbantian, S. (2011). Autobiographical memory in modernist literature and neuroscience. In S. Nalbantian, P. M. Matthews, & J. L. McClelland (Eds.), *The memory process: Neuroscientific and humanistic perspectives.* MIT Press.

Nam, S., & Lee, Y. (2021). Information Seeking and Behavior Change for the Smoking Cessation of College Students Utilizing Mobile Applications. *Journal of Korean Library and Information Science Society, 52*(1), 279-300.

National Association of Anorexia Nervosa and Associated Disorders. (2021). Eating disorder statistics. https://anad.org/eating-disorders-statistics/

National Center for Drug Abuse Statistics. (2022). Drug Abuse Statistics. https://drugabusestatistics.org/

National Center for Health Statistics. (2000). *Health United States, 2000 with adolescent health chartbook.* Author.

National Center for Health Statistics. (2021). NHANES interactive data visualizations. Division of Health and Nutrition Examination Surveys. https://www.cdc.gov/nchs/nhanes/visualization/index.htm

National Institute of Child Health and Human Development Early Child Care Research Network. (2001). Child-care and family predictors of preschool attachment and stability from infancy. *Development Psychology, 37,* 847-862.

National Institute of Mental Health. (2019). Suicide. https://www.nimh.nih.gov/health/statistics/suicide.shtml

National Institute on Drug Abuse. (2018). What is the scope of cocaine use in the United States? Downloaded from https://www.drugabuse.gov/publications/research-reports/cocaine/what-scope-cocaine-use-in-united-states.

National Institute on Drug Abuse. (2021). What are the signs of someone with a drug use problem? Bethesda, MD: National Institutes of Health. Retrieved from https://teens.drugabuse.gov/blog/post/what-are-signs-having-problem-drugs

National Institutes of Health. (2022). Talking with your doctor or health care provider. https://www.nih.gov/institutes-nih/nih-office-director/office-communications-public-liaison/clear-communication/talking-your-doctor

National Institutes of Health. (n.d.). Depression. https://www.nimh.nih.gov/health/topics/depression

Natsuaki, M. N., Samuels, D., & Leve, L. D. (2015). Puberty, identity, and context: A biopsychosocial perspective on internalizing psychopathology in early adolescent girls. In K. C. McLean & M. Syed (Eds.), *The Oxford handbook of identity development.* Oxford University Press.

Neal, D., Matson, J. L., & Belva, B. C. (2013). An examination of the reliability of a new observation measure for autism spectrum disorders: The autism spectrum disorder observation for children. *Research in Autism Spectrum Disorders, 7,* 29-34.

Neblett Jr, E. W. (2019). Diversity (psychological) science training: Challenges, tensions, and a call to action. *Journal of Social Issues, 75*(4), 1216-1239.

Neibergall, N. C., Swanson, A. J., & Sánchez, F. J. (2019). Hormones, sexual orientation, and gender identity. In L. L. Welling & T. K. Shackelford (Eds.), *The Oxford handbook of evolutionary psychology and behavioral endocrinology.* Oxford University Press.

Nelson, D. L., Kitto, K., Galea, D., McEvoy, C. L., & Bruza, P. D. (2013). How activation, entanglement, and searching a semantic network contribute to event memory. *Memory & Cognition, 41,* 797-819.

Nelson, G., & MacLeod, T. (2017). The evolution of housing for people with serious mental illness. In J. Sylvestre, G. Nelson, T. Aubry, J. Sylvestre, G. Nelson, & T. Aubry (Eds.), *Housing, citizenship, and communities for people with serious mental illness: Theory, research, practice, and policy perspectives.* Oxford University Press.

Nelson, T. D. (2013). The neurobiology of stereotyping and prejudice. In D. D. Franks & J. H. Turner (Eds.), *Handbook of neurosociology.* Springer Science + Business Media.

Nelson, W. M., III, & Finch, A. J., Jr. (2000). Managing anger in youth: A cognitive-behavioral intervention approach. In P. C. Kendall (Ed.), *Child & adolescent therapy: Cognitive-behavioral procedures* (2nd ed.). Guilford Press.

Neria, Y., DiGrande, L., & Adams, G. G. (2011). Posttraumatic stress disorder following the September 11, 2001, terrorist attacks. *American Psychologist, 66,* 429-446.

Nettles, M. T. (2019). History of testing in the United States: Higher education. *The ANNALS of the American Academy of Political and Social Science, 683*(1), 38-55.

Neubauer, A. B., Smyth, J. M., & Sliwinski, M. J. (2019). Age differences in proactive coping with minor hassles in daily life. *The Journals of Gerontology: Series B, 74*(1), 7-16.

Newman, C. F., Leahy, R. L., Beck, A. T., Reilly-Harrington, N. A., & Gyulai, L. (2002). *Bipolar disorder: A cognitive therapy approach.* American Psychological Association.

Newman, S. D., Willoughby, G., & Pruce, B. (2011). The effect of problem structure on problem-solving: An fMRI study of word versus number problems. *Brain Research, 30,* 88-96.

Newport, F. (2018). In U.S., estimate of LGBT population rises to 4.5%. *Gallup.* https://news.gallup.com/poll/234863/estimate-lgbt-population-rises.aspx

Newton, D. E. (2019). *Eating disorders in America: A reference handbook.* ABC-CLIO.

Ng, E., Lipsman, N., Hamani, C., Lozano, A., Kennedy, S., & Giacobbe, P. (2019). Adverse childhood experiences and deep brain stimulation outcomes for treatment resistant depression. *Brain Stimulation: Basic, Translational, and Clinical Research in Neuromodulation, 12*(2), 548.

Ng, Q. X., Venkatanarayanan, N., & Ho, C. X. (2017). Clinical use of *Hypericum perforatum* (St. John's wort) in depression: A meta-analysis. *Journal of Affective Disorders, 210,* 211-221.

Nguyen, T. T., Lee, E. E., Daly, R. E., Wu, T.-C., Tang, Y., Tu, X., Van Patten, R., Jeste, D. V., & Palmer, B. W. (2020). Predictors of loneliness by age decade: Study of psychological and environmental factors in 2,843 community-dwelling Americans aged 20-69 years. *The Journal of Clinical Psychiatry, 81*(6), 20M13378. https://doi.org/10.4088/JCP.20m13378

Nichols, E. S., Wild, C. J., Stojanoski, B., Battista, M. E., & Owen, A. M. (2020). Bilingualism affords no general cognitive advantages: A population study of executive function in 11,000 people. *Psychological Science, 31*(5), 548-567.

Nickerson, R. S., & Adams, M. J. (1979). Long-term memory for a common object. *Cognitive Psychology, 11,* 297.

Nicklaus, S., & Schwartz, C. (2019). Early influencing factors on the development of sensory and food preferences. *Current Opinion in Clinical Nutrition & Metabolic Care, 22*(3), 230-235.

Niedenthal, P. M. (2007). Embodying emotion. *Science, 316,* 1002-1005.

Nielsen, S. R., Boye, K., Bastiaanse, R., & Lange, V. M. (2019). The production of grammatical and lexical determiners in Broca's aphasia. *Language, Cognition and Neuroscience.* https://doi.org/10.1080/23273798.2019.1616104.

Nielsen, T. (2020, October). Infectious dreams. *Scientific American,* pp. 31-34.

Nielsen, T., O'Reilly, C., Carr, M., Dumel, G., Godin, I., Solomonova, E., et al. (2015). Overnight improvements in two REM sleep-sensitive tasks are associated with both REM and NREM sleep changes, sleep spindle features, and awakenings for dream recall. *Neurobiology of Learning and Memory, 122,* 88-97.

Nijboer, T. C. W., te Pas, S. F., & van der Smagt, M. J. (2011). Detecting gradual visual changes in colour and brightness agnosia: A double dissociation. *NeuroReport: For Rapid Communication of Neuroscience Research, 22,* 175-180.

Nimrod, G., & Kleiber, D. A. (2007). Reconsidering change and continuity in later life: Toward an innovation theory of successful aging. *International Journal of Human Development, 65,* 1-22.

Nisbet, E. K., Zelenski, J. M., & Murphy, S. A. (2011). Happiness is in our nature: Exploring nature relatedness as a contributor to subjective well-being. *Journal of Happiness Studies, 12,* 303-322.

Nisbett, R. E. (2019). Culture and intelligence. In D. Cohen & S. Kitayama (Eds.), *Handbook of cultural psychology.* Guilford Press.

Nishida, M., Pearsall, J., Buckner, R., & Walker, M. (2009). REM sleep, prefrontal theta, and the consolidation of human emotional memory. *Cerebral Cortex, 19,* 1158-1166.

Nishimura, T., Kawamura, S., & Sakurai, S. (2011). Autonomous motivation and meta-cognitive strategies as predictors of academic performance: Does intrinsic motivation predict academic performance? *Japanese Journal of Educational Psychology,59,* 77-87.

Nissley, G. E., & DeFreese, E. (2020). Thematic Apperception Test. In B. J. Carducci & C. S. Nave (Eds.), *The Wiley Encyclopedia of Personality and Individual Differences: Measurement and Assessment.* Wiley.

Nolen-Hoeksema, S. (2020). *Abnormal psychology* (8th ed.). McGraw Hill.

Nolen-Hoeksema, S. (2023). *Abnormal psychology* (9th ed.). McGraw Hill.

Norcross, J. C., & Lambert, M. (Eds.). (2019). *Psychotherapy relationships that work.* Oxford University Press.

Norman, A. (2021). *Mental immunity: Infectious ideas, mind-parasites, and the search for a better way to think.* HarperCollins.

Norman-Haignere, S. V., Long, L. K., Devinsky, O., Doyle, W., Irobunda, I., Merricks, E. M., Feldstein, N. A., McKhann, G. M., Schevon, C. A., Flinker, A., & Mesgarani, N. (2022). Multiscale temporal integration organizes hierarchical computation in human auditory cortex. *Nature Human Behaviour, 6*(3), 455-469.

Norrholm, S. D., & Jovanovic, T. (2018). Fear processing, psychophysiology, and PTSD. *Harvard review of psychiatry, 26*(3), 129-141.

North, M. M., & North, S. M. (2017). Virtual reality therapy for treatment of psychological disorders. In M. M. Maheu, K. P. Drude, & S. D. Wright (Eds.), *Career paths in telemental health.* Springer International Publishing.

Norton, D., Heath, D., & Ventura, D. (2013). Finding creativity in an artificial artist. *Journal of Creative Behavior, 47,* 106-124.

Nosek, C. L., Kerr, C. W., Woodworth, J., Wright, S. T., Grant, P. C., Kuszczak, S. M., et al. (2015). End-of-life dreams and visions: A qualitative perspective from hospice patients. *American Journal of Hospice & Palliative Medicine, 32,* 269-274.

Nourouzpour, N., Salomonczyk, D., Cressman, E. K., & Henriques, D. Y. (2015). Retention of proprioceptive recalibration following visuomotor adaptation. *Experimental Brain Research, 233,* 1019-1029.

Nouwens, P. G., Lucas, R., Embregts, P. M., & van Nieuwenhuizen, C. (2017). In plain sight but still invisible: A structured case analysis of people with mild intellectual disability or borderline intellectual functioning. *Journal of Intellectual and Developmental Disability, 42*, 36-44.

Novasky, M., & Rosales, T. (2020). Mental health and homelessness in the wake of Covid-19: The path to supportive and affordable housing. *UCLA Law Review Discourse, 68*, 130. https://www.uclalawreview.org/mental-health-and-homelessness-in-the-wake-of-covid-19-the-path-to-supportive-and-affordable-housing/

Novotney, A. (2017). A growing wave of online therapy. *Monitor on Psychology, 48*(2), 48.

Novotney, A. (2018, September). What happens to the survivors? *Monitor on Psychology*, pp. 36-44.

Nowakowski, M. E., McCabe, R. E., & Busse, J. W. (2019). Cognitive behavioral therapy to reduce persistent postsurgical pain following internal fixation of extremity fractures (COPE): Rationale for a randomized controlled trial. *Canadian Journal of Pain, 3*(2), 59-68.

Nutt, D. (2022). Psychedelic drugs–a new era in psychiatry? *Dialogues in Clinical Neuroscience, 21*(2), 139-147.

Nutt, D., and de Wit, H. (2021). Putting the MD back into MDMA. *Nature Medicine, 27*, 950-951.

Nygaard, E., Slinning, K., Moe, V., & Walhovd, K. B. (2017). Cognitive function of youths born to mothers with opioid and poly-substance abuse problems during pregnancy. *Child Neuropsychology, 23*, 159-187.

Nykamp, M. J., Zorumski, C. F., Reiersen, A. M., Nicol, G. E., Cirrito, J., & Lenze, E. J. (2022). Opportunities for drug repurposing of serotonin reuptake inhibitors: Potential uses in inflammation, infection, cancer, neuroprotection, and Alzheimer's disease prevention. *Pharmacopsychiatry, 55*(01), 24-29.

Oberauer, K., Awh, E., & Sutterer, D. W. (2017). The role of long-term memory in a test of visual working memory: Proactive facilitation but no proactive interference. *Journal of Experimental Psychology: Learning, Memory, and Cognition, 43*, 1-22.

Oberauer, K., & Greve, W. (2021). Intentional remembering and intentional forgetting in working and long-term memory. *Journal of Experimental Psychology: General*. Advance online publication. https://doi.org/10.1037/xge0001106

Oberhaus, D. (2020, April 27). A brain implant restored this man's motion and sense of touch. *Wired Science*. https://www.wired.com/story/a-brain-implant-restored-this-mans-motion-and-sense-of-touch/. Downloaded March 28, 2022.

Occhionero, M. (2004). Mental processes and the brain during dreams. *Dreaming, 14*, 54-64.

Oddie, G. A. (2021). Missionaries as social commentators: The Indian case. In M. Frederiks & D. Nagy (Eds.), *Critical Readings in the History of Christian Mission* (pp. 145-158). Brill.

Oeberst, A., Wachendörfer, M. M., Imhoff, R., & Blank, H. (2021). Rich false memories of autobiographical events can be reversed. *Proceedings of the National Academy of Sciences, 118*(13).

Oeztuerk, O. F., Pigoni, A., Wenzel, J., Haas, S. S., Popovic, D., Ruef, A., Dwyer, D. B., Kambeitz-Ilankovic, L., Ruhrmann, S., Chisholm, K., Lalousis, P., Griffiths, S. L., Lichtenstein, T., Rosen, M., Kambeitz, J. Shultze-Lutter, F., Liddle, P., Upthegrove, R., Salokangas, R. K. R., Pantelis, C., et al. (2022). The clinical relevance of formal thought disorder in the early stages of psychosis: Results from the PRONIA study. *European Archives of Psychiatry and Clinical Neuroscience, 272*(3), 403-413.

Offer, D., Kaiz, M., Howard, K. I., & Bennett, E. S. (2000). The altering of reported experiences. *Journal of the American Academy of Child & Adolescent Psychiatry, 39*, 735-742.

Ogbu, J. U. (2003). *Black American students in an affluent suburb: A study of academic disengagement.* Lawrence Erlbaum.

Ogden, J. (2022). Health psychology. In *Health Studies* (pp. 157-200). Palgrave Macmillan, Singapore.

Ojagbemi, A., Bello, T., & Gureje, O. (2018). Gender differential in social and economic predictors of incident major depressive disorder in the Ibadan Study of Ageing. *Social Psychiatry and Psychiatric Epidemiology: The International Journal for Research in Social and Genetic Epidemiology and Mental Health Services, 53*(4), 351-361.

Okada, K., Nakao, T., Sanematsu, H., Murayama, K., Honda, S., Tomita, M., Togao, O., Yoshiura, T., & Kanba, S. (2015). Biological heterogeneity of obsessive-compulsive disorder: A voxel-based morphometric study based on dimensional assessment. *Psychiatry and Clinical Neurosciences, 69*, 411-421.

Olson, D. H., & DeFrain, J. (2014). *Marriages and families: Intimacy, diversity, and strengths.* New York: McGraw Hill.

Onal Ertugrul, I., Ahn, Y. A., Bilalpur, M., Messinger, D. S., Speltz, M. L., & Cohn, J. F. (2022). Infant AFAR: Automated facial action recognition in infants. *Behavior Research Methods*, 1-12.

Ong, J. C. (2017). Insomnia: The problem of sleeplessness. In J. C. Ong, *Mindfulness-based therapy for insomnia*. Washington, DC: American Psychological Association.

Ono, D., Honma, K. I., & Honma, S. (2021). GABAergic mechanisms in the suprachiasmatic nucleus that influence circadian rhythm. *Journal of neurochemistry, 157*(1), 31-41.

Ooms, J., Hoeks, J., & Jansen, C. (2019). "Hey, that could be me": The role of similarity in narrative persuasion. *PLOS ONE, 14*(4), e0215359.

Opendak, M., Gould, E., & Sullivan, R. (2017). Early life adversity during the infant sensitive period for attachment: Programming of behavioral neurobiology of threat processing and social behavior. *Developmental Cognitive Neuroscience, 25*, 145-159.

Orben, A., and Przybylski, A. (2019). The association between adolescent well-being and digital technology use. *Nature Human Behavior, 3*, 173-182.

Organisation for Economic Co-operation and Development. (2018). *The resilience of students with an immigrant background: Factors that shape well-being, OECD Reviews of Migrant Education.* https://doi.org/10.1787/9789264292093-en.

Organisation for Economic Co-operation and Development. (2022). Employment: Time spent in paid and unpaid work, by sex. https://stats.oecd.org/index.aspx?queryid=54757

Ornat, S. L., & Gallo, P. (2004). Acquisition, learning, or development of language? Skinner's "verbal behavior" revisited. *Spanish Journal of Psychology, 7*, 161-170.

Ort, A., Siegenthaler, P., & Fahr, A. (2021). How positively valenced health messages can foster information selection: Evidence from two experiments. *Frontiers in Communication, 6*, 534496.

Ort, D., Moore, C., & Farber, B. A. (2022). Therapists' perspectives on positive regard. *Person-Centered & Experiential Psychotherapies*, 1-15. Advance online publication. https://doi.org/10.1080/14779757.2022.2104751

Orúzar, H., Miranda, R., Oriol, X., & Montserrat, C. (2019). Self-control and subjective-wellbeing of adolescents in residential care: The moderator role of experienced happiness and daily-life activities with caregivers. *Children and Youth Services Review, 98*, 125-131.

Orwin, R. G., & Condray, D. S. (1984). Smith and Glass' psychotherapy conclusions need further probing: On Landman and Dawes' re-analysis. *American Psychologist, 39*, 71-72.

Osth, A. F., & Farrell, S. (2019). Using response time distributions and race models to characterize primacy and recency effects in free recall initiation. *Psychological Review, 126*(4), 578-609.

Ostojic-Aitkens, D., Brooker, B., & Miller, C. J. (2019). Using ecological momentary assessments to evaluate extant measures of mind wandering. *Psychological Assessment, 31*(6), 817-827.

Ostroumov, A., Wittenberg, R. E., Kimmey, B. A., Taormina, M. B., Holden, W. M., McHugh, A. T., & Dani, J. A. (2020). Acute nicotine exposure alters ventral tegmental area inhibitory transmission and promotes diazepam consumption. *eNeuro, 7*(2), ENEURO.0348-19.2020. https://doi.org/10.1523/ENEURO.0348-19.2020

Otero, I., Salgado, J. F., & Moscoso, S. (2022). Cognitive reflection, cognitive intelligence, and cognitive abilities: A meta-analysis. *Intelligence, 90*, 101614.

Otgaar, H., Howe, M. L., & Muris, P. (2017). Maltreatment increases spontaneous false memories but decreases suggestion-induced false memories in children. *British Journal of Developmental Psychology, 35*(3), 376-391.

Otgaar, H., Howe, M. L., & Patihis, L. (2021). What science tells us about false and repressed memories. *Memory*, 1-6.

Otgaar, H., Schell-Leugers, J. M., Howe, M. L., Vilar, A. D. L. F., Houben, S. T., & Merckelbach, H. (2021). The link between suggestibility, compliance, and false confessions: A review using experimental and field studies. *Applied Cognitive Psychology, 35*(2), 445-455.

Otters, R. V., & Hollander, J. F. (2015). Leaving home and boomerang decisions: A family simulation protocol. *Marriage & Family Review, 51*, 39-58.

Ousdal, O. T., Brancati, G. E., Kessler, U., Erchinger, V., Dale, A. M., Abbott, C., & Oltedal, L. (2021). The neurobiological effects of electroconvulsive therapy studied through magnetic resonance: What have we learned, and where do we go? *Biological Psychiatry, 91*(6), 540-549.

Ouyang, F., & Xu, W. (2022). The effects of three instructor participatory roles on a small group's collaborative concept mapping. *Journal of Educational Computing Research, 60*(4), 930-959.

Owen, D. (2019, May 13). Volumetrics. *New Yorker*, pp. 26-31.

Owens, J., & Cribb, A. (2019). 'My Fitbit Thinks I Can Do Better!'do health promoting wearable technologies support personal autonomy?. *Philosophy & Technology, 32*(1), 23-38.

Ozana, A., & Ganel, T. (2019). Obeying the law: Speed-precision tradeoffs and the adherence to Weber's law in 2D grasping. *Experimental Brain Research, 237*(8), 2011-2021.

Özdemir, V., Dove, E. S., Gürsoy, U. K., Şardaş, S., Yıldırım, A., Yılmaz, Ş. G., Barlaws, Ö., Güngör, K. , Mete, A., & Srivastava, S. (2017). Personalized medicine beyond genomics: Alternative futures in big data–proteomics, environtome and the social proteome. *Journal of Neural Transmission, 124*, 25-32.

Özmete, E., & Pak, M. (2020). The relationship between anxiety levels and perceived social support during the pandemic of COVID-19 in Turkey. *Social Work in Public Health, 35*(7), 603-616.

Ozier, E. M., Taylor, V. J., & Murphy, M. C. (2019). The cognitive effects of experiencing and observing subtle racial discrimination. *Journal of Social Issues, 75*(4), 1087-1115.

Ozturk, M. B., & Berber, A. (2022). Racialised professionals' experiences of selective incivility in organisations: A multi-level analysis of subtle racism. *Human Relations, 75*(2), 213-239.

O'Brien, B., Kane, L., Houle, S. A., Aquilina, F., & Ashbaugh, A. R. (2022). Recall, response bias and recognition are differentially impacted by social anxiety irrespective of feedback modality. *Journal of Behavior Therapy and Experimental Psychiatry, 74*, 101694.

O'Brien, W. H., & Young, K. M. (2013). Assessment of psychopathology: Behavioral approaches. In J. R. Graham, J. A. Naglieri, & I. B. Weiner (Eds.), *Handbook of psychology: Assessment psychology* (pp. 583-599). John Wiley & Sons, Inc.

O'Connell, M., & Marks, G. N. (2021). Are the effects of intelligence on student achievement and well-being largely functions of family income and social class? Evidence from a longitudinal study of Irish adolescents. *Intelligence, 84*, 101511.

O'Leary, A. P., & Sloutsky, V. M. (2017). Carving metacognition at its joints: Protracted development of component processes. *Child Development, 88*, 1015-1032.

O'Leary, K. (2021). Psychiatry goes psychedelic. *Nature Medicine, 27*, 2056-2057.

O'Shea, B. A., Watson, D. G., Brown, G. D., & Fincher, C. L. (2020). Infectious disease prevalence, not race exposure, predicts both implicit and explicit racial prejudice across the United States. *Social Psychological and Personality Science, 11*(3), 345-355.

Paap, K. R. (2021). Bilingualism, executive function, and beyond: Questions and insights ed. by Irina A. Sekerina et al. *Language, 97*(4), 836-845.

Paciorek, A., & Williams, J. N. (2015). Semantic generalization in implicit language learning.

Journal of Experimental Psychology: Learning, Memory, and Cognition, 41, 989-1002.

Pagano, M. E., White, W. L., Kelly, J. F., Stout, R. L., & Tonigan, J. S. (2013). The 10-year course of Alcoholics Anonymous participation and long-term outcomes: A follow-up study of outpatient subjects in Project MATCH. *Substance Abuse, 34*, 51-59.

Pager, D., & Shepherd, H. (2008). The sociology of discrimination: Racial discrimination in employment, housing, credit, and consumer markets. *Annual Review of Sociology, 34*, 181-209.

Pakaluk, C. R., & Price, J. (2020). Are mothers and fathers interchangeable caregivers? *Marriage & Family Review, 56*(8), 784-793.

Paknahad, J., Loizos, K., Yue, L., Humayun, M. S., & Lazzi, G. (2021). Color and cellular selectivity of retinal ganglion cell subtypes through frequency modulation of electrical stimulation. *Scientific Reports, 11*(1), 1-13.

Pakpour, A. H., Griffiths, M. D., & Lin, C. Y. (2021). Assessing psychological response to the COVID-19: The fear of COVID-19 scale and the COVID stress scales. *International Journal of Mental Health and Addiction, 19*(6), 2407-2410.

Palamar, J. J., Rutherford, C., & Keyes, K. M. (2019). "Flakka" use among high school seniors in the United States. *Drug and Alcohol Dependence, 196*, 86-90.

Palfi, B., Moga, G., Lush, P., Scott, R. B., & Dienes, Z. (2019). Can hypnotic suggestibility be measured online? *Psychological Research.* https://doi.org/10.1007/s00426-019-01162-w

Palladino, J. J., & Carducci, B. J. (1984). Students' knowledge of sleep and dreams. *Teaching of Psychology, 11*(3), 189-191.

Palmiter, R. (2015). Hunger logic. *Nature Neuroscience, 18*, 789-791.

Pan, D. (2022, June 3). What drives mass shooters? Grievance, despair, and anger are more likely triggers than mental illness, experts say. *Boston Globe.* https://www.bostonglobe.com/2022/06/03/nation/what-drives-mass-shooters-grievance-despair-anger-are-more-likely-triggers-than-mental-illness-experts-say/

Panaite, V., Devendorf, A. R., Kashdan, T. B., & Rottenberg, J. (2021). Daily life positive events predict well-being among depressed adults 10 years later. *Clinical Psychological Science, 9*(2), 222-235.

Paplikar, A., Vandana, V. P., Mekala, S., Darshini, K. J., Arshad, F., Iyer, G. K., Kandukuri, R., Divyaraj, G., Varghese, F., Kaul, S., Patterson, K., & Alladi, S. (2022). Semantic memory impairment in dementia: A cross-cultural adaptation study. *Neurological Sciences, 43*(1), 265-273.

Papoiu, A., Nattkemper, L., Sanders, K., Kraft, R., Chan, Y-H, Coghill, R., & Yosipovitch, G. (2013). Brain's reward circuits mediate itch relief. A functional MRI study of active scratching. *PLOS ONE 8*(12), e82389.

Pappas, S. (2021, October). Rousing our motivation. *Monitor on Psychology,* pp. 53-59.

Pardini, D., White, H. R., Xiong, S., Bechtold, J., Chung, T., Loeber, R., et al. (2015). Unfazed or dazed and confused: Does early adolescent marijuana use cause sustained impairments in attention and academic functioning? *Journal of Abnormal Child Psychology, 43*(7), 1203-1217.

Parent, M. C., Gobble, T. D., & Rochlen, A. (2019). Social media behavior, toxic masculinity, and depression. *Psychology of Men & Masculinities, 20*(3), 277-287.

Park, A. (2011, March 7). Healing the hurt. *Time,* pp. 64-71.

Park, H., & Raymo, J. M. (2013). Divorce in Korea: Trends and educational differentials. *Journal of Marriage and Family, 75*, 110-126.

Park, H., Yun, I., & Walsh, A. (2017). Early puberty, school context, and delinquency among South Korean girls. *International Journal of Offender Therapy and Comparative Criminology, 61*, 795-818.

Park, P., Kang, H., Sanderson, T. M., Bortolotto, Z. A., Georgiou, J., Zhuo, M., Kaang, B-K., & Collingridge, G. L. (2019). On the role of calcium-permeable AMPARs in long-term potentiation and synaptic tagging in the rodent hippocampus. *Frontiers in Synaptic Neuroscience, 11*, 4.

Parkinson, J., Garfinkel, S., Critchley, H.,Dienes, Z., & Seth, A. K. (2017). Don't make me angry, you wouldn'tlike me when I'm angry: Volitional choices to act or inhibit are modulated by subliminal perception of emotional faces. *Cognitive, Affective & Behavioral Neuroscience, 17*, 252-268.

Parke, M. R., Seo, M., & Sherf, E. N. (2015). Regulating and facilitating: The role of emotional intelligence in maintaining and using positive affect for creativity. *Journal of Applied Psychology, 100*, 917-934.

Parma, V., Gordon, A. R., Cecchetto, C., Cavazzana, A., Lundström, J. N., & Olsson, M. J. (2017). Processing of human body odors. In A. Buettner (Ed.), *Springer handbook of odor* (pp. 127-128). Springer.

Parmar, M., Grealish, S., & Henchcliffe, C. (2020). The future of stem cell therapies for Parkinson disease. *Nature Reviews Neuroscience, 21*(2), 103-115.

Parra, A., & Argibay, J. C. (2007). Comparing psychics and non-psychics through a "token-object" forced-choice ESP test. *Journal of the Society for Psychical Research, 71*, 80-90.

Parris, B. A. (2017). The role of frontal executive functions in hypnosis and hypnotic suggestibility. *Psychology of Consciousness: Theory, Research, and Practice, 4*, 211-229.

Parrish, E. M., Kim, N. S., Woodberry, K. A., & Friedman, Y. M. (2019). Clinical high risk for psychosis: The effects of labelling on public stigma in a undergraduate population. *Early Intervention in Psychiatry, 13*(4), 874-881.

Parrott, A. C., Downey, L. A., Roberts, C. A., Montgomery, C., Bruno, R., & Fox, H. C. (2017). Recreational 3,4-methylenedioxymethamphetamine or 'ecstasy': Current perspective and future research prospects. *Journal of Psychpharmacology.* doi: 10.1177/0269881117711922.

Patel, K. K., Spertus, J. A., Chan, P. S., Sperry, B. W., Al Badarin, F., Kennedy, K. F., Thompson, R. C., Case, J. A., McGhie, A. I., & Bateman, T. M. (2020). Myocardial blood flow reserve assessed by positron emission tomography myocardial perfusion imaging identifies patients with a survival benefit from early revascularization. *European Heart Journal, 41*(6), 759-768.

Pathak, R., & Lata, S. (2018). Optimism in relation to resilience and perceived stress. *Journal of Psychosocial Research, 13*(2), 359-367.

Patihis, L., Ho, L. Y., Loftus, E. F., & Herrera, M. E. (2021). Memory experts' beliefs about repressed memory. *Memory, 29*(6), 823-828.

Patrick, M. E., Shaw, K. A., Dietz, P. M., Baio, J., Yeargin-Allsopp, M., Bilder, D. A., Kirby, R. S., Hall-Lande, J. A., Harrington, R. A., Lee, L-C., Lopez, M. L. C., Daniels, J., & Maenner, M. J. (2021). Prevalence of intellectual disability among eight-year-old children from selected communities in the United States, 2014. *Disability and Health Journal, 14*(2), 101023.

Patrick, S. W., Slaughter, J. C., Harrell Jr, F. E., Martin, P. R., Hartmann, K., Dudley, J., Stratton, S., & Cooper, W. O. (2021). Development and validation of a model to predict neonatal abstinence syndrome. *The Journal of Pediatrics, 229*, 154-160.

Patten, S. B., Williams, J. A., Lavorato, D. H., Bulloch, A. M., Fiest, K. M., Wang, J. L., et al. (2017). Seasonal variation in major depressive episode prevalence in Canada. *Epidemiology and Psychiatric Sciences, 26*, 169-176.

Patterson, P. D., Liszka, M. K., Mcilvaine, Q. S., Nong, L., Weaver, M. D., Turner, R. L., . . . & Callaway, C. (2021). Does the evidence support brief (< 30 mins), moderate (31-60 mins), or long duration naps (61+ mins) on the night shift? A systematic review. *Sleep Medicine Reviews, 59*, 101509.

Patterson, T. G., & Joseph, S. (2013). Unconditional positive self-regard. In M. E. Bernard (Ed.), *The strength of self-acceptance: Theory, practice and research.* Springer Science + Business Media.

Paulmann, S., Jessen, S., & Kotz, S. A. (2009). Investigating the multimodal nature of human communication: Insights from ERPs. *Journal of Psychophysiology, 23*, 63-76.

Paulson, K. L., Straus, E., Bull, D. M., MacArthur, S. K., DeLorme, J., & Dalenberg, C. J. (2019). Knowledge and views of psychological tests among psychiatrists and psychologists. *Journal of Forensic Psychology Research and Practice, 19*(2), 112-127.

Pauly, L., Bergmann, N., Hahne, I., Pux, S., Hahn, E., Ta, T. M. T., Rapp, M., & Böge, K. (2022). Prevalence, predictors and types of unpleasant and adverse effects of meditation in regular meditators: International cross-sectional study. *BJPsych Open, 8*(1), e11.

Pavão, R., Tort, A. L., & Amaral, O. B. (2015). Multifactoriality in psychiatric disorders: A computational study of schizophrenia. *Schizophrenia Bulletin, 41*, 980-988.

Pavlov, I. P. (1927). Conditioned reflexes: an investigation of the physiological activity of the cerebral cortex. Oxford Univ. Press.

Pawluski, J. L., Li, M., & Lonstein, J. S. (2019). Serotonin and motherhood: From molecules to mood. *Frontiers in Neuroendocrinology.* doi: 10.1016/j.yfrne.2019.03.001.

Payne, B. K., & Hannay, J. W. (2021). Implicit bias reflects systemic racism. *Trends in Cognitive Sciences, 25*(11), 927-936.

Pearson, A. R., Dovidio, J. F., & Pratto, E. (2007). Racial prejudice, intergroup hate, and blatant and subtle bias of whites toward blacks in legal decision making in the United States. *International Journal of Psychology & Psychological Therapy, 7*, 125-134.

Pearson, G. D. H., & Knobloch-Westerwick, S. (2019). Is the confirmation bias bubble larger online? Pre-election confirmation bias in selective exposure to online versus print political information. *Mass Communication & Society, 22*(4), 466-486.

Pecker, L. H., & Lanzkron, S. (2021). Sickle cell disease. *Annals of Internal Medicine, 174*(1), ITC1-ITC16.

Pedraza, O., & Mungas, D. (2008). Measurement in cross-cultural neuropsychology. *Neuropsychology Review, 18*, 184-193.

Peebles, A. T., van der Veen, S., Stamenkovic, A., France, C. R., Pidcoe, P. E., & Thomas, J. S. (2022). A virtual reality game suite for graded rehabilitation in patients with low back pain and a high fear of movement: Within-subject comparative study. *JMIR Serious Games, 10*(1), e32027.

Pekrun, R. (2017). Emotion and achievement during adolescence. *Child Development Perspectives, 11*(3), 215-221.

Pelletier, P., & Drozda-Senkowska, E. (2020). Towards a socially situated rumouring: Historical and critical perspectives of rumour transmission. *Social and Personality Psychology Compass, 14*(6), e12532.

Penhollow, T. M., Young, M., & Nnaka, T. (2017). Alcohol use, hooking-up, condom use: Is there a sexual double standard? *American Journal of Health Behavior, 41*, 92-103.

Penlington, C., Urbanek, M., & Barker, S. (2019). Psychological theories of pain. *Primary Dental Journal, 7*(4), 24-29.

Penn, D. L., Corrigan, P. W., Bentall, R. P., Racenstein, J. M., & Newman, L. (1997). Social cognition in schizophrenia. *Psychological Bulletin, 121*, 114-132.

Pennequin, V., Questel, F., Delaville, E., Delugre, M., & Maintenant, C. (2020). Metacognition and emotional regulation in children from 8 to 12 years old. *British Journal of Educational Psychology.* https://doi.org/10.1111/bjep.12305.

Pennisi, E. (2021, October 29). The simplest of slumbers. *Science, 374*, 526-529.

Pennisi, E. (2022). Most complete human genome yet is revealed. *Science, 376*(6588), 15-16.

Pennycook, G., & Rand, D. G. (2021). The psychology of fake news. *Trends in Cognitive Sciences, 25*(5), 388-402.

Perez, C. O., London, K., & Otgaar, H. (2022). A review of the differential contributions of language abilities to children's eyewitness memory and suggestibility. *Developmental Review, 63*, 101009.

Pérez-Leroux, A. T., Pirvulescu, M., & Roberge, Y. (2011). Topicalization and object omission in child language. *First Language, 31*, 280-299.

Perlstein, S., & Waller, R. (2022). Integrating the study of personality and psychopathology in the context of gene-environment correlations across development. *Journal of Personality, 90*(1), 47-60.

Perogamvros, L., & Schwartz, S. (2015). Sleep and emotional functions. In P. Meerlo, R. M. Benca, & T. Abel (Eds.), *Sleep, neuronal plasticity and brain function.* New York: Springer-Verlag Publishing.

Perovic, S., & Radenovic, L. (2011). Fine-tuning nativism: The "nurtured nature" and innate cognitive structures. *Phenomenology and the Cognitive Sciences, 10,* 399-417.

Perrier, M., & Ginis, K. M. (2017). Narrative interventions for health screening behaviours: A systematic review. *Journal of Health Psychology, 22,* 375-393.

Perrotta, G., & Fabiano, G. (2021). Behavioural disorders in children and adolescents: Definition, clinical contexts, neurobiological profiles and clinical treatments. *Open Journal of Pediatrics and Child Health, 6*(1), 5-15.

Perry, G. (2013). *Behind the shock machine.* New Press.

Perry, G., Polito, V., & Thompson, W. F. (2021). Rhythmic chanting and mystical states across traditions. *Brain Sciences, 11*(1), 101.

Persson, A., Flynn, T., Miniscalco, C., & Lohmander, A. (2021). Impact of auditory variables on consonant production in babbling and early speech in children with moderate hearing loss-a longitudinal study. *Clinical Linguistics & Phonetics, 36*(10), 833-848.

Pesonen, A. K., Lipsanen, J., Halonen, R., Elovainio, M., Sandman, N., Mäkelä, J. M., . . . & Kuula, L. (2020). Pandemic dreams: network analysis of dream content during the COVID-19 lockdown. *Frontiers in Psychology, 11,* 2569.

Pessin, L. (2018). Changing gender norms and marriage dynamics in the United States. *Journal of Marriage and Family, 80*(1), 25-41.

Pester, B. D., Crouch, T. B., Christon, L., Rodes, J., Wedin, S., Kilpatrick, R., Pester, M. S., Borckardt, J., & Barth, K. (2022). Gender differences in multidisciplinary pain rehabilitation: The mediating role of pain acceptance. *Journal of Contextual Behavioral Science, 23,* 117-124.

Peters, E., Hess, T. M., Västfjäll, D., & Auman, C. (2007). Adult age differences in dual information processes. *Perspectives on Psychological Science, 2,* 1-23.

Peters, E. N., Rosenberry, Z. R., Schauer, G. L., O'Grady, K. E., & Johnson, P. S. (2017). Marijuana and tobacco cigarettes: Estimating their behavioral economic relationship using purchasing tasks. *Experimental and Clinical Psychopharmacology, 25*(3), 208-215.

Peters, P., Van Der Heijden, B., Spurk, D., De Vos, A., & Klaassen, R. (2019). Please don't look at me that way: An empirical study into the effects of age-based (meta-) stereotyping on employability enhancement among supermarket workers. *Frontiers in Psychology, 10,* 249.

Petersen, A. (2011, August 23). A sleep battle of the sexes. *Wall Street Journal,* pp. D1, D4.

Petersen, A. (2022, January 13). To get a better night's sleep, first fix your day. *Wall Street Journal,* p. A13.

Peterson, C. J., Lee, B., & Nugent, K. (2022). COVID-19 vaccination hesitancy among healthcare workers—A review. *Vaccines, 10*(6), 948.

Peterson, L. R., & Peterson, M. J. (1959). Short-term retention of individual items. *Journal of Experimental Psychology, 58,* 193-198.

Petzel, Z. W., & Casad, B. J. (2022). Take a chance on STEM: Risk-taking buffers negative effects of stereotype threat. *The Journal of Experimental Education, 90*(3), 656-672.

Pezoulas, V. C., Zervakis, M., Michelogiannis, S., & Klados, M. A. (2017). Resting-state functional connectivity and network analysis of cerebellum with respect to crystallized IQ and gender. *Frontiers In Human Neuroscience, 11,* 1-10.

Pfaff, D. W. (2014). *The altruistic brain: How we are naturally good.* Oxford University Press.

Pfattheicher, S., Nielsen, Y. A., & Thielmann, I. (2022). Prosocial behavior and altruism: A review of concepts and definitions. *Current Opinion in Psychology, 44,* 124-129.

Pfefferbaum, B., & North, C. S. (2020). Mental health and the Covid-19 pandemic. *New England Journal of Medicine, 383*(6), 510-512.

Phadke, I., Karia, S., & De Sousa, A. (2015). Hallucinations in patients with schizophrenia attending a tertiary psychiatry hospital. *Arab Journal of Psychiatry, 26*(1), 68-73.

Phalen, P. L., Dimaggio, G., Popolo, R., & Lysaker, P. H. (2017). Aspects of Theory of Mind that attenuate the relationship between persecutory delusions and social functioning in schizophrenia spectrum disorders. *Journal of Behavior Therapy and Experimental Psychiatry, 56,* 65-70.

Philippi, C. L., Bruss, J., Boes, A. D., Albazron, F. M., Deifelt Streese, C., Ciaramelli, E., . . . & Tranel, D. (2021). Lesion network mapping demonstrates that mind-wandering is associated with the default mode network. *Journal of neuroscience research, 99*(1), 361-373.

Phillips, C. R., Miletich, D. M., & Mullins, L. (2022). Complex regional pain syndrome. In *Features and Assessments of Pain, Anaesthesia, and Analgesia* (pp. 117-125). Academic Press.

Phillips, W. L. (2019). Cross-cultural differences in visual perception of color, illusions, depth, and pictures. In K. D. Keith (Ed.), *Cross-Cultural Psychology: Contemporary Themes and Perspectives* (2nd ed., pp. 287-308). Wiley.

Phua, J., Jin, S. V., & Kim, J. (. (2017). Uses and gratifications of social networking sites for bridging and bonding social capital: A comparison of Facebook, Twitter, Instagram, and Snapchat. *Computers in Human Behavior, 72,* 115-122.

Phukhachee, T., Maneewongvatana, S., Angsuwatanakul, T., Iramina, K., & Kaewkamnerdpong, B. (2019). Investigating the effect of intrinsic motivation on alpha desynchronization using sample entropy. *Entropy, 21*(3), 237.

Piaget, J. (1970). Piaget's theory. In P. H. Mussen (Ed.), *Carmichael's manual of child psychology* (3rd ed., Vol. I). Wiley.

Piaget, J., & Inhelder, B. (1958). *The growth of logical thinking from childhood to adolescence* (A. Parsons & S. Seagrin, Trans.). Basic Books.

Picciotto, M. R., & Kenny, P. J. (2021). Mechanisms of Nicotine Addiction. *Cold Spring Harbor perspectives in medicine, 11*(5), a039610.

Pieper, J., Chang, D. G., Mahasin, S. Z., Swan, A. R., Quinto, A. A., Nichols, S. L., Diwakar, M., Huang, C., Swan, J., Lee, R. R., Baker, D. G., & Huang, M. (2019). Brain amygdala volume increases in veterans and active-duty military personnel with combat-related posttraumatic stress disorder and mild traumatic brain injury. *Journal of Head Trauma Rehabilitation, 35*(1), E1-E9.

Pietromonaco, P., & Collins, N. L. (2017). Interpersonal mechanisms linking close relationships to health. *American Psychologist, 72,* 531-542.

Pijnenborg, G. M., Timmerman, M. E., Derks, E. M., Fleischhacker, W. W., Kahn, R. S., & Aleman, A. (2015). Differential effects of antipsychotic drugs on insight in first episode schizophrenia: Data from the European First-Episode Schizophrenia Trial (EUFEST). *European Neuropsychopharmacology, 25,* 808-816.

Pike, A. F., Szabò, I., Veerhuis, R., & Bubacco, L. (2022). The potential convergence of NLRP3 inflammasome, potassium, and dopamine mechanisms in Parkinson's disease. *npj Parkinson's Disease, 8*(1), 1-9.

Pillai, A., Schooler, N. R., Peter, D., Looney, S. W., Goff, D. C., Kopelowicz, A., Lauriello, J., Manschreck, T., Mendelowitz, A., Miller, D. D., Severe, J. B., Wilson, D. R., Ames, D., Bustillo, J., Kane, J. M., & Buckley, P. F. (2018). Predicting relapse in schizophrenia: Is BDNF a plausible biological marker? *Schizophrenia Research, 193,* 263-268.

Pinal, D., Zurrón, M., & Díaz, F. (2015). Age-related changes in brain activity are specific for high order cognitive processes during successful encoding of information in working memory. *Frontiers in Aging Neuroscience, 7,* 88-97.

Pincus, T., & Morley, S. (2001). Cognitive processing bias in chronic pain: A review and integration. *Psychological Bulletin, 127,* 599-617.

Pinker, S. (1994). *The language instinct.* William Morrow.

Pinky, P. D., Bloemer, J., Smith, W. D., Moore, T., Hong, H., Suppiramaniam, V., et al. (2019). Prenatal cannabinoid exposure and altered neurotransmission. *Neuropharmacology, 149,* 181-194.

Pinquart, M., & Kauser, R. (2017). Do the associations of parenting styles with behavior problems and academic achievement vary by culture? Results from a meta-analysis. *Cultural Diversity and Ethnic Minority Psychology, 24*(1), 75-100.

Pisarik, C. T., Rowell, P., & Currie, L. K. (2013). Work-related daydreams: A qualitative content analysis. *Journal of Career Development, 40,* 87-106.

Piton, M., Hirtz, C., Desmetz, C., Milhau, J., Lajoix, A. D., Bennys, K., Lehmann, S., & Gabelle, A. (2018). Alzheimer's disease: Advances in drug development. *Journal of Alzheimer's Disease, 65*(1), 3-13.

Pizzagalli, D. A., & Roberts, A. C. (2022). Prefrontal cortex and depression. *Neuropsychopharmacology, 47*(1), 225-246.

Planalp, E. M., & Goldsmith, H. H. (2020). Observed profiles of infant temperament: Stability, heritability, and associations with parenting. *Child Development.* https://doi.org/10.1111/cdev.13277.

Plank, F., & Bergmann, J. (2021). The European Union as a security actor in the Sahel: Policy entrapment in EU foreign policy. *European Review of International Studies, 8*(3), 382-412.

Plante, C., & Anderson, C. A. (2017). Global warming and violent behavior. *APS Observer,* pp. 29-32.

Pluess, M., & Belsky, J. (2009). Differential susceptibility to rearing experience: The case of childcare. *Journal of Child Psychology and Psychiatry, 50,* 396-404.

Poirier, M., Saint-Aubin, J., Mair, A., Tehan, G., & Tolan, A. (2015). Order recall in verbal short-term memory: The role of semantic networks. *Memory & Cognition, 43,* 489-499.

Pols, H. (2019, November 8). Undercover in the asylum. *Science, 366,* 697.

Pontzer, H. (2017). Exercise paradox. *Scientific American, 316*(2), 28-31.

Pontzer, H., Yamada, Y., Sagayama, H., Ainslie, P. N., Andersen, L. F., Anderson, L. J., Arab, L., Baddou, I., Bedu-Addo, K., Blaak, E. E., Bonomi, A. G. Bouten, C. V. C., Bovet, P., Buchowski, M. S., Butte, N. F., Camps, S. G., Close, G. L., Cooper, J. A., et al. (2021). Daily energy expenditure through the human life course. *Science, 373*(6556), 808-812.

Pool, E., Rehme, A. K., Fink, G. R., Eickhoff, S. B., & Grefkes, C. (2013). Network dynamics engaged in the modulation of motor behavior in healthy subjects. *Neuroimage, 88,* 68-76.

Poormahdy, H., Najafi, M., & Khosravani, V. (2022). The effects of emotion dysregulation and negative affect on urge to smoke and nicotine dependence: The different roles of metacognitions about smoking. *Addictive Behaviors, 124,* 107108.

Popova, N. K., Kulikov, A. V., & Naumenko, V. S. (2020). Spaceflight and brain plasticity: Spaceflight effects on regional expression of neurotransmitter systems and neurotrophic factors encoding genes. *Neuroscience & Biobehavioral Reviews, 119,* 396-405.

Popov, V, Marevic, I., Rummel, J., & Reder, L.M. (2019). Forgetting is a feature, not a bug: Intentionally forgetting some things helps us remember others by freeing up working memory resources. *Psychological Science,* 1-15.

Population & Public Health. (2020, July 31). Global health disparities infographic. https://www.himss.org/resources/global-health-disparities-infographic

Porcerelli, J. H., Bornstein, R. F., Porcerelli, D., & Arterbery, V. E. (2015). The complex role of personality in cancer treatment: Impact of dependency-detachment on health status, distress, and physician-patient relationship. *Journal of Nervous and Mental Disease, 203,* 264-268.

Posada, G., & Trumbell, J. M. (2017). Universality and cultural specificity in child-mother attachment relationships: In search of answers. In S. Gojman-de-Millan, C. Herreman, & L. A. Sroufe (Eds.), *Attachment across clinical and cultural perspectives: A relational psychoanalytic approach.* Routledge/Taylor & Francis Group.

Possin, K. L., Tsoy, E., & Windon, C. C. (2021). Perils of race-based norms in cognitive testing: The case of former NFL players. *JAMA Neurology, 78*(4), 377-378.

Post, C., & Leuner, B. (2019). The maternal reward system in postpartum depression. *Archives of Women's Mental Health, 22*(3), 417-429.

Potash, J. S. (2015). Archetypal aesthetics: Viewing art through states of consciousness. *International Journal of Jungian Studies, 7,* 139-153.

Pottick, K. J., Kirk, S. A., Hsieh, D. K., & Tian, X. (2007). Judging mental disorder in youths: Effects of client, clinician, and contextual differences. *Journal of Consulting Clinical Psychology, 75,* 1-8.

Pow, A. M., & Cashwell, C. S. (2017). Posttraumatic stress disorder and emotion-focused coping among disaster mental health counselors. *Journal of Counseling & Development, 95*(3), 322-331.

Pow, J. L., Baumeister, A. A., Hawkins, M. F., Cohen, A. S., & Garand, J. C. (2015). Deinstitutionalization of American public hospitals for the mentally ill before and after the introduction of antipsychotic medications. *Harvard Review of Psychiatry, 23,* 176-187.

Powell, R. A., & Schmaltz, R. M. (2021). Did Little Albert actually acquire a conditioned fear of furry animals? What the film evidence tells us. *History of Psychology, 24*(2), 164-181.

Pozzan, L., & Valian, V. (2017). Asking questions in child English: Evidence for early abstract representations. *Language Acquisition: A Journal of Developmental Linguistics, 24,* 209-233.

Prasser, J., Schecklmann, M., Poeppl, T. B., Frank, E., Kreuzer, P. M., Hajak, G., Rupprecht, R., Landgrebe, M., & Langguth, B. (2015). Bilateral prefrontal rTMS and theta burst TMS as an add-on treatment for depression: A randomized placebo controlled trial. *World Journal of Biological Psychiatry, 16,* 57-65.

Pratkanis, A. R. (2007). Social influence analysis: An index of tactics. In A. R. Pratkanis (Ed.), *The science of social influence: Advances and future progress.* Psychology Press.

Pratkanis, A. R., Epley, N., & Savitsky, K. (2007). Issue 12: Is subliminal persuasion a myth? In J. A. Nier (Ed.), *Taking sides: Clashing views in social psychology* (2nd ed.). McGraw-Hill.

Pratt, M. W. & Matsuba, M. K. (2019). *The life story, domains of identity, and personality development in emerging adulthood.* Oxford University Press.

Pratto, F., Lee, I., Tan, J. Y., & Pitpitan, E. Y. (2011). Power basis theory: A psychoecological approach to power. In D. Dunning (Ed.), *Social motivation.* Psychology Press.

Prayag, A. S., Najjar, R. P., & Gronfier, C. (2019). Melatonin suppression is exquisitely sensitive to light and primarily driven by melanopsin in humans. *Journal of Pineal Research: Molecular, Biological, Physiological and Clinical Aspects of Melatonin, 66*(4), 1-8.

Preskorn, S. H. (2022). How an understanding of the function of the locus coeruleus led to use of dexmedetomidine to treat agitation in bipolar disorder: Example of rational development of psychiatric medications. *Journal of Psychiatric Practice, 28*(3), 227-233.

Prete, G., Croce, P., Zappasodi, F., Tommasi, L., & Capotosto, P. (2022). Exploring brain activity for positive and negative emotions by means of EEG microstates. *Scientific Reports, 12*(1), 1-11.

Preti, A., Piras, M., Cossu, G., Pintus, E., Pintus, M., Kalcev, G., Cabras, F., Moro, M. F., Romano, F., Balestrieri, M., Caraci, F., Dell'Osso, L., Di Sciascio, G., Drago, F., Hardoy, M. C., Roncone, R., Faravelli, C., Musu, M., Finco, G., Nardi, A. E., & Carta, M. G. (2021). The burden of agoraphobia in worsening quality of life in a community survey in Italy. *Psychiatry Investigation, 18*(4), 277-283.

Pretsch, J., Heckmann, N., Flunger, B., & Schmitt, M. (2013). Agree or disagree? Influences on consensus in personality judgments. *European Journal of Psychological Assessment.* http://psycnet.apa.org/psycinfo/2013-30588-001/

Price, M. (2008, September). Against doctors' orders. *Monitor on Psychology,* pp. 34-36.

Price, M. A., McKetta, S., Weisz, J. R., Ford, J. V., Lattanner, M. R., Skov, H., Wolock, E., & Hatzenbuehler, M. L. (2021). Cultural sexism moderates efficacy of psychotherapy: Results from a spatial meta-analysis. *Clinical Psychology: Science and Practice, 28*(3), 299-312. https://doi.org/10.1037/cps0000031

Priester, J. R., & Petty, R. E. (2011). The pot-holed path to happiness, possibly paved with money: A

research dialogue. *Journal of Consumer Psychology, 21,* 113-114.

Prieto, J. T., McEwen, D., Davidson, A. J., Al-Tayyib, A., Gawenus, L., Sangareddy, S. R. P., et al. (2019). Monitoring opioid addiction and treatment: Do you know if your population is engaged? *Drug and Alcohol Dependence, 202,* 56-60.

Prior, K. N., & Bond, M. J. (2017). Patterns of "abnormal" illness behavior among healthy individuals. *American Journal of Health Behavior, 41,* 139-146.

Priyanka, S. K. (2021). A cross-sectional study of mental wellbeing with practice of yoga and meditation during COVID-19 pandemic. *Journal of Family Medicine and Primary Care, 10*(4), 1576.

Proctor, C., Tweed, R. G., & Morris, D. B. (2021). Unconditional positive self-regard: The role of perceived parental conditional regard. *The Humanistic Psychologist, 49*(3), 400-422. https://doi.org/10.1037/hum0000168

Proctor, H. (2020). The synaesthete. In *Psychologies in Revolution* (pp. 211-238). Palgrave Macmillan.

Proto, E., & Quintana-Domeque, C. (2021). COVID-19 and mental health deterioration by ethnicity and gender in the UK. *PLOS ONE, 16*(1), e0244419.

Protoshhak, V. V., Andreev, E. A., Karpushhenko, E. G., Slepcov, A. V., Ovchinnikov, D. V., Alentev, S. A., Lazutkin, M. V., Mamaenko, A. V., & Mamaenko, T. V. (2019, December). Prostate cancer and dogs sense of smell: opportunities of noninvasive diagnostics. *Urologiia,* 22-26.

Proudfoot, D. (2009). Meaning and mind: Wittgenstein's relevance for the 'Does Language Shape Thought?' debate. *New Ideas in Psychology, 27*(2), 163-183.

Proudfoot, D., & Fath, S. (2021). Signaling creative genius: How perceived social connectedness influences judgments of creative potential. *Personality and Social Psychology Bulletin, 47*(4), 580-592.

Proyer, R. T., Gander, F., Wellenzohn, S., & Ruch, W. (2013). What good are character strengths beyond subjective well-being? The contribution of the good character on self-reported health-oriented behavior, physical fitness, and the subjective health status. *Journal of Positive Psychology, 8,* 222-232.

Przybylski, A. K., & Weinstein, N. (2019). Digital screen time limits and young children's psychological well-being: Evidence from a population-based study. *Child Development, 90*(1), e56-e65.

Ptak, R., & Lazeyras, F. (2019). Functional connectivity and the failure to retrieve meaning from shape in visual object agnosia. *Brain and Cognition, 131,* 94-101.

Pugliese, O. T., Solari, J. L., & Ferreres, A. R. (2014). The extent of surgical patients' understanding. *World Journal of Surgery, 38*(7), 1605-1609. https://doi.org/10.1007/s00268-014-2561-8

Purdy, S. C., Sharma, M. M., Munro, K. J., & Morgan, C. A. (2013). Stimulus level effects on speech-evoked obligatory cortical auditory evoked potentials in infants with normal hearing. *Clinical Neurophysiology, 124,* 474-480.

Purtill, C. (2022, May 9/May 16). The new science of forgetting. *Time,* pp. 74-77.

Qi, L., Gao, X., Pan, D., Sun, Y., Cai, Z., Xiong, Y., & Dang, Y. (2022). Research progress in the screening and evaluation of umami peptides. *Comprehensive Reviews in Food Science and Food Safety.* https://doi.org/10.1111/1541-4337.12916

Qu, C., Zhang, A., & Chen, Q. (2013). Monetary effects on fear conditioning. *Psychological Reports, 112,* 353-364.

Quillin, S. J., Tran, P., & Prindle, A. (2021). Potential roles for gamma-aminobutyric acid signaling in bacterial communities. *Bioelectricity, 3*(2), 120-125.

Quinn, K., Pacella, M. L., Dickson-Gomez, J., & Nydegger, L. A. (2017). Childhood adversity and the continued exposure to trauma and violence among adolescent gang members. *American Journal of Community Psychology, 59,* 36-49.

Quinn, P. C., Lee, K., & Pascalis, O. (2018). Perception of face race by infants: Five developmental changes. *Child Development, 12,* 204-209.

Quinn, P. D., López Pérez, D., Kennedy, D. P., Bölte, S., D'Onofrio, B., Lichtenstein, P., & Falck-Ytter, T.

(2022). Visual search: Heritability and association with general intelligence. *Genes, Brain and Behavior,* e12779.

Quintana, S. M., Aboud, F. E., & Chao, R. K. (2006). Race, ethnicity, and culture in child development: Contemporary research and future directions. *Child Development, 77,* 1129-1141.

Qu, Y., Jorgensen, N. A., & Telzer, E. H. (2021). A call for greater attention to culture in the study of brain and development. *Perspectives on Psychological Science, 16*(2), 275-293.

Rabin, R. C. (2013, August 13). A glut of antidepressants. *The New York Times,* p. D4.

Rabin, R. C. (2022, August 31). U.S. life expectancy falls again in "historic" setback. *The New York Times.* https://www.nytimes.com/2022/08/31/health/life-expectancy-covid-pandemic.html

Racine, N., McArthur, B. A., Cooke, J. E., Eirich, R., Zhu, J., & Madigan, S. (2021). Global prevalence of depressive and anxiety symptoms in children and adolescents during COVID-19: A meta-analysis. *JAMA Pediatrics, 175*(11), 1142-1150.

Racine, S. E., VanHuysse, J. L., Keel, P. K., Burt, S. A., Neale, M. C., Boker, S., & Klump, K. L. (2017). Eating disorder-specific risk factors moderate the relationship between negative urgency and binge eating: A behavioral genetic investigation. *Journal of Abnormal Psychology, 126,* 481-494.

Radvansky, G. A. (2010). *Human memory.* Psychology Press.

Radvansky, G. A. (2021). *Human memory.* (4th ed.). Routledge.

Radvansky, G. A., Doolen, A. C., Pettijohn, K. A., & Ritchey, M. (2022). A new look at memory retention and forgetting. *Journal of Experimental Psychology: Learning, Memory, and Cognition.* Advance online publication. https://doi.org/10.1037/xlm0001110

Radvansky, G. A., Pettijohn, K. A., & Kim, J. (2015). Walking through doorways causes forgetting: Younger and older adults. *Psychology and Aging, 30,* 259-265.

Rahman, Q., & Yusuf, S. (2015). Lateralization for processing facial emotions in gay men, heterosexual men, and heterosexual women. *Archives of Sexual Behavior, 44,* 1405-1413.

Railo, H., Piccin, R., & Lukasik, K. M. (2021). Subliminal perception is continuous with conscious vision and can be predicted from prestimulus electroencephalographic activity. *European Journal of Neuroscience, 54*(3), 4985-4999.

Rajecki, D. W., & Borden, V. M. H. (2011). Psychology degrees: Employment, wage, and career trajectory consequences. *Perspectives on Psychological Science, 6,* 321-335.

Ramchand, R., Gordon, J. A., & Pearson, J. L. (2021). Trends in suicide rates by race and ethnicity in the United States. *JAMA Network Open, 4*(5), e2111563-e2111563.

Ramchand, R., Jaycox, L., Ebener, P., Gilbert, M. L., Barnes-Proby, D., & Goutam, P. (2017). Characteristics and proximal outcomes of calls made to suicide crisis hotlines in California: Variability across centers. *Crisis: The Journal of Crisis Intervention and Suicide Prevention, 38*(1), 26-35.

Ramachandran, V. S., & Hubbard, E. M. (2006). Hearing colors, tasting shapes. *Scientific American, 16,* 76-83.

Ramos, R. A., Ferguson, C. J., Frailing, K., & Romero-Ramirez, M. (2013). Comfortably numb or just yet another movie? Media violence exposure does not reduce viewer empathy for victims of real violence among primarily Hispanic viewers. *Psychology of Popular Media Culture, 2,* 2-10.

Randolph-Seng, B., & Nielsen, M. E. (2009). Opening the doors of perception: Priming altered states of consciousness outside of conscious awareness. *Archivfür Religionspsychologie/Archive for the Psychology of Religions, 31,* 237-260.

Rangell, L. (2007). *The road to unity in psychoanalytic theory.* Jason Aronson.

Ranot, J. (2021). Vaccine Hesitancy in the Current Landscape of the COVID-19 Pandemic. *University of Ottawa Journal of Medicine, 11*(S1).

Ranscombe, P. (2019). The PET and the pendulum: investigating hypnosis and the brain. *The Lancet Psychiatry, 6*(6), 475-476.

Rao, G., Redline, S., Schilbach, F., Schofield, H., & Toma, M. (2021). Informing sleep policy through field experiments. *Science, 374*(6567), 530-533.

Rao, U., Hammen, C. L., & Poland, R. E. (2009). Ethnic differences in electroencephalographic sleep patterns in adolescents. *Asian journal of psychiatry, 2*(1), 17-24.

Raque, T. L., Mitchell, A. M., Coleman, M. N., Coleman, J. J., & Owen, J. (2021). Addressing racial equity in health psychology research: An application of the multicultural orientation framework. *American Psychologist, 76*(8), 1266-1279. https://doi.org/10.1037/amp0000888

Raskin, N. J., & Rogers, C. R. (1989). Person-centered therapy. In R. J. Corsini & D. Wedding (Eds.), *Current psychotherapies* (4th ed.). F. E. Peacock.

Rassin, E., & Muris, P. (2007). Abnormal and normal obsessions: A reconsideration. *Behaviour Research and Therapy, 45*, 1065-1070.

Ratner, K. G., Dotsch, R., Wigboldus, D. H. J., van Knippenberg, A., & Amodio, D. M. (2014). Visualizing minimal ingroup and outgroup faces: Implications for impressions, attitudes, and behavior. *Journal of Personality and Social Psychology, 106*(6), 897-911. https://doi.org/10.1037/a0036498

Ratz, D., Wiitala, W., Badr, M. S., Burns, J., & Chowdhuri, S. (2018). Correlates and consequences of central sleep apnea in a national sample of US veterans. *Sleep, 41*(9), zsy058.

Rauch, J. (2021). *The constitution of knowledge: A defense of truth.* Brookings Institution Press.

Raufelder, D., & Kulakow, S. (2022). The role of social belonging and exclusion at school and the teacher–student relationship for the development of learned helplessness in adolescents. *British Journal of Educational Psychology, 92*(1), 59-81.

Ravindran, A., Richter, M., Jain, T., Ravindran, L., Rector, N., & Farb, N. (2019). Functional connectivity in obsessive-compulsive disorder and its subtypes. *Psychological medicine*, 1-9.

Ray, J. V., Thornton, L. C., Frick, P. J., Steinberg, L., & Cauffman, E. (2015). Impulse control and callous-unemotional traits distinguish patterns of delinquency and substance use in justice involved adolescents: Examining the moderating role of neighborhood context. *Journal of Abnormal Child Psychology, 43*(9), 1190-1203.

Ray, L., Bryan, A., MacKillop, J., McGeary, J., Hesterberg, K., & Hutchison, K. (2009). The dopamine D4 receptor gene exon III polymorphism, problematic alcohol use and novelty seeking: Direct and mediated genetic effects. *Addiction Biology, 14*, 238-244.

Raz, A. (2007). Suggestibility and hypnotizability: Mind the gap. *American Journal of Clinical Hypnosis, 49*, 205-210.

Reardon, S. (2021). Genetic patterns offer clues to evolution of homosexuality. *Nature, 597*(7874), 17-18.

Reddy, P. H., Amakiri, N., Tran, J., & Kubosumi, A. (2019). Amyloid beta and microRNAs in Alzheimer's disease. *Frontiers in Neuroscience, 13*, 430.

Reddy, S. (2013, March 19). People who taste too much. *Wall Street Journal*, p. D1.

Reddy, S. (2015, May 19.) How doctors break bad news. *Wall Street Journal*, pp. D1, D4.

Reddy, S. (2016, May 10). When daydreaming becomes a problem. *Wall Street Journal*, pp. D1, D4.

Reddy, S. (2019, July 1). Challenging the stigma of "shock therapy." *Wall Street Journal*, p. A14.

Redford, M. A. (2017). Sound categories or phonemes? *British Journal of Psychology, 108*, 34-36.

Redick, T. S., Wiemers, E. A., & Engle, R. W. (2019). The role of proactive interference in working memory training and transfer. *Psychological Research*, 1-20.

Redshaw, M., & Martin, C. (2013). Babies, "bonding" and ideas about parental "attachment." *Journal of Reproductive and Infant Psychology, 31*, 219-221.

Reed, S. K. (2017). Problem solving. In S. F. Chipman, S. F. Chipman (Eds.), *The Oxford handbook of cognitive science*. Oxford University Press.

Rees, P., & Seaton, N. (2011). Psychologists' response to crises: International perspectives. *School Psychology International, 32*, 73-94.

Regnerus, M., Price, J., & Gordon, D. (2017). Masturbation and partnered sex: Substitutes or complements? *Archives of Sexual Behavior, 46*(7), 2111-2121.

Rehan, W., Antfolk, J., Johansson, A., & Santtila, P. (2019). Do single experiences of childhood abuse increase psychopathology symptoms in adulthood? *Journal of Interpersonal Violence, 34*(5), 1021-1038.

Reichenberg, A., & Harvey, P. D. (2007). Neuropsychological impairments in schizophrenia: Integration of performance-based and brain imaging findings. *Psychological Bulletin, 133*, 212-223.

Reichenberg, A., Harvey, P., Bowie, C., Mojtabai, R., Rabinowitz, J., Heaton, R., & Bromet, E. (2009). Neuropsychological function and dysfunction in schizophrenia and psychotic affective disorders. *Schizophrenia Bulletin, 35*, 1022-1029.

Reid, J. L., Martin, A., & Brooks-Gunn, J. (2017). Low-income parents' adult interactions at childcare centres. *Early Child Development and Care, 187*, 138-151.

Reid, J. R., MacLeod, J., & Robertson, J. R. (2010). Cannabis and the lung. *Journal of the Royal College of Physicians, 40*, 328-334.

Reilly, M. T., Noronha, A., Goldman, D., & Koob, G. F. (2017). Genetic studies of alcohol dependence in the context of the addiction cycle. *Neuropharmacology, 12*, 23-21.

Reinders, A. A., & Veltman, D. J. (2021). Dissociative identity disorder: Out of the shadows at last? *The British Journal of Psychiatry, 219*(2), 413-414.

Reiner, K. (2018). Least restrictive environments: Where segregated, self-contained special education classrooms fall on the continuum of placements and why mainstreaming should occur with same-age peers. *Michigan State Law Review, 3*, 743.

Reinisch, J. M., Mortensen, E. L., & Sanders, S. A. (2017). Prenatal exposure to progesterone affects sexual orientation in humans. *Archives of Sexual Behavior, 46*(5), 1239-1249.

Reinoso-Suárez, F., De Andrés, I., Rodrigo-Angulo, M. L., De la Roza, C., Nuñez, A., & Garzón, M. (2022). The anatomy of dreaming, and REM sleep. *European Journal of Anatomy, 3*(3), 163-175.

Reis, H., Regan, A., and Lyubomirsky, S. (2022). Interpersonal chemistry: What is it, how does it emerge, and how does it operate? *Perspectives on Psychological Science, 17*(2), 530-558.

Reisberg, D. (1997). *Cognition: Exploring the science of the mind.* Norton.

Reisberg, D. (2009). *Cognition: Exploring the science of the mind.* Norton.

Reisberg, D. (2013). Mental images. In D. Reisberg (Ed.), *The Oxford handbook of cognitive psychology.* Oxford University Press.

Reks, S., Sheaves, B., & Freeman, D. (2017, July 15.) Nightmares in the general population: Identifying potential causal factors. *Social Psychiatry and Psychiatric Epidemiology*. doi: 10.1007/s00127-017-1408-7.

Remington, G., Foussias, G., Fervaha, G., & Agid, O. (2014). Schizophrenia, cognition, and psychosis. *JAMA Psychiatry, 71*, 336-337.

Rendall, D. (2021). Aping language: Historical perspectives on the quest for semantics, syntax, and other rarefied properties of human language in the communication of primates and other animals. *Frontiers in Psychology*, 2888.

Renger, S., & Macaskill, A. (2021). Developing the foundations for a learning-based humanistic therapy. *Journal of Humanistic Psychology*, 00221678211007668.

Rentzou, K., Slutsky, R., Tuul, M., Gol-Guven, M., Kragh-Müller, G., Foerch, D. F., & Paz-Albo, J. (2019). Preschool teachers' conceptualizations and uses of play across eight countries. *Early Childhood Education Journal, 47*(1), 1-14.

Repp, B. H., & Knoblich, G. (2007). Action can affect auditory perception. *Psychological Science, 18*, 6-7.

Ressler, K., Berretta, S., Bolshakov, V. Y., Rosso, I. M., Meloni, E. G., Rauch, S. L., & Carlezon, W. A. (2022). Post-traumatic stress disorder: Clinical and translational neuroscience from cells to circuits. *Nature Reviews Neurology, 18*(5), 273-288.

Ressler, R. L., & Maren, S. (2019). Synaptic encoding of fear memories in the amygdala. *Current opinion in neurobiology, 54*, 54-59.

Retkoceri, U. (2022). Remembering emotions. *Biology & Philosophy, 37*(1), 1-26.

Reus-García, M. M., Sánchez-Campusano, R., Ledderose, J., Dogbevia, G. K., Treviño, M., Hasan, M. T., Gruart, M., & Delgado-García, J. M. (2021). The claustrum is involved in cognitive processes related to the classical conditioning of eyelid responses in behaving rabbits. *Cerebral Cortex, 31*(1), 281-300.

Reyna, V. F., Mills, B., Estrada, S., & Brainerd, C. J. (2017). False memory in children: Data, theory, and legal implications. In *Handbook of eyewitness psychology* (pp. 479-508). Psychology Press.

Reynolds, C. R., Altmann, R. A., & Allen, D. N. (2021). The problem of bias in psychological assessment. In *Mastering Modern Psychological Testing*. Springer. https://doi.org/10.1007/978-3-030-59455-8_15

Reynolds, C. R., & Ramsay, M. C. (2003). Bias in psychological assessment: An empirical review and recommendations. In J. R. Graham & J. A. Naglieri (Eds.), *Handbook of psychology: Assessment psychology* (Vol. 10). Wiley.

Rezai-Rashti, G. M., & Lingard, B. (2021). Test-based accountability, standardized testing and minority/racialized students' perspectives in urban schools in Canada and Australia. *Discourse: Studies in the Cultural Politics of Education, 42*(5), 716-731.

Reznikova, T. N., Seliverstova, N. A., Kataeva, G. V., Aroev, R. A., Ilves, A. G., & Kuznetsova, A. K. (2015). Functional activity of brain structures and predisposition to aggression in patients with lingering diseases of the CNS. *Human Physiology, 41*, 27-33.

Rhoads, T. W., & Anderson, R. M. (2021). Taking the long view on metabolism. *Science, 373*(6556), 738-739.

Rhue, L. (2019, January 3). Emotion-reading tech fails the racial bias test. *The Conversation*.

Rice, S. M., Kealy, D., Ogrodniczuk, J. S., Seidler, Z. E., Denehy, L., & Oliffe, J. L. (2020). The cost of bottling it up: Emotion suppression as a mediator in the relationship between anger and depression among men with prostate cancer. *Cancer Management and Research, 12*, 1039.

Richardson, D., & Hammock, G. S. (2011). Is it aggression? Perceptions of and motivations for passive and psychological aggression. In J. P. Forgas, A. W. Kruglanski, & K. D. Williams (Eds.), *The psychology of social conflict and aggression.* Psychology Press.

Richmond, A. S., Broussard, K. A., Sterns, J. L., Sanders, K. K., & Shardy, J. C. (2015). Who are we studying? Sample diversity in teaching of psychology research. *Teaching of Psychology, 42*, 218-226.

Richtel, M. (2022, April 24). "It's life or death": U.S. teenagers face a mental health crisis. *The New York Times*, p. A1.

Ricker, T. J., Sandry, J., Vergauwe, E., & Cowan, N. (2020). Do familiar memory items decay? *Journal of Experimental Psychology: Learning, Memory, and Cognition, 46*(1), 60-76. https://doi.org/10.1037/xlm0000719

Ridley, M., Rao, G., Schilbach, F., & Patel, V. (2020). Poverty, depression, and anxiety: Causal evidence and mechanisms. *Science, 370*(6522), 1289.

Riener, C. (2019). New approaches and debates on top-down perceptual processing. *Teaching of Psychology, 46*(3), 267-272.

Rigutto, C., Sapara, A. O., & Agyapong, V. I. (2021). Anxiety, depression and posttraumatic stress disorder after terrorist attacks: a general review of the literature. *Behavioral Sciences, 11*(10), 140.

Rimmele, J. M., Sussman, E., & Poeppel, D. (2015). The role of temporal structure in the investigation of sensory memory, auditory scene analysis, and speech perception: A healthy-aging perspective. *International Journal of Psychophysiology, 95*, 175-183.

Rinaman, L., Banihashemi, L., & Koehnle, T. J. (2011). Early life experience shapes the functional organization of stress-responsive visceral circuits. *Physiology & Behavior, 104*, 632-640.

Rindone, H. G. (2015). Methamphetamine addiction. In R. L. Smith (Ed.), *Treatment strategies for substance and process addictions*. Alexandria, VA: American Counseling Association.

Rinn, W. E. (1991). Neuropsychology of facial expression. In R. S. Feldman & B. Rimé (Eds.), *Fundamentals of non-verbal behavior*. Cambridge University Press.

Risen, J. (2015, August 8). Association bars psychologists from ties to U.S. national security interrogations. *The New York Times*, A11.

Ritchie, H, & Roser, M. (2018, April). Mental health. Our World in Data. https://ourworldindata.org/mental-health

Ritchie, H., & Roser, M. (2021, August). Mental health. Our World in Data. https://ourworldindata.org/mental-health

Rizzelli, L., Kassin, S. M., & Gales, T. (2021). The language of criminal confessions: A corpus analysis of confessions presumed true vs. proven false. *Wrongful Conviction Law Review, 2*, 205.

Rizzi, T. S., & Posthuma, D. (2013). Genes and intelligence. In D. Reisberg (Ed.), *The Oxford handbook of cognitive psychology*. Oxford University Press.

Robbins, M. L., Wright, R. C., Maria López, A., & Weihs, K. (2019). Interpersonal positive reframing in the daily lives of couples coping with breast cancer. *Journal of Psychosocial Oncology, 37*(2), 160-177.

Robbins, T. W., Vaghi, M. M., & Banca, P. (2019). Obsessive-compulsive disorder: Puzzles and prospects. *Neuron, 102*(1), 27-47.

Robbins, W. J. (1929). *Growth*. Yale University Press.

Roberts, R. L., Rhodes, J. R., & Elkins, G. R. (2021). Effect of hypnosis on anxiety: Results from a randomized controlled trial with women in postmenopause. *Journal of Clinical Psychology in Medical Settings, 28*(4), 868-881.

Roberts, R. M., Neate, G. M., & Gierasch, A. (2017). Implicit attitudes towards people with visible difference: Findings from an Implicit Association Test. *Psychology, Health & Medicine, 22*, 352-358.

Robinson, D. N. (2007). Theoretical psychology: What is it and who needs it? *Theory & Psychology, 17*, 187-198.

Robinson, T. N., Banda, J. A., Hale, L., Lu, A. S., Fleming-Milici, F., Calvert, S. L., & Wartella, E. (2017). Screen media exposure and obesity in children and adolescents. *Pediatrics, 140* (Supplement 2), S97-S101.

Rocco, I., Corso, B., Bonati, M., & Minicuci, N. (2021). Time of onset and/or diagnosis of ADHD in European children: A systematic review. *BMC Psychiatry, 21*(1), 1-24.

Röder, B., Kekunnaya, R., & Guerreiro, M. J. (2021). Neural mechanisms of visual sensitive periods in humans. *Neuroscience & Biobehavioral Reviews, 120*, 86-99.

Rodrigues, H., Valentin, D., Franco-Luesma, E., Rakotosamimanana, V. R., Gomez-Corona, C., Saldaña, E., & Sáenz-Navajas, M. P. (2022). How has COVID-19, lockdown and social distancing changed alcohol drinking patterns? A cross-cultural perspective between britons and spaniards. *Food Quality and Preference, 95*, 104344.

Rodrigues, L., & Girandola, F. (2017). Self-prophecies and cognitive dissonance: Habit, norms and justification of past behavior. *North American Journal of Psychology, 19*, 65-86.

Rodrigues-Amorim, D., Rivera-Baltanás, T., López, M., Spuch, C., Olivares, J. M., & Agís-Balboa, R. C. (2017). Schizophrenia: A review of potential biomarkers. *Journal of Psychiatric Research, 93*, 37-49.

Roe, D. G., Kim, S., Choi, Y. Y., Woo, H., Kang, M. S., Song, Y. J., Ahn, J-H., Lee, Y., & Cho, J. H. (2021). Biologically plausible artificial synaptic array: Replicating Ebbinghaus' memory curve with selective attention. *Advanced Materials, 33*(14), 2007782.

Roels, R., & Janssen, E. (2020). Sexual and relationship satisfaction in young, heterosexual couples: The role of sexual frequency and sexual communication. *The Journal of Sexual Medicine, 17*(9), 1643-1652.

Roen, K. (2019). Intersex or diverse sex development: Critical review of psychosocial health care research and indications for practice. *Journal of Sex Research, 56*(4-5), 511-528.

Roesler, C., & Ulyet, A. (2021). *C. G. Jung's archetype concept: Theory, research and applications*. Routledge.

Roesler, R., Parent, M. B., LaLumiere, R. T., & McIntyre, C. K. (2021). Amygdala-hippocampal interactions in synaptic plasticity and memory formation. *Neurobiology of Learning and Memory, 184*, 107490.

Rogers, B., & Naumenko, O. (2015). The new moon illusion and the role of perspective in the perception of straight and parallel lines. *Attention, Perception, & Psychophysics, 77*, 249-257.

Rogers, C. R. (1971). A theory of personality. In S. Maddi (Ed.), *Perspectives on personality*. Little, Brown.

Rogers, C. R. (1995). *A way of being*. Houghton Mifflin.

Rogers, J. M. (2009). Tobacco and pregnancy: Overview of exposures and effects. *Birth Defects Research Part C: Embryo Today, 84*, 152-160.

Rogers, S. (2007). The underlying mechanisms of semantic memory loss in Alzheimer's disease and semantic dementia. *Dissertation Abstracts International: Section B: The Sciences and Engineering, 67*(10-B), 5591.

Rogoff, B., Coppens, A. D., Alcalá, L., Aceves-Azuara, I., Ruvalcaba, O., López, A., & Dayton, A. (2017). Noticing learners' strengths through cultural research. *Perspectives on Psychological Science, 12*(5), 876-888.

Rohan, K. J., Meyerhoff, J., Ho, S.-Y., Roecklein, K. A., Nillni, Y. I., Hillhouse, J. J., et al. (2019). A measure of cognitions specific to seasonal depression: Development and validation of the Seasonal Beliefs Questionnaire. *Psychological Assessment, 31*(7), 925-938.

Roid, G., Nellis, L., & McLellan, M. (2003). Assessment with the Leiter International Performance Scale–Revised and the S-BIT. In R. S. McCallum & R. Steve (Eds.), *Handbook of nonverbal assessment*. Kluwer Academic/Plenum Publishers.

Rolles-Abraham, K. L. (2020, April 27). How my patients and I struggle with remote mental health treatment during circuit breaker. *Today*. https://www.todayonline.com/commentary/how-patients-and-i-struggle-remote-mental-health-treatment-covid-19-circuit-breaker

Rolls, E. T. (2011). Functions of human emotional memory: The brain and emotion. In S. Nalbantian, P. M. Matthews, & J. L. McClelland (Eds.), *The memory process: Neuroscientific and humanistic perspectives*. MIT Press.

Romani, C., Palermo, L., MacDonald, A., Limback, E., Hall, S. K., & Geberhiwot, T. (2017). The impact of phenylalanine levels on cognitive outcomes in adults with phenylketonuria: Effects across tasks and developmental stages. *Neuropsychology, 31*, 242-254.

Romer, D., & Jamieson, K. H. (2020). Conspiracy theories as barriers to controlling the spread of COVID-19 in the US. *Social Science & Medicine, 263*, 113356.

Romero-Guevara, R., Cencetti, F., Donati, C., & Bruni, P. (2015). Sphingosine 1-phosphate signaling pathway in inner ear biology. New therapeutic strategies for hearing loss? *Frontiers In Aging Neuroscience, 7*, 101-111.

Romero-Lebrón, E., Oviedo, D. M. A., Elias, D., Vrech, D. E., & Peretti, A. V. (2019). Effect of the mating plug on female chemical attractiveness and mating acceptance in a scorpion. *Ethology, 125*(4), 184-194.

Roncero, C., Daigre, C., Gonzalvo, B., Valero, S., Castells, X., Grau-López, L., et al. (2013). Risk factors for cocaine-induced psychosis in cocaine-dependent patients. *European Psychiatry, 28*, 141-146.

Ronconi, L., Casartelli, L., Carna, S., Molteni, M., Arrigoni, F., & Borgatti, R. (2017). When one is enough: Impaired multisensory integration in cerebellar agenesis. *Cerebral Cortex, 27*, 2041-2051

Roos, V., & Zaaiman, R. (2017). Active ageing as positive intervention: Some unintended consequences. In C. Proctor (Ed.), *Positive psychology interventions in practice*. Springer International Publishing.

Roostaei, N., & Hamidi, S. M. (2022). Two-dimensional biocompatible plasmonic contact lenses for color blindness correction. *Scientific Reports, 12*(1), 1-8.

Rorschach, H. (1924). *Psychodiagnosis: A diagnostic test based on perception*. Grune & Stratton.

Rosellini, A. J., Stein, M. B., Colpe, L. J., Heeringa, S. G., Petukhova, M. V., Sampson, N. A., Schoenbaum, M., Ursano, R. J., & Kessler, R. C. (2015). Approximating a DSM-5 diagnosis of PTSD using DSM-IV criteria. *Depression and Anxiety, 32*, 493-501.

Rosenberg, E. L., & Ekman, P. (Eds.). (2020). *What the face reveals: Basic and applied studies of spontaneous expression using the Facial Action Coding System (FACS)* (3rd ed.). Oxford University Press.

Rosenfeld, D. L., Balcetis, E., Bastian, B., Berkman, E. T., Bosson, J. K., Brannon, T. N., Burrow, A. L., Cameron, C. D., Chen, S., Cook, J. E., Crandall, C., Davidai, S., Dhont, K., Eastwick, P. W., Gaither, S. E., Gangestad, S. W., Gilovich, T., Gray, K., Haines, E. L., Haselton, M. G., et al. (2022). Psychological science in the wake of COVID-19: Social, methodological, and metascientific considerations. *Perspectives on Psychological Science, 17*(2), 311-333.

Rosenfeld, M. J., & Thomas, R. J. (2012). Searching for a mate: The rise of the Internet as a social intermediary. *American Sociological Review, 77*, 523-547.

Rosenfeld, M. J., Thomas, R. J., & Hausen, S. (2019). Disintermediating your friends: How online dating in the United States displaces other ways of meeting. *Proceedings of the National Academy of Sciences, 116*(36), 17753-17758.

Rosen, L. J., Galili, T., Kott, J., & Rees, V. (2021). Beyond "safe and effective": The urgent need for high-impact smoking cessation medications. *Preventive Medicine, 150*, 106567.

Rosen, M. G. (2021). I could do that in my sleep: skilled performance in dreams. *Synthese, 199*, 6495-6522.

Rosenhan, D. L. (1973). On being sane in insane places. *Science, 179*, 250-258.

Rosenström, T., Ystrom, E., Torvik, F. A., Czajkowski, N. O., Gillespie, N. A., Aggen, S. H., Krueger, R. F., Kendler, K. S., & Reichborn-Kjennerud, T. (2017). Genetic and environmental structure of DSM-IV criteria for antisocial personality disorder: A twin study. *Behavior Genetics, 47*, 265-277.

Rosenthal, N. F. (2003). *The emotional revolution: How the new science of feeling can transform your life*. Citadel.

Rosenthal-von der Pütten, A. M., Hastall, M. R., Köcher, S., Meske, C., Heinrich, T., Labrenz, F., & Ocklenburg, S. (2019). "Likes" as social rewards: Their role in online social comparison and decisions to like other people's selfies. *Computers in Human Behavior, 92*, 76-86.

Rossato, M., Pagano, C., & Vettor, R. (2008). The cannabinoid system and male reproductive functions. *Journal of Neuroendocrinology, 20*, 90-93.

Ross, C. A. (2015). When to suspect and how to diagnose dissociative identity disorder. *Journal of EMDR Practice and Research, 9*, 114-120.

Ross, E. D., Gupta, S. S., Adnan, A. M., Holden, T. L., Havlicek, J., & Radhakrishnan, S. (2019). Neurophysiology of spontaneous facial expressions: II. Motor control of the right and left face is partially independent in adults. *Cortex: A Journal Devoted to the Study of the Nervous System and Behavior, 111*, 164-182.

Ross, J. (2006). Sleep on a problem . . . It works like a dream. *The Psychologist, 19*, 738-740.

Ross, L. A., Molholm, S., Blanco, D., Gomez-Ramirez, M., Saint-Amour, D., & Foxe, J. J. (2011). The development of multisensory speech perception continues into the late childhood years. *European Journal of Neuroscience, 33*, 2329-2337.

Rossi-Arnaud, C., Cestari, V., Marques, V. S., Gabrielli, G. B., & Spataro, P. (2017). Collaboration in implicit memory: Evidence from word-fragment completion and category exemplar generation. *Psychological Research, 81*, 55-65.

Rotan, L. W., & Ospina-Kammerer, V. (2007). *Mindbody medicine: Foundations and practical applications.* New York: Routledge/Taylor & Francis Group.

Rouder, J. N., Morey, R. D., & Province, J. M. (2013). A Bayes factor meta-analysis of recent extrasensory perception experiments: Comment on Storm, Tressoldi, and Di Risio (2010). *Psychological Bulletin, 139,* 241-247.

Roughton, R. E. (2002). Rethinking homosexuality: What it teaches us about psychoanalysis. *Journal of the American Psychoanalytic Association, 50,* 733-763.

Rousseaux, F., Dardenne, N., Massion, P. B., Ledoux, D., Bicego, A., Donneau, A. F., Faymonville, M-E., Nyssen, A-S., & Vanhaudenhuyse, A. (2022). Virtual reality and hypnosis for anxiety and pain management in intensive care units: A prospective randomised trial among cardiac surgery patients. *European Journal of Anaesthesiology, 39*(1), 58-66.

Rousseaux, F., Faymonville, M. E., Nyssen, A. S., Dardenne, N., Ledoux, D., Massion, P. B., & Vanhaudenhuyse, A. (2020). Can hypnosis and virtual reality reduce anxiety, pain and fatigue among patients who undergo cardiac surgery: A randomised controlled trial. *Trials, 21*(1), 1-9.

Routtenberg, A., & Lindy, J. (1965). Effects of the availability of rewarding septal and hypothalamic stimulation on bar pressing for food under conditions of deprivation. *Journal of Comparative and Physiological Psychology, 60,* 158-161.

Rozek, D. C., Baker, S. N., Rugo, K. F., Steigerwald, V. L., Sippel, L. M., Holliday, R., Roberge, E. M., Held, P., Mota, N., & Smith, N. B. (2022). Addressing co-occurring suicidal thoughts and behaviors and posttraumatic stress disorder in evidence-based psychotherapies for adults: A systematic review. *Journal of Traumatic Stress, 35*(2), 729-745.

Rubin, D. C. (1985, September). The subtle deceiver: Recalling our past. *Psychology Today,* pp. 39-46.

Rubin, D. C., Schrauf, R. W., Gulgoz, S., & Naka, M. (2007). Cross-cultural variability of component processes in autobiographical remembering: Japan, Turkey, and the USA. *Memory, 15,* 536-547.

Ruch, W., Heintz, S., Gander, F., Hofmann, J., Platt, T., & Proyer, R. T. (2021). The long and winding road: A comprehensive analysis of 50 years of Eysenck instruments for the assessment of personality. *Personality and Individual Differences, 169,* 110070.

Rudrauf, D., Bennequin, D., & Williford, K. (2020). The moon illusion explained by the projective consciousness model. *Journal of Theoretical Biology, 507,* 110455.

Ruiz, M. R. (2015). Behaviourisms: Radical behaviourism and critical inquiry. In I. Parker & I. Parker (Eds.), *Handbook of critical psychology.* New York: Routledge/Taylor & Francis Group.

Rumas, R., Shamblaw, A. L., Jagtap, S., & Best, M. W. (2021). Predictors and consequences of loneliness during the COVID-19 pandemic. *Psychiatry Research, 300,* 113934.

Rumjaun, A., & Narod, F. (2020). Social learning theory–Albert Bandura. In B. Akpan & T. J. Kennedy (Eds.), *Science education in theory and practice.* Springer Texts in Education.

Russell, B. S., Tomkunas, A. J., Hutchison, M., Tambling, R. R., & Horton, A. L. (2022). The protective role of parent resilience on mental health and the parent-child relationship during COVID-19. *Child Psychiatry & Human Development, 53*(1), 183-196.

Russo, N. (1981). Women in psychology. In L. T. Benjamin, Jr. & K. D. Lowman (Eds.), *Activities handbook for the teaching of psychology.* American Psychological Association.

Rutland, A., & Killen, M. (2015). A developmental science approach to reducing prejudice and social exclusion: Intergroup processes, social-cognitive development, and moral reasoning. *Social Issues and Policy Review, 9,* 121-154.

Ryan, R. M., & Deci, E. L. (2017). *Self-determination theory: Basic psychological needs in motivation, development, and wellness.* Guilford Press.

Ryan, T. J., & Frankland, P. W. (2022). Forgetting as a form of adaptive engram cell plasticity. *Nature Reviews Neuroscience,* 1-14.

Sa, M. (2015). Mood and personality disorders. In G. M. Kapalka (Ed.), *Treating disruptive disorders: A guide to psychological, pharmacological, and combined therapies.* Routledge/Taylor & Francis Group.

Sabbagh, M., Sadowsky, C., Tousi, B., Agronin, M. E., Alva, G., Armon, C., Bernick, C., Keegan, A. P., Karatzoulis, S., Baror, E., Ploznik, M., & Pascual-Leone, A. (2019). Effects of a combined transcranial magnetic stimulation (TMS) and cognitive training intervention in patients with Alzheimer's disease. *Alzheimer's & Dementia.* Advance online publication. https://doi.org/10.1016/j.jalz.2019.08.197

Sabe, M., Zhao, N., & Kaiser, S. (2021). A systematic review and meta-analysis of the prevalence of cocaine-induced psychosis in cocaine users. *Progress in Neuro-psychopharmacology & Biological Psychiatry, 109,* 110263.

Sabet, K. (2021). Lessons learned in several states eight years after states legalized marijuana. *Current Opinion in Psychology, 38,* 25-30.

Sachs-Ericsson, N., Joiner, T., Plant, E. A., & Blazer, D. G. (2005). The influence of depression on cognitive decline in community-dwelling elderly persons. *American Journal of Geriatric Psychiatry,13,* 402-408.

Sachse, P., Beermann, U., Martini, M., Maran, T., Domeier, M., & Furtner, M. R. (2017). "The world is upside down"–The Innsbruck goggle experiments of Theodor Erismann (1883-1961) and Ivo Kohler (1915-1985). *Cortex: A Journal Devoted to the Study of the Nervous System and Behavior, 92,* 222-232.

Sachser, R. M., Haubrich, J., Lunardi, P. S., & de Oliveira Alvares, L. (2017). Forgetting of what was once learned: Exploring the role of postsynaptic ionotropic glutamate receptors on memory formation, maintenance, and decay. *Neuropharmacology, 112*(Part A), 94-103.

Sadeghi, B., Mashalchi, H., Eghbali, S., Jamshidi, M., Golmohammadi, M., & Mahvar, T. (2020). The relationship between hostility and anger with coronary heart disease in patients. *Journal of Education and Health Promotion, 9.*

Sadeh, N., Bounoua, N., & Javdani, S. (2019). Psychopathic traits, pubertal timing, and mental health functioning in justice-involved adolescents. *Personality and Individual Differences, 145,* 52-57.

Sadowsky, J. (2021). Before and after Prozac: Psychiatry as medicine, and the historiography of depression. *Culture, Medicine, and Psychiatry, 45*(3), 479-502.

Sagiv, L., & Schwartz, S. H. (2022). Personal values across cultures. *Annual Review of Psychology, 73,* 517-546.

Sahakian, B. J., & Gottwald, J. (2017). *Sex, lies, & brain scans: How fMRI reveals what really goes on in our minds.* Oxford University Press.

Sakr, R., Ghsoub, C., Rbeiz, C., Lattouf, V., Riachy, R., Haddad, C., & Zoghbi, M. (2022). COVID-19 detection by dogs: from physiology to field application–a review article. *Postgraduate Medical Journal, 98*(1157), 212-218.

Salles, A., Bohn, K. M., & Moss, C. F. (2019). Auditory communication processing in bats: What we know and where to go. *Behavioral Neuroscience, 133*(3), 305-319.

Samoilov, V., & Zayas, V. (2007). Ivan Petrovich Pavlov (1849-1936). *Journal of the History of the Neurosciences, 16,* 74-89.

Samuel, D. B., Carroll, K. M., Rounsaville, B. J., & Ball, S. A. (2013). Personality disorders as maladaptive, extreme variants of normal personality: Borderline personality disorder and neuroticism in a substance using sample. *Journal of Personality Disorders, 27,* 625-635.

Sanchez-Roige, S., Gray, J. C., MacKillop, J., Chen, C. H., & Palmer, A. A. (2018). The genetics of human personality. *Genes, Brain and Behavior, 17*(3), e12439.

Sanders, A. R., Beecham, G. W., Guo, S., Badner, J. A., Bocklandt, S., Mustanski, B. S., Hamer, D. H., & Martin, E. R. (2021). Genome-wide linkage study meta-analysis of male sexual orientation. *Archives of Sexual Behavior, 50*(8), 3371-3375.

Sandford, S. (2017). Freud, Bion and Kant: Epistemology and anthropology in The Interpretation of Dreams. *International Journal of Psychoanalysis, 98,* 91-110.

Sandman, C. A. (2015). Mysteries of the human fetus revealed. *Monographs of the Society for Research in Child Development, 80,* 124-137.

Sandstrom, G. M., & Dunn, E. W. (2014a). Is efficiency overrated? Minimal social interactions lead to belonging and positive affect. *Social Psychological and Personality Science, 5*(4), 437-442.

Sanes, J. R., & Masland, R. H. (2015). The types of retinal ganglion cells: Current status and implications for neuronal classification. *Annual Review of Neuroscience, 38,* 221-246.

Santomauro, D. F., Herrera, A. M. M., Shadid, J., Zheng, P., Ashbaugh, C., Pigott, D. M., Abbafati, C., Adolph, C., Amlag, J. O., Aravkin, A. Y., Bang-Jensen, B. L., Bertolacci, G. J., Bloom, S. S., Castellano, R., Castro, E., Chankrabarti, S., Chattopadhyay, J., Cogen, R. M., Collins, J. K., Dai, X., Dangel, W. J., et al. (2021). Global prevalence and burden of depressive and anxiety disorders in 204 countries and territories in 2020 due to the COVID-19 pandemic. *The Lancet, 398*(10312), 1700-1712.

Santos, B. G., Carey, R. J., & Carrera, M. P. (2017). The acquisition, extinction and spontaneous recovery of Pavlovian drug conditioning induced by post-trial dopaminergic stimulation/inhibition. *Pharmacology, Biochemistry and Behavior, 156,* 24-29.

Santos, T. (2021). Positive youth development in adolescence. *Journal of Mother and Child, 25*(3), 137-138.

Saper, C. B. (2013). The neurobiology of sleep. *CONTINUUM: Lifelong Learning In Neurology, 19,* 19-31.

Saracho, O. N. (2019). Motivation theories, theorists, and theoretical conceptions. *Contemporary Perspectives on Research in Motivation in Early Childhood Education, 21.*

Sarason, I. G. (2019). Cognitive processes, anxiety and the treatment of anxiety disorders. In *Anxiety and the anxiety disorders.* Routledge.

Sarsour, K., Sheridan, M., Jutte, D., Nuru-Jeter, A., Hinshaw, S., & Boyce, W. (2011). Family socioeconomic status and child executive functions: The roles of language, home environment, and single parenthood. *Journal of the International Neuropsychological Society, 17,* 120-132.

Sarubin, N., Hilbert, S., Naumann, F., Zill, P., Wimmer, A., Nothdurfter, C., Rupprecht, R., Baghai, T. C., Bühner, M., & Schüle, C. (2017). The sex-dependent role of the glucocorticoid receptor in depression: Variations in the NR3C1 gene are associated with major depressive disorder in women but not in men. *European Archives of Psychiatry and Clinical Neuroscience, 267,* 123-133.

Sasayama, D., Washizuka, S., & Honda, H. (2016). Effective treatment of night terrors and sleepwalking with ramelteon. *Journal of Child and Adolescent Psychopharmacology, 26*(10), 948.

Saucier, G., & Srivastava, S. (2015). What makes a good structural model of personality? Evaluating the Big Five and alternatives. In M. Mikulincer, P. R. Shaver, M. L. Cooper, & R. J. Larsen (Eds.), *APA handbook of personality and social psychology, Volume 4: Personality processes and individual differences.* American Psychological Association.

Sauer, J. D., Palmer, M. A., & Brewer, N. (2019). Pitfalls in using eyewitness confidence to diagnose the accuracy of an individual identification decision. *Psychology, Public Policy, and Law, 25*(3), 147.

Saul, J., Rodgers, R. F., & Saul, M. (2022). Adolescent eating disorder risk and the social online world: An update. *Child and Adolescent Psychiatric Clinics, 31*(1), 167-177.

Saulino, P. A., Greenwald, B. D., & Gordon, D. J. (2021). The changing landscape of the use of medical marijuana after traumatic brain injury: a narrative review. *Brain injury, 35*(12-13), 1510-1520.

Saunders, B. T., Yager, L. M., & Robinson, T. E. (2013). Preclinical studies shed light on individual variation in addiction vulnerability. *Neuropsychopharmacology, 38,* 249-250.

Sauter, S. L., & Hurrell, J. J. (2017). Occupational health contributions to the development and promise of occupational health psychology. *Journal of Occupational Health Psychology, 22,* 251-258.

Saywitz, K. J., Wells, C. R., Larson, R. P., & Hobbs, S. D. (2019). Effects of interviewer support on children's memory and suggestibility: Systematic review and meta-analyses of experimental research. *Trauma, Violence, & Abuse, 20*(1), 22-39.

Scalzo, S., Bowden, S., & Hillbom, M. (2015). Wernicke-Korsakoff syndrome. In J. Svanberg, A. Withall, B. Draper, & S. Bowden (Eds.), *Alcohol and the adult brain.* Psychology Press.

Scarborough, J. (2019). Understanding gendered realities: Mothers and father roles in family based therapy for adolescent eating disorders. *Clinical Social Work Journal,* 1-13.

Scarella, T. M., Boland, R. J., & Barsky, A. J. (2019). Illness anxiety disorder: Psychopathology, epidemiology, clinical cbnharacteristics, and treatment. *Psychosomatic Medicine, 81*(5), 398-407.

Scarpelli, S., Alfonsi, V., Mangiaruga, A., Musetti, A., Quattropani, M. C., Lenzo, V., . . . & Franceschini, C. (2021). Pandemic nightmares: Effects on dream activity of the COVID-19 lockdown in Italy. *Journal of sleep research,* e13300.

Scelfo, J. (2015, February 8). They. *The New York Times,* p. ED18.

Schachter, R. (2011). Using the group in cognitive group therapy. *Group, 35,* 135-149.

Schachter, S., & Singer, J. E. (1962). Cognitive, social, and physiological determinants of emotional state. *Psychological Review, 69,* 379-399.

Schachter, S., & Singer, J. E. (2001). Cognitive, social, and psychological determinants of emotional state. In W. G. Parrott, (Ed.), *Emotions in social psychology: Essential readings.* Psychology Press.

Schaefer, E. G., Halldorson, M. K., & Dizon-Reynante, C. (2011). TV or not TV? Does the immediacy of viewing images of a momentous news event affect the quality and stability of flashbulb memories? *Memory, 19,* 251-266.

Schäfer, L., Mehler, L., Hähner, A., Walliczek, U., Hummel, T., & Croy, I. (2019). Sexual desire after olfactory loss: Quantitative and qualitative reports of patients with smell disorders. *Physiology & Behavior, 201,* 64-69.

Schaie, K. W. (2005a). Longitudinal studies. In *Developmental influences on adult intelligence: The Seattle Longitudinal Study.* Oxford University Press.

Schaie, K. W. (2005b). What can we learn from longitudinal studies of adult development? *Research in Human Development, 2,* 133-158.

Schalock, R. L., Luckasson, R. & Tassé, M. J. (2021). *Intellectual disability: Definition, diagnosis, classification, and systems of supports* (12th Ed.). American Association on Intellectual and Developmental Disabilities.

Scharrer, E., & Ramasubramanian, S. (2015). Intervening in the media's influence on stereotypes of race and ethnicity: The role of media literacy education. *Journal of Social Issues, 71,* 171-185.

Schechter, E., & Bayne, T. (2021). Consciousness after split-brain surgery: The next challenge to the classical picture. *Neuropsychologia, 160,* 107987.

Scheier, M. F., Carver, C. S., & Bridges, M. W. (1994). Distinguishing optimism from neuroticism (and trait anxiety, self-mastery, and self-esteem): A reevaluation of the Life Orientation Test. *Journal of Personality and Social Psychology, 67,* 1063-1078.

Schermer, J. A., Krammer, G., Goffin, R. D., & Biderman, M. D. (2020). Using the 16PF to test the differentiation of personality by intelligence hypothesis. *Journal of Intelligence, 8*(1), 12.

Schickedanz, J. A., Schickedanz, D. I., Forsyth, P. D., & Forsyth, G. A. (2001). *Understanding children and adolescents* (4th ed.). Pearson Education.

Schier, L. A., Hyde, K. M., & Spector, A. C. (2019). Conditioned taste aversion versus avoidance: A re-examination of the separate processes hypothesis. *PloS one, 14*(6), e0217458.

Schiff, R., & Vakil, E. (2015). Age differences in cognitive skill learning, retention and transfer: The case of the Tower of Hanoi puzzle. *Learning and Individual Differences, 39,* 164-171.

Schilling, O. K., & Diehl, M. (2015). Psychological vulnerability to daily stressors in old age: Results of short-term longitudinal studies. *Zeitschrift Für Gerontologie Und Geriatrie, 48,* 517-523.

Schimmack, U. (2021). The Implicit Association Test: A method in search of a construct. *Perspectives on Psychological Science, 16*(2), 396-414.

Schirmer, L., Schafer, D. P., Bartels, T., Rowitch, D. H., & Calabresi, P. A. (2021). Diversity and function of glial cell types in multiple sclerosis. *Trends in Immunology, 42*(3), 228-247.

Schlichting, M. L., & Frankland, P. W. (2017). Memory allocation and integration in rodents and humans. *Current Opinion in Behavioral Sciences, 17,* 90-98.

Schlinger, H. R. (2011). Skinner as missionary and prophet: A review of Burrhus F. Skinner: Shaper of behaviour. *Journal of Applied BehaviorAnalysis, 44,* 217-225.

Schmidt, I. D., Pfeifer, B. J., & Strunk, D. R. (2019). Putting the "cognitive" back in cognitive therapy: Sustained cognitive change as a mediator of in-session insights and depressive symptom improvement. *Journal of Consulting and Clinical Psychology, 87*(5), 446.

Schmidt, J., Klusmann, U., Lüdtke, O., Möller, J., & Kunter, M. (2017). What makes good and bad days for beginning teachers? A diary study on daily uplifts and hassles. *Contemporary Educational Psychology, 48,* 85-97.

Schmied, A., Soda, T., Gerig, G., Styner, M., Swanson, M. R., Elison, J. T., Shen, M. D., McKinstry, R. C., Pruett Jr., J. R., Botteron, K. N., Estes, A. M., Dager, S. R., Hazlett, H. C., Schultz, R. T., Piven, J., Wolff, J. J., & IBIS Network. (2020). Sex differences associated with corpus callosum development in human infants: A longitudinal multimodal imaging study. *NeuroImage, 215,* 116821.

Schneider, D. W., & Logan, G. D. (2015). Chunking away task-switch costs: A test of the chunk-point hypothesis. *Psychonomic Bulletin & Review, 22*(3), 884-889.

Schneiderman, N., McIntosh, R. C., & Antoni, M. H. (2019). Psychosocial risk and management of physical diseases. *Journal of Behavioral Medicine, 42*(1), 16-33.

Schnell, K., & Herpertz, S. C. (2007). Effects of dialectic-behavioral-therapy on the neural correlates of affective hyperarousal in borderline personality disorder. *Journal of Psychiatric Research, 41,* 837-847.

Schoch, S. F., Cordi, M. J., Schredl, M., & Rasch, B. (2019). The effect of dream report collection and dream incorporation on memory consolidation during sleep. *Journal of Sleep Research, 28*(1), 1-8.

Schoeller, F., Bertrand, P., Gerry, L. J., Jain, A., Horowitz, A. H., & Zenasni, F. (2019). Combining virtual reality and biofeedback to foster empathic abilities in humans. *Frontiers in Psychology, 9.*

Schönenberg, A., Mühlhammer, H. M., Lehmann, T., & Prell, T. (2022). Adherence to medication in neuro-geriatric patients: Insights from the NeuroGerAd Study. *Journal of Clinical Medicine, 11*(18), 5353.

Schoenfeld, T. J., & Swanson, C. (2021). A Runner's high for new neurons? Potential role for endorphins in exercise effects on adult neurogenesis. *Biomolecules, 11*(8), 1077.

Schooler, L. J., & Hertwig, R. (2012). How forgetting aids heuristic inference. In G. Gigerenzer, R. Hertwig, & T. Pachur (Eds.), *Heuristics: The foundations of adaptive behavior.* Oxford University Press.

Schredl, M., & Bulkeley, K. (2020). Dreaming and the COVID-19 pandemic: A survey in a US sample. *Dreaming, 30*(3), 189.

Schultheiss, O. C., & Schiepe-Tiska, A. (2013). The role of the dorsoanterior striatum in implicit motivation: The case of the need for power. *Frontiers in Human Neuroscience, 7,* 141.

Schumm, W., & Crawford, D. (2019). Scientific consensus on whether LGBTQ parents are more likely (or not) to have LGBTQ children: An analysis of 72 social science reviews of the literature published between 2001 and 2017. *Journal of International Women's Studies, 20*(7), 1-12.

Schurger, A., Sarigiannidis, I., Naccache, L., Sitt, J. D., & Dehaene, S. (2015). Cortical activity is more stable when sensory stimuli are consciously perceived. *PNAS Proceedings of the National Academy of Sciences of the United States of America, 112,* E2083-E2092.

Schwartz, S. J., Meca, A., Ward, C., Szabó, Á., Benet-Martínez, V., Lorenzo-Blanco, E. I., Sznitman, G. A., Cobb, C. L., Szapocznik, J., Unger, J. B., Cano, M. A., Stuart, J., & Zamboanga, B. (2019). Biculturalism dynamics: A daily diary study of bicultural identity and psychosocial functioning. *Journal of Applied Developmental Psychology, 62,* 26-37. https://doi-org.silk.library.umass.edu/10.1016/j.appdev.2018.12.007

Schwarz, S. (2018). Resilience in psychology: A critical analysis of the concept. *Theory & Psychology, 28*(4), 528-541.

Schwarzer, R., & Luszczynska, A. (2013). Stressful life events. In A. M. Nezu, C. Nezu, P. A. Geller, & I. B. Weiner (Eds.), *Handbook of psychology, Vol. 9: Health psychology* (2nd ed.). John Wiley & Sons.

Schwemmer, C., Knight, C., Bello-Pardo, E. D., Oklobdzija, S., Schoonvelde, M., & Lockhart, J. W. (2020). Diagnosing gender bias in image recognition systems. *Socius, 6,* 2378023120967171.

Sciutto, M., & Eisenberg, M. (2007). Evaluating the evidence for and against the overdiagnosis of ADHD. *Journal of Attention Disorders, 11,* 106-113.

Scott, E. S., Ross, D. A., & Fenstermacher, E. (2021). Stand by or stand up: Exploring the biology of the bystander effect. *Biological Psychiatry, 90*(2), e3-e5.

Scott, K. M., de Jonge, P., Stein, D. J., & Kessler, R. C. (Eds.). (2018). *Mental disorders around the world: Facts and figures from the WHO World Mental Health Surveys.* Cambridge University Press.

Scuotto, C., Ilardi, C. R., Avallone, F., Maggi, G., Ilardi, A., Borrelli, G., Gamboz, N., La Marra, M., & Perrella, R. (2021). Objective knowledge mediates the relationship between the use of social media and COVID-19-related false memories. *Brain Sciences, 11*(11), 1489.

Seamon, J. G., Punjabi, P. V., & Busch, E. A. (2010). Memorising Milton's *Paradise Lost:* A study of a septuagenarian exceptional memoriser. *Memory, 18*(5), 498-503.

Searight, H. (2013). Deinstitutionalization of people with mental illness: A failed policy that could have succeeded. *PsycCRITIQUES, 58,* 88-94.

Searls, D. (2017). *The inkblots: Hermann Rorschach, his iconic test, and the power of seeing.* Crown Publishers/Random House.

Secerbegovic, A., Spahic, M., Hasanbasic, A., Mesic, V., Hadzic, H., & Mujcic, A. (2021, April). Wearable sensor for home-based biofeedback therapy for migraine. In *International Conference on Medical and Biological Engineering* (pp. 116-123). Springer.

Seeman, M. V. (2021). History of the dopamine hypothesis of antipsychotic action. *World Journal of Psychiatry, 11*(7), 355.

Segall, M. H., Campbell, D. T., & Herskovits, M. J. (1966). *The influence of culture on visual perception.* Bobbs-Merrill.

Segers, G. (2021, December 2). The Grimmest Milestone that America Ignored this Year. *The New Republic.* Downloaded from https://newrepublic.com/article/164884/opioid-crisis-2021-pandemic-health, January 3, 2022.

Segobin, S., & Pitel, A. L. (2021). The specificity of thalamic alterations in Korsakoff's syndrome: Implications for the study of amnesia. *Neuroscience & Biobehavioral Reviews, 130,* 292-300.

Sejunaite, K., Lanza, C., & Riepe, M. W. (2019). Everyday memory in healthy aging: Porous but not distorted. *Frontiers in Aging Neuroscience, 11.*

Seligman, M. (2018). *The hope circuit.* Hachette.

Seligman, M. E. P. (1995). The effectiveness of psychotherapy: The *Consumer Reports* study. *American Psychologist, 50,* 965-974.

Sell, C., Möller, H., & Taubner, S. (2017). Effectiveness of integrative imagery- and trance-based psychodynamic therapies: Guided imagery psychotherapy and hypnopsychotherapy. *Journal of Psychotherapy Integration.* http://psycnet.apa.org/record/2017-07863-001

Selsky, A. (1997, February 16). African males face circumcision rite. *Boston Globe*, p. C7.

Selye, H. (1993). History of the stress concept. In L. Goldberger & S. Breznitz (Eds.), *Handbook of stress: Theoretical and clinical aspects* (2nd ed.). Free Press.

Semin, G. R., & Garrido, M. V. (2013). A systemic approach to impression formation: From verbal to multimodal processes. In J. P. Forgas, K. Fiedler, & C. Sedikides (Eds.), *Social thinking and interpersonal behavior.* Psychology Press.

Semykina, A., & Linz, S. J. (2007). Gender differences in personality and earnings: Evidence from Russia. *Journal of Economic Psychology, 28,* 387-410.

Senden, M., Emmerling, T. C., Van Hoof, R., Frost, M. A., & Goebel, R. (2019). Reconstructing imagined letters from early visual cortex reveals tight topographic correspondence between visual mental imagery and perception. *Brain Structure and Function, 224*(3), 1167-1183.

Seo, E. H., Yang, H. J., Kim, S. G., Park, S. C., Lee, S. K., & Yoon, H. J. (2021). A Literature Review on the Efficacy and Related Neural Effects of Pharmacological and Psychosocial Treatments in Individuals With Internet Gaming Disorder. *Psychiatry Investigation, 18*(12), 1149.

Serretti, A. (2017). Genetics and pharmacogenetics of mood disorders. *Psychiatria Polska, 51,* 197-203.

Servick, K. (2014). New support for "gay gene." *Science, 346,* 900.

Sezgin, F., & Erdogan, O. (2015). Academic optimism, hope and zest for work as predictors of teacher self-efficacy and perceived success. *Kuram Ve Uygulamada Eğitim Bilimleri, 15,* 7-19.

Shafer, V. L., & Garrido-Nag, K. (2007). The neurodevelopmental bases of language. In E. Hoff & M. Shatz (Eds.), *Blackwell handbook of language development.* Blackwell Publishing.

Shah, A. S., Young, J., & Vieira, K. (2014). Long-term Suboxone treatment and its benefit on long-term remission for opiate dependence. *African Journal of Psychiatry, 17,* 1-4.

Shain, S. (2019, June 17). Making a decision doesn't have to be so hard. *The New York Times*, p. B7.

Shaked, A., & Clore, G. (2017). Breaking the world to make it whole again: Attribution in the construction of emotion. *Emotion Review, 9*(1), 27-35.

Shakya, H., & Christakis, N. (2017). Association of Facebook use with compromised well-being: A longitudinal study. *American Journal of Epidemiology, 185,* 203-211.

Shalom-Sperber, S., Chen, A., & Zaidel, A. (2022). Rapid cross-sensory adaptation of self-motion perception. *Cortex, 148,* 14-30.

Sham, J. (2022, February 1). Progressive Snapshot review. Downloaded from https://www.bankrate.com/insurance/car/progressive-snapshot/. April 12, 2022.

Shanahan, L., Copeland, W. E., Worthman, C. M., Erkanli, A., Angold, A., & Costello, E. (2013). Sex-differentiated changes in C-reactive protein from ages 9 to 21: The contributions of BMI and physical/sexual maturation. *Psychoneuroendocrinology, 38,* 2209-2217.

Shang, X., Kallmann, M., & Arif, A. S. (2019, March). Effects of virtual agent gender on user performance and preference in a VR training program. In K. Arai & R. Bhatia (Eds.), *Advances in information and communication.* Springer.

Shapira-Berman, O. (2019). That which was "not": Some thoughts regarding Oedipus's modern conflicts. *Psychoanalytic Review, 106*(3), 247-271.

Shariatgorji, M., Nilsson, A., Fridjonsdottir, E., Vallianatou, T., Källback, P., Katan, L., Sävmarker, J., Mantas, I., Zhang, X., Bezard, E., Svenningsson, P., Odel, L. R., & Andrén, P. E. (2019). Comprehensive mapping of neurotransmitter networks by MALDI-MS imaging. *Nature Methods, 16*(10), 1021-1028.

Sharifian, N., & Zahodne, L. B. (2019). Social media bytes: Daily associations between social media use and everyday memory failures across the adult life

span. *The Journals of Gerontology: Series B.* https://doi.org/10.1093/geronb/gbz005.

Sharp, C., & Wall, K. (2021). DSM-5 level of personality functioning: Refocusing personality disorder on what it means to be human. *Annual Review of Clinical Psychology, 17,* 313-337.

Shaw, P. M., Chandra, V., Escobar, G. A., Robbins, N., Rowe, V., & Macsata, R. (2018). Controversies and evidence for cardiovascular disease in the diverse Hispanic population. *Journal of Vascular Surgery, 67*(3), 960-969.

Sheahan, C. L., Pozzulo, J. D., Reed, J. E., & Pica, E. (2017). The role of familiarity with the defendant, type of descriptor discrepancy, and eyewitness age on mock jurors' perceptions of eyewitness testimony. *Journal of Police and Criminal Psychology.* Accessed from https://link.springer.com/article/10.1007/s11896-017-9232-2.

Shehab, A. S., Brent, D., & Maalouf, F. T. (2016). Neurocognitive changes in selective serotonin reuptake inhibitors—Treated adolescents with depression. *Journal of Child and Adolescent Psychopharmacology, 26,* 713-720.

Shehata-Dieler, W., Ehrmann-Mueller, D., Wermke, P., Voit, V., Cebulla, M., & Wermke, K. (2013). Pre-speech diagnosis in hearing-impaired infants: How auditory experience affects early vocal development. *Speech, Language and Hearing, 16,* 99-106.

Sheikh, H., Brezar, A., Dzwonek, A., Yau, L., & Calder, L. A. (2018). Patient understanding of discharge instructions in the emergency department: Do different patients need different approaches? *International Journal of Emergency Medicine, 11*(1), 5. https://doi.org/10.1186/s12245-018-0164-0

Sheldon, K. M., & Lucas, R. E., (Eds.). (2014). *Stability of happiness: Theories and evidence on whether happiness can change.* Elsevier Academic Press.

Shellenbarger, S. (2013, April 3). Tactics to spark creativity. *Wall Street Journal*, pp. D1-D2.

Shellenbarger, S. (2019, January 24). The secret benefits of forgetting. *Wall Street Journal*, p. A12.

Shepard, R. N., & Metzler, J. (1971). Mental rotation of three-dimensional objects. *Science, 171*(3972), 701-703.

Sheydaei, I. (2021). Gender identity and nonbinary pronoun use: Exploring reference strategies for referents of unknown gender. *Gender & Language, 15*(3), 369-393.

Shibata, K., Sasaki, Y., Bang, J. W., Walsh, E. G., Machizawa, M. G., Tamaki, M., Chang, L-H., & Watanabe, T. (2017). Overlearning hyperstabilizes a skill by rapidly making neurochemical processing inhibitory-dominant. *Nature Neuroscience, 20,* 470-475.

Shifren, J. L., Crandall, C. J., & Manson, J. E. (2019). Menopausal hormone therapy. *JAMA, 321*(24), 2458-2459.

Shillington, K. J., Vanderloo, L. M., Burke, S. M., Ng, V., Tucker, P., & Irwin, J. D. (2021). Not so sweet dreams: adults' quantity, quality, and disruptions of sleep during the initial stages of the COVID-19 pandemic. *Sleep medicine.*

Shin, D. W., Roter, D. L., Roh, Y. K., Hahm, S. K., Cho, B., & Park, H. (2015). Physician gender and patient centered communication: The moderating effect of psychosocial and biomedical case characteristics. *Patient Education and Counseling, 98,* 55-60.

Shin, H. B., & Kominski, R. A. 2010. *Language use in the United States: 2007.* American Community Survey Reports, ACS-12. U.S. Census Bureau.

Shin, J. E., Suh, E. M., Li, N. P., Eo, K., Chong, S. C., & Tsai, M. H. (2019). Darling, get closer to me: Spatial proximity amplifies interpersonal liking. *Personality and Social Psychology Bulletin, 45*(2), 300-309.

Shinohara, Y., & Iverson, P. (2021). The effect of age on English/r/-/l/perceptual training outcomes for Japanese speakers. *Journal of Phonetics, 89,* 101108.

Shirayama, Y., & Hashimoto, K. (2017). Effects of a single bilateral infusion of R-ketamine in the rat brain regions of a learned helplessness model of depression. *European Archives of Psychiatry and Clinical Neuroscience, 267,* 177-182.

Shnabel, N., Purdie-Vaughns, V., Cook, J. E., Garcia, J., & Cohen, G. L. (2013). Demystifying values-affirmation interventions: Writing about social belonging is a

key to buffering against identity threat. *Personality and Social Psychology Bulletin, 39,* 663-676.

Shogren, K. A., & Wehmeyer, M. L. (2017). Problem solving. In M. L. Wehmeyer, K. A. Shogren, T. D. Little, & S. J. Lopez (Eds.), *Development of self-determination through the life-course.* Springer Science + Business Media.

Short, C. E., Crutzen, R., Stewart, E. M., O'Rielly, J., Dry, M., Skuse, A., Quester, P., Rebar, A. L., Vandelanotte, C., Duncan, M. J., & Vincent, A. (2022). Exploring the interplay between message format, need for cognition and personal relevance on processing messages about physical activity: A two-arm randomized experimental trial. *International Journal of Behavioral Medicine,* 1-14.

Shrikant, N., Giles, H., & Angus, D. (2022). Language and Social Psychology Approaches to Race, Racism, and Social Justice: Analyzing the Past and Revealing Ways Forward. *Journal of Language and Social Psychology, 41*(1), 4-28.

Shulman, M. E. (2021). What use is Freud? *Journal of the American Psychoanalytic Association, 69*(6), 1093-1113.

Shurkin, J. N. (1992). *Terman's kids: The groundbreaking study of how the gifted grow up.* Little, Brown.

Sibunruang, H., Capezio, A., & Restubog, S. D. (2015). In pursuit of success: The differential moderating effects of political skill on the relationships among career-related psychological needs and ingratiation. *Journal of Career Assessment, 23,* 336-348.

Sicard-Cras, I., Rioualen, S., Pellae, E., Misery, L., Sizun, J., & Roué, J. M. (2022). A review of the characteristics, mechanisms and clinical significance of habituation in foetuses and newborn infants. *Acta Paediatrica, 111*(2), 245-258.

Sidiropoulos, G., Kiourt, C., Sevetlidis, V., & Pavlidis, G. (2021, November). Shaping the behavior of reinforcement learning agents. In *25th Pan-Hellenic Conference on Informatics* (pp. 448-453).

Sielski, R., Rief, W., & Glombiewski, J. A. (2017). Efficacy of biofeedback in chronic back pain: A meta-analysis. *International Journal of Behavioral Medicine, 24,* 25-41.

Siemerkus, J., Tomiello, S., & Stephan, K. E. (2019). Bayesian inference and hallucinations in schizophrenia. *Brain, 142*(8), 2178-2181.

Sifrit, K. J. (2006). The effects of aging and cognitive decrements on simulated driving performance. *Dissertation abstracts international: Section B: The sciences and engineering, 67,* 2863.

Sikkema, K. J., Ranby, K. W., Meade, C. S., Hansen, N. B., Wilson, P. A., & Kochman, A. (2013). Reductions in traumatic stress following a coping intervention were mediated by decreases in avoidant coping in people living with HIV/AIDS and childhood sexual abuse. *Journal of Consulting and Clinical Psychology, 81,* 274-283.

Silva, M. T. A., Gonçalves, E. L., & Garcia-Mijares, M. (2007). Neural events in the reinforcement contingency. *Behavior Analyst, 30,* 17-30.

Silva, R. C., Domingues, H. S., Salgado, A. J., & Teixeira, F. G. (2022). From regenerative strategies to pharmacological approaches: Can we fine-tune treatment for Parkinson's disease? *Neural Regeneration Research, 17*(5), 933-936.

Silverstein, M. L. (2007). Rorschach test findings at the beginning of treatment and 2 years later, with a 30-year follow-up. *Journal of Personality Assessment, 88,* 131-143.

Simões, C., Gomes, A. R., & Costa, P. (2019). A multigroup analysis of the effect of cognitive appraisal on nurses' psychological distress. *Nursing Research, 68*(3), E1-E11.

Šimić, G., Tkalčić, M., Vukić, V., Mulc, D., Španić, E., Šagud, M., Olucha-Bordonau, F. E., Vukšić, M., & R Hof, P. (2021). Understanding emotions: Origins and roles of the amygdala. *Biomolecules, 11*(6), 823.

Simms, S., Nicolazzo, Z, & Jones, A. (2023). Don't say sorry, do better: Trans students of color, disidentification, and internet futures. Journal of Diversity in Higher Education, 16(3), 297-308. https://doi.org/10.1037/dhe0000337

Simon, E. B., Maron-Katz, A., Lahav, N., Shamir, R., & Hendler, T. (2017). Tired and misconnected: A breakdown of brain modularity following sleep deprivation. *Human Brain Mapping, 38,* 3300-3314.

Simonton, D. K. (2014). The mad-genius paradox: Can creative people be more mentally healthy but highly creative people more mentally ill? *Perspectives on Psychological Science, 9,* 470-480.

Simonton, D. K. (2022). The development of creativity, expertise, talent, and giftedness: A bridge too far? In J. VanTassel-Baska (Ed.), *Talent Development in Gifted Education: Theory, Research, & Practice.* Routledge.

Sinclair, R. R., Allen, T., Barber, L., Bergman, M., Britt, T., Butler, A., Ford, M., Hammer, L., Kath, L., Probst, T., & Yuan, Z. (2020). Occupational health science in the time of COVID-19: Now more than ever. *Occupational Health Science, 4*(1), 1-22.

Sinclair, R. R., Waitsman, M. C., Oliver, C. M., & Deese, M. (2013). Personality and psychological resilience in military personnel. In R. R. Sinclair & T. W. Britt (Eds.), *Building psychological resilience in military personnel: Theory and practice.* American Psychological Association.

Singer, B. F., Bryan, M. A., Popov, P., Robinson, T. E., & Aragona, B. J. (2017). Rapid induction of dopamine sensitization in the nucleus accumbens shell induced by a single injection of cocaine. *Behavioural Brain Research, 324,* 66-70.

Singh, M. (2021). Heuristics in the delivery room. *Science, 374*(6565), 324-329.

Singh, P. (2022). Antisocial personality disorder and psychopathy: A brief overview. *Journal of Forensic Psychiatry & Psychology, 7*(1), 1000207.

Singh, R. D., Jimerson, S. R., Renshaw, T., Saeki, E., Hart, S. R., Earhart, J., et al. (2011). A summary and synthesis of contemporary empirical evidence regarding the effects of the Drug Abuse Resistance Education Program (D.A.R.E.). *Contemporary School Psychology, 15,* 93-102.

Singh, S., Wulf, D., Samara, R., & Cuca, Y. P. (2000). Gender differences in the timing of first intercourse: Data from 14 countries. *International Family Planning Perspectives, 26,* 21-28, 43.

Singla, D.R. (2021). Scaling up psychological treatments: Lessons learned from global mental health. *American Psychologist, 76,* 1457-1467.

Sivec, H. J., Montesano, V. L., Skubby, D., Knepp, K. A., & Munetz, M. R. (2017). Cognitive behavioral therapy for psychosis (CBT-p) delivered in a community mental health setting: A case comparison of clients receiving CBT informed strategies by case managers prior to therapy. *Community Mental Health Journal, 53,* 134-142.

Skałacka, K., & Gerymski, R. (2019). Sexual activity and life satisfaction in older adults. *Psychogeriatrics, 19*(3), 195-201.

Skinner, B. F. (1957). *Verbal behavior.* Appleton-Century-Crofts.

Skinner, B. F. (1975). The steep and thorny road to a science of behavior. *American Psychologist, 30,* 42-49.

Skorska, M. N., Yule, M. A., Bogaert, A. F., & Brotto, L. A. (2022). Patterns of genital and subjective sexual arousal in cisgender asexual men. *The Journal of Sex Research,* 1-18. Advance online publication. https://doi.org/10.1080/00224499.2022.2071411

Slater, E., & Meyer, A. (1959). Contributions to a pathography of the musicians: Robert Schumann. *Confinia Psychiatrica.* Reprinted in Jamison, K. R. (1996). *Touched with fire: Manic-depressive illness and the artistic temperament.* Free Press; reprinted in Jamison, K. R. (1995). *An unquiet mind: A memoir of moods and madness.* Knopf.

Śledziński, P., Zeyland, J., Slomski, R., & Nowak-Terpiłowska, A. (2019). The adverse effects of marijuana use: The present state and future directions. *Journal of Child & Adolescent Substance Abuse, 28*(2), 65-72.

Sleigh, J. W., Leslie, K., Davidson, A. J., Amor, D. J., Diakumis, P., Lukic, V., Lockhart, P. J., & Bahlo, M. (2019). Genetic analysis of patients who experienced awareness with recall while under general anesthesia. *Anesthesiology, 131*(5), 974-982. https://doi.org/10.1097/ALN.0000000000002877

Slobin, D. I. (2021). Imitation and grammatical development in children. In A. Bandura (Ed.), *Psychological modeling.* Routledge.

Ślusarczyk, E., & Niedźwieńska, A. (2013). A naturalistic study of prospective memory in preschoolers: The role of task interruption and motivation. *Cognitive Development, 28,* 179-192.

Smagorinsky, P. (2018). Is instructional scaffolding actually Vygotskian, and why should it matter to literacy teachers? *Journal of Adolescent & Adult Literacy, 62*(3), 253-257.

Smart, R. G. (2007). Review of introduction to addictive behaviours. *Addiction, 102,* 831.

Smederevac, S., Mitrović, D., Sadiković, S., Riemann, R., Bratko, D., Prinz, M., & Budimlija, Z. (2020). Hereditary and environmental factors of the Five-Factor model traits: A cross-cultural study. *Personality and andividual Differences, 162,* 109995.

Smith, A. T. (2021). Cortical visual area CSv as a cingulate motor area: a sensorimotor interface for the control of locomotion. *Brain Structure and Function, 226*(9), 2931-2950.

Smith, C. A., & Lazarus, R. S. (2001). Appraisal components, core relational themes, and the emotions. In W. G. Parrott (Ed.), *Emotions in social psychology: Essential readings.* Philadelphia: Psychology Press.

Smith, D. E., Springer, C. M., & Barrett, S. (2011). Physical discipline and socioemotional adjustment among Jamaican adolescents. *Journal of Family Violence, 26,* 51-61.

Smith, E. S., Geissler, S. A., Schallert, T., & Lee, H. J. (2013). The role of central amygdala dopamine in disengagement behavior. *Behavioral Neuroscience, 127,* 164-174.

Smith, I. A., & Griffiths, A. (2022). Microaggressions, everyday discrimination, workplace incivilities, and other subtle slights at work: A meta-synthesis. *Human Resource Development Review,* 15344843221098756.

Smith, M. L., Glass, G. V., & Miller, T. I. (1980). *The benefits of psychotherapy.* The Johns Hopkins University Press.

Smith, N. A., Folland, N. A., Martinez, D. M., & Trainor, L. J. (2017). Multisensory object perception in infancy: 4-month-olds perceive a mistuned harmonic as a separate auditory and visual object. *Cognition, 164,* 1-7.

Smith, R. A., & Weber, A. L. (2005). Applying social psychology in everyday life. In F. W. Schneider, J. A. Gruman, & L. M. Coutts (Eds.), *Applied social psychology: Understanding and addressing social and practical problems.* Sage Publications.

Smith, T. J., & Hillner, B. E. (2019). The cost of pain. *JAMA Network Open, 2*(4), e191532.

Snoswell, C. L., Chelberg, G., De Guzman, K. R., Haydon, H. H., Thomas, E. E., Caffery, L. J., & Smith, A. C. (2021). The clinical effectiveness of telehealth: A systematic review of meta-analyses from 2010 to 2019. *Journal of Telemedicine and Telecare,* 1357633X211022907.

Snowdon, C. T. (2017). Learning from monkey "talk." *Science, 355,* 1120-1122.

Snyder, M. D., & Dwyer, P. C. (2013). Altruism and prosocial behavior. In H. Tennen, J. Suls, & I. B. Weiner (Eds.). *Handbook of psychology, Vol. 5: Personality and social psychology (2nd ed.).* Hoboken, NJ: John Wiley & Sons.

So, J. (2021). Counterproductive effects of overfamiliar antitobacco messages on smoking cessation intentions via message fatigue and resistance to persuasion. *Psychology of Addictive Behaviors, 36*(8), 931-941.

Soares, C. N., & Shea, A. K. (2021). The midlife transition, depression, and its clinical management. *Obstetrics and Gynecology Clinics, 48*(1), 215-229.

Sodian, B. (2011). Theory of mind in infancy. *Child Development Perspectives, 5,* 39-43.

Sohlberg, J. (2019). Elections are (not) exciting: Need for cognition and electoral behaviour. *Scandinavian Political Studies, 42*(2), 138-150.

Šolcová, I. P., & Lačev, A. (2017). Differences in male and female subjective experience and physiological reactions to emotional stimuli. *International Journal of Psychophysiology, 117,* 75-82.

Sokol, Y., Gromatsky, M., Edwards, E. R., Greene, A. L., Geraci, J. C., Harris, R. E., & Goodman, M. (2021). The deadly gap: Understanding suicide among veterans transitioning out of the military. *Psychiatry Research, 300,* 113875.

Solesio-Jofre, E., Lorenzo-López, L., Gutiérrez, R., López-Frutos, J., Ruiz-Vargas, J., & Maestú, F. (2011). Age effects on retroactive interference during working memory maintenance. *Biological Psychology, 88,* 72-82.

Solomon, A. (2020, April 12). Don't ignore clinical mental illness. *The New York Times,* p. SR10.

Somers, J. (2021, December 6). Head space. *New Yorker,* pp. 30-35.

Somers, J. (2021, December 6). The science of mind reading. *New Yorker,* pp. 1-17.

Somers, T. J., Moseley, G., Keefe, F. J., & Kothadia, S. M. (2011). Neuroimaging of pain: A psychosocial perspective. In R. A. Cohen & L. H. Sweet (Eds.), *Brain imaging in behavioral medicine and clinical neuroscience.* Springer Science + Business Media.

Sonawane, K., Lin, Y. Y., Damgacioglu, H., Zhu, Y., Fernandez, M. E., Montealegre, J. R.,Cazaban, C. G., Li, R., Lairson, D. R., Lin, Y., Giuliano, A. R., & Deshmukh, A. A. (2021). Trends in human papillomavirus vaccine safety concerns and adverse event reporting in the United States. *JAMA Network Open, 4*(9), e2124502-e2124502.

Song, J., Yang, X., Zhou, Y., Chen, L., Zhang, X., Liu, Z., Niu, W., Zhan, N., Fan, X., Aziz Khan, A., Kuang, Y., Song, L., He, G., & Li, W. (2019). Dysregulation of neuron differentiation in an autistic savant with exceptional memory. *Molecular Brain, 12*(1), 1-12.

Song, X., & Vilares, I. (2021). Assessing the relationship between the human learned helplessness depression model and anhedonia. *PLOS ONE, 16*(3), e0249056.

Sonone, S. S., Jadhav, S., & Sankhla, M. S. (2021). A forensic aspect on drug facilitated sexual assault. *Forensic Res Criminol Int J, 9*(2), 59-63.

Sood, A. B., & Linker, J. (2017). Proximal influences on the trajectory of suicidal behaviors and suicide during the transition from adolescence to young adulthood. *Child and Adolescent Psychiatric Clinics of North America, 26,* 235-251.

Soorya, L. V., Carpenter, L., & Romanczyk, R. G. (2011). Applied behavior analysis. In E. Hollander, A. Kolevzon, & J. T. Coyle (Eds.), *Textbook of autism spectrum disorders.* American Psychiatric Publishing.

Sorek, Y. (2019). Children of divorce evaluate their quality of life: The moderating effect of psychological processes. *Children and Youth Services Review, 107,* 104533.

Sorokowski, P., Karwowski, M., Misiak, M., Marczak, M. K., Dziekan, M., Hummel, T., & Sorokowska, A. (2019). Sex differences in human olfaction: A meta-analysis. *Frontiers in Psychology, 10,* 242.

Sorokowski, P., Sorokowska, A., Karwowski, M., Groyecka, A., Aavik, T., Akello, G., Alm, C., Amjad, N., Anjum, A., Asao, K., Atama, C. S., Duyar, D. A., Ayebare, R., Batres, C., Bendixen, M., Bensafia, A., Bizumic, B., Boussena, M., Buss, D. M., Butovskaya, M., et al. (2021). Universality of the triangular theory of love: Adaptation and psychometric properties of the Triangular Love Scale in 25 countries. *The Journal of Sex Research, 58*(1), 106-115.

Soussignan, R. (2002). Duchenne smile, emotional experience, and automatic reactivity: A test of the facial feedback hypothesis. *Emotion, 2,* 52-74.

South, S., & Krueger, R. (2008). An interactionist perspective on genetic and environmental contributions to personality. *Social and Personality Psychology Compass, 2,* 929-948.

South, S. C., Reichborn-Kjennerud, T., Eaton, N. R., & Krueger, R. F. (2013). Genetics of personality. In H. Tennen, J. Suls, & I. B. Weiner (Eds.), *Handbook of psychology, Vol. 5: Personality and social psychology* (2nd ed.). John Wiley & Sons.

Soysal, Y., Radmard, S., & Murat, M. (2021). A critical examination of Turkish language teaching curriculum from an interactionist perspective. *Journal of Education, 201*(3), 183-197.

Spalding, K. L., Bergmann, O., Alkass, K., Bernard, S., Salehpour, M., Huttner, H. B., Boström, E., Westerlund, I., Vial, C., Buchholz, B. A., Possnert, G., Mash, D. C., Druid, H., & Frisén, J. (2013). Dynamics of hippocampal neurogenesis in adult humans. *Cell, 153*(6), 1219-1227.

Spandler, H., & Carr, S. (2022). Lesbian and bisexual women's experiences of aversion therapy in England. *History of the Human Sciences,* 09526951211059422.

Sparrow, E. P., Swirsky, L. T., Kudus, F., & Spaniol, J. (2021). Aging and altruism: A meta-analysis. *Psychology and Aging, 36*(1), 49-56. https://doi.org/10.1037/pag0000447

Speed, L. J., Atkinson, H., Wnuk, E., & Majid, A. (2021). The sound of smell: Associating odor valence with disgust sounds. *Cognitive Science, 45*(5), e12980.

Spence, C. (2022). What is the link between personality and food behavior? *Current Research in Food Science, 5,* 19-27.

Spence, C., Auvray, M., & Smith, B. (2015). Confusing tastes with flavours. In D. Stokes, M. Matthen, & S. Biggs (Eds.), *Perception and its modalities.* Oxford University Press.

Spence, M. J., & DeCasper, A. J. (1982, March). *Human fetuses perceive maternal speech.* Paper presented at the meeting of the International Conference on Infant Studies, Austin, TX.

Spencer, K. L. (2018). Transforming patient compliance research in an era of biomedicalization. *Journal of Health and Social Behavior, 59*(2), 170-184.

Spencer, S. J., Fein, S., Zanna, M. P., & Olson, J. M. (Eds.). (2003). *Motivated social perception: The Ontario Symposium* (Vol. 9). Erlbaum.

Speranza, L., Pulcrano, S., Perrone-Capano, C., di Porzio, U., & Volpicelli, F. (2022). Music affects functional brain connectivity and is effective in the treatment of neurological disorders. *Reviews in the Neurosciences, 33*(7), 789-801.

Sperling, G. (1960). The information available in brief visual presentation. *Psychological Monographs, 74,* 29.

Sperner-Unterweger, B., & Fuchs, D. (2015). Schizophrenia and psychoneuroimmunology: An integrative view. *Current Opinion in Psychiatry, 28,* 201-206.

Sperry, R. (1982). Some effects of disconnecting the cerebral hemispheres. *Science, 217,* 1223-1226.

Spiegel, D. (2014). Minding the body: Psychotherapy and cancer survival. *British Journal of Health Psychology, 19,* 465-485.

Spies, R., & Duschinsky, R. (2021). Inheriting Mary Ainsworth and the strange situation: Questions of legacy, authority, and methodology for contemporary developmental attachment researchers. *SAGE Open, 11*(3), 2158244021047577.

Spilsbury, J. C., Storfer-Isser, A., Rosen, C. L., & Redline, S. (2015). Remission and incidence of obstructive sleep apnea from middle childhood to late adolescence. *Sleep, 38*(1), 23-29.

Spitzer, R. L., Skodol, A. E., Gibbon, M., & Williams, J. B. W. (1983). *Psychopathology: A case book.* McGraw Hill.

Sprecher, S., & Hatfield, E. (1996). Premarital sexual standards among U.S. college students: Comparison with Russian and Japanese students. *Archives of Sexual Behavior, 25,* 261-288.

Sprecher, S., & Regan, P. C. (2002). Liking some things (in some people) more than others: Partner preferences in romantic relationships and friendships. *Journal of Social and Personal Relationships, 19,* 436-481.

Sprecher, S., Treger, S., & Sakaluk, J. K. (2013). Premarital sexual standards and sociosexuality: Gender, ethnicity, and cohort differences. *Archives of Sexual Behavior, 42*(8), 1395-1405.

Spreckley, M., Seidell, J., & Halberstadt, J. (2021). Perspectives into the experience of successful, substantial long-term weight-loss maintenance: A systematic review. *International Journal of Qualitative Studies on Health and Well-Being, 16*(1), 1862481.

Spring, B., Champion, K. E., Acabchuk, R., & Hennessy, E. A. (2021). Self-regulatory behaviour change techniques in interventions to promote healthy eating, physical activity, or weight loss: A meta-review. *Health Psychology Review, 15*(4), 508-539.

Squire, L. R., Clark, R. E., & Bayley, P. J. (2004). Medial temporal lobe function and memory. In M. S. Gazzaniga (Ed.), *Cognitive neurosciences* (3rd ed.). MIT Press.

Srinivasan, M., Al-Mughairy, S., Foushee, R., & Barner, D. (2017). Learning language from within: Children use semantic generalizations to infer word meanings. *Cognition, 159,* 11-24.

Srisavasdi, R. (2008, July 18). Here's a list of O.C. kids who killed their parents. *Orange County Register.* https://www.ocregister.com/2008/07/18/heres-a-list-of-oc-kids-who-killed-their-parents/

Srivastava, A., Dada, O., Qian, J., Al-Chalabi, N., Fatemi, A. B., Gerretsen, P., Graff, A., & De Luca, V. (2021). Epigenetics of schizophrenia. *Psychiatry Research, 305,* 114218.

St. Amant, K. (2021). Cognition, care, and usability: Applying cognitive concepts to user experience design in health and medical contexts. *Journal of Technical Writing and Communication, 51*(4), 407-428.

Stålhammar, J., Nordlund, A., & Wallin, A. (2015). An example of exceptional practice effects in the verbal domain. *Neurocase, 21,* 162-168.

Stallings, M. C., & Neppl, T. (2021). An examination of genetic and environmental factors related to negative personality traits, educational attainment, and economic success. *Developmental Psychology, 57*(2), 191.

Stam, G. (2015). Changes in thinking for speaking: A longitudinal case study. *Modern Language Journal, 99*(Suppl 1), 83-99.

Stamm, K., Lin, L., & Cristidis, P. (2016, June). Datapoint. *Monitor on Psychology,* p. 12.

Stangier, U., Schramm, E., Heidenreich, T., Berger, M., & Clark, D. M. (2011). Cognitive therapy vs. interpersonal psychotherapy in social anxiety disorder: A randomized controlled trial. *Archives of General Psychiatry, 68,* 692-700.

Staniewski, M. W., & Awruk, K. (2019). Entrepreneurial success and achievement motivation—A preliminary report on a validation study of the Questionnaire of Entrepreneurial Success. *Journal of Business Research, 101,* 433-440.

Stanley, M. L., Henne, P., Iyengar, V., Sinnott-Armstrong, W., & De Brigard, F. (2017). I'm not the person I used to be: The self and autobiographical memories of immoral actions. *Journal of Experimental Psychology: General, 146,* 884-895.

Stanton, S. J., Sinnott-Armstrong, W., & Huettel, S. A. (2017). Neuromarketing: Ethical implications of its use and potential misuse. *Journal of Business Ethics, 144*(4), 799-811.

Starcevic, V., Berle, D., Milicevic, D., Hannan, A., Pamplugh, C., & Eslick, G. D. (2007). Pathological worry, anxiety disorders and the impact of co-occurrence with depressive and other anxiety disorders. *Journal of Anxiety Disorders, 21,* 1016-1027.

Starkey, M. L. (2018). *The devil in Massachusetts: A modern inquiry into the Salem witch trials.* Pickle Partners Publishing.

Starr, S. B. (2022). Race-norming and statistical discrimination: Beyond the NFL. University of Chicago, Public Law Working Paper No. 805.

Staudt, M. D., Herring, E. Z., Gao, K., Miller, J. P., & Sweet, J. A. (2019). Evolution in the treatment of psychiatric disorders: from psychosurgery to psychopharmacology to neuromodulation. *Frontiers in Neuroscience, 13.*

Stech, E. P., Lim, J., Upton, E. L., & Newby, J. M. (2019, July 15). Internet-delivered cognitive behavioral therapy for panic disorder with or without agoraphobia: A systematic review and meta-analysis. *Cognitive Behaviour Therapy,* 1-24.

Steffens, N. K., Munt, K. A., van Knippenberg, D., Platow, M. J., & Haslam, S. A. (2021). Advancing the social identity theory of leadership: A meta-analytic review of leader group prototypicality. *Organizational Psychology Review, 11*(1), 35-72.

Stein, L. A. R., & Graham, J. R. (2005). Ability of substance abusers to escape detection on the Minnesota Multiphasic Personality Inventory-Adolescent (MMPI-A) in a juvenile correctional facility. *Assessment, 12,* 28-39.

Stein, R., & Swan, A. B. (2019). Evaluating the validity of Myers-Briggs Type Indicator theory: A teaching tool and window into intuitive psychology. *Social and Personality Psychology Compass.* https://doi-org.silk.library.umass.edu/10.1111/spc3.12434.

Steinbeis, N., Crone, E., Blakemore, S., & Kadosh, K. C. (2017). Development holds the key to understanding the interplay of nature versus nurture in shaping the individual. *Developmental Cognitive Neuroscience, 25,* 1-4.

Steinberg, L. (2016). Commentary on special issue on the adolescent brain: Redefining adolescence. *Neuroscience and Biobehavioral Reviews, 70,* 343-346.

Steinhubl, S. R., Wineinger, N. E., Patel, S., Boeldt, D. L., Mackellar, G., Porter, V., Redmond, J. T., Muse, E. D., Nicholson, L., Chopra, D., & Topol, E. J. (2015). Cardiovascular and nervous system changes during meditation. *Frontiers in Human Neuroscience, 9,* 88-97.

Steinmetz, K. (2015, March 6). States battle over bathroom access for transgender people. *Time.* http://time.com/3734714/transgender-bathroom-bills-lgbtdiscrimination/

Steinmetz, N. A., Aydin, C., Lebedeva, A., Okun, M., Pachitariu, M., Bauza, M., Beau, M., Bhagat, J., Böhm, C., Broux, M., Chen, S., Colonell, J., Gardner, R. J., Karsh, B., Kloosterman, F., Kostadinov, D., Mora-Lopez, C., O'Callaghan, J., Park, J., Harris, T. D. (2021). Neuropixels 2.0: A miniaturized high-density probe for stable, long-term brain recordings. *Science, 372*(6539), eabf4588.

Steins-Loeber, S., Madjarova, R., Lörsch, F., Herpertz, S. C., Flor, H., & Duka, T. (2019). An experimental study on spontaneous recovery of conditioned reward expectancies and instrumental responding in humans. *Behaviour Research and Therapy, 118,* 54-64.

Stemler, S. E., & Sternberg, R. J. (2006). Using situational judgment tests to measure practical intelligence. In J. A. Weekley & R. E. Ployhart (Eds.), *Situational judgment tests: Theory, measurement, and application.* Lawrence Erlbaum Associates.

Stemler, S. E., Sternberg, R. J., Grigorenko, E. L., Jarvin, L., & Sharpes, K. (2009). Using the theory of successful intelligence as a framework for developing assessments in AP physics. *Contemporary Educational Psychology, 34,* 195-209.

Stern, L. (2020, July.). What can bonobos teach us about the nature of language? *Smithsonian Magazine.* https://www.smithsonianmag.com/science-nature/bonobos-teach-humans-about-nature-language-180975191/

Stern, P. (2021). The many benefits of healthy sleep. *Science, 374,* 552-555.

Sternberg, R. J. (1998). *Successful intelligence: How practical and creative intelligence determine success in life.* Plume.

Sternberg, R. J. (2000). Intelligence and wisdom. In R. J. Sternberg (Ed.), *Handbook of intelligence.* Cambridge University Press.

Sternberg, R. J. (2011). Individual differences in cognitive development. In U. Goswami (Ed.), *The Wiley-Blackwell handbook of childhood cognitive development* (2nd ed.). Wiley-Blackwell.

Sternberg, R. J. (2013). What is cognitive education? *Journal of Cognitive Education and Psychology, 12*(1), 45-58.

Sternberg, R. J. (2015). Multiple intelligences in the new age of thinking. In S. Goldstein, D. Princiotta, & J. A. Naglieri (Eds.), *Handbook of intelligence: Evolutionary theory, historical perspective, and current concepts.* Springer Science + Business Media.

Sternberg, R. J. (2017). *Career paths in psychology: Where your degree can take you* (3rd ed.). Washington, DC: American Psychological Association.

Sternberg, R. J. (2018). Successful intelligence in theory, research, and practice. In R. J. Sternberg (Ed.), The nature of human intelligence (pp. 308-321). Cambridge University Press. https://doi.org/10.1017/9781316817049.020

Sternberg, R. J. (1986). A triangular theory of love. *Psychological Review, 93*(2), 119-135.

Sternberg, R. J., & Jarvin, L. (2003). Alfred Binet's contributions as a paradigm for impact in psychology. In R. J. Sternberg (Ed.), *The anatomy of impact: What makes the great works of psychology great.* American Psychological Association.

Sternberg, R. J., & Sternberg, K. (Eds.). (2018). *The new psychology of love.* Cambridge University Press.

Sternberg, R. J., Glaveanu, V., Karami, S., Kaufman, J. C., Phillipson, S. N., & Preiss, D. D. (2021). Meta-intelligence: Understanding, control, and interactivity between creative, analytical, practical, and wisdom-based approaches in problem solving. *Journal of Intelligence, 9*(2), 19.

Sternberg, R. J., Grigorenko, E. L., & Kidd, K. K. (2005). Intelligence, race, and genetics. *American Psychologist, 60,* 46-59.

Sternberg, R. J., Jarvin, L., & Grigorenko, E. L. (2011). *Explorations in giftedness.* Cambridge University Press.

Sternberg, R. J., Kaufman, J. C., & Roberts, A. M. (2019). The relation of creativity to intelligence and wisdom. In J. C. Kaufman & R. J. Sternberg (Eds.), *The Cambridge handbook of creativity* (2nd ed.). Cambridge University Press.

Sternson, S. M., Betley, J., & Cao, Z. (2013). Neural circuits and motivational processes for hunger. *Current Opinion in Neurobiology, 23,* 353-360.

Stevens, C. F. (2015). Novel neural circuit mechanism for visual edge detection. *PNAS Proceedings of The National Academy of Sciences of The United States of America, 112,* 875-880.

Stevens, G. (2015). Black psychology: Resistance, reclamation, and redefinition. In I. Parker & I. Parker (Eds.), *Handbook of critical psychology.* New York: Routledge/Taylor & Francis Group.

Stevens, T., Brevers, D., Chambers, C. D., Lavric, A., McLaren, I. L., Mertens, M., Noël, X., & Verbruggen, F. (2015). How does response inhibition influence decision making when gambling? *Journal of Experimental Psychology: Applied, 21,* 15-36.

Stewart, C. E., Lee, S. Y., Hogstrom, A., & Williams, M. (2017). Diversify and conquer: A call to promote minority representation in clinical psychology. *The Behavior Therapist, 40,* 74-79.

Stewart, J. (2021). *Revelations in air: A guidebook to smell.* Penguin Books.

Stey, P. C., Lapsley, D., & McKeever, M. O. (2013). Moral judgement in adolescents: Age differences in applying and justifying three principles of harm. *European Journal of Developmental Psychology, 10,* 206-220.

Stickgold, R. (2015). Why we sleep. *Scientific American, 313*(4), 52-57.

Stickgold, R., Malia, A., Maguire, D., Roddenberry, D., & O'Connor, M. (2000). Replaying the game: Hypnagogic images in normals and amnesics. *Science, 290*(5490), 350-353.

Stix, G. (2011). The neuroscience of true grit. *Scientific American, 304,* 28-33.

Stoll, O. (2019). Peak performance, the runner's high, and flow. In M. H. Anshel, S. J. Petruzzello, & E. E. Labbé (Eds.), *APA handbook of sport and exercise psychology, Vol. 2: Exercise psychology.* American Psychological Association.

Stöllberger, C., Koller, J., Finsterer, J., Schauer, D., & Ehrlich, M. (2019). Anterograde amnesia as a manifestation of acute type A aortic dissection. *International Journal of Angiology.* 10.1055/s-0039-1693029

Stolorow, R. D., & Stolorow, B. A. (2013). Blues and emotional trauma. *Clinical Social Work Journal, 41,* 5-10.

Stone, C. A. (2015). Neuro/cognitive and sociocultural perspectives on language and literacy disabilities: Moving from parallel play to productive cooperation. In R. H. Bahr & E. R. Silliman (Eds.), *Routledge handbook of communication disorders.* Routledge/Taylor & Francis Group.

Stone, J., Moskowitz, G. B., Zestcott, C. A., & Wolsiefer, K. J. (2019). Testing active learning workshops for reducing implicit stereotyping of Hispanics by majority and minority group medical students.

Stigma and Health. http://dx.doi.org/10.1037/sah0000179.

Stone, K. (2020, October 12). Don Pellmann Dies at 105; His 5 World Records in San Diego Made Global News. *Times of San Diego.* Downloaded from https://timesofsandiego.com/sports/2020/10/12/don-pellmann-dies-at-105-his-5-world-records-in-san-diego-made-global-news/, May 12, 2022.

Stopa, L., Denton, R., Wingfield, M., & Taylor, K. (2013). The fear of others: A qualitative analysis of interpersonal threat in social phobia and paranoia. *Behavioural and Cognitive Psychotherapy, 41,* 188-209.

Stoppelbein, L., McRae, E., & Greening, L. (2017). A longitudinal study of hardiness as a buffer for posttraumatic stress symptoms in mothers of children with cancer. *Clinical Practice in Pediatric Psychology, 5,* 149-160.

Storm, L., & Rock, A. J. (2015). Dreaming of psi: A narrative review and meta-analysis of dream-ESP studies at the Maimonides Dream Laboratory and beyond. In J. A. Davies & D. B. Pitchford (Eds.), *Stanley Krippner: A life of dreams, myths, and visions: Essays on his contributions and influence.* University Professors Press.

Stowell, J. R., Robles, T. F., & Kane, H. S. (2013). Psychoneuroimmunology: Mechanisms, individual differences, and interventions. In A. M. Nezu, C. Nezu, P. A. Geller, & I. B. Weiner (Eds.), *Handbook of psychology, Vol. 9: Health psychology* (2nd ed.). John Wiley & Sons.

Strathern, A., & Stewart, P. J. (2003). *Landscape, memory and history: Anthropological perspectives.* Pluto Press.

Straus, V. (2021, December 17). Why social-emotional learning isn't enough to help students today. *Washington Post.* https://www.washingtonpost.com/education/2021/12/17/why-socialemotional-learning-isnt-enough/

Strayer, D. L., & Drews, F. A. (2007). Cell-phone-induced driver distraction. *Current Directions in Psychological Science, 16,* 128-131.

Streeter, K. (2020). Chris Nikic, You Are an Ironman. And Your Journey Is Remarkable. *New York Times.* https://www.nytimes.com/2020/11/16/sports/ironman-triathlon-down-syndrome.html

Strenze, T. (2015). Intelligence and success. In S. Goldstein, D. Princiotta, & J. A. Naglieri (Eds.), *Handbook of intelligence: Evolutionary theory, historical perspective, and current concepts.* Springer Science + Business Media.

Stroup, T. S., Lieberman, J. A., Swartz, M. S., & McEvoy, J. P. (2022). Comparative effectiveness of antipsychotic drugs in schizophrenia. *Dialogues in Clinical Neuroscience, 2*(4), 373-379.

Struik, L. L., Dow-Fleisner, S., Belliveau, M., Thompson, D., & Janke, R. (2020). Tactics for drawing youth to vaping: Content analysis of electronic cigarette advertisements. *Journal of Medical Internet Research, 22*(8), e18943.

Strunk, K. K. (2021). Kinsey scale. In K. K. Strunk & S. A. Shelton (Eds.), *Encyclopedia of Queer Studies in Education.* Brill.

Su, N., Buchin, Z. L., & Mulligan, N. W. (2021). Levels of retrieval and the testing effect. *Journal of Experimental Psychology: Learning, Memory, and Cognition, 47*(4), 652-670. https://doi.org/10.1037/xlm0000962

Suárez-Orozco, M. M., & Suárez-Orozco, C. (2018, September 20). Like it or not, immigrant children are our future. *Washington Post.* https://www.washingtonpost.com/news/theworldpost/wp/2018/09/20/immigrant/

Substance Abuse and Mental Health Services Administration. (2019). Key substance use and mental health indicators in the United States: Results from the 2018 National Survey on Drug Use and Health (HHS Publication No. PEP19-5068, NSDUH Series H-54). Center for Behavioral Health Statistics and Quality, Substance Abuse and Mental Health Services Administration. https://www.samhsa.gov/data/

Substance Abuse and Mental Health Services Administration. (2021). *National Mental Health Services Survey (N-MHSS): 2020. Data on mental health treatment facilities.* Author.

Sue, D. W. (2017). Microaggressions and "evidence": Empirical or experiential reality? *Perspectives on Psychological Science, 12,* 170-172.

Sue, D. W., & Sue, D. (1990). *Counseling the culturally different: Theory and practice* (2nd ed.). John Wiley & Sons.

Sue, D., Sue, D. W., Sue, D. M., & Sue, S. (2021). *Understanding abnormal behavior.* Cengage Learning.

Suen, H. K. (2015). Technical Brief: Kuder Career Interests Assessment® - Likert 2015 (KCIA-L 2015). Kuder. https://www.kuder.com/webres/File/Technical%20Briefs/KCIA-L%202015%20Technical%20Brief.pdf

Sukhera, J., Miller, K., Milne, A., Scerbo, C., Lim, R., Cooper, A., & Watling, C. (2017). Labelling of mental illness in a paediatric emergency department and its implications for stigma reduction education. *Perspectives on Medical Education, 6*(3), 165-172.

Sullivan, E. L., Smith, S. M., & Grove, K. L. (2011). Perinatal exposure to high-fat diet programs energy balance, metabolism and behavior in adulthood. *Neuroendocrinology, 93,* 1-8.

Sulser, R. B., Patterson, B. D., Urban, D. J., Neander, A. I., & Luo, Z. X. (2022). Evolution of inner ear neuroanatomy of bats and implications for echolocation. *Nature,* 1-6.

Summa, K. C., & Turek, F. W. (2015). The clocks within us. *Scientific American, 312,* 51-55.

Summers, M. (2000). *Everything in its place.* Putnam.

Summers, S. J., Schabrun, S. M., Marinovic, W., & Chipchase, L. S. (2017). Peripheral electrical stimulation increases corticomotor excitability and enhances the rate of visuomotor adaptation. *Behavioural Brain Research, 322*(Part A), 42-50.

Sun, J., Schwartz, H. A., Son, Y., Kern, M. L., & Vazire, S. (2019). The language of well-being: Tracking fluctuations in emotion experience through everyday speech. *Journal of Personality and Social Psychology.* https://doi.org/10.1037/pspp0000244

Sun, L. H. (2019, September 5). Contaminant found in marijuana vaping products linked to deadly lung illnesses, tests show. *Washington Post.* https://www.washingtonpost.com/health/2019/09/05/contaminant-found-vaping-products-linked-deadly-lung-illnesses-state-federal-labs-show/

Sun, M., Oliwa, T., Peek, M. E., & Tung, E. L. (2022). Negative patient descriptors: Documenting racial bias in the electronic health record: Study examines racial bias in the patient descriptors used in the electronic health record. *Health Affairs, 41*(2), 203-211.

Sun, X., Niu, G., You, Z., Zhou, Z., & Tang, Y. (2017). "Gender, negative life events and coping on different stages of depression severity: A cross-sectional study among Chinese university students": Corrigendum. *Journal of Affective Disorders, 215,* 102.

Sun, Y., Giacobbe, P., Tang, C. W., Barr, M. S., Rajji, T., Kennedy, S. H., Fitzgerald, P. B., Lozano, A. M., Wong, W., & Daskalakis, Z. (2015). Deep brain stimulation modulates gamma oscillations and theta-gamma coupling in treatment resistant depression. *Brain Stimulation, 8,* 1033-1042.

Sundar, P. S., Chowdhury, C., & Kamarthi, S. (2021). Evaluation of human ear anatomy and functionality by axiomatic design. *Biomimetics, 6*(2), 31.

Sunshine, J. E., Meo, N., Kassebaum, N. J., Collison, M. L., Mokdad, A. H., & Naghavi, M. (2019). Association of adverse effects of medical treatment with mortality in the United States: A secondary analysis of the Global Burden of Diseases, Injuries, and Risk Factors Study. *JAMA Network Open, 2*(1), e187041. https://doi.org/10.1001/jamanetworkopen.2018.7041

Super, C. M. (1980). Cognitive development: Looking across at growing up. In C. M. Super & S. Harakness (Eds.), *New directions for child development: Anthropological perspectives on child development.* Jossey-Bass.

Suriagandhi, V., & Nachiappan, V. (2022). Protective effects of melatonin against obesity-induced by leptin resistance. *Behavioural Brain Research, 417,* 113598.

Surya, S., Bishnoi, R. J., & Shashank, R. B. (2019). Balancing medical ethics to consider involuntary administration of electroconvulsive therapy. *The Journal of ECT, 35*(3), 150-151.

Sutherland, S. (2016). The maddening sensation of itch. *Scientific American, 314*, 39-43.

Suzuki, L. A., Short, E. L., & Lee, C. S. (2011). Racial and ethnic group differences in intelligence in the United States: Multicultural perspectives. In R. J. Sternberg & S. Kaufman (Eds.), *The Cambridge handbook of intelligence.* Cambridge University Press.

Swaab, D. F., Wolff, S. E., & Bao, A. M. (2021). Sexual differentiation of the human hypothalamus: Relationship to gender identity and sexual orientation. *Handbook of Clinical Neurology, 181*, 427-443.

Swain, R. A., Kerr, A. L., & Thompson, R. F. (2011). The cerebellum: A neural system for the study of reinforcement learning. *Frontiers in Behavioral Neuroscience, 18*, 89-96.

Swanson, L. W., Hahn, J. D., & Sporns, O. (2020). Structure-function subsystem models of female and male forebrain networks integrating cognition, affect, behavior, and bodily functions. *Proceedings of the National Academy of Sciences, 117*(49), 31470-31481.

Sweeney, M. M., Meredith, S. E., Juliano, L. M., Evatt, D. P., & Griffiths, R. R. (2019). A randomized controlled trial of a manual-only treatment for reduction and cessation of problematic caffeine use. *Drug and Alcohol Dependence, 195*, 45-51.

Szapocznik, J., & Hervis, O. E. (2020). *Brief strategic family therapy.* American Psychological Association.

Szkody, E., Stearns, M., Stanhope, L., & McKinney, C. (2021). Stress-buffering role of social support during COVID-19. *Family Process, 60*(3), 1002-1015.

Tadmor, C. T. (2007). Biculturalism: The plus side of leaving home? The effects of second-culture exposure on integrative complexity and its consequences for overseas performance. *Dissertation Abstracts International Section A: Humanities and Social Sciences, 67*(8-A), 3068.

Tafesse, W. (2022). Social networking sites use and college students' academic performance: Testing for an inverted U-shaped relationship using automated mobile app usage data. *International Journal of Educational Technology in Higher Education, 19*(1), 1-17.

Tahara, M., Mashizume, Y., & Takahashi, K. (2021). Coping mechanisms: Exploring strategies utilized by Japanese healthcare workers to reduce stress and improve mental health during the COVID-19 pandemic. *International Journal of Environmental Research and Public Health, 18*(1), 131.

Taibbi, R. (2018). *Brief therapy with couples and families in crisis.* Routledge/Taylor & Francis Group.

Taitz, J. (2020, May 18). Reduce your risk of PTSD after lockdown. *The New York Times,* p. B7.

Tajfel, H., & Turner, J. C. (2004). The social identity theory of intergroup behavior. In J. T. Jost & J. Sidanius (Eds.), *Political psychology: Key readings.* Psychology Press.

Takamiya, S., Yuki, S., Hirokawa, J., Manabe, H., & Sakurai, Y. (2019). Dynamics of memory engrams. *Neuroscience Research.* https://doi.org/10.1016/j.neures.2019.03.005

Takehara-Nishiuchi, K. (2021). Neurobiology of systems memory consolidation. *European Journal of Neuroscience, 54*(8), 6850-6863.

Takeuchi, H., Taki, Y., Nouchi, R., Yokoyama, R., Kotozaki, Y., Nakagawa, S., . . . & Kawashima, R. (2018). Shorter sleep duration and better sleep quality are associated with greater tissue density in the brain. *Scientific Reports, 8*(1), 1-8.

Takizawa, T., Kondo, T., & Sakihara, S. (2007). Stress buffering effects of social support on depressive symptoms in middle age: Reciprocity and community mental health: Corrigendum. *Psychiatry and Clinical Neurosciences, 61*, 336-337.

Takooshian, H., Gielen, U.P., Plous, S., Rich, G.J., & Velayo, R.S. (2016). Internationalizing undergraduate psychology education: Trends, techniques, and technologies. *American Psychologist, 71*, 136-147.

Talarico, J., & Rubin, D. (2007). Flashbulb memories are special after all; in phenomenology, not accuracy. *Applied Cognitive Psychology, 21*, 557-578.

Talarico, J. M., Bohn, A., & Wessel, I. (2019). The role of event relevance and congruence to social groups in flashbulb memory formation. *Memory, 27*, 985-997.

Tam, S. E., Bonardi, C., & Robinson, J. (2015). Relative recency influences object-in-context memory. *Behavioural Brain Research, 281*, 250-257.

Tamannaeifar, M., & Shahmirzaei, S. (2019). Prediction of academic resilience based on coping styles and personality traits. *Journal of Practice in Clinical Psychology, 7*(1), 1-9.

Tamini, B., Bojhd, F., & Yazdani, S. (2011). Love types, psychological well-being and self-concept. *Journal of the Indian Academy of Applied Psychology, 37*, 169-178.

Tan, F. C. J. H., Oka, P., Dambha-Miller, H., & Tan, N. C. (2021). The association between self-efficacy and self-care in essential hypertension: a systematic review. *BMC Family Practice, 22*(1), 1-12.

Tan, G., Rintala, D. H., Jensen, M. P., Richards, J. S., Holmes, S. A., Parachuri, R., Lashgari-Saegh, S., & Price, L. R. (2011). Efficacy of cranial electrotherapy stimulation for neuropathic pain following spinal cord injury: a multi-site randomized controlled trial with a secondary 6-month open-label phase. *Journal of Spinal Cord Medicine, 34*, 285-296.

Tan, L., Yu, J., & Tan, L. (2015). Causes and consequences of microRNA dysregulation in neurodegenerative diseases. *Molecular Neurobiology, 51*, 1249-1262.

Tanaka-Matsumi, J. (2019). Culture and psychotherapy: Searching for an empirically supported relationship. In K. D. Keith (Ed.), *Cross-cultural psychology: Contemporary themes and perspectives* (2nd ed.). John Wiley & Sons.

Tandon, R., Gaebel, W., Barch, D. M., Bustillo, J., Gur, R. E., Heckers, S., Malaspina, D., Owen, M. J., Schultz, S., Tsuang, M., Van Os, J., & Carpenter, W. (2013). Definition and description of schizophrenia in the DSM-5. *Schizophrenia Research, 150*(1), 3-10.

Tanida, Y., Nakayama, M., & Saito, S. (2019). The interaction between temporal grouping and phonotactic chunking in short-term serial order memory for novel verbal sequences. *Memory, 27*(4), 507-518.

Tanner, J. M. (1978). *Education and physical growth* (2nd ed.). International Universities Press.

Tappin, B. M., McKay, R. T., & Abrams, D. (2017). Choosing the right level of analysis: Stereotypes shape social reality via collective action. *Behavioral and Brain Sciences, 40.*

Tariq, M. U., Poulin, M., & Abonamah, A. A. (2021). Achieving operational excellence through artificial intelligence: driving forces and barriers. *Frontiers in Psychology, 12*, 686624.

Tart, C. T. (2017). Measuring the depth of an altered state of consciousness, with particular reference to self-report scales of hypnotic depth. In E. Fromm & R. E. Shor (Eds.), *Hypnosis: Developments in research and new perspectives* (pp. 567-601). Routledge.

Tasca, G. A., Mikail, S. F., & Hewitt, P. L. (2021). Group therapy theory and group psychodynamic-interpersonal psychotherapy stages of development. In G. A. Tasca, S. F. Mikail, & P. L. Hewitt (Eds.), *Group psychodynamic-interpersonal psychotherapy.* American Psychological Association. https://doi.org/10.1037/0000213-005

Tassone, D., Reed, A. E., & Carstensen, L. L. (2019). Time may heal wounds: Aging and life regrets. *Psychology and Aging.* Advance online publication. http://dx.doi.org/10.1037/pag0000381.

Tauseef, S. (2022). Can money buy happiness? Subjective wellbeing and its relationship with income, relative income, monetary and non-monetary poverty in Bangladesh. *Journal of Happiness Studies, 23*(3), 1073-1098.

Taylor, C. L., & Barbot, B. (2021). Gender differences in creativity: Examining the greater male variability hypothesis in different domains and tasks. *Personality and Individual Differences, 174*, 110661.

Taylor, F., & Bryant, R. A. (2007). The tendency to suppress, inhibiting thoughts, and dream rebound. *Behaviour Research and Therapy, 45*, 163-168.

Taylor, M. A., & Bisson, J. B. (2019). Changes in cognitive function: Practical and theoretical considerations for training the aging workforce. *Human Resource Management Review.* Advance online publication. https://doi.org/10.1016/j.hrmr.2019.02.001.

Taylor, S. (2020). *Health psychology* (9th ed.). McGraw Hill.

Tazouti, Y., & Jarlégan, A. (2019). The mediating effects of parental self-efficacy and parental involvement on the link between family socioeconomic status and children's academic achievement. *Journal of Family Studies, 25*(3), 250-266.

Teague, R. (2013). The American view of Freud's couch. *PsycCRITIQUES, 58*, 12-21.

Teeuwen, R. R., Wacongne, C., Schnabel, U. H., Self, M. W., & Roelfsema, P. R. (2021). A neuronal basis of iconic memory in macaque primary visual cortex. *Current Biology, 31*(24), 5401-5414.

Teglasi, H. (2021). Thematic Apperception Test (TAT) for assessing disordered thought and perception. In I. B. Weiner & J. H. Kleiger (Eds.), *Psychological assessment of disordered thinking and perception.* American Psychological Association. https://doi.org/10.1037/0000245-011

Tellegen, A., Lykken, D. T., Bouchard Jr., T. J., Wilcox, K. J., Segal, N. L., & Rich, S. (1998). Personality similarity in twins reared apart and together. *Journal of Personality and Social Psychology, 54*, 1031-1039.

Tellis, G. J., MacInnis, D. J., Tirunillai, S., & Zhang, Y. (2019). What drives virality (sharing) of online digital content? The critical role of information, emotion, and brand prominence. *Journal of Marketing, 83*(4), 1-20.

ten Cate, C. (2017). Assessing the uniqueness of language: Animal grammatical abilities take center stage. *Psychonomic Bulletin & Review, 24*, 91-96.

Tendilla-Beltrán, H., del Carmen Sanchez-Islas, N., Marina-Ramos, M., Leza, J. C., & Flores, G. (2021). The prefrontal cortex as a target for atypical antipsychotics in schizophrenia, lessons of neurodevelopmental animal models. *Progress in Neurobiology, 199*, 101967.

Teovanović, P., Knežević, G., & Stankov, L. (2015). Individual differences in cognitive biases: Evidence against one-factor theory of rationality. *Intelligence, 50*, 75-86.

Terlizzi, E. P. , & Schiller, J.S. (2022, September). Mental health treatment among adults aged 18-44: United States, 2019-2021. *NCHS Data Brief, No. 444.* U.S. Department of Health and Human Services.

Termorshuizen, J. D., Watson, H. J., Thornton, L. M., Borg, S., Flatt, R. E., MacDermod, C. M., Harper, L. E., van Furth, E. F., Peat, C. M., & Bulik, C. M. (2020). Early impact of COVID-19 on individuals with self-reported eating disorders: A survey of~ 1,000 individuals in the United States and the Netherlands. *International Journal of Eating Disorders, 53*(11), 1780-1790.

Terrier, L. M., Lévêque, M., & Amelot, A. (2019). Brain lobotomy: A historical and moral dilemma with no alternative? *World Neurosurgery, 132*, 211-218.

Thaler, L. (2015). Using sound to get around: Discoveries in human echolocation. *APS Observer, 28*, 24-27.

Thaler, N. S., Thames, A. D., Cagigas, X. E., & Norman, M. A. (2015). IQ testing and the African American client. In L. T. Benuto & B. D. Leany (Eds.), *Guide to psychological assessment with African Americans.* Springer Science + Business Media.

Tharp, R. G. (1989). Psychocultural variables and constants: Effects on teaching and learning in schools [Special issue: Children and their development: Knowledge base, research agenda, and social policy application]. *American Psychologist, 44*, 349-359.

Thase, M. E. (2013). Comparative effectiveness of psychodynamic psychotherapy and cognitive-behavioral therapy: It's about time, and what's next? *American Journal of Psychiatry, 170*, 953-956.

Thayer, L. (2021, January February). An uneven playing field. *Psychological Science Observer,* p. 29.

Theriault, J., Krause, P., & Young, L. (2017). Know thy enemy: Education about terrorism improves social attitudes toward terrorists. *Journal of Experimental Psychology: General, 146*(3), 305-317.

Thomas, N. S., Salvatore, J. E., Gillespie, N. A., Aliev, F., Ksinan, A. J., Dick, D. M., & Spit for Science Working Group. (2021). Cannabis use in college: Genetic predispositions, peers, and activity participation. *Drug and alcohol dependence, 219*, 108489.

Thomeer, M. B., Moody, M. D., & Yahirun, J. (2022). Racial and ethnic disparities in mental health and mental health care during the COViD-19 pandemic. *Journal of Racial and Ethnic Health Disparities, 10*(2).

Thompson, A. E., Hart, J., Stefaniak, S., & Harvey, C. (2018). Exploring heterosexual adults' endorsement of the sexual double standard among initiators of consensually nonmonogamous relationship behaviors. *Sex Roles, 79*(3), 228-238.

Thompson, A. K., & Wolpaw, J. R. (2015). Restoring walking after spinal cord injury: Operant conditioning of spinal reflexes can help. *The Neuroscientist, 21*(2), 203-215.

Thompson, A. L. (2021). What is normal, healthy growth? Global health, human biology, and parental perspectives. *American Journal of Human Biology, 33*(5), e23597.

Thompson, D. (2021, October 1.) How the COVID Pandemic Made the Opioid Epidemic Worse, Even as Telehealth Helped. *US News and World Report.* Downloaded from https://www.usnews.com/news/health-news/articles/2021-10-01/how-the-covid-pandemic-made-the-opioid-epidemic-worse-even-as-telehealth-helped, January 3, 2022.

Thompson, M. (2015, April 6.) Unlocking the secrets of PTSD. *Time*, pp. 41-43.

Thompson, T., Terhune, D. B., Oram, C., Sharangparni, J., Rouf, R., Solmi, M., Veronese, N., & Stubbs, B. (2019). The effectiveness of hypnosis for pain relief: A systematic review and meta-analysis of 85 controlled experimental trials. *Neuroscience and Biobehavioral Reviews, 99*, 298-310.

Thorkildsen, T. A. (2006). An empirical exploration of language and thought. *PsycCRITIQUES, 51*, n.p.

Thorndike, E. L. (1932). *The fundamentals of learning.* Teachers College.

Thornicroft, G., Chatterji, S., Evans-Lacko, S., Gruber, M., Sampson, N., Aguilar-Gaxiola, S., Al-Hamzawi, A., Alonso, J., Andrade, L., Borges, G., Buffaerts, R., Bunting, B., Caldas de Almeida, J. M., Florescu, S., de Girolamo, G., Gureje, O., Haro, J. M., He, Y., Hinkov, H., Karam, E., et al.(2017). Undertreatment of people with major depressive disorder in 21 countries. *The British Journal of Psychiatry, 210*(2), 119-124.

Thrailkill, E. A., & Bouton, M. E. (2017). Effects of outcome devaluation on instrumental behaviors in a discriminated heterogeneous chain. *Journal of Experimental Psychology: Animal Learning and Cognition, 43*, 88-95.

Tillema, E. S. (2019). Students' solution of arrangement problems and their connection to Cartesian product problems. *Mathematical Thinking and Learning*, 1-33.

Tingley, K. (2016, March 20). Sixth sense. *The New York Times Magazine*, p. MM52.

Tingley, K. (2022, July 10). The time of your life. *New York Times Magazine*, p. 26-31, 45-47.

Tiwari, A. K., Zai, C. C., Müller, D. J., & Kennedy, J. L. (2022). Genetics in schizophrenia: Where are we and what next? *Dialogues in Clinical Neuroscience, 12*(3), 289-303.

Tiwari, A. K., Zai, C. C., Müller, D. J., & Kennedy, J. L. (2022). Genetics in schizophrenia: Where are we and what next? *Dialogues in Clinical Neuroscience.* Advance online publication. https://doi.org/10.31887/DCNS.2010.12.3/atiwari

Tobajas, J., Gómez-Ramírez, P., María-Mojica, P., Navas, I., García-Fernández, A. J., Ferreras, P., & Mateo, R. (2019). Selection of new chemicals to be used in conditioned aversion for non-lethal predation control. *Behavioural Processes, 166*, 103905.

Todes, D. P. (2014). *Ivan Pavlov: A Russian life in science.* Oxford University Press.

Todorov, A., Fiske, S., & Prentice, D. (Eds.). (2011). *Social neuroscience: Toward understanding the underpinnings of the social mind.* Oxford University Press.

Tokutsu, Y., Umene-Nakano, W., Shinkai, T., Yoshimura, R., Okamoto, T., Katsuki, A., Hori, H., Ikenouchi-Sugita, A., Hayashi, K., Atake, K., & Nakamura, J. (2013). Follow-up study on electroconvulsive therapy in treatment-resistant depressed patients after remission: A chart review. *Clinical Psychopharmacology and Neuroscience, 11*, 34-38.

Tolin, D. F., Lee, E., Levy, H. C., Das, A., Mammo, L., Katz, B. W., & Diefenbach, G. J. (2021). Psychophysiological assessment of stress reactivity and recovery in anxiety disorders. *Journal of Anxiety Disorders, 82*, 102426.

Tolman, E. C., & Honzik, C. H. (1930). Introduction and removal of reward and maze performance in rats. *University of California Publications in Psychology, 4*, 257-275.

Tolnai, S., Beutelmann, R., & Klump, G. M. (2017). Effect of preceding stimulation on sound localization and its representation in the auditory midbrain. *European Journal of Neuroscience, 45*, 460-471.

Tomasello, M. (2019). The role of roles in uniquely human cognition and sociality. *Journal for the Theory of Social Behaviour.* https://doi-org.silk.library.umass.edu/10.1111/jtsb.12223.

Tonnaer, F., Cima, M., & Arntz, A. (2019). Explosive matters: Does venting anger reduce or increase aggression? Differences in anger venting effects in violent offenders. *Journal of Aggression, Maltreatment & Trauma*, 1-17.

Tononi, G., & Cirelli, C. (2013). Perchance to prune. *Scientific American, 309*(2), 34-39.

Torre, J. B., & Lieberman, M. D. (2018). Putting feelings into words: Affect labeling as implicit emotion regulation. *Emotion Review, 10*(2), 116-124.

Torres, S. A., Sosa, S. S., Flores Toussaint, R. J., Jolie, S., & Bustos, Y. (2022). Systems of oppression: The impact of discrimination on Latinx immigrant adolescents' well-being and development. *Journal of Research on Adolescence.* Advance online publication. https://doi.org/10.1111/jora.12751

Torrey, E. F., & Yolken, R. H. (2019). Schizophrenia as a pseudogenetic disease: A call for more gene-environmental studies. *Psychiatry Research, 278*, 146-150.

Tosto, M. G., Hayiou-Thomas, M. E., Harlaar, N., Prom-Wormley, E., Dale, P. S., & Plomin, R. (2017). The genetic architecture of oral language, reading fluency, and reading comprehension: A twin study from 7 to 16 years. *Developmental Psychology, 53*, 1115-1129.

Toto, H. S. A., Piffer, D., Khaleefa, O. H., Bader, R. A. S. A. T., Bakhiet, S. F. A., Lynn, R., & Essa, Y. A. S. (2019). A study of the heritability of intelligence in Sudan. *Journal of Biosocial Science, 51*(2), 307-311.

Towns, C. R. (2017). The science and ethics of cell-based therapies for Parkinson's disease. *Parkinsonism & Related Disorders, 34*, 1-6.

Tracy, J. L., & Robins, R. W. (2004). Show your pride: Evidence for a discrete emotion expression. *Psychological Science, 15*, 194-197.

Tramontana, J. (2011). *Sports hypnosis in practice: Scripts, strategies and case examples.* Crown House Publishing Limited.

Trapido, D. (2022). The female penalty for novelty and the offsetting effect of alternate status characteristics. *Social Forces, 100*(4), 1592-1618.

Travis, F., Haaga, D. A., Hagelin, J., Tanner, M., Nidich, S., Gaylord-King, C., Grosswald, S., Rainforth, M., & Schneider, R. H. (2009). Effects of transcendental meditation practice on brain functioning and stress reactivity in college students. *International Journal of Psychopathy, 71*, 170-176.

Treatment Advocacy Center. (2016). Serious mental illness and homelessness. https://www.treatmentadvocacycenter.org/storage/documents/backgrounders/smi-and-homelessness.pdf

Triki, Z., Aellen, M., van Schaik, C. P., & Bshary, R. (2021). Relative brain size and cognitive equivalence in fishes. *Brain, Behavior and Evolution, 96*(3), 124-136.

Trindade, I. A., Mendes, A. L., & Ferreira, N. B. (2020). The moderating effect of psychological flexibility on the link between learned helplessness and depression symptomatology: A preliminary study. *Journal of Contextual Behavioral Science, 15*, 68-72.

Trollinger, L. M. (2021). Sex/gender research in music education: A review. *Visions of Research in Music Education, 16*(5), 5.

Trope, A., Anderson, B. T., Hooker, A. R., Glick, G., Stauffer, C., & Woolley, J. D. (2019). Psychedelic-assisted group therapy: A systematic review. *Journal of Psychoactive Drugs, 51*(2), 174-188.

Truc, A. (2021). Mapping behavioral economics and its interdisciplinary practices. *SSRN 3788167.*

Trujillo-Pisanty, I., Hernandez, G., Moreau-Debord, I., Cossette, M. P., Conover, K., Cheer, J. F., Shizgal, P. (2011). Cannabinoid receptor blockade reduces the opportunity cost at which rats maintain operant performance for rewarding brain stimulation. *Journal of Neuroscience, 31*, 5426-5430.

Tschentscher, N., & Hauk, O. (2017). Frontal cortex supports the early structuring of multiple solution steps in symbolic problem-solving. *Journal of Cognitive Neuroscience, 29*, 114-124.

Tse, V. V., Crabtree, J., Islam, S., & Stott, J. (2019). Comparing intellectual and memory abilities of older autistic adults with typically developing older adults using WAIS-IV and WMS-IV. *Journal of Autism and Developmental Disorders, 49*(10), 4123-4133.

Tsemberis, S., & Macnaughton, E. (2017). Homelessness and challenges of community care. In N. Okkels, C. B. Kristiansen, & P. Munk-Jørgensen (Eds.), *Mental health and illness in the city.* Springer Science + Business Media.

Tseng, W. S. (2003). *Clinician's guide to cultural psychiatry.* Elsevier Publishing.

Tsenkova, V., Boylan, J., & Ryff, C. (2013). Stress eating and health. Findings from MIDUS, a national study of US adults. *Appetite, 69*, 151-155.

Tsukahara, J. S., & Engle, R. W. (2021). Fluid intelligence and the locus coeruleus-norepinephrine system. *Proceedings of the National Academy of Sciences, 118*(46), e2110630118.

Tsukasaki, T., & Ishii, K. (2004). Linguistic-cultural relativity of cognition: Rethinking the Sapir-Whorf hypothesis. *Japanese Psychological Review, 47*, 173-186.

Tuan, L. T. (2022). Employee mindfulness and proactive coping for technostress in the COVID-19 outbreak: The roles of regulatory foci, technostress, and job insecurity. *Computers in Human Behavior, 129*, 107148.

Tucker, A. (2022, October). Sniffing out the science of smelling. *Smithsonian.* https://www.smithsonianmag.com/science-nature/scientific-mysteries-smelling-180980756/

Tucker-Drob, E. M., Brandmaier, A. M., & Lindenberger, U. (2019). Coupled cognitive changes in adulthood: A meta-analysis. *Psychological Bulletin,145*(3), 273-301.

Tuckey, M. R., Searle, B. J., Boyd, C. M., Winefield, A. H., & Winefield, H. R. (2015). Hindrances are not threats: Advancing the multidimensionality of work stress. *Journal of Occupational Health Psychology, 20*, 131-147

Tudor, K. (2022). There and back again: Re-envisioning "relationship therapy" as the center of a contemporary, cultural, and contextual person-centered therapy. *Person-Centered & Experiential Psychotherapies*, 1-19.

Tudor, K. (2022). There and back again: Re-envisioning "relationship therapy" as the center of a contemporary, cultural, and contextual person-centered therapy. *Person-Centered & Experiential Psychotherapies, 21*(2), 188-206.

Tuerk, P. W., Yoder, M., Grubaugh, A., Myrick, H., Hamner, M., & Acierno, R. (2011). Prolonged exposure therapy for combat-related posttraumatic stress disorder: An examination of treatment effectiveness for veterans of the wars in Afghanistan and Iraq. *Journal of Anxiety Disorders, 25*, 397-403.

Tullis, J. G., & Qiu, J. (2022). Generating mnemonics boosts recall of chemistry information. *Journal of Experimental Psychology: Applied, 28*(1), 71-84. https://doi.org/10.1037/xap0000350

Tummala-Narra, P. (2016). *Psychoanalytic theory and cultural competence in psychotherapy.* American Psychological Association.

Tunstall, B. J., Verendeev, A., & Kearns, D. N. (2013). Outcome specificity in deepened extinction may limit treatment feasibility: Co-presentation of a food cue interferes with extinction of cue-elicited cocaine seeking. *Drug and Alcohol Dependence, 133*(3).

Turban, J. L., Kraschel, K. L., & Cohen, I. G. (2021). Legislation to criminalize gender-affirming medical care for transgender youth. *JAMA, 325*(22), 2251-2252.

Turnbull, P. R., Khanal, S., & Dakin, S. C. (2021). The effect of cellphone position on driving and gaze behaviour. *Scientific Reports, 11*(1), 1-10.

Turner, C. W., & Leyens, J. P. (2019). The weapons effect revisited: The effects of firearms on aggressive behavior. *Psychology and Social Policy,* 201-222.

Turner, J. S., Tollison, A. C., Hopkins, B., Poloskey, L., & Fontaine, D. (2021). Sport-related concussion education and the elaboration likelihood model: Need for cognition as mediator between health literacy and concussion education efficacy. *Communication & Sport, 9*(4), 527-549.

Turri, M. G. (2015). Transference and katharsis, Freud to Aristotle. *International Journal of Psychoanalysis, 96,* 369-387.

Tversky, A., & Kahneman, D. (1987). Rational choice and the framing of decisions. In R. Hogarth & M. Reder (Eds.), *Rational choice: The contrast between economics and psychology.* University of Chicago Press.

Twenge, J., Haidt, J., and Cummins, K. (2022, February 16). Social media is riskier for kids than "screen time." *Washington Post.*

Twenge, J., Haidt, J., Lozano, J., and Cummins, K. (2022). Specification curve analysis shows that social media use is linked to poor mental health, especially among girls. *Acta Psychologica, 224,* 103512.

Twenge, J. M., Hisler, G. C., & Krizan, Z. (2019). Associations between screen time and sleep duration are primarily driven by portable electronic devices: Evidence from a population-based study of US children ages 0-17. *Sleep Medicine, 56,* 211-218.

Twenge, J. M., & Kasser, T. (2013). Generational changes in materialism and work centrality, 1976-2007: Associations with temporal changes in societal insecurity and materialistic role-modeling. *Personality and Social Psychology Bulletin, 34,* 17-31.

Twining, R. C., Wheeler, D. S., Ebben, A. L., Jacobsen, A. J., Robble, M. A., Mantsch, J. R., & Wheeler, R. A. (2015). Aversive stimuli drive drug seeking in a state of low dopamine tone. *Biological Psychiatry, 77,* 895-902.

Tyrer, H., Tyrer, P., Lisseman-Stones, Y., McAllister, S., Cooper, S., Salkovskis, P., Crawford, M. J., Dupont, S., Green, J., Murphy, D., & Wang, D. (2015). Therapist differences in a randomised trial of the outcome of cognitive behaviour therapy for health anxiety in medical patients. *International Journal of Nursing Studies, 52,* 686-694.

Tyrrell, P., Harberger, S., & Siddiqui, W. (2021). Stages of dying. StatPearls Publishing.

Updegraff, J. A., & Taylor, S. E. (2021). From vulnerability to growth: Positive and negative effects of stressful life events. In J. Harvey & E. Miller (Eds.), *Loss and Trauma.* Routledge.

Urban, J. B., & Linver, M. R. (Eds.). (2019). *Building a career outside academia: A guide for doctoral students in the behavioral and social sciences.* Washington, DC: American Psychological Association.

U.S. Bureau of Labor Statistics. (2022, April 20). Employment characteristics of families–2021. https://www.bls.gov/news.release/pdf/famee.pdf

U.S. Census Bureau. (2022, March 21). National Single Parent Day: March 21, 2022. https://www.census.gov/newsroom/stories/single-parent-day.html

U.S. Department of Education, National Center for Education Statistics. (2021). ChildStats.

U.S. Department of Health and Human Services. (2019, April 19). Data and statistics on children's mental health. https://www.cdc.gov/childrensmentalhealth/data.

U.S. Department of Health and Human Services. (2020). *Smoking cessation. A report of the Surgeon General.* Author.

U.S. Department of Veterans Affairs. (2021). *2021 national veteran suicide prevention annual report.* Office of Mental Health and Suicide Prevention. https://www.mentalhealth.va.gov/docs/datasheets/2021/2021-National-Veteran-Suicide-Prevention-Annual-Report-FINAL-9-8-21.pdf

Ustun, S. (2022). Ataque de nervios: A case report. *BJPsych Open, 8*(S1), S126-S126.

Vaccarino, F. J., Schiff, B. B., & Glickman, S. E. (2019). Biological view of reinforcement. *Contemporary Learning Theories: Volume II: Instrumental Conditioning Theory and the Impact of Biological Constraints on Learning,* 111.

Vadivel, R., & Ganesh, G. (2019). Enhancing the student's understanding of place theory of hearing using a sonometer. *International Journal of Physiology, 7*(1), 39-41.

Valencia, A., Zuma, B. Z., Spencer-Bonilla, G., López, L., Scheinker, D., & Rodriguez, F. (2021). The Hispanic paradox in the prevalence of obesity at the county-level. *Obesity Science & Practice, 7*(1), 14-24.

Valencia, R. R., & Suzuki, L. A. (2003). *Intelligence testing and minority students: Foundations, performance factors, and assessment issues.* Sage.

Valentine, K. E., Milling, L. S., Clark, L. J., & Moriarty, C. L. (2019). The efficacy of hypnosis as a treatment for anxiety: A meta-analysis. *International Journal of Clinical and Experimental Hypnosis, 67*(3), 336-363.

Valenzuela, V., Martínez, G., Duran-Aniotz, C., & Hetz, C. (2016). Gene therapy to target ER stress in brain diseases. *Brain Research, 1648*(Part B), 561-570.

Valkenburg, P. M., Meier, A., & Beyens, I. (2022). Social media use and its impact on adolescent mental health: An umbrella review of the evidence. *Current opinion in psychology, 44,* 58-68.

Vally, Z., & D'Souza, C. G. (2019). Abstinence from social media use, subjective well-being, stress, and loneliness. *Perspectives in Psychiatric Care.* https://doi.org/10.1111/ppc.12431.

Valyear, M. D., Villaruel, F. R., & Chaudhri, N. (2017). Alcohol-seeking and relapse: A focus on incentive salience and contextual conditioning. *Behavioural Processes, 141*(Part 1), 26-32.

Van Belle, V., Pelckmans, K., Suykens, J. A. K., & Van Huffel, S. (2011). Learning transformation models for ranking and survival analysis. *Journal of Machine Learning Research, 12,* 819-862.

Vandbakk, M., Olaff, H. S., & Holth, P. (2019). Conditioned reinforcement: The effectiveness of stimulus–stimulus pairing and operant discrimination procedures. *The Psychological Record, 69*(1), 67-81.

van de Blaak, F. L., & Dumont, G. J. (2021). Serotonin transporter availability, neurocognitive function and their correlation in abstinent 3, 4-methylenedioxy-methamphetamine users. *Human Psychopharmacology: Clinical and Experimental,* e2811.

Van De Graaff, K. (2000). Human anatomy (5th ed.). McGraw Hill.

Van Den Heuvel, M. I., Hect, J. L., Smarr, B. L., Qawasmeh, T., Kriegsfeld, L. J., Barcelona, J., Hijazi, K. E., & Thomason, M. E. (2021). Maternal stress during pregnancy alters fetal cortico-cerebellar connectivity in utero and increases child sleep problems after birth. *Scientific Reports, 11*(1), 1-12.

van der Heijden, M., & Vavakou, A. (2021). Rectifying and sluggish: Outer hair cells as regulators rather than amplifiers. *Hearing Research,* 108367.

Van Dessel, P., Mertens, G., Smith, C. T., & De Houwer, J. (2017). The mere exposure instruction effect: Mere exposure instructions influence liking. *Experimental Psychology, 64*(5), 299-314. https://doi.org/10.1027/1618-3169/a000376

Van Deurzen, E., Craig, E., Längle, A., Schneider, K. J., Tantam, D., & du Plock, S. (Eds.). (2019). *The Wiley world handbook of existential therapy.* Wiley Blackwell.

Vandierendonck, A., & Szmalec, A. (Eds.). (2011). *Spatial working memory.* Psychology Press.

Van Doesum, N. J., Karremans, J. C., Fikke, R. C., de Lange, M. A., & Van Lange, P. A. M. (2018). Social mindfulness in the real world: The physical presence of others induces other-regarding motivation. *Social Influence, 13*(4), 209-222.

Vanheule, S., Desmet, M., Rosseel, Y., & Meganck, R. (2006). Core transference themes in depression. *Journal of Affective Disorders, 91,* 71-75.

Van Lange, P. A. M., & Columbus, S. (2021). Vitamin S: Why is social contact, even with strangers, so important to well-being? *Current Directions in Psychological Science, 30*(3), 267-273.

Vanlessen, N., De Raedt, R., Koster, E. H., & Pourtois, G. (2016). Happy heart, smiling eyes: A systematic review of positive mood effects on broadening of visuospatial attention. *Neuroscience & Biobehavioral Reviews, 68,* 816-837.

van Marle, K., & Wynn, K. (2009). Infants' auditory enumeration: Evidence for analog magnitudes in the small number range. *Cognition, 111,* 302-316.

van Nieuwenhuijzen, M., Vriens, A., Scheepmaker, M., Smit, M., & Porton, E. (2011). The development of a diagnostic instrument to measure social information processing in children with mild to borderline intellectual disabilities. *Research in Developmental Disabilities, 32,* 358-370.

van Rooij, S. J. H., Sippel, L. M., McDonald, W. M., & Holtzheimer, P. E. (2021). Defining focal brain stimulation targets for PTSD using neuroimaging. *Depression and Anxiety.* https://doi.org/10.1002/da.23159

van Rosmalen, L., Luijk, M. P., & van der Horst, F. C. (2022). Harry Harlow's pit of despair: Depression in monkeys and men. *Journal of the History of the Behavioral Sciences, 58*(2), 204-222.

Van Rosmalen, L., Van Der Veer, R., & Van Der Horst, F. (2015). Ainsworth's strange situation procedure: The origin of an instrument. *Journal of the History of the Behavioral Sciences, 51,* 261-284.

Varkevisser, R. D. M., van Stralen, M. M., Kroeze, W., Ket, J. C. F., & Steenhuis, I. H. M. (2019). Determinants of weight loss maintenance: A systematic review. *Obesity Reviews, 20*(2), 171-211.

Varma, R. (2018). US science and engineering workforce: Underrepresentation of women and minorities. *American Behavioral Scientist, 62*(5), 692-697.

Vasile, C. (2021). Eclectic psychotherapy and case formulation. *Journal of Educational Sciences & Psychology, 11*(2), 162-168.

Vasileva, O., & Balyasnikova, N. (2019). (Re) Introducing Vygotsky's thought: From historical overview to contemporary psychology. *Frontiers in Psychology, 10,* 1515.

Vasilyeva, N., Eski, R., & Rothwell, J. (2023, 13 February.). Pictured: moments of hope as woman rescued 176 hours after devastating earthquakes. *The Telegraph.* Downloaded from https://www.telegraph.co.uk/news/2023/02/08/turkey-syria-earthquake-miracle-rescues-hopeful-searches/.

Vasudeva, K., Vodovotz, Y., Azhar, N., Barclay, D., Janjic, J. M., & Pollock, J. A. (2015). In vivo and systems biology studies implicate IL-18 as a central mediator in chronic pain. *Journal of Neuroimmunology, 28,* 343-349.

Vaughan-Graham, J., Patterson, K., Zabjek, K., & Cott, C. A. (2019). Important movement concepts: Clinical versus neuroscience perspectives. *Motor Control, 23*(3), 273-293.

Vaughn Becker, D., & Neuberg, S. L. (2019). Pushing archetypal representational systems further. *Psychological Inquiry, 30*(2), 103-109.

Vela, A., & Kamsickas, L. (2022). Happiness and social connectivity. In G. Merlo & K. Berra (Eds.), *Lifestyle Nursing.* CRC Press.

Velentzas, K., Heinen, T., & Schack, T. (2011). Routine integration strategies and their effects on volleyball serve performance and players' movement mental representation. *Journal of Applied Sport Psychology, 23,* 209-222.

Vella, E. J. (2020). Psychosocial factors in coronary heart disease. In K. Sweeny, M. L. Robbins, & L. M. Cohen (Eds.), *The Wiley Encyclopedia of Health Psychology.* John Wiley & Sons.

Velotti, P., Garofalo, C., Dimaggio, G., & Fonagy, P. (2019). Mindfulness, alexithymia, and empathy moderate relations between trait aggression and antisocial personality disorder traits. *Mindfulness, 10*(6), 1082-1090.

Vera-Estay, E., Dooley, J. J., & Beauchamp, M. H. (2015). Cognitive underpinnings of moral reasoning in adolescence: The contribution of executive functions. *Journal of Moral Education, 44*, 17-33.

Veraksa, N., & Samuelsson, I. P. (Eds.). (2022). *Piaget and Vygotsky in XXI century: Discourse in early childhood education* (Vol. 4). Springer Nature.

Verhaeghen, P., & Mirabito, G. (2021). When you are talking to yourself, is anybody listening? The relationship between inner speech, self-awareness, wellbeing, and multiple aspects of self-regulation. *International Journal of Personality Psychology, 7*, 8-24.

Verhoef, E., Shapland, C. Y., Fisher, S. E., Dale, P. S., & St Pourcain, B. (2021). The developmental origins of genetic factors influencing language and literacy: Associations with early-childhood vocabulary. *Journal of Child Psychology and Psychiatry, 62*(6), 728-738.

Verplanken, B., & Orbell, S. (2022). Attitudes, habits, and behavior change. *Annual Review of Psychology, 73*, 327-352.

Verschueren, M., Rassart, J., Claes, L., Moons, P., & Luyckx, K. (2017). Identity statuses throughout adolescence and emerging adulthood: A large-scale study into gender, age, and contextual differences. *Psychologica Belgica, 57*, 32-42.

Vicario, C. M., Kuran, K. A., & Urgesi, C. (2019). Does hunger sharpen senses? A psychophysics investigation on the effects of appetite in the timing of reinforcement-oriented actions. *Psychological Research, 83*(3), 395-405.

Vicari, S., Pontillo, M., & Armando, M. (2013). Neurodevelopmental and psychiatric issues in Down's syndrome: Assessment and intervention. *Psychiatric Genetics, 23*, 95-107.

Vilendrer, S., Brown-Johnson, C., Kling, S. M., Veruttipong, D., Amano, A., Bohman, B., Daines, W. P., Overton, D., Srivastava, R., & Asch, S. M. (2021). Financial incentives for medical assistants: A mixed-methods exploration of bonus structures, motivation, and population health quality measures. *The Annals of Family Medicine, 19*(5), 427-436.

Villafaina, S., Collado-Mateo, D., Cano-Plasencia, R., Gusi, N., & Fuentes, J. P. (2019). Electroencephalographic response of chess players in decision-making processes under time pressure. *Physiology & Behavior, 198*, 140-143. https://doi.org/10.1016/j.physbeh.2018.10.017.

Vincus, A. A., Ringwalt, C., Harris, M. S., & Shamblen, S. R. (2010). A short-term, quasi-experimental evaluation of D.A.R.E.'s revised elementary school curriculum. *Journal of Drug Education, 40*, 37-49.

Viswanathan, M., Golin, C. E., Jones, C. D., Ashok, M., Blalock, S. J., Wines, R. C., Coker-Schwimmer, E. J., Rosen, D. L., Sista, P., & Lohr, K. N. (2012). Interventions to improve adherence to self-administered medications for chronic diseases in the United States: A systematic review. *Annals of Internal Medicine,157*(11),785-795.https://doi.org/10.7326/0003-4819-157-11-201212040-00538

Vital, J. E. C., de Morais Nunes, A., New, B. S. D. A. C., de Sousa, B. D. A., Nascimento, M. F., Formiga, M. F., & Fernandes, A. T. N. (2021). Biofeedback therapeutic effects on blood pressure levels in hypertensive individuals: A systematic review and meta-analysis. *Complementary Therapies in Clinical Practice, 44*, 101420.

Vitello, P. (2006, June 12). A ring tone meant to fall on deaf ears. *The New York Times*, p. A1.

Vitriol, J. A., & Marsh, J. K. (2018). The illusion of explanatory depth and endorsement of conspiracy beliefs. *European Journal of Social Psychology, 48*(7), 955-969.

Vlassova, A., & Pearson, J. (2013). Look before you leap: Sensory memory improves decision making. *Psychological Science, 24*, 1635-1643.

Vogel, E. A., Rose, J. P., Okdie, B. M., Eckles, K., & Franz, B. (2015). Who compares and despairs? The effect of social comparison orientation on social media use and its outcomes. *Personality and Individual Differences, 86*, 249-256.

Vöhringer, I. A., Kolling, T., Graf, F., Poloczek, S., Fassbender, I., Freitag, C., Lamm, B., Suhrke, J., Teiser, J., Teubert, M., Keller, H., Lohaus, A., Schwarzer, G., & Knopft, M. (2017). The development of implicit memory from infancy to childhood: On average performance levels and interindividual differences. *Child Development, 89*(2), 370-382.

Voits, T., Robson, H., Rothman, J., & Pliatsikas, C. (2022). The effects of bilingualism on hippocampal volume in ageing bilinguals. *Brain Structure and Function, 227*(3), 979-994.

Voiß, P., Höxtermann, M. D., Dobos, G., & Cramer, H. (2019). The use of mind-body medicine among US individuals with sleep problems: Analysis of the 2017 National Health Interview Survey data. *Sleep Medicine, 56*, 151-156.

Volkow, N. D., & Blanco, C. (2021). The changing opioid crisis: development, challenges and opportunities. *Molecular psychiatry, 26*(1), 218-233.

von Stumm, S., & Plomin, R. (2021). Using DNA to predict intelligence. *Intelligence, 86*, 101530.

Vorgias, D., & Bernstein, B. (2021). Fetal alcohol syndrome. *StatPearls*. StatPearls Publishing.

Vosoughi, S., Roy, D., & Aral, S. (2018). The spread of true and false news online. *Science, 359*, 1146-1151.

Voznessenskaya, V. V., Klyuchnikova, M. A., & Laktionova, T. K. (2022). Evolution of pheromones in mammals. *Biology Bulletin Reviews, 12*(1), 49-64.

Vrieze, S. I., McGue, M., Miller, M. B., Hicks, B. M., & Iacono, W. G. (2013). Three mutually informative ways to understand the genetic relationships among behavioral disinhibition, alcohol use, drug use, nicotine use/dependence, and their co-occurrence: Twin biometry, GCTA, and genome-wide scoring. *Behavior Genetics, 43*, 97-107.

Vukasovic´, T., & Bratko, D. (2015). Heritability of personality: A meta-analysis of behavior genetic studies. *Psychological Bulletin, 141*, 769-785.

Vuust, P., Heggli, O. A., Friston, K. J., & Kringelbach, M. L. (2022). Music in the brain. *Nature Reviews Neuroscience, 23*(5), 287-305. https://doi.org/10.1038/s41583-022-00578-5

Vygotsky, L. S. (1926/1997). *Educational psychology*. St. Lucie Press.

Wagemans, J., Elder, J. H., Kubovy, M., Palmer, S. E., Peterson, M. A., Singh, M., & von der Heydt, R. (2012). A century of Gestalt psychology in visual perception: I. Perceptual grouping and figure-ground organization. *Psychological Bulletin, 138*, 1172-1217.

Wagner, R. K. (2011). Practical intelligence. In R. J. Sternberg & S. Kaufman (Eds.), *The Cambridge handbook of intelligence*. Cambridge University Press.

Wagstaff, G. (2009). Is there a future for investigative hypnosis? *Journal of Investigative Psychology and Offender Profiling, 6*, 43-57.

Wagstaff, G. F., Wheatcroft, J. M., & Jones, A. (2011). Are high hypnotizables especially vulnerable to false memory effects? A sociocognitive perspective. *International Journal of Clinical and Experimental Hypnosis, 59*, 310-326.

Wailoo, K. (2021). *Pushing cool: Big tobacco, racial marketing, and the untold story of the menthol cigarette*. University of Chicago Press.

Waismeyer, A., & Meltzoff, A. N. (2017). Learning to make things happen: Infants' observational learning of social and physical causal events. *Journal of Experimental Child Psychology, 162*, 58-71.

Waite, S. (2021). Should I stay or should I go? Employment discrimination and workplace harassment against transgender and other minority employees in Canada's federal public service. *Journal of Homosexuality, 68*(11), 1833-1859.

Walker, L., & Frimer, J. (2009). The song remains the same: Rebuttal to Sherblom's re-envisioning of the legacy of the care challenge. *Journal of Moral Education, 38*, 53-68.

Wallace, L. S., Chisolm, D. J., Abdel-Rasoul, M., & DeVoe, J. E. (2013). Survey mode matters: Adults' self-reported statistical confidence, ability to obtain health information, and perceptions of

patient-health-care provider communication. *Journal of Health Psychology, 18*, 1036-1045.

Walle, E. A., Lopez, L. D., & Castillo, A. (2022). Emotional development: A field in need of a (cognitive) revolution. In D. Dukes, A. C. Samson, & E. A. Walle (Eds.), *The Oxford Handbook of Emotional Development*. Oxford Academic.

Wallis, C. (2019, June). Is pot any good for pain? *Scientific American*, p. 20.

Wallis, C. (2021, March). 7 ways to tackle COVID vaccine hesitancy. *Scientific American*, p. 23.

Walter, K. V., Conroy-Beam, D., Buss, D. M., Asao, K., Sorokowska, A., Sorokowski, P., Aavik, T., Akello, G., Alhabahba, M. M., Alm, C., Amjad, N., Anjum, A., Atama, C. S., Duyar, D. A., Ayebar, R., Batres, C., Bendixen, M., Bensafia, A., Bizumic, B., Boussena, M., et al. (2020). Sex differences in mate preferences across 45 countries: A large-scale replication. *Psychological Science, 31*(4), 408-423.

Walton, G. M., & Cohen, G. L. (2011). A brief social-belonging intervention improves academic and health outcomes of minority students. *Science, 331*, 1447-1451.

Walton, J. R., Murphy, C., & Bartram, L. (2017). Childhood behavioral problems–Attention-deficit/hyperactivity disorder (ADHD). In W. O'Donohue, L. James, & C. Snipes (Eds.), *Practical strategies and tools to promote treatment engagement*. Springer International Publishing.

Wampold, B. E. (2019). A smorgasbord of PTSD treatments: What does this say about integration? *Journal of Psychotherapy Integration, 29*(1), 65.

Wampold, B. E. (2019). *The basics of psychotherapy: An introduction to theory and practice* (2nd ed.). American Psychological Association.

Wang, D. (2019). A study of the relationship between narcissism, extraversion, body-esteem, social comparison orientation and selfie-editing behavior on social networking sites. *Personality and Individual Differences, 146*, 127-129.

Wang, L. N., Wang, X. Z., Li, Y. J., Li, B. R., Huang, M., Wang, X-Y., Grygorczyk, R., Ding, G-H., & Schwarz, W. (2022). Activation of subcutaneous mast cells in acupuncture points triggers analgesia. *Cells, 11*(5), 809.

Wang, M., Chen, W., Zhang, C., & Deng, X. (2017). Personality types and scholarly creativity in undergraduate students: The mediating roles of creative styles. *Personality and Individual Differences, 105*, 170-174.

Wang, M. T., & Hofkens, T. L. (2020). Beyond classroom academics: A school-wide and multi-contextual perspective on student engagement in school. *Adolescent Research Review, 5*(4), 419-433.

Wang, M. T., & Kenny, S. (2013). Longitudinal links between fathers' and mothers' harsh verbal discipline and adolescents' conduct problems and depressive symptoms. *Child Development, 85*(3), 908-923.

Wang, M. Z., & Hayden, B. Y. (2021). Latent learning, cognitive maps, and curiosity. *Current Opinion in Behavioral Sciences, 38*, 1-7.

Wang, Q., & Conway, M. A. (2006). Autobiographical memory, self, and culture. In L-G. Nilsson & N. Ohta, *Memory and society: Psychological perspectives*. Psychology Press.

Wang, Q., Peterson, C., Khuu, A., Reid, C. P., Maxwell, K. L., & Vincent, J. M. (2019). Looking at the past through a telescope: Adults postdated their earliest childhood memories. *Memory, 27*(1), 19-27.

Wang, R., Liu, H., Jiang, J., & Song, Y. (2017). Will materialism lead to happiness? A longitudinal analysis of the mediating role of psychological needs satisfaction. *Personality and Individual Differences, 105*, 312-317.

Wang, X., Chao, F., Yu, G., & Zhang, K. (2022). Factors influencing fake news rebuttal acceptance during the COVID-19 pandemic and the moderating effect of cognitive ability. *Computers in Human Behavior, 130*, 107174.

Wang, Y., & Sloan, F. A. (2018). Present bias and health. *Journal of Risk and Uncertainty, 57*(2), 177-198.

Wang, Y., & Wagner, S. (2018, May). On groupthink in safety analysis: An industrial case study. In *Proceedings of the 40th International Conference on Software Engineering: Software Engineering in Practice*. Association for Computing Machinery.

Wang, Y., & Zhong, Z. (2015). Effects of frustration situation and resilience on implicit aggression. *Chinese Journal of Clinical Psychology, 23*, 209-212.

Wannez, S., Heine, L., Thonnard, M., Gosseries, O., & Laureys, S. (2017). The repetition of behavioral assessments in diagnosis of disorders of consciousness. *Annals of Neurology, 81*, 883-889.

Warach, B., Josephs, L., & Gorman, B. S. (2019). Are cheaters sexual hypocrites? Sexual hypocrisy, the self-serving bias, and personality style. *Personality and Social Psychology Bulletin, 45*(10), 1499-1511.

Ward, E. V. (2022). EXPRESS: Age and processing effects on perceptual and conceptual priming. *Quarterly Journal of Experimental Psychology*. Advance online publication, 17470218221090128.

Ward, L. M. (2011). The thalamic dynamic core theory of conscious experience. *Consciousness and Cognition: An International Journal, 20*, 464-486.

Ward-Baker, P. D. (2007). The remarkable oldest old: A new vision of aging. *Dissertation Abstracts International Section A: Humanities and Social Sciences, 67*(8-A), 3115.

Wark, B., Lundstrom, B., & Fairhall, A. (2007). Sensory adaptation. *Current Opinion in Neurobiology, 17*, 423-429.

Warmbold-Brann, K., Burns, M. K., Preast, J. L., Taylor, C. N., & Aguilar, L. N. (2017). Meta-analysis of the effects of academic interventions and modifications on student behavior outcomes. *School Psychology Quarterly, 32*(3), 291-305.

Warne, R. T. (2019). An evaluation (and vindication?) of Lewis Terman: What the father of gifted education can teach the 21st century. *Gifted Child Quarterly, 63*(1), 3-21.

Warne, R. T., & Liu, J. K. (2017). Income differences among grade skippers and non-grade skippers across genders in the Terman sample, 1936-1976. *Learning and Instruction, 47*, 1-12.

Wasserman, J. D. (2018). A history of intelligence assessment: The unfinished tapestry. In D. P. Flanagan & E. M. McDonough (Eds.), *Contemporary intellectual assessment: Theories, tests, and issues* (4th ed.) The Guilford Press.

Waters, A. M., Theresiana, C., Neumann, D. L., & Craske, M. G. (2017). Developmental differences in aversive conditioning, extinction, and reinstatement: A study with children, adolescents, and adults. *Journal of Experimental Child Psychology, 159*, 263-278.

Watkins, M. W., & Canivez, G. L. (2021). Assessing the psychometric utility of IQ scores: A tutorial using the Wechsler Intelligence Scale for Children-Fifth Edition. *School Psychology Review*, 1-15. Advanced online publication. https://doi.org/10.1080/23729 66X.2020.1816804

Watson, J. B. (1924). *Behaviorism*. New York: Norton.

Watters, E. (2010, January 10). The Americanization of mental illness. *The New York Times*, p. C2.

Wawrosz, P., & Jurásek, M. (2021). Developing intercultural efficiency: The relationship between cultural intelligence and self-efficacy. *Social Sciences, 10*(8), 312.

Waxman, S. (2009). Learning from infants' first verbs. *Monographs of the Society for Research in Child Development, 74*, 127-132.

Waxman, S. R. (2021). Racial awareness and bias begin early: Developmental entry points, challenges, and a call to action. *Perspectives on Psychological Science, 16*(5), 893-902.

Weber, J. M. (2019). Individuals matter, but the situation's the thing: The case for a habitual situational lens in leadership and organizational decision-making. *Organizational Dynamics*. https://doi.org/ 10.1016/j. orgdyn.2019.03.003.

Weber, L., & Dwoskin, E. (2014, September 30). As personality tests multiply, employers are split. *Wall Street Journal*, pp. A1, A12.

Wechsler Adult Intelligence Scale-Fourth Edition (WAIS-IV). (2008). Pearson Education, Inc.

Weeks, M., & Lupfer, M. B. (2004). Complicating race: The relationship between prejudice, race, and social class categorizations. *Personality and Social Psychology Bulletin, 30*, 972-984.

Wehrle, R., Kaufmann, C., Wetter, T. C., Holsboer, F., Auer, D. P., Pollmacher, T., et al. (2007). Functional microstates within human REM sleep: First evidence from fMRI of a thalamocortical network specific for phasic REM periods. *European Journal of Neuroscience, 25*, 863-871.

Weidemann, C. T., Kragel, J. E., Lega, B. C., Worrell, G. A., Sperling, M. R., Sharan, A. D., et al. (2019). Neural activity reveals interactions between episodic and semantic memory systems during retrieval. *Journal of Experimental Psychology: General, 148*(1), 1.

Weiland, N., & Sanger-Katz, M. (2022, May 12). Overdose deaths hit record levels, with fentanyl a key culprit. *New York Times*, P. A1, A21.

Weimann, J., Knabe, A., & Schöb, R. (2015). *Measuring happiness: The economics of well-being*. MIT Press.

Weiner, R. D., & Falcone, G. (2011). Electroconvulsive therapy: How effective is it? *Journal of the American Psychiatric Nurses Association, 17*, 217-218.

Weinschenk, A. C., Dawes, C. T., Kandler, C., Bell, E., & Riemann, R. (2019). New evidence on the link between genes, psychological traits, and political engagement. *Politics and the Life Sciences, 38*(1), 1-13.

Weir, K. (2016, April). New insights on eating disorders. *Monitor on Psychology*, 36-40.

Weir, K. (2016, March). The risks of earlier puberty. *Monitor on Psychology*, 41-44.

Weir, K. (2016). The science of naps. *Monitor on Psychology, 47*, 48-51.

Weller, P. D., Anderson, M. C., Gomez-Ariza, C. J., & Bajo, M. T. (2013). On the status of cue independence as a criterion for memory inhibition. *Journal of Experimental Psychology: Learning, Memory, and Cognition, 39*, 1232-1245.

Wellings, K., Palme, M. J., Machiyama, K., & Slaymaker, E. (2019). Changes in, and factors associated with, frequency of sex in Britain: Evidence from three National Surveys of Sexual Attitudes and Lifestyles (Natsal). *BMJ: British Medical Journal, 365*.

Wen, M., Butler, L. T., & Koutstaal, W. (2013). Improving insight and noninsight problem solving with brief interventions. *British Journal of Psychology, 104*, 97-118.

Wendt, D. C., Gone, J. P., & Nagata, D. K. (2015). Potentially harmful therapy and multicultural counseling: Bridging two disciplinary discourses ψ. *The Counseling Psychologist, 43*(3), 334-358.

Wenzel, A. (2011). Obsessions and compulsions. In A. Wenzel & S. Stuart (Eds.), *Anxiety in childbearing women: Diagnosis and treatment*. American Psychological Association.

Werfel, K. L., Reynolds, G., Hudgins, S., Castaldo, M., & Lund, E. A. (2021). The production of complex syntax in spontaneous language by 4-year-old children with hearing loss. *American Journal of Speech-Language Pathology, 30*(2), 609-621.

Werhane, P. H., Pincus Hartman, L., Archer, C., Englehardt, E. E., & Pritchard, M. S. (2013). *Obstacles to ethical decision-making: Mental models, Milgram and the problem of obedience*. Cambridge University Press.

Wertheimer, M. (1923). Untersuchungen zur Lehre von der Gestalt, II. *Psychologische Forschung., 5*, 301-350. In R. Beardsley & M. Wertheimer (Eds.) (1958), *Readings in perception*. Van Nostrand.

Wertz, J., Belsky, J., Moffitt, T. E., Belsky, D. W., Harrington, H., Avinun, R., Poulton, R., Ramrakha, S., & Caspi, A. (2019). Genetics of nurture: A test of the hypothesis that parents' genetics predict their observed caregiving. *Developmental Psychology, 55*(7), 1461-1472.

West, R. L., Bagwell, D. K., & Dark-Freudeman, A. (2007). Self-efficacy and memory aging: The impact of a memory intervention based on self-efficacy. *Neuropsychological Development and Cognition, B, Aging and Neuropsychological Cognition, 14*, 1-28.

Wester, A. J., van Herten, J. C., Egger, J. M., & Kessels, R. C. (2013). Applicability of the Rivermead Behavioural Memory Test-Third Edition (RBMT-3) in Korsakoff's syndrome and chronic alcoholics. *Neuropsychiatric Disease and Treatment, 9*, 202-212.

Westerhausen, R., Moosmann, M., Alho, K., Medvedev, S., Hämäläinen, H., & Hugdahl, K. (2009). Top-down and bottom-up interaction: Manipulating the dichotic listening ear advantage. *Brain Research, 1250*, 183-189.

Westerterp, K. R. (2006). Perception, passive overfeeding and energy metabolism. *Physiology & Behavior, 89*, 62-65.

Westgate, E., Riskind, R., & Nosek, B. (2015). Implicit preferences for straight people over lesbian women and gay men weakened from 2006 to 2013. *Collabra: Psychology, 1*(1).

Wettstein, M., Wahl, H.-W., Siebert, J., & Schröder, J. (2019). Still more to learn about late-life cognitive development: How personality and health predict 20-year cognitive trajectories. *Psychology and Aging, 34*(5), 714-728.

Whillans, A. V., & Dunn, E. W. (2019). Valuing time over money is associated with greater social connection. *Journal of Social and Personal Relationships, 36*(8), 2549-2565.

Whillans, A. V., Dunn, E. W., Smeets, P. I., Bekkers, R., & Norton, M. I. (2017). Buying time promotes happiness. *PNAS, 114*, 8523-8527.

Whisman, M., & Snyder, D. (2007). Sexual infidelity in a national survey of American women: Differences in prevalence and correlates as a function of method of assessment. *Journal of Family Psychology, 21*, 14-154.

Whitbourne, S. K. (2010). *The search for fulfillment: Revolutionary new research that reveals the secret to long-term happiness*. Ballantine Books.

Whitbourne, S. K., Zuschlag, M. K., Elliot, L. B., & Waterman, A. S. (1992). Psychosocial development in adulthood: A 22-year sequential study. *Journal of Personality and Social Psychology, 63*, 260-271.

White, B. A., Miles, J. R., & Frantell, K. A. (2021). Intergroup dialogue: A justice-centered pedagogy to address gender inequity in STEM. *Science Education, 105*(2), 232-254.

White, F. A., Harvey, L. J., & Abu-Rayya, H. M. (2015). Improving intergroup relations in the Internet Age: A critical review. *Review of General Psychology, 19*, 129-139.

White, K. (2013). Remembering and forgetting. In G. J. Madden, W. V. Dube, T. D. Hackenberg, G. P. Hanley, & K. A. Lattal (Eds.), *APA handbook of behavior analysis, Vol. 1: Methods and principles*. American Psychological Association.

White, R. G., Jain, S., Orr, D. R., & Read, U. M. (2017). *The Palgrave handbook of sociocultural perspectives on global mental health*. Palgrave Macmillan.

Whitebread, D., Coltman, P., Jameson, H., & Lander, R. (2009). Play, cognition and self-regulation: What exactly are children learning when they learn through play? *Educational and Child Psychology, 26*, 40-52.

Whitehurst, L. N., & Mednick, S. C. (2021). Psychostimulants may block long-term memory formation via degraded sleep in healthy adults. *Neurobiology of Learning and Memory, 178*, 107342.

Whitney, P. G., & Green, J. A. (2011). Changes in infants' affect related to the onset of independent locomotion. *Infant Behavior & Development,34*, 459-466.

Whorf, B. L. (1956). *Language, thought, and reality*. Wiley.

Wicks, S., Berger, Z., & Camic, P. M. (2019). It's how I am... it's what I am . . . it's a part of who I am: A narrative exploration of the impact of adolescent-onset chronic illness on identity formation in young people. *Clinical Child Psychology and Psychiatry, 24*(1), 40-52.

Widaman, K. (2009). Phenylketonuria in children and mothers: Genes, environments, behavior. *Current Directions in Psychological Science, 18*, 48-52.

Widiger, T. A. (2015). Assessment of DSM-5 personality disorder. *Journal of Personality Assessment, 97*, 456-466.

Wiech, K. (2016). Deconstructing the sensation of pain: The influence of cognitive processes on pain perception. *Science, 354*, 584-587.

Wiedman, C. (2019). Rewarding collaborative research: Role congruity bias and the gender pay gap in academe. *Journal of Business Ethics*. Advance online publication. https://doi.org/10.1007/s10551-019-04165-0.

Wierzbiński, B., Surmacz, T., Kuźniar, W., & Witek, L. (2021). The role of the ecological awareness and the influence on food preferences in shaping pro-ecological behavior of young consumers. *Agriculture, 11*(4), 345. https://doi.org/10.3390/agriculture11040345

Wiesel, I., Bigby, C., van Holstein, E., & Gleeson, B. (2022). Three modes of inclusion of people with intellectual disability in mainstream services: mainstreaming, differentiation and individualisation. *Disability & Society*, 1-22. https://doi.org/10.1080/09687599.2022.2060803

Wiesman, A. I., Christopher-Hayes, N. J., & Wilson, T. W. (2021). Stairway to memory: Left-hemispheric alpha dynamics index the progressive loading of items into a short-term store. *NeuroImage, 235*, 118024.

Wieth, M., & Zacks, R. (2011). Time of day effects on problem solving: When the non-optimal is optimal. *Thinking & Reasoning, 17*, 387-401.

Wijeratne, C., Johnco, C., Draper, B., & Earl, J. (2021). Doctors' reporting of mental health stigma and barriers to help-seeking. *Occupational Medicine, 71*(8), 366-374.

Wilcox, C. E., Calhoun, V. D., Rachakonda, S., Claus, E. D., Littlewood, R. A., Mickey, J., et al. (2017). Functional network connectivity predicts treatment outcome during treatment of nicotine use disorder. *Psychiatry Research: Neuroimaging, 26*, 545-53.

Wildavsky, B. (2000, September 4). A blow to bilingual education. *U.S. News & World Report*, pp. 22-28.

Wilde, D. J. (2011). *Jung's personality theory quantified*. Springer-Verlag.

Wiley, J., & Jarosz, A. F. (2012). Working memory capacity, attentional focus, and problem solving. *Current Directions in Psychological Science, 21*, 258-262.

Wilkin, L., & Haddock, B. (2011). Functional fitness of older adults. *Activities, Adaptation & Aging, 35*, 197-209.

Wilkinson, H. A. (2009). Cingulotomy. *Journal of Neurosurgery, 110*, 607-611.

Wilkinson, S. T., Kitay, B. M., Harper, A., Rhee, T. G., Sint, K., Ghosh, A., Lopez, M. O., Saenz, S., & Tsai, J. (2021). Barriers to the implementation of electroconvulsive therapy (ECT): Results from a nationwide survey of ECT practitioners. *Psychiatric Services, 72*(7), 752-757.

Willems, S. J., Castells, M. C., & Baptist, A. P. (2022). The magnification of health disparities during the COVID-19 pandemic. *The Journal of Allergy and Clinical Immunology: In Practice, 10*(4), 903-908.

Williams, C. L., & Butcher, J. N. (2011). The nuts and bolts: Administering, scoring, and augmenting MMPI-A assessments. In C. L. Williams & J. N. Butcher (Eds.), *A beginner's guide to the MMPI–A*. American Psychological Association.

Williams, I. L., & Mee-Lee, D. (2019). Inside the black box of traditional treatment programs: Clearing the air on the original literary teachings of Alcoholics Anonymous (AA). *Addiction Research & Theory, 27*(5), 412-419.

Williams, K. E., Krems, J. A., Ayers, J. D., & Rankin, A. M. (2022). Sex differences in friendship preferences. *Evolution and Human Behavior, 43*(1), 44-52.

Williams, M. T. (2019). Microaggressions: Clarification, evidence, and impact. *Perspectives on Psychological Science, 15*(1), 3-26.

Williams, M. T. (2021). Racial microaggressions: Critical questions, state of the science, and new directions. *Perspectives on Psychological Science, 16*(5), 880-885.

Williams, R. H., Black, S. W., Thomas, A. M., Piquet, J., Cauli, B., & Kilduff, T. S. (2019). Excitation of cortical nNOS/NK1R neurons by hypocretin 1 is independent of sleep homeostasis. *Cerebral Cortex, 29*(3), 1090-1108.

Willis, J. (2017). Moving toward extremism: Group polarization in the laboratory and the world. In S. C. Cloninger & S. A. Leibo, S. C. (Eds.), *Understanding*

angry groups: Multidisciplinary perspectives on their motivations and effects on society. Praeger/ABC-CLIO.

Wills, K. E. (2013). Sickle cell disease. In I. Baron & C. Rey-Casserly (Eds.), *Pediatric neuropsychology: Medical advances and lifespan outcomes*. Oxford University Press.

Wilmot, J. H., Puhger, K., & Wiltgen, B. J. (2019). Acute disruption of the dorsal hippocampus impairs the encoding and retrieval of trace fear memories. *Frontiers in Behavioral Neuroscience, 13*, 116.

Wilsnack, R. W., Wilsnack, S. C., Gmel, G., & Kantor, L. W. (2018). Gender differences in binge drinking: Prevalence, predictors, and consequences. *Alcohol research: current reviews*.

Winberg, M. (2019, July 5). Sonic devices target teenagers In Philadelphia. *National Public Radio*. https://www.npr.org/2019/07/05/738860218/sonic-devices-target-teenagers-in-philadelphia.

Winston, C. N., Maher, H., & Easvaradoss, V. (2017). Needs and values: An exploration. *Humanistic Psychologist, 45*(3), 295-311.

Winter, D. G. (2007). The role of motivation, responsibility, and integrative complexity in crisis escalation: Comparative studies of war and peace crises. *Journal of Personality and Social Psychology, 92*, 920-937.

Winter, D. G. (2016). Taming power: Generative historical consciousness. *American Psychologist, 71*, 160-174.

Wiryosutomo, H. W., Hanum, F., & Partini, S. (2019). History of development and concept of person-centered counseling in cultural diversity. *International Journal of Educational Research Review, 4*(1), 56-64.

Wiseman, R., & Greening, E. (2002). The mind machine: A mass participation experiment into the possible existence of extra-sensory perception. *British Journal of Psychology, 93*, 487-499.

Wiseman, R. (2019). Getting beyond rites of passage in archaeology: Conceptual metaphors of journeys and growth. *Current Anthropology, 60*(4), 449-474.

Wishart, D., Somoray, K., & Rowland, B. (2017). Role of thrill and adventure seeking in risky work-related driving behaviours. *Personality and Individual Differences, 104*, 362-367.

Wittig, S. M., & Rodriguez, C. M. (2019). Emerging behavior problems: Bidirectional relations between maternal and paternal parenting styles with infant temperament. *Developmental Psychology,55*(6), 1199-1210.

Witzel, C., & Gegenfurtner, K. R. (2018). Color perception: Objects, constancy, and categories. *Annual Review of Vision Science, 4*, 475-499.

Wixted, J. T. (2021). The role of retroactive interference and consolidation in everyday forgetting. In *Current Issues in Memory* (pp. 117-143). Routledge.

Wixted, J. T., & Wells, G. L. (2017). The relationship between eyewitness confidence and identification accuracy: A new synthesis. *Psychological Science in the Public Interest, 18*(1), 10-65.

Wojciechowska, L. (2017). Subjectivity and generativity in midlife. *Polish Psychological Bulletin, 48*, 38-43.

Wolf, A. J., Guyer, M. J., & Sharpe, L. (2010). Repressed memories in a controversial conviction. *Journal of the American Academy of Psychiatry Law, 38*, 607-609.

Wolman, D. (2012). The split brain: A tale of two halves. *Nature, 483*, 260-263.

Wombacher, K., Matig, J. J., Sheff, S. E., & Scott, A. M. (2019). "It just kind of happens": College students' rationalizations for blackout drinking. *Health Communication, 34*(1), 1-10.

Wong, N., Sarver, D. E., & Beidel, D. C. (2011). Quality of life impairments among adults with social phobia: The impact of subtype. *Journal of Anxiety Disorders, 14*, 88-95.

Wood, D., Crapnell, T., Lau, L., Bennett, A., Lotstein, D., Ferris, M., & Kuo, A. (2018). Emerging adulthood as a critical stage in the life course. In N. Halfon, C. B. Forest, R. M. Lerner, &E. M. Faustman (Eds.), *Handbook of life course health development*. SpringerLink.

Woodruff, S. I., Conway, T. L., & Edwards, C. C. (2007). Sociodemographic and smoking-related psychosocial

predictors of smoking behavior change among high school smokers. *Addictive Behaviors, 33*, 354-358.

Woods, S. C., Schwartz, M. W., Baskin, D. G., & Seeley, R. J. (2000). Food intake and the regulation of body weight. *Annual Review of Psychology, 51*, 255-277.

Workman, L., Taylor, S., & Barkow, J. H. (2022). Evolutionary perspectives on social development. In P. K. smith & C. H. Hart (Eds.), *The Wiley-Blackwell handbook of childhood social development* (3rd ed.). Wiley.

World Health Organization. (2019a). Guidelines on physical activity, sedentary behaviour and sleep for children under 5 years of age. World Health Organization. https://apps.who.int/iris/handle/10665/311664.

World Health Organization (2019b). *WHO report on the global tobacco epidemic*. Author.

World Health Organization. (2022, March 2). Mental health and COVID-19: Early evidence of the pandemic's impact. https://apps.who.int/iris/rest/bitstreams/1412184/retrieve

World Health Organization. (2022). Smoking fact sheet. https://www.who.int/news-room/fact-sheets/detail/tobacco

World Health Organization. (2022). WHO coronavirus (COVID-19) dashboard. https://covid19.who.int

Wretman, C. J. (2016). Saving Satir: Contemporary perspectives on the change process model. *Social Work, 61*, 61-68.

Wright, A. C. (2017). The current state and future of factor analysis in personality disorder research. *Personality Disorders: Theory, Research, and Treatment, 8*, 14-25.

Wright, A. C., Zalewski, M., Hallquist, M. N., Hipwell, A. E., & Stepp, S. D. (2016). Developmental trajectories of borderline personality disorder symptoms and psychosocial functioning in adolescence. *Journal of Personality Disorders, 30*, 351-372.

Wright, D. S., Nash, R. A., & Wade, K. A. (2015). Encouraging eyewitnesses to falsely corroborate allegations: Effects of rapport-building and incriminating evidence. *Psychology, Crime & Law, 21*, 648-660.

Wright, J. H., Owen, J. J., Richards, D., Eells, T. D., Richardson, T., Brown, G. K., Barnett, M., Rasku, M. A., Polser, G., & Thase, M. E. (2019). Computer-assisted cognitive-behavior therapy for depression: a systematic review and meta-analysis. *The Journal of Clinical Psychiatry, 80*(2), 3573.

Wróbel, M., & Królewiak, K. (2017). Do we feel the same way if we think the same way? Shared attitudes and the social induction of affect. *Basic and Applied Social Psychology, 39*, 19-37.

Wrosch, C., Bauer, I., & Scheier, M. (2005). Regret and quality of life across the adult life span: The influence of disengagement and available future goals. *Psychology and Aging, 20*, 657-670.

Wu, J., Harlow, A. F., Wijaya, D., Berman, M., Benjamin, E. J., Xuan, Z., Hong, T., & Fetterman, J. L. (2022). The impact of influencers on cigar promotions: A content analysis of large cigar and Swisher Sweets videos on TikTok. *International Journal of Environmental Research and Public Health, 19*(12), 7064.

Wu, J., Luan, S., & Raihani, N. (2022). Reward, punishment, and prosocial behavior: Recent developments and implications. *Current Opinion in Psychology, 44*, 117-123.

Wu, P., Song, L., & Meng, X. (2022). Temporal analysis of cellphone-use-involved crash injury severities: Calling for preventing cellphone-use-involved distracted driving. *Accident Analysis & Prevention, 169*, 106625.

Wu, Y. (2013). An empirical study of narrative imagery in implicit and explicit contexts. *Computers in Human Behavior, 29*, 1580-1589.

Wu, Y. (2021). Distinguishing the binary of news-fake and real: The illusory truth effect. *Journal of Applied Journalism & Media Studies*. https://doi.org/10.1386/ajms_00042_1

Wyatt, T. D. (2020). Reproducible research into human chemical communication by cues and pheromones:

Learning from psychology's renaissance. *Philosophical Transactions of the Royal Society B, 375*(1800), 20190262.

Wyrofsky, R. R., Reyes, B. A., Zhang, X. Y., Bhatnagar, S., Kirby, L. G., & Van Bockstaele, E. J. (2019). Endocannabinoids, stress signaling, and the locus coeruleus-norepinephrine system. *Neurobiology of Stress.* https://doi.org/10.1016/j.ynstr.2019.100176

Xi, J., Lee, M., LeSuer, W., Barr, P., Newton, K., & Poloma, M. (2017). Altruism and existential well-being. *Applied Research in Quality of Life, 12,* 67-88.

Xi, M., Shen, X., Guliyeva, K., Hancock-Howard, R., Coyte, P. C., & Chan, B. C. (2021). Cost-utility analysis of transcranial direct current stimulation therapy with and without virtual illusion for neuropathic pain for adults with spinal cord injury in Canada. *The Journal of Spinal Cord Medicine, 44*(sup1), S159-S172.

Xiang, J., & Stanley, S. J. (2017). From online to offline: Exploring the role of e-health consumption, patient involvement, and patient-centered communication on perceptions of health care quality. *Computers in Human Behavior, 70,* 446-452.

Xiang, P., Zhang, H., Geng, L., Zhou, K., & Wu, Y. (2019). Individualist-collectivist differences in climate change inaction: The role of perceived intractability. *Frontiers in Psychology, 10.*

Xiao, N. G., Quinn, P. C., Liu, S., Ge, L., Pascalis, O., & Lee, K. (2015). Eye tracking reveals a crucial role for facial motion in recognition of faces by infants. *Developmental Psychology, 51,* 744-757.

Xie, G., & Johnson, J. Q. (2015). Examining the third-person effect of baseline omission in numerical comparison: The role of consumer persuasion knowledge. *Psychology & Marketing, 32,* 438-449.

Xie, T. T., Wang, T. Z., Wei, Y. P., & Ye, E. C. (2019). Declarative memory affects procedural memory: The role of semantic association and sequence matching. *Psychology of Sport and Exercise, 43,* 253-260.

Xie, Y., Xu, E., & Al-Aly, Z. (2022). Risks of mental health outcomes in people with COVID-19: Cohort study. *The BMJ, 376.*

Xu, M., & Petty, R. E. (2022). Two-sided messages promote openness for morally based attitudes. *Personality and Social Psychology Bulletin, 48*(8), 1151-1166.

Yadav, R., Yadav, R. K., Sarvottam, K. & Netam, R. (2017). Framingham Risk Score and estimated 10-year cardiovascular disease risk reduction by a short-term yoga-based life-style intervention. *Journal of Alternative Complement Medicine, 23*(9), 730-737.

Yagi, M., Hirano, Y., Nakazato, M., Nemoto, K., Ishikawa, K., Sutoh, C., et al. (2017). Relationship between symptom dimensions and white matter alterations in obsessive-compulsive disorder. *Acta Neuropsychiatrica, 29,* 153-163.

Yagoda, B. (2018, September). Your lying mind: The cognitive biases tricking you brain. *The Atlantic.*

Yamada, R., & Itsukushima, Y. (2013). The schema provokes a disparity of false recollection between actions and objects in an everyday scene. *Scandinavian Journal of Psychology, 54,* 276-282.

Yanakieva, S., Polychroni, N., Family, N., Williams, L. T. J., Luke, D. P., & Terhune, D. B. (2019). The effects of microdose LSD on time perception: A randomised, double-blind, placebo-controlled trial. *Psychopharmacology, 236*(4), 1159-1170.

Yang, C., Crain, S., Berwick, R. C., Chomsky, N., & Bolhuis, J. J. (2017). The growth of language: Universal grammar, experience, and principles of computation. *Neuroscience and Biobehavioral Reviews, 81*(Part B), 103-119.

Yang, D., Bushnell, E. W., Buchanan, D. W., & Sobel, D. M. (2013). Infants' use of contextual cues in the generalization of effective actions from imitation. *Journal of Experimental Child-Psychology , 116,* 510-531.

Yang, M., Liou, K. T., Garland, S. N., Bao, T., Hung, T. K., Li, S. Q., Li, Y., & Mao, J. J. (2021). Acupuncture versus cognitive behavioral therapy for pain among cancer survivors with insomnia: An exploratory

analysis of a randomized clinical trial. *NPJ Breast Cancer, 7*(1), 1-7.

Yang, X., Liu, X., Zeng, Y., Wu, R., Zhao, W., Xin, F., Yao, S., Kendrick, K. M., Ebstein, R. P., & Becker, B. (2021). Secondary rewards acquire enhanced incentive motivation via increasing anticipatory activity of the lateral orbitofrontal cortex. *Brain Structure and Function, 226*(7), 2339-2355.

Yano, K., Shin, J., & Yasumura, A. (2022). Brain activity in the prefrontal cortex during cancelation tasks: Effects of the stimulus array. *Behavioural Brain Research,* 113744.

Yarkoni, T. (2015). Neurobiological substrates of personality: A critical overview. In M. Mikulincer, P. R. Shaver, M. L. Cooper, & R. J. Larsen (Eds.), *APA handbook of personality and social psychology, Volume 4: Personality processes and individual differences.* Washington, DC: American Psychological Association.

Yaros, J. L., Salama, D. A., Delisle, D., Larson, M. S., Miranda, B. A., & Yassa, M. A. (2019). A memory computational basis for the other-race effect. *Scientific Reports, 9*(1), 1-11.

Yeh, Y. J. Y., & Chen, M. H. (2021). Examining the primacy and recency effect on learning effectiveness with the application of interactive response systems (IRS). *Technology, Knowledge and Learning,* 1-14.

Yelderman, L. A., Joseph, J. J., West, M. P., & Butler, E. (2019). Mass shootings in the United States: Understanding the importance of mental health and firearm considerations. *Psychology, Public Policy, and Law, 25*(3), 212-223.

Yelderman, L. A., & Miller, M. K. (2017). Religious fundamentalism, religiosity, and priming: Effects on attitudes, perceptions, and mock jurors' decisions in an insanity defense case. *Psychology, Crime & Law,* 23, 147-170.

Yeomans, M. R., Tepper, B. J., & Ritezschel, J. (2007). Human hedonic responses to sweetness: Role of taste genetics and anatomy. *Physiology & Behavior, 91,* 264-273.

Yesilyaprak, B., Kisac, I., & Sanlier, N. (2007). Stress symptoms and nutritional status among survivors of the Marmara region earthquakes in Turkey. *Journal of Loss & Trauma, 12,* 1-8.

Yi, X., Plucker, J. A., & Guo, J. (2015). Modeling influences on divergent thinking and artistic creativity. *Thinking Skills and Creativity, 16,* 62-68.

Yildirim, F., & Barnett, R. V. (2017). Comparing the effects of specific variables on passionate love among young people: A cross-cultural study. In N. R. Silton (Ed.), *Family dynamics and romantic relationships in a changing society.* Information Science Reference/IGI Global.

Yildiz, G. Y., Sperandio, I., Kettle, C., & Chouinard, P. A. (2019). The contribution of linear perspective cues and texture gradients in the perceptual rescaling of stimuli inside a Ponzo illusion corridor. *PLOS ONE, 14*(10), e0223583.

Yıldız, M., Orak, U., Walker, M. H., & Solakoglu, O. (2019). Suicide contagion, gender, and suicide attempts among adolescents. *Death Studies, 43*(6), 365-371.

Yoder, R. M., Goebel, E. A., Köppen, J. R., Blankenship, P. A., Blackwell, A. A., & Wallace, D. G. (2015). Otolithic information is required for homing in the mouse. *Hippocampus, 25,* 890-899.

Yoo, H., & Pituc, S. T. (2013). Assessments of perceived racial stereotypes, discrimination, and racism. In K. F. Geisinger, B. A. Bracken, J. F. Carlson, J. C. Hansen, N. R. Kuncel, S. P. Reise, & M. C. Rodriguez (Eds.), *APA handbook of testing and assessment in psychology, Vol. 2: Testing and assessment in clinical and counseling psychology.* American Psychological Association.

Young, K. D., Misaki, M., Harmer, C. J., Victor, T., Zotev, V., Phillips, R., Siegle, G. J., Drevets, W. C., & Bodurka, J. (2017). Real-time functional magnetic resonance imaging amygdala neurofeedback changes positive information processing in major depressive disorder. *Biological Psychiatry, 82*(8), 578-586.

Young, R., Subramanian, R., Miles, S., Hinnant, A., & Andsager, J. L. (2017). Social representation of cyberbullying and adolescent suicide:

A mixed-method analysis of news stories. *Health Communication, 32*(9), 1082-1092.

Yu, M., & Hyun, S. S. (2021). Development of modern racism scale in global airlines: A study of Asian female flight attendants. *International Journal of Environmental Research and Public Health, 18*(5), 2688.

Yuen, E. K., Koterba, E. A., Stasio, M. J., Patrick, R. B., Gangi, C., Ash, P., Barakat, K., Greene, V., Hamilton, W., & Mansour, B. (2019). The effects of Facebook on mood in emerging adults. *Psychology of Popular Media Culture, 8*(3), 198-206.

Zadra, A., & Stickgold, R. (2021). *When brains dream: Exploring the science and mystery of sleep.* WW Norton & Company.

Zahl-Olsen, R., Thuen, F., & Espehaug, B. (2019). Divorce and remarriage in Norway: A prospective cohort study between 1981 and 2013. *Journal of Divorce & Remarriage, 60*(8), 600-611.

Zahnow, R., McVeigh, J., Ferris, J., & Winstock, A. (2017). Adverse effects, health service engagement, and service satisfaction among anabolic androgenic steroid users. *Contemporary Drug Problems: An Interdisciplinary Quarterly, 44,* 69-83.

Zahn, N., Sellbom, M., Pymont, C., & Schenk, P. W. (2017). Associations between MMPI-2-RF scale scores and self-reported personality disorder criteria in a private practice sample. *Journal of Psychopathology and Behavioral Assessment, 39*(4), 723-741.

Zajonc, R. B. (2001). Mere exposure: A gateway to the subliminal. *Current Directions in Psychological Science, 10,* 224-228.

Zamarian, L., Högl, B., Delazer, M., Hingerl, K., Gabelia, D., Mitterling, T., et al. (2015). Subjective deficits of attention, cognition and depression in patients with narcolepsy. *Sleep Medicine, 16,* 45-51.

Zambrano-Sánchez, E., Martínez-Cortés, J., Poblano, A., Dehesa-Moreno, M., Vázquez-Urbano, F., & del Río-Carlos, Y. (2021). Maternal smoking during pregnancy and physiological anxiety in children with attention deficit hyperactivity disorder. *Applied Neuropsychology: Child.* https://doi.org/10.1080/216 22965.2019.1632708.

Zeidan, J., Fombonne, E., Scorah, J., Ibrahim, A., Durkin, M. S., Saxena, S., Yusuf, A., Shih, A., & Elsabbagh, M. (2022). Global prevalence of autism: a systematic review update. *Autism Research, 15*(5), 778-790.

Zeigler, K., & Camarota, S. A. (2019). 67.3 million in the United States spoke a foreign language at home in 2018. *Center for immigration studies, 29.*

Zeng, L., Proctor, R. W., & Salvendy, G. (2011). Can traditional divergent thinking tests be trusted in measuring and predicting real-world creativity? *Creativity Research Journal, 23,* 24-37.

Zhang, D., Guo, T., Pan, H., Hou, J., Feng, Z., Yang, L., Lin, H., & Xia, F. (2019, May). Judging a book by its cover: The effect of facial perception on centrality in social networks. In *The World Wide Web Conference, WWW 2019.* https://doi.org/10.1145/3308558.3313527

Zhang, D., He, Z., Chen, Y., & Wei, Z. (2016). Deficits of unconscious emotional processing in patients with major depression: An ERP study. *Journal of Affective Disorders, 199,* 13-20.

Zhang, D. C. (2022). Horse-sized ducks or duck-sized horses? Oddball personality questions are likable (but useless) for organizational recruitment. *Journal of Business and Psychology, 37*(1), 215-233.

Zhang, J., Chen, H., Kornreich, R., & Yu, C. (2019). Prenatal diagnosis of Tay-Sachs disease. In B. Levy (Ed.), *Prenatal diagnosis.* Humana Press.

Zhang, W., & Guo, B. (2017). Resolving defence mechanisms: A perspective based on dissipative structure theory. *International Journal of Psychoanalysis, 98,* 457-472.

Zhang, W., Pan, Q., & Guo, B. (2022). The significance of infant research for psychoanalysis. *Humanities and Social Sciences Communications, 9*(1), 1-8.

Zhang, W., Wang, Y., Feng, Z., Zhu, S., Cui, J., Hao, W., & Wang, C. (2022). A method to improve the hazard perception of young novice drivers based on Bandura's observational learning theory: Supplement to expert commentary training. *Transportation Research Part F: Traffic Psychology and Behaviour, 85,* 133-149.

Zhang, X., Wan, Q., Lyu, S., Li, O., & Liu, Y. (2021). Overlearning is as ineffective as underlearning? A cross-culture study from PISA 2015. *Learning and Individual Differences, 88*, 102005.

Zhao, F., Li, S., Li, T., & Yu, G. (2019). Does stereotype threat deteriorate academic performance of high school students with learning disabilities? The buffering role of psychological disengagement. *Journal of Learning Disabilities, 52*(4), 312-323.

Zhao, K., & Smillie, L. D. (2015). The role of interpersonal traits in social decision making: Exploring sources of behavioral heterogeneity in economic games. *Personality and Social Psychology Review, 19*, 277-302.

Zheng, D., Ni, X. L., & Luo, Y. J. (2019). Selfie posting on social networking sites and female adolescents' self-objectification: The moderating role of imaginary audience ideation. *Sex Roles, 80*(5-6), 325-331.

Zhou, Y., Li, H., Siddiqui, N., Caudle, Y., Zhang, H., Elgazzar, M., & Yin, D. (2017). Hematopoietic stem progenitor cells prevent chronic stress-induced lymphocyte apoptosis. *Journal of Neuroimmunology, 309*, 72-76.

Zietsch, B. P. (2021). More evidence and context are needed to evaluate the possibility that scent perception is part of the same-sex sexual behavior story. *Archives of Sexual Behavior, 50*(6), 2313-2315.

Zimbardo, P. G. (2004). Does psychology make a significant difference in our lives? *American Psychologist, 59*, 339-351.

Zion, S. R., Louis, K., Horii, R., Leibowitz, K., Heathcote, L. C., & Crum, A. J. (2022). Making sense of a pandemic: Mindsets influence emotions, behaviors, health, and wellbeing during the COVID-19 pandemic. *Social Science & Medicine*, 114889.

Zizzari, Z. V., Engl, T., Lorenz, S., van Straalen, N. M., Ellers, J., & Groot, A. T. (2017). Love at first sniff: A spermatophore-associated pheromone mediates partner attraction in a collembolan species. *Animal Behaviour, 124*, 221-227.

Zmigrod, L., & Goldenberg, A. (2021). Cognition and emotion in extreme political action: Individual differences and dynamic interactions. *Current Directions in Psychological Science, 30*(3), 218-227.

Zografova, Y., Bakalova, D., Hristova, A., Andreev, B., Nedeva-Atanasova, V., Racheva, R., & Totkova, Z. (2019). Personality traits and family environment-antecedents of students' aggression. *Psychological Research, 22*(3), 689-711.

Zuberbühler, K. (2022). Event parsing and the origins of grammar. *Wiley Interdisciplinary Reviews: Cognitive Science, 13*(3), e1587.

Zuckerman, M. (1978, February). The search for high sensation. *Psychology Today*, pp. 30-46.

Zvyagintsev, M., Clemens, B., Chechko, N., Mathiak, K. A., Sack, A. T., & Mathiak, K. (2013). Brain networks underlying mental imagery of auditory and visual information. *European Journal of Neuroscience, 37*, 1421-1434.

Zyoud, S. H., Sweileh, W. M., Awang, R., & Al-Jabi, S. W. (2018). Global trends in research related to social media in psychology: Mapping and bibliometric analysis. *International Journal of Mental Health Systems, 12*, doi:10.1186/s13033-018-0182-6.

Name Index

Subject Index

Note: Page numbers followed by *f* indicate figures.

A

AA. *See* Alcoholics Anonymous
A-B-C model of rational-emotive behavior therapy, 504–505, 505*f*
Abnormal behavior, 457–466
  classification of, 463–465, 463*f*
  cultural differences in, 461, 490–491
  definitions of, 457–459
  as learned, 460, 500
  psychological perspectives on, 24, 459–462, 462*f*
Absolute thresholds, 87–88, 88*f*
Absorption, as personality trait, 405*f*
Academic success
  cultural differences in views on, 572–573
  intelligence in, 274–275
  stereotype vulnerability and, 554
Acceptance
  of death, 380
  in unconditional positive regard, 407, 509
Accommodation, 93
Accutane, 340*f*
Acetylcholine (ACh), 56*f*, 57
Achievement. *See also* Success
  cultural differences in views of, 574
  need for, 313–314
  as personality trait, 405*f*
Acquired immune deficiency syndrome (AIDS), 340*f*
Acrophobia, 467–468
Action potential, 52–54, 53*f*
Activation information modulation (AIM) theory, 141
Activation-synthesis theory, 139*f*, 141
Activity theory of aging, 379
Acupuncture, 111, 112, 113
Adaptation
  to light and dark, 95
  sensory, 90–91
Adaptive testing, 281
Adderall, 159
Addiction
  causes of, 156–158
  classical conditioning in, 177–178
  to drugs, 156–158
  to smoking, 436
ADHD. *See* Attention-deficit hyperactivity disorder
Adolescents, 359–369
  anxiety in, 483, 483*f*, 489
  definition of, 359
  disorders affecting, 483–485, 483*f*
  drug use by, 156, 157*f*
  egocentrism of, 366
  hearing of, 104, 104*f*
  mental health of, 483, 483*f*, 489
  moral development of, 361–363, 362*f*
  parents' relationship with, 365–366
  physical development of, 359–361, 360*f*
  smoking by, 436–438, 436*f*, 438*f*
  social development of, 363–369
  suicide by, 366–368, 367*f*

Adrenal glands, 65*f*
Adults, 370–381
  definition of, 370
  moral development of, 362
  older. *See* Older adults
  physical development of, 371–372
  psychosocial development of, 364–365
  rites of passage for, 368–369
  social development of, 372–374
  stages of adulthood, 370, 371*f*
Advertising, subliminal, 142
Aerobic exercise. *See* Exercise
Afferent neurons. *See* Sensory neurons
Affiliation, need for, 314
African Americans
  in COVID-19 pandemic, 440–441, 441*f*
  discrimination against. *See* Racism
  health disparities in, 438–439
  homicide rates for, 574
  intelligence testing of, 284–286
  microaggressions against, 562
  schemas for, 224
  sickle-cell anemia in, 339
  smoking by, 435
  stereotype vulnerability of, 553–554
  test norms for, 411
  use of term, 569, 570
Afterimages, 98–99, 98*f*
Age. *See also* Aging
  chronological, 277
  at marriage, 373
  maternal, 340*f*
  mental, 277
  at puberty, 360, 360*f*
  of viability, 337
Aggression, 560–563
  cultural differences in, 574–576
  definition of, 561, 561*f*, 574
  gender differences in, 575
  media violence and, 33, 34*f*, 198–200
  observational learning in, 198–200, 401, 563
  as personality trait, 405*f*
  physical punishment and, 185
  as reaction to frustration, 562–563
  as release, 562
Aggressive cues, 563
Aging. *See also* Older adults
  activity theory of, 379
  and cognitive abilities, 376–378, 377*f*
  and creativity, 257
  disengagement theory of, 379
  and emotional regulation, 324
  genetic programming theories of, 375
  and hearing, 104, 104*f*
  and smell, 107
  wear-and-tear theories of, 375
Agoraphobia, 468–469, 468*f*
Agreeableness, 398–399, 399*f*
AI. *See* Artificial intelligence

AIDS. *See* Acquired immune deficiency syndrome
AIM. *See* Activation information modulation
Ainsworth strange situation, 347
Alarm and mobilization stage, 426, 427*f*
Alcohol consumption, 161–164
  in binge drinking, 161–162, 162*f*
  effects of, 160*f*, 162–163, 163*f*
  in fetal alcohol syndrome, 282
  during pregnancy, 282, 340, 340*f*
  rates of, 161–162
  signs of abuse with, 167–168
Alcoholics Anonymous (AA), 511
Alcoholism, 163–164
  prevalence of, 163
  self-help therapy for, 511
  signs of, 167–168
  Wernicke-Korsakoff syndrome in, 236
Alcohol use disorders, 485, 487
Algorithms, 244–246
Alienation, 405*f*
All-or-none law, 52, 54
Alprazolam, 519
Altered states of consciousness, 130–131, 150–155. *See also* Drugs; Sleep
Alternation model of bicultural competence, 269
Altruism, 565
Alzheimer's disease, 56, 235, 377–378
Ambidexterity, 77
Ambivalence, about adulthood, 370, 371*f*
Ambivalent children, 347
American Academy of Pediatrics, 348, 441
American Indians. *See* Native Americans
American Journal of Psychoanalysis, 17
American Pediatric Association, 199
American Psychological Association (APA), 17, 25, 199, 312, 525
Amnesia, 235–236
  anterograde, 235–236
  dissociative, 472–473
  retrograde, 235
  source, 223
Amok, 491
Amphetamines, 159–161, 160*f*
Amplitude, of sound, 104
Amygdala
  in emotional experience, 323–324, 324*f*
  in memory, 216, 216*f*
  in prejudice, 551
  structure and functions of, 71–72, 71*f*
Analogies, 257–258
Anal stage, 388*f*, 389
Analytical intelligence, 275
Analytical learning style, 201, 201*f*
Androgens, 306
Anemia, sickle-cell, 339
Anger
  in aggression, 562–563
  in response to death, 380
  strategies for dealing with, 566